THIS EDITION WRITTEN AND RESEARCHED BY

Mark Be... Bush,

welcome to
Thailand

Sand between Your Toes

Thailand's beaches are mythical: tall palms angle over pearlescent sand, coral gardens flourish in the shallow seas and beach parties are liberally lubricated with alcohol and fun. With a long coastline (well, actually, two coastlines) and jungle-topped islands anchored in azure waters, Thailand is a tropical getaway for the hedonist and the hermit, the prince and the pauper. And in between the kissing cousins of sea and sky are dramatic limestone mountains standing sentinel. This paradise offers a varied menu of playing in the gentle surf of Bang Saphan Yai, diving with whale sharks in Ko Tao, scaling the sea cliffs of Krabi, learning to kiteboard in Hua Hin, recuperating at a health resort in Ko Samui and feasting on the beach wherever sand meets sea.

Sacred Spaces

The celestial world is a close confidant in this Buddhist nation, where religious devotion is a colourful and ubiquitous spectacle. Gleaming temples and golden Buddhas frame both the rural and modern landscape with exuberance. Ancient banyan trees are ceremoniously wrapped in sacred cloth to honour the resident spirits, fortune-bringing shrines decorate humble noodle houses as well as monumental malls, while garland-festooned dashboards ward off traffic accidents. The Thai's ongoing dialogue with the divine an-

Friendly and fun-loving, exotic and tropical, cultured and historic, Thailand beams with a lustrous hue from its gaudy temples and golden beaches to the ever-comforting Thai smile.

(left) Wat Phra That Doi Kong Mu (p384), Mae Hong Son.
(below) Terracotta sculptures, Chiang Mai (p234).

chors the day-to-day chaos to a solid base of tranquillity. Visitors can join in on the conversation through meditation retreats in Chiang Mai, noisy religious festivals in northeastern Thailand, peaceful underground cave shrines in Kanchanaburi and Phetchaburi or scenic hilltop temples in northern Thailand.

A Bountiful Table

No matter what draws you to the country first, a Thai meal will keep you hooked. Adored around the world, Thai cuisine expresses fundamental aspects of Thai culture: it is generous and warm, outgoing and nuanced, refreshing and relaxed. And it is much more delicious in its native setting.

Each Thai dish relies on fresh and local ingredients – from pungent lemongrass and searing chillies to plump seafood and crispy fried chicken. With a tropical abundance, a varied national menu is built around the four fundamental flavours: spicy, sweet, salty and sour. And then there are the regional differences, which propel travellers on an eating tour of Bangkok noodle shacks, seafood pavilions in Phuket, Burmese market stalls in Mae Hong Son, and luscious tropical fruit everywhere. Cooking classes reveal the simplicity behind the seemingly complicated dishes and mastering the markets becomes an important skill.

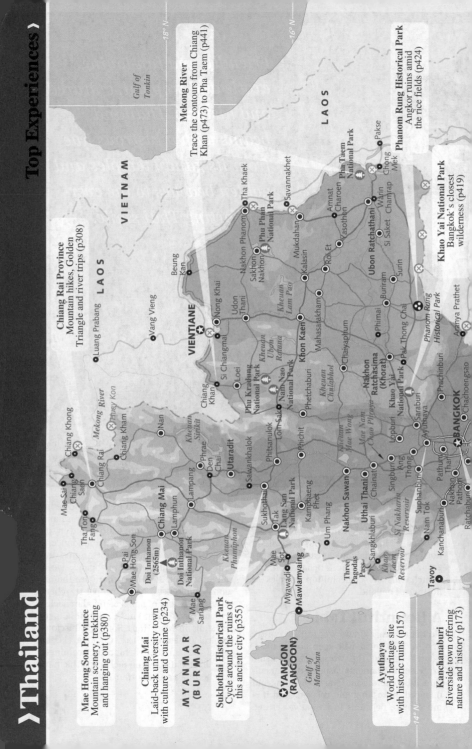

❭ Thailand

Top Experiences ❭

Mae Hong Son Province
Mountain scenery, trekking and hanging out (p380)

Chiang Mai
Laid-back university town with culture and cuisine (p234)

Sukhothai Historical Park
Cycle around the ruins of this ancient city (p355)

Ayuthaya
World heritage site with historic ruins (p157)

Kanchanaburi
Riverside town offering nature and history (p173)

Chiang Rai Province
Mountain hikes, Golden Triangle and river trips (p308)

Mekong River
Trace the contours from Chiang Khan (p473) to Pha Taem (p441)

Phanom Rung Historical Park
Angkor ruins amid the rice fields (p424)

Khao Yai National Park
Bangkok's closest wilderness (p419)

MYANMAR (BURMA)

LAOS

VIETNAM

Gulf of Tonkin

Gulf of Martaban

VIENTIANE

BANGKOK

YANGON (RANGOON)

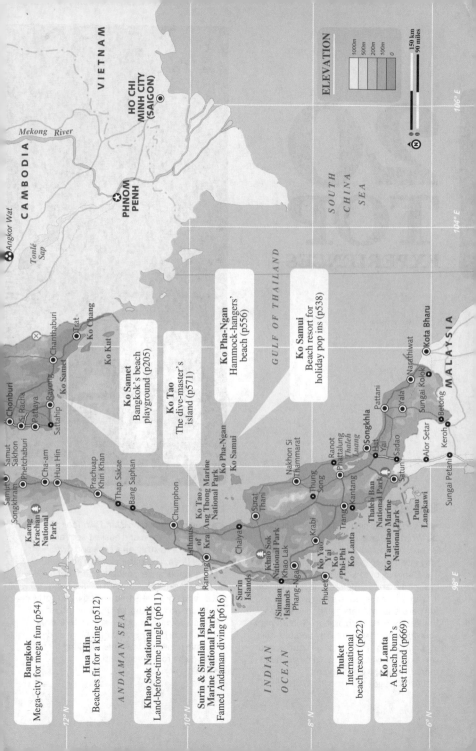

Bangkok
Mega-city for mega fun (p54)

Hua Hin
Beaches fit for a king (p512)

Khao Sok National Park
Land-before-time jungle (p611)

Surin & Similan Islands
Marine National Parks
Famed Andaman diving (p616)

Phuket
International beach resort (p622)

Ko Lanta
A beach bum's best friend (p669)

Ko Samet
Bangkok's beach playground (p205)

Ko Tao
The dive-master's island (p571)

Ko Pha-Ngan
Hammock-hangers' beach (p556)

Ko Samui
Beach resort for holiday pop ins (p538)

ELEVATION

1000m
500m
200m
100m
0

150 km
90 miles

VIETNAM

CAMBODIA

Mekong River

Angkor Wat

Tonlé Sap

PHNOM PENH

HO CHI MINH CITY (SAIGON)

SOUTH CHINA SEA

GULF OF THAILAND

ANDAMAN SEA

INDIAN OCEAN

MALAYSIA

Chonburi
Si Racha
Pattaya
Rayong
Chanthaburi
Trat
Ko Chang
Ko Kut
Ko Samet
Sattahip

Samut Songkhram
Samut Sakhon
Phetchaburi
Cha-am
Hua Hin
Kaeng Krachan National Park
Prachuap Khiri Khan
Thap Sakae
Bang Saphan
Chumphon

Isthmus of Kra
Ranong
Surin Islands
Similan Islands
Phang-Nga
Khao Lak
Khao Sok National Park
Phuket
Ko Yao Yai
Ko Phi-Phi
Ko Lanta
Krabi
Chaiya
Surat Thani
Ang Thong Marine National Park
Ko Tao
Ko Pha-Ngan
Ko Samui
Nakhon Si Thammarat
Thung Song
Ranot
Phatthalung
Thaleh Luang
Trang
Kantang
Thaleh Noi
Thaleh Ban National Park
Pulau Langkawi
Ko Tarutao Marine National Park
Satun
Sadao
Songkhla
Hat Yai
Pattani
Yala
Betong
Keroh
Alor Setar
Sungai Petani
Sungai Kolok
Naradhiwat
Kota Bharu

12° N
10° N
8° N
6° N

98° E
104° E
106° E

20 TOP
EXPERIENCES

Bangkok

1 Food, shopping, fun, temples, palaces... What isn't available in Bangkok (p54)? Be prepared to adjust your itinerary if you've only given Bangkok the requisite day or two. The Bangkok of today is tidier and easier to navigate than ever before, and will pull you in with one of the world's biggest markets, fun bars, sublime eats and endless opportunities for urban exploration. Supplement your fun with more scholarly pursuits such as a cooking or Thai massage course, and we're certain you'll see Bangkok as much more than just a transit point.

Wat Arun, beside the Chao Phraya River

Ko Tao

2 The dive-master's island, Ko Tao (p571) is the cheapest and easiest spot around to learn how to strap on a tank and dive into the deep. The water is warm and gentle and the underwater spectacles are not to be missed. Just offshore are scenic rocky coves and coral reefs frequented by all sorts of fish providing a snorkelling 'aperitif'. Ko Tao is a beautiful island even for nondivers. Its small size means you can explore all of its jungle nooks and crannies, looking for a sandy niche to call your own.

Ao Chalok, Ko Tao

Mae Hong Son Province

3 Tucked in the country's northwest corner, this province (p380) has a lot more in common with neighbouring Myanmar (Burma) than anywhere else in Thailand. In fact, with its remote location, intimidating mountains and unique culture and cuisine, Mae Hong Son can seem like an entirely different country. Exploration is the reason to make the schlep here, and can take the form of tramping through one of the province's many caves, taking a hairpin turn on your motorcycle, or doing a self-guided trek from Mae La-Na to Soppong.

Prayers during Poi Sang Long, Mae Hong Son

Ko Pha-Ngan

4 Famous for its sloppy Full Moon parties and all-night techno parties, Ko Pha-Ngan (p556) has graduated from a sleepy bohemian island to full-on attraction for migrating party-people. The beach shanties have been transformed into boutiques, meaning comfort seekers have an alternative to Ko Samui. And in the northern and eastern coasts, the ascetic hammock hangers can still escape enough of the modern life to feel like a modern castaway (well-fed ones, of course). Just offshore is Sail Rock, one of the gulf's best dive sites.

Hat Rin

GLENN VAN DER KNIJFF/LONELY PLANET IMAGES ©

Surin & Similan Islands Marine National Parks

5 These world-renowned dive sites (p616 and p617) have anchored Thailand as a global diving destination. Live-aboard trips set out from Khao Lak, allowing for more time at the famous sites where you can meet the local manta rays and whale sharks. There is the thrill of being far from land as the sun sinks into the sea and the night shows off its twinkling lights. The islands are an attraction in their own right with jungle-filled interiors and smooth white beaches surrounded by decent coral reefs.

Similan Islands Marine National Park

Ayuthaya

6 A once vibrant, glittering capital packed with hundreds of temples, Ayuthaya (p157) today only hints at its erstwhile glory. Cycle around the brick-and-stucco ruins, which form part of a Unesco World Heritage Site, and try to imagine how the city must have looked in its prime, when it greeted merchants from around the globe. On the outskirts of the city sit several more attractions, including an enormous handicraft centre, the most eclectic royal palace you'll ever see and a water theatre.

Wat Phra Si Sanphet

Ko Lanta

7 A beach bum's best friend, Ko Lanta (p669) sports a mellow island vibe and a parade of peachy sand. Social butterflies alight on the northern beaches for a same-same but different party scene. Solitude seekers migrate southward to low-key beach huts and a sleepy village ambience. Activities abound from hiking through a surreal landscape of limestone caves and crevices to diving to underwater hangouts for sharks and rays. Sprinkle in some culture with a stop at the local markets or Ban Lanta, the historic commercial centre.

Hat Nui

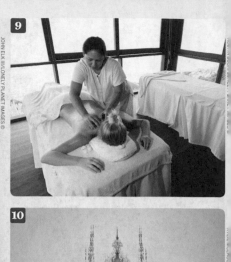

JOHN ELK III/LONELY PLANET IMAGES ©

Sukhothai Historical Park

8 Step back in time about 800 years at Thailand's most impressive historical park (p355). Exploring the ruins of this former capital by bicycle is the classic Thailand experience, and is a leisurely way to wind through the crumbling temples, graceful Buddha statues and fish-filled ponds. Worthwhile museums and good-value accommodation round out the package. Despite its popularity, Sukhothai rarely feels crowded, but for something off the beaten track, head to nearby Si Satchanalai-Chaliang Historical Park, where you might be the only one scaling an ancient stairway. Wat Mahathat

Ko Samui

9 Eager to please, Samui (p538) is a civilised beach-resort island for the vacationing masses, many of whom fly in and out having made hardly any contact with the local culture. Cha-weng is a luxurious stretch of sand where sun-worshippers come to see and be seen. However, there are still sleepy spits reminiscent of Samui's old moniker, 'Coconut Island', and a few gentle coves for families who need to get in and out quickly. Samui also boasts great amenities and a thriving health scene with yoga, meditation, detoxing and other yins to the island's partying yang.

Chiang Rai Province

10 The days of the Golden Triangle opium trade are over, but Chiang Rai (p308) still packs intrigue in the form of fresh-air fun such as trekking and self-guided exploration. It's also a great destination for unique cultural experiences, ranging from a visit to an Akha village to a stay at the Yunnanese-Chinese hamlet of Mae Salong. From the Mekong River to the mountains, Chiang Rai is arguably Thailand's most beautiful province, and if you've set your sights further, it's also a convenient gateway to Myanmar (Burma), Laos and China.
Wat Rong Khun

Hua Hin

11 The king's choice, Hua Hin (p512) is a fine fit for both city and sea creatures. The beaches are long and wide, the market meals are fantastic and there's even Thai culture (fancy meeting you here). Explore the quiet beaches south of the city for a more secluded feel, hike to the top of a headland shrine or master the sea and the wind with a kiteboard lesson. And of course feast like a Thai from morning, noon and night.
Kiteboarding, Hua Hin beach

Chiang Mai

12 Amid a jumble of mountains, Chiang Mai (p234) looks respectfully up to mighty Doi Suthep, whose sacred temple floats unnervingly on its forest bed. The old city, framed by a moat flopping with fish, is crammed with soaring temple peaks and twisting sois (lanes) best suited to exploration by bicycle. Stop for a temple 'monk chat', an intimate insight into those orange-robed figures. Browse the traditional handicraft outlets and when the sun sinks over Doi Suthep, feast on some of the north's best Burmese or Japanese cuisine. Wat Chiang Man

Phetchaburi

13 A delightful mix of culture and nature combine in this provincial capital (p505), a close and quiet alternative to the hectic streets of Bangkok. Explore an antique hilltop palace, sacred cave shrines and bustling temples. Wander the old shophouse neighbourhood filled with do-it-yourself businesses run by Thai aunties and grannies. Then head off to the wilds of Kaeng Krachan National Park to spot wild gibbons and exotic birds. Phetchaburi is also a smart layover for travellers returning from the south.

Cave shrine, Tham Khao Luang

Khao Sok National Park

14 A deep and dark jungle hugs the midsection of southern Thailand. This ancient rainforest (p611) is filled with long sweaty hiking routes up dramatic limestone formations that reward with postcard-perfect views. Just remember to wear leech-proof gear to prevent an involuntary blood donation. Birds and bats call this forest home as does the rare Rafflesia kerrii, one of the stinkiest flowers on the planet. Reward all your outdoor work with riverside camping and listen to the symphony of the jungle.

Accommodation among the trees

Kanchanaburi

15 Walks on the wild side are the main reason to visit Kanchanaburi (p173), where dragon-scaled limestone mountains gaze down upon dense jungle. Trek past silvery waterfalls and rushing rivers in search of elusive tigers and gibbons, then spend the night at a homestay organised through an ethnic group. Once you've explored this western province's wartime past – the infamous Bridge Over the River Kwai is here – hold on tight to experience the growing number of adventure activities, which include ziplining, kayaking and elephant rides.

Bridge Over the River Kwai

Phanom Rung Historical Park

16 Perched high atop an extinct volcano, the biggest and best Khmer ruin in Thailand (p424) is special. As you amble along the promenade, up the stairs and over the naga-flanked bridges, the sense of anticipation builds. And when you enter the temple, completely restored and still rich with Hindu sculpture, you will experience a moment of timelessness. While Phanom Rung is not as awe-inspiring as Cambodia's Angkor Wat, the experience here is impressive and different enough that you should visit both.

Mekong River

17 From the historic timber shophouses of Chiang Khan (p473) to the waterfalls of Pha Taem National Park (p441), northeastern Thailand's glorious arc of the Mekong River offers an incomparable smorgasbord of culture and beauty. This is not just the best of Isan; it's among the best of Thailand. Fishing villages, prehistoric rock paintings, holy temples, elephants, a bizarre sculpture park, and so much more are on offer for those who travel this little-known trail. Chase the meandering river aboard a rickety bus, long-tail boat or even a bicycle.

16

17

ANDERS BLOMQVIST/LONELY PLANET IMAGES ©

CHRISTIAN ASLUND/LONELY PLANET IMAGES ©

FRANK CARTER/LONELY PLANET IMAGES ©

Phuket

18 An international-strength beach resort, Phuket (p622) is an easy-peasy destination for all ages. You can fly in from Bangkok, cutting out the long land journey, and then retreat into a five-star resort or arty boutique hotel for a trouble-free tropical vacation. There are slinky stretches of sand, hedonistic party pits and all the mod-cons needed for 21st-century rest and recreation. Plus there are day trips to mangrove forests, monkey-rescue centres and a ton of watersports, from diving to surfing (when the weather is right).

Pool scene, Ko Yao Noi

Khao Yai National Park

19 Here you'll find elephants, monkeys, gibbons, hornbills, pythons, bears, a million bats and a few wily tigers. Wildlife sightings are almost at the mercy of chance, but your odds are excellent at this vast Unesco World Heritage–listed reserve (p419) just a few hours out of Bangkok. And even if you don't meet many big animals, the orchids, birds, waterfalls and sense of adventure that inevitably arises when trekking in the jungle guarantee a good day. Khao Yai's mix of scenery, accessibility and beauty is hard to beat.

Ko Samet

20 So close to Bangkok and oh so pretty, Samet (p205) is a perfect beach when your time is pinched. The jungle eclipses developments, the sand and sea are tropically proportioned and a wooded coastal trail skirts between rocky headlands and a string of beautiful coves. People-watch by day, party by night on the popular northern beaches or hide away on the southern beaches for a well-earned nap. When your vacation is done, board the boat and be back in Bangkok by lunchtime.

Jetty, Ao Cho

need to know

Currency
» Thai baht (B)

Language
» Thai

When to Go

Mae Hong Son
GO Nov-Mar

Chiang Mai
GO Nov-Feb

BANGKOK
GO Nov-Feb

Ko Samui
GO Dec-Aug

Phuket
GO Oct-Apr

Tropical climate,
Rain year round

Tropical climate,
Wet and dry season

High Season
(Nov–Mar)
» A cool and dry season follows the monsoons, meaning the landscape is lush and temperatures are comfortable.

» Western Christmas and New Year's holidays bring crowds and inflated rates to the beaches.

Shoulder Season
(Apr–Jun, Sep & Oct)
» Hot and dry (April to June) but less so in higher elevations.

» Beaches aren't crowded and ocean provides the air-con.

» September and October are ideal for the north and the Gulf coast.

Low Season
(Jul–Oct)
» Monsoon season can range from afternoon showers to multiday drenchers.

» Some islands shut down and boat service is limited during stormy weather.

» Be flexible with travel plans.

Your Daily Budget

Budget less than

1500B

» Basic guest house room: 300–800B

» Excellent market and street stall meals

» One or two evening drinks

» Get-around town with public transport

Midrange

1500– 3000B

» Flashpacker guest house or midrange hotel room: 800– 1500B

» Western food lunches and seafood dinners

» Several evening beers

» Motorbike hire

Top End over

3000B

» Boutique hotel room: 3000B

» Fine dining

» Private tours

» Car hire

Money

» ATMs widespread and charge a 150B foreign-account fee. Visa and MasterCard accepted at upmarket places.

Visas

» International air arrivals receive 30-day visa; 15-day visa at land borders; 60-day visas from a Thai consulate before leaving home.

Mobile Phones

» Thailand is on a GSM network through inexpensive pre-paid SIM cards. 3G is coming...soon.

Transport

» Extensive and affordable buses, cheap air connections, slow and scenic trains. Easy to rent cars and motorcycles.

Websites

» **Tourism Authority of Thailand** (TAT; www.tourismthailand .org) National tourism department covering info and special events.

» **Thaivisa** (www.thai visa.com) Expat site.

» **Lonely Planet** (www .lonelyplanet.com/ thailand) Country profile and what to do and see.

» **Bangkok Post** (www .bangkokpost.com) English-language daily.

» **Thai Language** (www.thai-language. com) Online dictionary, Thai tutorials.

» **Thai Travel Blogs** (www.thaitravelblogs .com) Thailand-based travel blogger.

Exchange Rates

Australia	A$1	32B
Canada	C$1	31B
China	Y10	40B
Euro zone	€1	44B
Japan	¥100	38B
New Zealand	NZ$1	25B
Russia	R10	10B
UK	£1	50B
USA	US$1	30B

For current exchange rates see www.xe.com.

Important Numbers

Thailand country code	☎66
Emergency	☎191
International access codes	☎001, 007, 008, 009 (different service providers)
Operator-assisted international calls	☎100
Tourist police	☎1155

Arriving in Thailand

» **Suvarnabhumi International Airport**

Airport Bus This service has been discontinued; there are local buses to the airport but the airport train is the better option.

Airport Rail Link Local service (45B, 30 minutes) to Phaya Thai station; express service (150B, 15 minutes) to Makkasan station.

Taxi Meter taxis 200B to 300B plus 50B airport surcharge and tolls; about an hour to the city, depending on traffic.

English in Thailand

Don't know a lick of Thai? In most places you don't need to. Tourist towns are well-stocked with English speakers. Bus drivers, market vendors and even taxi drivers are less competent speakers. If there is a communication problem, though, Thais will find someone to sort things out. In small untouristed towns, it helps to know how to order food and count in Thai. Thais are patient (and honoured) at attempts to speak their language. With just a few phrases, you'll be rewarded with big grins and heaps of praise.

Thais have their own script, which turns educated Westerners into illiterates. Street signs are always transliterated into English, but there is no standard system so spellings vary widely and confusingly. Not all letters are pronounced as they appear (ie 'ph' is 'p' and final 'l' is often 'n'). Confounding, huh?

what's new

For this new edition of Thailand, our authors have hunted down the fresh, the transformed, the hot and the happening. These are some of our favourites. For up-to-the-minute recommendations, see lonelyplanet.com/thailand.

Get to the Beach Faster

1 Recent transport routes have emerged directly from Thailand's Suvarnabhumi International Airport to the Eastern Seaboard beaches of Ko Samet and Ko Chang. That means you can bypass Bangkok and be beachside sooner.

Kiteboarding

2 If all the watersports mated and had an offspring, it would be kiteboarding. Riders harness the wind and the waves at Hua Hin, Pranburi and Phuket, the kiteboarding hot spots.

Stylish Sleep for All

3 Bangkok has sprouted hip hostels, such as NapPark Hostel and Lub*d, far removed from the functional dorms of yore.

Flying Through the Canopy

4 Why walk when you can fly through the forest on an elevated zip-line? Ropes courses have proliferated wherever trees meet tourists in such places as Ko Tao, Sangkhlaburi, Pattaya and Pai.

Extreme Diving

5 Ko Tao is no longer just for beginners. Technical divers are now exploring underwater caves and even casting off their scuba gear for lung-stretching free dives.

Cliff-hanging in Krabi

6 Everyone knows that Krabi is Thailand's rock-climbing capital but did you know that free-climbing is the latest trend? Assaults on overhanging sea cliffs are done without ropes and the ocean is there to catch you.

Hip Chiang Mai

7 Chiang Mai has its antique charms but happening Th Nimmanhaemin is a fountain of youth. Check out new restaurants such as Su Casa and the people-watching perch at At 9 Bar.

Isan Fashionista

8 More traditional than trendy, the northeast has graduated into the stylish world of boutique hotels with Khorat's V-One, Khao Yai's Hotel des Artists and Khon Kaen's Glacier Hotel.

Ringleaders: Muay Thai Warriors

9 Rather than packing on the pounds, train to be a lean, mean fighting machine at the new crop of *moo·ay tai* (muay thai) training and fitness camps, such as Pattaya's Fairtex Sports Club and Phuket's Promthep Muay Thai Camp.

Resort Beaches on the Cheap

10 Thailand's beaches have transformed quickly from bamboo huts to luxury villas. We can't turn back time but we've got more budget options on big-spender beaches, such as Ko Kut, Ko Chang and Hua Hin.

if you like...

Beaches

From intimate coves to leggy coastlines, Thailand's beaches are beauty queens and draw a steady crowd of international sun-seekers. Long gone are the days of having paradise to yourself but the scenery is still supreme.

Ko Phi-Phi A real looker, this Andaman island has craggy limestone sea cliffs and ribbons of cerulean water and a boozy party scene (p662)

Ko Pha-Ngan The original beach bum island hosts boisterous Full Moon parties and a whole lot of hammock hanging in between (p556)

Hua Hin City-meets-sea for beach lovers who need sand and sophistication (p512)

Trang Islands A family favourite with soaring limestone cliffs, blonde sands and techno-free nights (p680)

Bang Saphan Yai With a handful of cheap huts on the beach, this mainland spot is delightfully stuck in the '90s (p530)

Diving & Snorkelling

The warm clear waters of the Gulf of Thailand and the Andaman Sea harbour a variety of underwater landscapes and marine species that rank Thailand among the world's top diving destinations. The Andaman is the regional blockbuster, while the Gulf is good for beginners.

Surin & Similan Islands National Marine Parks One of the world's top diving spots, these Andaman islands have dramatic rocky gorges, hard and soft coral reefs and a laundry list of marine life; live-aboard trips depart from Khao Lak (p616)

Ko Lanta Nearby feeding stations for manta rays, whale sharks and other large pelagic fish earn this Andaman island high diving marks (p669)

Ko Tao With affordable dive schools, shallow waters and year-round conditions, Ko Tao remains the country's scuba-training island. Its near-shore reefs mean you can go snorkelling right after breakfast (p571)

Ko Kradan A snorkeller's paradise with pristine hard and soft corals just past the silky shore (p682)

Great Food

Thai food is fabulously flavoured, remarkably convenient and ridiculously cheap. Street stalls spring up wherever there are appetites, night markets serve everyone dinner, and family restaurants deliver colourful plates of traditional recipes.

Curries The soup that eats like a meal, Thai curry is pungent, fiery and colourful. Bangkok, southern Thailand and northern Thailand all whip up their own variations.

Isan cuisine The food that fuels labour, the northeast's triumvirate dishes – *gài yâhng* (grilled chicken), *sôm·đam* (spicy green papaya salad) and *kôw něe·o* (sticky rice) – have converts across the country.

Seafood Grilled prawns, spicy squid stir-fries, crab curries, fried mussels – get thee to the coast and dine on the fruits of the sea.

Fruits Whole meals are made up of the luscious variety of Thai fruits, which are sold in abundance at day markets or displayed like precious jewels in glass cases by roaming vendors.

Cooking Courses Learn how to replicate the tricks of the trade at cooking schools in Bangkok (p96) or Chiang Mai (p255)

If you like... learning, make your holiday smarter by studying Thai language, traditional massage or Buddhist meditation in Chiang Mai (p252)

Culture: Temples & Ruins

The Thai landscape is filled with monuments to the gods, be they glittering Buddhist temples or ancient Khmer sanctuaries. Many of the country's most famous temples are de facto museums, sheltering religious art, history and regional identities.

Bangkok The seat of the monarchy is also the seat of Thai Buddhism, and its most exalted Buddha figure resides comfortably in Wat Phra Kaew (p58)

Ayuthaya The ruins of this fabled city stand testament to the formative years of Thai history, identity and architecture (p157)

Sukhothai Cycle around the well-preserved grounds of this ancient city, the capital of one of Thailand's first home-grown kingdoms (p355)

Chiang Mai Northern Thailand boasts its own historic and artistic lineage and within Chiang Mai's old walled city are antique teak temples decorated with tinkling bells (p234)

Phanom Rung This Khmer outpost built in the Angkor style has surveyed this rural landscape for centuries (p424)

Outdoor Adventure

From the mountains in the north to the rainforests of the south, a variety of adventures allows visitors to trek, paddle and be carried by elephants through the tropical landscape. Along the mountain ridges, ethnic hill-tribe villages hold on to an ancient way of life.

Kanchanaburi Exert a little for a big reward at an outdoor buffet of waterfall spotting, rafting and elephant riding, just a short journey from Bangkok (p173)

Kaeng Krachan National Park Disappear into a wild landscape in this little-visited park, south of Bangkok (p509)

Khao Yai National Park Spot elephants, monkeys, snakes and creepy-crawlies in Thailand's oldest national park (p419)

Mae Hong Son Small-scale trekking groups head off into the mountainous frontier between Thailand and Burma (p380)

Ko Chang When you tire of the sea, plunge into the jungle-covered hills where local guides have played since childhood (p216)

Khao Sok National Park Canoe and hike through Thailand's ancient rainforest studded with limestone mountains (p611)

Festivals & Festivities

Thais love to turn up the tunes, fire up the grill and open a bottle of booze in honour of any occasion: home-grown festivals, imported holidays and even made-up excuses to party.

Full Moon Party Ko Pha-Ngan's lunar event turns sunbathers into all-night, day-glo revellers. Copy-cat moon parties and other lunar cycles are celebrated throughout the islands.

Music festivals From jazz to alt-rock, Thailand hosts an impressive playlist of music festivals. Bangkok's Fat Festival features indie bands, Hua Hin prefers jazz and Pattaya does international/Asian rock. Ko Samui hosts international DJs and occasionally Pai pays tribute to reggae.

Fruit festivals Provincial towns celebrate their signature agricultural product with genuine small-town charm. Chanthaburi pays homage to its orchards of mangosteens, durian and rambutan, while Chiang Rai celebrates the venerable lychee.

Songkran The festival begins with the use of water as a mark of respect then, in some locations, erupts into a water war where no one stays dry (p23)

month by month

Top Events

1 **Songkran**, April
2 **Loi Krathong**, November
3 **Ubon Ratchathani's Khao Phansaa**, July
4 **Vegetarian Festival**, September
5 **Surin Elephant Round-up**, November

January

The weather is cool and dry in Thailand, ushering in the peak tourist season when Europeans escape dreary winter weather.

 Chinese New Year

Thais with Chinese ancestry celebrate the Chinese lunar new year (dates vary) with a week of house-cleaning and fireworks. Phuket, Bangkok and Pattaya all host citywide festivities, but in general Chinese New Year (drùd jeen) is a family event.

February

Still in the high season swing, snowbirds flock to Thailand for sun and fun.

Makha Bucha

One of three holy days marking important moments of Buddha's life, Makha Bucha (mah·ká boo·chah) falls on the full moon of the third lunar month and commemorates Buddha preaching to 1250 enlightened monks who came to hear him 'without prior summons'. A public holiday, it's mainly a day for temple visits. Organisations and schools will often make merit as a group at a local temple.

Flower Festival

Chiang Mai displays its floral beauty during a three-day period. The festival highlight is the flower-decorated floats that parade through town.

March

Hot and dry season approaches and the beaches start to empty out. The winds kick up ushering in kite-flying and kiteboarding season. This is also Thailand's semester break (mid term), and students head out on sightseeing trips.

Pattaya International Music Festival

Pattaya showcases pop and rock bands from across Asia at this free music event, attracting bus loads of Bangkok university students.

Kite-Flying Festivals

During the windy season, colourful kites battle it out over the skies of Sanam Luang in Bangkok and elsewhere in the country.

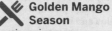 **Golden Mango Season**

Luscious ripe mangoes come into season from March to June and are sliced before your eyes, packed in a container with sticky rice and accompanied with a sweet sauce. Reason enough to visit in the 'summer'.

April

Hot, dry weather sweeps across the land and the tourist season is winding down, except for one last hurrah during Songkran. Make reservations well in advance since the whole country is on the move for this holiday.

Songkran

Thailand's traditional new year (12–14 April) starts out as a respectful affair then degenerates into a water war. Morning visits to the temple involve colourful processions of the sacred Buddha images, which are ceremoniously sprinkled with water. Elders are shown respect by younger family members by having water sprinkled on their hands. Afterwards Thais load up their water guns and head out to the streets for battle: water is thrown, catapulted and sprayed from roving commandos and outfitted pick-up trucks at willing and unwilling targets. Chiang Mai and Bangkok are the epicentres of the battles. Innocent bystanders shelter indoors until the ammunition runs out.

May

Leading up to the rainy season, festivals encourage plentiful rains and bountiful harvests. This is an under-appreciated shoulder season when prices are lower and tourists are few but it is still incredibly hot.

Royal Ploughing Ceremony

This royal ceremony employs astrology and ancient Brahman rituals to kick off the rice-planting season. Sacred oxen are hitched to a wooden plough and part the ground of Sanam Luang in Bangkok. The ritual was revived in the 1960s by the king, and Crown Prince Maha Vajiralongkorn has assumed the ceremony's helm.

Rocket Festival

In the northeast, where rain can be scarce, villagers craft bamboo rockets (*bâng fai*) that are fired into the sky to encourage precipitation so that the upcoming rice-planting season will be successful. This festival is celebrated in Yasothon, Ubon Ratchathani and Nong Khai.

Visakha Bucha

The holy day of Visakha Bucha (*wí·săh·kà boo·chah*) falls on the 15th day of the waxing moon in the sixth lunar month and commemorates the date of the Buddha's birth, enlightenment and *parinibbana* (passing away). Activities are centred around the temple.

June

In some parts of the country, the rainy season is merely an afternoon shower, leaving the rest of the day for music and merriment.

Hua Hin Jazz Festival

Jazz groups descend on this royal retreat for a musical homage to the king, an accomplished jazz saxophonist and composer.

Phi Ta Khon

The Buddhist holy day of Bun Phra Wet is given a Carnival makeover in Dan Sai village in northeastern Thailand. Revellers disguise themselves in garish 'spirit' costumes and parade through the village streets wielding wooden phalluses and downing rice whisky. The festival commemorates a Buddhist legend in which a host of spirits (*pĕe*, also spelt '*phi*') appeared to greet the Buddha-to-be (Prince Vessantara or Phra Wet), the penultimate birth. Dates vary.

July

With the start of the rainy season, the religious community and attendant

festivals prepare for Buddhist Lent, a period of reflection and meditation. If you can stand a little drizzle, this is an ideal time for rural sightseeing as rice planting begins and the parched landscape turns a verdant green.

Asahna Bucha

The full moon of the eighth lunar month commemorates Buddha's first sermon during Asahna (also spelt Asalha) Bucha (*ah·săhn·hà boo·chah*).

Khao Phansaa

The day after Asahna Bucha marks the beginning of Buddhist Lent (the first day of the waning moon in the eighth lunar month), the traditional time for men to enter the monkhood and when monks typically retreat inside the monastery for a period of study and meditation. During Khao Phansaa, worshippers make offerings of candles and other necessities to the temples and attend ordinations. In Ubon Ratchathani, the traditional candle offerings have grown into elaborately carved wax sculptures that are shown off during the Candle Parade.

August

Overcast skies and daily showers mark the middle of the rainy season. The predictable rains just adds to the ever-present humidity.

HM the Queen's Birthday

The Thai Queen's Birthday (12 August) is a public holiday and national mother's day. In Bangkok, the day is marked with cultural displays along Th Ratchadamnoen and Sanam Luang.

October

Religious preparations for the end of the rainy season and the end of Buddhist Lent begin. The monsoons are reaching the finish line (in most of the country).

Vegetarian Festival

A holiday from meat is taken for nine days (during the ninth lunar month) in adherence with Chinese Buddhist beliefs of mind and body purification. Cities with large Thai-Chinese populations, such as Bangkok, Hua Hin, Pattaya, Trang and Krabi, are festooned with yellow banners heralding vegetarian vendors, and merit-makers dressed in white shuffle off for meditation retreats. In Phuket the festival gets extreme, with entranced marchers turning themselves into human shish kebabs.

Ork Phansaa

The end of the Buddhist lent (three lunar months after Khao Phansaa) is marked by the *gà·tǐn* ceremony, in which new robes are given to the monks by merit-makers. The peculiar natural phenomenon known as the '*naga* fireballs' coincides with Ork Phansaa. In Mae Hong Son, the end of Buddhist Lent is marked by the Shan-style Jong Para festival, in which miniature castles are paraded on poles

(Above) The end of the rainy season is the time to explore beaches such as Ko Tarutao Marine National Park
(Below) Getting soaked at Songkran, Chiang Mai

to the temples. Localities near rivers and the ocean celebrate with traditional long-tail boat races. Nakhon Phanom's Illuminated Boat Festival electrifies an old-fashioned tradition.

★ King Chulalongkorn Day

Rama V is honoured on the anniversary of his death at the Royal Plaza in Dusit. Crowds of devotees come to make merit with incense and flower garlands. Held on 23 October.

November

The cool, dry season has arrived and if you get here early enough, you'll beat the tourist crowds. The beaches are inviting and the landscape is lush: perfect for trekking and waterfall-spotting.

★ Surin Elephant Round-up

Held on the third weekend of November, Thailand's biggest elephant show celebrates this northeastern province's most famous residents. The event in Surin

begins with a colourful elephant parade culminating in a fruit buffet for the pachyderms. Re-enactments of Thai battles showcase mahouts and elephants wearing royal military garb.

★ Loi Krathong

One of Thailand's most beloved festivals, Loi Krathong is celebrated on the first full moon of the 12th lunar month. The festival thanks the river goddess for providing life to the fields and forests and asks for forgiveness for the polluting ways of humans. Small handmade boats (called *kràthong* or *grà·tong*) are sent adrift in the country's waterways. The *grà·tong* are origami-like vessels made from banana leaves. They're decorated with flowers, and incense, candles and coins are placed in them. Loi Krathong is believed to have originated in Sukhothai, where it is celebrated today with much pomp. In Chiang Mai the festival is also called Yi Peng.

★ Lopburi Monkey Festival

During the last week of November, the town's

troublesome macaques get pampered with their very own banquet, while merit-makers watch merrily.

December

The peak of the tourist season has returned with fair skies, busy beach resorts and a holiday mood.

★ HM the King's Birthday

Honouring the king's birthday on 5 December, this public holiday hosts parades and merit-making events; it is also recognised as national father's day. Th Ratchadamnoen Klang in Bangkok is decorated with lights and regalia. Everyone wears pink shirts, pink being the colour associated with the monarchy.

★ Chiang Mai Red Cross and Winter Fair

A 10-day festival that displays Chiang Mai's cultural heritage with a country-fair atmosphere; expect food (lots of it) and traditional performances.

itineraries

Whether you've got six days or 60, these itineraries provide a starting point for the trip of a lifetime. Want more inspiration? Head online to lonelyplanet. com/thorntree to chat with other travellers.

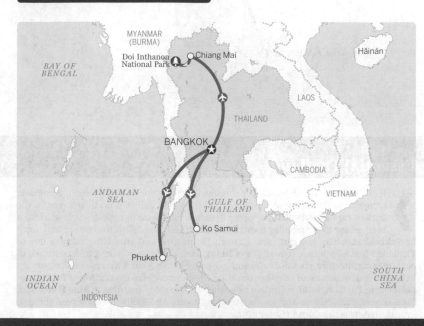

Two Weeks
Just A Quickie

> Even if you're only doing a Thailand 'pop-in', you can still pack in a full itinerary thanks to the affordability of domestic flights. Start off in **Bangkok** and then fly to the tropical beach resorts of **Ko Samui** or **Phuket**. Although both are international superstars, there are plenty of quiet corners if needed, and beaches with personalities to suit every sand hunter. If you find yourself on a spot that fits like a wet bathing suit, shop around the island before plotting your escape route to the next destination.

Once you've tired of sand and sun, fly up to **Chiang Mai** for a Thai cooking class and temple-spotting. Then explore the surrounding countryside filled with mountainous road trips and hill-tribe trekking. Pay homage to Thailand's highest peak at **Doi Inthanon National Park**.

Return to Bangkok with a tan, a Thai recipe book and lots of travel tales for the water cooler.

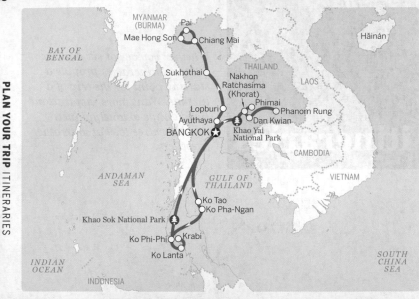

One Month
Essential Thailand

> If you've got a month to wander through Thailand, spend a few days in **Bangkok**, adjusting to the heat and the chaos, and then take the train north stopping in the ancient capital of **Ayuthaya**, where Thailand built a small regional empire. Make a brief detour to the monkey town of **Lopburi**. And then follow the culture trail north to **Sukhothai**, where you can cycle through the historic and crumbling ruins of one of Thailand's first kingdoms. Hightail it to **Chiang Mai**, made up of a delightful collection of old Lanna architecture, youthful cafes and easygoing living. A week may pass before you get itchy feet. Mountains await in either direction from Chiang Mai. Go northwest for the hippie scene in **Pai**. Follow the mountain ridge through the misty morning to **Mae Hong Son**, for a slice of Shan culture and low-key trekking tours. And follow the loop road through little dusty towns to return to Chiang Mai.

By now the beach is calling so transit back through Bangkok and then on to the classic Gulf of Thailand stops: **Ko Pha-Ngan** for beach bumming and partying and **Ko Tao** for deep-sea diving and snorkelling.

Hop over to the Andaman Coast to see those famous postcard views of limestone mountains jutting out of the sea. **Ko Phi-Phi** is the prettiest (and one of the priciest) of them all but **Ko Lanta** has the quintessential beach vibe and a thriving dive scene. Rock climbers opt for nearby **Krabi**. On the way back north detour through the rainforests of **Khao Sok National Park**.

Transit again through Bangkok to dip your toes into the northeast, the agricultural heartland. Crawl through the jungles of **Khao Yai National Park**. Then head to **Nakhon Ratchasima** (Khorat), a transit point for trips to the Angkor ruins at **Phimai** and the pottery village of **Dan Kwian**. Follow the Khmer trail east to **Phanom Rung**, the most important and visually impressive of the Angkor temples in Thailand. Surrounding Phanom Rung are a handful of smaller more remote temples known for their regal but forgotten ambiance.

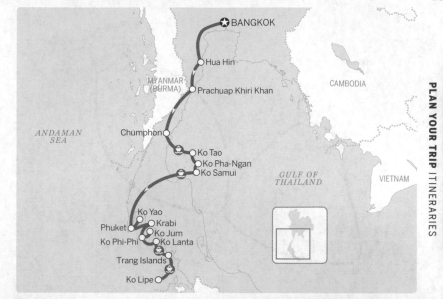

Southern Islands & Beaches

> If your bragging buddies back home have sent you to Thailand with a long list of must-see beaches, then prepare for a marathon beach binge. From Bangkok, dip south into **Hua Hin**, for wide sandy beaches and city amenities, and to **Prachuap Khiri Khan**, a mellow seaside town sheltered from the tourist crowds. Then slide down to **Chumphon** to island hop. Swim with the fishes in **Ko Tao**, howl at the full moon in **Ko Pha-Ngan** or hang-out with the bronzing bodies in **Ko Samui**.

Cross the peninsula to imbibe on the Andaman resort island of **Phuket** or pop over to mellow **Ko Yao** to rock climb the limestone mountains or just smile at the scenery. Scramble up or paddle around **Krabi's** scenic missile-shaped peaks planted in the sea. **Ko Phi-Phi** is a party-hard pretty girl and **Ko Lanta** is a kick-back island idyll. **Ko Jum** has a lot of nothing, a perfect perk these days.

The **Trang Islands** are an up-and-comer with karst scenery and cerulean seas. Time is getting tight but you might be able to squeeze in one last stop at **Ko Lipe**, that last grip of beach party mayhem this side of the Andaman.

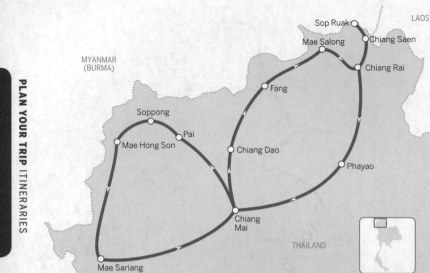

Two to Three Weeks
Northern Thailand

Climb into the bosom of lush mountains and the ethnic minority villages that cling to the border of Thailand, Myanmar and Laos.

Chiang Mai is an ideal base for northern culture and exploration with a menu of meditation, language and massage courses on offer. Follow the northwest spur to **Pai**, a mountain retreat with daytime strolls and night-time carousing, Next is **Soppong**, a mecca for caving. Continue to **Mae Hong Son** to immerse yourself in a remote region more akin to Burma than Bangkok. The last stop along the route is at **Mae Sariang**, a small river-side town developing a good reputation for sustainable trekking tours.

Return to civilisation in Chiang Mai and plot your next campaign towards Chiang Rai. More mountains await northwards in **Chiang Dao**, a sober alternative to Pai. Then take the backdoor to Chiang Rai through **Fang** and zigzagging up the mountain ridge to **Mae Salong**, a Yunnanese tea settlement. Slide into **Chiang Rai** for a hill-tribe homestay and culturally sensitive treks and continue on to the formerly infamous Golden Triangle towns of **Chiang Saen** and **Sop Ruak**. Bypass the crowds with a stop in **Phayao**, a pleasant northern town for temple-spotting, before returning to Chiang Mai.

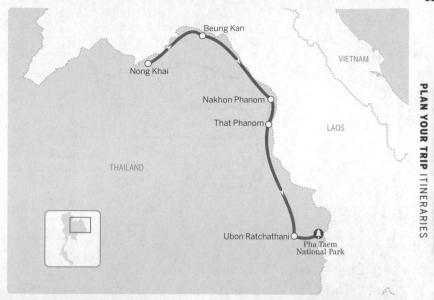

One to Two Weeks
Mekong River

> There aren't a lot of big-ticket attractions in Thailand's rural northeast (known as Isan) but cultural chameleons will find an old-fashioned way of life, easygoing people and interesting homestays that mix lodging with lounging around the rice fields. The most scenic route through the region is along the Mekong River, which divides Thailand and Laos. The border towns barely recognise the boundary and often share more cultural attributes with their foreign neighbours than with Bangkok.

Start in the charming town of **Nong Khai**, a rock-skipping throw from Laos and an easy border-crossing point. If the pace here is too fast, follow the river road east to **Bueng Kan**, a dusty speck of a town with a nearby temple built on a rocky outcrop and several neighbouring homestays with forays into wild-elephant territory. Pass through **Nakhon Phanom** for its picturesque river promenade and tiny **That Phanom**, with its famous Lao-style temple, honoured with a vibrant 10-day festival in January/February.

For a little urban Isan, check out **Ubon Ratchathani**, surrounded by the **Pha Taem National Park**, river rapids and handicraft villages. From here you can exit into Laos at Pakse or catch an overnight train to Bangkok.

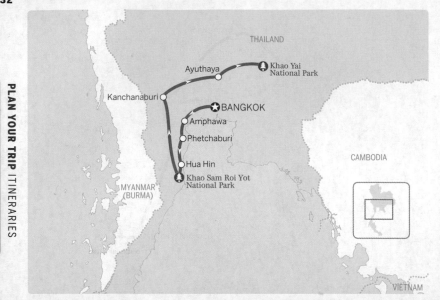

One to Two Weeks
Bangkok & Around

If you're pressed for time or don't want to waste time travelling, there is an amazing diversity of sites within 150km of Bangkok. Take the backdoor route aboard a scenic commuter rail line out of Bangkok to **Amphawa**, a canal-crossed community that hosts a floating market beloved by foodie Thais. Appreciate history away from the capital's hectic streets in **Phetchaburi**, once a royal retreat with a hilltop palace and fascinating cave shrines. Then rest and recreate in **Hua Hin** and the long and sandy coastline that stretches south all the way to **Khao Sam Roi Yot National Park** with its collection of interior karst mountains and mangrove swamps.

Backtrack north to **Kanchanaburi**, which played a minor but well-memorialised role in WWII. The forested mountains to the northwest are ideal for a variety of outdoor adventures. Skirt around the present-day capital to the once-glorious capital of **Ayuthaya** for a Thai history lesson. Then catch the train to **Khao Yai National Park**, for one last foray into nature's jungle before returning to Bangkok's concrete jungle.

» (above) Beach scene, Ko Lipe (p687)
» (left) Elephant trekking, Chiang Mai Province (p232)

Responsible Travel

Don'ts

Don't step on a dropped bill to prevent it from blowing away – Thai money bears a picture of the king.

Never step over someone or their personal belongings.

Avoid tying your shoes to the outside of your backpack where they might accidentally brush against someone.

Don't get a tattoo of the Buddha – the culture ministry is seeking to ban the practice and it is considered sacrilegious.

Dos

Stand respectfully for the national anthem (unless you're inside a home or building), which is played at 8am and 6pm.

Rise for the royal anthem, which is played in movie theatres before every screening.

Greet people with a smile and a cheery *sà·wàt·dee kráp* if you're male or *sà·wàt·dee kâ* if you're female.

Bring a gift if you're invited to a Thai home and take off your shoes when you enter.

Lower your head slightly when passing between two people having a conversation or when passing near a monk.

Dress modestly (cover to the elbows and ankles) for temple visits and always remove your shoes when entering any building containing a Buddha image.

Extend the right hand out while the left hand gently grips the right elbow when handing an object to another person or receiving something – truly polite behaviour.

Hair-raising adventures and postcard snapshots make great souvenirs from a trip, but the travel experiences that become lifelong companions are the moments when you stop being an invading alien and connect with someone who may not speak your language or share your culture. Stepping outside of the comfortable tourist zones and into the community can elevate you from an economic opportunity to an honoured guest and even a friend.

There are a number of ways to respectfully visit and interact with a host country: learning the language, customs and culture; volunteering your time and skills to disadvantaged people; and supporting businesses with environmental or social justice missions. The People & Culture chapter (p721) provides insights into Thailand's rich heritage and gives tips on culture.

Cultural Etiquette

The monarchy and the religion (which are often viewed as interconnected) are treated with extreme deference in Thailand. Thais avoid criticising or disparaging the royal family for fear of offending someone or, worse, being charged for lèse majesté, which carries a jail sentence. With the king's increasing frailness, lese-majesty charges have increasingly been doled out to foreigners, Thai expats, political rivals and academics.

Buddha images are sacred objects. Thais consider it bad form to pose in front of one for a photo or to clamber upon them (in the case of temple ruins), instead they would show respect by performing a *wâi* (a prayer-like gesture) to the figure no matter how humble it is. As part of their ascetic vows, monks are not supposed to touch or be touched by women. If a woman wants to hand something to a monk, the object is placed within reach of the monk or on the monk's 'receiving cloth'. Women don't sit next to monks on public transport and they cross out of the way on streets to avoid an accidental brush.

From a spiritual viewpoint, Thais regard the head as the highest and most sacred part of the body and the feet as the dirtiest and lowest. Many of the taboos associated with the feet have a practical derivation as well. Traditionally Thais ate, slept and entertained on the floor of their homes with little in the way of furniture. To keep their homes and eating surfaces clean, the feet (and shoes) contracted a variety of rules.

When sitting in a religious edifice, Thais sit in the 'mermaid' position with their legs folded to one side so that the bottoms of the feet or the toes aren't pointed at a Buddha image.

Shoes aren't worn inside private homes and temple buildings, as a sign of respect and for sanitary reasons. Thais can kick off their shoes in one fluid step and many lace-up shoes are modified by the wearer to become slip-ons. Thais also step over the threshold, which is where the spirit of the house is believed to reside. On some buses and 3rd-class trains, you'll see Thais prop up their feet on the adjacent bench; while this isn't the height of propriety, do notice that they always remove their shoes before doing so. Thais also take off their shoes if they need to climb up onto a chair or seat.

Thais don't touch each other's head or ruffle their hair as a sign of affection. Occasionally you'll see young people touching each other's head, which is a teasing gesture, maybe even a slight insult, between friends.

Social Conventions & Gestures

The traditional Thai greeting is made with a prayerlike palms-together gesture known as *wâi*. The depth of the bow and the placement of the fingers in relation to the face is dependent on the status of the person receiving the *wâi*. Adults don't *wâi* children and in most cases service people (when they are doing their jobs) aren't *wâi-ed*, though this is a matter of personal discretion.

In the more traditional parts of the country, it is not proper for members of the opposite sex to touch one another, either as lovers or as friends. Hand-holding is not acceptable behaviour outside of the major cities such as Bangkok. But same-sex touching is quite common and is typically a sign of friendship, not sexual attraction. Older Thai men might grab a younger man's thigh in the same way that buddies slap each other on the back. Thai women are especially affectionate with female friends, often sitting close to one another or linking arms.

Thais hold modesty in personal dress in high regard, though this is changing among the younger generation. The importance of modesty extends to the beach as well. Except for urban Bangkokians, most Thais swim fully clothed. For this reason, sunbathing nude or topless is not acceptable and in some cases is even illegal.

See p726 for other insights on dealing with Thai people.

Tourism

Most forms of tourism, despite the prevailing prejudices, have a positive economic effect on the local economy in Thailand: providing jobs for young workers and business opportunities for entrepreneurs. But in an effort to be more than just a consumer, many travellers look for opportunities to spend where their money might be needed, either on charitable causes or activities that preserve traditional ways of life. Thailand has done a surprisingly good job at adapting to this emerging trend by promoting village craft programs and homestays. Unfortunately, much of this is aimed at the domestic market rather than international visitors. But more and more, foreign tourists can engage in these small-scale tourism models that offer an insight into traditional ways.

Homestays

You can travel independently without isolating yourself from the culture by staying at one of Thailand's local homestays. More

TOP HOMESTAYS

» Ban Prasat, Nakhon Ratchasima

» Ban Kham Pia, Bueng Kan

» Ban Ta Klang, Surin

» Ban Mae Kampong, Chiang Mai

popular with domestic tourists, homestays differ from guest houses in that visitors are welcomed into a family's home, typically in a small village that isn't on the tourist trail. Accommodation is basic: usually a mat or foldable mattress on the floor, or occasionally a family will have a private room. Rates include lodging, meals with the family and cultural activities that highlight a region's traditional way of life, from rice farming to silk weaving. English fluency varies, so homestays are also an excellent way to exercise your spoken Thai.

Hill-Tribe Trekking

Though marginalised within mainstream society, the hill-tribe minorities remain a strong tourism draw with large and small businesses organising trekking tours to villages for cultural displays and interactions. Economically, it is unclear whether hill-tribe trekking helps alleviate the poverty of the hill-tribe groups and in turn helps to maintain their separate ethnic identity. Most agree that a small percentage of the profits from trekking filters down to individual families within hill-tribe villages, giving them a small source of income that might prevent urban migration. One guide we spoke to estimated that 50% of the tour budget was spent on purchasing food, lodging and supplies from hill-tribe merchants at the host village.

In general the trekking business has become more socially conscious than in previous decades. Most companies now tend to limit the number of visits to a particular area to lessen the impact of outsiders on the daily lives of ordinary villagers. But the industry still has a long way to go. It should be noted that trekking companies are Thai owned and employ Thai guides, another bureaucratic impediment regarding citizenship for ethnic minorities. Without an identification card, guides from the hill tribes do not qualify for a Tourist Authority of Thailand (TAT) tour guide

licence and so are less than desirable job candidates.

Trekkers should also realise that the minority tribes maintain their own distinct cultural identity and many continue their animistic traditions, which define social taboos and conventions. If you're planning on visiting hill-tribe villages on an organised trek, talk to your guide about dos and don'ts.

Here is a general prescription to get you started.

» Always ask for permission before taking any photos of tribes people, especially at private moments inside their dwellings. Many traditional belief systems regard photography with suspicion.

» Show respect for religious symbols and rituals. Don't touch totems at village entrances or sacred items hanging from trees. Don't participate in ceremonies unless invited to.

» Avoid cultivating the practice of begging, especially among children. Don't hand out candy unless you can also arrange for modern dentistry. Talk to your guide about donating to a local school instead.

» Avoid public nudity and be careful not to undress near an open window where village children might be able to peep in.

» Don't flirt with members of the opposite sex unless you plan on marrying them. Don't drink or do drugs with the villagers; altered states sometimes lead to culture clashes.

» Smile at villagers even if they stare at you. Ask your guide how to say 'hello' in the tribal language.

» Avoid public displays of affection, which in some traditional systems are viewed as offensive to the spirit world.

» Don't interact with the villagers' livestock, even the free-roaming pigs; these creatures are valuable possessions, not entertainment oddities. Also avoid interacting with jungle animals, which in some belief systems are viewed as visiting spirits.

» Don't litter.

TOP PLACES FOR HILL-TRIBE TREKKING

» Chiang Mai

» Chiang Rai

» Mae Hong Son

» Mae Sariang

» Adhere to the same feet taboos that apply to Thai culture (see p34). Don't step on the threshold of a house, prop your feet up against the fire or wear your shoes inside.

Elephant Encounters

Throughout Thai history, elephants have been revered for their strength, endurance and intelligence, working alongside their mahouts harvesting teak, transporting goods through mountainous terrain or fighting ancient wars.

But many of the elephant's traditional roles have either been outsourced to machines or outlawed (logging was banned in 1989), leaving the domesticated animals and their mahouts without work. Some mahouts turned to begging on the streets in Bangkok and other tourist centres, a dangerous practice that the government is working to curb through fines and incentive programs.

But most elephants, like many human migrants, found work in Thailand's burgeoning tourism industry, which varies from circus-like shows to elephant camps giving rides to tourists. Other elephant encounters include mahout-training schools, while sanctuaries and rescue centres provide modest retirement homes to animals that can no longer work and are no longer profitable to their owners. See the boxed text, p38 for more.

There is much debate within the animal welfare community as to how to prevent abuse and ensure humane conditions for domesticated elephants. Until an alternative is developed tourism at least helps to temporarily fix the elephant unemployment issue and with proper education conscientious tourists can ensure that safe working conditions for elephants are the industry norm.

Here are some questions to ask the elephant camps to make sure you've chosen a well-run operation. Also see Environment & Wildlife (p751) for recommended elephant centres and sanctuaries.

» Does the camp employ a veterinarian? Good camps keep their elephants under regular medical supervision.

» What is its policy on procuring new elephants? Many of the wild-caught animals come from the Thai–Burmese border.

» How many hours per day do the elephants work? A brisk-paced walk for about four hours per day (with breaks for eating and drinking in between) is considered adequate exercise.

» How many adults do the elephants carry? Elephants can carry a maximum of 150kg (330lb) of weight on its back, plus a mahout on its neck. Tally up you and your partner's combined weight and request a separate elephant if you tip the scales.

» Are the elephants kept in a shady spot near fresh water and a food source? What do they eat? A balanced diet includes a mixture of fruit, grasses, bamboo and pineapple shoots.

» Do the elephants have noticeable wounds? This is often a sign of mistreatment.

Diving

The popularity of Thailand's diving industry places immense pressure on fragile coral sites. To help preserve the ecology, adhere to these simple rules.

» Avoid touching living marine organisms, standing on coral or dragging equipment (such as fins) across the reef. Coral polyps can be damaged by even the gentlest contact.

» When treading water in shallow reef areas, be careful not to kick up clouds of sand, which can easily smother the delicate reef organisms.

» Take great care in underwater caves where your air bubbles can be caught within the roof and leave previously submerged organisms high and dry.

» Join a coral clean-up campaign that's sponsored by dive shops.

» Don't feed the fish or allow your dive operator to dispose of excess food in the water. The fish become dependent on this food source and don't tend to the algae on the coral, causing harm to the reef.

Volunteering

When you travel to another country it is easier to see the areas of suffering much more clearly than you can in your own country. And Thailand is still technically a developing country, lacking a tight-knit social safety net and an executed environmental protection program. There are a myriad of organisations in Thailand to address both the needs of the locals and visitors' desire to help.

PACHYDERM DILEMMA

Working elephants have a career of about 50 years and are trained at a young age by two mahouts, usually a father-and-son team, who can see the animal through its lifetime. Thai law requires that elephants be retired and released into the wild at age 61. They often live for 80 years or more. It costs about 30,000B (US$1000) per month to provide a comfortable living standard for an elephant; this amount is equivalent to the salary of Thailand's upper middle class.

Activists within the elephant welfare world disagree about the best way to handle the domesticated population, which numbers about 3500 elephants. At issue is the current solution to the problem of unemployed elephants, namely elephant treks and mahout programs. Some activists maintain that elephants should not be domesticated, bred or ridden because the process is cruel and painful for the animals. Instead the animals should live in as natural a state as possible, either in the wild or in wild-like sanctuary settings.

Proponents of working elephants believe that elephant tourism can provide these domesticated creatures and their human caretakers (the mahouts, who are often part of an extended elephant-herding tribe in Surin) with a respectable livelihood and comfortable working and living conditions that they otherwise wouldn't be able to afford. Many believe that there isn't enough wild space to 'free' the elephants and without the elephant camps the mahouts and the animals would return to a life of begging.

Another complicating factor is the buying of elephants to tourism-related businesses, including sanctuaries (the term used by sanctuaries is 'rescue' though there is often a monetary transaction with the elephant owner). According to Thai law, captive elephants can be bought, sold and transported as long as they have the proper permits and certificates verifying that the animal was born on a farm instead of in the forest. But the system is easily manipulated and it is more profitable to sell a 'free' forest elephant than to breed one. Poachers are typically local people with knowledge of elephant round-ups, the traditional process of corralling wild populations. In other cases, the animals are caught in Burma and transported across the border.

Conscientious elephant camps are aware of the practice and have a variety of methods of circumventing fraud. The Royal Elephant Kraal & Village in Ayuthaya has a successful breeding program and doesn't engage in the elephant trade. The Golden Triangle Asian Elephant Foundation, affiliated with the Anantara and Four Season resorts in Sop Ruak, hires elephants and their mahouts on a contractual basis instead of buying elephants. Wildlife Friends Foundation Thailand in Phetchaburi buys old and infirmed animals at below-market prices to prevent the mahout from buying a wild-caught replacement.

Humanitarian & Educational Work

Education is the primary source for volunteer opportunities. In Thailand, the public schools offer tuition-free education for 12 years to anyone living legally in the country. The definition of a legal resident excludes some hill-tribe villagers in the northern mountains and undocumented Burmese refugees and immigrants. Even for members of these groups who do have the proper documentation, the associated fees for attending school (such as uniforms, supplies and books) are often too expensive for families to afford. The incidental fees of an education

also exclude many fully recognised but poor citizens living in the northeast.

Not only is there a need for volunteer teachers but the teaching profession is a revered one and offers rewarding interactions into a supportive community. If you want more of a cultural challenge than just a job overseas, look into programs in rural areas where English is limited and foreigners are few. In these situations, you'll learn Thai more quickly and observe a way of life with deeper connections to the past.

Northern Thailand, especially Chiang Mai and Chiang Rai, has a number of volunteer opportunities working with disadvantaged hill-tribe groups. Chiang Mai, Mae Sot and Sangkhlaburi have distressed communities of Burmese refugees and migrants. There are also many volunteer teaching positions in northeastern Thailand, the country's agricultural heartland. The destination chapters also have reviews of small-scale volunteer opportunities at orphanages and drop-in centres.

The following organisations are worth investigating:

Akha Association for Education and Culture in Thailand (Afect; www.akhathai.org; Chiang Rai) A hill-tribe-run NGO that operates schools and public information programs in northern Thailand villages.

Andaman Discoveries (☑08 7917 7165; www.andamandiscoveries.com; Phang-Nga) Manages a learning centre for children of Burmese migrants, an orphanage and a school for disabled children in southern Thailand.

Cultural Canvas Thailand (☑08 6920 2451; www.culturalcanvas.com; Chiang Mai) Places volunteers in migrant learning centres, art programs and other social-justice projects in northern Thailand.

Dragonfly Volunteer Projects (☑08 7963 0056; http://thai-dragonfly.com; Nakhon Ratchasima) Trains and places volunteers in building, teaching and animal-welfare projects throughout the country.

Isara (☑0 4246 0827; www.isara.org; Nong Khai) Places English and computer teachers in underprivileged schools around Thailand; one of the few volunteer programs that are free, and includes housing and some meals.

LemonGrass Volunteering (☑08 1977 5300; www.lemongrass-volunteering.com; Surin) Places volunteer teachers in classrooms and student camps around Surin, in the northeast.

Open Mind Projects (☑0 4241 3578; www.openmindprojects.org; Nong Khai) Offers volunteer positions in IT, health care, education and community-based ecotourism throughout Thailand.

Redemptorist Foundation (www.fr-ray.org; Pattaya) Operates a variety of educational and outreach programs for disadvantaged people in Pattaya.

Travel to Teach (☑08 4246 0351; www.travel-to-teach.org; Chiang Mai) Offers flexible volunteering positions in schools, English camps or temples with placements in Mae Hong Son and Chiang Mai.

Volunthai (www.volunthai.com; Bangkok) A family-run operation that places volunteers in teaching positions at rural schools with homestay accommodation.

Environmental & Animal Welfare Work

As Thailand becomes industrialised, there are continued pressures on the natural environment and the wild populations of animals. Though the problems are apparent, clear answers are not. There is a strong environmental movement within the country but their efforts are often disparate and function on a small-scale. A number of NGOs undertake local conservation efforts, run rescue and sanctuary centres for wild animals that have been adopted as pets or veterinarian clinics that tend to the domesticated population of dogs and cats.

The following are centres and sanctuaries that rely on volunteer labour; your hard work is often rewarded with meaningful interactions with the animals.

Elephant Nature Park (☑0 5320 8246; www.elephantnaturepark.org; Mae Taeng) Accepts volunteers, including veterinarians, to help care for the resident elephants.

Highland Farm Gibbon Sanctuary (☑0 9958 0821; www.highland-farm.org; Mae Sot) Gives a permanent home to orphaned, abandoned and mistreated gibbons; volunteers are asked for a one-month commitment and to help with daily farm chores.

Starfish Ventures (☑44 800 1974817; www.starfishvolunteers.com) Places volunteers in conservation, teaching and animal welfare programs throughout Thailand, but mainly in Surin.

Wild Animal Rescue Foundation (WARF; www.warthai.org) Operates the Phuket Gibbon Rehabilitation Centre and a conservation education centre in Ranong Province on the Andaman Coast. Job placements include assisting with the daily care of gibbons that are being rehabilitated for life in the wild or counting and monitoring sea-turtle nests.

Wildlife Friends of Thailand Rescue Centre (www.wfft.org) Puts volunteers to work caring for sun bears, macaques and gibbons at its animal rescue centre outside of Phetchaburi.

Islands & Beaches

Best Beaches for Diving & Snorkelling

Ko Tao Gulf island where everyone learns to dive.

Ko Kradan Andaman snorkelling heaven; popular with daytrippers.

Khao Lak Gateway to the world-renowned Surin and Similan Islands and Burma Banks.

Ko Lanta Underappreciated Andaman dive sites, conveniently close.

Best Islands & Beaches for Kids

Dolphin Bay Low-key scenic bay close to Bangkok.

Hua Hin International Gulf mainland resort with a long coastline.

Ko Ngai (Trang Islands): Shallow tropical Andaman bay with coral reefs.

Ko Lanta Sand, sea, eat, repeat – and nap under a coconut tree.

Best Party Beaches

Ko Samui Get your beach drunk on in Hat Chaweng.

Ko Pha-Ngan The full moon turns everyone into a party werewolf.

Ko Phi-Phi The sauce-loving sorority sister of Thai party beaches.

Planning Your Trip

The monsoon rains and peak tourist season are two factors determining when to go and which islands and beaches to pick. The rainy weather varies between the two coasts and there are dry and wet microclimates as well as seasonal severity of rains.

When To Go

Best Times

» **March to April** The hot, dry season means that the days are mostly rain-free and the tourist crowds have mostly returned home.

» **Late October to November** In Ko Chang and the Andaman, this is an ideal shoulder season near the end of the rains and before the end-of-year holidaymakers arrive. The Gulf gets a second rainy season from October to December.

Times to Avoid

» **May to October** The monsoon rains arrive, some hotels shut-down and boat travel can be interrupted by storms. The Gulf tends to stay dry from May to June with rains typically starting in July.

» **December to February** Peak tourist season on Thai islands and beaches. Rates soar and beaches are packed. The Gulf coast gets a second rainy season from October to December.

All the tropical stereotypes apply to the Thai beaches: white stoles of sand punctuated by arcing palm trees and jewel-toned waters. The bays are shallow, warm and gentle and often fringed by coral reefs, making Thailand a major dive and snorkelling destination.

OVERVIEW OF THAILAND'S ISLANDS & BEACHES

BEACHES	PACKAGE, HIGH-END TOURISTS	BACK-PACKERS	FAMILIES	PARTIES	DIVING & SNORKELLING	PERSONALITY
Ko Chang & Eastern Seaboard						
Ko Samet	✓	✓	✓	✓		Easy to get to and pretty beach getaway from Bangkok
Ko Chang	✓	✓	✓	✓	✓	International resort, mediocre beaches, jungle interior
Ko Wai		✓	✓		✓	Primitive daytripper, deserted in the evening
Ko Mak	✓	✓	✓			Mediocre beaches, great island vibe
Ko Kut	✓	✓	✓			Pretty semi-developed island, great for solitude
Hua Hin & the Southern Gulf						
Hua Hin	✓	✓	✓			International resort, easy access to Bangkok
Pranburi & Around	✓		✓			Quiet and close to Bangkok
Ban Krut			✓			Low-key and popular with Thais
Bang Saphan Yai		✓	✓			Cheap and beachy
Ko Samui & the Lower Gulf						
Ko Samui	✓	✓	✓	✓		International resort for social beach-goers
Ko Pha-Ngan	✓	✓	✓	✓		Boho beach with boozy Hat Rin
Ko Tao	✓	✓	✓	✓	✓	Dive schools galore
Ang Thong		✓	✓			Gorgeous karst scenery, rustic
Ao Khanom		✓	✓			Quiet, little known
Phuket & the Andaman Coast						
Ko Chang (Ranong)		✓	✓		✓	Rustic
Ko Phayam		✓	✓			Quiet, little known
Surin & Similan Islands		✓			✓	Dive sites accessed by live-aboards
Ko Yao	✓	✓	✓			Poor beaches but nice vibe, great scenery
Phuket	✓	✓	✓	✓	✓	International resort for social beach-goers
Ao Nang	✓	✓	✓		✓	Touristy, close to Railay
Railay	✓	✓	✓			Rock-climbing centre
Ko Phi-Phi	✓	✓		✓	✓	Pretty party island
Ko Jum	✓	✓	✓			Mediocre beach, nice island vibe
Ko Lanta	✓	✓	✓		✓	Mediocre beach, nice island vibe
Trang Islands	✓	✓	✓		✓	Ko Ngai good for kids
Ko Bulon Leh		✓	✓		✓	Pretty beaches, little known
Ko Tarutao		✓	✓			Semi-developed national park
Ko Lipe	✓	✓	✓	✓	✓	Hot spot, handy for visa-runs
Ko Adang		✓			✓	Popular with daytrippers

Culture & Cuisine

Best Cities for Eating

Bangkok Great street eats, tasty international comfort food, high-end dining too.
Hua Hin Seafood, seafood and seafood, plus some noodles for a change.
Chiang Rai Nosh on northern cuisine like a local.
Chiang Mai Market meals, northern specialities, Burmese eats and sushi and salads.

Best Hill-Tribe Treks

Chiang Mai Well-developed trekking scene for organising a quick foray.
Chiang Rai Many hill-tribe outreach projects are funded through treks.
Mae Hong Son More remote setting with more involved experiences.
Mae Sariang Even more remote than Mae Hong Son but developing a responsible-tourism reputation.

Best Hang-Out Towns

Pai Hippie hang-out in a pretty mountain valley.
Prachuap Khiri Khan Escape the crowds in this seaside town.
Nong Khai Cycle around this pleasant Mekong River town.
Mae Salong Ethnic Chinese village sits atop a mountain ridge cultivated with tea plantations.

Planning Your Trip

The monsoon rains and seasonal temperatures are two factors determining when to go. The bulk of the country experiences one rainy season, followed by 'winter' (when it is cool and dry) then 'summer' (when it is hot and dry). High season in Chiang Mai and the north is during the winter months (November to February) and advance reservations on lodging and transport are recommended during Songkran in April.

When to Go

Best Times

» **November to February** The winter season has cool temperatures and the northern mountains are still green from the previous months' rains. In higher elevations it can be cold at night. This is the best time to do trekking or waterfall spotting.

» **June to October** The rainy season isn't the best time to do a northern trek but it is ideal for seeing rice-planting season, especially in the northeast, which gets less rain than the rest of the country.

Times to Avoid

» **March to May** The summer season is oppressively hot and dry. The landscape becomes parched and in Chiang Mai and northern Thailand the agricultural fields are burned for the next year's crop creating a smoky haze.

Though it might be poorly signed in English, Thailand is one massive museum for those who know how to look for it. Each

» (above) Street food (p123), Bangkok
» (left) Lisu woman and child, near Pai (p388)

TOP CULTURAL TOWNS

Bangkok First stop for culture vultures bulking up on Thai history.

Chiang Mai Northern Thailand's cultural repository of temples and architecture.

Ayuthaya Crumbling ruins from a once-great capital.

Sukhothai Can't do Ayuthaya without Sukhothai, a well-preserved ancient city.

Kanchanaburi Unlikely WWII sightseeing town plus cave temples and scenic drives.

Ubon Ratchathani Rewarding wandering, temples and museums in a pleasant Isan city.

Thai town follows the same blueprint – revolving around a temple and a day market, as food and religion are the centrepieces of daily life. The famous Thai temples exemplify the artistic evolution of the kingdom – the inheritance of Buddhism, which came from Sri Lanka, the imposing military style of the Khmer empire, and the emergence of a distinct Thai artistic personality.

The day market is another indicator of geography and cultural affiliations. Here you'll find the standard repertoire of colourful fruits piled up like miniature pyramids and standard vegetables that get shipped across the country in small pick-up trucks. A requisite visit to the local day market will reveal the region's agricultural specialities, quirky forest herbs and culinary toolkit. Antiquated coconut grinders appear in the southern markets while sugarcane pressers across the country squeeze out nature's original sweet drink from an unlikely looking source. Northern markets prepare blue-hued sticky rice desserts that look like something dreamed up by Willy Wonka.

Radiating out from the market is the commercial strip, typically where Thai-Chinese families have built mercantile enterprises selling utilitarian necessities ranging from paint to motorcycles. A few towns still boast the old wooden shophouses that once dominated the mercantile districts more than half a century ago. Roads in the commercial centre are divided into lanes (called soi) and lanes are divided into alleys; if you follow one or the other you'll eventually end up in someone's living room, usually an open-air porch where a child is being bathed from an earthenware basin or where a sarong-clad grandmother keeps tabs on neighbourhood gossip.

Regardless of the similarities seen across Thailand, every region has its own collective personality, which is reflected in the language, architecture and food that provide a new dimension to the familiar template of Thai towns. The border regions are unique cross-pollinations of cultures separated by arbitrary geopolitical lines. In the north, the cultures are akin to the mountainous regions of Burma and Laos, while the northeast shares its cultural heritage with the dry plains of Laos and Cambodia. Added to this, is the Chinese influence, most notably visible in the Chinatowns in a number of cities. Appreciating these different influences helps build a deeper cultural understanding of a superficially monolithic culture.

The best ways to explore these differences and the various attractions of mustsee towns is to go on a walk-about, sampling street food, poking around the commercial centre and catching local transport to outlying attractions. For more information on the food staples of different regions, see p738.

TOP HANDICRAFT VILLAGES & MARKETS

Ko Kret Little island near Bangkok makes pottery the old-fashioned Mon way.

Hang Dong Northern Thailand's centre for furniture and decorative arts, just outside Chiang Mai.

Ban Tha Sawang Renowned silk-weaving centre near Surin.

Mae Sot Border town selling Burmese handicrafts at local shops and markets.

Nan Textiles, jewellery and other northern handicrafts make for in-situ shopping.

Travel with Children

Best Regions for Kids

Eastern Seaboard & Ko Chang

Families with children flock to Ko Chang. Shallow seas are kind to young swimmers and the low evening tides make for good beachcombing. Older children will like the interior jungle, elephant camp and mangrove kayaking. Neighbouring islands Ko Wai and Ko Kut have clear water.

Southern Gulf

Hua Hin attracts an international crowd and has a long sandy coastline for pint-sized marathons and hillside temples for monkey spotting. Phetchaburi's cave temples often deliver a bat sighting. Ban Krut and Bang Saphan Yai are so casual you can wake up and play in the waves before breakfast.

Ko Samui & Lower Gulf

Older children can snorkel Ko Tao without worry. Ko Samui, especially its northern beaches, is a hit with pram-pushers and toddlers, while Chaweng appeals to older kids.

Phuket & Andaman Coast

As well as the beach, Phuket has amusements galore, though steer clear of the Patong party scene. There are at least a dozen islands along this coast where families can frolic in the sea.

Thailand for Children

Thais are serious 'cute' connoisseurs and exotic-looking foreign children rank higher on their adorable meter than stuffed animals and fluffy dogs. Children are instant celebrities and attract almost paparazzi-like attention that eclipses the natural shyness of Thai people.

Babies do surprisingly well with their new-found stardom, soaking up adoration from gruff taxi drivers who transform into loving uncles wanting to play a game of peekaboo (called '*já ăir'*). If you've got a babe in arms, the food vendors will often offer to hold the child while you eat, taking the child for a brief stroll to visit the other vendors.

At a certain age, kids develop stranger anxiety, which doesn't mix well with the Thai passion for children. The author's four-year-old spent a lot of time in Thailand hiding behind her skirt when the ladies would come a calling. Often she had to strategically shield him from their love pinches. In these cases, she would explain that he was 'shy' (*'ki aye'*), a polite way of bowing out of further interaction. For the preschool set, who are becoming self-conscious but still have major cute quotient, we recommend sticking to tourist centres instead of trotting off to far-flung places where foreigners, especially children, will attract too much attention.

To smooth out the usual road bumps of dragging children from place to place, check out Lonely Planet's *Travel with Children,*

EATING WITH KIDS AUSTIN BUSH

Dining with children, particularly with infants, in Thailand is a liberating experience as the Thais are so fond of kids. Take it for granted that your babies will be fawned over, played with, and more than not, carried around, by restaurant wait staff. Regard this as a much-deserved break, not to mention a bit of free cultural exposure.

Because much of Thai food is so spicy, there is also an entire art devoted to ordering 'safe' dishes for children, and the vast majority of Thai kitchens are more than willing to oblige.

In general Thai children don't start to eat spicy food until primary school, before then they seemingly survive on *kôw nĕe·o* (sticky rice) and jelly snacks. Other kid-friendly meals include chicken in all of its nonspicy permutations – *gài yâhng* (grilled chicken), *gài tôrt* (fried chicken) and *gài pàt mét má·môo·ang* (chicken stir-fried with cashew nuts) – as well as *kài jee·o* (Thai-style omelette). A mild option includes *kôw man gài*, Hainanese chicken rice.

which contains useful advice on how to cope with kids on the road, with a focus on travel in developing countries.

Children's Highlights

Of the many destinations in Thailand, children will especially enjoy the beaches, as most are shallow, gentle bays good for beginner swimmers. The further south you go, the clearer the water and where there are near-shore reefs curious fish will swim by for a visit.

Animal amusements abound in Thailand, but animal conditions and treatment are often sub-par compared with standards in the West. Elephant rides, bamboo rafting and other outdoor activities around Chiang Mai and Kanchanaburi are more animal- and kid-friendly. Many of the beach resorts, such as Phuket and Ko Chang, also have wildlife encounters, waterfall spotting and organised water sports ideal for children aged six years and older.

Bangkok is great fun for those in awe of construction sites: the city is filled with cranes, jackhammers and concrete-pouring trucks. Then there's the aboveground Skytrain and shopping malls complete with escalators (a preschool favourite). The city's immense shopping options will appeal to the tweens and teens. For sights that will interest kids, see the boxed text, p98.

Kids on a train kick might like an overnight journey. On the train they can walk around and they're assigned the lower sleeping berths with views of the stations. The author's son's favourite part of their five-week trip through Thailand was the speedboats they took to get around the Ko Chang archi-

pelago. The child also got very excited when the hotel had two soaps, a reminder that children are adorably easily pleased. And the mosquito net they slept under in Ko Kut became their very own 'bat cave'.

Even the temples can be engaging places for children. The climb to the hilltop temples are a great way to expend energy and some of the forested hills have resident monkeys and cave shrines. Merit-making at a Buddhist temple is surprisingly child-friendly – there's the burning joss sticks, the bowing in front of the Buddha and the rubbing of gold leaf on the central image. It is a very active process that kids can be a part of. Also most temples have a fortune-telling area, where you shake a bamboo container until a numbered stick falls out. The number corresponds to a printed fortune. A variation on this is to make a donation into a pot (or in some cases an automated machine) corresponding to the day of the week you were born and retrieve the attached fortune.

Planning & Practicalities

Amenities specially geared towards young children – such as child-safety seats for cars, high chairs in restaurants or nappy-changing facilities in public restrooms – are virtually nonexistent in Thailand. Therefore parents will have to be extra resourceful in seeking out substitutes or just follow the example of Thai families (which means holding smaller children on their laps much of the time).

Baby formula and nappies (diapers) are available at minimarkets and 7-Elevens in the larger towns and cities, but the sizes are usually small, smaller and smallish. If your kid wears size 3 or larger, head to Tesco Lotus, Big C or Tops Market stores. Nappy rash cream is sold at the pharmacies.

Hauling around little ones can be a challenge. Thailand's footpaths are often too crowded to push a pram, especially today's full-size SUV versions. Instead opt for a compact umbrella stroller that can squeeze past the fire hydrant and the mango cart and that can be folded up and thrown in a túk-túk. A baby pack is also useful but make sure that the child's head doesn't sit higher than yours: there are lots of hanging obstacles poised at forehead level.

Health & Safety

For the most part parents needn't worry too much about health concerns, although it pays to lay down a few ground rules (such as regular hand washing) to head off potential medical problems. Children should be warned not to play with animals as rabies is relatively common in Thailand and many dogs are better at barking and eating garbage than being pets.

Mosquito bites often leave big welts on children. If your child is bitten, there are a variety of locally produced balms that can reduce swelling and itching. All the usual health precautions apply (see p776).

Children familiar with urban environments will do well in Thailand's cities, where traffic is chaotic and pedestrian paths are congested. Thai cities are very loud and can be a sensory overload for young children. Be sure that your child cooperates with your safety guidelines before heading out as it will be difficult for them to focus on your instructions amid all the street noise.

regions at a glance

Bangkok

Food ✓✓✓
Nightlife ✓✓✓
Shopping ✓✓✓

Classic Siam

Beyond the modern veneer of this megacity are the flamboyant royal temples that cradle the revered symbols of Thai Buddhism. The great temples built along Chao Phraya River were a show of strength for the resurrected Siam after its ancient and devastating war with Burma. Today these temples are both national pilgrimage sites and the country's greatest displays of classical art and architecture.

More is Better

This multiwatt megacity peddles excess in every permutation, from the sky-scraper mountain ranges and luxe malls to the never-ending traffic jams and late-night after-hours clubs. Food can be found everywhere from pushcarts to grease-stained wok shops and it is all delicious. The city's cosmopolitan upbringing shines in fine dining and fashion-minded cafes. Shopping flourishes in crisp modern malls and humble streetside markets, including Chatuchak, a super-sized collection of tented stalls selling everything that can be peddled.

Toast the Stars

The quintessential night out in Bangkok is still a plastic table filled with sweating Beer Changs but this aspirational city capitalises on its skyscraper towers with half a dozen rooftop bars, where the breezes are cool and the cocktails are fizzy. Bangkok's legions of young and hip university students are always out on the town, filling music clubs with the latest indie beats or hangar-like entertainment zones that offer a buffet of eating, dancing and drinking.

p54

Central Thailand

Culture/History ✓✓✓
Mountains ✓✓
Festivals ✓

Mother Waters

This fertile river plain is Thailand's cultural heartland, which birthed the once-dominant ancient kingdom of Ayuthaya. Today the Ayuthaya ruins are a Unesco World Heritage Site and a must-stop along the culture trail. Amiable Lopburi and its ancient ruins, some of which are informally ruled by a troop of monkeys, can be visited in a day. Loi Krathong is celebrated in Bang Pa-In palace with great spectacle.

Mountain Journeys

The subdued town of Kanchanaburi played an unlikely role in WWII when Japanese forces used Allied POWs to build the infamous Death Railway. It is also the gateway to the misty mountains of southwestern Thailand leading all the way to the Burmese border. Rivers and waterfalls carve the contours and a collection of parks makes this one of Thailand's wildest corners.

p156

Ko Chang & Eastern Seaboard

Beaches ✓✓
Diving/Snorkelling ✓
Small Towns ✓✓

A Chain of Islands
Jungle-covered Ko Chang and a collection of smaller islands stake out one last territorial claim in the Gulf's warm waters before ceding to Cambodia. Overland travellers en route to coastal Cambodia and Russian package tourists claim Ko Chang for its tropical ambience, dive sites and thriving party scene. Further afield, quiet Ko Kut excels in seaside seclusion, Ko Mak boasts a laid-back island vibe and little Ko Wai, with its clear, reef-filled waters, has the prettiest views you've ever seen.

Provincial Prominence
Tourists often overlook the eastern seaboard's small towns of Chanthaburi, famous for a weekend gem market, and Trat, a transit link to Ko Chang. But these provincial towns are charming for their ordinariness and middle-class prosperity, not found on the islands.

p191

Chiang Mai Province

Culture/History ✓✓✓
Food ✓✓
Nightlife ✓✓

Lanna Latitudes
A refreshing counterpoint to Bangkok's mayhem, charming Chiang Mai proudly displays northern Thailand's unique history and culture in its antique fortified city. Culture geeks flock here for sightseeing, cooking courses, language classes and massage training. During Songkran the city goes famously wild in an all-out water war. Beyond the old city gates are hip hang-outs and clubs where the uni students keep the city pointed into the future.

Curries & Noodles
Northern Thailand has its own versions of standard Thai dishes, reflecting its cooler climate and proximity to Yunnan and Burma. The curries are hardy, and pork dominates the grill. The dining scene is down to earth, concentrating on flavours instead of fads.

p232

Northern Thailand

Culture/History ✓✓✓
Mountains ✓✓✓
Food ✓✓

Ancient Kingdoms
In olden times, rival city-states with their fortressed walls and sandstone Buddhist monuments sprang up throughout the upper plains of northern Thailand, defining important artistic and historical periods for the country. Sukhothai and its peaceful ancient city is the most atmospheric of them all and an easy detour north to Chiang Mai.

Misty Mornings
Further north the terrain becomes rugged as it climbs into the highlands shared with Laos and Burma. Winding roads and scenic vistas are highlights of Chiang Rai and Mae Hong Son Provinces. And tucked into high-altitude valleys are ethnic minorities whose traditional practices continue to fascinate modern globe-trekkers. The regional menu in the north is a melange of Thai, Shan and Yunnan, catered by small dusty markets.

p294

Northeastern Thailand

Culture/History ✓✓
Food ✓✓✓
Festivals ✓✓✓

Ancient Angkor

The northeast was once a remote frontier of the great Angkor empire, based in present-day Cambodia, which built miniature versions of fantastic Angkor Wat throughout the countryside, still a frontier in some ways.

Powered by Sticky Rice

This rice-growing region is intimately tied to the agricultural clock and draws a regional pride from the local staple. The rainy season heralds the planting of tender green shoots still done by hand. Homestays in the region place visitors smack dab in the middle of the paddies complete with impervious water buffaloes. Local festivals put on an authentic cultural displays of folk beliefs and traditional dancing and music that can't be found anywhere else in the country.

p406

Hua Hin & the Southern Gulf

Culture/History ✓
Beaches ✓✓
Small Towns ✓✓

Royal Coast

Successive Thai kings escaped Bangkok's stifling climate to this coastal getaway. Bangkok Thais follow in their footsteps today, stopping in Phetchaburi to tour an historic hilltop palace and cave shrines, and then on to Hua Hin, a modcon seaside retreat. The region's coastline is long and inviting and not nearly as crowded as every other beach resort in Thailand. Honeymooners and families will appreciate this short cut to the beach.

Surf & Turf

This coastal region is an excellent combination of sea and city for beach-lovers looking for a sense of place. Prachuap Khiri Khan is a mellow small town with stunning karst scenery, and Hua Hin and Phetchaburi both boast atmospheric shophouse districts indicative of Thailand's coastal cities settled by Chinese merchants.

p503

Ko Samui & the Lower Gulf

Beaches ✓✓✓
Diving/Snorkelling ✓✓

Diver Down

The three Samui sister islands, with their various charms, have been pursued by smitten island-hoppers for decades. The warm gentle seas and wallet-friendly prices keep Ko Tao as one of the globe's best places to learn how to dive. Just offshore are snorkelling spots that make fish-spotting fun and easy.

Bronzing Bodies

Next door is Ko Pha-Ngan, known for lunar parties and coastal loafing. Gone are the thatch shacks but the layabout vibe remains. And finally professional Samui caters to international tastes, high-end resorts and active vacationers who fly in and out with purpose. A daytrip dreamboat, Ang Thong National Park is a stunning collection of hulking limestone mountains jutting out of azure seas.

p535

Phuket & the Andaman Coast

Beaches ✓✓✓
Diving/Snorkelling ✓✓✓

Cousteau Territory
Big fish, pristine coral, clear waters – diving and snorkelling sites dot the coast all the way from the world-renowned Similan and Surin National Marine Parks to the Malaysian border. Most visitors pack a snorkel set in their day bags for impromptu sessions.

Karst Cathedrals
All along the Andaman limestone mountains fringed with beardlike vegetation jut out of jewel-coloured waters with monumental stature. The spectacle is breathtaking and enhanced by a variety of sports, based in Krabi and Ko Yao, that turns the landscape into an outdoor playground.

Just Phuket
Thailand's leading international beach destination excels in comfort for the holidaying masses. Resorts specialise in design and pampering and the modern convenience of an airport delivers time-crunched visitors from sky to shore faster.

p602

> **Every listing is recommended by our authors, and their favourite places are listed first**

> **Look out for these icons:**

 TOP CHOICE Our author's top recommendation

A green or sustainable option

FREE No payment required

See the Index for a full list of destinations covered in this book.

On the Road

Bangkok

Includes »

Best Places to Eat

Best Places to Stay

Why Go?

Formerly the epitome of the elderly Asian metropolis, in recent years Bangkok has gone under the knife and emerged as a rejuvenated starlet. Her wrinkles haven't totally been erased, but you might not notice them behind the ever-expanding public-transport system, air-conditioned mega-malls and international-standard restaurants.

But don't take this to mean that there's no more 'real' Bangkok. The Royal Palace and Wat Phra Kaew still sparkle just as they did more than 200 years ago, and the BTS (Skytrain) has had little impact on the shophouses of Banglamphu or the canals of Thonburi. To really experience the Bangkok of today, it's necessary to explore both of these worlds. Take the MRT (Metro) to hectic Chinatown or the *klorng* boat to the chic Central World mall, and along the way we're certain you'll find that the old personality and that new face culminate in one sexy broad indeed.

When to Go

According to the World Meteorological Organisation, Bangkok is one of the hottest cities in the world. To make things worse, there's very little fluctuation in the temperature, and the average high sways between a stifling 32°C and an incrementally more stifling 34°C. The rainy season runs from approximately May to October, during when the city receives as much as 300mm of rain a month.

Virtually the only break from the relentless heat and humidity comes during Bangkok's winter, a few weeks of relative coolness in December/January.

History

The centre of government and culture in Thailand today, Bangkok was a historical miracle during a time of turmoil. Following the fall of Ayuthaya in 1767, the kingdom fractured into competing forces, from which General Taksin emerged as a decisive unifier. He established his base in Thonburi, on the western bank of Mae Nam Chao Phraya (Chao Phraya River), a convenient location for sea trade from the Gulf of Thailand. Taksin proved more of a military strategist than a popular ruler. He was later deposed by another important military general, Chao Phraya Chakri, who in 1782 moved the capital across the river to a more defensible location in anticipation of a Burmese attack. The succession of his son in 1809 established the present-day royal dynasty, and Chao Phraya Chakri is referred to as Rama I.

Court officials envisioned the new capital as a resurrected Ayuthaya, complete with an island district (Ko Ratanakosin) carved out of the swampland and cradling the royal court (the Grand Palace) and a temple to the auspicious Emerald Buddha (Wat Phra Kaew). The emerging city, which was encircled by a thick wall, was filled with stilt and floating houses ideally adapted to seasonal flooding.

Modernity came to the capital in the late 19th century as European aesthetics and technologies filtered east. During the reigns of Rama IV (King Mongkut) and Rama V (King Chulalongkorn), Bangkok received its first paved road (Th Charoen Krung) and a new royal district (Dusit) styled after European palaces.

Bangkok was still a gangly town when soldiers from the American war in Vietnam came to rest and relax in the city's go-go bars and brothels. It wasn't until the boom years of the 1980s and '90s that Bangkok exploded into a fully fledged metropolis crowded with hulking skyscrapers and an endless spill of concrete that gobbled up rice paddies and green space. The city's extravagant tastes were soon tamed by the 1997 economic meltdown, the effects of which can still be seen in the numerous half-built skyscrapers.

◉ Sights

In recent years Bangkok has yet again started to redefine itself, and projects such as the BTS (Skytrain) and MRT (Metro) have begun to address the city's notorious traffic problems, while simultaneously providing the city with a modern face. A spate of giant air-conditioned mega-malls has some parts of the city looking a lot like Singapore,

---

BANGKOK IN...

One Day

Get up as early as you can and take the **Chao Phraya Express** north to **Nonthaburi Market**. On your way back, hop off at Tha Chang to explore the museums and temples of **Ko Ratanakosin**, followed by **lunch in Banglamphu**.

After freshening up, get a new perspective on the city with sunset cocktails at one of the **rooftop bars**, followed by an upscale Thai dinner at **nahm**.

Two Days

Allow the **BTS** to whisk you to various **shopping** destinations and a visit to **Jim Thompson House**, punctuated by a **buffet lunch** at one of the city's hotels. Wrap up the daylight hours with a **traditional Thai massage**. Then work off those calories at the dance clubs of **RCA**.

Three Days

Spend a day at **Chatuchak Weekend Market** or if it's a weekday, enrol in a **cooking school**. Now that you're accustomed to Bangkok's noise, pollution and traffic, you're ready for **a street-food dinner** in Chinatown.

Four Days

At this point you may be itching to get out of the city. Convenient escapes include **Ko Kret**, a car-less island north of Bangkok, or taking a long-tail boat to ride through **Thonburi's canals**.

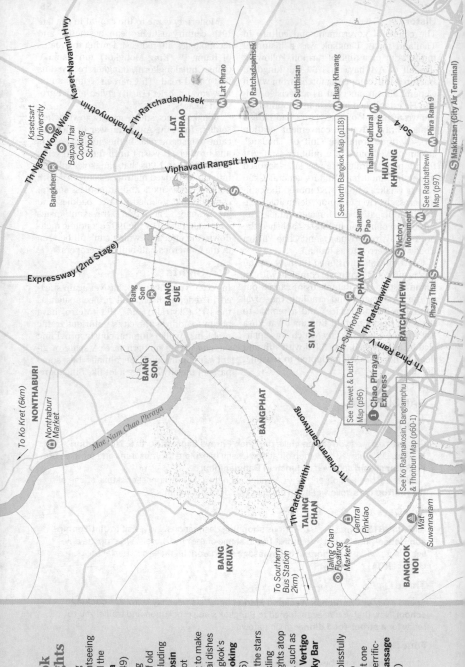

Bangkok Highlights

1 Skipping between sightseeing spots aboard the **Chao Phraya Express** (p149)

2 Exploring the streets of old Bangkok, including **Ko Ratanakosin** (p102), on foot

3 Learning to make authentic Thai dishes at one of Bangkok's numerous **cooking schools** (p96)

4 Toasting the stars and the twinkling skyscraper lights atop a rooftop bar, such as **Moon Bar at Vertigo** or **Sirocco Sky Bar** (p132)

5 Getting blissfully pounded into submission at one of the city's terrific-value **Thai massage centres** (p91)

6 Eating yourself into a stupor on the streets of **Chinatown** (p123)

7 Getting out of the city and visiting the nearby canalside town of **Amphawa** (p153)

Ko Ratanakosin 2

6 Eating in **Chinatown**

See Chinatown & Phahurat Map (p76)

See Siam Square & Pratunam Map (p86-7)

See Th Sukhumvit Map (p92-3)

Thai Massage Centres 5

Moon Bar at Vertigo 4

See Lumphini Park & Th Phra Ram IV Map (p90)

See Silom & Sathon Map (p82-3)

Cooking Schools 3

Sirocco Sky Bar 4

See Riverside Map (p80)

Manohra Cruises

THONBURI

KHLONG SAN

Wong Wian Yai

Krung Thonburi

Th Charoen Nakhon

Th Phetkasem

Wong Wian Yai

Th Taksin

Th Phra Ram II

Chalerm Mahanakhon Expwy

Th Suksawat

RATBURANA

PHRA PRADAENG

Th Phra Ram III

Wat Chong Nonsi

Museum of Counterfeit Goods

Mae Nam Chao Phraya

BANGNA

To Bearing Station (500m)

To On Nut Station (950m)

Phra Khanong

Th Rama IV

Th Sukhumvit

KHLONG TAN

KHLONG TOEY

PORT

Th Narathiwat Ratchanakharin

Phetchaburi

0   2 km
0   1 mile

and despite recent bouts of political unrest, the general atmosphere is hectic but stable. It seems like only a matter of time before Bangkok's modernisation reaches the lever of other leading Asian capitals.

KO RATANAKOSIN, BANGLAMPHU & THONBURI เกาะรัตนโกสินทร์/บางลำพู/ธนบุรี

Welcome to Bangkok's birthplace. The vast city we know today emerged from Ko Ratanakosin, a tiny virtual island ('Ko') made by dredging a canal around Mae Nam Chao Phraya during the late 18th century. Within this area you'll find the glittering temples and palaces that most visitors associate with the city. Ko Ratanakosin's riverfront setting is also home to several museums, markets and universities. All these sights are within walking distance of each other and are best visited early in the morning before the day comes to a boil.

Adjacent Banglamphu suffers from an extreme case of bipolar disorder, encompassing both the most characteristically old-school-Bangkok part of town as well as Th Khao San, a brash, neon-lit decompression zone for international backpackers. Depending on which one you fancy, it's not difficult to escape the other – another of Banglamphu's charms. The bulk of Bangkok's classic buildings are found in this area, as well as lots of authentic Bangkok cuisine and culture.

Directly across the river is Thonburi, which served a brief tenure as the Thai capital after the fall of Ayuthaya. Today the area along both sides of the river is easily accessed from Bangkok's cross-river ferries, and there are museums and temples in Thonburi that are historical complements to those in Ko Ratanakosin.

Despite the abundance of attractions, Ko Ratanakosin and Banglamphu are still isolated from the more modern forms of public transport. The Chao Phraya River Express is probably the most efficient way of reaching the area, and the *klorng* (canal; also spelt *khlong*) taxi along Khlong Saen Saeb to eastern Banglamphu is another convenient option if you're coming from the Siam Square or Sukhumvit areas. The closest BTS station is Ratchathewi (Map p86).

If you're planning on doing some extensive exploring in the area, consider borrowing one of the free Green Bangkok Bikes (see the boxed text, p151) available at five bike stations within the district.

Ko Ratanakosin

Bangkok's biggest and gaudiest tourist sites float regally on this artificial island. The river ferry pier at Tha Chang is the most convenient access point.

Wat Phra Kaew & Grand Palace   BUDDHIST TEMPLE, PALACE COMPOUND
(วัดพระแก้ว/พระบรมมหาราชวัง; Map p60; admission 350B; ⊗8.30am-3.30pm; bus 503, 508, river ferry Tha Chang) Also known as the Temple of the Emerald Buddha, **Wat Phra Kaew** is the colloquial name of the vast, fairy-tale compound that also includes the former residence of the Thai monarch, the Grand Palace.

This ground was consecrated in 1782, the first year of Bangkok rule, and is today Bangkok's biggest tourist attraction and a pilgrimage destination for devout Buddhists and nationalists. The 94.5-hectare grounds encompass more than 100 buildings that represent 200 years of royal history and architectural experimentation. Most of the ar-

TRAVELS OF THE EMERALD BUDDHA

The Emerald Buddha (Phra Kaew Morakot) holds a prominent position in Thai Buddhism in spite of its size (a mere 66cm) and original material (probably jasper quartz or nephrite jade rather than emerald). In fact, the Emerald Buddha was just another ordinary image, with no illustrious pedigree, until its monumental 'coming out' in 15th-century Chiang Rai. During a fall, the image revealed its luminescent interior, which had been covered with plaster (a common practice to safeguard valuable Buddhas from being stolen). After a few successful stints in various temples throughout northern Thailand, the image was stolen by Lao invaders in the mid-16th century and remained in that country for 200 years.

In 1778 Thailand's King Taksin waged war against Laos, retrieving the image and mounting it in Thonburi. Later, when the capital moved to Bangkok and General Chakri took the crown, the Emerald Buddha was honoured with one of the country's most magnificent monuments, Wat Phra Kaew.

chitecture, royal or sacred, can be classified as Ratanakosin (or old-Bangkok style).

Housed in a fantastically decorated *bòht* (*chapel*) and guarded by pairs of *yaksha* (mythical giants), the **Emerald Buddha** is the temple's primary attraction. It sits atop an elevated altar, barely visible amid the gilded decorations. The diminutive figure is always cloaked in royal robes, one for each season (hot, cool and rainy). In a solemn ceremony, the king (or in recent years, the crown prince) changes the garments at the beginning of each season. Recently restored **Buddhist murals** line the interior walls of the *bòht,* and the **murals of the Ramakian** (the Thai version of the Indian epic *Ramayana*) line the inside walls of the temple compound. Originally painted during the reign of Rama I (1782–1809) and also recently restored, the murals illustrate the epic in its entirety, beginning at the north gate and moving clockwise around the compound.

Except for an anteroom here and there, the buildings of the Grand Palace (Phra Borom Maharatchawong) are now put to use by the king only for certain ceremonial occasions, such as Coronation Day.

Borombhiman Hall (eastern end), a French-inspired structure that served as a residence for Rama VI, is occasionally used to house visiting foreign dignitaries. The building to the west is **Amarindra Hall**, originally a hall of justice but used today for coronation ceremonies.

The largest of the palace buildings is the **Chakri Mahaprasat**, the Grand Palace Hall. Built in 1882 by British architects using Thai labour, the exterior is a peculiar blend of Italian Renaissance and traditional Thai architecture. It's a style often referred to as *fa·ràng sài chá·dah* (Westerner in a Thai crown) because each wing is topped by a *mon·dòp* – a heavily ornamented spire representing a Thai adaptation of the Hindu *mandapa* (shrine). The tallest *mon·dòp*, in the centre, contains the ashes of Chakri kings; the flanking *mon·dòp* enshrine the ashes of Chakri princes. Thai kings housed their huge harems in the inner palace area, which was guarded by combat-trained female sentries.

Last, from east to west, is the Ratanakosin-style **Dusit Hall**, which initially served as a venue for royal audiences and later as a royal funerary hall.

ⓘ DRESS FOR THE OCCASION

Most of Bangkok's biggest tourist attractions are sacred places, and visitors should dress and behave appropriately. In particular at Wat Phra Kaew, the Grand Palace and in Dusit Park, you won't be allowed to enter unless you're well covered. Shorts, sleeveless shirts or spaghetti-strap tops, short skirts, capri pants – basically anything that reveals more than your arms (certainly don't show your shoulders) knees and head – are not allowed. This applies to men and women. Violators can expect to be shown into a dressing room and loaned a sarong before being allowed to go in.

For walking in the courtyard areas you are supposed to wear shoes with closed heels and toes, although these rules aren't as zealously enforced. Regardless, footwear should always be removed before entering any main *bòht* (chapel) or *wí·hǎhn* (sanctuary). When sitting in front of a Buddha image, tuck your feet behind you to avoid the highly offensive pose of pointing your feet towards a revered figure.

Guides can be hired at the ticket kiosk; ignore offers from anyone outside. An audio guide can be rented for 200B for two hours. Wat Phra Kaew and the Grand Palace are best reached either by a short walk south from Banglamphu, via Sanam Luang, or by Chao Phraya Express boat to Tha Chang. From the Siam Sq area – in front of the MBK Center (Th Phra Ram I), take bus 47.

Admission for the complex includes entrance to **Dusit Park** (p89), which includes Vimanmaek Teak Mansion and Abhisek Dusit Throne Hall.

Wat Pho BUDDHIST TEMPLE
(วัดโพธิ์ (วัดพระเชตุพน); Wat Phra Chetuphon; Map p60; Th Sanam Chai; admission 50B; ☺8am-9pm; bus 508, 512, river ferry Tha Tien) You'll find (slightly) fewer tourists here than at Wat Phra Kaew, but Wat Pho is our personal fave among Bangkok's biggest temples. In fact, the compound incorporates a host of superlatives: the largest reclining Buddha, the largest collection of Buddha images in Thailand and the country's earliest centre for public education.

Somdej Prapinklao Soi 2 — 45

Santichaiprakan Park

Tha Saphan Phra Pin Klao

Tha Phra Athit (Tha Banglamphu)

40 Th Phra Athit 79

Saphan Phra Pin Klao

42 51 Th Ram Buttri

55 41 Soi Ram Buttri

31 Th Rongmai

25

81 Th Chao Fa

7 65

Bangkok Noi Train Station

Khlong Bangkok Noi

10

THONBURI

13

Tha Rot Fai

8 73

Siriraj Hospital

Tha Phra Chan

Thammasat University

Sanam Luang

Th Phrannok

Tha Wang Lang

Soi Tambon Wanglang 1

Tha Maharaj

1

Th Phra Chan

Th Na Phra That

24

26

Th Maha Rat

Sanam Luang

Mae Nam Chao Phraya

BANGKOK NOI

Th Wat Rakhang

Tha Chang

57

Silpakorn University

Bangkok Smile Bike

Th Na Phra Lan

5 Th Lak Meuang

83

17

Th Sanam Chai

Grand Palace

KO RATANAKOSIN

Saranrom Royal Garden

Th Thai Wang

Wat Pho

Enlargement

0   200 m
0   0.1 miles

84

39

Th Tani

62

Th Rambuttri

49 50

85

66 23

69 77 67

80 47

61 64

32

Susie Walking Street

Th Khao San

Th Tanao

Tha Tien

Soi Pratu Nok Yung

28

Wat Arun

27

Th Chetuphon

Soi Pratu Nok Yung

86 78

15

29 33

6

Mae Nam Chao Phraya

BANGKOK

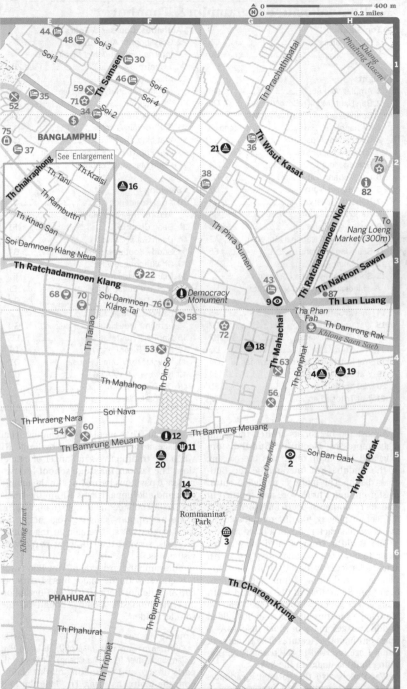

Ko Ratanakosin, Banglamphu & Thonburi

Almost too big for its shelter, the genuinely impressive **Reclining Buddha**, 46m long and 15m high, illustrates the passing of the Buddha into nirvana (ie the Buddha's death). The figure is modelled out of plaster around a brick core and finished in gold leaf. Mother-of-pearl inlay ornaments the feet, displaying 108 different auspicious *lák·sà·nà* (characteristics of a Buddha).

The **Buddha images** on display in the other four *wí·hăhn* (sanctuary) are worth a nod. Particularly beautiful are the Phra Chinnarat and Phra Chinnachai Buddhas, both from Sukhothai, in the west and south chapels. The galleries extending between the four chapels feature no less than 394 gilded Buddha images, many of which display Ayuthaya or Sukhothai features. The remains of Rama I are interred in the base of the presiding Buddha image in the *bòht*.

Wat Pho is also the national headquarters for the teaching and preservation of traditional Thai medicine, including Thai massage, a mandate legislated by Rama III when the tradition was in danger of extinction. The famous **massage school** has two massage pavilions located within the temple area and additional rooms within the training facility outside the temple (p93). Nearby stone inscriptions showing yoga and massage techniques still remain in the temple grounds, serving their original purpose as visual aids.

The rambling grounds of Wat Pho cover 8 hectares, with the major tourist sites occupying the northern side of Th Chetuphon and the monastic facilities found on the southern side.

Amulet Market   MARKET
(ตลาดพระเครื่องวัดมหาธาตุ; Map p60; Th Maha Rat; ☺7am-5pm; river ferry Tha Chang) This equal-parts bizarre and fascinating market claims both the footpaths along Th Maha Rat and

BANGKOK SIGHTS

Th Phra Chan, as well as a dense network of covered market stalls near Tha Phra Chan. The trade is based around small talismans carefully prized by collectors, monks, taxi drivers and people in dangerous professions. Potential buyers, often already sporting tens of amulets, can be seen bargaining and flipping through magazines dedicated to the amulets, some of which command astronomical prices.

Also along this strip are handsome shophouses overflowing with family-run herbalmedicine and traditional-massage shops, and additional street vendors selling used books, cassettes and, oddly enough, dentures.

Museum of Siam MUSEUM
(สถาบันพิพิธภัณฑ์การเรียนรู้แห่งชาติ; Map p60; www.museumsiam.com; Th Maha Rat; admission 300B; ⊙10am-6pm Tue-Sun; bus 32, 524, river ferry Tha Tien) This fun museum employs a variety of media to explore the origins and culture

of the Thai people. Housed in a Rama III-era palace, the exhibits are superinteractive, well balanced and entertaining. Highlights include the informative and engaging narrated videos in each exhibition room, and an interactive Ayuthaya-era battle game.

National Museum MUSEUM
(พิพิธภัณฑสถานแห่งชาติ; Map p60; 4 Th Na Phra That; admission 200B; ⊙9am-3.30pm Wed-Sun; bus 32, 123, 503, river ferry Tha Chang) Often touted as Southeast Asia's biggest museum, the National Museum is home to an impressive collection of religious sculpture, best appreciated on one the museum's twice-weekly guided **tours** (⊙9.30am Wed & Thu).

Most of the museum's structures were built in 1782 as the palace of Rama I's viceroy, Prince Wang Na. Rama V turned it into a museum in 1874, and the current museum consists of three permanent exhibitions spread out over several buildings.

ART ATTACK

Although Bangkok's hyper-urban environment seems to cater to the inner philistine in all of us, the city has a significant but low-key art scene. In recent years, galleries seem to have been opening on a weekly basis, and Bangkok also acts as something of a regional art hub, with works by emerging artists from places such as Myanmar and Cambodia. To find out what's happening while you're in town, pick up a free copy of the excellent **BAM!** (Bangkok Art Map; www.bangkokartmap.com).

Our picks of the better galleries:

» **100 Tonson Gallery** (Map p86; www.100tonsongallery.com; 100 Soi Tonson, Th Ploenchit; ☺11am-7pm Thu-Sun; BTS Chit Lom) Atmospheric gallery showcasing the work of domestic and international emerging and high-profile painters, sculptors and conceptual artists.

» **Bangkok Art and Culture Centre** (BACC; Map p86; www.bacc.or.th; cnr Th Phayathai & Th Phra Ram 1; ☺10am-9pm Tue-Sun; BTS Siam or National Stadium) This brand-new state-owned complex combines art and commerce in a multistorey building smack-dab in the centre of Bangkok.

» **H Gallery** (Map p82; www.hgallerybkk.com; 201 Soi 12, Th Sathon; ☺10am-6pm Wed-Sat, by appointment Tue; BTS Surasak) Leading commercial gallery for emerging Thai abstract painters.

» **Kathmandu Photo Gallery** (Map p82; www.kathmandu-bkk.com; 87 Th Pan; ☺11am-7pm Tues-Sun; BTS Surasak) Bangkok's only truly dedicated photography gallery is located in a restored Sino-Portuguese shophouse. The small upstairs gallery plays host to changing exhibitions by local and international artists and photographers.

» **Queen's Gallery** (Map p60; www.queengallery.org; 101 Th Ratchadamnoen Klang; admission 30B; ☺10am-7pm Thu-Tue; bus 2, 15, 44, 511, klorng taxi Tha Phan Fah) This royally funded gallery presents five floors of rotating exhibitions of modern and traditionally influenced art.

» **Surapon Gallery** (Map p90; www.rama9art.org/gallery/surapon/index.html; 1st fl, Tisco Tower, Th Sathon Neua; ☺11am-6pm Tue-Sat; MRT Lumphini) Unique contemporary Thai art.

» **Tang Gallery** (Map p82; basement, Silom Galleria, 919/1 Th Silom; ☺11am-7pm Tue-Sat; BTS Surasak) Bangkok's primary venue for modern artists from China has also edged its way up to become among the city's top contemporary galleries. Check the posters in the lobby of the Galleria to see what's on.

The **history wing** has made impressive bounds towards mainstream curatorial aesthetics with a succinct chronology of prehistoric, Sukhothai-, Ayuthaya- and Bangkok-era events and figures. Gems include King Ramakhamhaeng's inscribed stone pillar, said to be the oldest record of Thai writing; King Taksin's throne; the Rama V section; and the screening of the movie about King Prajadhipok, *The Magic Ring*.

The **decorative arts and ethnology exhibit** covers every possible handicraft: traditional musical instruments, ceramics, clothing and textiles, woodcarving, regalia and weaponry. The **archaeology and art history wing** has exhibits ranging from prehistoric to the Bangkok period.

In addition to the main exhibition halls, the **Buddhaisawan (Phutthaisawan) Chapel** includes some well-preserved original murals and one of the country's most revered Buddha images, Phra Phut Sihing. Legend says the image came from Sri Lanka, but art historians attribute it to 13th-century Sukhothai.

Lak Meuang (City Pillar)　　ANIMIST SHRINE
(ศาลหลักเมือง; Map p60; cnr Th Ratchadamnoen Nai & Th Lak Meuang; admission free; ☺6.30am-6.30pm; bus 2, 60, 507, river ferry Tha Chang) Serving as the spiritual keystone of Bangkok, Lak Meuang is a phallus-shaped wooden pillar erected by Rama I during the founding of the new capital city in 1782. Today the structure shimmers with gold leaf and is housed in a white cruciform sanctuary. Part of an animistic tradition, the pillar embodies the city's guardian spirit (Phra Sayam Thewathirat) and also lends a practical purpose as a

(Continued on page 73)

Thai Temples

Religion permeates Thailand from deep within the souls of the faithful to the unseen ethereal realm. Sacred spaces can be found in humble corners and exalted centres, and the Thai temple (wát) is the focal point of every community, the repository of traditional art and architecture and the primary counsellor for those with wishes and needs.

Wat Phra Kaew (p58), Bangkok

Top Temples

Thailand's most famous temples have earned adoration from the faithful both for their artistic beauty as well as for their resident Buddha or holy relics.

Wat Phra Kaew, Bangkok

1 The holiest of them all, this temple (p58) contains the country's most revered Buddha image, through which the exaltation of monarchy, nation and religion become one. The temple is a dazzling spectacle of mosaic-tiled facades, gilded spires and ornate murals.

Wat Phra That Doi Suthep, Chiang Mai

2 Sitting atop a sacred mountain, this picturesque temple (p251) is venerated by Thai Buddhists for its golden *chedi* (stupa) and Buddha relic buried inside. It is also a beautiful example of Lanna (northern Thai) architecture that gazes down at Chiang Mai.

Wat Phra Si Ratana Mahathat, Phitsanulok

3 In a land that prizes beauty, this temple (p349) is a major pilgrimage stop because of its resplendent Buddha. The seated figure glows with a heavenly lustre that is accented by an intricate and stylised halo.

Wat Pho, Bangkok

4 Wat Pho (p59) specialises in relaxation: it is the national repository for traditional massage and even its resident Buddha (a 46m long, 15m high reclining figure) assumes a slumbering pose. Dotting the shaded complex are giant Chinese sculptures.

Wat Phra Si Sanphet, Ayuthaya

5 Though time and war have taken its toll, Thailand's former capital of Ayuthaya survives with a gravity-defying elegance in Wat Phra Si Sanphet (p157). Its most striking feature is the picturesque profile of three tapered *chedi* spires – a feature of the era.

Clockwise from top left
1. *Prangs* at Wat Phra Kaew 2. Wat Phra That Doi Suthep
3. Seated Buddha statue, Wat Phra Si Ratana Mahathat
4. Reclining Buddha statue, Wat Pho

Thai Buddhism

The practice of Buddhism in Thailand is highly varied and individualised. For many it starts at dawn when the orange-robed barefoot monks solemnly process through town collecting food alms from the faithful. It is a genuinely touching ritual attesting to the religion's deep devotion and compassion. Daily devotions also occur in homes and businesses where small shrines to the site's guardian spirit are offered morning prayers, lit joss sticks and even treats in exchange for a prosperous and trouble-free day.

The formal aspects of the religion – funeral rites, meditation courses, merit-making and dharma talks – are carried out at the temples. But Thai temples are a jumble of strict orthodoxy and folk beliefs, often mixing religious guidance with luck-enhancing rituals. When in need, be it a broken heart or money troubles, Thais turn to the temple first beseeching the resident Buddha image for divine assistance. Some temples also host fortune-tellers and monks are trained in astrology.

Temples also serve a social function, as a destination for friends and families on a weekend tour. Stopping into a town's famous temple to make merit is the Western equivalent of visiting a regional museum. Paying respect to a temple's central Buddha usually involves offerings of lotus bud, joss sticks and small sheets of gold leaf.

TOP READS ON THAI BUDDHISM

» **A Still Forest Pool: The Insight Meditation of Achaan Chah**, Achaan Chah (2004)

» **Thailand: Into the Spirit World**, by Marlane Guelden (1995)

» **Phra Farang: An English Monk in Thailand**, by Phra Peter Pannapadipo (1999)

» **Buddhism Explained**, by Laurence-Khantipalo Mills (1999)

Clockwise from top left
1. Monks at Wat Phon Chai, Dan Sai (p476) 2. Lotus offering, Sukhothai Historical Park (p355) 3. Golden Buddha statues at Wat Phra That Doi Suthep (p251), Chiang Mai

Temple Tour

10 days

Temple buffs can get to know the ins and outs of Thai Buddhism on this journey from Bangkok north to Chiang Mai.

» Start in **Bangkok** (p54), the seat of the Thai triumvirate: nation, monarchy and religion. Tour the famous riverside temples of Wat Phra Kaew, Wat Pho and Wat Arun. If you long to see more, not too far away are interesting Wat Saket and Wat Suthat.

» Take a day trip to **Ayuthaya** (p157), a former empire where once gilded temples have become haunting ruins pockmarked by time. Here, Wat Phra Si Sanphet is a must-see on any temple tour. And why not tour the temples like royalty aboard an elephant.

» Take the train to **Phitsanulok** (p348) to pay homage to Thailand's stunning Buddha in Wat Phra Si Ratana Mahathat and the 700-year-old Buddha at interesting Wat Ratburana. Do as the Thais and eat at the famous noodle shop near Wat Phra Si Ratana Mahathat as a post-pilgrimage pit-stop.

» Bus over to **Sukhothai** (p355) to meditate among the fine ancient ruins of a now-deceased empire that heralded Thailand's golden era'. Be sure to see Wat Mahathat and Wat Si Chum. The ancient city is so vast that visiting the sites by bicycle is recommended.

» Bus north to **Chiang Mai** (p234) to immerse yourself in northern Thai architecture, visiting the old city and Wat Phra Doi Suthep, which overlooks the city. In the city itself, Wat Phra Singh and Wat Chedi Luang make fine venerable stops.

Clockwise from top left & following page
1. Wat Phra Kaew, Bangkok **2.** Wat Si Sawai, Sukhothai
3. Row of statues, Wat Mahathat, Sukhothai **4.** Elephant tour of Ayuthaya ruins **5.** Statue of the Buddha with protective *naga* (serpents) at Wat Phra That Doi Suthep, Chiang Mai **6.** Monks, Bangkok

(Continued from page 64)

marker of the town's crossroads and measuring point for distances between towns.

If you're lucky, a *lá·kon gâa bon* (commissioned dance) may be in progress. Brilliantly costumed dancers measure out subtle movements as gratitude to the guardian spirit for granting a worshipper's wish.

National Gallery   MUSEUM
(พิพิธภัณฑสถานแห่งชาติ หอศิลป์; Map p60; 4 Th Chao Fa; admission 200B; ⊘9am-4pm Wed-Sun; river ferry Tha Phra Athit) The humble National Gallery belies the country's impressive tradition of fine arts. Decorating the walls of this early Ratanakosin-era building are works of contemporary art, mostly by artists who receive government support. The permanent exhibition is rather dated and dusty, but the temporary exhibitions, held in spacious halls out back, can be good.

Banglamphu

Although slightly less grand than those of its neighbour, Banglamphu's sights are a window into the Bangkok of yesterday, a city that's largely starting to disappear.

Golden Mount   BUDDHIST TEMPLE
(วัดสระเกศ (ภูเขาทอง); Map p60; Th Boriphat; admission 10B; ⊘7.30am-5.30pm; bus 8, 37, 47, klorng taxi Tha Phan Fah) Even if you're wát-ed out, you should take a brisk walk to the Golden Mount. Like all worthy summits, the temple plays a good game of optical illusion, appearing closer than its real location. Serpentine steps wind through an artificial hill shaded by gnarled trees, some of which are signed in English, and past graves and pictures of wealthy benefactors. At the peak, you'll find a breezy 360-degree view of Bangkok's most photogenic side.

This artificial hill was created when a large stupa, under construction by Rama III, collapsed because the soft soil beneath would not support it. The resulting mud-and-brick hill was left to sprout weeds until Rama IV built a small stupa on its crest. Rama V later added to the structure and housed a Buddha relic from India (given to him by the British government) in the stupa. The concrete walls were added during WWII to prevent the hill from eroding. Every year in November there is a big festival on the grounds of Wat Saket, which includes a candlelit procession up the Golden Mount.

If you're coming from the eastern end of the city, the Golden Mount is a short walk south of the *klorng* boats' western terminus at Tha Phan Fah.

Wat Suthat & Sao
Ching-Cha   BUDDHIST TEMPLE & MONUMENT
(วัดสุทัศน์/เสาชิงช้า; Map p60; Th Bamrung Meuang; admission 20B; ⊘8.30am-9pm; bus 10, 12, klorng taxi Tha Phan Fah) Brahmanism predated the arrival of Buddhism in Thailand and its rituals were eventually integrated into the dominant religion. **Wat Suthat** is the headquarters of the Brahman priests who perform the Royal Ploughing Ceremony in May. Begun by Rama I and completed in later reigns, Wat Suthat boasts a *wí·hăhn* with gilded bronze Buddha images (including Phra Si Sakayamuni, one of the largest surviving Sukhothai bronzes) and incredibly expansive *jataka* (stories of the Buddha's previous lives) murals (see the boxed text, p74). The wát also holds the rank of Rachavoramahavihan, the highest royal-temple grade; the ashes of Rama VIII (Ananda Mahidol, the current king's deceased older brother) are contained in the base of the main Buddha image in the *wí·hăhn*.

Wat Suthat's priests also perform rites at two nearby Hindu shrines: **Thewa Sathaan** (Deva Sathan), which contains images of Shiva and Ganesh; and the smaller **Saan Jao Phitsanu** (Vishnu Shrine), dedicated to Vishnu.

The spindly red arch in the front of the temple is **Sao Ching-Cha** (Giant Swing), as much a symbol of Bangkok as Wat Phra Kaew. The swing formerly hosted a spectacular Brahman festival in honour of Shiva, in which participants would swing in ever-higher arcs in an effort to reach a bag of gold suspended from a 15m bamboo pole. Many died trying and the ritual was discontinued during the reign of Rama VII. In 2007 the decaying swing was ceremoniously replaced with the current model, made from six specially chosen teak logs from Phrae Province in northern Thailand.

The temple is within walking distance of the *klorng* boats' terminus at Tha Phan Fah.

Wat Bowonniwet   BUDDHIST TEMPLE
(วัดบวรนิเวศวิหาร; Map p60; cnr Th Phra Sumen & Th Tanao; admission free; ⊘8am-5.30pm; bus 56, 58, 516, river ferry Tha Phra Athit) Founded in 1826, Wat Bowonniwet is the national headquarters for the Thammayut monastic sect. King Mongkut, founder of this minority sect, began a royal tradition by residing here as a monk – in fact, he was the abbot

of Wat Bowonniwet for several years. King Bhumibol (Rama IX) and Crown Prince Vajiralongkorn, as well as several other males in the royal family, have been temporarily ordained as monks. The *ubosot* has some interesting wall murals (see the boxed text, below). Because of the temple's royal status, visitors should be particularly careful to dress properly for admittance to this wát – no shorts or sleeveless shirts.

Wat Ratchanatdaram Worawihan
BUDDHIST TEMPLE

(วัดราชนัดดารามวรวิหาร; Map p60; cnr Th Ratchadamnoen Klang & Th Mahachai; admission free; ☺9am-5pm; bus 2, 15, 44, 511, klorng taxi Tha Phan Fah) Across Th Mahachai from Wat Saket, Wat Ratchanatdaram dates from the mid-19th century and in addition to Loha Prasat, the metallic, castlelike monastery, is home to a well-known market selling Buddhist *prá pim* (magical charm amulets) in all sizes, shapes and styles. The amulets not only feature images of the Buddha, but also famous Thai monks and Indian deities. Buddha images are also for sale.

Ban Baht (Monk's Bowl Village)
NEIGHBOURHOOD

(บ้านบาตร; Map p60; Soi Ban Baht; ☺10am-6pm; bus 8, 37, 47, klorng taxi Tha Phan Fah) Just when you start to lament the adverse effects of tourism, pay a visit to this handicraft village. This is the only surviving village established by Rama I to make the *bàht* (rounded bowls) that the monks carry to receive food alms from faithful Buddhists every morning. Today the average monk relies on a bowl mass-produced in China, but the traditional technique survives in Ban Baht thanks to patronage by tourists.

About half a dozen families still hammer the bowls together from eight separate pieces of steel representing, they say, the eight spokes of the Wheel of Dharma (which symbolise Buddhism's Eightfold Path). The

---

TEMPLE MURALS

Because of the relative wealth of Bangkok, as well as its role as the country's artistic and cultural centre, the artists commissioned to paint the walls of the city's various temples were among the most talented around, and Bangkok's temple paintings are regarded as the finest in Thailand. Some particularly exceptional works:

» **Wat Bowonniwet** (see p73) Painted by an artist called In Kong during the reign of Rama II, the murals in the panels of the *ubosot* (chapel) of this temple include Thai depictions of Western life (possibly copied from magazine illustrations) during the early 19th century.

» **Wat Chong Nonsi** (วัดช่องนนทรี; Map p56; Th Nonsi, off Th Phra Ram III; admission free; ☺8am-6pm; MRT Khlong Toei & access by taxi) Dating back to the late Ayuthaya period, Bangkok's earliest surviving temple paintings are faded and missing in parts, but the depictions of everyday Thai life, including bawdy illustrations of a sexual manner, are well worth visiting.

» **Buddhaisawan (Phutthaisawan) Chapel** (p63) Although construction of this temple, located in the National Museum, began in 1795, the paintings were probably finished during the reign of Rama III (1824–51). Among other scenes, the graceful murals depict the conception, birth and early life of the Buddha – common topics among Thai temple murals.

» **Wat Suthat** (p73) Almost as impressive in their vast scale as for their quality, the murals at Wat Suthat are among the most awe-inspiring in the country. Gory depictions of Buddhist hell can be found on a pillar directly behind the Buddha statue.

» **Wat Suwannaram** (วัดสุวรรณาราม; Map p56; 33 Soi 32, Th Charoen Sanitwong, Khlong Bangkok Noi; admission free; ☺8am-6pm; klorng taxi from Tha Chang) These paintings inside a late Ayuthaya–era temple in Thonburi contain skilled and vivid depictions of battle scenes and foreigners, including Chinese and Muslim warriors.

» **Wat Tritosathep** (วัดตรีทศเทพ; Map p60; Th Prachathipatai; admission free; bus 12, 19, 56) Although still a work in progress, Chakrabhand Posayakrit's postmodern murals at this temple in Banglamphu have already been recognised as masterworks of Thai Buddhist art.

joints are fused in a wood fire with bits of copper, and the bowl is polished and coated with several layers of black lacquer. A typical output is one bowl per day. If you purchase a bowl, the craftsperson will show you the equipment and process used.

Thonburi

It's calm enough on the right bank of the Mae Nam Chao Phraya to seem like another province – there are relatively few, but *fàng ton* is a great area for aimless wandering among leafy streets.

Wat Arun   BUDDHIST TEMPLE

(วัดอรุณฯ; Map p60; Th Arun Amarin; admission 50B; ⊙8.30am-4.30pm; cross-river ferry from Tha Tien) Striking Wat Arun commands a martial pose as the third point in the holy trinity (along with Wat Phra Kaew and Wat Pho) of Bangkok's early history. After the fall of Ayuthaya, King Taksin ceremoniously clinched control here on the site of a local shrine (formerly known as Wat Jaeng) and established a royal palace and a temple to house the Emerald Buddha. The temple was renamed after the Indian god of dawn (Aruna) and in honour of the literal and symbolic founding of a new Ayuthaya.

It wasn't until the capital and the Emerald Buddha were moved to Bangkok that Wat Arun received its most prominent characteristic: the 82m-high *prang* (Khmer-style tower). The tower's construction was started during the first half of the 19th century by Rama II and later completed by Rama III. Not apparent from a distance are the ornate floral **mosaics** made from broken, multi-hued Chinese porcelain, a common temple ornamentation in the early Ratanakosin period, when Chinese ships calling at the port of Bangkok discarded tonnes of old porcelain as ballast.

Also worth an inspection is the interior of the *bòht*. The main Buddha image is said to have been designed by Rama II himself. The **murals** date from the reign of Rama V; particularly impressive is one that depicts Prince Siddhartha encountering examples of birth, old age, sickness and death outside his palace walls, an experience that led him to abandon the worldly life. The ashes of Rama II are interred in the base of the presiding Buddha image.

Cross-river ferries (3.50B) run over to Wat Arun every few minutes from Tha Tien.

Sunset views of the temple compound can be caught from across the river at the riverfront warehouses that line Th Maha Rat. Another great viewpoint is from Amorosa, the rooftop bar at the Arun Residence (p128).

Royal Barges National Museum   MUSEUM

(พิพิธภัณฑ์เรือพระที่นั่ง; Map p60; Khlong Bangkok Noi; admission 100B, photo permit 100B; ⊙9am-5pm; river ferry Tha Saphan Phra Pin Klao) The royal barges are slender, fantastically ornamented vessels used in ceremonial processions along the river. The tradition dates back to the Ayuthaya era, when most travel (for commoners and royalty) was by boat. Today the royal barge procession is an infrequent occurrence, most recently performed in 2006 in honour of the 60th anniversary of the king's ascension to the throne. When not in use, the barges are on display at this Thonburi museum.

Suphannahong, the king's personal barge, is the most important of the boats. Made from a single piece of timber, it's the largest dugout in the world. The name means 'Golden Swan', and a huge swan head has been carved into the bow. Lesser barges feature bows that are carved into other Hindu-Buddhist mythological shapes such as *naga* (mythical sea serpent) and *garuda* (Vishnu's bird mount). Historic photos help envision the grand processions in which the largest of the barges would require a rowing crew of 50 men, plus seven umbrella bearers, two helmsmen and two navigators, as well as a flagman, rhythm-keeper and chanter.

The most convenient way to get to the museum is by taking a taxi (ask the driver to go to *reu·a prá têe nâng*) from Tha Saphan Phra Pin Klao. Another alternative is walking from the Bangkok Noi train station (accessible by ferrying to Tha Rot Fai), but the walk is tricky and unpleasant and you'll encounter uninvited guides who will charge for their services. The museum is also an optional stop on long-tail boat trips through Thonburi's canals.

Church of Santa Cruz   CATHOLIC CHURCH

(โบสถ์ซางตาครูส; Map p76; Th Kuti Jiin; admission free; ⊙Sat & Sun; cross-river ferry from Tha Pak Talat/Atsadang) Dating back to 1913, this Catholic church holds relatively little interest unless you visit on a Sunday. But the surrounding neighbourhood, a former Portuguese concession dating back to the Ayuthaya period, is worth a wander for its old-school riverside atmosphere and Portuguese-inspired cakes, *kà·nŏm fa·ràng.*

Chinatown & Phahurat

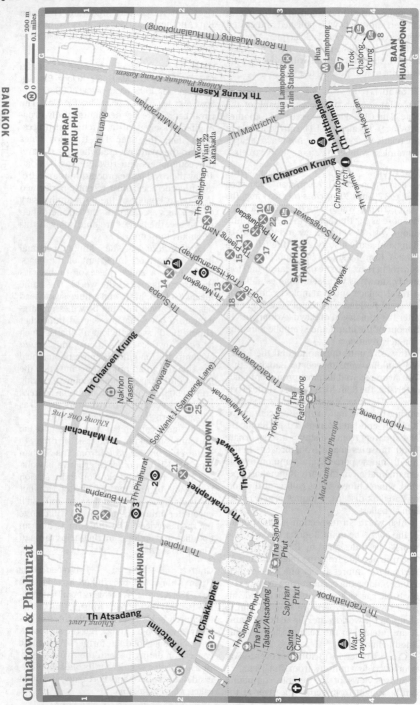

200 m
0.1 miles

Chinatown Phahurat

BANGKOK SIGHTS

CHINATOWN & PHAHURAT

เยาวราช (สำเพ็ง)/พาหุรัด

Bangkok's Chinatown (called Yaowarat after its main thoroughfare, Th Yaowarat) is the urban explorer's equivalent of the Amazon Basin. Unlike neighbouring Ko Ratanakosin and Banglamphu, the highlights here aren't tidy temples or museums, but rather a complicated web of tiny alleyways, crowded markets and delicious street stalls. And unlike other Chinatowns around the world, Bangkok's is defiantly ungentrified, and getting lost in it is probably the best thing that could happen to you.

The neighbourhood dates back to 1782 when Bangkok's Chinese population, many of them labourers hired to build the new capital, were moved here from today's Ko Ratanakosin area by the royal rulers. Relatively little has changed since then, and you can still catch conversations in various Chinese dialects, buy Chinese herbal cures or taste Chinese dishes not available elsewhere in Thailand. For those specifically interested in the latter, be sure to check out our food-based walk around the district (p123).

Getting in and out of Chinatown is hindered by horrendous traffic. The river ferry stop at Tha Ratchawong was previously the easiest way to reach the district; however, the advent of the MRT has put the area a brief walk from Hua Lamphong station.

At the western edge of Chinatown is a small but thriving Indian district, generally called Phahurat. Here, dozens of Indian-owned shops sell all kinds of fabric and clothes.

Wat Traimit   BUDDHIST TEMPLE

(วัดไตรมิตร; Temple of the Golden Buddha; Map p76; cnr Th Yaowarat & Th Charoen Krung; admission 40B; ⊙8am-5pm Tues-Sun; MRT Hua Lamphong, river ferry Tha Ratchawong) The attraction at Wat Traimit is undoubtedly the impressive 3m-tall, 5.5-tonne, **solid-gold Buddha image**, which gleams like, well, gold. Sculpted in the graceful Sukhothai style, the image was 'discovered' some 40 years ago beneath a stucco or plaster exterior, when it fell from a crane while being moved to a new building within the temple compound. It has been theorised that the covering was added to protect it from marauding hordes, either during the late Sukhothai period or later in the Ayuthaya period when the city was under siege by the Burmese. The temple itself is said to date from the early 13th century.

Donations and a constant flow of tourists have proven profitable, and the statue is now housed in a brand-new four-storey marble structure. The 2nd floor of the building is home to the **Phra Buddha Maha Suwanna Patimakorn Exhibition** (admission 100B; ⊙8am-5pm Tues-Sun), which has exhibits on how the statue was made, discovered and came to arrive at its current home, while the 3rd floor is home to the **Yaowarat Chinatown Heritage Center** (admission

WORTH A TRIP

OFFBEAT BANGKOK MUSEUMS

If looking at stuffed tigers and Buddha statues is not doing anything for you, then consider a visit to one of these quirky institutions.

» **Ancient City** (Muang Boran; Map p153; www.ancientcity.com; 296/1 Th Sukhumvit, Samut Prakan; adult/child 400/200B; ⊙8am-5pm) Claiming to be the largest open-air museum in the world, the site covers more than 80 hectares of peaceful countryside littered with 109 scaled-down facsimiles of many of the kingdom's most famous monuments. It's an excellent place to explore by bicycle (daily rental 50B), as it is usually quiet and never crowded. Ancient City lies outside Samut Prakan, which is accessible via air-conditioned bus 511 from Bearing BTS station at the east end of Th Sukhumvit. Upon reaching the bus terminal at Pak Nam, board minibus 36, which passes the entrance to Ancient City.

» **Bangkok Folk Museum** (Map p80; 273 Soi 43/Saphan Yao, Th Charoen Krung; admission free; ⊙10am-4pm Wed-Sun; river ferry Tha Si Phraya) Consisting of three wooden houses, this family-run museum is a window into Bangkok life during the 1950s and '60s. Particularly interesting is the traditional Thai kitchen.

» **Corrections Museum** (Map p60; 436 Th Mahachai; admission free; ⊙9am-4pm Mon-Fri; bus 508, klorng taxi to Tha Phan Fah) Learn about the painful world of Thai-style punishment at what's left of this former jail. Life-sized models re-enact a variety of horrendous executions and punishments, encouraging most visitors to remain law-abiding citizens for the remainder of their stay.

» **Museum of Counterfeit Goods** (Map p56; ✆0 2653 5555; www.tillekeandgibbins.com/museum/museum.htm; Tilleke & Gibbins, Supalai Grand Tower, 1011 Th Phra Ram III; admission free; ⊙8am-5pm Mon-Fri by appointment only; MRT Khlong Toei & access by taxi) This private collection displays all the counterfeit booty that has been collected by the law firm Tilleke & Gibbins over the years. Many of the fake items are displayed alongside the genuine ones.

» **Songkran Niyosane Forensic Medicine Museum & Parasite Museum** (Map p60; 2nd fl, Forensic Pathology Bldg, Siriraj Hospital, Th Phrannok, Thonburi; admission 40B; ⊙9am-4pm Mon-Sat; river ferry Tha Wang Lang) This gory institution contains the various appendages and remnants of famous murders, including the bloodied T-shirt from a victim who was stabbed to death with a dildo. The adjacent Parasite Museum is also worth a visit, much for the same reasons as above. The easiest way to reach the museum is by taking the river-crossing ferry to Tha Wang Lang (on the Thonburi side) from Tha Chang. At the exit of the pier, turn right to enter Siriraj Hospital, and follow the signs to the museum.

» **Thai Human Imagery Museum** (Map p153; www.rosenini.com/thaihumanimagery/english.htm; Nakhon Chais, Nakhon Pathom; admission 200B; ⊙9am-5.30pm Mon-Fri, 8.30am-6pm Sat & Sun) Contains an exhibition of 120 lifelike wax sculptures. A group of Thai artists reportedly spent 10 years studying their subjects and creating the figures, which range from famous Buddhist monks of Thailand to Winston Churchill. The museum is outside town at the Km 31 marker on Th Pinklao-Nakhon Chaisi. Any Nakhon Pathom–Bangkok bus or minivan can drop you off here.

100B; ⊙8am-5pm Tues-Sun), a small but engaging museum with multimedia exhibits on the history of Bangkok's Chinatown and its residents.

Talat Mai   MARKET
(ตลาดใหม่; Map p76; Soi 16/Trok Itsaranuphap, Th Yaowarat; bus 73, 159, 507, MRT Hua Lamphong, river ferry Tha Ratchawong) With nearly two centu-

ries of commerce under its belt, 'New Market' is no longer an entirely accurate name for this market. Essentially it's a narrow covered alleyway between tall buildings, but even if you're not interested in food the hectic atmosphere and exotic sights and smells culminate in something of a surreal sensory experience.

While much of the market centres on cooking ingredients, the section north of Th Charoen Krung (equivalent to Soi 21, Th Charoen Krung) is known for selling incense, paper effigies and ceremonial sweets – the essential elements of a traditional Chinese funeral.

FREE Wat Mangkon Kamalawat CHINESE TEMPLE

(วัดมังกรกมลาวาส; Neng Noi Yee; Map p76; Th Charoen Krung; ⏰9am-6pm; bus 73, 159, 507, MRT Hua Lamphong, river ferry Tha Ratchawong) Clouds of incense and the sounds of chanting form the backdrop at this Chinese-style Mahayana Buddhist temple. Dating back to 1871, it's the largest and most important religious structure in the area, and during the annual Vegetarian Festival (see the boxed text, p122), religious and culinary activities are particularly active here.

Phahurat Market MARKET

(ตลาดพาหุรัด; Map p76; Th Phahurat & Th Chakraphet; bus 82, 169, 507, river ferry Tha Saphan Phut) Hidden behind the new and astonishingly out of place India Emporium mall is Phahurat Market, an endless bazaar uniting flamboyant Bollywood fabric, photogenic vendors selling *paan* (betel nut for chewing) and several shops stocked with delicious northern Indian-style sweets.

Gurdwara Siri Guru Singh Sabha SIKH TEMPLE

(Map p76; Th Phahurat; ⏰9am-5pm) In an alley off Th Chakraphet is this large Sikh temple that's reminiscent of a mosque interior, devoted to the worship of the *Guru Granth Sahib*, the 16th-century Sikh holy book, which is itself considered to be a 'living' guru and the last of the religion's 10 great teachers. Reportedly, the temple is the second-largest Sikh temple outside India. Visitors are welcome, but they must remove their shoes.

RIVERSIDE ข้างแม่น้ำ

Talat Noi NEIGHBOURHOOD

(ตลาดน้อย; Map p80; Soi Phanurangsi; ⏰9am-6pm; river ferry Tha Si Phraya) Bordered by the river, Th Songwat, Th Charoen Krung and Th Yotha, this ancient neighbourhood is a fascinating jumble of tiny alleys, greasy machine shops and traditional architecture. Located opposite the River View Guest House, **San Jao Sien Khong** (Map p80; admission free; ⏰6am-6pm) is one of the city's oldest Chinese shrines and also one of the best areas to be

during the annual Vegetarian Festival (see the boxed text, p122).

SILOM & SATHON สีลม/สาธร

The business district of Th Silom has only a handful of tourist attractions scattered among the corporate hotels, office towers and wining-and-dining restaurants. As you get closer to the river, the area becomes spiced with the sights and smells of its Indian and Muslim residents. Moving north along Th Charoen Krung, the area adjacent to the river was the international mercantile district during Bangkok's shipping heyday.

Traffic is notorious in this part of town, but the BTS, MRT and Chao Phraya Express provide some transport relief.

MR Kukrit Pramoj House MUSEUM

(บ้านหม่อมราชวงศ์คึกฤทธิ์ปราโมช; Map p82; Soi 7/Phra Phinij, Th Narathiwat Rachananakharin; adult/child 50/20B; ⏰10am-4pm; BTS Chong Nonsi) Author and statesman Mom Ratchawong (MR, an honorary royal title) Kukrit Pramoj once resided in this charming Thai house, now open to the public as a museum. European-educated but devoutly Thai, MR Kukrit surrounded himself with the best of both worlds: five traditional teak buildings, Thai art, Western books and lots of heady conversations. A guided tour is recommended for a more intimate introduction to the former resident, who authored more than 150 books and served as prime minister of Thailand.

Queen Saovabha Memorial Institute (Snake Farm) SNAKE FARM

(สถานเสาวภา (สวนงู); Map p82; www.saovabha.com; cnr Th Phra Ram IV & Th Henri Dunant; adult/child 200/50B; ⏰9.30am-3.30pm Mon-Fri, to 1pm Sat & Sun; BTS Sala Daeng, MRT Si Lom) Snake farms tend to gravitate towards carnivalesque rather than humanitarian, except at the Queen Saovabha Memorial Institute. Founded in 1923, the snake farm prepares antivenin from venomous snakes. This is done by milking the snakes' venom, injecting it into horses, and harvesting and purifying the antivenom that they produce. The antivenoms are then used to treat human victims of snake bites.

The leafy grounds are home to a few caged snakes (and a constant soundtrack of Western rock music), but the bulk of the attractions are found in the Simaseng Building, at the rear of the compound. The ground floor houses several varieties of snakes in glass cages. Regular milkings (⏰11am Mon-Fri) and snake-handling performances (⏰2.30pm Mon-Fri & 11am Sat & Sun) are held at the outdoor ampitheatre.

Riverside

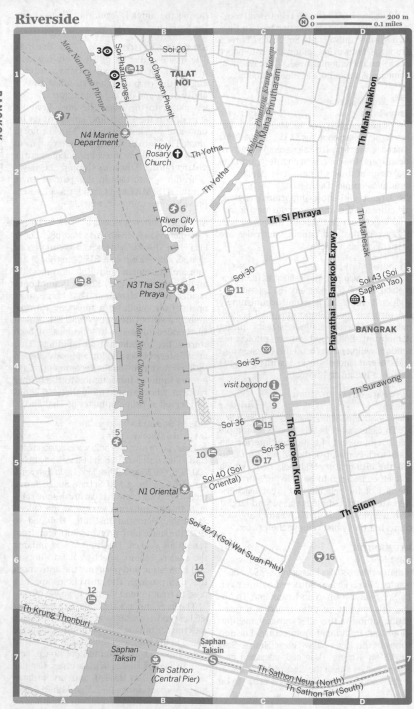

BANGKOK

0 ————— 200 m
0 ————— 0.1 miles

Mae Nam Chao Phraya

Soi Phanurangsi

Soi 20

TALAT NOI

Soi Charoen Phanit

N4 Marine Department

Holy Rosary Church

Th Yotha

Th Yotha

Khlong Phadung Krung Kasem

Th Maha Phrutharam

Th Maha Nakhon

Th Si Phraya

Th Mahesak

River City Complex

Mae Nam Chao Phraya

N3 Tha Sri Phraya

Soi 30

Soi 43 (Soi Saphan Yao)

BANGRAK

Soi 35

visit beyond

Soi 36

Th Surawong

Soi 38

Th Charoen Krung

Soi 40 (Soi Oriental)

N1 Oriental

Th Silom

Soi 42/1 (Soi Wat Suan Phlu)

Th Krung Thonburi

Saphan Taksin

Saphan Taksin

Tha Sathon (Central Pier)

Th Sathon Neua (North)

Th Sathon Tai (South)

Riverside

Sri Mahariamman Temple HINDU TEMPLE

(วัดศรีมหาอุมาเทวี (วัดแขกสีลม); Wat Phra Si Maha Umathewi; Map p82; cnr Th Silom & Th Pan; admission free; ⊘6am-8pm; bus 15, 504, BTS Surasak) Standing out, even among Bangkok's golden wát, this Hindu temple virtually leaps off the block. Built in the 1860s by Tamil immigrants in the centre of a still thriving ethnic enclave, the structure is a stacked facade of intertwined, full-colour Hindu deities. In the centre of the main shrine is Jao Mae Maha Umathewi (Uma Devi, also known as Shakti, Shiva's consort), and along the left interior wall sit rows of Shiva, Vishnu and other Hindu deities, as well as a few Buddhas, so that just about any non-Muslim, non-Judaeo-Christian Asian can worship here.

Thais call this temple Wat Khaek – *kàak* is a colloquial expression for people of Indian descent. The literal translation is 'guest', an obvious euphemism for a group of people that locals don't particularly want as permanent residents; hence most Indians living permanently in Thailand don't appreciate the term.

SIAM SQUARE & PRATUNAM
สยามสแควร์/ประตูน้ำ

Commerce, mainly in the form of multistorey mega-malls, forms the main attraction in this part of town, but there are a couple of sights that don't involve credit cards. The BTS and *klorng* taxis provide easy access to most attractions here.

Erawan Shrine BRAHMIN SHRINE

(ศาลพระพรหม; San Phra Phrom; Map p86; cnr Th Ratchadamri & Th Ploenchit; admission free; ⊘6am-11pm; BTS Chit Lom) The Erawan Shrine was originally built in 1956 as something of a last-ditch effort to end a string of misfortunes that occurred during the construction of the hotel, at that time known as the Erawan Hotel. After several incidents ranging from injured construction workers to the sinking of a ship carrying marble for the hotel, a Brahmin priest was consulted. Since the hotel was to be named after the elephant escort of Indra in Hindu mythology, the priest determined that Erawan required a passenger, and suggested it be that of Lord Brahma. A statue was built, and lo and behold, the misfortunes miraculously ended.

Although the original Erawan Hotel was demolished in 1987, the shrine still exists, and today remains an important place of pilgrimage for Thais, particularly those in need of some material assistance. Those making a wish from the statue should ideally come between 7am and 8am, or 7pm and 8pm, and should offer a specific list of items that includes candles, incense, sugar cane or bananas, all of which are almost exclusively given in multiples of seven. Particularly popular are teak elephants, the money gained through the purchase of which is donated to a charity run by the current hotel, the Grand Hyatt Erawan. And as the tourist brochures depict, it is also possible for you to charter a

Silom & Sathon

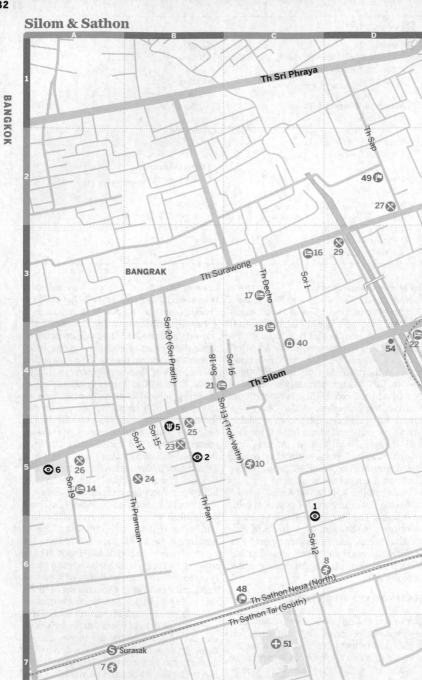

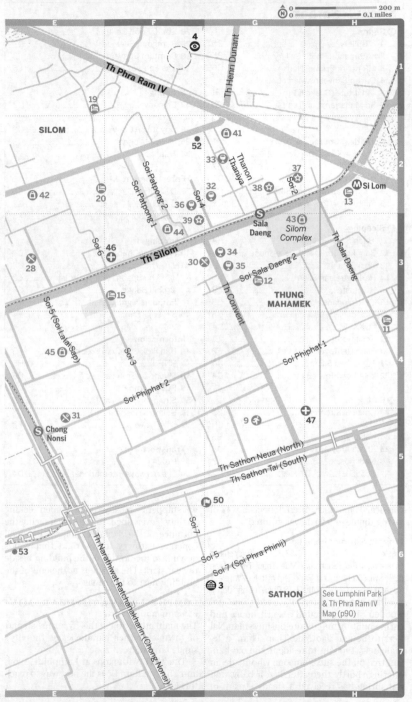

Silom & Sathon

classical Thai dance, often done as a way of giving thanks if a wish was granted.

Lingam Shrine at Nai Lert Park
ANIMIST SHRINE
(ศาลเจ้าแม่ทับทิม; Saan Jao Mae Thap Thim; Map p86; Swissôtel Nai Lert Park, Th Witthayu/Wireless Rd; admission free; ⏰24hr; BTS Phloen Chit, klorng taxi Tha Withayu) Clusters of carved stone and wooden phalli surround a spirit house and shrine built by millionaire businessman Nai Lert to honour Jao Mae Thap Thim, a female deity thought to reside in the old banyan tree on the site. Someone who made an offering shortly thereafter had a baby, and the shrine has received a steady stream of worshippers – mostly young women seeking fertility – ever since. To get here if facing the entrance of the Swissôtel, follow the small concrete pathway to the right that winds down into the bowels of the building beside the car park. The shrine is at the end of the building next to the canal.

LUMPHINI PARK & TH PHRA RAM IV
สวนลุมพินี/ถนนพระราม ๔
The main attraction in this hyper-urban part of town is, rather paradoxically, the city's single largest green zone.

The MRT, with stops at Lumphini, Silom and Th Phra Ram IV, is the best way to reach this area.

Lumphini Park   PARK

(สวนลุมพินี; Map p90; Th Phra Ram IV, btwn Th With-ayu/Wireless Rd & Th Ratchadamri; admission free; ◉4.30am-9pm; BTS Sala Daeng, MRT Lumphini or Si Lom) Named after the Buddha's place of birth in Nepal, Lumphini Park is the best way to escape Bangkok without leaving town. Shady paths, a large artificial lake and swept lawns temporarily blot out the roaring traffic and hulking concrete towers.

There are **paddleboats** (per 1/2 hr 40B) for lovers, **playgrounds** for the kids, open-air concerts on Sunday afternoon, and one of the best times to visit the park is before 7am when the air is fresh (well, relatively so for Bangkok) and legions of Thai-Chinese are practising *taijiquan* (t'ai chi). The park re-awakens with the evening's cooler tempera-tures – aerobics classes collectively sweat to a techno soundtrack. Late at night the borders of the park are frequented by street-walking prostitutes, both male and female.

SUKHUMVIT   สุขุมวิท

More time will be spent here eating, drink-ing and perhaps sleeping (as there is a high concentration of hotels in the area) rather than sightseeing.

The BTS is the primary public-transport option.

Ban Kamthieng   MUSEUM

(บ้านคำเที่ยง; Map p92; Siam Society, 131 Soi Asoke/Soi 21, Th Sukhumvit; admission adult/child 100/50B; ◉9am-5pm Tues-Sat; BTS Asok, MRT Sukhumvit) An engaging house museum, Ban Kamthieng transports visitors to a northern Thai village complete with informative dis-plays of daily rituals, folk beliefs and every-day household chores, all within the setting of a traditional wooden house. This museum is operated by and shares space with the Siam Society, the publisher of the renowned *Journal of the Siam Society* and a valiant preserver of traditional Thai culture.

Khlong Toey Market   FOOD MARKET

(ตลาดคลองเตย; Map p92; cnr Th Ratchadaphisek & Th Phra Ram IV; ◉5-10am; MRT Khlong Toei) This wholesale market, one of the city's largest, is inevitably the origin of many of the meals you'll eat during your stay in Bangkok. Get there early, and although some corners of the market can't exactly be described as pho-togenic, be sure to bring a camera to capture the stacks of durians or cheery fishmongers.

GREATER BANGKOK

Bangkok's 'burbs cover a lot of land, but a minimum of visit-worthy sites. The most worthwhile area is Dusit, the royal district of wide streets, monuments and greenery.

DON'T MISS

JIM THOMPSON HOUSE

This leafy **compound** (Map p86; www.jimthompsonhouse.com; 6 Soi Kasem San 2; adult/child 100/50B; ◉9am-5pm, compulsory tours in English & French every 20min; BTS National Stadium, klorng taxi Tha Saphan Hua Chang) is the former home of the eponymous American silk entrepreneur and art collector. Born in Delaware in 1906, Thompson briefly served in the Office of Strategic Services (forerunner of the CIA) in Thailand during WWII. Settling in Bangkok after the war, his neighbours' handmade silk caught his eye and piqued his business sense; he sent samples to fashion houses in Milan, London and Paris, gradually building a steady worldwide clientele.

In addition to exquisite Asian art, Thompson also collected parts of various derelict Thai homes in central Thailand and had them reassembled in their current location in 1959. One striking departure from tradition is the way each wall has its exterior side fac-ing the house's interior, thus exposing the wall's bracing system. His small but splendid Asian art collection and his personal belongings are also on display in the main house.

Thompson's story doesn't end with his informal reign as Bangkok's best-adapted foreigner. While out for an afternoon walk in the Cameron Highlands of western Malaysia in 1967, Thompson mysteriously disappeared. That same year his sister was murdered in the USA, fuelling various conspiracy theories. Was it communist spies? Business rivals? Or a man-eating tiger? The most recent theory – for which there is apparently some hard evidence – has it that the silk magnate was accidentally run over by a Malaysian truck driver who hid his remains. *Jim Thompson: The Unsolved Mystery,* by William War-ren, is an excellent book on Thompson, his career, residence and subsequent intriguing disappearance.

Siam Square & Pratunam

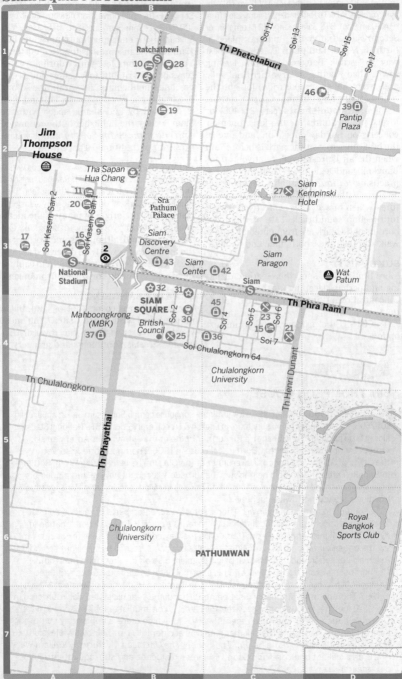

Th Phetchaburi

Soi 11
Soi 13
Soi 15
Soi 17

Ratchathewi
10 S
7
28
19

46

39
Pantip
Plaza

**Jim
Thompson
House**

Tha Sapan
Hua Chang

11
20
9

17
14
16
2

National
Stadium

Soi Kasem San 2
Soi Kasem San 1

Sra
Pathum
Palace

Siam
Discovery
Centre
43
Siam
Center 42

27
Siam
Kempinski
Hotel

44

Siam
Paragon

Wat
Patum

Siam

Th Phra Ram I

32 31
SIAM
SQUARE
30
25
36

Mahboongkrong
(MBK)
37
British
Council

Soi 2
45
23
15
21

Soi 4
Soi 5
Soi 6
Soi 7

Th Henri Dunant

Soi Chulalongkorn 64

Chulalongkorn
University

Th Chulalongkorn

Th Phayathai

Chulalongkorn
University

PATHUMWAN

Royal
Bangkok
Sports Club

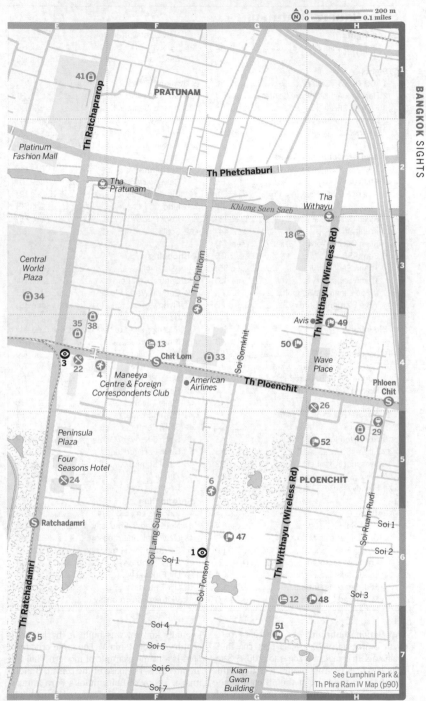

N
0 —————————— 200 m
0 —————————— 0.1 miles

PRATUNAM

Th Ratchaprarop

41

Platinum
Fashion Mall

Tha
Pratunam

Th Phetchaburi

Khlong Saen Saeb

Tha
Withayu

18

Central
World
Plaza

34

35
38

3

22

4

13

Chit Lom

33

Th Chitlom

8

Soi Somkhit

Avis

Th Witthayu (Wireless Rd)

49

50

Wave
Place

Phloen
Chit

Maneeya
Centre & Foreign
Correspondents Club

American
Airlines

Th Ploenchit

26

Peninsula
Plaza

Four
Seasons Hotel

24

40

29

52

PLOENCHIT

6

Ratchadamri

Soi Lang Suan

Soi 1

47

1

Soi Tonson

Th Witthayu (Wireless Rd)

Soi Ruam Rudi

Soi 1

Soi 2

Soi 3

12

48

Th Ratchadamri

5

Soi 4

Soi 5

Soi 6

Soi 7

51

Kian
Gwan
Building

See Lumphini Park &
Th Phra Ram IV Map (p90)

Siam Square Pratunam

Wat Benchamabophit BUDDHIST TEMPLE
(วัดเบญจมบพิตร (วัดเบญจฯ); Map p96; cnr Th Si
Ayuthaya & Th Phra Ram V; admission 20B; ⊙8am-
6pm; bus 72, 503) You might recognise this
temple from the back of the 5B coin. Made
of white Carrara marble, Wat Ben, as it's col-
loquially known, was built in the late 19th
century under Rama V. The large cruciform
bòht is a prime example of modern Thai wát
architecture. The base of the central Buddha
image, a copy of Phitsanulok's Phra Phuttha
Chinnarat, contains the ashes of Rama V. The

courtyard behind the *bòht* exhibits 53 Buddha images (33 originals and 20 copies) representing famous figures and styles from all over Thailand and other Buddhist countries.

Dusit Palace Park　　　ROYAL PALACE
(วังสวนดุสิต; Map p96; bounded by Th Ratchawithi, Th U-Thong Nai & Th Ratchasima; adult/child 100/50B or free with Grand Palace ticket; ⏱9.30am-4pm; bus 18, 28, 515) Following Rama V's first European tour in 1897 (he was the first Thai monarch to visit the continent), he returned home with visions of European castles swimming in his head and set about transforming these styles into a uniquely Thai expression, today's Dusit Palace Park. The royal palace, throne hall and minor palaces for extended family were all moved here from Ko Ratanakosin, the ancient royal court. Today the current king has yet another home and this complex now holds a house museum and other cultural collections.

Originally constructed on Ko Si Chang in 1868 and moved to the present site in 1910, **Vimanmaek Teak Mansion** contains 81 rooms, halls and anterooms, and is said to be the world's largest golden-teak building, allegedly built without the use of a single nail. The mansion was the first permanent building on the Dusit Palace grounds, and served as Rama V's residence in the early 1900s. The interior of the mansion contains various personal effects of the king and a treasure trove of early Ratanakosin art objects and antiques. Compulsory tours (in English) leave every half-hour between 9.45am and 3.15pm, and last about an hour.

The nearby **Ancient Cloth Museum** presents a beautiful collection of traditional silks and cottons that make up the royal cloth collection.

Originally built as a throne hall for Rama V in 1904, the smaller **Abhisek Dusit Throne Hall** is typical of the finer architecture of the era. Victorian-influenced gingerbread architecture and Moorish porticoes blend to create a striking and distinctly Thai exterior. The hall houses an excellent display of regional handiwork crafted by members of the Promotion of Supplementary Occupations & Related Techniques (Support) foundation, an organisation sponsored by Queen Sirikit.

Near the Th U-Thong Nai entrance, two large stables that once housed three white elephants – animals whose auspicious albinism automatically make them crown property – are now the **Royal Elephant Museum**. One of the structures contains artefacts and photos outlining the importance of elephants in Thai history and explaining their various rankings according to

THE CHINESE INFLUENCE

In many ways Bangkok is as much a Chinese city as it is Thai. The presence of the Chinese in Bangkok dates back to before the founding of the city, when Thonburi Si Mahasamut was little more than a Chinese trading outpost on the Chao Phraya River. In the 1780s, during the construction of the new capital under Rama I, Hokkien, Teochiew and Hakka Chinese were hired as coolies and labourers. The Chinese already living in the area were relocated to the districts of Yaowarat and Sampeng, today known as Bangkok's Chinatown.

During the reign of King Rama I, many Chinese began to move up in status and wealth. They controlled many of Bangkok's shops and businesses, and because of increased trading ties with China, were responsible for an immense expansion in Thailand's market economy. Visiting Europeans during the 1820s were astonished by the number of Chinese trading ships in the Chao Phraya River, and some assumed that the Chinese formed the majority of Bangkok's population.

The newfound wealth of certain Chinese trading families created one of Thailand's first elite classes that was not directly related to royalty. Known as *jôw sòo·a*, these 'merchant lords' eventually obtained additional status by accepting official posts and royal titles, as well as offering their daughters to the royal family. Today it is thought that more than half of the people in Bangkok can claim some Chinese ancestry.

During the reign of Rama III, the Thai capital began to absorb many elements of Chinese food, design, fashion and literature. The growing ubiquity of Chinese culture, coupled with the tendency of the Chinese men to marry Thai women and assimilate into Thai culture, meant that by the beginning of the 20th century there was relatively little that distinguished many Chinese from their Siamese counterparts.

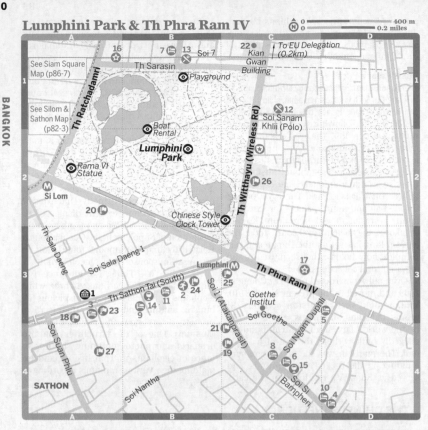

physical characteristics. The second stable holds a sculptural representation of a living royal white elephant (now kept at the Chitlada Palace, home to the current Thai king). Draped in royal vestments, the statue is more or less treated as a shrine by the visiting Thai public.

Because this is royal property, visitors should wear long pants (no capri pants) or long skirts and shirts with sleeves.

Rama V Memorial   MONUMENT

(พระบรมรูปทรงม้า; Map p96; Royal Plaza, Th U-Thong Nai; bus 18, 28, 515) A bronze figure of a military-garbed leader may seem like an unlikely shrine, but Bangkokians are comfortable with their expression of religious devotion. Most importantly, the figure is no forgotten general – this is Rama V (King Chulalongkorn; 1868–1910), who is widely credited for steering the country into the modern age and for preserving Thailand's independence from European colonialism. He is also con-

sidered a champion of the common person for his abolition of slavery and corvée (the requirement that every citizen be available for state labour when called). His accomplishments are so revered, especially by the middle class, that his statue attracts worshippers (particularly on Tuesdays, the day of his birth), who make offerings of candles, flowers (predominantly pink roses), incense and bottles of whisky. The statue is also the site of a huge celebration on 23 October, the anniversary of the monarch's death.

The domed neoclassical building behind the statue is **Ananta Samakhom Throne Hall** (Map p96; www.artsofthekingdom.com; Th U-Thong Nai; admission 150B; ☺10am-6pm Tue-Sun), originally built as a royal reception hall during the reign of Rama V, but not completed until 1915, five years after his death. Today the building houses an exhibit called Arts of the Kingdom, which like the nearby Abhisek Dusit Throne Hall, displays

Lumphini Park & Th Phra Ram IV

the products of Queen Sirikit's Support foundation.

FREE **National Library** LIBRARY, MUSEUM
(Map p96; ☑0 2281 5212; Th Samsen; ☺9am-6.30pm Mon-Fri, to 5pm Sat & Sun; river ferry Tha Thewet) Has few foreign-language resources, but the library's strength is in its astrological books and star charts, as well as recordings by the king and sacred palm-leaf writings and ancient maps.

Suan Phakkad Palace Museum MUSEUM
(วังสวนผักกาด; Map p97; ☑0 2245 4934; Th Sri Ayuthaya; admission 100B; ☺9am-4pm; BTS Phaya Thai) An overlooked treasure, Suan Phakkad is a collection of eight traditional wooden Thai houses that was once the residence of Princess Chumbon of Nakhon Sawan and before that a lettuce farm – hence the name. Within the stilt buildings are displays of art, antiques and furnishings, and the landscaped grounds are a peaceful oasis complete with ducks, swans and a semi-enclosed garden.

The diminutive **Lacquer Pavilion**, at the back of the complex, dates from the Ayuthaya period and features gold-leaf *jataka* and *Ramayana* murals, as well as scenes

from daily Ayuthaya life. The building originally sat in a monastery compound on Mae Nam Chao Phraya, just south of Ayuthaya. Larger residential structures at the front of the complex contain displays of Khmer-style Hindu and Buddhist art, Ban Chiang ceramics and a very interesting collection of historic Buddhas, including a beautiful late U Thong-style image.

🏃 Activities
Traditional Massage

A good massage is the birthright of every Bangkokian, and the joy of every visitor. Correspondingly, places offering massage are everywhere in Bangkok, and they range in quality, depending largely if they offer massage or 'massage'. To avoid the latter, stay clear of the places that advertise via scantily dressed women.

If it's your first time in the hands of a Thai masseur/masseuse, discard any preconceived notions, as many visitors find authentic Thai massage equal parts painful and relaxing. A traditional Thai massage often also involves herbal heat compresses (oil treatments are typically associated with 'sexy' massage).

BANGKOK

Th Sukhumvit

SUKHUMVIT

Th Phetchaburi

Th Ratchadaphisek

Th Sukhumvit

Soi 21 (Asoke)

TOBACCO
MONOPOLY

Benjakitti
Park

Lake
Ratchada

Benjasiri
Park

Phrom
Phong

Soi 55 (Thong Lor)

Kamphaeng Phet 7

Khlong Saen Saeb

To TAT Main
Office (1km)

Soi Ekamai 21

Soi Thong Lo 16

Soi Ekamai 5

Soi Thong Lor 10

Soi 9

Soi 5

Soi 53

Soi 51

Soi 49

Soi 45

Soi 43

Soi 41

Soi 39 (Phrom Phong)

Soi Promsri 2

Soi Promsri 1

Soi Phrommit

Soi Thong Lo 15

Thong Lor Soi 13

Soi 49

Soi 31 (Sawatdi)

Soi 33

Soi 31 (Sawatdi)

Soi 29
(Lak Khet)

Soi 27

Soi 23

Soi Cowboy

Sukhumvit

Asok

Jasmine
City

Soi 22

Soi 20

Soi 18

Soi 16

Soi 14

Soi 12

Soi 10

Soi 8

Soi 10

Soi 15

Soi 13

Soi 11

Soi 11/1

Soi 9

Soi 7

Soi 5

Soi 3 (Soi Nana Neua)

Soi Nana

One-
Two-Go

Soi 4 (Soi Nana Tai)

Soi 2 (Soi
Phasak)

Port-Din Daeng Expwy

Phloen
Chit

Landmark
Bangkok

Soi 1

400 m
0.2 miles

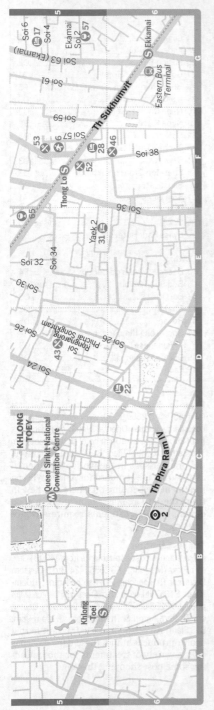

Health Land
SPA, MASSAGE

(www.healthlandspa.com; Thai massage 2 hours 450B) Ekamai (Map p92; ☑0 2392 2233; 96/1 Soi 10, Soi 63/Ekamai, Th Sukhumvit; ☺9am-11pm; BTS Ekkamai); Sathon (Map p82; ☑0 2637 8883; 120 Th Sathon Neua; ☺9am-11pm; BTS Chong Nonsi); Sukhumvit (Map p92; ☑0 2261 1110; 55/5 Soi 21/ Asoke, Th Sukhumvit; ☺9am-midnight; BTS Asok, MRT Sukhumvit) A winning formula of affordable prices, expert treatments and pleasant facilities has created a small empire of Health Land centres.

Wat Pho Thai Traditional Medical and Massage School
MASSAGE

(Map p60; ☑0 2622 3550; Soi Penphat, Th Sanam Chai; Thai massage per hr 220B; ☺8am-6pm; bus 123, 508, river ferry Tha Tien) The primary training ground for the masseuses who are deployed across the country; there are also massage pavilions inside the temple complex (see p59) and lessons are available (p100).

Asia Herb Association
MASSAGE

(www.asiaherbassociation.com; Thai massage per hr 350B) Phrom Phong (Map p92; ☑0 2260 8864; 33/1 Soi 24, Th Sukhumvit; ☺10am-9pm; BTS Phrom Phong); Sawastdi (Map p92; ☑0 2261 2201; 20/1 Soi 31/Sawatdi, Th Sukhumvit; ☺9am-midnight; BTS Phrom Phong); Thong Lor (Map p92; ☑0 2392 3631; 58/19-25 Soi 55/Thong Lor, Th Sukhumvit; ☺9am-midnight; BTS Thong Lo) With several branches along Th Sukhumvit, this Japanese-owned chain specialises in massage using *prà·kóp*, traditional Thai herbal compresses filled with 18 different herbs.

Ruen-Nuad Massage Studio
MASSAGE

(Map p82; ☑0 2632 2662; 42 Th Convent; Thai massage per hr 350B; ☺10am-9pm; BTS Sala Daeng, MRT Si Lom) Set in a refurbished wooden house, this charming place successfully avoids both the tackiness and New Agedness that characterise most Bangkok massage joints. Prices are affordable too.

Th Sukhumvit is home to several recommended and reputable massage studios, including:

Coran Boutique Spa
MASSAGE

(Map p92; ☑0 2651 1588; www.coranbangkok. com; 27/1-2 Soi 13, Th Sukhumvit; Thai massage per hr 400B; ☺11am-10pm; BTS Nana)

Lavana
MASSAGE

(Map p92; ☑0 2229 4510; www.lavanabangkok. com; 4 Soi 12, Th Sukhumvit; Thai massage per hr 450B; ☺9am-11pm; BTS Asok, MRT Sukhumvit)

Th Sukhumvit

Rakuten   MASSAGE
(Map p92; ☎0 2258 9433; www.rakutenspa.com;
94 Soi 33, Th Sukhumvit; Thai massage per hr
250B; ⊕noon-midnight; BTS Phrom Phong)

Baan Dalah   MASSAGE
(Map p92; ☎0 2653 3358; www.baandalahmind
bodyspa.com; 2 Soi 8, Th Sukhumvit; Thai massage per hr 350B; ⊕10am-midnight; BTS Nana)

Spas
Unless you've spent your entire visit in an
air-conditioned bubble (entirely possible in
today's Bangkok), at some point you're going
to need to rid yourself of the negative effects
of the city's urban environment. This can take
the form of a simple scrub or can involve
multistage treatments involving a customised
choice of aromas and oils, a team of staff and
possibly even acupuncture needles. There
are countless spas in Bangkok now, many of
them located in the city's high-end hotels with
high-end price tags to match. To round down
your choices, visit www.spasinbangkok.com
or consider one of the following:

Oriental Spa   SPA
(Map p80; ☎0 2659 9000; www.mandarinoriental.
com/bangkok/spa; Oriental Hotel; spa packages
from 2900B; ⊕9am-10pm; hotel shuttle boat from
Tha Sathon/Central Pier) Regarded as among
the premier spas in the world, the Oriental
Spa also set the standard for Asian-style spa
treatment. Depending on where you flew in
from, the Jet Lag Massage might be a good
option, but all treatments require advance
booking.

Thann Sanctuary   SPA
(www.thann.info; spa treatments from 1400B) Gaysorn Plaza (Map p86; ☎0 2656 1424; 3rd fl, Gaysorn
Plaza, cnr Th Ploenchit & Th Ratchadamri; ⊕10am-
10pm; BTS Chit Lom); Siam Discovery Center (Map
p86; ☎0 2258 0550; 5th fl, Siam Discovery Center,
cnr Th Phra Ram I & Th Phayathai; ⊕10am-9pm;
BTS Siam) An offshoot of the fragrant herbal
health products brand, these dark day spas
offer a variety of treatments for those needing some post-shopping therapy.

Spa 1930   SPA
(Map p86; ☑0 2254 8606; www.spa1930.com; Soi Tonson, Th Ploenchit; spa treatments from 3800B; ⊙9.30am-9.30pm; BTS Chit Lom) It rescues relaxers from the contrived spa ambience of New Age music and ingredients you'd rather see at a dinner party. The menu is simple (face, body care and body massage) and all scrubs and massage oils are based on traditional Thai herbal remedies.

Divana Massage & Spa   SPA
(Map p92; ☑0 2261 6784; www.divanaspa.com; 7 Soi 25, Th Sukhumvit; spa treatments from 2500B; ⊙11am-11pm Mon-Fri, 10-11am Sat & Sun; BTS Asok, MRT Sukhumvit) This place retains a unique Thai touch with a private and soothing setting in a garden house.

Sports & Yoga Facilities
If you're dedicated to the cause of athletic pusuits in this energy-sucking climate, you need access to an air-conditioned facility. Most membership gyms and top-end hotels have fitness centres and swimming pools.

Some hotels offer day-use fees but these policies vary per establishment.

Clark Hatch Physical Fitness Centers (www.clarkhatchthailand.com) is a top-class operation with more than 14 locations throughout the city. All branches have weight machines, aerobics classes, pool, sauna and massage.

Other commercial gyms include **California Wow** (www.californiawowx.com), with seven branches, and **Fitness First** (www.fitnessfirst.co.th), with 15.

Hash House Harriers   RUNNING
(www.bangkokhhh.com) One of Bangkok's longest-running sports groups is the Hash House Harriers, who pride themselves both on their dedication to running and their ability to subdue dehydration with massive amounts of beer. If you've got commitment issues with either pursuit, start with a simple jog at a local park, such as Lumphini (p85).

Yoga Elements Studio   YOGA
(Map p86; ☑0 2655 5671; www.yogaelements.com; 23rd fl, 29 Vanissa Bldg, Th Chitlom; BTS Chit

Thewet & Dusit

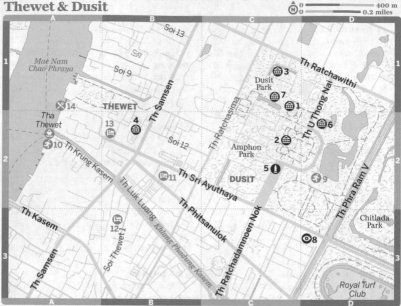

Thewet & Dusit

Lom) Emphasises a vinyasa flow practice with attractive rates.

Absolute Yoga   YOGA
(Map p86; ☎0 2252 4400; www.absoluteyoga bangkok.com; 4th fl, Amarin Plaza, Th Ploenchit; BTS Chit Lom) It offers yoga for the gym rat, not the spiritualist, with classes in hot yoga, Pilates and vinyasa.

🍃 Courses

Cooking and language courses dominate Bangkok's continuing-education syllabus.

Cooking

Imagine the points you'll rack up if you can make authentic Thai dishes for your friends back at home. A visit to a Thai cooking school has become a must-do for many Bangkok itineraries, and for some visitors it's a highlight of their trip.

Courses range in price and value, but a typical half-day course should include at least a basic introduction to Thai ingredients and flavours, and a hands-on chance to both prepare and cook several dishes. Most schools offer a revolving cast of dishes that changes on a daily basis, making it possible to study for a week without repeating the cooking of a dish. Many courses include a visit to a market, and nearly all lessons include a set of printed recipes and end with a communal lunch consisting of your handiwork.

Khao COOKERY COURSE
(Map p60; ☑08 9111 0947; www.khaocookingschool.com; D&D Plaza, 68-70 Th Khao San; lessons 1500B; ◷9.30am-12.30pm & 1.30-4.30pm) Although it's located smack dab in the middle of Khao San, this new cooking school was started up by an authority on Thai food and features instruction on a wide variety of authentic dishes. Located in the courtyard behind D&D Inn.

Helping Hands COOKERY COURSE
(☑08 4901 8717; www.cookingwithpoo.com) This popular cookery course was started by a native of Khlong Toey's slums and is held in her neighbourhood. Courses, which must be booked in advance, span four dishes and include a visit to Khlong Toey Market and transport to and from Emporium (p137).

Baipai Thai Cooking School COOKERY COURSE
(Map p56; ☑0 2561 1404; www.baipai.com; 8/91 Soi 54, Th Ngam Wong Wan; lessons 1800B; ◷9.30am-1.30pm & 1.30-5.30pm Tue-Sat) Housed in an attractive suburban villa, and taught by a small army of staff, Baipai offers two daily lessons of four dishes each. Transport is available.

BANGKOK COURSES

Ratchathewi

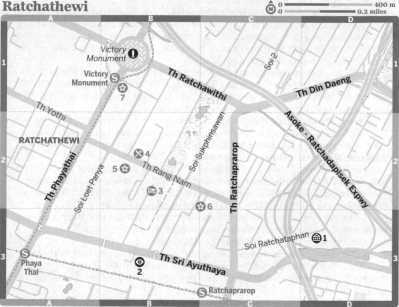

Ratchathewi

BANGKOK FOR CHILDREN

There aren't a whole lot of attractions in Bangkok meant directly to appeal to the little ones, but there's no lack of locals willing to provide attention. The website www.bambi web.org is a useful resource for parents in Bangkok.

Housing a colourful selection of traditional Thai dolls, both new and antique, is the **Bangkok Doll Factory & Museum** (Map p97; ☏0 2245 3008; 85 Soi Ratchaphataphan/ Mo Leng; admission free; ☺8am-5pm Mon-Sat; BTS Ratchaprarop). The downside is that it can be really hard to find. Approach via Th Si Ayuthaya heading east. Cross under the expressway past the intersection with Th Ratchaprarop and take the soi to the right of the post office. Follow this windy street until you start seeing signs.

Disguising learning as kid's play, most activities at the **Children's Discovery Museum** (Map p118; www.bkkchildrenmuseum.com; Queen Sirikit Park, Th Kamphaengphet 4; adult/child 70/50B; ☺9am-5pm Tue-Fri, 10am-6pm Sat & Sun) are geared to early elementary–aged children. There is also a toddler-aged playground at the back of the main building. Note that the museum was closed for revovations at the time of research, and was scheduled to re-open in late 2011. It's opposite Chatuchak Weekend Market.

Although not specifically child-targeted, the **Museum of Siam** (p63) has lots of interactive exhibits that will appeal to children.

Dusit Zoo (Map p96; Th Ratchawithi; adult/child 100/50B; ☺8am-6pm; bus 18, 28, 515) covers 19 hectares with caged exhibits of more than 300 mammals, 200 reptiles and 800 birds, including relatively rare indigenous species such as banteng, gaur, serow and some rhinoceros. There are shady grounds plus a lake in the centre with paddleboats for hire and a small children's playground.

A massive underwater world has been re-created at the **Siam Ocean World** (Map p86; www.siamoceanworld.co.th; basement, Siam Paragon, Th Phra Ram I; adult/child 900/700B; ☺10am-9pm; BTS Siam) shopping-centre aquarium. Gaze into the glass-enclosed deep-reef zone or view the daily feeding of penguins and sharks.

Lumphini Park (p85) is a trusty ally in the cool hours of the morning and evening for kite-flying (in season) as well as for stretching the legs and lungs. Nearby, kids can view lethal snakes become reluctant altruists at the adjacent antivenin-producing **Queen Saovabha Memorial Institute** (p79) snake farm.

Further Afield, **Siam Park City** (Map p153; 203 Th Suansiam, Khannayao; ☏0 2919 7200; www.siamparkcity.com; Th Ratchawithi; admission 100-600B; ☺10am-6pm) and **Dream World** (Map p153; ☏0 2533 1152; www.dreamworld-th.com; 62 Moo 1, Th Rangsit-Nakornnayok, Patumthani; admission from 450B; ☺10am-6pm) are expansive amusement parks. Siam Park City features more than 30 rides and a water park with the largest wave pool in the world, while Dream World features a snow room. Both lie north of Bangkok and are accessible by taxi from Mo Chit BTS station (Map p118).

Join the novice monks and other children as they sprinkle tiny pellets of fish food (which are sold on the pier) into the river at **Tha Thewet** (Map p96; Th Samsen; ☺7am-7pm, bus 32, 315, river ferry Tha Thewet), transforming the muddy river into a brisk boil of flapping bodies.

MBK Center (p136) and **Siam Paragon** (p137) both have bowling alleys to keep the older ones occupied. **Krung Sri IMAX** (Map p86; ☏0 2129 4631; www.imaxthai.com; Siam Paragon, Th Phra Ram I; tickets 350-450B; BTS Siam) screens special-effects versions of Hollywood action flicks and nature features.

Blue Elephant Thai Cooking School COOKERY COURSE
(Map p82; ☏0 2673 9353; www.blueelephant.com; 233 Th Sathon Tai; lessons 2943B; ☺8.45am-1pm & 1.15-4.30pm Mon-Sat; BTS Surasak) Bangkok's most chi-chi Thai cooking school offers two lessons daily. The morning class squeezes in a visit to a local market, while the afternoon session includes a detailed introduction to Thai ingredients.

Silom Thai Cooking School COOKERY COURSE
(Map p82; ☏08 4726 5669; www.bangkokthai cooking.com; 68 Soi 13/Trok Vaithi, Th Silom; lessons 1000B; ☺9.30am-1pm & 1.40-6pm; BTS

Chong Nonsi) The facilities are basic but Silom crams a visit to a local market and instruction of six dishes into three and a half hours, making it the best bang for your baht. Transportation is available.

Meditation

Although at times Bangkok may seem like the most un-Buddhist place on earth, there are several places where foreigners can practise Theravada Buddhist meditation. For background information on Buddhism, see p729; for temple etiquette, see p59 and p34. Additional sources of information include **Dharma Thai** (www.dhammathai.org), which has a rundown on several prominent wát and meditation centres.

House of Dhamma
MEDITATION

(Map p118; ☑0 2511 0439; www.houseofdhamma. com; 26/9 Soi 15, Th Lat Prao; MRT Lat Phrao) Helen Jandamit has opened her suburban Bangkok home to meditation retreats and classes in *vipassana* (insight meditation). Check the website to see what workshops are on offer, and be sure to call ahead before making a visit.

Wat Mahathat
MEDITATION

(Map p60; 3 Th Maha Rat; bus 32, 201, 503, river ferry Tha Maharaj or Tha Chang) This temple is home to two independently operating meditation centres. The **International Buddhist Meditation Center** (☑0 2222 6011; www.centermeditation.org; Section 5, Wat Mahathat; donations accepted) offers daily meditation classes at 7am, 1pm and 6pm. Taught by English-speaking Phra Suputh, classes last three hours. The **Meditation Study and Retreat Center** (☑0 223 6878; www.meditation-watmahadhat.com; Wat Mahathat; donations accepted) offers a regimented daily programme of meditation. With both of these programmes, longer stays, including accommodation and food can be arranged, but students are expected to follow a strict regmen of conduct.

World Fellowship of Buddhists
MEDITATION

(WFB; Map p92; ☑0 2661 1284; www.wfb-hq. org; 616 Benjasiri Park, Soi 24, Th Sukhumvit; ☺8.30am-4pm Sun-Fri; BTS Phrom Phong) On the first Sunday of the month, this centre of Theravada Buddhism hosts meditation classes in English from 2pm to 5pm. The fellowship also holds interesting forums on Buddhist issues.

Thai Boxing

Training in *moo·ay tai* (also spelt *muay thai*) for foreigners has increased in popularity in the past five years and many camps all over the country are tailoring their programs for English-speaking fighters. The following camps provide instruction in English and accept men and women. Food and accommodation can often be provided for an extra charge. The website www.muaythai. com contains loads of information on training camps.

Muay Thai Institute
THAI BOXING GYM

(Map p153; ☑0 2992 0096; www.muaythai-institute.net; Rangsit Stadium, 336/932 Th Prachatipat, Pathum Thani; tuition for 1st level 8000B; BTS Mo Chit & access by taxi) Associated with the respected World Muay Thai Council, the institute offers a fundamental course (consisting of three levels of expertise), as well as courses for instructors, referees and judges.

Sor Vorapin Gym
THAI BOXING GYM

(Map p60; ☑0 2282 3551; www.thaiboxings.com; 13 Th Kasab, Th Chakraphong; tuition per day/month 500/9000B; bus 2, 15, 44, 511, river ferry Tha Phra Athit) Specialising in training foreign students of both genders, this gym is sweating distance from Th Khao San. More serious training is held at a gym outside the city.

Fairtex Muay Thai
THAI BOXING GYM

(off Map p153; ☑0 2755 3329; www.fairtexbangplee. com; 99/5 Mu 3, Soi Buthamanuson, Th Thaeparak, Bangpli, Samut Prakan; tuition & accommodation per day from 1100B; BTS Chong Nonsi & access by taxi) A popular, long-running camp south of Bangkok.

Thai Language
Union Language School
THAI LANGUAGE LESSONS

(Map p86; ☑0 2214 6033; www.unionlanguageschool.com; 7th fl, 328 CCT Office Bldg, Th Phayathai; tuition from 7000B; BTS Ratchathewi) Generally recognised as having the best and most rigorous courses (many missionaries study here). Union employs a balance of structure- and communication-oriented methodologies in 80-hour, four-week modules.

American University Alumni Language Centre
THAI LANGUAGE LESSONS

(AUA; Map p86; ☑0 2252 8398; www.auathai.com; 179 Th Ratchadamri; tuition per hr 128B; BTS Ratchadamri) This longstanding institute features various levels of tuition that can be completed within a sliding timescale.

Pro Language THAI LANGUAGE LESSONS

(Map p92; ☑0 2250 0072; www.prolanguage. co.th; 10th fl, Times Square Bldg, 246 Th Sukhumvit; BTS Asok, MRT Sukhumvit; tuition from 10,00B) A favourite of expat professionals; Pro Language starts with the basics and increases in difficulty to the advanced level, which involves studying examples of Thai literature.

Siri-Pattana Thai Language School THAI LANGUAGE LESSONS

(Map p90; ☑0 2677 3150; siri_pattanathai@ hotmail.com; YWCA, 13 Th Sathon Tai; MRT Lumphini; tuition from 7500B) This institute offers Thai-language courses that cover 30 hours broken into one- or two-hour classes per day, as well as preparation for the *bor hòk* (teaching proficiency exam).

AAA Thai Language Center THAI LANGUAGE LESSONS

(Map p86; ☑0 2655 5629; www.aaathai.com; 6th fl, 29 Vanissa Bldg, Th Chitlom; BTS Chit Lom) Opened by a group of experienced Thai language teachers from other schools, good-value AAA Thai has a loyal following.

Thai Massage

Wat Pho Thai Traditional Medical and Massage School THAI MASSAGE

(Map p60; ☑0 2622 3550; www.watpomassage. com; 392/25-28 Soi Phen Phat; tuition from 5000B; ⊘8am-6pm; bus 508, 512, river ferry Tha Tien) Offers basic and advanced courses in traditional Thai massage; basic courses offer 30 hours spread out over five days and cover either general massage or foot massage. The advanced level spans 60 hours, requires the basic course as a prerequisite, and covers therapeutic and healing massage. Other advanced courses include oil massage and aromatherapy, and infant and child massage. The school is outside the temple compound in a restored Bangkok shophouse on unmarked Soi Phen Phat – look for Coconut Palm restaurant.

☞ Tours

If you would like a guide, recommended outfits include **Tour with Tong** (☑0 81835 0240; www.tourwithtong.com; day tour from 1000B), whose team conduct tours in and around Bangkok, and **Thai Private Tour Guide** (☑0 81860 9159; www.thaitourguide.com; day tour from 2000B), where Chob and Mee get good reviews.

See p104 for more specific guided tour experiences.

Boat Tours
RIVER & CANAL TRIPS

Glimpses of Bangkok's past as the 'Venice of the East' are still possible today, even though the motor vehicle has long since become the city's conveyance of choice. Along the river and the canals is a motley fleet of watercraft, from paddled canoes to rice barges. In these areas many homes, trading houses and temples remain oriented towards life on the water, providing a fascinating glimpse into the past when Thais still considered themselves *jôw nám* (water lords).

The most obvious way to commute between riverside attractions is the **Chao Phraya Express** (☑0 2623 6001; www.chaophrayaboat.co.th; tickets 9-32B). The terminus for most northbound boats is Tha Nonthaburi and for most southbound boats it's Tha Sathon (also called Central Pier), near the Saphan Taksin BTS station, although some boats run as far south as Wat Ratchasingkhon. See p149 for more information about boat travel.

For a more custom view, you might consider chartering a long-tail boat along the city's canals – see boxed text, p101 for details.

DINNER CRUISES

Perfect for romancing couples or subdued families, dinner cruises drift along Mae Nam Chao Phraya basking in the twinkling city lights at night, far away from the heat and noise of town. Cruises range from downhome to sophisticated, but the food generally ranges from mediocre to forgettable.

Loy Nava DINNER CRUISE

(Map p80; ☑0 2437 4932; www.loynava.com; set menu 1766B; ⊘6-8pm & 8.10-10.10pm) Operating since 1970, and quite possibly the original Bangkok dinner cruise, Loy Nava offers two daily excursions, both departing from the Tha Si Phraya, near River City. A vegetarian menu is available.

Manohra Cruises DINNER CRUISE

(Map p56; ☑0 2477 0770; www.manohracruises. com; Bangkok Marriott Resort & Spa, Thonburi; cocktail cruise, dinner cruise adult/child 2343/1712B; ⊘7.30-10pm) Commands a fleet of converted teak rice barges that part the waters with regal flair. Boats depart from the Marriott Resort, accessible via a free river shuttle that operates from Tha Sathon (near BTS Saphan Taksin; see map p80).

Wan Fah Cruises   DINNER CRUISE
(Map p80; ✆0 2222 8679; www.wanfah.in.th; cruises 1200B; ✆7-9pm; river ferry to Tha Si Phraya) Departing from the River City Complex, Wan Fah runs a buxom wooden boat that floats in style with accompanying Thai music and traditional dance. Dinner options include a standard or seafood set menu, and hotel transfer is available.

Yok Yor Restaurant   DINNER CRUISE
(Map p80; ✆0 2439 3477; www.yokyor.co.th; dinner à la carte plus adult/child 140/70B surcharge; ✆8-10pm; river-crossing ferry from Th Sri Phraya) This long-running floating restaurant on the Thonburi side of the river also runs a daily dinner cruise, as well as several boats that can be hired for private functions.

BANG PA-IN & AYUTHAYA CRUISES
A little faster than the days of sailing ships, river cruises from Bangkok north to the ruins of the former royal capital of Ayuthaya (p157) take in all the romance of the river. Most trips include a guided tour of Ayuthaya's ruins with a stop at the summer palace of Bang Pa In (p167). Normally only one leg of the journey between Bangkok and Ayuthaya is aboard a boat, while the return or departing trip is by bus.

Asian Oasis   RIVER CRUISE
(Map p86; ✆0 2655 6246; www.asian-oasis.com; 7th floor, Nai Lert Tower, 2/4 Th Witthayu/Wireless Rd; 2-day trip 6450-10,450B depending on season & direction) Cruise the Chao Phraya River aboard a fleet of restored rice barges with old-world charm and modern conveniences.

Trips include either an upstream or downstream journey to/from Ayuthaya with bus transfer in the opposite direction.

Manohra Cruises   RIVER CRUISE
(Map p56; ✆0 2477 0770; www.manohracruises.com; Bangkok Marriott Resort & Spa, Thonburi; 3-day trip 69,000B) The nautical equivalent of the *Eastern & Oriental Express* train, the *Manohra Song* is a restored teak rice barge decorated with antiques, Persian carpets and four luxury sleeping berths. The trip is a three-day, two-night excursion to Ayuthaya, and the package price is all-inclusive except for tax and service. The *Manohra Dream*, an even more luxurious boat for a maximum of two couples, is also available for longer excursions.

Bicycle & Segway Tours
Although some cycling tours tackle the city's urban neighbourhoods, many take advantage of the nearby lush, undeveloped district to the south known as Phra Pradaeng (Map p56), where narrow walkways crisscross irrigation canals that feed small-scale fruit plantations and simple villages.

To tour the sites of old Bangkok by free borrowed bicycle, see the boxed text, p151.

Grasshopper Adventures   BICYCLE TOURS
(Map p60; ✆0 2280 0832; www.grasshopperadventures.com; 57 Th Ratchadamnoen Klang; tours from 750B; ✆8.30am-6.30pm Mon-Fri; bus 2, 15, 44, 511, klorng taxi Tha Phan Fah) This lauded outfit runs a variety of unique bicycle tours in and

---

ROLLIN' ON THE...CANAL

For an up-close view of the city's famed canals, long-tail boats are available for hire at Tha Chang, Tha Tian, Tha Oriental and Tha Phra Athit. Prices at Tha Chang are the highest and allow little room for negotiation, but you stand the least chance of being taken for a ride or being hit up for tips and other unexpected fees.

Trips explore the Thonburi canals **Khlong Bangkok Noi** and, further south, **Khlong Bangkok Yai**, taking in the Royal Barges National Museum, Wat Arun and a riverside temple with fish feeding. Longer trips diverge into **Khlong Mon**, between Bangkok Noi and Bangkok Yai, which offers more typical canal scenery, including orchid farms. On weekends, you have the option of visiting the **Taling Chan floating market**. However it's worth pointing out that, to actually disembark and explore any of these sights, the most common tour of one hour (1000B, up to six people) is simply not enough time and you'll most likely need 1½ (1300B) or two hours (1600B). Most operators have set tour routes, but if you have a specific destination in mind, you can request it.

A cheaper alternative is to take the **commuter long-tail boat** (50B; one hour; ✆4pm-7pm) that also departs from Tha Chang, although it's one-way only and you'll have to find your own way back from Bang Yai, located at the distant northern end of Khlong Bangkok Noi.

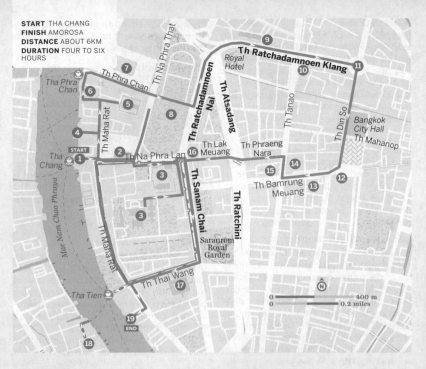

Walking Tour
Old Bangkok

❭ The bulk of Bangkok's 'must-see' destinations are found in the former royal district, Ko Ratanakosin, and Banglamphu, so this walking tour links the two, spanning major and minor attractions. It's best to start early to beat the heat and get in before the hordes have descended. Remember to dress modestly (long pants and skirts, shirts with sleeves and closed-toed shoes) in order to gain entry to the temples. Also ignore any strangers who approach you offering advice on sightseeing or shopping.

Start at ❶ **Tha Chang** and follow Th Na Phra Lan east with a quick diversion to ❷ **Silpakorn University**, Thailand's premier fine-arts university. Originally founded as the School of Fine Arts by Italian artist Corrado Feroci, the university campus includes part of an old palace built for Rama I. If you haven't already been, continue east to the main gate into ❸ **Wat Phra Kaew & Grand Palace**, two of Bangkok's most famous attractions.

Double back to Th Maha Rat and proceed north, through a gauntlet of herbal apoth-

ecaries and pavement amulet sellers. Immediately after passing the cat-laden newsstand (you'll know it when you smell it), turn left into ❹ **Trok Tha Wang**, a narrow alleyway holding a seemingly hidden classic Bangkok neighbourhood. Returning to Th Maha Rat, continue moving north. On your right is ❺ **Wat Mahathat** one of Thailand's most respected Buddhist universities.

Across the street, turn left into crowded Trok Mahathat to discover the cramped ❻ **amulet market**. Follow the alley all the way towards the river to appreciate how extensive the amulet trade is.

As you continue north alongside the river, amulets soon turn to food vendors. The emergence of white-and-black uniforms is a clue that you are approaching ❼ **Thammasat University**, known for its law and political-science departments. The campus was also the site of the bloody October 1976 prodemocracy demonstrations, when Thai students were killed or wounded by the military.

Exiting the market at Tha Phra Chan, cross Th Maha Rat and continue east, passing even more traditional Thai medicine shops and amulet vendors until you reach ❽ **Sanam Luang**, the 'Royal Field'. The park is the site for the annual Ploughing Ceremony, in which the King (or, lately, the Crown Prince) officially initiates the rice-growing season, and a large kite competition is also held here during the kite-flying season (mid-February to April).

Cross Th Ratchadamnoen Nai and go north, turning right at the Royal Hotel onto ❾ **Th Ratchadamnoen Klang**, Bangkok's own Champs Élysées. Continuing east, after the intersection Th Tanao, you'll see the ❿ **October 14 Memorial**, commemorating the civilian demonstrators who were killed on 14 October 1973 by the military during a prodemocracy rally. Ahead in the distance you'll see the four-pronged ⓫ **Democracy Monument**, erected in 1932 to commemorate Thailand's transformation from absolute to constitutional monarchy. In recent decades, the monument has been a site of huge demonstrations, most notably during 1973 and 1992.

Turn right down Th Din So and continue south until you reach the unmistakable ⓬ **Wat Suthat and Sao Ching-Cha**, both lesser-known Bangkok landmarks.

You're well overdue for lunch at this point, but thankfully you're only a couple of blocks west of Th Tanao, one of Bangkok's premier eating areas. Cut through the ⓭ **religious shops** along Th Bamrung Meuang for a pit stop at ⓮ **Poj Spa Kar** or ⓯ **Chote Chitr**.

After lunch, turn left on Th Phraeng Nara, crossing Khlong Lawt, and continue west along Th Lak Meuang until you reack the street's namesake and home of Bangkok's city spirit, ⓰ **Lak Meuang**.

After paying your respects, head south along Th Sanam Chai and turn right onto Th Thai Wang, which will escort you to the entrance of ⓱ **Wat Pho** home of the giant Reclining Buddha and lots of quiet nooks and crannies.

If you've still got the energy, head to adjacent Tha Tien to catch the cross-river ferry to Khmer-influenced ⓲ **Wat Arun**; otherwise end your journey with celebratory drinks at the Arun Residence's rooftop bar, ⓳ **Amorosa** – if you're there at the right time, you can catch one of Bangkok's premier sunset views.

around Bangkok, including a night tour and a tour of the city's green zones.

ABC Amazing Bangkok Cyclists
BICYCLE TOURS

(Map p92; ☑0 2665 6364; www.realasia.net; 10/5-7 Soi 26, Th Sukhumvit; tours from 1000B; ☺tours at 8am, 10am or 1pm; BTS Phrom Phong) Operating for more than a decade, the bike-based tours here purport to reveal the 'real' Asia by following the elevated walkways of the city's rural canals.

Segway Tour Thailand
SEGWAY TOURS

(Map p60; ☑0 2221 4525; www.segwaytourthai land.com; Maharaj Pier Building, Tha Maharaj, off Th Maha Rat; half-day tours from 3500B; ☺9.30am-6.30pm Tues-Sun; 32, 201, 503, river ferry Tha Maharaj) This outfit runs half-day and full-day Segway tours of Bangkok and elsewhere, including Ayuthaya.

Bangkok Bike Rides
BICYCLE TOURS

(Map p92; ☑0 2712 5305; www.bangkokbikerides. com; 14/1-B Soi Phromsi 2, off Soi 39/Phrompong, Th Sukhumvit; tours from 1000B; ☺8.30am-6.30pm Tue-Sun; BTS Phrom Phong) A division of the tour company Spice Roads, it offers a variety of tours, both urban and rural.

Walking & Speciality Tours

Although the pollution and heat are significant obstacles, Bangkok is a fascinating city to explore on foot. If you'd rather do it with an expert guide, **Bangkok Private Tours** (www.bangkokprivatetours.com; full-day walking tour 3400B) conducts customised walking tours of the city. And foodies may appreciate the offerings at **Bangkok Food Tours** (☑08 9126 3657; www.bangkokfoodtours.com; half-day tour adult/child 950/750B), which offer half-day culinary tours of Bangkok's Bang Rak neighbourhood.

⭐ Festivals & Events

In addition to the national holidays (see p759), there's always something going on in Bangkok. Check the website of **TAT** (www. tourismthailand.org) or the **Bangkok Information Center** (www.bangkoktourist.com) for exact dates. The cultural centres also host various international festivals.

February & March
Chinese New Year
NEW YEAR

Thai-Chinese celebrate the lunar New Year with a week of housecleaning, lion dances and fireworks. Most festivities centre on Chinatown. Dates vary.

Kite-Flying Season
KITE-FLYING

During the windy season (March), colourful kites battle it out over the skies of Sanam Luang and Lumphini Park.

April & May
Songkran
NEW YEAR

The celebration of the Thai New Year has morphed into a water war with high-powered water guns and water balloons being launched at suspecting and unsuspecting participants. The most intense water battles take place on Th Khao San. Held in mid-April.

Royal Ploughing Ceremony
PLANTING CEREMONY

His Majesty the King (or lately the Crown Prince) commences rice-planting season with a ceremony at Sanam Luang. Held in May; dates vary.

August
Queen's Birthday
MOTHER'S DAY

The queen's birthday is recognised as Mother's Day throughout the country. In Bangkok, festivities centre on Th Ratchadamnoen and the Grand Palace. Held on 12 August.

September & October
Vegetarian Festival
FOOD FESTIVAL

A 10-day Chinese-Buddhist festival wheels out yellow-bannered streetside vendors serving meatless meals. The greatest concentration of vendors is found in Chinatown. Dates vary.

International Festival of Music & Dance
MUSIC & DANCE FESTIVAL

(www.bangkokfestivals.com) An extravaganza of arts and culture sponsored by the Thailand Cultural Centre. Held September or October.

King Chulalongkorn Day
ROYAL EVENT

Rama V is honoured on the anniversary of his death at the Royal Plaza in Dusit. Crowds of devotees come to make merit with incense and flower garlands. Held on 23 October.

November
Loi Krathong
FULL-MOON FESTIVAL

A beautiful festival where, on the night of the full moon, small lotus-shaped boats made of banana leaf and containing a lit candle are set adrift on Mae Nam Chao Phraya. Held in early November.

Fat Festival
MUSIC FESTIVAL

Sponsored by FAT 104.5FM radio, Bangkok's indie-est indie bands gather for an annual fest. Held in early November.

Bangkok Pride GAY & LESBIAN
(www.bangkokpride.org) A week-long festival of parades, parties and awards is organised by the city's gay businesses and organisations. Held in mid-November.

Bangkok World Film Festival FILM FESTIVAL
(www.worldfilmbkk.com) Home-grown talent and overseas indies arrive on the silver screens. Held in mid-November.

December

King's Birthday FESTIVAL
Locals celebrate their monarch's birthday with lots of parades and fireworks. Held on 5 December.

🛏 Sleeping

At first glance, deciding where to lay your head in Bangkok appears an insurmountable task – there are countless hotels in virtually every corner of this sprawling city. Making this task slightly easier is the fact that where you stay is largely determined by your budget. Banglamphu and the tourist ghetto of Th Khao San still hold the bulk of Bangkok's budget accommodation, although the downside is that it can be difficult to get to other parts of town. Cheap rooms are also available around lower Th Sukhumvit, although you'll have to put up with sex tourists and touts. Chinatown also has its share of hotels in this category, with the added bonus of anonymity. And there's a decent selection of budget digs on Soi Ngam Duphli, near Th Sathon.

Those willing to spend a bit more can consider staying in 'downtown' Bangkok. Both Th Sukhumvit and Th Silom have heaps of midrange options, often within walking distance of the BTS or MRT. The sois opposite the National Stadium, near Siam Sq, have some good midrange options, and have the benefit of being close to the BTS.

Upper Sukhumvit is home to many of Bangkok's boutique and upscale designer hotels. And the city's most famous luxury hotels are largely found along the riverside near Th Silom.

KO RATANAKOSIN, BANGLAMPHU & THONBURI

Ko Ratanakosin, the most touristed area of Bangkok, was until relatively recently utterly devoid of lodging options. But with the advent of the boutique-hotel craze, a few riverside shophouses are being transformed into charming tourists' nests.

Although Banglamphu is ground zero for budget accommodation in Bangkok, this doesn't necessarily mean it's the only or even the best place to stay in town, but prices are generally low, and services such as internet cafes, travel agents and beer stalls are available in abundance, making it a convenient base.

In recent years many longstanding Banglamphu guest house owners have converted their former hovels into small hotels, leading to an abundance of new, good-value midrangers and posh backpacker hostels. Although some see this as the gentrification of Th Khao San, it's added a dimension of accommodation that was previously lacking.

It would be impossible to list all of Banglamphu's accommodation options in this book. Instead, we've chosen a select few that stand out, typically those away from the main strip, which can get pretty noisy. If you've got the time, explore a bit and check out a few guest houses before making a decision – there are increasingly attractive options spanning all price levels on outlying streets such as riverside Th Phra Athit, leafy Soi Ram Buttri and the residential side streets off Th Samsen. During the high season (December to February), however, it's probably a wise idea to take the first vacant bed you come across. The best time of day to find a vacancy is around check-out time, 10am or 11am.

Th Khao San & Around

Diamond House BOUTIQUE HOTEL $$
(Map p60; ☏0 2629 4008; www.thaidiamondhouse. com; 4 Th Samsen; r 2000-2800B; ste 3600B; ※@🕏; bus 32, 516, river ferry Tha Phra Athit) Despite sharing real estate with a rather brash Chinese temple, there's no conflict of design at this eccentric, funky hotel. Most rooms are loft style, with beds on raised platforms, and are outfitted with stained glass, dark, lush colours and chic furnishings. There's a lack of windows, and some of the suites aren't that much larger than the cheaper rooms, but a rooftop sunbathing deck and an outdoor Jacuzzi (!) make up for this.

NapPark Hostel HOSTEL $
(Map p60; ☏0 2282 2324; www.nappark.com; 8 Th Tani; dm 550-750B; ※@🕏; river ferry Tha Phra Athit) This exceedingly well-done hostel features dorm rooms of various sizes, the smallest and most expensive of which boasts six pod-like beds outfitted with power points, mini-TV, reading lamp, and wi-fi. Daily

PRICE RANGES IN BANGKOK

Hotel rooms are generally more expensive in Bangkok than elsewhere in Thailand, but don't fret as there's a huge variety and significant discounts can be had, making accommodation very good value overall. In this chapter, we have divided rooms into the following three categories:

» **Budget** less than 1000B
» **Midrange** 1000B to 3000B
» **Top End** more than 3000B

The prices listed are high-season walk-in rates, but it's worth noting that significant discounts can be found by booking online. See the boxed text, p114 for recommended sites.

So what do you get for your money? At the **budget** end, the days of 50B beds in Banglamphu are over, but those counting every baht can still get a fan-cooled dorm bed (or a closet-like room) for between 150B and 200B with a shared bathroom. The more you're willing to pay, the more likely you are to get a towel, hot water and air-con. If you require privacy and your own bathroom, paying in the realm of 700B or so can get you a capable, although generally characterless, room.

The biggest mixed bag of all, the **midrange** level starts out with the high-quality guest houses, then moves into a grey area of ordinariness. Above 1000B, the hotels have all the appearance of a hotel back home – a bellboy, uniformed desk clerks and a well-polished lobby – but without the predictability. If you're on a lower midrange budget, and aren't so keen on aesthetics, some very acceptable rooms can be had for between around 1500B and 2000B. If your budget is near the higher end of the scale, it really pays to book ahead, as online discounts here can be substantial.

Bangkok's growing array of **top-end** hotels typically include amenities such as pool, spa, fitness and business centres and overpriced internet connections. The famous brands generally provide more space, while 'boutique' hotels emphasise ambience. In the top tier, rooms start at more than 10,000B, but in most of the luxurious design and boutique hotels, and the vast majority of the international brands, you're looking at about 6000B to 9000B, before hefty online discounting. Keep in mind that the hotels in this category will generally add a 10% service charge plus 7% tax to hotel bills.

cultural-based activities including bike trips and volunteer opportunities, and inviting communal areas ensure that you may not actually get the chance to plug in.

Buddy Boutique Hotel   BOUTIQUE HOTEL **$$$**
(Map p60; ☑0 2629 4477; www.buddylodge.com; 256 Th Khao San; r incl breakfast 3500-4500B; ✳@☎⊠; bus 2, 15, 44, 511, river ferry Tha Phra Athit) This gigantic complex, which includes a pool, fitness room and, ahem, a branch of McDonald's, is, as far as we're aware, the most expensive place to stay on Th Khao San. Correspondingly, rooms are comfortable, well equipped and evocative of a breezy tropical manor house.

Villa Cha-Cha   HOTEL **$$**
(Map p60; ☑0 2280 1025; www.villachacha.com; 36 Th Tani; r 900-2900B; ✳@☎⊠; bus 53, 516, river ferry Tha Phra Athit) Wind between statues, lounging residents, an expansive restaurant

and an inviting pool to emerge at this seemingly hidden, but popular hotel. A few clumsy stabs have been made at interior design (think topless portraits), but the real draw is the social, resort-like atmosphere.

Rikka Inn   BUDGET HOTEL **$$**
(Map p60; ☑0 2282 7511; www.rikkainn.com; 259 Th Khao San; r 1150-1450B; ✳@☎⊠; bus 53, 516, river ferry Tha Phra Athit) Boasting tight but attractive rooms, a rooftop pool and a central location, the new Rikka is one of several great-value hotels changing the face of Th Khao San.

Lamphu House   BUDGET HOTEL **$**
(Map p60; ☑0 2629 5861; www.lamphuhouse.com; 75-77 Soi Ram Buttri; r 400-980B; ✳@☎; river ferry Tha Phra Athit) Tucked off Soi Ram Buttri, you'll forget how close to Th Khao San you are in this quiet, homey budget hotel.

Rooms are simple but clean, with the cheapies cooled by fan and sharing bathrooms.

Viengtai Hotel HOTEL **$$**
(Map p60; ☑0 2280 5434; www.viengtai.co.th; 42 Th Rambuttri; r 2200-4000B, ste 5200B; ❄@⊛⊠; bus 53, 516, ferry Tha Phra Athit) Long before Th Khao San was 'discovered', this was an ordinary Chinese-style hotel in a quiet neighbourhood. It now sits comfortably in the midrange with reliable but unstylish rooms. Prices include breakfast.

Outside the Th Khao San Area

TOP CHOICE **Lamphu Tree House** BOUTIQUE HOTEL **$$**
(Map p60; ☑0 2282 0991; www.lamphutree hotel.com; 155 Wanchat Bridge, Th Prachatipatai; r incl breakfast 1500-2100B; ❄@⊛; bus 56, 58, 516, klorng taxi Tha Phah Fah, river ferry Tha Phra Athit) Despite the name, this attractive midranger has its feet firmly on land and as such, represents brilliant value. Rooms are attractive and inviting, and the rooftop bar, pool, internet, restaurant and quiet canalside location ensure that you may never feel the need to leave. A new annexe a couple of blocks away increases your odds of snagging an elusive reservation.

Arun Residence BOUTIQUE HOTEL **$$$**
(Map p60; ☑0 2221 9158; www.arunresidence. com; 36-38 Soi Pratu Nok Yung, Th Maha Rat; r 3500-3800B, ste 5500B; ❄@⊛; bus 123, 508, river ferry Tha Tien) Although strategically located across from Wat Arun, this multilevel wooden house on the river boasts much more than just brilliant views. The six rooms here manage to feel both homey and stylish, some being tall and loftlike, while others cojoin two rooms (the best is the top-floor suite with its own balcony). There are inviting communal areas, including a library, a rooftop bar and a restaurant. Breakfast is included.

Praya Palazzo BOUTIQUE HOTEL **$$$**
(Map p60; ☑0 2883 2998; www.prayapalazzo.com; 757/1 Somdej Prapinklao Soi 2, Thonburi; r 6000-11,900B, ste 16,500-26,500B; ❄⊛⊠; hotel shuttle from Tha Phra Athit) After lying dormant for nearly 30 years, this elegant 19th-century mansion has been reborn as an attractive riverside boutique hotel. The 17 rooms can feel rather tight, and river views can be elusive, but the meticulous renovation, handsome antique furnishings and bucolic atmosphere convene in a hotel with genuine old-word charm. Prices include breakfast.

Chakrabongse Villas BOUTIQUE HOTEL **$$$**
(Map p60; ☑0 2622 3356; www.thaivillas.com; 396/1 Th Maha Rat; r 5000B, ste 10,000-40,00B; ❄@⊛; river ferry Tha Tien) The occasionally inhabited compound of Thai royalty dating back to 1908, this unique hotel incorporates three sumptuous but cramped rooms and six larger suites and villas. There's a pool, jungle-like gardens and an elevated deck for romantic riverside dining. Breakfast is included.

Fortville Guesthouse BUDGET HOTEL **$**
(Map p60; ☑0 2282 3932; www.fortvilleguesthouse. com; 9 Th Phra Sumen; r 650-970B; bus 32, 33, 64, 82; ❄@⊛; river ferry Tha Phra Athit) With an exterior that combines elements of a modern church and/or castle, and an interior that relies on mirrors and industrial elements, the design concept of this unique new hotel is a bit hard to pin down. Rooms are stylishly minimal, and the more expensive ones include perks such as fridge, balcony and free wi-fi.

Navalai River Resort HOTEL **$$$**
(Map p60; ☑0 2280 9955; www.navalai.com; 45/1 Th Phra Athit; r incl breakfast 2900-4800B; bus 32, 33, 64, 82; ❄@⊛⊠, river ferry Tha Phra Athit) The latest thing to go up on breezy Th Phra Athit, this chic hotel has 74 modern rooms, many looking out over the Chao Phraya River. There are attractive Thai design touches throughout, but you might end up spending much of your time checking out the views from the rooftop pool.

Old Bangkok Inn BOUTIQUE HOTEL **$$$**
(Map p60; ☑0 2629 1787; www.oldbangkokinn. com; 609 Th Phra Sumen; r incl breakfast 3190-6590B; klorng taxi to Tha Phan Fah; ❄@⊛) The 10 rooms in this refurbished antique shophouse are decadent and sumptuous, combining rich colours and heavy wood furnishings. All have computers for personal use, and some have semi-outdoor bathrooms. The perfect honeymoon hotel.

Baan Sabai BUDGET HOTEL **$**
(Map p60; ☑0 2629 1599; baansabai@hotmail. com; 12 Soi Rongmai; s 190, r 270-600B; ❄@; bus 53, 516, river ferry Tha Phra Athit) Truly living up to its name (Comfortable House), this rambling old building holds dozens of plain but comfy rooms, at a variety of prices. There's a palpable old-school atmosphere, particularly at the inviting open-air restaurant-bar area downstairs.

New Siam Riverside HOTEL **$$**
(Map p60; ☑0 2629 3535; www.newsiam.net; 21 Th Phra Athit; r incl breakfast 1390-2990B; ✳@☎; bus 32, 33, 64, 82, river ferry Tha Phra Athit) One of a couple of new places along Th Phra Athit taking advantage of the riverside setting, this hotel has comfortable rooms with tiny bathrooms. But the real value is the amenities (internet, travel agent, restaurant) and the location on one of the city's more pleasant streets.

Aurum: The River Place BOUTIQUE HOTEL **$$$**
(Map p60; ☑0 2622 2248; www.aurum-bangkok. com; 394/27-29 Soi Pansook, Th Maha Rat; r incl breakfast 3950-4900B; ✳@☎; bus 123, 508, river ferry Tha Tien) The 12 modern rooms here don't necessarily reflect the grand European exterior of this refurbished shophouse. Nonetheless they're comfortable and well appointed, and most offer fleeting views of the Chao Phraya.

Baan Chantra BOUTIQUE HOTEL **$$**
(Map p60; ☑0 2628 6988; www.baanchantra. com; 120 Th Samsen; r incl breakfast 2400-3500B; ✳@☎; bus 32, 516, river ferry Tha Phra Athit) This beautiful converted house is without pretensions, preferring to be comfortable and roomy rather than fashionable and pinched. Many of the house's original teak details remain, and the deluxe room boasts a sunny patio.

Wild Orchid Villa BUDGET HOTEL **$**
(Map p60; ☑0 2629 4378; www.wildorchidvilla.com; 8 Soi Chana Songkhram; r 280-1800B; ✳@☎; bus 32, 33, 64, 82, river ferry Tha Phra Athit) The cheapies here are some of the tiniest we've seen anywhere, but all rooms are clean and neat, and come in a bright, friendly package. This place is exceedingly popular, so it's best to book ahead.

Penpark Place BUDGET HOTEL **$-$$**
(Map p60; ☑0 2628 8896; www.penparkplace. com; 22 Soi 3, Th Samsen; r 300-1350B, ste 1800B; ✳@☎; bus 53, 516, river ferry Tha Phra Athit) This former factory has been turned into a good-value budget hotel. Rooms in the original building are little more than a bed and a fan, but a recent add-on sees a handful of well-equipped apartment-like rooms and suites.

Some other budget and midrange options:

Hotel Dé Moc HOTEL **$$**
(Map p60; ☑0 2282 2831; www.hoteldemoc.com; 78 Th Prachathipatai; r incl breakfast 1960-2520B; ✳@☎✳; bus 12, 56) The rooms at this classic hotel are large, with high ceilings and generous windows, but the furnishings could certainly use an update. Complimentary transport to Th Khao San and free bike rental are thoughtful perks.

Sam Sen Sam GUEST HOUSE **$**
(Map p60; ☑0 2628 7067; www.samsensam.com; 48 Soi 3, Th Samsen; r 590-2400B; river ferry to Tha Phra Athit; ✳@☎) One of the homiest places around, this bright, refurbished villa gets good reports about its friendly service and quiet location.

Rajata Hotel BUDGET HOTEL **$**
(Map p60; ☑0 2628 8084; www.rajatahotel.com; 46 Soi 6, Th Samsen; r 650-850B; ✳@☎; bus 53, 516, river ferry Tha Phra Athit) This old-skool hotel is a plain but comfortable choice for those who don't want to stay on Th Khao San, but who don't want to be too far away.

New Merry V Guest House BUDGET HOTEL **$**
(Map p60; ☑0 2280 3315; newmerry@gmail.com; 18-20 Th Phra Athit; s 150, r 290-700B; ✳@; bus 32, 33, 64, 82, river ferry Tha Phra Athit) The cheap rooms here are as bare as it gets, but are spotless and have ample natural light and the odd view or two.

CHINATOWN & PHAHURAT

Yaowarat, Bangkok's Chinatown, isn't the most hospitable part of town, but for those who wish to stay off the beaten track it's an area where travellers can remain largely anonymous. There's a decent selection of accommodation, much of it just off busy streets, so be sure to assess the noise situation before choosing your room. The area used to be a nightmare to get to, but the MRT stop at Hua Lamphong has improved things immensely.

If you're arriving in Bangkok by train and can't be bothered to search elsewhere for accommodation, there are several great budget choices near Hua Lamphong train station, including the **Baan Hualampong** (p109), **Siam Classic** (Map p76; ☑0 2639 6363; www.siamclassic-hostel.com; 336/10 Trok Chalong Krung; r 450-1400B; ✳@☎; MRT Hua Lamphong, river ferry Tha Ratchawong) and **@Hua Lamphong** (Map p76; ☑0 2639 1925; www.at-hualamphong.com; 326/1 Th Phra Ram IV; dm 200B, r 690-1000B; ✳@☎; MRT Hua Lamphong, river ferry Tha Ratchawong).

Shanghai Mansion BOUTIQUE HOTEL **$$$**
(Map p76; ☑0 2221 2121; www.shanghai-inn.com; 479-481 Th Yaowarat; r 2500-3500B, ste 4000B;

BANGKOK'S GRANDE DAME

The Oriental Hotel started out as a roughshod boarding house for European seafarers in the late 19th century, but was transformed into an aristocratic magnet by Hans Niels Anderson, the founder of the formidable East Asiatic Company (which operated between Bangkok and Copenhagen). He hired an Italian designer to build what is now known as the Authors' Wing, which was the city's most elaborate secular building; all other grand architecture at the time was commissioned by the king.

With a dramatic setting beside Mae Nam Chao Phraya, the hotel has gained its reputation from its famous guests. A Polish-born sailor named Joseph Conrad stayed here inbetween nautical jobs in 1888. W Somerset Maugham stumbled into the hotel with an advanced case of malaria contracted during his overland journey from Burma. In his feverish state, he heard the German manager arguing with the doctor about how a death in the hotel would hurt business. Maugham's recovery and completion of *Gentleman in the Parlour: A Record of a Journey from Rangoon to Haiphong* contributed to the long-lasting literary appeal of the hotel. Other notable guests have included Noël Coward, Graham Greene, John le Carré, James Michener, Gore Vidal and Barbara Cartland. Some modern-day writers even claim that a stay in the Oriental will overcome writer's block.

To soak up the ambience of old seafaring Bangkok, stop by for a cocktail at the Bamboo Bar or toast the 'swift river' as Noël Coward did from the riverside terrace. For teetotallers, an afternoon brew is served in a frilly Victorian lounge filled with black-and-white photographs of Rama V. To ensure its aristocratic leanings in a less formal age, the hotel enforces a dress code (no shorts, sleeveless shirts or sandals allowed).

✻@ 🛜; river ferry Tha Ratchawong) Easily the most consciously stylish place to stay in Chinatown, if not in all of Bangkok. This award-winning boutique hotel screams Shanghai circa 1935 with stained glass, an abundance of lamps, bold colours and tongue-in-cheek Chinatown kitsch. If you're willing to splurge, ask for one of the bigger streetside rooms with tall windows that allow more natural light.

Baan Hualampong GUEST HOUSE $
(Map p76; ☎0 2639 8054; www.baanhualampong. com; 336/20-21 Trok Chalong Krung; dm 250B, r 290-800B; ✻@🛜; MRT Hua Lamphong) Repeat visitors rave about the homey setting and warm, personal service at this guest house. Located a short walk from Hua Lamphong train station, it has kitchen and laundry facilities, and there are lots of chill-out areas and computers. Prices include breakfast.

China Town Hotel HOTEL $$
(Map p76; ☎0 2225 0204; www.chinatownhotel. co.th; 526 Th Yaowarat; r 880-2500B; ✻@🛜; MRT Hua Lamphong, river ferry Tha Ratchawong) Popular with Chinese tourists, the lobby here plays on the theme suggested by the hotel's name, but the rooms are largely devoid of any design concept. Nonetheless, they've recently been remodelled and offer decent value.

RIVERSIDE

Accommodation on either side of the Mae Nam Chao Phraya tends to diverge between upscale and hostel, with little in between.

Oriental Hotel LUXURY HOTEL $$$
(Map p80; ☎0 2659 9000; www.mandarinorien tal.com; 48 Soi 40/Oriental, Th Charoen Krung; r 12,799-14,799B, ste 23,999-140,999B; ✻@🛜🏊; hotel shuttle boat from Tha Sathon/Central Pier) For the true Bangkok experience, a stay at this grand old riverside hotel is a must. The majority of rooms are located in the modern and recently refurbished New Wing, but we prefer the old-world ambience of the Garden and Authors' Wings. The hotel is also home to the city's most longstanding fine dining restaurant, Le Normandie (p121), and across the river in Thonburi one of the region's most acclaimed spas (p94) and a cooking school. Breakfast is included. For background on the hotel's history, see the boxed text, above.

Shangri-La Hotel LUXURY HOTEL $$$
(Map p80; ☎0 2236 7777; www.shangri-la.com; 89 Soi 42/1/Wat Suan Phlu, Th Charoen Krung; r 6800-7700B; ste 8500-15,600B; ✻@🛜🏊; BTS Saphan Taksin) A recent facelift has the longstanding Shangri-La looking better than ever. Generous rates, breakfast included, a resort-like atmosphere and ample activities and amenities make this a good choice for families.

Swan Hotel
HOTEL $$

(Map p80; ☎0 2235 9271; www.swanhotelbkk. com; 31 Soi 36, Th Charoen Krung; s/d incl breakfast 1200/1500B; ✳@☎⌧; river ferry Tha Oriental) Despite its relatively large size, this classic Bangkok hotel is able to maintain a homey feel. Recent renovations has it looking better than ever, although the room furnishings are still stuck in the 1970s. The inviting pool area is a bit more timeless, and the entire place is virtually spotless.

Peninsula Hotel
LUXURY HOTEL $$$

(Map p80; ☎0 2861 2888; www.peninsula.com; off Th Charoen Nakhon, Thonburi; r 10,800-15,500B, ste 18,800-120,000B; hotel shuttle boat from Tha Sathon/Central Pier; ✳@☎⌧) After more than a decade in Bangkok, the Pen still seems to have it all: the location (towering over the river in Thonburi), the rep (it's consistently one of the highest-ranking luxury hotels in the world) and one of the highest levels of service in town. If money is no obstacle, stay on one of the upper floors (there are 38) where you literally have all of Bangkok at your feet. Prices include breakfast.

Millennium Hilton
HOTEL $$$

(Map p80; ☎0 2442 2000; www.bangkok.hilton. com; off Th Charoen Nakhorn, Thonburi; r 6200-7800B, ste 10,000B; ✳@☎⌧; hotel shuttle boat from River City & Tha Sathon/Central Pier) As soon as you enter the dramatic lobby, it's obvious that this is Bangkok's youngest, most modern riverside hotel. Rooms, all of which boast widescreen river views, follow this theme and are decked out with funky furniture and Thai-themed photos. A glass elevator and an artificial beach are just some of the fun touches.

River View Guest House
BUDGET HOTEL $

(Map p80; ☎0 2234 5429; www.riverviewbkk.com; 768 Soi Phanurangsi, Th Songwat; r 350-1500B; ✳☎; river ferry Marine Department) After 20 years, this towering budget staple is finally receiving a much-needed rennovation. The rooms that have been renovated are spacious and modern, although the halls and exterior are caught in a rather gritty time warp. To get there, heading north on Th Charoen Krung from Th Si Phraya, take a left onto Th Songwat (before the Chinatown Arch), then the second left onto Soi Phanurangsi. You'll start to see signs at this point.

New Road Guesthouse
HOSTEL $

(Map p80; ☎0 2630 9371; www.newroadguest house.com; 1216/1 Th Charoen Krung; dm fan/air-con 160/250B, r 900-2500B; ✳@☎; river ferry Tha Si Phraya) For those on tight budgets, the clean dorms with fan are among the cheapest accommodation in all of Bangkok. The attached travel agency, visit beyond (see p146), is reputable.

P&R Residence
BOUTIQUE HOTEL $$

(Map p80; ☎0 2639 6091-93; pandrresidence@ gmail.com; 34 Soi 30, Th Charoen Krung; r 900-1800B; ✳☎; river ferry Tha Si Phraya) There's nothing fancy about the P&R, but its rooms are comfortable and clean and it's very fairly priced for this atmospheric corner of town.

SILOM & SATHON

The city's financial district along Th Silom is not the most charming area of town, but it is convenient to nightspots and to the BTS and MRT for quick access to modern parts of Bangkok. There's a lack of budget accommodation around Th Silom, but some good-value boutique midrangers can be found on Th Sala Daeng. Some of Bangkok's most famous top-enders are also located along this stretch of the river and can be reached via the complimentary hotel ferries at Tha Sathon (Central Pier).

Th Sathon is home to several top-end hotels, but lacks atmosphere, the primary feature being the vast eponymous road. If you need to stay around this area also check out p115 for a few more hotel options around lower Th Sathon.

TOP CHOICE Siam Heritage
BOUTIQUE HOTEL $$$

(Map p82; ☎0 2353 6101; www.thesiamherit age.com; 115/1 Th Surawong; r 3000-3500B, ste 4500-9000B; ✳@☎⌧; BTS Sala Daeng, MRT Si Lom) Tucked off busy Th Surawong, this classy boutique hotel oozes with homey Thai charm – probably because the owners also live in the same building. The rooms are decked out in silk and dark woods with genuinely thoughtful design touches, not to mention thoughtful amenities. There's an inviting rooftop garden/pool/spa, which like the rest of the hotel, are cared for by a team of charming and professional staff. Breakfast is included. Highly recommended.

Heritage Baan Silom
BOUTIQUE HOTEL $$

(Map p82; ☎0 2236 8388; www.theheritagehotels. com; Baan Silom Shopping Centre, 669 Soi 19, Th Silom; r 2100-3400B; ✳@☎; BTS Surasak) Tucked behind a 'lifestyle arcade' (ie shopping centre), this wannabe top-ender is a modern interpretation of an English colonial-era mansion. Carefully designed with attractive wood and wicker furnishings, the rooms are bright and airy, each featuring a different colour theme and custom wall prints.

La Résidence Hotel
BOUTIQUE HOTEL **$$**

(Map p82; ☎0 2233 3301; www.laresidencebang kok.com; 173/8-9 Th Surawong; r 1200-2200B, ste 3200-3700B; ❄@⚛; BTS Chong Nonsi) La Résidence is a boutique inn with playfully and individually decorated rooms. A standard room is very small and fittingly decorated like a child's bedroom. The next size up is more mature and voluptuous with blood-red walls and modern Thai motifs. Breakfast is included.

Baan Saladaeng
BOUTIQUE HOTEL **$$**

(Map p82; ☎0 2636 3038; www.baansaladaeng. com; 69/2 Soi Sala Daeng 2; r incl breakfast 1300-2300B; ❄⚛; BTS Sala Daeng, MRT Si Lom) Of the handful of pint-sized boutique hotels along Th Sala Daeng, Baan Saladaeng is most welcoming. The lobby's cheery primary colour theme carries on into the 11 rooms, those on the upper floors being the largest and airiest.

Triple Two Silom
HOTEL **$$$**

(Map p82; ☎0 2627 2222; www.tripletwosilom.com; 222 Th Silom; r 3500-3800B, ste 5500B; ❄@⚛; BTS Chong Nonsi) Rooms here resemble sleek modern offices – in a good way. But don't worry, with huge bathrooms and inviting-looking beds, you'll be inspired to relax, not work. Guests can use the rooftop garden, but have to go next door to the sister Narai Hotel for the swimming pool and fitness centre. Prices include breakfast.

Dusit Thani
LUXURY HOTEL **$$$**

(Map p82; ☎0 2200 9000; www.dusit.com; 946 Th Phra Ram IV; r 7900-10,000B, ste 12,500-32,500B; ❄@⚛≋; BTS Sala Daeng, MRT Si Lom) At one point the tallest building in the country, this venerable luxury hotel is a testament to how much things have changed in Bangkok. A 2010 renovation has many of the rooms looking more modern than the flagrantly 1970s exterior, but the hotel remains notable more for its convenient location and city views than its hip factor. Breakfast is included.

Rose Hotel
HOTEL **$$$**

(Map p82; ☎0 2266 8268-72; www.rosehotelbkk. com; 118 Th Surawong; r 3200-3400B, ste 4000-4400B; ❄@⚛≋; BTS Sala Daeng, MRT Si Lom) Don't let the unremarkable exterior fool you – the convenient location, modern

rooms, pool, gym and sauna make this Vietnam War–era vet a pretty solid deal. Prices include breakfast.

HQ Hostel
HOSTEL **$**

(Map p82; ☎0 2233 1598; www.hqhostel.com; 5/3-4 Soi 3, Th Silom; dm 380-599B, r 1300-1700B; ❄@⚛; BTS Sala Daeng, MRT Si Lom) This new hostel combines basic but stylish rooms and dorms with inviting communal areas, smack dab in the middle of Bangkok's financial district.

Bangkok Christian Guest House
BUDGET HOTEL **$$**

(Map p82; ☎0 2233 2206; www.bcgh.org; 123 Soi Sala Daeng 2; s/d/tr incl breakfast 1100/1540/1980B; ❄@⚛⚐; BTS Sala Daeng, MRT Si Lom) This austere guest house is a great choice for families, as some rooms have as many as five beds and there's a 2nd-floor children's play area.

YHA Downtown Bangkok
HOSTEL **$**

(Map p82; ☎0 2266 4443; 395/4 Th Silom; dm 299B, r 699-1129B; ❄@⚛; BTS Chong Nonsi) Another tidy and conveniently located backpacker hostel.

SIAM SQUARE & PRATUNAM

For centrally located accommodation, there's really no better destination than the area surrounding Siam Square. Home to the intersection of the two BTS lines, and only a brief-ish (depending on traffic) taxi ride to Banglamphu, this is about as good as it gets in ever-expanding Bangkok.

For those on a budget who also need a central location, a low-key backpacker community exists along Soi Kasem San 1 (say 'gà·săirm'), across from the National Stadium.

TOP CHOICE Siam@Siam
HOTEL **$$$**

(Map p86; ☎0 2217 3000; www.siamatsiam.com; 865 Th Phra Ram I; r incl breakfast 5000-700B; ❄@⚛≋; BTS National Stadium) The lobby of this new hotel is more amusement park than accommodation, but that's what makes it so much fun. A seemingly random mishmash of colours and materials result in a style one could only describe as 'junkyard' – but in a good way, of course. The rooms, which continue the theme, and which are located between the 14th and 24th floors, offer terrific city views, free wi-fi and breakfast. There's also a spa, a rooftop restaurant and a pool on the 11th floor.

Lub*d HOSTEL $
(Map p86; ☑0 2634 7999; www.lubd.com; Th Pha Ram I; dm 550B, r 1350-1800B; ❄@🏠; BTS National Stadium) The title is a play on the Thai *làp dee*, meaning 'sleep well', but the fun atmosphere at this bright new backpacker hostel might make you want to stay up all night. There are 24 dorms (including women-only dorms), each with only four beds, and a few private rooms, both with and without bathrooms. There's an inviting communal area stocked with free internet, games and a bar, and thoughtful facilities ranging from washing machines to a theatre room. If this one's full, there's another branch (Map p82; ☑0 2634 7999; www.lubd.com; 4 Th Decho; dm 400B, r 1050-1400B; ❄@🏠; BTS Chong Nonsi) just off Th Silom.

Swisshôtel Nai Lert Park LUXURY HOTEL $$$
(Map p86; ☑0 2253 0123; www.swissotel.com/bangkok-nailertpark; 2 Th Witthayu/Wireless Rd; r 4100-4500B, ste 5200-6800B; ❄@🏠🏊; BTS Phloen Chit, klorng taxi Tha Withayu) This hotel has seen a few reincarnations during its 30-year history, but we like the current one. The suites follow the sleek design theme laid out in the lobby, while cheaper rooms follow a more conservative wood-heavy 'classic' theme. Regardless, all are huge and include balconies. Breakfast is included.

Conrad Hotel Bangkok HOTEL $$$
(Map p86; ☑0 2690 9999; www.conradhotels.com; 87 Th Witthayu/Wireless Rd; r 7298-10,005B, ste 14,242-17,185B; ❄@🏠🏊; BTS Phloen Chit) When built in 2003, the Conrad was one of the first hotels in Bangkok to consciously make an effort to appeal to the young and hip. It has since been surpassed in this area, but still offers attractive and comfortable accommodation. Breakfast is included.

Reno Hotel BUDGET HOTEL $$
(Map p86; ☑0 2215 0026; www.renohotel.co.th; 40 Soi Kasem San 1; r incl breakfast 1280-1890B; BTS National Stadium, klorng taxi to Tha Ratchathewi; ❄@🏠🏊) Most of the rooms reflect the renovations evident in the lobby and exterior, but the cafe and classic pool of this Vietnam War-era hotel still cling to the past.

Vie HOTEL $$$
(Map p86; ☑0 2309 3939; www.viehotelbangkok. com; 117/39-40 Th Phayathai; r/ste incl breakfast 4296/5030-12,530B; BTS Ratchathewi; ❄@🏠🏊) Vie combines a convenient location and a casual atmosphere in one attractive package. The service gets good reports, there's

an emphasis on wining and dining, and if you're considering upgrading, the duplex suites are spacious and offer great city views.

Asia Hotel HOTEL $$$
(Map p86; ☑0 2217 0808; www.asiahotel.co.th; 296 Th Phayathai; r 3700-4800B; ste 8000-10,000B; ❄@🏠🏊; BTS Ratchathewi, klorng taxi to Tha Ratchathewi) A recent renovation has this tourist-group staple looking slightly more modern than the 1970s-era lobby would suggest. Connoisseurs of kitsch don't fret: the hotel's Calypso Cabaret (see the boxed text, p133) and a nightly Elvis show are still in full effect. Breakfast is included.

Golden House HOTEL $$
(Map p86; ☑0 2252 9535; www.goldenhouses. net; 1025/5-9 Th Ploenchit; r incl breakfast 2000-2300B; ❄@🏠; BTS Chit Lom) With parquet flooring and built-in wooden furniture, the 27 rooms here are more like modern Thai condos than hotel rooms. The beds are huge, but just like those of Thai condos, they have the potential to sag.

Novotel Bangkok on Siam Square BUSINESS HOTEL $$$
(Map p86; ☑0 2255 6888; www.novotelbkk.com; Soi 6, Siam Sq; r 4049-6403B, ste 5449-11,403B; ❄@🏠🏊; BTS Siam) Appropriate for business or leisure, the soon-to-be-renovated Novotel Siam is conveniently located near the BTS and shopping. Breakfast is included.

A-One Inn BUDGET HOTEL $
(Map p86; ☑0 2215 3029; www.aoneinn.com; 25/13-15 Soi Kasem San 1; s/d/tr 600/750/950B; ❄@🏠; BTS National Stadium, klorng taxi to Tha Ratchathewi) The rooms here are tight and simple, but the wealth of backpacker amenities (computers, luggage storage, free ice and water) makes up for this.

Wendy House BUDGET HOTEL $$
(Map p86; ☑0 2214 1149; www.wendyguesthouse. com; 36/2 Soi Kasem San 1; r incl breakfast 900-1200B; ❄@🏠; BTS National Stadium, klorng taxi to Tha Ratchathewi) The rooms here are small and basic, but well stocked (TV, fridge) for this price range.

Bed & Breakfast Inn BUDGET HOTEL $
(Map p86; ☑0 2215 3004; Soi Kasem San 1; r incl breakfast 500-700B; ❄🏠; BTS National Stadium, klorng taxi to Tha Ratchathewi) This mazelike guest house has standard but comfortable rooms.

SUKHUMVIT

This seemingly endless urban thoroughfare is Bangkok's unofficial International Zone and also boasts much of the city's accommodation. There's a bit of everything here, from the odd backpacker hostel to sex tourist hovels and five-star luxury. The former two are largely located between Soi 1 and Soi 4, while the latter doesn't begin to appear until you reach Soi 12 or so.

In general, because visitors with larger budgets stay in Sukhumvit, tourist services are more expensive here than in Banglamphu. The trade-off is access to food from virtually every corner of the globe, heaps of nightlife options and easy access to both the BTS and MRT.

Lower Sukhumvit

TOP CHOICE AriyasomVilla BED & BREAKFAST **$$$**
(Map p92; ☑0 2254 880; www.ariyasom.com; 65 Soi 1, Th Sukhumvit; r incl breakfast 4248-9138B; ❋@❖☒; BTS Phloen Chit) Located at the end of Soi 1 behind a virtual wall of fragipani, this renovated 1940s-era villa is one of the worst-kept accommodation secrets in Bangkok. If you can score a reservation, you'll be privy to one of 24 spacious rooms, meticulously outfitted with thoughtful Thai design touches and beautiful antique furniture. There's a spa and an inviting tropical pool, and breakfast is vegetarian and served in the original villa's stunning glass-encased dining room.

Suk 11 BUDGET HOTEL **$**
(Map p92; ☑0 2253 5927; www.suk11.com; 1/33 Soi 11, Th Sukhumvit; s/d/tr incl breakfast from 535/749/1284B; ❋@❖; BTS Nana) Extremely well run and equally popular, this guest house is an oasis of woods and greenery in the urban jungle that is Th Sukhumvit. The cheaper rooms have shared bathrooms, and although the owners have somehow managed to stuff nearly 100 rooms in there, you'll still need to book at least two weeks ahead.

Stable Lodge BUDGET HOTEL **$$**
(Map p92; ☑0 2653 0017; www.stablelodge.com; 39 Soi 8, Th Sukhumvit; r 1495-1695B; ❋@❖☒; BTS Nana) To be honest, we were slightly disappointed that the faux-Tudor theme of the downstairs restaurant didn't carry on into the rooms, but could find no other faults. A recent renovation has given a bit of life to the simple rooms here, and the spacious balconies still offer great city views.

Golden Palace Hotel HOTEL **$$**
(Map p92; ☑0 2252 5115; www.goldenpalacehotel.com; 15 Soi 1, Th Sukhumvit; r 1110-1350B; ❋@❖☒; BTS Phloen Chit) The abundance of mirrors in the ground-floor rooms gives this away as a former tryst hotel, but for just a couple of hundred baht more, you can get one of the simple but airy rooms upstairs. A pool, coffeeshop and nearby spa ensure that you won't need to go very far to be entertained.

Federal Hotel HOTEL **$$**
(Map p92; ☑0 2253 0175; www.federalbangkok.com; 27 Soi 11, Th Sukhumvit; r incl breakfast 1050-1500B; ❋@❖☒; BTS Nana) You wouldn't know it from the exterior, but after 40 years 'Club Fed' finally decided to get a makeover. The upstairs rooms are comfortable and almost contemporary, but the rooms at ground level still scream 1967. The real draws are the frangipani-lined pool and time-warped US-style coffeeshop.

Atlanta BUDGET HOTEL **$**
(Map p92; ☑0 2252 1650; 78 Soi 2/Phasak, Th Sukhumvit; r/ste incl breakfast from 535/1820B; ❋@❖☒; BTS Phloen Chit) Defiantly antiquated and equally frumpy, this crumbling gem has changed very little since its construction in 1952. The opulent lobby stands in contrast to the simple rooms, but the inviting pool (allegedly the country's first hotel pool) and delightful restaurant are incentive enough.

Swiss Park Hotel HOTEL **$$**
(Map p92; ☑0 2254 0228; 155/23 Soi 11/1, Th Sukhumvit; r/ste from 1500/2900B; ❋❖☒; BTS Nana) The rooms here are workaday and largely forgettable, but the convenient location and friendly and competent staff make this a good midrange find.

Bed Bangkok HOSTEL **$**
(Map p92; ☑0 2655 7604; www.bedbangkok.com; 11/20 Soi 1, Th Sukhumvit; dm/r incl breakfast from 390/800B; ❋@❖; BTS Asok, MRT Sukhumvit) This brand-new hostel manages to maintain a homey feel despite the industrial-design theme. The friendly service makes up for the rather hard dorm beds.

Soi 1 Guesthouse HOSTEL **$**
(Map p92; ☑0 2655 0604; www.soi1guesthouse.com; 220/7 Soi 1, Th Sukhumvit; dm 400B; ❋@❖; BTS Phloen Chit) This slightly aged backpacker haven has four cluttered dorm rooms and a chummy communal area with pool table, TV and computers.

THINKING AHEAD

The rates listed in this chapter are high-season rack rates; ie the highest price a hotel will generally charge for a room. However, there's no reason you should be paying this much, especially if you know ahead of time when you'll be in town. Booking rooms online can lead to savings of at least 20%, and often more, at many of Bangkok's leading hotels. This can be done directly through the hotel websites or by sites such as **Lonely Planet's Hotels & Hostels** (hotels.lonelyplanet.com), which features thorough reviews from authors and traveller feedback, and a booking facility.

It can also work to your advantage to simply call the hotel and book ahead; sometimes desk staff collect a commission on walk-ins and are reluctant to discount, something that can be remedied by a pre-emptive phone call and an inquiry about the lowest possible rate.

Upper Sukhumvit

Middle Sukhumvit, Soi 19 in particular, is home to a handful of inexpensive yet attractive midrangers, including the surprisingly sophisticated **Sacha's Hotel Uno** (Map p92; ☎0 2651 2180; www.sachas.hotel-uno.com; 28/19 Soi 19, Th Sukhumvit; r incl breakfast 1800-2500B; ❄@⊛; BTS Asok, MRT Sukhumvit) and **Silq** (Map p92; ☎0 2252 6800; www.silqbkk.com; 54 Soi 19, Th Sukhumvit; r incl breakfast 2654-3560B; ❄@⊛; BTS Asok, MRT Sukhumvit), and the funky **Fusion Suites** (Map p92; ☎0 2665 2644; www.fusionbangkok.com; 143/61-62 Soi 21/Asoke, Th Sukhumvit; r incl breakfast 2100-2400B, ste incl breakfast 3200B; ❄@⊛; BTS Asok, MRT Sukhumvit).

72 Ekamai
BOUTIQUE HOTEL $$

(Map p92; ☎02 714 7327; www.72ekamai.com; 72 Soi 63/Ekamai, Th Sukhumvit; r 2100B, ste 2500-2850B; ❄@⊛; BTS Ekkamai) This fun, young-feeling, design-conscious hotel is a great choice. Reds, black and pop art prints define the look here, and perhaps we were mistaken, but on our visit, we swear the place smelled like candy. The junior suites are huge, and like all rooms, are well equipped and conveniently located. Breakfast is included.

Eugenia
BOUTIQUE HOTEL $$$

(Map p92; ☎0 2259 9017-19; www.theeugenia.com; 267 Soi 31/Sawatdi, Th Sukhumvit; ste incl breakfast 8107-9911B; ❄@⊛⊛; BTS Phrom Phong & access by taxi) Although Thailand was never anybody's colony, there's no doubt about the design influence of this character-laden hotel. Decked out in antique furniture and an abundance of animal skins, a stay here is like travelling to Burma circa 1936. Don't fear though; you won't have to ask the 'boy' to draw you a bath – modern amenities such as flat-screen TVs and free domestic and international calls are also provided (the baths are beautiful and are made of copper). Ask about the vintage-car airport transfers.

Napa Place
BED & BREAKFAST $$

(Map p92; ☎0 2661 5525; www.napaplace.com; 11/3 Yaek 2, Soi 36, Th Sukhumvit; r 2200-2400B, ste 3400B; ❄@⊛; BTS Thong Lo) Seemingly hidden in the confines of a typical Bangkok urban compound is what must be the city's homiest accommodation. The 12 expansive rooms here have been decorated with dark woods from the family's former business and light brown cloths from the hands of Thai weavers. The communal areas couldn't be much different from the suburban living room you grew up in.

S31
HOTEL $$$

(Map p92; ☎0 2260 1111; www.s31hotel.com; 545 Soi 31, Th Sukhumvit; r 6000B, ste 7000-9000B; ❄⊛⊛; BTS Phrom Phong) The bold patterns and graphics of its interior and exterior make the S31 a fun, young-feeling choice. Thoughtful touches such as kitchenettes with large fridge, superhuge beds and free courses (cooking, Thai boxing and yoga) prove that the style also has substance. Prices include breakfast. Branches can also be found on Soi 15 and Soi 33.

Ma Du Zi
BOUTIQUE HOTEL $$$

(Map p92; ☎0 2615 6400; www.maduzihotel.com; cnr Th Ratchadapisek & Soi 16, Th Sukhumvit; r 5000-12,000B, ste 12,000B; ❄@⊛; BTS Asok, MRT Sukhumvit) The name is Thai for 'come take a look,' somewhat of a misnomer for this reservations-only, no walk-ins hotel. If you've gained access, behind the gate you'll find an attractive midsized hotel steeped in dark, chic tones and designs. We fancied the immense bathrooms, with a walk-in tub and minimalist shower.

Seven   BOUTIQUE HOTEL **$$$**
(Map p92; ☑0 2662 0951; www.sleepatseven.com; 3/15 Soi 31/Sawatdi, Th Sukhumvit; r incl breakfast 3290-5290B; ✹@☎; BTS Phrom Phong) This tiny hotel somehow manages to be chic and homey, stylish and comfortable, Thai and international all at the same time. Each of the six rooms is decked out in a different colour that corresponds to Thai astrology, and thoughtful amenities abound.

Davis   BOUTIQUE HOTEL **$$$**
(Map p92; ☑0 2260 8000; www.davisbangkok. net; 88 Soi 24, Th Sukhumvit; r 2299-3599B, ste 5999-9999B; ✹@☎☲; BTS Phrom Phong) If it's hard to pinpoint the design of the Davis it's probably because it seems to have covered all the bases with Chinese-, Japanese-, Myanmar- and Balinese-themed rooms. Domestically speaking, there are also 10 Thai-style villas surrounding a pool. Breakfast is included.

Dream Bangkok   BOUTIQUE HOTEL **$$$**
(Map p92; ☑0 2254 8500; www.dreambkk.com; 10 Soi 15, Th Sukhumvit; r 3500-4000B, ste 6500-12,000B; ✹@☎☲; BTS Asok, MRT Sukhumvit) If your idea of interior design involves stuffed tigers, copious mirrors and slick leather, you'll feel at home here. The standard rooms are a tight fit, but include ample and quirky amenities such as the Dream signature blue light to aid in sleeping. Prices also include breakfast.

Sheraton Grande Sukhumvit   BUSINESS HOTEL **$$$**
(Map p92; ☑0 2649 8888; www.luxurycollection. com/bangkok; 250 Th Sukhumvit; r 3500-10,000B, ste 16,500-55,000B; ✹@☎☲; BTS Asok, MRT Sukhumvit) This conveniently located business-oriented hotel offers some of the most spacious rooms in town and fills them with a generous array of amenities. By the time you read this, an impending renovation may have already made what was already a very good hotel an excellent hotel. Prices include breakfast.

Baan Sukhumvit   BED & BREAKFAST **$$**
(Map p92; ☑0 2258 5622; www.baansukhumvit. com; 392/38-39 Soi 20, Th Sukhumvit; r incl breakfast 1430B; ✹@☎; BTS Asok, MRT Sukhumvit) One of three similarly priced hotels located on this small side street off Soi 20, Baan Sukhumvit's 12 rooms exude a homey, cosy atmosphere. A newer branch is located around the corner on Soi 18.

Despite the general upscale nature of this part of town, there's a decent selection of backpacker hostels:

Nana Chart Hotel   HOSTEL **$**
(Map p92; ☑0 2259 6908; www.thailandhostel. com; cnr Soi 25 & Th Sukhumvit; dm 390-550B, r 1200-1800B; ✹@☎; BTS Asok, MRT Sukhumvit) This tidy, newish backpacker hostel packs 68 plain but more-than-adequate budget rooms, as well as some of the better dorms around with private bathrooms. Prices include breakfast.

HI-Sukhumvit   HOSTEL **$**
(Map p92; ☑0 2391 9338; www.hisukhumvit.com; 23 Soi 38, Th Sukhumvit; dm/s/d/tr incl breakfast from 320/650/900/1200B; ✹@☎; BTS Thong Lo) Located in a quiet residential street a brief walk from the BTS, this friendly hostel excels with its neat dorms and accompanying immense bathrooms.

LUMPHINI PARK & TH PHRA RAM IV

If you were hitting the Asian hippie trail back in the 1970s, you would have laid your love beads at a guest house in Soi Ngam Duphli, off Th Phra Ram IV, not too far from Lumphini Park. Despite the decades that have passed, it's still a good area to go to for supercheap accommodation, particularly along Soi Si Bamphen. There are also more upmarket options. And getting there has been made even easier by the MRT stop at Lumphini.

TOP CHOICE **Metropolitan**   HOTEL **$$$**
(Map p90; ☑0 2625 3333; www.metropolitan. como.bz; 27 Th Sathon Tai, r 4951-5768B, ste 6945-21,186B; ✹@☎☲; MRT Lumphini) The exterior of the former YMCA has changed relatively little, but a peek inside reveals one of Bangkok's sleekest hotels. Urban minimalism rules here, except where it concerns the size of the two-storey penthouse suites. Breakfast (included in the price) is either US-style or 'organic' and the attached nahm (p125) is Bangkok's best upscale Thai restaurant.

LUXX XL   BOUTIQUE HOTEL **$$**
(Off map p90; ☑0 2684 1111; www.staywithluxx. com; 82/8 Soi Lang Suan; r 2500-7000B, ste 13,000-22,000B; ✹@☎☲; BTS Ratchadamri) Despite its location in a leafy Bangkok street, Luxx oozes with a minimalist hipness that wouldn't be out of place in London or New York. There's another slightly cheaper **branch** (Map p82; ☑0 2635 8800; 6/11 Th Decho; r/ste from 2200/4100B; ✹@☎; BTS Chong Nonsi)

on Th Decho, off Th Silom. Breakfast is included at both places.

Sukhothai Hotel
HOTEL $$$

(Map p90; ☑0 2344 8888; www.sukhothai.com; 13/3 Th Sathon Tai; r 11,000-14,000B, ste 15,000-90,000B; ✵@ 🛜 🌊; MRT Lumphini) As the name suggests, this hotel employs brick stupas, courtyards and antique sculptures to create a historical, temple-like atmosphere. The recently remodelled superior rooms contrast this with hi-tech TVs, phones and yes, toilets. Breakfast is included.

All Seasons Sathorn
HOTEL $$

(Map p90; ☑0 2343 6333; www.allseasons-sathorn. com; 31 Th Sathon Tai; r incl breakfast 1800-2500B; ✵@ 🛜; MRT Lumphini) The former king's Hotel has been reborn as this modern attractive budget choice, right in the middle of the embassy district. The primary colours and bold lines of the design scheme make up for the lack of natural light in some rooms.

Malaysia Hotel
BUDGET HOTEL $

(Map p90; ☑0 2679 7127; www.malaysiahotelbkk. com; 54 Soi Ngam Duphli; r incl breakfast 698-998B; ✵@ 🛜 🌊; MRT Lumphini) The Malaysia was once Bangkok's most famous budget lodge and even provided shelter for Maureen and Tony Wheeler on their maiden shoestring trip through Southeast Asia. Our sources tell us that the couple stay elsewhere when in Bangkok nowadays, but the Malaysia is still a good choice for the rest of us for its fair prices and frozen-in-time atmosphere.

Penguin House
BUDGET HOTEL $

(Map p90; ☑0 2679 9991; www.penguinhouses. com; 27/23 Soi Si Bamphen; r 800-950B; ✵ 🛜; MRT Lumphini) The oddly named Penguin is a breath of fresh air in this area of tired old-timers. The rear rooms are quieter, and there are a couple of interior rooms that sleep two couples.

ETZzz Hostel
BUDGET HOTEL $

(Map p90; ☑0 2286 9424; www.etzhostel.com; Soi Ngam Duphli; dm/r 200/900B; ✵ 🛜; MRT Lumphini) The rooms at this brand-new shophouse-based hostel are overpriced, but the tidy dorm, shiny facilities and convenient location are draws.

Ibis Sathon
BUDGET HOTEL $$

(Map p90; ☑0 2659 2888; 29/9 Soi Ngam Duphli; r incl breakfast 1800B; ✵@ 🛜 🌊; MRT Lumphini) The business-friendly Ibis delivers comfort and convenience without corporate expense-account prices.

Café des Arts Guest House
BUDGET HOTEL $

(Map p90; ☑0 2679 8438; 27/39 Soi Si Bamphen; r with fan/air-con 300/400B; ✵; MRT Lumphini) Run by a French-Thai couple, there's seemingly no cafe (nor art) here, but rather a downstairs noodle restaurant and eight simple rooms upstairs.

GREATER BANGKOK

Many of the following hotels require a little more effort to reach. This also means that they tend to be located in less hectic parts of the city, and are perfect for those who'd rather not stay in the thick of it.

If you need to stay near one of Bangkok's two airports, check the accommodation options in our boxed text, p117.

Phra-Nakorn Norn-Len
BOUTIQUE HOTEL $$

(Map p96; ☑0 2628 8188; www.phranakorn-norn len.com; 46 Soi Thewet 1, Th Krung Kasem; s/d incl breakfast from 1800/2200B; ✵@ 🛜; bus 32, 516, river ferry Tha Thewet) Set in an expansive garden compound decorated like the Bangkok of yesteryear, this bright and cheery hotel is an atmospheric if not necessarily great value place to stay. Rooms are simply furnished, but generously decorated with antiques and wall paintings, and there's wi-fi, massage and endless opportunities for peaceful relaxing. Breakfast originates from the hotel's organic rooftop garden.

Bangkok International Youth Hostel
HOSTEL $

(Map p96; ☑0 2282 0950; 25/15 Th Phitsanulok; dm 200B, r 600-900B; ✵@ 🛜; bus 32, 516, river ferry Tha Thewet) One of the only options if you want to stay in the quiet Dusit area, this recently refurbished hostel has cheaper rooms in the original building and new but cramped rooms in a tall structure facing Th Phitsanulok. There's a pleasant rooftop balcony and a travel library.

Refill Now!
HOSTEL $

(☑0 2713 2044; www.refillnow.co.th; 191 Soi Pridi Bhanom Yong 42, Soi 71, Th Sukhumvit, Phra Khanong; dm/s/d 480/928/1215B; ✵@ 🛜 🌊; BTS Phra Khanong & access by taxi) Sporting a look that blends the Habitat catalogue and a Kubrick movie, this is the kind of place that might make you think twice about sleeping in a dorm. The spotless white private rooms and dorms have flirtatious pull screens between each double-bunk; women-only dorms are also available. There's an achingly hip chill-out area, and a massage centre upstairs. If you decide you need to leave, there's a túk-túk (30B per passenger) to Thong Lo and Phra Khanong BTS stations.

Mystic Place
BOUTIQUE HOTEL **$$**
(Map p118; ☑0 2270 3344; www.mysticplacebkk.com; 224/5-9 Th Pradiphat; r incl breakfast 2250-3250B; ❊@♠; BTS Saphan Khwai & access by taxi) This hotel unites 36 rooms, each of which is individually and playfully designed. One of the rooms we checked out combined a chair upholstered with stuffed animals and walls covered with graffiti. Heaps of fun and perpetually popular, so be sure to book ahead.

Pullman Bangkok King Power
BUSINESS HOTEL **$$$**
(Map p97; ☑0 2680 9999; www.pullmanbangkokkingpower; 8/2 Th Rang Nam; r/ste incl breakfast 3861-4331/6803-7274B; ❊@♠❊; BTS Victory Monument) The Pullman is a great choice for those who want to stay in a business-class hotel, but would rather not stay downtown.

Th Si Ayuthaya, in Thewet, the district north of Banglamphu near the National Library, is a pleasant backpacker enclave, particularly popular with families and the over-30 crowd. It is a lovely leafy area, but during the rainy season it can be prone to flooding.

Sri Ayuttaya Guest House
BUDGET HOTEL **$**
(Map p96; ☑0 2282 5942; 23/11 Th Si Ayuthaya, Thewet; r 400-1000B; ❊@♠; bus 32, 516, river ferry Tha Thewet) The wood-and-brick theme here is a nice break from the usual, less permanent-feeling guest house design. The rooms, half of which share bathrooms, also feel sturdy and inviting.

Shanti Lodge
GUEST HOUSE **$**
(Map p96; ☑0 2281 2497; 37 Th Si Ayuthaya; dm 250B, r 400-1950B; ❊@♠; bus 32, 516, river ferry Tha Thewet) This family-run place exudes a peaceful, dharmic aura. Walls are bamboo-thin in the cheaper rooms, but there's a huge variety of accommodation; check out a few rooms before making a decision.

Taewez Guesthouse
BUDGET HOTEL **$**
(Map p96; ☑0 2280 8856; www.taewez.com; 23/12 Th Si Ayuthaya; r 250-530B; ❊@♠; bus

---

LATE-NIGHT TOUCHDOWN

A lot of nail-biting anxiety is expended on international flights arriving in Bangkok around midnight. Will there be taxis into town, will there be available rooms, will my family ever hear from me again? Soothe those nagging voices with the knowledge that most international flights arrive late and that Bangkok is an accommodating place. Yes, there are taxis and even an express train service (see p148).

If you haven't already made hotel reservations, a good area to look for a bed is lower Sukhumvit – it's right off the expressway and hotels around Soi Nana such as the **Swiss Park** (p113) and the **Federal** (p113) are used to lots of late-night traffic and won't break your bank. Alternatively, you could always go to Th Khao San, which stays up late, is full of hotels and guest houses, and sees a near-continuous supply of 'fresh-off-the-birds' just like you.

If, for some reason, you can't stray too far from the airport, these places provide a more than adequate roof.

Suvarnabhumi International Airport

The nearest good budget option is **Refill Now!** (see p116).

» **Grand Inn Come Hotel** (☑0 2738 8189-99; www.grandinncome-hotel.com; 99 Moo 6, Th Kingkaew, Bangpli; r incl breakfast from 1800B; ❊@♠) Solid midranger 10km west of the airport, with airport shuttle and 'lively' karaoke bar.

» **All Seasons Bangkok Huamark** (☑0 2308 7888; 5 Soi 15, Th Ramkhamhaeng; r 1366-2195B; ❊@♠❊) Less than 20km west of the airport, this midranger has 268 rooms to choose from.

» **Novotel Suvarnabhumi Airport Hotel** (☑0 2131 1111; www.novotel.com; r incl breakfast from 7146B; ❊@♠) Has 600-plus luxurious rooms in the airport compound.

Don Muang Airport

» **Amari Airport Hotel** (☑0 2566 1020; www.amari.com; 333 Th Choet Wutthakat; d incl breakfast from 2001-3350B; ❊@♠❊) Directly opposite Don Muang (Map p153).

North Bangkok

32, 516, river ferry Tha Thewet) Popular with French travellers, the cheapest rooms here are plain and share bathrooms, but are good value.

✕ Eating

Invariably the safest of Bangkok's infamous carnal pleasures, food is serious business in this city. Attracting hungry visitors from across the globe, Bangkok's eateries also draw natives from disparate ends of the city, happy to brave traffic or floods for a bowl of noodles or a plate of rice.

The selection is enormous, with eating places in Bangkok ranging from wheeled carts that set up shop on a daily basis to chic dining rooms in five-star hotels. In our experience the tastiest eats are generally found somewhere in-between, at family-run shophouse restaurants serving a limited repertoire of dishes.

The influences are also vast, and you'll find everything from Chinese-Thai to Muslim-Thai, not to mention most regional domestic cuisines. And if at some point you do tire of *gŏo·ay đĕe·o* (rice noodles) and curries, Bangkok has an ever-expanding selection of high-quality international restaurants, encompassing everything from upscale French to hole-in-the-wall Japanese ramen houses.

KO RATANAKOSIN, BANGLAMPHU & THONBURI

Despite its proximity to the faux *pàt tai* and tame *đôm yam* (a sour/spicy soup) of Th Khao San, Banglamphu is one of the city's most legendary eating areas. Decades-old restaurants and legendary hawkers line the streets in this leafy corner of Old Bangkok, and you could easily spend an entire day grazing the southern end of Th Tanao alone.

Although you'd be wisest to get your domestic nosh away from the main drag, the

North Bangkok

foreign influence on Th Khao San has led to a few import standouts.

In contrast, Bangkok's royal district has an abundance of sights but a dearth of restaurants – a pity, considering the potential views.

TOP CHOICE **Krua Apsorn** THAI $$
(Map p60; Th Din So; mains 70-320B; ⊙lunch & dinner Mon-Sat; ✻; bus 2, 25, 44, 511, klorng taxi to Tha Phan Fah) This homey dining room has served members of the Thai royal family and, back in 2006, was recognised as Bangkok's Best Restaurant by the *Bangkok Post*. Must-eat dishes include mussels fried with fresh herbs, the decadent crab fried in yellow chilli oil and the tortilla Española-like crab omelette.

Jay Fai THAI $$
Map p60; 327 Th Mahachai; mains 200-250B; ⊙3pm-2am; klorng taxi Tha Phan Fah) You wouldn't think so by looking at her barebones dining room, but Jay Fai is known far and wide for serving Bangkok's most expensive – and arguably most delicious – *pàt kêe mow* (drunkard's noodles). The price is justified by the copious fresh seafood, as well as Jay Fai's distinct frying style that results in a virtually oil-free finished product.

Poj Spa Kar THAI $$
(Map p60; 443 Th Tanao; mains 100-200B; ⊙lunch & dinner; ✻; bus 2, 25, 44, 511, klorng taxi to Tha Phan Fah) Pronounced *pôht sà·pah kahn*, this is allegedly the oldest restaurant in Bangkok, and continues to maintain recipes handed down from a former palace cook. Be sure to order the simple but tasty lemon-grass omelette or the deliciously sour/sweet *gaang sôm*, a traditional central Thai soup.

Shoshana ISRAELI $$
(Map p60; 88 Th Chakraphong; mains 90-220B; ⊙lunch & dinner; ✻; bus 32, 516, river ferry Tha Phra Athit) Although prices have gone up slightly since it began back in 1982, Shoshana still puts together a cheap but tasty Israeli meal. Feel safe ordering anything deep-fried – they do an excellent job of it – and don't miss the eggplant dip.

Nang Loeng Market THAI $
(off Map p60; Btw Soi 8-10, Th Nakhon Sawan; ⊙10am-2pm Mon-Sat; bus 72) Dating back to 1899, this atmospheric market, east of Banglamphu, is primarily associated with Thai sweets, but at lunchtime it's also an excellent place to fill up on savouries. Try a bowl of handmade egg noodles at Rung Reuang or the rich curries at Ratana.

Chote Chitr THAI $$
(Map p60; 146 Th Phraeng Phuthon; mains 30-200B; ⊙lunch & dinner Mon-Sat; bus 15, klorng taxi to Tha Phan Fah) This third-generation shophouse restaurant boasting just six tables is a Bangkok foodie landmark. The kitchen can be inconsistent, but when they're on, dishes such as *mèe gròrp* (crispy fried noodles) and *yam tòoa ploo* (wing-bean salad) are in a class of their own.

Thip Samai THAI $
(Map p60; 313 Th Mahachai; mains 25-120B; ⊙5.30pm-1.30am closed alternate Wednesdays; klorng taxi Tha Phan Fah) Brace yourself, but you should be aware that the fried noodles sold from carts along Th Khao San have nothing to do with the dish known as *pàt tai*.

DAVID THOMPSON: CHEF & AUTHOR

David Thompson is the Head Chef of both the London and Bangkok branches of the famed nahm restaurant. He is also the bestselling author of *Thai Food* and *Thai Street Food*.

HOW DO YOU DESCRIBE THE FOOD IN BANGKOK?

The food of Bangkok is more urbane, with the rough and rambunctious tastes of the wild and remote regions polished off. There's a huge Chinese influence here because Bangkok was a Chinese city. The central-plains food, which Bangkok is the epitome of, is refined and has the classic four flavours [sweet, sour, salty and spicy].

WHAT ARE SOME CLASSIC BANGKOK-STYLE DISHES?

I like some of the dishes in Chinatown, whether it be the oyster place I adore (Nay Mong; p123), or whether it be noodles with fish dumplings or with roast duck. Also *boo pàt pŏng gàrèe* [crab fried with curry powder], when done well, is easy, but is bloody delicious and accessible. And *pàt tai* – well, you can't really escape from the cliché, however delicious it might be.

THE BEST FOOD 'HOOD?

It depends on what I'm looking for. Chinatown, for smoked duck or noodles. But if you want to eat Thai food, you need to go to the markets. Bangkok still has some remnants of the city or villages that it was. For Muslim food you can go down to the area near Haroon Mosque, near the Oriental Hotel (p109), or for Portuguese cakes, you can go to Santa Cruz (p75). There's still those types of areas.

YOUR FAVOURITE RESTAURANT

It changes all the time. I like Krua Apsorn (p119). It's local. It's good. It's unreformed. It's not too precious. They cook for Thais, they feed Thais and it is Thai.

THE BEST MARKET

Of course, Or Tor Kor (p140). Even though it's sanitised, its soul has not been expunged from it as it's modernised. There's some great stuff there.

BEST EATING ADVICE FOR A FIRST-TIME VISITOR

Just bloody well eat it – don't think about it – just eat it. It's so unlikely you'll get sick, but you will kick yourself for not actually just diving in. Go to places that look busiest, because they're busy for a reason. And a bit of food poisoning, well that adds local colour, doesn't it?

As told to Austin Bush

Luckily, less than a five-minute túk-túk ride away lies Thip Samai, also known by locals as *pàt tai bràdoo pĕe*, and home to the most legendary *pàt tai* in town. For something a bit different, try the delicate egg-wrapped version, or the *pàt tai* fried with *man gûng* (decadent shrimp fat).

Khunkung　　　　　　　　THAI $$
(Khun Kung Kitchen; Map p60; 77 Th Maha Rat; mains 75-280B; ☺lunch & dinner; ※; bus 25, 32, 503, 508, river ferry Tha Chang) The restaurant of the Royal Navy Association has one of the few coveted riverfront locations along this stretch of the Chao Phraya. Locals come for the combination of riverfront views and cheap and tasty seafood-based eats. The

entrance to the restaurant is near the ATM machines at Tha Chang.

Hemlock　　　　　　　　THAI $$
(Map p60; 56 Th Phra Athit; mains 60-220B; ☺4pm-midnight; ※; bus 32, 33, 64, 82, river ferry Tha Phra Athit) Taking full advantage of its cosy shophouse setting, this white-tablecloth local is an excellent intro to Thai food. The vast menu has the usual suspects, but also includes some dishes you'd be hard pressed to find elsewhere, as well as a strong vegie section.

Ann's Sweet　　　　　　PASTRIES $
(Map p60; 138 Th Phra Athit; mains 75-150B; ☺lunch & dinner; ※; bus 32, 33, 64, 82, river ferry Tha Phra Athit) Ann, a native of Bangkok and a gradu-

ate of the Cordon Bleu cooking program, makes some of the most authentic Western-style cakes you'll find anywhere in town.

CHINATOWN & PHAHURAT

When you mention Chinatown, most Bang-kokians immediately dream of street food, the best of which we've included in our 'Eats Walk' on p123. The area is also famous as ground zero for the yearly Vegetarian Festival (see the boxed text, p122).

On the western side of the neighbour-hood is Bangkok's Little India, the fabric district of Phahurat, filled with small Indian and Nepali restaurants tucked into the soi off Th Chakraphet.

Old Siam Plaza
THAI $

(Map p76; ground fl, Old Siam Plaza, cnr Th Phahurat & Th Triphet; mains 15-50B; ⊙9am-6.30pm; river ferry Tha Saphan Phut) Sugar junkies, be sure to include this stop on your Bangkok eating itinerary. The ground floor of this shopping centre is a candyland of traditional Thai sweets and snacks, most made right before your eyes.

Royal India
NORTHERN INDIAN $$

(Map p76; 392/1 Th Chakraphet; mains 65-250B; ⊙lunch & dinner; river ferry Tha Saphan Phut) Yes, we realise that this legendary hole in the wall has been in every edition of our guide since the beginning, but after all these years it's still the most reliable place to eat in Bangkok's Little India. Try any of the deli-cious breads or rich curries, and don't forget to finish with a homemade Punjabi sweet.

RIVERSIDE

Le Normandie
FRENCH $$$

(Map p80; ☎0 2659 9000; www.mandarinoriental.com; 48 Soi Oriental/38, Th Charoen Krung; mains 750-3900B; ⊙noon-2.30pm & 7-11pm Mon-Sat, 7-11 Sun; ✦; hotel shuttle boat from Tha Sathon/Central Pier) As the menu, which boasts an entire foie gras section, suggests, this is classic French cuisine, and no fewer than 20 three-starred Michelin chefs have helped to prepare it over the years. Dress appropriately.

SILOM & SATHON

Th Silom has a bit of everything, from truly old-skool Thai to some of the city's best upscale international dining.

D'Sens
FRENCH $$$

(Map p82; ☎0 2200 9000; 22nd fl, Dusit Thani, 946 Th Phra Ram IV; set menu 1850-3100B; ⊙11.30am-2.30pm & 6-10pm, 6-10pm Sat; ✦; BTS Sala Daeng, MRT Si Lom) Arguably Bangkok's best upscale *fa·ràng* (foreign) fine-dining restaurant, D'Sens is perched like an air traffic control tower atop the Dusit Thani hotel. A venture of French wonder-twins Laurent and Jacques Pourcel, creators of the Michelin-starred Le Jardin des Sens in Montpellier, France, the menu draws from the traditions of the south of France, relying mainly on high-quality French imports for its ingredients.

VEGING OUT IN BANGKOK

Vegetarianism is a growing trend among urban Thais, but vegie restaurants are still generally few and far between.

Banglamphu has the greatest concentration of vegetarian-friendly restaurants, thanks to the nonmeat-eating *fa·ràng* (foregners); these are typically low-scale stir-fry shops that do something akin to what your hippie roommates have cooking in their kitchens. We like **May Kaidee** (Map p60; 33 Th Samsen; mains 50-100B; ⊙lunch & dinner; ✦; bus 32, 516, river ferry Tha Phra Athit), which in addition to three branches around Th Khao San, also offers a vegie Thai cooking school, and **Ranee's** (Map p60; 77 Trok Mayom; dishes 70-320B; ⊙breakfast, lunch & dinner; bus 32, 516, river ferry Tha Phra Athit), whose menu features a lengthy meat-free section.

Elsewhere in town, **Baan Suan Pai** (Map p118; Banana Family Park, Th Phahonyothin; mains 15-30B; ⊙7am-3pm; BTS Ari), the **MBK Food Court** (p124), **Chennai Kitchen** (p122) and **Arawy** (Map p60; 152 Th Din So, Phra Nakhon; dishes 20-30B; ⊙8am-8pm; bus 10, 12, klorng taxi to Tha Phan Fah) all offer cheap but tasty meat-free meals. East of the city, upscale-ish Thai- and Italian-style vegie eats can be found at **Anotai** (976/17 Soi Rama 9 Hospital, Rama 9; dishes 150-303B; ⊙10am-9pm Thu-Tue; ✦; MRT Phra Ram 9 & access by taxi).

During the vegetarian festival in October, the whole city goes mad for tofu (see the boxed text, p122). Stalls and restaurants indicate their nonmeat menu with yellow banners; Chinatown has the highest concentration of stalls.

Kalapapruek
THAI $$

(Map p82; 27 Th Pramuan; mains 80-120B; ☺8am-6pm Mon-Sat, to 3pm Sun; ✴; BTS Surasak) This venerable Thai eatery has numerous branches and mall spin-offs around town, but we still like the quasi-concealed original branch. The diverse menu spans regional Thai specialties from just about every region, daily specials and, occasionally, seasonal treats as well.

Scoozi
PIZZA $$

(Map p82; 174 Th Surawong; pizzas 100-425B; ☺lunch & dinner; ✴; BTS Sala Daeng, MRT Si Lom) Now boasting several locations across Bangkok, we still think the wood-fired pizzas taste best at this, the original branch. However, if you find yourself elsewhere with a dough craving, you can also get a pie at the Th Sukhumvit **branch** (Map p92; Windsor Hotel, Soi 20, Th Sukhumvit; ✴; BTS Asok, MRT Sukhumvit).

Somboon Seafood
CHINESE-THAI $$$

(Map p82; 169/7-11 Th Surawong; mains 120-900B; ☺dinner; ✴; BTS Chong Nonsi) Holy seafood factory: ascending the many staircases to a free table might make you nervous about the quality of so much quantity. But Somboon's famous crab curry will make you messy and full. Dainty eaters can opt for the slightly more surgical pursuit of devouring a whole fried fish.

The Foodie
THAI $$

(Map p82; Soi Phiphat 2; mains 80-150B; ☺lunch & dinner; ✴; BTS Chong Nonsi) This airy, cafeteria-like restaurant boasts a menu of hard-to-find central- and southern-style Thai dishes. Highlights include the *yam sôm oh* (a spicy/sour/sweet salad of pomelo), and the spicy *prík kïng 'blah dòok foo,* catfish fried in a curry paste until crispy.

Chennai Kitchen
INDIAN $

(Map p82; 10 Th Pan; mains 50-150B; ☺10am-3pm & 6-9.30pm; ✴; BTS Surasak) This thimble-sized restaurant puts out some of the most solid southern Indian vegetarian around. The arm-length dosas (a crispy southern Indian bread) are always a good choice, but if you're feeling indecisive go for the thali set that seems to incorporate just about everything in the kitchen.

Somtam Convent
THAI $

(Map p82; 2/4-5 Th Convent; mains 20-120B; ☺10.30am-9pm; BTS Sala Daeng, MRT Si Lom) Northeastern-style Thai food is usually relegated to less-than-hygienic stalls perched by the side of the road with no menu or English-speaking staff in sight. A less intimidating introduction to the wonders of *lâhp* (a minced meat 'salad'), *sôm·đam* (papaya salad) and other Isan delights can be had at this popular restaurant.

Soi 10 Food Centres
THAI $

(Map p82; Soi 10, Th Silom; mains 20-60B; ☺lunch Mon-Fri; BTS Sala Daeng, MRT Si Lom) These two adjacent hangarlike buildings tucked behind Soi 10 are the main lunchtime fuelling stations for this area's office staff. Choices range from southern-style *kôw gaang* (point-and-choose curries ladled over rice) to virtually every form of Thai noodle.

Nadimos
LEBANESE $$

Map p82; Baan Silom, cnr Th Silom & Soi 19; mains 70-400B; ☺lunch & dinner; ✴; BTS Surasak, bus 15, 504) This semiformal dining room does tasty versions of all the Lebanese standards, plus quite a few dishes you'd never expect to see this far from Beirut. There's lots of vegetarian options as well.

WAVING THE YELLOW FLAG

During the annual Vegetarian Festival in September/October, Bangkok's Chinatown becomes a virtual orgy of nonmeat cuisine. The festivities centre on Chinatown's main street, Th Yaowarat, and the Talat Noi area (see p79), but food shops and stalls all over the city post yellow flags to announce their meat-free status.

Celebrating alongside the ethnic Chinese are Thais who look forward to the special dishes that appear during the festival period. Most restaurants put their normal menus on hold and instead prepare soy-based substitutes for standard Thai dishes such as *đôm yam* (spicy, sour soup) and *gaang kĕe·o wăhn* (green curry). Even Thai regional cuisines are sold without the meat. Of the special festival dishes, yellow Hokkien-style noodles appear in stir-fried dishes along with meaty mushrooms and big hunks of vegetables.

Along with abstinence from meat, the 10-day festival is celebrated with special visits to a temple, often requiring worshippers to dress in white.

CHINATOWN EATS WALK

Street food rules in this part of town and many of Chinatown's best kitchens don't require walls or a roof, making the area ideal for a food-based stroll.

Although many vendors stay open until the wee hours, the more popular stalls tend to sell out quickly, and the best time to feast in this area is from about 7pm to 9pm. Avoid Mondays, when most of the city's street vendors stay at home. A dish at just about any of the following stalls should set you back no more than 50B. Access to the area is by MRT to Hua Lamphong, followed by a brief walk or taxi ride.

Start your walk at the intersection of Th Yaowarat and Th Phadungdao. Moving west, turn right into Th Plaeng Nam. Immediately on your right is **Burapa Birds Nest** (Map p76; Th Plaeng Nam), as good a place as any to try the very Chinatown dish, birds' nest soup. Directly across from Burapa you'll see a gentleman on the street working three coal-fired stoves. This stall, **Khrua Phornlamai** (ครัวพรละมัย; Map p76; Th Plaeng Nam), is a great place for greasy but delicious fried faves such as *pàt kêe mow* (wide rice noodles fried with seafood, chillies and Thai basil).

Continue down Th Plaeng Nam and cross Th Charoen Krung. Go straight, staying on the right-hand side for about 50m, until you reach **Nay Mong** (นายหมง; Map p76; 539 Th Phlap Phla Chai), a minuscule restaurant renowned for its delicious *hŏy tôrt*, mussels or oysters fried with egg in a sticky batter.

Backtrack to Th Charoen Krung and turn right. Upon reaching Th Mangkorn make a right and immediately on your left-hand side you're bound to see a row of people waiting in line, as well as several more sitting on plastic stools holding plates of rice and curry in their hands. This is **Jék Pûi** (เจ็กปุ๊ย; Map p76; Th Mangkorn), a stall known for its Chinese-style Thai curries and also for the fact that it has no tables.

Head left down Th Charoen Krung again and continue east until you reach Trok Itsaranuphap (Soi 16). This narrow alleyway is also known as **Talat Mai** (ตลาดใหม่), and is the area's most famous strip of commerce. Although morning is the best time to visit this market, if you're not too late you can still get a good idea of the exotic ingredients that define the area.

At the end of the alley you'll see a gentleman frying noodles with a brass wok and a spoon. He's making **gŏo·ay đĕe·o kôo·a gài** (ก๋วยเตี๋ยวคั่วไก่; Map p76), a simple but delicious dish of rice noodles fried with chicken, egg and garlic oil.

Upon emerging at Th Yaowarat, cross over to the busy market area directly across the street. The first vendor on the right, **Nay Lék Uan** (นายเล็กอ้วน; Map p76; Soi 11, Th Yaowarat), is among the most popular stalls in Bangkok, and sells *gŏo·ay jáp nám săi*, a thick, intensely peppery broth containing noodles and pork offal. There are several more stalls here, selling everything from *pàt tai* to satay.

Walk east down Th Yaowarat, and on the corner of Th Yaowaphanit and Th Yaowarat you'll see a stall with yellow noodles and barbecued pork. This is **Mangkorn Khăo** (มังกร ขาว; Map p76; cnr Th Yawarat & Th Yaowaphanit), a respected vendor of *bà·mèe*, Chinese-style wheat noodles, and delicious wontons.

Keep walking down Th Yaowarat and you'll be back to where you started. By now the two opposing seafood places, **Lek & Rut** (Map p76; cnr Th Yaowarat & Th Phadungdao) and **T&K** (Map p76; cnr Th Yaowarat & Th Phadungdao) should be buzzing. You could join the tourists for grilled prawns and fried rice, but hopefully by this point you've had your fill of what Chinatown *really* has to offer.

Krua 'Aroy-Aroy' THAI $
(Map p82; Th Pan; mains 30-70B; ⊗8am-8.30pm, closed 2nd & 4th Sun of each month; BTS Surasak) It can be crowded and hot, but Krua 'Aroy-Aroy' ('Delicious Kitchen') rarely fails to live up to its lofty name. Stop by for some of Bangkok's richest curries, as well as a revolving menu of daily specials.

SIAM SQUARE & PRATUNAM

If you find yourself hungry in this part of central Bangkok, you're largely at the mercy of shopping-mall food courts and chain

ℹ DAY OFF

Fans of street food be forewarned that all of Bangkok's stalls close on Monday for compulsory street cleaning (the results of which are not entirely evident come Tuesday morning). If you happen to be in the city on this day, take advantage of the lull to perhaps visit one of the city's upscale hotel restaurants, which virtually never close.

restaurants. However, this is still Thailand, and if you can ignore the prefabricated atmosphere, the food can often be quite good. If you don't need air-con, stop by the numerous **food stalls** (Map p86; btwn Sois 5 & 6, Siam Sq; dishes 30-40B; ⏱7am-6pm; BTS Siam) at Siam Sq for a quick Thai lunch.

TOP CHOICE MBK Food Court THAI $

(Map p86; 6th floor, MBK Center, cnr Th Phra Ram I & Th Phayathai; ⏱10am-9pm; ❄; BTS National Stadium) The granddaddy of Bangkok food courts offers dozens of vendors selling dishes from virtually every corner of Thailand and beyond. It's a great introduction to Thai food, and standouts include an excellent vegetarian food stall (stall C8) and a very decent Isan food vendor (C22). To pay you must first exchange your cash for a temporary credit card at one of several counters; your change is refunded at the same desk.

Crystal Jade La Mian Xiao Long Bao CHINESE $$

(Map p86; Urban Kitchen, basement, Erawan Bangkok, 494 Th Ploenchit; dishes 120-400B; ⏱lunch & dinner; ❄; BTS Chit Lom) The tongue-twistingly long name of this excellent Singaporean chain refers to the restaurant's signature wheat noodles (la mian) and the famous Shanghainese steamed dumplings (xiao long pao). If you order the hand-pulled noodles, allow the staff to cut them with kitchen shears, otherwise you'll end up with evidence of your meal on your shirt.

Erawan Tea Room THAI $$

Map p86; 2nd fl Erawan Bangkok, 494 Th Ploenchit; mains 170-450B; ⏱lunch & dinner; ❄; BTS Chit Lom) The oversized chairs, panoramic windows and variety of hot drinks make this one of Bangkok's best places to catch up with the paper. The lengthy menu, with an emphasis on regional Thai dishes, will likely encourage you to linger a bit longer.

Coca Suki THAI-CHINESE $$

(Map p86; 416/3-8 Th Henri Dunant; mains 60-200B; ⏱11am-11pm; ❄; BTS Siam) Immensely popular with Thai families, sù·gêe takes the form of a bubbling hotpot of broth and the raw ingredients to dip therein. Coca is one of the oldest purveyors of the dish, and the Siam Sq branch reflects the brand's efforts to appear more modern.

Sanguan Sri THAI $

(Map p86; 59/1 Th Witthayu/Wireless Rd; mains 40-150B; ⏱10am-3pm Mon-Sat; ❄; BTS Ploen Chit) If you don't manage to walk right past it, join the area's hungry office workers at this old-school Thai eatery. There's a limited English-language menu, but simply pointing to the delicious dishes being consumed around you is probably a better strategy.

New Light Coffee House INTERNATIONAL-THAI $$

(Map p86; 426/1-4 Siam Sq; dishes 60-200B; ⏱11am-2pm & 6-10pm; ❄; BTS Siam) Travel back in time to 1960s-era Bangkok at this vintage diner popular with students from nearby Chulalongkorn University. Try old-style Western dishes, all of which come accompanied by a soft roll and green salad, or choose from the extensive Thai menu.

SUKHUMVIT

This seemingly endless ribbon of a road is where to go if you wish to forget you're in Thailand. From Korean to Middle Eastern, just about every cuisine has an outpost here. We've mentioned a few Thai places following, but most domestic eats in this area are more miss than hit, and it's really the place to indulge in the flavours you left at home.

Lower Sukhumvit

Nasir al-Masri MIDDLE EASTERN $$

(Map p92; 4/6 Soi 3/1, Th Sukhumvit; mains 80-350B; ⏱24hr; ❄; BTS Nana) One of several similar Middle Eastern restaurants on Soi 3/1, Nasir al-Masri is easily recognisable by its genuinely impressive floor-to-ceiling stainless steel 'theme'. Middle Eastern food generally means meat, meat and more meat, but there are also several delicious vegie-based mezze.

Bed Supperclub INTERNATIONAL $$$

(Map p92; ✆0 2651 3537; 26 Soi 11, Th Sukhumvit; mains 450-990B, set meals 790-1850B; ⏱7.30-10pm Tue-Thu, dinner 9pm Fri & Sat; ❄; BTS Nana) Within this sleek and futuristic setting – beds instead of tables and contemporary performances instead of mood music – the food stands up to the distractions with a changing menu described as 'modern eclectic cuisine'. Dining is à la carte except on Fridays and Saturdays when there's a four-course surprise menu served at 9pm sharp.

Tapas Café   SPANISH $$
(Map p92; 1/25 Soi 11, Th Sukhumvit; mains 75-750B; ⊙11am-midnight; ✦; BTS Nana) If vibrant tapas, refreshing sangria and an open, airy atmosphere aren't reasons enough to eat here, consider that before 7pm dishes and drinks are buy-two, get-one-free.

Upper Sukhumvit

**Boon Tong Kiat Singapore
Hainanese Chicken Rice**   SINGAPOREAN $
(Map p92; 440/5 Soi 55/Thong Lor, Th Sukhumvit; dishes 60-150B; ⊙lunch & dinner; ✦; BTS Thong Lo) Order a plate of the restaurant's namesake and bear witness to how a dish can be

simultaneously simple and profound. And while you're here you'd be daft not order *rojak*, the spicy/sour fruit 'salad', which here is cheekily called 'Singapore Som Tam'.

Sukhumvit Plaza   KOREAN $$$
(Korean Town; Map p92; cnr Soi 12 & Th Sukhumvit; ⊙lunch & dinner; ✦; BTS Asok, MRT Sukhumvit) Known around Bangkok as 'Korean Town', this multistorey complex is the city's best destination for authentic 'Seoul' food. Expat Koreans swear by **Myeong Ga** (Map p92; ✆0 2229 4658; mains 200-550B; ⊙dinner; ✦) on the ground floor, although there are slightly cheaper places in the complex as well.

Le Beaulieu   FRENCH $$$
(Map p92; ✆0 2204 2004; 50 Soi 19, Th Sukhumvit; set lunch/dinner from 525/1950B; ⊙11.30am-3pm & 6.30-11pm; ✦; BTS Asok, MRT Sukhumvit) This tiny service hotel–bound restaurant is considered by many residents to be Bangkok's

---

PRETTY THAI FOR A WHITE GUY

Starting around 2009, a handful of foreigners decided to open up Thai restaurants in Bangkok. The Thais can be very, well, protective about their cuisine, and the chefs involved generated a huge amount of local and international press – not all of it positive (one Thai food critic accused a well known foreign restaurateur of 'slapping the faces of Thai people'). The storm has since passed, and in its wake we reap the benefit of several excellent Thai restaurants.

» **nahm** (Map p90; ✆0 2625 3333; Metropolitan Hotel, 27 Th Sathon Tai; set meal 1500B; ⊙dinner; ✦; MRT Lumphini) Australian chef/author David Thompson (see the boxed text, p120) is behind what is quite possibly the best Thai restaurant in Bangkok. Taking his inspiration largely from antique texts, the dishes range from the exotic (spicy stir-fried frog with chillies, turmeric holy basil and cumin leaves) to the adventurous (fermented fish simmered with minced prawns and pork with chillies, galangal and green peppercorn), with bold flavours and artful presentation as a unifying thread. If you're expecting bland, gentrified Thai food meant for foreigners, prepare to be disappointed. Reservations recommended.

» **Bo.lan** (Map p92; ✆0 2260 2962; 42 Soi Rongnarong Phichai Songkhram, Soi 26, Th Sukhumvit; set meal 1500B; ⊙dinner Tue-Sun; BTS Phrom Phong) Bo and Dylan (Bo.lan, a play on words that also means 'ancient'), former chefs at London's nahm, have provided Bangkok with a compelling reason to reconsider upscale Thai cuisine. The couple's scholarly approach to Thai cooking takes the form of seasonal set meals featuring dishes you're not likely to find elsewhere.

» **Soul Food Mahanakorn** (Map p92; ✆0 2714 7708; 56/10 Soi 55/Thong Lor, Th Sukhumvit; mains 120-250B; ⊙dinner; ✦; BTS Thong Lo) Started up by a native of Pennsylvania, this cosy bar-restaurant does tasty but pricey takes on rustic Thai dishes such as *gài tôrt Hat Yai* (southern-style fried chicken), and *gaeng hang lair*, a northern-style pork curry, not to mention great cocktails.

» **Sra Bua** (Map p86; ✆0 2162 9000; Siam Kempinski Hotel, 991/9 Th Rama I; set meal 2400B; ⊙noon-3pm & 6-11pm Mon-Fri, 6-11pm Sat & Sun; ✦; BTS Siam) Helmed by a Thai and a Dane whose Copenhagen restaurant, Kiin Kiin, scored a Michelin star, Sra Bua takes a correspondingly international approach to Thai food – think frozen red curry with lobster. It's behind the Siam Paragon.

BRUNCH BUFFET BONANZA

Sunday brunch has become something of a Bangkok institution among resident foreigners, and virtually every large hotel in town puts together decadent buffets on every other day as well. The following choices will leave you with more than simply a distended stomach.

The highly regarded restaurants at the **Four Seasons Hotel** (Map p86; ✆0 2250 1000; 155 Th Ratchadamri; buffet 2766B; ⏰11.30am-3pm Sun; ✵; BTS Ratchadamri) set up steam tables for their decadent Sunday brunch buffet – reservations are essential.

Even if you can't afford to stay at the Oriental Hotel, you should save up for the riverside seafood buffet at **Lord Jim's** (Map p80; ✆0 2659 9000; 48 Soi Oriental/38, Th Charoen Krung; buffet 1472-1943B; ⏰noon-2.30pm Mon-Fri, 11.30am-3pm Sat, 11am-3pm Sun; ✵; river ferry Tha Oriental).

The award-winning buffet at US chain **JW Marriott** (Map p92; ✆0 2656 7700; ground fl, JW Marriott Hotel, 4 Soi 2, Th Sukhumvit; buffet Sat/Sun 1285/1885B; ⏰11.30am-3pm Sat & Sun; ✵; BTS Nana) is likened to Thanksgiving all year-round, and generous options for free-flowing beer or wine are also available.

Rang Mahal (Map p92; ✆0 2261 7100; 26th fl, Rembrandt Hotel, 19 Soi 20, Th Sukhumvit; buffet 850B; ⏰11am-2.30pm Sun; ✵; BTS Asok, MRT Sukhumvit), on the top of the Rembrandt Hotel, couples great views with an all-Indian buffet every Sunday.

And for those who love the sweet stuff, the **Sukhothai Hotel** (Map p90; ✆0 2344 8888; 13/3 Th Sathon Tai; buffet 800B; ⏰2-5.30pm Fri-Sun; ✵; MRT Lumphini) offers a unique, entirely cocoa-based chocolate buffet.

best place for French cuisine. The menu ranges from the classic (steak tartare, bouillabaisse) to the modern (minuté of scrambled eggs and fresh sea urchin), with dishes prepared using both unique imported ingredients and produce from Thailand's Royal Projects. Reservations recommended.

Bei Otto GERMAN **$$$**
(Map p92; www.beiotto.com; 1 Soi 20, Th Sukhumvit; mains 220-590B; ⏰9am-midnight; ✵; BTS Asok, MRT Sukhumvit) Claiming a Bangkok residence for nearly 20 years, Bei Otto's major culinary bragging point is its pork knuckles, reputedly the best in town. A good selection of German beers and an attached delicatessen with brilliant breads and super sausages make it even more attractive to go Deutsch.

Serenade INTERNATIONAL **$$$**
(Map p92; ✆0 2713 8409; 264/1 Soi 12, Soi 55/ Thong Lor, Th Sukhumvit; mains 145-480B; ⏰lunch & dinner; ✵; BTS Thong Lo & access by taxi) This sexy new wine bar excels in tasty tapas-like dishes such as Greek olives and white anchovy sautée on baguette with melted Manchego cheese, or Grilled grass-fed Australian black angus strip loin with *jim jaew* demiglace.

Bharani THAI **$**
(Sansab Boat Noodle; Map p92; 96/14 Soi 23, Th Sukhumvit; mains 50-200B; ⏰10am-10pm; ✵; BTS Asok, MRT Sukhumvit) This cosy Thai restaurant dabbles in a bit of everything, from ox-tongue stew to rice fried with shrimp paste, but the real reason to come is for the rich, meaty 'boat noodles' – so called because they used to be sold from boats plying the *klorngs* (canals) of Ayuthaya.

Bacco – Osteria da Sergio ITALIAN **$$$**
(Map p92; 35/1 Soi 53, Th Sukhumvit; antipasti 100-1200B; mains 250-850B; ⏰lunch & dinner; ✵; BTS Thong Lo) The slightly cheesy interior of this osteria serves as something of a cover for one of Bangkok's better Italian menus. There's an abundance of delicious antipasti, but the emphasis here is breads, from pizza to piada, all of which are done exceedingly well.

Duc de Praslin CHOCOLATE **$**
(Map p92; ground fl, RSU Tower, Soi 31/1, Th Sukhumvit; mains 20-120B; ⏰8am-9pm; ✵; BTS Phrom Phong) Travel from sweaty Bangkok to Olde Europe in one step at this classy cafe-slash-chocolatier. Other than the spot-on bonbons and good coffee, try a hot cocoa, made in front of your eyes by combining steaming milk with shards of rich chocolate.

Face INTERNATIONAL **$$$**
(Map p92; ✆0 2713 6048; 29 Soi 38, Th Sukhumvit; mains 310-670B; ⏰lunch & dinner; ✵; BTS Thong Lo) This handsome dining complex is

essentially three very good restaurants in one: Lan Na Thai does solid upscale Thai, Misaki focuses on the Japanese end of things, while Hazara dabbles in exotic-sounding 'North Indian frontier cuisine'.

Thonglee THAI $
(Map p92; Soi 20, Th Sukhumvit; mains 40-100B; ☺lunch & dinner, closed 3rd Sun of the month; BTS Asok, MRT Sukhumvit) One of the few remaining mom-and-pop Thai places on Th Sukhumvit, this tiny kitchen offers a few dishes you won't find elsewhere, such as *mŏo pàt gà·bì* (pork fried with shrimp paste) and *mèe gròrp* (sweet-and-spicy crispy fried noodles).

Mokkori JAPANESE $
(Map p92; 8/3 Soi 55/Thong Lor, Th Sukhumvit; mains 70-130B; ☺lunch & dinner; ❄; BTS Thong Lo) You know you're in the right place if, upon entering this restaurant, the staff drop everything they're doing and scream at you. Tiny Mokkori serves Japanese-style ramen in a resoundingly authentic setting, and many agree they do one of the better bowls in town. In addition to noodles, be sure to order the wonderfully simple snack of cucumber chunks served with a spicy miso dipping sauce.

Soi 38 Night Market THAI-CHINESE $
(Map p92; Soi 38, Th Sukhumvit; mains 30-60B; ☺8pm-3am; BTS Thong Lo) After a hard night of clubbing, this gathering of basic Chinese-Thai hawker stalls will look like a shimmering oasis. If you're going sober, stick to the knot of 'famous' vendors tucked into an alley on the right-hand side as you enter the street.

LUMPHINI PARK & TH PHRA RAM IV

TOP CHOICE **Kai Thort Jay Kee** THAI $
(Soi Polo Fried Chicken; Map p90; 137/1-3 Soi Sanam Khlii (Polo), Th Withayu/Wireless Rd; mains 40-280B; ☺lunch & dinner; ❄; MRT Lumphini) Although the *sôm·đam*, sticky rice and *lâhp* (a Thai-style 'salad' of minced meat) give the impression of a northeastern Thai-style eatery, the restaurant's namesake deep-fried bird is more southern in origin. Regardless, smothered in a thick layer of crispy deep-fried garlic, it is none other than a truly Bangkok experience.

Ngwan Lee Lang Suan CHINESE-THAI $$
(Map p90; cnr Soi Lang Suan & Soi Sarasin; mains 50-900B; ☺7am-3am; BTS Ratchadamri) This cavernous food hall is centrally located and open late, making it a perfect post-clubbing destination. It's also a great place to try those dishes you never dare to order elsewhere such as *jàp chài,* Chinese-style stewed vegies, or the delicious *ʼbèt đǔn,* duck stewed in Chinese spices.

Café 1912 FRENCH-THAI $$
(Map p90; Alliance Française, 29 Th Sathon Tai; dishes 50-185B; ☺7am-7pm Mon-Sat, to 2pm Sun; ❄; MRT Lumphini) Part of the French cultural centre, and with food provided by a good local bakery, this cafeteria is a great place to fuel up while on an embassy run. Both French and Thai dishes are available, as well as coffee and delicious cakes and sweets.

GREATER BANGKOK

Mallika SOUTHERN THAI $$
(Map p97; 21/36 Th Rang Nam; mains 70-480B; ☺10am-10pm Mon-Sat; ❄; BTS Victory Monument) A dream come true: authentic regional Thai (southern, in this case), with a legible English menu, good service and a tidy setting. The prices are slightly high for a mom-and-pop Thai joint, but you're paying for quality.

Kaloang Home Kitchen THAI $$
(Map p96; 503-505 Th Samsen; mains 60-170B; ☺11am-11pm; bus 32, 516, river ferry Tha Thewet) Don't be alarmed by the peeling paint and the dilapidated deck – Kaloang Home Kitchen certainly isn't. The laid-back atmosphere and seafood-heavy menu will quickly dispel any concerns about sinking into the Mae Nam Chao Phraya, and a beer and the breeze will temporarily erase any scarring memories of Bangkok traffic. To reach the restaurant, follow Th Si Ayuthaya until you reach the river.

Phat Thai Ari THAI $
(no roman-script sign; Map p118; 2/1-2 Soi Ari/7, Th Phahonyothin; mains 45-100B; ☺11am-10pm; BTS Ari) One of the city's better-known *pàt tai* shops is located a couple of blocks from the eponymous soi. Try the innovative 'noodle-less' version, where long strips of crispy green papaya are substituted for the traditional rice noodles from Chanthaburi. Phat Thai Ari is located on the narrow soi that leads to Phaholyothin Center, north of BTS Ari.

Pathé THAI $
(Map p118; cnr Th Lat Phrao & Th Viphawadee; mains 75-160B; ☺2pm-1am; ❄; MRT Phahon Yothin) The Thai equivalent of a 1950s-era US diner, this popular place combines solid Thai food, a fun atmosphere and a jukebox playing scratched records. Don't miss the deep-fried ice cream.

THE WHISKY SET

Thai beer is generally more miss than hit, so the next time you're out on the town, why not drink like the Thais do and order a bottle of whisky?

Your first step is to choose a brand. For a particularly decadent night out, the industry standard is a bottle of *blåak* (Johnnie Walker Black Label). Those on a budget can go for the cheaper imported labels such as Red Label or Benmore, and a rock-bottom but fun night can be had on domestic spirits such as 100 Pipers or Sang Som. And it's not unusual to bring your own bottle to many Thai bars, although some might charge a modest corkage fee.

As any Thai can tell you, your next immediate concern is mixers. These will take the form of several bottles of soda water and a bottle or two of Coke, along with a pail of ice. Most waiters will bring these to you as a matter of course.

Mixing is the easiest step and requires little or no action on your part; your skilled waiter will fill your glass with ice, followed by a shot of whisky, a splash of soda, a top-off of Coke and, finally, a swirl with the ice tongs to bring it all together.

If you can't finish your bottle, shame on you, but don't fret, as it's perfectly normal to keep it at the bar. Simply tell your trusted waiter, who will write your name and the date on the bottle and keep it for your next visit.

River Bar Café　　　　　　　　THAI $$

(405/1 Soi Chao Phraya, Th Ratchawithi, Thonburi; mains 130-350B; ⊗5pm-midnight; ❀; klorng taxi to Tha Krung Thon Bridge pier) Sporting a picture-perfect riverside location, good food and live music, the River Bar Café combines all the essentials for a perfect Bangkok night out.

🍷 Drinking

Once infamous as an anything-goes nightlife destination, in recent years Bangkok has been edging towards teetotalism with strict regulations limiting the sale of alcohol and increasingly conservative closing times. Regardless, the city still boasts a diverse and fun bar scene, and there are even a few places to go if you find 1am too early to get back on the wagon.

Keep in mind that smoking has been outlawed at all indoor (and some quasi-outdoor) entertainment places since 2008. Surprisingly for Thailand, the rule is strictly enforced.

KO RATANAKOSIN, BANGLAMPHU & THONBURI

During the day, Th Khao San is dominated by just about everybody but Thais. At night the natives deem it safe to join the crowds, giving the area an entirely different atmosphere. In addition to the main strip, Th Rambuttri and Th Phra Athit also draw drinkers and fun seekers from across the city, and the world.

Hippie de Bar　　　　　　　　BAR

(Map p60; 46 Th Khao San; ⊗6pm-2am; river ferry Tha Phra Athit) Popular with the domestic crowd, Hippie boasts several levels of fun, both indoor and outdoor. There's food, pool tables and a soundtrack you're unlikely to hear elsewhere in town.

Amorosa　　　　　　　　　　　BAR

Map p60; www.arunresidence.com; rooftop, Arun Residence, 36-38 Soi Pratu Nok Yung; ⊗6-11pm; bus 123, 508, river ferry Tha Tien) It may be the only bar in the area, but that doesn't mean it's any sort of compromise; Amorosa's rooftop location packs killer views of Wat Arun, making it one of the best spots in Bangkok for a riverside sundowner.

Rolling Bar　　　　　　　　　BAR

(Map p60; Th Prachathipatai; ⊗6pm-midnight; klorng taxi Tha Phan Fah) An escape from hectic Th Khao San is a good enough excuse to shlep to this quiet canal-side boozer. Tasty bar snacks and live music are excuses to stay.

Taksura　　　　　　　　　　　BAR

(Map p60; 156/1 Th Tanao; ⊗5pm-midnight; klorng taxi Tha Phan Fah) There are no signs to lead you to this seemingly abandoned century-old mansion in the heart of old Bangkok, which is all the better, according to the cool uni-artsy crowd who frequent the place.

Phranakorn Bar　　　　　　　BAR

(Map p60; 58/2 Soi Damnoen Klang Tai; ⊗6pm-midnight; klorng taxi Tha Phan Fah) It must have taken a true visionary to transform this characterless multilevel building into a warm, fun destination for a night out. Students and arty types make Phranakorn Bar a home away from hovel with eclectic decor and changing gallery exhibits.

Bars tend to segregate into foreigner and Thai factions, but you can always reverse that trend. Here are a few popular options:

Center Khao San
BAR

(Map p60; Th Khao San; ⊘24hr; river ferry Tha Phra Athit) One of many front-row views of the human parade on Th Khao San. The upstairs bar hosts late-night bands.

Mulligans
BAR

(Map p60; 1st fl, Buddy Lodge, 265 Th Khao San; ⊘3pm-4am; river ferry Tha Phra Athit; ✸) Irish/colonial-themed bar for when only air-con will do.

Molly Bar
BAR

(Map p60; Th Rambutri; ⊘8pm-1am; river ferry Tha Phra Athit) Packed on weekends for live music; it's more mellow on weekdays with outdoor seating.

Roof Bar
BAR

(Map p60; Th Khao San; ⊘5pm-midnight; river ferry Tha Phra Athit) Although the live acoustic soundtrack is hit and miss, the views of Th Khao San are solid from this elevated pub.

SILOM & SATHON

Barbican Bar
BAR

(Map p82; 9/4-5 Soi Thaniya, Th Silom; ⊘4pm-1am; BTS Sala Daeng, MRT Si Lom; ✸) Surrounded by massage parlours with teenage prom queens cat-calling at Japanese businessmen, this is a straight-laced yuppie bar where office crews come for some happy-hour drinks and stay until closing time.

Coyote on Convent
BAR

(Map p82; 1/2 Th Convent, Th Silom; ⊘11am-midnight; BTS Sala Daeng, MRT Si Lom; ✸) Forget the overpriced Tex-Mex cuisine; the real reason to visit Coyote is for its 75-plus varieties of margaritas. On Wednesdays from 6pm to 8pm and Saturdays from 10pm to midnight, the icy drinks are distributed free to all women who pass through the door.

Molly Malone's
IRISH BAR

(Map p82; 1/5-6 Th Convent, Th Silom; ⊘11am-1am; BTS Sala Daeng, MRT Si Lom; ✸) A recent makeover has this longstanding local leaning perilously towards Irish kitsch, but it still pulls a fun crowd and the service is friendly and fast.

SIAM SQUARE & PRATUNAM

Co-Co Walk
BAR, LIVE MUSIC

(Map p86; 87/70 Th Phayathai; ⊘6pm-1am; BTS Ratchathewi) This covered compound is a smorgasbord of pubs, bars and live music popular with Thai university students. **The Tube** left its heart in London, and is heavy on the Brit Pop, **Chilling House Café** features Thai

---

OUT ALL NIGHT

With most pubs and dance clubs closing around 1am, One Night in Bangkok is not quite what it used to be. Thankfully, there are a few places around town that have gained sufficient 'permission' to stay open until the morning hours.

Off Soi Ngam Duphli, **Wong's Place** (Map p90; 27/3 Soi Si Bamphen, Th Phra Ram IV; ⊘8pm-late; MRT Lumphini; ✸), a longstanding backpacker bar, is so late-night, it's best not to show up before midnight.

Vaguely Middle Eastern-themed **Gazebo** (Map p60; 3rd fl, 44 Th Chakraphong; river ferry Tha Phra Athit) represents the posh side of the Th Khao San area. This bar's elevated setting appears to lend it some leniency with the city's strict closing times.

On Th Sukhumvit, **Club Insomnia** (Map p92; Soi 12, Th Sukhumvit; admission 200B; ⊘8pm-late; BTS Asok, MRT Sukhumvit) and **Scratch Dog** (Map p92; ☏0 2262 1234; Windsor Suites Hotel, 8-10 Soi 20, Th Sukhumvit; ⊘8pm-late; BTS Asok, MRT Sukhumvit) employ a Top 40 hip-hop and R&B soundtrack to propel partiers into the morning hours.

For something a bit edgier, ask your friendly taxi driver to escort you to any of the following: **Shock 39, Spicy, Spice Club, Boss** or **Bossy**. These creatively named late-night clubs are all located in central Bangkok and stay open until well past sunrise. We'd tell you a bit more about them and put them on our maps, but our experience and research suggest that these clubs exist in an alternate late-night reality that only Bangkok taxi drivers can navigate...

hits played by live acoustic guitar and a few pool tables, and **69** sets the pace with cover bands playing Western rock staples and current hits.

Hyde & Seek
BAR

(Map p86; ground fl, Athenee Residence, 65/1 Soi Ruam Rudi; ⊙11am-1am; BTS Phloen Chit; ✸) The tasty and comforting English-inspired bar snacks and meals have earned Hyde & Seek the right to call itself a 'gastro bar', but we reckon the real reasons to come here are arguably Bangkok's most well-stocked bar and some of the city's best cocktails.

To-Sit
RESTAURANT-BAR

(Map p86; Soi 3, Siam Sq, Th Phra Ram 1; ⊙6pm-midnight; BTS Siam; ✸) To-Sit epitomises everything a Thai university student could wish for on a night out: sappy Thai music and cheap, spicy eats.

SUKHUMVIT
WTF
GALLERY, BAR

(Map p92; www.wtfbangkok.com; 7 Soi 51, Th Sukhumvit; ⊙6pm-1am Tue-Sun; BTS Thong Lo; ✸) No, not that WTF; Wonderful Thai Friendship combines a cozy bar and an art gallery in one attractive package. Throw in some of Bangkok's best cocktails and some delicious Spanish-influenced bar snacks, and you won't need another destination for the evening.

Bangkok Bar
BAR

(Map p92; Soi Ekamai 2, Soi 63/Ekamai, Th Sukhumvit; ⊙8pm-1am; BTS Ekkamai; ✸) Bounce with Thai indie kids at this fun, but astonishingly uncreatively named bar. There's live music, and the eats are strong enough to make Bangkok Bar a dinner destination in itself. And we double-dog dare you to walk a straight line after two Mad Dogs, the infamous house drink.

GAY & LESBIAN BANGKOK

Bangkok is so gay it makes San Francisco look like rural Texas. With out-and-open nightspots and annual pride events, the city's homosexual community enjoys an unprecedented amount of tolerance considering attitudes in the rest of the region. It should be mentioned, however, that recent years have seen a sharp rise in HIV and other STDs among gay men in Bangkok; when in town, be sure to play it safe.

Utopia (www.utopia-asia.com) is an online resource for the Southeast Asian gay community, listing Bangkok entertainment venues, news and views, and providing travel services. **Dreaded Ned** (www.dreadedned.com) and **Fridae** (www.fridae.com) also have up to date listings and events. The **Lesbian Guide to Bangkok** (www.bangkoklesbian.com) is the only English-language tracker of the lesbian scene.

Gay women and men are well advised to visit Bangkok in mid-November, when the city's small but fun **Pride Festival** (www.bangkokpride.org) is in full swing. Dinners, cruises, clubbing and contests are the order of the week.

Bed Supperclub (see p134) hosts the hugely popular 'Confidential Sundays', and other posh locales often play host to weekend-long 'circuit parties'. Visit **G Circuit** (www.gcircuit.com) to find out when and where the next one is.

Soi 2 on Th Silom is lined with dance clubs, such as **DJ Station** (Map p82; 8/6-8 Soi 2, Th Silom; ⊙8pm-late; BTS Sala Daeng, MRT Si Lom), where the crowd is a mix of Thai guppies (gay professionals), money boys and a few Westerners. Just half a soi over is **G.O.D.** (Guys on Display; Map p82; Soi 2/1, Th Silom; cover 280B; ⊙8pm-late; BTS Sala Daeng, MRT Si Lom), which as the name suggests is not averse to a little shirtless dancing. Traipse on over to Soi 4 to find the old-timer conversation bars, such as **Balcony** (Map p82; www.balconypub.com; 86-88 Soi 4, Th Silom; ⊙5.30pm-1am; BTS Sala Daeng, MRT Si Lom) and **Telephone** (Map p82; 114/11-13 Soi 4, Th Silom; ⊙5pm-1am; BTS Sala Daeng, MRT Si Lom).

Further out of town is a more local scene, where a little Thai will make you feel more welcome. Several of the bars along Th Kamphaeng Phet, including **Fake Club** (Map p118; Th Kamphaeng Phet, Chatuchak; ⊙9pm-2am; BTS Mo Chit, MRT Kamphaeng Phet) and **el Ninyo** (Map p118; Th Kamphaeng Phet, Chatuchak; ⊙9pm-2am; BTS Mo Chit, MRT Kamphaeng Phet), are popular on weekends for loud and lushy behaviour.

Zeta (29/67 Royal City Ave/RCA, off Phra Ram IX; admission 100B; ⊙8pm-2am; MRT Phra Ram 9 & access by taxi) is an easy-going club for the girls with a nightly band doing Thai and Western covers.

Cheap Charlie's
BAR

(Map p92; Soi 11, Th Sukhumvit; ⊘Mon-Sat; BTS Nana) There's never enough seating, and the design concept is best classified as 'junkyard,' but on most nights this chummy open-air beer corner is a great place to meet everybody, from package tourists to resident English teachers.

Iron Fairies
PUB, WINE BAR

(Map p92; www.theironfairies.com; Soi 55/Thong Lor, Th Sukhumvit; ⊘5pm-midnight Mon-Sat; BTS Thong Lo; ❀) Imagine, if you can, an abandoned fairy factory in Paris c 1912, and you'll get an idea of the design theme at this popular pub–wine bar. If you manage to wrangle one of a handful of seats, the staff claim to serve Bangkok's 'best burgers' and there's live music after 9.30pm.

Tuba
BAR

(Off map p92; 34 Room 11-12 A, Soi Ekamai 21, Soi Ekamai/63, Th Sukhumvit; BTS Ekkamai; ❀) Part storage room for over-the-top vintage furniture, part friendly local boozer, this bizarre bar certainly doesn't lack in character. Indulge in a whole bottle for once and don't miss the delicious chicken wings.

Bull's Head
PUB

(Map p92; ☎0 2259 4444; 595/10-11 Soi 33/1, Th Sukhumvit; ⊘5pm-1am; BTS Phrom Phong; ❀) Bangkok boasts several English-style pubs but this is probably the most authentic of the lot. With friendly management and staff, and more events and activities than a summer camp, it's also a good place to meet people, particularly those of the British persuasion.

HOBS
PUB

(House of Beers; Map p92; 522/3 Soi Thong Lo 16, Soi 55/Thong Lor, Th Sukhumvit; ⊘11am-midnight; BTS Thong Lo; ❀) Arguably the word's best brews, Belgian beers have been fleetingly available around Bangkok for a while now, but have found a permanent home at this new pub. Be sure to accompany your beer with a bowl of crispy *frites*, served here Belgian-style with mayonnaise.

☆ Entertainment

Shame on you if you find yourself bored in Bangkok. And even more shame if you think the only entertainment options involve the word 'go-go'. Nowadays Bangkok's nightlife is as diverse as that of virtually any modern city. And even if you're usually in bed by 9pm, Bangkok still offers interesting post-dinner diversions, from flash cinemas to traditional cultural performances.

Live Music

Music is an essential element of a Thai night out, and just about every pub worth its salted peanuts has a house band of varying quality. For the most part this means perky Thai pop covers or tired international standards (if you've left town without having heard a live version of *Hotel California*, you haven't really been to Bangkok), but an increasing number of places are starting to deviate from the norm with quirky and/or inspired bands and performances.

Brick Bar
BAR, LIVE MUSIC

(Map p60; basement, Buddy Lodge, 265 Th Khao San; ⊘8pm-1am; river ferry Tha Phra Athit; ❀) This cavelike pub hosts a nightly revolving cast of live music for an almost exclusively Thai crowd. Come at midnight, wedge yourself into a table a few inches from the horn section, and lose it to Teddy Ska, one of the most energetic live acts in town.

Living Room
HOTEL LOUNGE, JAZZ

(Map p92; ☎0 2649 8888; Level I, Sheraton Grande Sukhumvit, 250 Th Sukhumvit; ⊘6.30pm-midnight; BTS Asok, MRT Sukhumvit; ❀) Don't let looks deceive you; every night this bland hotel lounge transforms into the city's best venue for live jazz. Contact ahead of time to see which sax master or hide hitter is currently in town.

Diplomat Bar
HOTEL LOUNGE

(Map p86; ground fl, Conrad Hotel, 87 Th Witthayu/Wireless Rd; ⊘6pm-midnight; BTS Phloen Chit; ❀) This is one of the few hotel lounges that the locals make a point of visiting. Choose from an expansive list of innovative martinis and sip to live jazz (from 6.30pm to midnight), played gracefully at conversation level.

Parking Toys
LIVE MUSIC

(☎0 2907 2228; 17/22 Soi Mayalap, Kaset-Navamin Hwy; ⊘6pm-1am; BTS Mo Chit & access by taxi; ❀) Essentially a rambling shed stuffed with vintage furniture, Parking Toys hosts an eclectic revolving cast of fun bands ranging in genre from acoustic/classical ensembles to electro-funk jam acts. To get here, take a taxi heading north from BTS Mo Chit and tell the driver to take you to Th Kaset-Navamin. Upon passing the second stop light on this road, look for the small Heineken sign on your left.

DRINKING WITH THE STARS

Bangkok is one of the few big cities in the world where nobody seems to mind if you set up the odd bar or restaurant on the top of a skyscraper. Note that reservations are recommended for the more restaurant-like of the following, and none allow shorts or sandals wearers.

» **Moon Bar at Vertigo** (Map p90; Banyan Tree Hotel, 21/100 Th Sathon Tai; ⊙5.30pm-1am; MRT Lumphini) Precariously perched on the top of 61 floors of skyscraper, Moon Bar offers a bird's-eye view of Bangkok. Things can get a bit crowded here come sunset, so be sure to show up a bit early to get the best seats.

» **Sirocco Sky Bar** (Map p80; The Dome, 1055 Th Silom; ⊙6pm-1am; BTS Saphan Taksin) Descend the sweeping stairs like a Hollywood diva to the precipice bar of this rooftop restaurant that looks over the Mae Nam Chao Phraya.

» **Nest** (Map p92; ☑0 2255 0638; www.nestbangkok.com; 8th fl, Le Fenix Hotel, 33/33 Soi 11, Th Sukhumvit; ⊙5pm-2am; BTS Nana) Perched on the roof of the Le Fenix Hotel, Nest is a chic maze of cleverly concealed sofas and inviting daybeds. A DJ soundtrack and one of the most interesting pub grub menus in town bring things back down to ground level.

» **Long Table** (Map p92; ☑0 2302 2557; 25th fl, 48 Column Building, Soi 16, Th Sukhumvit; ⊙5pm-2am; BTS Asok, MRT Sukhumvit; ❋) Not exactly a roof-topper, but the open-air section of this upscale Thai restaurant-slash-bar provides great views over one of Bangkok's busiest central districts.

» **RedSky** (Map p86; ☑0 2100 1234; 55th fl, Centara Grand, Central World Plaza; ⊙5pm-1am; BTS Siam & Chit Lom) Bangkok's most recent rooftop dining venture is probably the most formal of the lot, and boasts an extensive martini menu.

» **Roof** (Map p86; 25th fl, Siam@Siam, 865 Th Phra Ram I; ⊙5.30pm-12.30am; BTS National Stadium) In addition to views of central Bangkok, the Roof offers a dedicated personal martini sommelier and an extensive wine and champagne list.

Saxophone Pub & Restaurant   LIVE MUSIC
(Map 60; www.saxophonepub.com; 3/8 Th Phayathai; ⊙6pm-2am; BTS Victory Monument; ❋) This nightlife staple is the big stage of Bangkok's live-music scene. It's a bit too loud for a first date, but the quality and variety of the music makes it a great destination for music-loving buddies on a night out.

Ad Here the 13th   BAR, LIVE MUSIC
(Map p60; 13 Th Samsen; ⊙6pm-midnight; river erry Tha Phra Athit; ❋) Beside Khlong Banglamphu, Ad Here is everything a neighbourhood joint should be: lots of regulars, cold beer and heart-warming tunes delivered by a masterful house band starting at 10pm. Everyone knows each other, so don't be shy about mingling.

Tawandang German Brewery   BAR, RESTAURANT
(cnr Th Phra Ram III & Th Narathiwat Ratchanakharin; BTS Chong Nonsi & access by taxi; ❋) It's Oktoberfest all year-round at this hangar-sized music hall, south of the city. The Thai-German food is tasty, the house-made brews are entirely potable, and the nightly stage shows make singing along a necessity. Music starts at 8.30pm.

Brown Sugar   PUB, LIVE MUSIC
(Map p90; 231/20 Th Sarasin; ⊙6pm-midnight; BTS Ratchadamri; ❋) Plant yourself in a corner of this cosy, mazelike pub, and bump to Zao-za-dung, the nine-piece house band. The tables are so close that you can't help but make new friends.

Titanium   LIVE MUSIC
(Map p92; 2/30 Soi 22, Th Sukhumvit; ⊙8pm-1am; BTS Phrom Phong; ❋) Some come to this slightly cheesy 'ice bar' for the chill and the flavoured vodka, but we come for Unicorn, an all-female rock band.

Raintree   PUB, LIVE MUSIC
(Map 60; 116/63-64 Soi Th Rang Nam; ⊙6pm-1am; BTS Victory Monument; ❋) This atmospheric pub is one of the few remaining places in town to hear 'songs for life', Thai folk music with roots in the communist insurgency of the 1960s and '70s.

Bamboo Bar   HOTEL LOUNGE, JAZZ
(Map p80; ☑0 2236 0400; Oriental Hotel, 48 Soi 40/Oriental, Th Charoen Krung; ⊙11am-1am; river ferry Tha Oriental; ❋) The Oriental's Bamboo Bar is famous for its live lounge jazz, which holds court inside a colonial-era cabin of lazy fans, broad-leafed palms and rattan decor.

Fat Gut'z   LIVE MUSIC
(Map p92; www.fatgutz.com; 264 Soi 12, Soi 55/ Thong Lor, Th Sukhumvit; ⊙6pm-2am; BTS Thong Lo; ❋) This closet-sized 'saloon' combines live music and, er, fish and chips. Despite (or perhaps thanks to) the odd whiff of chip oil, the odd combo works. Live blues every night from 9pm to midnight.

Rock Pub   PUB, LIVE MUSIC
(Map p86; www.therockpub-bangkok.com; 93/26-28 Th Phayathai; ⊙9.30pm-2am; BTS Ratchathewi; ❋) If you thought the days of heavy metal were long gone, step back in time at this cave-like pub where posters of Iron Maiden pass for interior design and black jeans and long hair are the unofficial dress code.

Dance Clubs

Bangkok's discos are largely fly-by-night outfits, and that really fun club you found on your last trip two years ago is most likely history today. To find out what is going on, check **Dude Sweet** (www.dudesweet.org), organisers of hugely popular monthly parties, and **Bangkok Recorder** (www.bangkokrecorder.com) for rotating theme nights and visiting celeb DJs.

Other sources of info. include listings mag **BK** (http://bk.asia-city.com/nightlife), or if you're partial to the Th Sukhumvit scene, www.thonglor-ekamai.com has a good rundown of the area's clubs.

Cover charges for clubs and discos range from 100B to 600B and usually include a drink. Don't even think about showing up before 11pm, and always bring ID. Most clubs close at 2am. For places that open late, see p129.

RCA   DANCE CLUBS
(Royal City Avenue; off Th Phra Ram IX; MRT Phra Ram 9 & access by taxi) RCA is well and truly Club Alley. Formerly a bastion of the teen scene, this Vegas-like strip has finally graduated from high school and hosts partiers of every age. Worthwhile destinations include **808 Club** (www.808bangkok.com; admission from 300B), **Flix/Slim**, **Route 66** (www. route66club.com; admission free) and **Cosmic Café** (admission free).

Tapas Room   DANCE CLUB
(Map p82; www.tapasroom.net; 114/17-18 Soi 4, Th Silom; admission 100B; BTS Sala Daeng, MRT Si Lom) You won't find food here, but the name is an accurate indicator of the Spanish/Moroccan-inspired vibe of this multilevel den. Come from Wednesday to Saturday when the combination of DJs and live percussion brings the body count to critical level.

Ekamai Soi 5   CLUB
(Map p92; cnr Soi Ekamai 5 & Soi 63/Ekamai, Th Sukhumvit; BTS Ekkamai & access by taxi) This open-air entertainment zone is the destination of choice for Bangkok's young and beautiful – for the moment at least. **Demo** (admission free), with blasting beats and a NYC warehouse vibe, is the epitome of the Alpha Club, while **Funky Villa** (admission free), with its outdoor seating and Top 40 soundtrack, boasts more of a chill-out vibe. Also accessible via Soi Thong Lor 10.

Glow   CLUB
(Map p92; www.glowbkk.com; 96/4-5 Soi 23, Th Sukhumvit; admission from 200B; MRT Asok, MRT Sukhumvit) Glow is a small venue with a big reputation. Boasting a huge variety of vodkas and a recently upgraded sound system, the tunes range from hip-hop to electronica and just about everything in between.

GÀ-TEU-I CABARET

Watching men dressed as women perform tacky show tunes has, not surprisingly, become the latest 'must-do' fixture on the Bangkok tourist circuit. Both **Calypso Cabaret** (Map p86; ☑0 2653 3960; www.calypsocabaret. com; Asia Hotel, 296 Th Phayathai; tickets 1200B; ⊙show times 8.15pm & 9.45pm; BTS Ratchathewi) and **Mambo Cabaret** (☑0 2294 7381; www.mambocabaret.com; 59/28 Yannawa Tat Mai; tickets 800-1000B; ⊙show times 7.15pm, 8.30pm & 10pm; BTS Chong Nonsi & access by taxi) host choreographed stage shows featuring Broadway high kicks and lip-synched pop tunes by the most well-endowed dudes you'll find anywhere. Mambo is located near Phra Ram III, in far southern Bangkok.

Nung-Len   CLUB
(Map p92; www.nunglen.net; 217 Soi 63/Ekamai; admission free; BTS Ekkamai & access by taxi) Young, loud and Thai, Nung-Len (literally 'sit and chill') is a ridiculously popular sardine tin of live music and uni students on popular Th Ekamai. Make sure you get in before 10pm or you won't get in at all.

Bed Supperclub   CLUB
(Map p92; www.bedsupperclub.com; 26 Soi 11, Th Sukhumvit; admission from 600B; BTS Nana) This illuminated tube has been a literal highlight of the Bangkok club scene for a good while now. Arrive early to squeeze in dinner (p124), or if you've only got dancing on your mind, come on Tuesday for the popular hip-hop nights.

Q Bar   CLUB
(Map p92; www.qbarbangkok.com; 34 Soi 11, Th Sukhumvit; admission from 700B; BTS Nana) The club that introduced Bangkok to the lounge scene in 1999 is still alive and writhing. This darkened industrial space sees a revolving cast of somebodies, nobodies and working girls. Various theme nights fill the weekly calendar.

Club Culture   CLUB
(Map p60; www.club-culture-bkk.com; admission from 200B; off Th Ratchadamnoen Klang; klorng taxi Tha Phan Fah) Housed in a seemingly abandoned four-storey building, Club Culture is the quirkiest member of Bangkok's club scene. Opening dates and times can depend on events, so check the website to see what's going on.

Traditional Arts Performances

As Thailand's cultural repository, Bangkok offers an array of dance and theatre performances. For background information about these ancient traditions, see p734 and p736.

**Chalermkrung Royal
Theatre**   TRADITIONAL PERFORMANCE
(Sala Chalerm Krung; Map p76; ☑0 2222 0434; www.salachalermkrung.com; cnr Th Charoen Krung & Th Triphet; tickets 800-1200B; ☺showtime 7.30pm; river ferry Tha Saphan Phut) In a Thai art deco building at the edge of the Chinatown-Phahurat district, this theatre provides a striking venue for *kŏhn* (masked dance-drama based on stories from the *Ramakian*, the Thai version of the *Ramayana*). When it opened in 1933, the royally funded Chalermkrung was the largest and most modern theatre in Asia. Today, *kŏhn* performances are held every Thursday and Friday and last about two hours plus intermission. The theatre requests that patrons dress respectfully, which means no shorts, tank tops or sandals.

Aksra Theatre   PUPPET SHOW
(Map 60; ☑0 2677 8888, ext 5730; www.aksratheatre.com; 3rd fl, King Power Complex, 8/1 Th Rang Nam; tickets 400-600B; ☺shows 7.30-8.30pm Mon-Wed,

CINEMA STRATEGY

Going to the movies is a big deal in Bangkok. Every mall has its own theatre and it's unlikely that any other city in the world has anything like EGV's Gold Class, a ticket that grants you entry into a cinema with fewer than 50 seats, and where you're plied with blankets, pillows, foot-warming stockings and, of course, a valet food-and-drink service. There's also Major Cineplex's Emperor Class seat, which for the price of a sticky stool back home entitles you to a sofa-like love seat designed for couples. And if you find Paragon Cineplex's 16 screens and 5000 seats a bit plebeian, you can always apply for Enigma, a members-only theatre.

For something a bit more intimate, try the old-skool stand-alone theatres at Siam Sq, including **Scala** (Map p86; ☑0 2251 2861; Siam Sq, Soi 1, Th Phra Ram I; BTS Siam) and **Lido** (Map p86; ☑0 2252 6498; Siam Sq, Th Phra Ram I; BTS Siam), or for something artsier, RCA's **House** (Map p92; ☑0 2641 5177; www.houserama.com; UMG Bldg, Royal City Ave, near Th Petchaburi; MRT Phra Ram 9 & access by taxi) or Bangkok's **foreign cultural centres**; for contact details of the latter, see p144.

Nearly all movies in Thailand offer screenings with English subtitles – visit **Movie Seer** (www.movieseer.com) for show times. All films are preceded by the Thai royal anthem and everyone is expected to stand respectfully for its duration. And despite the heat and humidity on the streets, keep in mind that all of Bangkok's movie theatres pump the air-con with such vigour that a jumper is an absolute necessity – unless you're going Gold Class, that is.

dinner shows 6.30-7pm Thu-Sun; BTS Victory Monument) A variety of performances are now held at this modern theatre, but the highlight is performances of the *Ramakian* by using knee-high puppets that require three puppeteers to strike humanlike poses. Come early in the week for a performance in the Aksra Theatre, or later for a Thai buffet dinner coupled with a show.

National Theatre   TRADITIONAL PERFORMANCE
(Map p60; ☑0 2224 1352; 2 Th Rachini; tickets 60-100B; river ferry Tha Chang) After a lengthy renovation, the National Theatre is again open for business. Performances of *kŏhn* are held on the first and second Sundays of the month, *lá·kon*, Thai dance-dramas, are held on the first Friday of the month, and Thai musical performances are held on the third Friday of the month.

Thai Boxing (Moo·ay tai)
Thai boxing's best of the best fight it out at Bangkok's two boxing stadiums: **Lumphini Stadium** (Sanam Muay Lumphini; Map p90; ☑0 2251 4303; Th Phra Ram IV; tickets 3rd/2nd class/ ringside 1000/1500/2000B; MRT Lumphini) and **Ratchadamnoen Stadium** (Sanam Muay Ratchadamnoen; Map p60; ☑0 2281 4205; Th Ratchadamnoen Nok; tickets 3rd/2nd class/ringside 1000/1500/2000B; bus 70, 503, 509, klorng taxi Tha Phan Fah). You'll note that tickets are not cheap, and these prices are exponentially more than what Thais pay. To add insult to injury, the inflated price offers no special service or seating, and at Ratchadamnoen Stadium foreigners are sometimes corralled into an area with an obstructed view. As long as you are mentally prepared for the financial jabs from the promoters, you'll be better prepared to enjoy the real fight.

Fights are held throughout the week, alternating between the two stadiums. Ratchadamnoen hosts the matches at 6.30pm on Monday, Wednesday, Thursday and Sunday. Lumphini hosts matches at 6.30pm on Tuesday and Friday and Saturday at 5pm and 8.30pm. Aficionados say the best-matched bouts are reserved for Tuesday nights at Lumphini and Thursday nights at Ratchadamnoen. There is a total of eight to 10 fights of five rounds a piece. The stadiums don't usually fill up until the main events, which normally start around 8pm or 9pm.

There are English-speaking 'staff' standing outside the stadium who will practically tackle you upon arrival. Although there have been a few reports of scamming, most

of these assistants help steer visitors to the foreigner ticket windows and hand out a fight roster; they can also be helpful in telling you which fights are the best match-ups between contestants. (Some say that welterweights, between 135lb and 147lb – 61.2kg to 66.7kg, are the best.) To keep everyone honest, though, remember to purchase tickets from the ticket window, not from a person outside the stadium.

As a prematch warm-up, grab a plate of *gài yâhng* (grilled chicken) and other northeastern dishes from the restaurants surrounding the Ratchadamnoen Stadium.

🔒 Shopping
Welcome to a true buyer's market. Home to one of the world's largest outdoor markets, numerous giant upscale malls, and sidewalk-clogging bazaars on nearly every street, it's impossible not to be impressed by the amount of commerce in Bangkok. However, despite the apparent scope and variety, Bangkok really excels in one area when it comes to shopping: cheap stuff. The city is not the place to buy a new Nikon SLR or a (real) Fendi handbag – save those for online warehouses in the US or bargain-basement sales in Hong Kong. Ceramics, dirt-cheap T-shirts, fabric, Asian knick-knackery and yes, if you can deal with the guilt, pirated software and music – are the things for sale in Bangkok.

The difficulty is finding your way around, since the city's intense urban tangle sometimes makes orientation difficult. A good shopping companion is *Nancy Chandler's Map of Bangkok*, with annotations on all sorts of small and out-of-the-way shopping venues and *dà·làht* (markets).

Antiques
Real Thai antiques are rare and costly. Most Bangkok antique shops keep a few authentic pieces for collectors, along with lots of pseudo-antiques or traditionally crafted items that look like antiques.

River City   ANTIQUES MALL
(Map p80; www.rivercity.co.th; Th Yotha, off Th Charoen Krung; ◎10am-10pm; river ferry Tha Si Phraya) Near the Royal Orchid Sheraton Hotel, this multistorey shopping centre is an all-in-one stop for old-world Asiana. Several high-quality art and antique shops occupy the 3rd and 4th floors. Although the quality is high, the prices are too, as many wealthy tourists filter in and out. Many stores here close on Sunday.

House of Chao ANTIQUES
(Map p82; 9/1 Th Decho; ☻9.30am-7pm; BTS Chong Nonsi) This three-storey shop, housed, appropriately, in an antique house, has everything necessary to deck out your fantasy colonial-era mansion. Particularly interesting are the various weatherworn doors, doorways, gateways and trellises behind the showroom.

Bookshops

For a decent selection of English-language books and magazines, branches of **Bookazine** (www.bookazine.co.th) and **B2S** (www.b2s.co.th) can be found at nearly every mall in central Bangkok. The Banglamphu area is home to nearly all of Bangkok's independent bookstores, and Th Khao San is virtually the only place in town to go for used English-language books. You're not going to find any deals there, but the selection is decent.

Asia Books (Map p92; www.asiabook.com; Soi 15, 221 Th Sukhumvit; ☻8am-9pm; BTS Asok, MRT Sukhumvit) Also a branch in the Emporium Shopping Centre (p136) and Siam Discovery Center (p136).

Book Lover (Map p60; Soi Rambuttri; ☻noon-10.30pm Tue-Sun; bus 2, 15, 44, 511, river ferry Tha Phra Athit) Well-stocked used bookstore.

Dasa Book Café (Map p92; 710/4 Th Sukhumvit, btwn Soi 26 & 28; ☻10am-8pm; BTS Phrom Phong) Multilingual used bookstore.

Kinokuniya (www.kinokuniya.com) Siam Paragon (Map p86; 3rd fl, Th Phra Ram I; ☻10am-10pm; BTS Siam); Emporium (Map p92; 3rd fl, Th Sukhumvit; ☻10am-10pm; BTS Phrom Phong) The country's largest book store has two branches, both featuring multilanguage selections, magazines and children's books.

Orchid Books (Map p82; www.orchidbooks.com; 4th fl, Silom Complex, 191 Th Silom; ☻11am-7pm Tue-Sun; BTS Sala Daeng, MRT Si Lom) Bangkok showroom of eponymous publishing house, with titles from other local imprints, with emphasis on Asian topics.

RimKhobFah Bookstore (Map p60; 78/1 Th Ratchadamnoen Klang; ☻10am-7pm; bus 2, 15, 44, 511, klorng taxi to Tha Phan Fah) This shop has a brief collection of scholarly publications in English on Thai art and architecture.

Saraban (Map p60; 106/1 Th Rambuttri; ☻9.30am-10.30pm; bus 2, 15, 44, 511, river ferry Tha Phra Athit) Large selection of international newspapers and Lonely Planet guides.

Shaman Bookstore Susie Walking Street (Map p60; Susie Walking St, off Th Khao San; ☻9am-11pm); Th Khao San (Map p60; Th Khao San; ☻9am-11pm) With two locations on Th Khao San, Shaman has the area's largest selection of used books.

Department Stores & Shopping Centres

Bangkok may be crowded and polluted, but its department stores are modern oases of order. They're also downright frigid, and Sunday afternoons see a significant part of Bangkok's population crowding into the city's indoor malls to escape the heat. By no accident, the BTS stations also have shaded walkways delivering passengers directly into nearby stores without ever having to set foot on ground level. Most shopping centres are open from 10am or 11am to 9pm or 10pm.

The selection is surprisingly good at Bangkok's shopping centres, but don't expect any bargains – most imported items cost more than they would elsewhere. Another quirk is that shop assistants follow you around the store from rack to rack. This is the definition of Thai 'service' rather than an indication that they've sniffed you out as a shoplifter. And be sure you're satisfied with an item, as returns are largely unheard of.

MBK Center MALL
(Mahboonkhrong; Map p86; www.mbk-center.co.th/en; cnr Th Phra Ram I & Th Phayathai; BTS National Stadium & Siam) This colossal mall has become a tourist destination in its own right. Swedish and other languages can be heard as much as Thai, and on any given weekend half of Bangkok can be found here combing through an inexhaustible range of small stalls and shops. This is the cheapest place to buy mobile phones and accessories (4th floor) and name-brand knock-offs (nearly every other floor). It's also one of the better places to stock up on camera gear (ground floor and 5th floor), and the expansive food court (6th floor) is one of the best in town.

Siam Center & Siam Discovery Center MALL
(Map p86; cnr Th Phra Ram I & Th Phayathai; BTS National Stadium or Siam) These linked sister centres feel almost monastic in their hushed hallways compared to frenetic MBK, just across the street. Siam Discovery Center excels in home decor, with the whole 3rd floor devoted to Asian-minimalist styles and jewel-toned fabrics; we love the earthy, Thai-influenced designs at **Doi Tung**. The

MARKETING STRATEGY

Bangkok's shopping options can be a bit overwhelming. So to help you burn your baht more efficiently, we've put together a brief cheat sheet.

Malls

» **Gaysorn Plaza** (p137) Great for upscale handicrafts and souvenirs.

» **Siam Center** (p136) A goldmine of local fashion labels.

» **MBK Center** (p136) Cheap mobile phones and other electronics.

» **Pantip Plaza** (p137) Several floors of computer gear.

» **Siam Paragon** (p137) Luxury labels, from Lamborghini to Fendi.

» **Siam Discovery Center** (p136) Funky home furnishings.

Markets

» **Chatuchak Weekend Market** (p140) Souvenirs or a vintage tracksuit – they're all here.

» **Nonthaburi Market** (p142) The most picturesque fresh market in the area, but get there early – ideally before 7am.

» **Pak Khlong Market** (p142) Show up late-late for the visual poetry that is the nightly flower market.

» **Pratunam Market** (p142) Acres of cheap togs, much of it for less than you'd pay for a pair of socks at home.

» **Talat Rot Fai** (p142) Bangkok's version of the *Antiques Road Show*.

---

attached Siam Center, Thailand's first shopping centre built in 1976, has recently gone under the redesign knife for a younger, hipper look. Youth fashion is its new focus, and several local labels, ranging from **anr** to **senada***, can be found on the 2nd floor.

Siam Paragon   MALL
(Map p86; Th Phra Ram I; BTS Siam) The biggest and glitziest of Bangkok's shopping malls, Siam Paragon is more of an urban park than shopping centre. Astronomically luxe brands occupy most floors, while the majority of shoppers hang out in the reflecting pool atrium or basement-level food court. The 3rd floor is home to **Kinokuniya**, Thailand's largest English-language bookstore.

Gaysorn Plaza   MALL
(Map p86; cnr Th Ploenchit & Th Ratchadamri; BTS Chit Lom) A haute couture catwalk, Gaysorn's spiralling staircases and all-white halls preserve all of fashion's beloved designers in museum-curatorship style. Local fashion leaders occupy the 2nd floor 'Thai Fashion Chic', while the top floor is a stroll through home decor, highlights of which are the eclectic **D&O Shop**, the fragrant soaps at **Thann** and the Asian-influenced ceramics at **Lamont**.

Central World Plaza   MALL
(Map p86; cnr Th Ratchadamri & Th Phra Ram I; BTS Chit Lom). Bangkok's hippest mall suffered greatly during the unrest of April 2010, but the vast majority of shops are open again and **Zen** department store was being rebuilt at research time. There's an extrahuge branch of bookstore **B2S**, and you could spend an hour sniffing around the fragrances at **Karmakamet**.

Emporium   SHOPPING CENTRE
(Map p92; 622 Th Sukhumvit, cnr Soi 24; BTS Phrom Phong; ☺10am-10pm) You might not have access to the beautiful people's nightlife scene, but you can observe their spending rituals at this temple to red hot and classic cool. For something cheekily local, check out **Propaganda**, home to Mr P, brainchild of Thai designer Chaiyut Plypetch, and who appears in anatomically correct cartoon lamps and other products.

Pantip Plaza   IT MALL
(Map p86; 604 Th Petchaburi; BTS Ratchathewi) North of Siam Sq, this place is five storeys of computer and software stores ranging from legit to flea market. Many locals come here to buy 'pirated' software and computer peripherals, but the crowds and touts ('DVD sex?') make it among the more tiring shopping experiences in town.

BARGAINING 101

Many of your purchases in Bangkok will involve an ancient skill that has long been abandoned in the West: bargaining. Contrary to what you'll see on a daily basis on Th Khao San, bargaining (in Thai, *dòr rahkah*) is not a terse exchange of numbers and animosity. Rather, bargaining Thai style is a generally friendly transaction where two people try to agree on a price that is fair to both of them.

The first rule of bargaining is to have a general idea of the price. Ask around at a few vendors to get a rough notion. When you're ready to buy, it's generally a good strategy to start at 50% of the asking price and work up from there. If you're buying several of an item, you have much more leverage to request and receive a lower price. If the seller immediately agrees to your first price you're probably paying too much, but it's bad form to bargain further at this point. In general, keeping a friendly, flexible demeanour throughout the transaction will almost always work in your favour. And remember, only begin bargaining if you're really planning on buying the item. Most importantly, there's simply no point in getting angry or upset over a few baht. The locals, who inevitably have less money than you, never do this.

Central Chit Lom DEPARTMENT STORE
(Map p86; www.central.co.th; 1027 Th Ploenchit; BTS Chit Lom) Generally regarded as the all-round best for quality and selection, Central has 13 branches in Bangkok in addition to this chi-chi flagship.

Fashion & Textiles

In recent years Bangkok has become something of a fashion-conscious and, increasingly, fashion-generating city. Local designers such as senada*, Flynow and Tango have shown that the city harbours a style scene that can compete on the international catwalk. More affordable looks are exhibited by the city's trendy teens who strut their distinctive 'Bangkok' look in the various shopping areas.

Siam Square OPEN-AIR MALL
(Map p86; btwn Th Phra Ram I & Th Phayathai, BTS Siam) This low-slung commercial universe is a network of some 12 soi lined with trendy, fly-by-night boutiques, many of which are the first ventures of young designers. It's a great place to pick up designs you're guaranteed not to find anywhere else, not to mention the best place for urban naturalists to observe Bangkok teens in their natural habitat.

**It's Happened to be
a Closet** WOMEN'S FASHION
(Map p86; 1st fl, Siam Paragon, Th Phra Ram I; BTS Siam) Garbled grammar aside, this is a brilliant place to stock up on locally designed and made togs – think Th Khao San meets Siam Paragon. Also available at Emporium and Siam Square.

Flynow WOMEN'S FASHION
(Map p86; www.flynowbangkok.com; 2nd fl, Gaysorn Plaza, cnr Th Ploenchit & Th Ratchadamri; BTS Chit Lom) A longstanding leader in Bangkok's home-grown fashion scene, Flynow creates feminine couture that has caught the eyes of several international shows. There are branches at Siam Center and Central World Plaza.

Tango LEATHER GOODS
(Map p86; www.tango.co.th; 2nd fl, Gaysorn Plaza, cnr Th Ploenchit & Th Ratchadamri; BTS Chit Lom) This home-grown brand specialises in funky leather goods, but you may not even recognise the medium under the layers of bright embroidery and chunky jewels. Also available at Siam Center.

Jim Thompson SILK
(Map p82; www.jimthompson.com; 9 Th Surawong; ☺9am-9pm; BTS Sala Daeng, MRT Si Lom) The surviving business of the international promoter of Thai silk, this, the largest Jim Thompson shop, sells colourful silk handkerchiefs, placemats, wraps and pillow cushions. Just up the road is the company's **factory outlet** (Map p82; 149/4-6 Th Surawong; ☺9am-6pm) that sells discontinued patterns at a significant discount.

Handicrafts & Decor

The tourist markets have tons of factory-made pieces that pop up all along the tourist route. The shopping centres sell products with a little better quality at proportionally higher prices, but the independent shops sell the best items all round.

A bi-monthly **Thai Craft Fair** (Map p92; www.thaicraft.org; 3rd fl, Jasmine City Building, Soi 23, Th Sukhumvit; ⊘9am-6pm; BTS Asok, MRT Sukhumvit) is held in Bangkok, featuring the wares of more than 60 Thai artisans.

Thai Home Industries   HANDICRAFTS
(Map p80; 35 Soi 40/Oriental, Th Charoen Krung; ⊘9am-6.30pm Mon-Sat; river ferry Tha Oriental) A visit to this temple-like building, a former monks' quarters, is like discovering an abandoned attic of Asian booty. Despite the odd assortment of items (our last visit revealed items ranging from elegant handmade flatware to wooden model ships) and lack of order, it's heaps more fun than the typically faceless Bangkok handicraft shop.

Nandakwang   HANDICRAFTS
(Map p92; 108/2-3 Soi 23, Th Sukhumvit; ⊘9am-5pm Mon-Sat & 10am-5pm Sun; BTS Asok, MRT Sukhumvit) A Bangkok satellite of a Chiang Mai–based store, Nandakwang sells a fun and handsome mix of cloth, wood and glass products. The cheery hand-embroidered pillows and bags are particularly attractive. There is also a branch on the 4th floor of Siam Discovery Center.

Sop Moei Arts   HANDICRAFTS
(Map p92; www.sopmoeiarts.com; Soi 49/9, Th Sukhumvit; ⊘9.30am-5pm Sun-Fri; BTS Phrom Phong & access by taxi) The Bangkok showroom of this nonprofit organisation features the vibrant cloth creations of Karen weavers in Mae Hong Son, northern Thailand. It's located near the end of Soi 49/9, in the large Racquet Club complex.

Taekee Taekon   HANDICRAFTS
(Map p60; 118 Th Phra Athit; ⊘9am-6pm Mon-Sat; bus 32, 33, 64, 82, river ferry Tha Phra Athit) Representing Thailand's main silk-producing regions, this charming store has a beautiful selection of table runners and wall hangings. Alongside silk products, you will also find small examples of celadon pottery and a terrific selection of postcards.

Narai Phand   HANDICRAFTS
(Map p86; www.naraiphand.com; ground fl, President Tower, 973 Th Ploenchit; ⊘10am-8pm; BTS Phloen Chit) Souvenir-quality handicrafts are given fixed prices and comfortable air-con at this government-run facility. You won't find anything here that you haven't already seen at all of the tourist street markets, but it is a good stop if you're pressed for time or spooked by haggling.

Markets

Although air-conditioned malls have better PR departments, open-air markets are the true face of commercial Bangkok, and are where you'll find the best bargains.

7-ELEVEN FOREVER

Be extremely wary of any appointment that involves the words 'meet me at 7-Eleven'. According to the company's website there are 3912 branches of 7-Eleven in Thailand alone (there will inevitably be several more by the time this book has gone to print) – more than half the number found in the entire USA. In Bangkok, 7-Elevens are so ubiquitous that it's not uncommon to see two branches staring at each other from across the street.

The first *sewên* (as it's known in Thai) in Thailand was installed in Patpong in 1991. The brand caught on almost immediately and today Thailand ranks behind only Japan and Taiwan in the total number of branches in Asia. The stores are either owned directly by the company or are franchises, owned and managed by private individuals.

Although the company claims that its stores carry more than 2000 items, the fresh flavours of Thai cuisine are not reflected in the wares of a typical Bangkok 7-Eleven, whose food selections are even junkier than those of its counterparts in the West. Like all shops in Thailand, alcohol is only available from 11am to 2pm and 5pm to 11pm, and branches of 7-Eleven located near hospitals, temples and schools do not sell alcohol or cigarettes at all (but do continue to sell unhealthy snack food).

We love 7-Eleven for the wide selection of drinks, a godsend in sweltering Bangkok. You can conveniently pay most of your bills at the Service Counter, and all manner of phone cards, prophylactics and 'literature' (although, oddly, not most newspapers) are also available. And sometimes the blast of air-conditioning alone is enough reason to stop by. But our single favourite 7-Eleven item must be the dirt-cheap chilled scented towels for wiping away the accumulated grime and sweat before your next appointment.

ALL-PURPOSE MARKETS

Chatuchak Weekend Market MARKET
(Talat Nat Jatujak; location on Map p118, plan of market p141; ☺9am-6pm Sat & Sun; BTS Mo Chit, MRT Chatuchak Park & Kamphaeng Phet) Among the largest markets in the world, Chatuchak seems to unite everything buyable, from used vintage sneakers to baby squirrels. Plan to spend a full day, as there's plenty to see, do and buy. But come early, ideally around 9am to 10am, to beat the crowds and the heat.

There is an information centre and a bank with **ATMs** and **foreign-exchange booths** at the **Chatuchak Park offices**, near the northern end of the market's Soi 1, Soi 2 and Soi 3. Schematic maps and toilets are located throughout the market.

There are a few vendors on weekday mornings, and a daily vegetable, plant and flower market opposite the market's southern side. One section of the latter, known as the **Or Tor Kor Market** (Map p118; Th Kamphaeng Phet; ☺8am-6pm; MRT Kamphaeng Phet 1), sells fantastically gargantuan fruit and seafood, and has a decent food court as well.

Once you're deep in the bowels of Chatuchack, it will seem like there is no order and no escape, but the market is arranged into relatively coherent sections. Use the clocktower as a handy landmark.

Antiques, Handicrafts & Souvenirs
Section 1 is the place to go for Buddha statues, old LPs and other random antiques. More secular arts and crafts, such as musical instruments and hill-tribe items can be found in Sections 25 and 26. **Baan Sin Thai** (Map p141; Section 24, Stall 130, Soi 1) sells a mixture of *kŏhn* masks and old-school Thai toys, all of which make fun souvenirs, and **Kitcharoen Dountri** (Map p141; Section 8, Stall 464, Soi 15) specialises in Thai musical instruments, including flutes, whistles, drums and CDs of classical Thai music.

Other quirky gifts include the life-like plastic Thai fruit and vegetables at **Marché** (Map p141; Section 17, Stall 254, Soi 1), or their scaled-down miniature counterparts nearby at **Papachu** (Map p141; Section 17, Stall 23, Soi 1).

Clothing & Accessories
Clothing dominates most of Chatuchak, starting in Section 8 and continuing through the even-numbered sections to 24. Sections 5 and 6 deal in used clothing for every Thai youth subculture, from punks to cowboys, while Soi 7, where it transects Sections 12

and 14 is heavy on the more underground hip-hop and skate fashions. Tourist-sized clothes and textiles are found in sections 10 and 8.

For accessories, several shops in Sections 24 and 26, such as **Orange Karen Silver** (Map p141; Section 26, Stall 246, Soi 8) specialise in chunky silver jewellery and semiprecious uncut stones.

Eating & Drinking
Lots of Thai-style eating and snacking will stave off Chatuchak rage (cranky behaviour brought on by dehydration or hunger), and numerous food stalls set up shop between Sections 6 and 8. Longstanding standouts include **Foon Talop** (Map p141; Section 26, Stall 319, Soi 8), an incredibly popular Isan restaurant, **Café Ice** (Map p141; Section 7, Stall 267, Soi 3), a Western-Thai fusion joint that does good *pàt tai* and tasty fruit shakes, and **Saman Islam** (Map p141; Section 16, Stall 34, Soi 24), a Thai-Muslim restaurant that serves a tasty chicken biryani.

If you need air-con, pop into **Toh-Plue** (Map p141; Th Kamphaengphet 2; ☺11am-8pm; MRT Kamphaeng Phet; ❋) for all the Thai standards. And as evening draws near, down a beer at **Viva's** (Map p141; Section 26, Stall 149, Soi 6), a cafe-bar that features live music or, if it's dark, cross to Th Kamphaeng Phet 2 to the cozy whisky bars near Fake Club (p130).

Housewares & Decor
The northern and northwestern edge of the market, particularly sections 8 to 26, specialises in all manner of housewares, from cheap plastic buckets to expensive brass woks. This area is a particularly good place to stock up on inexpensive Thai ceramics, ranging from celadon to the traditional rooster-themed bowls from Lampang.

N & D Tablewares (Map p141; Section 25, Stall 185, Soi 4) has a huge variety of stainless-steel flatware, and **Tan-Ta-Nod** (Map p141; Section 22, Stall 061, Soi 5) deals in coconut and sugar palm–derived plates, bowls and other utensils.

Those looking to spice up the house should stop by **Spice Boom** (Map p141; Section 26, Stall 246, Soi 8), were you can find dried herbs and spices for both consumption and decoration. Other notable olfactory indulgences include the hand-made soaps, lotions, salts and scrubs at **D-narn** (Map p141; Section 19, Stall 204, Soi 1) and the fragrant perfumes and essential oils at **Karmakamet** (Map p141; Section 2, Soi 3).

Chatuchak Market

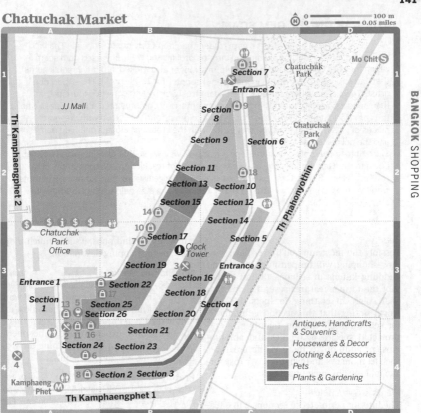

Chatuchak Market

⊗ Eating
1	Café Ice	C1
2	Foon Talop	A4
3	Saman Islam	B3
4	Toh-Plue	A4

⊜ Drinking
5	Viva's	A3

⊕ Shopping
6	Baan Sin Thai	A4
7	D-narn	B3
8	Karmakamet	A4
9	Kitcharoen Dountri	C1
10	Marché	B3
11	Meng	A4
12	N & D Tablewares	B3
13	Orange Karen Silver	A3
14	Papachu	B2
15	Pariwat A-nantachina	C1
16	Spice Boom	A4
17	Tan-Ta-Nod	B3
18	Tuptim Shop	C2

For less utilitarian goods, Section 7 is a virtual open-air gallery – we particularly liked **Pariwat A-nantachina's** (Map p141; Section 7, Stall 118, Soi 2) for Bangkok-themed murals. Several shops in Section 10, including **Tuptim Shop** (Map p141; Section 10, Shop 261, Soi 19) sell new and antique Burmese lacquer ware. **Meng** (Map p141; Section 26, Stall 195, Soi 8) features a dusty mish-mash of quirky antiques from both Thailand and Burma.

THE WAR ON THE GEM SCAM

We're begging you, if you aren't a gem trader, then don't buy unset stones in Thailand – period. Countless tourists are sucked into the prolific and well-rehearsed gem scam in which they are taken to a store by a helpful stranger and tricked into buying bulk gems that can supposedly be resold in their home country for 100% profit. The expert con artists (part of a well-organised cartel) seem trustworthy and convince tourists that they need a citizen of the country to circumvent tricky customs regulations. Guess what, the gem world doesn't work like that; and what most tourists end up with are worthless pieces of glass. By the time you sort all this out, the store has closed, changed names and the police can do little to help.

Want to know more or want to report a scam? Visit www.2bangkok.com and navigate down to the 'Gem Scam' page for five years' worth of tracking the phenomenon, or go to **Thai Gems Scam Group** (www.geocities.com/thaigemscamgroup) for photos of touts who troll the temples for victims. The tourist police can also help to resolve some purchase disputes, but don't expect miracles.

Pets

Possibly the most fun you'll ever have window shopping will be petting puppies and cuddling kittens in sections 13 and 15. Soi 9 of the former features several shops that deal solely in clothing for pets. It's also worth noting that this section is infamous for selling illegal wildlife, mainly rare and protected species of reptiles and amphibians, in addition to more exotic creatures such as monkeys and what not. We discourage making any such purchases.

Plants & Gardening

The interior perimeter of sections 2 to 4 feature a huge variety of potted plants, flowers, herbs, fruits, and the accessories needed to maintain them. Many of these shops are also open on weekday afternoons.

Pak Khlong Market　　　MARKET
(Flower Market; Map p76; Th Chakkaphet & Th Atsadang; ⊙24hr; river ferry Tha Saphan Phut) Every night this market near the Chao Phraya river becomes the city's largest depot for wholesale flowers. Arrive as late as you're willing to stay up, and be sure to take a camera, as the technicolour blur of roses, lotuses and daisies on the move is a sight to behold. During the day, Pak Khlong is a wholesale vegetable market.

Talat Rot Fai　　　MARKET
(Map p118; Th Kamphaeng Phet; ⊙6pm-midnight Sat & Sun; MRT Kamphaeng Phet) Set in a sprawling abandoned rail yard, this market is all about the retro, from antique enamel platters to secondhand Vespas. With mobile snack vendors, VW van-based bars and even

a few land-bound pubs, it's also much more than just a shopping destination.

Nonthaburi Market　　　MARKET
(Map p56; Tha Nam Non, Nonthaburi; ⊙5am-8am; river ferry Tha Nonthaburi) Located a short walk from Nonthaburi Pier, the northernmost extent of the Chao Phraya Express boats, this is one of the most expansive and atmospheric produce markets in the area. Come early, as most vendors are gone by 9am.

Pratunam Market　　　MARKET
(Map p86; cnr Th Petchaburi & Th Ratchaprarop; ⊙10am-9pm; klorng taxi to Tha Pratunam) The city's biggest wholesale clothing market, Pratunam is a tight warren of stalls trickling deep into the block. In addition to cheap T-shirts and jeans, luggage, bulk toiletries and souvenirs are also available.

Soi Lalai Sap　　　STREET MARKET
(Map p82; Soi 5/Lalai Sap, Th Silom; ⊙8am-6pm; BTS Chong Nonsi) The 'money-melting' street has a number of vendors selling all sorts of cheap clothing, watches and homewares during the day. Regular perusers say that imperfections from name-brand factories often appear in the stacks.

Sampeng Lane　　　MARKET
(Map p76; Soi Wanit 1/Sampeng Lane; river ferry Tha Ratchawong) This wholesale market runs roughly parallel to Th Yaowarat, bisecting the two districts of Chinatown and Phahurat. Pick up the narrow artery from Th Ratchawong and follow it through its many manifestations – from handbags, homewares, hair decorations, stickers, Japanese-animation gear, plastic beeping key chains.

TOURIST MARKETS

The souvenir sellers have an amazing knack for sniffing out what new arrivals want to haul back home – perennial favourites include raunchy T-shirts, *mŏrn kwăhn* (traditional Thai wedge-shaped pillow), CDs and synthetic sarongs.

Th Khao San Market   STREET MARKET
(Map p60; Th Khao San; ☉11am-11pm; bus 2, 15, 44, 511, river ferry Tha Phra Athit) The main guest house strip in Banglamphu is a day-and-night shopping bazaar for serious baht pinchers,

with cheap T-shirts, 'bootleg' CDs, wooden elephants, hemp clothing, fisherman pants and other goods that make backpackers go ga-ga.

Th Sukhumvit Market   STREET MARKET
(Map p92; Th Sukhumvit btwn Soi 2 & 12, 3 & 15; ☉11am-11pm; BTS Nana) Knock-off bags and watches, stacks of skin-flick DVDs, Chinese throwing stars and other questionable gifts for your high-school-aged brother dominate at this market peddling to package and sex tourists.

ONE NIGHT IN BANGKOK... IS NOT ENOUGH TO HAVE A SUIT MADE

Many tourists arrive in Bangkok with the notion of getting clothes custom-tailored at a bargain price. Which is entirely possible. Prices are almost always lower than what you'd pay at home, but common scams ranging from commission-hungry túk-túk drivers to shoddy workmanship and inferior fabrics make bespoke tailoring in Bangkok a potentially disappointing investment. To maximise your chances of walking away feeling (and looking) good, read on...

The golden rule of custom tailoring is that you get what you pay for. If you sign up for a suit, two pants, two shirts and a tie, with silk sarong thrown in for US$169 (a very popular offer in Bangkok), the chances are it will look and fit like a sub-US$200 wardrobe. Although an offer may seem great on the surface, the price may fluctuate significantly depending on the fabric you choose. Supplying your own fabric won't necessarily reduce the price by much, but it should ensure you get exactly the look you're after. If it's silk you fancy, go straight to the Jim Thompson outlet (p138) for quality at good prices.

Have a good idea of what you want before walking into a shop. If it's a suit you're after, should it be single- or double-breasted? How many buttons? What style trousers? Of course, if you have no idea then the tailor will be more than happy to advise. Alternatively, bring a favourite garment from home and have it copied.

Set aside a week to get clothes tailored. Shirts and trousers can often be turned around in 48 hours or less with only one fitting, but no matter what a tailor may tell you, it takes more than one and often more than two fittings to create a good suit. Most reliable tailors will ask for two to five sittings. Any tailor that can sew your order in less than 24 hours should be treated with caution.

Reputable tailors include:

» **Pinky Tailors**   TAILOR
(Map p86; 888/40 Mahatun Plaza Arcade, Th Ploenchit; ☉10am-7.30pm Mon-Sat; BTS Phloen Chit) Custom-made suit jackets have been Mr Pinky's speciality for more than 35 years. Located behind the Mahatun Building.

» **Marco Tailors**   TAILOR
(Map p86; 430/33 Soi 7, Siam Sq; ☉9am-7pm Mon-Sat; BTS Siam) Dealing solely in men's suits, this longstanding and reliable tailor has a wide selection of banker-sensibility wools and cottons.

» **Raja's Fashions**   TAILOR
(Map p92; 1/6 Soi 4, Th Sukhumvit; ☉10.30am-8.30pm Mon-Sat; BTS Nana) One of Bangkok's more famous tailors, Raja's gets a mixed bag of reviews, but the majority swear by the service and quality.

» **Nickermann's**   TAILOR
(Map p92; www.nickermanns.net; basement, Landmark Hotel, 138 Th Sukhumvit; ☉10am-9pm; BTS Nana) Corporate ladies rave about Nickermann's tailor-made power suits: pants and jackets that suit curves and busts. Formal ball gowns are another area of expertise.

Patpong Night Market STREET MARKET

(Map p82; Patpong Soi 1 & 2, Th Silom; ⏰7pm-1am; BTS Sala Daeng, MRT Si Lom) Drawing more crowds than the ping-pong shows, this market continues the street's illicit leanings with a deluge of cheap and pirated goods, particularly watches and clothing. Bargain with intensity as first-quoted prices tend to be astronomically high.

❶ Information

Dangers & Annoyances

You are more likely to be charmed rather than coerced out of your money in Bangkok. Practised con artists capitalise on Thailand's famous friendliness and a revolving door of clueless tourists. Bangkok's most heavily touristed areas – Wat Phra Kaew, Wat Pho, Jim Thompson House, Th Khao San, Erawan Shrine – are favourite hunting grounds for these scallywags. The best prevention is knowledge, so before hitting the ground, become familiar with the more common local scams listed in the boxed text below.

If you've been scammed, the tourist police can be effective in dealing with some of the 'unethical' business practices and crime. But in general you should enter into every monetary transaction with the understanding that you have no consumer protection or recourse.

Cultural Centres

Various international cultural centres in Bangkok organise film festivals, lectures, language classes and other educational liaisons.

Alliance Française (Map p90; ☎0 2670 4200; www.alliance-francaise.or.th; 29 Th Sathon Tai; MRT Lumphini) Leafy compound includes a **library** (⏰10am-7pm Mon-Fri, 8.30am-5.30pm Sat, 10am-1pm Sun), **bookshop** (⏰9am-7pm Mon-Sat) and **Café 1912** (p127).

British Council (Map p86; ☎0 2657 5678; www.britishcouncil.or.th; 254 Soi Chulalongkorn 64, Th Phra Ram I; ⏰8.30am-7pm; BTS Siam)

Foreign Correspondents Club of Thailand (FCCT; Map p86; ☎0 2652 0580; www.fccthai. com; Penthouse, Maneeya Center, 518/5 Th Ploenchit; BTS Chit Lom)

Goethe Institut (Map p90; ☎0 2287 0942; www.goethe.de; 18/1 Soi Goethe, btwn Th Sathon Tai & Soi Ngam Duphli; ⏰9.30am-6pm Tues-Thurs, 9.30am-3pm Wed, 8am-1pm Sat & Sun; MRT Lumphini)

Emergency

If you have a medical emergency and need an ambulance, contact the English-speaking hos-

---

COMMON BANGKOK SCAMS

Commit these classic rip-offs to memory and join us in our ongoing crusade to outsmart Bangkok's crafty scam artists. For details on the famous gem scam, see the boxed text, p142.

» **Closed today** Ignore any 'friendly' local who tells you that an attraction is closed for a Buddhist holiday or for cleaning. These are set-ups for trips to a bogus gem sale.

» **Túk-túk rides for 10B** Say goodbye to your day's itinerary if you climb aboard this ubiquitous scam. These alleged 'tours' bypass all the sights and instead cruise to all the fly-by-night gem and tailor shops that pay commissions.

» **Flat-fare taxi ride** Flatly refuse any driver who quotes a flat fare (usually between 100B and 150B for in-town destinations), which will usually be three times more expensive than the reasonable meter rate. Walking beyond the tourist area will usually help in finding an honest driver. If the driver has 'forgotten' to put the meter on, just say, 'Meter, *kâ/kráp*' (for female/male).

» **Tourist buses to the south** On the long journey south, well-organised and connected thieves have hours to comb through your bags, breaking into (and later resealing) locked bags, searching through hiding places and stealing credit cards, electronics and even toiletries. This scam has been running for years but is easy to avoid simply by carrying valuables with you on the bus.

» **Friendly strangers** Be wary of smartly dressed men who approach you asking where you're from and where you're going. Their opening gambit is usually followed with: 'Ah, my son/daughter is studying at university in (your city)' – they seem to have an encyclopaedic knowledge of major universities. As the tourist authorities here pointed out, this sort of behaviour is out of character for Thais and should be treated with suspicion.

pitals listed below. In case of a police or safety issue, contact the following emergency services:

Fire (☏199)

Police/Emergency (☏191)

Tourist police (☏1155; ⊗24hr) An English-speaking unit that investigates criminal activity involving tourists, including gem scams. It can also act as a bilingual liaison with the regular police.

Internet & Telephone Access

There's no shortage of internet cafes in Bangkok competing to offer the cheapest and fastest connection. Rates vary depending on the concentration and affluence of net-heads – Banglamphu is cheaper than Sukhumvit or Silom, with rates as low as 20B per hour. Many internet shops are adding Skype and headsets to their machines so that international calls can be made for the price of surfing the web.

A convenient place to take care of your communication needs in the centre of Bangkok is the **TrueMove Shop** (Soi 2, Siam Sq; ⊗7am-10pm; BTS Siam). It has high-speed internet computers equipped with Skype, sells phones and mobile subscriptions, and can also provide information on city-wide wi-fi access for computers and phones.

Wi-fi, provided mostly free of charge, is becoming more and more ubiquitous around Bangkok and is available at more businesses and public hot spots than we have space to list here. For relatively authoritative lists of wi-fi hot spots in Bangkok, go to www.bkkpages.com (under 'Bangkok Directory') or www.stickmanweekly.com/WiFi/BangkokFreeWirelessInternetWiFi.htm.

Media

Daily newspapers are available at streetside newsagents. Monthly magazines are available in most bookstores.

Bangkok 101 (www.bangkok101.com) A monthly city primer with photo essays and reviews of sights, restaurants and entertainment.

Bangkok Post (www.bangkokpost.net) The leading English-language daily with Friday and weekend supplements covering city events.

BK (http://bk.asia-city.com) Free weekly listings mag for the young and hip.

CNNGo (www.cnngo/bangkok) The Bangkok pages of this online listings mag are a good source for the lowdown on restaurants and events.

The Nation (www.nationmultimedia.com) English-language daily with a heavy focus on business.

Medical Services

Thanks to its high standard of hospital care, Bangkok is fast becoming a destination for medical tourists shopping for more affordable dental check-ups, elective surgery and cosmetic procedures. Pharmacists (chemists) throughout the city can diagnose and treat most minor ailments (Bangkok belly, sinus and skin infections etc). The following hospitals offer 24-hour emergency services, and the numbers below should be contacted if you need an ambulance or immediate medical attention. Most of these hospitals also have daily clinics with English-speaking staff.

Bangkok Christian Hospital (Map p82; ☏0 2235 1000; www.bkkchristianhosp.th.com; 124 Th Silom; BTS Sala Daeng, MRT Si Lom)

BNH (Map p82; ☏0 2686 2700; www.bnh hospital.com; 9 Th Convent, off Th Silom; BTS Sala Daeng, MRT Si Lom)

Bumrungrad Hospital (Map p92; ☏0 2667 1000; www.bamrungrad.com; 33 Soi 3/Nana Neua, Th Sukhumvit; BTS Phloen Chit)

Samitivej Hospital (Map p92; ☏0 2711 8000; www.samitivejhospitals.com; 133 Soi 49, Th Sukhumvit; BTS Phrom Phong & access by taxi)

St Louis Hospital (Map p82; ☏0 2210 9999; www.saintlouis.or.th; 215 Th Sathon Tai; BTS Surasak)

Money

Regular bank hours in Bangkok are generally 8.30am to 3.30pm, although branches in busy areas and shopping malls are open later. ATMs are common in all areas of the city. Many Thai banks also have currency-exchange bureaus; there are also exchange desks within eyeshot of most tourist areas. Go to 7-Eleven shops or other reputable places to break 1000B bills; don't expect a vendor or taxi to be able to change a bill 500B or larger.

Post

Main post office (Map p80; Th Charoen Krung; ⊗8am-8pm Mon-Fri, to 1pm Sat & Sun; river ferry Tha Si Phraya) Near Soi 35, services include poste restante and packaging within the main building. Branch post offices throughout the city also offer poste restante and parcel services.

Toilets

Public toilets in Bangkok are few and far between and your best bet is to head for a shopping centre, fast-food restaurant, or our favourite, a luxury hotel. Shopping centres might charge 2B to 5B for a visit; some newer shopping centres have toilets for the disabled. Despite what you'll hear, squat toilets are a dying breed in Bangkok.

Tourist Information

Official tourist offices distribute maps, brochures and advice on sights and activities. Don't confuse these free services with the licensed travel agents that book tours and transport

THE INSIDE SCOOP

Several Bangkok residents, both local and foreign, have taken their experiences to the 'small screen' and maintain blogs and websites about living in Bangkok. Some of the more informative or entertaining include:

» **2Bangkok** (www.2bangkok.com) News sleuth and history buff follows the city headlines from today and yesterday.

» **Austin Bush Food Blog** (www.austinbushphotography.com/category/foodblog) Written by the author of this chapter, the blog focuses on food culture and eating in Bangkok and elsewhere.

» **Global Post** (www.globalpost.com/bio/patrick-winn/articles) Patrick Winn, this online news agency's Southeast Asia Correspondent, is based in Bangkok and has a knack for uncovering all the wacky things that go on there.

» **Greg To Differ** (www.gregtodiffer.com) 'Stories, rants and obersvations on expat life in Asia's craziest city.' Also has an accompanying podcast.

» **Newley Purnell** (www.newley.com) This Bangkok-based US freelance writer comments on everything from local politics to his profound love of *pàt gà·prow* (a type of spicy stir-fry).

» **Not The Nation** (www.notthenation.com) Thailand's answer to *The Onion*.

» **Stickman** (www.stickmanbangkok.com) Formerly associated with naughty Bangkok nightlife, the 'new' Stickman is a more general blog about life, work and love in Bangkok.

on a commission basis. Often, travel agencies incorporate elements of the official national tourism organisation name (Tourism Authority of Thailand; TAT) into their own to purposefully confuse tourists.

Bangkok Information Center (Map p60; ☑0 2225 7612-4; www.bangkoktourist.com; 17/1 Th Phra Athit; ⊗8am-7pm Mon-Fri & 9am-5pm Sat & Sun; bus 32, 33, 64, 82, river ferry Tha Phra Athit) City-specific tourism office that provides maps, brochures and directions; yellow information booths staffed by student volunteers are located throughout the city. They also operate 20 **tourist information booths** (⊗9am-5pm Mon-Sat) in touristed areas.

Tourism Authority of Thailand (TAT; ☑1672; www.tourismthailand.org) Head Office (off Map p92; ☑0 2250 5500; 1600 Th Petchaburi Tat Mai; ⊗8.30am-4.30pm; MRT Phetchaburi); Banglamphu (Map p60; ☑0 2283 1500; cnr Th Ratchadamnoen Nok & Th Chakrapatdipong; klorng taxi Phan Fah; ⊗8.30am-4.30pm); Suvarnabhumi International Airport (☑0 2134 0040; 2nd fl, btwn Gates 2 & 5; ⊗24hr).

Travel Agencies

Bangkok is packed with travel agencies where you can book bus and air tickets. Some are reliable, while others are fly-by-night scams issuing bogus tickets or promises of (undelivered) services. Ask for recommendations from fellow travellers before making a major purchase from a travel agent. Generally, it's best to buy bus and train tickets directly from the station rather than through travel agents.

The following are some reputable agencies:
Diethelm Travel (Map p90; ☑0 2660 7000; www.diethelmtravel.com; 14th fl, Kian Gwan Bldg II, 140/1 Th Witthayu/Wireless Rd; BTS Phloen Chit)

STA Travel (Map p82; ☑0 2236 0262; www.statravel.co.th; 14th fl, Wall Street Tower, 33/70 Th Surawong; ⊗9am-5pm Mon-Fri, to noon Sat; BTS, MRT Si Lom)

visit beyond (Map p80; ☑0 2630 9371; www.visitbeyond.com; New Road Guest House, 1216/1 Th Charoen Krung; river ferry Tha Oriental; ⊗8am-noon & 3-7pm)

☉ Getting There & Away

Air

Bangkok has two airports. **Suvarnabhumi International Airport** (Map p153; ☑0 2132 1888; www.bangkokairportonline.com), 30km east of central Bangkok, began commercial international and domestic service in 2006 after several years of delay. The airport's name is pronounced *sù·wan·ná·poom,* and it inherited the airport code (BKK) previously used by the old airport at Don Muang. The unofficial airport website has practical information in English, as well as real-time details of arrivals and departures.

Bangkok's former international and domestic **Don Muang Airport** (Map p153; ☑0 2535 1111; www.donmuangairportonline.com), 25km north of central Bangkok, was retired from commercial service in September 2006, only to be partially reopened five months later to handle overflow from Suvarnabhumi. At the time of research, rumours of the airport's imminent closure had been circulating, but for now it's still serving some domestic flights.

For hotels near either airport, see the boxed text, p117. For details on getting to and from the airports, see p148.

AIRLINES The following carriers service domestic destinations; a few also fly to international destinations. For a list of international carriers, see p768.

Air Asia (⬛nationwide 0 2515 9999; www. airasia.com) Suvarnabhumi International Airport (4th fl, Suvarnabhumi International Airport); Th Khao San (Map p60; 127 Th Tanao; ⬤11am-10pm) Flies from Suvarnabhumi to Chiang Mai, Chiang Rai, Hat Yai, Krabi, Nakhon Si Thammarat, Narathiwat, Phuket, Ranong, Surat Thani, Ubon Ratchathani and Udon Thani.

Bangkok Airways (⬛nationwide 1771; www. bangkokair.com) Head Office (Map p118; 0 2270 6699; 99 Moo 14, Th Viphawadee; ⬤8am-5.30pm Mon-Fri) Suvarnabhumi International Airport (Map p153; ⬛02 134 3960; 4th fl, Suvarnabhumi International Airport) Suvarnabhumi to Chiang Mai, Ko Samui, Krabi, Lampang, Phuket, Sukhothai and Trat.

Nok Air (⬛nationwide call centre 1318; www. nokair.com) Don Muang Airport (1st fl, Don Muang Airport) Head Office (Map p82; ⬛02 627 2000; 17th fl, Rajanakarn Bldg, 183 Th Sathon; ⬤) This subsidiary of Thai flies from Don Muang to Buriram, Chiang Mai, Hat Yai, Loei, Mae Sot, Nakhom Phanom, Nakhon Si Thammarat, Nan, Narathiwat, Phitsanulok, Phuket, Roi Et, Sakon Nakhon, Surat Thani, Trang, Ubon Ratchathani and Udon Thani.

One-Two-Go (⬛nationwide 1126; www.fly orientthai.com) Don Muang Airport (1st fl, Don Muang Airport; ⬤5am-8pm); Head Office (Map p92; ⬛0 2229 4260; 18 Th Ratchadaphisek; ⬤8.30am-5.30pm Mon-Fri, to noon Sat) Domestic arm of Orient Thai; flies from Don Muang to Chiang Mai, Chiang Rai, Hat Yai, Nakhon Si Thammarat, Phuket, Trang and Udon Thani.

Solar Air (⬛nationwide 02 535 2455; www. solarair.co.th) Don Muang Airport (1st fl, Don Muang Airport) Solar Air flies 19-seat airplanes between Don Muang and Chumphon, Hua Hin, Loei, Mae Sot, Phrae Nan and Roi Et.

Thai Airways International (THAI; ⬛nationwide 02 356 1111; www.thaiair.com) Banglamphu (Map p60; ⬛0 288 7000; 6 Th Lan Luang; ⬤8am-5pm Mon-Sat & 9am-1pm Sun); Silom (Map p82; ⬛0 2288 7000; 485 Th Silom; ⬤8am-5pm Mon-Sat); Suvarnabhumi International Airport (⬛02 134 5483; 4th fl, Suvarnabhumi International Airport) Operates domestic air services between Suvarnabhumi and Chiang Mai, Chiang Rai, Hat Yai, Khon Kaen, Ko Samui,

Krabi, Phuket, Surat Thani, Ubon Ratchathani and Udon Thani.

Bus

Bangkok is the centre for bus services that fan out all over the kingdom. For long-distance journeys to popular tourist destinations it is advisable to buy tickets directly from the bus companies located at the bus stations, rather than through travel agents in tourist centres such as Th Khao San. See the boxed text p144, for common transport scams to keep an eye open for.

BUS STATIONS There are three main bus terminals – two of which are located an inconvenient distance from the centre of the city – and a terminal at the public transport centre at Suvarnabhumi Airport with inter-provincial departures. Allow an hour to reach all terminals from most parts of Bangkok.

Eastern bus terminal (Ekamai; Map p92; ⬛0 2391 2504; Soi Ekamai/40, Th Sukhumvit; BTS Ekkamai) The departure point for buses to Pattaya, Rayong, Chanthaburi and other points east, except for Aranya Prathet. Most people call it sà·tăh·nee èk·gà·mai (Ekamai station). It's near the Ekkamai BTS station.

Northern & Northeastern bus terminal (Mo Chit; Map p118; ⬛for northern routes 0 2936 2841, ext 311/442, for northeastern routes 0 2936 2852, ext 611/448; Th Kamphaeng Phet) Located just north of Chatuchak Park, this hectic bus station is also commonly called kŏn sòng mŏr chít (Mo Chit station) – not to be confused with Mo Chit BTS station. Buses depart from here for all northern and northeastern destinations. Buses to Aranya Prathet (near the Cambodian border) also leave from here, not from the Eastern bus terminal as you might expect. To reach the bus station, take BTS to Mo Chit or MRT to Chatuchak Park and transfer onto city bus 3, 77 or 509, or hop on a motorcycle taxi.

Southern bus terminal (Sai Tai Mai; off Map p56; ⬛0 2435 1199; Th Bromaratchachonanee, Thonburi) The city's new terminal lies a long way west of the centre of Bangkok. Commonly called săi đâi mài, it's among the more pleasant and orderly in the country. Besides serving as the departure point for all buses south of Bangkok, transport to Kanchanaburi and western Thailand also departs from here. The easiest way to reach the station is by taxi, or you can take bus 79, 159, 201 or 516 from Th Ratchadamnoen Klang or bus 40 from the Victory Monument.

Suvarnabhumi public transport centre (p153; ⬛0 2132 1888; Suvarnabhumi Airport) Located 3km from Suvarnabhumi International Airport, this terminal has relatively frequent departures to points east and northeast including Aranya Prathet (for the Cambodian border),

Chanthaburi, Ko Chang, Nong Khai (for the Lao border), Pattaya, Rayong, Trat and Udon Thani. It can be reached from the airport by a free shuttle bus.

Minivan

Privately run minivans, called *rót đôo*, are a fast and relatively comfortable way to get between Bangkok and its neighbouring provinces. The biggest minivan stop is just north of the Victory Monument (Map p97), with departures for Aranya Prathet (for the Cambodian border; 230B, 3½ hours, from 6am to 6pm), Lopburi (130B, two hours, 4.30am to 9pm), Mae Klong (Samut Songkhram – for Amphawa; 70B, one hour, from 5.30am to 9pm), Muak Lek (for Khao Yai; 120B, 2½ hours, from 8am to 8pm), Nakhon Pathom (60B, one hour, 6am to 9pm) and the Southern bus terminal (35B, one hour, 6.30am to 9pm).

Directly east of the monument are lines to Ayuthaya (60B, one hour, from 5am to 8.30pm), Ban Phe (for Ko Samet; 200B, 2½ hours, from 6am to 9pm), Pattaya (97B, two hours, from 6am to 8pm) and Suvarnabhumi International Airport (40B, one hour, from 5am to 10.30pm).

Train

Hua Lamphong station (Map p76; ☎ 0 2220 4334, general information & advance booking 1690; www.railway.co.th; Th Phra Ram IV; MRT Hua Lamphong) Hua Lamphong is the terminus for the main rail services to the south, north, northeast and east. See p776 for information about train classes and services.

Bookings can be made in person at the advance booking office (just follow the signs; open from 8.30am to 4pm). The other ticket windows are for same-day purchases, mostly 3rd class. From 5am to 8.30am and 4pm to 11pm, advance bookings can also be made at windows 2 to 11. You can obtain a train timetable from the information window. Avoid smiling 'information' staff who try to direct all arrivals to a travel agency in the mezzanine level.

Hua Lamphong has the following services: shower room, mailing centre, luggage storage, cafes and food courts. To get to the station from Sukhumvit take the MRT to the Hua Lamphong stop. From western points (Banglamphu, Thewet), take bus 53.

Bangkok Noi station (Map p60; next to Siriraj Hospital, Thonburi) Bangkok Noi handles infrequent (and overpriced for foreigners) services to Nakhon Pathom, Kanchanaburi and Nam Tok. The station can be reached by river ferry to Tha Rot Fai. Tickets can be bought at the station.

Wong Wian Yai station (Map p56) This tiny station is the jumping off point of the Mahachai Shortline commuter line to Samut Sakhon (see p152).

ℹ Getting Around

Although Bangkok's rush-hour traffic is the stuff of nightmares, seemingly random acts of *embouteillage* can impede even the shortest trip, any day, any time. If it's an option, going by river, canal or BTS is always the best choice; otherwise assume a 45-minute journey for most outings.

To/From the Airport

At the time of research were still two functioning airports in Bangkok; the vast majority of flights are from the shiny new Suvarnabhumi, but some domestic flights still fly in and out of the old Don Muang Airport. If you need to transfer between the two, pencil in *at least* an hour, as the two airports are at opposite ends of town. Minivans run between the two airports from 6am to 5pm (30B to 50B).

SUVARNABHUMI INTERNATIONAL AIRPORT

The following ground transport options leave directly from the Suvarnabhumi terminal to in-town destinations: metered taxis, hotel limousines, airport rail link, private vehicles and private buses. If there are no metered taxis available kerbside or if the line is too long, you can take the airport shuttle to the taxi stand at the public-transport centre.

The public-transport centre is 3km from Suvarnabhumi and includes a public bus terminal, metered taxi stand and long-term parking. A free airport shuttle bus running both an ordinary and express route connects the transport centre with the passenger terminals.

LOCAL BUS Several other air-conditioned local buses serve the airport's public-transport centre. Bus lines that city-bound tourists are likely to use include 551 (Victory Monument), 554 (Don Muang) and 556 (Th Khao San), and minivan line 552 (to On Nut BTS station) – fares start at 25B. From these points, you can continue on public transport or by taxi to your hotel.

Intercity buses to destinations east including Pattaya, Rayong and Trat stop at the public-transport centre, also reached via the free shuttle from the airport.

From town, you can take the BTS to On Nut, then from near the market entrance opposite Tesco take minivan 522 (25B, about 40 minutes, 6am to 9pm) or AE3 (150B) to the airport.

AIRPORT RAIL LINK In 2010 the much-delayed elevated train service linking central Bangkok and Suvarnabhumi International Airport was finally completed. The system is comprised of a local service, which makes six stops before terminating at Phaya Thai station (Map p97; 30 minutes, 45B), connected by a walkway to BTS at Phaya Thai station, and an express service that runs, without stops, between Phaya Thai and Makkasan stations and the airport (15 minutes, 150B). Makkasan, also known as Bangkok City Air Terminal (Map p56), is a short walk from MRT Phetchaburi, and if you arrive at least three hours before your departure, also has check-in facilities for two different airlines (Thai Airways and Lufthansa). Both train lines run from 6am to midnight.

The Airport Rail Link is located on floor B1 of Suvarnabhumi Airport.

TAXI As you exit the terminal, ignore the touts and all the signs pointing you to 'official airport taxis' (which cost 700B flat); instead, descend to the 1st floor to join the generally fast-moving queue for a public taxi. Cabs booked through these desks should always use their meter, but they often try their luck so insist by saying, 'Meter, please'. Typical metered fares from the airport are as follows: 200B to 250B to Th Sukhumvit; 250B to 300B to Th Khao San; 500B to Mo Chit. Toll charges (paid by the passengers) vary between 25B and 45B. Note also that there's an additional 50B surcharge added to all fares departing from the airport, payable directly to the driver.

DON MUANG AIRPORT

There are no longer any express airport buses to/from Don Muang.

BUS Slow, crowded public bus 59 stops on the highway in front of the airport and carries on to Banglamphu, passing Th Khao San and the Democracy Monument; luggage is not allowed. Air-conditioned buses are faster, and you might actually get a seat. Useful routes with air-conditioned buses:

Bus 510 Victory Monument and Southern bus terminal.

Bus 513 Th Sukhumvit and Eastern bus terminal.

Bus 29 Northern bus terminal, Victory Monument, Siam Square and Hua Lamphong train station.

TAXI As at Suvarnabhumi, public taxis leave from outside the arrivals hall and there is a 50B airport charge added to the meter fare. A trip to Banglamphu, including airport change and tollway fees, will set you back about 400B. The fare will be slightly less for a trip to Sukhumvit or Silom.

TRAIN The walkway that crosses from Terminal 1 to the Amari Airport Hotel also provides access to Don Muang train station, which has trains to Hua Lamphong train station every one to 1½ hours from 4am to 11.30am and then roughly every hour from 2pm to 9.30pm (3rd-class 5B to 10B, one hour).

Boat

Once the city's dominant form of transport, public boats still survive along the mighty Mae Nam Chao Phraya and on a few interior *klorng*.

CANAL ROUTES

Over the years boat services along Bangkok and Thonburi's *klorng* have diminished, but with mounting traffic woes there may be plans to revive these water networks. For now, canal taxi boats run along Khlong Saen Saeb (Banglamphu to Ramkhamhaeng) and are an easy way to get from Banglamphu to Jim Thompson House, the Siam Square shopping centres (get off at Tha Hua Chang for both), and other points further east along Sukhumvit – after a mandatory change of boat at Tha Pratunam. These boats are mostly used by daily commuters and pull into the piers for just a few seconds – jump straight on or you'll be left behind. Fares range from 9B to 21B and boats run from approximately 6am to 7pm.

RIVER ROUTES

Chao Phraya Express (☎0 2623 6001; www. chaophrayaboat.co.th) This company provides one of the city's most scenic (and efficient) transport options, running passenger boats

---

WORTH A TRIP

BANGKOK'S ISLAND GETAWAY

Soothe your nerves with a half-day getaway to **Ko Kret**, a car-free island in the middle of Mae Nam Chao Phraya, at Bangkok's northern edge. Actually an artificial island, the result of dredging a canal in a sharp bend in the river, the island is home to one of Thailand's oldest settlements of Mon people, who were the dominant culture in central Thailand between the 6th and 10th centuries AD. The Mon are also skilled potters, and Ko Kret continues the culture's ancient tradition of hand-thrown earthenware, made from local Ko Kret clay.

If you come on a weekday you'll likely to be the only visitor. There are a couple of temples worth peeking into and a few places to eat, but the real highlight is taking in the bucolic riverside atmosphere. On weekends, things change drastically and Ko Kret is an extremely popular destination for urban Thais. There's heaps more food, drink and things for sale, but with this come the crowds.

The most convenient way to get there is by bus (33 from Sanam Luang) or taxi to Pak Kret, before boarding the cross-river ferry that leaves from Wat Sanam Neua.

along Mae Nam Chao Phraya to destinations both south and north of Bangkok. The central pier is known varyingly as Tha Sathon and Saphan Taksin, and connects to the Saphan Taksin BTS station, at the southern end of the city. Visitors are most likely to go northwards, to the stops designated with an N prefix.

Tickets range from 13B to 32B and are generally purchased on board the boat, although some larger stations have ticket booths. Either way, hold on to your ticket as proof of purchase.

The company operates express (indicated by an orange, yellow or yellow and green flag), local (without a flag) and tourist boat (larger boat) services. During rush hour, pay close attention to the flag colours to avoid an unwanted journey to a foreign province. Ask for one of the route maps provided at some of the larger piers.

Local (☺6-8.30am & 3-6pm Mon-Fri; 9-13B) The local line (no flag) serves all company piers between Wat Ratchasingkhon, in south-central Bangkok, north to Nonthaburi, stopping frequently.

Tourist (☺9.30am-3.30pm; 19B, one-day pass child/adult 80/150B) The more expensive tourist boat offers heaps of seating and English-language commentary (though it may be hard to comprehend); it operates from Tha Sathon to 10 major sightseeing piers, only going as far north as Tha Phra Athit (Banglamphu).

Orange Express (☺5.50am-6.40pm Mon-Fri, 6am-6.40pm Sat & Sun; 14B) This, the most frequent line, operates between Wat Ratchasingkhon and Nonthaburi with frequent stops.

Yellow Express (☺6.10-8.40am & 3.45-7.30pm Mon-Fri; 19-28B) The yellow express line operates between Ratburana to Nonthaburi with stops at major piers.

Green-Yellow Express (☺6.15-8.05am & 4.05-6.05pm Mon-Fri; 11-31B) This rush-hour-only boat takes commuters directly to Pakkret Pier, in the far north of Bangkok.

Blue Express (☺7-7.45am & 5.05-6.25pm Mon-Fri; 11-32B) Another rush-hour-only boat takes commuters directly to Nonthaburi.

There are also flat-bottomed cross-river ferries that connect Thonburi and Bangkok. These piers are usually next door to the Chao Phraya Express piers and cost 3.5B per crossing.

BTS (Skytrain)

The most comfortable option for travelling in 'new' Bangkok (Silom, Sukhumvit and Siam Square) is the *rót fai fáh*, BTS or Skytrain, an elevated rail network that sails over the city's notorious traffic jams. The BTS has revolutionised travel in the modern parts of Bangkok. Trips that would have taken an hour now take 15 minutes. Another advantage of the BTS is that it offers a pleasant bird's-eye view of the city, allowing

glimpses of greenery and historic architecture not visible at street level.

So far two lines have been built by the **Bangkok Mass Transit System** (BTS; ☎0 2617 7300; www.bts.co.th) – the Sukhumvit and Silom lines.

The Sukhumvit Line terminates in the north of the city at the Mo Chit station, next to Chatuchak Park, and follows Th Phayathai south to the Siam interchange station at Th Phra Ram I and then swings east along Th Ploenchit and Th Sukhumvit to terminate at Bearing station, at Soi 107, Th Sukhumvit.

The Silom Line runs from the National Stadium station, near Siam Square, and soon after makes an abrupt turn to the southwest, continuing above Th Ratchadamri, down Th Silom to Th Narathiwat Ratchanakharin, then out Th Sathon until it terminates at Wong Wian Yai across the Mae Nam Chao Phraya in Thonburi.

Trains run frequently from 6am to midnight along both lines. Fares vary from 15B to 40B, depending on your destination. Most ticket machines accept 5B and 10B coins only, but change is available from the information booths. The staffed booths are also where you buy value-stored tickets. Brochures available at the information booths detail the various commuter and tourist passes.

Bus

The city's public bus system is operated by **Bangkok Mass Transit Authority** (☎184; www.bmta.co.th); the website is a great source of information on all bus routes, but this doesn't really help the fact that Bangkok's bus system is confusing and generally lacks English. If you're determined, or are pinching pennies, fares for air-conditioned buses typically start at 11B and ordinary (fan) buses start at 6.5B. Smaller privately operated green buses cost 5B.

Most of the bus lines run between 5am and 10pm or 11pm, except for the 'all-night' buses, which run from 3am or 4am to midmorning.

Bangkok Bus Guide by thinknet, available at Kinokuniya and Asia Books (p136), is the most up-to-date route map available. The following bus lines are useful for tourists travelling between Banglamphu and the Siam Square area:

Bus 15 From Tha Phra, on the Thonburi side of the river, to Sanam Luang (accessible to Wat Phra Kaew) with stops at MBK Center (connect to BTS) and Th Ratchadamnoen Klang (accessible to Th Khao San).

Bus 47 Khlong Toei Port to Department of Lands, along Th Phahonyothin, in northern Bangkok, with stops along Th Phra Ram IV, MBK Center, Th Ratchadamnoen and Sanam Luang.

Car

For short-term visitors, you will find parking and driving a car in Bangkok more trouble than it is

FREE RIDE

Launched in 2008, **Bangkok Smile Bike** is a municipally sponsored program encouraging visitors to explore parts of old Bangkok and Thonburi by bicycle. The small green bikes can be borrowed for free, and an expansive tourist route encompassing the areas' major sites has been marked by relatively clear road signs and occasional green bike lanes.

There are five stations spread out between Ko Ratanakosin and Banglamphu, and the suggested starting/ending point is at the southwest corner of Sanam Luang (Map p60), across from the main entrance to Wat Phra Kaew. On the Thonburi side, there are six stations and the suggested starting point is at the base of Saphan Phra Pin Klao Bridge, with the route ending at Saphan Phut, also known as Memorial Bridge. Bikes are available from 10am to 5pm, and you'll need some form of ID to borrow one.

worth. If you need private transport, consider hiring a car and driver through your hotel or hire a taxi driver that you find trustworthy. One reputable operator is **Julie Taxi** (⏰08 1846 2014; www.julietaxitour.com), which offers a variety of vehicles and excellent service.

If you're not dissuaded, cars and motorcycles can be rented throughout town, including through such international chains as **Avis** (Map p86; ⏰0 2251 2011; www.avisthailand.com; 2/12 Th Withayu/Wireless Rd; ☺8am-6pm; BTS Phloen Chit), opposite the Swiss embassy, or local chains such as **Thai Rent A Car** (⏰0 2318 8888; www.thairentacar.com; 2371 Th Petchaburi; MRT Phetchaburi & access by taxi), both of which also have branches at/near Suvarnabhumi airport. Rates start at around 1200B per day, excluding insurance. An International Driving Permit and passport are required for all rentals.

MRT (Metro)

Bangkok's first subway line opened in 2004 and is operated by the **Metropolitan Rapid Transit Authority** (MRTA; ⏰0 2624 5200; www.mrta.co.th). Thais call the metro *rót fai fáh dâi din*.

The 20km Blue Line goes from Hua Lamphong train station to Bang Sue, stopping at 18 stations, including four that link up with the BTS, and one that connects with the airport link. Fares cost 16B to 41B; child and concession fares can be bought at ticket windows. The trains run every seven minutes from 6am to midnight, except during peak hours – 6am to 9am and 4.30pm to 7.30pm – when frequency is less than five minutes. The main advantage for visitors is that the Sukhumvit hotel area is now easily connected to Hua Lamphong train station and Chinatown at one end, and Chatuchak weekend market and the Northern bus terminal at the Bang Sue end.

There are ambitious plans to extend the MRT by more than four times its present length with stabs into northern Bangkok, Samut Prakan and Th Ramkhamhaeng, although if the airport link is anything to judge by, it could be a very long wait indeed.

Motorcycle Taxi

Forming the backdrop of modern Bangkok, teams of cheeky, numbered and vested motorcycle-taxi drivers can be found at the end of just about every long street. A ride to the end (*sùt soy*) or mouth (*bàhk soy*) of an average soi usually costs 10B to 15B. Longer journeys should be negotiated in advance, and can range from 20B to 100B.

Helmets are occasionally available upon request, although considering the way some of these guys drive, any body part is at risk. In particular, keep your legs tucked in – the drivers are used to carrying passengers with shorter legs than those of the average Westerner. Women wearing skirts should sit side-saddle and gather any extra cloth to avoid it catching in the wheel or drive chain.

Taxi

Táak·see mee·đêu (metered taxis) were introduced in Bangkok in 1993 and the current flag fare of 35B is only a slight increase from that time, making us wonder how these guys (and there are a lot of them) earn any money. Although many first-time visitors are hesitant to use them, in general, Bangkok's taxis are new and spacious and the drivers are courteous and helpful, making them an excellent way to get around. Fares to most places within central Bangkok cost 60B to 80B, and freeway tolls – 20B to 45B depending where you start – must be paid by the passenger.

Taxi Radio (⏰1681; www.taxiradio.co.th) and other 24-hour 'phone-a-cab' services are available for 20B above the metered fare. Taxis are usually plentiful except during peak commute hours, when bars are closing (1am to 2am), or when it is raining and your destination requires sitting in too much traffic.

It's generally a good idea to get in taxis that pull up, rather than parked taxis, as the latter often refuse to use their meters. And simply exit any taxi that refuses to use the meter.

Túk-Túk

A ride on Thailand's most emblematic three-wheeled vehicle is an experience particularly sought after by new arrivals, but it only takes a few seconds to realise that most foreigners are too tall to see anything beyond the low-slung roof.

Túk-túk drivers also have a knack for smelling crisp bills and can potentially take you and your wallet far away from your desired destination. In particular, beware of drivers who offer to take you on a sightseeing tour for 10B or 20B – it's a touting scheme designed to pressure you into purchasing overpriced goods. A short trip on a túk-túk should cost at least 50B.

AROUND BANGKOK

If you're itching to get out of the capital city, but don't have a lot of time, consider a day trip to one of the neighbouring towns and provinces. On Bangkok's doorstep are all of Thailand's provincial charms – you don't have to go far to find ancient religious monuments, floating markets, architectural treasures and laid-back fishing villages.

Bangkok to Amphawa

The quaint canalside village of Amphawa in Samut Songkhram is only 70km southwest of Bangkok, but if you play your cards right, you can reach the town via a multihour journey involving trains, boats and a short ride in the back of a truck. Why? Because sometimes the journey is just as important as the destination.

Your adventure begins when you take a stab into Bangkok's Thonburi looking for the **Wong Wian Yai train station** (Map p56; BTS Wong Wian Yai). Just north of the traffic circle (Wong Wian Yai) is a fairly ordinary food market that camouflages the unceremonious terminal of this commuter line, known in English as the Mahachai Shortline. Hop on one of the hourly trains (10B, one hour, from 5.30am to 8.10pm) to Samut Sakhon and you're on your way.

Only 15 minutes after you leave the station the city density yields to squatty villages where you can peek into homes, temples and shops, many of which are only arm's length from the tracks. Further on, palm trees, small rice fields and marshes filled with giant elephant ears and canna lilies line the route, tamed only briefly by little whistle-stop stations. The backwater farms

evaporate quickly as you enter **Samut Sakhon**, also known as Mahachai, a bustling port town several kilometres from the Gulf of Thailand and the end of the first rail segment.

After working your way through what must be one of the most hectic fresh markets in the country, you'll come to a vast harbour clogged with water hyacinth and wooden fishing boats. Before the 17th century, the town was known as Tha Jiin (Chinese Pier) because of the large number of Chinese junks that called here.

Occupying the imposing ferry building, the seafood **Tarua Restaurant** (no roman-script sign; 859 Th Sethakit, Samut Sakhon; dishes 60-200B; ⊙lunch & dinner) offers views over the harbour and an English-language menu. Board the ferry to **Ban Laem** (3B to 5B).

Arriving on the opposite side, the Jao Mae Kuan Im Shrine at **Wat Chong Lom** is a 9m-high fountain in the shape of the Mahayana Buddhist Goddess of Mercy. To get here, take a motorcycle taxi (10B) from the pier for the brief ride to Wat Chong Lom. Conveniently located just beside the shrine is Tha Chalong, a train station with departures for your next destination, Samut Songkhram at 10.10am, 1.30pm and 4.40pm (10B, one hour).

You'll know when you've reached **Samut Songkhram**, also known as Mae Klong, when it looks like you've crashed into the town's wet market. In fact, the market is held directly on the train tracks, and vendors must frantically scoop up their wares as the trains come through.

At the mouth of Mae Nam Mae Klong river is the province's most famous tourist attraction: a bank of fossilised shells known as **Don Hoi Lot**. The shell bank can really only be seen during the dry season when the river surface has receded to its lowest level (typically April and May), but most visit for the perennial seafood restaurants (open lunch and dinner) that have been built at the edge of Don Hoi Lot. To get there you can hop into a *sŏrng·tăa·ou* in front of Somdet Phra Phuttalertla Hospital at the intersection of Th Prasitpattana and Th Tamnimit; the trip takes about 15 minutes (15B). Or, if it's afternoon and the water is high enough, you can charter a boat from the Mae Klong Market pier (*tâh dà·làht mâa glorng*), a scenic round-trip journey of around 45 minutes (1000B).

Around Bangkok

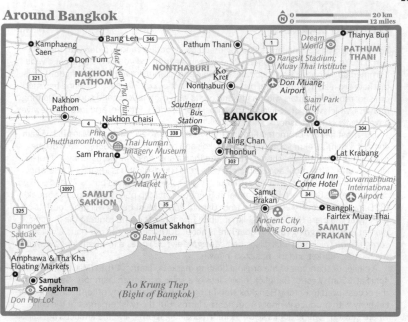

To reach your final destination, charter a boat (800B) or hop in a *sŏrng·tăa·ou* (8B) near the market for the 10-minute ride to **Amphawa**.

Amphawa   อัมพวา

This canalside village has become a popular destination for city folk who seek out its quintessentially 'Thai' setting. This urban influx has sparked a few signs of gentrification, but the canals, old wooden buildings, atmospheric cafes and quaint waterborne traffic still retain heaps of charm. From Friday to Sunday, Amphawa puts on a floating market (p154). Alternatively, visit on a weekday and you'll proably be the only tourist.

◎ Sights

Steps from Amphawa's central footbridge is **Wat Amphawan Chetiyaram**, a graceful temple believed to be located at the place of the family home of Rama II, and which features accomplished murals. A short walk from the temple is **King Buddhalertla (Phuttha Loet La) Naphalai Memorial Park** (admission 20B; ☺8.30am-5pm), a museum housed in a collection of traditional central Thai houses set on 1.5 landscaped hectares. Dedicated to Rama II, the museum

contains a library of antiques from early-19th-century Siam.

At night long-tail boats zip through Amphawa's sleeping waters to watch the Christmas light–like dance of the *hìng hôy,* fireflies, most populous during the wet season. From Friday to Sunday, several operators from several piers lead tours, charging 60B for a seat. Outside of these days, it costs 500B for a two-hour charter.

🛏 Sleeping & Eating

Amphawa is popular with Bangkok's weekend warriors, and it seems like virtually every other house has opened its doors to tourists in the form of homestays. These can range from little more than a mattress on the floor and a mosquito net to upscale guest house-style accommodation. Rooms with fan start at about 200B while rooms with air-con, many of which share bathrooms, begin at about 1000B. Prices are half this on weekdays.

If you prefer something a bit more private, consider **Ploen Amphawa Resort** (☎08 1458 9411; www.ploenamphawa.com; Th Rim Khlong; r incl breakfast 1400-2500B; ❄✿), or **ChababaanCham Resort** (☎08 1984 1000; Th Rim Khlong; r incl breakfast 1900-2400B; ❄✿), an attractive but somewhat overpriced

WORTH A TRIP

FLOATING MARKETS

(ตลาดน้ำ)

The photographs of Thailand's floating markets – wooden canoes laden with multicoloured fruits and vegetables, paddled by women wearing indigo-hued clothes and wide-brimmed straw hats – have become an iconic and alluring image for the kingdom. The markets are also a sentimental piece of history. In the past 20 years, Thailand has modernised, replacing canals with roads, and boats with motorcycles and cars. The floating markets, which were once lively trading posts for produce farmers and local housewives, have mostly crawled ashore.

The most heavily promoted floating market is **Damnoen Saduak** (Map p153; ⊙7am-4pm Sat & Sun), 104km southwest of Bangkok and north of Samut Songkhram on the road to Nakhon Pathom. Though little more than a souvenir market catering to tourists, it is one of the most accessible markets from Bangkok and is ideal for those who haven't yet filled their suitcases with touristy gifts. Air-conditioned buses 78 and 996 go direct from the Southern bus terminal in Thonburi (off Map p56) to Damnoen Saduak (80B, two hours, every 20 minutes from 6am to 9pm). Most buses will drop tourists off directly at the piers that line Th Sukhaphiban 1, which is the land route to the floating market area. The going rate for boat hire is about 300B per person per hour. A yellow *sŏrng·tăa·ou* (pick-up truck, also spelt *săwngthăew*; 5B) does a frequent loop between the floating market and the bus stop in town.

A closer descendant of the original floating markets, **Taling Chan** (Map p56; ⊙7am-4pm Sat & Sun), west of Bangkok, offers less of a sales pitch than Damnoen Saduak. On the access road to Khlong Bangkok Noi, Taling Chan looks like any other fresh-food market busy with produce vendors from nearby farms. But the twist emerges at the canal where several floating docks serve as informal dining rooms, and the kitchens are canoes tethered to the docks. Many local Thai families come to feast on grilled shrimp and noodles, all produced aboard a bobbing boat. Taling Chan is in Thonburi and can be reached from any bus stop along Bangkok's Th Ratchadamnoen Klang in Banglamphu, via air-con bus 79 (16B, 25 minutes). Long-tail boats from any large Bangkok pier can also be hired for a trip to Taling Chan and the nearby Khlong Chak Phra.

Not technically a swimmer, **Don Wai Market** (Map p153; Talat Don Wai; ⊙6am-6pm) claims a riverbank location in Nakhon Pathom Province, having originally started out in the early 20th century as a floating market for pomelo and jackfruit growers and traders. Like many tourist attractions geared towards Thais, the main draw here is food, such as fruit, traditional sweets and *bèt pálóh* (five-spice stewed duck), which can be consumed onboard large boats that cruise the Nakhon Chaisi River (60B, one hour). The easiest way to reach Don Wai Market is to take a minibus (45B, 35 minutes) from beside Central Pinklao (Map p56) in Thonburi.

The **Amphawa Floating Market** (ตลาดน้ำอัมพวา; ɖalat nám ampáwah; Map p153; ⊙4-9pm Fri-Sun), about 7km northwest of Samut Songkhram, is a popular weekend destination for Bangkok residents. There are other floating markets nearby that meet in the mornings on particular lunar days, including **Tha Kha Floating Market** (Map p153; ⊙7am-noon weekends on 2nd, 7th & 12th day of waxing & waning moons). Tha Kha convenes along an open, breezy *klorng* lined with greenery and old wooden houses. Call Amphawa's **Tourism Authority of Thailand office** (☑0 3475 2847) for specific dates.

---

resort just off the canal, or **Baan Ku Pu** (☑0 3472 5920; Th Rim Khlong; d 1000B; ❋), a collection of wooden bungalows.

Amphawa has basic restaurants and a simple night market open each evening. If you're in town on a weekend, get your eats at the fun **Amphawa Floating Market** (ɖà·làht nám am·pá·wah; dishes 20-40B; ⊙4-9pm Fri-Sun), where *pàt tai* and other noodle dishes are served directly from boats.

❶ Getting There & Away

See p152 for an enjoyable itinerary for getting to Amphawa. You can return the same way; however, it's much more convenient to hop on one of the frequent minivans that depart from Samut Songkhram's market (and on weekends, from Amphawa) to Bangkok's Victory Monument (70B, one hour, from 5.30am to 8pm) in Ratchathewi. Alternatively, you can flag down one of several buses to/from Damnoen Saduak that ply the highway near Amphawa, terminating at Bangkok's Southern bus terminal (80B, one hour).

Nakhon Pathom นครปฐม

POP 120,000

Nakhon Pathom is a typical central Thai city, with the Phra Pathom Chedi as a visible link to its claim as the country's oldest settlement. The town's name, which derives from the Pali 'Nagara Pathama' meaning 'First City', appears to lend some legitimacy to this boast.

The modern town is quite sleepy, but it is an easy destination to see everyday Thai ways and practise your newly acquired language skills on a community genuinely appreciative of such efforts.

◉ Sights

Phra Pathom Chedi BUDDHIST TEMPLE
(พระปฐมเจดีย์; admission free) In the centre of town, rising to 127m, is one of the tallest Buddhist monuments in the world. The original stupa, which is buried within the massive orange-glazed dome, was erected in the early 6th century by the Theravada Buddhists of Dvaravati (possibly at the same time as Myanmar's famous Shwedagon stupa). But, in the early 11th century the Khmer king, Suriyavarman I of Angkor, conquered the city and built a Brahman *prang* (Hindi/Khmer-style stupa) over the sanctuary. The Burmese of Bagan, under King Anawrahta, sacked the city in 1057 and the *prang* lay in ruins until Rama IV (King Mongkut) had it restored in 1860. The temple is best visited on weekends when local families come to make merit.

On the eastern side of the monument, in the *bòht,* is a **Dvaravati-style Buddha** seated in a European pose similar to the one in Wat Phra Meru in Ayuthaya. It may, in fact, have come from there.

Also of interest are the many examples of Chinese sculpture carved from a greenish stone that came to Thailand as ballast in the bottom of 19th-century Chinese junks. Opposite the *bòht* is a **museum** (admission by donation; ◷9am-4pm Wed-Sun), with some interesting Dvaravati sculpture and lots of old junk. Within the chedi complex is **Lablae Cave**, an artificial tunnel containing the shrine of several Buddha figures.

The **wát** surrounding the stupa enjoys the kingdom's highest temple rank, Rachavoramahavihan; it's one of only six temples so honoured in Thailand. King Rama VI's ashes are interred in the base of the Sukhothai-era Phra Ruang Rochanarit, a large standing Buddha image in the wát's northern *wí·hǎhn.*

Phutthamonthon BUDDHIST TEMPLE
(พุทธมณฑล) Southeast of the city stands this Sukhothai-style standing Buddha designed by Corrado Feroci. At 15.8m, it is reportedly the world's tallest, and it's surrounded by a 400-hectare landscaped park that contains sculptures representing the major stages in the Buddha's life (eg a 6m-high dharma wheel, carved from a single slab of granite).

All Bangkok–Nakhon Pathom buses pass by the access road to the park at Phra Phutthamonthon Sai 4; from there you can walk, hitch or flag down a *sŏrng·tǎa·ou* into the park itself. From Nakhon Pathom you can also take a white-and-purple Salaya bus; the stop is on Th Tesa across from the post office.

Don Wai Market MARKET
(ตลาดดอนหวาย) On the banks of Mae Nam Nakhon Chaisi, is another worthwhile destination. See p154 for details on getting here.

✕ Eating

Nakhon Pathom has an excellent market along the road between the train station and Phra Pathom Chedi; its *kôw lǎhm* (sticky rice and coconut steamed in a length of bamboo) is reputed to be the best in Thailand. There are many good, inexpensive food vendors and restaurants in this area.

❶ Getting There & Away

Nakhon Pathom is 64km west of Bangkok. The city doesn't have a central bus station, but most transport arrives and departs from near the market and train station.

The most convenient and fastest way to get to Nakhon Pathom is on a *rót đôo* (shared minivan) from Bangkok's Victory Monument (60B; Map p97). Vans leave when full, generally from 6am to about 6pm.

There are also more frequent trains from Bangkok's Hua Lamphong station in Chinatown (14B to 60B, one hour) throughout the day. Nakhon Pathom is also on the spur rail line that runs from Thonburi's Bangkok Noi station (Map p60) to Kanchanaburi's Nam Tok station, although because of the route's status as a 'tourist line' the fares are exorbitantly high for foreigners.

Central Thailand

Includes »

Best Places to Eat

» Blue Rice (p181)

» Sai Thong (p165)

» Baan Watcharachai (p166)

» Khao Tom Hor (p172)

» Jukkru (p181)

Best Places to Stay

» Baan Lotus Guest House (p165)

» Tony's Place (p165)

» Noom Guest House (p171)

» Jolly Frog (p179)

» Sabai@Kan (p179)

Why Go?

Overflowing with nearly as much history as it is nature, Central Thailand offers everything from cascading waterfalls to ancient temple ruins. Nature lovers are drawn to the cloud-canopied mountain ranges that separate Thailand from Myanmar (Burma) and the untamed jungle that shelters tigers, elephants and leopards. History buffs head north of Bangkok to Ayuthaya, the former capital of Siam. Once one of the world's most splendid cities, today visitors can cycle around its well-preserved ruins. Further north is the tiny town of Lopburi, where monkeys scamper among the Khmer-style temples.

Northwest from Bangkok is Kanchanaburi, where trekking and adventure activities are the big draw. Visitors also come to remember those who died in WWII building the 'Death Railway'.

In the northwest mountains sit Thong Pha Phum and Sangkhlaburi, home to several ethnic groups.

When to Go

Central Thailand experiences the country's three seasons in equal measure; Kanchanaburi can have baking sunshine while torrential rain buffets Sangkhlaburi. It is hot in the region from February to June, rainy from June to October, and cool (relatively speaking) from October to January: the one constant is the humidity.

Because of altitude, it can be cooler in Sangkhlaburi and surrounding national parks than in other areas. Ayuthaya and Lopburi sit in a wide-open plain that receives similar amounts of rain and heat as Bangkok.

AYUTHAYA PROVINCE

Ayuthaya

พระนครศรีอยุธยา

POP 137,553

Ayuthaya was once one of the most dazzling and dynamic cities in Asia; today, its temple ruins largely offer just tantalising hints of this former majesty. The city's most famous sites have been partially restored so it is easy to imagine how they must have looked in their prime, while others remain fully functioning temples.

Between 1350 and 1767 Ayuthaya was the capital of Siam. As a major trading port during the time of the trade winds, international merchants visited and were left in awe of the hundreds of glittering temples and treasure-laden palaces. At one point the empire ruled over an area larger than England and France combined. Ayuthaya had 33 kings who engaged in more than 70 wars during its 417-year period; however, fine diplomatic skills also ensured no Western power ever ruled Siam.

The last of the empire's battles was in 1767, when an invading Burmese army sacked the city, looting most of its treasures. What was left continued to crumble until major restoration work began. In 1991 Ayuthaya's ruins were designated a Unesco World Heritage Site.

Away from the temples, Ayuthaya has a growing number of attractions that focus on locally made produce and handicrafts.

◉ Sights

At one time, 400 glittering temples stood proudly in Ayuthaya. Today, more than a dozen restored ruins can be found within the heart of the city, while there are also several working temples. The headless Buddha images, crumbling columns and battered balustrades recreate images of a once mighty city.

For simpler navigation, we've divided up the sites into 'on the island' and 'off the island' sections. It is easy to get between the sites by bicycle, and hiring a guide for some historical detail is useful.

Most temples are open from 8am to 4pm; the more famous sites charge an entrance fee. A one-day pass for most sites on the island is available for 220B and can be bought at the museums or ruins.

The ruins are symbols of royalty and religion, two fundamental elements of Thai society, and so please show respect (see p34).

ON THE ISLAND

The following sites are in central Ayuthaya.

TOP CHOICE Wat Phra Si Sanphet
TEMPLE

(วัดพระศรีสรรเพชญ์; admission 50B) The three *chedi* (stupas) at Wat Phra Si Sanphet are perhaps the most iconic image in Ayuthaya. Built in the late 14th century, it was the city's largest temple and was used by several kings. It once contained a 16m-high standing Buddha (Phra Si Sanphet) covered with 250kg of gold, which was melted down by Burmese conquerors.

AYUTHAYA IN...

Two Days

Rise early to beat the Ayuthaya sun and cycle around the **Historical Park**. Stop for lunch at **Lung Lek's** noodle emporium before heading north of the island to catch a late-afternoon performance at **Ayuthaya Klong Sabua Floating Market and Water Theatre**. The following day hop on an elephant for a short ride among the ruins then finish your visit by sampling locally made produce at the **Ayothaya Floating Market**.

Four Days

Head out of the city to visit **Bang Pa In Palace** and the nearby **Bang Sai Arts and Crafts Centre**. On the way back, drop by at **Wat Phanan Choeng** and ensure good luck by releasing fish back to the river.

One Week

A week gives you plenty of time to see the temples and the nearby countryside. Cycle to **Wat Yai Chai Mongkhon** and mingle in the neighbouring Muslim markets before returning to the island for a sunset boat trip. With a few extra days spare, you can learn how to be a mahout at the **Ayuthaya Elephant Palace**.

Central Thailand Highlights

1 Exploring remote national parks, such as **Si Nakharin** (p186), to look for elusive tigers, elephants and gibbons

2 Clambering up the seven levels at **Erawan** (p183), one of Thailand's most impressive waterfalls

3 Cycling around the temple and palace ruins in **Ayuthaya** (p167)

4 Sampling the laid-back vibe of **Sangkhlaburi** (p188) and spending time with ethnic groups that live there

5 Watching monkeys scurrying around the temple ruins in **Lopburi** (p168)

6 Visiting the WWII museums and remembering the past in **Kanchanaburi** (p174)

7 Flying across zip-lines, riding elephants through the jungle, kayaking along rivers and enjoying other **adventure activities** (p188) around Sangkhlaburi

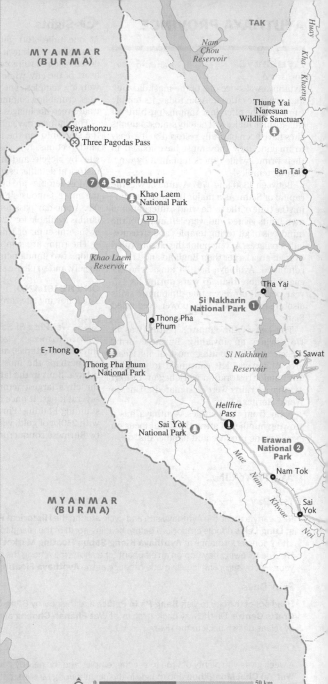

CENTRAL THAILAND AYUTHAYA PROVINCE

Ayuthaya

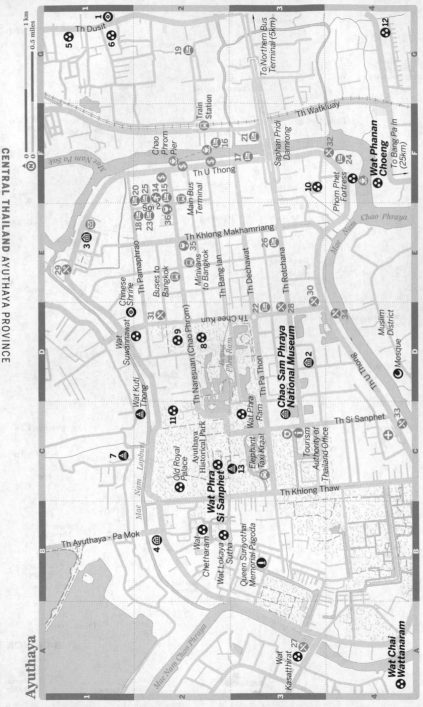

Th Dusit

Train Station

Th Watkluay

To Northern Bus Terminal (5km)

Saphan Pridi Damrong

Wat Phanan Choeng

To Bang Pa In (25km)

Chao Phrom Pier

Th U Thong

Mae Nam Pa Sak

Phom Phet Fortress

Soi 2

Main Bus Terminal

Th Khlong Makhamriang

Chao Phraya

Mae Nam

Th Pamaphrao

Buses to Bangkok

Th Bang Ian

Minivans to Bangkok

Th Dechawat

Th Rotchana

Chinese Shrine

Wat Suwannawat

Th Naresuan (Chao Phrom)

Th Chee Kun

Khu Phra Ram

Th Pa Thon

Chao Sam Phraya National Museum

Th Thong

Muslim District

Mosque

Wat Kuti Thong

Ayuthaya Historical Park

Wat Phra Ram

Tourism Authority of Thailand Office

Th Si Sanphet

Old Royal Palace

Wat Phra Si Sanphet

Elephant Taxi Kraal

Th Khlong Thaw

Wat Chetharam

Wat Sutha

Wat Lokaya Sutha

Queen Suriyothai Memorial Pagoda

Th Ayuthaya - Pa Mok

Mae Nam Lopburi

Wat Kasatthrat

Wat Chai Wattanaram

Mae Nam Chao Phraya

1 km
0.5 miles

Ayuthaya

◎ Top Sights

◎ Sights

◎ Activities, Courses & Tours

◎ Sleeping

◎ Eating

◎ Drinking

TOP CHOICE **Chao Sam Phraya National
Museum** MUSEUM
(พิพิธภัณฑสถานแห่งชาติเจ้าสามพระยา; adult/child
150B/free; ⊙9am-4pm Wed-Sun) The largest
museum in the city has 2400 items on show,
ranging from a 2m-high bronze-cast Buddha head to glistening treasures found in
the crypts of Wat Phra Mahathat and Wat
Ratburana.

**Wihaan Mongkhon
Bophit** HISTORICAL BUILDING
(วิหารมงคลบพิตร) Next to Wat Phra Si Sanphet
is this sanctuary hall, which houses one of
the largest bronze Buddha images in Thailand. This 17m-high figure has undergone
several facelifts due to lightning strikes and
fire.

In 1955 the Burmese Prime Minister visited the site and donated 200,000B to help
restore the building, an act of belated atone-
ment for his country's sacking of the city 200
years before.

Wat Phra Mahathat TEMPLE
(วัดพระมหาธาตุ; admission 50B) The most photographed image in Ayuthaya is here; a sandstone Buddha head that lies mysteriously
tangled within a tree's entwined roots. Built
in 1374 during the reign of King Borom Rachathirat I, Wat Phra Mahathat also has a
central *prang* (Khmer-style chedi) and rows
of headless Buddha images. Nobody knows

TAILOR-MADE TÚK-TÚKS

Túk-túks (pronounced '*đúk dúk*';
motorised transport) in Ayuthaya are
different from the classic Thai design
thanks to their strange dome-shaped
fronts. Resembling Darth Vader's iconic
mask, they zip around in a variety of
colours and designs. One veteran driver
remembers these distinctive taxis have
looked the same for more than 50
years. It is thought they may have first
been made in Japan, which could explain the samurai-like curved front.

Audio guides (150B) can be hired at Wat Phra Si Sanphet, Wat Phra Mahathat and Wat Chai Wattanaram. The English-language guides provide excellent background information and vivid detail that help visitors imagine exactly what once stood on these sites.

for sure how the Buddha head ended up in the tree. Some say the head was abandoned after the Burmese sacked Ayuthaya, and trees subsequently grew around it. Others believe thieves tried to steal the image, but gave up as it was too heavy.

Wat Ratburana TEMPLE

(วัดราชบูรณะ; Ratcha-burana; admission 50B) The *prang* in this temple is one of the best extant versions in the city, with detailed carvings of lotus and mythical creatures. The temple, just north of Wat Phra Mahathat, was built in the 15th century by King Borom Rachathirat II on the cremation site for his two brothers who both died while fighting each other for the throne. Looters raided the site in 1957 and stole many treasures. Some of the culprits were arrested and a subsequent official excavation of the site uncovered many rare Buddha images in the crypt.

Wat Thammikarat TEMPLE

(วัดธรรมิกราช) To the west of Wat Ratburana, this temple is a pleasant place to sit among the ruins. The most prominent feature is a central *chedi* surrounded by *singha* (guardian lion) sculptures. Local people believe that the temple predated the Ayuthaya period, a claim unsupported by architectural evidence.

Wat Suwan Dararam TEMPLE

(วัดสุวรรณดาราราม) This temple is not one of the most-visited sites but its different architectural styles make it worth seeing. Set in the southeast of the island, King Rama I designed the exterior of the older-style

---

AYUTHAYA'S TOP FIVE SITES

---

uposatha while Rama III was responsible for the interior. The slightly bowed line along the temple's edge and its plain finish are typical of the late Ayuthaya period. Next to it is a *wi·hǎhn* from Rama IV's reign, resplendent with a glittering external mosaic.

Ayuthaya Historical Study Centre MUSEUM

(ศูนย์ศึกษาประวัติศาสตร์อยุธยา; Th Rotchana; adult/student 100/50B; 9am-4.30pm Mon-Fri, to 5pm Sat & Sun) An impressive diorama of the city's former glories illustrates how spectacular Ayuthaya once was. Other features in this open-plan museum include timelines, examples of traditional village life and videos.

Chantharakasem National Museum MUSEUM

(พิพิธภัณฑสถานแห่งชาติจันทรเกษม; Th U Thong; admission 100B; 9am-4pm Wed-Sun) Inside this national museum is a collection of Buddhist art, sculptures, ancient weapons and lacquered cabinets. The museum is within the grounds of Wang Chan Kasem (Chan Kasem Palace), which was built for King Naresuan by his father in 1577.

Million Toy Museum TOY MUSEUM

(พิพิธภัณฑ์สถานของเล่นเกริกยุ้นพันธ์; adult/child 50/20B; daily 9am-4pm) Godzilla, tin soldiers and a life-size Superman make this magical museum a fascinating place to wander around. The brainchild of associate professor Krirk Yoonpun, the collection of toys from around the world includes both old and new items, along with a display of Buddhist amulets and old Thai currency.

OFF THE ISLAND

On the opposite side of the water that envelops central Ayuthaya are several famous temples. You can reach some sites by bicycle, but others require a motorbike. Evening boat tours around the island are another way to see the highlights.

TOP CHOICE Wat Phanan Choeng TEMPLE

(วัดพนัญเชิง; admission 20B) Inside this bustling temple is one of Ayuthaya's most revered Buddha images. The 19m-high Phra Phanan Choeng was created in 1325 and sits in the *wi·hǎhn* (large hall), surrounded by 84,000 Buddha images that line the walls.

The grounds have a Chinese shrine, where firecrackers rip through the air for good fortune, and a riverfront area where bags of fish are bought and then released for good luck.

Wat Phanan Choeng, southeast of the old city, can be reached by ferry (5B) from the pier near Phom Phet Fortress. Your bicycle can accompany you across.

TOP CHOICE Wat Chai Wattanaram TEMPLE
(วัดไชยวัฒนาราม; admission 50B) Just 40 years ago this temple was immersed in thick jungle. Today it is one of Ayuthaya's most-photographed sites thanks to its impressive Khmer-style central *prang*, which stands 35m high. Built in 1630 by King Prasat Thong, the temple is a great place to watch sunsets. The site is west of the island and can be reached on bicycle via a nearby bridge.

FREE Ayuthaya Floating Market MARKET
(ตลาดน้ำอโยธยา; ⊗9am-8pm) Popular with Thais as well as tourists, the floating market sells a range of snacks, artwork and clothes. Set on wooden platforms above the water, the market is covered and so is ideal if the city's fierce heat gets too much. Traditional shows take place throughout the day and longboats (20B) can be hired. The market is to the east of the old city off Th Dusit, near Wat Kudi Dao.

Foreign Quarter HISTORICAL SITE
(หมู่บ้านชาวต่างประเทศ) Ayuthaya's leaders were brilliant diplomats. As a result of their tolerance towards other religions and cultures, up to 40 ethnic groups settled in the city. The Portuguese were first to arrive in 1511, followed by the Dutch, British and Japanese. Up to 2000 Portuguese traders and diplomats lived in the area and there were three Catholic churches. A small group of group Thai Catholics still lives near the site today.

The Portuguese brought guns with them, and this modern weapon helped the Thais defeat the Burmese in 1520. As a result of this victory, the Portuguese were given land on which to build. In 1767 the Burmese invaders burned down the settlement and it wasn't until 1985 that a Portuguese foundation came to restore the village.

Just south of the island, the **Portuguese Settlement** displays the skeletal remains of 40 Portuguese settlers in an open pit. Look for the unusual spirit house with figures of St Joseph and St Paul. To the west of the Portuguese Settlement is a **Muslim quarter**, where an evening market is held

WAT A SIGHT BY NIGHT

The temple ruins look good during the day, but they are spectacular by night. Many of the main ruins are illuminated after dark and take on an ethereal glow. Wat Ratburana, Wat Chai Wattanaram, Wat Phra Ram and Wat Mahathat are lit up from 7pm to 9pm. The grounds are closed, but it is still worth strolling past or finding a nearby restaurant for dinner.

on Wednesdays and Saturdays. The area is picturesque and ideal for cycling. Along the way, stop at **Wat Phutthai Sawan** to see a reclining Buddha and Khmer-style *prang*.

Japanese Village MUSEUM
(หมู่บ้านญี่ปุ่น; adult/child 50/20B; ⊗8.30am-4.30pm) Up to 1500 Japanese settled in Ayuthaya. Some came to trade while others were fleeing the persecution of Christians in their homeland during the 16th century. This Japanese Village includes a video presentation that sets the scene and a giant electronic image of an oil painting by Dutch artists of the old city at its zenith. The village is 5km south from the Portuguese Settlement.

Phu Khao Thong MONUMENT
(เจดีย์ภูเขาทอง) At the top of this *chedi's* 79 steps are splendid views of the city. Originally built by the Burmese during a 15-year occupation, the top section was added later by Thais. The statue at the front is a memorial to the all-conquering King Naresuan. Surrounding him are dozens of statues of fighting cockerels. Legend says that when Naresuan was a hostage in Burma his invincible fighting cockerels secured his fearsome reputation. Phu Khao Thong is northwest of the island.

Wat Na Phra Meru TEMPLE
(วัดหน้าพระเมรุ; Phra Mehn; admission 20B) This temple was one of only a few to escape the wrath of Burma's invading army in 1767 as it was used as their base.

Inside the *wi·hǎhn* is a magnificent 1500-year-old green sandstone Buddha from Sri Lanka. Its prominent facial features and joined eyebrows are typical of the Dvaravati period. The *bòht* (central sanctuary) houses a carved wooden ceiling showing the Buddhist heavens.

HELPING AN OLD FRIEND

Elephants helped Thailand win wars, build cities and transport kings. However, today these animals are the ones needing help, as their natural habitat has been slashed back and they are reduced to begging for food in the street. With only 4000 domestic and wild elephants remaining in Thailand, they need all the assistance they can get.

The **Ayuthaya Elephant Palace** (☏0 8066 87727; www.elephantstay.com) does its part by running a hugely successful breeding program and providing brief tourist rides around the ruins. This nonprofit organisation protects elephants by buying sick or abused animals, including bulls that have killed villagers.

Laithongrien Meepan opened the centre in 1996 after buying his daughter an elephant as a present. Australians Michelle Reedy, a former zoo keeper, and Ewa Nakiewicz run an Elephant Stay program (12,000B for three nights minimum) where visitors learn how to ride, bathe and earn the trust of the animals.

Paying for a pachyderm is not cheap, as they can munch their way through 150kg of food a day, so the taxi rides and Elephant Stay help cover costs. In turn, some elephants help earn their keep by turning their trunks to art, appearing in movies such as Oliver Stone's *Alexander* and even providing dung – which is made into paper, bookmarks and photo albums.

The site is not designed for walk-in tourists, but those that do spend time living with the elephants usually come away with a new-found admiration for Thailand's national animal.

Elephant Kraal ELEPHANT STOCKADE
(เพนียดคล้องช้าง) Wild elephants were once rounded up and kept in this *kraal* (stockade). Each year the king would look on as the finest beasts were chosen and either put to work or used as war machines. This restored *kraal,* which has 980 teak logs, is northeast of the island.

Bahn Thanon Dusit TEMPLES
(บ้านถนนดุสิต) For a more scenic side to the city, grab a bicycle and peddle around this rural patch, east of the island. **Wat Maheyong** is a popular weekend meditation retreat in a leafy courtyard near the temple ruins. Slightly further down the road is **Wat Kudi Dao**, which nature has taken a hold of and **Wat Ayuthaya**, which dates from the early Ayuthaya period and has a modest market on Wednesday evenings.

Wat Yai Chai Mongkhon TEMPLE
(วัดใหญ่ชัยมงคล; admission 20B) A 7m-long reclining Buddha is the main feature at Wat Yai Chai Mongkhon. Rumour has it that if you can get a coin to stick to the Buddha's feet good luck will come your way. King U Thong built the monastery in 1357 to house monks from Sri Lanka. The bell-shaped *chedi* was built later to honour King Naresuan's victory over Burma.

Activities & Tours
Pedalling around the island is the best way to see the ruins. To see more of the surrounding countryside, guides are available and two-day trips are possible. Try **Tour With Thai** (☏0 3523 1084; www.tourwiththai.com; Th Naresuan).

Boat tours (200B per hour) can be arranged at the pier near the night market or at guest houses. Guest houses offer two-hour sunset tours of the ruins (200B) but they can be cancelled if numbers are too low.

For in-depth coverage of Ayuthaya's history, talk to staff at TAT (p167) about hiring a guide.

Festival & Events
Loi Kratong CULTURAL FESTIVAL
In November, the Bang Sai Arts and Crafts Centre is the place to be for the Loi Kratong festival. Hundreds of beautiful lotus-shaped vessels containing candles and incense sticks are set afloat from the riverside. In late January, the centre holds its annual fair, showcasing its work.

Swan Boat Races BOAT RACES
The Thailand International Swan Boat Races take place on the Mae Nam Chao Phraya at the Bang Sai Arts and Crafts Centre every September. It involves long-boats pitting international and domestic crews.

Songkran
WATER FESTIVAL

Unlike the water mayhem at places such as Bangkok and Chiang Mai, the Thai New Year festival here is more of a time for merit-making and paying homage to the elderly. It is held around April 12 to 14.

🛏 Sleeping

Backpackers head for Soi 2, Th Naresuan, where there is a handful of guest houses. Midrange and top-end options can be found along the more scenic riverfront. Look for substantial discounts during the low season (April to November).

⭐ TOP CHOICE Baan Lotus Guest House
GUEST HOUSE $

(📞0 3525 1988; 20 Th Pamaphrao; s 200B, d 400-600B; ❄️🛜) Set in large, leafy grounds, this converted teak schoolhouse has a cool, clean feel and remains our favourite place to crash. Staff are as charmingly old-school as the building itself.

⭐ TOP CHOICE Tony's Place
GUEST HOUSE $$

(📞0 3525 2578; www.tonyplace-ayutthaya.com; 12/18 Soi 2, Th Naresuan; r 200-1200B; ❄️🛜) Budget rooms still offer just the basics, but the true flashpacker can hang out in renovated rooms that verge on the palatial, relatively speaking.

Promtong Mansion
GUEST HOUSE $$

(📞0 3524 2459; www.promtong.com; off Th Dechawat; s/d/tr 500/700/1100B; ❄️🛜) Tucked away off the main road, Promtong Mansion is a four-storey guest house that has a distinctive buzz, thanks to its enthusiastic staff.

Baan Thai House
BOUTIQUE HOTEL $$$

'(📞0 35245 555; off Th Dusit; r 2100-2800B; P❄️🛜🏊) A gorgeous boutique resort set just off the island. Each of the dozen Thai-style villas is immaculate and set amid lush gardens. A túk-túk (pronounced 'dúk dúk'; motorised transport) to the old city costs 80B.

PU Inn Ubonpon
GUEST HOUSE $

(📞0 3525 1213; www.puguesthouse.com; 20/1 Soi Thaw Kaw Saw; r 200-900B; ❄️@🛜) The upbeat staff here give the place a vibrant air and can also help arrange trips. Rooms are bright and clean. If you need a Japanese-speaking local, this is a good choice.

Chantana Guest House
GUEST HOUSE $

(📞0 3532 3200; chantanahouse@yahoo.com; 12/22 Soi 2, Th Naresuan; r 400-500B; ❄️) Standing out from the more ramshackle rooms along this strip is the Chantana with its helpful staff, clean rooms and a balcony – it's worth forking out an extra 50B to get the latter.

Baan Khun Phra
GUEST HOUSE $

(📞0 3524 1978; www.bannkunpra.com; 48/2 Th U Thong; dm/d 250/600B; 🛜) A charming riverside teak property, built about 100 years ago, which is teeming with antiques; where else are you going to find Thai swords next to your bed? Dorms sleep up to four.

Krungsri River Hotel
HOTEL $$$

(📞0 3524 4333; www.krungsririver.com; 27/2 Th Rotchana; r1800-5738B; ❄️@🛜🏊)Splendid river views and simple but stylish rooms make this four-star hotel the best spot in town.

Baan Are Gong
GUEST HOUSE $

(📞0 3523 5592; siriporntan@yahoo.com.sg; off Th Rotchana; s 150B, d 350-500B; ❄️🛜) Tucked away in the soi facing the train station is this 100-year-old teak guest house, run by a welcoming Thai-Chinese family. The 3B ferry to the island is nearby.

Wiang Fa Hotel
GUEST HOUSE $

(📞0 3524 3252; 1/8 Th Rotchana; r 500B; P❄️🛜) Rooms are small in this two-storey guest house, but an outdoor patio, coffee and waffle shop and laid-back feel help compensate.

Ayothaya Hotel
HOTEL $$$

(📞0 3523 2855; www.ayothayahotel.com; 12 Soi 2, Th Naresuan; r 650-3800B; ❄️@🛜🏊) Located within range of the ruins, this hotel has friendly staff and plenty of facilities. The retro rooms to the rear are worth exploring. Look for low-season discounts.

River View Place Hotel
HOTEL $$$

(📞0 3524 1444; www.riverviewplacehotel.com; 35/5 Th U Thong; r from 2000B; ❄️@🛜🏊) As the name suggests, this is in one of the most scenic on-island spots. Rooms are large and cosy.

🍴 Eating

Ayutthaya's rich heritage has resulted in an equally diverse range of food, from sweet Muslim snacks to seafood. As well as Western-friendly restaurants on Soi 2, Th Naresuan, there are excellent options along the southern part of Th U Thong.

⭐ TOP CHOICE Sai Thong
THAI $

(Th U Thong; dishes 90-150B; ⏱9.30am-10pm) With 180 items on the menu, live music and spectacular food, this old-school restaurant is the best place to eat on the island. As well as the regular fare, there are interesting variations, such as chicken marinated in whisky.

TOP CHOICE **Baan Watcharachai** THAI $$
(no roman-script sign; off Th Worachate; dishes 100-200B) Located next to Wat Kasatthirat, take a seat on the wooden boat moored outside and feast on *yam 'blah dùk fòo* (crispy catfish salad).

Hua Raw Night Market MARKET $
(Th U Thong) This evening market offers simple riverside seating and a range of Thai and Muslim dishes; for the latter look for the green star and crescent.

Roti Sai Mai Stalls DESSERTS $
(Th U Thong; ⊙10am-8pm) Ayuthaya is famous for the Muslim dessert *roh-đee săi măi*. This is created by rolling together thin strands of melted palm sugar and wrapping them inside the roti. Stalls can be found opposite Ayuthaya Hospital.

Lung Lek NOODLES $
(no roman-script sign; Th Chee Kun; dishes 30-40B; ⊙8.30am-4pm) For the tastiest, most slurpable noodles around, visit this long-established restaurant opposite Wat Ratburana. The perfect spot for a between-temples meal.

Gahn Glooay THAI $
(no roman-script sign; cnr Th Rotchana & Th Chee Kun; dishes 120-150B; ⊙5pm-midnight) If you want to see Thais unwind, head to this relaxed restaurant where karaoke sessions often take centre stage.

Tony's Place WESTERN $
(Soi 2, Th Naresuan; dishes 60-100B) Set at the front of the guest house of the same name, this is an ideal pit stop as it comes with simple Thai/Western dishes, a few veggie nibbles and plenty of fellow travellers.

Krua Nai Pan THAI $$
(no roman-script sign; cnr Th U Thong & Th Chee Kun; dishes 80-250B) Serving up superb northeastern cuisine is this stylish, wood-panelled restaurant, where the speciality is the super-spicy soup.

Pae Krung Gao THAI $$
(Th U Thong; dishes 100-200B) A well-established riverside restaurant serving top-notch Thai food. The English-language menu is more limited than the Thai version so if you know what you like, just ask.

♥ Drinking & Entertainment

Nightlife on the island is restricted due to the proximity of the revered ruins. Backpackers hang out along Soi 2, Th Naresuan, listening to live music at Street Lamp. Young Thais sip fruit/vodka combos at **Spin** (cnr Th Naresuan & Th Khlong Makhamriang).

Off the island, a collection of bars can be found just off Th Rotchana, near the northern bus terminal. Khlawng Phleng (no roman-script sign) is the best, and least salacious, of these with live music and a lively crowd.

Ayuthaya Klong Sabua Floating Market and Water Theatre THEATRE
(ตลาดน้ำอยุธยาคลองสระบัว; www.ayutthayafloating market.com; admission 99-199B; ⊙10am-5.30pm Sat & Sun) Billed as the only water theatre in the kingdom, performers seemingly glide across the water's surface while staging traditional shows with a few dramatic touches, such as fire-breathing. There are five daily performances between 11am and 4.30pm. Tickets, which include a buffet, are cheaper after 2.30pm. Despite the name, don't expect much of a market. To reach the water theatre, follow the road that goes past Wat Na Phra Meru for 2km.

ℹ Information

Dangers & Annoyances
Traffic lights are often absent from road junctions in Ayuthaya where they would seem a prudent choice. This means extra care is needed, especially when on a bicycle. Remember Thailand's unofficial road rules: if you're faster and larger, you have right of way. When cycling, put bags around your body, not in baskets where they could be snatched.

At night several packs of dogs roam the streets. Avoid eye contact and be sure to keep your distance.

Emergency
Tourist police (✆emergency 1155; Th Si Sanphet)

Internet Access
Several shops on and around Soi 2, Th Naresuan have connections for 30B per hour.

Medical Services
Ayuthaya Hospital (✆emergency 1669, 0 3532 2555-70; cnr Th U Thong & Th Si Sanphet) Has an emergency centre and English-speaking doctors.

Money

ATMs are plentiful along Th Naresuan, near the Amporn Shopping Centre.

Bank of Ayuthaya (Th U Thong near Th Naresuan)
Kasikorn Bank (Th Naresuan)
Siam City Bank (Th U Thong)
Siam Commercial Bank (Th Naresuan)

Post

Main post office (Th U Thong; ⊙8.30am-4.30pm Mon-Fri, 9am-noon Sat & Sun)

Tourist Information

Tourist Authority of Thailand (TAT; ⊡0 3524 6076; 108/22 Th Si Sanphet; ⊙8.30am-4.30pm) The TAT office, next to the police station, has a good selection of free maps and brochures.

❶ Getting There & Away

Boat

Several tour companies run boats along the river to Bangkok (see p100).

Bus

Ayuthaya's provincial bus stop is on Th Naresuan, a short walk from the guest-house area. Destinations include:
Bang Pa In (25B, hourly every 20 minutes; via *sŏrng·tăa·ou*)
Lopburi (40B, two hours, every 45 minutes)
Suphanburi (60B, two hours, every 30 minutes) Transfer in town for buses to Kanchanaburi.

Bangkok-bound buses and minivans leave from stops on Th Naresuan to the following areas of the city:
Victory Monument (60B, 1½ hours, every hour from 5.30am to 7pm)
Rangsit (40B, one hour, every 15 minutes)
Southern (Sai Tai Mai) station (70B, one hour, every 30 minutes from 4.30am to 7pm)
Northern (Mo Chit) station (50B, 1½ hours, every 20 minutes) Also stops at Don Muang airport.

The bus terminal servicing northern Thailand is 5km east of the old city, off Th Rotchana. A túk-túk from the terminal to the old city will cost 100B. Destinations include:
Chiang Mai (403B to 806B, nine hours, frequent)
Nan (386B to 497B, eight hours, one morning and two evening departures)
Phitsanulok (224B to 227B, five hours, frequent)

Sukhothai (255B to 328B, six hours, every two hours)

Train

The train station is east of central Ayuthaya. Destinations include:
Bang Pa In (3B)
Bangkok's Hua Lamphong station (ordinary/rapid/express 15B/20B/315B, 1½ hours, frequent morning and night departures)
Bangkok's Bang Sue station (ordinary/rapid/express 15B/20B/315B, 1½ hours, frequent morning and night departures) A convenient station to the Th Khao San area.
Chiang Mai (ordinary/rapid/express 586B/856B/1198B, six departures a day)
Khon Kaen (ordinary/rapid/express 173B/265B/375B, six hours, four departures a day)
Pak Chong (ordinary/rapid/express 23B/73B/130B, frequent) The nearest station to Khao Yai National Park.

The train station is accessible by a quick cross-river ferry from the centre of town (4B) or *sŏrng·tăa·ou* (50B).

❶ Getting Around

Săhm·lór (three-wheeled pedicabs; also spelt săamláw) or túk-túk are readily available. Always agree on a price before you get on. For trips on the island, the rate is 30B to 40B.

As most of the ruins are close together, the most environmentally friendly way to see them is by bicycle or elephant. Guest houses rent bicycles (30B) and motorcycles (200B). You can take brief rides around the historical park by elephant (200B to 500B) or by horse and carriage (300B). The elephants stay at a *kraal* on Th Pa Thon.

See p164 for information on hiring a long-tail boat for trips around the island.

Around Ayuthaya

BANG PA IN PALACE   บางปะอิน

An intriguing assortment of architectural styles makes up Thailand's most eclectic **palace** (admission 100B; ⊙8am-4pm). Originally built in the 17th century, the palace was restored during the reign of Rama V (King Chulalongkorn; 1868–1910). The European, Chinese and Thai buildings may seem incongruous, but they reflect the broad influences of Rama V.

Highlights of the palace include a replica of the Tiber Bridge in Rome, the quite stunning Chinese-style **Wehut Chamrun**, the

Victorian-influenced observatory **Withun Thatsana** and a Thai pavilion in the middle of a pond housing a statue of Rama V.

In 1880, Queen Sunanta drowned during a journey to the palace. Thai law at the time forbid courtiers from touching the queen, and so nobody dared jump in and save her. As a result of the tragedy King Rama V changed the law. A marble obelisk in memory of the queen is in the palace grounds.

Self-drive carts (400B for one hour, 100B per hour thereafter) are available to get around.

Wat Niwet Thamaprawat, located to the rear of the palace car park, is the most unlikely of temples. Designed to resemble a cathedral, its Gothic style, stained-glass windows and knights in armour stand in contrast to the Buddha images. Take a free, monk-operated cable car to the other side of the water.

To reach the palace, take a public *sŏrng·tăa·ou* (25B, one hour, frequent) from the provincial bus stop on Th Naresuan in Ayuthaya. Once the *sŏrng·tăa·ou* drops you at the Bang Pa In bus station, jump on a motorbike taxi (30B) to the palace, which is 4km away. Trains run from Ayuthaya (3rd class 3B, 30 minutes). The train station is closer to the palace than the bus station, but you'll still need a motorbike taxi (20B) to complete the last leg. Another option is to charter a túk-túk for about 400B return.

BANG SAI ARTS & CRAFTS CENTRE
ศูนย์ศิลปาชีพบางไทร

Another 17km southwest of the palace is **Bang Sai Arts and Crafts Centre** (◷9am-5pm). The centre preserves traditional Thai art by offering 30 training courses, ranging from ceramics, silk weaving and mask making. Launched in 1984 with support from Queen Sirikit, this 180-hectare site includes **Sala Phra Ming Kwan** pavilion, which sells a wide range of goods, and an excellent arts and crafts village. A **bird park** (20B) and Thailand's largest freshwater fish **aquarium** (adult/child 100/50B) will keep younger visitors hooked. Avoid coming here on a Monday, when some attractions are closed.

To reach the arts centre, take a train to Bang Pa In then hire a motorbike taxi or *sŏrng·tăa·ou*.

LOPBURI PROVINCE
POP 26,500

Lopburi
ลพบุรี

Languid Lopburi is a pleasant town notable mainly for its temple ruins – and an infamous troop of monkeys.

Lopburi had a role in the Dvaravati, Khmer, Sukhothai and Ayuthaya empires and the ruins, all within the old part of town, reflect this.

As one of Thailand's oldest cities, Lopburi was first developed during the Dvaravati period (6th to 10th centuries), when it was known as Lavo. The enormous influence of the Khmer empire can still be seen in the architecture and artwork. During the Ayuthaya period, Lopburi was a second capital and hosted many foreign dignitaries, which led to advances in architecture, astronomy and literature.

Today, it is the monkeys that take centre stage as they scamper, scavenge and swing around town. These macaques live among the ruins, but don't be surprised if their mischievous faces also peer through your hotel window.

Lopburi, which is 150km north of Bangkok, is renowned for its sunflower fields, coconut jelly and rattan furniture, while sugar cane and rice are the main crops.

◉ Sights

TOP
CHOICE **Phra Narai Ratchaniwet**   MUSEUM
(วังนารายณ์ราชนิเวศน์; entrance Th Sorasak; admission 150B; ◷gallery 8.30am-4pm Wed-Sun, palace grounds 8am-5.30pm) Start your tour of Lopburi at this former royal palace. Inside the palace grounds is the **Lopburi Museum** (officially called Somdet Phra Narai National Museum), which houses displays of local history. The museum is divided into three separate buildings. In Phiman Mongkut Pavilion there are sculptures and art from the Lopburi, Khmer, Dvaravati, U Thong and Ayuthaya periods. The Chantara Phisan Throne Hall contains paintings and artefacts in memory of King Narai, while the European-style Phra Pratiab Building has a small display of traditional handicraft and hunting tools.

Built between 1665 and 1677, with help from French and Italian engineers, the palace was used to welcome foreign dignitaries. The main entry point is through **Pratu Phayakkha** gate, off Th Sorasak. To your left are the remains of the palace reservoir and former reception hall.

Ahead of these are the elephant stables and towards the rear of the compound is the Suttha Sawan throne hall, where King Narai died.

A 150B one-day pass to the main ruins can be bought here.

TOP CHOICE **Prang Sam Yot**   MONUMENT
(ปรางค์สามยอด; Th Wichayen; admission 50B; ◷8am-6pm) Prang Sam Yot is the most famous and most photographed attraction in Lopburi. The three linked towers originally symbolised the Hindu Trimurti of Shiva, Vishnu and Brahma. Now two of them contain ruined Lopburi-style Buddha images. The towers are accessible and offer relief from the heat and monkeys.

Young guides show visitors around for a small donation and, while their English is minimal, their catapults keep the monkeys at bay. The monument is the best example of Khmer-Lopburi architecture, and looks especially good at night when illuminated.

Wat Phra Si Ratana Mahathat   TEMPLE
(วัดพระศรีรัตนมหาธาตุ; Th Na Phra Kan; admission 50B; ◷7am-5pm) Opposite the train station is this 13th-century Khmer wát. Once the town's largest monastery, it has been heavily renovated and makes for a great photo opportunity. The central Phra Prang has bas-relief depicting the life of the Buddha while its arched gate has images in the style of the Lawo period. The northwestern prang has U Thong–style angels; their oblong faces and unusual halos are rare.

Ban Wichayen   HISTORICAL BUILDING
(บ้านวิชาเยนทร์; Th Wichayen; admission 50B; ◷9am-4pm) King Narai built this Thai-European palace as a residence for foreign ambassadors. Greek diplomat and trader Constantine Phaulkon was its most famous resident. The palace is across the street and northeast of Wat Sao Thong Thong.

Prang Khaek   RUINS
(ปรางค์แขก) The oldest monument in Lopburi, this 11th-century tower is on a triangular piece of land bordered by Th Wichayen to the north. The structure has Khmer-style brickwork and was possibly once a temple to the Hindu god Shiva.

Lopburi

◉ **Top Sights**

◉ **Sights**

⚘ **Activities, Courses & Tours**

⬒ **Sleeping**

⊗ **Eating**

◉ **Drinking**

Wat Nakhon Kosa   RUINS
(วัดนครโกษา; Th Na Phra Kan) Just along from the train station is Wat Nakhon Kosa. Built in the 12th century it may have originally been a Hindu shrine. The main *chedi* was built during the Dvaravati period, while the *wí·hăhn* was added later by King Narai. To the rear is a collection of headless Buddha images.

MONKEY MAGIC

Grown men arm their catapults, old women grab 2m-long poles and toy crocodiles peer out from shop windows. Welcome to Lopburi, where these methods are used in a vain attempt to prevent the iconic monkeys from taking over.

Every day the monkeys put on a public performance as they swing, somersault and scamper across town. Residents make up the supporting cast as they lay their hands on anything they can to keep the creatures at bay.

The monkeys are a type of macaque that are an integral part of Lopburi's character. Stay in one of the old town's hotels and you will see them scurrying across power cables, pounding over corrugated roofs or squabbling over a tomato.

Their favourite haunts are **San Phra Kan** (Kala Shrine; Th Wichayen) and **Prang Sam Yot** (Th Wichayen). While visiting these places, put bottles of water and anything that may be mistaken for food inside a bag. Any bottles on display will be considered fair game. It is also wise to only take your camera, and not its carrying bag.

While locals may seem to dislike their simian neighbours, the monkeys are never harmed due to the Buddhist belief of preserving all life. In addition, some feel the animals are 'descendants' of the Hindu god Kala and so to injure one would be seriously bad karma. Monkey souvenirs are nearly as omnipresent as the real thing; there is even now a 'monkey beer' brewed by the Lopburi Inn Hotel and Resort.

A feeding station has been set up to discourage the monkeys from pilfering tourists' food, and so at 10am and 4pm every day heaps of vegetables and fruit are distributed, and quickly scoffed down, next to San Phra Kan.

Care should be taken when being around the monkeys. They may look cute but they are wild animals, and wherever there is a sweet baby monkey, you can bet a protective mother is not far behind. Take a look at the arms of the young guides who offer to show you around for proof that the monkeys can, and sometimes do, bite.

Wat Sao Thong Thong
RUINS

(วัดเสาธงทอง; Th Wichayen) Northwest of the palace centre, Wat Sao Thong Thong is remarkable for its unusual Gothic-style windows, which were added by King Narai so it could be used as a Christian chapel.

Wat Khao Wong Kot
TEMPLE, CAVES

(วัดเขาวงกต) About 30km west of Lopburi is Wat Khao Wong Kot, home to an enormous bat cave. At sunset hundreds of thousands of bats emerge for their nocturnal hunt. To find the cave, take the 280 steps to the right of the temple entrance. The temple can be reached by taking a train (6/26B) north from Lopburi to Ban Mee station and then catching a motorbike taxi. Buses (23B) also run hourly to Ban Mee. However, the last train to Lopburi departs at 4.45pm while the last bus is at 5.30pm so you will need private transport to witness the bat exodus.

Pa Sak Jolasid Dam
PICNIC SPOT

(เขื่อนป่าสักชลสิทธิ์) This 4860m-long dam is a popular picnic spot and has several food and drink stalls. Trams (25B) take visitors for short rides by the water's edge. Camping and bungalows are available. Buses running the 50km east from Lopburi to Wang Moung

(33B, two hours, every 30 minutes) stop by the dam.

🏃 Activities

Khao Chin Lae
ROCK CLIMBING

This 240m mountain has more than 40 climbing routes, meaning there is a way up for just about anyone. Those who conquer the mountain are rewarded with views of Lopburi's famous sunflower fields (providing they come between November to January when the flowers are in bloom). If you want to just see the sunflowers, take the bus east from Lopburi to Khao Noi (15B) and ask the driver to stop at Khao Chin Lae. The fields are a short walk away, and most are free to enter. The mountain is 20km from Lopburi.

For more details on Khao Chin Lae, contact **Nature Adventure** (☑0 3642 7693; www. noomguesthouse.com; 15-17 Th Phraya Kamjat).

🎆 Festivals & Events

King Narai Festival
TRADITIONAL FESTIVAL

Held from 16–22 February every year at the Phra Narai Ratchaniwet. Locals don traditional clothes and stage a colourful parade that leads to the former palace. Highlights include a demonstration of *lá·kon ling* (a traditional drama performed by monkeys).

Monkey Festival   MONKEY FESTIVAL
The real macaques take centre stage during the last week of November for their very own Monkey Festival. Thousands gather to watch the simians devour their banquet.

🛏 Sleeping
Options in the old town are limited to budget rooms, but staying there does mean you can stroll to all the main ruins. A few mid-range options can be found in the new part of town; most have access to local buses that can take you to the attractions.

TOP CHOICE Noom Guest House   GUEST HOUSE $
(📞0 3642 7693; www.noomguesthouse.com; Th Phraya Kamjat; r 150-300B; ❉🛜) Bamboo-roofed bungalows facing a leafy garden make this one of the more pleasant places to stay. Upstairs rooms have shared bathrooms. A sister guest house around the corner takes any overspill.

Nett Hotel   GUEST HOUSE $
(📞0 3641 1738; netthotel@hotmail.com; 17/1-2 Th Ratchadamnoen; r 300-550B; ❉🛜) Still one of the best-value spots, the renovated rooms are clean and the location couldn't be more central. Cheaper rooms are fan-only and have cold-water showers.

Thepthani Hotel   GUEST HOUSE $
(📞0 3641 1029; Th Phra Narai Maharat; r 400B; ❉) Run by the Rajabhat University's tourism and hospitality department, rooms are spotless and staff are friendly. A 10B blue bus stops outside and runs to the old and new towns.

Sri Indra Hotel   GUEST HOUSE $
(📞0 3641 1261; 3-4 Th Na Phra Kan; r 200-350B; ❉) Opposite the train station, the Sri Indra has views of the San Phra Kan, simple rooms and great service. Cheaper options are fan-only.

Residence 1   HOTEL $$
(📞0 3661 3410; Th Kanklorngchonbratahn; r 600-1200B; ❉🛜▥) On the outskirts of town but within walking distance of the bus station, the main perk here is the swimming pool. Some rooms lack natural light, so ask to see before choosing one.

Lopburi Inn Hotel   HOTEL $$
(📞0 3641 2300; www.lopburiinnhotel.com; 28/9 Th Phra Narai Maharat; r 700-950B; ❉🛜▥) If you haven't had enough of monkeys, a 3m-bronze one and 30 small simian statues greet guests here. The top rooms come with enormous bathrooms.

Lopburi Inn Resort   RESORT $$
(📞0 3642 0777; www.lopburiinnresort.com; 1144 M.3 Th Pahonyohtin, Tambon Tha Sala; r 900-1300B; ❉🛜▥) Lopburi's fanciest resort offers a pool and spacious grounds, but the rooms

CENTRAL THAILAND LOPBURI

WORTH A TRIP

SARABURI SIGHTS

Nestled between its more well-known neighbours of Ayuthaya and Lopburi, **Saraburi** is a small province with a handful of attractions. Fortunately, two of the best spots are next to each other.

Wat Phra Puttachai

In this cave temple a silhouette said to be of the Buddha can be seen on one of its hillside walls. Behind six Buddha images are prehistoric paintings dating back 3000 years. If you look closely, chickens and religious images can just be made out. Clamber to the top of the hill and you'll be rewarded with magnificent views of the plains down below. The temple is on Rte 3042, 5km from Hwy 1.

Nam Tok Sam Lan National Park

(📞0 2562 0760; www.dnp.go.th; adult/child 200/100B) Just 2km down the road from the temple is this national park. Covering 44 sq km, the park has a central plain and offers good trekking opportunities and the chance to see pheasants, barking deer, wild boar and butterflies. While the park doesn't quite match its 'three million waterfall' moniker, Nam Tok Sam Lan, Nam Tok Rak Sai and Nam Tok Pho Hin Dat are all near the main entrance and worth a visit. Guides from the main office can lead visitors on a three-hour trek. Tents (200B to 400B) and bungalows (600B to 2400B) are available.

need a makeover. A minibus makes the 5km run to the old town.

✖ Eating & Drinking

Lopburi's street markets are great places to discover new snacks. On Wednesdays a market fills Th Phraya Kamjat, while in the evenings vendors selling noodles and desserts line up along Th Na Phra Kan.

TOP CHOICE Khao Tom Hor   THAI-CHINESE $
(cnr Th Na Phra Kan & Th Ratchadamnoen; dishes 30-80B) The busiest place in town offers excellent Thai-Chinese dishes, including *salid tôrd* (deep-fried salted fish) and *pàd gàprow gài* (chicken with kaprao leaf). Service is speedy and efficient.

Teu   THAI $
(no roman-script sign; Th Pratoo Chai; dishes 40-70B; ⊙3pm-12.30am) To eat with the locals, pull up a plastic stool and snack on the fantastic *gaang 'bàh néua* (curry) and slushy frozen beer. Seating is opposite the restaurant by a grassy verge or inside, next to the chaotic kitchen. Look for the big red sign.

Central Market   MARKET $
(off Th Ratchadamnoen & Th Surasongkhram; ⊙6am-5pm) Wander through the narrow alleyways and take in the sights and smells of this local market. Blood-red strawberries, orange prawns and silver fish are laid out alongside *kôw đom mùd* (rice wrapped in coconut leaves), *đa·go peu·ak* (taro custard with coconut milk) and *gài tôrt* (fried chicken). In the centre is a vegetarian pavilion.

Thaisawang House   THAI-VIETNAMESE $
(Th Sorasak; dishes 60-100B; ⊙8.30am-8pm) Opposite Phra Narai Ratchaniwet, the Thai-Vietnamese menu here is extensive and portions are generous. Steamed pancakes are a particular favourite. Check out the 'shrine' surrounded by toy action figures behind the counter.

Noom Guesthouse   BAR
(Th Phraya Kamjat) One of a couple of old town options, where expats cradle their Changs and Leos.

Sahai Phanta   BAR
(Th Sorasak) Around the corner from Noom, this is a popular venue with its Karabao-style house band. There's no English sign, so look for the giant 'Benmore' banner on the roof.

Good View   BAR
(Th Naresuan; dishes 80-150B; ⊙5pm-1am) With its split-level design and great seafood, the best of the open-air restaurants and bars on Th Naresuan in the new town.

❶ Information

There are several banks in the old part of Lopburi and some next to the bus station. Several internet cafes and online game shops sit shoulder to shoulder along Th Na Phra Kan. The going rate is 15B to 20B per hour. Free wi-fi is available at the **Zon Coffee Bar** (Th Naresuan).

Communications Authority of Thailand (CAT; Th Phra Narai Maharat; ⊙8.30am-4.30pm)

Muang Narai Hospital (☏0 3661 6300; Th Pahonyohtin)

Police (☏0 3678 0042) The police station is 2km west of the old town.

Post office (Th Phra Narai Maharat)

TAT (☏0 3642 2768-9; Th Phra Narai Maharat; ⊙8.30am-4.30pm) The office is a rather inconvenient 5km east of the old town, along Th Phra Narai Maharat, but it is worth finding for TAT's excellent free map.

❶ Getting There & Away

Bus & Minivans

Lopburi's **bus station** (Th Naresuan) is 2km from the old town. Destinations include:

Ayuthaya (40B, two hours, every 30 minutes)

Bangkok's Northern (Mo Chit) bus terminal (80B, three hours, every 30 minutes)

Khorat (Nakhon Ratchasima) (2nd/1st class 120/155B, 3½ hours, hourly)

Suphanburi (60B, three hours, every 90 minutes) Transfer in town for buses to Kanchanaburi.

Other nearby destinations include Singburi and Ang Thong. Motorbike taxis from the station to the old town cost 30B.

Bangkok-bound **minivans** (KO Travel; ☏0 3661 8755) leave every 20 minutes from Th Na Phra Kan between 3.30am and 8pm and drop passengers by the Victory Monument (110B). Vans leave from the capital between 5am and 8pm. If your bag is too big, it will also need a ticket.

Train

The **train station** (Th Na Phra Kan) is conveniently located within walking distance of the old town. Destinations include:

Ayuthaya (ordinary/rapid/express 13/20/336B, frequent daytime departures)

Bangkok's Hua Lamphong station (ordinary/rapid/express 28/50/345B, frequent daytime departures) Express trains take three hours, ordinary trains take four hours. Get off at Bangkok's Bang Sue station and take the nearby subway to the city centre.

Phitsanulok (ordinary/rapid/express 49/99/393B, frequent)

If you are not stopping long, luggage can be stored at the station for 10B per bag per day.

ℹ Getting Around

Sŏrng·tăa·ou and city buses run along Th Wichayen and Th Phra Narai Maharat between the old and new towns for 10B per passenger; *săhm·lór* will go anywhere in the old town for 30B.

KANCHANABURI PROVINCE

POP 849,361

Despite being Thailand's third-largest province, Kanchanaburi remains blissfully undeveloped.

The area, which boasts a rugged mountain range along its border with Myanmar, attracts nature lovers thanks to its tumbling waterfalls, national parks and numerous crystal-lined caves.

Visitors tend to spend a few days in the provincial town visiting its WWII memorials before heading northwest to camp in the national parks, where tigers, elephants and gibbons live.

In the far northwest are remote towns that are home to ethnic groups who have fled the military regime in Myanmar. These frontier towns are sleepy, sedentary sanctuaries of calm that often detain visitors for longer than they had planned.

Kanchanaburi กาญจนบุรี

POP 47,147

The provincial town of Kanchanaburi is an ideal base from which to explore Thailand's wild west.

Today the town is busy and alive but the WWII memorials and museums are a reminder of darker times. Japanese forces used Allied prisoners of war (POWs) and conscripted Southeast Asian labourers to build a rail route to Myanmar. The harrowing story was told in Pierre Boulle's book *The Bridge Over the River Kwai* and in the 1957 movie based on the book. The bridge is one of the main attractions in Kanchanaburi. Roads in the guest-house area are named after countries that were involved in the conflict.

Sitting in the slightly elevated valley of Mae Nam Mae Klong, the town is surrounded by fields filled with tapioca, sugar cane and corn. Being just 130km from Bangkok, many city folk come here for the weekend, though they prefer to board booming karaoke boats than enjoy the serenity.

Travellers congregate around Th Mae Nam Khwae, which is now a mini version of Bangkok's Th Khao San. The street is centrally located and a 10-minute walk from the

KANCHANABURI IN...

Two Days

Fortunately, many of the main attractions are all centrally located, so it is possible to see most of them within 48 hours. Begin at the **Thailand-Burma Railway Centre** before crossing the road to see the **Allied War Cemetery**. Spend the afternoon around the **Death Railway Bridge** and then head to the other side of town for a coffee and stroll along the charming **Heritage Walking Street**. For your second day, take a train ride along the Death Railway to **Sai Yok Noi Waterfall** and see some of the verdant countryside.

Four Days

Head north of the provincial town to visit **Erawan National Park** and the must-see **Hellfire Pass**.

One Week

Seven days gives you the opportunity to explore more remote towns such as **Sangkhlaburi**, where misty morning boat rides and zip-lining await. Ensure you have one night spare to stay in the treetop huts at **Thong Pha Phum National Park**, where giant hornbills are regular visitors.

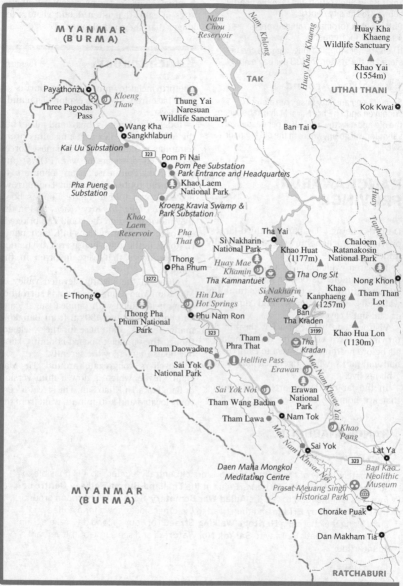

train station. Most accommodation is built beside or floating on the river, although there are some midrange options on Th Saengchuto. In-town attractions are too spread out to cover on foot, so you'll need a bicycle or motorbike.

◉ Sights

TOP CHOICE **Death Railway Bridge (Bridge Over the River Kwai)** HISTORICAL SITE

(สะพานข้ามแม่น้ำแคว; Th Mae Nam Khwae) The 300m railway bridge is an iconic symbol that

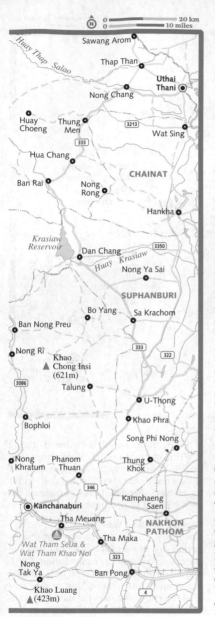

day only the outer curved spans are original. Once you make it to the other side there are cafes and greenery by the waterfront.

The first version of the bridge, completed in 1943, was wooden and was later replaced by a steel bridge. During the last week of November and first week of December a nightly sound-and-light show marks the Allied attack on the Death Railway in 1945. Rooms are hard to come by at this time, so book ahead.

The bridge spans Mae Nam Khwae Yai, which is 2.5km from the centre of Kanchanaburi. This means it is walkable from Th Mae Nam Khwae or you can jump on a northbound *sŏrng·tăa·ou* (10B) along Th Saengchuto. A mini train runs regular trips (20B) over the bridge from the nearby train station.

TOP CHOICE Allied War Cemetery HISTORICAL SITE
(สุสานทหารพันธมิตรดอนรัก; Th Saengchuto; ⊗8am-6pm) Across the street from the Thailand-Burma Railway Centre is the Allied War Cemetery, which is immaculately maintained by the War Graves Commission. Of the 6982 POWs buried here, nearly half were British; the rest came mainly from Australia and the Netherlands. It is estimated that at least 100,000 people died while working on the railway, the majority being labourers from nearby Asian countries, though not one of these has an identifiable grave. If you are looking for the resting place of a loved one, a small office to the side has lists of names and their locations within the cemetery.

TOP CHOICE Thailand-Burma Railway Centre MUSEUM
(ศูนย์รถไฟไทย-พม่า; www.tbrconline.com; 73 Th Chaokanen; adult/child 100/50B; ⊗9am-5pm) This informative museum uses video footage, models and detailed display panels to explain Kanchanaburi's role in WWII. Nine galleries tell the story of the railway, how prisoners were treated and what happened after the line was completed. Upstairs is a display of wartime artefacts, including one POW's miniature chess set, and an excellent collection of related books. A poignant video from POW survivors ensures that the deaths remain a tragedy, not merely a statistic.

Jeath War Museum MUSEUM
(พิพิธภัณฑ์สงคราม; Th Wisuttharangsi; admission 30B; ⊗8am-5pm) This small museum resembles the bamboo-*ata* in which POWs were kept. Newspaper cuttings, letters and artwork

represents the efforts of those who toiled to build a crossing here. It is also the biggest attraction in town, so side-step the numerous hawkers and walk, carefully, along the wooden and metal slats. The centre of the bridge was destroyed by Allied bombs in 1945 so to-

Kanchanaburi

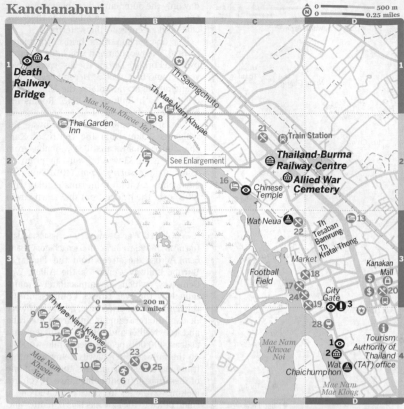

line the sides of the long hut and offer harsh reminders of the brutal punishments meted out by Japanese troops. The archives focus heavily on surgeon Sir Edward 'Weary' Dunlop, who saved hundreds of lives by operating on injured soldiers and fighting to improve basic medical conditions. The museum is run by the monks of the adjacent **Wat Chaichumphon** (Wat Tai), which in itself is worth a visit. Jeath is an acronym of the countries involved in the railway: Japan, England, Australia/USA, Thailand and Holland. The war museum is at the west end of Th Wisuttharangsi (Visutrangsi).

Heritage Walking Street HISTORICAL STREET

Set within the heart of the old town, more than 20 yellow signs tell the history and architecture of this fascinating street. Set aside at least an hour to stroll and note the variety of buildings, which include Sino-Portuguese, Thai and Chinese styles. Former residents include Boonpong Sirivejabhand, who helped

POWs send messages back home during WWII using secret codes. Many shops date from the turn of the 20th century and are still owned by the same family. Look out for the erstwhile hotel that, back in the good old days, charged 1B per night.

Chung Kai Allied War Cemetery HISTORICAL SITE

(สุสานทหารพันธมิตรช่องไก่) Chung Kai was the site of a major prisoner camp during WWII, and Allied prisoners built their own hospital and church close to here. Most graves have brief, touching epitaphs for the 1400 Commonwealth and 300 Dutch soldiers buried here.

The cemetery is 4km south of central Kanchanaburi across the Mae Nam Khwae Noi and can be reached by bicycle.

Lak Meuang LANDMARK

(ศาลหลักเมือง; City Pillar; Th Lak Meuang) The city pillar is at the centre of the old town and is

Kanchanaburi

said to give shelter to local spirits. Just down the road is a statue of King Rama III and the renovated city wall, which used to stretch for more than 400m and had six fortresses. Three original cannons remain.

Wat Tham Seua & Wat Tham Khao Noi
TEMPLES

(วัดถ้ำเสือ/วัดถ้ำเขาน้อย) These neighbouring hill-top monasteries are of interest due to their vastly different styles. Wat Tham Khao Noi (Little Hill Cave Monastery) has an intricately designed Chinese-style pagoda while next door the larger Wat Tham Seua (Tiger Cave Monastery) has several styles of *chedi* and an 18m-tall Buddha covered in a golden mosaic. In front of the Buddha image a conveyor belt has small silver trays into which donations are made and then tipped into a central pot. You can walk to the top or take the easy option and go by cable car (10B).

The temples are around 14km south of the town centre. If coming by motorbike, take the right fork of the highway when you reach Tha Meuang, turn right across the Kheuan Meuang (City Dam) and right again on the other side. By bicycle, avoid the highway by using back roads that follow the river. Follow Th Pak Phraek and cross the bridge towards Wat Tham Mangkon Thong. Once over the bridge, turn left and follow the river for 14km, at which point you should see the hilltop pagodas on your right. Buses (10B) leave from Kanchanaburi bus station to Ratchaburi every 20 minutes. Get off at Tha Meuang Hospital and hire a motorbike taxi (40B).

WWII Museum
MUSEUM

(พิพิธภัณฑ์สงครามโลกครั้งที่สอง; admission 40B; ⊗8am-6pm) One of the most eclectic and downright odd sites, this museum houses everything from wartime artefacts to paintings of former beauty queens.

The museum is divided into two buildings. Inside one is a display of Japanese wagons used to transport prisoners, old photographs and unconvincing waxwork POWs. Notes about the area's history are scrawled on the walls, but the translations sometimes go badly awry, with unfortunately comic results. One sign about the victims of an Allied bombing raid reads: 'the bodies lay higgledy-piggledy beneath the bridge'. Another says simply: 'England was pushed into the sea by Dunkirk'.

The larger building resembles a Chinese temple and is far more opulent, or garish, depending on your viewpoint. The top level is the best place to see the nearby Death Railway Bridge at sunset.

Between the two buildings is a pyramid-shaped family shrine with coloured bowls decorating the exterior. The museum is immediately south of the Death Railway Bridge.

Wat Bahn Tham
TEMPLE

(วัดบ้านถ้ำ) The web of hillside caves for which this temple is famous holds many ancient secrets, according to folklore. Getting to the caves involves ascending a flight of steps that passes through a 'dragon's mouth' entrance. Of the five caves near the top, one has a standing Buddha image which is illuminated by a single shaft of sunlight breaking through the top of the hill. A stone in one cave is said to resemble an innocent woman, Bua Khli, who was killed by her husband 400 years ago. The stone is painted and given different dresses throughout the year as her soul was once thought to inhabit there. Another blocked-off passageway leads to a village inhabited by giants, or so legend says.

To find the temple, which is 15km south of the town, cross the Kheuan Meuang (City Dam) and go right on the other side of the river. Follow the road parallel to the river and look for the temple to your left.

🏃 Activities & Courses

Thai Cooking

Apple & Noi's Thai Cooking Course
COOKING COURSE

(www.applenoi-kanchanaburi.com; Apple's Retreat, Bahn Tamakahm; course 1250B) If you don't know your *sôm·dam* from your *dôm yam* then Khun Noi can assist. The one-day course starts at the local market and ends, four dishes later, at the dining table.

Trekking & Cycling

Elephant rides, trips to Thailand's best waterfalls and bamboo rafting are all easily booked with tour agents.

More adventurous experiences, including cycling tours, canoeing, and overnight jungle trekking, can also be arranged. As a rule of thumb, the further north you go, the wild-

---

WHY BRIDGE THE RIVER KHWAE?

The construction of the 'Death Railway' was an astonishing feat of engineering. However, the prisoners and conscripted workers who toiled to build it paid a terrible price. Around 100,000 labourers died due to the extreme conditions.

The railway was built during the WWII-era Japanese occupation of Thailand (1942–43) and its objective was to link 415km of rugged terrain between Thailand and Burma (Myanmar) to secure an alternative supply route for the Japanese conquest of other west Asian countries. Some considered the project impossible but the track was completed despite a lack of equipment and appalling conditions.

Construction began on 16 September 1942 at existing stations at Thanbyuzayat in Myanmar and Nong Pladuk (Ban Pong) in Thailand. Japanese engineers estimated it would take five years to link Thailand and Burma by rail. In reality, the Japanese army forced the POWs to complete the 1m-gauge railway in 16 months. Much of the work was done by hand with simple tools used to build bridges and carve cuttings into the sides of the mountains.

As the Japanese demand for faster construction grew, so conditions worsened. The meagre rice supplies were often laced with kerosene, a by-product of Allied bombing raids over rice stocks. Cholera, malaria and dysentery were rife, and Japanese guards employed barbaric punishments for anyone who stepped out of line.

The rails were finally joined 37km south of Three Pagodas Pass; a Japanese brothel train inaugurated the line.

The bridge that spans the River Kwai near Kanchanaburi (dubbed the 'Death Railway Bridge') was used for just 20 months before the Allies bombed it in 1945. Rather than a supply line, the route quickly became an escape path for Japanese troops. After the war the British took control of the railway on the Burmese side and ripped up 4km of the tracks leading to Three Pagodas Pass for fear of the route being used by Karen separatists.

On the Thai side, the State Railway of Thailand (SRT) assumed control and continues to operate trains on 130km of the original route between Nong Pladuk, south of Kanchanaburi, to Nam Tok. See p182 for transport information.

er things get. Most of Kanchanaburi's roads are in good condition and perfect for bicycle or motorbike touring, while some off-road routes lead to rarely visited waterfalls and caves. Several trips stay overnight in a Mon or Karen village and involve a combination of rafting, trekking and elephant rides.

For those with less time, the countryside close to Kanchanaburi is replete with wonderful vistas and a bicycle is an ideal way to see them. One particularly scenic route lies immediately behind the backpacker guest houses. From the northern end of Th Mae Nam Khwae, cross Sutjai Bridge and head right. Explore Bahn Thamakham and Bahn Hua Hin, where lemongrass, corn, tapioca and teak trees soak up the sun while in the distance mist-covered mountains serve as a breathtaking backdrop.

Some package tours are cancelled if not enough people sign up, so check before booking. The following agencies are reputable.

AS Mixed Travel TREKKING, CYCLING
(📞0 3451 2017; www.applenoi-kanchanaburi. com; Apple's Retreat) A well-organised company with knowledgeable staff. Trips can be tailor-made depending on travellers' preferences, and pockets.

Good Times Travel TREKKING, CYCLING
(📞0 3462 4441; www.good-times-travel.com; 63/1 Tha Mae Nam Khwae) All the normal day trips are available, plus adventure packages to more remote areas. Cycling tours can be arranged from here.

Kayaking
Paddle power is one of the most fun ways to get around.

River Kwai Canoe Travel Services KAYAKING
(📞0 3451 2017; riverkwaicanoe@yahoo.com; Th Mae Nam Khwae) Arranges one- or two-day trips that include visits to the main attractions.

🛏 Sleeping

Most of Kanchanaburi's sleeping spots are along a 1km stretch of Th Mae Nam Khwae. Many budget places offer riverfront views, sometimes on raft houses, and easy access to the main attractions. Across the river and out of town are the top-end resorts. The erstwhile backpacker hub along Soi Th Rong Hip Oi now has only a few options thanks partly to the noise from passing karaoke boats, but the disturbances are fleeting and some good budget rooms are available.

DON'T BE A BUFFALO

The movie *The Bridge on the River Kwai* made the waterway famous, and also left a generation pronouncing it incorrectly. You should talk about the River Khwae (sounds like 'square' without the 's') and not Kwai (sounds like 'why'). Get it wrong and you'll be referring to the River Buffalo, which the Thais always find amusing.

Th Saengchuto has a handful of midrange hotels that are favoured by Thais coming for the weekend. Check out **Kanchanaburi Info** (www.kanchanaburi-info.com) for more choices.

TOP CHOICE **Apple's Retreat** GUEST HOUSE $
(📞0 3451 2017; www.applenoi-kanchanaburi.com; 153/4 M.4 Bahn Tamakahm; r 490-690B; 🌐) With the most welcoming smiles in town, friendly and knowledgeable staff give the place a homely feel. All the compact, clean rooms look out over a well-maintained garden. In a bid to be ecofriendly, the rooms lack a TV and fridge. Noi's one-day Thai cooking courses are popular.

TOP CHOICE **Jolly Frog** GUEST HOUSE $
(📞0 3451 4579; 28 Soi China; s 70B, d 150-400B; 🌐🛜) A favourite for those just off the bus from Th Khao San, this place lacks certain luxuries, such as organised staff and flushing toilets, but does compensate by having a large communal garden and a range of rooms. The Frog gets bonus points for free wi-fi and a good restaurant.

TOP CHOICE **Sabai@Kan** HOTEL $$
(📞0 3462 5544; www.sabaiatkan.com; 317/4 Th Mae Nam Khwae; r 1300-1600B; 🌐🛜🏊) This two-level boutique resort is handily located along the main drag. Rooms overlook a swimming pool and have heaps of natural light.

Pong Phen GUEST HOUSE $$
(📞0 3451 2981; www.pongphen.com; Th Mae Nam Khwae; r 150-1000B; 🌐🛜🏊) The best-value option if you need a pool, Pong Phen has rooms that range from backpacker simplicity to more spacious options with balconies. The restaurant offers decent Western and Thai dishes.

Sam's House GUEST HOUSE **$$**
(☑0 3451 5956; www.samsguesthouse.com; Th Mae Nam Khwae; d 400-800B; ✱) A walkway set over a bed of hyacinths leads off to basic but clean rooms, most of which have balconies. The A-frame designs and gnarly wood patterns add character.

Blue Star Guest House GUEST HOUSE **$**
(☑0 3451 2161; bluestar_guesthouse@yahoo.com; 241 Th Mae Nam Khwae; r 150-650B; ✱🛜) This collection of wooden bungalows is enveloped by trees, giving it a natural, out-of-the-way feel. The more expensive rooms are down by the riverfront. The variety of rooms makes it a good idea to see a few before deciding on one.

U Inchantree Kanchanaburi HOTEL **$$$**
(☑0 3452 1584; www.ukanchanaburi.com; 443 Th Mae Nam Khwae; r from 2825B; ✱🛜🌀) This gorgeous boutique resort 1km north of the bridge has thought of just about everything. Clever touches include a free mp3 player in every room (you choose the tunes in advance), infinity pool, split-level riverside seating, a gym and library. Service is impeccable, while the rooms have subtle hints of the famous bridge a few metres away.

Bamboo House GUEST HOUSE **$**
(☑0 3462 4470; bambooguesthouse@hotmail. com; 3-5 Soi Vietnam, Th Mae Nam Khwae; r 200-500B; ✱) For a sense of truly being away from the maddening crowds, this is ideal. Set in large, open grounds, the river raft rooms have stunning sunset views of the Death Railway Bridge. Cheaper rooms have shared bathrooms.

VN Guest House GUEST HOUSE **$**
(☑0 3451 4082; www.vnguesthouse.net; 44 Soi Th Rong Hip Oi; r 280-450B; ✱🛜) Still the best option along this strip, VN remains popular due to the beautiful river views and floating raft houses. Prepare for a few passing karaoke rafts if you stay at the weekend.

Ploy Guesthouse GUEST HOUSE **$$**
(☑0 3451 5804; www.ploygh.com; 79/2 Th Mae Nam Khwae; r 750-1000B; ✱🌀) If you manage to find the rather elusive receptionists, Ploy has stylish rooms, some open-air bathrooms and a pleasant rooftop terrace.

Felix River Kwai Resort HOTEL **$$$**
(☑0 3455 1000; www.felixriverkwai.co.th; 9/1 M.3 Bahn Tamakahm; s 4800B, d 5300B, ste from 8700B; ✱🛜🌀) Felix markets itself as the only five-star resort in Kanchanaburi, and it has the facilities, opulence and panache to back up such a claim. Renovation work means Felix, which is 2km west of the bridge, is still the king of Kanchanaburi's resorts.

Kasem Island Resort HOTEL **$$**
(☑0 3451 3359, in Bangkok 0 2254 8871; r 1000-1800B; ✱🌀) Set on its very own island on Mae Nam Mae Klong, this relaxed resort offers a variety of slightly dated wooden rooms, all river-facing and with private balconies. A free shuttle boat runs to and from Th Chaichumphon.

River Kwai Hotel HOTEL **$$$**
(☑0 3451 3348; www.riverkwai.co.th; 284/15-16 Th Saengchuto; r from 1800B; ✱🛜🌀) A major renovation has breathed new life into this hotel, and its pastel-coloured rooms, lift, gym and spa make it ideal for those wanting to stay in the town centre. Also here is 'Glitzy', the only nightclub in town.

Royal River Kwai Resort & Spa HOTEL **$$$**
(☑0 3465 3342; www.royalriverkwairesort.com; 88 Kanchanaburi-Saiyok Rd; r 1750-3360B; ✱🛜🌀) Beautiful Thai-style rooms, enormous grounds and an equally huge pool make this one of the finest resorts in town. The spa, with riverfront rooms, provides a range of treatments. The resort is located 4km north of town.

SINGING THE KARAOKE BLUES

One minute you're sitting with your toes dipped in the cool river, listening to the rustle of branches overhead. The next the silence is splintered by the booming beats of a passing karaoke boat.

During the evenings, especially at weekends, Bangkokians and mainly Korean tourists are bussed in for a trip along the river. The commotion used to make guest houses along Soi Rong Hip Oi unappealing, but now the all-nighters have virtually stopped and the boats are just a temporary nuisance. Bridges prevent the boats from going too far, so guest houses along Th Mae Nam Khwae are unaffected. If you want to experience the floating karaoke, boats can be hired for 4000B. Food and drink are extra.

✕ Eating

From market snacks to riverside restaurants, Kanchanaburi is not short of eating options. Sprinkled along Th Mae Nam Khwae is a string of restaurants serving pizzas, burgers and standard Thai dishes. For more authentic food, check out the **night market** (Th Saengchuto; ⊘Thu-Tue) near the train station, which is packed with stalls serving fried treats and blended drinks. Several good-quality **floating restaurants** (Th Song Khwae) are often full of Korean or Thai package-company tourists. The **market** (Th Saengchuto) near the bus station is well-known for its excellent *hŏy tôrt* (fried mussels in an egg batter).

TOP CHOICE **Blue Rice** THAI $
(153/4 M.4 Bahn Tamakahm; dishes 50-100B) Along with standard Thai dishes, chef Apple has created some ingenious culinary twists, such as the eponymous rice and the wonderful *yam sôm oh.*

TOP CHOICE **Jukkru** THAI $
(no roman-script sign; Th Song Khwae; dishes 60-100B) This well-established restaurant has a regular nightly crowd thanks to its simple but delicious dishes. Look for the blue tables and chairs outside. The collection of Burmese artefacts and shrine to the rear is fascinating.

Sri Rung Rueng THAI, WESTERN $
(Th Mae Nam Khwae; dishes 60-150B) With pasta, steak, vegetarian and nine pages of drinks to pick from, the menu defines comprehensive. Thai food comes with some Western compromise, but remains tasty and fresh.

Saisowo NOODLES $
(no roman-script sign; Th Chaokunen; dishes 20-25B; ⊘8am-4pm) When a place is this popular with locals, it must be doing something right. This long-established noodle spot has a few surprise options, such as the excellent *gŏoay dĕeo đôm yam kài kem* (noodle soup with salty eggs).

Thai Seri THAI-CHINESE $
(no roman-script sign; dishes 80-150B) Set away from the noisy karaoke boats, this pleasant floating restaurant has a mix of Thai/Chinese cuisine with a few surprises thrown in, such as the excellent *tôrt man ʼblah mèuk* (squid cakes).

LEAF IT ALONE

The tapioca fields dotted throughout Kanchanaburi don't look remarkable, yet sometimes they get special attention from travellers. Tour guides have spotted visitors surreptitiously picking the leaves and stuffing them into their bags. The guides then have to patiently explain that while the leaves may closely resemble a marijuana plant, they really are just plain old tapioca.

🍺 Drinking

Tourists tend to spend their evenings along Th Mae Nam Khwae, where there are bars, pool tables and an increasing number of prostitutes, though the latter are largely at the southern end. For true budget drinking, street-side bars offer shots of local spirits for a mere 10B. Thais head to Th Song Khwae, which has a handful of bars and clubs.

Tham Naan BAR
(Th Song Khwae) The best of the bars along this strip, with live music and a country vibe.

Sugar Member BAR
(Th Mae Nam Khwae) Has hip, friendly staff who will sip whisky buckets with you all night.

No Name Bar BAR
(Th Mae Nam Khwae) Gets the expat crowd.

Buddha Bar BAR
(Th Mae Nam Khwae) Attracts dreadlocked backpackers.

ℹ Information

Emergency
Tourist police (✆0 3451 2668, 1155; Th Saengchuto)

Internet Access
Internet cafes can be found along Th Mae Nam Khwae for 30B per hour.

Medical Services
Thanakarn Hospital (✆0 3462 2366, emergency 0 3462 2811; Th Saengchuto) Near the junction of Th Chukkadon, this is the best-equipped hospital to deal with foreign visitors.

Money
Several major Thai banks can be found on Th Saengchuto near the market and the bus terminal.

AS Mixed Travel (☎0 3451 2017; Apple's Retreat) Foreign-exchange service available out of bank hours.

Bangkok Bank (Th U-Thong) Near the market.

Krung Thai Bank (Th Saengchuto) Near the River Kwai Bridge.

Thai Military Bank (Th Saengchuto) Near the bus station.

Post

Main post office (Th Saengchuto; ⊗8.30am-4.30pm Mon-Fri, 9am-noon Sat & Sun)

Telephone

Many private shops along Th Mae Nam Khwae offer long-distance calls.

Communications Authority of Thailand (CAT; ⊗8.30am-4.30pm Mon-Fri)

Tourist Information

Tourism Authority of Thailand (TAT; ☎0 3451 2500; Th Saengchuto; ⊗8.30am-4.30pm) Pick up free copies of town and regional maps from here.

❶ Getting There & Away

Bus

Kanchanaburi's bus station is to the south of the town on Th Saengchuto. Destinations include:

Bangkok's Northern (Mo Chit) bus terminal (2nd/1st class 95/122B, two hours, every 90 minutes between 6.30am and 6pm) Go here if heading to northern Thailand.

Bangkok's Southern (Sai Tai Mai) bus terminal (2nd/1st class 84B/99B, two hours, every 15 minutes between 4am and 8pm)

Ratchaburi (2nd/1st class 47B/65B, two hours, frequent) Use this to head south then change to a Hua Hin or Phetchaburi-bound bus.

Sangkhlaburi (2nd/1st class 180/192B, four hours, frequent from 7.30am to 4.30pm)

Suphanburi (47B, two hours, every 20 minutes until 5.30pm) Connections to Ayuthaya and Lopburi.

Minibuses also run from the bus station. Destinations include:

Bangkok's Victory Monument (110B, two hours, every 10 minutes until 8pm) Stops at the Southern (Sai Tai Mai) bus terminal.

Northern (Mo Chit) terminal (120B, two hours, every 90 minutes until 6pm)

Srimongkol Transport (☎08 4471 8282, 350B) runs air-conditioned buses to Rayong, stopping at Pattaya.

Train

Kanchanaburi's train station is 2km northwest of the bus station and near the guest house area. Kanchanaburi is on the Bangkok Noi-Nam Tok

rail line, which includes a portion of the historic Death Railway built by WWII POWs during the Japanese occupation of Thailand. The SRT promotes this as a historic route, and so charges foreigners 100B for any one-way journey along the line, regardless of the distance. Coming from Bangkok Noi station (located in Thonburi), 100B is reasonable, but for short trips in Kanchanaburi it seems steep. The most historic part of the journey begins north of Kanchanaburi as the train crosses the Death Railway Bridge and terminates at Nam Tok station. Destinations include:

Nam Tok (two hours, 5.30am, 10.30am and 4.19pm) Return journeys from Nam Tok leave at 5.20am, 12.55pm and 3.15pm. Sai Yok Noi waterfall is within walking distance.

Thonburi's Bangkok Noi station (three hours, 7.19am and 2.44pm) Trains leave Bangkok at 7.44am and 1.55pm.

The SRT runs a daily **tourist train** (☎0 3451 1285) from Kanchanaburi to Nam Tok (300B one way). This is the same train that carries the 100B passengers. For those who simply want to cross the Death Railway Bridge, a rainbow-coloured mini train (20B, 15 minutes, frequent) runs trips from 8am to 10am and noon to 3pm.

❶ Getting Around

Boat

The river ferry that crosses Mae Nam Mae Klong costs 5B per person for a one-way trip. Long-tail boats offer 1½-hour trips to various attractions by the riverside. Prices start at 800B but are negotiable. Boats leave from the pier off Th Chukkadon or from the Jeath War Museum.

Motorcycle

Motorcycles can be rented at guest houses and shops along Th Mae Nam Khwae for 150B a day. Bicycle rentals cost 50B.

Public Transport

Trips from the bus station to the guest-house area will cost 50B on a *săhm·lór* and 30B on a motorcycle taxi. Public *sŏrng·tăa·ou* run up and down Th Saengchuto for 10B per passenger (get off at the cemetery if you want the guest-house-area). The train station is within walking distance of the guest-house area.

Around Kanchanaburi

Away from the provincial town the area's natural beauty is abundant. It's possible to see some of the highlights on one-day outings from Kanchanaburi, but you will need to stay overnight elsewhere to reach some parts.

The waterfalls outside of Kanchanaburi are best visited during the rainy season from June to October or in November and December, when water levels are at their peak.

In the north of the province, the tiny towns of **Thong Pha Phum** and **Sangkhlaburi** are completely unspoiled, slow-paced places from which to plan excursions into the nearby national parks. These parks give visitors the opportunity to explore thick jungle, stay with ethnic groups and visit incredible waterfalls and caves. This is all part of the **Western Forest Complex**, one of Asia's largest protected areas.

Entry to the parks is 200B for foreigners. Bungalows and camping facilities are available at most sites, but it is important to book ahead (☑0 2562 0760; www.dnp.go.th).

Park headquarters have free booklets and maps, and most have guides that can lead trekking trips. Temperatures range from 8°C to 45°C depending on the time of year, so bring appropriate clothing.

Some tour companies in Kanchanaburi town can arrange tours of the parks with English-speaking guides.

ERAWAN NATIONAL PARK อุทยานแห่งชาติเอราวัณ
The majestic seven-tiered **waterfall** within **Erawan National park** (☑0 3457 4222; admission 200B; ☺8am-4pm, levels 1-2 5pm) is one of the most popular in Thailand. The top level is so-called due its resemblance to Erawan, the three-headed elephant of Hindu mythology. Walking to the first three tiers is easy work, but after that good walking shoes and some endurance are needed to complete the 1.5km hike. Levels 2 and 4 are impressive, but be wary of monkeys who may snatch belongings while you're taking a dip.

Elsewhere in this 550-sq-km park, **Tham Phra That** is a cave with a variety of limestone formations. Guides carrying paraffin lamps lead visitors through the gloom, pointing out the translucent rocks, glittering crystals and bat-covered caverns. Geologists find the caves of interest due to a clearly visible fault line. You will need your own transport or a guide to reach the cave, which is 12km northwest of the park entrance, or you can negotiate a ride with park staff. The approach road is a dirt track and there is a stiff walk up to the cave entrance. Another 5km north is the enormous and scenic **Si Nakharin Reservoir**.

Around 80% of Erawan is forest, and many of the park's various trees can be seen along three nature trails, which range from 1km to 2km. Bird-watchers try to spy hornbills, woodpeckers and parakeets from the camping areas and observation trails. Tigers, elephants, cobras and gibbons also call the park home.

Park bungalows (☑0 2562 0760; www.dnp.go.th; bungalows 800-5000B, camping 150-300B) sleep between two and 50 people. If you bring your own tent, there is a 30B service fee.

Buses from Kanchanaburi stop by the entrance of the Erawan waterfall (50B, 1½ hours, every hour from 8am to 5.20pm). The last bus back to Kanchanaburi is at 4pm. Within the park, you can rent bicycles for 20B to 40B per day.

HELLFIRE PASS MEMORIAL ช่องเขาขาด
To truly understand the suffering that occurred along the Burma-Thailand Railway in WWII, a visit to this **war memorial** (www.dva.gov.au/commem/oawg/thailand.htm; admission by donation; ☺9am-4pm) is imperative. Start at the museum on the top level, look out over the contemplation deck, then walk along the trail that runs alongside the original rail bed.

Near the start of the route is the infamous cutting known as **Hellfire Pass** (locally referred to as Konyu Cutting). The area earned its name following the three-month 'Speedo' construction period where shifts of 500 prisoners worked 16 to 18 hours a day. The glow from burning torches cast eerie shadows of the Japanese guards and of the gaunt prisoners' faces, so that the scene was said to resemble Dante's *Inferno*.

Poor hygiene, a lack of medical equipment and the brutal treatment of prisoners claimed the lives of around 15,000 Allied prisoners of war and tens of thousands of civilian labourers from Southeast Asian countries.

At the time of writing, Thai officials had blocked off about one-third of the walking route, so the **Pack of Cards Bridge**, which earned its name after collapsing three times, was off limits.

A walking trail map and excellent audio guide are available. The museum is 80km northwest of Kanchanaburi on Hwy 323 and can be reached by the Sangkhlaburi-Kanchanaburi bus (60B, 1½ hours, frequent departures). The last bus back to Kanchanaburi passes here at 4.45pm.

SAI YOK NATIONAL PARK
อุทยานแห่งชาติไทรโยค

This 500-sq-km **national park** (☎0 3468 6024; www.dnp.go.th; admission 200B) is home to limestone mountains, waterfalls, caves – and some extremely rare animals.

The park is well signposted and free leaflets provide information about hiking trails and how to hire canoes, rafts or bicycles. A cycling route is available to the Kitti's hog-nosed bat cave where the eponymous creature, the smallest mammal in the world, was first spotted in 1973.

Near the visitors centre is Nam Tok Sai Yok Yai (Sai Yok Yai waterfall), which is more of a creek than a waterfall. It empties into Mae Nam Khwae Noi near a suspension bridge. The park was the setting for the famous Russian-roulette scenes in the 1978 movie *The Deer Hunter*.

Among the animals to keep an eye out for in the teak forest are elephants, tigers, wild pigs, wreathed hornbills, gibbons, and the red, white and blue queen crab, first discovered in the park in 1983.

Forestry department **bungalows** (☎0 2562 0760; bungalows 800-2100B) are available and sleep up to seven. Several raft guest houses near the suspension bridge offer fantastic views, while eating is never an issue as there are floating restaurants nearby and rows of food stalls near the visitors' centre.

Around 18km south of Sai Yok Noi is **Tham Lawa** (admission 200B), which runs for 500m and has five large caverns with imposing stalactites and stalagmites. To get here private transport is best, or you can take the train to Nam Tok station and try to find a motorcycle taxi.

The entrance to the park is 100km northwest of Kanchanaburi and 5km from Hwy 323. The Sangkhlaburi–Kanchanaburi bus (55B, two hours, frequent departures) goes past the turn-off to the park, and from there a motorcycle taxi is needed to reach the entrance. Tell the driver you want '*nám dòk sai yôhk yài*'. The last bus back to Kanchanaburi passes at 5.10pm.

Long-tail boats near the suspension bridge can be hired for sightseeing trips along the river, and also to **Tham Daowadung**. It is wise to take a guide and torch with you before entering the cave. Chartering a long-tail costs about 800B per hour, but rates are negotiable.

SAI YOK NOI WATERFALL
น้ำตกไทรโยคน้อย

Not so much a waterfall as a paddling pool, this is where Thais come to have fun. These gentle falls within the park are a minute's walk from the main road and are hugely popular at weekends, when Thais sit on mats, snack on *sôm·dam* and clamber over the sloping rocks. Buy some bags of deep-fried taro or sweet potato from the snack shops on the main road, then eat them by the waterfall.

The waterfall is 60km northwest from Kanchanaburi on Hwy 323 and can be reached by using the Sangkhlaburi–Kanchanaburi bus (50B, one hour, frequent departures); tell your driver you're going to '*nám dòk sai yôhk nóy*'. The last bus back is at 5.30pm. Nam Tok train station is 2km away (100B; see p182 for train departure times).

TIGER SANCTUARY OR TOURIST TRAP?

Having once started as a refuge for abandoned cubs, nowadays the **Tiger Temple** seems more about Disney than *dhamma*. How many other temples have a giant cartoon tiger over the entrance and charge 600B to get in? Still, the tourists still flock here, enticed by the chance to sit in a canyon and have their photographs taken next to chained-up tigers.

The temple has been dogged by claims that the animals are drugged, ill-treated and even traded, all allegations that are strongly refuted by the temple.

One explanation given for the tigers' placid manners is that they eat and are exercised immediately before their public appearances, and that they have been trained from birth to be used to human contact.

Schemes to build a temple, education centre and reforestation scheme have been discussed for years, but progress seems slow. Some tour operators now decline to take visitors to the Tiger Temple, and Lonely Planet no longer recommends visiting.

It is important to do some research before deciding whether to go. See www.care-forthewild.org for a detailed report about alleged abuses.

PRASAT MEUANG SINGH HISTORICAL PARK อุทยานประวัติศาสตร์ปราสาทเมืองสิงห์

This **historical park** (admission 100B; ⊙8.30am-5pm) preserves the remains of a 13th-century Khmer outpost that may have been a relay point for trade along Mae Nam Khwae Noi. The restored ruins show a Bayon style of architecture and cover 73.6 hectares.

All the park's shrines are constructed of laterite bricks and are situated in a huge grassy compound surrounded by layers of laterite ramparts and city walls. Sections of the ramparts show seven additional layers of earthen walls, suggesting cosmological symbolism.

Meuang Singh, or City of the Lion, has two main monuments and two ruins where little more than the bases remain. The principal shrine **Prasat Meuang Singh** is in the centre and faces east (the cardinal direction of most Angkor temples). Walls surrounding the shrine have gates in each of the cardinal directions; the ponds and ditches around it represent the continents and oceans.

Also within the grounds is a **burial site**, excavated in 1986, that shows skeletons and pottery thought to date back 2000 years.

Prasat Meuang Singh is 40km west of Kanchanaburi and is best reached by private transport. Trains heading from Kanchanaburi to Nam Tok stop nearby at Tha Kilen station (100B; see p182 for train departure times). From here it is a 1km walk to the entrance, but it's best having some form of transport as the grounds are large.

DAEN MAHA MONGKOL MEDITATION CENTRE แดนมหามงคล

Should you dream of a stress-free world without mobile phones, reality TV and email, then you are in luck. This **meditation centre** (⊙7am-5pm), founded in 1986, is a popular retreat set within well-kept and spacious grounds. Tamara, an English woman who has lived there for several years, leads two-hour meditation classes, which take place at 4am and 6pm. Cross the teak bridge over the Mae Nam Khwae Noi to get in, and first pay respects before the wooden Buddha image in the meditation pavilion. About 300 people stay at the centre, most of them permanently. Most are nuns, but there is a separate area for men. There is no charge for visiting or even staying here, but donations are appreciated. Day visitors

MAKE MINE A SPIRIT

The abandoned Pilok mine in E-Thong gained its name thanks to the supernatural. When an outbreak of malaria hit the tin and wolfram mine, several workers died. Afterwards, villagers began to see strange apparitions near the mine and believed that the spirits of the miners (*pĕe*) were playing tricks (*lok*) on them. They would cry out 'pilok' and the name stuck. Pilok is also the name of the subdistrict.

are welcome, while basic accommodation is available for those who want to stay longer. White shirts and trousers are provided free at the entrance and should be worn.

The centre is off Hwy 323, 12km from the Tiger Temple, and is well signposted. By train, get off at Maha Mongkol station.

THONG PHA PHUM NATIONAL PARK อุทยานแห่งชาติทองผาภูมิ

This **park** (☎0 3453 2114; Thong Pha Phum district) includes the **Jorgrading** waterfall and simple tree-top **accommodation** (☎0 2562 0760; www.dnp.go.th; 600-1200B).

The 62km ride from Thong Pha Phum to the park is along a serpentine but well-made road shaded by soaring hillside trees. The main waterfall is 5km from the park entrance.

Keep going for another 8km along Hwy 3272 to visit the frontier village of **E-Thong**, where most of the population is Burmese. It may not be a second Pai quite yet, but its reputation for tranquil living is spreading. If you stay at **Nao Prai Homestay** (mrtripop@hotmail.com; r 600-1200B) ask for Khun Tripop, as he speaks English and can arrange treks. Entrepreneurial children offer their own brief guided tour of the village, the old Pilok mine and Burmese quarter.

Yellow *sŏrng·tăa·ou* (170B, 1½ hours, 10.30am, 11.30am and 12.30pm) run from Thong Pha Phum's market to E-Thong. The return trip leaves at 6.30am and 7.30am.

KHAO LAEM NATIONAL PARK อุทยานแห่งชาติเขาแหลม

With the mighty Khao Laem Reservoir at its heart, this 1497-sq-km **park** (☎0 3453 2099; Thong Pha Phum district) is particularly picturesque.

HELPING TO NURTURE NATURE

The largest mainland conservation area in Southeast Asia is comprised of **Thung Yai Naresuan Wildlife Sanctuary** and **Huay Kha Khaeng Wildlife Sanctuary**. Designated a Unesco World Heritage Site in 1991, the sanctuaries, which cover 6200 sq km, host an incredible range of fauna and flora.

Set in the northeastern corner of Kanchanaburi and sprawling into neighbouring provinces, the sanctuaries are largely a mountainous wilderness with rivers and streams separating the grassy lowlands and valleys.

The sanctuaries are protected areas, not national parks, and so visitors require prior permission to enter. One way to do this is via P Guest House in Sangkhlaburi (see p189).

The sanctuaries are one of the last natural habitats for around 700 tigers, who share space with 400 types of bird, 96 reptiles and 120 mammals, including leopards, gaur, bears and maybe even the Javan rhinoceros.

Thung Yai Naresuan (large field) takes its name from its enormous central grassland plain and the fact that King Naresuan once used the area as a temporary army base. Huay Kha Khaeng has more amenities and camping sites, though there are no restaurants or bungalows. The park includes the Khao Hin Daeng nature study route, which can be reached by private transport via Uthai Thani by following Hwy 333, then Hwy 3438.

There are two **camping areas** within Huay Kha Khaeng: Cyber Ranger Station and Huay Mae Dee. Cyber Ranger Station is 7km from the main office and has several waterfalls and valleys within trekking distance. The 37km off-road track to Huay Mae Dee passes a Karen village and is set within thick forest. Thai-speaking guides can be hired from both sites. Camping (30B per tent) sites are available, but you will need to bring all your own equipment.

The main office is best reached by private transport. The closest buses or trains run is to Lan Sak, from where it is a 35km drive to the office.

Ornithologists flock to **Kroeng Kravia Swamp** to see the birdlife, which includes the Asian fairy bluebird and green-billed malkoha. To reach the swamp, go to the Kroeng Kravia substation 45km south of Sangkhlaburi.

More than 260 species of wildlife have been recorded at the park, including gibbons, deer and wild boar. The dam is surrounded by several waterfalls and huge limestone mountains.

Kra Teng Jeng waterfall begins 400m from the park entrance and has a 4km shaded trail leading towards the main falls. A guide is required.

Approximately 1km north from the park entrance is **Pom Pee substation**. From here you can hire long-tail boats to cross the reservoir to Pha Pueng or Kai Uu substations, or head back to the Mon settlement of Wang Kha (or Ka). Hiring a boat with eight people costs around 2000B. Pom Pee also has a campsite and **bungalows** (☑0 2562 0760; www.dnp.go.th; r from 900B) whereas the main park only offers camping facilities.

Approximately 12km south from the park entrance is the 15m-high **Dai Chong Thong** waterfall. The park headquarters are 28km south of Sangkhlaburi. From Thong Pha

Phum, *sŏrng·tǎa·ou* go to Kroeng Kravia Swamp (35B, one hour, every 45 minutes).

The **Lake House Adventure** (www.lakehouseadventure.com; adult/child/dm 15,900/12,000/12,900B) houseboat includes kayaking, elephant rides and a visit to a Karen village on its laid-back five-day trip that goes to Sangkhlaburi.

SI NAKHARIN NATIONAL PARK อุทยานแห่งชาติศรีนครินทร์

The seven-tiered **Huay Mae Khamin** waterfall, close to the **park** (☑0 3451 6667; Si Sawat district) entrance, is one of Thailand's most beautiful falls. In addition, the park has hot springs, limestone caves and a hiking route. At the heart of the 1500-sq-km park is the Si Nakharin Reservoir, which is fed by surrounding streams and tributaries.

For many years getting here has involved arduous off-road travel or boat trips, but the times are changing. An improved road linking the park to **Erawan National Park** is being completed, meaning you can visit both falls in one day. If you still want to take the old school route, a car ferry crosses the reservoir between Tha Ong Sit in the east and Tha Kamnantuet in the west. The ferry runs from 6am to 8pm and leaves once it is full, or you can charter it for 300B per vehicle. After the 45-minute crossing, the park entrance is 7km from Tha Kamnantuet. Alternatively, charter a speedboat on the east side from Tha Kradan pier (about 1500B).

Camping (☎0 2562 0760; www.dnp.go.th; r 150-700B) and bungalows (900-2700B) are available.

CHALOEM RATANAKOSIN NATIONAL PARK

อุทยานแห่งชาติเฉลิมรัตนโกสินทร์

The area's smallest park (☎0 3451 9606; Nong Preu district) manages to pack a lot in to its 59 sq km. Highlights include Tham Than Lot Noi and Tham Than Lot Yai. The former is unremarkable but leads to a pleasant 2.5km nature trail. At the end of the trail is Tham Than Lot Yai, an enormous opening with jagged stalactites.

Sleeping options include bungalows (☎0 2562 0760; www.dnp.go.th; r 600-2700B) or tents (250-600B). Another option is to stay nearby with a friendly Karen family at the solar-powered Khao Lek Homestay (100-300B). Contact tour agents in Kanchanaburi for details. Most visitors arrive by private transport along Hwy 3086.

Thong Pha Phum   ทองผาภูมิ

POP 62,848

Overlooked by mountains – and often tourists – Thong Pha Phum is a tranquil town that enjoys a slower way of life.

The town, used as a stop-off point on the way to Sangkhlaburi, has its own charm and is easy to get around as there is only one main street. Mae Nam Khwae Noi runs parallel to the east of the town. Facilities are sparse although there are now some banks and a handful of guest houses.

The market, at the epicentre of the town, is the perfect place to find breakfast. Browse the dozens of stalls and choose from deep-fried banana, sugary snacks or noodles. Behind the market is the three-tiered Krua Tom Nam restaurant, with views of the river. Other restaurants reflect the large Burmese and ethnic communities that live here; the large metal pots full of tempting curries are typically Mon.

At night the illuminated hilltop temple casts an ethereal glow over a town that has long gone to bed. To reach the temple, follow the riverfront road towards the main highway, cross a footbridge and walk up.

As well as being within reach of Sangkhlaburi, the town is close to a growing number of adventure activities. Phuiyara Resort (www.phuiyararesort.com; r 1000-1500B) has a zip-line, rope bridge and climbing net course, along with ATV and trekking tours. It can also arrange trips to Thung Yai Naresuan Wildlife Sanctuary (see the boxed text, p186).

South of Thong Pha Phum town is Hin Dat Hot Springs (admission 50B; ☺6am-10pm). If the effects of its two geothermal pools aren't sufficiently soothing, there is a massage pavilion nearby.

The bòr nám rórn (hot springs) is accessible via the Sangkhlaburi–Kanchanaburi bus on Hwy 323 (Km 105 marker) and is 1km from the main road.

Along the same road as the hot springs is Nam Tok Pha That, (200B), a pretty, multi-level waterfall that doesn't get many visitors.

Kheuan Khao Laem, known locally as Vachiralongkorn Dam, is 9km northwest of the town. Some bungalows (☎0 3459 8030; r 600-800B; ☒) are set within the grounds. Activities include golf, tennis, a shooting range and a boat tour of the dam.

Of the in-town accommodation, Som Jainuk Hotel (☎0 3459 9001; 29/10 Mu 1; r 200-500B; ☒) has simple fan rooms or stone-walled bungalows with balconies. The real bonus is June, the owner, who speaks English and can offer invaluable travel tips. Barn Cha Daan (☎0 3459 9035; Mu 1; r 450B; ☒) is near the entrance to town and has split-level rooms set among a wooded courtyard.

❶ Getting There & Away

Air-conditioned buses leave from opposite Siam City Bank on the main road. Tickets are sold at the back of the Krua Ngobah (☎0 3459 9377) restaurant, opposite Siam City Bank. Destinations include:

Bangkok's Northern (Mo Chit) terminal (2nd/1st class 179/227B, five hours, every 90 minutes) Depart until 3.40pm.

Sangkhlaburi (2nd/1st class 62/79B, two hours, four times a day)

Local buses leave from the market.

❶ Getting Around

You can try your bartering skills on the motorbike taxi drivers at the market, who may let you rent their bikes out for around 300B a day. Sŏrng·tǎa·ou run up and down the main road and should cost about 10B for rides within town.

Sangkhlaburi
สังขละบุรี

POP 47,147

For many travellers Sangkhlaburi is the end of the line, but for many residents it represents the start of a new journey. Few places in Thailand have such a blend of ethnic identities, with Burmese, Karen, Mon, Thai and some Lao each calling this home.

Many cross the Burmese border driven by economic need or through fear of oppression. The result is a melange of cultures, beliefs and even languages.

Remote Sangkhlaburi overlooks the vast Kheuan Khao Laem (Khao Laem Reservoir), and owes its existence to the waters. It was founded after an old village, near the confluence of the three rivers that feed the reservoir, was flooded.

Several NGOs in town help the ethnic communities survive and fight for what few rights they have. As a result, there is a constant need for volunteers (p188).

In the last week of July the town is abuzz due to **Mon National Day**.

⊙ Sights & Activities

Wang Kha
MON SETTLEMENT

(วังคา) A rickety **wooden bridge** (Saphan Mon), said to be the longest of its kind in Thailand, leads to this Mon settlement. The village relocated here after the dam's construction flooded the original settlement. Burma's conflicts forced many Mon into Thailand and now Wang Kha has its own unmistakable character. Children play a form of cricket, women smoke giant cheroots and many wear traditional white face powder.

At the end of the bridge is **Dok Bua Homestay** (☑08 6168 6655; r 300-500B), which has rafthouses and regular rooms. A **day market** in the village centre is always busy, while north of this is **Wat Wang Wi-wekaram** (Wat Mon), the spiritual centre of the Mon people in Thailand. The temple has

two complexes 640m apart. To the right of the T-junction is the multiroofed *wi-hăhn* with heavy, carved wooden doors and marble banisters. To the left of the T-junction is the Chedi Luang Phaw Uttama, constructed in the style of the Mahabodhi *chedi* in Bodhgaya, India. At night the 6kg of gold that cover it are illuminated. Men only may climb to the top. In the same courtyard are an ageing *chedi* and a handicrafts market.

The temple was the home of a highly respected monk, Luang Phaw Uttama. Born in Burma in 1910, he fled to Thailand in 1949 to escape the civil war and was a cornerstone of the Mon community. He helped secure this area after the Mon village's previous location was flooded by the construction of the dam. In 2006 he died aged 97 at Bangkok's Srirat Hospital and his medical bills were covered by the queen.

Be sure to hire a **private boat** (400B) and immerse yourself in the pre-dawn mist that envelops the dam. Trips go under the wooden bridge and past the old Mon temple, which is sometimes submerged depending on the time of year.

Khao Laem Reservoir
LAKE

(เขื่อนเขาแหลม) This enormous lake was formed when the Vachiralongkorn Dam (known locally as Khao Laem Dam) was constructed across Mae Nam Khwae Noi in 1983. The lake submerged an entire village at the confluence of the Khwae Noi, Ranti and Sangkhalia Rivers. In the dry season **Wat Sam Prasop** is clearly visible.

The pre-dawn hour is a magical time, when the grey and blue mists and sounds of nature envelop the water.

Baan Unrak
ORPHANAGE, VOLUNTEERING

(บ้านอนุรักษ์; House of Joy; www.baanunrak.org) The large orange building overlooking the town is Baan Unrak, which cares for orphaned or abandoned children from ethnic groups.

As well as the children's home, Baan Unrak runs a weaving centre to provide an income for local women, helps single mothers, and works with HIV/AIDS patients.

Most of the children at Baan Unrak are Karen and all follow the home's neohumanist philosophy of vegetarianism, universal love and meditation.

Due to the large refugee numbers in Sangkhlaburi there is great demand for such services, and volunteers are always needed. The home usually only accepts helpers for six months or longer, but visitors are wel-

---

LIVING ON THE EDGE

On the way up the steps of **Chedi Luang Phaw Uttama**, visitors face a challenge. A footprint of the Buddha is in the middle of the stairs and resting on it are dozens of coins. The task is simple and the reward immense – if you can make your coin balance on its edge, good luck will follow you everywhere.

WHO ARE THE MON?

The Mon people have a proud history, but today they are in danger of being lost forever. As well as introducing Theravada Buddhism to the region, their Dvaravati kingdom covered much of the central plains of Thailand and Burma between the 6th and 11th centuries.

Many Mon have fled the oppressive regime in Burma and live as refugees around Sangkhlaburi. Less than a million people speak the Mon language and they face a fight to preserve their heritage, beliefs and independence.

For centuries there has been conflict between the Burmese and the Mon. The British exploited this tension during its colonisation of Burma by promising the Mon independence in return for their support. Once Burma achieved independence in 1948, the Mon launched a campaign for self-determination but protests were swiftly crushed, with Mon leaders killed and their villages razed. In 1974 a semi-autonomous state, Monland, was created and a ceasefire was declared in 1996, but clashes continue to this day.

Lai Phipit, who is in his 60s, is one of many who left their homeland due to violence. He said: 'When I was a child, soldiers came and told all the men and boys to come and help carry weapons to fight the communists. Anybody who refused would be shot. My family decided to flee to Thailand.'

Of Sangkhlaburi's 47,000 residents, 23,800 are from ethnic groups. Thailand does little more than tolerate their presence. The Mon are given Thai ID cards that offer virtually no rights, travel is restricted and there are checkpoints all around Sangkhlaburi and Three Pagodas Pass. Many Mon and Karen work for 150B a day or less, below the Thai minimum wage but still more than they would receive in Burma. They fear being fined, deported or even attacked and so often have a self-imposed curfew.

The Mon people in Burma continue to suffer and reports of rape, beatings and arrests are common. They are stuck between a country where they are repressed and a country where they have few rights. Because of this, there are fears their once proud traditions and culture could eventually become completely assimilated and lost forever.

A Mon village close to E-Thong preserves its culture by offering a **homestay** (450B) and performing a traditional show. Contact **Phuiyara Resort** (⌨0 3468 5632) for details.

come. The children stage yoga performances at the home every Wednesday at 6pm.

Hilltribe Learning Centre
SCHOOL, VOLUNTEERING
(ศูนย์การศึกษาตามอัธยาศัยไทยภูเขา) Set on a remote hillside 10km south of Sangkhlaburi is the Hilltribe Learning Centre. When Buddhist nun Pimjai Maneerat went to meditate in the forest in 1997 she was soon asked by ethnic groups to teach them. The centre she founded has grown and now has a rudimentary school for its 70 children, but remains an extremely remote outreach program. Students are mostly Karen and learn Thai language and basic life skills. Without the centre, they would have no education. Nun Pimjai, who runs the place virtually singlehandedly, welcomes any volunteers who can teach or help with daily chores. English teachers are particularly needed.

Basic accommodation is available for anyone wanting to stay a few days. For details contact P Guest House.

🛏 Sleeping

P Guest House GUEST HOUSE **$$**
(⌨0 3459 5061; www.pguesthouse.com; 8/1 Mu 1; r 250-950B; ❄) With English-speaking staff and fabulous views, it is no surprise that you need to call in advance to guarantee a room. Fan-rooms are simple affairs with shared bathrooms. Trips out can be arranged from here, along with motorbike, bicycle and canoe hire.

The Nature Club ADVENTURE RESORT **$$$**
(⌨0 3459 5596; www.thenatureclubresort.com; r 800-2500B, tents 300B) Catering for the thrill-seeking, nature-loving market, this giant resort on the outskirts of Sangkhlaburi features reputedly Thailand's longest zip-line (at 800m), lakes and kayaking. Nonguests can also try out the activities.

Ban Thor Phan HEALTH RESORT **$$$**
(⌨0 3459 5018; r 2500-36,000B; ❄❄) Crystal healing, chlorophyll baths and yoga are a

few of the holistic treatments on offer in this stunning retreat. Rooms are cool and calming.

Burmese Inn　　　　　GUEST HOUSE　$$
(☎0 3459 5146; www.sangkhlaburi.com; 52/3 Mu 3; r 400-800B; ❉) Having undergone a facelift, even the cheapest rooms are now rather pleasant and come with TV and hot water. The on-site restaurant has a range of Burmese and Thai dishes.

✗ Eating & Drinking

Guest houses tend to be the favourite eating venues, thanks largely to their scenic waterfront locations. As with most Thai towns, the market offers the greatest variety of food. Be sure to sample some of the delicious Thai and Burmese curries (20B). Nightlife consists of a beer in your guest house or the Western Bar and Country, which does great burgers and most Thai dishes.

Baan Unrak Bakery　　　　　BAKERY　$
(snacks 25-90B) Vegetarians will love this meat-less cafe, which has fine pastries. The bakery is part of the Baan Unrak organisation.

🛍 Shopping

Visitors interested in Karen weaving can pick up authentic products at the Baan Unrak Bakery or at a shop outside P Guest House; the products are made by the Baan Unrak women's cooperative.

Weaving for Women　　CLOTHING, HANDICRAFTS
(www.weavingforwomen.org) Along the same road as P Guest House, it sells hand-woven goods made by Mon and Karen refugee women.

ℹ Information

For money matters go to Siam Commercial Bank (ATM), near the market. Internet shops are also near the market and charge 15B to 20B per hour. There is an international phone in front of the post office (located on the main street).

ℹ Getting There & Away

Across from the market is a bare patch of land that serves as Sangkhlaburi's bus station. Destinations include:

Kanchanaburi (150B, five hours) Bus 8203 leaves at 6.40am, 8.15am, 9.45am and 1.15pm, stopping at Sai Yok and Kanchanaburi.
For Bangkok-bound transport, head to the booking office near the market or the minivan office behind the market.

Bangkok's Northern (Mo Chit) terminal (2nd/1st class 228/293B, seven hours) Buses depart at 7.30am, 9am, 10.30am and 2.30pm. The 2.30pm bus is the only 1st-class option.
Kanchanaburi (175B, 3½ hours, every 30 minutes from 6am to 4pm). Minibuses stop at Thong Pha Phum (80B).

A motorbike taxi to guest houses will cost about 15B. Sangkhlaburi is about 230km from Kanchanaburi and and 74km from Thong Pha Phum.

Around Sangkhlaburi

THREE PAGODAS PASS　　ด่านเจดีย์สามองค์
The eponymous pagodas (*prá jair·dee săhm ong*) may be unremarkable, but the border town is worth visiting for its heavy Burmese influence.

Across the border is the town of Payathonzu, with a **souvenir market** and **teahouses**. If you plan on seeing it, check before heading out as the Myanmar government habitually shuts its side of the border due to fighting between Burmese military and ethnic armies. At the time of writing, the border was open for the first time in three years, but only for Thai nationals.

If there is no way through, then the **market** on the Thai side is full of traders selling Burmese whisky, jewellery, cigars and bizarre health treatments involving goats' heads. At the entrance to one noodle restaurant is a time capsule that was buried in 1995 by Allied POWs to mark the 50th anniversary of the 'Death Railway'. Come here on 20 April 2045 and you can see it being opened.

If the border is accessible, foreigners can obtain a day pass, but not visa extensions. You will need to temporarily surrender your passport and provide a passport photo to the Thai immigration office. At the Myanmar immigration office, a copy of the photo page of your passport and a passport photo is needed, plus 500B or US$10. When you return to Thailand, you will receive your passport back. There is a small photocopy shop near the Thai immigration office.

The pass has a history of violence and smuggling, and even today it is rumoured to be an important drug smuggling route, notably for wood, semiprecious stones and amphetamines.

Green *sŏrng·tăa·ou* leave from Sangkhlaburi's bus station (30B, 40 mintes) every 40 minutes. The border is a short walk from the *sŏrng·tăa·ou* stop in Three Pagodas Pass.

Ko Chang & Eastern Seaboard

Best Places to Eat

» Mum Aroi (p201)

» Barrio Bonito (p226)

» Cool Corner (p215)

» Pan & David Restaurant (p197)

Best Places to Stay

» Birds & Bees Resort (p201)

» Tubtim Resort (p208)

» Ban Jaidee Guest House (p214)

» Bang Bao Sea Hut (p224)

» Paradise Cottages (p224)

Why Go?

Bangkok Thais have long escaped the urban grind with weekend escapes to the eastern seaboard. Some of the country's first beach resorts sprang up here, starting a trend that has been duplicated wherever sand meets sea. As the country became industrialised, only a few, like Ko Samet beaches, remain spectacular specimens within reach of the capital. Further afield, Ko Chang and its sister islands offer the best 'tropical' ambience in the region but expect crowds.

Just beyond the foothills and the curving coastline is Cambodia, and the east coast provides a convenient, cultural link between the two countries. Many of the mainland Thai towns were at some point occupied by the French during the shifting border days of the colonial era. Migrating travellers who take the time to explore these lesser-known spots will find remnants of Old Siam, tasty market meals and an easygoing prosperity that defines ordinary Thai life.

When to Go

The best time to visit is at the end of the rainy season (usually around November) but before the start of high season (December to March). The weather is cool, the landscape is green and rates are reasonable. Peak season on Ko Chang is during the Christmas and New Year holiday period. Crowds thin in March but this is the start of the hot season.

The rainy season runs from May to October. Some businesses on Ko Chang close for the season and the nearby islands of Ko Wai, Ko Mak and Ko Kut shut completely. Your best monsoon bet is Ko Samet, which is relatively drier.

Ko Chang & Eastern Seaboard Highlights

1 Beachcombing and jungle trekking on **Ko Chang** (p218)

2 Floating the day away on the crystalline waters of **Ko Kut** (p230)

3 Swimming with the fishes in the gin-clear coves of **Ko Wai** (p228)

4 Cove-hopping on pretty **Ko Samet** (p205), so close to Bangkok but so far away

5 Strolling the old city and watching the gem traders in **Chanthaburi** (p210)

6 Running errands with the Thai housewives in the day markets of **Trat** (p213)

7 Avoiding Bangkok's hustle and bustle with an alternative layover in **Si Racha** (p194) and a day trip to **Ko Si Chang** (p196)

8 Admiring the modern masterpiece of Pattaya's **Sanctuary of Truth** (p198), an elaborately carved testament to the artistry of Buddhism and Hinduism

9 Dining on seafood beside the sea everywhere, the primary reason Thais travel to the beach

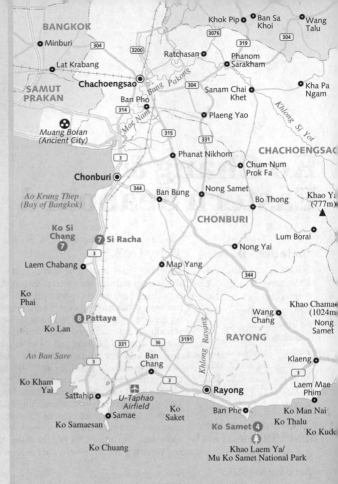

Si Racha

ศรีราชา

POP 68,292

A subdued seaside town, Si Racha is a mix of fishing-village roots and modern industry. Waterfront condo towers eclipse a labyrinth of rickety piers and the cargo ships docking at the Laem Chabang port share the shipping channels with simple, multicoloured fishing boats.

Thai towns, especially those with a modern veneer, are adept at disguising themselves to look like every other Thai town. In Si Racha's case, you need a bit of backstory to know that the many Japanese restaurants in town are catering to the international workforce of the nearby Japanese car manufacturers, and the BMWs that are cruising the streets indicate that those too are being produced nearby. In fact, surrounding the Laem Chabang port, Thailand's busiest deep-water port, is a host of industrial factories, petrochemical facilities and chemical plants – the muscle of the Thai manufacturing economy. As a result there's money in this town: the new municipal building is landscaped like a resort and the health park is impeccably maintained.

From a tourism perspective, Si Racha is attractive for what it doesn't have; there are no guest houses, girlie bars or traffic jams. It is also an easy commute to Bangkok's Suvarnabhumi airport if you're looking for a quiet and untouristed place to layover.

⊙ Sights

Si Racha's attractions are limited, but the town makes for a pleasant stroll.

Ko Loi
ISLAND

This small rocky island is connected to the mainland by a long jetty at the northern end of Si Racha's waterfront and lauded as a local highlight. It has a festival atmosphere centred around a **Thai-Chinese temple** (⊙daylight hrs), decorated by a couple of giant ponds with turtles of every size, from tiny hatchlings to seen-it-all-before seniors. This is also where you can catch the boat to offshore Ko Si Chang.

Health Park
GARDEN

The town's waterfront Health Park is possibly one of the best-maintained municipal parks in the country. There are sea breezes, a playground, shady coffee shop with wi-fi, a jogging track and a lot of evening activity.

🛏 Sleeping

The most authentic (read: basic) places to stay are the wooden hotels on the piers.

COCK SAUCE BY ANY OTHER NAME

Judging by the phenomenal popularity of Sriracha Hot Chili sauce in the USA, you'd expect the eponymous town to be a veritable sauce temple. But no one in the town of Si Racha seems to know much about the sauce, much less that US haute chefs are using it on everything from cocktails to marinades and that food magazines, like *Bon Appetit,* are profiling it alongside truffle oil as a must-have condiment. (Curiously the culinary world also mispronounces the name of the sauce: Sriracha, an alternative spelling of 'Si Racha', is pronounced 'see-rach-ah' not 'sir-rach-ah'.)

There's a good explanation for all this: the stuff sold in the US was actually invented on home soil. A Vietnamese immigrant living in a suburb of Los Angeles concocted a chilli sauce to accompany noodles based on his memory of Vietnamese hot sauces. His first batches were sold out of his car but eventually his business grew into the Huy Fong Foods company.

Today the company's distinctive rooster logo bottles are distributed in the US and Australia, but not in any Asian countries, according to a company spokesperson. But every now and then you might spot it at a Thai noodle shop. How it is this US-born, Thainamed, Vietnamese-inspired sauce got here, the Huy Fong Foods company does not know.

But that doesn't mean Thailand doesn't have its own version of a vinegar-based chilli sauce (*nám prík sĕe rah·chah*). In fact, many believe that the condiment must have originated in Si Racha and then migrated across Asia to undergo various permutations. In Thailand, Si Racha–style sauces, including such popular brands as Golden Mountain or Sriraja Panich, are used with *kài jee·o* (omelette) and *hŏy tôrt* (fried mussel omelette) and tend to be more homogenous and of a thinner consistency than the rooster brand.

Siriwatana Hotel

HOTEL **$**

(✆0 3831 1037; Soi Siriwatana, Th Jermjompol; r 200B) This wooden stilt hotel sits above the sea – in fact, you can look straight through the squat toilet's hole to the ocean. It's simple, but the basic rooms are cheap.

Samchai

HOTEL **$**

(✆0 3831 1800; Soi 10, Th Jermjompol; r 300B) Look for the sign that says 'Hotel' and you'll find another wooden pier hotel that creeps up the comfort scale. It feels a bit like a port: cement floors with yellow lines wind through the large complex.

Seaview Sriracha Hotel

HOTEL **$$**

(✆0 3831 9000; 50-54 Th Jermjompol; r 900-1200B; ❋@) Rooms are large and comfortable, and some have views of the sea and piers. Rooms facing the street can be a tad noisy, but Si Racha is not Times Square, and a gentle hush settles relatively early.

✖ Eating & Drinking

Si Racha is famous for seafood.

Moom Aroy

SEAFOOD **$$**

(no roman-script sign; dishes 100-350B; ⊙lunch & dinner) Moom Aroy delivers on its name, meaning 'delicious corner'. This is *the* place to enjoy a Si Racha seafood meal with views of the pier and squid rigs. It is north of town; turn left at Samitivet Sriracha Hospital and look for the tank with the 2m fish out front.

Bang Saen

SEAFOOD **$$**

(dishes 100-250B; ⊙lunch & dinner) Do as the Thais do and judge your beach by its seafood restaurants. This beach resort, 18km north of town, isn't good for swimming but weekending Bangkokians and local university students love it for its food and views. You'll need private transport to reach it.

Ko Loi Seafood Stalls

SEAFOOD **$**

(dishes 40-160B; ⊙lunch & dinner) Perched on the Ko Loi jetty, these humble spots specialise in fresh seafood. There is no English menu but it's all good.

Night Square

MARKET **$**

(Th Jermjompol & Th Si Racha Nakorn; dishes from 50B; ⊙5pm) This evening market is a bit small but big enough to feed a street-stall appetite.

Picha Cake Garden

BAKERY **$**

(cnr Th Jermjompol & Th Surasak 1; coffee 40B; ⊙breakfast, lunch & dinner) Baked goodies, coffee and spotless air-con surroundings make

this a convenient haven from Si Racha's busy streets. Plus there's wi-fi.

Asami Sriracha

JAPANESE **$$**

(Th Jermjompol; dishes 150-250B; ⊙lunch & dinner) Catering to the local Japanese community, this sit-down restaurant does sushi, udon noodle dishes and katsu sets.

Pop Pub

BAR

(Th Jermjompol; dishes 60-220B; ⊙5-11pm) More like 'Rock', this waterfront beer-hall-meets-music-club boasts a menu ranging from salty snacks to full meals and plenty of liquid sustenance.

ℹ Information

Krung Thai Bank (cnr Th Surasak 1 & Th Jermjompol)

Post office (Th Jermjompol) A few blocks north of the Krung Thai Bank.

Samitivet Sriracha Hospital (☑0 3832 4111; Soi 8, Th Jermjompol) Regarded as Si Racha's best.

ℹ Getting There & Around

Si Racha doesn't have a consolidated bus station but most companies operate near each other on Th Sukhumvit (Hwy 3). Government buses serve Bangkok's Eastern (Ekamai) station (88B to 155B, two hours), Northern (Mo Chit) station (100B, 1½ hours) and Suvarnabhumi (airport) station (100B, one hour) with hourly arrivals and departures from an office beside IT Mall (Tuk Com) on Th Sukhumvit.

Bangkok-bound minivans stop in front of Robinson department store on Th Sukhumvit and have frequent services to Bangkok's various bus stations (100B to 120B) and Victory Monument (100B).

All the arriving Bangkok buses continue on to Pattaya (50B) and points east. White *sŏrng·tǎa·ou* (small pick-up trucks) leave from Si Racha's clock tower to near Pattaya's Naklua market (25B, 30 minutes).

Private bus companies have offices on Th Sukhumvit south of the intersection with Th Surasak and serve the following long-distance destinations: Nong Khai (506B, 12 hours, one evening departure), Khorat (380B, five hours, two evening departures) and Phuket (848B to 1138B, one evening departure).

There is one daily train from Bangkok to Pattaya that stops at Si Racha. It leaves Hua Lamphong station at 6.55am and returns from Si Racha at 2.50pm (3rd class 100B, three hours). Si Racha's train station is 3km east of the waterfront.

Túk-túks (motorised three-wheeled pedicab) go to points around town for 30B to 40B.

Ko Si Chang   เกาะสีชัง

POP 5012

Once a royal beach retreat, Ko Si Chang has a fishing-village atmosphere and enough attractions to fill a day's excursion from Si Racha. Bangkok Thais come on weekends to eat seafood, pose in front of the sea and make merit at the local temples.

◉ Sights

FREE **Phra Chudadhut Palace**   HISTORICAL SITE

(◉9am-5pm Tue-Sun) This former royal palace was used by Rama V (King Chulalongkorn) over the summer months, but was abandoned when the French briefly occupied the island in 1893. The main throne hall – a magnificent golden teak structure known as Vimanmek Teak Mansion – was moved to Bangkok in 1910 (see p89).

What remains today are fairly subdued Victorian-style buildings indicative of the king's architectural preferences. **Ruen Vadhana** and **Ruen Mai Rim Talay** contain historical displays about the king's visits to the island and his public works programs, including a lecture to the local people on Western tea parties. Up the hill is **Wat Asadang Khanimit**, a temple containing a small, consecrated chamber where Rama V used to meditate. The unique Buddha image inside was fashioned more than 50 years ago by a local monk. Nearby is a stone outcrop wrapped in holy cloth, called Bell Rock because it rings like a bell when struck.

Because this is royal property, proper attire (legs and arms should be covered) is technically required but this place doesn't have an administrative presence so the rules aren't enforced. Sadly, the grounds have fallen into disrepair, which is surprising considering the site's proximity to Bangkok and the reverence usually afforded this revered king.

Cholatassathan Museum   AQUARIUM

(admission by donation; ◉9am-5pm Tue-Sun) Just before you reach the palace, this aquatic museum has a few marine exhibits and a dash of English-language signage. The touch tank is interesting because Thais stand around remarking about which animals are delicious to eat. The Aquatic Resources Research Institute conducts coral research here.

San Jao Phaw Khao Yai   TEMPLE

(◉daylight hrs) The most imposing sight on the island is the ornate Chinese temple, dating back to the days when Chinese traders anchored in the sheltered waters. During Chinese New Year in February, the island is overrun with visitors from the Chinese mainland. There are also shrine caves, multiple platforms and a good view of the ocean. It's east of the town, overlooking the modern-day barges waiting silently in the sea.

Wat Tham Yai Phrik TEMPLE

(วัดถ้ำยายปริก; donation appreciated; ⊙dawn-dusk) This Buddhist monastery is built around several meditation caves running into the island's central limestone ridge and offers fine views from its hilltop *chedi* (stupa). Monks and *mâa chee* (nuns) from across Thailand come to take advantage of the caves' peaceful environment. Someone is usually around to give informal tours and talk about Buddhism; you can also arrange multi-day meditation retreats.

Hat Tham Phang BEACH

On the southwest side of the island, Hat Tham Phang (Fallen Cave Beach) has simple facilities with deckchair and umbrella rental. Swimming isn't recommended but you can soak up all the sun you desire.

🏃 Activities

Several locals run **snorkelling** trips to nearby Koh Khang Khao (Bat Island). Ask at Pan & David Restaurant for details.

Sea kayaks are available for rent (150B per hour) on Hat Tham Phang. A nice paddle is down the coast to Koh Khang Khao, which is also a good spot for snorkelling.

Si Chang Healing House MASSAGE

(⌨0 3821 6467; 167 Mu 3 Th Makham Thaew; ⊙8am-6pm Thu-Tue) Offers massage and beauty treatments (400B to 800B) in a garden labyrinth opposite Pan & David Restaurant.

🍴 Eating

The town has several small restaurants, with simply prepared seafood being your best bet.

⭐ TOP CHOICE Pan & David Restaurant INTERNATIONAL $$

(⌨0 3821 6629; 167 Mu 3 Th Makham Thaew; dishes 50-260B; ⊙breakfast, lunch & dinner Wed-Mon) With free-range chicken, homemade ice cream, French-pressed coffee and excellent Thai dishes, the menu can't go wrong. Phoning ahead for a booking is recommended. The restaurant is 200m from the palace.

Lek Tha Wang SEAFOOD $

(dishes 60-150B; ⊙lunch & dinner) Near the entrance to the palace, this famous restaurant is where Thais go to eat conch and other shellfish. For the rest of us, there's always *dôm yam gûng* (spicy and sour prawn soup) and fried fish.

ⓘ Information

The island's one small settlement faces the mainland and is the terminus for the ferry. A bumpy road network links the village with all the other sights.

Kasikornbank (99/12 Th Atsadang) Has an ATM and exchange facilities.

Post office (Th Atsadang) Near the pier.

www.koh-sichang.com An excellent source of local information.

ⓘ Getting There & Around

Boats to Ko Si Chang leave hourly from 7am to 8pm from the Ko Loi jetty in Si Racha (one way 40B). From Ko Si Chang boats shuttle back hourly from 6am to 6pm. Boats leave promptly.

Ko Si Chang's túk-túks will take you anywhere for 40B to 60B. Island tours are available for 250B to 300B: you might need to haggle.

Motorbikes are available to rent on the pier.

Pattaya พัทยา

POP 215,888

Synonymous with prostitution, Pattaya is unapologetic about its bread-and-butter industry. Go-go clubs, massage parlours and girlie bars occupy block after block of the central city, making Bangkok's red-light districts look small and provincial. The city is slightly less seedy in the daylight hours, when families from Russia and Eastern Europe, fresh off a charter flight, might outnumber stiletto-wearing drag queens. More recently, Bangkok Thais have adopted Pattaya as an affordable weekend getaway. They dine beside the sea from a dry location, remarking how much cheaper it is and how much clearer the water is here than in Hua Hin. Does this mean that Sin City is becoming Something-For-Everybody City? Hardly, but there are a few pockets of wholesomeness amid the vice (though it is doubtful that anyone but a missionary would be lured by such a claim).

The city is built around **Ao Pattaya**, a wide crescent-shaped bay that was one of Thailand's first beach resorts in the 1960s. The surrounding area is now Thailand's manufacturing base, transforming the bay from fishing and swimming pool into an industrial port. Some provincial Thais still swim here but we don't think you should as the water is dirty. The oceanfront promenade does, however, provide a scenic stroll under shady trees and a lovely coastal view.

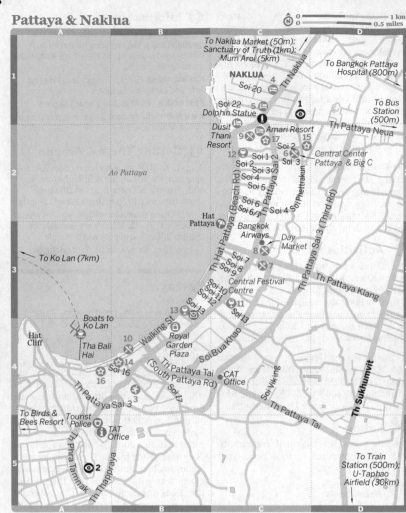

N
0 — 1 km
0 — 0.5 miles

To Naklua Market (50m);
Sanctuary of Truth (1km);
Mum Aroi (5km)

NAKLUA
Soi 20   4
To Bangkok Pattaya
Hospital (800m)

Soi 22   5
Dolphin Statue   1   To Bus
Station
(500m)
Dusit   Th Pattaya Neua
Thani   9   Amari Resort
Resort   17   Soi 2   15
12   Soi 1   6   Central Center
Soi 2   Soi 3   Soi 3   Pattaya & Big C
Soi 4
Soi 5
Soi 6   Soi 4
Soi 6/1

Ao Pattaya

Hat
Pattaya   Bangkok
Airways   Day
Market
8
To Ko Lan (7km)   Soi 7   7
Soi 8
Soi 9
Central Festival
Soi 10   Centre
Soi 11   11
Soi 12   Soi 13
13   Soi 13

Boats to   Soi 13
Ko Lan
Hat   10   Royal
Cliff   Tha Bali   Garden
Hai   Plaza   Soi Bua Khao
14   Walking St
Soi 16   Th Pattaya Tai
16   (South Pattaya Rd)   CAT
Office
Th Pattaya Sai 3   Sor Viking
To Birds &   Th Pattaya Tai
Bees Resort   Tourist
Police
TAT
Office

2
To Train
Station (500m);
U-Taphao
Airfield (30km)

Th Phra Tamnak
Th Thappraya
Th Hat Pattaya (Beach Rd)
Pattaya Sai 2
Soi Phettrakun
Th Pattaya Sai 3 (Third Rd)
Th Pattaya Klang
Th Pattaya Neua
Th Sukhumvit

KO CHANG & EASTERN SEABOARD

Optimists claim that Hat Jomtien, south of the centre, is a family-friendly scene. True, there are fewer girlie bars, but minus that Jomtien is about two decades away from being retro and in the meantime is decidedly dated with a lot of mediocre tour-group hotels and restaurants. North Pattaya (Pattaya Neua) is fashioning itself as a mini-Bangkok with modern condo towers and respectable corporate hotels. North of the city is **Naklua**, which is a little glossier than Jomtien and a little more promising for Pattaya's alternative tourists.

⊙ Sights & Activities

Sanctuary of Truth   MONUMENT
(ปราสาทสัจธรรม; ☏0 3836 7229; www.sanctuary oftruth.com; 206/2 Th Naklua; admission 500B; ⊗8am-6pm) Made entirely of wood (no metal nails) and commanding a celestial view of the ocean, the Sanctuary of Truth is best described as a visionary environment: part art installation, religious shrine and cultural monument. The ornate temple-like complex was conceived by Lek Viriyaphant, a Thai millionaire who spent his fortune on this and other heritage projects (such as Ancient City near Bangkok) that revived and

Pattaya & Naklua

preserved ancient building techniques and architecture in danger of extinction. In this case, the building will continue to support hand-hewn woodworking skills because it has been under construction for 30 years and still isn't finished.

The sanctuary is constructed in four wings dedicated to Thai, Khmer, Chinese and Indian religious iconography. Every inch of the 20-storey-tall building is covered with wood carvings of Hindu and Buddhist gods and goddesses – an artistic consolidation of centuries of religious myths under one unifying roof for greater spiritual enlightenment. For non-Buddhists the experience will be more educational than transcendent as much of the symbolism will be unfamiliar. Regardless, the building and setting are beautiful and the architecture is impressive.

Compulsory tours are led through the building every half hour from 8.30am to 5pm. Thai dancing is on display at 11.30am and 3.30pm. Motorcycle taxis can be hired from Pattaya for 50B to 70B.

Anek Kusala Sala (Viharn Sien) MUSEUM
(อเนกกุศลศาลา (วิหารเซียน); ☏0 3823 5250; off Th Sukhumvit; admission 50B; ⊙9am-5pm) A popular stop for tour groups, this museum contains more than 300 pieces of Chinese artwork, mainly bronze and brass statues depicting historical figures as well as Buddhist, Confucian and Taoist deities. Founded by Sa-nga Kulkobkiat, a Thai national who grew up in China, the museum was founded as a friendship-building project between the two countries, but its greatest success is an impressive collection of art with an unusu-

ally high degree of English-language signage (supplemented by a helpful bilingual guidebook available at the ticket office).

The 1st floor is a crowded pavilion of Chinese immortals, from Pangu, the cosmic giant, to Guan Yin, the goddess of mercy. The 2nd-floor terrace is the museum's most dramatic, with larger-than-life-sized statues of Shaolin monks depicting different martial arts poses. Nearby is a touching collection of daily life statues (a fortune teller, dress maker, liquor seller) that visitors place one baht coins on.

The museum is 16km south of central Pattaya; take Th Sukhumvit to the turn-off for Wat Yan Sangwararam. There is a Pattaya-Sattahip *sŏrng·tăa·ou* (25B) that will take you to the turn-off; from there you can hire a motorcycle the remaining 3km to the museum (50B) but finding a ride back to the main road is difficult. You can either negotiate with the driver to wait or come with your own transport.

Ko Lan BEACH
(เกาะล้าน) Day trippers flock to this small island, 7km offshore of central Pattaya, for sun and sand. On weekends, Bangkok's visiting party people bake off hangovers in beach chairs, and the aquamarine sea is sliced and diced by jet-skis, banana boats and other marine merriment. There are about five beaches on the island, easily accessible by motorcycle, but don't expect to find complete seclusion. Boats leave Pattaya's Bali Hai pier (30B, five daily departures) at the southern end of Walking St. The last boat back from Ko Lan is at 6pm.

Hat Jomtien

N 0 ————— 500 m
   0 ————— 0.25 miles

Hat Jomtien

🛏 **Sleeping**
1 Rabbit Resort A1
2 RS Seaside B3
3 Summer Beach Inn B3

🍴 **Eating**
4 Sam's Mexican & American
  Grill A1

Khao Phra Tamnak VIEWPOINT
(เขาพระตำหนัก; Map p198; ⊙daylight hrs) A giant golden Buddha sits on top of this forested hill between Jomtien and South Pattaya (Pattaya Tai) as a reminder that religion has not forsaken this modern-day Gomorrah. The serene Buddha figure of Wat Phra Yai dates back to the days when Pattaya was a small fishing village and from this lofty position you can almost imagine a time before mini-skirts and Beer Chang happy hours. You can walk to the top of the hill from the southern end of Walking St, passing a small Chinese shrine en route.

Fairtex Sports Club FITNESS, MOO·AY TAI
(Map p198; ☎0 3825 3888; www.fairtex-muaythai. com; 179/185-212 Th Pattaya Neua; per session 800B) Burned-out professionals, martial arts fans and adventurous athletes flock to this resort-style sports camp for *moo·ay tai* (Thai boxing; also spelt *muay thai*) training and a sweat-inducing vacation. Daily sessions include pad work, sparring and clinching, exercise drills and body sculpting work. There are also occasional brushes with fame: domestically famous *moo·ay tai* champions and international mixed martial arts fighters also train here.

Fairtex has been training *moo·ay tai* fighters for 40 years. In 2005, the company opened this sports club to provide Western-style comfort for international visitors interested in fighting and fitness courses. Accommodation packages are available and use of the club's pool and other sports facilities are included.

Flight of the Gibbon OUTDOOR ADVENTURE
(☎08 9970 5511; www.treetopasia.com; tours from 3000B) This zip-line course extends 3km with 26 platforms through the forest canopy of Khao Kheeo Open Safari in Chonburi, 50 minutes from Pattaya. It is an all-day tour with additional add-on activities, like a jungle obstacle course and a visit to the neighbouring animal zoo. Children 1m tall can do the zip-line independently while younger, shorter kids can ride tandem with an adult.

🎉 Festivals

Pattaya International Music Festival MUSIC
In mid-March, Pattaya's oceanfront esplanade is transformed into an outdoor concert venue running for three days of live music. In 2011, bands from Korea, Japan, Malaysia and Laos topped the billing along with Thai favourites such as Modern Dog and Tattoo Colour.

🛏 Sleeping

If you're an 'alternative' Pattaya tourist (meaning you aren't a sex tourist or a package tourist), then you should avoid staying in central Pattaya and opt instead for Naklua, Jomtien or parts of Pattaya Neua. Even if you have no desire to visit Pattaya, you might consider an overnight here if you're transiting to Suvarnabhumi International Airport, 110km away, and don't want to layover in Bangkok.

RS Seaside HOTEL $$
(Map p200; ☎0 3823 1867; www.rs-seaside.com; Th Hat Jomtien; r from 650B; ❉❉) With small rooms and nice desk staff, RS is a good-value

spot in the package-tour part of town. Two breakfasts are included in the room rate.

Summer Beach Inn
HOTEL **$$**

(Map p200; ✆0 3823 1777; Th Hat Jomtien; r 650-1500B; ❄@) Clean, comfortable rooms come with most of the modern conveniences in a high-rise hotel far from Pattaya's vice.

Rabbit Resort
HOTEL **$$$**

(Map p200; ✆0 3825 1730; www.rabbitresort.com; Hat Dongtan; r from 4000B; ❄@≋) Rabbit Resort has stunning bungalows and villas set in beachfront forest hidden between Jomtien and Pattaya Tai. Furnishings showcase Thai design and art and bathrooms are especially stylish with accents of river stone and granite. It is a lovely escape from Pattaya.

TOP CHOICE Birds & Bees Resort
HOTEL **$$$**

(✆0 3825 0556; www.cabbagesandcondoms.co.th; Soi 4, Th Phra Tamnak; r from 4500B; ❄@≋) Retreat into a tropical garden resort bisected by meandering paths and decorated with tongue-in-cheek artwork. Resident rabbits crouch behind the shrubs and kids splash in the pool until they wrinkle like prunes. There's a semi-private beach and an incongruous wholesomeness for a resort affiliated with PDA, the Thai NGO responsible for the country's successful adoption of condom-use and family-planning services.

Garden Lodge Hotel
HOTEL **$$**

(Map p198; ✆0 3842 9109; cnr Soi 20 & Th Naklua; r 950-1450B; ❄≋) Quality rooms with balconies occupy a landscaped garden and shady swimming pool.

Woodlands Resort
HOTEL **$$$**

(Map p198; ✆0 3842 1707; www.woodland-resort.com; cnr Soi 22, 164/1 Th Naklua; r from 3700B; ❄@≋) A surprisingly affordable resort, Woodlands Resort is low-key and professional with a tropical garden and two swimming pools, one with a 'beach' entry for young swimmers. The rooms are light and airy with teak furniture.

✖ Eating

It is a tourist town and there are a lot of overpriced, mediocre restaurants so lower your standards. Most menus are bilingual (usually English and Russian).

TOP CHOICE Mum Aroi
THAI **$$**

(✆0 3822 3252; 83/4 Soi 4, Th Naklua; dishes 180-240B; ☉dinner) 'Delicious corner' is a contemporary glass-and-concrete restaurant perched beside the sea in the fishing village end of Naklua. Old fishing boats sit marooned offshore and crisp ocean breezes envelope diners as they greedily devour fantastic Thai food. Try *sôm-đam ʉoo* (spicy papaya salad with crab) and *ɓlah mèuk nêung ma-now* (squid steamed in lime juice). You'll need to charter a baht bus to get here (one way 100B).

Central Festival Food Hall & Park
INTERNATIONAL **$**

(Map p198; Th Pattaya Sai 2; dishes from 60B; ☉lunch & dinner) The glitziest place to eat a plate of *pàt tai* is in this new Bangkok-style shopping mall.

MOO·AY TAI CHAMPION: YODSAENKLAI FAIRTEX

Khun Yod is a famous *moo·ay tai (muay thai)* fighter but you'd never know it. He is humble and as he is passing into the sunset of his career he is a little stockier than the sinewy kids that can high-kick their opponents in the head. Yod started fighting at eight years old, partly to help his struggling farming family. His first fight was at a temple fair in his home province of Nong Banglamphu and he lost. But since then he earned the nickname 'Computer Wizard' for his technical and methodical fighting style, was a three-time Lumphini champion and has now expanded into the international circuit, winning the super welterweight WBC Muay Thai championship. In the last two years, he has fought in 12 countries and always travels with a supply of Mama noodles and a rice cooker, preferring something akin to Thai food than the local delicacies.

While in Pattaya, Yod recommends an early morning run along the beach road and up Khao Phra Tamnak or a dish of *sôm·đam lao* (Lao-style spicy green papaya salad) from the stand opposite the municipal building. As is customary, Yod adopted the last name of the gym he trains with (Fairtex) where he can be found preparing for a match.

CHARITY SQUAD

A natural counterpoint to the city's prominent debauchery is the city's solid network of charitable organisations. Among the many benevolent servants in Pattaya, Father Ray Brennan, an American priest with the Redemptorist Order who died in 2003, established a lasting and inspiring legacy that today includes six charitable programs under the umbrella of the Redemptorist Foundation. He also founded the Pattaya Orphanage and School for the Deaf, both of which are now operated by the Catholic diocese. All of them succeed thanks to the generosity of benefactors and volunteers.

Pattaya Orphanage (✆0 3842 3468; www.thepattayaorphanage.org; Th Sukhumvit, North Pattaya) was founded in the 1970s when Father Ray was given a baby by a parishioner who could not care for the child. This first child led to many more as word spread that the priest could care for the unintended consequences of the US military presence in the area during the Vietnam War. Today the orphanage cares for children orphaned by modern misfortunes (poverty, drug abuse, HIV/AIDS) and helps find adoptive parents. Those interested in helping the orphanage can sponsor a meal, donate useful items and volunteer for an extended period of time.

Redemptorist Foundation (volunteer@fr-ray.org) operates schools for the blind and disabled and a home and drop-in centre for street children, many of whom may be involved in Pattaya's child-sex industry. The foundation also runs a day-care centre for children of labourers who would otherwise accompany their parents to dangerous work sites. Volunteers rotate through the different centres, teaching English, playing with the children and leading art projects. A six-month commitment is required; contact the foundation for a volunteer handbook that outlines the application process.

If you don't have the time to commit to volunteering, at least stop by **Thais 4 Life** (www.thais4life.com; Soi Yen Sabai Condotel, Th Phra Tamnak; ◷noon-6pm Mon-Sat), a charity bookstore whose proceeds go to medical treatments for destitute patients, orphanages and school uniform scholarships.

Sam's Mexican & American Grill   MEXICAN-AMERICAN **$$**
(Map p200; ✆08 6142 8408; 472/9 Th Tha Phraya, Jomtien Plaza; dishes 80-200B; ◷closed Sun) When it comes to expat cuisine, Thailand does not excel in Mexican food even though there is a common love of chillies and limes. But Sam's gets the formula right and comes recommended by a displaced Los Angeleno.

Nang Nual   THAI **$$**
(Map p198; ✆0 3842 8478; Walking St; dishes 100-200B; ◷lunch & dinner) Pattaya's most famous seafood restaurant could be a major tourist trap but it keeps its prices affordable and the dishes are pleasant if not spectacular. The outdoor deck gulps in a big view of the bay and you don't have to use sign language to talk to your waiter.

Mae Sai Tong   THAI **$**
(Map p198; Th Pattaya Klang; dishes 50B) Next to the day market, this stand is famous for selling *kôw něe·o má·môo·ang* (ripe mango with sticky rice) all year round. Everyone else has to wait for the hot-dry season to compete.

Leng Kee   THAI-CHINESE **$**
(Map p198; Th Pattaya Klang; dishes 50-80B; ◷lunch & dinner) Like Bangkok and other coastal Thai towns, Pattaya has a thriving Chinatown operated by second- and third-generation families who expertly balance their Thai and Chinese heritage. This basic restaurant is a popular lunch stop for duck over rice, but is city-renowned during Chinese New Year when the menu goes vegetarian and includes the festival's golden good-luck noodles.

La Baguette   BAKERY **$**
(Map p198; ✆0 3842 1707; 164/1 Th Naklua; dishes from 120B; ◷breakfast, lunch & dinner) Part of the Woodlands Resort, this sleek cafe has yummy pastries, espresso, and even better crepes. You can also link into its wi-fi network.

Mantra   INTERNATIONAL **$$$**
(Map p198; ✆0 3842 9591; Th Hat Pattaya; dishes 240-800B; ◷dinner Mon-Sat, brunch & dinner Sun) Industrial cool, Mantra is fun even if you can only afford a classy cocktail. The bar is swathed in raw silk and the expansive dining room is cloaked in dark wood. The

menu combines Japanese, Thai and Indian flavours, and everyone comes here for Sunday brunch.

Ban Amphur THAI $
(dishes from 100B; ⊙lunch & dinner) This fishing village 15km south of Pattaya is a dinner destination for Thais. A half-dozen seafood restaurants line the beach road and some are so large the waiters use walkie-talkies. Pick one that doesn't seem lonely or overwhelmed and order all the seafood specialities. You'll have to hire transport to get here.

🍺 Drinking

Despite the profusion of noisy, identikit beer bars, there are still some good places for a no-strings-attached drink.

Hopf Brew House BAR
(Map p198; ☑0 3871 0650; Th Hat Pattaya) Moodily authentic in dark wood, the Hopf Brew House is a haven for middle-aged beer aficionados. Beers and pizza are brewed and wood-fired on-site.

Gulliver's BAR
(Map p198; ☑0 3871 0641; Th Hat Pattaya) The neo-colonial facade belies the laid-back sports-bar inside.

Green Bottle BAR
(Map p198; ☑0 3842 9675; 216/6-20 Th Pattaya 2) Cheap beer and lots of cheer can be found at dressed-down Green Bottle, which has been filling glasses since 1988.

☆ Entertainment

Aside from the sex scene, Pattaya does have a youthful club scene centred on Walking St, a semi-pedestrian area with bars and clubs for every predilection.

Lima Lima NIGHTCLUB
(Map p198; Walking St) International DJ scene and a mix of Russian and Western tourists, locals and expats.

Differ NIGHTCLUB
(Map p198; Soi Phettrakun) Popular with weekending Bangkokians, this dance club's slogan is 'feel fun, feel differ'. It's across from Big C.

Blues Factory LIVE MUSIC
(Map p198; ☑0 3830 0180; www.thebluesfactorypattaya.com; Soi Lucky Star, Walking St) This is Pattaya's best venue for no-nonsense live music.

Tiffany's THEATRE
(Map p198; ☑08 4362 8257; www.tiffany-show.co.th; 464 Th Pattaya 2; admission 500-800B; ⊙6pm, 7.30pm & 9pm) Established in 1974, Pattaya probably invented the transvestite cabaret, a show tune-style spectacle of sequins, satin and sentimental songs.

ⓘ Information

Dangers & Annoyances
So many people are so drunk in this town that all sorts of mayhem ensues (fighting, pickpocketing and reckless driving) after dark. Try to have your wits about you and exit any volatile situation as quickly as possible.

Emergency
Tourist police (☑emergency 1155) The head office is beside the Tourism Authority of Thailand office on Th Phra Tamnak with police boxes along Pattaya and Jomtien beaches.

Internet Access
There are internet places throughout the city and most hotels offer wi-fi or internet terminals.

Media
Explore Pattaya, a free fortnightly magazine, contains information on events, attractions and hotel and restaurant listings. *What's On Pattaya* is a similar monthly publication. *Pattaya Mail* (www.pattayamail.com) is the city's English-language weekly. Pattaya 24 Seven (www.pattaya24seven.com) is an online guide to the city.

Medical Services
Bangkok Pattaya Hospital (☑0 3842 9999; www.bph.co.th; 301 Th Sukhumvit, Naklua; ⊙24hr) For first-class health care.

Money
There are banks and ATMs conveniently located throughout the city.

Post
Post office (Map p198; Soi 13/2, Th Pattaya Sai 2)

Tourist Information
Tourism Authority of Thailand (TAT; Map p198; ☑0 3842 8750; 609 Th Phra Tamnak; ⊙8.30am-4.30pm) Located at the northwestern edge of Rama IX Park. The helpful staff have brochures and maps.

ⓘ Getting There & Away

Air
Pattaya's airport is U-Taphao International Airport, located 33km south of town; it is an old military base that now receives some commercial flights, especially charters. **Bangkok**

ℹ️ **BYPASSING BANGKOK**

An expanding network of bus and mini-van services now connect the eastern seaboard with Suvarnabhumi airport, meaning that you don't have to transit through Bangkok upon a flight arrival or departure. This is especially alluring to winter-weary visitors or newlyweds eager for a beach retreat. With a little advance planning, Ko Samet is the closest prettiest beach to the airport and its southeastern beaches are serene enough for honeymooners. From the airport bus terminal, check the schedule for Rayong-bound buses and then catch a *sŏrng·tăa·ou* to reach the ferry pier to Ko Samet.

Airways (📞0 3841 2382; www.bangkokair.com; 179/85-212 Th Pattaya Sai 2) flies from here to Phuket (from 3000B) and Ko Samui (3600B).

Boat

A new high-speed ferry service links Pattaya to Hua Hin (adult/child 1500/900B, 3½ hours). Ferries leave Pattaya at 8.30am three times a week in high season (two times in low season) and leave Hua Hin at 12.30pm on the same days. Contact **Thai Living Ferry** (📞0 3836 4515; www.thailivingferry.com) for bookings and info.

Bus

Pattaya's main bus station is on Th Pattaya Neua. Buses serve the following destinations:
Bangkok's Eastern (Ekamai) station (91B, 1½ hours, frequently from 6am to 9pm)
Bangkok's Northern (Mo Chit) station (105B, two hours, frequently from 6am to 9pm)
Bangkok's Suvarnabhumi (airport) station (124B, 1½ hour, hourly 7am to 3pm)

Many 2nd-class provincial buses make stops along Th Sukhumvit (not the bus station); from here you can flag down buses heading to Rayong (83B, 1½ hours) and Si Racha (65B, 30 minutes). You can also catch a white *sŏrng·tăa·ou* from the Naklua market to Si Racha (25B, 30 minutes).

Minibuses go to Ko Chang and Ko Samet for about 250B; travel agencies sell tickets and arrange pick-ups.

Train

One train per day travels between Pattaya and Bangkok's Hualamphong station (3rd class 31B, 3¾ hours). It leaves Bangkok at 6.55am and returns at 2.20pm. Schedules for this service can change, so it's wise to check with the **Pat-**taya train station (📞0 3842 9285), off Th Sukhumvit just north of Th Hat Pattaya Neua, before travelling.

ℹ️ **Getting Around**

Locally known as 'baht buses', *sŏrng·tăa·ou* do a loop along the major roads; just hop on and pay 10B when you get off. If you're going all the way from Jomtien to Naklua you might have to change vehicles at the dolphin roundabout in Pattaya Neua. You can also take a baht bus to the bus station from the dolphin roundabout as well. If you're going further afield, you can charter a baht bus; establish the price beforehand.

Rayong & Ban Phe   ระยอง/บ้านเพ

POP 106,737/16,717

You're most likely to be in either of these towns as a transit link en route to Ko Samet. Rayong has frequent bus connections to elsewhere and the little port of Ban Phe has ferry services to Ko Samet. Blue *sŏrng·tăa·ou* link the two towns (25B, 45 minutes, frequent departures).

🛏️ **Sleeping**

Rayong President Hotel   GUEST HOUSE **$**
(📞0 3861 1307; Th Sukhumvit, Rayong; r from 550B; ❄️) From the bus station, cross to the other side of Th Sukhumvit. The hotel is down a side street that starts next to the Siam Commercial Bank; look for the sign.

Christie's Guesthouse   GUEST HOUSE **$**
(📞0 3865 1976; fax 0 3865 2103; 280/92 Soi 1, Ban Phe; r from 500B; ❄️) Christie's is a comfortable place near the pier if you need a room, meal or a book.

ℹ️ **Getting There & Away**

Buses from Rayong go to/from the following:
Bangkok's Eastern (Ekamai) station (127B to 146B, three hours, hourly 6am to 9.30pm)
Bangkok's Northern (Mo Chit) station (146B, four hours, hourly 6am to 7pm)
Bangkok's Southern (Sai Tai Mai) station (150B, five hours, five daily departures)
Bangkok's Suvarnabhumi (airport) station (165B, 2½ hours, eight daily departures)
Chanthaburi (80B, 2½ hours, frequent)

Buses from Ban Phe's bus station (near Tha Thetsaban) go to/from Bangkok's Eastern (Ekamai) station (157B, four hours, hourly 6am to 6pm). Ban Phe also has frequent minivan services to the following destinations:
Pattaya (250B, two hours, three daily departures)

Bangkok's **Victory Monument** (250B, four hours, hourly 7am to 6pm)
Laem Ngop (350B, four to five hours, two daily departures) For boats to Ko Chang.
For information about boats to/from Ko Samet see p209.

Ko Samet

เกาะเสม็ด

An island idyll, Ko Samet bobs in the sea with a whole lot of scenery: small sandy coves bathed by clear aquamarine water. You'll have to share all this prettiness with other beach lovers as it's an easy weekend escape from Bangkok as well as a major package-tour destination.

But considering its proximity and popularity, Ko Samet is surprisingly underdeveloped with a thick jungle interior crouching beside the low-rise hotels. Most beachfront buildings adhere to the government setback regulations and are discreetly tucked behind the tree line. There are no high-rises or traffic jams (the interior road still isn't paved) and most beach-hopping is done the old-fashioned way, by foot along wooded trails skirting the coastline.

◉ Sights & Activities

On some islands, you beach-hop while on Ko Samet you cove-hop. The coastal footpath traverses rocky headlands, cicada-serenaded forests and one stunning cove after another where the mood becomes successively more mellow the further south you go.

Hat Sai Kaew   BEACH
Starting in the island's northeastern corner, Hat Sai Kaew, or 'Diamond Sand', is the island's widest and whitest stretch of sand and has all the hubbub you'd expect of a top-notch beach resort. With sunbathers, sarong-sellers, anchored speedboats loading day-trippers, and restaurants galore – the people-watching here is part of the appeal. At night the scene is equally rambunctious with late-night parties and karaoke sessions.

At the southern end of Hat Sai Kaew are the **prince and mermaid statues** that memorialise Samet's literary role in *Phra Aphaimani,* the great Thai epic by Sunthorn Phu. The story follows the travails of a prince exiled to an undersea kingdom ruled by a lovesick female giant (who has her own lonely statue in Hat Puak Tian in Phetchaburi). A mermaid aids the prince in his escape to Ko Samet, where he defeats the giant by playing a magic flute.

Ao Hin Khok & Ao Phai   BEACHES
More subdued than their northern neighbour, Ao Hin Khok and Ao Phai are two gorgeous bays separated by rocky headlands. The crowd here tends to be younger and more stylish than the down-to-earth crew in Hat Sai Kaew and the parties are late-nighters. These two beaches are the traditional backpacker party centres of the island.

Ao Phutsa (Ao Tub Tim)   BEACH
Further still is wide and sandy Ao Phutsa (Ao Tub Tim), a favourite for solitude seekers, families and couples who need access to 'civilisation' but not a lot of other stimulation.

Ao Wong Deuan   BEACH
A smaller sister to Hat Sai Kaew, Ao Wong Deuan is a long, crescent-shaped bay packed with people, mainly package tourists.

Ao Thian   BEACH
Ao Thian (Candlelight Beach) is punctuated by big boulders that shelter small sandy spots creating a castaway ambience. It is one of Samet's most casual, easygoing beaches and is deliciously lonely on weekdays. On weekends, Bangkok university students serenade the stars with all-night guitar sessions.

Ao Wai   BEACH
The cove 'caboose' is Ao Wai, a lovely beach far removed from everything else (in reality it is 1km from Ao Thian).

Ao Prao   BEACH
On the west coast, Ao Prao is worth a visit for a sundowner cocktail but the small beach is outsized by the high-end resorts that promise (but don't deliver) solitude.

KO CHANG & EASTERN SEABOARD KO SAMET

BEACH ADMISSION FEE

Ko Samet is part of a national park and charges all visitors an entrance fee (adult/child 200/100B) upon arrival. The fee is collected at the National Parks office in Hat Sai Kaew; *sŏrng·tăa·ou* from the pier will stop at the gates for payment. Hold on to your ticket for later inspections.

Ko Samet

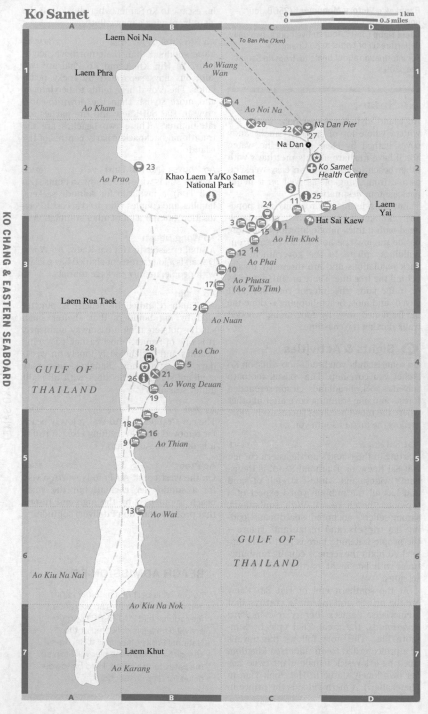

0 — 1 km
0 — 0.5 miles

Laem Noi Na

Laem Phra

Ao Kham

Ao Wiang Wan

To Ban Phe (7km)

Ao Noi Na

Na Dan Pier

Na Dan

Ko Samet Health Centre

Ao Prao

Khao Laem Ya/Ko Samet National Park

Laem Yai

Hat Sai Kaew

Ao Hin Khok

Ao Phai

Ao Phutsa (Ao Tub Tim)

Laem Rua Taek

Ao Nuan

GULF OF THAILAND

Ao Cho

Ao Wong Deuan

Ao Thian

Ao Wai

GULF OF THAILAND

Ao Kiu Na Nai

Ao Kiu Na Nok

Laem Khut

Ao Karang

Ko Samet

☞ Tours

Ko Samet, along with nine neighbouring islands, is part of the Khao Laem Ya/Mu Ko Samet National Park. While there is some development on the other islands, most visitors come for day trips. **Ko Kudee** has a small, pretty sandy stretch, clear water for decent snorkelling and a nice little hiking trail. Ko Man Nai is home to the **Rayong Turtle Conservation Centre**, which is a breeding place for endangered sea turtles and has a small visitor centre.

Agents for boat tours camp out on the popular beaches and have a couple of different boat trips on offer (from 1500B).

🛏 Sleeping

Though resorts are replacing bungalows, Ko Samet's accommodation is still surprisingly simple and old-fashioned compared to Thailand's other beach resorts. Weekday rates don't rank well on the value scale (fan rooms start at 800B), but look incredibly attractive considering that weekend and holiday rates increase by as much as 100%.

A word of caution to early risers: Hat Sai Kaew, Ao Hin Khok, Ao Phai and Ao Wong Deuan are the most popular beaches and host well-amplified night-time parties.

HAT SAI KAEW

Laem Yai Hut Resort GUEST HOUSE $
(☏0 3864 4282; Hat Sai Kaew; r 800-1000B; ❄) A colourful collection of weather-worn huts are camped out in a shady garden on the north end of the beach. The laid-back vibe creates an alternative backpacker universe in a firmly rooted package-tour beach.

Saikaew Villa HOTEL $$
(☏0 3864 4144; Hat Sai Kaew; r 800-2000B; ❄) The closest option to the pier, Saikaew Villa has big rooms or small rooms, fan or air-con and conjures up a holiday-camp atmosphere. Quality and privacy varies with each room.

AO HIN KHOK & AO PHAI

Tok's HOTEL $$
(☏0 3864 4072; Ao Hin Khok; r 1500B; ❄) Snazzy villas climb up a landscaped hillside with plenty of shade and flowering plants, making Tok's a respectable midranger.

Jep's Bungalows GUEST HOUSE $$
(☏0 3864 4112; www.jepbungalow.com; Ao Hin Khok; r 500-1600B; ❄@) Good old Jep's still has cheapie fan huts spread across a forested hillside, just like the old days (a mere five years ago). Air-conditioned rooms are the same, just with cooler interior temps.

A WORKING HOLIDAY

You can volunteer to work at Rayong's Turtle Conservation Centre through **Starfish Ventures** (www.starfishven tures.co.uk; 4 weeks incl accommodation £800). Activities include monitoring the progress of the turtles, releasing young turtles into the ocean and explaining the project to tourists on day trips from Ko Samet. Accommodation is in a fishing village, and every day you'll go to work in a speedboat across to Ko Man Mai. It's pretty leisurely – you'll be expected to work from 8am to 3pm or 4pm, four days a week – and in your downtime there are good beaches nearby to explore.

Ao Pai Hut
GUEST HOUSE $
(✆0 3864 4075; Ao Hin Khok; r 600-1000B; ✹) Same, same as Jep's, this guest house has basic wooden bungalows perched amid the trees.

Silver Sand
HOTEL $$
(✆0 3864 4300; www.silversandsamed.com; Ao Phai; r 1500-2200B; ✹@) Contemporary villas with luscious beds and sleek bathrooms provide a needed slice of sophistication to simple Ko Samet. The after-hours action in the Silver Sands bar can be disorderly and is popular with gay travellers.

Samed Villa
HOTEL $$
(✆0 3864 4094; www.samedvilla.com; Ao Phai; r 1800-2500B; ✹) Handsome bungalows gaze at the ocean or at a manicured garden and boast a lot of comfort without a lot of hassles.

AO PHUTSA & AO NUAN

TOP CHOICE Tubtim Resort
HOTEL $$
(✆0 3864 4025; www.tubtimresort.com; Ao Phutsa; r 800-2500B; ✹@) Ranging from fan to fab, Tubtim has a little of everything. More expensive bungalows are pretty and polished, while the cheapies are spare but still within walking distance to the same dreamy beach.

Pudsa Bungalow
GUEST HOUSE $$
(✆0 3864 4030; Ao Phutsa; r 700-1500B; ✹) The nicer bungalows near the beach are trimmed with driftwood, but sit beside the main footpath within earshot of late-night blathering. A good option if you are doing the blathering.

Ao Nuan
GUEST HOUSE $$
(r 700-2000B) The inventor of chillaxin' on Ko Samet, quirky Ao Nuan has simple wooden bungalows hidden among vegetation. Everyone cool enough to score a room here hangs out in the relaxed restaurant. No phone means no reservations, so just walk on over; it is the only place to stay on a supremely secluded beach.

AO WONG DEUAN & AO THIAN (CANDLELIGHT BEACH)

Ferries run between Ao Wong Deuan and Ban Phe (50B each way), with increased services at the weekend.

To get to Ao Thian, catch a ferry to Ao Wong Deuan and walk south over the headland. It's also a quick walk from here to the west side of the island – look for the marked trail near Tonhard Bungalow.

Blue Sky
GUEST HOUSE $
(✆08 1509 0547; r 600-1200B; ✹) A rare budget spot on Ao Wong Deuan, Blue Sky has simple bungalows set on a rocky headland. Though we love cheapies in all their simplicity, budgeters will get better value on other beaches.

Candlelight Beach
GUEST HOUSE $
(✆08 1762 9387; r 700-1200B; ✹) On the beach, these fan and air-con bungalows with sea-facing porches have a natural, woody ambience.

Lung Dam Apache
GUEST HOUSE $
(✆08 1452 9472; r 800-1200B; ✹) Air-con bungalows sit right smack on the sand and the whole basic collection favours the Thai-country aesthetic of recycled materials.

Tonhard Bungalow
GUEST HOUSE $$
(✆08 1435 8900; r 700-1500B; ✹) On a wooded part of the beach, this place has bungalows that vary from basic to less basic. But in return you get a friendly and relaxing setting.

Viking Holiday Resort
HOTEL $$
(✆0 3864 4353; www.sametvikingresort.com; r 1200-2000B; ✹@) Ao Thian's most 'upscale' spot with large and comfortable rooms; there's only nine of them so book ahead.

AO WAI

Ao Wai is about 1km from Ao Thian but can be reached from Ban Phe by chartered speedboat.

Samet Ville Resort
HOTEL **$$$**

(☎0 3865 1682; www.sametvilleresort.com; r incl breakfast 2000-5300B; 🖼) Under a forest canopy, it's a case of 'spot the sky' at the only resort on this secluded beach. It is an unpretentious sort of place and a tad shabby for resort aficionados. But there is a huge range for all budgets and a great beach.

AO NOI NA

Baan Puu Paan
GUEST HOUSE **$$**

(☎0 3864 4095; r 700-1200B; 🖼 @) This English-run spot has a breezy setting between the main road and the sea, northwest of the Na Dan pier. If the rates were higher, this would be boutique with its cute cottage colours and a few stand-alone huts squatting above the ocean. Bring a fat book – it's a good place to get away. You'll need private transport to come and go.

✖ Eating & Drinking

Most hotels and guest houses have restaurants that moonlight as bars after sunset. The food and the service won't blow you away, but there aren't many alternatives. Nightly beach barbecues are an island favourite but try to pick one that looks professionally run – meaning that there is a steady stream of dishes being served and people eating rather than looking bored.

On weekends Ko Samet is a boisterous night-owl with provincial tour groups crooning away on karaoke machines or the young ones slurping down beer and buckets to a techno beat. The bar scene changes depending on who is around but there is usually a crowd on Hat Sai Khao, Ao Hin Khok, Ao Phai and Ao Wong Deuan.

Jep's Restaurant
INTERNATIONAL **$$**

(Ao Hin Khok; dishes 60-150B; ☺breakfast, lunch & dinner) Canopied by the branches of an arching tree decorated with pendant lights, this pretty place does a little of everything right on the beach.

Summer Restaurant
INTERNATIONAL **$$$**

(Baan Puu Paan, Ao Noi Na; dishes 250-400B; ☺dinner) In a crisp setting overlooking the harbour, Summer savours a globetrotters' culinary scrapbook, from Indian-style chicken tikka to Cajun chicken breasts.

Ban Ploy Samed
THAI **$$$**

(☎0 3864 4188; Ao Noi Na; dishes 300-600B; ☺dinner) Better than having to haul in your meal, you are hauled to this floating restaurant by a boat-and-pulley system. Fresh seafood dishes, especially the whole steamed fish variety, await.

Rabeang Bar
THAI **$**

(Na Dan; dishes 50-100B; ☺breakfast, lunch & dinner) Right by the ferry terminal, this over-the-water spot has good enough food to make you forget you have to leave the island.

Naga Bar
BAR

(Ao Hin Khok; drinks from 60B) The beachfront bar specialises in drinking games: coin tosses, *moo·ay tai* bouts and whisky buckets to give you courage.

Silver Sand Bar
BAR

(Ao Phai; drinks from 60B) Silver Sands progresses (regresses?) from dinner to cocktail buckets and dance floor gyrations and is a popular gay spot.

Baywatch Bar
BAR

(Ao Wong Deuan; drinks from 80B) There are a number of chill-out spaces for after-dark beach-gazing. The cocktails are strong and it's a fun evening crowd.

Ao Prao Resort
BAR

(Ao Prao; drinks from 80B) On the sunset-side of the island, this resort has a lovely sea-view restaurant perfect for an evening sundowner. You'll need to take private transport here.

❶ Information

There are several ATMs on Ko Samet, including near the Na Dan pier and Ao Wong Deuan.

Internet terminals or wi-fi are available at hotels on most beaches.

Ko Samet Health Centre (☎0 3861 1123; ☺8.30am-9pm Mon-Fri, 8.30am-4.30pm Sat & Sun) On the main road between Na Dan and Hat Sai Kaew. On-call mobile numbers are posted for after-hours emergencies.

National Parks main office (btwn Na Dan & Hat Sai Kaew) Has another office on Ao Wong Deuan.

Police station (☎1155) On the main road between Na Dan and Hat Sai Kaew. There's a substation on Ao Wong Deuan.

❶ Getting There & Away

Ko Samet is accessible from the mainland piers in Ban Phe. There are dozens of piers in Ban Phe, each used by different ferry companies, but they all charge the same fares (one way/return 50/100B, 40 minutes, hourly 8am to 4pm) and dock at Na Dan, the main pier on Ko Samet. Boats return to the mainland with the same frequency.

If you're staying at Ao Wong Deuan or further south, catch a ferry from the mainland directly to the beach (one way 50B, one hour, two daily departures).

When you buy your ticket on the mainland, you'll get the hard sell for a speedboat trip (2500B for the boat). The boat can hold 10 passengers (250B each) but it is never clear how long you have to wait for that price. But it is always an option if you're in a hurry; the boats go directly to your beach of choice.

Ticket agents on the mainland will also pressure you into pre-booking accommodation with a hefty commission tacked on. You'll be fine if you just show up on the island and start hunting for a room.

ⓘ Getting Around

Ko Samet's small size makes it a great place to explore on foot. A network of dirt roads connects most of the western side of the island.

Green *sŏrng·tăa·ou* meet arriving boats at the pier and provide drop-offs at the various beaches (20B to 80B, depending on the beach). If drivers don't have enough people to fill the vehicle, they either won't go or they will charge passengers 200B to 500B to charter the whole vehicle.

You can rent motorcycles nearly everywhere along the northern half of the island. Expect to pay about 300B per day. The dirt roads are rough and hazardous, and larger vehicles can leave behind blinding dust clouds. At any rate, make sure to test the brakes before you decide, and drive slowly around curves.

Chanthaburi จันทบุรี

POP 99,819

Chanthaburi is proof that all that glitters is not gold. Here, gemstones do the sparkling, attracting international traders, including Southeast Asians and Africans, dealing in sapphires, rubies, jade and other coloured stones. Thanks to the gem trade and its multicultural history (French, Vietnamese and Chinese), the so-called 'City of the Moon' is surprisingly diverse for a typical Thai town and worth visiting for an appreciation of the economic and religious sanctuary Thailand has long provided in the region.

The old city (also known as the Chantaboon Waterfront community) is the best place to chart the course of immigration and international involvement in the city. The Vietnamese began arriving in the 19th century when Christian refugees escaped religious and political persecution in Cochin China (southern Vietnam). A second wave of Vietnamese refugees followed in the 1920s and 1940s, fleeing French rule, and a third arrived after the 1975 communist takeover of southern Vietnam. The French occupied Chanthaburi from 1893 to 1905, while disputing with Siam over the borders of Indochina.

LOCAL KNOWLEDGE

LIVING WITH HISTORY

Pratapan Chatmalai is the community leader of the Chantaboon Waterfront Community Association. She grew up here and fondly remembers the tight-knit community of culturally diverse people. Today she works to save the stories and the character of the community.

What does your organisation do?

Now this community is a 'grandma' city. The old city is losing life and the young people have moved away. I want to keep the culture for the next generation to learn about and I'm trying to help the people in the area have a good life. We run the Learning House so that people can come look at the daily life of the past.

What do you recommend tourists see or do in the old city?

There is unique history and lifestyle of the past here. Come look at the cathedral, Chinese shrines and old houses. Each house is different and mixes Thai, Chinese and Western styles. Eat at the local restaurants. There are seafood noodles, old-style ice cream and dim sum. If you get tired, you can have a massage in an old Thai-style house.

What is your favourite part of the old city?

I love the whole place because it is a living museum and I can walk along and talk to the people about the past and make them happy.

As told to China Williams

Chanthaburi

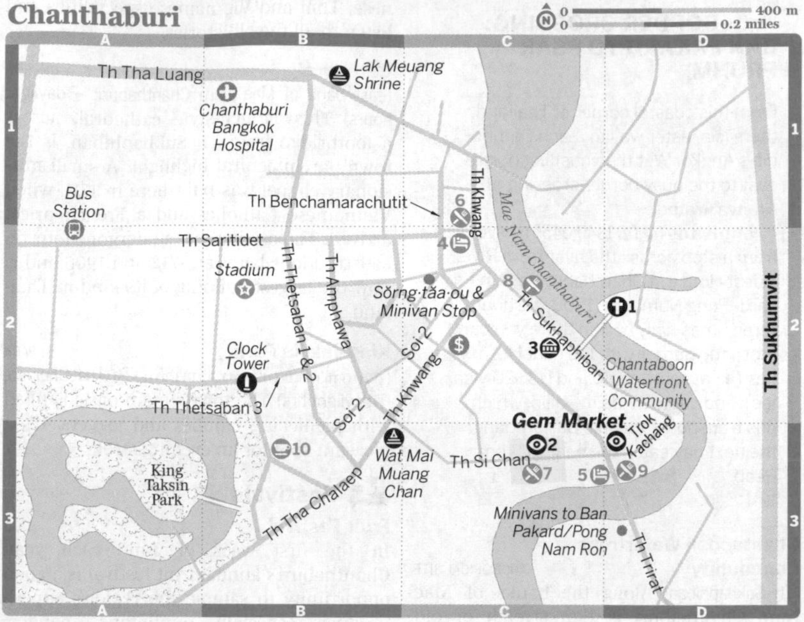

Chanthaburi

Top Sights
Gem Market D3

Sights
1 Cathedral D2
2 Gem Shops C3
3 Learning House C2

Sleeping
4 Kasemsarn Hotel C2
5 River Guest House C3

Eating
6 Chanthorn Phochana C1
7 Muslim Restaurant C3
8 Seafood Noodle Shop C2
9 Sony Yadaw D3

Drinking
10 Coffee Room B3

Sights & Activities

TOP CHOICE **Gem Market** MARKET

(ตลาดพลอย; Th Si Chan & Trok Kachang; Fri, Sat & Sun) On weekends, the streets and side streets near Th Si Chan (or 'Gem Rd') are overflowing with the banter and intrigue of the hard sell. It has the feel of an average Thai market, incongruously humble considering the preciousness of the commodity. People cluster around makeshift tables or even a trader's outstretched palm, examining small piles of unset stones. In the formal shops, hardnosed inspectors examine the gemstones under magnifying glasses looking for quality and authenticity. This is strictly a spectator sport and not recommended for the uninitiated, but it is a fascinating glimpse at a relatively private trade.

In the hills surrounding Chanthaburi, several sapphire and ruby mines once supplied the palace with fine ornaments prior to the mid-19th century when the mines were developed into commercial operations by Shan (Burmese) traders. These days, locally mined gems are of inferior international quality but the resourceful Chanthaburi traders roam the globe acquiring precious and semi-precious stones, which are in turn traded here to other globetrotters.

The last remaining mine in the area is **Khao Phloi Waen**, 6km from town, which is famous locally for its 'Mekong Whiskey' yellow-coloured sapphire.

ℹ️

BORDER CROSSING: BAN PAKARD TO PSAR PRUHM

From this coastal corner of Thailand, there is a faster way to reach Cambodia's Angkor Wat than hustling northeast to the busy border crossing of Aranya Prathet.

Minivans (☎08 1949 0455) leave from a stop across the river from River Guest House in Chanthaburi to Ban Pakard/Pong Nam Ron (150B, 1½ hours, three times daily). From there you can cross the border with the usual formalities (a passport photo and US$20 visa fee), and catch a ride to Pailin, which has transport to scenic Battambang; the next day catch the boat to Siem Reap.

Chantaboon Waterfront Community
HISTORICAL SITE

(Th Sukhaphiban) Along the banks of Mae Nam Chanthaburi is 1km stretch of old wooden shophouses that are valiantly being promoted and preserved as a living history museum. It is an atmospheric stroll through time and place with a uniquely Thai twist: food features more prominently than facts and figures.

Stop by the Learning House (☎08 1945 5761; ⊙9am-5pm) for an educational introduction to the community. The 2nd floor displays historic photographs of daily life as well as architectural drawings of the homes' beautifully carved ventilation panels. Much of the community's immigrant past is revealed in these unique panels: there are carvings of Chinese characters and even French fleurs-de-lis.

Farmers and merchants first settled on the fertile river banks some 300 years ago, establishing the area as an agricultural trading post. Chinese traders and economic migrants sought refuge here, thus diversifying the local population. Vietnamese Catholics fled from religious persecution in their home country. And before long the different groups had intermarried until everyone claimed a little bit of each.

Today, the older generation remains in the rickety old houses but through Khun Pratapan's efforts, many domestic tourists are coming for weekend outings to eat Chi-

nese, Thai and Vietnamese specialities and listen to all the old stories.

Cathedral
CHURCH

(east bank of Mae Nam Chanthaburi; ⊙daylight hours) This French-style cathedral, across a footbridge from Th Sukhaphiban, is the town's architectural highlight. A small missionary chapel was built here in 1711, when Vietnamese Catholics and a French priest arrived. The original has undergone four reconstructions between 1712 and 1906 and is now the largest building of its kind in Thailand.

King Taksin Park
PARK

(สวนสาธารณะสมเด็จพระเจ้าตากสิน; Th Tha Chalaep; ⊙daylight hrs) The town's main oasis is filled with picnicking families and joggers. It's a pleasant spot for an evening stroll.

✷ Festivals

Fruit Festival
FOOD

In the first week of June each year, Chanthaburi's annual fruit festival is a good opportunity to sample the region's superb produce, especially rambutans, mangosteens and the ever-pungent durian.

🛏 Sleeping

Accommodation can get very busy. Try to book ahead, especially from Friday to Sunday when the gem traders are in town.

River Guest House
HOTEL $

(☎0 3932 8211; 3/5-8 Th Si Chan; r 150-400B; ❄@) Standard hotel boxes aren't much to get excited about, but this is as good as it gets in the budget range. The relaxed sitting area and friendly staff are a plus. Try to score a room away from the highway.

Kasemsarn Hotel
HOTEL $$

(☎0 3931 1100; www.kasemsarnhotel.net; Th Benchamarachutit 98/1; r 1200-1500B; ❄@) Good enough for visiting Bangkokians, Kasemsarn has large modern rooms with generous weekday discounts.

🍴 Eating & Drinking

Seafood Noodle Shop
THAI $

(Th Sukhaphiban; dishes 25-50B; ⊙lunch & dinner) The old city, along Mae Nam Chanthaburi, is where you'll find most sightseeing Thais eating this Chanthaburi variation of the basic rice-noodle theme; nearby are other homemade snacks.

Sony Yadaw
INDIAN $

(Th Si Chan; dishes 30-100B; ⊖breakfast, lunch & dinner; ♪) Many South Asian gem dealers stop into this hole-in-the-wall vegetarian restaurant for a home-away-from-home meal.

Chanthorn Phochana
THAI-CHINESE $

(✐0 3931 2339; 102/5-8 Th Benchamarachutit; dishes 30-120B; ⊖breakfast, lunch & dinner) A dazzling array of Thai-Chinese meals includes such specialities as stir-fried papaya and local mangosteen wine. Try the Vietnamese spring rolls, and buy a bag of local durian chips (tastier than you think) for your next bus ride. It is totally packed on weekends.

Muslim Restaurant
MUSLIM THAI $

(✐08 1353 5174; cnr Soi 4, Th Si Chan; dishes 25-50B; ⊖9.30am-9pm) This tiny place has excellent paratha, *biryani*, curries and chai tea.

Coffee Room
CAFE $

(Th Tha Chalaep; drinks from 50B; ⊖breakfast & lunch) Across from King Taksin Park, this urban-style coffee shop is where upscale traders and visitors from Bangkok come to feel a little less provincial.

ⓘ Information

Banks with change facilities and ATMs can be found across town.

Bank of Ayudhya (Th Khwang)

Chanthaburi Bangkok Hospital (✐0 3935 1467; Th Tha Luang; ⊖6am-9pm) Part of the Bangkok group; handles emergencies.

ⓘ Getting There & Around

Buses operate from Chanthaburi's bus station to the following destinations:

Bangkok's Eastern (Ekamai) station (187B, 3½ hours, hourly 6am to 11.30pm)

Bangkok's Northern (Mo Chit) station (187B, four hours, two daily departures)

Trat (70B, 1½ hours, every 1½ hours 6.30am to 11.30pm)

Khorat (266B, hourly 6am to 6pm) Gateway to the northeast.

Sa Kaew (106B to 137B, hourly 6am to 10pm) Transfer point for buses to Aranya Prathet border crossing.

Minivans leave from a stop near the market and go to Trat (80B) and Rayong (100B). For Ko Samet–bound travellers, take the minivan directly to Ban Phe (120B).

Motorbike taxis around town cost 20B to 30B.

Trat
ตราด

POP 21,590

A major mainland transit point for Ko Chang and coastal Cambodia, Trat is underappreciated for its provincial charms. The guest-house neighbourhood occupies an atmospheric wooden shophouse district bisected by winding sois and filled with typical Thai street life: kids riding bikes, housewives running errands, small businesses selling trinkets and necessities. Since your destination is still so far away, why not stay a little longer and enjoy all the things you can't get on the islands: fresh, affordable fruit; tasty noodles; and tonnes of people-watching.

NATIONAL PARKS NEAR CHANTHABURI

Two small national parks are easily reached from Chanthaburi, and make good day trips. Both are malarial, so take the usual precautions.

Khao Khitchakut National Park (อุทยานแห่งชาติเขาคิชฌกูฏ; ✐0 3945 2074; admission 200B; ⊖8.30am-4.30pm) is 28km northeast of town. The cascade of **Nam Tok Krathing** is the main attraction; though it is only worth a visit just after the rainy season.

To get to Khao Khitchakut, take a *sŏrng·tăa·ou* from next to the post office, near the northern side of the market in Chanthaburi (35B, 45 minutes). The *sŏrng·tăa·ou* stops 1km from the park headquarters on Rte 3249, from which point you'll have to walk. Returning transport is a bit thin so expect to wait or hitch.

Nam Tok Phlio National Park (อุทยานแห่งชาติน้ำตกพลิ้ว; ✐0 3943 4528; admission 200B; ⊖8.30am-4.30pm), off Hwy 3, is 14km to the southeast of Chanthaburi and is much more popular. A pleasant, 1km nature trail loops around the waterfalls, which writhe with soro brook carp. To get to the park, catch a *sŏrng·tăa·ou* from the northern side of the market in Chanthaburi to the park entrance (40B, 30 minutes). You'll get dropped off about 1km from the entrance.

Accommodation is available at both parks; book with the **park reservation system** (✐0 2562 0760; www.dnp.go.th).

⊙ Sights

Trat's signature product is a **medicinal herbal oil** (known in Thai as *nám·man lěu·ang*), touted as a remedy for everything from arthritis to bug bites and available at local pharmacies. It's produced by resident Mae Ang-Ki (Somthawin Pasananon), using a secret pharmaceutical recipe that has been handed down through her Chinese-Thai family for generations. It's said if you leave Trat without a couple of bottles of *nám·man lěu·ang,* then you really haven't been to Trat.

Another booming business in the city is **swiftlet farming**. Walk down Th Lak Meuang and you'll soon figure out that the top floors of a shophouse have been purposefully converted into a nesting site for a flock of birds who produce the edible nests considered a delicacy among Chinese populations. Swiftlets' nests were quite rare (and expensive) because they were only harvested from precipitous sea caves by trained, daring climbers. But in the 1990s, entrepreneurs figured out how to replicate the cave atmosphere in multi-storey shophouses and the business has been a turn-key operation throughout Southeast Asia and here in Trat. Now many municipalities are dealing with the noise pollution of these moneymakers; have a listen for yourself.

Trat Province

Indoor Market MARKET

The indoor market sprawls east from Th Sukhumvit to Th Tat Mai and has a little bit of everything, especially all the things that you forgot to pack. Without really noticing the difference you will stumble upon the **day market**, selling fresh fruit, vegetables and takeaway food.

🛏 Sleeping

Trat has many budget hotels housed in traditional wooden houses on and around Th Thana Charoen. You'll find it hard to spend more even if you want to.

🏆 Ban Jaidee Guest House GUEST HOUSE $

(☑0 3952 0678; 6 Th Chaimongkol; r 200B; 🛜) In a charming neighbourhood, this relaxed traditional wooden house has simple rooms with shared bathrooms (hot-water showers). Paintings and objets d'art made by the artistically inclined owners decorate the common spaces. It's very popular and booking ahead is essential.

Residang Guest House GUEST HOUSE $

(☑0 3953 0103; www.trat-guesthouse.com; 87/1-2 Th Thana Charoen; r 260-600B; ❄🛜) Thick mattresses, hot-water showers, wi-fi – what more do you need? Fan rooms come with breezes and balconies. The owners keep an extensive list of transport information.

Garden Guest House GUEST HOUSE $

(☑0 3952 1018; 87/1 Th Sukhumvit; r 120-200B) A lovely grandmotherly type runs this guest house festooned with flowers and the flotsam of Thai life. Of the eight rooms, only one has a private bathroom.

Rimklong HOTEL $$

(☑08 1861 7181; 194 Th Lak Meuang; r 800B; ❄) Trat's first boutique hotel was under construction when we visited; but everything looked promising for the espresso-sipping crowd.

Sawadee GUEST HOUSE $

(☑0 3951 2392; sawadee_trat@yahoo.com; 90 Th Lak Meuang; r 100-300B) In a converted shophouse, this simple family-run place has fan rooms with shared bathroom.

Pop Guest House GUEST HOUSE $

(☑0 3951 2392; 1/1 Th Thana Charoen; r 150-500B; ❄@) You'll probably end up at Pop without intending to since the owners are generous with their taxi commissions and aggressive in procuring guests. The rooms are clean and cheap, but if you're an idealistic consumer, promote competition.

✖ Eating & Drinking

Trat is all about market eating: head to the day market on Th Tat Mai for *gah·faa boh·rahn* (ancient coffee), the indoor market for lunchtime noodles and the night market for a stir-fried dinner.

Cool Corner
TOP CHOICE · CAFE **$**

(☑08 4159 2030; 49-51 Th Thana Charoen; dishes 50-150B; ⊙breakfast, lunch & dinner) Run by Khun Morn, a modern Renaissance woman (writer, artist and traveller) from Bangkok, Cool Corner is an anchor of Trat's creative expats (both domestic and international) who moved to the city because of its small size, proximity to Bangkok and easygoing way of life. The cafe has a degree of sophistication that you don't usually find in provincial towns and serves up a great vibe, *phat* (cool) beats and darn good mango lassies.

Kluarimklong Cafe
THAI **$**

(☑0 3952 4919; cnr Soi Rimklong & Th Thana Charoen; dishes 70-90B; ⊙lunch & dinner) The winning combination here is delicious Thai food served in modern air-conditioned surroundings. The dishes are surprisingly affordable given the slick decor.

Oscar Bar
BAR

(Th Thana Charoen) Trat's artist and expat business owners can be found at this corner bar welcoming the end of the work day.

🛍 Shopping

Tratosphere Books
BOOKSHOP

(23 Soi Rimklong; ⊙8am-10pm) A good place to browse for secondhand titles and Thai handicrafts. Owner Serge is a fan and promoter of Trat and can point you to some unexplored corners.

ℹ Information

Th Sukhumvit runs through town, though it's often referred to as Th Ratanuson.

Bangkok Trat Hospital (☑0 3953 2735; Th Sukhumvit; ⊙24hr) Best health care in the region. It's 400m north of the town centre.

Krung Thai Bank (Th Sukhumvit) Has an ATM and currency-exchange facilities.

Police station (☑1155; cnr Th Santisuk & Th Wiwatthana) A short walk from Trat's centre.

Post office (Th Tha Reua Jang) East of Trat's commercial centre.

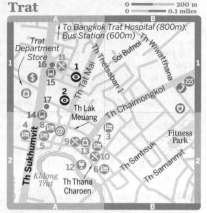

Trat

◉ Sights

1	Day Market	A1
2	Indoor Market	A1

🛏 Sleeping

3	Ban Jaidee Guest House	B2
4	Garden Guest House	A2
5	Pop Guest House	A2
6	Residang Guest House	A2
7	Rimklong	A2
8	Sawadee	A2

🍽 Eating

9	Cool Corner	A2
	Day Market	(see 1)
10	Kluarimklong Cafe	A2
11	Night Market	A1

🍷 Drinking

12	Oscar Bar	A2

🛍 Shopping

13	Tratosphere Books	A2

ℹ Transport

14	Family Tour (Minivans to Bangkok)	A2
15	Minivans to Chanthaburi	A1
16	Sŏrng·tăa·ou to bus station, Laem Ngop	A1
17	Sŏrng·tăa·ou to Tha Centrepoint (Laem Ngop)	A1

Sawadee@Cafe Net (☑0 3952 0075; Th Lak Meuang; per min 1B; ⊙10am-10pm) Internet and Skype are both available.

Telephone office (Th Tha Reua Jang) Near the post office.

WORTH A TRIP

SCRATCHING THE BEACH ITCH

If you're going through coastal withdrawal, the sliver of Trat Province that extends southeast towards Cambodia is fringed by sandy beaches. One of the easiest beaches to reach is **Hat Mai Rut**, roughly halfway between Trat and the border crossing of Hat Lek. Nearby is a traditional fishing village filled with colourful wooden boats and the sights and smells of a small-scale industry carried on by generations of families. **Mairood Resort** (☎08 414858; www.mairood-resort.com; Km 53; r 500-1000B; ✴@✶) is a lovely spot to stay overnight and is run by an English-speaking Thai who lived for many years in the US. After being abroad for so long, he is able to explain the unique aspects of this area to foreigners. The resort has simple huts by the sea and in the mangroves.

You can get to Hat Mai Rut from the Trat bus station via Hat Lek–bound *sŏrng·tăa·ou*. The resort is 3km from the Km 53 highway marker.

Trat Map (www.Tratmap.com) An online directory of businesses and attractions in Trat.

ℹ Getting There & Around

Air

The airport is 40km from town; a taxi to the airport from Trat town costs a ridiculous 500B. **Bangkok Airways** (☎Trat airport 0 3955 1654-5, in Bangkok 0 2265 5555; www.bangkokair.com) flies to the following destinations:

Bangkok (one way from 2090B, three times daily)

Ko Samui (one way from 3390B, three times weekly) Via Bangkok.

Phuket (one way from 4090B, three times weekly) Via Bangkok.

Bus & Minivans

Trat's bus station is outside of town and serves the following destinations:

Bangkok's Eastern (Ekamai) station (248B, 4½ hours, hourly 6am to 11.30pm)

Bangkok's Northern (Mo Chit) station (248B, 5½ hours, two morning departures)

Bangkok's Suvarnabhumi (airport) station (248B, four to 4½ hours, five daily departures)

Chanthaburi (70B, 1½ hours, every 1½ hours 6.30am to 11.30pm)

Hat Lek (120B to 150B, one hour) Minivans depart when full; morning departures are more frequent.

There are also many in-town options. Minivans to Chanthaburi (80B) leave when full from a stop on Th Sukhumvit north of the indoor market. **Family Tour** (☎08 1996 2216; Th Sukhumvit cnr Th Lak Meuang) runs minivans to Bangkok's Victory Monument (300B, five hours, hourly 8am to 5pm) and continues on to Th Khao San (350B).

Local *sŏrng·tăa·ou* leave from Th Sukhumvit near the market for the bus station (20B to 60B, depending on number of passengers).

Boat

The piers that handle boat traffic to/from Ko Chang are located in Laem Ngop, about 30km southwest of Trat.

There are three piers in Laem Ngop each used by different boat companies, but the most convenient services are through Koh Chang Ferry (from Tha Thammachat) and Centrepoint Ferry (from Tha Centrepoint). See p227 for price and departure details on these ferry services.

From Trat town, shared *sŏrng·tăa·ou* leave from a stop on Th Sukhumvit to Laem Ngop's Tha Centrepoint (50B per person for six passengers, 45 minutes). To reach Tha Thammachat, inquire about pier transfers when you buy your ticket or charter a *sŏrng·tăa·ou* (60B per person for six people or 300B for the vehicle). It should be the same charter price if you want to go directly from Trat's bus station to the pier.

From Bangkok, you can catch a bus from Bangkok's Eastern (Ekamai) station all the way to Tha Centrepoint (250B, five hours, three morning departures). This route includes a stop at Suvarnabhumi (airport) bus station as well as Trat's bus station. In the reverse direction, buses have two afternoon departures from Laem Ngop.

If you want to skip Ko Chang and head straight to the neighbouring islands (Ko Wai, Ko Mak and Ko Kut), see those sections for mainland transport options.

Ko Chang   เกาะช้าง

POP 7033

With steep, jungle-covered peaks erupting from the sea, picturesque Ko Chang (Elephant Island) retains its remote and rugged spirit despite its current status as a package-tour resort akin to Phuket. The island's swathes of sand are girl-next-door pretty but not beauty-queen gorgeous. What it lacks in sand, it makes up for in an unlikely combination: accessible wilderness with a thriving party scene. Convenient forays into a verdant jungle or underwater coral gardens can be enthusiastically toasted at one of Lonely Beach's many beer and bucket parties.

A little more than a decade ago, Ko Chang didn't have 24-hour electricity, was still considered malarial, had few paved roads and fewer motorised vehicles. Today it is still a slog to get here, but there is a constant migration of visitors: Russian package tourists, Cambodia-bound backpackers and beach-hopping couples funnelling through to more remote islands in the Mu Ko Chang National Marine Park. Along the populous west coast are virtual mini-cities with a standard of living that has noticeably outpaced the island's infrastructure, a common problem on many Thai islands: Ko Chang struggles to provide decent sanitation and alternative means of transport to an ever-expanding nonresident population.

◉ Sights

Though Thailand's second-largest island has accelerated into modernity with some understandable growing pains, Ko Chang still has tropically hued seas, critter-filled jungles and a variety of water sports for athletic beach bums.

WEST COAST

The west coast has the island's widest and sandiest beaches and the greatest amount of development. Frequent public *sŏrng·tăa·ou* make beach-hopping easy and affordable. It is a good idea to bring swim shoes, especially for children, as many of the beaches are rocky in spots. These shallow, gentle seas are great for inexperienced swimmers, but do be careful of riptides during the storms and the rainy season (May to September).

Hat Sai Khao (White Sand Beach)   BEACH
(หาดทรายขาว) The longest, most luxurious stole of sand on the island is packed with package-tour hotels and serious sunbathers. Finding a blanket's-worth of sand can be tough during the high season, unless you wait until the hot hours of the afternoon or hike past KC Grande Resort towards the remarkably low-key backpacker area in the far northern section of the beach. Along the main road, the village is busy, loud and brash – but the extremities provide a convenient break.

Hat Kai Mook (Pearl Beach)   BEACH
(หาดไข่มุก) The pearls here are large pebbles that pack the shore and culminate in fish-friendly headlands. Swimming and sunbathing are out but there's good snorkelling. The stylish restaurant Saffron by the Sea is a scenic perch should you prefer to wet your palette instead.

Ao Khlong Prao   BEACH
(อ่าวคลองพร้าว) A relaxed counterpoint to Hat Sai Khao's energy, Khlong Prao's beach is a pretty sweep of sand pinned between hulking mountainous headlands and bisected by two estuaries. At low tide, beachcombers stroll the rippled sand eyeing the critters left naked by the receding water. Sprawling luxury resorts dominate Khlong Prao and the primary pastime is sunbathing at seaside pools since high tide tends to gobble up most of the beach.

KO CHANG & EASTERN SEABOARD KO CHANG

BORDER CROSSING: HAT LEK TO KRONG KOH KONG

For coastal border crossers, the closest Thai-Cambodian crossing is at the Thai town of Hat Lek into the Cambodian town of Krong Koh Kong. This crossing poises you for transit to Sihanoukville (via Krong Koh Kong) or Ko Chang (via Trat).

If you're leaving Thailand, catch a minivan from Trat's bus station to Hat Lek (120B to 150B) and continue on to Cambodian immigration.

Cambodian tourist visas are available at the border for 1200B (though other borders charge only US$20); payment is only accepted in baht at this border. If you try to debate the issue, be prepared for an argument. Be sure to bring a passport photo and try to avoid some of the runner boys who want to issue a health certificate or other 'medical' paperwork.

From the Cambodian border, take a private taxi (US$10) or moto (US$3) to Koh Kong where you can catch onward transport to Sihaunokville (four hours, one or two departures per day) and Phonm Penh (five hours, two or three departures till 11.30am). You can also use this border to renew your Thai visa, but do note that visas at land borders have been shortened to 15 days. This border crossing closes at 8pm.

Ko Chang

With hired transport, you can depart the beach for some waterfall-spotting. The island's biggest is **Nam Tok Khlong Plu** (park fee 200B; ⊗8am-5pm), a three-tiered cascade with a swimmable pool. It is reached via a 600m jungle path and is most stunning just after the rainy season months and in the morning before the crowds arrive.

Hat Kaibae
BEACH

(หาดไก่แบ้) A companion beach to Khlong Prao, Hat Kaibae is a great spot for families and thirty-something couples. A slim strip of sand unfurls around an island-dotted bay far enough removed from the package tour scene that you'll feel self-righteously independent. There's kayaking to the outlying island and low tide provides hours of beachcombing.

Lonely Beach
BEACH

The island's backpacker hang-out is the five-o'clock shadow of beaches, a bit scruffy but ready for fun. During the day, most sunbathers are baking off a hangover earned the night before when Lonely Beach becomes the most social place on the island. The music is loud, the drinks are strong and the crowd is youthful and carefree.

Ban Bang Bao
VILLAGE

(บ้านบางเบ้า) Nearly at the end of the west coast road, Bang Bao is a former fishing community built in the traditional fashion of interconnected piers. The villagers have swapped their nets for the tourist trade by renting out portions of their homes to souvenir shops and restaurants. Though it isn't a traditional experience, the resulting commercialism is extremely Thai, much like a mainland market with every possible space dedicated to selling something. Follow the pier all the way to the end and you'll find a big blue ocean and boats waiting to take you past the horizon. Most visitors come for a seafood meal and some decide to stay overnight. Wrap up your visit before sunset as taxis become scarcer and more expensive after dark.

Khlong Kloi BEACH
At the eastern end of Ao Bang Bao, Khlong Kloi is a sandy beach that feels a lot like a secret though there are other people here and all the requisite amenities (beer, fruit, food, massage) and a few guest houses if you want the place to yourself. You'll need private transport to get out here.

NORTHERN INTERIOR
Ko Chang's mountainous interior is predominately protected as a national park. The forest is lush and alive with wildlife and threaded by silver-hued waterfalls. For information about hiking tours, see p220).

Ban Kwan Chang ELEPHANT CAMP
(บ้านควาญช้าง; ☎08 1919 3995; changtone@yahoo.com; ⊗8.30am-5pm) In a beautiful forested setting, this camp offers a quiet and intimate experience with its nine resident elephants. A one-hour visit (900B) involves feeding, bathing and riding an elephant and hotel transfer is included. Be sure to wear mozzie spray.

Pittaya Homkrailas is the camp owner and a well-regarded conservation enthusiast who works to preserve a humane relationship between the elephant and mahout. His interest in environmental and community issues also includes efforts to preserve the southeastern mangroves in Ao Salak Kok on the island's east coast.

EAST COAST
The east coast is still peaceful and undeveloped, mainly undulating hills of coconut and palm trees and low-key fishing villages that have resisted the resort rush of the west coast. You'll need private transport to explore this lost coast of scenic bays and mangrove forests.

Nam Tok Than Mayom WATERFALL
(น้ำตกธารมะยม; park fee 200B; ⊗8am-5pm) A series of three falls along the stream of Khlong Mayom can be reached via the park office near Tha Than Mayom. The view from the top is superb and nearby there are inscribed stones bearing the initials of Rama V, Rama VI and Rama VII.

Ao Salak Kok MANGROVE BAY
(อ่าวสลักคอก) From a hotel developers' perspective, this thick tangle of mangroves is an unprofitable wasteland. But the local population of fisherfolk recognises that its beauty and profit is in its environmental fertility. Mangroves are the ocean's nurseries, fostering the next generation of marine species as well as resident birds and crustaceans.

Thanks to its natural state, the bay is now Ko Chang's leading example of ecotourism. Villagers, working in conjunction with Khun Pittaya, of Ban Kwan Chang elephant park, operate an award-winning program to preserve the environment and the traditional way of life. They rent kayaks through the Salak Kok Kayak Station and run an affiliated restaurant.

Ban Salak Phet VILLAGE
(บ้านสลักเพชร) In the southeast pocket of the island is Ban Salak Phet, a surprisingly bustling Thai community of fisherfolk and merchants plus lots of bike-riding kids and yawning dogs. This is what most of Ko Chang looked like less than a generation ago. Just beyond the commercial heart of the village is Ao Salak Phet, a beautiful blue bay serenely guarded by humpbacked islands. Most visitors come for the seafood

---

ⓘ ECO VS FUN: DON'T FEED THE ANIMALS

On many of the around-the-island boat tours, operators amaze their guests with a stop at a rocky cliff to feed the wild monkeys. It seems innocent enough and even entertaining but there's an unfortunate consequence. The animals become dependent on this food source and when the boats don't come as often during the low season the young and vulnerable ones are ill-equipped to forage in the forest.

The same goes for the dive or boat trips that feed the fish leftover lunches or bread bought on the pier specifically for this purpose. It is a fantastic way to show young children a school of brilliantly coloured fish but the downside is that the fish forsake the coral reefs for an easier meal. Without the fishes' daily grooming efforts the coral is soon overgrown with algae and will eventually suffocate. Sorry to ruin the fun.

KO CHANG IN...

Four Days

Lay on the beach, roll over to the other side and repeat. Do this until you get sunburned or bored and then rouse yourself out of the sun-induced stupor to explore the island. Do a **day hike** through the jungle or view the island from aboard a **kayak**. Catch a *sŏrng·tăa·ou* to **Bang Bao** for lunch or an early dinner and work off your meal with some souvenir shopping. The next day rent a motorbike and explore the **east coast**.

One Week

Devote a few days to giving back to the island by volunteering at **Koh Chang Animal Project** or **Koh Chang Pony Rehabilitation Project**. Migrate to the nearby islands of **Ko Wai** or **Ko Kut** for a little island sightseeing.

restaurants or to cruise the lonely byways for a secluded beach.

Nam Tok Khiri Phet   WATERFALL

(น้ำตกคีรีเพชร) This small waterfall, 2km from Ban Salak Phet, is a 15-minute walk from the road and rewards you with a small, deep plunge pool. It's usually quieter than many of the larger falls and is easily reached if you're in the neighbourhood of Ao Salak Phet.

🏃 Activities

Kayaking

Ko Chang cuts an impressive and heroic profile when viewed from the sea aboard a kayak. The water is generally calm and off-shore islands provide a paddling destination that is closer than the horizon. Most hotels rent open-top kayaks (from 300B per day) that are convenient for near-shore outings and noncommittal kayakers.

KayakChang   KAYAKING

(☑08 7673 1923; www.kayakchang.com; Amari Emerald Cove Resort, Khlong Prao) For more serious paddlers, KayakChang rents high-end, closed-top kayaks (from 1000B per day) that handle better and travel faster. They also lead one- and multi-day trips to other islands in the archipelago.

Salak Kok Kayak Station   KAYAKING

(☑08 1919 3995; kayak rentals per hr 100B) On the east side of the island, explore the island's mangrove swamps of Ao Salak Kok while supporting an award-winning eco-tour program. Salak Kok Kayak Station rents self-guided kayaks and is a village-work project designed to promote tourism without deteriorating the traditional way of

life. The kayak station can also help arrange village homestays and hiking tours.

Hiking

Ko Chang is unusual in Thailand for having a well-developed trekking scene. The island is blessed with lush forests filled with birds, monkeys, lizards and beautiful flowers. Best of all there are a handful of guides who speak English that know and love the forest so that it can be shared with tourists.

Mr Tan from **Evolution Tour** (☑0 3955 7078; www.evolutiontour.com) or Lek from **Jungle Way** (☑08 9247 3161; www.jungleway.com) lead one-day treks (800B to 1400B) through Khlong Son Valley. The trip works up a sweat and then rewards the work with a waterfall swim and a stop at the Ban Kwan Chang elephant camp. Multi-day trips can be arranged through both. Mr Tan also has family-friendly treks and a hike that heads west from Khlong Son to Hat Sai Khao.

Koh Chang Trekking   HIKING, BIRD-WATCHING

(☑08 1588 3324; www.kohchangtrekking.info) Bird-watchers should contact Koh Chang Trekking which runs one- and two-day trips (1000B to 2000B) into the national park and hikes to the top of Khao Chom Prasat, two nearby rocky tipped peaks.

Salak Phet Kayak Station   HIKING

(☑08 7834 9489; from 1500B) Guides overnight treks on Khao Salak Phet, Ko Chang's highest peak, which rises 744km into the heavens and provides a sunrise and sunset view. Though the altitude might be modest, this is one of the few places in Thailand where you can combine such serious exertion with a coastal landscape; you can choose to sleep in a tent or under the stars.

Volunteering

Koh Chang Animal Project   VOLUNTEERING

(☑08 9042 2347; www.kohchanganimalproject.org; Ban Khlong Son) Abused, injured or abandoned animals receive medical care and refuge at this nonprofit centre, established in 2002 by American Lisa McAlonie. The centre also works with local people on spaying, neutering and general veterinarian services, and Lisa is well-known on the island by concerned pet owners and flea-ridden dogs. Volunteers, especially travelling vets and vet nurses, are welcome to donate a bit of TLC and elbow grease for the cause. Call to make an appointment. Most *sŏrng·tăa·ou* drivers know how to get here; tell them you're going to 'Ban Lisa' (Lisa's House) in Khlong Son.

Koh Chang Pony Rehabilitation Project   VOLUNTEERING

(☑08 9723 4278; ponyproject.org; Ban Khlong Son) On the same street as Ban Lisa, this centre works to rescue and rehabilitate abused and neglected equines. Volunteers can help feed, clean and exercise the ponies and horses that are recovering from injuries or awaiting adoption in caring environments.

🍽 Courses

Break up your lazy days with classes designed to enhance mind and body. Khlong Prao hosts two well-regarded culinary schools. Cooking classes at both are typically four to five hours, include a market tour and cost 1200B per person; book ahead.

Koh Chang Thai Cookery School   COOKING

(☑0 3955 7243; Blue Lagoon Bungalows, Khlong Prao) Slices, dices and sautés in a shady open-air kitchen beside the estuary.

KaTi   COOKING

(☑0 3955 7252; main road, Khlong Prao) Across from Tropicana Resort, is run by a mother and daughter team teaching family recipes.

Baan Zen   YOGA, MEDITATION

(☑08 6530 9354; www.baanzen.com; Khlong Prao; classes from 5500B) Hidden down an unpaved road between Noren Resort and Coco Massage in Khlong Prao. It is a peaceful and relaxing setting for classes in yoga, reiki and meditation.

Sima Massage   MASSAGE

(☑08 1489 5171; main road, Khlong Prao; massage per hr 250B; ⊗8am-10pm) Across from Tropicana Resort, and regarded by locals as the best massage on the island – quite an accolade in a place where a massage is easier to find than a 7-Eleven.

Bailan Herbal Sauna   SAUNA

(☑08 6252 4744; Ban Bailan, across from Bailan Inn; ⊗4-9pm) Sweating on purpose might seem like a free and unintended consequence of tropical living but, just south of Lonely Beach, Bailan continues an old-fashioned Southeast Asian tradition of the village sauna. Set amid lush greenery, the earthen huts are heated with a health-promoting stew of herbs. There's also massage, facial treatments and a post-steam juice bar.

🛏 Sleeping

Ko Chang's package-tour industry has distorted accommodation pricing. In general rates have risen while quality has not, partly because hotels catering to group tours are guaranteed occupancy and don't have to maintain standards to woo repeat visitors or walk-ins. There is also a lot of copy-cat pricing giving value-oriented visitors little to choose from.

A few places close down during the wet season (April to October) and rates drop precipitously. Consider booking ahead and shopping for online discounts during peak season (November to March), weekends and holidays.

WEST COAST

On the west coast, Lonely Beach is still the best budget option, Hat Kai Bae is the

---

ℹ **NATIONAL PARK STATUS**

Parts of Ko Chang are protected and maintained as a national park. Though their conservation efforts are a bit amorphic, you will be required to pay a 200B park entrance fee when visiting some of the waterfalls (entrance fees are stated in the reviews and payable at the site). **National Park headquarters** (☑0 3955 5080; Ban Than Mayom; ⊗8am-5pm) is on the eastern side of the island near Nam Tok Than Mayom.

Do also be aware that nudity and topless sunbathing are forbidden by law in Mu Ko Chang National Marine Park; this includes all beaches on Ko Chang, Ko Kut, Ko Mak etc.

DON'T MISS

DIVING & SNORKELLING

The dive sites near Ko Chang offer a variety of coral, fish and beginner-friendly shallow waters on par with other Gulf of Thailand dive sites.

The seamounts off the southern tip of the island within the Ko Chang marine park are reached within a 30-minute cruise. Popular spots include **Hin Luk Bat** and **Hin Rap**, rocky, coral-encrusted seamounts with depths of around 18m to 20m. These are havens for schooling fish and some turtles.

By far the most pristine diving in the area is around **Ko Rang**, an uninhabited island protected from fishing by its marine park status. Visibility here is much better than near Ko Chang and averages between 10m and 20m. Everyone's favourite dive is **Hin Gadeng**, spectacular rock pinnacles with coral visible to around 28m. On the eastern side of Ko Rang, **Hin Kuak Maa** (also known as Three Finger Reef) is another top dive and is home to a coral-encrusted wall sloping from 2m to 14m and attracting swarms of marine life.

Ko Yak, **Ko Tong Lang** and **Ko Laun** are shallow dives perfect for both beginners and advanced divers. These small rocky islands can be circumnavigated and have lots of coral, schooling fish, puffer fish, morays, barracuda, rays and the occasional turtle.

Reef-fringed **Ko Wai** features a good variety of colourful hard and soft corals and is great for snorkelling. It is a popular day-tripping island but has simple overnight accommodation for more alone time with the reef.

Dive operators estimate that about 30% of the area's coral reefs were destroyed during the global bleaching phenomenon of 2010. In response park officials closed some areas of the Ko Rang marine park; ask the dive operators which sites are open.

Diving trips typically cost around 2800B to 3500B. PADI Open Water certification costs 14,500B per person. Recently dive shops remain open during the rainy season (June to September) but visibility and sea conditions can be poor. The following are recommend dive operators:

» **BB Divers**
(☑0 3955 8040; www.bbdivers.com) Based at Bang Bao with branches in Lonely Beach, Khlong Prao and Hat Sai Khao.

» **Scuba Zone**
(☑0 3961 9035; www.scuba-kohchang.com) Based at Hat Sai Khao; the instructors come highly recommended.

---

best-value option and Hat Sai Khao is the most overpriced.

HAT SAI KHAO

The island's prettiest beach is also its most expensive. The northern and southern extremities have some budget and midrange options worth considering if you need proximity to the finest sand. There's a groovy backpacker enclave north of KC Grande Resort accessible only via the beach. We've listed two here but there are more further north.

At the southern end, you can find some good value budget and midrangers but this end of the beach is rocky and lacking sand during high tide.

If you want to splash out, don't do it on Hat Sai Khao where good money will be wasted.

Independent Bo's   GUEST HOUSE $
(☑08 5283 5581; r 350-550B) A colourful place on the jungle hillside exuding a creative, hippie vibe that Ko Chang used to be famous for. All bungalows are funky and different. The cheapest rooms are 'way, way' up in the jungle. First come, first served.

Rock Sand Beach Resort   GUEST HOUSE $$
(☑08 4781 0550; www.rocksand-resort.com; r 550-2000B; ❋) Just past Bo's, Rock Sand takes budget accommodation up a notch. Simple fan bungalows share bathrooms, while the highest-priced air-con rooms look out over the sea. The restaurant is popular and hovers over the clear blue water.

Koh Chang Hut Hotel   HOTEL $$
(☑08 1865 8123; r 600-1500B; ❋☎) Next to Plaloma Cliff Resort at the southern end of the beach, this cliff-side hotel puts you

within walking distance of the beach without spending a lot of baht. More expensive oceanfront rooms drink in the view, while cheaper streetside rooms are noisier.

Keereeelé HOTEL **$$**
(☏0 3955 1285; www.keereeele.com; r 2000B; ✳☎☀) An excess of 'e's in the name doesn't detract from the merits of this new multi-storey hotel on the interior side of the road. The rooms are modern and comfortable and some have views of the verdant mountains behind. Beach access is 300m via sidewalks so you don't have to play chicken with traffic.

Sai Khao Inn GUEST HOUSE **$$**
(☏0 3955 1584; www.saikhaoinn.com; r 800-1800B; ✳) A garden setting on the interior side of the road, Sai Khao Inn has a little bit of everything – bungalows, concrete bunkers, big rooms, even rooms for taxi drivers (according to the brochure).

AO KHLONG PRAO
Ao Khlong Prao is dominated by high-end resorts and just a few budget spots peppered in between. There is a handful of cheapies on the main road that are within walking distance to the beach, though traffic can be treacherous and noisy.

Blue Lagoon Bungalows GUEST HOUSE **$**
(☏08 6330 0094; r 600-1000B; ✳) An exceedingly friendly garden spot, Blue Lagoon has simple wooden bungalows with private decks beside a peaceful estuary. A wooden walkway leads to the beach.

Tiger Huts GUEST HOUSE **$**
(☏08 1762 3710; r 600B) The only thing that separates these wooden huts from labourer shanties is indoor plumbing. They are low on comfort and hospitality, but high on location claiming the widest and prettiest part of the beach. The neighbouring resorts must be very jealous.

Aana HOTEL **$$$**
(☏0 3955 1539; www.aanaresort.com; r from 7000B; ✳☎☀) Private villas perch prettily above the forest and Khlong Prao, kayaking distance from the beach. The rooms are effortlessly romantic and have verandahs and views.

Lin Bungalows GUEST HOUSE **$$**
(☏08 4120 1483; r 800-1200B; ✳) Opposite Blue Lagoon, a variety of sealed concrete bungalows facing the beach.

Baan Rim Nam GUEST HOUSE **$$**
(☏08 7005 8575; www.iamkohchang.com; r from 1100B; ✳☎) Converted fisherman's-house-turned-guest house teeters over a mangrove-lined river; kayaks and dialled-in advice free of charge.

Sofia Resort GUEST HOUSE **$$**
(☏0 3955 7314; www.jussinhotel.net; r 900-1200B; ✳☎☀) Great price for the comfort factor but the trade-off is the location on the main road without direct beach access.

Boonya Resort GUEST HOUSE **$**
(☏0 3955 7361; r from 800B; ✳☎☀) Another main road option that would be a fab find if the beds weren't bare springs.

HAT KAIBAE
Hat Kaibae has some of the island's best variety of accommodation, from boutique hotels to budget huts and midrange bungalows. It is a great beach for families and flashpackers.

TOP CHOICE **KB Resort** HOTEL **$$**
(☏0 1862 8103; www.kbresort.com; r 2000-3500B; ✳@☀) Lemon yellow bungalows have cheery bathrooms and pose peacefully beside the sea. Listen to the gentle lapping surf while the kids construct mega-cities in the sand. Skip the overpriced fan bungalows, though.

Buzza's Bungalows GUEST HOUSE **$**
(☏08 7823 6674; r from 400B; ✳@) Solid concrete bungalows with porches face each other creating a laid-back travellers ambience. It is a short and hassle-free stroll to the beach.

Kaibae Hut Resort HOTEL **$$**
(☏0 3955 7142; r 700-2500B; ✳) Sprawling across a scenic stretch of beach, Kaibae Hut has sane prices and a variety of lodging options – slightly worn fan huts, fancier concrete bungalows and modern hotel-style rooms. A large open-air restaurant fires up nightly barbecues and there's plenty of room for free-range kids.

Garden Resort HOTEL **$$**
(☏0 3955 7260; www.gardenresortkohchang.com; r from 2500B; ✳@☀) On the interior side of the main road, Garden Resort has picture-window bungalows blossoming in a shady garden with a salt-water swimming pool. The owners are friendly and kid-oriented, thanks to their own child.

GajaPuri Resort & Spa   HOTEL $$$

(☑0 2713 7689; www.gajapuri.com; r from 6900B; ❄@☎) Polished wooden cottages gleam with quintessential Thai touches so that you have a sense of place and pampering. Oversized beds with crisp linens, sun-drenched reading decks and a pretty beach are even more luxurious if you score an online discount.

Porn's Bungalows   GUEST HOUSE $

(☑08 9251 9233; www.pornsbungalows-kohchang. com; r 800-900B) Kaibae's resident rasta scene hangs out in a shady coconut grove beside the beach; wooden fan bungalows with hot-water showers. First come, first served.

Siam Cottage   GUEST HOUSE $

(☑08 9153 6664; www.siamcottagekohchang.com; r 500-800B; ❄) Rickety wooden bungalows packed perpendicular to the beach don't afford much privacy but a nice slice of sand is right at your feet.

LONELY BEACH

A backpacker party fave, Lonely Beach is one of the cheapest places to sleep on the island, though oceanfront living has mostly moved upmarket, pushing the penny-pinchers into the interior village. If you've been flashpackerised, there are several creative midrangers that will save you from carbon-copy resorts. This end of the island is less developed and the jungle broods just over the squatty commercial strip.

TOP CHOICE Paradise Cottages   HOTEL $$

(☑08 5831 4228; www.paradisecottagekohchang. com; r 700-1200B; ❄☎) A whole lot of chillin'-out happens at this mellow flashpacker spot. Dining hammocks hang over the water for guests to savour a meal with a view. The usual concrete huts are dressed up with style and function. Though it is oceanfront, the beach is too muddy and rocky for swimming.

Oasis Bungalows   GUEST HOUSE $

(☑08 1721 2547; www.oasis-khochang.com; r from 350B; ☎) Sitting at the end of an interior soi, Oasis has basic wooden bungalows in a pretty fruit and flower garden. The hillside restaurant peeks at the ocean above the tree tops and is a pleasant place for traveller camaraderie. You'll have to walk through the village and down the main road to get to the beach. If Oasis is full, this soi is filled with comparable options.

Warapura Resort   HOTEL $$

(☑08 3987 4777; www.warapuraresort.com; r 2000-3500B; ❄@☎) Chic for relatively cheap, Warapura has a collection of adorable cottages tucked in between the village and a mangrove beach. The oceanfront pool is perfect for people who would rather gaze at the ocean than frolic in it.

Kachapura   GUEST HOUSE $

(☑08 60500754; www.kachapura.com; r 500-1800B; ❄☎) Warapura's modest sister, Kachapura does budget with care. Wooden walkways navigate a shady garden to clean and tidy bungalows that are basic but not busted up. It sits right in the middle of the village; no direct beach access.

🌿 Mangrove   HOTEL $

(☑08 1949 7888; r 1000B) South of Lonely Beach is the real deal when it comes to an eco-lodge committed to a smaller footprint. Cascading down a forested hill to a private beach, Mangrove has beautiful yet simple bungalows purposefully designed with accordion-style doors that open to the views and the breezes (a natural air-con). The ambience is a pleasing combo of private rustic-chic.

BAN BANG BAO

Despite its touristy veneer, Ban Bang Bao is still a charming place to stay for folks who prefer scenery to swimming. Accommodation is mainly converted pier houses overlooking the sea with easy access to departing inter-island ferries. Daytime transport to a swimmable beach is regular thanks to the steady arrival and departure of day trippers. Night owls should either hire a motorbike or stay elsewhere as *sŏrng·tăa·ou* become rare and expensive after dinnertime.

TOP CHOICE Bang Bao Sea Hut   HOTEL $$

(☑08 1285 0570; r 2500B; ❄) With individual bungalows built on the edge of Bang Bao's pier, this is one of Ko Chang's most unusual places to stay. Each 'hut' (actually much flasher than it sounds) is surrounded by a private deck where breakfast is served, with wooden shutters opening to the sea breeze.

Bang Bao Cliff Cottage   GUEST HOUSE $

(☑08 5904 6706; www.cliff-cottage.com; r 350-700B) Partially hidden on a verdant hillside west of the pier are a few dozen simple thatch huts overlooking a rocky cove. Most have sea views and a couple offer spectacular vistas. There's easy-access snorkelling down below.

Ocean Blue GUEST HOUSE $
(☎08 1889 2348; www.oceanbluethailand.com; r 800B) Simple fan rooms line a long, polished-wood hallway at this traditional pier house. Toilets are the bucket variety, and showers are cold, but the rooms are clean and you can hear the ocean slosh beneath you. The crew running the place are quirky and funny.

Nirvana HOTEL $$$
(☎0 3955 8061; www.nirvanakohchang.com; r 3500-7000B; ❄️🛜❄️) Ko Chang's premium resort is its own private universe hidden away on a rocky, jungle-filled peninsula. Come to get away from it all, including everything else on the island, and to enjoy the stunning sea views from the comfort of the individually decorated Balinese-style bungalows. The adjacent beach is scenic but not swimmable.

NORTHERN INTERIOR & EAST COAST
The northern and eastern part of the island is less developed than the west coast and feels more isolated. You'll need your own transport and maybe even a posse not to feel lonely out here, but you'll be rewarded with a quieter, calmer experience.

Jungle Way GUEST HOUSE $
(☎08 9247 3161; www.jungleway.com; Khlong Son Valley; r 200-400B) Ko Chang's un-sung attribute is its jungle interior and the English-speaking guides who grew up playing in it. Lek, a local guide, and his family run this friendly guest house, deep in the woods and beside a babbling brook. Bungalows are simple but adequate and the on-site restaurant will keep you well fed. Free pier pick-up.

Amber Sands HOTEL $$
(☎0 3958 6177; www.ambersandsbeachresort.com; Ao Dan Kao; r 2000-2700B; ❄️@❄️) Sandwiched between mangroves and a quiet red sand beach, Amber Sands has eight comfortable bungalows with picture windows facing a high-definition sea view. South Africans Cheryl and Julian run the place with a professional and family touch. The location feels a world away but it is only 15 minutes from the pier.

The Souk GUEST HOUSE $
(☎08 1553 3194; Ao Dan Kao; r 700B; @) Next door to Amber Sands, this funky spot has seven pop-art cool (fan only) bungalows at a pleasant price. There are lots of chill-out spaces and an urban vibe in the open-deck restaurant and cocktail bar. Young couples

and long-stay visitors rave about this low-key find. Easy access to the ferry pier.

Salak Phet Homestay HOMESTAY $
(☎08 1294 1650; Ban Salak Phet; r incl meals 300B) Part of a village ecotour program, accommodation is provided in one of several pier homes in the fishing village of Salak Phet. Expect simple lodgings: a bedroll on the floor of a small room, and shared, basic bathrooms. You'll dine with the family and knowing some Thai is helpful. The **Salak Phet Kayak Station** (☎08 7834 9489) can help arrange the stay for you.

Treehouse Lodge GUEST HOUSE $
(☎08 1847 8215; Hat Yao; r 300B) The original Treehouse Lodge on Lonely Beach created the initial buzz about Ko Chang as a laid-back paradise. But civilisation arrived and the original owners defected to Ko Pha Ngan in 2009. Adopting the name and the ambience, the new Treehouse moved to remote Hat Yao (Long Beach), on the far southeastern peninsula. Basic huts (with basic bathrooms) chill along a hillside, looking down to a softly sanded slice of beach. The road to Hat Yao is well-sealed to the lookout point but poorly maintained past that, so plan on staying awhile. Inquire in Trat about a taxi service that goes all the way to Long Beach.

The Spa Koh Chang Resort HOTEL $$
(☎0 3955 3091; www.thespakohchang.com; Ao Salak Kok; r 1200-3000B; ❄️🛜❄️) In a lush garden setting embraced by the bay's mangrove forests, this spa resort specialises in all the popular health treatments (yoga, meditation, fasting etc) that burned-out professionals need. Elegantly decorated bungalows scramble up a flower-filled hillside providing a peaceful getaway for some quality 'me' time. No beach access.

🍴 Eating & Drinking

Virtually all of the island's accommodation has attached restaurants with adequate but not outstanding fare. Parties abound on the beaches and range from the older and surlier scene on Hat Sai Khao to the younger and sloppier on Lonely Beach.

WEST COAST

Oodie's Place INTERNATIONAL $$
(☎0 3955 1193; Hat Sai Khao; dishes 150-280B; ⏱️lunch & dinner) Local musician Oodie runs a nicely diverse operation with excellent French food, tasty Thai specialities and live

music from 10pm. After all these years, it is still beloved by expats.

Norng Bua
THAI $$
(Hat Sai Khao; dishes 80-200B; ⊙breakfast, lunch & dinner) This popular stir-fry hut makes everything fast and fresh and with chillies and fish sauce (praise the culinary gods).

Invito Al Cibo
ITALIAN $$$
(✉03955 1326; Koh Chang Hut, Hat Sai Khao; dishes 250-550B; ⊙lunch & dinner) Upscale Invito is no more but the executive chef has migrated to this start-up with a lovely sea view.

Saffron on the Sea
THAI $$
(✉0 3955 1253; Hat Kai Mook; dishes 150-350B; ⊙breakfast, lunch & dinner) Owned by an arty escapee from Bangkok, this friendly boutique hotel has a generous portion of oceanfront dining and a relaxed, romantic atmosphere. All the Thai dishes are prepared in the island-style, more sweet than spicy.

KaTi Culinary
THAI $
(✉08 1903 0408; Khlong Prao; dishes 80-150B; ⊙lunch & dinner) This popular Thai cooking school is equally popular for its attached restaurant. Apart from Thai dishes, on the menu are also creative smoothies, such as lychee, lemon and peppermint.

Iyara Seafood
SEAFOOD $$
(✉0 3955 1353; Khlong Prao; dishes 150-300B; ⊙lunch & dinner) Iyara isn't your standard island seafood warehouse: after dining in the lovely bamboo pavilion, guests are invited to kayak along the nearby estuary.

Nid's Kitchen
THAI $
(Hat Kaibae; dishes 30-80B; ⊙lunch & dinner) A sweaty little restaurant north of GajaPuri Resort, Auntie Nid's does all the Thai standards like a wok wizard. Plus the beers are cold.

Porn's Bungalows Restaurant
THAI $
(Hat Kaibae; dishes 40-150B; ⊙lunch & dinner) This wooden tree-house restaurant affiliated with a Rasta-style guest house is the quintessential beachside lounge. Feel free to have your drinks outsize your meal and don't worry about dressing for dinner.

TOP CHOICE Barrio Bonito
MEXICAN $$
(✉08 0092 8208; Lonely Beach; dishes 150-250B; ⊙breakfast, lunch & dinner) This breezy, hip place has all the island raving about its seriously good Mexican fare. A French-Mexican couple runs the place with flair

and there's a plunge pool should the salsa induce sweating.

Magic Garden
THAI $
(✉0 3955 8027; Lonely Beach; dishes 60-120B; ⊙dinner) Magic Garden is a pagoda to Lonely Beach's special variety of chill-laxin'. Grab some grub, polish off some Beer Changs, watch a movie and then wander down to the beach for some DJ beats.

Bailan Bay Resort Restaurant
THAI $$
(Ao Bailan; dishes 150-250B; ⊙lunch & dinner) Our taxi driver recommended this hilltop restaurant south of Lonely Beach that serves spicy *sôm·dam* with a view.

Ruan Thai
SEAFOOD $$
(Ban Bang Bao; dishes 100-300B; ⊙lunch & dinner) It's about as fresh as it gets (note your future dinner greeting you in tanks as you enter) and the portions are large. The doting service is beyond excellent – they'll even help you crack your crabs.

Buddha View Restaurant
INTERNATIONAL $$
(✉0 3955 8157; Ban Bang Bao; dishes 250-350B; ⊙breakfast, lunch & dinner) Dangle your toes within teasing distance from the nibbling fish at the creative pier-side seating of this new addition to Bang Bao's restaurant scene. The view is nearly panoramic and the fare is mainly steak and pastas with Thai seafood as well.

NORTHERN INTERIOR & EAST COAST

Blues Blues Restaurant
THAI $
(✉08 5839 3524; Ban Khlong Son; dishes 50-100B; ⊙lunch & dinner) Through the green screen of tropical plants is an arty stir-fry hut that is beloved for expertise, efficiency and economy. The owner's delicate watercolour paintings are on display too. The restaurant is about 600m from the turn-off to Ban Kwan Chang.

Jungle Way Restaurant
THAI $
(✉08 9247 3161; Ban Khlong Son; dishes 60-70B; ⊙breakfast, lunch & dinner; ✉) Enjoy the natural setting and home-style cooking of this guest house restaurant. Meal preparation takes a leisurely pace so climb up to the elevated wildlife-viewing platform to spot some jungle creatures while the wok is sizzling.

Paradise Behind the Sea Restaurant
THAI $$
(✉08 1900 2388; Ban Hat Sai Daeng; dishes 110-280B; ⊙breakfast, lunch & dinner) If you're cruising the east coast for scenery, stop in for a

view and a meal at this cliffside restaurant. Vietnamese and Thai dishes crowd the tables and cool breezes provide refreshment. In Thai, this is called 'Lang Talay'.

ℹ️ Information

Dangers & Annoyances

It is not recommended to drive between Ban Khlong Son south to Hat Sai Khao as the road is steep and treacherous with several hairpin turns. There are mudslides and poor conditions during storms. If you do rent a motorbike, stick to the west coast beaches and take care when travelling between Hat Kaibae and Lonely Beach. Wear protective clothing when riding or driving a motorcycle to reduce injury if you do have an accident.

The police conduct regular drug raids on the island's accommodation. If you get caught with narcotics, you could face heavy fines or imprisonment.

Be aware of the cheap minibus tickets from Siem Reap to Ko Chang; these usually involve some sort of time- and money-wasting commission scam.

Ko Chang is considered a low-risk malarial zone, meaning that liberal use of mosquito repellent is probably an adequate precaution.

Emergency

Police station (☎0 3958 6191; Ban Dan Mai)
Tourist police office (☎1155) Based north of Ban Khlong Prao. Also has smaller police boxes in Hat Sai Khao and Hat Kaibae.

Internet Access

Internet access is easy to find all the way down the west coast and most guest houses have free wi-fi.

Medical Services

Bang Bao Health Centre (☎0 3955 8088; Ban Bang Bao; ⏱8.30am-6pm) For the basics.
Ko Chang Hospital (☎0 3952 1657; Ban Dan Mai) Public hospital with a good reputation and affordably priced care; south of the ferry terminal.
Ko Chang International Clinic (☎0 3955 1151; Hat Sai Khao; ⏱24hr) Related to the Bangkok Hospital Group; accepts most health insurances and has expensive rates.

Money

There are banks with ATMs and exchange facilities along all the west coast beaches.

Post

Ko Chang post office (☎0 3955 1240; Hat Sai Khao) At the far southern end of Hat Sai Khao.

Tourist Information

The free magazine *Koh Chang Guide* (www.white sandsthailand.com) is widely available on the island and has handy beach maps.

The comprehensive website I Am Koh Chang (www.iamkohchang.com) is a labour of love from an irreverent Brit living on the island. His 'KC Essentials A-Z' section is jam-packed with opinion and information.

ℹ️ Getting There & Away

Whether originating from Bangkok or Cambodia, it is an all-day haul to reach Ko Chang.

TO/FROM MAINLAND: Ko Chang-bound boats depart from the mainland piers collectively referred to as Laem Ngop (see p216 for more information), southwest of Trat. You'll arrive in Ko Chang at either Tha Sapparot or Tha Centrepoint, depending on which pier and boat company you used on the mainland.

Tha Sapparot is the closest to the west coast beaches and receives vehicle ferries from the mainland pier of Tha Thammachat. **Koh Chang Ferry** (☎0 3955 5188) runs this service (one way 80B, 30 minutes, hourly 6.30am to 7pm).

At the time of writing, the car ferry associated with Tha Centrepoint was competing aggressively for business by offering cheaper prices, more commissions and a Bangkok–Laem Ngop bus service. You cut out some of the land transfers with the new bus service but Tha Centrepoint (on Ko Chang) is further from the west coast beaches, so the time-saving is negligible. **Centrepoint Ferry** (☎0 3953 8196) runs this service (one way/round-trip 80/100B, 45 minutes, hourly 6am to 7.30pm). Weekend service in high season runs until 9pm.

There is also a new bus route directly from Bangkok's Suvarnabhumi (airport) station to Ko Chang (308B, six hours) via the car ferry with stops on the mainland at Trat and Chanthaburi. The bus leaves Suvarnabhumi at 7.30am and departs Ko Chang at 1.30pm. On Ko Chang, the bus arrives and departs from Khlong Son. Another option is a minivan service from Bangkok's Victory Monument that goes all the way to Ko Chang's Tha Sapparot (one way 300B, four hours, hourly departures).

TO/FROM NEIGHBOURING ISLANDS: Tha Bang Bao in the southern part of the island is the pier used for boat trips to neighbouring islands. There is a daily inter-island ferry (known conflictingly as 'express' or 'slow' boat) operated by **Bang Bao Boats** (www.bangbaoboat.com) that does a loop to Ko Wai, Ko Mak, Ko Kut and back. Faster and more frequent speedboat departures do the same circuit. The slow boat is the smartest option when seas are rough and for ocean sightseeing as the speedboat ride is like a James Bond martini: shaken not stirred.

See the respective islands for getting there and away information.

ℹ Getting Around

Shared *sŏrng·tăa·ou* meet arriving boats to shuttle passengers to the various beaches (Hat Sai Khao 50B, Khlong Prao 60B and Lonely Beach 100B). Compared to other islands, *sŏrng·tăa·ou* drivers are almost invariably honest and reliable in their pricing, especially during the day when demand is high. Most hops between neighbouring west coast beaches should cost around 40B to 50B.

Businesses along the west coast charge 150B to 200B per day for motorbike hire. Ko Chang's hilly and winding roads are quite dangerous (see p227 for road safety considerations); make sure the bike is in good working order.

Ko Wai
เกาะหวาย

Stunning Ko Wai is teensy and primitive, but endowed with gin-clear waters, excellent coral reefs for snorkelling and a handsome view across to Ko Chang. Expect to share the bulk of your afternoons with day trippers but have the remainder of your time in peace.

Most bungalows close during the May-to-September low season when seas are rough and flooding is common.

🛏 Sleeping

Ko Wai Paradise   GUEST HOUSE $
(r 300-500B) Simple wooden bungalows (some with shared bathroom) on a postcard-perfect beach. You'll share the coral out front with day trippers.

Good Feeling   GUEST HOUSE $
(☑08 8503 3410; r 300-500B) Wooden huts (some with shared bathroom) spread out along a rocky headland interspersed with private sandy coves.

Grandma Hut   GUEST HOUSE $
(☑08 1841 3011; r 250-500B) On the rocky northeastern tip of the island is this simple and remote place; speedboat operators know it by the nearby bay of Ao Yai Ma.

Ko Wai Pakarang   GUEST HOUSE $$
(☑08 4113 8946; www.kohwaipakarang.com; r 600-2500B; ✳🔄@) The closest Ko Wai comes to modernity with concrete air-con bungalows and lots of day trippers milling about.

ℹ Getting There & Around

Boats will drop you off at the nearest pier to your guest house; otherwise you'll have to walk 15 to 30 minutes along a narrow forest trail.

Bang Bao Boat (www.bangbaoboat.com) is the archipelago's inter-island ferry running a daily loop from Ko Chang to Ko Kut. Boats depart Ko Chang at 9am and arrive at Ko Wai (one way 300B, one hour) and continue on to Ko Mak (one way 300B, one hour) and Ko Kut (500B, three hours). You can return to Ko Chang at 1pm.

Several speedboat companies run from Ko Wai to the following destinations:
Ko Chang (one way 400B, 15 minutes, two daily departures)
Ko Mak (one way 350B, 30 minutes, two daily departures)
Ko Kut (one way 700B, one hour, two daily departures)
Laem Ngop (450B, two to three hours, one daily departure)

Ko Mak
เกาะหมาก

Little Ko Mak is only 16 sq km and doesn't have speeding traffic, wall-to-wall development, noisy beer bars or crowded beaches. The palm-fringed bays are bathed by gently lapping water and there's an overall relaxed island vibe. But Ko Mak is not destined for island super-stardom as the interior is a utilitarian landscape of coconut and rubber plantations and reports of sand flies make visitors a little nervous.

Visiting the island is easier in the high season; during the low season (May to September) many boats stop running and bungalow operations wind down. Storms also deposit uninvited litter on the exposed southern beaches.

🏃 Activities

Swimming and beach strolling are best on the northwestern bay of **Ao Suan Yai**, which is a wide arc of sand and looking-glass clear water; it is easily accessible by bicycle or motorbike if you stay elsewhere on the island. Offshore is **Ko Kham**, a private island that sold in 2008 for a reported 200 million baht. It used to be a popular day-trippers' beach but is currently under construction for its next incarnation as a super-luxury resort.

Koh Mak Divers (☑08 3297 7723; www.kohmakdivers.com; dive trips 2200-3000B) runs dive trips to the Mu Ko Chang National Marine Park, about 45 minutes away.

🛏 Sleeping & Eating

Most budget guest houses are located on Ao Khao, a decent strip of sand on the southwestern side of the island, while the resorts sprawl on the more scenic northwestern bay of Ao Suan Yai.

There is a handful of homey stir-fry shacks on the main road between Monkey Island and Makathanee Resort. And if you feel like a journey, use a meal or a sundowner as an excuse to explore different bays.

Monkey Island GUEST HOUSE **$$**
(☑08 9501 6030; www.monkeyislandkohmak.com; Ao Khao; r 350-3000B; 🕸@) The troop leader of guest houses, Monkey Island has earthen or wooden bungalows in three creatively named models – Baboon, Chimpanzee and Gorilla – with various amenities (shared or private bathroom or private deck). All have fun design touches and the hip restaurant does respectable Thai cuisine in a leisurely fashion. In true Thai beach style, the affiliated bar rouses the dead with its nightly parties.

Baan Koh Mak GUEST HOUSE **$$**
(☑08 9895 7592; www.baan-koh-mak.com; Ao Khao; r from 1200B; 🕸) Bright and funky, Baan Koh Mak provides a respectable flashpacker abode with colourful paint jobs and soft mattresses.

Island Huts GUEST HOUSE **$**
(☑08 7139 5537; Ao Khao; r 350-450B) Rickety shacks camp out on the beach with all the bare necessities: beach, bathroom and mattress.

Ao Kao Resort GUEST HOUSE **$$**
(☑08 3152 6564; www.aokaoresort.com; r 1200-2500; 🕸) In a pretty crook of the bay, Ao Kao has an assortment of stylish and basic bungalows. Opt for a traditional Thai-style house complete with carved wood flourishes and handsome balconies. Families congregate here as there is front-yard swimming and the rocky headland harbours sea creatures.

Lazy Day Resort GUEST HOUSE **$$**
(☑08 1882 4002; www.kohmaklazyday.com; r 2250-2700B; 🕸) Next door to Ao Kao Resort this professionally run operation has picture-window bungalows posing in a grassy garden; rates include breakfast.

Koh Mak Resort HOTEL **$$**
(☑0 3950 1013; www.kohmakresort.com; Ao Suan Yai; r 1700-5400B; 🕸🕸) Though it isn't the island's best value, you can cut out your com-

mute to the prettiest beach without much financial sacrifice.

SEARCHING FOR MR(S) RIGHT?

Still can't seem to find your island idyll? Give Ko Rayang a try. It is a private island with one tiny resort. **Rayang Island Resort** (☑0 3950 1000; www.rayang-island.com; r 2500-3800B) has 15 simple one- and two-bedroom bungalows (no air-con, no hot-water showers) with limited electricity and snorkelling outside your door. You can catch a speedboat shuttle (170B) from Ko Mak's Tha Makathanee and check it out if you're commitment shy.

ℹ Information

There are no banks or ATMs on the island, so stock up on cash before visiting. Speedboats arrive at Koh Mak Resort pier on Ao Suan Yai. The main cargo pier is at Ao Nid, on the eastern side of the island.

Ball's Cafe (☑08 1925 6591; Ao Nid Pier; ⊙9am-6pm) Has internet access, travel agent and coffee shop. Khun Ball is an active island promoter and runs www.kohmak.com as well as environmental initiatives.

Ko Mak Health Centre (☑08 9403 5986; ⊙8.30am-4.30pm) Can handle basic first-aid emergencies and illnesses. It's on the cross-island road near Ao Nid Pier.

Police (☑0 3952 5741) Near the health centre.

ℹ Getting There & Around

There are different piers used by different companies on the island but you don't have to worry about sorting it out; pier transfers are usually handled by guest houses and hotels free-of-charge.

A slow ferry leaves Ko Mak for Laem Ngop (mainland pier; one way 200B, three hours, one morning departure on certain days); on alternate days it departs from the mainland. Check with an agent about departure days and times, which are subject to change.

Ao Thai Marine Express (☑08 1863 3525; www.kohkoodspeedboat.com) runs speedboats from the mainland pier of Tha Dan Kao, 5km east of Trat, to Ko Mak (450B). Departure times are dependent upon demand.

Bang Bao Boat (www.bangbaoboat.com) is the archipelago's inter-island ferry running a daily loop from Ko Chang to Ko Kut. Boats depart Ko Chang at 9am and arrive at Ko Mak (one way

400B, 1½ to two hours) and continue on to Ko Kut (one way 300B, one to two hours, departs 1pm). In the opposite direction, you can catch it to Ko Wai (one way 300B, 45 minutes) and Ko Chang (400B, 2½ hours).

Several speedboat companies run from Ko Mak to the following destinations:

Ko Chang (one way 550B, 45 minutes, three daily departures)

Ko Kut (one way 400B, 45 minutes, two daily departures)

Laem Ngop (mainland pier; one way 450B, one hour, four daily departures)

Ko Wai (one way 350B, 30 minutes, two daily departures)

Once on the island, you can pedal (40B per hour) or motorbike (200B per day) your way around.

Ko Kut   เกาะกูด

All the paradise descriptions apply to Ko Kut: the beaches are graceful arcs of sand, the water is gin clear, coconut palms outnumber buildings, and a secluded, unhurried atmosphere embraces you upon arrival. There's nothing in the form of nightlife or even dining, really, but those are the reasons for visiting.

Half as big as Ko Chang and the fourth-largest island in Thailand, Ko Kut has long been the domain of package-tour resorts and a seclusion-seeking elite. The most recent news on the island was that the Beckhams had bought a vacation home here. Even more noteworthy is Six Senses' new Soneva Kiri resort, which is accessible by private plane and has base rates starting at US$2000 per night. But the island is becoming more egalitarian and independent travellers, especially families and couples, will find home sweet home here.

🏃 Sights & Activities

Beaches   BEACHES
Blonde beaches with gorgeous aquamarine water are along the western side of the island. **Hat Khlong Chao** is one of the island's best and could easily compete with Samui's Hat Chaweng in a beach beauty contest; the clear water is shallow and bathtub smooth. **Ao Noi** is a pretty boulder-strewn beach with a steep drop-off and steady waves for strong swimmers. **Ao Prao** is another lovely sweep of sand. There is no public transport on Ko Kut but you can rent motorbikes for exploring the west coast beaches as traffic is mini-

mal and the road is paved from Khlong Hin in the southwest to Ao Noi in the northeast.

With its quiet rocky coves and mangrove estuaries, Ko Kut is great for **snorkelling** and **kayaking**. Most resorts have equipment on offer.

Nam Tok Khlong Chao   WATERFALL
Two waterfalls on the island make good short hiking destinations. The larger and more popular Nam Tok Khlong Chao is wide and pretty with a massive plunge pool. Expect to share it with dozens of other visitors, especially on weekends. It's a quick jungle walk to the base, or you can kayak up Khlong Chao. Further north is **Nam Tok Khlong Yai Ki**, which is smaller but also has a large pool to cool off in.

🛌 Sleeping

During low season (May to September) many boats stop running and bungalow operations wind down. On weekends and holidays during the high season, vacationing Thais fill the resorts. Call ahead during busy periods so you can be dropped off at the appropriate pier by the speedboat operators.

You can scrimp your way into the neighbourhood of beautiful Hat Khlong Chao by staying at one of the village guest houses, which are a five- to 15-minute walk to the beach. Families might like the midrange and budget options on Ao Ngam Kho, which has a small sandy section in the far northern corner of the bay, though the rest is an old coral reef and very rocky. Bring swim shoes.

Ao Bang Bao is another popular spot for independent travellers though the beach is mediocre and so is the accommodation.

If you're itching to splurge, Ko Kut is the place to do it.

TOP CHOICE **Bann Makok**   HOTEL **$$**
(☑08 1934 5713; Khlong Yai Ki; r 2500-3000B; ❄@) Be the envy of the speedboat patrons when you get dropped off at this boutique hotel tucked into the mangroves. Recycled timbers painted in vintage colours have been constructed into a maze of eight rooms designed to look like a traditional pier fishing village. Common decks and reading nooks provide a peaceful space to listen to birdsong or get lost in a book.

Tinkerbell Resort   HOTEL **$$$**
(☑08 1813 0058; www.tinkerbellresort.com; Hat Khlong Chao; r incl meals from 7900B; ❄@⛱) Natural materials, like towering bamboo

privacy fences and thatched roof villas, sew this resort seamlessly into the landscape. The rooms are bright and airy and smack dab on the prettiest beach you've ever seen.

Mangrove Bungalows
GUEST HOUSE $$

(☑08 5279 0278; Ban Khlong Chao; r 600-1200B; ✳) Lounging pleasantly along mangrove-forested Khlong Chao, this place has large bungalows sporting polished wood floors and hot-water showers. A restaurant hangs above the lazy canal, and it is a 10-minute walk to the beach.

Mark House Bungalows
GUEST HOUSE $$

(☑08 6133 0402; www.markhousebungalow.com; Ban Khlong Chao; r 800-1200B; ✳) Right behind the beachside resorts, Mark House is the closest cheapie to the beach. The bungalows sit beside the canal and the ambience feels like you're halfway through a nap.

Koh Kood Ngamkho Resort
GUEST HOUSE $

(☑08 1825 7076; www.kohkood-ngamkho.com; Ao Ngam Kho; r 650B; @) Uncle Joe along with his niece and nephew run one the best budget options around. Rustic huts outfitted with new linens, creatively decorated bathrooms and accordion-style front doors perch on a forested hillside. The restaurant is fabulous (fresh coconut milk curries, spicy stir-fries). At the time of writing, Uncle Joe was looking to sell the land, and we selfishly hope that he reconsiders.

Dusita
HOTEL $$

(☑08 1523 7369; Ao Ngam Kho; r 700-1200B; ✳) Solid bungalows spaciously occupy a shady oceanfront garden ideally suited for families who need running space for young ones.

Ao Noi Resort
GUEST HOUSE $$

(☑0 3952 4979; www.kohkoodaonoi.com; Ao Noi; r 1200-2000B; ✳) This village of thatched-roof huts is adequate yet unremarkable. In return for lacklustre lodging you get a semi-private palm-fringed beach with vigorous surf. Skip the overpriced fan ones, though.

The Beach Natural Resort
HOTEL $$

(☑08 6009 9420; www.thebeachkohkood.com; Ao Bang Bao; r incl breakfast 1200-2600B; ✳@) Bun-galows sit among a shady garden on a rocky stretch of beach. The customer service is beyond Thai-friendly. Thais pack this place for karaoke-fuelled fun at the weekend, so opt for a weekday.

Siam Beach
GUEST HOUSE $$

(☑08 4332 0788; Ao Bang Bao; r incl breakfast 1200-2000B; ✳@) With a monopoly on the sandiest part of the beach, Siam Beach hasn't put much effort into its bungalows. But location is what you get.

❶ Information

There are no banks or ATMs, though major resorts can exchange money. A small **hospital** (☑0 3952 5748; ☺8.30am-4.30pm) can handle minor emergencies and is located inland at Ban Khlong Hin Dam. The **police station** (☑0 3952 5741) is nearby. Internet access is still a bit spotty, though many resorts have at least a common terminal.

❶ Getting There & Around

Ko Kut is accessible from the mainland pier of Laem Sok, 22km southeast of Trat, the nearest bus transfer point.

Ninmoungkorn Boat (☑08 6126 7860) runs an air-con boat (one way 350B, two hours, one daily departure) that docks at Ao Salad, in the northeastern corner of the island; free land transfer (about 45 minutes each way) is available on each side of the journey.

Speedboats also make the crossing to/from Laem Sok (one way 450B to 600B, 1½ hours, three daily departures), and will drop you off at your hotel's pier.

Bang Bao Boat (www.bangbaoboat.com) is the archipelago's inter-island ferry running a daily loop from Ko Chang, departing at 9am, to Ko Kut (one way 700B, five to six hours). In the opposite direction, you can catch it to Ko Mak (one way 300B, one to two hours) and Ko Wai (one way 400B, 2½ hours).

Several speedboat companies run from Ko Kut to Ko Chang (one way 900B, 45 minutes, three daily departures) with stops in Ko Mak and Ko Wai.

To get around, you should rent a motorbike (300B per day) or mountain bike (100B to 150B per day).

Chiang Mai Province

Best Places to Eat

» New Delhi (p266)
» Lert Ros (p266)
» Palaad Tawanron (p271)
» Ai Sushi (p271)
» Chiang Dao Nest (p286)

Best Places to Stay

» Villa Duang Champa (p258)
» Mo Rooms (p261)
» Riverside House (p263)
» Sakulchai (p263)
» Chiang Dao Nest (p285)

Why Go?

The province of Chiang Mai, with its cooling mist-shrouded mountains bursting with dense jungle, has long enticed travellers intent on exploring this southern slice of the great Himalayan mountain range.

Highlights include the laid-back city of Chiang Mai, with its moated, partially walled old city; its celebrated ancient temples, built with teak money reflecting the aesthetics of an ancient trade dependent on the forest; and a traveller-friendly scene catering for those here to party through to those who prefer their cocktails by the saltwater pool.

Outside of the urban sphere is very accessible country-side and two of Thailand's highest mountain peaks: Doi Inthanon (2565m) and Doi Chiang Dao (2195m). Boasting more natural forest cover than any other province in the north, activities such as cycling, hiking, elephant trekking, birdwatching and river rafting offer an escape from the steaming plains.

When to Go

The weather in Chiang Mai province is best for travel during the cool season, roughly from November to February, when temperatures are mild and rain is scarce. Temperatures can be cool enough to warrant a jacket at night and in the early morning, particularly at higher elevations.

During the hot season, from March until June, Chiang Mai often experiences a 'fire season', when a thick haze forms over the city, a combination of dust and smoke from the burning off of nearby rice fields. April is a great time to be around for the Songkran Festival.

Chiang Mai Highlights

1 Taking in the sacred **Wat Phra Singh** (p238) and **Wat Chedi Luang** (p238)

2 Picking up bargains at the **Saturday Walking Street** (p245) and **Sunday Walking Street** (p235)

3 Stretching out for a traditional **massage** or **meditation course** (p256)

4 Dodging the relentless city traffic on a **river cruise** (see boxed text, p244) and floating lazily past stilted houses

5 Escaping the brutal city heat in cool, lush **Doi Suthep-Pui National Park** (p250)

6 Exploring the mystical cave at **Doi Chiang Dao**

(p284), and tucking into fine cuisine afterwards

7 Getting nice and wrinkly in the curative hot spring waters of **Doi Pha Hompok National Park** (p287)

8 Scaling the heights of **Doi Inthanon** (p291), and posing for pics among the conifers and rhododendrons

CHIANG MAI

เชียงใหม่

POP 174,000

Are you here yet? OK, good, breathe a sigh of relief – you're in Thailand's second city, but it ain't Bangkok. Now, have a look around you, because this nonchalant city encapsulates much of what is unique and breathtaking about Thailand.

Piercing the foothills of northern Thailand, and snuggling up to Doi Suthep, Chiang Mai contains hundreds of sacred temples, with *chedi* and gabled rooftop tiers soaring skyward, and then billowing out protectively as they swoop to the ground. The city's enduring Lanna characteristics are evident in these revered, merit-making houses of worship, along with the quaint, moated old city where so many temples are housed. The surrounding mountains, their legendary, mystical attributes ever watchful over the steamy metropolis, loom large over the city.

Chiang Mai is laid-back, creative and reverential. It's a city with heart – most NGOs working with Burmese refugees have their headquarters here. In reality, the city is dynamic and modern without having lost its down-to-earth charm. There's certainly traffic, pollution and ugly concrete buildings, but this is a very Thai place – Thai culture overwhelmingly pervades a city wrapped up in Western sensibilities and striving for advancement. Fortunately the university students keep Chiang Mai looking and feeling youthful. Head down to Th Nimmanhaemin and you'll glimpse the city's future movers and shakers, intent now on moving and shaking it in the nightclubs, bars and discos that crown this area as Chiang Mai's nightlife headquarters.

Oh, and don't forget the eating scene. Specialities of the city include Japanese sushi bars around the university, Burmese curries and salads, and of course Thai: from delicious street food to white-linen riverside dining where fine wines and twinkling candles floating on the water create a special Chiang Mai indulgence.

History

Chiang Mai and Thailand's other northern provinces share more of their early development with the Shan state of present-day Myanmar (Burma), neighbouring parts of Laos and even the southern mountains of China than with Bangkok and Thailand's central plains.

King Phaya Mengrai (also spelt Mangrai) is credited for founding the Lanna kingdom and expanding it into the Ping River valley. Once he reached the valley, he built a temporary capital at Wiang Kum Kam (p243). Around 1296, King Mengrai relocated the Lanna capital to a more picturesque spot between Doi Suthep and the Ping River and named the auspicious city Nopburi Si Nakhon Ping Chiang Mai (shortened to Chiang Mai, meaning the 'New Walled City'). Traces of the original 1296 earthen ramparts can still be seen today along Th Kamphaeng Din in Chiang Mai.

In the 14th and 15th centuries, the Lanna kingdom expanded as far south as Kamphaeng Phet and as far north as Luang Prabang in Laos. During this time, Chiang Mai became an important religious and cultural centre and the eighth world synod of Theravada Buddhism was held here in 1477.

The Lanna kingdom was soon confronted by challenges from Ayuthaya, the powerful city-state that had flourished in Thailand's central plains and that would later consolidate the region under Siamese control and help shape the broader 'Thai' identity. But it was the Burmese who would overtake the city and the kingdom in 1556, an occupation that lasted 200 years.

The fall of Ayuthaya in 1767 to the Burmese marked another turning point in Chiang Mai's history. The defeated Thai army reunited under Phraya Taksin south of Ayuthaya in present-day Bangkok and began a campaign to push out the occupying Burmese forces. Chao Kavila, a chieftain (known as *jôw meu·ang*) from nearby Lampang principality, helped 'liberate' northern Thailand from Burmese control, which led to the eventual integration of the Lanna kingdom into the expanding Thai kingdom based in Bangkok.

Under Kavila, Chiang Mai became an important regional trade centre. In 1800 Kavila built the monumental brick walls around Chiang Mai's inner city and expanded the city in southerly and easterly directions, establishing a river port at the end of what is today Th Tha Phae (*tha phae* means 'raft pier'). Many of the later Shan- and Burmese-style temples were built by wealthy teak merchants who emigrated from Burma during this period.

There were many political and technological factors that ultimately led to the demise of an independent Lanna state. The

Bangkok-based government designated Chiang Mai as an administrative unit in 1892 during the expansion of colonial rule in neighbouring Burma and Laos. The completion of the northern railway to Chiang Mai in 1921 finally linked the north with central Thailand. In 1927, King Rama VII and Queen Rambaibani rode into the city at the head of an 84-elephant caravan, becoming the first central Thai monarchs to visit the north. In 1933, Chiang Mai officially became a province of Siam.

In 2001, then prime minister and Chiang Mai native Thaksin Shinawatra sought to make Chiang Mai one of the nation's primary centres of information technology by expanding the airport and building superhighways. The political demise of the Thaksin administration by the military coup of 2006 and the ongoing political ramifications (such as the red shirt protests in Bangkok and the north, including Chiang Mai, in 2010), together with the global economic downturn, have put the brakes on these plans. The city is warily expecting more protests in the future as discontent about Thaksin's overthrow and the wider political ramifications continue to simmer.

Maps

A copy of Nancy Chandler's *Map of Chiang Mai*, available in bookshops, is a worthwhile investment. It shows the city's main points of interest, shopping venues and oddities that you will be pleased to stumble upon. Groovy Map's *Chiang Mai Map'n'Guide*, also in bookshops, adds Thai script and more nightspots.

◉ Sights

Chiang Mai is a very manageable city to navigate. Most visitors base themselves in the old city, which is easily covered on foot or by bike – the famous temples are spread out along Th Ratchadamnoen.

The old city has four gates, often referred to as markers for direction around the city: the easternmost gate is Pratu Tha Phae, which leads to Th Tha Phae, a main drag that links the riverside area with the old city; Pratu Suan Dok exits the western moat and connects the old city to the leafy environs of Chiang Mai University and Doi Suthep; the northern gate is Pratu Chang Pheuak; and the southern gate is Pratu Chiang Mai.

OLD CITY เมืองเก่า

Chiang Mai's historic quarter has buildings that are human-scaled and reserves the highest elevation for the temple stupas that peak out over the rooftops. Small bells decorating the eaves tinkle in the morning wind before the motorcycle engines awake.

One of the best ways to explore the old city is to jump on a bicycle and head off into the lanes, sois and smaller roads that infest this ancient urban space – traffic is minimal, and a lot of backstreets are surprisingly green and residential. All roads eventually lead to the old city wall, in some parts preserved or rebuilt and in other parts worn and rounded by time.

Sunday Walking Street MARKET
(ถนนเดินวันอาทิตย์; Map p240; Th Ratchadamnoen; ☉4pm-midnight Sun) A unique shopping experience, the Sunday Walking Street offers all manner of products and a good dose of provincial culture. It is also a reminder of an itinerant merchant tradition of the ancient Chinese caravans.

Vendors line Th Ratchadamnoen all the way from the square in front of Pratu Tha Phae to Wat Phra Singh and stretching a few blocks down both sides of Th Phra Pokklao. Many of the products are handmade in and

---

SOI BAN HAW

A remnant from the days when Chiang Mai was a detour on the Silk Road is the Thai-Muslim community along Soi 1 off Th Chang Khlan, near Chiang Mai Night Bazaar. The 100-year-old **Matsayit Chiang Mai** (Map p240; Soi 1, Th Charoen Prathet), also known as Ban Haw Mosque, was founded by *jeen hor* ('galloping Chinese'), the Thai expression for Yunnanese caravan traders. Within the past two centuries, the city's Muslim community has also grown to include ethnic Yunnanese Muslims escaping unrest in neighbouring Laos and Burma.

There are also a number of simple restaurants and vendors selling Thai-Muslim curries, *kôw soy* (curried chicken and noodles), *kôw mòk gài* (chicken biriani), and *néu·a òp hörm* ('fragrant' dried beef), a speciality of Chiang Mai's Yunnanese Muslim community. An evening food vendor does delicious *roh·đee* (Indian flat bread).

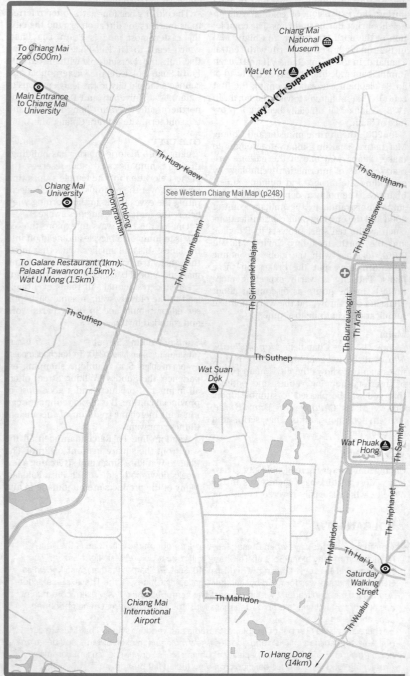

To Chiang Mai
Zoo (500m)

Chiang Mai
National
Museum

Wat Jet Yot

Hwy 11 (Th Superhighway)

Main Entrance
to Chiang Mai
University

Th Huay Kaew

Th Santitham

Chiang Mai
University

Th Khlong
Chonpathan

See Western Chiang Mai Map (p248)

Th Nimmanhaemin

Th Sirimankhalajan

Th Huttsadisawee

To Galare Restaurant (1km);
Palaad Tawanron (1.5km);
Wat U Mong (1.5km)

Th Suthep

Th Suthep

Th Bunreuangrit

Th Arak

Wat Suan
Dok

Wat Phuak
Hong

Th Samlan

Th Mahidon

Th Thiphanet

Th Hai Ya

Saturday
Walking
Street

Chiang Mai
International
Airport

Th Mahidon

Th Wualai

To Hang Dong
(14km)

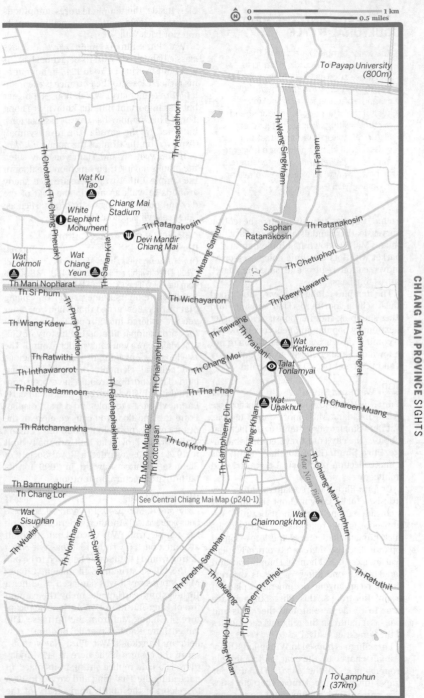

bles. Inside, the temple features sumptuous *lai-krahm* (gold pattern) stencilling on its interior back wall.

Wat Phra Singh's main *chedi* displays classic Lanna style with its octagonal base. It was built by King Pa Yo in 1345 in honour of his father. Closer to the entrance is the main *wí·hăhn* (sanctuary), which houses a bigger but less important Buddha known as Thong Thip. This temple has royal associations, indicated by the garuda (the royal symbol) displayed on the front of the main *wí·hăhn*.

If you visit around 11am you may catch the monks having their lunch on the floor of the temple. Either way, there are nice, shady grounds to walk around in the heat of the day and poignant slogans to digest, such as: 'The real evil is ignorance'.

Chiang Mai City Arts & Cultural Centre
MUSEUM

(หอศิลปวัฒนธรรมเชียงใหม่; Map p240; ☑0 5321 7793; Th Ratwithi; adult/child 90/40B; ☺8.30am-5pm Tue-Sun) The Chiang Mai City Arts & Cultural Centre offers a fine primer on Chiang Mai history. Be warned that when you enter you are ushered into a room for the obligatory promotional film on the history of Chiang Mai, before you can wander around. The 1st floor has engaging displays on religious and cultural elements of northern Thailand. The 2nd floor rooms have been converted into historic settings: there's an early Lanna village, a temple and a train display. From the 2nd floor you can see more of the beauty of this postcolonial building, Chiang Mai's former Provincial Hall, originally built in 1924. It was awarded a Royal Society of Siamese Architects award in 1999 for its faithful architectural restoration.

Wat Chedi Luang
TEMPLE

(วัดเจดีย์หลวง; Map p240; Th Phra Pokklao; donations appreciated) Another venerable stop on the temple trail, Wat Chedi Luang is built around a partially ruined Lanna-style *chedi* dating from 1441 that was believed to be one of the tallest structures in ancient Chiang Mai. Stories say it was damaged by either a 16th-century earthquake or by the cannon fire of King Taksin in 1775 during the recapture of Chiang Mai from the Burmese. The famed Phra Kaew (Emerald Buddha), now held in Bangkok's Wat Phra Kaew (p58), sat in the eastern niche here in 1475. Today there is a jade replica sitting in its place, financed by the Thai king and carved in 1995 to celebrate the 600th anniversary of the

around Chiang Mai, including the cotton scarves, leather sandals and wood carvings. Chiang Mai lets down its hippie hair at this market with lots of ethnic chic accessories, undyed cotton T-shirts and 'save the planet' canvas tote bags.

The temples along the way host food stalls selling northern Thai cuisine and other shopping-stamina boosts. The market is extremely popular and gets very crowded, so coming early is a good idea. If you're not in town on Sunday, check out the **Saturday Walking Street** (p245) on Th Wualai.

TOP CHOICE Wat Phra Singh
TEMPLE

(วัดพระสิงห์; Map p240; Th Singharat; donations appreciated) Chiang Mai's most visited temple, Wat Phra Singh owes its fame to the fact that it houses the city's most revered Buddha image, **Phra Singh** (Lion Buddha), and it has a fine collection of **classic Lanna art** and architecture.

Despite Phra Singh's exalted status, very little is actually known about the image. It is considered one of the most beautiful examples of Lanna religious art thanks to its thick human-like features and lotus-shaped topknot. Because there are two nearly identical images in Nakhon Si Thammarat and Bangkok, no one knows if this is the real one, nor can anyone document its place of origin. Regardless, this Phra Singh image came to reside here around the 1360s and today is a fixture in the religious ceremonies of the Songkran festival.

Phra Singh is housed in Wihan Lai Kham, a small chapel to the rear of the temple grounds next to the *chedi*. The exterior chapel displays the Lanna characteristics of a three-tiered roofline and carved ga-

chedi (according to some reckonings), and the 700th anniversary of the city.

A restoration of the impressive *chedi* was financed by Unesco and the Japanese government. Despite their good intentions, the restoration work is easily spotted: new porticoes and *naga* (mythical serpent) guardians and new Buddha images in three of the four directional niches. On the southern side of the monument, five elephant sculptures in the pediment can be seen. Four are cement restorations; only the one on the far right – without ears and trunk – is original brick and stucco. The restoration efforts also stopped short of creating a new spire, since no one knows for sure how the original superstructure looked. Regardless, a slow stroll around the massive walls of the chedi is quite meditative.

Wat Chedi Luang's other prominent attraction is the *làk meu·ang* (city pillar, believed to house the city's guardian deity) enshrined in a small building to the left of the compound's main entrance.

In the main *wí·hăhn* is the standing Buddha, known as Phra Chao Attarot, flanked by two disciples, both renowned for meditation and mysticism.

Have a chat to the monks while you are here (see boxed text, p250).

Wat Phan Tao   TEMPLE
(วัดพันเตา; Map p240; Th Phra Pokklao; donations appreciated) Near Wat Chedi Luang, Wat Phan Tao contains a beautiful old teak *wí·hăhn* that was once a royal residence and is today one of the unsung treasures of Chiang Mai. Constructed entirely of moulded teak panels fitted together and supported by 28 gargantuan teak pillars, the *wí·hăhn* features *naga* bargeboards inset with coloured mirror mosaic. On display inside are **old temple bells**, some ceramics, a few old northern-style gilded wooden Buddhas, and **antique cabinets** stacked with **old palm-leaf manuscripts**. The front panel of the building displays a mirrored **mosaic** of a peacock standing over a dog, representing the astrological year of the former royal resident's birth, making this temple a necessary pilgrimage site for those born in the year of the dog.

Wat Chiang Man   TEMPLE
(วัดเชียงมั่น; Map p240; Th Ratchaphakhinai; donations appreciated) Considered to be the oldest wát in the city, Wat Chiang Man, is believed to have been established by the city's found-

er, Phaya Mengrai. The wát features typical northern Thai temple architecture.

Two important Buddha images are kept in a glass cabinet inside the smaller sanctuary to the right of the main chapel. Phra Sila is a marble bas-relief Buddha that stands about 30cm high and reportedly came from Sri Lanka or India. The well-known Phra Sae Tang Khamani, a **crystal seated-Buddha** image, is thought to have come from Lavo (Lopburi) 1800 years ago and stands just 10cm high. The chapel housing the venerated images is open between 9am and 5pm.

In front of the *bòht* (ordination hall) a stone slab, engraved in 1581, bears the earliest known reference to the city's 1296 founding.

Wat Phuak Hong   TEMPLE
(วัดพวกหงส์; Map p236; off Th Samlan; donations appreciated) This neighbourhood wát, located behind Suan Buak Hat (Buak Hat Park), contains the locally revered Chedi Si Pheuak. The *chedi* is more than 100 years old and features the 'stacked spheres' style seen only here and at Wat Ku Tao, and most likely influenced by Thai Lü *chedi* in China's Xishuangbanna (also spelled Sipsongpanna) district, Yunnan.

Anusawari Sam Kasat   MONUMENT
(อนุสาวรีย์สามกษัตริย์; Map p240; Th Phra Pokklao) Proudly wearing 14th-century royal garb, the bronze Three Kings Monument commemorates the alliance forged between the three northern Thai-Lao kings (Phaya Ngam Meuang of Phayao, Phaya Mengrai of Chiang Mai and Phaya Khun Ramkhamhaeng of Sukhothai) in the founding of Chiang Mai. The statues mark one of the city's spiritual centres and have become a shrine to local residents, who regularly leave offerings of flowers, incense and candles at the bronze feet in return for blessings from the powerful spirits of the three kings.

EAST OF THE OLD CITY & RIVERSIDE
Passing through Pratu Tha Phae leads to a standard-issue commercial neighbourhood of two-storey concrete shophouses and busy mult-laned roads. South of Talat Warorot, on Th Chang Khlan, is the Chiang Mai Night Bazaar (see boxed text, p277). The meandering Mae Ping is another historical attraction.

Wat Chetawan, Wat Mahawan & Wat Bupparam   TEMPLE
(วัดเชตวัน/วัดมหาวัน/วัดบุปผาราม; Map p240) These three wát along Th Tha Phae feature highly

Central Chiang Mai

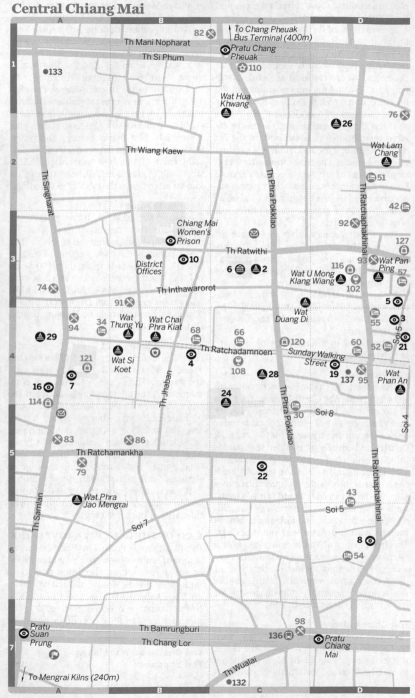

82

To Chang Pheuak
Bus Terminal (400m)

Th Mani Nopharat

Th Si Phum

Pratu Chang
Pheuak

110

133

Wat Hua
Khwang

26

Th Wiang Kaew

Wat Lam
Chang

Th Phra Pokklao

Th Ratchaphakhinai

51

42

92

127

Chiang Mai
Women's
Prison

Th Ratwithi

10

93

Wat Pan
Ping

116

57

District
Offices

6   2

Wat U Mong
Klang Wiang

102

Th Inthawarorot

74

5

91

Wat
Duang Di

55

94

34

Wat
Thung Yu

Wat Chai
Phra Kiat

68

3

Soi 5

21

29

Wat Si
Koet

4

66

Th Ratchadamnoen

120

60

52

Sunday Walking
Street

121

108

28

19

137   95

Wat
Phan An

16   7

24

114

30   Soi 8

Soi 4

83

86

Th Ratchamankha

22

79

Wat Phra
Jao Mengrai

43

Soi 5

Soi 7

8

54

Th Samlan

Th Ratchaphakhinai

Pratu
Suan
Prung

Th Bamrungburi

98

136

Th Chang Lor

Pratu
Chiang
Mai

To Mengrai Kilns (240m)

Th Wualai

132

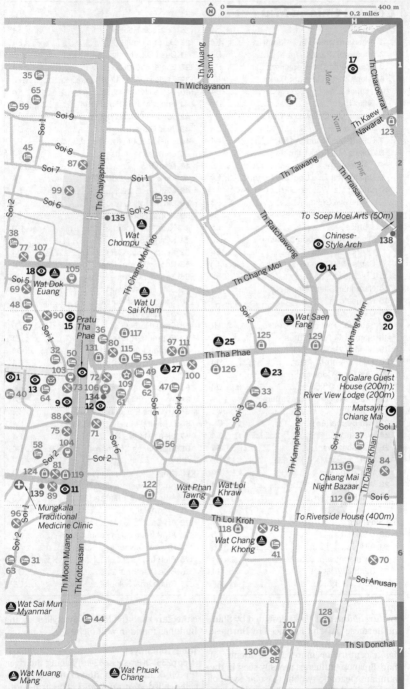

Central Chiang Mai

ornate *wí·hǎhn* and *chedi* designed by Shan and Burmese artisans. Financed by Burmese teak merchants who immigrated to Chiang Mai a century or more ago, evidence of Shan/Burmese influence is easily seen in the abundant peacock symbol (a solar symbol common in Burmese and Shan temple ar-

chitecture) and the Mandalay-style standing Buddhas found in wall niches.

Talat Tonlamyai MARKET
(Map p236; Th Praisani; ◷24hr) Facing the river, the city's main fresh **flower market** is lo-cally called *gàht dòrk mái*. The arm-width

bundles of asters, roses and coreopsis are ripened in the cooler climate of the surrounding highlands and brought to market at night to avoid the wilting daytime heat. Varieties that need even colder temperatures, such as pussy willow, are grown by hill-tribe villages perched at higher altitudes. Then there are the voluptuous tropical flowers, like jasmine, orchids and lotus buds, which flourish in the heat. The flower market is always busy but even more so during citywide festivals, such as Loi Krathong and, of course, the Flower Festival.

Wiang Kum Kam   HISTORICAL RUINS
(เวียงกุมกาม; ⊙8am-5pm) These excavated ruins offer an easy trip into the country. Climb aboard one of the horse-drawn carriages

(200B) and relax into the mellow pace of an old-fashioned conveyance. The driver typically passes pleasantries with the locals who live among the old ruins, which are mainly half-buried brick foundations spread out over 3 sq km. The actual ruins are of more historical importance than spectacle but it is the peaceful surrounding village that completes the attraction.

Wiang Kum Kam was the earliest historical settlement in the Chiang Mai area and was established by the Mon as a satellite town for the Hariphunchai kingdom. It was occupied by Phaya Mengrai in 1286 and used as the Lanna capital for 10 years before the construction of Chiang Mai. The city was abandoned in the 16th century due to massive flooding when Mae Ping changed its course.

Over 1300 inscribed stone slabs, bricks, bells and *chedi* have been excavated at the site. The most important archaeological discovery has been a four-piece inscribed stone slab, now on display in the Chiang Mai National Museum. The early 11th-century inscriptions on this slab indicate that the Thai script predates King Ramkhamhaeng's famous Sukhothai inscription (introduced in 1293) by 100 or more years.

One way to reach Wiang Kum Kam is to hire a bicycle; follow Th Chiang Mai-Lamphun (Rte 106) southeast for approximately 3km and look for a sign to the ruins on the right. From this junction it's another 2km. You could also hire a túk-túk or red *sŏrng·tăa·ou* for around 100B (one way).

Chinatown   HISTORICAL DISTRICT

West of the market, along Th Chang Moi, is the city's small Chinatown, most obviously marked by a flamboyant Chinese-style arch and the typical two-storey shophouses of Southeast Asia's mercantile districts. Most stores are family-owned businesses selling bulk household products and yellow-gold jewellery. There are also the old apothecaries smelling of tree bark and dried herbs. The area is home to two Chinese temples and clan houses and hosts an annual Chinese New Year parade. A small population of Sikhs also live in this area and specialise in selling bolts of fabric. They worship at the nearby Namdhari Sikh Temple (Map p240; Th Ratchawong), catering to the Namdhari sect of Sikhism.

Talat Warorot   MARKET

(ตลาดวโรรส; Map p240; cnr Th Chang Moi & Th Praisani; ⊙6am-5pm) Following Th Chang Moi towards the river you'll discover a beehive of activity around Chiang Mai's oldest and most famous marketplace, Talat Warorot. In northern Thai dialect, the market is known as *gàht lŏo·ang* (northern Thai for 'great market'). Technically there are two multistorey buildings that comprise the market, but so much activity surrounds these enclosures and spreads into the neighbouring area that it is hard to define Talat Warorot's specific boundaries.

Outside the market buildings are fruit and vegetable vendors selling highland varieties that are considered exotic to central Thais. Parked nearby are an extinct species in Bangkok: sǎhm·lór (also spelt sǎamláw)

RIVER CRUISES

Mae Ping is rural and rustic in most parts with grassy banks and small stilted houses crouching alongside. There are several day and evening boat tours that explore this waterway.

» Scorpion Tailed River Cruise (Map p240; ☑08 1960 9398; www.scorpiontailed.com; Th Charoenrat; fare 500B) focuses on the history of the river using traditional-style craft, known as scorpion-tailed boats. Informative cruises (five daily) last 1½ hours. They depart from Wat Srikhong pier near Rim Ping Condo and stop for a snack at the affiliated Scorpion Tailed Boat Village.

» Mae Ping River Cruises (☑0 5327 4822; www.maepingrivercruise.com; Wat Chaimongkhon, 133 Th Charoen Prathet) offers two-hour daytime cruises (450B) in roofed long-tail boats. The boats stop at a small farm for fruit snacks after touring the countryside. The 1½-hour Thai dinner cruise (550B) offers a set menu, and departs daily at 7pm. The departure point is across the river from Ban Kaew Guest House; it's well signposted.

» Riverside Bar & Restaurant (p270) also has a post-dinner cruise.

drivers who shuttle home shoppers burdened with produce.

If you push your way through the thick barrier of vendor stalls, you'll find the interior market selling pickled products, premade curries and packaged *kâap mŏo* (pork rinds). It's an especially good market for cheap clothes, fabrics and cooking implements, as well as inexpensive cosmetics and handicrafts.

Wat Ketkaram   NEIGHBOURHOOD
(แม่ปิง/วัดเกตการาม; Map 237; Th Charoenrat) Chiang Mai's exalted river is **Mae Ping** (see boxed text, p244). A community of Chinese traders and Western missionaries populated the eastern riverbank directly across from Talat Warorot. Today the neighbourhood is called Wat Ket, the nickname of the nearby temple, Wat Ketkaram. The temple was built in the 15th century and houses an eclectic museum of attic-like treasures.

If Th Charoenrat had footpaths, this area would rival the old city for its ancient ambience and tourist appeal. But speeding traffic claims the narrow space between buildings. Instead, it's best to dive deeper into the neighbourhood by going along one of the little lanes off Th Charoenrat and behind the temple.

SOUTH OF THE OLD CITY
The southern part of the city is a mix of quaint antique districts and impersonal modern spaces. Th Wualai is renowned for its **silver shops** and is often filled with the tapping sound of a decorative pattern being imprinted onto a plate of silver (or, more often, aluminium). One of the best ways to observe Th Wualai is to come at the start of the Saturday Walking Street when traffic is blocked off for pedestrians.

Saturday Walking Street   MARKET
(ถนนเดินวันเสาร์; Map p236; Th Wualai; ☺4pm-midnight Sat) The Saturday Walking Street has developed a reputation of having more authentic handicrafts and being less commercial than the Sunday Walking Street. This might be a bit of an exaggeration as most vendors work both markets without exclusion. But the atmospheric old neighbourhood with its silver shops and old ladies wrapped up in Thai silk does give it an authenticity. It's also slightly less hectic, making an evening stroll a bit more pleasant.

Wat Sisuphan   TEMPLE
(วัดศรีสุพรรณ; Map p240; Soi 2, Th Wualai; donations appreciated) This *wát* was founded in 1502, but little remains of the original structures except for some teak pillars and roof beams in the *wí·hǎhn*. The **murals** inside show an interesting mix of Taoist, Zen and Theravada Buddhist elements. The *ubosot* (chapel) next door is allegedly the only silver ordination hall in Thailand (although technically they were using a mix of aluminium, compounded silver and pure silver), and the result of the recent renovation is magnificent. The temple hosts a monk chat and meditation instruction (see boxed text, p250). Wat Sisuphan is one of the few *wát* in Chiang Mai where you can see the Poy Luang (also known as Poy Sang Long) Festival, a Shan-style group ordination of young boys as Buddhist novices, in late March.

WEST OF THE OLD CITY
Th Nimmanhaemin is the city's most stylish avenue, a busy multilane road with a number of small residential lane offshoots, where 1970s garden houses have been converted into style-conscious commercial concerns, mainly nightlife.

THE PLIGHT OF CHIANG MAI'S MIGRANT WORKERS

When travelling in the 'land of smiles', exactly whose smiles do we encounter? Thailand is not only home to a diverse range of indigenous ethnic groups, but also to an estimated three million migrant workers from neighbouring countries, notably Laos, Cambodia and, especially, Myanmar (Burma).

Refugees from Myanmar (Burma) have fled across the Thai border since the 1980s, fleeing the armed conflict taking place in ethnic areas and the persecution of pro-democracy activists. Eight IDP (internally displaced persons) camps on the Burmese side of the border provide a little security to 20,000 people and nine camps in Thailand provide more security, but few rights to 100,000, mostly Karen, refugees. There is also an estimated half a million IDPs still in Burma.

In the absence of formal migration channels, many more Burmese live and work in Thailand as undocumented migrant workers – now a significant feature of the Thai economy and society. Over the last 20 years the Thai government has allowed migrants who entered the country without documents to register annually for a temporary work permit. More recently the government has embarked on a complicated process to request the countries of origin to verify the nationality of the migrants and issue them with temporary passports.

Many migrant workforces, often consisting entirely of Burmese, work in exploitative conditions: employers do not bother to pay the minimum wage, with full knowledge of the difficulties their employees will face if they attempt to seek redress. Undocumented migrant workers also live in constant fear of arrest, detention and deportation from the authorities.

There are an estimated 150,000 to 200,000 migrant workers in Chiang Mai Province alone. The vast majority are from Shan State, which borders northern Thailand. Shan migrants find work on construction sites in Chiang Mai, building housing estates, condominiums, shopping malls and prisons. Take a glimpse at the makeshift shelters on the next construction site you pass and you'll get an idea of the conditions migrants are forced to live in. If the building has no safety nets, if there is flimsy bamboo scaffolding, and if the workers are barefooted, then it is migrant workers doing the building for little more than US$3 a day. And don't be surprised to see women working on construction sites – it is very common in Thailand.

Women migrants also find employment as domestic workers in private households in Chiang Mai. Their living and working conditions are totally dependent on their employer as they have no protection under the labour laws. But they are not all prepared to be exploited and abused: one clever young lady noticed how her employer, who hadn't paid her for two years, always proudly showed off a trophy to visitors. Unable to read Thai, she had no idea what it said, but she laboriously copied down each letter and carefully hid it away. One day she made a run for it, and showed some NGO workers what she had written. It was an award to the president of a respected local club giving his full name. Needless to say, she gained a little leverage in her negotiations with him for her unpaid salary.

A large number of migrants also work in the sprawling orange and lychee orchards that stretch across northern Chiang Mai's Fang district. They live in bamboo huts in small communities and work taking care of the trees, and picking and sorting the fruit. A lot of the work involves dangerous pesticides, and proper training or protective clothing is rarely given.

The needs of migrant communities range from information about their rights, to assistance with their health, education and welfare needs. Several NGOs offer dedicated services and/or carry out advocacy work to try and meet these needs. **MAP Foundation** (www.mapfoundationcm.org) and **Migrants from Mekong Neighbourhood** (MMN; www.mekongmigration.org) are two such organisations based in Chiang Mai. If you are interested in helping migrant workers, or in learning more about these issues, contact these organisations via their websites.

Reiko Harima – Migrants from Mekong Neighbourhood
Jackie Pollock – MAP Foundation

TOP CHOICE Best Friend Library LIBRARY
(Map p248; 302/2 Soi 13, Th Nimmanhaemin; ⏱11.30am-8pm Mon-Sat) A nonprofit lending library and resource centre for Myanmar (Burma), this place also sells books, videos and other items about Myanmar (Burma) with profits being ploughed back into charities working directly with Burmese refugees and street children.

Wat U Mong TEMPLE
(วัดอุโมงค์; Map p236; Soi Wat U Mong, Th Khlong Chonprathan; donations appreciated) If you've never visited a forest wát, you should make the trek to this temple. Not only does it offer a secluded sylvan setting, considered an important component for meditation in the forest wát tradition, it is also famous for its interconnecting tunnels built underneath the main chedi terrace.

The temple was first used during Phaya Mengrai's rule in the 14th century. The brick-lined tunnels were allegedly fashioned around 1380 for the clairvoyant monk Thera Jan. The monastery was abandoned at a later date and wasn't reactivated until a local Thai prince sponsored a restoration in the late 1940s. The since-deceased Ajan Buddhadasa Bhikkhu, a well-known monk and teacher at southern Thailand's Wat Suanmok, sent a number of monks to re-establish a monastic community at Wat U Mong in the 1960s.

A marvellously grisly image of the fasting Buddha – ribs, veins and all – can be seen in the grounds on top of the tunnel hill, along with a very large and highly venerated chedi. Also on the grounds is a small artificial lake, surrounded by gù·dì (monastic cottages).

Wat U Mong is accessible from a series of small lanes off Th Suthep near Chiang Mai University. Once you reach the university, keep an eye out for signs pointing the way. Note that there is another temple named Wat U Mong in Chiang Mai. To make sure a sŏrng·tăa·ou or túk-túk driver understands you want this one ask for 'Wat U Mong Thera Jan'.

Wat Suan Dok TEMPLE
(วัดสวนดอก; Map p236; Th Suthep; donations appreciated) Built on a former flower garden in 1373, this temple is not as architecturally interesting as the temples in the old city but it does have a very powerful photographic attribute: the temple's collection of whitewashed chedi sit in the foreground while the blue peaks of Doi Suthep and Doi Pui loom in the background.

Wat Suan Dok is also spiritually united with the temple that sits upon Doi Suthep thanks to an auspicious relic brought to Chiang Mai by Phra Sumana Thera, a visiting monk from Sukhothai. According to legend, the relic miraculously duplicated itself: one piece was enshrined in the temple's large central chedi (recently wrapped in gold sheet), while the other was used as a 'guide' for the founding of Wat Doi Suthep. This main chedi is a textbook example of the Lanna period that began to be influenced by Sukhothai. The other chedi on the grounds contain the ashes of various members of the Lanna royal family.

Today Wat Suan Dok is home to a large population of resident monks and novices, many of them students at the monastery's Mahachulalongkorn Buddhist University. Foreigners often come to Wat Suan Dok for the popular monk chat (see boxed text, p250) and the English-language meditation retreats.

Chiang Mai University UNIVERSITY
(มหาวิทยาลัยเชียงใหม่; CMU; Map p236; Th Huay Kaew) The city's principal public university was established in 1964. The main campus occupies a 2.9 sq km wedge of land about 2km west of the city centre that has preserved much of its original forest character. Architecturally the campus buildings are soot-stained boxes, but the verdant environment achieves a distinctively Thai version of an idyllic collegiate setting. The best way for visitors to enjoy the campus is to ride a bicycle through it – there are bike lanes throughout, and cafes to stop at for a refreshment break.

There are two main entrances into the campus on Th Suthep and Th Huay Kaew. When giving directions, Thais often refer to the university area on Th Suthep as 'lăng mor' (behind the university) and on Th Huay Kaew as 'nâh mor' (in front of the university).

Chiang Mai University Art Museum
(Th Nimmanhaemin; admission free; ⏱9am-5pm Tue-Sun) The museum displays temporary exhibitions of contemporary Thai and international art. Local artists, such as Tanakarn Songlin and Tiwawan Srisombat, were the best of the bunch we saw, bringing everyday activity to life with poignancy and joy. Although the temporary exhibits can be a bit hit and miss (there's no permanent collection), we saw a lot of creativity in the works

Western Chiang Mai

on display. The exhibits in the university grounds outside the museum shop are permanent – we like the crab-creature made of old wood and rusted metal. The museum is near the intersection of Th Suthep and Th Klorng Chonprathan.

Chiang Mai Zoo
ZOO

(สวนสัตว์/แหล่งเพาะพันธุ์ไม้ป่าเขตร้อนเชียงใหม่; off Map p236; ☎0 5322 1179; www.chiangmaizoo.com; 100 Th Huay Kaew; adult/child 100/50B; ◷8am-5pm) At the foot of Doi Suthep, the Chiang Mai Zoo occupies a lush park setting and boasts a fairly comprehensive assortment of animals plus two special attractions (pandas and an aquarium) that require separate admission fees. The **aquarium** (adult/child 520/390B) reportedly has Asia's longest viewing tunnel (measuring 113m) and replicates the water environments of Thailand, from the northern rivers to the mangrove swamps and coastal oceans, as well as the Amazon basin.

Except for the baby elephant on a walkway for entertainment of visitors (with leg chained, which was disturbing) and some animals obviously in distress (ie walking around in circles) in their concrete enclosures, most animals seem fairly well treated here.

The zoo also has a parking garage that costs 10B for motorcycles and bicycles and 50B for cars or trucks.

Chiang Mai Night Safari
ZOO

(เชียงใหม่ในท์ซาฟารี; ☎0 5399 9000; www.chiang mainightsafari.com; Rte 121/Th Klorng Chonprathan; ◷11am-11pm) This attraction is open during the day but the real action happens at night during the **Predator Prowl** and '**Savannah Safari**' (adult/child 500/300B), when an open-sided tram transports visitors through the parkland. The English-language tram leaves at 7.45pm and 9.30pm and the tour takes about two hours. The night safari differs from the Chiang Mai Zoo in that some animals – like wildebeests, giraffes, white rhinoceroses and zebras – are allowed to roam and often come right up to the bus. In the 'Predator Prowl' section, the tigers, lions, Asiatic black bears and crocodiles are kept at a safe distance by deep trenches.

During the day you can visit the **Jaguar Trail** (adult/child 100/50B) encircling Swan Lake, a 1.2km walk where over 50 species (ranging from rabbits to cranes) are generally not in cages, except of course the trail's namesake animal.

The Night Safari is about 12km from central Chiang Mai and a *sŏrng·tăa·ou* should

Western Chiang Mai

cost about 100B. You can also book this through a tour agency that handles hotel transfer.

NORTH OF THE OLD CITY
Sights north of the old city through Pratu Chang Pheuak (the 'white elephant gate', a reference to the elephant who carried the sacred relic to Doi Suthep) are less of a tourist draw, which is a draw in itself for some. These sights tend to be too far spread out to visit on foot; it is advisable to hire your own transport.

Wat Jet Yot   TEMPLE
(วัดเจ็ดยอด; Map p236; Th Superhighway) Dedicated temple-spotters are the prime candidates for Wat Jet Yot. It was built to host the eighth World Buddhist Council in 1477, a momentous occasion for the Lanna capital. To the back of the temple compound are the ruins of the old *wí·hǎhn,* which was supposed to be a replica of the Mahabodhi Temple in Bodhgaya, India, but the proportions don't match up. Some scholars assume that the blueprint for the temple must have come from a small votive tablet depicting the Mahabodhi in distorted perspective.

Although much of the decorative stucco work is gone, you can still count the *jèt yôrt* (seven spires) that represent the seven weeks Buddha was supposed to have spent in Bodhgaya after his enlightenment. Of the original stucco relief, a few intact Bodhisattva (Buddhist saints, usually associated with Mahayana Buddhism) depictions remain on the outer walls.

Wat Chiang Yeun   TEMPLE
(วัดเชียงยืน; Map p236; Th Mani Nopharat) Another unique local temple is 16th-century Wat Chiang Yeun, just northeast of Pratu Chang Pheuak. Besides the large northern-style *chedi* here, the main attraction is an old **Burmese colonial-style gate** and **pavilion** on the eastern side of the school grounds attached to the wát. This area of Chiang Mai was historically settled by Shan people and the shops still maintain that ethnic identity, catering to Shan and Burmese temple-goers with such products as pickled tea leaves (*mêe·ang* in Thai) and Shan-style noodles.

MONK CHAT

If you're curious about Buddhism, Chiang Mai is a great place to learn about its teachings and rituals, as well as Thai culture and the life of a monk. Some of the temples in town offer a 'monk chat', where a resident monk or novice fields questions from foreigners. This simple exchange gives them a chance to practise their English while answering questions about daily routines, Buddhist teachings or even how monks stay wrapped up in their robes. Remember that it is respectful to dress modestly: cover your shoulders and knees. Women should take care not to touch the monks or their belongings or to pass anything directly to them.

Wat Suan Dok (Map p236; www.monkchat.net; Th Suthep; ⏰5-7pm Mon, Wed & Fri) has a dedicated room for foreigners to interact with the monastic students. To find the room, enter the wát from the main entrance and walk 100m or so into the temple grounds.

Wat Chedi Luang (Map p240; Th Phra Pokklao; ⏰1-6pm Mon-Fri) and **Wat Sisuphan** (Map p236; 100 Th Wualai; ⏰5.30-7pm Tue, Thu & Sat) both have monk chat tables.

Wat Ku Tao   TEMPLE
(วัดกู่เต้า; Map p236; Soi 6, Th Chang Pheuak) North of the moat, Wat Ku Tao dates from 1613 and has a unique *chedi* that looks like a pile of diminishing spheres, a Tai Lü design common in Yunnan, China. The *chedi* is said to contain the ashes of Tharawadi Min, a son of the Burmese king Bayinnaung, ruler of Lanna from 1578 to 1607.

Chiang Mai National Museum   MUSEUM
(พิพิธภัณฑสถานแห่งชาติเชียงใหม่; Map p236; ☎0 5322 1308; www.thailandmuseum.com; off Th Superhighway; admission 100B; ⏰9am-4pm Wed-Sun) Operated by the Fine Arts Department and established in 1973, the Chiang Mai National Museum functions as the primary caretaker of Lanna artefacts and as the curator of northern Thailand's history. This museum is a nice complement to the municipally run Chiang Mai City Arts & Cultural Centre (p238) because you'll find more art and artefacts here and the scope of the exhibits reaches beyond the city limits. The best curated section of the museum is the **Lanna art** section, which displays a selection of Buddha images in all styles, and explains the different periods and influences. Apart from this upstairs exhibit, the museum is a bit lacklustre, although worth a visit to orient your historical perspective of northern Thailand.

Tribal Museum   MUSEUM
(พิพิธภัณฑ์ชาวเขา; ☎0 5321 0872; tribalmuseum-chiangmai.com; off Th Chang Pheuak) Overlooking a lake in Suan Ratchamangkhala on the northern outskirts of the city, this octagonal museum houses a collection of handicrafts, costumes, jewellery, ornaments, household utensils, agricultural tools, musical instruments and ceremonial paraphernalia. The museum was closed for renovations at the time of research.

Huay Teung Thao Reservoir   RESERVOIR
(อ่างเก็บน้ำห้วยตึงเฒ่า; admission 20B; ⏰8am-sunset) Thais love lounging by the water and this sizeable reservoir, at the northwestern foot of Doi Suthep-Pui National Park, has become more than just a piece of infrastructure. The banks are dotted with floating bamboo huts (10B per person), where Thais come to snack on fried bugs (another reservoir pastime), share a bottle of whisky and perfect the art of relaxation. The reservoir is about 12km northwest of the city. Travelling by car or motorcycle you can reach Huay Teung Thao by driving 10km north on Rte 107 (follow signs towards Mae Rim), then west 2km past an army camp to the reservoir.

DOI SUTHEP-PUI NATIONAL PARK   อุทยานแห่งชาติดอยสุเทพ – ปุย
Looming over the city like guardian spirits and providing a sanctuary of forest and mountain cool air, Chiang Mai's sacred peaks, **Doi Suthep** (1676m) and **Doi Pui** (1685m) were used by the city's founders as a divine compass in locating an auspicious position. Suthep was named after the hermit Sudeva, who lived on the mountain's slopes for many years, and is the site of Chiang Mai's holy temple Wat Phra That Doi Suthep.

Portions of the mountains form a 265-sq-km **national park** (☎0 5321 0244; adult/child under 14yr 100/50B, car 30B; ⏰8am-sunset) that contains a mix of wilderness, **hill-tribe villages** and tourist attractions, including Wat Phra That Doi Suthep. Despite human encroachment, the park is still an excellent forest playground for city dwellers. Most people stick to the main road, visiting the temple, the winter palace and one of the touristy Hmong villages, altogether bypassing the forested interior.

The eastern side of the mountain stays green and cool almost year-round. The mountain ascends from the humid lowlands into the cool (and sometimes even cold) cloud belt with moss growing on the curbs and mist wafting across the road. Thriving in the diverse climate are more than 300 **bird species** and nearly 2000 species of **ferns** and **flowering plants**. During the rainy season, **butterflies** bloom as abundantly as the flowers.

There are **hiking** and **mountain-biking** trails as well as **camping**, **birdwatching** and waterfall spotting. One of the most scenic waterfalls is **Nam Tok Monthathon** (the park admission fee is collected here), 2.5km off the paved road to Doi Suthep. Pools beneath the falls hold water year-round, although swimming is best during or just after the annual monsoon. Close to the base of the mountain, **Nam Tok Wang Bua Bahn** is free, and full of frolicking locals, although it is more of a series of rapids than a falls.

For off-road mountain biking, the park has technical single-track trails that were old hunting and transport routes used by hill-tribe villagers. The routes are never crowded and provide hours of downhill. Because the trails aren't well marked it is advisable to join a guided mountain-biking tour; see p252 for more information on activities.

The park fee is collected at some of the park's waterfalls. There is no park fee charged to visit the attractions along the main road, though the attractions have their own admission prices.

Accommodation (www.dnp.go.th; camping 60-90B, bungalows 400-2500B) in the national park includes smart bungalows, about 1km north of the temple by the park headquarters and the Doi Pui campground, near the mountain summit.

The park is about 16km northwest of central Chiang Mai and is accessible via shared *sŏrng·tăa·ou* that leave from the main entrance of Chiang Mai University on Th Huay Kaew. One-way fares start at 40B and increase from there depending on the destination within the park and the number of passengers. You can also charter a *sŏrng·tăa·ou* (passenger pick-up truck) for about 500B (round-trip) or rent a motorcycle (check your travel insurance) for much less. *Sŏrng·tăa·ou* also depart from Pratu Chang Pheuak and the Chiang Mai Zoo. Cyclists (who are very fit) can also make the 13km ascent to the temple – preferably either early in the morning or in the late evening when traffic is diminished.

⬛ TOP CHOICE **Wat Phra That Doi Suthep**   TEMPLE
(วัดพระธาตุดอยสุเทพ; admission 30B) Like a beacon projecting a calming blanket on the urban plains below, Wat Suthep is seen clearly from Chiang Mai, majestically perched atop Doi Suthep's summit. It is one of the north's most sacred temples, and Thai pilgrims flock here to make merit to the Buddhist relic enshrined in the picturesque golden *chedi*. Offering sublime city views, when the clouds and smoke-dust haze (March-June) permit, the temple also has an interesting collection of Lanna art and architecture.

The temple was first established in 1383 under King Keu Naone and enjoys a fantastically mystical birth story. A visiting monk from Sukhothai instructed the Lanna king to take the twin of a miraculous relic (enshrined at Wat Suan Dok) to the mountain and establish a temple. The relic was mounted on the back of a white elephant, which was allowed to wander until it 'chose' a site on which a *wát* could be built to enshrine it. The elephant stopped and died at a spot on Doi Suthep, 13km west of Chiang Mai, where the temple was built in the year of the goat.

The temple is reached by a strenuous *naga*-balustrade staircase of 306 steps, a feature that incorporates aspects of medita-

CHIANG MAI PROVINCE SIGHTS

THE LONG WALK

At the start of every academic year in July, the freshman class from Chiang Mai University makes the annual pilgrimage on foot to Wat Suthep. It is a long-time tradition that fills the winding mountain road with close to 10,000 exuberant students and faculty members. The purpose of the trek is to introduce the new students to the spirit of the city, believed to reside in the mountain, and to make merit to the revered Buddha relic at Wat Suthep. But it is also a chance for the students to introduce themselves to each other and make friends that might last a lifetime.

tion with a cardio workout. (For the less fit, there's a tram for 20B.) You'll first reach an open-air terrace filled with important statues and shrines documenting the history of the temple. Near a signed jackfruit tree is a shrine to Sudeva, the hermit who lived on the mountain, and nearby is a statue of the white elephant who carried the relic up the mountain slope. Follow the walkway around in the clockwise direction to reach a viewpoint and a small sanctuary dedicated to the king who established the temple.

A second set of stairs leads to the main cloister and the temple's famously photographed **gold-plated chedi**, topped by a five-tiered umbrella erected in honour of the city's independence from Burma and its union with Thailand. It is the *chedi* (and the sacred Buddha relic enshrined inside) not a resident Buddha image that attracts the majority of worshippers.

Within the monastery compound, the **International Buddhism Center** conducts a variety of religious outreach programs for visitors; see p255 for more information.

Phra Tamnak Bhu Bhing   TEMPLE
(พระตำหนักภูพิงค์; Bhu Bhing Palace; admission 50B; ◷8.30-11.30am & 1-3.30pm) About 4km beyond the temple is Phra Tamnak Phu Bhing, a winter palace for the royal family surrounded by gardens that are open to the public. It closes if the royal family is visiting, but that's not very often. The gardens specialise in cool-weather flowers, like roses, which are exotic to Thais. More interesting is the **water reservoir** brought to life by dancing fountains moving in sync to musical compositions by the king. Though not a must, the **gardens** are good for 'nature sightseers' who like their forests to have paved footpaths.

Hmong Villages   CULTURAL
หมู่บ้านชาวม้ง
The road that passes the palace splits off to the left, stopping at the peak of Doi Pui. From there, a road proceeds for a couple of kilometres to **Ban Doi Pui**, a Hmong hilltribe village. Don't expect much evidence of village life here though – it is basically a tourist market selling Hmong crafts and souvenirs. There is a tiny **museum** (admission 10B) giving some information about hill tribes and opium production.

A more interesting Hmong village is **Ban Kun Chang Kian**, north of the Doi Pui campground. Instead of going left on the road past the palace head right. The road is paved just past the campground and then for the last 500m or so it is a bumpy dirt track. To save wear and tear, you can park at the campground's visitor centre and walk from there to enjoy the ridgeline and the pink flowering trees (called '*pá·yah sĕua krôhng*'). You'll find a basic village-run coffee house surrounded by coffee plants that are harvested in January.

🏃 Activities
The surrounding mountains, rivers and byways boast a wave of adrenaline sports that have begun to eclipse the traditional trekking tour.

The countryside surrounding Chiang Mai is exceptional for two-wheeled outings. The city's closest green space, Doi Suthep (p250) is gaining its own fame for off-road **mountain biking**. For **motorcyclists** and long-distance **cyclists**, the Mae Sa–Samoeng loop (p284) is the closest and most stunning escape into the mountains.

Chiang Mai is one of Thailand's most famous destinations for **elephant 'encounters'**. In the past, most elephant attractions were circus-like sideshows. But there has been a new sensitivity in recent times towards the quality of life for Thailand's emblematic animal, resulting in a diversification of attractions towards nature preserves and mahout-training schools.

Rock climbers head to Crazy Horse Buttress, an impressive set of limestone cliffs located behind Tham Meuang On, near Sankamphaeng, 45km east of Chiang Mai. While the scenery isn't as stunning as Krabi's seaside cliffs, the ascents reward with pastoral views.

White-water rafting is also possible. Mae Taeng is north of Chiang Mai and carves a path through the Doi Chiang Dao National Park and the Huai Nam Dang National Park. The river is a wild and frothy white-water ride for nine months of the year (roughly from July to March), a surprisingly long season in this monsoonal climate. The 10km rafting route travels through grade II to grade IV, and some grade V, rapids. In one particularly thrilling stretch, the river drops almost 60m in about 1.5km. Following a heavy rain, especially in September, the river can become swollen and ferocious and drownings do occur. When choosing a white-water outfitter, ask about their safety standards and training (and check your travel insurance).

TREKKING IN CHIANG MAI

Thousands of visitors trek into the hills of northern Thailand each year hoping to see fantastic mountain scenery, interact with primitive cultures and ride elephants. Most come with an Indiana Jones sense of adventure but leave with disappointment: the actual walk through the jungle lasted less than an hour, the hill-tribe villagers were disinterested in the lowlanders and the other trekkers were boring.

Most companies operating out of Chiang Mai offer the same type of tour: a one-hour mini-bus ride to Mae Taeng or Mae Wang (depending on the duration of the trip), a brief hike to an elephant camp, a one-hour elephant ride to a waterfall, another hour rafting down a river and an overnight in or near a hill-tribe village. The day goes by pretty quickly and then you've got to entertain yourself among strangers from sunset to bedtime, without the usual social lubricants.

Chiang Mai is not the only base for hill-tribe treks but it is the most accessible. Most guest houses in Chiang Mai act as booking agents in exchange for a commission, which in turn subsidises the cheap room rates. One-day treks usually cost around 1000B, while multiday treks (three days and two nights) cost 1500B. Both prices include transport, guide and lunch; in the case of overnight trips, the price also includes lodging (prices will be a bit more in high season). More expensive treks that offer a better experience may be available; ask around.

For general tips on choosing a trekking company and places to go trekking, see boxed text, p253.

Flight of the Gibbon ZIPLINING
(☎08 9970 5511; www.treetopasia.com; Mae Kampong; 3hr tours 3000B) This adventure outfit in Chiang Mai operates a zipline through the forest canopy some 1300m above sea level. Nearly 2km of wire with 18 staging platforms follow the ridgeline and mimic the branch-to-branch route a gibbon might take down the mountain. You can also tack on mountain biking (5800B), rock climbing (6300B), rafting (6500B) or hiking (7900B) over two days, which includes an overnight at a homestay in Mae Kampong (see p290), a pretty high-altitude village an hour's drive east from Chiang Mai.

Elephant Nature Park ELEPHANT PARK
(Map p240; booking office ☎0 5320 8246; www.elephantnaturepark.org; 1 Th Ratchamankha; 1-/2-day tours 2500/5800B) Khun Lek (Sangduen Chailert) has won numerous awards for her elephant sanctuary in the Mae Taeng valley, 60km (1½-hour drive) from Chiang Mai. The forested area provides a semi-wild environment for the elephants that have been rescued from abusive situations or retired from a lifetime of work. Visitors can help wash the elephants and watch the herd but there is no show or riding. Volunteer work for up to four weeks (that includes helping to wash the elephants and provide their health care) is available – see the website for details.

Patara Elephant Farm ELEPHANT PARK
(☎08 1992 2551; www.pataraelephantfarm.com; full-day tours 5800B) More expensive and more hands-on, Patara's farm has a slightly different focus than the Elephant Nature Park. The first mission is to combat the declining numbers of elephants in Thailand through a breeding program and to develop a safe tourism model. The six resident elephants are 'adopted' by the guests for the day. Activities with your elephant include feeding, bathing, learning basic mahout commands and riding to a waterfall. Tours are limited to six people and the fee includes hotel transfers. The farm is a 30-minute drive south of Chiang Mai in the Hang Dong area.

Baan Chang Elephant Park ELEPHANT PARK
(☎0 5381 4174; www.baanchangelephantpark.com; full-day 1-2 person tours 4200B) Another good option, this place concentrates on educating visitors about elephants and their preservation – we've had good feedback about Baan Chang. Tours involve taking care of an elephant for a day and some training to learn about their behaviour and lifestyle (including feeding and bathing). While you'll ride bareback through the jungle, the centre is firmly against teaching elephants to perform tricks. The training program is in Mae Taeng, 50 minutes north of Chiang Mai.

PAMPERING & PUMMELLING

While there are a few truly exceptional spas in Chiang Mai, the city excels in a more modest category: old-fashioned Thai massage. The massage centre might be just a few mattresses on the floor, but the practitioner can bend, stretch and pummel knotted bodies into jelly without New Age gimmicks.

Many of the temples in the old city have a massage *săh·lah* (often spelt *sala*) on the grounds, continuing an ancient tradition of the monasteries being a repository for traditional knowledge and healing.

Chiang Mai Women's Prison Massage Centre (Map p240; 100 Th Ratwithi; foot/traditional massage 150-180B; ⊙8am-4.30pm) offers fantastic full body and foot massages, performed by inmates at the women's prison as a part of their rehabilitation training program. Despite their incarceration, those working in the massage centre are due for release within six months. The money earned from these treatments goes directly to the prisoners for use after their release. Other rehabilitation initiatives include teaching sewing and cake baking – the results of which you'll find in the same building.

Ban Hom Samunphrai (⊘0 5381 7362; www.homprang.com; 93/2 Moo 12; treatments 500-1300B) is a unique time capsule of old folk ways, 9km from Chiang Mai near the McKean Institute. Maw Hom ('Herbal Doctor') is a licensed herb practitioner and massage therapist. She runs a traditional herbal steam bath recreating what was once a common feature of rural villages. Traditional Thai massage is also available.

Thai Massage Conservation Club (Map p240; 99 Th Ratchamankha; massages 150-250B) employs only blind masseuses, who are considered to be expert practitioners because of their heightened sense of touch.

Dheva Spa (⊘0 5388 8888; www.mandarinoriental.com/chiangmai/spa/; Mandarin Oriental Dhara Dhevi, 51/4 Th Chiang Mai-San Kamphaeng; treatments from 3500B), the grandest spa in all of Chiang Mai, is also a cheaper passport into the exclusive and stunning grounds of the luxurious Mandarin Oriental Dhara Dhevi resort than a night's stay there would be. Try the *tok sen* massage, an old Lanna technique that uses a wooden gavel to tap on pressure points. Now you'll know how a piece of carved wood feels.

Oasis Spa (Map p240; ⊘0 5392 0111; www.chiangmaioasis.com; 4 Th Samlan; treatments 1900-6500B) has a tranquil garden setting navigated by elevated walkways hosting private villas for single or couples treatments. If you've spa-ed elsewhere in Thailand, the Oasis will be a familiar friend, offering scrubs, wraps, massage and ayurvedic treatments.

Chiang Mai Rock Climbing Adventures ROCK CLIMBING

(Map p240; ⊘08 6911 1470; www.thailandclimbing.com; 55/3 Th Ratchaphakhinai; climbing course 2000-6500B) Maintains many of the climbing routes at Crazy Horse Buttress, and the expat owner publishes a guide to rock climbing in northern Thailand. If you prefer subterranean cliffs, it also leads caving trips in the same area. The office on Th Ratchaphakhinai has gear sales and rental, a partner-finding service and a bouldering wall for practice sessions. It offers introductory climbing courses for beginners and advanced training for multipitch climbs; trips include guides, gear, hotel transfers and lunch.

Peak ROCK CLIMBING

(⊘0 5380 0567; www.thepeakadventure.com; climbing course 1800-2500B) Teaches introductory and advanced rock-climbing courses at Crazy Horse Buttress. The Peak also leads a variety of soft adventure trips, including quad biking, as well as trekking, white-water rafting and a jungle survival cooking course. Note it's best to book directly with the company, and not through a travel agent.

Siam River Adventures RAFTING

(Map p240; ⊘089 515 1917; www.siamrivers.com; 17 Th Ratwithi; tours from 1800B) Has the best safety reputation. The guides have swiftwater rescue training and additional staff are located at dangerous parts of the river with throw ropes. Trips can be combined with elephant trekking and village overnights. It also operates kayak trips.

Chiang Mai Mountain Biking MOUNTAIN BIKING

(Map p240; ⊘08 1024 7046; www.mountainbikingchiangmai.com; 1 Th Samlan; tours from 1450-2700B) Offers a variety of guided mountain biking (as well as hike-and-bike) tours through Doi Suthep for all levels.

Click and Travel
CYCLING

(✐0 5328 1553; www.clickandtravelonline.com; tours 950-1500B; ⊛) Specialises in half-day and full-day bicycle tours of Chiang Mai. It is a pedal-powered (and family friendly) cultural trip, visiting temples and attractions outside of the city centre. Hotel transfer is included in the price; make arrangements online or via phone.

700-Year Anniversary Stadium
SWIMMING

(✐0 5311 2301; 185 Th Klorng Chonprathan) Modern sports complex with Olympic-sized swimming pool.

Anantasiri Tennis Courts
TENNIS

(✐0 5322 2210; off Th Superhighway; ⊗6am-8pm daily) The best public tennis facility in Chiang Mai. It's just off the Superhighway near the Chiang Mai National Museum.

Gymkhana Club
SPORTS CLUB

(✐0 5324 1035; www.chiengmaigymkhana.com; Th Ratuthit) Scenic sports and social club with squash and tennis courts, golf and driving range open to nonmembers for a day-use fee. It's just of the Chiang Mai-Lamphun Rd.

Centre of the Universe
SWIMMING

(www.therealcentreoftheuniverse.com) Chiang Mai's only saltwater swimming pool; it's 6km north of the city centre.

Namo
YOGA

(Map p240; ✐0 5332 6648; www.namochiangmai. com; 109/1 Th Moon Muang; classes 200B) Tucked away down a quiet lane near Tha Pae Gate, Namo has drop-in yoga classes at 10.30am and 6pm from Monday to Friday. Also runs a half-day massage workshop.

⮌ Courses

Buddhist Meditation

The following temples offer *vipassana* meditation courses and retreats to English-language speakers. Participants here should dress in modest white clothes, which can typically be purchased from the temple. Following Buddhist precepts, there is no set fee but donations are appreciated. Peruse the various websites for course descriptions and daily routines.

International Buddhism Center
MEDITATION

(IBC; ✐0 5329 5012; www.fivethousandyears. org; Wat Phra That Doi Suthep) Headquartered within the temple grounds on Doi Suthep.

It offers beginner to advanced meditation retreats, lasting from three to 21 days.

Northern Insight Meditation Centre
MEDITATION

(✐0 5327 8620; www.watrampoeng.com; Wat Ram Poeng) Located 4km south of Chiang Mai and offers an intensive 26-day or longer course. Days start at 4am and meals are taken in silence. The formal name for Wat Ram Poeng is Wat Tapotaram. Requirements include bringing your own white underwear, an alarm clock, passport and passport photos; and an understanding and acceptance of the strict rules governing a stay here. See website for more.

Wat Sisuphan
MEDITATION

(Map p236; ✐0 5320 0332; 100 Th Wualai) Offers a two-hour introduction to meditation using the four postures: standing, walking, sitting and lying down.

Wat Suan Dok
MEDITATION

(Map p236; ✐0 5380 8411 ext 114; www.monkchat. net; Th Suthep) Offers a two-day meditation retreat every Tuesday to Wednesday. At the end of each month, the temple extends the retreat to a four-day period (Tuesday to Friday). Participants should register in advance and meet at Wat Suan Dok for transfer to the meditation centre, 15km northeast of Chiang Mai. Check the website for cancellation notices.

Cooking

Courses in Thai cuisine are another staple of Chiang Mai's vacation learning scene. Dozens of schools offer cooking classes, typically costing around 1000B a day, either at an in-town location, like an atmospheric old house, or out of town in a garden or farm setting. Classes are usually offered five or more times a week and the menu might vary each day. Students will learn about Thai culinary herbs and spices, tour a local market and prepare a set menu. Of course, you also get to eat the Thai food and travel home with a recipe booklet.

Asia Scenic Thai Cooking
COOKING

(Map p240; ✐0 5341 8657; www.asiascenic.com; 31 Soi 5, Th Ratchadamnoen) Run by Khun Gayray who speaks great English and has done some backpacking herself.

Baan Thai
COOKING

(Map p240; ✐0 5335 7339; www.baanthaicookery. com; 11 Soi 5, Th Ratchadamnoen) Has an in-town location where you can select which dishes to prepare; most of their courses include a tour of a local market – very useful for identifying local fruit and veg.

Chiang Mai Thai Cookery School COOKING
(Map p240; ☑0 5320 6388; www.thaicookery school.com; booking office, 47/2 Th Moon Muang) One of Chiang Mai's first cooking schools holds classes in a rural setting outside of Chiang Mai. The school also has a 'masterclass' with a northern Thai menu. A portion of the profits funds education of disadvantaged kids.

Gap's Thai Culinary Art School COOKING
(Map p240; ☑0 5327 8140; www.gaps-house.com; 3 Soi 4, Th Ratchadamnoen) Affiliated with the guest house Gap's House (where you can make your booking) and holds its classes out of town at the owner's house.

Thai Farm Cooking School COOKING
(Map p240; ☑08 7174 9285; www.thaifarmcooking. com; booking office, 2/2 Soi 5, Th Ratchadamnoen) Teaches cooking classes at its organic farm, located 17km outside of Chiang Mai.

Language

Being a university town, Chiang Mai fosters continuing education opportunities in Thai language.

American University Alumni LANGUAGE
(AUA; Map p240; ☑0 5327 8407; www.learnthai inchiangmai.com; 73 Th Ratchadamnoen; group course 4200B) Conducts six-week Thai courses that work on mastering tones, small talk and basic reading and writing. Classes meet for two hours, Monday to Friday. Private instruction is also available.

Payap University LANGUAGE
(off Map p236; http://ic.payap.ac.th; Kaew Nawarat Campus, Th Kaew Nawarat) A private university founded by the Church of Christ of Thailand and offers an academic Thai course through the **foreign language centre** (☑0 5385 1478 ext 475), which covers all levels in 60/120-hour modules (8000/20,200B).

Thai Boxing

Lanna Muay Thai Boxing Camp BOXING
(Kiatbusaba; ☑0 5389 2102; www.lannamuaythai. com; 161 Soi Chang Khian, Th Huay Kaew; fees per day/month 400/8000B) Offers *moo·ay tai* (Thai boxing, also spelt *muay thai*) instruction to foreigners and Thais. Several Lanna students have won stadium bouts, including the famous transvestite boxer Parinya Kiat-

busaba. The camp is difficult to find; get a ride on a túk-túk or *sŏrng·tăa·ou*.

Thai Massage

The following are government accredited programs that will provide students with the fundamentals to practise Thai massage professionally. Some schools are also recognised as continuing education options by international body-work organisations.

**Chetawan Thai Traditional
Massage School** MASSAGE
(☑0 5341 0360; www.watpomassage.com; 7/1-2 Soi Samud Lanna, Th Pracha Uthit; basic traditional course 8500B) Bangkok's Wat Pho massage school established the Chiang Mai branch outside of town near Rajabhat University.

Lek Chaiya MASSAGE
(Map p240; ☑0 5327 8325; www.nervetouch.com; 27-29 Th Ratchadamnoen; course from 5000B, 11/2 hr massage 550B) Khun Lek learned *jàp sên* (literally 'nerve touch'), a northern Thai massage technique akin to acupressure, from her mother and became a well-known practitioner before retiring and passing the business and the technique on to her son. Courses last from three to five days and cover about 50% of a traditional Thai massage course with the remainder dedicated to the nerve-touch technique and herbal therapies. To experience *jàp sên*, stop in for a massage either from an assistant (550B) or from Lek's son Jack (950B).

Old Medicine Hospital MASSAGE
(OMH; ☑0 5327 5085; www.thai massageschool. ac.th; 78/1 Soi Siwaka Komarat, Th Wualai; 5-day course 6000B) The curriculum is very traditional, with a northern-Thai slant, and was one of the first to develop massage training for foreigners. There are two 10-day massage courses a month, as well as shorter foot and oil massage courses. Classes tend to be large from December to February, but smaller the rest of the year.

**Thai Massage School of
Chiang Mai** MASSAGE, YOGA
(TMC; Map p240; ☑0 5385 4330; www.tmc school.com; 203/6 Th Chiang Mai-Mae Jo; courses 6500-7500B) Northeast of town, has a solid, government-licensed massage curriculum. There are three foundation levels and an intensive teacher-training program. There's also a one-day Thai yoga program.

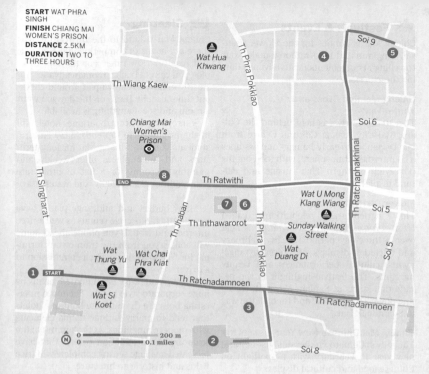

START WAT PHRA SINGH
FINISH CHIANG MAI WOMEN'S PRISON
DISTANCE 2.5KM
DURATION TWO TO THREE HOURS

Walking Tour
Old City Temple Tour

❯ No visit to Chiang Mai is complete without spending a sweaty day temple-spotting. This walking tour takes you to the old city's most famous temples. Start early before the day gets hot so that you can see the everyday uses of a temple: the comings and goings of monks, the prayer rituals of merit-makers and spotting which meditators are really asleep. Remember to dress modestly (covering shoulders and knees), take off your shoes when you enter a building and sit in the 'mermaid' position (with your legs tucked behind you) while you are observing the interior of a sanctuary.

Starting with the best, **❶ Wat Phra Singh** is home to the city's most revered Buddha image (Phra Singh) and is an excellent example of Lanna architecture. Trot down Th Ratchadamnoen and turn right on Th Phra Pokklao to **❷ Wat Chedi Luang**, another venerable temple. If you're starting to wonder what Buddhism is all about, go and have a chat with the monks at the north side of the *chedi*. Backtrack to charming **❸ Wat Phan Tao**, a teak temple that is more photogenic than venerated. If it isn't too

hot, squeeze in one more temple by turning right on Th Ratchadamnoen and left on Th Ratchaphakhinai to **❹ Wat Chiang Man**, the oldest *wát* in the city.

So much merit-making works up an appetite, but you're a little far from the city's main rice breaks. Instead you can use this opportunity to indulge your wheat tooth by continuing north on Th Ratchaphakhinai, and then turning right on Soi 9 to reach **❺ Blue Diamond**, a popular expat antidote to rice. After fuelling up, head south on Th Ratchaphakhinai and turn right at Th Ratwithi where you can nod to the **❻ Anusawari Sam Kasat**, the Three Kings Monument, on your way to the informative and air-conditioned **❼ Chiang Mai City Arts & Cultural Centre**.

If your feet are aching, carry on along Th Ratwithi until you reach Chiang Mai Women's Prison, where you'll find the **❽ Chiang Mai Women's Prison Massage Centre**. Don't attempt to enter the prison itself (unless you have something to confess!) but go to the building on the south side of the road with the 'Prison Shop' sign.

★ Festivals & Events

Chiang Mai is famous for the Flower Festival, Songkran and Loi Krathong; make your travelling arrangements far in advance during these periods.

Chiang Mai Red Cross and Winter Fair   FAIR

This 10-day festival is held behind the Chiang Mai City Arts & Cultural Centre from late December to early January and assumes a country-fair atmosphere, with food booths purveying northern Thai cuisine and cultural displays.

Flower Festival   FLOWERS

This agricultural celebration (called *têt·sà·gahn mái dòrk mái prà·dàp*) is held over a three-day period in early February and includes displays of flower arrangements, cultural performances and beauty pageants. The festival highlight is the parade that starts at Saphan Nawarat, travelling down Th Tha Phae and then all the way to Suan Buak Hat.

Chiang Mai Chinese New Year   NEW YEAR

The city's Chinatown heralds its cultural new year in February with a spotlight on Chinese food and cultural displays.

Songkran   NEW YEAR

The traditional Thai New Year is celebrated in Chiang Mai in mid-April with an enthusiasm that borders on pandemonium. Thousands of revellers line up along all sides of the moat to throw water on any passerby in the city (and each other). It is virtually impossible to stay dry during the five days of this festival.

Intakin Festival   RELIGIOUS

Held at Wat Chedi Luang in mid-May, this religious festival (known as *ngahn tam bun sŏw in·tá·gin*) is centred on the *làk meu·ang* (city pillar) and propitiates the city's guardian deity to ensure that the annual monsoon will arrive on time.

Loi Krathong   RIVER

From late October to early November Chiang Mai's riverbanks are alive with people floating the small lotus-shaped boats honouring the spirit of the river. In Chiang Mai this festival is also known as Yi Peng, and some *kon meu·ang* (people of northern Thailand) celebrate by launching cylindrical hot-air balloons, lighting up the night skies with hundreds of pinpoints of fire.

🛏 Sleeping

Chiang Mai is kind to the thrifty traveller: there are heaps of competing guest houses, and resulting low rates. For the real cheapies, you cannot book a room in advance: instead you have to show up at around checkout time (usually 11am) on the day you want a room and see if anything is available.

A crop of concept/boutique hotels fill in the midrange to top end. Many cultural students come to Chiang Mai for long-term stays and most places offer weekly or monthly discounts or a flat monthly rate with additional electricity and water usage fees.

Many budget and midrange places have bicycle and motorcycle rentals as well as free internet and wi-fi. If you phone ahead, some will collect you from the train or bus terminal for free to avoid paying a commission to a driver.

The top-end range is dominated mainly by huge corporate-style hotels. The more interesting ones are the intimate boutique hotels that tend to marry antique Lanna elements with modern amenities. At the summit of the scale are the destination resorts that have recreated a village setting complete with rice fields and historic architecture.

OLD CITY

There are heaps of guest houses in the residential sois off Th Moon Muang, especially in Soi 7 and Soi 9. There are also a few guest houses in the southeastern corner of the old city off Th Ratchamankha and in the lower numbered sois off Th Moon Muang.

TOP CHOICE Mini Cost   HOTEL $

(Map p240; ☑0 5341 8787; www.minicostcm.com; 19/4 Soi 1, Th Ratchadamnoen; r 750-1050B; ❄@) We're very impressed with this place. Apartment-style, contemporary rooms with easy chairs, calming colours and a few touches of Thai-style decor are unusual in Chiang Mai in this price range. It's in a terrific spot too, quiet but accessible to everything around Pratu Tha Phae. A real bargain – one of the few genuine midrange accommodations in the city with rooms priced (mostly) under 1000B.

Villa Duang Champa   HOTEL $$

(Map p240; ☑0 5332 7199; www.duangchampa.com; 82 Th Ratchadamnoen; r 2500B, guest-house r 700B; ❄@) Duang Champa is an excellent small hotel with simple, beautifully furnished concrete rooms that have tasteful modern fittings. The hotel occupies a colonial-style building marked by its simplicity, airiness and shuttered windows. Most rooms have an extra sitting area, although No 1 has its own private enclosed balcony with lounge seating – it's a beauty. Stick to the hotel as the dark, cramped guest house rooms are not a good deal.

Gap's House GUEST HOUSE $

(Map p240; ☑0 5327 8140; www.gaps-house.com; 3 Soi 4, Th Ratchadamnoen; r 500-750B; ✳@☞) A profusion of greenery wrapping itself around Lanna architecture meets guests at Gap's House, a quirky little gem. Thai-style wooden rooms are planted in a thick jungle garden and nature's air-con works well – it's definitely cooler in here than on the streets. Some rooms have antiquey furnishings but can be a tad musty with thin walls. The cheaper, sturdier concrete rooms are more basic. Bring your mozzie spray. Gap's is also famous for its Thai cooking course (p256) and nightly vegetarian buffet.

Vieng Mantra HOTEL $$$

(Map p240; ☑0 5332 6640; www.viengmantra. com; 9 Soi 1, Th Ratchadamnoen; r 2000-4500B; ✳@☞≋) This oasis, nestled into its own luxurious gardens, is a class act along bustling Soi 1. Smooth, clean lines and a marriage of concrete and wood dominate the Lanna-style building, while rooms are set around an inner courtyard pool and have balconies with sink-in-and-smile cushioned seating. The beautiful outdoor areas, complete with bar and pool, mean you may never want to leave. Walk-in rates are cheaper if they're not busy.

Safe House Court GUEST HOUSE $

(Map 240; ☑0 5341 8955; www.safehousecourt. com; 178 Th Ratchaphakhinai; r 350-550B; ✳@☞) There's something about this cheapie that makes it a cut above others in this price category. It may be its leafy location along a main drag, the excellent food at its restaurant next door, or its art deco appeal and friendly service. In any case, rooms are light and bright and those upstairs come with a small balcony taking in the roofs of nearby temples. Internet, cable TV and a smile are all part of the package.

3 Sis HOTEL $$

(Map p240; ☑0 5327 3243; www.the3sis.com; 1 Soi 8, Th Phra Pokklao; d 1300-1800B; ✳@☞) Good-sized rooms with double-glazed windows overlooking the street, in the front building,

may be the best deal here. However, those in the 'vacation lodge' have lovely wooden floors, clean white walls, fridge and cable TV. En suites are OK but check the condition of the shower. Wood, water and beanbags greet visitors in the open foyer communal area, which has a relaxing vibe.

Tamarind Village HOTEL $$$

(Map p240; ☑0 5341 8896-9; www.tamarindvillage. com; 50/1 Th Ratchadamnoen; r 6000-18,000B; ✳@☞≋) Considered to be one of the first of the 'Lanna revival' hotels, Tamarind Village has recreated the quiet spaces of a temple with galleried buildings and garden courtyards on the grounds of an old tamarind orchard. It's the size of a resort but retains a feeling of intimacy and is a fine option for some serious self-indulgence. The bamboo-shrouded walkway and whitewashed perimeter wall shut out the distracting modern world. Regular exhibitions are a bonus including, recently, on Thai jewellery.

Nice Apartments GUEST HOUSE $

(Map p240; ☑0 5321 8290; 15 Soi 1, Th Ratchadamnoen; r 320B; ✳) This old stalwart is a decent deal with cheap, clean rooms that come with fridge, air-con and a fan in a top old city location. The friendly service is a bonus and you need to drop by after 11am (check-out time) to see if they have a room. Its outdoor seating area provides free tea, coffee and fruit.

Wanasit Guesthouse GUEST HOUSE $

(☑0 5381 4042; 6 Soi 8, Th Rachamankha; s with fan/air-con 250/350B, d 300/400B) In a quiet soi and well signed, this homely guest house is a quiet alternative and not recommended for party animals. Attributes include rooftop terrace and rooms that are clean and well kitted out, if a little battered by age. Rooms also have their own balcony. The friendly, softly-spoken owner has lots of practical info about Chiang Mai on hand.

Sa Thu Boutique House HOTEL $$

(Map p240; ☑0 5390 3737; www.sathuboutique. com; 31 Soi Prapokklao, Th Ratchaphakhinai; superior/deluxe r 1200/1800B; ✳) Tucked away off busy Ratchaphakhinai Rd, this small boutique gem is freshly opened and beautifully designed, and has eager staff. The deluxe rooms are much better value with small outdoor courtyards accessed through French doors. Furnishings are in sympathy with the minimalist environment and fittings are funky and fun. The only drawback is the poky en suites. Walk-in rates are often better than those posted on the website.

Julie Guesthouse
GUEST HOUSE $

(Map p240; ☑0 5327 4355; www.julieguesthouse. com; 7 Soi 5, Th Phra Pokklao; dm 80B, r 100-350B; ☜) Part hostel, part guest house, Julie has cornered the young backpackers' social scene. The garden cafe is full of enthusiastic first-timers swapping tips and tales. In the evenings, folks retire to the covered roof terrace strung up with hammocks. No air-con, TV or fridge in rooms.

Lamchang House
GUEST HOUSE $

(Map p240; ☑0 5321 0586; 24 Soi 7, Th Moon Muang; r 200B) One of Chiang Mai's cheapest, this old wooden house has basic fan rooms with some Thai decorations and shared bath. The downstairs rooms are a little dark but there's a pleasant front-yard garden and attached restaurant.

Smile House 1
GUEST HOUSE $

(Map p240; ☑0 5320 8661; www.smileguesthouse. com; 5 Soi 2, Th Ratchamankha; r 300-1000B; ☀☜) A little backpacker village flourishes around an old Thai house here. It's tucked away in a small nook of the old city, on a tranquil little soi. We get good reports from travellers about Smile House – it's popular with young backpackers, especially for lounging around the pool with cold drink in hand. The atmosphere is friendly and the owner confirmed that the old house once served as the 'safe house' of Kun Sa, the infamous Shan-Chinese opium warlord.

Rachamankha
HOTEL $$$

(☑0 5390 4111; www.rachamankha.com; 6 Th Ratchamankha; r from 6000B; ☀@☜☀) The encore effort by architect Ong-ard Satrabhandu to Tamarind Village, Rachamankha imitates an ancient monastery in Lampang. Considering its reputation, rooms aren't opulent and the superiors are quite small. The deluxe rooms are more generous, however, with four-poster beds and bathrooms that double the living space. The highlight of the hotel is the library, a light-strewn room smelling of polished wood and musty paper. It's well signed near Pratu Suan Dokr.

Siri Guesthouse
GUEST HOUSE $

(Map p240; ☑0 5332 6550; 31/3 Soi 5, Th Moon Muang; r with fan/air-con 350/450B; ☀) Go for one of the upstairs rooms here as they have more light and space. The cheaper rooms are fine, although boxy and small on the ground floor. It's a good, quiet old city location with cafe on-site.

Thapae Gate Lodge
GUEST HOUSE $

(Map p240; ☑0 5320 7134; www.thapaegatelodge. com; 38/7 Soi 2, Th Moon Muang; r 350-500B; ☀@) Across the street from All in 1, this German-Thai guest house is a good choice. Rooms are compact but neatly furnished and some (even the cheaper ones) come with small balcony. Spending more here gives you air-con, TV and extra space. Check the beds as they can be a little saggy.

Awanahouse
GUEST HOUSE $

(Map p240; ☑0 5341 9005; www.awanahouse.com; 7 Soi 1, Th Ratchadamnoen; r 225-850B; ☀@☀) What started out as a small guest house has grown into a standard multistorey apartment building on a quiet soi. Awana is a bit institutional, but has large and bright rooms, some with balconies, TV and fridge. The cheapest rooms have fan and shared bathroom; the more you pay, the more space, views and luxuries such as air-con you'll get. The bonus here is the rooftop chill-out area with views of the nearby mountains.

Rendezvous Guest House
GUEST HOUSE $

(Map p240; ☑0 5321 3763; 3/1 Soi 5, Th Ratchadamnoen; r 500-900B; ☀) The clean rooms here are a mixed bag with nice modern furnishings, but some en suites could do with an upgrade; all rooms have TV, safety box and fridge. It flaunts its backpacker credentials via traveller info such as the cost of taxis around town, minibuses to places like Pai, details on visa runs and of course lots of activities. Some rooms have small balconies – request one when you check in.

RCN Court
GUEST HOUSE $

(Map p240; ☑0 5341 8280-2; www.rcnguesthouse.com; 35 Soi 7, Th Moon Muang; r with fan/air-con 350/550B; ☀@☜) This basic place is well known for its affordable monthly rates (from 6300B) and peaceful central location opposite a wát and plenty of trees. Rooms are nothing special but have cable TV and fridge. There is an outdoor kitchen for guests, a small front patio and a fitness room.

Montri Hotel
HOTEL $$

(Map p240; ☑0 5321 1069/70; 2-6 Th Ratchadamnoen; r 2100; ☀) If you're looking for comforts, you've found the right spot. Rooms are modern and well sized, have muted tones and are well-kitted out with safes, minibars, and sparkling en suites. Brix bar-and-restaurant here is a built-for-tourists place with nothing authentic about it. Still at least it doesn't pretend – dishes are Western in content and price. The attached outdoor area is perfect for an afternoon beer and people-watching on this busy corner (although you'll no doubt inhale the odd lungful of exhaust from the relentless traffic hurtling past). There's a 20% discount on room tariff if paying by credit card!

Top North Hotel HOTEL **$$**
(Map p240; ✆0 5327 9623; www.topnorthgroup.com; 41 Th Moon Muang; standard/superior/deluxe r 850/1200/1500B; ❄❀) This place feels quite resortish and seems to have far too much room for the old city. Standard and superior rooms are in the older building and are a bit of a mixed bag (en suites in particular should be carefully examined). Deluxe rooms in the newer wing are a much better option. The real pull here is the central salt-water swimming pool and bar.

Buri Gallery GUEST HOUSE **$$**
(Map p240; ✆0 5341 6500; www.burigallery.com; 102 Th Ratchadamnoen; superior/deluxe r 1000/2000B; ❄@❀❅) Buri Gallery occupies a converted teak building decorated with Lanna handicrafts. Some superior rooms are pretty cramped, dingy and vary in size, so check out a few; the walls are also too thin to block out noise. The upstairs deluxe rooms are quieter and have small terraces. Though the rates are a tad high, the staff provide the kind of services you'd find at fully fledged hotels.

Charcoa House HOTEL **$$**
(Map p240; ✆0 5321 2681; www.charcoa.com; 4 Soi 1, Th Si Phum; r 1400-2500B; ❄@❀) Small but beautifully-presented rooms rely on an imported heritage style with exposed timbers and whitewashed walls.

U Chiang Mai HOTEL **$$$**
(Map p240; ✆0 5332 7000; www.uchiangmai.com; 70 Th Ratchadamnoen; superior/deluxe r 4800/6000B; ❄❀❅) Corporate-friendly hotel with a 24-hour checkout policy: you leave at the same time you arrived.

Tri Gong Residence GUEST HOUSE **$$**
(Map p240; ✆0 5321 4754; www.trigong.com; 8 Soi 1, Th Si Phum; r 700-1000B; ❄@❀) It offers large rooms with decent furnishings, cable TV and fridge.

All In 1 GUEST HOUSE **$**
(Map p240; ✆0 5320 7133; www.allin1gh.com; 31 Soi 2, Th Moon Muang; r 400-700B; ❄@❀) Clean rooms with cable TV. Outdoor garden bar is an attractive feature fronting the street.

Supreme House GUEST HOUSE **$**
(Map p240; ✆0 5322 2480; 44/1 Soi 9, Th Moon Muang; r 150B) Relaxed atmosphere and you'll have plenty of money left over to hit the nearby bars.

Jonadda Guest House GUEST HOUSE **$**
(Map p240; ✆0 5322 7281; 23/1 Soi 2, Th Ratwithi; r 250-450B; ❄) Has spotless, basic rooms.

EAST OF THE OLD CITY
Traffic is more intense outside of the old city and the roar of engines often detracts from Chiang Mai's low-key ambience. While it isn't as quaint as the old city, Th Tha Phae is just as convenient for sightseeing and nightlife and even closer to the night bazaar. Corporate hotels with business centres and conference capacity occupy the area near the Chiang Mai Night Bazaar.

TOP CHOICE **Mo Rooms** HOTEL **$$**
(Map p240; ✆0 5328 0789; www.morooms.com; 263/1-2 Th Tha Pae; small/medium/large r 2800/3200/3500B; ❄@❅) This outrageous design hotel is completely unique in Chiang Mai and a great choice if you are inspired by art – 'art you can live in'. The 12 rooms are all individually designed according to the animals of the Chinese zodiac. Each is an inspiration from a local artist born under that zodiac sign. Our favourites are the rat, goat and monkey rooms but ask to see a few; it's great fun and more like walking around a gallery than a hotel. Arguably it's a bit overpriced but does that matter when the mangaer here tells you: 'You don't just choose a hotel, it must choose you'? There's also a suave cocktail bar overlooking the street at the front of the building.

TOP CHOICE **Baan Kaew Guest House** GUEST HOUSE **$**
(✆0 5327 1606; www.baankaew-guesthouse.com; 142 Th Charoen Prathet; r 800B; ❄❀) We like this place. The two-storey apartment building is set back from the road behind the owner's own residence. Rooms are fairly standard with fridge and cable TV, but upstairs rooms also have small balconies, and are light and airy. It's a good honest deal, very friendly, and in a quiet part of town in

its own green patch. It's also conveniently opposite a departure point for river cruises, and elegant Wat Chaimongkhon (Map p236) with its lovely riverside setting.

DusitD2 Chiang Mai
HOTEL $$$

(Map p240; ✆0 5399 9999; www.dusit.com; 100 Th Chang Khlan; r from 3500B; ✳@☎☀) Designed to impress and overwhelm, the gleaming white and blinding orange of the lobby in this slick hotel version of an urban hipster is dizzying. The rooms with moulded furnishings, an intelligent design, thoughtful features such as reading lights and a warmth that defies the modern decor, don't disappoint. The deluxe rooms with couch and cushions alongside windows overlooking Doi Suthep are very good but we'd recommend an upgrade to a suite, which is like a mini apartment – in this crowded city you can't help but feel spoilt by walk-in wardrobes.

Yaang Come Village
BOUTIQUE HOTEL $$$

(✆0 5323 7222; www.yaangcome.com; 90/3 Th Si Donchai; r 5000-10,000B; ✳@☎☀) A clever twist on the Lanna reproduction hotel is this homage to a Tai Lue village, based on the owner's travels to the Yunnan region of China. Deluxe rooms are much better than the superior, having the right combination of tradition, luxury and home comfort. All rooms are spacious with murals, textiles and teak furniture and have balconies overlooking the 'village' with cushioned seating so you can drink in the ambience at your leisure. For what you actually get the rooms are a tad overpriced, however walk-in rates can be heavily discounted. It's about 300m west of the Chedi on a main thoroughfare.

Banthai Village
HOTEL $$$

(Map p240; ✆0 5325 2789; www.banthaivillage. com; 19 Soi 3, Th Tha Phae; superior/deluxe r 3100/4100B; ✳@☎☀) The village action is centred on a long narrow pool and outside bar at this relaxing stylised-rice-village boutique lodge. With only 33 rooms, it strikes the right balance between intimacy and privacy. Superior rooms are smaller but better located in a separate building with garden views – ask for an upstairs one. Rooms occupy several Lanna-style terraced houses with funky fittings, huge stone bathtubs and dinner-plate-sized showerheads. Note that floors are a bit wonky for people with movement disabilities.

Daret's House
GUEST HOUSE $

(Map p240; ✆0 5323 5440; 4/5 Th Chaiyaphum; s/d 160/220B) A long-time backpackers' fave with a great location and stacks of basic, well-worn rooms, Daret's looks like many of Th Khao San's backpacker flops. But because this is Lanna-land, Kun Daret is an amiable guy often found in the cafe downstairs. You pay more for the luxury of hot water.

Micasa Guest House
GUEST HOUSE $

(Map p240; ✆0 5320 9127; 2/2 Soi 4, Th Tha Pae; r 300-1000B; ✳@☎) Trying hard to fabricate an air of sophistication, and with its dinky common area spilling out onto the soi, Micasa is a wanabee-boutique guest house. What is does best though is slightly higher standard, cheap rooms. Pluses include free internet, book exchange, quality bicycles for rent, and a helpful tour office with good info for getting around northern Thailand.

Roong Ruang Hotel
HOTEL $

(Map p240; ✆0 5323 4746; www.roongruanghotel. com; 398 Th Tha Phae; r 450-900B; ✳@) With a prime location near Pratu Tha Phae, Roong Ruang is a great deal for an older-style hotel. It doesn't look like much from the outside but the interior courtyard is cocooned from traffic noise. Go for a room in the new building as they are spacious and have huge showers. Cheaper rooms are fine to crash, just a bit cell-like and dark.

Tawan Guesthouse
GUEST HOUSE $

(Map p240; ✆0 5320 8077; 4 Soi 6, Th Tha Phae; r 200-300B) This simple guest house stands out from the pack with its stunning garden filled with fountains and kòi ponds, all woven together by the flowering vines of bougainvillea and a big shade tree with hairlike tendrils. Rooms are nothing special: some occupy an old wooden house while others are in a flimsy bamboo hut.

Eagle House
GUEST HOUSE $

(Map p240; ✆0 5387 4126; www.eaglehouse.com; 16 Soi 3; Th Chang Moi Kao; r 150-380B; ✳) In a shady location just outside the old city, the rooms here, with fan or air-con, and en suites, are pretty basic but clean and secure. There's also a laundry, book exchange and safety deposit boxes. The owners conduct eco-sensitive tours, which we get good feedback about; lots of info about Chiang Mai and beyond is available too. There is another branch of Eagle House in the old city.

Sarah Guest House GUEST HOUSE $
(Map p240; ✆0 5320 8271; http://sarahgh.hyper
mart.net; 20 Soi 4, Th Tha Phae; s 250-400B, d 300-
450B; 🐾@🛜) A long-running backpacker
spot, Sarah's sits in a quiet garden and is
run by the original English owner. There are
only 12 simple rooms, which have chunky
wood furniture and large bathrooms, and
the option of fan or air-con.

Manathai HOTEL $$$
(Map p240; ✆0 5328 1666; www.manathai.com;
39/9 Soi 3, Th Tha Phae; r from 3500B; 🐾@🖂)
Boutique Manathai has an Arabian-nights
feel and merges Lanna and colonial elements.

Thapae Boutique House GUEST HOUSE $$
(Map p240; ✆0 5328 4295, www.thapaeboutique
house.com; 4 Soi 5, Th Tha Phae; r superior/deluxe
1000/1200B; 🐾@) Superior rooms are the
best deal.

Lai-Thai Guesthouse GUEST HOUSE $
(Map p240; ✆0 5327 1725; www.laithai.com; 111/4-
5 Th Kotchasan; r 600-700B; 🐾🛜🖂) Rooms are
comfortable if a little cramped, with cable
TV and mini-fridge. They're a decent price
but the location is right beside a busy, traffic-
filled street.

Imperial Mae Ping Hotel HOTEL $$
(Map p240; ✆0 5328 3900; www.imperialhotels.
com; 153 Th Si Donchai; r from 2400B; 🐾@🛜🖂)
Best combination of Asian quirks and con-
temporary fashion for this large, modern
hotel near the night bazaar. Superior rooms
are better value than deluxe.

RIVERSIDE
Riverside House GUEST HOUSE $
(off Map p240; ✆0 5324 1860; www.riversidehouse
chiangmai.com; 101 Th Chiang Mai-Lamphun; r
500-800B; 🐾@🛜) Next door to the Tourism
Authority of Thailand, this friendly and
professional set-up has great cheap rooms
arranged around a pretty garden. The best
rooms are of course the most expensive,
but they are well worth the extra, being in
a new building at the rear of the property.
You share a common balcony out front and
have your own private balcony at the rear.
All rooms are extremely well presented, very
clean and recommended.

River View Lodge HOTEL $$
(off Map p240; ✆0 5327 1109; www.riverviewlodgch.
com; 25 Soi 4, Th Charoen Prathet; r 1500-2200B;
P🐾@🖂) The simple, spacious rooms are a
bit overpriced at this breezy riverside lodge
with its emphasis on charm and some old-
fashioned hospitality. But you aren't paying
for a spectacular room – go and sit by the
pool and drink in the extensive and beautiful gardens, and you'll appreciate the quiet
nature of the dead-end soi location. In our
opinion it makes it well worthwhile for short
visits. And you'll definitely fall for the place
when you're entertained by chirping red bul-
buls on your balcony in the morning.

Galare Guest House GUEST HOUSE $$
(off Map p240; ✆0 5381 8887; www.galare.com;
7 Soi 2, Th Charoen Prathet; r 1100B; 🐾P) Right
next to River View Lodge, Galare is a mod-
ern place with less ambience but more
change left in your wallet after a night's stay.
You can dine on tables set on grass virtu-
ally on the waterfront creating your own
river panorama of Chiang Mai. Rooms are
a bit sterile but very clean and spacious, if
a tad dated, and open on to a wide shared
veranda.

Baan Orapin B&B $$
(✆0 5324 3677; www.baanorapin.com; 150 Th
Charoenrat; r from 2100-3400B; 🐾@🖂) It's a
family affair at Baan Orapin, a pretty garden compound anchored by a stately teak
house, which has been in the family since
1914. Luxurious guest residences (a total of
15 rooms) are in separate and modern buildings spread throughout the property. It's
right next to Sop Moei Arts.

Hollanda Montri GUEST HOUSE $
(✆0 5324 2450; http://hollandamontri.com; 365
Charoenrat Rd; r with fan/air-con 450/550B; 🐾)
We get a lot of readers' letters recommend-
ing this place. It's a bit out of town and the
accommodation is fairly rudimentary but
the riverside setting is nice if you feel like
getting away from the crush of the old city.
We're not really sure what all the fuss is
about, but then there aren't many cheapies
to choose from on the river. Free use of bicycles is great. This place is right on the river
just north of Saphan Ratanakosin.

WEST OF THE OLD CITY
Prices tend to be a little higher here than
in the backpacker areas but you're closer to
Chiang Mai University and in the best area
of town for local nightlife.

Sakulchai HOTEL $
(Map p248; ✆0 5321 1982; Soi Plubpueng, Th Huay
Kaew; r 450-650B; 🐾🛜) The Sakulchai recently underwent extensive renovations and is
now one of the bargain options in Chiang

Mai. Located down a quiet, dead-end soi and within walking distance of both the old city and Th Nimmanhaemin, contemporary spacious hotel rooms are priced very cheaply for what you get. It's basically a midrange option at budget prices. It's a popular hotel with Thais, not so much for foreigners and there's not much English spoken.

H
HOTEL **$$**

(Map p248; ☑0 5322 0444; www.h-designhotel. com; 1 Th Sirimungklajarn; r from 1590B; ❋❀) This new concrete, cubist, monolith style-hotel is quite a find. Although calling itself a letter of the alphabet swings somewhere between pretentious and moronic, don't be discouraged. Staff are tripping over themselves to be helpful, and the architect has gone for space – and a lot of it. The rooms are huge (even the smaller ones) and bathrooms are modern and spacious. Huge windows let in plenty of light and the furnishings have a minimalist intent accentuating the feeling of space. The bright colours inside probably take things a bit too far, but overall this is an impressive and unique place for Chiang Mai. To find H, look out for the Mango Chilli Restaurant below.

Sweet Room
GUEST HOUSE **$**

(Map p248; ☑0 5321 4668; sweet_room_cafe@ hotmail.com; 81 Th Huay Kaew; s/d 700/1000B; ❀) Sweet it is indeed – it's also unique and personal. Not looking much from the outside, the narrow street frontage hides six very spacious and individually furnished rooms. Considering that two rooms share an outside bathroom on each level, the price is a bit cheeky, but rooms are beautifully kitted out in very contemporary styles, and we dare say a bit of bargaining would probably bring the price down, especially for longer stays. Definitely go for a room at the back of the building to avoid street noise. The 1st floor is given over to a kitchen and small living area. Great little cafe downstairs.

Uniserv-International Center Hostel
HOSTEL **$**

(☑0 5394 2881; 239 Th Nimmanhaemin; r 600B; ❋@) Looking for a place to stay close to the university? You can't get much closer than this hostel, which shares space with CMU's busy International Center. Rates include breakfast and monthly rates are available. Large old-fashioned rooms come with comfy armchairs and modern bathrooms; request a room with a view. It's signposted off Th Nimmanhaemin, just north of Th Suthep.

Dome
HOTEL **$$**

(Map p248; ☑0 5340 5400; www.thedomechiang mai.com; 1 Soi Plubpueng, Th Huay Kaew; standard/ deluxe/suite r 700/900/1200B; ❋❀) What you see here is what you get: modern, comfortable accommodation. Standard rooms are OK, but it's worth upgrading to deluxe for the extra space. Cheaper weekly and monthly rates are available. It's a good long-term option if you're going to be in the area for a while. The new downstairs restaurant-bar is a fine addition.

Baan Say-La
GUEST HOUSE **$$**

(Map p248; ☑08 1930 0187; www.baansaylaguest house.com; Soi 5, Th Nimmanhaemin; r 500-1500B; ❋) In the old city, a room with shared bathroom would be half the price or less but this is the Nimmanhaemin district, and prices reflect the hippest of Chiang Mai locations. Rooms in this bohemian-chic guest house with shared bathroom are very basic, but do come with cable TV and decent linen although mattresses have seen better days. Other rooms have four-poster beds and rattan furnishing. Black-and-white photography decorates the walls, and the shared seating areas have large easy chairs.

Miso
GUEST HOUSE **$**

(Map p248; ☑0 5389 4989; 9 Soi 7, Th Nimmanhaemin; r from 500B) Primarily a Korean restaurant and travel agent, Miso also lets cheap rooms in the building above. Admittedly they're a pretty disorganised crew here, but the friendly owner will probably cut you a deal on a decent room – good news as long as you can stand the garish colours of the bathrooms. It's pretty basic digs but clean and you won't find cheaper this close to Nimmanhaemin road. Long term stays also possible.

International Hotel Chiangmai
HOSTEL **$**

(☑0 5322 1819; www.ymcachiangmai.org; 11 Soi Sermsak, Th Hutsadisawee; r 600-1800B; ❋@ ❀❄) Quite possibly the ugliest building in a country where the competition is fierce, this local branch of the YMCA redeems itself with some excellent bargains for rooms with a view of Doi Suthep. Skip their overpriced dorm beds. Warm and cordial inside with an extensive range of well worn but clean rooms, this place has standard rooms that are fine, although for 100B more you get great views from the 6th floor. Some rooms also come with leather armchairs. Check the shower recess in bathrooms. To get here, turn onto Th Hutsadisawee from corner of

Th Huay Kaew and Th Mani Nopharat and then take your first left.

Pann Malee Home
GUEST HOUSE $$

(Map p248; ✉0 5328 9147; www.pannmalee.com; off Soi 17, Th Nimmanhaemin; r 1000-1400B; ✱) This converted townhouse really is like staying in somebody's house, the rooms are all individually furnished with the owner's eclectic taste and feel very homely. Apparently each room reflects the personalities of her family members. The extra baht basically buys you more space, less stairs and a slightly nicer setting.

Yesterday the Village
BOUTIQUE HOTEL $$

(Map p248; ✉0 5321 3809; www.yesterday.co.th; 24 Th Nimmanhaemin; r from 2000B; ✱@) Yesterday does a quick trip backwards to the near past. The common spaces of the converted apartment building are artistically decorated with vintage prints, old phonographs and the soon-to-be-extinct tube televisions. Rooms are plush, bathroom fittings impressive, and superior rooms come with balcony but no view; deluxe rooms have more panache than superiors and overall are a better deal.

SpicyThai Backpackers
HOSTEL $

(Map p248; ✉0 5340 0444; www.spicyhostels.com/spicythai-backpackers.html; 4/80 Nanthawan Village, Th Nimmanhaemin; dm 250B; ✱@) This place offers female-only as well as male dorms in the former US Ambassador residence. It's recommended by readers. You'll find it near the corner of Th Nimmanhaemin and Th Huay Kaew.

ELSEWHERE

Tri Yaan Na Ros
BOUTIQUE HOTEL $$$

(✉0 5327 3174; www.triyaannaros.com; 156 Th Wualai; r from 2500B; ✱✱) A honeymoon candidate of superb qualifications, this pint-size boutique hotel on what's called the Saturday Walking Street, creates a romantically antique world with its artfully restored house, galleried chambers and narrow walkways. It's quite a warren inside and just off a busy road with rooms set well back from the relentless screech of the traffic. Rooms are intimate, old-fashioned Lanna affairs with sink-in-and-smile four-poster beds. There are only eight rooms and you'll probably get a few hundred baht discount if you walk in off the street. The charming owner will soon win your affections.

Viangbua Mansion
APART-HOTEL $$

(✉0 5341 1202; www.viangbua.com; 3/1 Soi Viangbua, Th Chang Pheuak; r/apt per week 5600/1400B; ✱@✆) North of Pratu Chang Pheuak, this multi-storey hotel doesn't have the best location for sightseers but it has plenty of amenities for long-term guests and is a classy setup. The rooms have contemporary furnishings, fridge, small lounge, some also have a kitchen. Nightly rates are available.

Four Seasons Chiang Mai
RESORT $$$

(✉0 5329 8181; www.fourseasons.com; Th Mae Rim-Samoeng Kao; r from 18,000B; ✱@✆✱) Chiang Mai's first premier destination resort features vaulted pavilion suites and residences spread amid eight hectares of landscaped gardens and rice terraces worked by water buffalo. The resort is north of the city in the forested foothills and includes all the necessary self-contained distractions: cooking school, award-winning spa, swimming pool and tennis courts.

Mandarin Oriental Dhara Dhevi
RESORT $$$

(✉0 5388 8888; www.mandarinoriental.com; 51/4 Th Chiang Mai-San Kamphaeng; r from 16,000B; ✱@✆✱) Almost a kingdom unto itself, the Dhara Dhevi is an amazing resort destination that has recreated a miniature Lanna village with footpaths through walled residence compounds surrounding terraced rice fields. So much architectural history has been reproduced here that the resort fancies itself a cultural attraction, offering guided tours to guests as well as craft demos. The rooms are of course aristocratic and the grounds host many wedding parties. There's also a slightly cheaper and less imposing colonial wing. It's 5km east of the old city.

✖ Eating

The restaurant scene in Chiang Mai is surprisingly down to earth and wholesome. Modest family-run establishments and open-air food courts dominate the city's hot dining spots. As the sun sets on the city, evening food stalls emerge (from about 6pm), peddling all sorts of delicious, cheap street food. It's hard to go wrong but locals recommend the stalls on the corner of Th Mani Nopharat and Th Chang Pheuak with chairs and tables sprawling on the wide street frontage along Th Mani Nopharat.

Plus there are loads of vegetarian restaurants, ranging from backpacker cafes to religious society outreaches. You can also explore the local markets and small shopfronts for the regional speciality of *kôw soy* (sometimes written as *khao soi*), a curried noodle dish claiming Shan-Yunnanese heritage. It's usually accompanied by pickled vegetables and a thick red chilli sauce.

OLD CITY

Residents pick up *gàp kôw* (pre-made food served with rice) from evening vendors lining the stretch of Th Samlan south of Th Ratchadamnoen.

TOP CHOICE New Delhi INDIAN $$

(Map p240; Th Ratwithi; mains 100-180B; ☺dinner) This basic eatery serves up some of the most delicious Indian food we've tasted in northern Thailand. Lovingly and expertly prepared, predominantly northern Indian food dominates the menu. The deliciously spiced 'Handi' dishes are among our favourites. Note that the service is poor, but all will be forgiven when you're tucking into the delectable curries.

Pum Pui Italian Restaurant ITALIAN $$

(Map p240; ☑0 5327 8209; 24 Soi 2, Th Moon Muang; dishes 150-250B; ☺lunch, dinner) Fresh ingredients and an intimate knowledge of Italian cooking ensures the food here tastes just like Mama used to make...well almost. Pum Pui has a romantic garden setting, ideal for an intimate dinner. Pasta, pizza and risotto dishes feature on the extensive menu and there are some fine Italian beverages to linger over.

Jerusalem Falafel MIDDLE EASTERN $$

(Map p240; 35/3 Th Moon Muang; meze 100B, mains 220B, meze platters from 500B; ☺9am-11pm) You might yawn at the thought of yet another Middle Eastern restaurant in a backpacker ghetto but let us sing the praises of this exotic import. The restaurant is a lively place to assemble with friends and nosh on a meze platter of falafel, shashlik, hummus and tabouli. Yoghurt, haloumi and feta cheese are home-made here.

Safe House Court THAI $

(Map p240; 178 Th Ratchaphakhinai; dishes 50-80B; ☺7am-10pm) Steer away from Western offerings such as sandwiches and go for the cheap and well-prepared Thai dishes here, including regional specialities, spicy salads and good veggie options. It's a friendly, family-run affair in a leafy garden setting – well designed for a book read and slow consumption (watch the mozzies in the evening). Lip-curling fruit shakes too.

Baan Nok Noodle NOODLES $

(Map p240; Th Singharat; noodles 25-35B; ☺10am-6pm, closed Wed) For a quick bite on the street, perhaps after a visit to nearby Wat Phra Singh, locals recommend this Thai noodle place. Various types of noodles are served in spicy or clear soup (pork) but the signature dish is *tom yum baan nok* with small noodles. Vegetarian noodle dishes also served.

Lert Ros NORTHEASTERN THAI $

(Map p240; Soi 1, Th Ratchadamnoen; small/large dish 30/50B; ☺1-9pm) Whole fish frying on top of cooking drums at the front of this restaurant alerts passers-by to this simple Thai restaurant. Cooking food in the northeastern style, there are various meat and rice dishes strongly spiced, whole tilapia fish, and *sôm·dam* (spicy green papaya salad) to choose from. It's very popular so try early or late for dinner – it's the best cheapie in the area. Helpful picture menu.

Angel's Secrets VEGETARIAN $

(Map p240; cnr Soi 1 & 5; dishes 60-90B; ☺breakfast, lunch, closed Mon; ☑) Shielded from the roadside by a fast-growing fence of greenery and simply, but warmly, furnished, this outdoor eatery has a touchy-feely goodness flowing from the kitchen in the form of tasty and freshly prepared vegetarian dishes. There's lots of healthy alternatives for breakfast including crepes with fresh fillings or a bowl of fruit. The friendly service will make you smile, and your happy stomach will be nudging you back for more.

House ASIAN FUSION $$$

(Map p240; ☑0 5341 9011; 199 Th Moon Muang; dishes 200-800B; ☺6pm-11pm) This restaurant is definitely the place to treat yourself. It occupies a mid-20th-century house (it once belonged to an exiled Burmese prince) that's now outfitted with colonial accoutrements. The House menu is a pan-Pacific affair, combining imported lamb and salmon with local spices and cooking techniques. If you're after something lighter, stop in and enjoy a few mouth-watering tapas dishes at the outdoor Moroccan-themed bar, or even in the 'tents' set up outside.

Rachamankha THAI $$$

(Map p240; ☑0 5390 4111; Rachamankha Hotel, 6 Th Rachamankha; dishes 300-1000B) Tucked away behind Wat Phra Singh, in the sumptuous grounds of the boutique hotel of the same name, one dines at the Rachamankha to enjoy the crisp white linens and antique atmosphere just as much as the food. The menu is Thai-centred, along with hints of Myanmar (Burma), Yunnan and Europe at the periphery.

Pak Do Restaurant
THAI $

(Map p240; Th Samlan; dishes 30-35B; ☺7am-early afternoon) Across the street from Wat Phra Singh, this morning curry shop displays its dishes in big metal bowls out front. Do as the Thais do and lift the lids to survey the contents. If your stomach has developed a hankering for rice in the morning, you'll be glad you peaked into the pots.

Heuan Phen
NORTHERN THAI $

(Map p240; ✉0 5327 7103; 112 Th Ratchamankha; dishes 50-150B; ☺lunch & dinner) At this well-known restaurant everything is on display, from the northern Thai food to the groups of culinary visitors and the antique-cluttered dining room. Try the young jackfruit with a spicy paste. Daytime meals are served in a large canteen out front.

Dada Kafe
JUICE BAR $

(Map p240; Th Ratchamankha; breakfast 60-80B; ☺8am-10pm) Promoting itself as a healthy alternative, this eatery is very popular for breakfast. There are simple but comfy chairs and tables and a menu featuring freshly prepared food that has a good stab at sandwiches, pasta dishes and Thai mains. It specialises in juices and claims to have the liquid fruit answer to many ailments including acne, heart disease and high-blood pressure. True or not, they are delicious.

Nayok Fa
RESTAURANT $

(Map p240; Th Ratchaphakhinai; dishes 30-35B; ☺10am-6pm) This ma-and-pa place cooks up fresh food in the massive woks out front. Try *pàt see-éw* (stir-fried wide noodles with a choice of beef, pork or chicken) or the suckling pig and rice.

Fern Forest Cafe
CAFE $

(Map p240; 2/2 Soi 4, Th Singharat; desserts 70B; ☺8.30am-8.30pm) Indeed it is set among ferns and plenty of other greenery too. Add to that the quiet soi location, the sound of running water, cushioned seating and yummy desserts, and you're onto a winner. Delectable Western-style desserts (try the carrot cake) or sandwiches are available, and you can also loll about in the beautiful garden setting over a fruit drink or coffee. The cool of the garden makes it the perfect

place to wait out the heat of the afternoons too. From the top of Th Singharat in the old city, head south and before you reach Th Ratwithi you will see this place signposted down a soi on your left.

AUM Vegetarian Food
VEGETARIAN $

(Map p240; 66 Th Moon Muang; dishes 50-60B; ☺8am-5pm; ✐) Aiming square at the health-conscious traveller is AUM's vegetarian delights. There's organic coffee from Laos, seasonal juices and a range of all-veggie Thai-style stir-fries, soups, salads and rice dishes. The restaurant has an eating area with floor cushions and low tables. A more expensive, limited Japanese menu (that includes sweet chilli maki) is also available.

Blue Diamond
BAKERY $

(Map p240; 35/1 Soi 9, Th Moon Muang; mains 50-60B; ☺7am-9pm Mon-Sat) Always popular but a bit less frenetic than other traveller eating spots around here. Evidence of the quality of the food is in the return clientele. Blue Diamond bakes its own bread and pours fresh local coffee; breakfast is the meal to go for, or possibly a vegetable salad for lunch (Thai vegetarian is big on the menu). Trickling water and a shady garden setting complement the morning munchies.

Bierstube
GERMAN $

(Map p240; 33/6 Th Moon Muang; dishes 60-150B; ☺breakfast, lunch & dinner) This cosy, slightly dingy wooden place is the restaurant version of an old German uncle. It has been cooking up German comfort fare for so many years that its age can be measured by the regulars' expanding waistlines. In Bangkok such dinosaurs would be shunned, but here in Chiang Mai this is considered family. Thai and Western dishes are also available and it's popular for a drink in the evening, being slightly classier than many other places on this strip.

Chiangmai Saloon
INTERNATIONAL, BAR $$

(Map p240; 30 Th Ratwithi; mains 120-200B; ☺breakfast, lunch & dinner; ✇) Welcome to the Wild West, Thai style. Although very kitsch this friendly old joint, serves plenty of comfort food and mixes Aussie beef with southern American know-how. While the odd veg dish can be found, it's a real carnivore's delight – get your iron fix. If that's not enough, there's free popcorn, a pool table, internet and peanuts! The original branch is on Th Loi Kroh.

CHIANG MAI PROVINCE EATING

MARKET MEALS

Market mavens will love Chiang Mai's covered food and grocery centres, which offer everything from morning noodles to daytime snacking and evening supping. To impress a Thai friend, pick up a bag of *man gâa·ou,* a roasted acorn-like nut harvested at the end of the rainy season.

North of the Th Ratwithi intersection, **Talat Somphet** (Map p240; Soi 6, Th Moon Muang; ⊙6am-6pm) sells all the fixings for a Thai feast, including takeaway curries, sweets and fruit. Many of the cooking schools do their market tours here. Unfortunately, the market's proximity to the tourist area has encouraged the fruit sellers to be creative with their prices.

In the early morning, **Talat Pratu Chiang Mai** (Map p240; Th Bamrungburi; ⊙4am-noon & 6pm-midnight) is Chiang Mai's communal larder, selling foodstuffs and ready-made dishes. If you want to make merit to the monks, come early and find the woman who sells pre-assembled food donations (20B). Things quiet down by lunchtime, but the burners are re-ignited for a large and popular night market that sets up across the road.

Market aficionados will be impressed by **Talat Thanin** (off Th Chang Pheuak; ⊙5am-early evening), an efficient and clean covered market. The meat vendors are segregated into their own glass-enclosed area preventing an accidental tour by sensitive stomachs. The fruit and vegetable section is a beautiful display of tropical bounty. In the prepared food section you'll find Chiang Mai's recent food trends. Continue deeper to the covered food centre for made-to-order noodles and stir-fries. Easy to find, Th Chang Pheuak is the main thoroughfare heading north out of the city.

Talat Ton Phayom (Th Suthep) acts as both a local market and a souvenir stop for Thais visiting from other provinces. Take a look at the packaged food area to see the kinds of edible gifts (like bags of *kâap mŏo* and *sâi òo·a*) that make a visit to Chiang Mai complete. Because CMU students make up a good portion of the clientele, prices tend to be low. This place is just off Th Suthep near the corner of Th Khlorng Chonprathan.

Pho Vieng Chane　　STREET FOOD $
(Map p240; Th Ratchadamnoen; dishes 30-70B; ⊙lunch, dinner) Vietnamese street food behind Wawee Coffee. The steamed rolls and noodle soups are recommended.

Mangsawirat Kangreuanjam　VEGETARIAN $
(Map p240; Th Inthawarorot; dishes 25-35B; ⊙8am-2pm; 🌱) The cooks put out several pots of fresh, 100% Thai vegetarian dishes daily.

Juicy 4U　　JUICE BAR $
(Map p240; 5 Th Ratchamankha; breakfast 60-80B; juices 50-80B; ⊙8.30am-5.30pm) Serves hangover-fighting juices. Make-your-own vegetarian sandwiches and tasty breakfasts.

Coffee Lovers　　CAFE $
(Map p240; 175/1 Th Ratchamankha; mains 40-60B; ⊙7am-6pm) This place knows how to cook eggs and makes a top breakfast spot. Delicious juices too.

Ginger Kafe　　CAFE $$
(Map p240; 199 Th Moon Muang; dishes 100-250B; ⊙10am-11pm) In the same grounds as the House.

EAST OF THE OLD CITY

Chiang Mai's small Chinatown, along Th Chang Moi, is a tasty quarter to investigate early in the morning. On Th Khang Mehn, you'll find *kà·nŏm jeen* and other noodle dishes. An alley next to the Top Charoen Optical shop, wakes up early thanks to a popular *nám đow·hôo* (soy milk) stall, serving warm soy milk accompanied with Chinese-style deep-fried doughnuts.

🌱**Taste From Heaven**　VEGETARIAN $
(Map p240; 237-239 Th Tha Phae; dishes 60-110B; ⊙lunch, dinner; 🌱) This fine vegetarian restaurant makes delectable curries and fusion dishes incorporating Indian cuisine (such as veg samosas). It's also very friendly, ethically sound – with proceeds going towards the Elephant Nature Park (p253) – and has a cooling garden out the back for outside dining.

da Stefano　　ITALIAN $$
(Map 240; 🕿0 5387 4187; 2/1-2 Th Changmoi Kao; mains 180-250B; ⊙11.30am-11pm) This unassuming Italian eatery, with its portraits of the Mediterranean hanging on its walls, is tucked into a soi just outside of the old city.

It's one of the best Italian restaurants in Chiang Mai, and you can't really go wrong with the menu, but we'd recommend the rich lasagne, and richer tiramisu.

Aroon Rai
THAI $

(Map p240; 45 Th Kotchasan; mains 40-80B; ⊗8am-10pm) The Aroon Rai is a basic, Thai-style, open-air eatery proclaiming to have the best curries in town. It certainly does have variety: soup, noodle and rice dishes along the curries, even frog dishes, appear on the menu. It's very popular with Thais and budget travellers, and is an excellent cheapie; peruse the northern Thai sausage and pots of curry on the way in to warm-up your appetite.

Antique House
NORTHERN THAI $$

(71 Th Charoen Prathet; dishes 80-200B; ⊗lunch, dinner) Antique House is a quaint two-storey teak house and garden filled with wooden antiques and mellow nightly music. Better to come for dinner rather than lunch – it's a much better time to experience the magic of this beautiful setting. Excellent fish dishes especially the tab-tim fish in both Chinese and Thai style. Also available is cook it yourself BBQs and *rod duen* (fried crispy worm!). This place is just north of the old city, off Th Chang Pheuak.

Whole Earth Restaurant
RESTAURANT $$

(Map p240; 88 Th Si Donchai; dishes 150-350B; ⊗11am-10pm) This confectionery-coloured teak house wears a garden of hanging vines, kòi ponds and orchids growing in the crooks of tree limbs. It is the sort of place Thais go to treat someone special – where the staff will treat you like royalty and the dishes seem exotic (Thai Indian and vegetarian) without being demanding.

Just Khao Soy
KÔW SOY $

(Map p240; 108/2 Th Charoen Prathet; mains 100-150B, tapas 50B; ⊗lunch, dinner) This is the gourmet version of *kôw soy*. Served on a wooden artist's palette, this delightful eatery specialises in noodle dishes, which are prepared to order via a step-by-step process. First you order your meat (or vegies) with free range, grain-fed chicken favoured on the menu, then choose your level of spice, your type of noodles, sauce and a delicious, hearty broth is born. Although the food is beautifully presented it's probably a bit expensive for what you get. Lanna art decorates the bamboo walls.

La-Own
THAI $

(Th Charoen Prathet; dishes 40-80B; ⊗lunch, dinner) Tempting aromas waft down the street from this affable restaurant. Its grill-BBQ out front often seems empty; usually a bad sign. Not on this occasion. Dishes are thoughtfully prepared and include lots of seafood and chicken options. We enjoyed the seafood fried-rice with basil. Although it advertises itself as a 'grilled chicken restaurant' in fact the excellent Thai menu is much more extensive. This place is close to the river, on busy Th Charoen Prathet, just near the corner of Th Tha Phae.

Anusan Night Market
FOOD MARKET $$

(Map p240; Anusan Night Bazaar, Th Chang Khlan; dishes 100-350B; ⊗dinner) Anusan is a buzzing food market best known for its Thai-Chinese seafood restaurants. Stalls surround a large cluster of tables where each 'restaurant' has a section allocated with its own waiters. Nearby are other stand-alone restaurants, some of which have their own prawn holding ponds acting as centrepieces for their menu speciality. The prices are higher than they ought to be but these are special-occasion splash-out restaurants for Thais. Try **Lena Restaurant** here, where a kilo of succulent grilled prawns will set you back 300B. Or have a stab at the fish in Thai spices and basil leaves.

Tianzi Tea House
HEALTH $

(Map p240; Th Kamphaeng Din; dishes 60-120B; ⊗10am-10pm) Such hard-core health food is usually found in dirt-floor hippy shacks, but Tianzi has adopted the ascetic's meal to an aesthetic surrounding. Pretty open-air *săh·lah,* decorated with flowers and dappled with sunlight, host a range of organic and macrobiotic dishes, such as Yunnanese tofu cheese.

Ratana's Kitchen
INTERNATIONAL-THAI $

(Map p240; 320-322 Th Tha Phae; dishes 30-150B; ⊗7.30am-11.30pm) For all the talk of Chiang Mai having cool temperatures, it still gets hot by midday. Jump out of the oven and into Ratana's kitchen. It isn't a culinary legend but the dishes and prices are sensible and it's got a prime spot near Pratu Tha Phae for wilting tourists.

Good Health Store
HEALTH FOOD $

(Map p240; Th Si Donchai; set breakfast 75-120B; ⊗7am-2pm Mon-Sat) Sells mainly chemical-free products as well as herbal remedies, and does healthy breakfasts.

Art Cafe
INTERNATIONAL $$

(Map p240; cnr Th Tha Phae & Th Kotchasan; dishes 80-200B; ◎breakfast, lunch & dinner) Popular meeting spot just outside Tha Pae Gate, serving Thai, Italian, Mexican and American dishes.

Moxie
INTERNATIONAL-THAI $$$

(Map p240; ✆0 5399 9999; DusitD2 Chiang Mai, 100 Th Chang Khlan; dishes 200-450B; ◎6.30am-10.30pm) In the DusitD2 hotel; offers edible sculptures of Thai, Japanese and Italian components.

RIVERSIDE

Past Saphan Nakhon Ping, is Th Faham, known as Chiang Mai's *kôw soy* ghetto. Situated here are **Khao Soi Lam Duan** (Th Faham; dishes 40-60B), which also serves *kà·nŏm rang pêung* (literally beehive pastry – a coconut-flavoured waffle), **Khao Soi Samoe Jai** (Th Faham; dishes 30-65B) and **Khao Soi Ban Faham** (Th Faham; dishes 35-55B). *Kôw soy* foodies sometimes spend the day sampling a bowl at each place to select their favourite.

Chedi
THAI-INDIAN $$$

(✆0 5325 3333; 123 Th Charoen Prathet; mains 500-1000B; ◎dinner) Chiang Mai's most ambitious homage to modernism, the Chedi has transformed the former British Consulate into a minimalist sculpture with restrained Zen-like grounds. Fine Indian cuisine is available (the jinga masala is recommended by readers) as well as one of Chiang Mai's few quality wine lists. Shockingly expensive but swamped with first-class service, enjoy gorgeous white-linen dining on the riverbank with floating candles twinkling on the water. This is the place to impress. Even coming here for a drink in the bar allows you to enjoy the setting without having to take out a loan.

Love at First Bite
BAKERY $

(28 Soi 1, Th Chiang Mai-Lamphun; desserts 50-90B; ◎10.30am-6pm, closed Mon) Tucked deep into a residential soi on the east bank of the river, this famous dessert shop is filled with middle-class, cake-confident Thais. Don't be surprised to see folks posing in front of the dessert display case for a souvenir photo. It's on the eastern side of the river about 500m north of the tourist office.

Riverside Bar & Restaurant
INTERNATIONAL-THAI $$

(Th Charoenrat; dishes 100-200B; ◎10am-1am) This rambling set of wooden buildings has been the most consistently popular riverside place for over 20 years. The food – Thai, Western and vegetarian – is just a minor attraction compared to the good-times ambience. The clientele is a mix of Thais and *fa·ràng*. There's inside and outside dining: the bar area inside is musty and worn, and rather boisterous, while outside by the river is more sedate. Some veterans opt to dine on the docked boat before the nightly 8pm river cruise. It's right on the river just 300m north of Saphan Nawarat.

Good View
THAI $$

(13 Th Charoenrat; dishes 100-250B; ◎10am-1am) Next door to the Riverside, Good View lives up to its name with open-air seating in a contemporary setting. The formula is similar to the Riverside, except the menu focuses more on Thai food and the nightly music covers a broader genre range. Try to nab a table beside the river for a romantic evening.

Mahanaga
INTERNATIONAL-THAI $$$

(✆0 5326 1112; 431 Th Charoenrat/Faham; dishes 30-500B; ◎5.30pm-midnight) The Chiang Mai branch of a Bangkok-based fusion restaurant, Mahanaga is all style and romance with flickering candles, traditional Lanna-style buildings and tall trees. The menu features Thai food: classic recipes using high-end, imported meats, such as grilled Australian chilled ribeye with spicy Thai sauce. It's on the same street as Riverside Bar, about 1km further north.

Huan Soontaree
THAI $

(✆0 5387 2707; 46/2 Th Wang Singkham; dishes 120-150B; ◎4pm-1am) Visiting Thais from Bangkok make the pilgrimage to this rustic restaurant, built on the west bank of the river, partly for the food but mainly for the owner, Soontaree Vechanont, a famous northern singer popular in the 1970s. She performs at the restaurant from 8.30pm to 10pm Monday to Saturday. The menu is a pleasant blend of northern, northeastern and central Thai specialities. This place is on the river about 4km north of the city.

WEST OF THE OLD CITY

The area west of Wat Suan Dok on Th Suthep has several popular vegetarian (*ah·hăhn jair*) restaurants. Th Nimmanhaemin and the surrounding sois are an incredibly fast-growing area with new restaurants and cafes popping up every month. Step across culinary continents with the best Burmese and Japanese food in the city; there are adventures to be had in Mexican, fine Thai in the foothills of Doi Suthep, and some upmarket cafes, where students like to preen and imagine a tomorrow when they really can afford all this.

TOP CHOICE **Palaad Tawanron** THAI $$

(☏0 5321 6039; Th Suthep; dishes 120-320B; ☺lunch, dinner) Set into a rocky ravine next to a waterfall (in wet season) near Doi Suthep, this is a spectacularly sited restaurant. The Thai menu is extensive and includes plenty of seafood such as serpent-head fish, freshwater prawns, and sea bass. There's an extensive outdoor seating area overlooking a small reservoir and the city of Chiang Mai beyond. It's a magical spot in the evenings and much cooler than in the city. Follow the signs at the end of Th Suthep.

Khun Churn VEGETARIAN $

(Map p248; Soi 17, Th Nimmanhaemin; buffet 100B; ☺lunch; ✒) Thais love their buffets – it's the all-you-can-eat allure for these food-loving people. This place is certainly one of the best going around. There's a plethora of well-prepared vegetarian dishes and salads to choose from and basic fruit drinks are included. The shady outdoor setting will entice you to linger.

Hong Tauw Inn THAI $

(Map p248 95/17-18 Nantawan Arcade, Th Nimmanhaemin; dishes 70-130B; ☺11am-11pm) It's a relief to step through the doors at this old-fashioned, intimate Thai inn, decked out in an old-fashioned costume of aged pendulum clocks and antiques, and escape the fashionable haunts that have devoured this area. It's a really good spot to begin your Thai culinary adventures – there's an extensive menu that includes regional specialities such as *naem mog sai ou* (spicy grilled northern sausage with herbs). Relaxed dining, staff who speak English and decent quality, inexpensive Thai food – it ticks a lot of boxes for newbies. It's popular with Thais as well and the food is genuinely spicy. The *sôm·đam*, and curries are spot on.

Su Casa TAPAS $$

(Map p248; ☏0 5381 0088; 28 Soi 11, Th Nimmanhaemin; tapas 70-100B; ☺lunch, dinner) The chef at this vivacious Mediterranean gem invites Chiang Mai's fresh produce and imported ingredients to tango with him in the kitchen, preparing tapas standards and artful entrees. Try the baby octopus in lemon citrus dressing, the chorizo is also very good here. The outside eating area is perfect for breezy evenings as are the jugs of margarita.

Ai Sushi JAPANESE $

(Map p248; Th Huay Kaew; dishes 50-100B; ☺dinner) This sushi bar could well be the best Japanese in the city. The pace gets furious later in the evening as diners in-the-know pack it out. Watch the sushi chefs at work at the bar or sit at small tables inside or out right on Huay Kaew Rd. The food is fresh and delicious, and highly recommended is the *ebi tem maki* (crispy dragon sushi with prawns) – very morish. Salmon dishes are also a highlight. Service is very fast.

Pun Pun THAI, VEGETARIAN $

(Wat Suan Dok, Th Suthep; mains 30-40B; ☺breakfast & lunch; ✒) This shady outdoor eatery quietly churns out top quality Thai vegetarian dishes with little fuss. Food is simple, spicy and delicious. It does an excellent *sôm·đam* and the fruit shakes are also superb. Enter Wat Suan Dok from Suthep road, walk past the temple, and it's on your right after the 'monk chat' office.

▨ Royal Project Restaurant NORTHERN THAI $$

(Th Huay Kaew; mains 70-300B; ☺9am-6pm) Fine dining Thai-style is dished out at this outlet for the Royal Project, which supports various agricultural initiatives in Thailand. It's popular with Thais for a special occasion, university staff from across the road, and families. Unusually for a Thai restaurant rainbow trout features on the menu, which focuses predominantly on Northern Thai specialties, some only available during certain months of the year. It's located opposite the Huay Kaew Fitness Park and next to the CM Animal Quarantine station. Also on-site is a top class supermarket selling fruit & veg, grown organically where possible, as part of the Royal Project and packaged smoked trout.

Salsa Kitchen MEXICAN $$

(Map p248; Th Huay Kaew; mains 130-150B; ☺11am-11pm) Churns out authentic south-of-the-border dishes including burritos, enchiladas, fajitas and tacos; our favourites here are the chicken quesadillas – be warned the portions are huge. It's an expat favourite but Thais indulge here also, and it's often busy in the evening; certainly it's the best Mexican in town.

Burmese Restaurant BURMESE $

(Map p248; cnr Th Nimmanhaemin & Soi 14; dishes 30B; ☺lunch, dinner) This basic eatery behind another eatery with plastic chairs selling fried foods on the pavement, sells delicious Burmese food very cheaply. The food comes quick, goes down even quicker and at these prices you should be able to afford to sample a few of its offerings. Try the tamarind leaf salad (our favourite), goat offal curry or catfish balls in gravy.

100% Isan Restaurant NORTHERN THAI $

(Th Huay Kaew; dishes 60-200B; ☺lunch & dinner) Directly in front of CMU's main gate, this fluorescent-lit shop does a bumping business of northeastern standards: *sôm·đam*, *kôw něe·o* and *gài yâhng*. From the looks of it, everyone who leaves the university gets hungry when they hear the mortar-and-pestle music of *sôm·đam*.

Implaphao Restaurant THAI $

(Rte 121; dishes 700-160B; ☺11am-10.30pm) Dining by the water is an appetising feature for Thais and this barn-like restaurant lures in the supping parties for *plah pŏw* (broiled fish stuffed with aromatic herbs) and *đôm yam gûng*. It isn't the easiest restaurant to reach, 10km southwest of Chiang Mai, across from Talat Mae Huay, but it is an undiluted Thai experience.

NinjaRamen & Japanese Food JAPANESE $

(Map p248; Th Sirimungklajarn; mains 60-110B; ☺lunch & dinner) Ramen-based soups such as wanton dumplings and ramen topped with pork slices in soybean are some of the dishes on the extensive menu at this excellent Japanese restaurant. It also serves soba and udon noodle dishes, and fancy versions of sashimi and sushi. It's often full and turning people away, so nab a table early.

Galare Restaurant NORTHERN THAI $$

(off Map p236; 65 Th Suthep; dishes 100-220B; ☺10am-10pm) Out on the outskirts of Chiang Mai, Galare is a terraced, open-air restaurant nestled by a small lake and a green park that overlooks the city. A carpet of flowers fills in the spaces between the wooden picnic tables. The menu is mainly northern

Thai, and though it's not spectacular, you'll hardly notice more than the tranquil setting. Its a great way to escape the frenetic traffic of the city.

D-Lo BURMESE $

(soi off Th Huay Kaew; mains 30-50B; ☺lunch & dinner) This is a new Burmese restaurant and according to local Burmese food aficionados it serves up very authentic versions of the cuisine. Curries and salads feature on the small menu – try the fishball salad or one of the goat curries. Expect attentive service and warm smiles at no charge. It's located in a lane off Huay Kaew road, look for the sign to the Holiday Garden Hotel – it's about halfway down on the right-hand side.

Amazing Sandwich CAFE $

(Map p248; 20/2 Th Huay Kaew; sandwiches 100B; ☺daily) A self-described island in a sea of rice, Amazing Sandwich delivers bread to the wheat-deprived. Expats rank the make-your-own sandwiches right up there with sliced bread. Has recently expanded into pizza, hamburgers, and breakfasts. Rely on takeaway; the dining room does not win any awards.

I-Berry ICE-CREAM PARLOUR $

(Map p248; lane off Soi 17, Th Nimmanhaemin; ice cream from 60B) A Bangkok-based ice-cream store has churned a pretty wooden lot into a hip phenomenon. Students and locals flock here with cameras in tow hoping to run into the famous owner, comedian Udom Taepanich (nicknamed 'Nose'). If he's not around they'll settle for the huge yellow sculpture out front, said to mimic the star's signature feature (his big nose). The ice cream is pretty good, but watching Chiang Mai's celebrity worship is even better.

Salad Concept SALAD $

(Map p248; Th Nimmanhaemin; basic salad dishes 50B; ☺lunch, dinner; 🛜) Build your own fresh salad, which consists of eight types of greens, five optional toppings and a dressing. Some toppings are a little light on.

Boat THAI $

(Th Huay Kaew; mains 30-40B; ☺breakfast, lunch, dinner) Popular with Thais for its comfy seating and cheap food – the real puller is the local people-watching. It's about 300m northwest of Th Khlorng Chonprathan on the left hand side of Huay Kaew as you head towards Doi Suthep from the city.

CHIANG MAI PROVINCE CHIANG MAI

A TASTE OF MYANMAR (BURMA) IN CHIANG MAI

You don't need to travel to Myanmar (Burma) to experience it. More and more tourists head to Mae Sot to partake of breakfasts of nan bread and beans, shop at the border market, marvel at the official and unofficial crossings going on above and below the bridge and wander around the bilingual, bicultural town. But you can also have a Burmese experience here in Chiang Mai. Visit the Shan temples **Wat Pa Pao** or **Wat Ku Tao**. If you are lucky, you may chance upon the colourful and fascinating Poy Sanlong (Novice Ordination) festival. Wat Pa Pao also hosts a pilot project school for Shan children jointly organised by the Ministry of Education and the Shan community. Or you can visit the Burmese temple, **Wat Sai Moon**, on the moat. To experience the flavours of Burmese food, do not miss **D-Lo restaurant** (p272), there is usually an interesting gathering of people there too! Or a little further afield, but equally delicious, is the **Mee Mee Shan Burmese** at Ruamchoke market on the way to Mae Joe. On a Friday morning you can pop into the market off Chang Klan Soi 1, opposite the mosque, for Burmese noodles (*mohinga*) or Shan soft tofu and a whole host of other ethnic delights.

Jackie Pollock – MAP Foundation

Lemontree
THAI $
(Map p248; Th Huay Kaew; mains 40-70B; ⊙11am-10pm) The well-worn dining room tells you it's been around for a long time – plenty of local Thais eat here. Does good curries serving up a piping hot meal nice and quick. Servings are large and mains are much better than appetizers.

Smoothie Blues
CAFE $
(Map p248; 32 Th Nimmanhaemin; dishes 100-150B; ⊙7.30am-9pm) Expat favourite; and known for its breakfasts, as well as its sandwiches, baguettes and namesake drink.

ELSEWHERE

Chiang Mai reveals its Chinese heritage with its devotion to pork products, most obvious in the northern Thai speciality of *sâi ò·a* (pork sausage). Good quality *sâi ò·a* should be zesty and spicy with discernible flavours of lemongrass, ginger and turmeric. Two famous sausage makers are **Mengrai Sai Ua** (Th Chiang Mai-Lamphun), near the Holiday Inn on the east bank of the river, and **Sai Ua Gao Makham** (Rte 121), a small stall in Talat Mae Huay (Mae Huay market), which is a few kilometres south of the Night Safari on the way to Hang Dong.

Wrap & Roll
INTERNATIONAL-THAI $$
(88 Soi 2, Th Wualai; mains 60-130B; ⊙lunch, dinner) If you're checking out the Saturday Walking Street market, and want to get off your legs for a breather, this place offers the perfect respite. Cold beer, wine by the glass, ice-cold soda water with fresh lime, and well-prepared dishes like fresh spring rolls, or healthier wraps, can be consumed at out-door tables while you keep an eye on all the goings-on of the market.

Vegetarian Centre of Chiang Mai
VEGETARIAN $
(14 Th Mahidol; dishes 15-30B; ⊙6am-2pm Mon-Fri; ☑) Sponsored by the Asoke Foundation, an ascetic Buddhist movement, this restaurant serves inexpensive cafeteria-style veg. It's about 500m south of the old city.

Spirit House
INTERNATIONAL-THAI $$
(Soi Viangbua, Th Chang Pheuak; dishes 100-200B; ⊙from 5pm) Sometimes the most charming restaurants are just display cases for an eccentric personality. This antique-filled dining room is the creative outlet for the American owner who's a master of many trades, from antique dealer to classical musician. A former chef in New Orleans, he's a self-described 'nut about food' and builds the daily menu around what looks interesting at the market. The leafy surrounds and rustic feel add to the charm. This place is just off busy Th Chang Pheuak, near the market.

Drinking

See p270 for **Riverside**, a bar-restaurant that is a great drinking option right on the river, especially recommended at sunset.

Pub
PUB
(189 Th Huay Kaew) In an old Tudor-style cottage set well off the road, this venerable Chiang Mai institution semi-successfully calls up the atmosphere of an English country pub. The Friday-evening happy hour assembles all the old expats who claim to have arrived in the city on the back of elephants.

Ice-cold Tiger beer on tap. It's a couple of hundred metres past Th Nimmanhaemin on the west side of Th Huay Kaew.

Writer's Club & Wine Bar
BAR

(Map p240; 141/3 Th Ratchadamnoen) Run by an ex-foreign correspondent, this unassuming traveller hangout is popular with expats and serves a good range of cold beer and cocktails. There's also English pub grub to help anchor a liquid meal.

Archers
BAR

(Map p240; 33/4 Th Ratchaphakhinai; 🛜) Come to this chilled-out restaurant-bar for the cold beer and the people-watching – not the food. It's a good spot to knock back a couple in the afternoon with the newspaper and maybe your laptop (free wi-fi). Popular with expats and travellers.

Dayli
BAR

(Map p248; Soi 11, Th Nimmanhaemin) This ginormous outdoor bar-eatery is frankly a bit grotty. But it serves cheap, cold beer and service is attentive. The plastic chairs and tables on your right as you enter are a bit newer and cleaner – the further to the left you stray the more you invite trouble with hygiene. Has a rickety feel and the shady trees and palms give it a certain kitsch ambience. We like it! It's certainly party-central late Friday and Saturday nights.

Rooftop Bar
BAR

(Map p240; Th Kotchasan) This grungy backpacker bar is a good place to party. It's set out in rasta colours with plenty of graffiti and the inebriated sit around small, low tables on a bamboo floor admiring the views over Pratu Tha Phae and Doi Suthep beyond – until the dancing starts that is...

UN Irish Pub
PUB

(Map p240; 24/1 Th Ratwithi) A two-storey bar and restaurant, and stalwart on the Chiang Mai traveller scene, this is an old favourite for its Thursday quiz night and boozy nights. There's Guinness on tap, a beer garden and TV screens – sporting events are popular, especially rugby and football games.

At 9 Bar
BAR

(Map p240; Th Nimmanhaemin & Soi 9; ⊗6pm-midnight) For a bird's-eye view of all the action on Th Nimmanhaemin, pop into this upstairs, open-air bar. A great spot for a people watch, it's a perfect perch while you slug back a Chang (on tap).

Pinte Blues Pub
BAR

(Map p240; 33/6 Th Moon Muang) This place deserves some sort of award for staying in business so long (more than 20 years) while serving only espresso and beer, and for sticking to a blues-music format the whole time. It is easy to walk by and not notice it, so you'll have to use your ears as your guide.

John's Place
BAR

(Map p240; Th Moon Muang) Another old-school spot, John's dominates the triangular wedge of Th Ratchamankha and Soi 2 with neon and beer bellies. Climb the stairs past the faded posters of Thai scenery to the roof deck where a cold beer is good company at sunset and beyond. The downstairs bar is the place to park yourself if you want a chat with the locals (local expats that is).

Kafe
BAR

(Map p240; Th Moon Muang) A cute wooden affair with a couple of sunny, outdoor tables snuggled in beside Soi 5, Kafe is often crowded with Thais and backpackers when every other place is empty. It offers a simple formula: cheap cold beer and efficient service.

Mix Bar
BAR

(Map p240; DusitD2 Chiang Mai, 100 Th Chang Khlan) Looking for a night out on a town that is more cosmopolitan than Chiang Mai? Chart a course to DusitD2 hotel's slinky cocktail bar, a swish elixir after roving the night market. The last weekend of the month hosts gay-friendly rainbow parties.

Glass Onion
BAR

(Map p248; Rooms Boutique Mall, Th Nimmanhaemin; ⊗8pm-late) Tucked away at the far end of the walking mall is this small lounge bar outfitted in '60s-style mod fashions. While the barely legals try to blow their eardrums out at Nimmanhaemin's dance clubs, this is the domain of grown-ups desiring cocktails and conversation. The bar also enjoys a gay-friendly reputation. Friday night is ladies night and 7pm to 9pm is happy hour.

Pinocchio's (Map p248; Soi 7, Th Nimmanhaemin) and **Outdoors** (Map p248; Soi 7, Th Nimmanhaemin) are two large outdoor bars where the weekend action really hots up. They are deserted in the afternoon, but drop by in the evening if you want to see the young and beautiful at play. Pinocchio's is more upmarket, and gets packed with younger Thai students while Outdoors is a bit more mixed with Thais, expats and tourists. Be warned, though, the large screen TVs at both places take away any pretence at ambience.

Cafes & Teashops

Chiang Mai's creative and sociable temperament has eagerly adopted the global phenomenon of cafe culture, largely supplied by local coffee chains and home-grown Arabica beans. Almost an attraction in its own right, Soi Kaafae (Coffee Lane on Soi 9, Th Nimmanhaemin) is populated by two bustling coffee shops with lush garden seating and lots of laptop-tapping Thais. On one side of the street is **Wawee Coffee** (Map p248; Soi 9, Th Nimmanhaemin), a local chain that originally started at Mae Sa Elephant Camp and has since expanded to the point of Starbucks saturation. (There's also a Wawee on Th Ratchadamnoen in the old city.) Across the street is **94° Coffee** (Map p248; Soi 9, Th Nimmanhaemin).

Black Canyon Coffee   CAFE
(Map p240; 1-3 Th Ratchadamnoen) Local chain with multiple branches in the city and a high energy 'see-and-be-seen' location in front of Pratu Tha Phae that is always packed with people-watchers.

Impresso Espresso Bar   CAFE
(Map p248; 28/1 Soi 11, Th Nimmanhaemin; coffee 50B) If you want to get away from the bigger chain coffeeshops try this gem, in a top spot for some people-watching too (inside the cafe and outside on the street). Staff know their way around a coffee machine and it also pours smoothies, mocktails and teas such as jasmine dragon pearl.

Tea House   TEAHOUSE
(Map p240; Th Tha Phae; ☺9.30-6pm) The mountains of the north also produce Assam tea, served in the Victorian-era Tea House, which shares space with Siam Celadon. It's a beautiful setting for a cup of jasmine tea and a snack.

☆ Entertainment

🄯 Sudsanan   LIVE MUSIC
(Map p248; Th Huay Kaew) Down a driveway opposite a Shell Service Station, this warmly lit wooden house is filled with a lot of local soul. Long-haired Thais and expats, especially from local NGOs, come here to applaud the adept performances that jog from samba to *pleng pêu·a chee·wít* (songs for life). Oozing with character it's one of the best spots in the city to take in some local Thai bands. Be

prepared for some bowed heads and sniffles during particularly tear-jerking songs.

Bridge Bar   LIVE MUSIC
(Map p248; Soi 11, Th Nimmanhaemin) In their words, chic, retro and ready. Chic? Ummm, yes a little. Retro? Not really. Ready? Ready for what?! Well, anyway, this is a very cool, local small bar (a nice change from the sprawling bar-restaurants in these sois) that hosts local bands in the evenings on most weekend nights and sometimes during the week too. Be warned the music is loud, so bring earplugs if you're a little sensitive to throbbing decibel levels.

North Gate Jazz Co-Op   JAZZ
(Map p240; Th Si Phum) This tight little jazz club packs in more musicians, both local and foreign, than patrons, especially for its Tuesday open-mic night.

Riverside Bar & Restaurant   LIVE MUSIC
(9-11 Th Charoenrat) In a twinkly setting on Mae Ping, Riverside is a one of the longest-running live-music venues in Chiang Mai. The cover bands made up of ageing Thai hippies stake out centre stage and fill the room with all the singalong tunes from the classic-rock vault. It is the perfect antidote for electronica overload. Also good as an eatery (see p270).

Inter   LIVE MUSIC
(Map p240; 271 Th Tha Phae) A small band space in a wooden house spilling out onto the roadside, it's popular with travellers and backpackers staying around Pratu Tha Phae – it really ramps up some nights. There are opportunities to get involved if you've any musical talent.

Warm-Up   NIGHTCLUB
(Map p248; ☎0 5340 0676, 306 253; 40 Th Nimmanhaemin) The hippest joint in own, and a perennial favourite for the young and beautiful, Warm-Up is one of Chiang Mai's best dance houses. Hip-hop is spun by DJs in the main room, the electronic beat of house reverberates in the lounge and bands playing rock/indie music can be found in the garden. Young hipsters arrive in their coolest duds: tight jeans, spiked wolf hair-dos, sparkly shirt dresses and pointy heels. But ever youthful *fa·ràng* join the crowd as well.

Monkey Club   NIGHTCLUB
(Map p248; 7 Soi 9, Th Nimmanhaemin) Merging dinner with dancing and live music in the beautifully-lit tropical garden and featuring

local, crooning live bands, Monkey Club attracts a tribe of affluent Thai students and a few expats who might migrate from the garden seats to the glassed-in, all-white bar and club. It's a very happening place for the younger set.

Discovery
NIGHTCLUB

(12 Th Huay Kaew) This is the place to carve up the dance floor and show the locals your latest moves. And fortunately, you don't have to be hip to have fun at this disco. It is big, loud and totally cheesy – the perfect recipe for joining the massive blob of gyrating bodies. Discovery is across the street from Kad Suan Kaew.

Bubbles
NIGHTCLUB

(Pornping Tower Hotel, Th Charoen Prathet). A tad sleazy but Bubbles still mysteriously wins the affections of the prowlers and the ravers alike. Pretty much anything goes on the dance floor, including techno-trance, which is usually jammed full of tourists.

Thapae Boxing Stadium
BOXING

(Map p240; ☏08 6187 7655; Th Moon Muang; standard/VIP ticket 400/600B; ☺9pm various nights) Right in the heart of the backpacker scene, this stadium caters to foreign audiences, complete with a cabaret.

Kawila Boxing Stadium
BOXING

(off Th Charoen Muang) Near Talat San Pakoy, this is the locals' stadium for *moo·ay tai* (also spelt as *muay thai*) and has a very good reputation. Unfortunately fire gutted the building and it was being refurbished during research: it should reopen in 2012. Ask a local for directions.

Chiang Mai University Art & Culture Center
CINEMA

(Map p236; Faculty of Media Art & Design; admission free; ☺7pm Sun) Feed your art-flick hunger at the university's weekly showings of foreign films, often showcasing a certain theme; screenings are in the main auditorium.

Good View
LIVE MUSIC

(13 Th Charoenrat) Modern interpretation of cover tunes; it's next to Riverside Bar & Restaurant.

Le Brasserie
LIVE MUSIC

(37 Th Charoenrat) A popular late-night spot filled with devotees of local guitarist legend Took. Rock and blues from all the dead legends fill the set. It's about 500m north of Saphan Nawarat, right on the river.

Gallery
LIVE MUSIC

(27 Th Charoenrat) Traditional Thai music from 7pm to 9pm nightly. The beautiful, leafy, riverside setting marries well with the sounds. It's next to La Brasserie.

Major Cineplex
CINEMA

(Central Airport Plaza, 2 Th Mahidol)

Vista Movie Theatre
CINEMA

(Kad Suan Kaew Shopping Centre, Th Huay Kaew)

🔒 Shopping

Chiang Mai is Thailand's handicraft centre, ringed by small cottage factories and workshops. There are several shopping corridors throughout the city: the Chiang Mai Night Bazaar, east of the old city; Saturday Walking Street on Th Wualai; Sunday Walking Street on Th Ratchadamnoen; and Th Charoenrat, alongside the river, for high-quality ethnic textiles. Th Nimmanhaemin, west of the old city near Chiang Mai University, has a handful of contemporary boutiques haunted by trend-conscious Thais.

Handicraft villages lie just outside of the city to the south and to the east. Hang Dong (p291) is widely regarded as the area's furniture capital.

OLD CITY

Mengrai Kilns
POTTERY

(off Map p240; ☏0 5327 2063; www.mengraikilns.com; 79/2 Th Arak) In the southwestern corner of the inner moat, Mengrai Kilns are particularly focused on keeping the old Thai celadon-pottery traditions alive.

HQ Paper Maker
PAPER

(Map p240; ☏0 5381 4718; www.hqpapermaker.com; 3/31 Th Samlan; ☺8.30am-5.30pm) Mainly an art paper retailer, this small shop sells handmade mulberry paper *(săh)*, another Chiang Mai handcrafted speciality. There's a variety of colours and designs, including sheets printed with the northern Thai alphabet.

Herb Basics
HERBAL PRODUCTS

(Map p240; ☏0 5323 4585; Th Ratchadamnoen; ☺9am-6pm Mon-Sat, 2-9pm Sun) All of these good-smelling products – such as herbal lip balm, soap and shampoo – were made in Chiang Mai.

Lost Book Shop
BOOKS

(Map p240; 34/3 Th Ratchamankha) Secondhand books free of plastic wrap for easy browsing; same owner as Backstreet Books.

NIGHT TIME SHOPPING

Chiang Mai Night Bazaar (Map p240; Th Chang Khlan; ☉7pm-midnight) is one of the city's main night-time attractions, especially for families, and is the modern legacy of the original Yunnanese trading caravans that stopped here along the ancient trade route between Simao (in China) and Mawlamyaing (on Myanmar's Gulf of Martaban coast). Today the night bazaar sells the usual tourist souvenirs, like what you'll find at Bangkok's street markets. In true market fashion, vendors form a gauntlet along the footpath of Th Chang Khlan from Th Tha Phae to Th Loi Kroh. In between are dedicated shopping buildings: the **Chiang Mai Night Bazaar Building** is filled mainly with antique and handicraft stores. Across the street is the **Galare Night Bazaar** selling upmarket clothes and home decor. Behind the collection of shops is the **Galare Food Centre** (Map p240). The **Anusan Market** is less claustrophobic and filled with tables of vendors selling knitted caps, carved soaps and other cottage-industry goods. Deeper into the market is the **Anusan Food Centre** (p269).

The quality and bargains aren't especially impressive, but the allure is the variety and concentration of stuff and the dexterity and patience it takes to trawl through it all.

On the Road Books   BOOKS
(Map p240; 38/1 Th Ratwithi) A long-running secondhand shop with a small selection of good-quality reads.

EAST OF THE OLD CITY
Elements   GIFTS, JEWELLERY
(Red Ruby; Map p240; 400-402 Th Tha Phae) Located next to Roong Ruang Hotel, Elements stocks embroidered bags, a diverse collection of fun jewellery and other trinkets.

Nova   JEWELLERY
(Map p240; www.nova-collection.com; 201 Th Tha Phae; ☉10am-8pm Mon-Sat, 12.30-8.30pm Sun) For contemporary jewellery, this studio hand-makes high-quality rings (7000B to 8000B), pendants and earrings using silver, gold and precious stones. Pieces can be custom made and are very classy.

Lost Heavens   TRIBAL ARTS
(Map 240; 228-234 Th Tha Phae) This store specialises in museum-quality tribal arts, including textiles, carpets and antiques, as well as ritual artefacts from the Yao (also known as Mien) tribe.

Kesorn   TRIBAL ARTS
(Map p240; 154-156 Th Tha Phae) A collector's best friend, this cluttered shop has been trading old stuff for years. It specialises mainly in hill-tribe textiles, beads and crafts.

Siam Celadon   CERAMICS
(Map p240; www.siamceladon.com; 158 Th Tha Pae; ☉8am-6pm) This established company sells its fine collection of cracked-glazed celadon ceramics in a lovely teak building. Enjoy the Victorian-era structure and its dainty fret-

work longer with a proper English tea at the attached Tea House Siam Celadon (p273).

KukWan Gallery   TEXTILES, GIFTS
(Map p240; 37 Th Loi Kroh) Set slightly back from the road, this charming teak building houses natural cotton and silk by the metre. It's a great place to shop for gifts, with scarves, bedspreads and tablecloths available in subtle colours.

Pantip Plaza   ELECTRONICS
(Map p240; Th Chang Khlan) Near the night bazaar, this shiny shopping centre is a more legitimate version than its grey-market counterpart in Bangkok. Mainly licensed suppliers of electronic hardware, such as computers and cameras, fill the space without a single bootleg software vendor in sight.

Suriwong Book Centre   BOOKS
(Map p240; 54 Th Si Donchai; ☉8am-8pm) A Chiang Mai institution carrying mainly magazines and Thai titles with a small but sturdy English-language section of Thai and Southeast Asian nonfiction.

Backstreet Books   BOOKS
(Map p240; 2/8 Th Chang Moi Kao) In a rambling shop next to Gecko Books, Backstreet has a good selection of crime and thriller novels. Also a reasonable map section, although some are waaaaay out of date.

Book Zone   BOOKS
(Map p240; Th Tha Phae) Directly opposite Wat Mahawan; new travel guides and travel literature, plus contemporary fiction.

Gecko Books BOOKS
(Map p240; 2/6 Th Chang Moi Kao) A Chiang Mai chain, Gecko Books has several branches, including those at Th Ratchamankha and Th Loi Khro; includes new and used books sheathed in annoying plastic wrap.

RIVERSIDE

La Luna Gallery ART
(Map p240; ☑0 5330 6678; www.lalunagallery.com; 190 Th Charoenrat) In the old shophouse row on the east bank of the river, this professional gallery picks a fine bouquet of emerging Southeast Asian artists. Many canvases have a social commentary angle and give the viewer a window into the different artistic styles in the region. The handpainted elephants (1000B) make great gifts.

Vila Cini TEXTILES
(☑0 5324 6246; www.vilacini.com; 30-34 Th Charoenrat) Vila Cini sells high-end, handmade silks and cotton textiles that are reminiscent of the Jim Thompson brand. Perhaps the real draw is the store's atmospheric setting: a beautiful teak house with marble floors and a narrow, rickety staircase that leads to a galleried courtyard. It's on the eastern side of the road about 400m north of Saphan Nawarat.

Sop Moei Arts TEXTILES
(Map p240; ☑0 5330 6123; www.sopmoeiarts. com; 150/10 Th Charoenrat) Lots of shops sell hill-tribe crafts, but this one has put a modern makeover on the traditional crafts of the Pwo Karen, a tribal group living in Mae Hong Son Province. The result is some genuinely exquisite textiles including cushion covers, table pieces and wall hangings. The shop's directors began working with the people in the village through a health program some 30 years ago, but have since harnessed the craft traditions of textile weaving and basketry as an economic-development project.

Thai Tribal Crafts TRIBAL CRAFTS
(☑0 5324 1043; www.ttcrafts.co.th; 208 Th Bamrungrat) Peruse the ornate needle-work of the various hill tribes at this tribe-owned store near the McCormick Hospital. It operates by the principals of a fair-trade organisation. It's just south of cnr Th Bamrungrat and Th Kaew Nawarat.

SHOPPING FOR A CAUSE

Chiang Mai is Thailand's conscience in part because the city is the de facto caretaker of struggling immigrants from Myanmar (Burma) and hill-tribe villagers who lack the proper citizenship to get an education, good paying jobs and medical care. This close proximity to poverty prods the average resident out of complacency and into action, resulting in a myriad of nongovernmental organisations (NGOs) that help develop legitimate sources of income.

Dor Dek Gallery (Map p240; ☑08 9859 6683; Th Samlan) sells the craft projects of street children employed by the Volunteers for Children Development Foundation. This private organisation runs an orphanage and work-training program for displaced children. The profits from sales are divided among the child artist, the program's educational fund and future supply purchases. It's particularly good for handmade bags, purses and prezzies for the kids.

Or what about something novel, like a gift that doesn't need to be carried home? At **Freedom Wheel Chairs Workshop** (Map p240; ☑0 5321 3941; www.freedomwheelchairs. org; 133/1 Th Ratchaphakhinai) you can purchase a wheelchair (9500B) that will be donated to a disabled person who cannot afford such an expense. Run by a Thai survivor of polio and her husband, the workshop purchases and customises wheelchairs and mobility aids for needy recipients.

Would you rather treat yourself to something pretty with a social-justice hook? **Adorn with Studio Naenna** (p279) is the in-town showroom of a village weaving project that gives young women in the Chom Thong district of Chiang Mai a viable economic income without having to leave their families and migrate to the city for work. It also preserves traditional weaving techniques and aims for a softer environmental footprint through the use of natural fibres and dyes.

Other handicraft outlets for village-weaving projects include **KukWan Gallery** (p277), **Sop Moei Arts**, **Thai Tribal Crafts** and the **Hill-Tribe Products Promotion Centre** (p279).

WEST OF THE OLD CITY

Close to Chiang Mai University, Th Nimmanhaemin is often referred to as the trendy part of town. It has several malls filled with closet-sized clothing and gift boutiques. Don't miss the home-grown art and decor shops lining Soi 1 off Th Nimmanhaemin and its art and design festival every December.

Elephants
WOOD CARVING

(Map p248; 8 Soi 1, Th Nimmanhaemin) Founded by Mr Phet Wiriya, who has a passion for the art of wood carving, for elephants, and for developing new methods of carving, such as using local Cassia wood and changing the postures of the elephant. The results can be see (and bought) at his excellent shop.

Hill-Tribe Products Promotion Centre
TRIBAL CRAFTS

(21/17 Th Suthep) This royally sponsored project sells handmade hill-tribe crafts and touristy souvenirs. There are tribal costumes available from six hill-tribes. All the profits from sales go to hill-tribe welfare programs. It's right next to the entrance of Wat Suan Dok.

Srisanpanmai
SILK

(Map p248; 6 Soi 1, Th Nimmanhaemin) The display cases here show a visual textbook of the textiles of the Lanna people. From the technicolour rainbow patterns of Myanmar (Burma) to the wide-hem panel style of Chiang Mai, Srisanpanmai specialises in silks made in the old tradition.

Adorn with Studio Naenna
TEXTILES

(Map p248; 22 Soi 1, Th Nimmanhaemin) The pensive colours of the mountains have been woven into these naturally dyed silks and cottons, part of a village weaving project pioneered by Patricia Cheeseman, an expert and author on Thai-Lao textiles. This is the in-town shop, but you can see the production process at the studio. This is one of the best places in Chiang Mai for textiles – the quality is excellent. A quick browse and you'll be sold.

Studio Naenna
TEXTILES

(www.studio-naenna.com; 138/8 Soi Chang Khian, Th Huay Kaew) If you liked what you saw at Adorn with Studio Naenna, then head out of town to the main gallery of this textile cooperative. It's about 1km northwest of the intersection of Th Huay Kaew and Th Khlorng Chonprathan, along Soi Chang Khian.

Shinawatra
SILK

(Map p248; www.shinawatrathaisilk.co.th; 18 Th Huay Kaew) This venerable family-owned silk shop was already a household name before the owners' nephew, Thaksin Shinawatra, became the controversial prime minister. The colours and styles are a little dowdy for foreign tastes, but reconsider the selection should you happen to be elected mayor of Chiang Mai.

Koland
KITSCH ART

(Map p248; Soi 1, Th Nimmanhaemin) Chairman Mao greets visitors to the hippest store on the block, which sells a mix of locally made ceramics and kitsch art from China.

Kachama
TEXTILES

(Map p248; www.kachama.com; 10 Soi 1, Th Nimmanhaemin) If you're planning on hanging textiles instead of wearing them, visit this upmarket textile studio featuring the artist's traditionally inspired weavings.

Gongdee Gallery
GALLERY

(Map p248; gongdeegallery.com; 30 Soi 1, Th Nimmanhaemin) With one of the largest showrooms on the block, Gongdee is the soi's primary incubator for young artistic talent. There's a mix of home decor, furniture and paintings. Keep an eye out for the Byzantine icon-like Buddhas and altars painted by Chiang Mai artist Barinya.

Aka
FURNITURE

(Map p248; www.aka-aka.com; Soi 1, Th Nimmanhaemin) Thai furniture and decorative arts designer Eakrit Pradissuwana has created a contemporary look for modern Asia-philes. The furniture is slick and minimalist but distinctively 'Eastern' in character.

Chabaa
CLOTHING

(Map p248; www.atchabaa.com; Nimman Promenade, 14/32 Th Nimmanhaemin) If Putumayo put out clothes instead of music, you'd have Chabaa, which specialises in global ethnochic. You'll find brightly coloured embroidered tops and skirts plus big-statement jewellery.

Ginger
CLOTHING, ACCESSORIES

(Map p248; 6/21 Th Nimmanhaemin) For something more night-on-the-townish, check out the shimmery dresses, sparkly mules, fabulous jewellery and colourful accessories offered in this place.

❶ Information

Dangers & Annoyances

Compared to Bangkok, Chiang Mai is a breeze for tourists. The hassles from *sŏrng·tăa·ou* and túk-túk drivers are minimal.

A major annoyance is the traffic, but if you've just come from Bangkok you'll probably find it a relief as it's nowhere near as bad, and although very busy the main arteries do generally flow pretty well.

In March and April Chiang Mai can be enveloped in a smoky, dusty haze caused in large part by farmers burning off their fields in nearby districts.

Many less expensive guest houses in Chiang Mai will sometimes evict guests who don't engage trekking tours. Most places are pretty forthcoming with their policies on this and will usually offer rooms to nontrekking guests for a limited period.

Emergency

Tourist police (☎0 5324 7318, 24hr emergency 1155; Th Faham; ⏰6am-midnight) Has a volunteer staff of foreign nationals who speak a variety of languages; some volunteers are posted at the Sunday Walking Street. It's on the eastern side of the river, just south of the superhighway.

Internet Access

Most of the guest houses in Chiang Mai have free internet access, including wi-fi. You'll also find plenty of internet centres along Th Tha Phae, Moon Muang and Ratchamankha.

Internet Resources

1 Stop Chiang Mai (www.1stopchiangmai. com) Website covering city attractions with an emphasis on day trips and outdoor activities.

Chiang Mai Sawadee (http://chiangmai. sawadee.com) A useful website guide to Chiang Mai, especially when first arriving with airport information, accommodation and maps.

Guidelines (www.guidelineschiangmai.com) Monthly advertorial magazine that features respectable historical essays on the north; also a visitors guide.

Media

Chiangmai Mail (www.chiangmai-mail.com) Weekly English-language newspaper covering local and regional news and politics.

Citylife (www.chiangmainews.com) Lifestyle magazine profiling restaurants, bars local culture, politics and people; also has classified section.

Irrawaddy News Magazine (www.irrawaddy. org) A well-respected journal covering news in Myanmar (Burma), northern Thailand and other parts of Southeast Asia.

Medical Services

Chiang Mai Ram Hospital (☎0 5322 4880; www.chiangmairam.com; 8 Th Bunreuangrit) The most modern hospital in town; recommended by most expats.

Lanna Hospital (☎0 5399 9777; www.lanna -hospital.com; Th Superhighway) One of the better hospitals in town and less expensive than Chiang Mai Ram.

Malaria Centre (☎0 5322 1529; 18 Th Bunreuangrit) Offers blood checks for malaria.

Mungkala Traditional Medicine Clinic (Map p240; ☎0 5327 8494; 21-27 Th Ratchamankha; ⏰9am-12.30pm, 2.30-7pm) Government-licensed clinic using acupuncture, massage and Chinese herbal remedies.

McCormick Hospital (☎0 5392 1777; www. mccormick.in.th; 133 Th Kaew Nawarat) Former missionary hospital; good for minor treatments.

Money

All major Thai banks have several branches and ATMs throughout Chiang Mai; many of them along Th Tha Phae.

Western Union (☎0 5322 4979) Send or receive money by wire; counters at Central Airport Plaza, Kad Suan Kaew Shopping Centre, Th Huay Kaew and also available at any post office.

Post

Main post office (☎0 5324 1070; Th Charoen Muang; ⏰8.30am-4.30pm Mon-Fri, 9am-noon Sat & Sun) Other convenient branches are at Th Singharat/Samlan, Th Mahidon at Chiang Mai International Airport, Th Charoen Prathet, Th Phra Pokklao, Th Ratchadamnoen, Th Chotana and Chiang Mai University. The branch at Th Ratchadamnoen is a good place to organise packages home – staff are happy to wrap up boxes and awkward packages.

Telephone

Many internet cafes are outfitted with headsets so that customers can use Skype. There are also some direct-dial shops in the tourist sections of Chiang Mai and numerous phonecard booths in shops and bars around town.

Communications Authority of Thailand (CAT; ☎0 5324 1070; Th Charoen Muang; ⏰24hr) Out of the way, by the main post office.

Tourist Information

Tourism Authority of Thailand (TAT; ☎0 5324 8604; www.tourismthailand.org; Th Chiang Mai-Lamphun; ⏰8.30am-4.30pm) English-speaking staff provide maps and recommendations for tour guides; TAT doesn't make hotel reservations. It's just over Saphan Lek on the eastern side of the river.

Travel Agencies
Travel Shoppe (✆0 5387 4280; www.travel
-shoppe.com; 2/2 Th Chaiyaphum) Excellent
travel agency, just outside of Pratu Tha Phae.
Used to dealing with foreigners.

❶ Getting There & Away
Air
Regularly scheduled flights arrive into and
depart from **Chiang Mai International Airport**
(Map p236; www.chiangmaiairportonline.com),
which is 3km south of the centre of the old city.
Unless otherwise noted the following airlines use
the Suvarnabhumi Airport for travel from and to
Bangkok.
Air Asia (✆0 2515 9999; www.airasia.com)
Flies to Bangkok and Kuala Lumpur daily.
Bangkok Airways (✆0 5328 9338-9; www.
bangkokair.com) Flies daily to Bangkok and
continues to Samui.
Korean Air (✆662-620 6900; www.koreanair.
com) Flies between Chiang Mai and Seoul twice
weekly in either direction; direct flights.
Lao Airlines (✆0 5322 3401; www.laoairlines.
com) Flies to Luang Prabang daily.
Nok Air (✆1318; www.nokair.com) Flies to
Bangkok's Don Muang Airport; note that Nok
Air is a subsidiary of Thai Airways. Also flies to
Udon Thani.
Orient Thai Airlines (✆1126; www.flyorient
thai.com) Flies to Bangkok's Don Muang Airport
four times a day; and three times weekly to Pai
(operated by Kan Air).
Silk Air (✆0 5390 4985; www.silkair.com)
Flies to Singapore three times weekly.
Thai Airways International (THAI; ✆0 5321
1044/7; www.thaiair.com) Flies to Bangkok at
least six times daily. Also flies to many other
domestic destinations, although few are direct.

Bus
Chiang Mai's long-distance terminal is known
as **Arcade Bus Terminal** (Th Kaew Nawarat)
and is about 3km from the old city. From the
town centre, a túk-túk or chartered sŏrng·tăa·ou
should cost 50B to 80B. Green Bus Thailand is
the biggest company at the Arcade terminal. The
ticket counters that serve Pai, Mae Hong Son
and Mae Sariang are beyond the main terminal.

Minibuses also depart from the terminal,
and can be quicker than the buses, although
they are potentially more hair-raising journeys:
destinations include Mae Hong Son (250B) and
Pai (150B).

Do note that from Bangkok, the most reliable companies use Bangkok's Northern and
Northeastern bus terminal (Mo Chit). It is not
advisable to go north with a bus company that
leaves from Bangkok's tourist centres, like Th

Khao San. These invariably over-promise and
under-deliver.

For buses to destinations within Chiang Mai
Province, use the **Chang Pheuak Bus Terminal**
(off Map p240; Th Chang Pheuak), which is north
of the old city. Destinations served by the Chang
Pheuak terminal include Chiang Dao (40B, 1½
hours, every 30 minutes), Chom Thong (34B,
two hours, every 20 minutes), Fang (80B, three
hours, every 30 minutes), Hang Dong (15B, 30
minutes, every 20 minutes) and Tha Ton (90B,
five daily, four hours).

There is also a sŏrng·tăa·ou stop on Th Praisani
between Talat Warorot and Mae Ping serving
nearby towns, such as Lamphun, Bo Sang, San
Kamphaeng and Mae Rim. Sŏrng·tăa·ou and
buses also park on the east side of the river
near Saphan Lek and make the trip to Lamphun,
Lampang and Chiang Rai (via an older and
slower road).

Train
Chiang Mai's **train station** (off Map p236; Th
Charoen Muang) is about 2.5km east of the old
city. The train station has an ATM, a left-luggage
room (20B per piece) and an advance-booking
counter at the regular ticket window. For information on schedules and fares contact the
State Railway of Thailand (✆free hotline 1690;
www.railway.co.th) or grab a timetable from the
station.

All Chiang Mai–bound trains originate from
Bangkok's Hua Lamphong station. At the time
of research there were six daily departures from
Bangkok to Chiang Mai (and the same number
in the opposite direction) and the journey took
between 12 and 15 hours. The following fare
information indicates seats in air-con cars; if
there is no designation this means that the seats
are in fan-cooled cars.

Rapid trains leave Bangkok at 2.30pm arriving
at 5.10am the next day. Fares are 391/251B for
2nd-/3rd-class seats and 541/491B for lower/
upper sleeping berths in the 2nd-class cars.

Express trains leave Bangkok at 10pm and
arrive in Chiang Mai at 12.45pm the following
afternoon. Fares are 431/291B for 2nd-/3rd-
class seats, 541B for 2nd-class air-conditioned
seats, 581/531B for lower/upper sleeping berths
in 2nd-class cars, and 821/751B for lower/upper
sleeping berths for 2nd-class air-condioned cars.

Sprinter (special express diesel) trains leave
Bangkok at 8.30am and 7.20pm arriving in
Chiang Mai at 8.30pm and 7.40am, respectively.
Fares are 611B for 2nd-class air-conditioned
seats.

Special Express trains leave at 6pm and
7.20pm, arriving the next day at 7.15am and
9.45am. Fares are 1253B for a 1st-class air-conditioned sleeper and 881/791B for lower/upper
2nd-class air-conditioned sleeper.

BUS SERVICES FROM CHIANG MAI'S ARCADE TERMINAL

DESTINATION	FARE (B)	DURATION (HR)	FREQUENCY
Bangkok	605-810	9½	every 30min (6.30am-9.30pm)
Chiang Khong	215-275	6½	3 daily
Chiang Rai	135-265	3-4	every 30min (5.30am-5pm)
Chiang Saen	165-220	3½-4	2 daily
Khon Kaen	505	12	10 daily
Khorat	560-660	12	11 daily
Lampang	20-100	2	hourly (6.30am-9.30pm)
Lamphun	35	1	hourly (6.30am-9.30pm)
Mae Hong Son (via Pai)	145-170	7-8	8 daily
Mae Hong Son (via Mae Sariang)	180-340		6 daily
Mae Sai	165	5	2 daily
Mae Sariang	100-200	4-5	6 daily
Mae Sot	240-310	6-6½	2 daily
Nan	150-420	6	11 daily
Pai	75-85	4	12 daily
Phayao	115-150	2½-3	6 daily
Phrae	140-280	3½-4	7 daily
Phitsanulok (2nd class)	210-320	5-6	very frequently
Sukhothai (2nd class)	220	5-6	very frequently
Udon Thani (2nd class)	410-620	12	4 daily

Trains from Chiang Mai to Bangkok include the following services: express (departing 2.50pm, arriving 5.30am), special express (departing 4.30pm and 5.55pm, arriving 6.40am and 7am, respectively), sprinter (departing 9pm and 8.45am, arriving 9.10am and 8.25pm) and rapid (departing 6.45am, arriving 9.10pm).

Sleeping berths are increasingly hard to reserve without booking well in advance; tour groups sometimes book entire cars and available spots are even more scarce during holidays such as Songkran (mid-April), Chulalongkorn Day (October) and Chinese New Year (late February to early March). See p776 for information about advance bookings.

ⓘ Getting Around

To/From Airport

There is only one licensed airport taxi service, charging a flat 150B fare. Public bus number 6 (15B) goes from the airport to points west en route to Chiang Mai University; it isn't a convenient option if you're staying in the old city. Many guest houses and hotels also provide airport transfers.

From any point within the city, you can charter a túk-túk or red *sŏrng·tăa·ou* to the airport for about 60B to 80B; you can usually get one from the airport into the old city too, although you may have to wait around for a while until one shows up.

Bicycle

Cycling is a good way to get around Chiang Mai. Rickety cruiser bikes with a fixed gear can be rented for around 60B a day from some guest houses or from various places along the east moat. Check the bike carefully before you hire – brakes in particular can be dodgy. **Chiang Mai Mountain Biking** (Map p236; ☏0 5381 4207; www.mountainbikingchiangmai.com; 1 Th Samlan) rents well-maintained mountain bikes and city bikes for the day, and runs mountain bike tours of the area.

If you want to buy a bike or you need repairs, your best bet is **Cacti Bike** (Map p236; ☏0 5321 2979; 94/1 Th Singharat), which also offers reliable bike hire (80B to 350B daily depending on type of bike), from simple cruisers to serious mountain bikes with all the accessories. For the really good mountain bikes a deposit of US$250 or passport is required. An alternative, handily located option, is **SM Travel** ((Map p240; ✆0 5320 6844; 87 Th Ratchadamnoen), which also hires bikes and is a bit cheaper, reflective of the quality of their bikes (mountain bikes 100B to 200B).

Car & Truck

Private transport is available from rental agencies throughout the city, mainly along Th Moon Muang. Be sure that the vehicle you rent has insurance (liability) coverage, which usually includes a 5000B excess. This does not cover personal injury and medical payments of anyone injured in a traffic accident. Ask to take a look at the terms of the insurance policy so you're clear on what is and isn't included.

One of the most well-regarded agencies is **North Wheels** (Map p240; ✆0 5387 4478; www.northwheels.com; 70/4-8 Th Chaiyaphum), which offers hotel pick-up and delivery, 24-hour emergency road service, and comprehensive insurance. Another good bet is **Thai Rent a Car** (Petchburee Car Rent; ✆0 5328 1345; www.thairentacar.com; 81/1 Th Arak), located in the southwestern corner of the old city.

Standard rental rates per day are: small 1.5 litre cars such as Toyota Yaris or Honda Jazz are 900B to 1300B. Weekly and monthly rates are available and petrol is not included in the price. Unlimited kilometres should be included.

Other car-rental agencies in town:

Budget Car Rental (✆0 5320 2871; 201/2 Th Mahidol) Across from Central Airport Plaza.

Motorcycle

One of the most popular options for getting about on your own is to rent a scooter or motorcycle. Agencies along Th Moon Muang and even some guest houses rent Honda Dream 100cc step-through manual bikes for between 130B and 150B a day (automatic 200B); and Honda or Yamaha 125cc to 150cc rent for 250B a day. A few places rent 400cc motorcycles (600B to 900B), while a 650cc can go for 1300B.

Most agencies offer motorcycle insurance for around 50B a day; ask what this insurance coverage actually includes. Some policies will cover free repairs if the bike breaks down, but will charge a 1500B excess in case of accident and a 10,000B excess if the motorbike is stolen.

If you're renting a motorcycle for touring the countryside around Chiang Mai, check out the tips and routes at **Golden Triangle Rider** (www.gt-rider.com).

Among the more established and more reliable outlets:

Dang Bike Hire (Map p236; ✆0 5327 1524; 23 Th Kotchasan; ◷9am-5pm daily)

Mr Mechanic (Map p236; ✆0 5321 4708; www.mr-mechanic1994.com; 4 Soi 5, Th Moon Muang) There are also two other branches in the old city.

Tony's Big Bikes (Map p236; ✆0 5320 7124; 17 Th Ratchamankha) Rents well-maintained 125cc to 400cc motorbikes that all have license plates. Also offers riding lessons, can give touring advice and repairs motorcycles.

Sŏrng·tăa·ou, Túk-Túk & Săhm·lór

Chiang Mai residents who don't have their own wheels rely on the *sŏrng·tăa·ou* (also called *rót daang*) or túk-túk.

The *sŏrng·tăa·ou* are shared taxis: you can flag them down, tell them your destination and if they are going that way they'll nod. Along the way they might pick up other passengers if the stops are en route or close by. Short trips should cost 20B per person (eg between the old city and the river or Th Nimmahemin to the west) and longer trips from 40B per person, and more depending on the distance and your negotiation skills. If you travel from the riverside area to Th Nimmahemin you'll probably have to pay around 30B to 40B. By and large you hopefully shouldn't have a problem with *sŏrng·tăa·ou* drivers being too greedy about fares. Most quote honest prices and it seems to be something of a tradition for the drivers to scoot around town in the evenings and on weekends with their wives in the front seat for company.

Túk-túks work only on a charter basis and are more expensive than *sŏrng·tăa·ou*. In entertainment areas at night most túk-túk drivers will ask for an optimistic 100B.

Chiang Mai still has a few săhm·lór (pedicabs), typically parked at Talat Warorot. Săhm·lór cost around 20B to 30B for most trips.

Taxi

It is very rare to see a metered taxi to flag down in Chiang Mai. Call **Taxi Meter** (✆0 5326 2878; www.taxichiangmai.com) for a pick-up if you want one – most fares within greater Chiang Mai are no more than 150B. You can also organise tours in and around the city.

TÚK-TÚKS VERSUS SŎRNG·TĂA·OU

Túk túks are more expensive and their drivers are likely to rip you off, but they do offer a direct service and most drivers speak English. *Sŏrng·tăa·ou* drivers are cheaper, less inclined to rip off passengers (because many Thais use them too), but English can be a problem and routes are not always direct. Riding in a *sŏrng·tăa·ou* is an excellent way to meet local Thais.

NORTHERN CHIANG MAI PROVINCE

North of Chiang Mai the province becomes mountainous and rugged as it bumps against Myanmar's (Burma's) frontier. Among the highlights are the beautiful Mae Sa Valley and the forested peaks around Chiang Dao.

Mae Sa Valley & Samoeng

น้ำตกแม่สา/สะเมิง

One of the easiest mountain escapes, the Mae Sa–Samoeng loop travels from the lowland's concrete expanse into the highlands' forested frontier. The 100km route makes a good day trip with private transport or a country getaway with an overnight in Samoeng. **Golden Triangle Rider** (www.gt-rider.com) publishes a detailed map of the area.

Head north of Chiang Mai on Rte 107 (Th Chang Pheuak) toward Mae Rim, then left onto Rte 1096. The road becomes more rural but there's a steady supply of tour-bus attractions: orchid farms, butterfly parks, snake farms, you name it. Also lots of all-terrain vehicle (ATV) and offroad buggy hire.

Only 6km from the Mae Rim turn-off, **Nam Tok Mae Sa** (adult/child 100/50B, car 30B) is part of the Doi Suthep-Pui National Park. The cascade is a picturesque spot to picnic or tramp around in the woods for a bit and it is a favourite weekend getaway for locals. The falls are more a series of pools and a great place to cool off during the build-up (March to June); get there early and stake out your waterhole.

The road starts to climb and twist after the waterfall entrance. Not far past an elephant camp is the **Queen Sirikit Botanic Gardens** (☑0 5384 1000; www.qsbg.org; Rte 1096; adult/child 30/10B; ☉8.30am-5pm), featuring a shorn mountainside displaying 227 hectares of various exotic and local flora for conservation and research purposes. The best part of the collection is the glasshouse complex sitting near the mountain peak. The drive to the glasshouse affords some wonderful views and once up here highlights include: the waterlily and lotus collections with some enormous leafy examples, and beautiful two-, even three-tier flowers; and the huge **tropical rainforest glasshouse** complete with indoor waterfall, where you can walk around on a raised platform giving a bird's eye view of the forest below. Take the provided bus (30B) or your own car (100B) to get around the whole facility. Motorbikes are not allowed in the gardens.

Opposite the botanic gardens and set high on the hillside, the **Botanic Resort** ([☑0 5381 8628; www.botanicresort.org; Rte 1096; r 1500-4800B; ❋❋]) is all about fresh mountain air, views and relaxation in semi-luxurious rooms.

After the botanic gardens the road climbs up into the fertile Mae Sa Valley, once a high-altitude basin for growing opium poppies. Now the valley's hill-tribe farmers have re-seeded their **terraced fields** with sweet peppers, cabbage, flowers and fruits – which are then sold to the royal agriculture projects under the Doi Kham label. The royal project at the Hmong village of **Nong Hoi** sits some 1200m above sea level and is accessible by a turn-off road in the village of Pong Yeang.

Sitting at the western wedge of the valley, **Proud Phu Fah** (☑0 5387 9389; www.proudphufah.com; Km17, Rte 1096; r 4500-7000B; ❋@❋❋) is a small boutique hotel with creature-comfort villas designed to give the illusion of sleeping amid the great outdoors. Each villa also has a patio area right on the water's edge. The open-air restaurant serves healthy Thai food (dishes 100B to 150B) with a panoramic view of the valley.

After Proud Phu Fah, the road swings around the mountain ridge and starts to rise and dip until it reaches the conifer zone. Beyond, the landscape unfolds in a cascade of mountains. Eventually the road spirals down into **Samoeng**, a pretty village. If you want to stay overnight, try the simple, rather rundown **Samoeng Resort** (☑0 5348 7074; Rte 6033; r 400-500B; ❋), which is not a resort at all but rather a bunch of OK concrete bungalows in a bushy setting, about 2.5km outside the village. To get here take Rte 1349 from Samoeng (a right-hand turn in the town).

❶ Getting There & Away

Only part of the route is accessible via public transport. *Sŏrng·tăa·ou* go to Samoeng (70B, 2¾ hours, two morning departures) from the Chang Pheuak bus terminal in Chiang Mai. In Samoeng, the vehicles stop near the market, across from Samoeng Hospital.

Chiang Dao

เชียงดาว

In a lush, jungle setting and slammed up against the limestone cliffs of a mighty *doi* (mountain), Chiang Dao is a very popular escape from the steaming urban plains of Chiang Mai. Local accommodation plays on this theme attracting families and 30-something travellers looking for good eating, plenty of relaxing and northern rural ambience. The star attraction in this mountainous playground is **Doi Chiang Dao**, allegedly Thailand's highest limestone mountain. It is a thickly forested peak with a revered **cave shrine** burrowed into the base, and trails popular with birders and trekkers.

Chiang Dao town isn't much but a dusty crossroads that hosts a colourful **Tuesday morning market** (☉7am-12am), when hill tribes come to sell their wares. The more charming part of town is 5km west along the road that leads to Tham Chiang Dao (Chiang Dao Cave). The surrounding village and guest houses are smack up against the mountain.

From the main four-way junction at Chiang Dao, those with their own wheels can head eastwards to visit Lahu, Lisu and Akha villages, which are all within 15km. Roughly 13.5km east from Rte 107 is the Lisu village of Lisu Huay Ko, where rustic accommodation is available. Without independent transportation, you can arrange **hill-tribe treks** through the guest houses at Chiang Dao.

◉ Sights

Some guest houses rent mountain bikes for 100B a day – not much of a bargain but an improvement over two feet.

Tham Chiang Dao　　　　　　　CAVES
(ถ้ำเชียงดาว; admission 20B) In the heat of the day, the coolest place in town is the Chiang Dao Cave, a complex said to extend some 10km to 14km into Doi Chiang Dao. There are four interconnected caverns that are open to the public. Tham Phra Non (360m) is the initial segment and is electrically illuminated and can be explored on one's own. It contains several religious shrines, a common feature of Thailand's caves, which are regarded as holy meditation sites. There are also some surreal-looking stalactites reminiscent of a Salvador Dali painting.

To explore the other caves – Tham Mah (735m), Tham Kaew (474m) and Tham Nam (660m) – you can hire a guide with a pressurised gas lantern for 100B for up to five people. Local village ladies lead the guided tours and can point out the interior cave formations that have been named.

Local legend says this cave complex was the home of a *reu·sĕe* (hermit) for a thousand years and that the sage was on such intimate terms with the deities that he convinced some *tair·wá·dah* (the Buddhist

equivalent of angels) to create seven magic wonders inside the caverns: a stream flowing from the pedestal of a solid-gold Buddha; a storehouse of divine textiles; a mystical lake; a city of *naga* (mythical serpents); a sacred immortal elephant; and the hermit's tomb. Such fantastical wonders are said to be much deeper inside the mountain, beyond the last of the illuminated caverns.

There is a temple complex outside the cavern, and a stream with huge carp and catfish you can feed (which handily counts as making merit via a donation). Vendors by the parking lot sell medicinal roots and herbs harvested in the nearby forests.

Doi Chiang Dao　　　　　　　MOUNTAIN
(ดอยเชียงดาว) Part of the Doi Chiang Dao National Park, Doi Chiang Dao (also called Doi Luang) pokes into the heavens at 2195m above sea level. From the summit, reachable by a two-day hike, the views are spectacular. The southern side of the mountain is believed to be one of the most accessible spots in the world to see the giant nuthatch and Hume's pheasant. **Bird-watching** and **overnight treks** can be arranged through local guest houses.

If you just want to wander by yourself, continue to the end of the cave road to **Samnak Song Tham Pha Plong** (Tham Pha Plong Monastic Centre), where Buddhist monks sometimes meditate. A long, steep stairway leads up the mountain to a large *chedi* framed by forest and limestone cliffs.

🛏 Sleeping

Many of the guest houses are spread out along the road leading to Tham Chiang Dao and enjoy a view of the mountain and butterfly-filled gardens.

Chiang Dao Nest　　　　BUNGALOWS $$
(☑08 6017 1985; http://nest.chiangdao.com; r 550-1600B; @🛜☒) Simple, great-value A-frame bungalows get the basics right – comfy beds, privacy and immaculate interiors. Those closest to the restaurant have terrific views from the rickety rear porches. Bungalows further away have limited views but plenty of privacy and a lush garden setting. There's a secluded swimming pool in a forest setting with mountain views; and this place has a great feel to it, generated at least in part by the friendly owners and staff, and evidenced by the large return clientele – especially expats from Chiang Mai. However, the accommodation here is really window dressing for the sensational restaurant.

Malee's Nature Lovers Bungalows BUNGALOWS $$
(☎08 1961 8387; www.maleenature.com; r 650-1150B; @) Malee's has a more rustic traveller vibe than the Nest next door with its old-fashioned backpacker camaraderie. The cheaper bungalows are pretty basic but come with high ceilings, fans and decent bathrooms. The more expensive 'honeymoon bungalows' are excellent, with soaring ceilings, fridge and wrap-around porch, and set high off the ground, so they catch the breeze. There's also lots of info on stuff to do around Chiang Dao, and on public transport.

Chiang Dao Rainbow BUNGALOWS $$
(☎08 4803 8116; small/large bungalows 650/750B, r 380B) The two recycled teak bungalows are a great size, have suitably creaky floors, four-poster beds, and shuttered windows overlooking rice fields and mountains. There are also cheaper rooms in the house at the back and plenty of info on things to do around Chiang Dao, such as visiting hill-tribe villages or waterfalls. It's a difficult place to find: look for the turn-off, not far from where the bypass road meets Rte 107 (almost opposite Aurora Resort on the bypass road). There's a small sign and a lot of Thai banners.

Nature Guest House BUNGALOWS $
(☎08 9955 9074; r 550B; @ 🖥) Closer to town than the other guest houses, this quiet place is set in a neat garden with mountain views. The brick and wood A-frame bungalows with terraces are simple yet stylish. A very peaceful option. Motorbike and mountain bike hire available.

Hobby Hut BUNGALOWS $
(☎08 0034 4153; r 250B) These simple huts are the real backpacker option in Chiang Dao. Promoting itself as accommodation to experience a simple life on a Thai farm and enjoy 'Mum's home cooking', meals with the family are available. Very basic wooden huts raised off the ground to catch the breeze share a bathroom. It's very friendly and bike rental for 80B a day is available.

Chiang Dao Nest 2 BUNGALOWS $$
(☎0 5345 6242; nest.chiangdao.com; r 500-950B; @) The overflow site for Chiang Dao Nest, about 600m past the cave turn-off on the left side of the road.

Chiang Dao Hut BUNGALOWS $
(☎0 5345 6384; www.chiangdaohut.com; r 500B) There's something very cute about this place near Chiang Dao Nest 2. There are just three huts, all spacious, clean and with fans, hot water and TV.

✕ Eating

Chiang Dao has a lovely assortment of farm-fresh produce – mostly chemical free – thanks to the nearby royal agriculture projects.

There is a **daily food market** off the main street through Chiang Dao. The **Tuesday morning market** is the most colourful, with hill tribes bringing wares to sell.

TOP CHOICE Chiang Dao Nest INTERNATIONAL $$$
(☎0 6017 1985; dishes 300-500B; ⊗breakfast, lunch, dinner) The Nest's restaurant serves sophisticated fusion-European food in a relaxed garden setting. Wicha, the owner and chef, received her culinary training in the UK and creates a menu that reflects the seasons and the best of the local produce. Dishes such as double baked cheese souffle with spinach cream and roasted-veg salad; and baked passionfruit cheesecake grace the menu. The food ain't cheap but definitely comes with the wow factor.

Chiang Dao Rainbow THAI/MEDITERRANEAN $$
(☎08 4803 8116; set menu 250B) This highly recommended restaurant offers two menus – northern Thai and Greek-Mediterranean. There is an à la carte or set menu and plenty of vegetarian options, too.

❶ Getting There & Around

Chiang Dao is 72km north of Chiang Mai along Rte 107. Buses to Chiang Dao (40B, 1½ hours, frequent) leave from Chiang Mai's Chang Pheuak terminal. The buses arrive and depart from Chiang Dao's bus station from where you can catch a sŏrng·tǎa·ou to your guest house. Most drivers charge 150B to deliver passengers to guest houses on the cave road. Buses also travel to Fang (60B). Most accommodation hires mountain bikes, and some organise scooters and cars. Or, you can hire a sŏrng·tǎa·ou for about 1000B a day to drive you round the area.

Doi Ang Khang ดอยอ่างขาง

Welcome to Thailand's 'Little Switzerland', so called for its cool climate and mountain scenery. Tucked away in the northern corner of the province, motoring up here is a good chance to escape the brutal heat of the plains 1300m below. Doi Ang Khang supports the cultivation of many species of temperate flowers, fruits and vegetables that are considered exotic in Thailand and were introduced as substitutes for opium. But it is the sensation of winter that draws many Thais here, especially in January when they might spot frost or even a dusting of snow and get the rare opportunity to bundle up in heavy jackets and hats. Doi Ang Khang borders Myanmar (Burma) and offers the illusion of peeping over the border into that country's vast frontier.

The Tourism Authority of Thailand in Chiang Mai has a basic map of Doi Ang Khang outlining cycling routes and treks to hill-tribe villages, many of whom participate in royal agriculture projects. Another source of information on Doi Ang Khang is the ecofriendly Angkhang Nature Resort, which arranges cycling, mule riding and trekking to hill-tribe villages.

The main way to the summit is via Rte 1249 (there are great views from this route, but keep your eyes on the road as there are also some very steep switchbacks), but a more scenic back road is Rte 1178, which winds along a ridge to the mountain's western slopes. The village of **Ban Luang** is an interesting stopover for the Yunnanese atmosphere. Nineteen kilometres south of the park's turn-off on Rte 107, you can make a 12km detour west to visit **Ban Mai Nong Bua**, a Kuomintang (KMT) village with an old-fashioned Yunnanese feel.

Near the summit of Doi Ang Khang and the Yunnanese village of **Ban Khum**, is the **Royal Agricultural Station** (www.angkhang. com; admission 50B), showcasing fruit orchards and other flora (such as a bonsai garden). The restaurant serves Thai standards and there are several places to stay.

Close to the station's entry **Angkhang Nature Resort** (☑05345 0110; www.oamhotels. com/angkhang; r from 2500B; @❄) has accommodation in the way of large bungalows set in a slope behind the main reception building. They are quite plush, kitted out more like hotel rooms and a good size. The best feature is the small, wooden outdoor porches giving lovely garden views. In the resort itself, the attractive lobby boasts stone fireplaces to complete the winter-lodge atmosphere. The lodge can arrange lots of outdoor activities – there's a map of what's available on the lobby wall. The on-site restaurant uses locally-grown organic produce.

At the base of the slope are a couple of open-air restaurants serving a variety of dishes with an emphasis on Thai and Yunnanese Muslim cuisine.

❶ Getting There & Away

Doi Angkhang is about 25km from the intersection of Rte 107 and 1249; from this turn-off it's a further 13km to Fang. It is possible to get to Doi Ang Khang via public transport, but travelling to points along the mountain will be difficult. You can catch a bus heading to Fang (90B, three hours, every 30 minutes) from Chiang Mai's Chang Pheuak terminal. Tell the driver that you want to get off at the Rte 1249 turn-off. From there you can take a *sŏrng·tăa·ou* to Ban Khum (1500B chartered), which is near the summit.

Fang & Tha Ton   ฝาง/ท่าตอน

For most people Fang is just a road marker on the way to Tha Ton, the launching point for river trips to Chiang Rai. If you do hang around this large, bustling town, there are some quiet backstreets lined with little shops in wooden buildings and the Shan/Burmese-style **Wat Jong Paen** (near the New Wiang Kaew Hotel), which has an impressive stacked-roof *wí·hăhn*. The city of Fang was originally founded by Phaya Mengrai in the 13th century, although the locale dates back at least 1000 years as a stop for *jeen hor* caravans. Being so close to Myanmar (Burma), the surrounding district is an 'underground' conduit for *yah bâh* (methamphetamine).

Along the main street in Fang there are banks offering currency exchange and ATMs.

Tha Ton is a petite settlement plonked on the banks of a pretty bend in Mae Nam Kok, which is lined with a few riverside restaurants and the boat launch for river trips to Chiang Rai.

In Tha Ton, there is a **tourist police office** (☑1155) near the bridge on the boat-dock side.

◎ Sights & Activities

Wat Tha Ton   TEMPLE
(☑05345 9309; www.wat-thaton.org) In Tha Ton, this temple climbs up the side of a wooded hill. There are nine different levels punctuated by shrines, Buddha statues and a *chedi*. Each level affords stunning views of the mountainous valley towards Myanmar (Burma) and the plains of Tha Ton. From the base to the ninth level, it is about 3km or a 30-minute walk. The short walk to the first level has a statue of Kuan Yin, the Chinese

goddess of compassion; the international liaison monk has his office here too. There's also a herbal medical centre with traditional massage, acupuncture and public saunas.

Local Villages
ETHNIC VILLAGES

Within 20km of Fang and Tha Ton you can visit local villages, inhabited by Palaung (a Karennic tribe that arrived from Myanmar (Burma) around 16 years ago), Black Lahu, Akha and Yunnanese, on foot, mountain bike or motorcycle. Treks and rafting trips can be arranged through any of Tha Ton's guest houses or hotels.

Boat Trip to Chiang Rai
BOAT TRIP

(☑0 5305 3727; fare 350B; ⊙departs 12.30pm) From Tha Ton you can make a half-day long-tail boat trip to Chiang Rai. The regular passenger boat takes up to 12 travellers. The trip is a bit of a tourist trap as the passengers are all tourists, and the villages along the way sell cola and souvenirs. The best time to go is at the end of the rainy season in November when the river level is high. The travel time down river depends on river conditions and the skill of the pilot, taking anywhere from three to five hours. You could actually make the boat trip in a day from Chiang Mai, catching a bus back from Chiang Rai as soon as you arrive, but it's better to stay overnight in Tha Ton so that you aren't rushed.

Some travellers take the boat to Chiang Rai in two or three stages, stopping first in **Mae Salak** (90B), a large Lahu village, or **Ban Ruammit** (300B), a Karen village. Both are well touristed, but you can get off the path by joining a **hill-tribe trek** from here to other Shan, Thai and hill-tribe villages or longer treks south of Mae Salak to Wawi, a large multi-ethnic community of *jeen hor,* Lahu, Lisu, Akha, Shan, Karen, Mien and Thai peoples. The Wawi area has dozens of hill-tribe villages of various ethnicities, including the largest Akha community in Thailand (Saen Charoen) and the oldest Lisu settlement (Doi Chang). Another alternative is to trek south from Mae Salak all the way to the town of Mae Suay, where you can catch a bus on to Chiang Rai or back to Chiang Mai.

You can also make the trip (much more slowly) upriver from Chiang Rai – this is possible despite the rapids. The boats are also available for charter hire (2200B, six people).

🛏 Sleeping

Most visitors who do stay overnight prefer to stay in Tha Ton.

Apple Resort
TOP CHOICE
GUEST HOUSE $$

(☑0 5337 3144; garden bungalows with fan/air-con 350/500B, river bungalows 1000/1200B; ❄) Newly opened and right on the river opposite the boat launch (across the other side of the river), Apple Resort is a feel-good place with stylishly decorated riverfront bungalows that are light, bright and breezy and come with fantastic front porches right on the waterfront. The garden bungalows are well worth the price and quite roomy; the only downside is the very small twin beds. Bathrooms, with separate shower recess in all rooms, are excellent. Tariff includes breakfast.

Old Tree's House
HOTEL $$

(☑08 5722 9002; www.oldtreeshouse.net; bungalows 1200-1400B; ❄🛜🏊) Up a steep driveway and nestled into a hillside, this place is a great find, offering luxury bungalows in a garden setting. It's a cleverly designed mini-resort with lots of nooks and crannies and even a platform set in a tree where you can enjoy the views while drying off from the pool. What you give up at this place in riverside setting you more than make up for with spectacular views of mountains across the border in Myanmar (Burma). Included in the tariff is a stocked minibar and breakfast. It's 400m past Tha Ton, and well signed off the road.

Thaton Garden Riverside
GUEST HOUSE $

(☑0 5345 9286; r 300-600B) Next to Thaton Chalet by the bridge, this is not the friendliest place around, but has Tha Ton's best budget choice of air-con and fan rooms. It's worth paying the extra baht for an air-con room as you get a river terrace. Conveniently located close to the centre of town.

Garden Home
HOTEL $$

(☑0 5337 3015; r 600-1800B) A tranquil place along the river, about 150m from the bridge, with thatch-roofed bungalows spaced among lychee trees and bougainvillea. There are also a few stone bungalows, and three larger, more luxurious bungalows on the river with lovely verandahs, a TV and fridge. From the bridge, turn left at the Thaton River View Hotel sign.

Thaton River View
HOTEL $$

(☑0 5337 3173; thatonriverview@hotmail.com; r 1700B; ❄) You are really paying for the location here not the rudimentary comforts – with bungalow rooms peeping out of green thickets along the riverfront, joined by wooden walkways lined with frangipani trees. Rooms are fairly basic, although clean and serviceable, but sitting out on the common porch areas where you're almost falling into the water, is a real pleasure especially with a cold drink in the evening. If you want a quiet, comfortable spot to while away a couple of days staring at the river, this is it.

Thaton Chalet   HOTEL **$$$**
(☎0 5337 3155/7; www.thatonchalet.com; r 1400-2200B; ※) A bit more institutional, this four-storey hotel next to the bridge is called a chalet, but the rooms here are far more like a hotel – there's nothing rustic about the place. Deluxe rooms however have huge balconies overlooking the river and heaps of space inside too with plenty of cane sitting chairs. Where the rooms fall down is in the bathrooms, which could really do with an upgrade. Try to get a corner deluxe room, they have wall-to-wall windows providing magnificent vistas of the river and beyond.

Areeya Phuree   HOTEL **$$**
(☎0 5305 3658; http://areeyaphuree.com; r 1000B, hostel dm 225B; ※) On the boat-dock side, downstream along the river, this sprawling place was undergoing a change of ownership and major renovations when we passed through. We saw cute rooms that are a bit dark but have 'garden bathrooms' complete with plants and built mainly from stone. There is also hostel-style accommodation with shared sleeping arrangements. The hotel has a beautiful, quiet riverside location not far from town.

✖ Eating

The food stalls on the main street in Fang are good places to eat. There are also a few restaurants serving Yunnanese specialities such as *kôw soy*, *man·toh* (steamed buns; *mantou* in Mandarin) and *kôw mòk gài*, plus *gŏo·ay dĕe·o* (rice noodles) and other standards.

In Tha Ton, most of the top-end hotels have riverside restaurants. There is a row of basic **Thai-Chinese restaurants** (dishes 25-35B) by the boat dock.

Chankasen   THAI **$**
(209 Rimnumkok, Tha Ton; mains 60-80B; ⊙breakfast, lunch, dinner) The food is fine at this friendly, entrepreneurial Thai spot, but the real puller is the seating right on the river. Conveniently located right alongside the boat dock.

Sunshine Cafe   CAFE **$**
(Tha Ton; breakfast 70B; ⊙breakfast, lunch) This is the place to come for freshly brewed coffee (30B) in the morning. It also does a wide selection of Western breakfasts including muesli, fresh fruit and yoghurt. Located on the main road, just before the bridge.

CHIANG MAI PROVINCE FANG & THA TON

DON'T MISS

A CHANCE TO SOAK YOUR CARES AWAY

Doi Pha Hompok National Park (☎0 5345 3517; adult/child 200/100B) has a hot-springs complex (*bòr nám rórn; bor náam hórn* in northern Thai) that lies about 10km west of Fang at Ban Meuang Chom, near the agricultural station, off Rte 107 at the end of Rte 5054 (the park is sometimes referred to as Doi Fang or Mae Fang National Park). At the top of the mountain average temperatures are a mere 2°C during winter and 14°C during summer. From November to February average temperatures in the park are 14°C to 19°C.

Set amidst a boulder-strewn field, the 40 or so springs are in a very picturesque spot, and if you arrive early in the morning, before the tour buses, it's very tranquil too. The temperature of the water is between 50°C and 87°C: boiling eggs is a popular pastime for Thai visitors.

After walking the network of paths around streams and vents shooting steam (sometimes 30m) and bubbling water into the air you can immerse yourself in the good stuff, taking advantage of the water's curative powers. A public bath is just 20B with no time limit so you can get properly wrinkly. If you're a bit shy about these things, a private bath is 50B.

Accommodation (tent for 3/6/8 persons 225/450/600B, 4-/6-/10-person bungalows 600/1000/2000B) is available through the park headquarters; and sleeping bag, pillows, blankets etc, are also offered for campers.

① Getting There & Away

Bus & sŏrng·tăa·ou

Buses to Fang (90B, three hours, every 30 minutes) leave from the Chang Pheuak bus terminal in Chiang Mai. Air-con minivans make the trip to Fang (150B, three hours, every 30 minutes), leaving from behind the Chang Pheuak bus terminal on the corner of Soi Sanan Kila.

From Fang it's about 23km to Tha Ton (30B). Yellow sŏrng·tăa·ou leave from the market for the 40-minute trip between 5.30am and 5pm.

The river isn't the only way to get to points north of Tha Ton. Yellow sŏrng·tăa·ou leave from the northern side of the river in Tha Ton for Mae Salong (70B, 1½ hours, mornings only).

To get to Mai Sai (80B to 90B) or Chiang Rai (100B to 110B) directly, take the afternoon bus from the bridge.

If you're heading west to Mae Hong Son Province, it's not necessary to dip all the way south to Chiang Mai before continuing on. At Mae Malai, the junction of Rte 107 (the Chiang Mai–Fang highway) and Rte 1095, you can pick up a bus to Pai for 70B; if you're coming from Pai, be sure to get off at this junction to catch a bus north to Fang.

Motorcycle

Motorcycle trekkers can travel between Tha Ton and Doi Mae Salong, 48km northeast, over a fully paved but sometimes treacherous mountain road. There are a couple of Lisu and Akha villages on the way. The 27km or so between the village of Muang Ngam and Doi Mae Salong is very steep and winding – take care, especially in the rainy season. When conditions are good, the trip can be done in 1½ hours.

SOUTHERN CHIANG MAI PROVINCE

To the immediate south of Chiang Mai is the Ping Valley, a fertile agricultural plain that has also grown some noteworthy handicraft villages. Further to the southwest is Thailand's highest peak, Doi Inthanon.

Bo Sang & San Kamphaeng

บ่อสร้าง/สันกำแพง

Southeast of Chiang Mai is Bo Sang, known throughout the country as the 'umbrella village'. It is mainly a tourist market filled with craft shops selling painted umbrellas (often produced elsewhere), fans, silverware, statuary, celadon pottery and lacquerware. You'll find many of the same items at the Chiang Mai Night Bazaar but there's a greater concentration and variety here.

In late January the **Bo Sang Umbrella Festival** (têt·sà·gahn rôm) features a colourful umbrella procession during the day and a night-time lantern procession. Although it sounds touristy, this festival is actually a very Thai affair; a highlight are the many northern-Thai music ensembles that perform in shopfronts along Bo Sang's main street.

Further down Rte 1006 is **San Kamphaeng**, known for its cotton and silk weaving shops. The main street is lined with textile showrooms while the actual weaving is done in small factories down side streets. You can take a peek if you like.

① Getting There & Away

White sŏrng·tăa·ou to Bo Sang (20B) and San Kamphaeng (20B) leave Chiang Mai frequently during the day from the sŏrng·tăa·ou stop on Th Praisani near Talat Warorot. Bo Sang is 10km from Chiang Mai and San Kamphaeng is 14km.

Mae Kampong   แม่กำปอง

If you plough across the Ping Valley on Rte 1317 past the rice fields and cow pastures to Mae On district, the road begins to narrow and climb into the forested hills of Mae Kampong, an area that entices visitors for a day or overnight excursion because of its interesting combination of nature and cultural activities. Most visitors are first introduced to the area on daytrips with **Flight of the Gibbon** (p253), a zipline canopy tour.

Sitting at an altitude of about 1300m, **Ban Mae Kampong** is a Thai village that produces mêeang (pickled tea leaves), the northern Thai equivalent of betel nut. Most villagers make their living in this small-scale industry and head out into the forest to collect the tea leaves. In the early mornings the pickers stop by the local temple where the monk has prepared a restorative brew of medicinal herbs.

The village itself is a gravity-defying collection of maze-like huts hugging the steep hillside. Flowers bow in the cool breezes and the jungle insects screech at each other. Several families participate in a **homestay program** (⌚0 5331 5111, 08 9559 4797; per person 1/2 nights 550/900B) that includes three meals and basic lodging.

The narrow road through the village summits the hill and winds down into **Chae Son**

National Park, where you'll find waterfalls and hot springs.

If the natural solitude is appealing, stay awhile at one of the nature lodges south of the village. **Tharnthong Lodge** (☑08 6420 5354; www.tharnthonglodges.com; r 1200-4000B) is bisected by a pebble-strewn stream crossed by a wooden bridge to the six houses dotting the property. If you don't need a bed, stop by the restaurant to enjoy the affordable Thai food (dishes 80B to 160B).

Or try **Baan Chom Nok Chom Mai** (☑08 9559 9371; r 600B), a simple set-up with very good rooms.

Mae Kampong is 48km east of Chiang Mai and can be reached by following Rte 1317 toward San Kamphaeng. At the T-junction at Ban Huay Kaew, turn right towards the signs for Ban Mae Kampong.

Hang Dong, Ban Wan & Ban Thawai   หางดงบ้านวันบ้านถวาย

Just 15km south of Chiang Mai is a veritable 'furniture highway' where stores and workshops specialise in decorative arts, woodcarving, antiques and contemporary furniture.

The shops along Rte 108 in Hang Dong are impossible to explore on foot and still a bit of a pain in a car. North of Hang Dong centre, near Amarin Place, **Siam Lanna Art** (☑0 5382 3419; Rte 108; ⊙closed Sun) is an eccentric stop for junk aficionados. We're told it is a great spot for browsing, but impossible to buy from as no one knows the prices.

A greater concentration of stores can be found in Ban Wan on Th Thakhilek, the first left turn after Talat Hang Dong. A cluster of stores near the intersection sells antique reproductions using new wood; in times past they used salvaged teak but most of that is now gone. Further down the road is **Chili Antiques & Arts** (☑08 9952 7898; chiliantiques.com; 125 Th Thakhilek), a massive showroom of bronze and wooden Buddhas, sculptures, wood carvings and fine decor. Across the street is **Piak Antiques** (☑0 5344 1157; www.piakantique.com; Th Thakhilek) selling reclaimed, chunky wooden furniture. **Crossroads Asia** (☑0 5343 4650; Chaiyo Plaza, 214/7 Th Thakhilek) sells ethnic art and antiques from across Asia; our favourites are the brass lanterns and tribal masks upstairs. With its folk art, bronze statues and buddha collection, **World Port Services** (☑0 5343 4200; Th Thakhilek) is a bit quirkier than most. If you're after something for the kids, pop into **Kala Design** (☑08 1034 5495; Th Thakhilek). It's a bit more downmarket but there are some wonderful animal interpretations in wood: the goggle-eyed owls are adorable.

Continue toward the right fork in the road to **Ban Thawai Tourism Village**, which is a pedestrian-friendly market with 3km of shops selling all sorts of home decor. Past Zone 5 is Sriboonmuang's workshop, an example of what made Ban Thawai famous in the first place. In the factory's covered sheds, workers sand and polish small armies of wooden elephants, hobby horses and dolls.

When you need a break from the browsing, call into **Pana Botanicals** (www.panabo tanicals.com; Th Thakhilek; dishes 80-90B) where, in this fine wooden house, you can sit out on a deck overlooking extensive gardens and sip a peppermint tea or iced coffee; alternatively indulge in some well-prepared Thai food. Afterwards you can pick up some organic, locally made bathing products.

Many of the shops here deal in wholesale as well as retail, and shipping can be arranged.

It is advisable to come with private transport, but you can catch a *sŏrng·tăa·ou* from Pratu Chiang Mai to Hang Dong (20B) and to Ban Thawai (30B).

Doi Inthanon National Park   อุทยานแห่งชาติดอยอินทนนท์

Thailand's highest peak is Doi Inthanon (often abbreviated as Doi In), which measures 2565m above sea level, an impressive altitude for the kingdom, but a tad diminutive compared to its cousins in the Himalayan range. The 1000-sq-km **national park** (☑0 5328 6730; adult/child 200/100B, car/motorbike 30/20B; ⊙8am-sunset) surrounding the peak has hiking trails, waterfalls and two monumental stupas erected in honour of the king and queen. It is a popular day trip from Chiang Mai for tourists and locals, especially during the New Year's holiday when there's the rarely seen phenomenon of frost.

There are eight waterfalls that dive off the mountain. **Nam Tok Mae Klang** (at Km8) is the largest and the easiest to get to. **Nam Tok Wachiratan** (at Km20.8) is another popular stop with food vendors at its base and a huge frothy mane that plummets 50m. If you'd rather be a part of the cascade, try abseiling with the Peak (p254). **Nam Tok Siriphum** (at Km30) looks like a

SAN PA THONG

สันป่าตอง

Further south on Rte 108, on the outskirts of San Pa Thong, **Kaomai Lanna Resort** (☎0 5383 4470; www.kaomailanna.com; Km29, Th Chiang Mai-Hot; r 2400-3500B; ❉≋) is almost reason enough to travel this far. The resort has turned many of the property's abandoned tobacco-curing sheds into comfortable lodgings amid a lush garden setting. With plant-covered walkways and creeper covered buildings, this place is brimming with character and is a Thai version of English cottage accommodation. The cute rooms have comfy futons and wooden floors. The yoga studio, spa and swimming pool mean you can easily spend a few relaxing days here.

This used to be one of many northern Thai tobacco farms supplying the international cigarette market before China supplanted the local growers. The resort also arranges tours to the nearby **handicraft villages** (which are truly villages instead of souvenir markets). Even if you don't stay here, the outdoor restaurant serves superb Thai food.

If you want to stay out here, you really need your own wheels – whether you're heading into Chiang Mai, or out to Doi Inthanon.

river of silver from the vantage point of Ban Mong Khun Klang, a Hmong village. In February the village builds and races wooden carts down a steep incline. Along the road to the top are terraced rice fields and covered greenhouses tended by Hmong and Karen tribespeople.

About 3km before the summit of Doi Inthanon, **Phra Mahathat Naphamethanidon** and **Nophamethanidon** (admission to both 40B) at Km41-42 are two *chedi* built by the Royal Thai Air Force to commemorate the king's and queen's 60th birthdays in 1989 and 1992, respectively. In the base of the octagonal *chedi* is a hall containing a stone Buddha image.

The whole point of the park is to get as high as you can to see life in a colder climate, and the coolness is such a relief from the sweltering plains below. Thais relish bundling up in hats and jackets and posing for pictures among conifers and rhododendrons. Almost at the exact summit there's a *chedi* dedicated to one of the last Lanna kings (Inthawichayanon). From there, a lovely boardwalk through the thick, cool forest leads to a cafe, obligatory souvenir shop and the start of the **Ang Ka nature trail**, a 360m platform walkway through a moss-festooned bog. Walking through the forest on the nature trail is an enchanting experience (if devoid of crowds).

The views from Doi Inthanon are best in the cool dry season from November to February. But don't expect a rewarding view from the summit, as for most of the year a mist, formed by the condensation of warm humid air below, hangs around the top of the mountain creating an eerie effect. You can expect the air to be quite chilly towards the top, so take a jacket or sweater. The views on the way to the summit are much better.

The park is one of the top destinations in Southeast Asia for naturalists and birdwatchers. The mist-shrouded upper slopes produce abundant orchids, lichens, mosses and epiphytes, while supporting nearly 400 **bird species**, more than any other habitat in Thailand. Most of the park's bird species are found between 1500m and 2000m; the best bird-watching season is from February to April, and the best spots are the *beung* (bogs) near the top. The mountain is also home to Assamese macaques, Phayre's leaf monkeys, and a selection of other rare and not-so-rare monkeys and gibbons as well as the more common Indian civet, barking deer and giant flying squirrel – around 75 mammal species in all.

🍴 Sleeping & Eating

Park **accommodation** (reservations ☎08 8587 5680; www.dnp.go.th) is available in comfortable bungalows (from 1000B) located next to the information centre (the best ones overlook the water) and at Km31 there's a **restaurant** (mains 30-80B) that has decent Thai mains but is really a dining hall for tour bus patrons. There is camping (sites 60B to 90B) in front of the information centre too, or at Nam Tok Mae Pan.

Outside the park there are a number of accommodation options lining Rte 1009, none of which are outstanding but all perfectly OK for a night or two.

Touch Star Resort BUNGALOWS $$$
(✆0 5303 3594; www.touchstarresort.com; bungalows 1600-2200B; ✳) A step up in comfort, and luxury, the cheapest bungalows here are fairly small and rudimentary inside, but have lovely little outside porches overlooking the extensive gardens, which are the best feature of this place. It's well signed down a small lane off Rte 1009, just before entry into the park. Good restaurant serving Thai standards on site.

Ratchaphruek Hotel HOTEL $
(✆0 5334 1901; www.ratchaphruekhotel.com; superior/deluxe r 550/650B; ✳🖤) Close to the turn-off with Rte 108. Has straight up-and-down rooms, comfortable and no fuss. Warning: karaoke bar on site.

**Little Home Inthanon
Resort** BUNGALOWS $
(✆0 5303 3555; www.littlehomeinthanonresort.com; bungalow with fan/air-con 400/600B; ✳) These boxy bungalows are good value for the price, although a bit dark inside. You can park your car right alongside, like a motel

❶ Getting There & Away

Although most visitors come with private transport or on a tour from Chiang Mai, you can reach the park via public transport. Buses leave from Chang Pheuak terminal and yellow *sŏrng·tăa·ou* leave from Pratu Chiang Mai for Chom Thong (70B), 58km from Chiang Mai and the closest town to the park. Some buses go directly to the park's entrance near Nam Tok Mae Klang and some are bound for Hot and will drop you off in Chom Thong.

From Chom Thong there are regular *sŏrng·tăa·ou* to the park's entrance gate at Nam Tok Mae Klang (30B), about 8km north. *Sŏrng·tăa·ou* from the turn-off to Mae Klang, just outside the park gates, to the summit of Doi Inthanon (90B) leave almost hourly until late afternoon.

Northern Thailand

Best Places to Eat

Best Places to Stay

Why Go?

Northern Thailand's 'mountainous' reputation may cause residents of Montana or Nepal to chuckle, but it's the fertile river valleys between these glorified hills that served as the birthplace of much of what is associated with Thai culture. The mountains may not be large, but their impact and significance are immense.

Not surprisingly, these old hills are the ideal destination for a unique Thai experience. Exploring a Buddhist temple in Phrae, taking part in a homestay in rural Sukhothai, or sampling a dish at Lampang's evening market – northern Thailand's cultural attractions are generally low-key but are eminently rewarding. And for those seeking something more vigorous, the region's rugged geography ensures that there is also ample opportunity for more active pursuits such as rafting in Nan, visiting a national park in Phitsanulok or a road trip to Phayao.

When to Go

Northern Thailand is the place to head in winter (November to January), when daytime temperatures at the higher elevations are a relatively comfortable 20°C to 23°C and nighttime temperatures can, in some places, dip perilously close to freezing.

From March to May, the hottest time of year, daytime temperatures climb close to 40°C and smoke from slash-and-burn agriculture can fill the skies. The rainy season, June to October, should generally be avoided if you plan to do any trekking.

History

Northern Thailand's history has been characterised by the shifting powers of various independent principalities. One of the most significant early cultural influences in the north was the Mon kingdom of Hariphunchai (modern Lamphun), which held sway from the late 8th century until the 13th century. Hariphunchai art and Buddha images are particularly distinctive, and many good examples can be found at the Hariphunchai National Museum in Lamphun.

The Thais, who are thought to have migrated down from China since around the 7th century, united various principalities in the 13th century – this resulted in the creation of Sukhothai and the taking of Hariphunchai from the Mon. In 1238 Sukhothai declared itself an independent kingdom under King Si Intharathit and quickly expanded its sphere of influence. Because of this, and the influence the kingdom had on modern Thai art and culture, Sukhothai is considered by Thais to be the first true Thai kingdom. In 1296 King Mengrai established Chiang Mai after conquering Hariphunchai.

Later, Chiang Mai, in an alliance with Sukhothai in the 14th and 15th centuries, became a part of the larger kingdom of Lan Na Thai (Million Thai Rice Fields), popularly referred to as Lanna. This extended as far south as Kamphaeng Phet and as far north as Luang Prabang in Laos. The golden age of Lanna was in the 15th century. For a short time the Sukhothai capital was moved to Phitsanulok (1448–86), and Chiang Mai became an important religious and cultural centre. However, many Thai alliances declined in the 16th century. This weakness led to the Burmese capturing Chiang Mai in 1556 and their control of Lanna lasted for the next two centuries. The Thais regrouped after the Burmese took Ayuthaya in 1767, and under King Kawila, Chiang Mai was recaptured in 1774 and the Burmese were pushed north.

In the late 19th century Rama V of Bangkok made efforts to integrate the northern region with the centre to ward off the colonial threat. The completion of the northern railway to Chiang Mai in 1921 strengthened those links until the northern provinces finally became part of the kingdom of Siam in this early period of the 20th century.

Language

Thailand's regional dialects vary greatly and can even be unintelligible to native speakers of Thai not familiar with the vernacular being spoken. *Găm méuang*, the northern Thai dialect, is no exception and, in addition to an entirely different set of tones to master, possesses a wealth of vocabulary specific to the north. The northern dialect also has a slower rhythm than Thailand's three other

SPEAKING NORTHERN

Northerners used to take offence when outsiders tried speaking *găm méuang* to them, an attitude that dates back to a time when central Thais considered northerners to be very backward, and made fun of their dialect. Nowadays most northerners are proud of their native language and there was even a popular Bangkok-based TV series in which many characters spoke the northern dialect.

To help you win some smiles from the locals, we've provided a brief lexicon of the local lingo.

» *Ôo găm méuang bòr jâhng*	I can't speak northern Thai
» *A yăng gór?*	What did you say?
» *An née tôw dai?*	How much is this?
» *Mee kôw nêung bòr?*	Do you have sticky rice?
» *Lám ɖáa ɖáa*	Delicious
» *Mâan lâ*	Yes/That's right
» *Bòr mâan*	No
» *Sow*	20
» *Gàht*	Market
» *Jôw*	(A polite word used by women; equivalent to the central Thai *ka*)
» *ɓàht só! Nôrng née ngáhm kànàht!*	Hey, you're really cute!

Northern Thailand Highlights

1 Exploring one of the region's numerous and diverse national parks, such as Phitsanulok's historical **Phu Hin Rong Kla National Park** (p353) or Mae Hong Song's rugged **Salawin National Park** (p404)

2 Hiking and rafting in Um Phang, where the end of the road leads to **Nam Tok Thilawsu** (p376), Thailand's biggest, most beautiful waterfall

3 Learning to be a mahout (elephant caretaker) at Lampang's **Thai Elephant Conservation Center** (p307)

4 Phayao

5 Chiang Khong to Phayao

6 Mae Hong Son Loop

LAO

PHITSANULOK

Phu Hin Rong Kla National Park **1**

Khao Kho

PHETCHABURI

LOPBURI

Ban Mi

Mae Nam Nan

Utaradit

Nakhon Thai

Thung Salaeng Luang Wildlife Sanctuary **23**

Lam Nam Khek

Wang Thong

Phichit

Nong Bua

11

NAKHON SAWAN

Tak Fa

Ta Khli

311

CHAINAT

Ban Mi

11

Mae Nam Nan

Si Satchanalai

102

Sukhothai **5**

Phitsanulok

1063

PHICHIT

Mae Nam Yom

117

225

Nakhon Sawan

1

Uthai Thani

Chainat

CHAINAT

Ban Hat Siaw **5**
Si Satchanalai-Chaliang Historical Park

LAMPANG

Sawankhalok

Sukhothai Historical Park **5**

SUKHOTHAI

101

Mae Nam Yom

115

Thoen

12

Kamphaeng Phet

KAMPHAENG PHET

NAKHON SAWAN

Huay Thap Salao

UTHAI THANI

Mae Ping National Park

Mae Nam Ping

1

TAK

Tak

105

KAMPHAENG PHET

Nam Tok Thilawsu **2**

Huay Kha Kaeng National Park **44**

Thung Yai Naresuan Wildlife Reserve

Huay Kha Khaeng

Mae Ramat

Mae Sot

1090

Um Phang

Palatha

TAK

Um Phang Wildlife Sanctuary **23**

Poeng Kloeng

Ban Tha Song Yang

Mae Salit

Tha Song Yang

Myawadi

Mae Nam Moei

Letongkhu

Three Pagodas Pass

Sangkhlaburi

Payathonzu

M Y A N M A R (B U R M A)

---

4 Getting off the beaten path to the little-visited but atmospheric northern cities such as **Phayao** (p334) or **Phrae** (p336)

5 Cycling around the awesome ruins of Thailand's golden age at **Sukhothai** (p355) and **Si Satchanalai-Chaliang Historical Parks** (p363)

6 Renting a vehicle and driving the legendary **Mae Hong Son Loop** (p380) or the extraordinary route from **Chiang Khong to Phayao** (p334)

main dialects, an attribute reflected in the relaxed, easygoing manner of the people who speak it.

Northern Thai also has its own writing system, based on an old Mon script that was originally used only for Buddhist scripture. The script became so popular during the Lanna period that it was exported for use by the Thai Lü in China, the Khün in the eastern Shan State and other Thai-Kadai-speaking groups living between Lanna and China. Although few northerners nowadays can read the northern Thai script – often referred to as 'Lanna script' – it is occasionally used in signage to add a northern Thai cultural flavour.

For some useful northern Thai words and phrases, see the boxed text, p295.

LAMPHUN PROVINCE

Lamphun   ลำพูน

POP 14,000

Essentially a culture stop for Chiang Mai sightseers, this provincial capital sits quietly along the banks of the Mae Kuang, a tributary of the Mae Ping, without much fanfare regarding its superlative as one of Thailand's oldest cities. The old fortress wall and ancient temples are surviving examples of Lamphun's former life as the northernmost outpost of the ancient Mon Dvaravati kingdom then known as Hariphunchai (AD 750–1281). For a period, the city was ruled by Chama Thewi, a Mon queen who has earned legendary status among Thailand's constellation of historic rulers.

The 26km ride between Chiang Mai and Lamphun is one of the city's primary attractions. It's along a beautiful country road, stretches of which are canopied by tall dipterocarp trees.

NORTHERN SLEEPING PRICE RANGES

We list high-season rack rates in this book. See the boxed text, p106 for more details on the different sleeping categories used in this book.

» **Budget** under 600B

» **Midrange** 600B to 1500B

» **Top End** more than 1500B

◉ Sights

Wat Phra That Hariphunchai   TEMPLE

(วัดพระธาตุหริภุญชัย; Th Inthayongyot; admission 20B) This Buddhist temple enjoys an exalted status because it dates back to the Mon period, having been built on the site of Queen Chama Thewi's palace in 1044 (1108 or 1157 according to some datings). It lay derelict until Khru Ba Sriwichai, a famous northern Thai monk, made renovations in the 1930s. It boasts some interesting architecture, a couple of fine Buddha images and two old *chedi* (stupas) in the original Hariphunchai style. The tallest of the ancient *chedi*, Chedi Suwan, is a narrow brick spire dating from 1418 that sits 21m high. The newer *chedi*, 46m-high Phra Maha That Chedi, is regarded as a textbook example of 15th-century Lanna architecture with its square pedestal rising to a rounded bell shape.

Behind the temple is **Kad Khua Moong Tha Sing**, a small souvenir market on a covered bridge selling local OTOP (One Tambon, One Product) items such as dried *lam yai* (longan) and silk.

Hariphunchai National Museum   MUSEUM

(พิพิธภัณฑสถานแห่งชาติหริภุญไชย; Th Inthayongyot; admission 100B; ⏰9am-4pm Wed-Sun) Across the street from Wat Phra That Hariphunchai is the informative Hariphunchai National Museum. Run by the national Fine Arts Department, this museum has a collection of Mon and Lanna artefacts and Buddhas from the Dvaravati kingdom, as well as a stone inscription gallery with Mon and Thai Lanna scripts. The curator's passion for the museum and Lamphun's heritage is infectious. There is a small bookshop with some English titles.

Wat Chama Thewi   TEMPLE

(วัดจามเทวี) A more unusual Hariphunchai *chedi* can be seen at Wat Chama Thewi (popularly called Wat Kukut) and dates to around the 13th century. Known as Chedi Suwan Chang Kot, it has been restored many times since then, so it is now a mixture of several schools of architecture but is widely regarded as one of the most recent examples of Dvaravati architecture. Each side of the *chedi* has five rows of three Buddha figures, diminishing in size on each higher level. The standing Buddhas, although made recently, are in Dvaravati style.

The temple is about 1.5km from Wat Phra That Hariphunchai; you can take a motorcycle taxi (20B) from in front of the museum.

✫ Festivals

Songkran   WATER FESTIVAL

In mid-April, this is a milder, more tradition-al affair in Lamphun should Chiang Mai's water fight be too wet and wild.

Lam Yai Festival   LONGAN FESTIVAL

During the second week of August, Lamphun hosts the annual festival spotlighting its primary agricultural product. The festival features floats made of fruit and, of course, a Miss Lam Yai contest.

🛏 Sleeping & Eating

You're unlikely to stay overnight as Lamphun is so close to Chiang Mai. But in a pinch, try the very capable **Lamphun Will** (☎0 5353 4865; Th Chama Thewi; r 1200-1750B; ❄✿❃), op-posite Wat Chama Thewi.

Noodle and Rice Shops   NOODLES $

(Th Inthayongyot) There is a string of decent noodle shops south of Wat Phra That on the main street.

TRANSPORT IN THE NORTH

Public Transport

Going by train is the most comfortable way to get up north, although there's only one northern line and it is comparatively quite slow. For those in a hurry, there are now air-ports in almost every provincial capital in northern Thailand. Just about everywhere in the region is accessible by bus or minivan, except to the communities along the Myan-mar (Burma) border where the *sŏrng·tăa·ou* (pick-up truck, also spelt *săwngthăew*) is typically the transport of choice.

Car & Motorcycle

Car and motorcycle rental are available at most urban centres. If you don't know how to ride a motorcycle, it's easy to learn and you'll be glad you did.

One of the increasingly popular ways of exploring northern Thailand is from the sad-dle of a rented motorcycle. Despite the obvious risks of driving in Thailand, motorcycle touring is one of the best ways to explore the countryside at your own pace, and pro-vides the opportunity to leave the beaten track at any moment.

Unless you're specifically intending to go off-road or plan on crossing unpaved roads during the wet season, it's highly unlikely you'll need one of the large dirt bikes you'll see for rent in Chiang Mai. The automatic transmission 110cc to 150cc scooterlike motor-cycles found across Thailand are fast and powerful enough for most roads. If you want something a bit larger and more comfortable on those long straight-ways, an alternative is the 200cc Honda Phantom, a Thai-made chopper wannabe.

Rental prices in Chiang Mai start at about 150B per day for a 125cc Honda Wave/Dream, all the way to 1200B per day for a Honda CB1000. For general renting informa-tion and safety considerations, see p773.

A good introduction to motorcycle touring in northern Thailand is the 100km Samo-eng loop, which can be tackled in half a day. The route extends north from Chiang Mai and follows Rtes 107, 1096 and 1269, passing through excellent scenery and ample curves, and providing a taste of what a longer ride up north will be like. The 470km Chi-ang Rai loop, which passes through scenic Fang and Tha Ton along Rtes 107, 1089 and 118, is another popular ride that can be broken up with a stay in Chiang Rai. The classic northern route is the Mae Hong Son loop (see the boxed text, p380), a 950km ride that begins in Chiang Mai and takes in Rte 1095's 1864 curves with possible stays in Pai, Mae Hong Son and Mae Sariang, before looping back to Chiang Mai via Rte 108. A lesser known but equally fun ride is to follow Rtes 1155 and 1093 from Chiang Khong in Chiang Rai Province to the little-visited city of Phayao, a day trip that passes through some of the most dramatic mountain scenery in the country.

The best source of information on motorcycle travelling in the north, not to mention publishers of a series of terrific motorcycle touring-based maps, is **Golden Triangle Rider** (GT Rider; www.gt-rider.com). Their website includes heaps of information on rent-ing bikes (including recommended hire shops in Chiang Mai and Chiang Rai) and bike insurance, plus a variety of suggested tours with maps and an interactive forum.

ⓘ Getting There & Away

Blue *sŏrng·tăa·ou* and white buses to Lamphun (20B, every 30 minutes) leave Chiang Mai from a stop on Th Praisani in front of Talat Warorot and from another stop on the east side of the river on Th Chiang Mai-Lamphun, just south of the Tourist Authority of Thailand (TAT). Transport also leaves from Chiang Mai's Chang Pheuak terminal. Both can drop you off on Th Inthayongyot at the stop in front of the national museum and Wat Phra That Hariphunchai.

Purple minibuses (20B, every 20 minutes from 6am to 5pm) and blue *sŏrng·tăa·ou* (15B) return to Chiang Mai from the stop in front of the national museum or from the city's bus terminal on Th Sanam.

Around Lamphun

DOI KHUN TAN NATIONAL PARK
อุทยานแห่งชาติดอยขุนตาล

This 225-sq-km **national park** (☎0 5354 6335; admission 200B) straddles the mountains between Lamphun and Lampang Provinces. It ranges in elevation from 350m at the bamboo forest lowlands to 1363m at the pine-studded summit of Doi Khun Tan. Wildflowers, including orchids, ginger and lilies, are abundant. At the park headquarters there are maps of well-marked trails that range from short walks around the headquarters' vicinity to trails covering the mountain's four peaks; there's also a trail to **Nam Tok Tat Moei** (7km round trip). Intersecting the mountain slopes is Thailand's longest train tunnel (1352m), which opened in 1921 after six years of manual labour by thousands of Lao workers (several of whom are said to have been killed by tigers).

Bungalows (☎0 2562 0760; www.dnp.go.th; bungalows 1500-2700B) are available near the park headquarters. There is a restaurant by the bungalows. The park is very popular on cool-season weekends.

The main access to the park is from the Khun Tan train station. To check timetables and prices for other destinations call the **State Railway of Thailand** (☎nationwide call centre 1690; www.railway.co.th) or look at its website. Once at the Khun Tan station, cross the tracks and follow a steep, marked path 1.3km to the park headquarters. By car take the Chiang Mai-Lampang highway to the Mae Tha turn-off then follow the signs along a steep unpaved road for 18km.

LAMPANG PROVINCE

Lampang
ลำปาง

POP 59,000

Boasting lumbering elephants, the elegant mansions of former lumber barons and impressive (and in many cases, lumber-based) Lanna-era temples, Lampang seems to unite every northern Thai cliché – but in a good way. Despite all this, the city sees relatively few visitors, giving it more of an 'undiscovered' feel than some of the more touristed destinations in the north.

History

Although Lampang Province was inhabited as far back as the 7th century in the Dvaravati period, legend has it that Lampang city was founded by the son of Hariphunchai's Queen Chama Thewi, and played an important part in the history of the Hariphunchai Kingdom (8th to 13th centuries).

Like Chiang Mai, Phrae and other older northern cities, modern Lampang was built as a walled rectangle alongside a river (in this case Mae Wang). At the end of the 19th and beginning of the 20th century Lampang, along with nearby Phrae, became an important centre for the domestic and international teak trade. A large British-owned timber company brought in Burmese supervisors familiar with the teak industry in Burma to train Burmese and Thai loggers in the area. These well-paid supervisors, along with independent Burmese teak merchants who plied their trade in Lampang, sponsored the construction of more than a dozen temples in the city, a legacy that lives on in several of Lampang's most impressive *wáts*.

◉ Sights

Wat Phra Kaew Don Tao TEMPLE
(วัดพระแก้วดอนเต้า; admission 20B; ◷6am-6pm)
From 1436 to 1468, this *wát* was among four in northern Thailand to previously house the Emerald Buddha (now in Bangkok's Wat Phra Kaew). The main *chedi* shows Hariphunchai influence, while the adjacent *mon·dòp* (the small square, spired building in a *wát*) was built in 1909. The *mon·dòp*, decorated with glass mosaic in typical Burmese style, contains a Mandalay-style Buddha image. A display of Lanna artefacts (mostly religious paraphernalia and woodwork) can be viewed in the *wát*'s **Lanna Museum** (admission by donation; ◷7am-6pm).

Adjacent to the temple complex, pretty **Wat Suchadaram** dates back to 1809 and is named after Mae Suchada, the central figure in a local legend.

Wat Pongsanuk Tai   TEMPLE
(วัดปงสนุกใต้; Th Pongsnook; admission free; ☺5.30am-8.30pm) Despite having lost much of its character in a recent renovation, the *mon·dòp* at Wat Pongsanuk is still one of the few remaining local examples of original Lanna-style temple architecture, which emphasised open-sided wooden buildings. To get an idea of what it was like previously, look at the carved wooden gateway at the entrance to the north stairway.

There are a couple of informal museums on the temple grounds showing local artefacts, but with little English explanation.

Baan Sao Nak   MUSEUM
(บ้านเสานัก; 85 Th Radwattana; admission 50B; ☺10am-5pm) In the old Wiang Neua (North City) section of town, Baan Sao Nak was built in 1895 in the traditional Lanna style. A huge teak house supported by 116 square teak pillars, it was once owned by a local *kun·yĭng* (a title equivalent to 'Lady' in England); it now serves as a local museum. The entire house is furnished with Burmese and Thai antiques, but structure itself and its manicured garden are particularly magnificent.

Wat Chedi Sao   TEMPLE
(วัดเจดีย์ซาว; admission free; Th Pratuma) Located about 6km north of town, via Th Pamaikhet, this temple is named for the *sow* (northern Thai for 20) whitewashed Lanna-style *chedi* on its grounds. But the wát's real treasure is a solid-gold, 15th-century seated Buddha on display in a glassed-in **pavilion** (☺8am-5pm), built over a square pond. The image is said to contain a piece of the Buddha's skull in its head and an ancient Pali-inscribed golden palm leaf in its chest; precious stones decorate the image's hairline and robe. A farmer reportedly found the figure next to the ruins of nearby Wat Khu Kao in 1983. Monks stationed at Wat Chedi Sao make and sell herbal medicines; the popular *yah mòrng* is similar to tiger balm.

Wat Si Rong Meuang & Wat Si Chum   TEMPLES
(วัดศรีรองเมือง/วัดศรีชุม) Wat Si Rong Meuang, on Th Thakhrao Noi, and Wat Si Chum, on Th Thipawan, were built in the late 19th century by Burmese artisans. The temple buildings are constructed in the Burmese 'layered' style, with tin roofs gabled by intricate woodcarvings.

🏃 Activities

Horse Carts   GUIDED TOUR
Lampang is known throughout Thailand as Meuang Rot Mah (Horse Cart City) because it's the only town in Thailand where horse carts are still found, although nowadays they are exclusively used for tourists. You can't miss the brightly coloured carts that drip with nylon flowers, and are handled by Stetson-wearing drivers. A 15-minute horse-cart tour around town costs 150B; for 200B you can get a half-hour tour that goes along the Mae Wang. For 300B a one-hour tour stops at Wat Phra Kaew Don Tao and Wat Si Rong Meuang. Horse carts can be found near the larger hotels and just east of the market on Th Boonyawat.

Samakhom Samunphrai Phak Neua   MASSAGE
(no roman-script sign; ☎08 9758 2396; 149 Th Pratuma; massage per hr 300B, sauna 150B; ☺8am-7.30pm) Next to Wat Hua Khuang in the Wiang Neua area, accessible via Th Pamaikhet, this rustic place offers traditional northern-Thai

---

USE YOUR MELON

Diminutive Wat Suchadaram, at Wat Phra Kaew Don Tao, is said to be located on the former melon patch *(dorn dôw)* of Mae (Mother) Suchada, a pious local woman. It is said that during a time of famine, a monk appeared and was given an unusually shaped melon by Mae Suchada. Upon opening the melon, the monk found a large green gem inside, and with the help of Mae Suchada, as well as the divine intervention of Indra, the gem was shaped into a Buddha image.

Villagers suspected the collaboration between the monk and Mae Suchada of being a bit too friendly, and in a fit of rage, beheaded Suchada. Upon realising their mistake later (the beheading led to yet another famine), a temple was built in the woman's honour. Today, the emerald Buddha image is held at Wat Phra That Lampang Luang.

Lampang

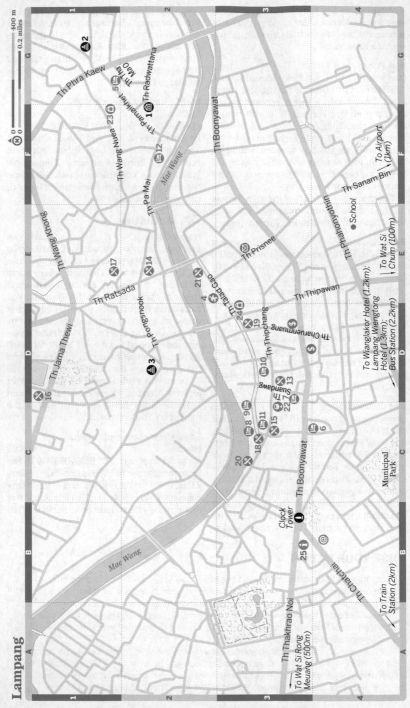

Lampang

massage and herbal saunas. A motorcycle taxi ride here should cost about 20B.

Thai Massage Shops MASSAGE
(Th Talad Gao; ◷8am-9pm) Several places at the far eastern end of Th Talad Gao offer Thai massage for about 150B per hour.

🛏 Sleeping

TOP CHOICE Riverside Guest House GUEST HOUSE $$
(🗗0 5422 7005; www.theriverside-lampang.com; 286 Th Talad Gao; r 350-900B, ste 1800B; ❋🛜) Although still within budget range, this leafy compound of refurbished wooden houses is by far the most pleasant place to stay in Lampang. Try to score one of the two upstairs rooms in the main structure that feature vast balconies overlooking the Mae Wang, or the huge two-room suite. Shaded tables for chatting or eating abound, and motorcycle rental and other tourist amenities are available.

Wienglakor Hotel HOTEL $$$
(🗗0 5431 6430-5; www.wienglakor.com; 138/35 Th Phahonyothin; r incl breakfast 1000-1700B, ste incl breakfast 3000B; ❋@🛜) If you're going to go upscale, this is Lampang's best choice. The lobby is tastefully decorated in a teak and northern Thai temple theme, a design that continues into the rooms. Deluxe rooms feature an added sitting area and walk-in clos-

et, and the hotel's attractive outdoor dining area with carp pond is a nice touch.

Pin Hotel HOTEL $$
(🗗0 5422 1509; 8 Th Suandawg; r incl breakfast 600-900B, ste incl breakfast 1300-1800B; ❋@🛜) Spotless, spacious and secluded, the rooms here come decked out with cable TV, minibar and large bathrooms. A travel agent is attached who books domestic and international flights. A solid midrange choice.

R-Lampang GUEST HOUSE $
(🗗0 5422 5278; www.r-lampang.com; Th Talad Gao; r 350-1000B; ❋🛜) Cute is the underlying aesthetic at these two wooden houses by the Mae Nam Wang. Wind through brightly coloured halls decked with teddy bears to emerge at spacious air-con rooms and rather tight fan-cooled, shared-bathroom budget rooms. An attached shop sells light eats, drinks and souvenirs.

Akhamsiri Home HOTEL $
(🗗0 5422 8791; www.akhamsirihome.com; 54/1 Th Pahmaikhet; r 450B; ❋@🛜) The tagline here ought to be 'Midrange amenities at a budget price'. The large cool rooms are located in a tidy residential compound and all have TV, fridge and a garden/balcony. There's an attached cafe and motorcycles and bicycles are available for hire.

NORTHERN NOSH

Much like the language, Thailand's food seems to take a slightly different form every time you cross a provincial border. The cuisine of Thailand's northern provinces is no exception and is indicative of the region's seasonal and relatively cool climate, not to mention a love for pork, veggies and all things deep-fried. Traditionally, the residents of Thailand's north ate almost exclusively *kôw nĕe·o*, sticky rice, known in the local dialect as *kôw nêung*. Coconut milk rarely makes its way into the northern kitchen, and northern Thai cuisine is probably the least spicy of Thailand's regional schools of cooking, often relying on bitter or bitter/hot flavours instead.

Paradoxically (and unfortunately), it can be quite difficult to find authentic local food outside of Chiang Mai and the other large cities in northern Thailand. There are relatively few restaurants serving northern-style dishes, and the vast majority of authentic local food is sold from stalls in 'to go' bags. However, if you manage to come across a local restaurant, some must-try dishes include:

» *Gaang hang·lair* – Burmese in origin (*hang* is a corruption of the Burmese *hin,* meaning curry), this rich pork curry is often seen at festivals and ceremonies.

» *Kâap mŏo* – deep-fried pork crackling is a common – and delicious – side dish in northern Thailand.

» *Kôw gân jîn* – banana leaf packets of rice mixed with blood that are steamed and served with garlic oil.

Lampang Wiengtong Hotel HOTEL **$$**
(☑0 5422 5801/2; www.lampangwiengthonghotel.com; 138/109 Th Phahonyothin; r incl breakfast 700-1500B; ste incl breakfast 2500-3200B; ❋@🎧⛱) Not surprisingly, Lampang's largest hotel also boasts some of the largest rooms we've seen anywhere. The budget rooms, on the other hand, are cramped and have the tiniest bathtubs we've seen outside of Tokyo.

Asia Lampang Hotel HOTEL **$$**
(☑0 5422 7844; www.asialampang.com; 229 Th Boonyawat; r incl breakfast 550-850B; ❋@🎧) The cheaper rooms on the ground floor are starkly plain and a bit dark, but for a tiny bit more go up a couple of floors where the wood-panelled rooms represent decent value.

Ton Nam Guest House GUEST HOUSE **$**
(☑0 5422 1175; wannaka_123@hotmail.com; 175/2 Th Talad Gao; r 500B; ❋@) This old wooden house unites four cosy rooms, all with air-con and private bathroom.

Tip Inn Guest House GUEST HOUSE **$**
(☑0 5422 1821; 143 Th Talad Gao; r fan/air-con 450/350B; ❋@🎧) Tip Inn is a homey alternative to the city's overwhelmingly characterless budget hotels. It's also the only accommodation to be located smack-dab in the middle of historic Th Talad Gao.

TT&T Back Packers Guesthouse GUEST HOUSE **$**
(☑0 5422 1303; 82 Th Pa Mai; r 200-400B; ❋@) Bathrooms are shared here, but this is made up for by the riverfront location and expansive chill-out areas downstairs.

✗ Eating

For a relatively small town, Lampang boasts a pretty strong repertoire of restaurants, ranging from northern Thai to Western fare, and a few things in between.

Self-caterers or those interested in local eats will want to check out Lampang's **evening market** (Th Ratsada; ⊙4-8pm) where steaming baskets of sticky rice and dozens of sides to dip it in are on daily display.

Aroy One Baht THAI **$**
(cnr Th Suandawg & Th Thipchang; mains 15-40B; ⊙4pm-midnight) Some nights it can seem like just about everybody in Lampang has gathered at this rambling wooden house, and understandably so: the food is tasty and embarrassingly cheap, the service lightning fast, and the setting in a wooden house-cum-balcony-cum-garden heaps of fun.

Papong NORTHERN THAI **$**
(125 Th Talad Gao; mains 30-40B; ⊙lunch & dinner) Be sure to stop by this popular local haunt serving *kà·nŏm jeen* (fresh rice noodles topped with various curries). You can't miss

» *Kôw soy* – this popular curry-based noodle dish is most likely Burmese in origin, and was probably introduced to northern Thailand by travelling Chinese merchants.

» *Kà·nŏm jeen nám ngée·o* – fresh rice noodles served with a spaghetti-like pork- and tomato-based broth.

» *Lâhp kôo·a* – literally 'fried *lâhp*', this dish takes the famous Thai minced-meat 'salad' and fries it with a mixture of local bitter/hot dried spices and herbs.

» *Lôo* – raw blood mixed with a curry paste and served over deep-fried intestines and crispy noodles – the most hardcore northern dish of all.

» *Nǎam* – fermented raw pork, a sour delicacy that tastes much better than it sounds.

» *Nám prík nùm* – green chillies, shallots and garlic that are grilled then mashed into a paste served with sticky rice, parboiled veggies and deep-fried pork crackling.

» *Nám prík òrng* – a chilli dip of Shan origin made from tomatoes and minced pork – a northern Thai bolognese of sorts.

» *Sâi òo·a* – a grilled pork sausage supplemented with copious fresh herbs.

» * Đam sôm oh* – the northern Thai version of *sôm·đam* substitutes pomelo for green papaya.

» *Đôm yam* – the northern Thai version of this Thai staple is flavoured with some of the same bitter/spicy dried spices featured in *lâhp kôo·a*.

it (simply look for a row of bubbling curries in earthenware pots), and ordering is a snap (simply point to whatever looks good). Auntie Pong's speciality is *kà·nŏm jeen nám ngée·o,* a delicious northern-style broth of pork and tomato.

Riverside Bar & Restaurant
INTERNATIONAL-THAI **$$**
(328 Th Thipchang; mains 80-210B; ☺lunch & dinner) This wooden shack that appears to be on the verge of tumbling into the Mae Wang is extremely popular with visiting and resident foreigners. Live music, a full bar and an expansive menu of local and Western dishes bring in the crowds. You'd be wise to plan your visit around the homemade pizza nights (Tuesday, Thursday, Saturday and Sunday).

Khawng Kin Ban Haw
NORTHERN THAI **$$**
(no roman-script sign; 72 Th Jama Thewi; mains 50-110B; ☺lunch & dinner) Located just outside the centre of town but worth the trip, this local favourite is most popular after dark when a bottle of whisky is regarded as a typical side dish. This is a good place to try northern Thai staples such as *gaang kaa gòp* (a herb-laden soup with frog) or *lâhp kôo·a* (*lâhp* that has been stir-fried with local spices).

Grandma's Café
THAI **$**
(361 Th Thipchang; mains 30-70B; ☺10am-6pm) Well-worn teak chairs and doily window

shades suggest grandma's influence, but we doubt she had any role in the slate greys and minimalist feel of this trendy coffee shop. Regardless, stop by for decent java and a menu of rice dishes that rarely exceeds the 50B barrier.

Krua 312
THAI **$**
(Th Thipchang; mains 45-80B; ☺lunch & dinner) Set in a charming wooden shophouse and surrounded by black-and-white pictures of Lampang and the king, this tiny, simple restaurant serves foreigner-friendly curries, noodle and rice dishes.

Vegetarian Food
VEGETARIAN-THAI **$**
(Th Talad Gao; mains 25-35B; ☺8am-6pm Mon-Sat; 🖉) A wide selection of Thai-style veggie dishes is served at this shophouse restaurant.

🍷 Drinking
The strip of Th Thipchang near Riverside Bar & Restaurant is Lampang's nightlife district, and includes a few friendly open-air restaurant/pubs such as **Relax Bar & Restaurant** (Th Thipchang; ☺6pm-midnight) and the curiously named **Gibbon** (Th Thipchang; ☺7pm-midnight).

🔒 Shopping
Walking Street
MARKET
Perhaps wanting to emulate the success of Chiang Mai's street markets, Lampang now

DON'T MISS

KHUN MANEE

Lampang is known for its addictive *kôw đaan*, deep-fried rice cakes drizzled with palm sugar, the making of which can be observed at this homey **factory** (no roman-script sign; 35 Th Ratsada) off Th Ratsada – look for the yellow arrow.

has its own along the charming Th Talad Gao (also known as Kat Korng Ta). Dotted with old shophouses showcasing English, Chinese and Burmese architectural styles, the street is closed to traffic on Saturday and Sunday from 4pm to 10pm and fills up with souvenir, handicraft and food stalls. A similar **Cultural Street** is also held on Th Wang Nuea from 6am to 9am on Sunday and 6pm to 9pm on Friday.

ⓘ Information

There are many banks with ATMs along Th Boonyawat, including Siam City Bank and Krung Thai Bank.

M@cnet (Th Chatchai; per hr 15B; ⊙9am-10pm) Internet access.

Post office (Th Prisnee; ⊙8.30am-4.30pm Mon-Fri, 9am-noon Sat)

Sanuksabai (8 Th Suandawg; ⊙8am-5pm Mon-Sat) Next door to Pin Hotel, this agency can arrange air tickets, saving you the trouble of a trip to the airport.

Tourism Authority of Thailand office (TAT; ☑nationwide call centre 1672, Lampang 0 5423 7229; Th Thakhrao Noi; ⊙10am-4pm Mon-Sat) The helpful folks here can provide a decent map of the area and details about local sights and activities.

ⓘ Getting There & Away

Air

Lampang's airport is about 1.5km from the centre of town, at the east end of Asia 1 Hwy. *Sŏrng·tăa·ou* from the airport to downtown cost 50B.

Bangkok Airways (☑nationwide call centre 1771, Lampang 0 5482 1522; www.bangkokair. com; Lampang airport) conducts flights between Lampang and Bangkok's Suvarnabhumi International Airport (2405B, one hour, once daily), and Lampang and Sukhothai (1915B, 30 minutes, once daily).

Bus

The bus terminal in Lampang is nearly 2km from the centre of town, at the corner of Asia 1 Hwy and Th Chantarasurin – 20B by shared *sŏrng·tăa·ou*. Minivans also depart from here, including frequent departures to Phrae (85B, two hours) from 7am to 4.30pm.

DESTINA-TION	FARE (B)	DURATION (HR)	FREQUENCY
Bangkok	347-625	9	frequent departures 7.30-11.30am & 6.30-9pm
Chiang Mai	67-134	2	every hr 8am-8.30pm
Chiang Rai	143	3½	3.30pm, 6.30pm & 9.30pm
Mae Sot	181-232	4	every hr 9am-midnight
Nan	150-300	4	every hr 9am-midnight
Phitsanulok	193	4½	every hr 5am-7pm
Phrae	78-157	2	every hr 9am-midnight
Sukhothai	162	3½	every hr 5am-7pm

Train

Lampang's historic **train station** (☑0 5421 7024; Th Phahonyothin) dates back to 1916 and is a fair hike from most accommodation. Major destinations from Lampang include Bangkok (256B to 1272B, 12 hours, six times daily) and Chiang Mai (23B to 50B, three hours, six times daily). To check timetables and prices for other destinations call the **State Railway of Thailand** (☑nationwide call centre 1690; www.railway. co.th) or look at its website.

Around Lampang

WAT PHRA THAT LAMPANG LUANG วัดพระธาตุลำปางหลวง

This ancient **Buddhist temple compound** (admission free) houses several interesting religious structures, including what is arguably the most beautiful wooden Lanna temple in northern Thailand, the open-sided **Wihan Luang**. Dating back to 1476, and thought to be the oldest-standing wooden structure in the country, the impressive *wí·hăhn* (large hall in a Thai temple, usually open to laity) features a triple-tiered wooden roof supported by immense teak pillars and early-19th-century *jataka* murals (stories of the Buddha's previous lives) painted on wooden panels around the inside upper perimeter. A huge, gilded *mon·dòp* in the back of the *wí·hăhn* contains a Buddha image cast in 1563.

The small and simple **Wihan Ton Kaew**, to the north of the main *wí·hăhn*, was built in 1476, while the tall Lanna-style *chedi* behind the main *wí·hăhn*, raised in 1449 and restored in 1496, is 45m high.

The *wí·hăhn* to the north of the *chedi*, **Wihan Nam Taem**, was built in the early 16th century and, amazingly, still contains traces of the original murals, making them among the oldest in the country.

Wihan Phra Phut, which is south of the main *chedi*, dates back to the 13th century and is the oldest structure in the compound.

Unfortunately, only men are allowed to see a camera obscura image of the *wí·hăhn* and *chedi* in the **Haw Phra Phutthabaht**, a small white building behind the *chedi*. The image is projected (upside down) onto a white cloth, and clearly depicts the colours of the structures.

The lintel over the entrance to the compound features an impressive dragon relief – once common in northern Thai temples but rarely seen these days. This gate supposedly dates to the 15th century.

In the arboretum outside the southern gate of the wát, there are now three **museums**. One displays mostly festival paraphernalia and some Buddha figures. Another, called 'House of the Emerald Buddha', contains a miscellany of coins, banknotes, Buddha figures, silver betel-nut cases, lacquerware and other ethnographic artefacts, along with three small, heavily gold-leafed Buddhas placed on an altar behind an enormous repoussé silver bowl. The third, a fine, small museum, features shelves of Buddha figures, lacquered boxes, manuscripts and ceramics, all well labelled in Thai and English.

Wat Phra That Lampang Luang is 18km southwest of Lampang in Ko Kha. To get there by public transport from Lampang, flag an eastbound *sŏrng·tăa·ou* (20B) on Th Boonyawat. From the Ko Kha *sŏrng·tăa·ou* stop, it's a 3km chartered motorcycle taxi ride to the temple (40B). A *sŏrng·tăa·ou* from Lampang's bus station will make the trip for 350B.

If you're driving or cycling from Lampang, head south on the Asia 1 Hwy and take the Ko Kha exit, then follow the road over a bridge and bear right. Follow the signs and continue for 3km over another bridge until you see the temple on the left.

THAI ELEPHANT CONSERVATION CENTER & AROUND ศูนย์อนุรักษ์ช้างไทย

Located in Amphoe Hang Chat, 33km from Lampang, this **elephant centre** (TECC; ☎0 5424 7876; www.thailandephant.org; child/adult incl shuttle bus 40/80B; ☯elephant bathing 9.45am & 1.15pm, public shows 10am, 11am & 1.30pm) promotes the role of the Asian elephant in ecotourism, and also provides medical treatment and care for sick elephants from all over Thailand. For more information on the plight of Thailand's elephants, see the boxed text, p38.

The elephant show at this 122-hectare centre is less touristy and more educational than most, focusing on how elephants work with logs, as well as the usual painting of pictures and playing oversized xylophones. There is an exhibit on the history and culture of elephants, an elephant art gallery, an elephant graveyard, and oh yes, **elephant rides** (10/30/60min 50/400/800B; ☯8am-3.30pm) through the surrounding forest.

For those keen on delving deeper into pachyderm culture, the TECC's **Mahout Training School** (☎0 5424 7875; www.thailandelephant.org;

WORTH A TRIP

WAT LAI HIN วัดไหล่หิน

If you're visiting Wat Phra That Lampang Luang and you've got your own transport, you might also consider a visit to beautiful **Wat Lai Hin** (admission free), also near Ko Kha. Built by artists from Chiang Tung, Myanmar, the tiny temple is one of the most characteristically Lanna temples around, and was an influence on the design of the Mandarin Oriental Dhara Dhevi hotel in Chiang Mai, not to mention a set for the 2001 Thai blockbuster, *Suriyothai*. There's an interesting **folk museum** on the grounds that the monks can unlock for you.

If coming from Ko Kha, the temple is located about 6km down a road that turns off 1km before reaching Wat Phra That Lampang Luang.

1/2/3/6/10/30 days 3500/5800/8500/20,000/ 35,000/100,000B) offers an array of scholarships ranging in duration from one day to one month, all with the aim of making you a bona-fide *kwahn cháhng* (elephant caretaker) or mahout. The popular one-day course involves learning a few simple commands for leading an elephant, experimenting with dung paper, riding an elephant in the jungle and a tour of the elephant hospital. A more involved three-day, two-night homestay program includes all meals, a night's lodging in a well-equipped wood-and-bamboo bungalow and another night at a jungle camp, plus a general introduction to elephant care and training.

Accommodation at the centre is available in the form of activity-packed homestays with mahouts in basic huts, or in bungalows at the centre's **Chang Thai Resort** (bungalows 1-/2-bedroom 1000/1500B). There are three restaurants on the centre grounds.

All proceeds from the entrance fee and souvenir shops go to the elephant hospital on-site, which cares for old, abandoned and sick elephants from all over Thailand, as well as working for the preservation of elephants by various research and breeding programs.

Nearby, but not affiliated with the TECC, is the **FAE's Elephant Hospital** (Friends of the Asian Elephant; ☑08 1914 6113; www.elephant-soraida.com; ◎8am-5pm), which claims to be the first of its kind in the world. Although visitors are appreciated and provided for, keep in mind that this is a functioning medical facility, and there are no guided tours and certainly no elephant art. Donations are greatly appreciated. In June 2008 the centre reached another first when it successfully provided an elephant with a prosthetic leg.

Both facilities can be reached by Chiang Mai-bound bus or *sŏrng·tăa·ou* (26B, 40 minutes) from Lampang's main bus terminal. Let the driver know where you are headed and get off at the Km 37 marker. The centre is 1.5km from the highway, and shuttle buses will take you inside. Alternatively, you can charter a blue *sŏrng·tăa·ou* for 600B at Lampang's bus terminal.

If you have your own transport, on the way to the elephant camp, 25km from Lampang, is the **Thung Kwian market**. Very popular with Thais, this market is a crash course in northern Thai food and handicrafts, offering everything from *rót dòo·an* (deep-fried worms, a northern speciality), to the distinctive rooster bowls made in Lampang.

CHIANG RAI PROVINCE

Chiang Rai, Thailand's northernmost province, has a bit of everything: the mountains in the far east of the province are among the most dramatic in the country, the lowland Mekong River floodplains to the northeast are not unlike those one would find much further south in Isan, and the province shares borders with Myanmar and Laos, allowing relatively easy access to China.

In terms of people, it's also among Thailand's most ethnically diverse provinces, and is home to a significant minority of hill tribes, Shan and other Tai groups, and relatively recent Chinese immigrants.

Chiang Rai เชียงราย

POP 62,000

Chiang Rai Province has such a diversity of attractions that its capital city is often overlooked. If you take the time to know it, Chiang Rai is a small but delightful city with a relaxed atmosphere, good value accommodation and some tasty eats. It's also the logical base from which to plan excursions to the more remote corners of the province.

Founded by Phaya Mengrai in 1262 as part of the Lao-Thai Lanna kingdom, Chiang Rai didn't become a Siamese territory until 1786, then a province in 1910.

◉ Sights

Oub Kham Museum MUSEUM

(พิพิธภัณฑ์อูบคำ; www.oubkhammuseum.com; 81/1 Military Front Rd; adult/child 300/200B; ◎8am-6pm) This privately owned museum houses an impressive collection of paraphernalia from virtually every corner of the former Lanna kingdom. The items, some of which truly are one of a kind, range from a monkey bone food taster used by Lanna royalty to an impressive carved throne from Chiang Tung, Myanmar. Guided tours (available in English) are obligatory, and include a walk through a gilded artificial cave holding several Buddha statues, complete with disco lights and fake torches! The grounds of the museum are equally kitschy, and include a huge golden *naga* (mythical serpentlike being with magical powers) statue and countless waterfalls and fountains. Truly an equal parts bizarre and enlightening experience.

The Oub Kham Museum is 2km outside of the centre town and can be a bit tricky to find; túk-túks (pronounced *dúk dúk*) will go here for about 50B.

Hilltribe Museum & Education Center
MUSEUM

(พิพิธภัณฑ์และศูนย์การศึกษาชาวเขา; www.pdacr.org; 3rd fl, 620/25 Th Thanalai; admission 50B; ☺9am-6pm Mon-Fri, 10am-6pm Sat & Sun) This museum and handicrafts centre is a good place to visit before undertaking any hill-tribe trek. The centre, run by the nonprofit Population & Community Development Association (PDA), is underwhelming in its visual presentation, but contains a wealth of information on Thailand's various tribes and the issues that surround them. A visit begins with a 20-minute slide show on Thailand's hill tribes, and exhibits include typical clothing for six major tribes, examples of bamboo usage, folk implements and other anthropological objects. The curator is passionate about his museum, and will talk about the different hill tribes, their histories, recent trends and the community projects that the museum helps fund. The PDA also runs highly recommended treks.

Wat Phra Kaew
TEMPLE

(วัดพระแก้ว; admission free) Originally called Wat Pa Yia (Bamboo Forest Monastery) in the local dialect, this is the city's most revered Buddhist temple. Legend has it that in 1434 lightning struck the temple's octagonal *chedi,* which fell apart to reveal the Phra Kaew Morakot, or Emerald Buddha (actually made of jade). After a long journey that included a long stopover in Vientiane, Laos (see the boxed text, p58), this national talisman is now ensconced in the temple of the same name in Bangkok.

In 1990 Chiang Rai commissioned a Chinese artist to sculpt a new image from Canadian jade. Named the Phra Yok Chiang Rai (Chiang Rai Jade Buddha), it was intentionally a very close but not exact replica of the Phra Kaew Morakot in Bangkok, with dimensions of 48.3cm across the base and 65.9cm in height, just 0.1cm shorter than the original. The image is housed in the impressive **Haw Phra Yoke**, the walls of which are decorated with beautiful modern murals, some depicting the journey of the original Phra Kaew Morakot, as well as the elaborate ceremony that saw the current image arrive at its new home in Chiang Rai.

The main prayer hall is a medium-sized, well-preserved wooden structure. The *chedi* behind it dates from the late 14th century

and is in typical Lanna style. The adjacent two-storey wooden building is a **museum** (admission free; ☺9am-5pm) housing various Lanna artefacts.

Tham Tu Pu & Buddha Cave
TEMPLE

(ถ้ำตุ๊ปู่/ถ้ำพระ) If you follow Th Winitchaikul across the bridge to the northern side of Mae Nam Kok, you'll come to a turn-off for both Tham Tu Pu and the Buddha Cave. Follow the road 1km, then turn off onto a dirt path 200m to the base of a limestone cliff where there is a steep set of stairs leading to a main chamber holding a dusty Buddha statue; this is Tham Tu Pu. Continue along the same road for 3km more and you'll reach Buddha Cave, a cavern by the Mae Nam Kok containing a tiny but active Buddhist temple, a lone monk and several cats. The temple was one of several destinations on a visit to the region by King Rama V in the early 20th century.

Neither attraction is particularly amazing on its own, but the surrounding country is beautiful and would make an ideal destination for a lazy bike ride. Bikes can be rented at Fat Free.

Wat Phra Singh
TEMPLE

(วัดพระสิงห์; Th Singhaclai; admission free) Housing yet another copy of a famous Buddha image, this temple was built in the late 14th century during the reign of Chiang Rai's King Mahaphrom. A sister temple to Chiang Mai's Wat Phra Singh, its original buildings are typical northern Thai-style wood structures with low, sweeping roofs. The impressive wooden doors are thought to have been carved by local artists. The main *wí·hǎhn* houses a copy of Chiang Mai's Phra Singh Buddha.

Wat Jet Yot
TEMPLE

(วัดเจ็ดยอด; Th Jet Yod; admission free) The seven-spired *chedi* at Wat Jet Yot is similar to that of its Chiang Mai namesake, but without stucco ornamentation. Of more aesthetic interest is the wooden ceiling of the front veranda of the main *wí·hǎhn,* which features a unique Thai astrological fresco.

Wat Klang Wiang
TEMPLE

(วัดกลางเวียง; cnr Th Ratanaket & Th Utarakit; admission free) This Buddhist temple appears thoroughly modern, but dates back at least 500 years. Extensive remodelling in the early 1990s has left several structures in the temple with a unique 'modern Lanna' style, but the elegant *hǒr drai* (manuscript depository) appears to retain its original form.

Chiang Rai

Wat Phra That Doi Chom Thong   TEMPLE

(วัดพระธาตุดอยจอมทอง; admission free) The Buddhist hilltop Wat Phra That Doi Chom Thong has partial views of the river and gets an occasional river breeze. The Lanna-style *chedi* here most likely dates from the 14th to 16th centuries, and may cover an earlier Mon *chedi* inside. King Mengrai, Chiang Rai's founder, first surveyed the site for the city from this peak. It's located just west of town on Th Kraisorasit.

🏃 Activities

Trekking

Nearly every guest house and hotel in Chiang Rai offers trekking trips, typically in the Doi Tung, Doi Mae Salong and Chiang Khong areas. Many of the local travel agencies merely act as brokers for guides associated with one of the local guest houses, so it may be cheaper to book directly through a guest house. As elsewhere in northern

Thailand, you're more assured of a quality experience if you use a TAT-licensed guide.

Trek pricing depends on the number of days and participants, and the type of activities. Rates at the places below range from 2500B to 4300B per person for two people for a two-night trek. Generally everything from accommodation to transport and food is included in this price.

For details on rules and taboos when visiting a hill-tribe village, see p36.

The following agencies have a reputation for operating responsible treks and cultural tours, and in some cases profits from the treks go directly to community-development projects.

Mirror Foundation   TREKKING

(☎0 5373 7616; www.themirrorfoundation.org; 106 Moo 1, Ban Huay Khom, Tambon Mae Yao) Although its rates are higher than others', trekking with this nonprofit NGO helps support the training of its local guides. Treks range

Chiang Rai

from one to three days, and traverse the Akha, Karen and Lahu villages of Mae Yao, north of Chiang Rai.

PDA Tours & Travel   TREKKING
(📞0 5374 0088; www.pda.or.th/chiangrai/package_tour.htm; 3rd fl, 620/25 Th Thanalai, Hilltribe Museum & Education Center; ⊙9am-6pm Mon-Fri, 10am-6pm Sat & Sun) One- to three-day treks are available through this NGO, the profits from which go back into community projects that include HIV/AIDS education, mobile health clinics, education scholarships and the establishment of village-owned banks.

Akha Hill House   TREKKING
(📞08 9997 5505; www.akhahill.com; Akha Hill House) This outfit does one- to seven-day treks. They begin with a long-tail boat up the river, before trekking to and around their Akha Hill House about 23km from Chiang Rai, at a height of 1500m. A portion of the profits from the guest houses and their activities go into a local school. Inquiries can be made at Akha Hill House.

Dragon Sabaii Tours   TREKKING
(📞08 548 0884; www.thailandhilltribeholidays.com; Mae Sariang) Based in southern Mae Hong Son, this outfit also leads responsible treks and guided tours in Chiang Rai upon request. Refer to the website for details.

Eagle Adventure Tour   TREKKING
(📞08 7265 0527; www.thaieagletour.com; City Home, Th Phahonyothin) A Chiang Rai–based outfit offering the usual variety of treks and guided tours.

Smiling Albino   TREKKING, CYCLING
(www.smilingalbino.com) This long-standing company conducts several tours in Chiang Rai, the majority of which include trekking, cycling and motorbiking.

NORTHERN THAILAND CHIANG RAI

Other Activities

Suwannee
COOKERY COURSE

(☎08 4740 7119; www.chiangraicookingclass.com; lessons 950B; ☺9.30am-2pm) Suwannee offers nearly day-long cooking courses that involve a visit to a local market and instruction in cooking four dishes. Suwanee's house is about 3km outside of the city centre, but she can pick you up at most centrally located hotels and guest houses.

Boomerang Adventure Park
ROCK CLIMBING

(☎08 4173 2757; www.thailandrocks.com; rock climbing half/full day 500/900B; ☺10am-7pm) In addition to rock climbing, this outdoor facility also offers zip-lines, Frisbee golf and self-guided trekking. Call ahead on weekdays to ensure that staff are there. The park is 3km from Chiang Rai, between Tam Tu Pu and the Buddha Cave.

Kamlar
HERBAL SAUNA

(Th Thanalai; herbal sauna per half hour 100B, Thai massage per hour 150B; ☺9am-6pm Mon-Sat, 1-6pm Sun) Traditional Thai herbal sauna and Thai massage are available at this wooden house. Kamlar is near the corner of Th Thanalai and Th Baanpa Pragarn.

Jao Nang Studio
PORTRAIT STUDIO

(645/7 Th Utarakit; ☺10am-7pm) Dress up like a member of Lanna royalty and have your portrait taken for posterity – a must-do activity for Thai visitors to Chiang Mai and Chiang Rai. Has a huge array of costumes and backdrops.

🛏 Sleeping

Chiang Rai has a good selection of accommodation, and prices seemed to have climbed little in the last couple of years, making the town good value. The two main areas for accommodation are in the centre, clustered around Th Jet Yod and off Th Phahonyothin.

Legend of Chiang Rai
HOTEL $$$

(☎0 5391 0400; www.thelegend-chiangrai.com; 124/15 Moo 21, Th Kohloy; r 3900-5900B; villa 8100B; ✳@☎🏊) One of the few hotels in town to take advantage of a river location, this upscale resort feels like a traditional Lanna village. Rooms feel romantic and luxuriously understated with furniture in calming creams and rattan. Each has a pleasant outdoor sitting area, frosted glass for increased privacy and a cool, outdoorlike bathroom with an oversized shower; villas have a small private pool. The riverside infinity pool and spa are the icing

on the comfort-filled cake. The resort is about 500m north of Th Singhaclai.

Ben Guesthouse
HOTEL $$

(☎0 5371 6775; www.benguesthousechiangrai.com; 351/10 Soi 4, Th Sankhongnoi; r 250-850B, ste 1500-3000B; ✳@☎🏊) The bland name and distance from the centre of town may not work in its favour, but if you can get past these, Ben is one of the best budget places we've encountered in the north. The absolutely spotless compound has a bit of everything, from fan-cooled cheapies to immense suites, not to mention an entire house (12,000B). It's 1.2km from the centre of town, at the end of Soi 4 on Th Sankhongnoi (the street is called Th Sathanpayabarn where it intersects with Th Phahonyothin) – a 60B túk-túk ride.

Baan Warabordee
HOTEL $$

(☎0 5375 4488; baanwarabordee@hotmail.com; 59/1 Th Sanpannard; r 600-800B; ✳@☎) A delightful small hotel has been made from this modern three-storey Thai villa. Rooms are cool and come decked out in dark woods and light cloths. The owners are friendly and can help with local advice.

Jansom House
HOTEL $

(☎0 5371 4552; 897/2 Th Jet Yod; r incl breakfast 450-500B; ✳@☎) This three-storey hotel offers spotless, spacious rooms set around a small courtyard filled with plants. You normally wouldn't expect frills at this price, but amazingly the rooms here are equipped with cable TV, well-designed bathrooms and tiled floors. An excellent value.

Moon & Sun Hotel
HOTEL $$

(☎0 5371 9279; www.moonandsun-hotel.com; 632 Th Singhaclai; r 500-800B, ste 1100B; ✳☎) Bright and sparkling clean, this little hotel offers large modern rooms. Some come with four-poster beds, while all come with desk, cable TV and refrigerator. Suites have a separate, spacious sitting area.

Mantrini
HOTEL $$$

(☎0 5360 1555; www.mantrini.com; 292 Moo 13, Robwiang on the Superhighway; r incl breakfast 2650-3190B; ste incl breakfast 9600B; ✳@☎🏊) This is the place to stay if design is your most important consideration. A highlight is the two 'Sweet Rooms', which are decked out in a faux-Victorian motif that somehow successfully combines an African mask and a rocking horse. The hotel is about 1km outside the city centre near Central Plaza, but operates a shuttle downtown.

Diamond Park Inn   HOTEL $$
(📞0 5375 4960; www.diamondparkinn.com; 74/6 Moo 18, Th Sanpannard; r incl breakfast 1100B, ste incl breakfast 1400-1500B; ✳@🛜☇) Aggressive marketing strategy aside ('When ever you are at Chiang Rai. Stay at The Diamond Park Inn'), this new hotel is a terrific midrange choice. Rooms are large and attractive, with modern furniture and beds on an elevated platform. The more expensive rooms have tubs, wide balconies, and are big enough to feel slightly empty.

Le Meridien Chiang Rai Resort   HOTEL $$$
(📞0 5360 3333; www.lemeridien.com; 221/2 Moo 20, Th Kwaewai; r 7500-8000B, ste 15,500-22,250B; ✳@🛜☇) Chiang Rai's newest upscale digs is about 2km outside of the city centre on a beautiful stretch of the Mae Nam Kok. Rooms are immense and decked out in greys, whites and blacks, and the compound includes two restaurants and an infinity pool, in addition to the usual amenities of a hotel with these prices.

Golden Triangle Inn   HOTEL $$
(📞0 5371 1339; www.goldentriangleinn.com; 590 Th Phahonyothin; s/d incl breakfast 700/800B; ✳🛜) Resembling an expansive Thai home (including the occasional lived-in untidiness this can involve), the 31 rooms here have tile or wood floors and wooden furniture. The compound includes a restaurant, a Budget car-rental office and an efficient travel agency. It's a popular place so book in advance.

Wiang Inn   HOTEL $$$
(📞0 5371 1533; www.wianginn.com; 893 Th Phahonyothin; r incl breakfast 2826-3226B, ste incl breakfast 7062-11,770B; ✳@🛜☇) The large, modern lobby sets the stage for this centrally located, business-class hotel. Despite the hotel's 30-plus years, the rooms are well maintained and have a few Thai decorative touches.

Lek House   HOTEL $
(📞0 5371 1550; lekhousehotel@live.co.uk; cnr Th Ratyotha & Th Baanpa Pragarn; r incl breakfast 350-550B, ste incl breakfast 1350B; ✳@🛜☇) This purple compound is home to a handful of tight but attractive air-con rooms, although there's little separating the bathrooms. The fan-cooled rooms are much simpler, and everybody gets to use the inviting pool. Lek House is near the corner of Th Ratyotha (the continuation of Th Thanalai) and Th Baanpa Pragarn.

The North   HOTEL $
(📞0 5371 9873; www.thenorth.co.th; 612/100-101 Sirikon Market; r with fan/air-con 350/450B;

✳@🛜) Located steps away from the bus station, this hotel has provided the drab market area with a bit of colour. The 18 rooms here combine both Thai and modern design, and the more expensive ones open to inviting chill-out areas.

Baan Bua Guest House   HOTEL $
(📞0 5371 8880; www.baanbuaguesthouse.com; 879/2 Th Jet Yod; r 300-500B; ✳@🛜) This quiet guest house consists of a strip of 17 bright green rooms surrounding an inviting garden. Rooms are simple, but clean and cosy.

Orchids Guest House   HOTEL $
(📞0 5371 8361; www.orchidsguesthouse.com; 1012/3 Th Jet Yod; r 400B; ✳@🛜) This collection of spotless rooms in a residential compound is a good budget catch. Various services are available here, including internet and airport transfer (250B).

Baan Rub Aroon Guesthouse   GUEST HOUSE $$
(📞0 5371 1827; www.baanrubaroon.net; 893 Th Ngam Meuang; dm 300B, r 550-850B; ✳@🛜) The rooms in this handsome villa may not be as nice as the exterior suggests, and all share bathrooms, but if you're looking for a quiet homey stay, this is the place.

Buffalo Hill Guesthouse   HOTEL $$
(Pankled Villa; 📞0 5371 7552; www.pankledvilla.com; Th Prachasanti; bungalows incl breakfast 600-700B; ✳🛜) Finding Chiang Rai city life too hectic? Then head to this wooded compound of rustic bungalows. Buffalo Hill is about 1km down Th Prachasanti, at the southern end of Th Phahonyothin.

Jitaree Guest House   HOTEL $
(📞0 5371 9348; Soi Flat Tamruat; r 200B; 🛜) Cool fan rooms in an apartmentlike complex. Jitaree is in the tiny backpacker enclave off Th Singhaclai, near the new bridge.

✕ Eating

The night market has a decent collection of food stalls offering snacks and meals, from deep-fried won tons to fresh fish. Choose a dish and sit at the nearby tables, or step inside one of several restaurants on and off Th Phahonyothin by the night market.

TOP
CHOICE **Lung Eed Locol Food**   NORTHERN THAI $
(Th Watpranorn; mains 30-60B; ⏱11.45am-9pm Mon-Sat) To eat like an authentic locol (!), look no further than this rustic but delicious northern-style food shack. There's an English-language menu on the wall, but don't miss

the sublime *lâhp gài*, minced chicken fried with herbs and topped with crispy deep-fried shallots and garlic. The restaurant is on Th Watpranorn near the intersection with the Superhighway.

Nam Ngiaw Paa Nuan
VIETNAMESE-THAI $

(Vietnamese Restaurant; Th Sanpannard; mains 10-100B; ☺9am-5pm) This somewhat concealed place serves a unique mix of Vietnamese and northern Thai dishes. Tasty food, friendly service and a barnlike atmosphere make us wish they were open for dinner as well.

Paa Suk
NORTHERN THAI $

(noroman-scriptsign;ThSankhongnoi;mains10-25B; ☺8am-3pm Mon-Sat) This immensely popular third-generation restaurant specialises in the local dish *kà·nŏm jeen nám ngée·o*, a thin broth of pork or beef and tomatoes served over fresh rice noodles. The restaurant is between Soi 4 and Soi 5 of Th Sankhongnoi (the street is called Th Sathanpayabarn where it intersects with Th Phahonyothin); look for the yellow sign.

Phu-Lae
NORTHERN THAI $$

(673/1ThThanalai;mains80-320B;☺lunch&dinner; ❄) This air-conditioned restaurant is exceedingly popular with Thai tourists for its tasty, but slightly gentrified northern Thai fare. Recommended local dishes include the *gaang hang·lair*, pork belly in a rich Burmese-style curry, here served with pickled garlic, and *sâi òo·a*, herb-packed sausages.

Old Dutch
DUTCH-INTERNATIONAL $$

(541 Th Phahonyothin; mains 150-300B; ❄) This cosy, foreigner-friendly restaurant is a good choice if you're tired of rice. There's a variety of well-done Dutch and other Western-style dishes, as well as a good attached bakery.

Somkhuan Khao Soi
NORTHERN THAI $

(no roman-script sign; Th Singhaclai; mains 25B; ☺8am-3pm Mon-Fri) Friendly Mr Somkhuan serves a tasty bowl of *kôw soy*, a northern Thai curry noodle dish, from a basic street stall under two giant trees.

Muang Thong
CHINESE-THAI $

(cnr Th Sanpannard & Th Phahonyothin; mains 20-90B; ☺24hr) Comfort food for Thais and travellers alike: this long-standing open-air place serves the usual repertoire of tasty, salty, spicy Chinese-Thai dishes.

Rosprasoet
MUSLIM-THAI $

(Th Itsaraphap; mains 25-50B; ☺7am-8pm) This Thai-Muslim restaurant next to the mosque on Th Itsaraphap dishes up delicious Thai-Muslim favourites, including *kôw mòk gài*, the Thai version of chicken *biryani*.

🍷 Drinking & Entertainment

Th Jet Yot is Chiang Rai's drinking strip. Standouts include **Cat Bar** (1013/1 Th Jet Yod; ☺5pm-1am), which has a pool table and live music, and **Easy House** (cnr Th Jet Yod & Th Pemavipat; ☺11am-midnight), with a friendly, open-air vibe.

🛍 Shopping

Walking Street
MARKET

(Th Thanalai; ☺4-10pm Sat) If you're around on a Saturday evening be sure not to miss the open-air Walking Street, an expansive street market focusing on all things Chiang Rai, from handicrafts to local dishes. The market spans Th Thanalai from the Hilltribe Museum to the morning market.

Fair Trade Shop
HANDICRAFTS

(www.ttcrafts.co.th; 528/8 Th Baanpa Pragarn; ☺9am-5pm Mon-Sat) Bright hill-tribe cloths and knick-knacks are available at this shop, the profits of which go to various development projects.

Night Bazaar
MARKET

(☺6-11pm) Adjacent to the bus station off Th Phahonyothin is Chiang Rai's night market. On a much smaller scale than Chiang Mai's, it is nevertheless a decent place to find an assortment of handicrafts.

Orn's Bookshop
BOOKSHOP

(off Soi 1, Th Jet Yod; ☺8am-8pm) The superb collection of books here spans many languages.

ℹ Information

Emergency

Tourist police (✆nationwide call centre 1155, Chiang Rai 0 5374 0249; Th Phahonyothin; ☺24hr) English is spoken and police are on stand-by 24 hours a day.

Internet Access

Internet access is readily available around town and costs around 30B per hour. It's especially abundant around the night market. Most internet places offer international call services.

Easy Fly (Th Phahonyothin; ☺8.30am-9pm) Across from Wiang Inn, this place has several computers.

CAFE CULTURE, CHIANG RAI STYLE

For such a relatively small town, Chiang Rai has an abundance of high-quality, Western-style cafes. This is largely due to the fact that many of Thailand's best coffee beans are grown in the more remote corners of the province. Some of the more interesting choices include the following:

BaanChivitMai Bakery (www.baanchivitmai.com; Th Prasopsook; ☺7am-9pm Mon-Sat; ✳@☎) In addition to a very well-prepared cup of local joe, you can snack on amazingly authentic Swedish-style sweets at this popular bakery. Profits go to BaanChivitMai, an organisation that runs homes and education projects for vulnerable, orphaned or AIDS-affected children.

Doi Chaang (542/2 Th Ratanaket; ☺7am-11pm; ✳@☎) Doi Chaang is the leading brand among Chiang Rai coffees, and its beans are now sold as far abroad as Canada and Europe.

Wawee Coffee (cnr Th Singhaclai & Th Srikerd; ☺7am-9pm; ✳@☎) Another local brand done well, this expansive, modern cafe serves a variety of creative coffee drinks using Chiang Rai beans.

Pangkhon Coffee (Th Singhaclai; ☺7am-7pm; ☎) Tiny coffee bar serving local beans.

Medical Services

Overbrook Hospital (☏0 5371 1366; www.overbrookhospital.com; Th Singhaclai) English is spoken in this modern hospital.

Money

There is an abundance of banks with foreign exchange and ATMs on both Th Phahonyothin and Th Thanalai.

Post

Main post office (Th Utarakit; ☺8.30am-4.30pm Mon-Fri, 9am-noon Sat & Sun) South of Wat Phra Singh.

Tourist Information

Tourism Authority of Thailand office (TAT; ☏nationwide call centre 1672, Chiang Rai 0 5374 4674; tatchrai@tat.or.th; Th Singhaclai; ☺8.30am-4.30pm) English is limited, but staff here do their best to give advice, and can provide a small selection of maps and brochures.

⊙ Getting There & Away

Air

Chiang Rai airport (☏0 5379 8000) is approximately 8km north of the city. Taxis run into town from the airport for 200B. Out to the airport you can get a taxi or túk-túk for approximately 250B. The terminal has restaurants, a money exchange, a post office and several car-rental booths.

In town, **Air Agent** (☏0 5374 0445; 869/18 Th Phahonyothin; ☺8am-10pm) can book domestic and international flights in advance.

Bangkok's Don Muang Airport (1550B, 1¼ hours, twice daily) via **One-Two-Go** (Orient Thai; ☏nationwide call centre 1126; www.flyorientthai.com; Chiang Rai airport)

Bangkok's Suvarnabhumi International Airport (2164B to 3120B, 1¼ hours, six times daily) via **Air Asia** (☏nationwide call centre 02 515 9999, Chiang Rai 0 5379 3543; www.airasia.com; Chiang Rai airport) and **THAI** (☏nationwide call centre 02 356 1111; www.thaiair.com) City Centre (☏0 5371 1179; 870 Th Phahonyothin; ☺8am-5pm Mon-Fri) Airport Office (☏0 5379 8202; ☺8am-8pm)

Chiang Mai (1399B, 40 minutes, twice daily) via **Kan Air** (☏nationwide call centre 02 551 6111, Chiang Rai 0 5379 3339; www.kanairlines.com; Chiang Rai airport)

Boat

Another way to reach Chiang Rai is by boat on the Mae Nam Kok from Tha Ton (see p287).

For boats heading upriver, go to **CR Pier** (☏0 5375 0009), 2km northwest of town, via Th Kraisorasit. Passenger boats embark daily at 10.30am with stops in Ban Ruammit (80B, one hour) and Tha Ton (350B, four hours), otherwise you can charter an entire boat to Ban Ruammit for 700B or all the way to Tha Ton for 3800B at the pier.

A túk-túk to CR Pier should cost about 50B.

⊙ Getting Around

A túk-túk ride anywhere within central Chiang Rai should cost around 40B. Shared *sǒrng·tǎa·ou* cost 20B per person.

BUSES & MINIVANS IN CHIANG RAI

Buses bound for destinations within Chiang Rai Province, as well as slow fan-cooled buses bound for Chiang Mai, Lampang, Nan and Phayao, depart from the bus station in the centre of town.

To Bangkok, **Sombat Tour** (☏0 5371 4971; Th Prasopsook; ⏱6am-7pm) has an office across from the inter-provincial bus terminal, but only VIP buses can be boarded here; all other Bangkok-bound buses depart from the new terminal.

DESTINATION	FARE (B)	DURATION (HR)	FREQUENCY
Ban Huay Khrai (for Doi Tung)	23	½	every 20min 6am-8pm
Ban Pasang (for Doi Mae Salong)	20	½	every 20min 6am-4pm
Chiang Khong	65	2½	every hour 5.20am-5.45pm
Chiang Mai	142	7	every 45min 6.30am-noon
Chiang Saen	32	1½	every 20min 6.20am-6.30pm
Lampang	102	5	every 45min 6.30am-noon
Mae Sai	39	1½	every 20min 6am-8pm
Nan	164	6	9.30am
Phayao	44	2	every 30min 9.30am-3.10pm

If you're heading beyond Chiang Rai (or are in a hurry), you'll have to go to the **new bus station** (☏0 5377 3989), 5km south of town on Hwy 1. *Sŏrng·tǎa·ou* linking it and the old station run from 5am to 9pm (10B, 20 minutes). Minivans also depart from here, including departures for Phayao (68B, 1½ hours, every 45 minutes from 6am to 7.30pm) and Phrae (150B, four hours, every 45 minutes from 6am to 5pm).

DESTINATION	FARE (B)	DURATION (HR)	FREQUENCY
Bangkok	448-716	11-12	every hr 7-11.30am & 6.30-9pm
Chiang Mai	142-263	3-7	every hr 6.30am-5.45pm
Kamphaeng Phet	280	7	7am, 8.30am, 1pm
Khon Kaen	316-553	11-12	9am, 10.15am, every 2hr 2pm-9pm
Nakhon Ratchasima (Khorat)	473-710	12-13	6.15am, 11.30am, 1.30pm, 3.30pm, 5pm, 7pm
Lampang	102-286	4-5	every hr 6am-3.45pm
Mae Sai	26-84	1-1½	every 15min 6am-6pm
Mae Sot	354-455	12	7.45am, 8.15am
Phayao	44-141	1½-2	every hr 6am-7.30pm
Phrae	148-244	4	every hr 6am-7.30pm
Phitsanulok	249-374	6-7	every hr 6am-7.30pm
Sukhothai	223-244	8	7.30am, 8.30am, 10.30am, 2.30pm

Bicycle rental can be arranged at **Fat Free** (☏0 5375 2532; 542/2 Th Baanpa Pragarn; per day 80-450B; ⏱8.30am-6pm). Motorcycles can be hired at **ST Motorcycle** (☏0 5371 3652; 1025/34-35 Th Jet Yod; per day 150-1000B;

⏱8am-8pm) – they take good care of their bikes. Many guest houses also rent out motorcycles and bikes.

The following car rental companies have offices in Chiang Rai.

Avis Rent-A-Car (✆0 5379 3827; www.
avisthailand.com; Chiang Rai airport;
🕗8am-6pm)

Budget Rent-A-Car (✆0 5374 0442/3; www.
budget.co.th; 590 Th Phahonyothin; 🕗8am-
6pm) At Golden Triangle Inn.

National Car Rental (✆0 5379 3683; Chiang
Rai airport; 🕗8am-6pm)

North Wheels (✆0 5374 0585; www.north
wheels.com; 591 Th Phahonyothin;
🕗8am-6pm)

Thai Rent A Car (✆0 5379 3393; www.thairent
acar.com; Chiang Rai airport; 🕗7am-6pm)

Around Chiang Rai

WAT RONG KHUN   วัดร่องขุ่น

About 13km south of Chiang Rai is the
unusual and popular **Wat Rong Khun**
('White Wat'; admission free). Whereas most
temples have centuries of history, this
one's construction began in 1997 by noted
Thai painter-turned-architect Chalermchai
Kositpipat.

Seen from a distance, the temple appears to be made of glittering porcelain;
a closer look reveals that the look is due
to a combination of whitewash and clear-
mirrored chips. Walk over a bridge and
sculpture of reaching arms (symbolising
desire) to enter the sanctity of the wát
where instead of the traditional Buddha
life scenarios, the artist has painted contemporary scenes representing *samsara*
(the realm of rebirth and delusion). Images such as a plane smashing into the
Twin Towers and, oddly enough, Keanu
Reeves as Neo from *The Matrix,* dominate the one finished wall of this work in
progress. If you like what you see, an adjacent gallery sells reproductions of Chalermchai Kositpipat's rather New Age–looking works.

To get to the temple, hop on one of the
regular buses that run from Chiang Rai to
Chiang Mai or Phayao and ask to get off at
Wat Rong Khun (20B).

Mae Salong (Santikhiri)

แม่สลอง (สันติคีรี)

POP 20,000

For a taste of China without crossing any
international borders, head to this atmospheric village perched on the back hills of
Chiang Rai. Although Mae Salong is now

thoroughly on the beaten track, its hilltop
setting, Chinese residents, and abundance
of hill tribes and tea plantations converge
in a unique destination not unlike a small
town in southern China's Yunnan Province.
It's a great place to kick back for a couple
of days, and the surrounding area is ripe
for exploration.

◉ Sights

Markets

A tiny but quite interesting **morning market** convenes from 6am to 8am at the T-
intersection near Shin Sane Guest House.
The market attracts town residents and
tribespeople from the surrounding districts.
An **all-day market** forms at the southern
end of town, and unites vendors selling hill-
tribe handicrafts, shops selling tea and a
few basic restaurants.

Temples

To soak up the great views from **Wat Santikhiri** go past the market and ascend 718
steps (or drive if you have a car). The wát
is of the Mahayana tradition and Chinese
in style.

Past the Khumnaiphol Resort and further up the hill is a **viewpoint** with some
teashops, and a famous Kuomintang (KMT)
general's **tomb**. It is sometimes guarded by
a soldier who will describe (in Thai or Yunnanese) the history of the KMT in the area.
In the same vein and south of the turn-off
to the tomb is the **Chinese Martyr's Memorial Museum**, an elaborate Chinese-
style building that is more memorial than
museum.

🏃 Activities

Trekking

Shin Sane Guest House and Little Home
Guesthouse have free maps showing ap-
proximate trekking routes to Akha, Lisu,
Mien, Lahu and Shan villages in the area.
Nearby Akha and Lisu villages are less than
half a day's walk away.

The best hikes are north of Mae Salong
between Ban Thoet Thai and the Myanmar
border. Ask first about political conditions
before heading off in this direction; Shan
and Wa armies competing for control over
this section of the Thailand–Myanmar
border do occasionally clash in the area. A
steady trade in methamphetamine and, to a
lesser extent, heroin, flows across the border via several conduit villages.

NORTHERN THAILAND AROUND CHIANG RAI

Golden Triangle & Around

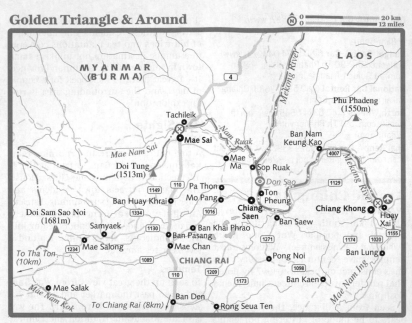

Shin Sane Guest House arranges four-hour **horseback treks** to four nearby villages for 500B for about three or four hours.

🛏 Sleeping

Since the road from Mae Salong to Tha Ton opened, fewer visitors are opting to stay overnight in Mae Salong. The resulting surplus of accommodation often makes prices negotiable, except during the high season (November to January).

IN TOWN
All accommodation is located on, or just off, the main road.

Little Home Guesthouse GUEST HOUSE $$
(☎0 5376 5389; www.maesalonglittlehome.com; r/bungalows 300/800B; @令) Located near the market intersection, this delightful wooden house holds a few basic but cosy rooms and large and tidy bungalows out back. An attached restaurant does local dishes. The owner is extremely friendly and has put together one of the more accurate maps of the area.

Baan Hom Muen Li HOTEL $$
(Boutique Hotel; ☎08 4045 8031; osmanhouse@ hotmail.com; r incl breakfast 1000-1500B) Located in the middle of town, across from Sweet Maesalong, this new place consists of five rooms artfully decked out in modern and classic Chinese themes. Go for the upstairs rooms that have huge windows with views over the surrounding tea plantations.

Saeng Aroon Hotel HOTEL $
(☎0 5376 5029; r 300B; ❄@) Next to the teashop of the same name, this new hotel has friendly staff, spacious tiled-floor rooms and great views of the hills. The cheaper rooms share spick-and-span hot-water bathrooms.

Shin Sane Guest House HOTEL $
(☎0 5376 5026; www.maesalong-shinsane.blogs pot.com; r 50-100B, bungalows 200-300B; @令) The rooms at Mae Salong's first hotel are bare but spacious with shared bathrooms, while the bungalows are much more comfortable and have private bathrooms and cable TV. It's located near the morning market intersection.

OUTSIDE OF TOWN
Phu Chaisai Resort & Spa HOTEL $$$
(☎0 5391 0500; www.phu-chaisai.com; r incl breakfast 4000-11,720B; ❄@令☎) Approximately 7km from Pasang on a remote bamboo-covered hilltop, this resort is an exceptional place to stay in the area. The rustic adobe/

bamboo duplex bungalows fittingly lack TV, but have amazing views of the surrounding mountains, and a host of activities including spa treatment, massage, yoga, day hikes and swimming should keep you occupied.

Maesalong Mountain Home   HOTEL $$$
(☑08 4611 9508; www.maesalongmountainhome.com; bungalows 800-2500B; ☎) Down a dirt road 1km east of the town centre (look for the orange sign), this boutique hotel is a great choice if you've got your own wheels. The nine bungalows here are in the middle of a working farm and are bright and airy, with enviable balconies and huge bathrooms. Another bonus is its location near a tea farm with gigantic teapot and lion statues – a bizarre but fun photo op.

Maesalong Flower Hills Resort   HOTEL $$$
(☑0 5376 5496; www.maesalongflowerhills.com; r incl breakfast 1800B, bungalows incl breakfast 2300-7000B; ❋☎❋) Located 2km east of the town centre, you can't miss this monument to flower-based landscaping. There's a variety of rooms and bungalows, and the huge

pool and larger bungalows make this a great choice for families.

✖ Eating

The very Chinese breakfast of *ƀah·tôrng·gŏh* (deep-fried fingers of dough) and hot soybean milk at the morning market is an inspiring way to start the day.

In fact, many Thai tourists come to Mae Salong simply to eat Yunnanese dishes such as *màn·tŏh* (steamed Chinese buns) served with braised pork leg and pickled vegetables, or black chicken braised with Chinese-style herbs. Homemade wheat and egg noodles are another speciality of Mae Salong, and are served with a local broth that combines pork and a spicy chilli paste. They're available at several places in town.

Countless teahouses sell locally grown teas (mostly oolong and jasmine) and offer complimentary tastings.

TOP CHOICE Sue Hai   CHINESE $
(mains 60-150B; ☉7am-9pm) This very simple family-run teashop-cum-Yunnanese place has

---

HOME AWAY FROM HOME

Mae Salong was originally settled by the 93rd Regiment of the Kuomintang (KMT), who had fled to Myanmar from China after the 1949 Chinese revolution. The renegades were forced to leave Myanmar in 1961 when the Yangon government decided it wouldn't allow the KMT to remain legally in northern Myanmar. Crossing into northern Thailand with their pony caravans, the ex-soldiers and their families settled into mountain villages and re-created a society like the one they'd left behind in Yunnan.

After the Thai government granted the KMT refugee status in the 1960s, efforts were made to incorporate the Yunnanese KMT and their families into the Thai nation. Until the late 1980s they didn't have much success. Many ex-KMT persisted in involving themselves in the Golden Triangle opium trade in a three-way partnership with alleged opium warlord Khun Sa and the Shan United Army (SUA). Because of the rough, mountainous terrain and lack of sealed roads, the outside world was rather cut off from the goings-on in Mae Salong, so the Yunnanese were able to ignore attempts by the Thai authorities to suppress opium activity and tame the region.

Infamous Khun Sa made his home in nearby Ban Hin Taek (now Ban Thoet Thai) until the early 1980s when he was finally routed by the Thai military. Khun Sa's retreat to Myanmar seemed to signal a change in local attitudes and the Thai government finally began making progress in its pacification of Mae Salong and the surrounding area.

In a further effort to separate the area from its old image as an opium fiefdom, the Thai government officially changed the name of the village from Mae Salong to Santikhiri (Hill of Peace). Until the 1980s packhorses were used to move goods up the mountain to Mae Salong, but today the 36km road from Pasang is paved and well travelled. But despite the advances in infrastructure, the town is unlike any other in Thailand. The Yunnanese dialect of Chinese still remains the lingua franca, residents tend to watch Chinese, rather than Thai, TV, and you'll find more Chinese than Thai food.

In an attempt to quash opium activity, and the more recent threat of *yah bâh* (methamphetamine) trafficking, the Thai government has created crop-substitution programs to encourage hill tribes to cultivate tea, coffee, corn and fruit trees.

an English-language menu of local specialities including local mushroom fried with soy sauce, or the delicious air-dried pork fried with fresh chilli. They also do filling and tasty bowls of homemade noodles. It's roughly in the middle of town.

Nong Im Phochana CHINESE $
(mains 60-150B; ☉lunch & dinner) Located directly across from Khumnaiphol Resort at the southern end of town, the menu at this open-air restaurant emphasises dishes using local veggies.

Sweet Maesalong CAFE $
(mains 45-185B; ☺8.30am-6pm) If you require a considerably higher degree of caffeine than the local tea leaves can offer, stop by this cosy modern cafe with an extensive menu of coffee drinks using local beans. Surprisingly sophisticated baked goods and dishes are also available. Sweet Maesalong is roughly in the middle of town.

Mae Salong Villa CHINESE $
(mains 60-150B; ☉lunch & dinner) With dishes such as duck smoked over tea leaves, the restaurant at this hotel, located east of the town centre, is said to do the most authentic Yunnanese food in town.

❶ Information

There is an ATM at the Thai Military Bank opposite Khumnaiphol Resort, at the southern end of town. An **internet cafe** (per hr 20B; ☉9am-11pm) can be found next door.

❶ Getting There & Away

Mae Salong is accessible via two routes. The original road, Rte 1130, winds west from Ban Pasang. Newer Rte 1234 approaches from the south, allowing easier access from Chiang Mai. The older route is more spectacular.

To get to Mae Salong by bus, take a Mae Sai-bound bus from Chiang Rai to Ban Pasang (20B, 30 minutes, every 20 minutes from 6am to 4pm). From Ban Pasang, blue *sŏrng·tăa·ou* head up the mountain to Mae Salong (60B, one hour, 7am to 5pm). To get back to Ban Pasang, *sŏrng·tăa·ou* park near the 7-Eleven. *Sŏrng·tăa·ou* stop running at around 5pm but you can charter one in either direction for about 500B.

You can also reach Mae Salong by road from Tha Ton (see p287). Yellow *sŏrng·tăa·ou* bound for Tha Ton stop near Little Home Guesthouse at 8.20am, 10.20am, 12.20pm and 1.50pm (60B, one hour).

Mae Sai แม่สาย
POP 22,000

At first glance, Thailand's northernmost town, Mae Sai, appears to be little more than a large open-air market. But the city serves as a convenient base for exploring the Golden Triangle, Doi Tung and Mae Salong, and its position across from Myanmar also makes it a stepping-off point for those wishing to explore some of the more remote parts of Shan State.

Because occasional fighting within Myanmar or disputes between the Thai and Myanmar governments can lead to the border being closed temporarily, it's always a good idea to check the current situation before travelling to Mae Sai.

◉ Sights & Activities

Wat Phra That Doi Wao TEMPLE
(วัดพระธาตุดอยเวา) Take the steps up the hill near the border to Wat Phra That Doi Wao, west of the main street, for superb views over Mae Sai and Myanmar. This wát was reportedly constructed in memory of a couple of thousand Burmese soldiers who died fighting the KMT here in 1965 (you'll hear differing stories around town, including a version wherein the KMT are the heroes).

⊨ Sleeping

Khanthongkham Hotel HOTEL $$
(☑0 5373 4222; www.kthotel.com; 7 Th Phahonyothin; r 800-950B, ste 1300-1650B; ❊@❈) This hotel features huge rooms that have been tastefully decorated in light woods and brown textiles. Suites are exceptionally vast, and like all rooms, have flat-screen TVs and truly user-friendly bathrooms. A downside is that many rooms don't have windows.

Maesai Guest House HOTEL $
(☑0 5373 2021; 688 Th Wiengpangam; bungalows r 200-600B; ❈) Located at the end of the narrow lane that stretches behind Mai Sai Riverside Resort, this collection of A-frame bungalows ranges from simple rooms with shared cold water showers to bungalows on the river with terraces and private bathrooms. There is a riverside restaurant onsite serving Thai and Western dishes.

Maekhong Delta Boutique Hotel HOTEL $$$
(☑053642517; www.maekhonghtel.com; 230/5-6 Th Phahonyothin; r incl breakfast 1200-3500B; ❊@❈) It's an odd name, considering that the Me-

Mae Sai

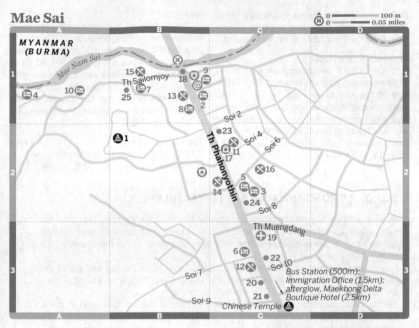

Mae Sai

◎ Sights

1 Wat Phra That Doi Wao	B2

🛏 Sleeping

2 Khanthongkham Hotel	B1
3 Little Bear	C2
4 Maesai Guest House	A1
5 Maesai Hotel	C2
6 Piyaporn Place Hotel	C3
7 S-House Hotel	B1
8 Top North Hotel	B1
9 Wang Thong Hotel	B1
10 Yeesun Guesthouse	A1

🍴 Eating

11 Bismillah Halal Food	C2
12 Kik Kok Restaurant	C3
13 Night Market	B1
14 Snack and Drink Vendors	C2
15 Sukhothai Cuisine	B1
16 Ying Ping Yunnan Restaurant	C2

🛍 Shopping

17 Gem Market	C2

ℹ Information

18 Immigration	B1
19 Overbrook Clinic	C3

ℹ Transport

20 Chok-Roong Tawee Tour	C3
Motorcycle Taxis to Bus Station	(see 17)
21 Pornchai	C3
22 Sŏrng·tǎa·ou to Ban Huay Khrai	C3
23 Sŏrng·tǎa·ou to Bus Station	C2
24 Sŏrng·tǎa·ou to Sop Ruak & Chiang Saen	C2
25 Toom Motorbike	B1

kong delta is way down in Vietnam. Odder still that the rooms here are somehow reminiscent of a ski lodge. Regardless, they're both cosy and comfortable, albeit nearly 4km from the centre of town.

Wang Thong Hotel HOTEL **$$$**
(☏0 5373 3389-95; www.wangthong-maesai. com; 299 Th Phahonyothin; r/ste incl breakfast 900/2500B; ❄@🛜🏊) The nine-storey Wang Thong is a comfortable business hotel, minutes from the border crossing. The rooms are

nothing special, but they're spacious and the hotel has a pub, disco and popular restaurant. Discounts available in the low season.

Piyaporn Place Hotel　　　HOTEL $$
(☎0 5373 4511-3; www.piyaporn-place.com; 77/1 Th Phahonyothin; r/ste incl breakfast 800/1800B; ✳@☎) On the main road by Soi 7, this seven-storey business hotel is good value. The large, contemporary-styled rooms have wooden floors, a small sofa and the usual four-/five-star amenities like bathroom, cable TV and minibar.

afterglow　　　HOTEL $$
(☎0 5373 4188; www.afterglowhostel.com; 139/5 Th Phahonyothin; r 690-990B; ✳☎) This place calls itself a hostel, but the dorms were not yet finished when we visited. Nonetheless, boasting a ground-floor cafe and rooms with a minimalist feel, it's probably the hippest place to stay in Mae Sai. Located about 4km from the border, across from Maekhong Delta Boutique Hotel.

Top North Hotel　　　HOTEL $
(☎0 5373 1955; topnorth_hotel@hotmail.com; 306 Th Phahonyothin; r 400-700B; ✳@☎)

BORDER CROSSING: MAE SAI TO TACHILEIK

Mae Sai, located opposite the Burmese town of Tachileik, is a legal crossing point for foreign tourists. Yet as with all of Myanmar's land crossings, there are several caveats involved and the following information is liable to change, so check the situation locally before you travel.

In general, it's very straightforward to cross to Tachileik for the day and slightly more complicated to get a two-week visa and permission to visit Kengtung, a quiet but interesting outpost of Tai culture 160km north of Tachileik.

The Thai immigration office is just before the bridge and is officially open from 7am to 6.30pm. After taking care of the usual formalities, cross the bridge and head to the Myanmar immigration office. Here you pay 500B and your picture is taken for a temporary ID card that allows you to stay in town for the day; your passport will be kept at the office. On your return to Thailand, the Thai immigration office will give you a new 15-day visa (see p766).

There is little to do in **Tachileik** apart from sample Burmese food and shop – the prices are about the same as on the Thai side and everyone accepts baht. There's an interesting morning market and it can be fun to hang about in the teashops.

If you'd like to stay longer or visit Kengtung, proceed directly to the adjacent tourist information office. There you'll need three photos, $10 and 50B to process a border pass valid for 14 days; your passport will be kept at the border. It's also obligatory to hire a guide for the duration of your stay. Guides cost 1000B per day (400B of this goes to Myanmar Travels & Tours, a state-run travel agency), and if you haven't already arranged for a Kengtung-based guide to meet you at the border, you'll be assigned one by MTT and will also have to pay for your guide's food and accommodation during your stay. Recommended Kengtung-based guides include **Sai Leng** (☎+95 9490 31470; sairoctor.htunleng@ gmail.com), **Freddie** (Sai Yot; ☎+95 9490 31934; yotkham@gmail.com) and **Paul** (Sai Lon; ☎+95 9490 30464, +95 842 2812).

Kengtung (called Chiang Tung by the Thais and usually spelt Kyaingtong by the Burmese) is a sleepy but historic capital for the Shan State's Khün culture. The Khün speak a northern Thai language related to Shan and Thai Lü, and use a writing script similar to the ancient Lanna script. Built around a small lake and dotted with ageing **Buddhist temples** and crumbling British **colonial architecture**, it's a much more scenic town than Tachileik and one of the most interesting towns in Myanmar's entire Shan State.

Places to stay include the **Princess Hotel** (☎+95 842 1319; kengtung@mail4u.com.mm; s/d $30/50; ✳), or the budget-oriented but inconveniently located **Harry's Trekking House** (☎+95 842 1418; 132 Mai Yang Rd; r $7-20).

Buses bound for Kengtung (K10,000, five hours) depart from Tachileik's dusty bus station, 2km and a 10B *sŏrng·tǎa·ou* ride or a 40B motorcycle taxi ride from the border, at about 8am and noon. Alternatively, you can charter a taxi for about 2500B, or if you're willing to wait, get a front/back seat in a share taxi for K15,000/10,000.

For more info on Kengtung, see Lonely Planet's *Myanmar (Burma)* guidebook.

A brief walk to the bridge to Myanmar, this older hotel has spacious rooms and friendly staff. Stick with the rooms at the back of the building to avoid street noise.

Yeesun Guesthouse   HOTEL $
(✆0 5373 3455; www.yeesunguesthouse.com; 816/13 Th Sailomjoy; r 400B; ❋🖥) This four-storey family-run hotel has great-value if rather characterless rooms with comfortable furniture and beds.

S-House Hotel   HOTEL $
(✆0 5373 3811; www.s-house-hotel-maesai.com; 384 Th Sailomjoy; r with fan/air-con 500/600B; ❋) At the end of the covered part of Th Sailomjoy, away from the border crossing, this hotel has spacious rooms with balconies overlooking the hills.

Maesai Hotel   HOTEL $
(✆0 5373 1462; 125/5 Th Phahonyothin; r with fan/air-con 250/450B) Located in a green building just off Th Phahonyothin, the rooms with fan here are decent value and have beds on an elevated concrete pedestal. The more expensive air-conditioned rooms have flimsy beds and cheap furniture.

Little Bear   HOTEL $
(✆0 5364 0933; off Soi 6, Th Phahonyothin; r 280-480B; ❋@🖥) The basic but tidy rooms here are given life by the attached bar/cafe lobby.

✖ Eating

An expansive **night market** (⊙5-11pm) unfolds every evening along Th Phahonyothin. During the day, several **snack and drink vendors** (Th Phahonyothin) can be found in front of the police station.

Bismillah Halal Food   MUSLIM-THAI $
(Soi 4, Th Phahonyothin; mains 25-40B; ⊙6am-6pm) Run by Burmese Muslims, this tiny restaurant does an excellent *biryani,* not to mention virtually everything else Muslim, from roti to samosa.

Sukhothai Cuisine   NOODLES $
(399/9 Th Sailomjoy; mains 30-40B; ⊙7am-4pm) This open-air restaurant serves the namesake noodles from Sukhothai, as well as satay and a few other basic dishes. A picture menu shows the varieties of noodles available, and the pictures on the wall are of the owner's daughter.

Ying Ping Yunnan Restaurant   CHINESE $$
(Soi 6, Th Phahonyothin; mains 100-350B; ⊙11am-10pm; ❋) For a special night out, head to this banquet-style Chinese restaurant. The menu here features a variety of exotic-sounding dishes you're unlikely to find elsewhere, as well as humble Yunnan-style noodle soup.

Kik Kok Restaurant   THAI $
(Th Phahonyothin; mains 30-120B; ⊙6am-8pm; ✎) This restaurant prepares a huge selection of Thai dishes, including several vegetarian options, and has an English menu.

🛍 Shopping

Commerce is ubiquitous in Mae Sai, although most of the offerings are of little interest to Western travellers. One popular commodity is gems, and dealers from as far away as Chanthaburi frequent the small gem market that is opposite the police station. A walk down Soi 4 will reveal several open-air gem dealers diligently counting hundreds of tiny semiprecious stones on the side of the street.

ℹ Information

There are several banks with ATM near the border.

Immigration Main Office (✆0 5373 1008; Rte 110; ⊙8.30am-4.30pm Mon-Fri); Border (⊙7am-6.30pm) There's a main office about 3km from the border near Soi 17 and another at the entrance to the border bridge.

Internet cafe (per hr 40B) Behind the Wang Thong Hotel by its car park.

Overbrook Clinic (✆0 5373 4422; 20/7 Th Phahonyothin; ⊙8am-5pm) Connected to the modern hospital in Chiang Rai, this small clinic on the main road has doctors who can speak English.

Tourist police (✆115) With a booth in front of the border crossing before immigration.

ℹ Getting There & Away

On the main Th Phahonyothin road, by Soi 8, is a sign saying 'bus stop'. From here *sŏrng·tǎa·ou* stop in Sop Ruak (45B, every 40 minutes, 8am to 1pm), terminating in Chiang Saen (50B). *Sŏrng·tǎa·ou* to Ban Huay Khrai (Doi Tung) park by Soi 10 (25B, 6.30am to 5pm).

Mae Sai's government **bus station** (✆0 5371 1224; Rte 110) is 1.5km from the border; getting there from the border involves a 15B shared *sŏrng·tǎa·ou* ride from the corner of Th Phahonyothin and Soi 2 or a 40B motorcycle taxi ride from the stand at the corner of Th Phahonyothin and Soi 4. If you're headed to Bangkok, you can avoid going all the way to the bus station by buying your tickets at **Chok-Roong Tawee Tour** (no roman-script sign; ☑0 5364 0123; near cnr Th Phahonyothin & Soi 9; ☺8am-5.30pm) – it's next door to the motorcycle dealership.

Destinations from Mae Sai:

Bangkok (483B to 966B, 13 hours, frequent departures from 4pm to 5.45pm)

Chiang Mai (165B to 320B, five hours, five departures from 6.45am to 3.30pm)

Chiang Rai (39B, 1½ hours, every 20 minutes from 5.45am to 8pm)

Fang (81B, three hours, 7am)

Mae Sot (388B to 499B, 12 hours, 6.15am and 6.45am)

Nakhon Ratchasima (Khorat) (507B to 760B, 15 hours, six departures)

Tha Ton (61B, two hours, 7am)

❶ Getting Around

Sŏrng·tăa·ou around town are 15B shared. Motorcycle taxis cost 20B to 40B.

Motorcycles can be rented at **Pornchai** (☑0 5373 1136; 4/7 Th Phahonyothin; per day 250-300B; ☺8am-5pm) and at **Toom Motorbike** (☑08 2106 8131; Th Sailomjoy; per day 200B; ☺9am-5pm).

Around Mae Sai

DOI TUNG & AROUND   ดอยตุง

About halfway between Mae Chan and Mae Sai on Rte 110 is the turn-off (west) for Doi Tung. The name means 'Flag Peak', from the northern Thai word for flag (*dung*). King Achutarat of Chiang Saen ordered a giant flag to be flown from the peak to mark the spot where two *chedi* were constructed in AD 911; the *chedi* are still there, a pilgrimage site for Thai, Shan and Chinese Buddhists.

But the main attraction at Doi Tung is getting there. The 'easy' way is via Rte 1149, which is mostly paved to the peak of Doi Tung. But it's winding, steep and narrow, so if you're driving or riding a motorcycle, take it slowly.

◉ Sights

Doi Tung Royal Villa   HISTORICAL BUILDING

(☑0 5376 7011; www.doitung.org; admission 70B; ☺6.30am-5pm) On the theory that local hill tribes would be so honoured by a royal presence that they would stop cultivating opium, the late Princess Mother (the king's mother) built the Doi Tung Royal Villa, a summer palace on the slopes of Doi Tung near Pa Kluay Reservoir, which is now open

to the public as a museum. The royal initiative also provided education on new agricultural methods to stop slash and burn practices. Opium has now been replaced by crops such as coffee, macadamia nuts and various fruits. The rest of the property, including the **Mae Fah Luang Garden** and **Mae Fah Luang Arboretum** (admission 70B; ☺7am-5pm), is also open to the public. There is also a top-end hotel, a restaurant, coffee kiosk and a Doi Tung craft shop up here. Near the parking lot, the **Doi Tung Bazaar** is a small open-air market with local agricultural products, prepared food and hill-tribe handicrafts. This entire complex is popular with bus tour groups.

Wat Phra That Doi Tung   TEMPLE

At the peak, 1800m above sea level, Wat Phra That Doi Tung is built around the twin Lanna-style *chedi*. The *chedi* were renovated by Chiang Mai monk Khruba Siwichai, famous for his prodigious building projects, early in the 20th century. Pilgrims bang on the usual row of temple bells to gain merit. Although the wát isn't that impressive, the forested setting will make the trip worthwhile. From the walled edge of the temple you can get an aerial view of the snaky road you've just climbed. A walking path next to the wát leads to a spring and there are other short walking trails in the vicinity.

A bit below the peak is the smaller **Wat Noi Doi Tung**, where food and beverages are available from vendors.

🛏 Sleeping & Eating

If you want to spend the night, try **Ban Ton Nam 31** (☑0 5376 7003; www.doitung.org; Doi Tung Development Project, Mae Fah Luang District; r incl breakfast 2500-3000B; ✳🛜). It consists of 46 comfortable rooms that formerly served as the living quarters of the Princess Mother's staff. The more expensive rooms have better views. A self-service **restaurant** (dishes 80-250B; ☺7am-9pm) offers meals made with local produce, and there's also a Doi Tung cafe.

❶ Getting There & Away

Sŏrng·tăa·ou from Mae Sai (25B) go to Ban Huay Khrai, the turn-off for Doi Tung. From there *sŏrng·tăa·ou* are available to Doi Tung (60B, one hour).

Alternatively, if you've got your own wheels, you can travel between Doi Tung and Mae Sai along the even more challenging, 24km, sealed but narrow Rte 1149. From Doi Tung Royal Villa simply follow the signs to Wat Phra That Doi Tung. The road hugs the Thai–Burma border behind the large limestone mountains you may have seen from Rte 110, and emerges at Soi 7 in Mae Sai. There are at least three military checkpoints along the way, so be sure to bring ID.

If you want to do a full loop from Mae Sai, ride/drive via Rte 110 south of Mae Sai, then Rte 1149 up to Doi Tung. Once you've had a look around the summit, return to Mae Sai via aforementioned roads; this means you'll be travelling downhill much of the way.

If you're coming from Mae Salong, Rte 1334 weaves from steep hills to a lush valley, before climbing again to Rte 1149 and Doi Tung. The road is fully sealed and in good shape, although it can be quite steep and windy in parts.

Chiang Saen   เชียงแสน

POP 11,000

The dictionary definition of a sleepy river town, Chiang Saen was the site of a Thai kingdom thought to date back to as early as the 7th century. Scattered throughout the modern town are the ruins of the former empire – surviving architecture includes several *chedi,* Buddha images, *wí·hăhn* pillars and earthen city ramparts. Chiang Saen later became loosely affiliated with various northern Thai kingdoms, as well as 18th-century Myanmar, and never became a Siamese possession until the 1880s.

Today huge river barges from China moor at Chiang Saen, carrying fruit, engine parts and all manner of other imports, keeping the old China-Siam trade route open. Despite this trade, and despite commercialisation of the nearby Sop Ruak, the town hasn't changed too much over the last decade, and because of this is a pleasanter base than the latter.

Only locals are allowed to cross the Mekong River into the Lao town of Ton Pheung, but foreigners who already hold a Chinese visa can use the town as a base for river trips to Jinghong in China's Yunnan Province.

◎ Sights & Activities

Wat Phra That Pha Ngao   TEMPLE

(วัดพระธาตุผาเงา; admission free) Located 3km south of town in the village of Sop Kham, this Buddhist temple complex contains a large prayer hall built to cover a partially excavated Chiang Saen-era Buddha statue. The walls of the brick building are partially covered by stucco relief murals that have been painted, giving the surface the impres-

sion of polished wood or copper. There is a beautiful golden teak *hŏr đrai,* and a steep road leads to a hilltop pagoda and temple with views over the area and the Mae Nam Khong.

Wat Chedi Luang   TEMPLE

(วัดเจดีย์หลวง; admission free) Behind the museum to the east are the ruins of the Buddhist Wat Chedi Luang, which features an 18m octagonal *chedi* in the classic Chiang Saen or Lanna style. Archaeologists argue about its exact construction date but agree it dates to some time between the 12th and 14th centuries.

Wat Pa Sak   TEMPLE

(วัดป่าสัก; admission free) About 200m from the **Pratu Chiang Saen** (the historic main gateway to the town's western flank) are the remains of Wat Pa Sak, where the ruins of seven monuments are visible in a **historical park** (admission 50B). The main mid-14th-century *chedi* combines elements of the Hariphunchai and Sukhothai styles with a possible Bagan influence, and still holds a great deal of attractive stucco relief work.

Wat Phra That Chom Kitti & Wat Chom Chang   TEMPLE

(วัดพระธาตุจอมกิตติ; admission free) The remains of Wat Phra That Chom Kitti and Wat Chom Chang can be found about 2.5km north of Wat Pa Sak on a hilltop. The round *chedi* of Wat Phra That Chom Kitti is thought to have been constructed before the founding of the kingdom. The smaller *chedi* below it belonged to Wat Chom Chang. There is nothing much to see at these *chedi,* but there is a good view of Chiang Saen and the river.

Wat Pha Khao Pan   TEMPLE

(วัดผาขาวป้าน; admission free) Inside the grounds of Wat Pha Khao Pan, a living *wát* near the river, stands a magnificent Lanna-period *chedi.* The large, square base contains Lanna-style walking Buddhas in niches on all four sides. The Buddha facing east is sculpted in the *mudra* ('calling for rain') pose, with both hands held pointing down at the image's sides – a pose common in Laos but not so common in Thailand.

Chiang Saen National Museum   MUSEUM

(พิพิธภัณฑสถานแห่งชาติเชียงแสน; 702 Th Phahonyothin; admission 100B; ◎8.30am-4.30pm Wed-Sun) Near the town entrance, this museum is a

Chiang Saen

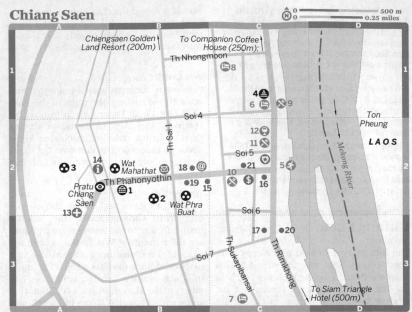

N 0 _____ 500 m
0 _____ 0.25 miles

Chiang Saen

◎ Sights
1	Chiang Saen National Museum	B2
2	Wat Chedi Luang	B2
3	Wat Pa Sak	A2
4	Wat Pha Khao Pan	C1

◎ Activities, Courses & Tours
5	Boats to Sop Ruak & Chiang Khong	C2

◎ Sleeping
6	Chiang Saen Guest House	C1
7	Chiang Saen River Hill Hotel	C3
8	Sa Nae Charn Guest House	C1

◎ Eating
9	Evening Food Vendors	C1
10	Food Stalls	C2
11	Kiaw Siang Hai	C2

◎ Drinking
12	2 be 1	C2

◎ Information
13	Chiang Saen Hospital	A2
14	Visitors Centre	A2

◎ Transport
15	Angpao Chaingsaen Tour	B2
16	Bus Stop	C2
17	Chiang Saen Tour and Travel	C3
18	Motorcycle Rental	B2
19	Sombat Tour	B2
20	Sŏrng·tăa·ou to Chiang Khong	C3
21	Sŏrng·tăa·ou to Sop Ruak & Mae Sai	C2

great source of local information considering its relatively small size.

Mekong River Trips   RIVER CRUISE
Five-passenger speedboats leave from the waterfront jet to Sop Ruak (per boat one way/return 500/600B, one hour), or all the way to Chiang Khong (per boat one way/return 2000/2500B, 1½ hours).

It's also possible to take a passenger boat to Jinghong, in China's Yunnan Province. For details, see the boxed text, p329.

🛏 Sleeping

Chiang Saen lacks quality accommodation, particularly of the upscale type. If you require a higher level of service and standards, then your best bet is to base yourself in nearby Sop Ruak.

Viang Yonok HOTEL $$$
(📞0 5365 0444; www.viangyonok.com; Chiang Saen Lake; bungalows incl breakfast 2000-2400B; ❄@🛜🏊) The emphasis at this well-manicured compound of seven bungalows is activities, and if a swimming pool, weight room, bicycles, kayaks and birdwatching aren't enough, well, you're a pretty tough customer. The only downsides we noticed were the stuffy furniture and distance from town. Viang Yonok is approximately 5km west of Chiang Saen along the road that leads to Mae Chan. The hotel sign isn't clear; take the turn-off about 1km after the Esso station.

Chiang Saen River Hill Hotel HOTEL $$
(📞0 5365 0826; www.chiangsaenriverhill.net; 714 Th Sukapibansai; r incl breakfast 1200B; ❄) Although the pink exterior and floor tiles don't exactly complement the northern-Thai furnishing touches, this is still probably the best place in town. Rooms are large, and equipped with TV, fridge and a small area for relaxing.

Chiengsaen Golden Land Resort HOTEL $$
(📞0 5365 1100; www.chengsanresort.com; 663 Th Sai 1; r incl breakfast 800B, bungalows incl breakfast 1200-2000B; ❄🛜🏊) At this resort hotel you can choose from large well-equipped rooms in a two-storey building or several attractive wooden bungalows surrounding a garden and a covered swimming pool. There is another branch with 10 similarly priced bungalows in the village of Sop Kham, 3km south along the Mekong.

Siam Triangle Hotel HOTEL $$$
(📞0 5365 1115; www.siamtriangle.com; 267 Th Rimkhong; r/ste incl breakfast 2500-4500/8000B; ❄@🛜🏊) Chiang Saen's newest and biggest hotel lacks atmosphere, but the gigantic suites, with river-view Jacuzzi tubs, laptop and free laundry are pretty good value. The hotel is just outside Chiang Saen, about 500m south of the former city wall.

Chiang Saen Guest House HOTEL $
(📞0 5365 0196; 45/2 Th Rimkhong; r 150-650B, bungalows 200B; ❄🛜) In a handy location opposite the river and night stalls, this long-running place has basic but good-value rooms and A-frame bungalows. Conveniently located within walking distance of both the river and 'downtown' Chiang Saen.

Sa Nae Charn Guest House HOTEL $
(📞0 5365 1138; 641 Th Nhongmoon; r 200-500B; ❄) Run by an elderly Singaporean gentleman, the rooms here start basic, but increasingly include amenities such as TV and air-con as you pay more.

🍴 Eating & Drinking

Cheap noodle and rice dishes are available at food stalls in and near the market on the river road and along the main road through town from the highway, near the bus stop. Evening food vendors set up at the latter location and stay open till around midnight.

Jinda's Kitchen NORTHERN THAI $
(Rte 1290; mains 20-130B; ⏱8am-4pm) This cosy roadside restaurant has been serving up local dishes for more than 50 years. Try the famous northern noodle dishes *kôw soy* or *kà·nŏm jeen nám ngèe·o*, or choose a curry or homemade sausage from the English-language menu. Jinda's Kitchen is roughly halfway between Chiang Saen and Sop Ruak.

Kiaw Siang Hai CHINESE $$
(no roman-script sign; 44 Th Rimkhong; mains 50-200B; ⏱8am-8pm) Serving the workers of Chinese boats that dock at Chiang Saen, this authentic Chinese restaurant prepares a huge menu of dishes in addition to the namesake noodle and wonton dishes. Try the spicy Szechuan-style fried tofu, or one of the Chinese herbal soups. The restaurant can be located by the giant ceramic jars out front.

Evening Food Vendors THAI $
(Th Rimkhong; mains 30-60B; ⏱4-11pm) During the dry months these vendors sell sticky rice, green papaya salad, grilled chicken, dried squid and other fun foods for people to eat while sitting on mats along the riverbank in front of Chiang Saen Guest House – a very pleasant way to spend an evening. Local specialities include fish or chicken barbecued inside thick joints of bamboo, eaten with sticky rice and *sôm·đam* (green papaya salad).

2 be 1 BAR
(Th Rimkhong; ⏱6pm-1am) By the river, this funky bar with inside and outside seating has colourful lamps and plays house music.

ℹ️ Information

Chiang Saen Hospital (☏0 5377 7017-7035) This government hospital is just south of Wat Pa Sak. Staff speak little English.

Companion Coffee House (Th Rimkhong; ⏰8am-7pm; 📶) This coffee shop also has a computer and wi-fi. Located north of town near Soi 2.

Internet (Th Phahonyothin; per hr 20B; ⏰10am-8pm) There are two internet shops, located across from each other, a block east of Wat Chedi Luang.

Post office (Th Phahonyothin) Located roughly across from Wat Chedi Luang.

Siam Commercial Bank (Th Phahonyothin) On the main street leading from the highway to the Mekong River. Has an ATM and currency exchange.

Visitors centre (☏0 5377 7084; Th Phahonyothin; ⏰8.30am-4.30pm) Has a good relief display showing the major ruin sites as well as photos of various *chedi* before, during and after restoration.

ℹ️ Getting There & Away

Blue *sŏrng·tăa·ou* that travel to Sop Ruak (20B) and Mae Sai (50B) wait at a stall at the eastern end of Th Phahonyothin from 7.20am to noon. The green *sŏrng·tăa·ou* bound for Chiang Khong (100B) park at a stall on Th Rimkhong, south of the riverside immigration office, from 7.30am to noon. After noon it's only possible to charter the entire vehicle, which costs between 800B and 1000B.

Chiang Saen has no proper bus terminal, rather there is a covered bus shelter at the eastern end of Th Phahonyothin where buses pick up and drop off passengers. From this stop there are frequent buses to Chiang Rai (37B, 1½ hours, 5.30am to 5pm) and two daily departures to Chiang Mai (2nd class air-con/1st class 165/212B, five hours, 7.15am and 9am).

To Bangkok, **Sombat Tour** (☏08 1595 4616; Th Phahonyothin) offers approximately 12 seats in a daily VIP bus (920B, 12 hours, 5pm), departing from a small office adjacent to Krung Thai Bank.

ℹ️ Getting Around

Motorbike taxis and sǎhm·lór will do short trips around town for 20B. They congregate near and across from the bus stop.

A good way to see the Chiang Saen area is on two wheels. Mountain bikes and motorcycles can be rented at **motorcycle rental** (☏08 9429 5798; 247/1 Th Phahonyothin; ⏰9am-5pm) and **Angpao Chiangsaen Tour** (☏0 5365 0143; www.angpaochiangsaentour.com; Th Phahonyothin; ⏰9am-8pm). The latter can also provide

a vehicle with driver, and conducts a variety of local tours.

Around Chiang Saen

SOP RUAK   สบรวก

The borders of Myanmar, Thailand and Laos meet at Sop Ruak, the official 'centre' of the Golden Triangle, at the confluence of Nam Ruak and the Mekong River.

In historical terms, 'Golden Triangle' actually refers to a much larger geographic area, stretching thousands of square kilometres into Myanmar, Laos and Thailand, within which the opium trade was prevalent. Nevertheless, hoteliers and tour operators have been quick to cash in on the name by referring to the tiny village of Sop Ruak as 'the Golden Triangle', conjuring up images of illicit adventure, exotic border areas and opium caravans.

But that's all history, and today the only caravan you're likely to see is the endless parade of huge buses carrying package tourists. The opium is now fully relegated to museums, and even the once-beautiful natural setting has largely been obscured by ATMs, countless stalls selling tourist tat, and the loud announcements from the various temples.

On the good side, the two opium-related museums, the House of Opium and Hall of Opium, are both worth a visit, and a boat trip is an enjoyable way to pass an hour. But the only reason to consider a stay here is if you've already booked a room in one of the area's outstanding luxury hotels.

◉ Sights & Activities

Hall of Opium   MUSEUM

(หอฝิ่น; admission 200B; ⏰8.30am-4pm Tue-Sun) One kilometre north of Sop Ruak on a plot of about 40 hectares opposite the Anantara Golden Triangle Resort & Spa, the Mah Fah Luang Foundation has established the 5600-sq-metre Hall of Opium. The goal of this impressive facility is to become the world's leading exhibit and research facility for the study of opiate use around the world. The multimedia exhibition includes a fascinating history of opium, and examines the effects of abuse on individuals and society. Well balanced and worth seeing.

House of Opium   MUSEUM

(บานฝิ่น; www.houseofopium.com; admission 50B; ⏰7am-7pm) This small museum with historical displays pertaining to opium culture is

NORTHERN THAILAND CHIANG RAI PROVINCE

DAY BOAT TO JINGHONG

Although it was once possible to travel by cargo ship from Chiang Saen to Jinghong in China, now it's only permitted via passenger boat through **Maekhong Delta Travel** (☎0 5364 2517; www.maekhongtravel.com; Maekhong Delta Boutique Hotel, 230/5-6 Th Phahonyothin, Mae Sai; one way 820 yuan/3500B; ☺9am-5pm) in Mae Sai.

The trip from Chiang Saen to Jinghong takes 15 hours when conditions are good. During drier months (typically March to May) boats don't run, as rocks and shallows can hamper the way. Boats usually depart from Chiang Saen on Monday, Wednesday and Friday at 5am, but this is not set in stone and it's important to call ahead before you make plans.

To do this trip you must already have your visa for China – several guest houses in town can arrange this for you, but it's quicker to arrange from Chiang Mai or Bangkok. If you already have a visa, tickets can be arranged at most local guest houses and hotels, or through **Chiang Saen Tour and Travel** (☎0 5377 7051; chiangsaen2004@yahoo.com; 64 Th Rimkhong; ☺8am-6pm).

worth a peek. Exhibits include all the various implements used in the planting, harvest, use and trade of the *Papaver somniferum* resin, including pipes, weights, scales and so on, plus photos and maps with labels in English. The museum is at the southeastern end of Sop Ruak, virtually across from Phra Chiang Saen Si Phaendin.

Phra Chiang Saen Si Phaendin MONUMENT (พระเชียงแสนสี่แผ่นดิน; admission free; ☺7am-9pm) The first sight you'll inevitably see in Sop Ruak is Phra Chiang Saen Si Phaendin, a giant Buddha statue financed by a Thai-Chinese foundation. The statue straddles a boat-like platform, and visitors here are encouraged to donate by rolling coins from an elevated platform behind the statue.

Wat Prathat Pukhao TEMPLE (วัดพระธาตุภูเขา; admission free) Next to the House of Opium are some steps up to the Buddhist Wat Prathat Pukhao, from where you get the best viewpoint of the Mekong meeting of Laos, Myanmar and Thailand.

Mekong River Cruises RIVER CRUISE (1hr cruise max 5 people per boat 400B) Local long-tail boat trips can be arranged through several local agents or at the various piers. The typical trip involves a circuit around a large island and upriver for a view of the Burmese casino hotel.

You can also arrange to stop off at a Lao village on the large river island of **Don Sao**, roughly halfway between Sop Ruak and Chiang Saen. The Lao immigration booth here is happy to allow day visitors onto the island without a Lao visa. A 20B arrival tax is collected from each visitor. There's not a lot to

see, but there's an official post office where you can mail letters or postcards with a Laos PDR postmark, a few shops selling T-shirts and Lao handicrafts, and the Sala Beer Lao, where you can quaff Beer Lao and munch on Lao snacks.

🍴 Sleeping & Eating

The only reason to stay in or around Sop Ruak is to take advantage of some of northern Thailand's best upscale lodgings. Those on a budget are advised to go to Chiang Saen. There are several tourist-oriented restaurants overlooking the Mekong River.

Four Seasons Tented Camp HOTEL $$$ (☎0 5391 0200; www.fourseasons.com; minimum 3-night stay 225,450-255,450B; ※@⊚≋) If you can fit it into your schedule (and budget), this safari-inspired 'tented camp' resort is among the most truly unique accommodation experiences in Thailand. Located at a secluded spot of riverside jungle outside Sop Ruak, a brief boat ride is necessary to reach the vast compound of 15 hillside tents. The tents are luxurious and decked out in colonial-era safari paraphernalia, the focus of which is an incredibly inviting copper and resin bathtub. There's no TV or iPod dock, rather guests are encouraged to take in the natural setting (tip: tent 15 looks over an elephant bathing area) and take part in daily activities, which range from mahout training to spa treatment. A minimum stay of at least three nights is required, and the fee covers every aspect of the stay, from airport pick-up to food and drink.

Anantara Golden Triangle Resort & Spa
HOTEL $$$

(☎0 5378 4084; www.anantara.com; r/ste incl breakfast 16,500/18000B; ✴@☜❋) This award-winning resort takes up a large patch of beautifully landscaped ground directly opposite the Hall of Opium. The rooms combine Thai and international themes, and all have balconies looking over the Mekong. A Jacuzzi, squash and tennis courts, gym, sauna and spa round out the luxury amenities. Special attractions include the King's Cup Elephant Polo Tournament and one- to three-day mahout-training packages.

❶ Getting There & Away

There are frequent *sŏrng·tăa·ou* to Chiang Saen (20B, every 20 minutes from 7am to noon) and Mae Sai (45B, every 40 minutes from 8am to 1pm), both of which can be flagged down along the main strip. It's an easy bicycle ride of 9km from Chiang Saen to Sop Ruak.

Chiang Khong
เชียงของ

POP 12,000

More remote yet livelier than its neighbour Chiang Saen, Chiang Khong is historically an important market town for local hill tribes and for trade with northern Laos. At one time the city was part of a small *meuang* (city-state) called Juon, founded in AD 701 by King Mahathai. Over the centuries Juon paid tribute to Chiang Rai, then Chiang Saen and finally Nan before being occupied by the Siamese in the 1880s. The territory of Chiang Khong extended all the way to Yunnan Province in China until the French turned much of the Mekong River's northern bank into French Indochina in 1893.

Today the riverside town is a popular travellers' gateway into Laos (see the boxed text, p333). From Huay Xai, on the opposite side of the Mekong, it's a two-day slow boat trip to Luang Prabang. And for those who have set their sights even further, Huay Xai is only an eight-hour bus ride from Boten, a legal border crossing to and from China.

🛏 Sleeping

The vast majority of accommodation in Chiang Khong is geared towards the budget market.

Rai Saeng Arun
HOTEL $$$

(☎0 5391 8255; www.raisaengarun.com; 2 Moo 3, Ban Phakub; bungalows incl breakfast 3000-3750B;

✴☜) Located 22km from Chiang Khong on Rte 4007, which leads to Chiang Saen, this resort brings together 14 bungalows in an attractive, natural setting. Some are perched on a hillside, while others are near stream-bordered rice fields, and three are at the edge of the Mekong River. All are stylish and comfortable, feature balconies and open-air showers, and are connected by bridged walkways over rice fields. The restaurant looks over the Mekong and serves dishes using vegetables and herbs from the resort's organic farm. Considerable discounts are available during the low season.

Baanrimtaling
GUEST HOUSE $

(☎0 5379 1613; maleewan_th@yahoo.com; 99/2 Moo 3; dm 100-120B, r 150-450B; @☜) The rooms here are pretty run-of-the-mill for this price range, and the location isn't exactly ideal, but the homelike atmosphere and gentle service may have you staying a bit longer than you planned. Great river views certainly don't hurt, and extras like free wi-fi, free bicycle use, free delivery to the pier, and Thai cooking lessons seal the deal.

Namkhong Riverside Hotel
HOTEL $$

(☎0 5379 1796; www.namkhongriverside.com; 174-176 Th Sai Klang; r incl breakfast 800-1200B; ✴@☜) This modern three-storey hotel holds heaps of clean, neat rooms, most with private balconies overlooking the river. The cheaper rooms are at ground level, and all rooms suffer from the noise pollution of nightly karaoke parties.

Portside Hotel
HOTEL $

(☎0 5365 5238; portsidehotel@hotmail.com; 546 Th Sai Klang; r with fan/air-con 300/500B; ✴@☜) This good-value hotel features two floors of tidy but slightly cramped rooms. There are no river views, but a communal rooftop area makes up for this.

Chiang Khong Green Inn
HOTEL $

(☎0 5379 1009; www.chiangkhong-greeninn.com; 89/4 Th Sai Klang; r with fan/air-con 200/580B; ✴@☜) The cheaper rooms in this new backpacker place are tight and share bathrooms, but the rooms with air-con are large and have TVs. All guests have free access to computers and wi-fi.

Chiang Khong Teak Garden Hotel
HOTEL $$$

(☎0 5379 2008; www.chiangkhongteakgarden. com; 666 Th Sai Klang; r 1500-1800B; ✴@☜) The

Chiang Khong

0 |====| 250 m
0 |====| 0.1 miles

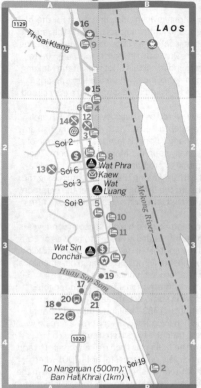

Chiang Khong

🛏 Sleeping
1. Baan-Fai Guest House A2
2. Baanrimtaling.................................B4
3. Ban Tammila A2
4. Boom House..................................A2
5. Chiang Khong Green Inn.....................A3
6. Chiang Khong Teak Garden
   Hotel.......................................A2
7. Chiangkhong River View Hotel...........B3
8. Namkhong Riverside Hotel................B2
9. Portside Hotel A1
10. PP Home....................................B3
11. Rimnaum Guest House.....................B3

🍴 Eating
12. Bamboo Mexican House...................A2
13. Khao Soi Pa Orn...........................A2
14. Lomtawan A2
    Rim Nam ....(see 11)

ℹ Information
15. Easy Trip.................................A1
16. Immigration Office.......................A1
17. Market....................................A3
18. Market....................................A4
19. Market....................................B3

🚌 Transport
20. Buses to Bangkok..........................A4
21. Buses to Chiang Mai & Chiang
    Rai.......................................A4
22. Sŏrng·tǎa·ou to Chiang Saen.............A4

NORTHERN THAILAND CHIANG KHONG

new duplex bungalows at Chiang Khong's newest, most expensive digs are well outfitted and cosy, if lacking in atmosphere. The price depends on garden or river view.

PP Home GUEST HOUSE $
(Baan Pak Pon; ☎0 5365 5092; baanpakpon@hotmail.co.th; r 350-600B; ❋@☎) One of a dwindling number of accommodation places still owned by locals, this attractive wooden house features large rooms with wood panelling, each with a private balcony looking over the river, and a couple of new rooms in an adjacent cement add-on.

Chiangkhong River View Hotel HOTEL $
(☎0 5379 1375; www.chiangkhong.com/riverviewhotel.htm; 141 Moo 12; r 500B; ❋☎) At the southern end of town, this tall building holds several virtually identical tiny rooms, all with air-con, TV and fridge. Locally owned, and good value.

Rimnaum Guest House HOTEL $
(☎0 5365 5680; suti_ja@hotmail.com; 166 Moo 12; r with fan/air-con 350/500B; ❋☎) This riverside place unites 20 identical, but spacious and clean rooms.

Baan-Fai Guest House GUEST HOUSE $
(☎0 5379 1394; 108 Th Sai Klang; r 100-200B; ☎) Located in an attractive wooden Thai home, the rooms don't quite live up to the exterior, but they're clean and represent a decent choice if funds are running low.

Ban Tammila HOTEL $
(☎0 5379 1234; baantammila@hotmail.com; 113 Th Sai Klang; r & bungalows 350-650B; ❋☎) Although the exterior looks a bit ragged, the stylish rooms and bungalows here are neat and decorated in warm colours.

Boom House HOTEL $
(☎0 5365 5136; www.boomhouseresort.com; 406/1 Th Sai Klang; dm 100B, r 250-400B; ❋☎) This multilevel place has a variety of plain

MEKONG'S GIANT CATFISH

The Mekong River stretch that passes Chiang Khong is an important habitat for the *blah bèuk* (giant Mekong catfish, Pangasianodon gigas to ichthyologists), among the largest freshwater fish in the world. A *blah bèuk* takes at least six and possibly 12 years (no one's really sure) to reach full size, when it will measure 2m to 3m in length and weigh up to 300kg. Although the adult fish have only been found in certain stretches of the Mekong River, it's thought that the fish originate in Qinghai Province (where the Mekong originates) in northern China and swim all the way to the middle Mekong, where they spend much of their adult lives.

In Thailand and Laos the mild-tasting flesh is revered as a delicacy and the fish are taken between late April and June when the river depth is just 3m to 4m and the fish are swimming upriver. Ban Hat Khrai, 1.5km from Chiang Khong, is famous as being one of the few places where *blah bèuk* are still occasionally caught. Before netting them, Thai and Lao fishermen hold a special annual ceremony to propitiate Chao Mae Pla Beuk, a female deity thought to preside over the giant catfish. Among the rituals comprising the ceremony are chicken sacrifices performed aboard the fishing boats. After the ceremony is completed, fishing teams draw lots to see who casts the first net, and then take turns casting.

In recent years only a few catfish have been captured in a typical season (some years have resulted in no catches at all). The catfish hunters' guild is limited to natives of Ban Hat Khrai, and the fishermen sell the meat on the spot for up to 500B or more per kilo (a single fish can bring 100,000B in Bangkok); most of it ends up in Bangkok, since local restaurants in Huay Xai and Chiang Khong can't afford such prices.

Although the *blah bèuk* is on the Convention on International Trade in Endangered Species (CITES) list of endangered species, there is some debate as to just how endangered it is. Because of the danger of extinction, in 1983 Thailand's Inland Fisheries Department developed a program to breed the fish in captivity. Every time a female was caught, it was kept alive until a male was netted, then the eggs were removed (by massaging the female's ovaries) and put into a pan; the male was then milked for sperm and the eggs fertilised in the pan. The program was largely unsuccessful until 2001 when 70,000 hatchlings survived. The fish were distributed to fishery centres elsewhere in the country, some of which have had moderate success breeding the fish, mostly in ponds in the central Thai province of Suphanburi. Because of this, *blah bèuk* is again being seen on menus around the country.

At the moment the greatest threats to the wild Mekong catfish's survival are the planned construction of 11 dams across the Mekong River, a potential obstacle to the fish's migration, and the blasting of Mekong River rapids in China, which is robbing the fish of important breeding grounds.

but tidy rooms, the more expensive of which have air-con, TV and fridge.

🍴 Eating & Drinking

Khao Soi Pa Orn　　NORTHERN THAI **$**
(no roman-script sign; Soi 6; mains 15-30B; ⏰8am-4pm) You may think you know *kôw soy*, the famous northern curry noodle soup, but the version served in Chiang Khong forgoes the coconut milk and replaces it with a rich minced pork and tomato mixture. There's no English-language sign here; look for the gigantic highway pillar at the eastern end of Soi 6.

Nangnuan　　THAI **$$**
(Ban Hat Khrai; mains 30-150B; ⏰8am-9pm) The menu here boasts that the restaurant is 'At the first great catfish's reproduction place', but it isn't all about sexy locality; they also do some tasty food. Freshwater fish from the Mekong is the emphasis here, and it's prepared in a variety of ways, as the extensive English-language menu describes.

Bamboo Mexican House　　INTERNATIONAL **$**
(Th Sai Klang; mains 30-180B; ⏰7am-8pm) Run by the manager of a now-defunct guest house, the chef of this tiny restaurant/bakery learned to make Mexican dishes from her American and Mexican guests. To be

honest, though, we never got past the delicious homemade breads and cakes. Opens early, and boxed lunches can be assembled for the boat ride to Luang Prabang.

Rim Nam
THAI $$

(mains 30-120B; ⊙11am-9pm) Part of Rimnaum Guest House is this simple indoor-outdoor restaurant that overlooks the Mekong. The bilingual menu is much shorter than the Thai menu; *yam* (spicy salads) are the house specialities, but the kitchen can whip up almost anything.

Lomtawan
THAI $$

(354 Th Sai Klang; mains 60-180B; ⊙lunch & dinner) If you don't require river views, this cosy, candlelit home is a great dinner option. The English-language menu is extensive and includes daring options such as green curry with salmon. Stay late, and the soundtrack becomes live and the place gradually transforms into an intimate bar.

ⓘ Information

A handful of banks have branches in town with ATMs and foreign-exchange services.

Easy Trip (☎0 5365 5174, 0 86997 7246; www. discoverylaos.com; Th Sai Klang; ⊙9am-7pm) This professional travel agency organises boats

and buses to Laos, as well as minibuses to Chiang Mai (250B) and Pai (450B). Flights in Thailand and to Laos can be booked here. Many guest houses in Chiang Khong offer similar services.

Internet (Th Sai Klang; per hr 30B; ⊙10am-10pm) On the main street roughly across from Bamboo Mexican House.

ⓘ Getting There & Away

Chiang Khong has no official bus terminal; buses pick up and drop off passengers at various points near the market, south of the centre of town. Arrive at the bus stop at least 30 minutes early or buy tickets in advance from the office or from Easy Trip. *Sŏrng·tăa·ou* bound for Chiang Saen (100B, frequent departures from 7.30am to noon) also depart from this area.

Bangkok (493B to 888B, 14 hours, frequent departures from 3.05pm to 4.10pm)

Chiang Mai (211B to 272B, 2½ hours, every 30 minutes from 4.30am to 3.45pm)

Chiang Rai (65B, 2½ hours, every 30 minutes from 4.30am to 3.45pm)

Phayao (111B to 142B, three hours, every 30 minutes from 4.30am to 3.45pm)

ⓘ Getting Around

A săhm·lór from the bus station to Tha Reua Bak, the border crossing to Laos, costs 30B.

BORDER CROSSING: CHIANG KHONG TO HUAY XAI

Long-tail boats to Huay Xai, Laos (30B), leave frequently from Tha Reua Bak, a pier at the northern end of Chiang Khong, from 8am to 6pm. A vehicle ferry also crosses a few times daily (except Sundays) between the main Thai immigration point and the slowboat landing in Huay Xai costing 500B for motorcycles, 1000B for cars (or 1500B on the 5pm sailing).

Foreigners can purchase a 30-day visa for Laos upon arrival in Huay Xai for US$30 to US$42, depending on nationality. There is an extra US$1 charge after 4pm and on weekends, and if you don't have a passport-style mugshot they'll charge 40B extra. On your return to Thailand, immigration will stamp your passport with a new 15-day visa (see p766).

Once on the Lao side you can continue by road to Luang Nam Tha and Udomxai, or by boat down the Mekong River to Luang Prabang. If you're bound for the capital, **Lao Airlines** (☎+856 211 026, +856 211 494; www.laoairlines.com) has flights from Huay Xai to Vientiane three times a week for US$94.

If time is on your side, the daily slow boat (900B, 10am) to Luang Prabang takes two days, including a night in the village of Pak Beng. Avoid the noisy fast boats (1450B, six to seven hours) that ply the Huay Xai to Luang Prabang route, as there have been reports of bad accidents. Booking tickets through an agent such as Easy Trip (p333) costs slightly more, but they arrange tickets for you, provide transport from your guest house and across the Mekong River, and provide a boxed lunch for the boat ride.

If you already hold a Chinese visa, it's now also possible to go more or less directly to China from Chiang Khong. After obtaining a 30-day Laos visa-on-arrival in Huay Xai, simply board one of the buses that go directly to the Xishuangbanna town of Mengla (110,000K, eight hours, 8.30am daily) or Jinghong (150,000K, 10 hours, 7.30am Tuesday, Thursday and Saturday) via the Lao border town of Boten.

PHAYAO PROVINCE

Phayao   พะเยา
POP 20,000

Few people, including many Thais, are aware of this quiet but attractive northern city. Perhaps in an overzealous effort to remedy this, a tourist brochure we came across described Phayao as 'The Vienna of South East Asia'. Although this is just *slightly* stretching the truth, Phayao is certainly one of the more pleasant towns in northern Thailand. Its setting on Kwan Phayao, a vast wetland, gives the town a back-to-nature feel that's utterly lacking in most Thai cities, and the tree-lined streets, temples and old wooden houses of 'downtown' Phayao provide a pleasing old-school Thai touch.

The little-visited town is the perfect place to break up your journey to/from Chiang Rai, or as a bookend to our suggested driving trip from Chiang Khong.

◉ Sights & Activities

Kwan Phayao   WETLANDS
(กว๊านพะเยา) This vast body of water is the largest swamp in northern Thailand, and is a symbol of Phayao. Although naturally occurring, the water level is artificially controlled, otherwise the wetlands would tend to go dry outside of the wet season. Framed by mountains, the swamp is in fact more scenic than the name suggests, and is the setting for what must be among the most beautiful sunsets in Thailand. Rowing crews can be seen practising in the evenings, and there's a pier at the southern end of Th Chai Kwan where there are **boat rides** (20B) to what remains of **Wat Tiloke Aram**, a submerged 500-year-old temple. There are ambitious plans to rebuild the temple, one of many submerged religious structures in Kwan Phayao. In addition to lost Buddhist artefacts, there are at least 50 types of fish native to these waters, and there's a small **fish breeding area** where for 5B you can feed the fish.

Wat Sri Khom Kham   TEMPLE
(วัดศรีโคมคำ) Phayao's most important temple is thought to date back to 1491, but its present structure was finished in 1923. The immense prayer hall holds the Phra Jao Ton Luang, the largest Chiang Saen-era Buddha statue in the country. Standing 18m high, legend has it that the construction of the statue took more than 30 years. It's not the

---

WORTH A TRIP

THE LONG WAY TO PHAYAO

If you're in Chiang Khong and happen to have your own wheels, we have an excellent suggestion for a drive. Rtes 1155 and 1093 are among Thailand's most dramatic land routes, hugging steep mountainsides along the Thai–Lao border and passing waterfalls, incredible vistas and national parks. If you need a destination you can continue all the way to Phayao, a little-visited province and town with ample accommodation and good food.

From Chiang Khong, the trip is as straightforward as heading south on Rte 1020 and following the signs to **Phu Chi Fa**, a national park near the Lao border. For Thailand, the signs are surprisingly clear, but a good companion is the Golden Triangle Rider's *Golden Triangle* map.

At the mountaintop village of Doi Pha Tang, consider a quick detour to **Pratu Siam**, at 1653m one of Thailand's most impressive viewpoints. There is basic lodging and food here.

Rte 1093 narrows and becomes markedly less populated as you approach Phu Chi Fa, a mountaintop that offers high-altitude views into Laos. There are a few different ways to approach the peak, the most popular being via Ban Rom Fah Thai. There is a variety of accommodation and some basic restaurants on either side of Phu Chi Fa.

Upon passing Phu Chi Fa, stay on Rte 1093 and follow the signs to **Ban Huak**. This is a picturesque village in Phayao Province, 2km from the Lao border. There's a border market on the 10th and 30th of every month, homestay-style accommodation in the town, and nearby **Nam Tok Phu Sang** is a unique waterfall of thermally heated water.

From Ban Huak, follow signs to Chiang Kham, then take Rte 1021 to Chun, from where it's a straight shot to Phayao (via Dok Kham Tai), itself another worthwhile destination.

If you do the drive in one go, allow at least six hours, including stops for taking photos, coffee and a meal.

most beautiful or well-proportioned Buddha image in Thailand, but it certainly is impressive. The ordination hall that is elevated over Kwan Phayao features graceful modern wall paintings. Also on the grounds of the wát is a Buddhist sculpture garden, which includes gory, larger-than-life depictions of Buddhist hell.

Next door to the temple is the **Phayao Cultural Exhibition Hall** (Th Phahonyothin; admission 40B; ☺8.30am-4.30pm), a two-storey museum packed with artefacts and a good amount of information on local history and culture in English. Standout items include a unique 'black' Buddha statue, and a fossil of two embracing crabs labelled 'Wonder Lover'. The temple and museum are about 2km from the northern end of Th Chaykawan.

Wat Li
TEMPLE

(วัดลี) Just off Rte 1 opposite the turn-off to Phayao, Wat Li features a small **museum** (admission by donation; ☺9am-3pm) with a decent variety of items from the previous Chiang Saen eras.

Wat Phra That Jom Thong
TEMPLE

(วัดพระธาตุจอมทอง) This is an attractive *chedi* on a wooded hilltop 3km from the centre of town.

🛏 Sleeping

Huean Phak Jum Jai
GUEST HOUSE $

(☎0 548 2659; 37/5-6 Th Phrasart; r 600B; ✻⎙☎) Of the handful of hotel-like places near Kwan Phayao calling themselves homestays, this one is the nicest. Rooms are spacious and clean and decked out in handsome wood. The sign says 'Home Stay & Guest House' and it's just off Th Chaykawan, a short walk from the waterfront.

Gateway Hotel
HOTEL $$$

(☎0 5441 1333; 7/36 Soi 2, Th Pratu Khlong; r incl breakfast 1000-1200B; ste incl breakfast 2500B; ✻@☎⎙) Despite being the city's most upmarket hotel, the rooms here are a bit on the tired side, although the 'sea view' rooms on the upper floors do boast great views of Kwan Phayao. It's next door to the bus terminal.

Tharn Thong Hotel
HOTEL $

(☎0 5443 1302; 56-59 Th Donsanam; d 170-300B; ✻☎) Stark fan-cooled rooms are available in the main building, while more comfortable air-con rooms can be found in the

complex behind it. It's near the town's police station.

Wattana Hotel
HOTEL $

(☎0 5443 1203; 69 Th Donsanam; fan/air-con 150/280B; ✻) Next to the Tharn Thong, Wattana offers a nearly identical package, but the rooms aren't quite as tidy as its neighbour's.

🍴 Eating & Drinking

For such a small town, Phayao has an amazing abundance of food, much of it quite good. During the day, dozens of vendors sell similar repertoires of grilled fish and papaya salad along the northern end of Th Chaykawan. Kaat Boran, a largely food-based night market, sets up every evening from 6pm to 10pm around the King Ngam Muang monument. Another extensive **night market** (Th Rob Wiang) convenes along the north side of Th Rob Wiang every evening.

There are literally dozens of lakefront restaurants along Kwan Phayao, beginning at Th Thakawan and extending all the way to the public park.

Chue Chan
THAI $$

(Th Chaykawan; dishes 80-240B; ☺lunch & dinner; ✻) This place has received the most acclaim from the various Thai food authorities. The lengthy menu, which has both pictures and English, spans dishes you won't find elsewhere, such as stuffed pig leg or sour fish fried with egg. The restaurant is the tallest building on the busy restaurant stretch of Th Chaykawan.

Khao Soi Saeng Phian
NORTHERN THAI $

(no roman-script sign; Th Thakawan; dishes 25-40B; ☺9am-3pm) One of the better bowls of *kôw soy* in this neck of the north is available at this family-run restaurant, a block from the waterfront. *Kà·nŏm jeen nám ngée·o* and various other noodle dishes are also available. Fans of northern-style noodles will be happy to know that there are at least four other shops boasting similar menus within a block radius of the intersection of Th Thakawan and Th Rajchawong.

ℹ Information

There are several banks along Th Donsanam, near the town's morning market, many with ATM and exchange services.

Internet@Cafe (Th Pratu Khlong; per hr 20B; ☺10am-10pm) Other shops offering internet access dot Th Donsanam.

Post office (Th Donsanam; ⊙8.30am-4.30pm Mon-Fri, 9am-noon Sat & Sun)

❶ Getting There & Away

Phayao's bus station, at the northern end of Th Chaykawan, is quite busy, primarily because the city lies on the main north–south highway. Because of this, if you're bound for Bangkok, it's possible to hop on one of the 40 or so buses that pass through the station from points further north.

There are also minivans to Chiang Rai (62B, one hour) and Phrae (98B, two hours), both departing approximately every hour from 7am to 7pm.

Destinations from Phayao include:

Bangkok (400B to 801B, 11 hours, frequent departures from 8.45am to 9.30am and 7.45pm to 8pm)

Chiang Mai (115B to 230B, three hours, every hour from 7.30am to 5.30pm)

Chiang Rai (62B to 99B, two hours, every 40 minutes from 7am to 5pm)

Nan (123B, four hours, 1.30pm)

PHRAE PROVINCE

Phrae is a rural, mountainous province most often associated with teak. Despite a nationwide ban on logging, there's not a whole lot of the hardwood left, and the little that does exist is under threat.

Phrae   แพร่

POP 18,000

Walking around the old city of Phrae one is struck by similarities with the historical Lao city of Luang Prabang: ample greenery, traditional wood buildings and scenic temples dominate the scenery, and monks form a significant part of the traffic. The city's residents must be among the friendliest folks in Thailand, and Phrae's location on the banks of the Mae Nam Yom and its ancient wall invite comparisons with Chiang Mai. Despite all this, Phrae is a little-visited city and a great destination for those who require little more than a few low-key attractions, good local food and cheery company.

◉ Sights

Wat Luang   TEMPLE

(วัดหลวง) This is the oldest wát in Phrae, probably dating from the founding of the city in the 12th or 13th century. **Phra That Luang Chang Kham**, the large octagonal Lanna-style *chedi,* sits on a square base with elephants supporting it on all four sides. As is sometimes seen in Phrae and Nan, the *chedi* is occasionally swathed in Thai Lü fabric.

The verandah of the main *wí·hǎhn* is in the classic Luang Prabang-Lan Xang style but has unfortunately been bricked in with laterite. Opposite the front of the *wí·hǎhn* is **Pratu Khong**, part of the city's original entrance gate. No longer used as a gate, it now contains a statue of Chao Pu, an early Lanna ruler.

Also on the temple grounds is a **museum** displaying temple antiques, ceramics and religious art dating from the Lanna, Nan, Bago and Mon periods. A 16th-century, Phrae-made sitting Buddha on the 2nd floor is particularly exquisite. There are also some 19th-century photos with English labels on display, including some gruesome shots of a beheading. The museum is usually open weekends only, but the monks will sometimes open it on weekdays on request.

Vongburi House   MUSEUM

(บ้านวงศ์บุรี; 50 Th Kham Leu; admission 30B; ⊙9am-5pm) The two-storey teak house of the last prince of Phrae has been converted into a private museum. It was constructed between 1897 and 1907 for Luang Phongphibun and his wife Chao Sunantha, who once held a profitable teak concession in the city. Elaborate carvings on gables, eaves, balconies and above doors and windows are in good condition. Inside, many of the house's 20 rooms display late-19th-century teak antiques, documents (including early-20th-century slave concessions), photos and other artefacts from the bygone teak-dynasty era. Most are labelled in English as well as Thai.

Wat Phra Non   TEMPLE

(วัดพระนอน) Located west of Wat Luang is a 300-year-old wát named after its highly revered reclining *prá norn* (reclining Buddha image). The *bòht* (central sanctuary) was built around 200 years ago and has an impressive roof with a separate, two-tiered portico and gilded, carved, wooden facade with Ramayana scenes. The *wí·hǎhn* behind the *bòht* contains the Buddha image, swathed in Thai Lü cloth with bead and foil decoration.

Wat Jom Sawan   TEMPLE

(วัดจอมสวรรค์) Outside the old city on Th Ban Mai, this Buddhist temple was built by local Shan in the late 19th and early 20th centuries, and shows Shan and Burmese influences throughout. An adjacent copper-crowned

THE DANCING TIGER

Kaeng Sua Ten (Dancing Tiger Rapids) are a series of rocky outcrops along the Mae Nam Yom, in Phrae's Song district. Part of Mae Yom National Park, the rapids are wild and beautiful, and are also the site of one of the more long-standing environmental conflicts in Thailand.

Since the early 1980s, the Thai government has repeatedly announced plans to build a dam across the Mae Nam Yom at Kaeng Sua Ten. Villagers in Tambon Sa-lab, the closest settlement to Kaeng Sua Ten, have vocally, and occasionally violently, objected to the plan. They claim that the dam would irrevocably alter their traditional lifestyle, forcing an estimated 2700 families to move away from their homes, and flood 3200 hectares of land, some of which includes Thailand's last remaining natural stands of golden teak.

Many elsewhere in Phrae and northern Thailand would like to see the dam built, as it is claimed that it will help control rampant flooding of the Mae Yom during the wet season and manage water during frequent droughts. Politicians in Bangkok say that the dam will provide additional power for the country and irrigation for farmers in provinces south of Phrae. And perhaps most significantly, dam building has been an important part of the king's rural development policy for several decades, and as recently as 1995 the monarch publicly pushed for the dam to be built.

In reality, the government's reasons for proposing the dam have inconsistently fluctuated between a need for power and irrigation, relying on whichever argument is more popular at the time. At one point the World Bank declined to fund the project, stating that the government's environmental impact assessment was incomplete. And many opponents have pointed out that the proposed site for the dam lies directly on a fault line.

In 2008 Samak Sundaravej became one of the more recent prime ministers to revive plans to build the dam. When confronted with concerns of the dam's potential environmental impact, Samak claimed that there were no teak trees and only 'three stupid peacocks' left in the area (the comments were made on World Environment Day, and Samak also claimed that the dam would reduce the effects of global warming). Villagers in Sa-lab reacted to the comments by burning an effigy of Samak and 'ordaining' several golden teak trees near Kaeng Sua Ten with orange monastic robes, a method of environmental protest that makes the trees 'sacred' and thus less likely to be cut down.

As recent as 2010 there has been talk of reviving the project, but for now plans are at a stalemate, largely the result of political instability rather than any change in government policy. What is certain is that plans to build a dam at Kaeng Sua Ten have caused many to question the concept of development in Thailand, and will continue to embody the struggle between poor rural Thais, who have little say in the development of their own environment, and the often authoritarian rule of the Bangkok-based central Thai government.

chedi has lost most of its stucco to reveal the artful brickwork beneath. Since a recent renovation, Wat Jom Sawan is more of a museum piece than a functioning temple.

Wat Phra Baht Ming Meuang TEMPLE

(วัดพระบาทมิ่งเมือง) Across from the post office within the old city, Wat Phra Baht Ming Meuang combines two formerly separate temple compounds (one of which contains a **museum** that is sporadically open), a Buddhist school, an old *chedi,* an unusual octagonal drum tower made entirely of teak and the highly revered Phra Kosai, which closely resembles the Phra Chinnarat in Phitsanulok.

Baan Pratubjai MUSEUM

(บ้านประทับใจ; admission 40B; ⊙8am-5pm) On the outskirts of the town is Baan Pratubjai (Impressive House), a large northern Thai-style teak house that was built using more than 130 teak logs, each over 300 years old. Opened in 1985, the house took four years to build, using timber taken from nine old rural houses. The interior pillars are ornately carved. The house is also filled with souvenir vendors and is rather tackily decorated, so don't take the moniker 'impressive' too seriously.

Pratubjai House is somewhat difficult to find; your best bet is to exit at the west gate of the former city wall and follow the signs,

Phrae

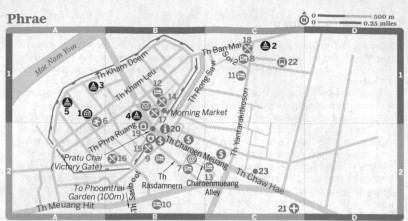

Phrae

◎ Sights
1 Vongburi House A1
2 Wat Jom Sawan C1
3 Wat Luang A1
4 Wat Phra Baht Ming Meuang B1
5 Wat Phra Non A1

🎯 Activities, Courses & Tours
6 Phrae Adventure A1

🛏 Sleeping
7 Bua Khao B2
8 Maeyom Palace Hotel C1
9 Nakhon Phrae Hotel B2
10 Nakhon Phrae Tower B2
11 Paradorn Hotel C1
12 Priwan's Homestay B1
13 Thep Vong Place C2

✗ Eating
14 Khao Soi Nok Noy B1
15 Night Market B2
16 Nok Bin B2
17 Pan Jai B1
18 Sod Cheon C1

◎ Shopping
19 Maw Hawm Anian B2

ⓘ Information
20 Loving Hut B2
21 Phrae Hospital C2

ⓘ Transport
22 Bus Terminal C1
23 Sŏrng·tăa·ou to Wat Phra That
    Cho Hae C2

turning right after the school. A săhm·lór here should cost about 60B.

🏃 Activities

Trekking & Rafting
Phrae has a burgeoning outdoor scene, largely revolving around the Mae Yom National Park and Kaeng Sua Ten areas.

Phrae Adventure TREKKING
(☏08 1033 9317; wa_divers@hotmail.com; 2 person min, per person per day 1000B; ⏱8am-8pm) Wa and his team lead a variety of trekking expeditions, ranging from one to seven days in Phrae's Mae Yom National Park, as well as rafting trips in Nan.

🛏 Sleeping

Phoomthai Garden HOTEL $$
(☏0 5462 7359; www.phoomthaitravel.com; 31 Th Sasiboot; r incl breakfast 900-1500B, bungalows incl breakfast 1500B; ❄@⏾) Although it's a bit of a hike from the old town, this boutique hotel is the best all-around choice in town. The rooms are modern and comfortable, and all have balconies overlooking the hotel's attractive garden. There are even a few wooden bungalows with huge bathrooms and inviting tubs. The hotel is about 300m south of the old walls on Th Sasiboot.

Bua Khao HOTEL $
(☏0 5451 1372; 8 Soi 1, Th Charoen Meuang; r 350-600B; ❄⏾) Tucked just off the main road, this

teak monstrosity has mostly small rooms, but heaps of character. Service is great and there's an inviting communal area (involving even more wood) on the ground floor.

Paradorn Hotel   HOTEL **$$**
(📞0 5451 1177; www.phraeparadorn.ob.tc; 177 Th Yantarakitkoson; r incl breakfast 360-650B; ste incl breakfast 800B; ❄@🐕) Probably the best budget option in town, you can't miss this place with its Burmese-style facade. The fan-cooled rooms have private balconies, and all rates include a simple breakfast. The hotel is on both sides of Th Yantarakitkoson, and there's also a museum dedicated to the Free Thai movement.

Maeyom Palace Hotel   HOTEL **$$$**
(📞0 5452 1028-34; wccphrae@hotmail.com; 181/6 Th Yantarakitkoson; r incl breakfast 1600-2000B, ste incl breakfast 3500-4000B; ❄@🐕🏊) Opposite the bus terminal, Phrae's top-end option has all the modern amenities: carpeted rooms with cable TV, sofa and minibar, and the city's only hotel pool. Discounts of up to 30% are typical in the low season.

Thep Vong Place   HOTEL **$**
(📞0 5452 1985; www.thepvongplace.com; 346/2 Th Charoen Meuang; r 350-500B; ❄@🐕) The large rooms here are outfitted with fittingly large TVs and fridges – the more expensive rooms pack in even more furniture. Thep Vong Place is in the tiny side street labelled Charoenmeuang Alley.

Priwan's Homestay   GUEST HOUSE **$**
(📞08 1764 8447; 1 Th Weera; s/d 150/200B; @) This enterprising local language teacher has opened up her vast wooden house to foreign guests. The six rooms are simply furnished and share a bathroom and a rambling vegetarian restaurant.

Nakhon Phrae Hotel   HOTEL **$**
(📞0 5451 1122; nkphrae@phrae.ksc.co.th; 69 Th Rasdamnern; r 290-400B; ❄@🐕) Being the closest accommodation to the old city has made this large hotel the most popular, but not necessarily the best budget option. Rooms definitely look their age and have tiny bathrooms, but are mostly clean and comfortable.

Nakhon Phrae Tower   HOTEL **$$**
(📞0 5452 1321; nakornphrae@yahoo.com; 3 Th Meuang Hit; r incl breakfast 550-650B; ste incl breakfast 1800-2500B; ❄@🐕) A large business-class hotel, this sister to the Nakhon Phrae lies a bit further from the old city.

🍴 Eating & Drinking

A small but fun night market convenes just outside the Pratu Chai (Victory Gate) intersection every evening. The vendor in front of the Chinese shrine makes tasty *sôm·đam,* tiny but tasty bowls of *kà·nŏm jeen nám ngée·o* and dishes of *kôw sôm,* a northern dish of rice cooked with tomatoes.

There are several restaurants serving local dishes along Rte 1022 as one approaches Wat Phra That Cho Hae.

Pan Jai   NORTHERN THAI **$**
(no roman-script sign; 2 Th Weera; mains 20-40B; ⊙7am-4pm) This open-air place combines everything we like in a restaurant; delicious local eats, attractive setting, good service and low prices. The emphasis is on *kà·nŏm jeen,* fresh rice noodles served with various curries and herbs, but there are a couple of different kinds of noodle soups, a variety of rice dishes and more. Everything's on display, so simply point to whatever looks tastiest.

Sod Cheon   CHINESE-THAI **$**
(Th Yantarakitkoson; mains 30-90B; ⊙11am-4am) On the crossroads, 50m north of the Maeyom Palace Hotel, is this simple but very popular Chinese/Thai restaurant. Choose from the big pots of Chinese-style soups or go for your usual Thai dishes. Good for late-night eats.

Loving Hut   VEGETARIAN **$**
(Th Charoen Meuang; mains 25-55B; ⊙10am-8.30pm; 🍴) At the entrance to the old town, this bright yellow place has a thick English-language menu of Thai-style veggie dishes.

Khao Soi Nok Noy   NORTHERN THAI **$**
(no roman-script sign; Th Weera; dishes 25-55B; ⊙10am-3pm) Just *kôw soy* – served with chicken, beef or pork – is served in this garden restaurant.

🛍 Shopping

Phrae is known for the distinctive *sêua môr hôrm,* the indigo-dyed cotton farmer's shirt seen all over northern Thailand. The cloth is made in Ban Thung Hong, just outside of the city.

Maw Hawm Anian   CLOTHING
(no roman-script sign; 36 Th Charoen Meuang; ⊙7am-8.30pm) A good place to buy *môr hôrm* in town, about 60m from the south-eastern gate (Pratu Chai) into the old city.

❶ Information

Government Savings Bank (Th Rong Saw; ⊘8.30am-3.30pm Mon-Fri) The ATM is next to the police station.

Krung Thai Bank (Th Charoen Meuang; ⊘8.30am-3.30pm Mon-Fri) Foreign-exchange service and ATM.

Internet cafe (Soi 1, Th Charoen Meuang; per hr 15B; ⊘10am-10pm) An internet/online games shop on the same soi as Bua Khao hotel.

Nok Bin (24 Th Wichairacha; ⊘10am-6pm) Khun Kung, a local journalist, and her husband have created a cheery cafe that also functions as an informal information centre for visitors. The couple prints a tourist map of Phrae that is updated regularly and can also arrange bicycle or motorcycle rental.

Phrae Hospital (☎0 5452 2444) Just east of Th Chaw Hae, southeast of town.

Post office (Th Charoen Meuang; ⊘8.30am-4.30pm Mon-Fri, 9am-noon Sat)

❶ Getting There & Away

Air

Solar Air (☎nationwide call centre 02 535 2455; www.solarair.co.th; Phrae airport) flies to Bangkok's Don Muang Airport every Monday and Friday, and the reverse on Sunday and Friday (2790B, 1½ hours).

Bus & Minivan

Unlike most cities in Thailand, Phrae's bus terminal is conveniently within walking distance of a few accommodation choices. There are also frequent minivans to Lampang (85B, two hours, 7am to 5pm) and Nan (78B, two hours, 6am to 6.15pm).

Bus destinations include:

Bangkok (318B to 636B, eight hours, frequent departures from 9.15am to noon and 6.30pm to 10.30pm)

Chiang Mai (137B to 274B, four hours, every hour from 6am to 5pm)

Chiang Rai (114B to 320B, four hours, frequent departures from 7am to 4pm)

Lampang (76B to 157B, two hours, every hour from 6am to 5pm)

Mae Sai (152B to 349B, five hours, frequent departures from 7am to 4pm)

Nan (58B to 162B, two hours, every hour from 7am to 8.30pm)

Phayao (70B to 196B, two hours, frequent departures from 7am to 4pm)

Train

Den Chai train station (☎0 5461 3260) is 23km from Phrae. There are frequent blue *sŏrng·tăa·ou* between Phrae's bus station and Den Chai (40B) from 6am to 5.30pm.

Major destinations from Den Chai station include Bangkok (155B to 1291B, nine to 11 hours, eight times daily) and Chiang Mai (72B to 549B, four to six hours, seven times daily). For other destinations call the **State Railway of Thailand** (☎nationwide call centre 1690; www.railway.co.th) or look at its website.

❶ Getting Around

A sǎhm·lór anywhere in the old town costs 30B. Motorcycle taxis are available at the bus terminal; a trip from here to Pratu Chai should cost around 40B.

Around Phrae

WAT PHRA THAT
CHO HAE   วัดพระธาตุช่อแฮ

On a hill about 9km southeast of town off Rte 1022, this *wát* (admission free) is famous for its 33m-high gilded *chedi*. Cho Hae is the name of the cloth that worshippers wrap around the *chedi* – it's a type of satin thought to have originated in Xishuangbanna (Sipsongpanna, literally '12,000 Rice Fields' in northern Thai), China. Like Chiang Mai's Wat Doi Suthep, this is an important pilgrimage site for Thais living in the north. Tiered *naga* stairs lead to the temple compound.

The interior of the *bòht* is rather tackily decorated with a gilded wooden ceiling, rococo pillars and walls with lotus-bud mosaics. The **Phra Jao Than Jai** Buddha image here, which is similar in appearance to the Phra Chinnarat in Phitsanulok, is reputed to impart fertility to women who make offerings to it.

The scenery along the road leading to the *wát* is picturesque and there is also an abundance of restaurants serving local dishes. *Sŏrng·tăa·ou* between Phrae and Phra That Cho Hae (20B) depart from near Talat Phrae Preeda, on Th Chaw Hae, from 6am to 4.30pm; outside of these hours a *sŏrng·tăa·ou* can be chartered for 400B.

PHAE MEUANG PHI   แพะเมืองผี

The name **Phae Meuang Phi** (admission free) means 'Ghost-Land', a reference to this strange geological phenomenon approximately 18km northeast of Phrae off Rte 101. Erosion has created bizarre pillars of soil and rock that look like giant fungi. The area has been made a provincial park; a few walking trails and viewpoints are recent additions. There are picnic pavilions in the park and food vendors selling *gài yâhng* (grilled, spiced chicken), *sôm·đam* and sticky rice near the entrance.

Getting to Phae Meuang Phi by public transport is complicated; you can charter a *sŏrng·tăa·ou* for about 600B or talk to Khun Kung at Nok Bin (p340) for alternatives.

NAN PROVINCE

Tucked into Thailand's northeastern corner, Nan is a remote province to be explored for its natural beauty. Nan's unique ethnic groups are another highlight and differ significantly from those in other northern provinces. Outside the Mae Nam Nan valley, the predominant hill tribes are Mien, with smaller numbers of Hmong, and dispersed throughout Nan are four lesser-known groups seldom seen outside this province: the Thai Lü, Mrabri, Htin and Khamu.

It's now also possible for foreign travellers to cross into Laos at the village of Ban Huay Kon, 140km north of Nan (see p348).

Nan น่าน

POP 20,000

Due to its remote location, Nan is not the kind of destination most travellers are going to stumble upon. And its largely featureless downtown isn't going to inspire many postcards home. But if you've taken the time to get here, you'll be rewarded by a city rich in both culture and history. Many of Nan's residents are Thai Lü, the ancestors of immigrants from Xishuangbanna, in southern China. This cultural legacy is seen in the city's art and architecture, particularly in its exquisite temples. A Lanna influence on the town can also be seen in the remains of the old city wall and several early wát.

History

For centuries Nan was an isolated, independent kingdom with few ties to the outside world. Ample evidence of prehistoric habitation exists, but it wasn't until several

---

THE MURALS OF WAT PHUMIN

Wat Phumin is northern Thailand's Sistine Chapel, and the images on its walls are now found on everything from knick-knacks at Chiang Mai's night bazaar to postcards sold in Bangkok. However, despite the happy scenes depicted, the murals were executed during a period that saw the end of Nan as a semi-independent kingdom. This resulted in several examples of political and social commentary manifesting themselves in the murals – a rarity in Thai religious art.

The murals commissioned by Jao Suliyaphong, the last king of Nan, include the *Khaddhana Jataka*, a relatively obscure story of one of the Buddha's lives that, according to Thai historian David K Wyatt in his excellent book, *Reading Thai Murals*, has never been illustrated elsewhere in the Buddhist world. The story, which is on the left side of the temple's northern wall, depicts an orphan in search of his parents. Wyatt argues that this particular tale was chosen as a metaphor for the kingdom of Nan, which also had been abandoned by a succession of 'parents', the Thai kingdoms of Sukhothai, Chiang Mai and Ayuthaya. At roughly the same time as the murals were painted, Nan was fully incorporated into Siam by King Rama V, and much of its territory was allotted to France. Apparent discontent with this decision can be seen in a scene on the west wall that shows two male monkeys attempting to copulate against a background that, not coincidentally according to Wyatt, resembles the French flag.

The murals are also valuable purely for their artistic beauty, something that is even more remarkable if one steps back and considers the limited palette of colours that the artist, Thit Buaphan, had to work with. The paintings are also fascinating for their fly-on-the-wall depictions of local life in Nan during the end of the 19th century. A depiction of three members of a hill tribe on the west wall includes such details as a man's immense goitre and a barking dog, suggesting this group's place as outsiders. Multiple depictions of a man wearing a feminine shawl, often seen performing traditionally female-only duties, are among the earliest depictions of a *gà·teu·i* (transsexual). And in what must be one of the art world's most superfluous cameos, the artist painted himself on the west wall, flirting with a woman. Considering that the murals took Thit Buaphan more than 20 years to complete, we'll allow him this excess.

Nan

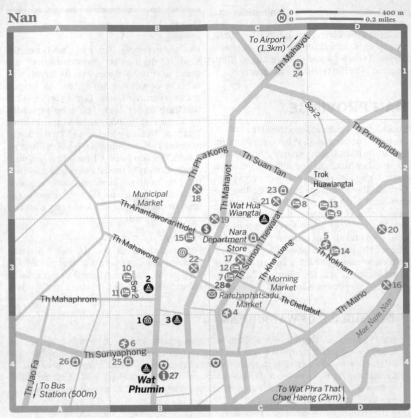

N 0 / 0 — 400 m / 0.2 miles

small *meuang* consolidated to form Nanthaburi in the mid-14th century that the city became a power to contend with. Towards the end of the 14th century Nan became one of the nine northern Thai-Lao principalities that comprised Lan Na Thai. The city-state flourished throughout the 15th century under the name Chiang Klang (Middle City), a reference to its position approximately midway between Chiang Mai (New City) and Chiang Thong (Golden City, which is today's Luang Prabang). The Burmese took control of the kingdom in 1558 and transferred many of the inhabitants to Burma as slaves; the city was all but abandoned until western Thailand was wrested from the Burmese in 1786. The local dynasty then regained local sovereignty and it remained semi-autonomous until 1931, when Nan finally (and reluctantly) accepted full Bangkok sponsorship.

⊙ Sights

Wat Phumin TEMPLE

(วัดภูมินทร์; admission free) Nan's most famous Buddhist temple is celebrated for its exquisite murals that were executed during the late 19th century by a Thai Lü artist called Thit Buaphan. For an insight into the historical significance of the murals, see the boxed text, p341.

The exterior of the temple takes the form of a cruciform *bòht* that was constructed in 1596 and restored during the reign of Chao Anantavorapitthidet (1867–74). The *bòht* exemplifies the work of Thai Lü architects, and the ornate altar sitting in the centre of the *bòht* has four sides, with four Sukhothai-style sitting Buddhas in *mahn wí·chai* ('victory over Mara' – with one hand touching the ground) posture, facing in each direction.

Nan

Nan National Museum   MUSEUM
(พิพิธภัณฑสถานแห่งชาติน่าน; Th Pha Kong; admission 100B; ⊙9am-4pm) Housed in the 1903-vintage palace of Nan's last two feudal lords, this museum first opened its doors in 1973. In terms of collection and content, it's one of the country's better provincial museums, and has English labels for most items.

The ground floor has ethnological exhibits covering the various ethnic groups found in the province. Among the items on display are silverwork, textiles, folk utensils and tribal costumes. On the 2nd floor are exhibits on Nan history, archaeology, local architecture, royal regalia, weapons, ceramics and religious art. Of the latter, the museum's collection of Buddha images includes some rare Lanna styles as well as the floppy-eared local styles. Also on display on the 2nd floor is a rare 'black' elephant tusk said to have been presented to a Nan lord over 300 years ago by the Khün ruler of Chiang Tung (Kengtung).

Wat Phra That Chae Haeng   TEMPLE
(วัดพระธาตุแช่แห้ง; admission free) Two kilometres past the bridge that spans Mae Nam Nan, heading southeast out of town, this Buddhist temple dating from 1355 is the most sacred wát in Nan Province. It's set in a square, walled enclosure on top of a hill with a view of Nan and the valley. The Thai Lü-influenced *bòht* features a triple-tiered roof with carved wooden eaves and dragon reliefs over the doors. A gilded Lanna-style *chedi* sits on a large square base next to the *bòht;* visit late in the day and the structure practically glows in the afternoon light.

Wat Phra That Chang Kham   TEMPLE
(วัดพระธาตุช้างค้ำ; admission free; Th Mahayot) This is the second-most important temple in the city after Wat Phra That Chae Haeng. The founding date is unknown, but the main *wí-hǎhn,* reconstructed in 1458, has a huge seated Buddha image and faint murals that have been partially recovered. (Sometime in the mid-20th century an abbot reportedly ordered the murals to be whitewashed because he thought they were distracting worshippers from concentrating on his sermons!)

Also in the *wí-hǎhn* is a set of Lanna-period scrolls inscribed (in Lanna script) not only with the usual Buddhist scriptures but with the history, law and astrology of the time. A *tam-mâht* (a '*dhamma* seat' used by monks when teaching) sits to one side.

The *chedi* behind the *wí·hǎhn* dates to the 14th century, probably around the same time as the temple was founded. It features elephant supports similar to those seen in Sukhothai and Si Satchanalai.

Next to the *chedi* is a small, undistinguished *bòht* from the same era. Wat Chang Kham's current abbot tells an interesting story involving the *bòht* and a Buddha image that was once kept inside. According to the abbot, in 1955 art historian AB Griswold offered to purchase the 145cm-tall Buddha inside the small *bòht*. The image appeared to be a crude Sukhothai-style walking Buddha moulded of plaster. After agreeing to pay the abbot 25,000B for the image, Griswold began removing the image from the *bòht* – but as he did it fell and the plaster around the statue broke away to reveal an original Sukhothai Buddha of pure gold underneath. Needless to say, the abbot made Griswold give it back, much to the latter's chagrin. Did Griswold suspect what lay beneath the plaster? The abbot refuses to say. The image is now kept behind a glass partition in the *hǒr đrai* (Tripitaka library) adjacent to the *wí·hǎhn,* the largest of its type in Thailand.

Wat Hua Khuang TEMPLE
(วัดหัวข่วง; admission free) Located diagonally opposite Wat Phra That Chang Kham, this temple features a distinctive Lanna/Lan Xang-style *chedi* with four Buddha niches, an attractive wooden *hǒr đrai* and a noteworthy *bòht* with a Luang Prabang-style carved wooden veranda. Inside is a carved wooden ceiling and a huge *naga* altar. The temple's founding date is unknown, but stylistic cues suggest this may be one of the city's oldest *wát*.

🏃 Activities

Trekking & Rafting
Nan has nothing like the organised trekking industry found in Chiang Rai and Chiang Mai, and most visitors, particularly Thais, opt to float rather than walk. White-water rafting along Mae Nam Wa, in northern Nan, is only possible when the water level is high (September to December), and is said to be best during the early part of the rainy season. The rapids span from levels I to IV, and pass through intact jungle and remote villages.

Nan Adventure Tour RAFTING
(☑08 6701 4777; Th Nokham; 2 days & 1 night per person 3500B, 3 days & 2 nights per person from 4500B) Run by the amicable Mr Boy, this outfit conducts from two- to three-day, all-inclusive, rafting and/or kayaking trips.

Nan Touring RAFTING
(☑08 1961 7711; www.nantouring.com; Th Suriyaphong; 3 days & 2 nights per person 5500B) This outfit offers a variety of rafting trips for groups of at least five people.

Other Activities

Nan Seeing Tour CYCLING TOURS
(☑0 81472 4131; www.nanseeingtour.com; Nan Coffee, Th Sumon Thewarat; 4 person min, 2 days & 1 night per person 1850B, 3 days & 2 nights per person 3850B) This locally run start-up conducts two-wheeled expeditions in and around Nan. A three-day package starts with mountain bikes in Nan city and finishes with dirt bikes in the countryside. Prices are all-inclusive, and Nan Coffee functions as the office.

Fhu Travel TREKKING
(☑0 5471 0636, 08 1287 7209; www.fhutravel.com; 453/4 Th Sumon Thewarat; 2-person min, per person 'soft' trek 1 day 1600B, 2 days & 1 night 2800B, 3 days & 2 nights 3700B) Offers treks to Mabri, Hmong, Mien, Thai Lü and Htin villages, and can also arrange elephant trekking, rafting and kayaking trips and city tours. The operators have been leading tours for more than 20 years.

🛏 Sleeping

TOP CHOICE Pukha Nanfa Hotel HOTEL $$$
(☑0 5477 1111; www.pukhananfahotel.com; 369 Th Sumon Thewarat; r 2500-4600B; ❉@🖥) A recent ownership change has transformed the formerly forgettable Nan Fah Hotel into a charming boutique hotel. Rooms are cosy and classy, with aged wood accentuated by touches such as local cloth, handicrafts and art. Old adverts and pictures add to the old-world feel, and to top it off, the place is conveniently located and has capable staff.

Fah Place HOTEL $
(☑0 5471 0222; 237/8 Th Sumon Thewarat; r 400-500B; ❉🖥) This new family-run hotel is by far the best deal in town, if not in this part of northern Thailand. The huge rooms have been decorated with attractive teak furniture, including the kind of puffy inviting beds you'd normally find at places that charge 10 times this much. Bathrooms are also big enough to get lost in, and like the rooms, are outfitted with attractive tiles. The same people also run the similar **Sukkasem**

Hotel (☏0 5471 0222; 119-121 Th Anantaworarit-tidet; r 400-800B; ❄🔊).

Nan Guest House
HOTEL $
(☏08 1288 8484; 57/15 Th Mahaphrom; r 250-400B; ❄@🔊) In a quiet residential area a short walk from most of Nan's famous temples, this long-standing and well-maintained place has spotless spacious rooms, half of which have private hot-water bathrooms. There's a nearby cafe run by the same people with homemade baked goods and other eats. Nan Guest House is at the end of Soi 2, just off Th Mahaphrom.

Srinual Lodge
HOTEL $$
(no roman-script sign; ☏0 5471 0174; 40 Th Nokham; r/ste 400/1300B; ❄🔊) This two-storey brick structure holds 25 rooms decked out in *faux rustique* style with logs, bamboo and local textiles. Despite the design theme, the rooms look comfortable and are about as close as you'll get to sleeping near the Mae Nam Nan.

Nan Boutique Hotel
HOTEL $$$
(☏0 5477 5532; www.nanboutiquehotel.com; Th Kha Luang; r 1400-2800B; ❄🔊) This super tidy suburban-feeling compound lacks the character of some of Nan's other choices, but makes up for this with some of the city's most modern and well-equipped rooms.

Dhevaraj Hotel
HOTEL $$
(☏0 5471 0078; www.dhevarajhotel.com; 466 Th Sumon Thewarat; r incl breakfast 900-1500B; ste incl breakfast 3500B; ❄@🔊☰) Not all the rooms here live up to the retro-yet-tidy exterior, with some of the cheaper ones feeling somewhat aged and musty. It's OK value, though, and conveniently located.

Phai Lueng Guest House
HOTEL $
(☏08 1594 2062; Th Mahaphrom; r 250-550B; ❄🔊) The rooms in this old wooden house are pretty bare, but the place has heaps of old-school character and is ideal for those who favour atmosphere over comfort.

Amazing Guest House
GUEST HOUSE $
(☏0 5471 0893; 23/7 Th Rat Amnuay/Suntisuk; r 150-450B; ❄🔊) Rooms in the main building have wooden floors, clean beds and shared hot-water showers. Rooms in concrete rooms out the back have private bathrooms. Amazing is about 1km north of town. After heading north on Th Mahayot, turn left on Th Prempracharat then another left on Th Rat Amnuay, which is also labelled as Th Suntisuk.

SP Guest House
HOTEL $$
(☏0 5477 4897; www.fornan.com/spguesthouse.html; Trok Huawiangtai; r 400-700B; ❄🔊) This place boasts a homey feel, with 14 mostly spacious rooms equipped with cheap but bright furnishings.

Numchock Guest House
GUEST HOUSE $
(☏08 1998 1855; 37 Th Rat Amnuay/Suntisuk; fan/air-con 200/350B; ❄🔊) Located across from Amazing Guest House, another local family has turned part of its tidy residential compound into an inviting guest house.

✖ Eating & Drinking

Despite its other charms, Nan has one of the least inspiring dining scenes in northern Thailand.

The town's **night market** (Th Pha Kong; ⏾5-11pm) provides a few decent food stall offerings.

Pu Som Restaurant
NORTHERN THAI $
(no roman-script sign; 203/1 Th Mano; mains 30-70B; ⏾lunch & dinner) Like a misplaced Texas barnhouse, this popular local restaurant is decked out in cowboy hats, cow skulls, gun holsters, and a plethora of images of the Marlboro Man. Fittingly, the emphasis here is on beef, served in the local style as *lâhp*, or as *néu·a nêung*, steamed over herbs and served with an incredibly delicious galangal dip.

Yota Vegetarian Restaurant
VEGETARIAN THAI $
(Th Mahawong; mains 10-35B; ⏾7am-3pm; 🖉) Run by the friendliest lady in town who will not let you leave hungry, this is perhaps the best deal in Nan. It's popular and once the food is gone after lunch, that's it for the day.

Som Tam Thawt
THAI $
(no roman-script sign; Th Sumon Thewarat; mains 15-30B; ⏾10am-9pm) This tiny restaurant is known for its *sôm·dam tôrt,* deep-fried *sôm·dam.* It's an equal parts crunchy and refreshing snack. They also do great fruit smoothies and other basic dishes.

Goodview Nan
THAI $
(203/1 Th Mano; dishes 35-150B; ⏾11am-midnight) One of the few places in town to take advantage of the views over the Mae Nam Nan, this place works equally well as a dinner date locale or a riverside pub. There's an English-language menu and at night, a live music soundtrack.

NORTHERN THAILAND NAN

Pizza Da Dario   ITALIAN-THAI **$**
(Th Mahayot; pizza 100-160B; ⊗lunch & dinner; ❊)
This Italian restaurant does pizza and pasta,
as well as other Western treats and Thai
dishes.

Nan Coffee   CAFE **$**
(Th Sumon Thewarat; coffee drinks 25-35B;
⊗7.30am-7pm) This conveniently located cafe
does good coffee drinks and light meals.
There are also a few souvenirs for sale and
the restaurant is also the unofficial headquarters for Nan Seeing Tour.

🛍 Shopping

Nan is one of the best places in northern
Thailand to pick up some souvenirs, and
good buys include local textiles, especially
the Thai Lü weaving styles. Typical Thai
Lü fabrics feature red and black designs on
white cotton in floral, geometric and animal designs. A favourite is the *lai nám lǎi*
(flowing-water design) that shows stepped
patterns representing streams, rivers and
waterfalls. Local Hmong appliqué and Mien
embroidery are of excellent quality. Htin
grass-and-bamboo baskets and mats are
worth a look, too.

Kad-Nan   MARKET
(www.kad-nan.com; Th Mahayot; ⊗10am-10pm)
This open-air market is Nan's answer to
Bangkok's Chatuchak Weekend Market.
Here you'll find shops selling local knick-
knacks, art, clothing, restaurants (including
one selling Greek food), coffee shops and
bars. The market is technically open from
10am, but evening, when most shops and
restaurants are open and live music gives
the place a fairlike atmosphere, is the best
time to visit.

Amnouy Porn & Jangtrakoon   HANDICRAFTS
(Th Sumon Thewarat; ⊗8am-7pm) These
adjacent shops sell a variety of local goods
with an emphasis on textiles and clothing.

OTOP   HANDICRAFTS
(Th Suriyaphong; ⊗8am-7pm) The showroom
of this government-funded development
initiative has everything from local snacks
to silverware.

Peera   TEXTILES
(26 Th Suriyaphong; ⊗8am-7pm) A short
walk from Wat Phumin, this place offers
high-quality local textiles, mostly women's
skirts and blouses.

Nan Silver   SILVER
(430/1 Th Sumon Thewarat; ⊗7.30am-7pm) This
small but classy shop sells a huge variety of
locally designed and produced silver items.

ⓘ Information

Kan Internet (Th Mahayot; per hr 15B; ⊗9am-
10pm) Other places offering internet services
are available around town for about 20B per
hour.

Main post office (Th Mahawong; ⊗8.30am-
4.30pm Mon-Fri, 9am-noon Sat & Sun) In the
centre of town.

Phunan Holiday (⊘0 5477 2018; 494 Th
Sumon Thewarat; ⊗9am-6.30pm Mon-Sat)
This cheery travel agency can arrange plane
tickets, as well as other local services, from
trekking to hiring a car and driver.

Siam Commercial Bank (Th Anantaworarit-
tidet) ATM and foreign-exchange service. There
are also multiple ATMs near Pukha Nanfa Hotel.

Tourist Information Centre (⊘0 5475 1169;
Th Pha Kong; ⊗8.30am-4.30pm) Opposite Wat
Phumin, this helpful information centre is hid-
den behind vendors and coffee shops.

ⓘ Getting There & Away

Air
Taxis from the airport to town run from about
100B per person; contact **Mr Klay** (⊘08 6188
0079).

Destinations from Nan include:

Bangkok's Don Muang Airport (1690B, one
hour 20 minutes, one to two times daily) via
Nok Air (⊘nationwide call centre 1318, Nan
0 5477 1308; www.nokair.co.th; Nan airport)
and **Solar Air** (⊘nationwide call centre 02 535
2455; www.solarair.co.th; Nan airport)

Chiang Mai (990B, 45 minutes, twice daily) via
Kan Air (⊘nationwide call centre 02 551 6111,
Nan 0 5477 1308; www.kanairlines.com; Nan
airport) and **Nok Mini** (⊘nationwide call centre
0 5328 0444; www.nokmini.com; Nan airport)

Bus
From Nan all buses, minivans and *sŏrng·tăa·ou*
leave from the bus station at the southwestern
edge of town. A motorcycle taxi from the station
to the centre of town costs 25B.

If you're connecting to the train station at Den
Chai in Phrae, you can hop on any bus bound for
Chiang Mai or Bangkok.

Bangkok (424B to 773B, 10 to 11 hours,
frequent departures from 8am to 10am and
6.10pm to 7.45pm)

Chiang Mai (223B to 412B, five hours, frequent
departures from 7.30am to 10.30pm)

Chiang Rai (176B, five hours, 9am)

Lampang (120B, four hours, frequent departures from 7.30am to 10.30pm)

Phayao (123B, three hours, 1.30pm)

Phrae (85B, two hours, frequent departures from 7.30am to 10.30pm)

ⓘ Getting Around

Săhm·lór around town cost 20B to 30B.

Several businesses, including Amazing Guest House, Fah Place, **Oversea Shop** (✉0 5471 0258; 488 Th Sumon Thewarat; bicycles per day 80B, motorcycles per day 200B; ⊙8.30am-5.30pm) and Nan Guest House rent out bikes for about 50B per day and motorcycles from about 180B to 300B per day.

Around Nan

THAM PHAH TUP FOREST
RESERVE   ถ้ำผาตูบ

This limestone **cave complex** is about 10km north of Nan and is part of a relatively new wildlife reserve. Some 17 caves have been counted, of which nine are easily located by means of established (but unmarked) trails.

From Nan you can catch a bus or *sŏrng·tăa·ou* bound for Pua or Thung Chang; it will stop at the turn-off to the caves for 30B. The vehicles leave from the bus station.

NAN RIVERSIDE GALLERY หอศิลป์ริมน่าน

Twenty kilometres north of Nan on Rte 1080, this private **art gallery** (www.nanart gallery.com; Km 20, Rte 1080; admission 20B; ⊙9am-5pm Thu-Tue) exhibits contemporary Nan-influenced art in a peaceful setting. Established in 2004 by Nan artist Winai Prabipoo, the two-storey building holds the more interesting temporary exhibitions downstairs – sculpture, ceramics and drawings – as well as a permanent painting collection upstairs – which seems to be mainly inspired by the Wat Phumin murals. The unusual building is a light-filled converted rice barn with an arrow-shaped turret. The shop and cafe have seats right on the Mae Nam Nan and the beautiful manicured gardens are nice to wander around. From Nan, take any northbound bus or *sŏrng·tăa·ou* (30B) to the gallery.

WAT NONG BUA   วัดหนองบัว

The neat and tidy Thai Lü village of Nong Bua, near the town of Tha Wang Pha, approximately 30km north of Nan, is famous for Lü-style **Wat Nong Bua** (admission free). Featuring a typical two-tiered roof and

carved wooden portico, the *wí·hăhn* design is simple yet striking – note the carved *naga* heads at the roof corners. Inside the *wí·hăhn* are some noteworthy *jataka* murals thought to have been painted by Thit Buaphan, the same mural artist whose work can be seen at Wat Phumin. Be sure to leave a donation at the altar for the temple's upkeep and restoration.

There is a model Thai Lü house directly behind the wát where weaving is done and you can buy attractive local textiles.

To get there, northbound buses and *sŏrng·tăa·ou* (35B) to Tha Wang Pha leave from the bus terminal. Get off at Samyaek Longbom, a three-way intersection before Tha Wang Pha, and walk west to a bridge over Mae Nam Nan and turn left. Continue until you reach another small bridge, after which Wat Nong Bua will be on your right. It's a long 3km from the highway to the wát.

DOI PHU KHA NATIONAL
PARK   อุทยานแห่งชาติดอยภูคา

This **national park** (✉0 5470 1000; admission 200B) is centred on 2000m-high Doi Phu Kha, the province's highest peak, in Amphoe Pua and Amphoe Bo Kleua in northeastern Nan Province (about 75km from Nan). There are several Htin, Mien, Hmong and Thai Lü **villages** in the park and vicinity, as well as a couple of **caves** and **waterfalls**, and endless opportunities for forest **walks**. The park headquarters has a basic map and staff can arrange a local guide for walks or more extended excursions around the area, as well as rafting on the Nam Wa. The park is often cold in the cool season and especially wet in the wet season.

The park offers a variety of **bungalows** (✉0 2562 0760; www.dnp.go.th; 2-7 people 300-2500B), and there is a nearby restaurant and basic shop.

To reach the national park by public transport you must first take a bus or *sŏrng·tăa·ou* north of Nan to Pua (50B). Get off at the 7-Eleven then cross the highway to board one of the three daily *sŏrng·tăa·ou* (50B, 30 minutes) that depart at 7.30am, 9.30am and 11.30am.

BAN BO LUANG   บ้านบ่อหลวง

Ban Bo Luang (also known as Ban Bo Kleua, or Salt Well Village) is a picturesque Htin village southeast of Doi Phu Kha National Park where the long-standing occupation has been the extraction of salt from local salt wells. It's easy to find the main community salt wells, more or less in the centre of the village.

If you have your own transport, the village is a good base for exploring the nearby national parks, Doi Phu Kha and **Khun Nan National Park** (📞08 4483 7240; admission free). The latter is located a few kilometres north of Ban Bo Luang, and has a 2km walk from the visitor centre that ends in a viewpoint looking over local villages and nearby Laos.

There is a handful of places to stay in Ban Bor Luang. The best of these, **Boklua View** (📞08 1809 6392; www.bokluaview.com; Ban Bo Luang; r & bungalows incl breakfast 1850B; ❄@🛜🏊), is an attractive and well-run hillside resort overlooking the village and the Nam Mang that runs through it. The resort has its own garden and serves good food (be sure to try Chef Toun's chicken deep-fried with northern Thai spices). If Boklua View is full or beyond your budget, just downhill **Oon Ai Mang** (no roman-script sign; 📞08 1374 7994; Ban Bo Luang; bungalows incl breakfast 500-650B) has some very basic tents and bamboo bungalows with shared bathrooms at the edge of the Nam Mang. There are some similar 'homestay' set-ups outside of the town.

There are a few small restaurants serving basic dishes in Ban Bo Luang.

To reach Ban Bo Luang from Nan, take a bus or *sŏrng·tăa·ou* north of Nan to Pua

(50B). Get off at the 7-Eleven, cross the highway to take the *sŏrng·tăa·ou* that terminates in the village (80B, one hour), departing at 7.30am, 9.30am and 11.30am.

PHITSANULOK PROVINCE

Phitsanulok พิษณุโลก

POP 84,000

Phitsanulok sees relatively few independent travellers, but a fair amount of package tourists, perhaps because the city is a convenient base from which to explore the attractions of historical Sukhothai, Si Satchanalai and Kamphaeng Phet. Due to large parts of the town being burned down by a massive fire in 1957, Phitsanulok's architecture is pretty nondescript. Yet this vibrant and extremely friendly city boasts some interesting sites and museums, chief of which is Wat Phra Si Ratana Mahathat, which contains one of Thailand's most revered Buddha images.

Those willing to forge their own path can also use the city as a base to visit the nearby national parks and wildlife sanctuaries of Thung Salaeng Luang and Phu Hin Rong Kla, the former strategic headquarters of the Communist Party of Thailand (CPT).

BORDER CROSSING: BAN HUAY KON TO MUANG NGEUN

Located 140km north of Nan, Ban Huay Kon is a very quiet village in the mountains near the Lao border. There's a fun **border market** on Saturday mornings, but most will come here because of the town's recent status as an international border crossing to Laos – it's allegedly only 35km to the Lao town of Hongsa, 152km to Luang Prabang (90km by boat), 295km to the Chinese town of Mengla and 406km to Dien Bien Phu in Vietnam.

After passing the **Thai immigration booth** (📞0 5469 3530; ⏰8am-5pm), foreigners can purchase a 30-day visa for Laos for US$30 to US$42, depending on nationality. There is an extra US$1 or 50B charge after 4pm and on weekends. You can then proceed 2.5km to the Lao village of Muang Ngeun, where you could stay at the **Phouxay Guesthouse** (📞020-214 2826; Nan-Hongsa Rd; r 50,000K), or if you're heading onward, to the tiny **'Passenger Car Station'** (📞020-245 0145, 020-244 4130) beside the market, from where *sŏrng·tăa·ou* leave for Hongsa (40,000K, 1½ hours) between 2pm and 4pm, and to Pak Kaen (35,000K, one hour) at around 7.30am and 2pm arriving in time for the Mekong slowboats to Huay Xai and Pak Beng respectively.

To get to Ban Huay Kon, there are three daily minivans (100B, three hours) from Den Chai, in Phrae, pulling into Nan at around 5am, 8am and 9am. The only other option is to hop on a bus from Nan to Pon (105B, 2½ hours), which departs every 30 minutes from 6am to 6pm. From Pon you'll need to transfer to one of two daily *sŏrng·tăa·ou* that go the remaining 30km to Ban Huay Kon (100B, one hour) at 9.30am and noon. In the opposite direction, minivans leave Ban Huay Kon at 10am, 1pm and 2.30pm.

There's basic bungalow-style accommodation between Ban Huay Kon and the border. Ask in the village for details.

FOLK MUSEUM, BUDDHA-CASTING FOUNDRY & BIRD GARDEN

A nationally acclaimed expert on Thai folkways, a former military cartographer and Buddha statue caster, and apparent bird aficionado, Sergeant Major Thawee Buranakhet has taken from his diverse experiences and interests to create three very worthwhile attractions in Phitsanulok.

The **Sergeant Major Thawee Folk Museum** (26/43 Th Wisut Kasat; adult/child 50/20B; ☺8.30am-4.30pm) displays a remarkable collection of tools, textiles and photographs from Phitsanulok Province. This fascinating museum is spread throughout five traditional-style Thai buildings with well-groomed gardens, and the displays are all accompanied by informative and legible English descriptions. Those interested in cooking will find much of interest in the display of a traditional Thai kitchen and the various traps used to catch game. Male visitors will be undoubtedly disturbed by a display that describes traditional bull castration – a process that apparently involves no sharp tools.

Across the street and also belonging to Dr Thawee is a small **Buddha Casting Foundry** (admission free; ☺8am-5pm) where bronze Buddha images of all sizes are cast. Visitors are welcome to watch and there are even detailed photo exhibits demonstrating the lost-wax method of metal casting. Some of the larger images take a year or more to complete. There is a small gift shop at the foundry where you can purchase bronze images of various sizes.

In addition to the bronze foundry, there is also a display of fighting cocks, which are bred and sold all over the country. (The official English name for this part of the facility is 'The Centre of Conservative Folk Cock'.)

Attached to the foundry is Dr Thawee's latest project, **Garden Birds of Thailand** (adult/child 50/20B; ☺8.30am-5pm). This collection of aviaries contains indigenous Thai birds including some endangered species, such as the very pretty pink-chested jamu fruit-dove, and the prehistoric-looking helmeted hornbill. Unfortunately, the cages are generally rather small and don't reflect the birds' natural environments.

The museums are south of Phitsanulok on Th Wisut Kasat; a túk-túk here should cost about 60B.

◉ Sights

Wat Phra Si Ratana Mahathat   TEMPLE
(วัดพระศรีรัตนมหาธาตุ; admission free; ☺6am-9pm)
The full name of this temple is Wat Phra Si Ratana Mahathat, but the locals call it Wat Phra Si or Wat Yai. The main *wí·hǎhn* appears small from the outside, but houses the Phra Phuttha Chinnarat, one of Thailand's most revered and copied Buddha images. This famous bronze statue is probably second in importance only to the Emerald Buddha in Bangkok's Wat Phra Kaew.

The story goes that construction of this wát was commissioned under the reign of King Li Thai in 1357. When it was completed, King Li Thai wanted it to contain three high-quality bronze images, so he sent for well-known sculptors from Si Satchanalai, Chiang Saen and Hariphunchai (Lamphun), as well as five Brahman priests. The first two castings worked well, but the third required three attempts before it was decreed the best of all. Legend has it that a white-robed sage appeared from nowhere to assist in the final casting, then disappeared. This last image was named the Chinnarat (Victorious King) Buddha and it became the centrepiece in the *wí·hǎhn*. The other two images, Phra Chinnasi and Phra Si Satsada, were later moved to the royal temple of Wat Bowonniwet in Bangkok.

The image was cast in the late Sukhothai style, but what makes it strikingly unique is the flamelike halo around the head and torso that turns up at the bottom to become dragon-serpent heads on either side of the image. The head of this Buddha is a little wider than standard Sukhothai, giving the statue a very solid feel.

Another sanctuary to one side has been converted into a free **museum** (☺9am-5.30pm Wed-Sun), displaying antique Buddha images, ceramics and other historic artefacts.

Despite the holiness of the temple, endless loud broadcasts asking for donations, Thai musicians, a strip of vendors hawking everything from herbs to lottery tickets, several ATM machines and hundreds of visitors

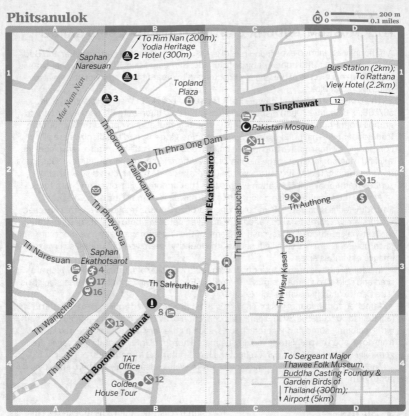

all contribute to a relentlessly hectic atmosphere. Come early (ideally before 7am) if you're looking for quiet contemplation or simply wish to take photos, and regardless of the time be sure to dress appropriately – no shorts or sleeveless tops.

Near Wat Yai, on the same side of the river, is another temple of the same period – **Wat Nang Phaya**.

Wat Ratburana   TEMPLE
(วัดราชบูรณะ; admission free; ⊘6am-8.30pm) Across the street from Wat Phra Si Ratana Mahathat, Wat Ratburana draws fewer visitors but in some ways is more interesting than its famous neighbour. In addition to a *wí·hăhn* with a 700-year-old gold Buddha, an *ùbohsòt* chapel with beautiful murals thought to date back to the mid-19th century, and two *hŏr đrai,* the temple is also home to a few quirky attractions that offer a fascinating insight into the practices of Thai Buddhism.

The most obvious of these is a large wooden boat decked with garlands that originally served to transport King Rama V on an official visit to Phitsanulok. Today the boat is thought to grant wishes to those who make an offering and crawl under its entire length three or nine times. Next to the *wí·hăhn* is a sacred tree with ladders on either side that visitors climb up, leave an offering, then ring a bell and descend, again repeating the action a total of three or nine times. And directly adjacent to the tree is an immense gong that, when rubbed the right way, creates a unique ringing sound. Near each of these attractions you'll find somebody stationed who, in addition to selling the coins, incense and flowers used in offerings, will also instruct visitors in exactly how to conduct each particular ritual, including how many times to pass, what to offer, and what prayer to say.

Phitsanulok

Sights
1 Wat Nang Phaya B1
2 Wat Phra Si Ratana Mahathat............... B1
3 Wat Ratburana B1

Activities, Courses & Tours
4 Phae Hatha Thai Massage................... A3

Sleeping
5 Golden Grand Hotel................................ C2
6 Grand Riverside Hotel........................... A3
7 Kraisaeng Place C1
8 Lithai Guest House B3

Eating
9 Ban Mai... C2
10 Daeng.. B2
11 Fah-Ke-Rah.. C2
12 Jaroen Tham... B4
13 Night Bazaar... B4
14 Night Market... C3
15 Night Market... D2

Drinking
16 Calito... A3
17 Sabai Boat... A3
18 Wood Stock... C3
Wow! ....(see 17)

Activities

Phae Hatha Thai Massage　　　MASSAGE
(Th Wangchan; massage per hr with fan/air-con
150/180B; ⏰10am-9pm) Relaxation takes an
entirely new form at this Thai massage
centre housed on a floating raft.

Sleeping

Lithai Guest House　　　HOTEL $
(☎0 5521 9626; 73/105 Th Phayalithai; r incl breakfast 250-460B; ❋@☎) This place is so clean it
gleams. The light-filled 60 or so rooms don't
have much character but they are excellent
value. Most have large private bathrooms
with hot water, cable TV, plentiful furniture and a fridge. Rates include breakfast
and free bottled water. There is an air ticket
agent, coffee shop and restaurant on site.

Golden Grand Hotel　　　HOTEL $$
(☎0 5521 0234; www.goldengrandhotel.com; 66 Th
Thammabucha; r incl breakfast 690-850B; ❋@☎)
Mint green went out of style a long time
ago, but this is about the only fault we can
find with the Golden Grand. The rooms are
so tidy we're wondering if they've ever even
been slept in, and friendly staff and great
views of the city from the upper floors are
even more incentive to stay here.

Yodia Heritage Hotel　　　HOTEL $$$
(☎08 1613 8496; www.yodiaheritage.com; 89/1
Th Phuttha Bucha; r incl breakfast 2950B; ste incl
breakfast 4200-8900B; ❋@☎) This new boutique hotel takes the crown as Phitsanulok's most upscale accommodation. Located
along a quiet stretch of the Mae Nam Nan,
suites are huge, and feature similarly large
tubs and a semi-private swimming pool.

Rattana View Hotel　　　HOTEL $$
(☎0 5522 1999; 847 Th Mitraphap; r incl breakfast
450-1400B; ❋☎❋) A block east of the main
bus station, this hotel is an attractive choice.
The handsome rooms exude a crisp, clean
feel, and all include wide balconies. There's
a restaurant on the ground floor and a spa
is located in the Amway Building directly in
front of the hotel.

Kraisaeng Place　　　HOTEL $
(☎0 5521 0509; 45 Th Thammabucha; r 350-
450B; ❋☎) Appearing more like a small
apartment building than a hotel, the well-
equipped rooms here are a good bargain. Be
sure to look at the double rooms, which for
only a bit more are gigantic and feature an
additional seating area. Be prepared for a
fair bit of traffic noise.

Grand Riverside Hotel　　　HOTEL $$$
(☎0 5524 8333; www.tgrhotel.com; cnr Th Nare-
suan & Th Wangchan; r incl breakfast 1600-1800B,
ste incl breakfast 3000B; ❋@☎) Overlooking
the Mae Nam Nan from its west bank, this
towering business hotel offers all the amenities you'd expect in a relatively new, top-end
hotel. Deluxe rooms offer an additional sitting area and river views.

Eating

Phitsanulok takes its cuisine seriously. The
city is particularly obsessive about night
markets, and there are no fewer than three
dotted in various locations around town.
The most well known, Phitsanulok's **Night
Bazaar** (mains 40-80B; ⏰5pm-3am), focuses
mainly on clothing, but a few riverfront
restaurants specialise in *pàk bûng loy fáh*
(literally 'floating-in-the-sky morning glory

vine'), where the cook fires up a batch of *pàk bûng* in the wok and then flings it through the air to a waiting server who catches it on a plate. If you're lucky, you'll be here when a tour group is trying to catch the flying vegetables, but is actually dropping *pàk bûng* all over the place. Another **night market** (mains 20-40B; ⊙5pm-midnight) lines either side of Th Phra Ong Dam north of Th Authong, and there's a very busy **night market** (mains 20-60B; ⊙4-8pm) just south of the train station that features mostly takeaway items including *kôw nĕe·o hòr,* tiny banana-leaf parcels of sticky rice with various toppings; there are two vendors opposite each other near the Th Ekathotsarot entrance to the market.

Another dish associated with Phitsanulok is *gŏoay·dĕe·o hôy kăh* (literally meaning, 'legs-hanging' noodles). The name comes from the way customers sit on the floor facing the river, with their legs dangling below. **Rim Nan** (no roman-script sign; 5/4 Th Phaya Sua; mains 20-35B; ⊙9am-4pm), north of Wat Phra Si Ratana Mahathat, is one of a few similar restaurants along Th Phutta Bucha that offer noodles and 'alternative' seating.

TOP CHOICE **Ban Mai**　　　　　　　THAI $$
(93/30 Th Authong; mains 60-150B; ⊙11am-2pm & 5-10pm; 🕸) Dinner at this local favourite is like a meal at your grandparents': opinionated conversation resounds, frumpy furniture abounds, and an overfed Siamese cat appears to rule the dining room. Don't

expect home cooking though; Ban Mai specialises in unusual but perfectly executed dishes that aren't easily found elsewhere, like the *gaang pèt ʿbèt yâhng,* a curry of smoked duck, or *yam dà·krái,* lemongrass 'salad'.

Fah-Ke-Rah　　　　　　MUSLIM-THAI $
(786 Th Phra Ong Dam; mains 5-20B; ⊙6am-2pm) There are several Thai-Muslim cafes near the mosque on Th Phra Ong Dam, and this is a popular one. Thick *roh·ɖee* (crispy dough 'pancakes') is served up with *gaang mát·sà·màn* (Muslim curry), fresh yoghurt is made daily and the *roh·ɖee gaang* (*roh·ɖee* served with a small bowl of curry) is a steal at 20B.

Daeng　　　　　　VIETNAMESE-THAI $
(no roman-script sign; Th Borom Trailokanat; dishes 40-120B; ⊙lunch & dinner; 🕸) Across from Pailyn Hotel (the English-language sign says 'Food & Drink'), this small shop is part of a popular chain of Thai/Vietnamese food that originated in Nong Khai. Be sure to order the restaurant's signature dish, *năam neu·ang,* grilled pork balls served with fresh herbs and rice paper sheets to wrap it all up in.

Jaroen Tham　　　　VEGETARIAN-THAI $
(Vegetarian Food; Th Sithamatraipidok; dishes 15-20B; ⊙8am-3pm; 🖋) Around the corner from the TAT office, this simple place serves a choice of vegetarian dishes paired with husky brown rice.

PHITSANULOK'S BUSES & MINIVANS

Transport options out of Phitsanulok are good as it's a junction for several bus routes. Phitsanulok's **bus station** (📞0 5521 2090) is 2km east of town on Hwy 12. Minivans also depart from the bus terminal, including frequent departures to Mae Sot (163B, four hours, 7am to 2.30pm).

DESTINATION	FARE (B)	DURATION (HR)	FREQUENCY
Bangkok	224-380	5	every hr 7.20am-midnight
Chiang Rai	249-320	5	every hr 8am-midnight
Mae Sai	280-456	6	every hr 5.30am-midnight
Nan	238	6	midnight, 2am
Phrae	150	4	midnight, 2am
Mae Sot	210	5	1am, 3am
Chiang Mai	211-317	6	every hr 8am-midnight
Lampang	155-265	4	every hr 8am-midnight
Sukhothai	28-50	1	every hr 5.40am-6pm
Kamphaeng Phet	53-74	3	every hr 5am-6pm

🍸 Drinking & Entertainment

A few floating pubs can be found along the strip of Th Wangchan directly in front of the Grand Riverside Hotel including **Sabai Boat** (no roman-script sign; Th Wangchan; dishes 40-140B; ⊙11am-11pm) and **Wow!** (Th Wangchan; dishes 50-150B; ⊙5pm-midnight), both proffering food as well as drink.

Wood Stock   BAR
(148/22-23 Th Wisut Kasat; dishes 35-70B; ⊙5pm-midnight) Wood Stock combines funky '60s and '70s-era furniture, live music, and a brief and cheap menu of *gàp glâam* (Thai-style nibbles).

Calito   BAR
(🖉08 1953 2629; 84/1 Th Wangchan; dishes 70-100B; ⊙6pm-midnight) Located on firm ground, Calito has an extensive menu of Thai eats and cold draught beer.

ⓘ Information

Shops offering internet access dot the streets around the train station, near Topland Plaza and on the western bank of the river near Saphan Ekathotsarot. Several banks in town offer foreign-exchange services and ATMs. There are also several ATMs inside the Wat Phra Si Ratana Mahathat compound.

Golden House Tour (🖉0 5525 9973; 55/37-38 Th Borom Trailokanat; ⊙7am-7pm Mon-Sat) This experienced travel agency can book airline tickets and arrange ground transport in and around Phitsanulok.

Krung Thai Bank (35 Th Naresuan; ⊙until 8pm) An after-hours exchange window.

Main post office (Th Phaya Sua; ⊙8.30am-4.30pm Mon-Fri, 9am-noon Sat & Sun)

Tourism Authority of Thailand office (TAT; 🖉nationwide call centre 1672, Phitsanulok 0 5525 2742; tatphlok@tat.or.th; 209/7-8 Th Borom Trailokanat; ⊙8.30am-4.30pm) Off Th Borom Trailokanat, with helpful staff who hand out free maps of the town and a walking-tour sheet.

Tourist police (🖉1155; Th Ekathotsarot)

ⓘ Getting There & Away

Air

Phitsanulok's **airport** (🖉0 5530 1002) is 5km south of town. Golden House Tour has a board at the airport indicating its minivan service from the airport to hotels (200B per person). Túk-túk go to the airport from town for 150B.

Nok Air (🖉nationwide call centre 1318; www.nokair.co.th; Phitsanulok airport) operates flights between Phitsanulok and Bangkok's Don Muang airport (1290B, 50 minutes, twice daily).

Train

Phitsanulok's train station is within walking distance of accommodation and offers a left-luggage service. The station is a significant train terminal, and virtually every northbound and southbound train stops here; major destinations from Phitsanulok include Bangkok (80B to 1164B, five to seven hours, 11 times daily) and Chiang Mai (143B to 1145B, seven to nine hours, six times daily). To check the most up-to-date timetables and prices in advance call the **State Railway of Thailand** (🖉free 24hr hotline 1690; www.railway.co.th) or look at its website.

ⓘ Getting Around

Rides on the town's Darth Vaderlike sähm·lór start at about 60B. Outside the train station there's a sign indicating túk-túk prices for different destinations around town.

Budget (🖉0 5530 1020; www.budget.co.th) has a car-rental office at the airport that charges from 1500B per day.

Around Phitsanulok

PHU HIN RONG KLA NATIONAL PARK

อุทยานแห่งชาติภูหินร่องกล้า

Between 1967 and 1982, the mountain that is known as **Phu Hin Rong Kla** (🖉0 5523 3527; admission 200B; ⊙8.30am-5pm) served as the strategic headquarters for the Communist Party of Thailand (CPT) and its tactical arm, the People's Liberation Army of Thailand (PLAT). The remote, easily defended summit was perfect for an insurgent army. China's Yunnan Province is only 300km away and it was here that CPT cadres received their training in revolutionary tactics. (This was until the 1979 split between the Chinese and Vietnamese communists, when the CPT sided with Vietnam.)

For nearly 20 years the area around Phu Hin Rong Kla served as a battlefield for Thai troops and the communists. In 1972 the Thai government launched an unsuccessful major offensive against the PLAT. The CPT camp at Phu Hin Rong Kla became especially active after the Thai military killed hundreds of students in Bangkok during the October 1976 student-worker uprising. Many students subsequently fled here to join the CPT, setting up a hospital and a school of political and military tactics. By 1978 the PLAT ranks here had swelled to 4000. In 1980 and 1981 the Thai armed forces tried again and were able to recapture some parts of CPT territory. But the decisive blow to the CPT came in 1982, when the government declared an amnesty for all the students who had joined the communists after 1976. The departure of most of the students broke the spine of the movement, which had become dependent on their membership. A final military push in late 1982 resulted in the surrender of the PLAT, and Phu Hin Rong Kla was declared a national park in 1984.

◉ Sights & Activities

The park covers about 307 sq km of rugged mountains and forest, much of it covered by rocks and wildflowers. The elevation at park headquarters is about 1000m, so the area is refreshingly cool even in the hot season. The main attractions don't tend to stray too far from the main road through the park and include the remains of the CPT stronghold – a rustic meeting hall, the school of political and military tactics – and the CPT admin-istration building. Across the road from the school is a water wheel designed by exiled engineering students.

Phu Hin Rong Kla can become quite crowded on weekends and holidays; schedule a more peaceful visit for midweek.

Pha Chu Thong   HISTORICAL SITE

A 1km trail leads to Pha Chu Thong (Flag Raising Cliff, sometimes called Red Flag Cliff), where the communists would raise the red flag to announce a military victory. Also in this area is an **air-raid shelter**, a **lookout** and the remains of the main **CPT headquarters** – the most inaccessible point in the territory before a road was constructed by the Thai government. The buildings in the park are made out of wood and bamboo and have no plumbing or electricity – a testament to how primitive the living conditions were.

There is a small **museum** at the park headquarters that displays relics from CPT days, although there's not a whole lot of Eng-

NORTHERN THAILAND PHITSANULOK PROVINCE

WORTH A TRIP

THE GREEN ROUTE

Rte 12 between Phitsanulok and Lom Sak is known as the 'Green Route', and runs along the scenic, rapid-studded Lam Nam Khek. Off this route are waterfalls, resorts, and the Phu Hin Rong Kla and Thung Salaeng Luang National Parks.

The Phitsanulok TAT office distributes a map of the attractions along this 130km stretch of road. You may want to bypass the first two waterfalls, **Nam Tok Sakhunoth-ayan** (at the Km 33 marker) and **Kaeng Song** (at the Km 45 marker), which on weekends can be overwhelmed with visitors. The third, **Kaeng Sopha** at the Km 72 marker, is a larger area of small falls and rapids where you can walk from rock formation to rock formation – there are more or fewer rocks depending on the rains. When there's enough water (typically from September to November) any of the resorts along this section can organise **white-water rafting** trips on the Lam Nam Khek.

Further east along the road is the 1262-sq-km **Thung Salaeng Luang National Park** (☏ 5526 8019; admission 200B; ⊙8am-5pm), one of Thailand's largest and most important wildlife sanctuaries. The entrance is at the Km 80 marker, where the park headquarters here has information on walks and accommodation.

If you have your own wheels, you can turn south at the Km 100 marker onto Rte 2196 and head for **Khao Kho** (Khow Khor), another mountain lair used by the CPT during the 1970s.

If you've made the side trip to Khao Kho you can choose either to return to the Phitsanulok-Lom Sak highway, or take Rte 2258, off Rte 2196, until it terminates at Rte 203. On Rte 203 you can continue north to Lom Sak or south to Phetchabun.

Resort-style accommodation can be found along most of the Green Route, with budget accommodation clumping near Kaeng Song, around Km 45, and at the various **national parks** (☏0 2562 0760; www.dnp.go.th; tent site 30B, 2-8 person tent 150-600B, bungalows 300-5000B). Several restaurants are located on the banks of the Nam Khek, most taking full advantage of the views and breezes.

For more freedom it's best to do this route with your own wheels. Buses between Phitsanulok and Lom Sak cost 50B for ordinary and 70B for air-con, each way. During daylight hours it's possible to flag down another bus to continue your journey, but after 4pm it gets a little chancy.

lish explanation. At the end of the road into the park is a small **White Hmong village**.

Walking Trails
WALKING

If you're not interested in the history of Phu Hin Rong Kla, there are **waterfalls**, **hiking trails** and **scenic views**, as well as some interesting rock formations – jutting boulders called **Lan Hin Pum**, and an area of deep rocky crevices where PLAT troops would hide during air raids, called **Lan Hin Taek**. Ask at the **visitor centre** (☉8.30am-4.30pm) for maps.

🛏 Sleeping & Eating

Golden House Tour, near the TAT office in Phitsanulok, can help book accommodation.

Thailand's Royal Forest Department
CAMPING GROUND $$

(☏0 2562 0760; www.dnp.go.th; 2-8 person tent 150-600B, bungalows 300-2100B) Bungalows for three to 15 people, in three different zones of the park, must be booked in advance via this organisation. You can also pitch a tent or rent one, and rent sleeping bags (60B). Near the camping ground and bungalows are restaurants and food vendors. The best are Duang Jai Cafeteria – try its famous carrot *sôm·đam* – and Rang Thong.

ℹ Getting There & Away

The park headquarters is about 125km from Phitsanulok. To get here, first take an early bus to Nakhon Thai (46B to 97B, two hours, every hour from 5am to 6pm). From there you can charter a *sŏrng·tăa·ou* to the park (800B) from near the market. From Phitsanulok, Golden House Tour charges 1700B for car and driver; petrol is extra. This is a delightful trip if you're on a motorcycle since there's not much traffic along the way, but a strong engine is necessary to conquer the hills to Phu Hin Rong Kla.

SUKHOTHAI PROVINCE

Sukhothai
สุโขทัย

POP 37,000

The Sukhothai (Rising of Happiness) Kingdom flourished from the mid-13th century to the late 14th century. This period is often viewed as the 'golden age' of Thai civilisation – the religious art and architecture of the era are considered to be the most classic of Thai styles. The remains of the kingdom, today known as the *meuang gòw* (old city), feature around 45 sq km of partially rebuilt

THE FIRST?

The establishment of Sukhothai in 1238 is often described as the formation of the first Thai kingdom. But the kingdom of Chiang Saen had already been established 500 years earlier, and at the time of Sukhothai's founding, other Thai kingdoms such as Lanna and Phayao also existed. Sukhothai's profound influence on the art, language, literature and religion of modern Thai society, not to mention the immense size of the kingdom at its peak in the early 13th century, are doubtlessly reasons for the proliferation of this convenient, but technically incorrect, historical fact.

ruins, which are one of the most visited ancient sites in Thailand.

Located 12km east of the historical park on the Mae Nam Yom, the market town of New Sukhothai is not particularly interesting. Yet its friendly and relaxed atmosphere, good transport links and attractive accommodation make it a good base from which to explore the old city ruins.

History

Sukhothai is typically regarded as the first capital of Siam, although this is not entirely accurate (see the boxed text above). The area was previously the site of a Khmer empire until 1238, when two Thai rulers, Pho Khun Pha Muang and Pho Khun Bang Klang Hao, decided to unite and form a new Thai kingdom.

Sukhothai's dynasty lasted 200 years and spanned nine kings. The most famous was King Ramkhamhaeng, who reigned from 1275 to 1317 and is credited with developing the first Thai script – his inscriptions are also considered the first Thai literature. Ramkhamhaeng eventually expanded his kingdom to include an area even larger than that of present-day Thailand. But a few kings later in 1438, Sukhothai was absorbed by Ayuthaya.

◎ Sights

SUKHOTHAI HISTORICAL PARK
อุทยานประวัติศาสตร์สุโขทัย

The Sukhothai ruins are one of Thailand's most impressive World Heritage Sites. The park includes remains of 21 historical sites and four large ponds within the old walls,

Sukhothai Historical Park

Sukhothai Historical Park

⊙ Sights
1 Ramkhamhaeng National Museum	C2
2 Wat Chang Lom	D2
3 Wat Mahathat	C2
4 Wat Phra Phai Luang	B1
5 Wat Sa Si	B2
6 Wat Si Chum	B1
7 Wat Si Sawai	B2
8 Wat Trapang Thong	C2

🛏 Sleeping
9 Old City Guest House	C2
10 Orchid Hibiscus Guest House	D3
11 PinPao Guest House	D2
Thai Thai	(see 10)
12 Tharaburi Resort	C3
Vitoon Guest House	(see 9)

✗ Eating
Coffee Cup	(see 9)
Food Stalls	(see 9)

with an additional 70 sites within a 5km radius.

The architecture of Sukhothai temples is most typified by the classic lotus-bud *chedi*, featuring a conical spire topping a square-sided structure on a three-tiered base. Some sites exhibit other rich architectural forms introduced and modified during the period, such as bell-shaped Sinhalese and double-tiered Srivijaya *chedi*.

Despite the popularity of the park, it's quite expansive, and solitary exploration is usually possible. Some of the most impressive ruins are outside the city walls, so a

bicycle or motorcycle is essential to fully appreciate everything.

The ruins are divided into five zones, the central, northern and eastern of which each has a separate 100B admission fee.

Central Zone
This is the historical park's main **zone** (Map p356; admission 100B, plus per bicycle/motorcycle/car 10/30/50B; ⊙6.30am-8pm) and is home to what are arguably some of the park's most well-preserved and impressive ruins. An audio tour, available in English, Japanese and Thai, can be rented at the ticket booth for 150B.

Wat Mahathat TEMPLE

(วัดมหาธาตุ; Map p356) Completed in the 13th century, the largest wát in Sukhothai is surrounded by brick walls (206m long and 200m wide) and a moat that is believed to represent the outer wall of the universe and the cosmic ocean. The *chedi* spires feature the famous lotus-bud motif, and some of the original stately Buddha figures still sit among the ruined columns of the old *wí·hǎhn*. There are 198 *chedi* within the monastery walls – a lot to explore in what many consider was once the spiritual and administrative centre of the old capital.

Ramkhamhaeng National Museum MUSEUM

(พิพิธภัณฑสถานแห่งชาติรามคำแหง; Map p356; ☎0 5561 2167; admission 150B; ☺9am-4pm) A good starting point for exploring the historical park ruins is Ramkhamhaeng National Museum. A replica of the famous Ramkhamhaeng inscription, said to be the earliest example of Thai writing, is kept here among an impressive collection of Sukhothai artefacts.

Wat Si Sawai TEMPLE

(วัดศรีสวาย; Map p356) Just south of Wat Mahathat, this Buddhist shrine (dating from the 12th and 13th centuries) features three Khmer-style towers and a picturesque moat. It was originally built by the Khmers as a Hindu temple.

Wat Sa Si TEMPLE

(วัดสระศรี; Map p356) Also known as 'Sacred Pond Monastery', Wat Sa Si sits on an island west of the bronze monument of King Ramkhamhaeng (the third Sukhothai king). It's a simple, classic Sukhothai-style wát containing a large Buddha, one *chedi* and the columns of the ruined *wí·hǎhn*.

Wat Trapang Thong TEMPLE

(วัดตระพังทอง; Map p356) Next to the museum, this small, still-inhabited wát with its fine stucco reliefs is reached by a footbridge across the large lotus-filled pond that surrounds it. This reservoir, the original site of Thailand's Loi Krathong festival, supplies the Sukhothai community with most of its water.

Northern Zone

This zone (Map p356; admission 100B, plus per bicycle/motorcycle/car 10/30/50B; ☺7.30am-5.30pm), 500m north of the old city walls, is easily reached by bicycle.

Wat Si Chum TEMPLE

(วัดศรีชุม; Map p356) This wát is northwest of the old city and contains an impressive *mon·dòp* with a 15m, brick-and-stucco seated Buddha. This Buddha's elegant, tapered fingers are much photographed. Archaeologists theorise that this image is the 'Phra Atchana' mentioned in the famous Ramkhamhaeng inscription. A passage in the *mon·dòp* wall that leads to the top has been blocked so that it's no longer possible to view the *jataka* inscriptions that line the tunnel ceiling.

Wat Phra Phai Luang TEMPLE

(วัดพระพายหลวง; Map p356) Outside the city walls in the northern zone, this somewhat isolated wát features three 12th-century Khmer-style towers, bigger than those at Wat Si Sawai. This may have been the centre of Sukhothai when it was ruled by the Khmers of Angkor prior to the 13th century.

Western Zone

This zone (Map p356; admission 100B, plus per bicycle/motorcycle/car 10/30/50B; ☺7.30am-5.30pm), at its furthest extent 2km west of the old city walls, is the most expansive, and in addition to Wat Saphan Hin, several mostly featureless ruins can be found. A bicycle or motorcycle is necessary to explore this zone.

Wat Saphan Hin TEMPLE

(วัดสะพานหิน; Map p356) Located on the crest of a hill that rises about 200m above the plain, the name of the wát, which means 'stone bridge', is a reference to the slate path and staircase that leads up to the temple, which are still in place. The site is 3km west of the former city wall and gives a good view of the Sukhothai ruins to the southeast and the mountains to the north and south.

All that remains of the original temple are a few *chedi* and the ruined *wí·hǎhn,* consisting of two rows of laterite columns flanking a 12.5m-high standing Buddha image on a brick terrace.

Other Sites

A few more worthwhile sites lie just outside the more popular paid zones.

Wat Chang Lom TEMPLE

(วัดช้างล้อม; Map p356) Off Hwy 12 in the east zone, Wat Chang Lom (Elephant Circled Monastery) is about 1km east of the main

SANGKALOK MUSEUM

This small but comprehensive **museum** (off map p360; ☑0 5561 4333; 203/2 Mu 3, Th Muangkao; adult/child 100/50B; ⊙8am-5pm) is an excellent introduction to ancient Sukhothai's most famous product and export, its ceramics. It displays an impressive collection of original 700-year-old Thai pottery found in the area, plus some pieces traded from Vietnam, Burma and China. The 2nd floor features examples of non-utilitarian pottery made as art, including some beautiful and rare ceramic Buddha statues.

park entrance. A large bell-shaped *chedi* is supported by 36 elephants sculpted into its base.

Wat Chetupon TEMPLE
(วัดเชตุพน; off Map p356) Located 1.4km south of the city walls, this temple once held a four-sided *mon·dòp* featuring the four classic poses of the Buddha (sitting, reclining, standing and walking). The graceful lines of the walking Buddha can still be made out today.

Wat Chedi Si Hong TEMPLE
(วัดเจดีย์สี่ห้อง; off Map p356) Directly across from Wat Chetupon, the main chedi here has retained much of its original stucco relief work, which shows still vivid depictions of elephants, lions and humans.

🏃 Activities

Cycling Sukhothai BICYCLE TOURS
(off map p360; ☑0 5561 2519; www.cycling-suk hothai.com; half-/full day 600/750B, sunset tour 300B) Belgian cycling enthusiast Ronny Hanquart offers a variety of fun and educational bicycle tours of the area. A resident of Sukhothai for nearly 20 years, his rides follow themed itineraries such as the Dharma & Karma Tour, which includes a visit to bizarre **Wat Tawet**, a temple with statues depicting Buddhist hell, or the Historical Park Tour, which includes stops at lesser-seen *wát* and villages. Personalised itineraries can also be arranged.

Ronny is based near Sabaidee House, and he also offers free transport for peopel who are his customers.

✹ Festivals

Loi Krathong TRADITIONAL
Celebrated for five days in November in historical Sukhothai; the city is one of the most popular destinations in Thailand to celebrate the holiday. In addition to the magical floating lights, there are fireworks, folk-dance performances and a light-and-sound production.

🛏 Sleeping

Most accommodation is still in New Sukhothai, which is home to some of the best-value budget-level accommodation in northern Thailand. Clean, cheerful hotels and guest houses abound, with many places offering attractive bungalows, free pick-up from the bus station, free wi-fi and free use of bicycles.

There are an increasing number of options near the park, many of them in the upscale bracket. Prices tend to go up during the Loi Krathong festival.

NEW SUKHOTHAI

TOP CHOICE Ruean Thai Hotel HOTEL $$$
(Map p360; ☑0 5561 2444; www.rueanthaihotel. com; 181/20 Soi Pracha Ruammit; r 1200-3600B; ❄@🛜🏊) At first glance, you may mistake this eye-catching complex for a temple or museum. The rooms on the upper level are very Thai, and feature worn teak furnishings and heaps of character. Poolside rooms are slightly more modern, and there's a concrete building with simple air-con rooms out the back. Service is both friendly and flawless. Call for free pick-up from the bus station.

At Home Sukhothai HOTEL $$
(Map p360; ☑0 5561 0172; www.athomesukhothai. com; 184/1 Th Vichien Chamnong; r incl breakfast 400-800B; ❄@🛜) Located in the 50-year-old childhood home of the proprietor, the attractive structure could easily pass as a newborn after recent renovations. Combining original wooden furnishings with new, the results blend seamlessly, and the simple but comfortable rooms really do feel like home. There's a lotus pond out back, and virtually every other service, from food to Thai massage, in front.

Lotus Village HOTEL $$$
(Map p360; ☑0 5562 1484; www.lotus-village.com; 170 Th Ratchathani; r & bungalows incl breakfast 720-2850B; ❄@🛜) Village is an apt label for

this peaceful compound of elevated wooden bungalows. Smaller rooms in an attractive wooden building are also available, and a Burmese/Indian design theme runs through the entire place. An on-site spa offers a variety of services.

Sila Resort HOTEL **$$**

(Map p360; ☎0 5562 0344; www.sila-resort@hotmail.com; 3/49 Th Kuhasuwan; r 400B, bungalows 500-1000B; ❄@📶) We couldn't help but think of Disneyland when we first encountered this villagelike compound of cosy wood bungalows, resortlike A-frames, clean rooms, a Thai villa and a restaurant. And like Disneyland, it comes together in a cheerful, colourful package, the only downside being that it's a fair hike from the centre of New Sukhothai.

Ananda HOTEL **$$$**

(off Map p360; ☎0 5562 2428-30; www.anandasukhothai.com; 10 Moo 4, Th Muangkao; r incl breakfast 2600-3300B, ste incl breakfast 5500B; ❄@📶) The label 'Museum Gallery Hotel' may cause some to wonder what actually goes on here, but this architecturally striking boutique hotel is straightforwardly attractive. Resembling something of a suburban church with Sukhothai influences, the 32 rooms combine dark woods and earth-coloured silks, and the hotel also houses a spa and antique shop. Located about 2km outside the centre of town, Ananda is directly next door to the Sangkalok Museum.

Ban Thai HOTEL **$**

(Map p360; ☎0 5561 0163; banthai_guesthouse@yahoo.com; 38 Th Prawet Nakhon; r with shared bathroom 200B, bungalows 300-500B; ❄@📶) Centred around an inviting garden, this mish-mash of rooms and tiny bungalows is among the more popular budget places in town. None of the accommodation is particularly remarkable in itself, but the combination of friendly atmosphere and low prices culminate in a winner.

Sabaidee House HOTEL **$**

(off Map p360; ☎0 5561 6303; www.sabaideehouse.com; 81/7 Moo 1, Tambol Banklouy; r 200-600B; ❄@📶) Having graduated from homestay status, this cheery guest house has followed the route of much of Sukhothai's budget accommodation and boasts five attractive bungalows. Cheaper accommodation is still

LOCAL KNOWLEDGE

RONNY HANQUART: MANAGER OF CYCLING SUKHOTHAI

Best Temple

Wat Mahathat (p357) and the majestic Buddha statue at Wat Si Chum (p357) are two temples you should not miss.

Best Museum

If you are visiting Si Satchanalai Historical Park (p363) then I recommend the excavated kilns along the Yom river (p364).

Best Time to Visit

Early in the morning is cooler and there are fewer visitors. After a siesta under one of the big trees in the park, you can continue till evening. Sukhothai is green during the monsoon (May to October) and nice and cool during the cool season (December to February).

Best Place to Escape the Crowds

The Western Zone (p357) is quite large and has a beautiful natural background. Few tourists go there.

Best Sunset

Wat Sa Si (p357) in the Central Zone is a good spot for sunset.

Secret Spot

Wat Tawet, where Buddhist and Hindu morals are explained through a display of about 200 statues, is an interesting place for people who like art and kitsch.

Best Non-Temple Activity

Why not go on a countryside tour by mountain bike? Paddy fields and villages – it's simple and beautiful.

New Sukhothai

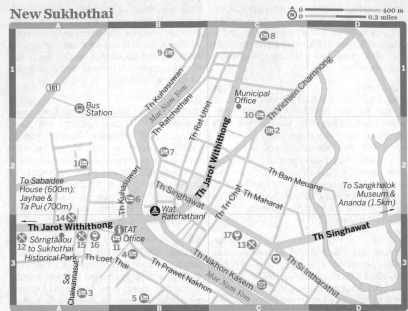

New Sukhothai

available in the main house, not to mention perks such as free bicycles and transport from the bus station. Sabaidee is 1.5km west of the Mae Nam Yom, on a side street about 200m before the intersection with Rte 101 – look for the sign.

Baan Georges Hotel HOTEL $$
(Map p360; ☑08 6100 7651; www.baan-georges.com; 28/54 Soi Chaiwannasut; r incl breakfast 700-1500B; ※@☞≋) The proprietors of the Poo Restaurant have opened their new three-storey villa to guests. Rooms are large and equipped with TV, fridge, air-con and rather hi-tech-looking bathrooms. Highlights in-

clude family rooms with bunk beds, a pool, and an open-air rooftop kitchen/dining room.

TR Room & Bungalow HOTEL $
(Map p360; ☑0 5561 1663; www.sukhothaibudgetguesthouse.com; 27/5 Th Prawet Nakhon; r 250-400B, bungalows 400B; ※@☞) The rooms here are basic but extremely tidy, and there are five spacious bungalows out back for those needing leg room. A cosy terrace provides even more incentive. An excellent budget choice.

4T Guesthouse HOTEL $$
(Map p360; ☑0 5561 4679; www.4tguesthouse.ob.tc; 122 Soi Mae Ramphan; r 300-400B, bunga-

lows 600-900B; ❋❀@☏☸) Hardly a leaf is out of place at this expansive resortlike guest house. A smorgasbord of bungalows and spacious rooms spans just about every budget, and the swimming pool makes the decision even easier.

Hung Jeng
GUEST HOUSE $

(Map p360; ☏0 5561 0585; hangjeng@hotmail.com; 44/10 Th Prawet Nakhon; r 150-350B; ❋@☏) A sign above the door here reads 'Welcome with open arms' and one gets the impression they really mean it. Maintained by an exceptionally lovely family, the rooms are in a rambling and colourful house and share toilets and balconies.

Sukhothai Guest House
HOTEL $$

(Map p360; ☏0 5561 0453; www.sukhothaiguesthouse.com; 68 Th Vichien Chamnong; r 450-750B; ❋@☏) This long-running guest house has 12 bungalows with terraces packed into a shaded garden. The communal area is filled with an eclectic mix of bric-a-brac and the owners are friendly and conduct local tours.

J&J Guest House
HOTEL $

(☏0 5562 0095; www.jjguest-house.com; 12 Th Kuhasuwan; bungalows with fan/air-con 500/600B; ❋@☏) Located in a tidy garden by the river, the eight bungalows here are new, cool and relatively spacious.

SUKHOTHAI HISTORICAL PARK

Orchid Hibiscus Guest House
HOTEL $$

(Map p356; ☏0 5563 3284; orchid_hibiscus_guest_house@hotmail.com; 407/2 Rte 1272; r/bungalows 900/1300B; ❋❀@☏☸) This collection of rooms and bungalows is set in relaxing, manicured grounds with a swimming pool as a centrepiece and the self-professed 'amazing breakfast' as a highlight. Rooms are spotless and fun, featuring various design details and accents. The guest house is on Rte 1272 about 500m off Rte 12 – the turn-off is between Km 48 and Km 49 markers.

Thai Thai
HOTEL $$

(Map p356; ☏08 4932 1006; thai_thai_guesthouse@hotmail.com; Rte 1272; bungalows incl breakfast 1000-1200B; ❋@☏) Next door to Orchid Hibiscus, Thai Thai takes the form of 10 wooden bungalows in an attractive garden and fully outfitted with TV, fridge, hot water and air-con.

Vitoon Guesthouse
GUEST HOUSE $

(Map p356; ☏0 5569 7045; www.vitoonguesthouse.com; 49 Moo 3; r with fan/air-con 300/600B; ❋@)

One of only two budget options within walking distance of the old city, the fan rooms here are showing their age, but the air-con rooms, in a newer building, are spotless and represent a good deal.

PinPao Guest House
HOTEL $$

(Map p356; ☏0 5563 3284; orchid_hibiscus_guest_house@hotmail.com; Hwy 12; r 900B; ❋❀@☏☸) Affiliated with the Orchid Hibiscus Guest House, this is a large building with 10 of the most gaily coloured rooms we've seen anywhere, although many lack windows and can be rather dark. The guest house is on Rte 12, directly opposite the turn-off to Rte 1272.

Tharaburi Resort
HOTEL $$$

(Map p356; ☏0 5569 7132; www.tharaburiresort.com; 321/3 Moo 3, Rte 1272; r incl breakfast 1200-4200B; ste 5000-6500B; ❋❀@☏☸) This slightly overpriced boutique hotel features three main structures divided up into 20 individually styled rooms and suites. Some are themed (Moroccan, Japanese, Chinese) and this is done with fine antiques, lush silks and exquisite attention to detail. The cheaper rooms are simpler, the suites feel like a small home, and there are also two-floor family rooms.

Old City Guest House
HOTEL $

(Map p356; ☏0 5569 7515; 28/7 Moo 3; r 150-700B; ❋☏) This vast complex features heaps of rooms in a variety of styles and budgets, most with air-con and TV; ask to see a few before you make a decision.

✗ Eating & Drinking

Sukhothai's signature dish is *gŏo·ay děe·o sù·kŏh·tai*, 'Sukhothai-style noodles', which feature a slightly sweet broth with different types of pork, ground peanuts and thinly sliced green beans. The dish is available at **Jayhae** (off Map p360; Th Jarot Withithong; dishes 25-40B; ☺7am-4pm) and **Ta Pui** (off Map p360; Th Jarot Withithong; dishes 25-35B; ☺7am-3pm), located across from each other on Th Jarot Withithong, about 1.3km west of the Mae Nam Yom.

Don't miss New Sukhothai's tiny **night market** (Map p360; Th Jarot Withithong). Most vendors here are accustomed to accommodating foreigners and even provide bilingual, written menus. Near the ticket kiosk in the historical park, there is a collection of food stalls (Map p356) and simple open-air restaurants.

NORTHERN THAILAND SUKHOTHAI

BUSES & MINIVANS FROM SUKHOTHAI

Sukhothai's **bus station** (☎0 5561 4529; Rte 101) is almost 1km northwest of the centre of town. There are frequent departures south to Bangkok, which also make stops in Phitsanulok, Kamphaeng Phet and Ayuthaya, and frequent departures north to Chiang Mai, with stops in Lampang.

There are also minivans to Mae Sot (130B, three hours, every two hours from 9.15am to 4.15pm) and frequent *sŏrng·tǎa·ou* to Kamphaeng Phet (39B, two hours) during the day.

If you're going to the bus station and don't want to succumb to profit-seeking túk-túk drivers, simply hop on the *sŏrng·tǎa·ou* bound for Sukhothai Historical Park, which makes a stop at the bus station (20B, 10 minutes) from 6am to 5.30pm. Alternatively, if you're staying near the historical park, buses for Bangkok (262B to 380B, six hours, 9am and 8.20pm) and Chiang Mai (300B, five hours, frequent departures from 7.30am to 8.30pm) can be boarded near Vitoon Guesthouse.

DESTINATION	FARE (B)	DURATION (HR)	FREQUENCY
Bangkok	255-380	6-7	every 30min 7.50am-11pm
Chiang Mai	218	6	every 30min 7.15am-4.30pm
Chiang Rai	249	9	6.40am, 9am, 11.30am
Kamphaeng Phet	55-70	1½	7.50am-11pm
Khon Kaen	234	7	8.30am-4pm
Lampang	162	3	every 30min 7.15am-4.30pm
Nan	185	4	3pm, 4pm
Phitsanulok	28-39	1	every 30min 6am-6pm
Sawankhalok	19-27	1	every hr 6am-6pm
Si Satchanalai	46	1½	11am

Dream Café   THAI $
(Map p360; 86/1 Th Singhawat; dishes 80-150B; ⊙lunch & dinner; ✹) A meal at Dream Café is like dining in a museum or an antique shop. Eclectic but tasteful furnishings and knick-knackery abound, staff are equal parts competent and friendly, and most importantly of all, the food is good. The helpful menu lays down the basics of Thai food, explaining what to order and how to eat it. Try one of the well-executed *yam* (Thai-style 'salads'), or one of the dishes that feature freshwater fish, a local speciality.

Chula   THAI $
(Map p360; Th Jarot Withithong; dishes 30-90B; ⊙lunch & dinner) It has all the charm of an airport hangar, but the food at this local favourite is solid. Pick-and-choose from prepared dishes, or do the same with the raw ingredients displayed out front, which will be fried before your eyes.

Poo Restaurant   INTERNATIONAL-THAI $
(Map p360; 24/3 Th Jarot Withithong; dishes 30-150B) Unfortunately named and deceptively simple, this restaurant offers a diverse menu of breakfasts, hearty sandwiches, Belgian beers and even a few Thai dishes.

Coffee Cup   INTERNATIONAL-THAI $
(Map p356; Moo 3, Old Sukhothai; dishes 30-150B; ⊙7am-10pm) If you're staying in the old city or are an early riser, come here for breakfast; the coffee is strong and the bread is fresh.

Chopper Bar   BAR
(Map p360; Th Prawet Nakhon; ⊙5pm-12.30am) Both travellers and locals congregate from dusk till hangover for food, drinks, live music and flirtation at this place, within spitting distance of Sukhothai's tiny guesthouse strip.

Terrace & Trees   BAR
(Map p360; Th Singhawat; ⊙5pm-12.30am) Directly behind the Sawasdipong Hotel, this bar/restaurant features live music of varying quality and is one of the trendier places in town to put back a few.

❶ Information

There are banks with ATMs scattered all around the central part of New Sukhothai, particularly in the area west of the Mae Nam Yom, and now a few in Old Sukhothai as well. Internet is easy to find in New Sukhothai, and is available at many guest houses.

Police station (☑0 5561 1010) In New Sukhothai.

Post office (Th Nikhon Kasem, New Sukhothai; ☺8.30am-noon & 1-4.30pm Mon-Fri, 9am-noon Sat & Sun)

Sukhothai Hospital (☑0 5561 0280; Th Jarot Withithong, New Sukhothai)

Tourism Authority of Thailand office (TAT; ☑nationwide call centre 1672, Sukhothai 0 5561 6228; Th Jarot Withithong; ☺8.30am-4.30pm) Near the bridge in New Sukhothai, this new office has a pretty good selection of maps and brochures.

Tourist police (Sukhothai Historical Park) Call 1155 for emergencies or go to the tourist police station opposite the Ramkhamhaeng museum.

ⓘ Getting There & Away

Air

Sukhothai's airport is 27km from town off Rte 1195, about 11km from Sawankhalok. There is a minivan service (180B) between the airport and new Sukhothai. **Bangkok Airways** (☑nationwide call centre 1771, Sukhothai 0 5564 7224; www.bangkokair.com; Sukhothai airport) operates flights to Bangkok's Suvarnabhumi International Airport (3480B, 80 minutes, twice daily) and Lampang (2115B, 30 minutes, once daily).

ⓘ Getting Around

A ride by săhm-lór within New Sukhothai should cost no more than 40B. Sŏrng·tăa·ou run frequently between New Sukhothai and Sukhothai Historical Park (20B, 30 minutes, 6am to 5.30pm), leaving from Th Jarot Withithong near Poo Restaurant, and making a stop at Sukhothai's bus station.

Transport from the bus terminal into the centre of New Sukhothai costs 60B in a chartered vehicle. Motorbike taxis charge 40B. If going directly to Old Sukhothai, sŏrng·tăa·ou charge 180B and motorcycle taxis 150B.

The best way to get around the historical park is by bicycle, which can be rented at shops outside the park entrance for 30B per day. The park operates a tram service (80B, one hour, 8am to 5pm) through the central zone, although explanation is in Thai only.

Motorbikes can be rented starting at about 250B for 24 hours and are available at Poo Restaurant and nearly every guest house in New Sukhothai.

Around Sukhothai

SI SATCHANALAI-CHALIANG HISTORICAL PARK

อุทยานประวัติศาสตร์ศรีสัชนาลัย

Don't skip this portion of the Sukhothai site. With your imagination and sense of adventure you're sure to love this more rustic collection of truly impressive ruins.

Set among hills, the 13th- to 15th-century ruins of the old cities of Si Satchanalai and Chaliang, 50km north of Sukhothai, are in the same basic style as those in the Sukhothai Historical Park, but the setting is more peaceful. The park covers roughly 720 hectares and is surrounded by a 12m-wide moat. Chaliang, 1km southeast, is an older city site (dating to the 11th century), though its two temples date to the 14th century.

The nearby towns of Ban Hat Siaw and Sawankhalok are the main centres for the area.

Si Satchanalai

This **zone** (admission 100B, plus car 50B; ☺8am-4.30pm) contains the majority of ruins. An **information centre** (☺8.30am-5pm) at the park distributes free maps and has a small exhibit outlining the history and attractions. Bikes can be rented near the entrance gate (20B).

Wat Chang Lom   TEMPLE
(วัดช้างล้อม) This fine temple, marking the centre of the old city of Si Satchanalai, has elephants surrounding a bell-shaped *chedi* that is somewhat better preserved than its counterpart in Sukhothai. An inscription states that the temple was built by King Ramkhamhaeng between 1285 and 1291.

Wat Khao Phanom Phloeng   TEMPLE
(วัดเขาพนมเพลิง) On the hill overlooking Wat Chang Lom are the remains of Wat Khao Phanom Phloeng, including a *chedi,* a large seated Buddha and stone columns that once supported the roof of the *wí·hăhn.* From this hill you can make out the general design of the once-great city. The slightly higher hill west of Phanom Phloeng is capped

ⓘ GOOD DEAL

An admission fee of 220B allows entry to Si Satchanalai, Wat Chao Chan (at Chaliang) and the Si Satchanalai Centre for Study & Preservation of Sangkalok Kilns.

by a large Sukhothai-style *chedi* – all that remains of Wat Khao Suwan Khiri.

Wat Chedi Jet Thaew TEMPLE

(วัดเจดีย์เจ็ดแถว) Next to Wat Chang Lom, these ruins contain seven rows of *chedi*, the largest of which is a copy of one at Wat Mahathat in Sukhothai. An interesting brick-and-plaster *wí·hǎhn* features barred windows designed to look like lathed wood (an ancient Indian technique used all over Southeast Asia). A *prasat* (small ornate building with a cruciform ground plan and needlelike spire) and *chedi* are stacked on the roof.

Wat Nang Phaya TEMPLE

(วัดนางพญา) South of Wat Chedi Jet Thaew, this *chedi* is Sinhalese in style and was built in the 15th or 16th century, a bit later than the other monuments at Si Satchanalai. Stucco reliefs on the large laterite *wí·hǎhn* in front of the *chedi* – now sheltered by a tin roof – date from the Ayuthaya period when Si Satchanalai was known as Sawankhalok. Goldsmiths in the district still craft a design known as *nahng pá·yah*, modelled after these reliefs.

Chaliang

This older **site** (Map p365), a short bike ride from Si Satchanalai, has two temples of note. Admission isn't always collected at Wat Chao Chan.

Wat Phra Si Ratana Mahathat TEMPLE

(วัดพระศรีรัตนมหาธาตุ; admission 20B; ⊙8am-5pm) These ruins consist of a large laterite *chedi* (dating back to 1448–88) between two *wí·hǎhn*. One of the *wí·hǎhn* holds a large seated Sukhothai Buddha image, a smaller standing image and a bas-relief of the famous walking Buddha, exemplary of the flowing,

SAWANWORANAYOK NATIONAL MUSEUM

In Sawankhalok town, near Wat Sawankhalam on the western river bank, this state-sponsored **museum** (✆0 5564 1571; 69 Th Phracharat, Sawankhalok; admission 50B; ⊙9am-4pm) houses an impressive collection of 12th- to 15th-century artefacts. The ground floor focuses on the area's ceramic legacy, while the 2nd floor features several beautiful bronze and stone Sukhothai-era Buddha statues.

boneless Sukhothai style. The other *wí·hǎhn* contains some less distinguished images.

Wat Chao Chan TEMPLE

(วัดเจ้าจันทร์; admission 100B; ⊙8am-5pm) These wát ruins are about 500m west of Wat Phra Si Ratana Mahathat. The central attraction is a large Khmer-style tower similar to later towers built in Lopburi and probably constructed during the reign of Khmer King Jayavarman VII (1181–1217). The tower has been restored and is in fairly good shape. The roofless *wí·hǎhn* on the right contains the laterite outlines of a large standing Buddha that has all but melted away from exposure and weathering.

Sawankhalok Kilns

At one time, more than 200 huge pottery **kilns** (admission free) lined the banks of Mae Nam Yom in the area around Si Satchanalai. In China – the biggest importer of Thai pottery during the Sukhothai and Ayuthaya periods – the pieces produced here came to be called 'Sangkalok', a mispronunciation of Sawankhalok. Ceramics are still made in the area, and a local ceramic artist even continues to fire his pieces in an underground wood-burning oven.

In addition to the centre, several barely recognisable kiln sites can be found along the road that runs north of Si Satchanalai.

Si Satchanalai Centre for Study & Preservation of Sangkalok Kilns MUSEUM

(ศูนย์ศึกษาและอนุรักษ์เตาสังคโลก; admission 100B; ⊙9am-4pm) Located 5km northwest of the Si Satchanalai ruins, this centre has large excavated kilns and many intact pottery samples. The exhibits are interesting despite the lack of English labels.

🛏 Sleeping & Eating

There's very little accommodation or food near the park. If you have your own transport, a better alternative is to be based in Sawankhalok, 20km south of the park, or Ban Hat Siaw, about 9km south of the park.

Sukhothai Heritage Resort HOTEL $$$

(✆0 5564 7564; www.sukhothaiheritage.com; 999 Moo 2, Sukhothai airport; r incl breakfast 4000-5900B, ste incl breakfast 11,600B; ❄@🛜🏊) Owned by Bangkok Airways and near its airport approximately 32km from Si Satchanalai Historical Park, this resort is now the area's most upscale accommodation. A virtual continuation of the historical park, the low-lying brick and peak-roofed structures are interspersed by calming

Si Satchanalai-Chaliang Historical Park

N ⊙ 0 ⎯⎯⎯ 500 m
0 ⎯⎯⎯ 0.25 miles

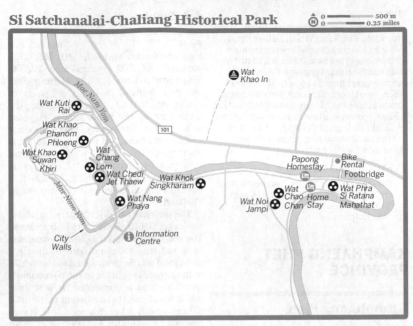

lotus-filled ponds, culminating in a templelike environment. The rooms take you back to the secular world with large flat-screen TVs and modern furniture.

Home Stay
GUEST HOUSE **$**

(☎08 1935 2835; r & bungalow 500B; Chaliang; ❄ 🛜 ≋) Located a minute's walk from Wat Phra Si Ratana Mahathat at Chaliang, the three rooms in this large house share bathrooms and are tidy and comfortable. There's also a poolside bungalow. The only thing lacking is food, which is best obtained near the entrance of the park, ideally before 6pm.

Papong Homestay
GUEST HOUSE **$**

(☎0 5563 1557, 08 7313 4782; r 500B; Chaliang; ❄) Another locally run outfit near the historical park, the three rooms here include private bathrooms and are tidy and comfortable.

Si Satchanalai Hotel and Resort
HOTEL **$**

(☎0 5567 2666; 247 Moo 2, Rte 101; r 200-500B, bungalows 1200B; ❄) Resembling neither hotel nor resort, nonetheless this is virtually the only formal accommodation to be located relatively near the historical park. Rooms are featureless but tidy, and the expansive bungalows would be great for families. It's approximately 6km north of the park on the west side of Rte 101.

Mukda
HOTEL **$**

(no roman-script sign; ☎0 5567 1024; Ban Hat Siaw; r 200-500B; ❄) The pink bungalows here are basic, but work if you want to stay relatively close to the historical park. It's at the northern end of Ban Hat Siaw, just down the turn-off to Utaradit.

Saengsin Hotel
HOTEL **$**

(☎0 5564 1259/1424; 2 Th Thetsaban Damri, Sawankhalok 3; s/d 220/360B; ❄) Located 1km south of the train station on the main street that runs through Sawankhalok, this long-standing hotel has clean, comfortable rooms and a coffee shop. A couple of other options also line the main drag.

❶ Getting There & Away

BUS

Si Satchanalai-Chaliang Historical Park is off Rte 101 between Sawankhalok and Ban Hat Siaw. From New Sukhothai, take a Si Satchanalai bus (46B, 1½ hours, 11am) or one of three buses to Chiang Rai (46B) at 6.40am, 9am and 11.30am, and ask to get off at 'meuang gòw' (old city). The last bus back to New Sukhothai leaves at 4.30pm.

From Sawankhalok, you can hop on just about any line from the town's roadside bus terminal (24B to 50B, frequent departures from 7am to 5pm).

TRAIN

Sawankhalok's original train station is one of the local sights. King Rama VI built a 60km railway spur from Ban Dara (a small town on the main northern trunk) to Sawankhalok just so that he could visit the ruins. Amazingly, there's a daily special express from Bangkok to Sawankhalok (482B, seven hours, 10.50am). The train heads back to Bangkok at 7.40pm, arriving in the city at 3.30am. You can also take this train to Phitsanulok (328B, 3½ hours, 5.55pm). It's a 'Sprinter' – 2nd class air-con and no sleepers. The fare includes dinner and breakfast.

ⓘ Getting Around

You can rent bicycles (per day 20B) from a shop at the gateway to Wat Phra Si Ratana Mahathat as well as near the food stalls at the entrance to the historical park.

KAMPHAENG PHET PROVINCE

Kamphaeng Phet กำแพงเพชร

POP 30,000

Located halfway between Bangkok and Chiang Mai, Kamphaeng Phet literally means 'Diamond Wall', a reference to the apparent strength of this formerly walled city's protective barrier. This level of security was necessary, as the city previously helped to protect the Sukhothai and later Ayuthaya kingdoms against attacks from Burma or Lanna. Parts of the wall can still be seen today, and the impressive ruins of several religious structures also remain. The modern city stretches along a shallow section of the Mae Nam Ping and is one of Thailand's pleasanter provincial capitals.

◉ Sights

Kamphaeng Phet Historical Park HISTORICAL PARK

(อุทยานประวัติศาสตร์กำแพงเพชร; ☏0 5571 1921; admission 100-150B, motorbike/car 20/50B; ☉8am-5pm) A Unesco World Heritage Site, this park features the ruins of structures dating back to the 14th century, roughly the same time as the better-known kingdom of Sukhothai. Kamphaeng Phet's Buddhist monuments continued to be built until the Ayuthaya period, nearly 200 years later, and thus possess elements of both Sukhothai and Ayuthaya styles, resulting in a school of Buddhist art quite unlike anywhere else in Thailand.

The park has two distinct parts; an inclusive ticket (150B) allows entry to both areas. The **old city** (admission 100B) is surrounded by a wall (the 'Diamond Gate' of the city's name) and was formerly inhabited by monks of the *gamavasi* ('living in the community') sect. This area is dominated by **Wat Phra Kaew**, which used to be adjacent to the royal palace (now in ruins). It's not nearly as well restored as Sukhothai, but it's smaller, more intimate and less visited. Weather-corroded Buddha statues have assumed slender, porous forms that remind some visitors of the sculptures of Alberto Giacometti. About 100m southeast of Wat Phra Kaew is **Wat Phra That**, distinguished by a large round-based *chedi* surrounded by columns.

The majority of Kamphaeng Phet's ruins are found about 1.5km north of the city walls in an area previously home to monks of the *arani* ('living in forests') sect (admission 100B). An inclusive ticket purchased at the old city also allows entrance here, and there is an excellent **visitor centre** (☉8.30am-4.30pm) at the entrance. There are more

---

WORTH A TRIP

BAN NA TON CHAN

Ban Na Ton Chan, a picturesque village in rural Sukhothai, has created a worthwhile and award-winning **homestay program** (☏08 9885 1639; http://homestaynatonchan.blogspot.com; per person 350B). Approximately 20 households participate in the program, and the fee includes breakfast and dinner (for lunch you can try *kôw bóep*, a local noodle dish), and involvement in local activities such as cooking, furniture making and weaving. The locals are keen to open their homes and share their knowledge, but it must be noted that the level of English ability among the villagers is low.

The village is 15km east of Rte 101, down a signed turn-off north of Ban Hat Siaw. A motorcycle taxi from near the 7-Eleven in Ban Hat Siaw will take people here for 150B, sǎhm·lór for 350B.

than 40 temple compounds in this area, including **Wat Phra Si Iriyabot**, which has the shattered remains of standing, sitting, walking and reclining Buddha images all sculpted in the classic Sukhothai style.

Northwest of here, **Wat Chang Rawp** (Elephant-Encircled Temple) is just that – a temple with an elephant-buttressed wall. Several other temple ruins – most of them not much more than flat brick foundations, with the occasional weather-worn Buddha image – can be found in the same general vicinity.

Wat Phra Borommathat   TEMPLE

(วัดพระบรมธาตุ; admission free) Across Mae Nam Ping are the neglected ruins of Wat Phra Borommathat, in an area that was settled long before Kamphaeng Phet's heyday, although visible remains are post-classical Sukhothai. The compound has a few small *chedi* and one large *chedi* of the late Sukhothai period which is now crowned with a Burmese-style umbrella added early in the 20th century.

Kamphaeng Phet National
Museum   MUSEUM

(พิพิธภัณฑสถานแห่งชาติกำแพงเพชร; ☎0 5571 1570; Th Pindamri; admission 100B; ☺9am-noon & 1-4pm Wed-Sun) The national museum has the usual survey of Thai art periods downstairs. Upstairs there is a collection of artefacts from the Kamphaeng Phet area including an immense Shiva statue that is the largest bronze Hindu sculpture in the country. The image was formerly located at the nearby **San Phra Isuan** (Shiva Shrine) until a tourist stole the idol's hands and head in 1886 (they were later returned). Today a replica stands in its place.

Phra Ruang Hot Springs   HOT SPRINGS

(บ่อน้ำร้อนพระร่วง; admission 30B; ☺8.30am-6pm) Located 20km outside Kamphaeng Phet along the road to Sukhothai, this complex of natural hot springs is the Thai version of a rural health retreat. The reputedly therapeutic hot waters have been diverged into seven private bathing rooms (50B), and there's also an outdoor foot pool and several places offering traditional Thai massage. There is no public transport to the hot springs, but transport can be arranged at Three J Guest House.

Kamphaeng Phet Regional
Museum   MUSEUM

(พิพิธภัณฑ์เฉลิมพระเกียรติกำแพงเพชร; ☎0 5572 2341; Th Pindamri; admission 10B; ☺9am-4pm) The regional museum is a series of Thai-style wooden structures on stilts set among nicely landscaped grounds. There are three main buildings in the museum featuring displays ranging from history and prehistory to the various ethnic groups that inhabit the province.

Wat Khu Yang   TEMPLE

(วัดคูยาง; admission free) This Buddhist temple contains a handsome wooden *hŏr đrai* dating back to the 19th century.

🛏 Sleeping

Three J Guest House   GUEST HOUSE **$$**

(☑0 5571 3129; www.threejguesthouse.com; 79 Th Rachavitee; r 250-700B; ❉@⊛) This pleasant collection of bungalows in a pretty garden has a very hospitable and friendly host. Pathways lead to clean log bungalows with terraces. The cheapest ones share a clean bathroom and the more expensive have aircon. There's heaps of local information; bicycles and motorcycles are available for rent, and the owner can also arrange visits to his country resort near Klong Wang Chao.

Chakungrao Riverview   HOTEL **$$$**

(☑0 5571 4900-8; www.chankungraoriverview.com; 149 Th Thesa; r incl breakfast 1000-1300B; ste incl breakfast 5000B; ❉@⊛) Kamphaeng Phet's poshest digs has some nice rooms despite its unremarkable facade. Rooms are tastefully decked out in dark woods and forest green and feature balconies with river or city views. Suites are huge and available at a considerable discount.

Navarat   HOTEL **$$**

(☑0 5571 1211; 2 Soi Prapan; r 700-1100B; ❉⊛) The '70s-era Navarat has undergone a recent renovation, which has erased some but not all signs of the hotel's true age. The 'new' rooms are slightly overpriced, but are clean and cosy, some boasting nice views.

Ko Chokchai Hotel   HOTEL **$**

(no roman-script sign; ☑0 5571 1531; 19-43 Soi 8, Th Ratchadamnoen 1; r 260-320B; ❉@⊛) This egg cartonlike building is a good budget choice with its smallish but tidy rooms. Popular with Thai businessmen, it's conveniently in the centre of the new town.

There are also several Thai-style riverside 'resorts' at Nakhon Chum, along the east bank of the Mae Nam Ping.

Grand View Resort   HOTEL **$$$**

(no roman-script sign; ☑0 5572 1104; www.grandviewresortkpp.com; 34/4 Moo 2, Nakhon Chum; r incl breakfast 290-5000B; ❉⊛) The

NORTHERN THAILAND KAMPHAENG PHET

Kamphaeng Phet

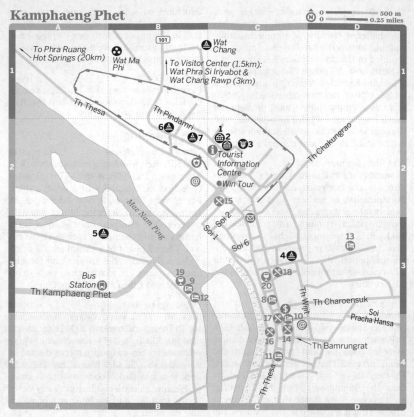

first one you'll come to on the left-hand side, it's similar to many others in quality and price.

Techno River Resort HOTEL $$$
(no roman-script sign; ✆0 5579 9800; 27/27 Moo 2, Nakhon Chum; r incl breakfast 450-2500B; ❄️🛜) This is the poshest of the lot, and offers a huge variety of clean, though generally characterless rooms.

✗ Eating & Drinking

Kamphaeng Phet is definitely not a culinary destination, but there are a few mildly interesting offerings. A busy night market sets up every evening near the river just north of the Navarat Hotel.

[TOP CHOICE] **Bamee Chakangrao** THAI $
(no roman-script sign; Th Ratchadamnoen; dishes 25-30B; ⏰8.30am-3pm) Thin wheat and egg noodles (*bà·mèe*) are a speciality of Kam-

phaeng Phet, and this famous restaurant is one of the best places to try them. The noodles are made fresh every day behind the restaurant, and pork satay is also available.

Kamphaeng Phet Phochana THAI $
(no roman-script sign; dishes 25-50B; ⏰6am-1am) This popular place puts out just about every Thai fave from *pàt tai* to *kôw man gài* (Hainanese-style chicken rice). It's also a good place to try *chŏw gŏoay*, grass jelly, a product made in Kamphaeng Phet. There's no English-language sign, so look for the rainbow-coloured facade near the roundabout.

Piggy THAI $
(no roman-script sign; Th Ratchadamnoen; per person 70B; ⏰dinner) *Mŏo gà·tá*, pork grilled over a hotpot, is one of the more popular dishes in these parts. Simply choose your ingredients from the buffet, then grill your meats, adding your veggies and other ingredients

Kamphaeng Phet

to the broth. There's no English sign, but Piggy is found on the corner and usually boasts several grilling customers.

Phayao Bakery INTERNATIONAL-THAI $
(Th Thesa; dishes 45-120B; 🔆) It may look closed with its heavily tinted windows, but inside you'll find a casual, family-friendly atmosphere with real coffee, a variety of baked goods and ice cream. Air-conditioned, it's a great place to escape from the heat.

Mae Ping Riverside RESTAURANT, BAR
(no roman-script sign; 50/1 Moo 2, Nakhon Chum; dishes 40-120B; ⊗lunch & dinner) Offers draught beer, live music, decent eats and cool breezes. It's one of the first places along the road that parallels the river.

Rong Tiam BAR
(no roman-script sign; Soi 9, Th Thesa 1; ⊗5pm-1am) Live music (from 8.30pm), snacks and beer are available at this friendly pub located in a converted antique shophouse.

ℹ Information

Most of the major banks also have branches with ATMs along the main streets near the river and on Th Charoensuk. There are a couple of internet cafes in town on Th Thesa and Th Ratchadamnoen.

Main post office (Th Thesa) Just south of the old city.

Police station (☏0 5571 1199, emergency 1155)

Tourist Information Centre (⊗8am-4.30pm) Across from the national museum; has some maps and pamphlets. There is another more history-focused centre at the group of ruins north of the city wall.

ℹ Getting There & Away

The **bus station** (☏0 5579 9844) is about 1km west of the Mae Nam Ping. From the same station, minivans run frequent departures to Mae Sot (140B, 2½ hours, 8am to 6pm) and *sŏrng·tǎa·ou* depart for Sukhothai (39B, two hours, every hour from 1pm to 8pm). If coming from Sukhothai or Phitsanulok get off in the old city or at the roundabout on Th Thesa to save getting a *sŏrng·tǎa·ou* back into town. You can also book tickets to Bangkok in advance and board buses near the traffic circle at **Win Tour** (☏0 5571 3971; Th Kamphaeng Phet).

DESTINA-TION	FARE (B)	DURATION (HR)	FREQUENCY
Bangkok	210-315	5	11.30am-1am
Chiang Rai	280	9	11.30am-1.30am
Chiang Mai	268-313	5	noon-1am
Mae Hong Son	468-838	11	8pm, 10pm, 11pm, midnight
Sukhothai	70	1	every hr 1-8pm
Phitsanu-lok	56-78	2½	every hr 5am-6pm

ℹ Getting Around

The least expensive way to get from the bus station into town is to hop on a red *sŏrng·tǎa·ou* (15B per person) to the roundabout across the river. From there take a *sǎhm·lór* anywhere in town for 20B to 30B. Motorcycle taxis from the bus station to most hotels downtown cost 40B.

It is worth renting a bicycle or motorbike to explore areas outside of the old city – Three J Guest House has both for rent (per day bicycle/motorcycle 50/200B).

TAK PROVINCE

Tak is a wild and mountainous province. Its proximity to Myanmar has resulted in a complex history and unique cultural mix.

The majority of Tak is forested and mountainous and is an excellent destination for those wanting to trek. There are Hmong, Musoe (Lahu), Lisu and White and Red Karen settlements throughout the west and north. In the 1970s many of these mountains were a hotbed of communist guerrilla activity. Since the 1980s the former leader of the local CPT movement has been involved in resort-hotel development and most of Tak is open to outsiders, but the area still has an untamed feeling about it.

Western Tak in particular has always been in distinct contrast with other parts of Thailand because of strong Karen and Burmese cultural influences. The Thailand–Myanmar border districts of Mae Ramat, Tha Song Yang and Mae Sot are dotted with refugee camps, an outcome of fire fights between the Karen National Union (KNU) and the Myanmar government.

Mae Sot   แม่สอด
POP 120,569

Despite its remote location and relatively small size, Mae Sot is among the most culturally diverse cities in Thailand. Walking down the streets of the town, you'll see a fascinating ethnic mixture: Burmese men in their *longyi* (sarongs), Hmong and Karen women in traditional hill-tribe dress, bearded Muslims, Thai army rangers and foreign NGO workers. Burmese and Karen are spoken more than Thai, shop signs along the streets are in Thai, Burmese and Chinese, and most of the temple architecture in Mae Sot is Burmese. Mae Sot has also become the most important jade and gem centre along the border, with most of the trade controlled by Chinese and Indian immigrants from Myanmar.

Although there aren't many formal sights in Mae Sot, and most tourists just come for a visa run, many end up staying longer than expected. A vibrant market, several good restaurants and a fun nightlife scene have become attractions in their own right.

◉ Sights & Activities

Border Market & Myawadi   MARKET
(ตลาดริมน้ำเมย/เมียวดี) There is an expansive covered market alongside the Mae Nam Moei on the Thai side that legally sells a mixture of workaday Burmese goods and cheap Chinese electronics.

However, the real reason most come here is to cross to Myawadi in Myanmar (Burma) – when the border is open (p375). *Sŏrng·tăa·ou* frequently go to the border (20B, frequent departures from 6.30am to 5.30pm), 5km west of Mae Sot: ask for Rim Moei (Edge of the Moei). The last *sŏrng·tăa·ou* going back to Mae Sot leaves Rim Moei at 5.30pm.

Herbal Sauna   SAUNA
(admission 20B; ⊘3-7pm) Wat Mani has separate herbal sauna facilities for men and women. The sauna is towards the back of the monastery grounds, past the monks' *gù·dì* (living quarters).

Cookery Course   COOKERY COURSE
(☏0 5554 6584; borderlineshop@yahoo.com; 674/14 Th Intharakhiri; lessons 1000B; ⊘8.30am-noon & 1-4pm Tue-Sun) Held at Borderline shop, this course teaches Shan, Burmese and Karen dishes, and includes a trip to the market, food and drink preparation, a cookbook, and sharing the results in the adjoining cafe. Courses decrease in price with bigger groups.

⭐ Festivals & Events

Thai-boxing Competition   THAI BOXING
Around April, Thai and Burmese boxers meet for a competition, held somewhere outside town in the traditional style. Five-round matches are fought in a circular ring; the first four rounds last three minutes, the fifth has no time limit. With their hands bound in hemp, boxers fight till first blood or knockout. You'll have to ask around to find the changing venue for this annual slugfest.

Thai-Burmese Gem Fair   GEM FAIR
Held in April.

🛏 Sleeping

Many places in Mae Sot fit in the budget range and cater for NGO workers that are staying longer-term.

Around Tak & Mae Sot

Ban Thai Guest House HOTEL $$
(☑0 5553 1590; banthai_mth@hotmail.com; 740 Th Intharakhiri; r 250-800B; ❀@🔊) This tiny neighbourhood of five converted Thai houses down a hibiscus-lined alley has spacious, very stylish wooden rooms with Thai-style furniture, axe lounging pillows and Thai textiles. Shared sitting areas have cable TV, DVDs and free wireless internet. There are bicycles and motorbikes to rent and a laundry service. The place is popular with long-stay NGO workers, so booking ahead is a good idea.

Rujira HOTEL $$
(☑0 5554 4969; rujira_tom@hotmail.com; 3/18 Th Buakjoon; r incl breakfast 350-1000B; ❀@🔊) This great-value place has spacious, apartmentlike rooms with lots of homey touches. There's also a pleasant communal feeling, with lots of shaded outdoor seating, a restaurant and a cute coffee shop. The only downside is that it's a long walk to the town centre.

Irawadee Resort HOTEL $$$
(☑0 5553 5430; www.irawadee.com; 758/1-2 Th Intharakhiri; r/ste incl breakfast 850/1800B; ❀🔊) This new brick monstrosity has rooms decked out in a Burmese – or is it an imperial Chinese – theme. Bathrooms are spacious with open-air showers. Gaudy, but fun and comfortable.

Bai Fern Guesthouse HOTEL $
(☑0 5553 1349; www.bai-fern.com; 660 Th Intharakhiri; r 150-300B; ❀@) Set just off the road in a large house, the rooms here are tidy, but plain. All have well-equipped shared bathrooms. The service is very friendly with the use of a kitchen, fridge and wireless internet in the communal area.

Poon Na Gunn Hotel HOTEL $$
(☑0 5553 4732; www.poonnagunn.com; 10/3 Th Intharakhiri; r incl breakfast 780-975B; ❀🔊) This is the kind of hotel you wish you could take with you everywhere; rooms are clean and

Mae Sot

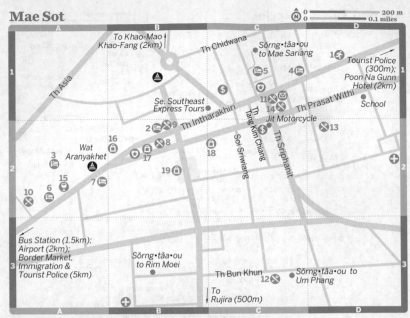

Mae Sot

Activities, Courses & Tours
- Cookery Course .... (see 16)
- 1 Herbal Sauna D1

Sleeping
- 2 Bai Fern Guesthouse B2
- Ban Pruk Sa Guesthouse ....(see 2)
- 3 Ban Thai Guest House A2
- 4 DK Mae Sot Hotel C1
- 5 Green Guest House C1
- 6 Irawadee Resort A2
- 7 Phan Nu House A2

Eating
- 8 Aiya B2
- 9 Bai Fern B2

- 10 Casa Mia A2
- 11 Khrua Canadian C1
- 12 Lucky Tea Garden C3
- 13 Night Market D2
- 14 Phat Thai Mae Sot C1

Drinking
- 15 Mali Bar A2
- Water Bar ....(see 15)

Shopping
- 16 Borderline Shop B2
- 17 Fair Trade Shop B2
- 18 Gem Shops C2
- 19 Municipal Market B2

large and tastefully decked out with attractive furnishings, and include a small verandah. The hotel is about 2km east of town.

DK Mae Sot Hotel HOTEL $
(☏0 5554 2648; 298/2 Th Intharakhiri; r with fan or air-con 250-450B; ❄☎) If the beds, towels and sheets here were upgraded, it would be a fantastic budget deal. Until then the large

rooms in this long-standing three-storey hotel are average, but conveniently located.

Ban Pruk Sa Guesthouse GUEST HOUSE $
(☏0 5553 2656; www.banpruksa.com; 740 Th Intharakhiri; r 200-500B; ❄☎) Opposite Ban Thai Guest House, this tidy villa unites a handful of unassuming but spacious and comfortable rooms.

Phan Nu House HOTEL **$**
(☑08 1972 4467; 563/3 Th Intharakhiri; r 250-500B; ❄☎) This place consists of 19 large rooms in a residential compound just off the street. Most are equipped with air-con, TV, fridge and hot water, making them a good deal.

Green Guest House HOTEL **$**
(☑0 5553 3207; krit.sana@hotmail.com; 406/8 sub-soi off Th Intharakhiri; dm 100B, r 270-250B) Run by a teacher and her husband, this peaceful, friendly guest house offers a variety of good-sized rooms with TV and decent furniture. It's great value, centrally located and has a pretty garden.

✗ Eating

Mae Sot is a virtual culinary crossroads with a diversity of cuisines not seen in most other Thai towns. For a fun breakfast head to the area directly south of the mosque where several buzzing Muslim restaurants serve sweet tea, roti and *nanbya,* tandoor-style bread. The town's vibrant day market is the place to try Burmese dishes such as *mohinga,* the country's unofficial national dish, or Burmese-style curries served over rice. Mae Sot's night market features mostly Thai/Chinese-style dishes.

Khao-Mao Khao-Fang THAI **$$**
(no roman-script sign; ☑0 5553 2483; 382 Moo 5, Mae Pa; mains 80-220B; ⊙lunch & dinner) Like dining in a gentrified jungle, this place, designed by a Thai botanist, replaces chandeliers with hanging vines, orchids and lots of running water. It also has one of the more interesting Thai menus you'll find anywhere, with dishes featuring local ingredients such as fish from the Mae Nam Moei or local herbs and veggies. Try one of the several delicious-sounding *yam* (Thai-style spicy salads), featuring ingredients ranging from white turmeric to local mushrooms. The restaurant is north of town between the Km 1 and Km 2 markers on the road to Mae Ramat.

Lucky Tea Garden BURMESE **$**
(Th Bun Khun; mains 10-50B; ⊙5.30am-9pm) For the authentic Burmese teashop experience without crossing over to Myawadi, visit this friendly cafe equipped with sweet tea, tasty snacks, and of course, bad Burmese pop music. Or come with an empty stomach and try one of the better *biryani* in town.

Phat Thai Mae Sot THAI **$**
(no roman-script sign; Th Prasat Withi; mains 25-45B; ⊙noon-9pm) This cosy place serves *pàt tai* with a local twist: toppings of pork rind and barbecued pork. It's a bit tricky to find, so look for the wooden house with the old-school advertisements.

Casa Mia INTERNATIONAL-THAI **$$**
(Th Don Kaew; mains 30-180B; ⊙7.30am-10pm) Tucked down a side street, this simple restaurant serves the cheapest homemade pasta dishes you'll find anywhere. And better yet, they're right tasty. They also do Thai and Burmese, and some exceptional desserts, including a wicked banoffee pie.

Aiya BURMESE-THAI **$**
(533 Th Intharakhiri; dishes 40-90B; ⊙lunch & dinner Tue-Sun; ✔) Opposite Bai Fern Guest House, Aiya is a simple place that serves good Burmese food, which is particularly strong on vegetarian options.

Khrua Canadian INTERNATIONAL-THAI **$$**
(3 Th Sriphanit; dishes 40-280B; ⊙7am-10pm; ☎) This is the place to go if you want to forget you're in Asia for one meal. Dave, the Canadian, brews his own coffee and also offers homemade bagels, deli meats and cheeses, in addition to a huge breakfast menu. The servings are large, the menu is varied, and when you finally remember you're in Thailand again, local information is also available.

Bai Fern INTERNATIONAL-THAI **$$**
(☑0 5553 3343; Th Intharakhiri; dishes 45-300B; ⊙8am-10pm) The cosy, wood-furnished Bai Fern has a pleasant atmosphere and is popular all day long.

🍷 Drinking & Entertainment

Mae Sot has a lively nightlife that heats up at the weekends. The strip of Th Intharakhiri that runs west from Wat Aranyakhet is where a handful of open-air bars are located.

Mali Bar BAR
(Th Intharakhiri; ⊙6pm-midnight) Staffed by Burmese and popular with the NGO set, this rather dark bar has a pool table and a world music soundtrack.

Water Bar BAR
(Th Intharakhiri; ⊙5pm-midnight) More of a Thai scene, this place has open-air tables, draught beer, snacks and a big screen for the big game.

🛍 Shopping

Mae Sot is most famous for its gems trade, and is the most important jade and gem centre along the border. Check out the hustle and bustle among the glittering treasures in the gem shops along Th Prasat Withi, just east of the morning market. If looking to buy be prepared to bargain hard.

Municipal Market   MARKET
Mae Sot's municipal market is among the largest and most vibrant we've encountered anywhere in Thailand. In addition to the usual Thai wet market veggies and dry goods, there's heaps of exotic stuff from Myanmar, including Burmese bookshops, sticks of *thanaka* (the source of the yellow powder you see on most faces), bags of pickled tea leaves, bizarre cosmetics from across the border and velvet thong slippers from Mandalay. Unlike most markets in Thailand it doesn't require a 6am wake-up call. It's also a great place to try authentic Burmese food.

Borderline Shop   HANDICRAFTS
(www.borderlinecollective.org; 674/14 Th Intharakhiri; ⊙10am-6pm Tue-Sat, 2-6pm Sun) Selling arts and craft items made by refugee women, the profits of this shop go back into a women's collective and a child-assistance foundation. Upstairs a gallery sells paintings, and a cookery course and an outdoor 'tea garden' (⊙9am-6pm Tue-Sun) are also here.

Fair Trade Shop   HANDICRAFTS
(www.weave-women.org; 656 Th Intharakhiri; ⊙9am-5pm Mon-Sat) One of three branches in northern Thailand, this shop specialises in bright handcrafted cloth goods crafted by displaced women from Burma.

ℹ Information

Several centrally located banks have ATMs. There aren't many internet cafes in central Mae Sot, but a couple can be found along Th Intharakhiri, west of Se. Southeast Express Tours. There is no official tourist information office in Mae Sot, but Khrua Canadian is a good source of local information.

Immigration (☏0 5556 3000; ⊙8.30am-noon & 1-4.30pm Mon-Fri) Located next to the Friendship Bridge, this office can do visa extensions.

Tourist police (☏1155; 738/1 Th Intharakhiri) Has an office east of the centre of town and at the market by the Friendship Bridge.

ℹ Getting There & Away

Air
Mae Sot's tiny airport is about 2km outside of town along the road to the Friendship Bridge. A motorcycle taxi to the airport costs 40B. The airline offices are located there, but tickets can be purchased from agents in town such as **Se. Southeast Express Tours** (522/3 Th Intharakhiri).

Destinations from Mae Sot:

Bangkok's Don Muang Airport (1890B to 2690B, 90 minutes, twice daily) via **Nok Air** (☏nationwide call centre 1318, Mae Sot 0 5556 3883; www.nokair.co.th; Mae Sot airport) and **Solar Air** (☏0 5556 3608; www.solarair.co.th; Mae Sot airport)

Chiang Mai (1899B, 50 minutes, three times weekly) via **Kan Air** (☏nationwide call centre 02 551 6111, Mae Sot 08 1585 4489; www.kanairlines.com; Mae Sot airport)

Bus & Minivan
All long-distance buses leave from the bus station 1.5km west of the town on Th Intharakhiri. Minivans bound for Phitsanulok (157B, four hours) and Sukhothai (125B, three hours) also depart from the bus station, with frequent departures from 7am to 2pm.

Bus destinations from Mae Sot:

Bangkok (307B to 613B, eight hours, frequent departures from 8am to 9.45pm)

Chiang Mai (253B to 326B, six hours, 6am and 8am)

Chiang Rai (379B to 488B, 10 hours, 6am and 8am)

Lampang (193B to 248B, four hours, 6am and 8am)

Mae Sai (416B to 535B, 12 hours, 6am and 8am)

Sŏrng·tăa·ou
Sŏrng·tăa·ou depart from various places around town. Orange *sŏrng·tăa·ou* bound for Mae Sariang (200B, six hours, six departures from 6.20am to 12.20pm) depart from the old bus station near the centre of town, while blue *sŏrng·tăa·ou* to Um Phang (120B, four hours, every hour from 6.30am to 3.30pm) leave from an office on Th Bun Khun. *Sŏrng·tăa·ou* to Rim Moei (20B, 15 minutes, frequent departures from 6am to 5.30pm) also leave from a spot just west on Th Bun Khun.

ℹ Getting Around

Most of Mae Sot can be seen on foot. Motorcycle taxis and săhm·lór charge 20B for trips around town.

Several tourism-related business around town, including Bai Fern restaurant, rent out vehicles.

BORDER CROSSING: MAE SOT TO MYAWADI

Mae Sot is – at least when things are calm – a legal border crossing to Myanmar. Yet as with all of Myanmar's land crossings, the situation is volatile, and on our visit, the border was firmly shut due to fighting between the Myanmar Armed Forces and splinter groups of the Democratic Karen Buddhist Army (DKBA). Yet even when the border is open, visits to Myanmar are restricted to a limited number of days within a limited area, and travellers are required to leave their passport at the border and are expected return the same way they came in.

If things change by the time you read this, immigration procedures are taken care of at the **Thai immigration booth** (☑0 5556 3000; ☻6.30am-6.30pm) at the Friendship Bridge. It takes a few minutes to finish all the paperwork to leave Thailand officially, and then you're free to walk across the arched 420m Friendship Bridge.

At the other end of the bridge is the **Myanmar immigration booth**, where you'll fill out permits for a one-day stay, pay a fee of US$10 or 500B and leave your passport as a deposit. Then you're free to wander around Myawadi as long as you're back at the bridge by 5.30pm Myanmar time (which is a half-hour behind Thai time) to pick up your passport and check out with immigration. On your return to Thailand, the Thai immigration office at the bridge will give you a new 15-day visa (p766).

Myawadi is a fairly typical Burmese town, with a number of monasteries, schools, shops and so on. The most important temple is **Shwe Muay Wan**, a traditional bell-shaped *chedi* gilded with many kilos of gold and topped by more than 1600 precious and semiprecious gems. Another noted Buddhist temple is **Myikyaungon**, called Wat Don Jarakhe in Thai and named for its crocodile-shaped sanctuary. Myawadi's 1000-year-old earthen city walls, probably erected by the area's original Mon inhabitants, can be seen along the southern side of town.

Ban Thai Guest House, Ban Pruk Sa Guesthouse and Bai Fern restaurant all rent out motorbikes. Bicycles are available for rent at Borderline, which also includes a suggested tour of the area. **Jit Motorcycle** (☑0 5553 2099; 127/4-6 Th Prasat Withi; motorcycles per day 150B; ☻8am-5pm) Rents out motorcycles.

Mae Sot to Um Phang

Rte 1090 goes south from Mae Sot to Um Phang, 150km away. This stretch of road used to be called the 'Death Highway' because of the guerrilla activity in the area that hindered highway development. Those days ended in the 1980s, but lives are still lost because of brake failure or treacherous turns on this steep, winding road through incredible mountain scenery.

Along the way there are short hikes off the highway to two waterfalls, **Nam Tok Thararak** (26km from Mae Sot) and **Nam Tok Pha Charoen** (41km). Nam Tok Thararak streams over limestone cliffs and calcified rocks with a rough texture that makes climbing the falls easy. It's been made into a park of sorts, with benches right in the stream at the base of the falls for cooling off and a couple of outhouse toilets nearby; on weekends food vendors set up here.

Just beyond Ban Rom Klao 4 – roughly midway between Mae Sot and Um Phang – is Um Piam, a very large Karen and Burmese refugee village with around 20,000 refugees that were moved here from camps around Rim Moei. There are also several Hmong villages in the area.

There are frequent *sŏrng·tǎa·ou* between Mae Sot and Um Phang to Mae Sot (120B, four hours).

Um Phang & Around   อุ้มผาง

Sitting at the junction of Mae Nam Klong and Huay Um Phang, **Um Phang** is an overgrown village populated mostly by Karen. Many Karen villages in this area are very traditional, and elephants are a common sight, especially in **Palatha**, a traditional Karen village 25km south of Um Phang. *Yaeng* (elephant saddles) and other tack used for elephant wrangling are a common sight on the verandahs of the houses in this village.

South of Um Phang, **Um Phang Wildlife Sanctuary** is a Unesco World Heritage Site. Nearby is the largest waterfall in Thailand.

◉ Sights

Nam Tok Thilawsu
WATERFALL

(น้ำตกทีลอซู) This waterfall is Thailand's largest, measuring an estimated 200m high and up to 400m wide during the rainy season. Thais, particularly fanatical about such things, consider Nam Tok Thilawsu to be the most beautiful waterfall in the country. There's a shallow cave behind the falls and several levels of pools suitable for swimming. The best time to visit is after the rainy season (November and December) when the 200m to 400m limestone cliffs alongside the Mae Nam Klong are streaming with water and Nam Tok Thilawsu is at its best.

The vast majority of people visit the falls as part of an organised tour, but it's also possible to go independently. If you've got your own wheels, take the turn-off to Rte 1167 just north of Um Phang. After 12km, turn left at the police checkpoint onto Rte 1288. Continue 6km until you reach the sanctuary checkpoint, where you're expected to pay the entry fee. It's another 30km along a rough road to the sanctuary headquarters.

If you're without transport, it's easy to book a truck just about anywhere in Um Phang (round trip 1800B to 2500B). Alternatively, you can take a Poeng Kloeng-bound *sŏrng·tăa·ou* to the sanctuary checkpoint (30B, every hour 6.30am to 3.30pm), and organise transport from there, although it's not always certain that trucks will be waiting.

Um Phang Wildlife Sanctuary
WILDLIFE SANCTUARY

(เขตรักษาพันธุ์สัตว์ป่าอุ้มผาง; ☏0 5557 7318; admission 200B) The Nam Tok Thilawsu falls are near the headquarters of the Um Phang Wildlife Sanctuary, which is about 50km from Um Phang, towards Sangkhlaburi in Kanchanaburi Province. The 2km path between the headquarters and falls has been transformed into a self-guided nature tour, with the addition of well-conceived educational plaques. Surrounding the falls on both sides of the river are Thailand's thickest stands of natural forest, and the hiking in the vicinity of Nam Tok Thilawsu can be superb. The forest here is said to contain more than 1300 varieties of palm; giant bamboo and strangler figs are also commonplace.

The wildlife sanctuary links with the Thung Yai Naresuan National Park and Huay Kha Kaeng Wildlife Sanctuary (another Unesco World Heritage Site), as well as Khlong Lan and Mae Wong National Parks

to form Thailand's largest wildlife corridor and one of the largest intact natural forests in Southeast Asia.

You can camp (50-100B) at the sanctuary headquarters at any time of year, although it's best to book ahead from November to January, when the falls are a particularly popular destination for Thais. This is also the only time of year when food is generally available at the headquarters, and if you visit at any other time you'll have to bring your own.

Tham Ta Khu Bi
CAVE

(ถ้ำตะโค๊ะบิ) From Ban Mae Klong Mai, just a few kilometres north of Um Phang via the highway to Mae Sot, Rte 1167 heads southwest along the Thai–Myanmar border. Along the way is the extensive cave system of Tham Ta Khu Bi, which in Karen allegedly means 'Flat Mango'. There are no guides here, so be sure to bring your own torch.

Poeng Kloeng
VILLAGE

(บ้านเปิงเคลิ่ง) After 12km, turn left onto Rte 1288, which leads to the checkpoint for Um Phang Wildlife Sanctuary. Past this point the road deteriorates in quality, yet continues more than 70km, terminating in Poeng Kloeng – a Karen, Burmese, Indo-Burmese, Talaku and Thai trading village where buffalo carts are more common than motorcycles. The picturesque setting among spiky peaks and cliffs is worth the trip even if you go no further. From the *sŏrng·tăa·ou* station in Um Phang there are *sŏrng·tăa·ou* to Poeng Kloeng (100B, 2½ hours, every hour 6.30am to 3.30pm).

Letongkhu & Sangkhlaburi
VILLAGES

(เลตองคุ) Roughly 12km south of Poeng Kloeng along a rough track (passable by 4WD in the dry season), near the Myanmar border on the banks of Mae Nam Suriya next to Sam Rom mountain, is the village of Letongkhu. According to what little anthropological information is available, the villagers, although for the most part Karen in language, belong to the Lagu or Talaku sect, said to represent a form of Buddhism mixed with shamanism and animism. Letongkhu is one of only six such villages in Thailand; there are reportedly around 30 more in Myanmar. Each village has a spiritual and temporal leader called a *pu chaik* (whom the Thais call *reu·sĕe* – 'rishi', or 'sage') who wears his hair long – usually tied in a topknot – and dresses in white, yellow or brown robes, depending on the subsect.

Um Phang

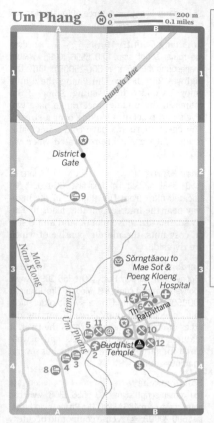

Evangelistic Christian missionaries have infiltrated the area and have tried to convert the Talaku, thus making the Talaku sensitive to outside visits. If you do visit Letongkhu, take care not to enter any village structures without permission or invitation. Likewise, do not take photographs without permission. If you treat the villagers with respect then you shouldn't have a problem.

Sangkhlaburi is 90km or a four- to five-day trek from Poeng Kloeng. The route to Sangkhlaburi has several branches; the main route crosses over the border into Myanmar for some distance before crossing back into Thailand.

Because of the overall sensitive nature of this border area and the very real potential for becoming lost, ill or injured, a guide is highly recommended for any sojourn south of Um Phang. If you speak Thai, you may be able to arrange a guide for this route in Poeng Kloeng. Otherwise, a few trekking agen-

cies in Um Phang have previously arranged such trips with advance notice. The best time of year to do the trek is October to January.

Activities

Trekking & Rafting

Virtually every guest house in Um Phang can arrange combination trekking and rafting trips in the area. Yet because Um Phang is dominated by Thai tourists, only a handful of guides have experience in dealing with foreign visitors, and likewise, few speak English. The agencies we list below have English-speaking guides.

A typical three-day, two-night trip involves both rafting and hiking, with a popular optional activity being elephant rides. The majority involve trips to Nam Tok Thilawsu and beyond, and longer or shorter trips, and trips to other local destinations, may also be arranged.

Rafting trips range from one-day excursions along the Mae Klong from Um Phang to Nam Tok Thilawsu, to three-day trips from Palatha to Nam Tok Thi Lo Re. Most rafting is only possible between November and February.

Um Phang Khi is a 'new' area for rafting, northeast of Um Phang. Officially there are 47 (some rafting companies claim 67) sets of rapids rated at class III (moderate) and class IV (difficult) during the height of the rainy season. The rafting season for Um Phang

NORTHERN THAILAND UM PHANG & AROUND

Khi is short – August to October only – as at other times of the year the water level isn't high enough.

Costs are all-inclusive and start at about 4000B per person (two or more people) for a three-day rafting and trekking excursion. Elephant rides and other extras will bring the price up.

Trekker Hill TREKKING, RAFTING
(☎0 5556 1090; 620 Th Pravitpaiwan, Um Phang) This recommended outfit has the greatest number of English-speaking guides and offers a variety of treks running from one-to four-days.

BC Adventure Tour TREKKING, RAFTING
(☎0 5556 1020; www.boonchuaytour.com) Offers a similar selection of treks and rafting trips, and guides with experience in dealing with foreign trekkers.

Napha Tour TREKKING, RAFTING
(☎0 5556 1287; Th Pravitpaiwan, Um Phang) This outfit offers a variety of programs and English-speaking guides.

Tu Ka Su Cottage TREKKING, RAFTING
(☎0 5556 1295; www.tukasu.net; 40 Moo 6, Um Phang) If none of the above work, contact this resort for help in arranging English-speaking guides.

Weera Tour TREKKING, RAFTING
(no roman-script sign; ☎0 5556 1368) Located just off the main road, this company arranges excellent tours, although the number of English-speaking guides is limited.

🛏 Sleeping

Most places in Um Phang cater to large groups of Thai visitors, so individual foreign travellers are met with a bit of confusion. Likewise, many of the rooms in town are designed for four or more people, and singles or couples can usually negotiate lower rates, especially in the wet season.

Tu Ka Su Cottage HOTEL $$$
(☎0 5556 1295; www.tukasu.net; 40 Moo 6, Um Phang; r incl breakfast 600-2000B; ❄@🛜) This is the cleanest and best-run accommodation in Um Phang. The attractive collection of brick-and-stone, multiroom cottages is surrounded by flower and exotic fruit gardens. All bathrooms have hot-water showers with an outdoor feel. The cheaper bungalows are also vast and comfortable, and terrific value.

The owner is a great source of local information and there's free wi-fi.

Umphang Country Huts HOTEL $$$
(no roman-script sign; ☎0 5556 1079; www.umphangcountryhut.com; r 500-2500B) Off the highway 2km before Um Phang, these huts enjoy a wooded hilly setting. Some of the rooms in the middle price range have two levels and balconies looking over a stream. The cheapest rooms have cold-water bathrooms. All were being renovated when we stopped by.

Baan Farang HOTEL $$
(☎08 3388 4223; r incl breakfast 700-1200B; 🛜) Located 3km from Um Phang, off the highway near the intersection that leads to Thilawsu, this attractive plot of land unites seven cosy huts, the more expensive of which are riverside.

Garden Huts HOTEL $$
(Boonyaporn Garden Hut; ☎0 5556 1093; www.boonyapornresort.com; 8/1 Moo 6, Um Phang; r 200-1500B) Operated by a sweet older lady, this collection of bungalows of varying degrees of comfort and size fronts the river. It features pleasant sitting areas and a well-cared-for garden. A new building has several spacious rooms with TV.

Ban Phurkchaya HOTEL $$$
(no roman-script sign; ☎0 5556 1308; www.banphurkchaya.com; 186 Moo 6, Um Phang; r incl breakfast 600-2000B; ❄) A cute compound of cutesy rooms. The rooms in the main structure are slightly less cute, but like all, appear clean and comfortable. There's no English sign here, but you'd have to struggle to miss it.

Phudoi Camp Site & Resort HOTEL $
(☎0 5556 1049; www.phudoi.com; 637 Th Pravitpaiwan, Um Phang; tent 150B, bungalow with fan/air-con 400/500B; ❄@) Primarily catering to its prebooked tour clients, Phudoi has bungalows set on a well-landscaped hillside near the village centre. The log cabin-style bungalows are spacious and have verandas. There's also a camping area and a restaurant with the same name.

Trekker Hill HOTEL $
(☎0 5556 1090; 620 Th Pravitpaiwan; dm/r 100/300B; 🛜) You may have ended up here even though it wasn't your choice – we're told that *sŏrng·tăa·ou* drivers are sometimes paid to drop passengers off here. Nonetheless, this rustic collection of huts on a steep hillside is a good place to stay, and

rooms have hot water and views of the valley and Um Phang. The restaurant serves three meals a day and also has satellite TV.

Ban Suansak Resort   HOTEL $
(☑08 9839 5308; r 300-500B) Just outside the town on the road to Palatha, this 'resort' has 13 rooms in a new two-storey building and three bungalows that can sleep up to 10 people. The beds look pretty thin, but the place is spotless and has its own restaurant.

✕ Eating

Um Phang has several very simple restaurants, morning and evening markets and a couple of small shops.

Khrua Ton Makham   THAI $
(no roman-script sign; mains 30-70B; ☺lunch & dinner) This rustic place has a brief English-language menu, although the Thai menu is much more expansive. The restaurant is under a huge tamarind tree ('Ton Makham'), next door to the internet cafe.

Phudoi Restaurant   THAI $$
(mains 40-170B; ☺8am-10pm) When open, this restaurant has decent food. There's a bilingual menu and it's often the only place open past 9pm.

Bankrusun   CAFE $
(mains 20-35B; ☺6.30am-8.30pm) Owned by a Thai musician, this souvenir shop/cafe offers good coffee, drinks and basic breakfasts.

ℹ Information

There are two ATMs in Um Phang, although it's still probably a good idea to bring cash. **Internet** (per hr 15B; ☺4-9pm Mon-Fri, 7am-9pm Sat & Sun) is available at a large cafe on the way to Ban Palatha.

ℹ Getting There & Away

There are frequent *sŏrng·tǎa·ou* from Um Phang to Mae Sot (120B, four hours, every hour from 6.30am to 1.30pm), departing from a stop at the top of Th Ratpattana.

Mae Sot to Mae Sariang

Rte 105 runs north along the Myanmar border from Mae Sot all the way to Mae Sariang (226km) in Mae Hong Son Province. The winding, paved road passes through the small communities of **Mae Ramat**, **Mae Salit**, **Ban Tha Song Yang** and **Ban Sop Ngao** (Mae Ngao). The thick forest in these

parts still has a few stands of teak and the Karen villages continue to use the occasional work elephant.

Nam Tok Mae Kasa, between the Km 13 and Km 14 markers, is an attractive waterfall fronting a cave. There's also a hot spring in the nearby village of Mae Kasa.

In Mae Ramat, don't miss **Wat Don Kaew**, behind the district office, which houses a large Mandalay-style marble Buddha.

At Km 58, after a series of roadblocks, you'll pass the immense refugee village of **Mae La** where it's estimated that 60,000 Burmese refugees live. The village is at least 3km long and takes a couple of minutes to drive past, bringing home the significant refugee problem that Thailand faces.

There are extensive limestone caverns at **Tham Mae Usu**, at Km 94 near Ban Tha Song Yang (there's another village of the same name further north). From the highway it's a 2km walk to Tham Mae Usu; note that it's closed in the rainy season, when the river running through the cave seals off the mouth.

At the northern end of Tak province, you'll reach **Ban Tha Song Yang**, a Karen village attractively set at the edge of limestone cliffs by the Mae Nam Moei. This is the last significant settlement in Tak before you begin climbing uphill and into the dense jungle and mountains of Mae Ngao National Park, in Mae Hong Son Province.

Ban Sop Ngao, little more than a roadside village that is home to the park headquarters, is the first town you'll come to in Mae Hong Son. From there it's another 40km to Mae Sariang, where there's ample food and accommodation.

🛏 Sleeping & Eating

There aren't too many places to stay and eat along this route. The most convenient base is Tha Song Yang (the town near Km 90 - not the village of the same name at the northern edge of Tak Province), as there are a few restaurants in town. Mae Salit, slightly further north, also has basic accommodation and food.

Thasongyang Hill Resort   HOTEL $$
(☑0 5558 9088; www.thasongyanghill.9nha.com; Km 85, Rte 105, Ban Tha Song Yang; r 200-800B; ❄☎) North of Tha Song Yang, accommodation here takes the form of large modern rooms in a long building, or attractive bungalows in a flower-lined garden. There are a couple of similar hotels in the area, but this place is the nicest.

Per-pron Resort HOTEL $
(☎08 1774 5624; 110 Moo 2, Mae Salit; bungalows 300-350B) Just south of Mae Salit, this place has a few rustic bungalows looking over the Mae Nam Moei.

ⓘ Getting There & Away

Sŏrng·tǎa·ou to Mae Sariang (200B, six hours, six departures from 6.20am to 12.20pm) depart from Mae Sot's old bus station, close to downtown.

MAE HONG SON PROVINCE

Accessible only by incredibly windy mountain roads or a dodgy flight to the provincial capital, this is Thailand's most remote province. Although it's undergone a tourist miniboom over the past decade, with many resorts opening in the area around the capital, few visitors seem to make it much further than Pai.

Mae Hong Son   แม่ฮ่องสอน
POP 6000

Mae Hong Son, with its remote setting and surrounding mountains, fits many travellers' preconceived notion of how a northern Thai city should be. A palpable Burmese influence and a border town feel don't dispel this image, and best of all, there's hardly a túk-túk or tout to be seen. This doesn't mean Mae Hong Son is uncharted territory; the tour groups have been coming here for years, but the city's potential as a base for activities, from spa treatment to trekking, ensures that your visit can be quite unlike anyone else's.

Mae Hong Son is best visited between November and March when the town is at its most beautiful. During the rainy season (June to October) travel to the more remote corners of the province can be difficult because there are few paved roads. During the hot season, the Mae Nam Pai valley fills with smoke from slash-and-burn agriculture. The only problem with going in the cool season is that the nights are downright cold – you'll need at least one thick sweater and a good pair of socks for mornings and evenings, and a sleeping bag or several blankets.

History

Mae Hong Son has been isolated from Thailand geographically, culturally and politically for most of its short existence. The city was founded as an elephant training centre in the early 19th century, and remained little more than this until 1856, when fighting in Burma caused thousands of Shan to pour into the area. In the years following, Mae Hong Son prospered as a centre for logging and remained an independent kingdom until 1900, when King Rama V incorporated the area into the Thai kingdom.

WORTH A TRIP

MAE HONG SON LOOP

One of the most popular motorcycle riding tours in northern Thailand is the circuitous route that begins in Chiang Mai and passes through the length of Mae Hong Son Province before looping back to the city – a round trip of nearly 1000km.

The Mae Hong Son loop really begins 34km north of Chiang Mai when you turn onto Rte 1095 and lean into the first of its 1864 bends. It's slow going, and you start climbing almost immediately; however, the good thing about this route is that potential overnight stops are frequent – many of the towns with good accommodation and food are less than 70km apart – giving riders ample chance to reclaim the blood flow to their bottoms. Convenient overnight stops include Pai, 130km from Chiang Mai, Soppong, another 40km up the road, and Mae Hong Son, 65km from Soppong.

Upon reaching Khun Yuam, 70km south of Mae Hong Son, you can opt to take Rte 1263 to Mae Chaem, before continuing back to Chiang Mai via Doi Inthanon, the country's highest peak, or you can continue south to Mae Sariang and follow Rte 108 all the way back to Chiang Mai via Hot, although the distances between towns here are greater and best done on a more powerful and more comfortable motorcycle.

An excellent driving companion is Golden Triangle Rider's *Mae Hong Son Loop Guide Map,* available at most bookshops in Chiang Mai. The map shows accurate distances between locations along the loop, as well as potential side trips and other helpful information.

⊙ Sights

With their bright colours, whitewashed stupas and glittering zinc fretwork, Mae Hong Son's Burmese- and Shan-style temples will have you scratching your head wondering just which country you're in anyway.

Wat Jong Kham & Wat Jong Klang TEMPLES
(วัดจองคำ/วัดจองกลาง; admission free) Wat Jong Kham was built nearly 200 years ago by Thai Yai (Shan) people, who make up about half of the population of Mae Hong Son Province. Wat Jong Klang houses 100-year-old glass *jataka* paintings and a **museum** (admission by donation; ☯8am-6pm) with 150-year-old wooden dolls from Mandalay that depict some of the more gruesome aspects of the wheel of life. Wat Jong Klang has several areas that women are forbidden to enter – not unusual for Burmese-Shan Buddhist temples.

The temples are lit at night and reflected in Nong Jong Kham – a popular photo op for visitors.

Wat Hua Wiang TEMPLE
(วัดหัวเวียง; Th Phanit Wattana; admission free) This *wát*, east of Th Khunlum Praphat, is recognised for its *bòht* boasting an elaborate tiered wooden roof and a revered bronze Buddha statue from Mandalay.

Other Temples TEMPLES
Other notable temples include **Wat Kam Kor** (admission free), known for its unique covered walkway, and **Wat Phra Non** (admission free) home to the largest reclining Buddha in town.

🏃 Activities

Trekking & Boat Trips

Mae Hong Son's location at the edge of mountainous jungle makes it an excellent base for treks into the countryside. Trekking here is not quite the large-scale industry it is elsewhere, and visitors willing to get their boots muddy can expect to find relatively untouched nature and isolated villages. Trekking trips can be arranged at several guest houses and travel agencies.

Long-tail boat trips on the nearby Mae Pai are gaining popularity, and the same guest houses and trekking agencies that organise treks from Mae Hong Son can arrange river excursions. The most common trip sets off from **Tha Pong Daeng**, 4km southwest of Mae Hong Son. Boats travel 15km downstream to the 'long-neck' village of **Huay Pu Keng** followed by a stop at the border

Mae Hong Son Province

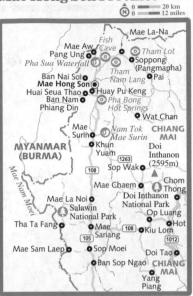

town of **Ban Nam Phiang Din**, 20km from the pier, before returning. It takes approximately 1½ hours to reach Ban Nam Phiang Din and costs 1000B per boat, with boats holding a maximum of eight passengers.

Multiday treks in groups of two people start at 1000B per person, per day. As with elsewhere in Thailand, the per-day rates drop significantly with a larger group and a longer trek.

Nature Walks TREKKING
(☏0 5361 1040, 08 9552 6899; www.trekkingthailand.com; natural_walks@yahoo.com) Although the treks here cost more than elsewhere, John, a native of Mae Hong Son, is the best guide in town. Treks range from day-long nature walks to multiday journeys across the province. John can also arrange custom nature-based tours, such as the orchid-viewing tours he conducts from March to May. John has no office; email and phone are the only ways to get in touch with him.

Friend Tour TREKKING
(☏0 5361 1647; PA Motorbike, 21 Th Pradit Jong Kham; ☯7.30am-7.30pm) With nearly 20 years' experience, this recommended outfit offers trekking, elephant riding and rafting, as well as day tours. Located at PA Motorbike.

Mae Hong Son

Long Time Tours TREKKING
(☑08 9838 6865; 21 Th Pradit Jong Kham;
☺8am-5pm) Another locally based outfit
that can arrange a variety of tours.

Nam Rin Tour TREKKING
(☑0 5361 4454; 21 Th Pradit Jong Kham) Mr
Dam advertises 'Bad sleep, bad jokes', but
his treks get good reports.

Mud Spa

Pooklon Country Club SPA
(☑08 6198 0722; Ban Mae Sanga; ☺8am-6.30pm)
This self-professed 'country club' is touted as
Thailand's only mud treatment spa. Discovered by a team of geologists in 1995, the mud
here is pasteurised and blended with herbs
before being employed in various treatments (facial 60B). There's thermal mineral
water for soaking (60B), and on weekends,
massage (per hour 200B).

Pooklon is 16km north of Mae Hong Son
in Mok Champae District. If you haven't got
your own wheels, you can take the daily Mae
Aw-bound *sŏrng·tăa·ou*, but this means you
might have to find your own way back.

☞ Tours

Rosegarden Tours TOURS
(☑0 5361 1681; www.rosegarden-tours.com;
86/4 Th Khunlum Praphat; tours from 600B) Its
English- and French-speaking guides focus
on cultural and sightseeing tours.

Tour Merng Tai TOURS
(☑0 5361 1979; www.tourmerngtai.com; 89 Th
Khunlum Praphat; van tours per day 1800B) This
outfit mostly does city-based van tours and
cycling tours, but can also arrange treks.

☆☆ Festivals & Events

Poi Sang Long Festival ORDINATION CEREMONY
Wat Jong Klang and Wat Jong Kham are
the focal point of this March festival, where
young Shan boys are ordained as novice

Mae Hong Son

monks in the ceremony known as *boòat lôok gâaou*. As part of the Shan custom, the boys are dressed in ornate costumes (rather than simple white robes) and wear flower headdresses and facial make-up.

Jong Para Festival BUDDHIST FESTIVAL
Another important local event, it is held towards the end of the Buddhist Rains Retreat around October – three days before the full moon of the 11th lunar month, so it varies from year to year. The festival begins with local Shan bringing offerings to monks in the temples in a procession marked by the carrying of models of castles on poles. An important part of the festival is the folk theatre and dance, which is performed on the wát grounds, some of it unique to northwest Thailand.

Loi Krathong TRADITIONAL
During this national holiday in November – usually celebrated by floating *grà·tong* (small lotus floats) on the nearest pond, lake or river – Mae Hong Son residents launch balloons called *grà·tong sà·wān* (heaven *grà·tong*) from Doi Kong Mu.

🛏 Sleeping

Mae Hong Son generally lacks in inspiring accommodation, although there are a couple of standout midrange options. Because it's a tourist town, accommodation prices fluctuate with the seasons, and outside of the high season (November to January) it's worth pursuing a discount.

IN TOWN

Baiyoke Chalet Hotel HOTEL $$$
(☎0 5361 3132; trv1864@hotmail.com; 90 Th Khunlum Praphat; r incl breakfast 1280-1800B; ❋@❂) This place combines both a convenient location and comfortable lodging. As established in the lobby, the rooms are tastefully outfitted in hardwood and local themes. A downside is that the restaurant/lounge downstairs can get quite loud, so request a room away from the street or on an upper level. Low-season rates are 50% less.

Residence@MaeHongSon HOTEL $$
(☎0 5361 4100; www.theresidence-mhs.com; 41/4 Th Ni-wet Pi-sarn; r 900-1400B; ❋@❂) One of the more recent places to go up, this cheery yellow building houses 11 inviting rooms. Teak furnishings abound, and lots of windows ensure ample natural light. There's also a sunny communal rooftop area, a friendly English-speaking owner, and bicycles provided free of charge.

Romtai HOTEL $$$
(☎0 5361 2437; www.maehongson-romtai.com; Th Chamnansathit; r 600-1200B, bungalows 1500-1700B; ❋❂) Hidden behind both the lakeside

DON'T MISS

WAT PHRA THAT DOI KONG MU

Climb the hill west of town, Doi Kong Mu (1500m), to visit this Shan-built *wát* (วัดพระธาตุดอยกองมู; admission free), also known as Wat Plai Doi. The view of the sea of fog that collects in the valley each morning is impressive; at other times of the day you get wonderful views of the town and surrounding valleys. Two Shan *chedi*, erected in 1860 and 1874, enshrine the ashes of monks from Myanmar's Shan State. Around the back of the *wát* you can see a tall, slender, standing Buddha and catch views west of the ridge.

temples and a bland-looking reception area, this place has a huge variety of accommodation, ranging from spacious, clean rooms to bungalows looking over a lush garden with fishponds.

Jongkham Place　　　GUEST HOUSE $$$
(☑0 5361 4294; 4/2 Th Udom Chao Ni-Thet; bungalows/ste 800/2000B; ❄🛜) This family-run place by the lake has four attractive wooden bungalows and two penthouselike suites. All accommodation includes TV, fridge and air-con.

Mountain Inn & Resort　　HOTEL $$$
(☑0 5361 1802; www.mhsmountaininn.com; 112/2 Th Khunlum Praphat; r incl breakfast 1500-2800B, ste incl breakfast 4500B; ❄🛜) This hotel has clean, cosy rooms with Thai decorative touches. There is a pretty courtyard garden with small ponds, benches and parasols. Standard rooms are a better deal than deluxe as you get a terrace overlooking the garden.

Coffee Morning　　　　HOTEL $
(☑0 5361 2234; 78 Th Singhanat Bamrung; r 300-500B; @🛜) This old wooden house unites an attractive cafe/bookshop and four basic but cosy rooms. Considering that bathrooms are shared, the high-season rates aren't exactly a deal, but free internet and the fun cafe atmosphere make up for this.

Palm House　　　　　HOTEL $
(☑0 5361 4022; 22/1 Th Chamnansathit; r 350-600B; ❄🛜) This two-storey cement building offers several characterless but clean rooms with TV, hot water and fan/air-con.

The helpful owner speaks English and can arrange transport when he's not napping.

Friend House　　　　HOTEL $
(☑0 5362 0119; 20 Th Pradit Jong Kham; r 150-400B; 🛜) Superclean rooms run from the ultra basic that share hot-water bathrooms to larger rooms with private bathrooms.

Jongkam GH　　　GUEST HOUSE $
(☑08 1594 5323; 7 Udom Chao Ni-Thet; r 200-400B) Fan-cooled, mattress-on-the-floor rooms in a lakeside garden.

OUTSIDE OF TOWN
Southwest of town, a few kilometres towards Ban Huay Deua and Ban Tha Pong Daeng on the river, are a few 'resorts', which in the Thai sense of the term means any hotel near a rural or semirural area. Discounts of up to 40% are common in the low season and online discounts can be found any time of year.

TOP CHOICE Fern Resort　　　HOTEL $$$
(☑0 5368 6110; www.fernresort.info; 64 Moo 10, Tambon Pha Bong; bungalows incl breakfast 2500-3500B; ❄@🛜🏊) This long-standing eco-friendly resort is one of the more pleasant places to stay in northern Thailand. The 40 Shan-style wooden bungalows are set among tiered rice paddies and streams and feature stylishly decorated interiors. Nearby nature trails lead to the adjacent Mae Surin National Park, and to encourage community-based tourism, most of the employees come from local villages. The downside is that the resort is 7km south of town, but free pick-up is available from the airport and bus terminal, and regular shuttles run to/from town stopping at the Fern Restaurant.

Sang Tong Huts　　　　HOTEL $$$
(☑0 5362 1680; www.sangtonghuts.com; Th Makhasanti; bungalows 800-3000B; @🛜🏊) This popular set of bungalows in a wooded area just outside of town is one of the more character-filled places to stay. There's a huge variety of bungalows, all of them spacious and well designed. And the tasty baked goods and a pool make up for the distance from the centre of town. It's popular among repeat visitors to Mae Hong Son, so it pays to book ahead. Sang Tong Huts is about 1km northeast of Th Khunlum Praphat, just off Th Makhasanti – if going towards Pai, turn left at the town's northernmost stoplight and follow the signs.

Imperial Tara Mae Hong Son Hotel
HOTEL $$$

(☎0 5368 4444-9; www.imperialhotels.com/tara maehongson; 149 Moo 8; r incl breakfast 2200-2800B, ste incl breakfast 2900-5400B; ✳@☀) Rooms in this upmarket, 104-room hotel all have wooden floors and are tastefully decorated. French windows that open onto a terrace make a change from the standard business hotel layout. Facilities include a sauna, swimming pool and fitness centre. It's about 2km south of town.

Pana Huts
HOTEL $$

(☎0 5361 4331; www.panahuts.com; 293/9 Moo 11, Th Makhasanti; r & bungalows 700-800B; ☎) Set in a wooded area outside of town, the six slightly overpriced bamboo huts all have hot-water bathrooms and terraces. The communal area feels appropriately rustic, with its thatched teak leaf roof, wooden benches and enclosed campfire for chilly nights. Pana Huts is about 1km northeast of Th Khunlum Praphat, just off Th Makhasanti – if going towards Pai, turn left at the town's northernmost stoplight and follow the signs.

🍴 Eating & Drinking

Mae Hong Son's morning market is a fascinating place to have breakfast. Several vendors at the north end of the market sell unusual dishes such as *tòo·a òon*, a Burmese noodle dish supplemented with thick chickpea porridge and deep-fried bits of vegetables, chickpea flour cakes and tofu. Other vendors along the same strip sell a local version of *kà·nǒm jeen nám ngée·o*, often topped with *kahng pòrng*, a Shan snack of battered and deep-fried vegetables.

The city also has two good night markets; the night market near the airport offers mostly takeaway northern Thai-style food while the night market at the southern end of Th Khunlum Praphat has more generic Thai food.

Ban Phleng
NORTHERN THAI $

(no roman-script sign; 108 Th Khunlum Praphat; mains 45-100B; ⊘lunch & dinner Mon-Sat) This popular open-air restaurant does a handful of very tasty local dishes – you're safe going with anything that says 'Maehongson style' on the English-language menu. Ban Phleng is just south of town – look for the white banners at the side of the road.

No-Name Restaurant
THAI $$

(Th Khunlum Praphat; mains 30-170B; ⊘lunch & dinner) There really is no name here (it's a tax thing), but this has no negative repercussions on the tasty, central Thai-style dishes. There's a limited English-language menu, or you can simply choose from the fresh veggies out front.

Mae Si Bua
NORTHERN THAI $

(51 Th Singhanat Bamrung; mains 20-30B; ⊘lunch) Like the Shan grandma you never had, Auntie Bua prepares a huge variety of different Shan curries, soups and dips on a daily basis. Try her delicious *gaang hang·lair*, an incredibly rich curry of pork belly with a flavour not unlike American-style barbecue sauce.

Fern Restaurant
INTERNATIONAL-THAI $$

(Th Khunlum Praphat; mains 70-180B; ⊘10.30am-10pm) The Fern is almost certainly Mae Hong Son's most upscale restaurant, but remember, this is Mae Hong Son. Nonetheless, service is professional and the food is decent. The expansive menu covers Thai, local and even European dishes. There is live lounge music some nights.

La Tasca
ITALIAN $$

(Th Khunlum Praphat; mains 89-209B; ⊘lunch & dinner) This cosy place has been serving homemade pasta, pizza and calzone for as long as we can remember and is one of the few places in town to serve relatively authentic Western food.

Baan Tua Lek
CAFE $

(51 Th Singhanat Bamrung; mains 20-30B; ⊘7am-9pm; ✳☎) This tiny, modern cafe serves good coffee drinks and a few sweets and cakes.

Crossroads
BAR

(61 Th Khunlum Praphat; ⊘8am-1am) This friendly bar-restaurant is a crossroads in every sense, from its location at one of Mae Hong Son's main intersections to its clientele that ranges from wet-behind-the-ears backpackers to hardened locals. Oh, and there's steak.

Sunflower Café
BAR

(Th Pradit Jong Kham; ⊘7am-midnight) This open-air place combines draught beer, live lounge music and views of the lake. Sunflower also does meals (35B to 180B) and runs tours.

Shopping

From October to February the walkway around the Jong Kham Lake becomes a lively **night market** (⊙5-10pm).

A few well-stocked souvenir shops can be found near the southern end of Th Khunlum Praphat, including **Maneerat** (80 Th Khunlum Praphat; ⊙8am-9pm), which features an extensive array of Shan and Burmese clothing, as well as Burmese lacquerware boxes.

ℹ Information

Most of the banks at the southern end of Th Khunlum Praphat have ATMs. Foreign-exchange services are available at Bangkok Bank and Kasikornbank, among others.

A few internet shops can be found around the southern end of Th Khunlum Praphat.

Mae Hong Son Internet (88 Th Khunlum Praphat; per hr 30B; ⊙8.30am-11pm)

Main post office (Th Khunlum Praphat; ⊙8.30am-4.30pm Mon-Fri)

Srisangwal Hospital (☑0 5361 1378; Th Singhanat Bamrung) A full-service facility that includes an emergency room.

Tourism Authority of Thailand office (TAT; ☑nationwide call centre 1672, Mae Hong Son 0 5361 2982; www.travelmaehongson.org; Th Niwet Pi-sarn; ⊙8.30am-4.30pm) Basic tourist brochures and maps can be picked up here.

Tourist police (☑nationwide call centre 1155, Mae Hong Son 0 5361 1812; Th Singhanat Bamrung; ⊙8.30am-4.30pm)

ℹ Getting There & Away

Air

For many people the time saved flying from Chiang Mai to Mae Hong Son versus bus travel is worth the extra baht. There are four flights daily (1590B to 1890B, 35 minutes), operated by **Kan Air** (☑nationwide call centre 02 551 6111, Mae Hong Son 0 5361 3188; www.kanairlines.com; Mae Hong Son airport) and **Nok Air** (☑nationwide call centre 1318, Mae Hong Son 0 5361 2057; www.nokair.co.th; Mae Hong Son airport).

A túk-túk into town costs about 80B.

Bus

Mae Hong Son's bus station is 1km south of the city. **Prempracha Tour** (☑0 5368 4100) conducts bus services within the province and **Sombat Tour** (☑0 5361 3211) conducts services between Mae Hong Son and Bangkok.

Other bus destinations from Mae Hong Son include:

Bangkok (718B to 838B, 15 hours, three departures from 2pm to 4pm)

Chiang Mai (northern route, 127B, eight hours, 8.30am and 12.30pm)

Chiang Mai (southern route, 178B, nine hours, frequent departures from 6am to 9pm)

Khun Yuam (50B, two hours, frequent departures from 6am to 9pm)

Mae Sariang (95B, four hours, frequent departures from 6am to 9pm)

Pai (70B, 4½ hours, 8.30am and 12.30pm)

Soppong (40B, two hours, frequent departures from 6am to 9pm)

Minivan

Air-conditioned minivans, a popular way to get around the province, also depart from the bus station.

Chiang Mai (250B, six hours, every hour from 7am to 3pm)

Pai (150B, 2½ hours, every hour from 7am to 4pm)

Soppong (150B, 1½ hours, every hour from 7am to 4pm)

ℹ Getting Around

The centre of Mae Hong Son can easily be covered on foot, and it is one of the few towns in Thailand that doesn't seem to have a motorcycle taxi at every corner. However, some can be found near the entrance to the morning market, and charge 20B to 30B for trips within town; to Doi Kong Mu it costs 100B return. There are also a few túk-túk in town; most are at the bus stop and charge 40B per trip within town and 80B to/from the airport or bus station.

Because most of Mae Hong Son's attractions are outside of town, renting a motorcycle or bicycle is a wise move.

PA Motorbike (☑0 5361 1647; 21 Th Pradit Jong Kham; ⊙7.30am-7.30pm) Opposite Friend House, rents motorbikes (250B per day) and trucks (1500B to 2500B per day).

PJ (☑08 4372 6967; Th Khunlum Praphat; ⊙8am-7.30pm) Rents motorbikes (150B per day).

Titan (Th Khunlum Praphat; ⊙10am-10pm) Rents good-quality mountain bikes (80B per day).

Around Mae Hong Son

PHA BONG HOT SPRINGS บ่อน้ำร้อนผาบ่อง Eleven kilometres south of the capital in the Shan village of Pha Bong is this public park with **hot springs** (private bath/bathing room 50/400B; ⊙8am-sunset). You can take a private bath or rent a room, and there's also massage (per hour 150B). The springs can be reached on any southbound bus.

THAM PLA FOREST PARK อุทยานแห่งชาติถ้ำปลา

(adult/child 100/50; ☺6am-6pm) This **provincial park**, 16km north of Mae Hong Son, is centred around Tham Pla, or Fish Cave, a water-filled cavern where hundreds of soro brook carp thrive. The fish grow up to 1m long and are found only in the provinces of Mae Hong Son, Ranong, Chiang Mai, Rayong, Chanthaburi and Kanchanaburi. The fish eat vegetables and insects, although the locals believe them to be vegetarian and feed them only fruit and vegetables, which can be purchased at the park entrance.

A 450m path leads from the park entrance to a suspension bridge that crosses a stream and continues to the cave. A **statue** of a Hindu *rishi* called Nara, said to protect the holy fish from danger, stands nearby. It's a bit anticlimactic, but the park grounds are a bucolic, shady place to hang out; food and picnic tables are available.

Buses to Pai pass by, but renting a motorcycle is the best way to get here.

LONG-NECKED KAYAN VILLAGES หมู่บ้านกะเหรี่ยงคอยาว

These villages are Mae Hong Son's most touted – and most controversial – tourist attraction. The 'long-necked' moniker stems from the habit of some Kayan (sometimes also referred to as Padaung, a Shan term) women of wearing heavy brass coils around their necks. The coils depress the collarbone and rib cage, which makes their necks look unnaturally stretched. A common myth claims if the coils are removed, the women's necks will fall over and the women will suffocate. In fact the women attach and remove the coils at will and there is no evidence that this deformation impairs their health at all.

Nobody knows for sure how the coil custom got started. One theory is that it was meant to make the women unattractive to men from other tribes. Another story says it was so tigers wouldn't carry the women off by their throats; most likely it is probably nothing more than a simple fashion accessory. Until relatively recently the custom was largely dying out, but money from tourism, and quite possibly the influence of local authorities eager to cash in on the Kayan, have reinvigorated it.

Regardless of the origin, the villages are now on every group tour's itinerary, and have become a significant tourist draw for Mae Hong Son. The villages are often derided as human zoos, and there are certainly elements of this, but we find them more like bizarre rural markets, with the women earning much of their money by selling tacky souvenirs and drinks. The Kayan we've talked to claim to be happy with their current situation, but the stateless position they share with all Burmese refugees is nothing to be envied, and these formerly independent farmers are now reliant on aid and tourists to survive. A report on the villages by journalist Patrick Winn can be seen at www.globalpost.com/dispatch/thailand/110128/thailand-tourism-burma-refugee-chiang-mai.

If you want to see any of the three Kayan settlements in Mae Hong Son, any travel agency in Mae Hong Son can arrange a tour. The most-touted Kayan village is **Huai Seua Thao**, about 7km from Mae Hong Son. More remote, but definitely not off the beaten track, is **Kayan Tayar**, near the Shan village of Ban Nai Soi, 35km northwest of Mae Hong Son. Both collect an entry fee from non-Thais of 250B per person. Another 'long-necked' community is based at **Huay Pu Keng** and is included on longtail boat tours departing from Tha Pong Daeng.

MAE AW & AROUND แม่ออ

A worthwhile day trip from the provincial capital is to Mae Aw, an atmospheric Chinese outpost right at the Myanmar border, 43km north of Mae Hong Son.

The road to Mae Aw is a beautiful route that passes through tidy riverside Shan communities such as **Mok Champae** before suddenly climbing and winding through impressive mountain scenery. Stops can be made at **Pha Sua Waterfall**, about 5km up the mountain, or **Pang Tong Summer Palace**, a rarely used royal compound a few kilometres past the waterfall.

For an interesting detour, at Ban Na Pa Paek take a left and continue 6km to the Shan village of **Ban Ruam Thai**. There are several basic places to stay and eat here, and the road ends 500m further at **Pang Ung**, a peaceful mountain reservoir surrounded by pines that is immensely popular among Thai day trippers in search of a domestic Switzerland.

Drive back to Ban Na Pa Paek the way you came. From there it is 6km further north past hills holding tea and coffee plantations to Mae Aw. The modern Thai name for the town is Ban Rak Thai (Thai-Loving Village) and the town was established by Yunnanese

KMT fighters who fled from communist rule in 1949. The town sits on the edge of a large reservoir and the faces and signs are very Chinese. The main industry here has become tea, and there are numerous places to taste the local brew, as well as several restaurants serving Yunnanese cuisine.

There's a brief dirt road to the border crossing, but it's not advisable to do any unaccompanied trekking here, as the area is an infamous drug route.

🛏 Sleeping & Eating

Ban Din Guest House HOTEL $$
(☎08 4854 9397; Mae Aw/Ban Rak Thai; r 300-750B) This place and other similar outfits ringing Mae Aw's reservoir offer basic accommodation in adobe-style bungalows.

Guest House and Home Stay GUEST HOUSE $$
(☎0 5307 0589, 08 3571 6668; Ban Ruam Thai; r 400-1500B) The first guest house in Ban Ruam Thai (there are now numerous 'homestays' offering accommodation from 200B to 400B), this place consists of several simple bamboo huts positioned on a slope surrounded by coffee plants, tea plants and fruit trees. Even if you're not staying, stop here for a brew; the owner is passionate about coffee, and there is a roasting room where visitors can roast and grind their own beans.

Gee Lee Restaurant CHINESE $$
(no roman-script sign; Mae Aw/Ban Rak Thai; mains 40-250B; ☺8am-7pm) This was one of the first places in Mae Aw to serve the town's Yunnanese-style Chinese dishes to visitors. Stewed pork leg and stir-fried local veggies are the specialities. It's at the corner of the lake, just before the intersection that leads to the centre of the village.

❶ Getting There & Away

There are three daily *sŏrng·tăa·ou* that head towards Mae Aw: two that only go as far as Ban Ruam Thai (80B, one hour, 9am and 3pm), and another that terminates in Mae Aw (70B, one hour, 2pm). Both depart from Mae Hong Son's municipal market only when full, which can sometimes be a couple of hours after the scheduled departure time. Because of this, it's probably worth getting a group of people together and chartering a vehicle; the *sŏrng·tăa·ou* drivers we talked to quoted 1000B for either destination, while any tour agency in Mae Hong Son will arrange a vehicle for around 1500B.

Alternatively, the route also makes a brilliant motorcycle ride – just make sure you have enough petrol, as the only station is in Ban Na Pa Paek, at the end of a very long climb.

Pai ปาย
POP 2000

Spend enough time in northern Thailand and eventually you'll hear rumours that Pai is the Khao San Rd of northern Thailand. Although this is definitely a stretch, in recent years the small town has started to resemble a Thai island getaway – without the beaches. Guest houses appear to outnumber private residences in the 'downtown' area, the internet is never more than a few steps away and the nights buzz with the sound of live music and partying.

However, unlike the islands, Pai (pronounced more like the English 'bye' not 'pie') is now just as popular among Thais as foreigners. During the peak of the cool season (December and January), thousands of Thais from Bangkok crowd the town, making parts of it feel more like Chatuchak Weekend market than a remote valley town in Mae Hong Son. Traffic jams aren't unusual during this time of year, and accommodation becomes so scarce that many are forced to rough it in tents.

Despite all this, the town's popularity has yet to impact on its setting in a nearly picture-perfect mountain valley. There's heaps of quiet accommodation outside the main drag, a host of natural, lazy activities to keep visitors entertained, a vibrant art and music scene, and the town's Shan roots can still be seen in its temples, quiet back streets and fun afternoon market.

◉ Sights

Many of Pai's sights are found just outside the city centre and in the surrounding areas.

Buddhist Temples

Wat Phra That Mae Yen TEMPLE
(วัดพระธาตุแม่เย็น) This temple sits atop a hill and has good views overlooking the valley. Walk 1km east from the main intersection in town, across a stream and through a village, to get to the stairs (353 steps) that lead to the top. Or take the 400m sealed road that follows a different route to the top.

Wat Nam Hoo TEMPLE
(วัดน้ำฮู) Wat Nam Hoo is about 2km from Pai and houses a sacred Buddha image said to have once emitted holy water from its head. The place is popular with visiting Thais and there's a small market on the grounds.

Pai

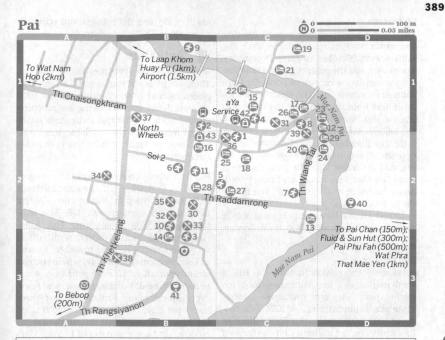

Pai

🟢 Activities, Courses & Tours
1	Back Trax	C2
2	Duang Trekking	B1
3	Mam Yoga House	B3
4	Pai Adventure	C1
5	Pai Cookery School	C2
6	Pai Kayak	B2
7	Pai Traditional Thai Massage	C2
8	Pai Zip Line	C1
9	Rose Gym	B1
	Taste of Pai	(see 1)
10	Thai Adventure Rafting	B2
11	Thom's Pai Elephant Camp	B2

🛌 Sleeping
12	Baan Pai Village	D1
13	Baan Tawan Guest House	C2
14	Blue Lagoon Hotel	B3
15	Breeze of Pai Guesthouse	C1
16	Charlie's House	B2
17	Hotel des Artists	C1
18	Mr Jan's Guest House	C2
19	Pai Country Hut	C1
20	Pai Fah	C2
21	Pai Nai Fun	C1
22	Pai River Villa	C1
23	Pai RiverCorner	D1
24	Pai Vimaan Resort	D2
25	Pravee's House	C2

🍽 Eating
26	Rim Pai Cottage	C1
27	Tayai's House	C2
28	TTK	B2
29	Villa De Pai	D2
30	Amido's Pizza Garden	B2
31	Big's Little Cafe	C1
32	Burger House	B2
33	Charlie & Lek Health Restaurant	B2
34	Evening Market	A2
	Good Life	(see 39)
35	Je-In Pai	B2
	Khanom Jeen Nang Yong	(see 4)
36	Mama Falafel	C2
37	Nong Beer	B1
38	Saengthongaram Market	B3
	TTK	(see 28)
39	Witching Well	C2

🍸 Drinking
40	Don't Cry	D2
41	Ting Tong	B3

🛍 Shopping
42	Siam Books	C1
43	Walking Street	B2

Waterfalls

There are a few waterfalls around Pai that are worth visiting, particularly after the rainy season (October to early December). The closest and the most popular, **Nam Tok Mo Paeng**, has a couple of pools that are suitable for swimming. The waterfall is a total of 8km from Pai along the road that also leads to Wat Nam Hoo – a long walk indeed, but suitable for a bike ride or short motorcycle trip. Roughly the same distance in the opposite direction is **Nam Pembok**, just off the road to Chiang Mai. The most remote is **Nam Tok Mae Yen**, a couple of hours' walk down the rough road east of Pai, just before the turn-off to Fluid.

Motorcycle and bike rentals are available at several guest houses, as well as at aYa Service.

Other Sights

Ban Santichon   VILLAGE

(บ้านสันติชน) About 4km outside of Pai, a small market, delicious Yunnanese food, tea tasting, pony rides and Yunnanese **adobe-style accommodation** (☏08 1024 3982; bungalows 1000-1500B) make the KMT village of Ban Santichon not unlike a Chinese-themed amusement park.

Tha Pai Hot Springs   HOT SPRINGS

(บ่อน้ำร้อนท่าปาย; adult/child 200/100B; ⊗6am-7pm) Across the Mae Nam Pai and 7km southeast of town via a paved road is the springs, a well-kept local park 1km from the road. A scenic stream flows through the park; the stream mixes with the hot springs in places to make pleasant bathing areas. The water is also diverted to a couple of nearby spas; see opposite.

Pai Canyon   CANYON

(เหวปาย) Located 8km from Pai along the road to Chiang Mai, a paved stairway here culminates in an elevated lookout over high rock cliffs and the Pai valley. The latter can be followed by a dirt trail, but lacking shade, is best tackled in the morning or afternoon.

Memorial Bridge   LANDMARK

(สะพานประวัติศาสตร์ท่าปาย) It may look like an antiquated bridge to us, but to thousands of Thai tourists who stop here during the tourist season, it's one of several crucial photo ops along the '762 curves' to Pai. Located 9km from Pai, the bridge was originally built by Japanese soldiers during WWII. Other crucial Pai-themed photo ops include the huge sign at Coffee in Love, about 3km

south of Pai, and the cutesy shops selling T-shirts along Th Chaisongkhram.

🏃 Activities

Massage & Spa Treatments

There are plenty of traditional Thai massage places around town charging around 150B an hour. Reiki, crystal healing acupuncture, reflexology and other non-indigenous methods of healing are also available; keep your eyes open for signs or refer to the monthly *Pai Events Planner*.

Pai Traditional Thai Massage   MASSAGE

(PTTM; ☏0 5369 9121; www.pttm1989.com; 68/3 Soi 1, Th Wiang Tai; massage per 1/1½/2hr 180/270/350B, sauna per visit 80B, 3-day massage course 2500B; ⊗9am-9pm) This long-standing and locally owned outfit offers very good northern-Thai massage, as well as a sauna (cool season only) where you can steam yourself in *sà·mǔn·prai* (medicinal herbs). Three-day massage courses begin every Monday and Friday and last three hours per day. The friendly couple that do the massages and teach the course are accredited and are graduates of Chiang Mai's Old Medicine Hospital.

A few local businesses near Tha Pai Hot Springs have taken advantage of the healing thermal waters.

Pai Hotsprings Spa Resort   SPA

(☏0 5306 5748; www.paihotspringsparesort. com; 84-84/1 Moo 2, Ban Mae Hi; 1hr massage 300B, thermal water soak 100B; ⊗7am-10pm) A resort-style hotel that also offers massages and thermal water soaks.

Aroma Pai Spa   SPA

(☏0 5306 5745; www.aromapaispa.com; 110 Moo 2, Ban Mae Hi; thermal water soak 50B, spa treatments from 850B; ⊗7am-9pm) Offers soaks in private rooms and a communal pool, as well as a variety of spa treatments.

Spa Exotic   SPA

(☏0 5306 5722; www.spaexotic.com; 86 Moo 2, Ban Mae Hi; ⊗7am-7pm) Next door to Aroma, this place goes a step further and channels the hot water into its bungalow bathrooms; nonguests can soak for 80B.

Rafting & Kayaking

Rafting and to a lesser extent, kayaking, along the Mae Nam Pai during the wet season (approximately June to February) is also a popular activity. The most popular trip

TROUBLE IN PAIRADISE?

In September 2005, a series of mudslides and floods devastated Pai, wiping away entire guest-house complexes and destroying the city's bridges. In a few short days it seemed that the town's tourism infrastructure, which had been growing steadily since the 1980s, would suffer a major, if not permanent, setback.

It certainly didn't take long to recover. The next year it's estimated that 367,869 tourists visited Pai. Many were foreign tourists, drawn to the town's cheap accommodation and reputation as a peaceful, natural destination. But in 2006, for the first time, the majority of visitors were Thai, largely inspired by the Thai love flicks *Rak Jang* and *Happy Birthday*, both of which were filmed in the town.

Despite its immense popularity, Pai has largely been able to remain a positive example of tourism development in Thailand. Unlike elsewhere in the country, the residents of Pai have maintained a significant role in the development of their town. Natural and cultural conservation have long been fundamental aspects of Pai's tourism sector. And the town has been able to remain loyal to its rural roots, which form the basis of a lively art and music scene that leave most visitors with an overwhelmingly positive impression.

Tourism has also brought prosperity to the formerly isolated farming community. Land in desirable parts of the town is said to sell for as much as US$65,000 an acre, and many locals are now employed in various tourist service-related jobs, or supplement their income by selling handicrafts. Roads and other infrastructure have improved, and in 2007 Pai's commercial airport commenced flights. And the general consensus among residents is that they welcome the tourists and the income they bring.

On the other hand, the huge influx of visitors to Pai has also resulted in a host of new problems. The town is beginning to experience difficulties in dealing with increasing amounts of rubbish and sewage. Locals complain of being kept awake by the sound of live music and partying. Drug use is widespread. And the city's police force has garnered considerable negative press where it concerns tourists and tourism, ranging from a brief crackdown on so-called 'illegal dancing' in the city's bars to the controversial shooting death of a Canadian tourist in early 2008.

In some ways the 2005 floods have been something of a wake-up call for the residents of Pai. Closing times at the town's bars are now strictly enforced, waste-water treatment is in the process of being made mandatory, and a new dump is being considered. But if Pai continues to maintain its current level of popularity, it remains to be seen whether or not the town can maintain the same level of responsible development that made it such an attractive destination to begin with.

runs from Pai to Mae Hong Son, which depending on the amount of water, can traverse rapids in scale from grade one to grade five. Rates are all-inclusive (rafting equipment, camping gear, dry bags and insurance) and run from about 1200B to 1500B per person for a one-day trip and from 1800B to 2500B per person for two days. Outfitters include:

Pai Adventure RAFTING
(☎0 5369 9385; www.thailandpai.net; Th Chaisongkhram) The one- to three-day white-water rafting trips offered by this recommended outfit can be combined with trekking and other activities. Can also offer a jungle survival course upon request.

Thai Adventure Rafting RAFTING
(☎0 5369 9111; www.thairafting.com; Th Chaisongkhram) This French-run outfit leads

one- and two-day trips. On the way, rafters visit a waterfall, a fossil reef and hot springs; one night is spent at the company's permanent riverside camp. Thai Adventure has two offices along Th Chaisongkhram.

Back-Trax RAFTING
(☎0 5369 9739; backtraxinpai@yahoo.com; Th Chaisongkhram) With more than a decade of experience, this company offers multiday rafting excursions, as well as inner tubing trips and, of course, reiki lessons.

Pai Kayak KAYAKING
(☎0 5306 4426; www.paikayak.com; Pai Let's Go Tour, Th Rangsiyanon) During the wet season, this outfit conducts two daily two-hour kayaking excursions along the Mae Nam Pai at 10am and 3pm.

Trekking

Guided treks range in cost from about 700B to 1000B per person per day, in groups of two or more, and are all-inclusive. Most treks focus on the Lisu, Lahu and Karen villages in and around neighbouring Soppong. Treks can be booked through guest-house-based agencies such as the long-standing **Duang Trekking** (☑0 5369 9101; http://sites.google. com/site/lungtangtrekking/; Duang Guest House, Th Chaisongkhram), or through specific outfitters, including all of the rafting outfits listed above.

Other Activities

Fluid   SPORTS FACILITY

(Ban Mae Yen; admission 60B; ☺9am-6.30pm) Pool/gym complex just outside of town, roughly across from Sun Hut. Includes a herbal steam room during the cool season (per hour 80B).

Pai Zip Line   ZIP-LINE

(☑0 5404 9010; Th Chaisongkhram; 800B; ☺8am-6pm) This new attraction, 7km from Pai near Pembok Waterfall, features a zip-line above forest canopy. The whole thing takes about two hours and concludes with a dip in the falls.

Thom's Pai Elephant Camp   ELEPHANT RIDES

(☑0 5369 9286; www.thomelephant.com; Th Rangsiyanon; elephant rides per person 500-1500B) The most established company and with an office in town. You can choose between riding bareback or in a seat, and some rides include swimming with the elephants – a barrel of laughs on a bouncing elephant in the river. Rides include a soak in the hot-spring-fed tubs afterwards.

🍴 Courses

Lessons in Thai massage are available at Pai Traditional Thai Massage, and Thai cooking lessons are also available at Sipsongpanna hotel.

Pai Cookery School   THAI COOKING

(☑08 1706 3799; Soi Wanchaloem; lessons 600-1000B; ☺11am-1pm & 2-6.30pm) With a decade of experience, this outfit offers a variety of courses spanning three to six dishes. The course typically involves a trip to the market for ingredients. Contact a day in advance.

Taste of Pai   THAI COOKING

(☑0 5369 9453; Th Chaisongkhram; lessons 700B; ☺9am-3.30pm) This new outfit conducts nearly day-long lessons in Thai

cookery. Classes involve a visit to the fresh market followed by instruction in six dishes.

Rose Gym   THAI BOXING

(☑08 7855 6433; www.muaythaibox.com; Ban Mae Hi; tuition per half-day/day 250/400B; ☺8-10am & 4-6pm) Offers scholarship in Thai boxing, just across the Nam Pai.

Mam Yoga House   YOGA

(☑08 9954 4981; www.mamyoga.paiexplorer. com; Th Rangsiyanon; 1-day course from 200B; ☺10am-noon & 3-5pm) Just north of the police station, Mam offers Hatha Yoga classes and courses in small groups.

S Wirasut   THAI BOXING

(☑08 0678 5269; lessons 400B; ☺8am-noon & 2-5pm) Chalee and Kot lead instruction in Thai boxing at this rustic gym about 1km outside of town, on the turn-off just before Fluid.

🛏 Sleeping

In the couple of years since we were last here, Pai has seemingly undergone an explosion in accommodation, and the rumour on the ground during our visits was that there are more than 500 hotels, guest houses and resorts. Although 'downtown' Pai has seen relatively little change in this respect, there are tens of new resorts in an approximate 3km circle around the town. Despite the glut of accommodation, during the height of the Thai tourist season (December to January), accommodation in Pai can be nearly impossible to come by and tents are available for about 100B.

Keep in mind that prices fluctuate significantly in Pai, and nearly all the mid-range and top-end accommodation cut their prices, sometimes by as much as 60%, during the off season. We've listed high-season walk-in rates here.

IN TOWN

Pai used to be an exceedingly inexpensive place to stay and we still recall the days of the 50B riverside bungalow. But the 2005 flood demolished most of the truly cheap places, most of which have been replaced by upper-budget or midrange choices. There are still some cheap places just outside of the centre of town, which is where you should base yourself if you're coming to Pai with preconceived notions of an idyllic, rural stay.

Rim Pai Cottage
HOTEL $$$

(☑0 5369 9133; www.rimpaicottage.com; Th Chaisongkhram; bungalows incl breakfast 1300-5000B; ❄️🛜) The homelike bungalows here are spread out along a secluded and beautifully wooded section of the Nam Pai. The interiors have a romantic feel with their mosquito nets and Thai decorating details, and the open bathrooms are particularly nice. There are countless cosy riverside corners to relax at, and a palpable villagelike feel about the whole place. Rim Pai is an excellent deal in the low season when the prices drop dramatically.

Baan Pai Village
HOTEL $$

(☑0 5369 8152; www.baanpaivillage.com; Th Wiang Tai; bungalows incl breakfast 500-1500B; ❄️@🛜) This well-maintained place has a collection of wooden bungalows set among winding pathways. The bungalows don't leave heaps of room to stretch, but have floor-to-ceiling sliding windows, large, quite plush bathrooms, rattan mats and axe cushions for relaxing, plus spacious terraces to enjoy the garden. There are also a few cheaper, but simpler, bamboo huts.

Hotel des Artists
HOTEL $$$

(☑0 5369 9539; www.hotelartists.com; Th Chaisongkhram; r incl breakfast 3600-4000B; ❄️🛜) It took years, but finally somebody saw the potential in this beautiful wooden Shan-style mansion. The 14 slightly crowded rooms mingle pan-Asian and Western design elements in a tasteful, attractive package. Twin beds are on an elevated platform, and all rooms have balconies, those with riverside views being the more expensive.

Pai River Villa
HOTEL $$$

(☑0 5369 9796; www.wangchangpuek.com; r incl breakfast 1000B, bungalows incl breakfast 1200-2500B; ❄️🛜) This place boasts some of the more attractive midrange riverside bungalows in town. The air-con bungalows are spacious and attractive, and have wide balconies that encourage lazy riverside relaxing and mountain viewing. The fan bungalows are a significantly tighter fit, and there's an adjacent house with 11 rooms.

Pai RiverCorner
HOTEL $$$

(☑0 5369 9049; www.pairivercorner.com; Th Chaisongkhram; r incl breakfast 3270-6540B; ❄️@🛜🏊) The nine rooms here include beautiful Thai furniture, gorgeous colours and lots of deluxe details. Definitely the place for the design-conscious, all rooms have river-facing balconies and some have lounges and interior spa pools.

Pai Vimaan Resort
HOTEL $$$

(☑0 5369 9403; www.paivimaan.com; Th Wiang Tai; r incl breakfast 3500-4500B, bungalows incl breakfast 8000B; ❄️🛜) The highlight here is the five riverside tented bungalows. Huge, and equipped with air-con, TV and other modern amenities, they redefine camping. The resort's three-storey bungalows are bright and airy, with the top-floor rooms allowing great views of the river, and there are also rooms in the main wooden structure.

Baan Tawan Guest House
HOTEL $$

(☑0 5369 8116; www.pai-baantawan.com; 117 Moo 4, Th Wiang Tai; r incl breakfast 1000-3000B, bungalows incl breakfast 1800-3000B; ❄️@🛜) The older, more charming, more expensive, riverside two-storey bungalows made with salvaged teak are the reason to stay here, but there are also spacious rooms in a large two-storey building.

Breeze of Pai Guesthouse
HOTEL $$

(☑08 1998 4597; helendavis2@yahoo.co.uk; Soi Wat Pa Kham; r 400B, bungalows with fan/air-con 500/800B; ❄️🛜) This well-groomed compound near the river consists of nine attractive and spacious rooms and six large A-frame bungalows. It's close to the action without the noise pollution, and the friendly English owner can provide good local advice.

Pai Country Hut
HOTEL $

(☑08 4046 4458; Ban Mae Hi; bungalows incl breakfast 500B; 🛜) The bamboo bungalows here are utterly simple, but are tidy and have bathrooms and inviting hammocks. Although it's not exactly riverside, it's the most appealing of several similar places in the area.

Pai Nai Fun
HOTEL $$$

(☑08 9123 5042; www.painaifun.com; Ban Mae Hi; bungalows incl breakfast 600-2200B; ❄️🛜) Located across the river, this place boasts a variety of accommodation, ranging from A-frame huts to adobe bungalows. It's no longer new, but is quieter than staying in town and bicycles can be borrowed for free.

Blue Lagoon Hotel
HOTEL $$$

(☑0 5369 9998; www.paibluelagoon.com; Th Rangsiyanon; r 1000-1800B; ❄️🛜🏊) This two-storey suburban-feel hotel, complete with pool and tropical plants, is more Las Vegas than Pai. Large rooms are available for travelling families.

Pai Fah HOTEL $$$
(☎0 5306 4446; www.paifahhotel.com; Th Wiang Tai; r with fan 1500B, with air-con 1800-2500B; ❄@📶) This self-professed 'boutique house' takes the form of simple but bright and clean rooms in a two-storey villa steps from all the action.

Villa De Pai HOTEL $$$
(☎0 5369 9109; 87/1 Th Wiang Tai; bungalows incl breakfast 1400-3000B; 📶) Slightly aged, but clean and conveniently located riverside bungalows.

TTK GUEST HOUSE $
(☎0 5369 8093; 8/10 Th Raddamrong, also spelt Ratchadamnoen; r 400-600B; ❄📶) Set behind the Israeli restaurant of the same name, the rooms here lack any effort at interior design, but are spotless and conveniently located.

Tayai's House GUEST HOUSE $
(☎0 5369 9579; off Th Raddamrong; r 400-600B; ❄) Simple but clean fan and air-con rooms in a leafy compound a short walk from the main drag.

Pravee's House HOTEL $
(☎0 5369 9368; Soi Wanchaloem; r with fan/air-con 500/600B; ❄📶) The rooms in this garden compound aren't as nice as their exterior suggests, but will do in a pinch.

Charlie's House GUEST HOUSE $
(☎0 5369 9039; Th Rangsiyanon; r 200-600B; ❄) This long-standing and locally run place offers a range of options in a suburban compound.

Mr Jan's Guest House GUEST HOUSE $$$
(☎0 5369 9554; Soi Wanchaloem 18; r 300-2000B; 📶) Owned by a native of Pai, the rooms here are set around a medicinal herb garden, although they can be plain and somewhat dark.

OUTSIDE OF TOWN

If you've got your own wheels, there are far more options outside of the centre of Pai than we have room to list here. The vast majority are targeted towards domestic, rather than foreign, tourists, which means they fall in the mid and upper range of the price spectrum and typically take the form of air-con-equipped bungalow compounds.

Bulunburi HOTEL $$$
(☎0 5369 8302; www.bulunburi.com; 28 Moo 5 Ban Pong; bungalows incl breakfast 1350-3300B; ❄@) Set in a tiny secluded valley of rice fields and streams, the seductively bucolic location is as much a reason to stay here as the attractive accommodation. The compound's most apparent structure, the conelike open-air lobby, is decorated with attractive murals and boasts a central fireplace. The bungalows mostly continue the tasteful design theme established in the lobby, and are large, well equipped and stylish. The hotel is about 2.5km from the centre of town along the road to Mae Hong Son – look for the well-posted turn-off, about 1km from Pai.

Bueng Pai Resort RESORT HOTEL $$$
(☎08 9265 4768; www.paifarm.com; 185 Moo 5 Ban Mae Hi; bungalows 400-1800B; 📶🏊) Uniting yoga enthusiasts and fisherfolk, the 12 simple bungalows here are strategically and attractively positioned between a functioning farm and a pond stocked with freshwater fish. During the tourist season Run and Orn serve meals made with their own organic produce, and fishing equipment is available for rent year-round. Bueng Pai is 2.5km from Pai, off the road that leads to Tha Pai Hot Springs – look for the sign.

Pairadise HOTEL $$
(☎0 5369 8065; www.pairadise.com; 98 Moo 1 Ban Mae Hi; bungalows 800-1500B; ❄📶) Popular with the Western yoga-and-meditation set, this tidy resort looks over the Pai Valley from atop a ridge just outside town. The bungalows are stylish, spacious and include gold leaf lotus murals, beautiful rustic bathrooms and terraces with hammocks. All surround a waterfall-fed pond that is suitable for swimming. The hotel is nearly 1km east of Pai – look for the sign just after the bridge.

Sipsongpanna HOTEL $$$
(☎0 5369 8259, 08 1881 7631; 60 Moo 5, Ban Juang, Wiang Neua; bungalows incl breakfast 1000-2500B; @📶) This fun place boasts a chilled-out atmosphere that feels authentically local rather than contrived. The adobe-style riverside bungalows are rustic and a bit quirky with a mix of bright colours, beds on elevated platforms and sliding-glass doors opening to wide balconies. There are also still a few original wooden bungalows, although these are being phased out. There is a vegetarian cafe and Thai vegetarian cooking lessons are available. The hotel is about 2.5km from the centre of town off the road to Mae Hong Son – look for the well-posted turn-off, about 1km from Pai.

Phu Pai HOTEL **$$$**

(📞0 5306 5111; www.phupai.com; 93 Moo 1, Mae Na Theung; bungalows incl breakfast 3500-7500B; ✳🎧🐾) This self-professed 'Art Resort' is a well-done and attractive gathering of locally styled luxury bungalows. Views are the focus here, with most bungalows edging rice fields, and the infinity pool sporting a terrific view of the Pai Valley. The hotel is about 4km from the centre of town off the road to Mae Hong Son – look for the well-posted turn-off just after the airport runway, about 1.3km from Pai.

Pai Chan HOTEL **$$$**

(📞08 1180 3064; www.paichan.com; 191 Moo 1 Ban Mae Hi; bungalows incl breakfast 600-2000B; 🎧🐾) Pai Chan doesn't look like much from the parking lot, but a closer look reveals attractive and comfortable heavy wooden bungalows, each with a spacious balcony overlooking rice fields or an inviting pool. The hotel is 300m east of Pai off the road that leads to Tha Pai Hot Springs – look for the sign just after the bridge.

Sun Hut HOTEL **$$$**

(📞0 5369 9730; www.thesunhut.com; 28/1 Ban Mae Yen; bungalows incl breakfast 900-1900B; 🎧) Located in a junglelike setting with a stream running through it, this long-standing and rustic resort is one of the more unique places in the area. Bungalows are nicely spaced apart and more expensive ones have porches and lots of charm. Service is friendly and gentle, there's an organic garden, a vegetarian restaurant, and an attractive communal area with hammocks and napping guests. The hotel is 300m east of the Mae Nam Pai along the road that leads to Tha Pai Hot Springs.

PuraVida HOTEL **$$$**

(📞08 9635 7556; www.puravidapai.com; 65 Moo 3 Wiang Nua; bungalows 1600B; ✳🎧) A friendly Dutch-Thai couple look after these eight cute bungalows on a well-manicured hillside in the quiet Wiang Nua area. The 'honeymoon' bungalow offers a bit more privacy, and all rooms are similarly equipped with air-con, TV, fridge and hot water. The hotel is about 4km from the centre of town off the road to Mae Hong Song – look for the well-posted turn-off, about 1km from Pai.

Lychee Garden Bungalow GUEST HOUSE **$$**

(📞08 5471 9220; 159 Moo 2 Wiang Nua; bungalows 500-1500B; ✳🎧) The four bungalows here, located in an overflowing garden and shaded by lychee trees, may not be the most luxurious accommodation in the area, but they're clean, with good bedding, TV, air-con and hot water. The Israeli-Thai couple who run the place will do their best to make you feel like family. The hotel is about 2.5km from the centre of town off the road to Mae Hong Song – look for the well-posted turn-off, about 1km from Pai.

Amy's Earth House GUEST HOUSE **$**

(📞08 6190 2394; www.amyshouse.net; Ban Mae Khong; bungalows 600B; 🎧) Amy's claims to have been the first adobe accommodation in Pai. Mud bungalows are simple, but spacious, and have open-air showers, and are on a landscaped hillside looking over the valley. The hotel is about 3.5km from the centre of town off the road to Mae Hong Song – look for the well-posted turn-off just after the airport runway, about 1.3km from Pai.

Pai Treehouse HOTEL **$$$**

(📞08 1911 3640; www.paitreehouse.com; 90 Moo 2 Mae Hi; bungalows incl breakfast 1200-12,000B; ✳@🎧) It's every child's fantasy hotel: wooden bungalows suspended from a giant old tree. Even if you can't score one of the three elusive tree-house rooms (they're popular), there are several other attractive bungalows, many near the river. On the vast grounds you'll also find elephants and floating decks on the Mae Nam Pai, all culminating in a family-friendly atmosphere. The resort is 6km from Pai, just before Tha Pai Hot Springs.

Pai Phu Fah HOTEL **$$$**

(📞08 1906 2718; www.paiphufah.com; 178/1 Moo 1 Ban Mae Hi; r & bungalows 900-1900B; 🎧) There's a decent range of accommodation here, from bungalows to rooms, nearly all of it good value. It's about 500m east of the Mae Nam Pai along the road to Thai Pai Hot Springs (which is 7km east of Th Raddamrong).

🍴 Eating

At first glance, Pai has a seemingly impressive range of restaurants for such a small town, but a few meals will reveal that the quality of food is generally pretty mediocre. Even the Thai food is fairly dull, and your best dining options are, quite paradoxically, probably Chinese and Israeli. And to make things worse, if you're here outside of the tourist season (approximately November to February), many of the town's better restaurants can be closed, although the options listed here should be open year-round.

During the day, there's takeaway food at **Saengthongaram market** (Th Khetkelang). For tasty take-home local eats, try the **evening market** (gàht láang; Th Raddamrong) that unfolds every afternoon from about 3pm to sunset. And every evening during the tourist season several vendors set up along Th Chaisongkhram and Th Rangsiyanon, selling all manner of food and drink from stalls and refurbished VW vans.

Laap Khom Huay Pu TOP CHOICE NORTHERN THAI $
(no roman-script sign; Ban Huay Pu; mains 35-60B; ⊙9am-10pm) Escape the dreadlocks and tofu crowd and get your meat on at this unabashedly carnivorous local eatery. The house special, and the dish you must order, is *lâhp kôo·a*, minced meat (beef or pork) fried with local herbs and spices. Accompanied by a basket of sticky rice, a plate of bitter herbs and a cold Singha, it's the best meal in Pai. The restaurant is on the road to Mae Hong Son, about 1km north of town, just past the turn-off to Sipsongpanna.

Yunnanese Restaurant CHINESE $$
(no roman-script sign; Ban Santichon; mains 25-200B; ⊙8am-8pm) This open-air place in the Chinese village of Ban Santichon serves the traditional dishes of the town's Yunnanese residents. Standouts include *màntŏ* (steamed buns), here served with pork leg stewed with Chinese herbs. There are several dishes using unique local crops and other dishes involving exotic ingredients such as black chicken. Or you could always go for the excellent noodles, made by hand and topped with a delicious mixture of minced pork, garlic and sesame. The restaurant is in an open-air adobe building behind the giant rock in Ban Santichon, about 4km west of Pai.

Mama Falafel ISRAELI $
(Soi Wanchaloem; set meals 80-90B; ⊙11am-8pm) This friendly native of Pai has been cooking up tasty felafel, hummus, schnitzel and other Jewish/Israeli faves since 2002. Set meals win in both quality and quantity. Come on Friday and Saturday when she does hamin, the Jewish stew, accompanied by challah bread.

Khanom Jeen Nang Yong THAI $
(no roman-script sign; Th Chaisongkhram; mains 20B; ⊙lunch & dinner) This place specialises in

kà·nŏm jeen – thin rice noodles served with a currylike broth. They do a particularly rich and spicy *kà·nŏm jeen nám ngée·o*, great with deep-fried pork rinds, but don't worry about getting the names right – simply point to whichever clay pot looks the tastiest. It's in the same building as Pai Adventure.

Burger House AMERICAN $$
(Th Rangsiyanon; mains 80-210B; ⊙9am-8.30pm) If you are hankering after a big juicy burger this is the place to come. Try the super-high Barbarian Burger with its two quarter pounders, two cheeses and special sauce. Or if you need a fortifying breakfast, go for the Truck Driver Special, which will probably take most of the morning to get through.

Je-In Pai VEGETARIAN $
(Pure Vegetarian Food; Th Raddamrong; mains 40-80B; ⊙10am-8pm; ✍) Opposite the District Office, this simple open-air place serves tasty and cheap vegan and vegetarian Thai food. During lunch, choose from the metal trays out front. There's good fruit and soy milk shakes too.

Nong Beer THAI $
(cnr Th Khetkalang & Th Chaisongkhram; mains 30-60B; ⊙10am-8pm) The atmosphere at this extremely popular place is akin to a food court (you have to exchange cash for tickets, and everything is self-serve), but it's a good place for cheap and authentic Thai eats ranging from *kôw soy* to curries ladled over rice. Open until they run out of food – usually about 8pm.

Big's Little Cafe INTERNATIONAL $
(Th Chaisongkhram; mains 55-100B) Big does largely English-influenced Western dishes, from bacon butties to burgers, not to mention breakfasts and a tasty homemade sausage.

Witching Well INTERNATIONAL $
(Th Wiang Tai; dishes 40-80B) This foreigner-run place is where to come if you're looking for authentic sandwiches, pasta, cakes and pastries. They also do the kind of breakfasts you're not going to find elsewhere in Pai.

TTK ISRAELI $
(The Thai Kebab; Th Raddamrong; dishes 40-150B; ⊙8.30am-8.30pm; ✍) The expansive menu here spans Israeli dishes from standards to surprises, with breakfast options and Thai vegetarian thrown in for good measure.

Good Life
INTERNATIONAL $

(Th Wiang Tai; dishes 60-140B; 🛜📶) Wheat grass and secondhand books (sample title: *The Aloe Answer*) function as interior design at this eclectic and popular cafe. In addition to heaps of teas, coffees, 'juice joints' and other tasty drinks, they also do breakfasts and vegetarian Thai dishes.

Amido's Pizza Garden
PIZZA $$

(Th Raddamrong; pizzas 150-340B; ⊘dinner) Considering how far Pai is from Naples, we reckon they do a pretty damn good pizza here.

Charlie & Lek Health Restaurant
THAI $

(Th Rangsiyanon; mains 30-140B; ⊘11am-2pm & 6-9pm) This popular place does central Thai-style fare for foreigners: lots of veggie options and light on the flavours.

🍷 Drinking & Entertainment

There are tens of bars in Pai – too many to list here – and given the fickleness of the local drinking scene, few would likely still be around by the time this goes to print. Instead, below we list some of the more longstanding places found outside of town.

As a general guide to 'downtown' Pai's entertainment scene, most of the open-air and VW van-based cocktail bars are along Th Chaisongkhram; Th Wiang Tai is where you'll find the mostly indoor and chilled reggae-type places; the 'guest house' style restaurant/bars with a diverse soundtrack are mostly found on Th Rangsiyanon; and a few live music bars can be found along the eastern end of Th Raddamrong.

Bebop
LIVE MUSIC

(Th Rangsiyanon; ⊘6pm-1am) This legendary box is popular with travellers and has live music nightly (from about 9pm), playing blues, R&B and rock.

Ting Tong
BAR

(Th Rangsiyanon; ⊘7pm-1am) A sprawling compound of bamboo decks, concrete platforms, hidden tables and towering trees, this is one of the larger bars in town. Reggae/dub defines but doesn't rule the play list, and there's occasional live music.

Don't Cry
BAR

(Th Raddamrong; ⊘6pm-late) Located just across the river, this is the kind of reggae bar you thought you left behind on Ko Phangan. Soporifically chilled out and open (albeit quietly) until the last guy goes home.

🛍 Shopping

Every evening during the tourist season, from November to February, a walking street forms along Th Chaisongkhram and Th Rangsiyanon. The western end of the former is home to a particular abundance of shops selling Pai-themed tat aimed at domestic tourists.

Siam Books
BOOKSHOP

(📷0 5369 9075; Th Chaisongkhram) Boasts the town's largest selection of new and used books.

ℹ Information

There are plenty of places around town, especially at the western end of Th Raddamrong, that offer internet services (20B to 30B per hour).

Several exchange booths and ATMs can be found along Th Rangsiyanon and Th Chaisongkhram.

Pai Explorer (www.paiexplorer.com) is the free local English-language map. The *Pai Events Planner* (PEP) is a free monthly map that covers cultural events, travel destinations and some restaurant and bar openings, and can be picked up around town.

ℹ Getting There & Away

Air

Pai's airport is around 1.5km north of town along Rte 1095 and offers a daily connection to Chiang Mai (1890B, 25 minutes) on **Kan Air** (📷nationwide call centre 02 551 6111, Pai 0 5369 9955; www.kanairlines.com; Pai airport).

Bus

Pai's tiny bus station runs ordinary (fan-cooled) and minibus (propane-fuelled) departures to Chiang Mai and destinations in Mae Hong Son.

Chiang Mai (72B to 150B, three to four hours, frequent departures from 8am to 4pm)

Mae Hong Son (70B, 4½ hours, 11am and 1pm)

Soppong (40B, 1½ hours, 11am and 1pm)

Minivan

Minivans also depart from Pai's bus terminal. You can also book tickets at **aYa Service** (📷0 5369 9940; www.ayaservice.com; 22/1 Moo 3 Th Chaisongkhram), which runs hourly air-con minivan buses to Chiang Mai (150B, three hours, frequent departures from 8am to 4pm), as well as a single departure to Chiang Rai (550B, five hours) and Mae Sai (850B, six hours) at 5.30am, and Chiang Khong (650B, seven hours) at 8pm.

Chiang Mai (150B, three hours, every hour from 7am to 4.30pm)

Mae Hong Son (150B, 2½ hours, every hour from 8.30am to 5.30pm)

Soppong (100B, one hour, every hour from 8.30am to 5.30pm)

❶ Getting Around

Most of Pai is accessible on foot. Motorcycle taxis wait at the taxi stand across from the bus station. Fares are 100B to Ban Santichon and 120B to Nam Tok Mo Paeng.

For local excursions you can rent bicycles or motorcycles at several locations around town.

aYa Service (☎0 5369 9940; www.ayaserv ice.com; Th Chaisongkhram; bikes per 24hr 80-700B) This busy outfit has more than 100 bikes. There are a couple of similar places in the immediate vicinity.

North Wheels (www.northwheels.com; Th Khetkelang; motorcycle/car per 24hr 150/1500B; ⏰7am-8pm)

Soppong   สบป่อง

Soppong (also sometimes known as Pang-mapha, actually the name of the entire district) is a small market village a couple of hours northwest of Pai and about 70km from Mae Hong Son. There's not much to see in town, but the surrounding area is defined by dense forests, rushing rivers and dramatic limestone outcrops and is *the* place in northern Thailand for caving. The best source of information on caving and trekking in the area is the owner of Cave Lodge in nearby Tham Lot, the most accessible cave in the area.

There are also several Shan, Lisu, Karen and Lahu villages that can easily be visited on foot.

If you're here on Tuesday morning, check out the town's rustic **market**.

🏃 Activities

Trekking & Rafting

Cave Lodge near Tham Lot, 9km from Soppong, has experienced local guides and arranges recommended kayaking, trekking and caving trips in the area.

Poodoi Namfaa Tour & Trekking   TREKKING, RAFTING
(☎08 4372 5295) This new outfit can arrange various outdoor pursuits, all led by local Musoe, Lisu and Karen guides. The emphasis is on two-day rafting trips along the Nam Khong and Nam Pai rivers (1500B per person, at least four people, all-inclusive). Two-day treks start at 800B per person (at least two people). The office is at the far western edge of town.

🛏 Sleeping & Eating

All accommodation, much of which is found along Soppong's main road, is clearly marked by signs. There's little in the way of food in Soppong, but virtually every guest house has a restaurant attached.

TOP CHOICE Soppong River Inn   HOTEL $$
(☎0 5361 7107; www.soppong.com; bungalows 300B, r 700-1500B; ❄@🌐) Combining nine rooms in a rambling riverside structure and a handful of free-standing basic bungalows, this is the most attractive place in Soppong. Set among lush gardens with winding paths, the rooms have heaps of character and are all slightly different. The River Rim Cottage is our fave, as it has a private balcony situated right over the river. Soppong River Inn is at the western edge of town, within walking distance of the bus station.

Little Eden Guesthouse   HOTEL $$$
(☎0 5361 7054; www.littleeden-guesthouse.com; r & bungalows 450-2000B; ❄@🏊) The five A-frame bungalows around a pleasant, grass-decked pool are well kept with hot-water showers. And four new rooms in a new building should be finished by the time you read this. Yet, it's the beautiful two-storey 'houses' that make this place special. Perfect for families or a group of friends, they are stylishly decorated, have living rooms, interesting nooks and crannies, and terraces with hammocks.

Baan Café   HOTEL $$
(☎0 5361 7081; khunjui@yahoo.com; r/bungalows 600/1200B) Located near the bridge, about 750m west of Soppong's bus stop, this place combines spotless rooms and houselike bungalows in a parklike setting by the Nam Lang. The bungalows include fireplaces, have balconies looking over the river and are terrific value. Baan Café is also one of the better restaurants in town and serves locally grown coffee.

Rock   HOTEL $$$
(☎0 5361 7134; www.therockresort.com; r & bungalows incl breakfast 1500-5000B; ❄🌐) Located about 1.5km west of town, you can't miss this place. The new bungalows are scattered across a manicured riverbank pockmarked with rock formations. Rooms are equipped with TV, fridge and air-con, and a suspension bridge links the grounds with adjacent flower gardens. This place is geared towards

THE CAVES OF PANGMAPHA

The 900-sq-km area of Pangmapha district is famous for its high concentration of cave systems, where over 200 have been found. Apart from Tham Lot (p400), one of its most famous is Tham Nam Lang, which is 20km northwest of Soppong near Ban Nam Khong. It's 8.5km long and said to be one of the largest caves in the world in terms of volume.

Many of the caves are essentially underground river systems, some of which boast waterfalls, lakes and 'beaches'. *Cryptotora thamicola,* an eyeless, waterfall-climbing troglobitic fish that forms its own genus, is found in only two caves in the world, both of which are in Pangmapha, Thailand. Other caves contain little or no life, due to an abundance of noxious gases or very little oxygen.

More than 85 of the district's 200 limestone caverns are known to contain ancient teak coffins carved from solid teak logs. Up to 9m long, the coffins are typically suspended on wooden scaffolds inside the caves. The coffins have been carbon-dated and shown to be between 1200 and 2200 years old. The ends are usually carved and Thai archaeologists have identified at least 50 different design schemes. Pottery remains found in coffin caves are on display in the Nature Education Centre at Tham Lot (p400).

The local Shans know these burial caves as *tâm pěe* (spirit caves), or *tâm pěe maan* (coffin caves). It is not known who made them or why they were placed in caves, but as most caves have fewer than 10 coffins it indicates that not everyone was accorded such an elaborate burial. Similar coffins have been found in karst areas west of Bangkok and also in Borneo, China and the Philippines, but the highest concentration of coffin caves from this period is in Pangmapha.

The easiest coffin caves to visit are found just past Pangmapha Hospital, 2km west of Soppong, and the coffin caves in Tham Lot, 9km from Soppong. Several caves that scientists are investigating at the moment are off limits to the public, but John Spies at Cave Lodge (p400) may know which caves are possible to explore. His book, *Wild Times,* is also a great informal guide to the area's caves.

Thai tourists and communicating in English might be a problem.

Lemon Hill Guest House　　GUEST HOUSE $$
(☑0 5361 7039, 0 5361 7213; r & bungalows 300-1500B; ✳✿) Due to its location across from the town bus stop, this guest house is probably the most popular place in town, although it must be said that there are nicer places to stay. There's a mish-mash of accommodation ranging from rooms to bungalows – check out a few before coming to a decision.

Rim Doi　　HOTEL $
(☑08 8413 9964; r & bungalows 200-650B) About 2km from Soppong, along the road to Tham Lot, this place unites bamboo huts and more permanent-feeling rooms on a grassy hillside. Rooms are large and comfortably furnished.

Northern Hill Guest House　　HOTEL $$
(☑0 5361 7081; khunjui@yahoo.com; r & bungalows 800-1500B) This place combines several cramped but tidy bungalows on a hill looking over Soppong. Some rooms include TV and fridge. Northern Hill is at the eastern extent of town, opposite the turn-off to Tham Lot.

Baanlek Guest House　　GUEST HOUSE $
(☑08 9485 7596; r 250B; ✿) Two very simple rooms in a small house (Baanlek) at the eastern end of Soppong. The owner also conducts **cooking courses** (www.flyingturtle cooking.com; half/full day 700/900) at her farm.

Baankeawmora　　THAI $
(dishes 40-160B; ☺8am-6pm) Good food and real coffee can be had at this cute wooden house along the road to Tham Lot. Early morning breakfasts and late dinners can be arranged in advance.

ⓘ Information

Soppong's police station is 1.5km west of the town. The town's only ATM is found there.

ⓘ Getting There & Around

Motorcycle taxis stationed at the bus stop in Soppong will take passengers to Tham Lot or the Cave Lodge for 80B per person; private pick-up trucks will take you and up to five other people for 300B.

Buses and minivans stop near the town's market.

Bus

Chiang Mai (95B, six hours, 10.30am and 2.30pm)

Mae Hong Son (40B, two hours, 12.30pm and 2.30pm)

Pai (40B, 1½ hours, 10.30am and 2.30pm)

Minivan

Chiang Mai (250B, five hours, every hour from 8.30am to 5.30pm)

Mae Hong Son (150B, 1½ hours, every hour from 9.30am to 6.30pm)

Pai (100B, one hour, every hour from 8.30am to 5.30pm)

Around Soppong

THAM LOT   ถ้ำลอด

About 9km north of Soppong is Tham Lot (pronounced *tâm lôrt* and also known as *tâm nám lôrt*), a large limestone cave with impressive stalagmites and 'coffin caves' (see the boxed text, p399), and a wide stream running through it. Along with Tham Nam Lang further west, it's one of the largest known caves in Thailand. The total length of the cave is 1600m, and for 600m the stream runs through it.

At the **Nature Education Centre** (☺8am-5.30pm) and entrance, you must hire a gas lantern and guide for 150B (one guide leads one to four people) to take you through the caverns; visitors are not permitted to tour the caves alone. Tham Lot is a good example of community-based tourism as all of the guides at the cave are from local Shan villages.

Apart from the main chamber, there are also three side chambers – Column Cavern, Doll Cave and Coffin Cave – that can be reached by ladders. It takes around two hours to explore the whole thing. Depending on the time of year it is necessary to take a bamboo raft for some or all of the journey through the caves. Access to parts of the cave may be limited between August and October because of water levels.

From the entrance to the exit and taking in the Column Cavern, Doll Cave and Coffin Cave, the rafts (up to four adults) cost 400B return, or 300B one way. If going one way you can walk back from outside the cave (20 minutes), only possible during the dry season. In the dry season it may be possible to wade to the Doll Cave and then take a raft through to the exit (300B return, 200B one way). Try to be at the exit at sunset when hundreds of thousands of swifts pour into Tham Lot and cling to their bedtime stalagmites.

🛏 Sleeping & Eating

A row of **outdoor restaurants** (dishes 15-40B; ☺9am-6pm) outside the Tham Lot park entrance offers simple Thai fare.

Cave Lodge   HOTEL **$$$**

(☎0 5361 7203; www.cavelodge.com; dm 90-120B, r 250B, bungalows 300-2000B) Open since 1986, this is one of the more legendary places to stay in northern Thailand (and probably the first guest house in Mae Hong Son). Run by the unofficial expert on the area, John Spies, the 19 rooms here are basic but unique and varied. The setting on a wooded hillside above the Nam Lang is beautiful and options for adventure abound. Choose from caving and kayaking trips, guided or unguided treks (good maps are available) or just hang out in the beautiful communal area. The traditional Shan herbal sauna is an experience and the custom ovens bake bread and other treats. Tham Lot is a short walk away.

MAE LA-NA   แม่ละนา

Set in an incredibly picturesque mountain valley 6km off Rte 1095, this tiny Shan village feels like a lost corner of the world. The most famous local attraction is **Tham Mae La-Na**, a 12km-long cavern with a stream running through it. Although local guides are willing to take people inside, in reality the cave lacks the appropriate infrastructure to support visitors, who run a serious risk of permanently damaging delicate cave formations and disturbing the habitat of sensitive cave fish. A better bet is to check out the nearby **Tham Pakarang** (Coral Cave) and **Tham Phet** (Diamond Cave), both of which feature good wall formations. Guides (200B) can be found during the day at the *săh·lah* (often spelt as *sala;* open-sided, covered meeting hall) and at the main village shop. Some of the caves may not be accessible during the rainy season.

Mae La-Na is also a good base for some inspiring **walks**. Some of Mae Hong Son's most beautiful scenery is within a day's ramble, and there are several Red and Black Lahu villages nearby. It's also possible to walk a 20km half-loop all the way from Mae La-Na to Tham Lot and Soppong. Khun Ampha at Maelana Garden Home can provide a basic map and advice. Experienced riders can do this route on a sturdy dirt bike – but not alone or during the rainy season.

The Mae La-Na junction is 13km west of Soppong. A motorcycle taxi here from Soppong costs 200B. Along the way you'll pass the Black Lahu village of Jabo, which also boasts a coffin cave.

🛏 Sleeping & Eating

A dozen homes in Mae La-Na have collaborated to form a **homestay program** (per person per night 100B) where the money goes back into a community fund. Meals can be prepared for 70B per person. Inquire at the sporadically staffed wooden house at the entrance to town.

Maelana Garden Home HOTEL **$**
(📞08 1706 6021; r & bungalows 200-500B) At the edge of town towards Tham Mae La-Na, this attractive farmlike compound combines two wooden houses and a few A-frame bamboo bungalows. The rooms are basic but clean and comfy. Authentic Shan meals can be prepared (100B per person), and the lady who runs it speaks a bit of English and is a good source of information. Call ahead – transport can be arranged for 100B from Rte 1095 or from Soppong for 400B – or ask for Khun Ampha at the village shop/petrol station.

Khun Yuam จุนยวม
POP 7000

About halfway between Mae Sariang and Mae Hong Son, where all northbound buses make their halfway stop, is the quiet hillside town of Khun Yuam. This little-visited town is a nice break from more 'experienced' destinations nearby. There are a couple of places to stay and a few notable sights.

◎ Sights

Thai-Japan Friendship Memorial Hall MUSEUM
(admission 50B; ⊗8am-4pm) At the northern end of town, a collection of rusted military trucks marks the Thai-Japan Friendship Memorial Hall. The centre was being renovated on our most recent visit, but in past years housed weapons, military equipment, personal possessions and fascinating black-and-white photographs that document the period when the Japanese occupied Khun Yuam in the closing weeks of the war with Burma. After they had recovered, some of the Japanese soldiers stayed in Khun Yuam and married. The last Japanese soldier who settled in the area died in 2000.

Wat To Phae TEMPLE
About 6km to the west of Khun Yuam, the atmospheric Wat To Phae sits alongside a country stream and boasts a Mon-style *chedi* and an immaculate Burmese-style *wí·hăhn*. Inside the latter, take a look at the large, 150-year-old Burmese *kalaga* (embroidered and sequined tapestry) that's kept behind curtains to one side of the main altar. The tapestry depicts a scene from the *Vessantara Jataka* and local devotees believe one accrues merit simply by viewing it.

Ban Mae U Khaw VILLAGE
On the slopes of Doi Mae U Khaw, 25km from Khun Yuam via Rte 1263, is the Hmong village of Ban Mae U Khaw. During late November the area blooms with scenic Mexican sunflowers, known locally as *dòrk booa torng*. This event is incredibly popular among Thais and accommodation in the town is booked out. Continue another 25km along the same route and you'll reach the 100m **Nam Tok Mae Surin** (admission 200B), part of the Mae Surin National Park and reportedly Thailand's highest cataract.

🛏 Sleeping & Eating

There are also a few homestay options in Ban To Phae.

Ban Farang HOTEL **$$**
(📞0 5362 2086; janny5alisa@hotmail.com; 499 Th Ratburana; dm incl breakfast 150B, r incl breakfast 700-800B, bungalows incl breakfast 800-1600B; ❊) Off the main road towards the north end of town (look for the signs near the bus stop). The tidy bungalows are set on a wooded hillside. The cheaper fan bungalows are plain and dark but have a terrace. The more expensive ones come with air-con, fridge, cable TV and a terrace. Herbal massage is available and the restaurant on-site is reasonable.

Mithkhoonyoum Hotel HOTEL **$$**
(📞0 5369 1057; 61 Rte 108; r 150-1000; ❊) On the main road through the town centre, Mithkhoonyoum Hotel has simple, clean rooms, some with private bathrooms.

In Khun Yuam you'll find a collection of modest rice and noodle shops along the east side, or Rte 108, towards the southern end of town. Most of these close by 5pm or 6pm.

❶ Information

There are a couple of banks with ATMs along the main strip.

❶ Getting There & Away

Buses stop regularly at Khun Yuam on their runs between Mae Sariang and Mae Hong Song. The bus station is just north of town.

Chiang Mai (145B to 258B, seven to eight hours, frequent departures from 6.30am to 10.30pm)

Mae Hong Son (50B to 80B, 1½ to two hours, five departures from 3am to 5.30pm)

Mae Sariang (60B to 100B, three to four hours, frequent departures from 6.30am to 10.30pm)

Mae Sariang   แม่สะเรียง

POP 20,000

Little-visited Mae Sariang is gaining a low-key buzz for its attractive riverside setting and potential as a launching pad for sustainable tourism and trekking opportunities. There are several hill-tribe settlements nearby, particularly around Mae La Noi, 30km north of the city, and the area south of Mae Sariang is largely mountainous jungle encompassing both Salawin and Mae Ngao National Parks.

◉ Sights

Wat Jong Sung & Wat Si Bunruang TEMPLES
(วัดจองสูง/วัดศรีบุญเรือง) Two adjacent Burmese-Shan temples, Wat Jong Sung and Wat Si Bunruang, just off Mae Sariang's main street, are definitely worth a visit if you have time. Built in 1896, Wat Jong Sung is the more interesting of the two temples and has slender, Shan-style *chedi* and wooden monastic buildings.

⚡ Activities

Trekking & Rafting

The area surrounding Mae Sariang is probably one of the country's best for trekking and tours. This is not only due to the area's natural beauty and cultural diversity, but also because of a new breed of responsible, sustainable and community-based touring and trekking outfits. Prices below are for groups of at least two people.

Dragon Sabaii Tours   TREKKING
(☑08 5548 0884; www.thailandhilltribeholidays.
com; Th Mongkolchai; 1-day tour max four people 2500B) Emphasises eco- and cultural tour-ism primarily in the Mae La Noi area just north of Mae Sariang. This new outfit offers a variety of tours aimed at giving a genuine introduction to the local way of life and hill-tribe culture. Activities range from nonintrusive tours of hill-tribe villages to homestays, 'volunteerism', and cooking and farming with hill tribes, all of which are designed to benefit local communities directly.

Mae Sariang Tours   TREKKING, RAFTING
(☑08 2032 4790, 08 8404 8402; www.maesari
angtravel.multiply.com; 1-day/2-day/3-day trek per person 1600/2200/2600B, plus expenses, min 2 people) Mae Sariang Man, as the owner of this company prefers to be known, is an experienced trekker who leads environmentally conscious and community-based treks and rafting trips in the jungles and national parks surrounding his native city. To ensure that the communities receive what they deserve, trekkers can opt to pay all expenses outside of the guide fee directly to the villagers themselves. He can be contacted at Northwest Guest House.

Salawin Tour & Trekking   TREKKING, RAFTING
(☑08 1024 6146; Th Laeng Phanit; per person per day 800B) Mr Salawin and his brothers have been leading tours in the area for years. Their trips typically involve activities such as elephant riding, rafting and hiking. At research time Mr Salawin could be found at River Bank Guest House, but had plans to move next door to the soon-to-be River View Guesthouse.

🛏 Sleeping

Riverhouse Hotel   HOTEL $$
(☑0 5362 1201; www.riverhousehotels.com; 77 Th Laeng Phanit; r incl breakfast 750-1300B; ❋@◈) The combination of nostalgia-inducing teak and stylish decor makes this riverside boutique hotel the best spot in town. Air-conditioned 2nd-floor rooms have huge verandas overlooking the river, as well as floor-to-ceiling windows.

River Bank Guest House   HOTEL $$
(☑0 5368 2787; Th Laeng Phanit; r 600-800B; ❋◈) Rooms in this attractive riverside house are decked out in hardwood and have lots of natural light. It's worth shelling out 200B more for the rooms on the upper floor as the cheaper rooms feel cramped and have comically small TVs.

Mae Sariang

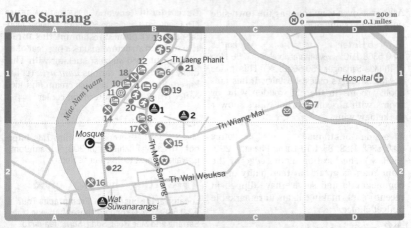

Mae Sariang

Northwest Guest House   HOTEL $
(☏08 9700 9928; www.northwestgh.blogspot. com; 81 Th Laeng Phanit; r 250-450B; ❄@🛜) The rooms in this cosy wooden house are simple (think mattress on the floor) but get natural light and are a good size. To make up for it, the guest house offers a huge variety of services, ranging from motorcycle rental to fish spa (!).

Mitaree Guesthouse & Garden House Resort   HOTEL $$
(☏0 5368 1109; www.mitareehotel.com; 24 Th Wiang Mai; r 150-1200B; ❄🛜) Located by the post office and owned by the same people who run Mitaree Hotel, it has a mish-mash

of nicer rooms, the more expensive of which have hot water, air-con and cable TV.

Huean Kham Khong   HOTEL $$
(no roman-script sign; ☏0 5368 2416; Th Laeng Phanit; bungalows 800B; ❄🛜) The five cute bungalows appear comfortable, and are equipped with TV, fridge and air-con, but the plot of land they're on certainly doesn't have much atmosphere.

Riverhouse Resort   HOTEL $$$
(☏0 5368 3066; www.riverhousehotels.com; Th Laeng Phanit; r incl breakfast 1800-2800B; ❄@🛜) Located virtually next door to Riverhouse Hotel, and run by the same people, this place is similar but lacks its sister's charm.

Ask for a river view room as the town-side ones are the same price.

Mitaree Hotel   HOTEL $
(📞0 5368 1110; www.mitareehotel.com; 256 Moo 2, Th Mae Sariang; r 250-500B; ❄) This place is Mae Sariang's oldest hostelry. It has fan-cooled rooms in the old wooden wing or rooms with air-con and hot-water shower in the new wing.

Riverside Guesthouse   HOTEL $
(📞0 5368 1188; 85/1 Th Laeng Phanit; r 200-550B; ❄) The location at the edge of the Nam Yuam is great, but the quality of accommodation and service have dipped in recent years, making it an unremarkable budget choice.

🍴 Eating & Drinking

Inthira Restaurant   THAI $
(Th Wiang Mai; mains 30-150B; ⊘8am-10pm) Probably the town's best restaurant, this place features a strong menu of dishes using unusual ingredients such as locally grown shiitake mushrooms and fish from the Mae Nam Moei. Everything's tasty, the prices are low and the setting cosy and informal.

Kai Yang Rai Khwan   THAI $$
(mains 30-180B; ⊘lunch) Head here for the Isan trinity of grilled chicken, papaya salad and sticky rice. This simple place is at the foot of the bridge crossing.

Leelawadee   THAI $
(cnr Th Wiang Mai & Th Mae Sariang; mains 40-180B; ⊘7am-9pm; 🕸) This cosy and friendly place has an English-language menu of both one-dish meals and mains, as well as real coffee and free wi-fi.

Sawadee Restaurant & Bar   THAI $
(Th Laeng Phanit; mains 40-150B; ⊘8am-midnight; 🕸🍴) Like a beachside bar, this is a great place to recline with a beer and watch the water (in this case the Mae Nam Yuam). There's a lengthy menu with lots of options for vegetarians.

Ban Rao   THAI $
(Th Laeng Phanit; mains 30-140B; ⊘dinner) For an authentic Thai dinner minus the spice, head to this homey riverside restaurant. The English-language menu touches on just about everything, from familiar curries to the more exotic *yam sôm oh*, a Thai-style salad of pomelo.

Coriander in Redwood INTERNATIONAL-THAI $$
(Th Laeng Phanit; dishes 50-180B; ⊘dinner Mon-Sat) The city's poshest restaurant, this attractive wooden structure makes a big deal of its steaks, but we'd suggest sticking with Thai dishes such as the various *nám prík* (chilli-based dips). There's also ice cream and iced coffee drinks for an afternoon cooler.

ℹ Information

Mae Sariang has several banks with ATMs. **Internet** (Th Laeng Phanit; per hr 20B; ⊘10am-9pm) is available next to Riverhouse Hotel.

ℹ Getting There & Around

Located at the bus station, **Prempracha Tour** (📞0 5368 1347) conducts buses between Mae Sariang and Mae Hong Song. *Sŏrng·tǎa·ou* to Mae Sot (200B, six hours, frequent departures from 6.30am to 12.30pm) also depart from the bus station when full.

With an office just north of the bus station, **Sombat Tour** (📞0 5368 1532; Th Mae Sariang) handles buses to Bangkok.

Motorcycles and bicycles are available for rent at a **rental shop** (📞08 1181 3695; ⊘8am-5pm) near Th Laeng Phanit, as well as at Northwest Guest House.

Destinations anywhere in town are 20B by motorcycle taxi.

Bus destinations from Mae Sariang:
Bangkok (444B to 571B, 13 hours, four departures from 4pm to 7.30pm)
Chiang Mai (95B to 171B, four to five hours, five departures from 7am to 3pm)
Khun Yuam (60B to 100B, two to three hours, six departures from 7am to 1am)
Mae Hong Son (95B to 171B, three to four hours, six departures from 7am to 1am)

Around Mae Sariang

SALAWIN NATIONAL PARK & MAE SAM LAEP อุทยานแห่งชาติสาละวิน/แม่สามแลบ
This **national park** (📞0 5307 1429; admission 200B) covers 722 sq km of protected land in Mae Sariang and Sop Moei districts. The park is heavily forested in teak, Asian redwood and cherrywood, and is home to the second-largest teak tree in Thailand. There are numerous hiking trails, and it's also possible to travel by boat along the Mae Nam Salawin to the park's outstation at Tha Ta Fang.

The main headquarters are 6km from Mae Sariang and have bungalow-style accommodation (300B to 1200B), which can be booked via the **Royal Forest Department** ([phone]0 2562 0760; www.dnp.go.th).

The riverside trading village of **Mae Sam Laep** is nearly at the end of a 50km winding mountain road from Mae Sariang, within the park boundaries. Populated by Burmese refugees, many of whom are Muslims, the town has a raw, border-town feel and is a launching point for **boat trips** along the Mae Nam Salawin. The trips pass through untouched jungle, unusual rock formations along the river and, occasionally, enter Myanmar.

From the pier at Mae Sam Laep it's possible to charter boats south to Sop Moei (1500B, 1½ hours), 25km from Mae Sam Laep, and north to the Salawin National Park station at Tha Ta Fang (1200B, one hour), 18km north of Mae Sam Laep. There are passenger boats as well, but departures are infrequent and, unless you speak Thai, difficult to negotiate.

There are frequent *sŏrng·tǎa·ou* from Mae Sariang to Mae Sam Laep (70B, 1½ hours, frequent departures from 6.30am to 3.30pm), departing from Th Laeng Phanit near the morning market.

Northeastern Thailand

Best Places to Eat

» Bao Phradit (p494)

» Turm-Rom (p448)

» Nagarina (p466)

Best Places to Stay

» Ban Kham Pia homestay (p481)

» Mut Mee Garden Guesthouse (p465)

» Poonsawasdi Hotel (p474)

» Kirimaya (p421)

Why Go?

For travellers and Thais alike, the northeast is Thailand's forgotten backyard. Isan *(ee·săhn)*, as it's called, offers a glimpse of the Thailand of old: rice fields run to the horizon, water buffalo wade in muddy ponds, silk weavers work looms under their homes, and pedal-rickshaw drivers pull passengers down city streets. If you have a penchant for authentic experiences, it will surely be satisfied here.

Spend even just a little time in this colossal corner of the country and you'll discover as many differences as similarities to the rest of Thailand. The language, food and culture are more Lao than Thai, with hearty helpings of Khmer and Vietnamese thrown into the mix.

And spend time here you should because it's home to some of Thailand's best historic sites, national parks and festivals. Thailand's tourist trail is at its bumpiest here (English is rarely spoken), but the fantastic attractions and daily interactions could end up being highlights of your trip.

When to Go

Only 1% of foreign travellers who come to Thailand visit Isan, so you don't need to worry about high and low seasons. The relatively cool dry season from November through February is the most comfortable time to visit, and the Surin Elephant Round-up in November is one festival worth planning your travels around. As the March-to-May hot season (when temperatures can climb over 40°C) comes to a close, towns and villages across the region, most famously Yasothon, launch giant homemade rockets into the sky to call for rain.

Isan is at its most beautiful during the June-to-October rainy season because the forests and rice paddies turn green and the waterfalls run wild. Dan Sai's Phi Ta Khon Festival (June) and Ubon Ratchathani's Candle Parade (July) attract hordes of Thai tourists.

History

The social history of this enigmatic region stretches back some 5600 years, to the hazy days of the Ban Chiang culture, which, by at least 2100 BC, had developed bronze tools to till fields. Though Ban Chiang was a very advanced society, the Khorat Plateau, over which Isan spreads, was a sparsely populated region for most of its history due to poor soils and frequent droughts, and no major powers were ever based here – it was usually under the control of empires based around it.

The name Isan comes from Isanapura (now known as Sambor Prei Kuk), the 7th-century capital of the Chenla kingdom, which at the time included what is now northeast Thailand and is now the general term used to classify the region *(pâhk ee·săhn)*, people *(kon ee·săhn)* and food *(ah·hăhn ee·săhn)* of the northeast.

Evidence shows that the Dvaravati held sway here and then the Khmers came in the 9th century and occupied it for some 500 years. After the Khmer empire waned, Isan was under the thumb of Lan Xang and Siam kings, but remained largely autonomous.

But as the French staked out the borders of colonial Laos, Thailand was forced to define its own northeastern boundaries. Slowly but surely, for better and worse, Isan fell under the mantle of broader Thailand.

Long Thailand's poorest area, the northeast became a hotbed of communist activity. Ho Chi Minh spent some years proselytising in the area, and in the 1940s a number of Indochinese Communist Party leaders fled here from Laos and helped bolster Thailand's communists. From the 1960s until an amnesty in 1982, guerrilla activity was rife across Isan. But the various insurgencies evaporated as the Thai government, with considerable help (and most of the money) from the US, began to take an interest in developing the region, resulting in an improved economy and increased opportunity. Despite rapid improvement since then, the per capita income here remains only one-third the national average.

Language & Culture

Isan is a melting pot of Thai, Lao and Khmer influences. The Isan language, still a more common first language than Thai, is very similar to Lao. In fact, there are probably

---

EATING ISAN

Isan's culinary creations are a blend of Lao and Thai cooking styles that make use of local ingredients. The holy trinity of northeastern cuisine, *gài yâhng* (grilled chicken), *sôm·dam* (spicy papaya salad) and *kôw něe·o* (sticky rice), is integral to the culture. Also essential are chillies, and a fistful of potent peppers find their way into most dishes, especially *lâhp* (spicy meat salad). Outsiders, including most other Thais, are not fans of *b̶lah ráh*, a fermented fish sauce (that looks like rotten mud), but Isan people *(kon ee·săhn)* consider it almost essential to good cooking.

Fish dominates Isan menus, with *b̶lah dùk* (catfish), *b̶lah chôrn* (striped snake-head) and *b̶lah boo* (sand goby) among the most popular. These are mostly caught in the Mekong and other large rivers. Fish that families catch themselves are usually small (sometimes so tiny they're eaten bones and all) because they come from streams and rice paddies, as do crabs, frogs and eels. The most famous fish associated with the northeast is *b̶lah bèuk* (giant Mekong catfish), but it's seldom eaten here because it's expensive. Fish farming, however, is slowly bringing it back to menus.

To both Westerners and other Thais, nothing stands out in Isan cuisine as much as insects. Even as recently as the 1970s insects composed a large part of the typical family's diet, though it became a fading tradition when the government promoted chicken and pig farming, thus lowering the prices of these now popular meats. Insects are still very common as snacks and chilli-sauce ingredients. Purple lights shining out in the countryside are for catching giant water bugs, which, along with crickets, grasshoppers, cicadas, *něrn mái pài* (bamboo worms) and more, are sold in most night markets. In fact, there's still enough of a demand that imports come from Cambodia. Thailand has no shortage of silkworm larvae, which, after they're dropped into boiling water to remove the silk threads from the cocoon, are popped into the mouth. If they stay in the water long enough to get crispy on the outside, you're in for a literal taste explosion: try one when you visit a weaving village and you'll see what we mean.

Northeastern Thailand Highlights

1 Getting awestruck by the scenery in **Pha Taem National Park** (p441)

2 Having a blast at a **Rocket Festival** (p464)

3 Looking for elephants, tigers, pythons, monkeys and more in **Khao Yai National Park** (p419)

4 Stepping back in time at the restored Angkor-era temple complexes of **Phanom Rung Historical Park** (p424) and **Phimai** (p417)

5 Climbing the rickety walkways up the mountain at **Wat Phu Tok** (p480)

6 Travelling along the **Mekong River** (p474)

7 Making friends with elephants in **Ban Ta Klang** (p429)

8 Eating *sôm·đam* (spicy papaya salad) and drinking *lôw kŏw* (white whisky) with the locals

9 Succumbing to the surreal at **Wat Pa Non Sawan** (p500)

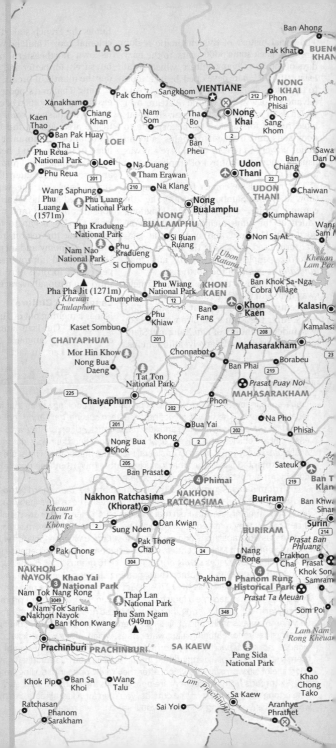

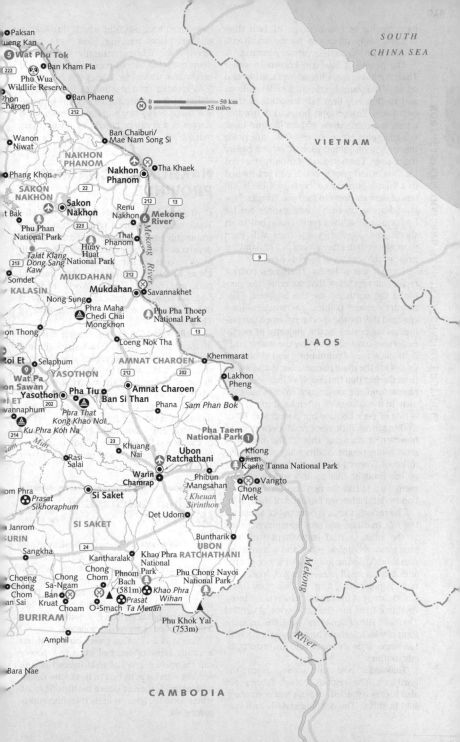

Paksan
ueng Kan
5 Wat Phu Tok
222
Phu Wua
Wildlife Reserve
Ban Kham Pia
Ban Phaeng
212
hon
Charoen
Wanon
Niwat
Ban Chaiburi/
Mae Nam Song Si
Phang Khon
NAKHON
PHANOM
Nakhon
Phanom
Tha Khaek
SAKON
NAKHON
22
Sakon
Nakhon
t Bak
Renu
Nakhon
212
13
Mekong
River
223
Phu Phan
National Park
That
Phanom
Huay
Huat
National Park
9
Talat Klang
Dong Sang
Kaw
213
Somdet
KALASIN
MUKDAHAN
212
Mukdahan
Savannakhet
Nong Sung
Phra Maha
Chedi Chai
Mongkhon
Phu Pha Thoep
National Park
on Thong
Loeng Nok Tha
13
LAOS
oi Et
Selaphum
AMNAT CHAROEN
Khemmarat
YASOTHON
212
202
Lakhon
Pheng
Wat Pa
on Sawan
Pha Tiu
Yasothon
Amnat Charoen
9
Ban Si Than
Phana
Sam Phan Bok
ET
vannaphum
Phra That
Kong Khao Noi
23
Khuang
Nai
Pha Taem
National Park
1
214
Ku Phra Koh Na
m
Muri
Rasi
Salai
Ubon
Ratchathani
Khong
Jiam
Kaeng Tanna National Park
Warin
Chamrap
Phibun
Mangsahan
Vangto
Si Saket
Prasat
Sikhoraphum
Kheuan
Sirinthon
Chong
Mek
om Phra
SI SAKET
Det Udom
Janrom
URIN
Buntharik
UBON
Sangkha
24
Khao Phra
RATCHATHANI
National
Kantharalak
Park
UBON
Chong
Chom
Phnom
Bach
(581m)
Phu Chong Nayoi
National Park
Choeng
Chong
Chong
Sa-Ngam
Khao Phra
Wihan
Mekong
Chom
an Sai
Ban
Kruat
Choam
O-Smach
Prasat
Ta Meuan
BURIRAM
Phu Khok Yai
(753m)
Amphil
River
Bara Nae
CAMBODIA

SOUTH
CHINA SEA

VIETNAM

N 0   50 km
  0   25 miles

more people of Lao heritage in Isan than in Laos. Many villages in the far south still maintain Khmer as their primary tongue.

The people of Isan are known by other Thais for their friendliness, work ethic and sense of humour: flip through radio stations and you'll surely hear DJs laughing at their own jokes. Respect and hospitality towards guests is a cornerstone of Isan life and most villagers, plus plenty of city folk, still pride themselves on taking care of others before themselves. The best food is usually reserved for monks and guests, and if you get invited to a village home, your hosts will likely kill one of their chickens to feed you (vegetarians should speak up early). Isan people are far less conservative than most Thais, but short shorts and spaghetti-strap tops will earn more stares than other places in Thailand because of the scarcity of tourists here.

Though this is by far Thailand's poorest region, surveys show that generally the people of the northeast are the happiest. (The country's recent political shenanigans have changed this for the short term since the politicians supported by the majority of northeasterners have come out on the losing end.) A strong sense of community and close family ties are the main reasons, but it also stems from the fact that the people of Isan seek happiness from the inside, not from what they own. In the villages it's often hard to tell who is rich or poor because big homes and fancy clothes garner little respect. Modern culture, however, is changing this in the minds of most young people. Additionally, the massive influx of Western men marrying local women has brought changes too and these days many Isan village women and their families hope to land a foreign husband of their own.

The region's music is born out of a distinctive folk tradition and uses instruments such as the *kaan* (a reed instrument with two long rows of bamboo pipes and a hardwood sound-box), *ʰohng·lahng* (like a xylophone) and *pin* (a small three-stringed lute). The most popular song form is *lôok tûng* (literally 'children of the fields'), which is far more rhythmic than the classical styles of central Thailand. Also huge is *mǒ lam,* the modern form of which features huge stage shows with Las Vegas–style showgirls and lowbrow comedy routines.

Thailand's best silk comes from the northeast. The region's cotton fabrics are also highly regarded, though less commonly sold in shops. The defining style is *mát·mèe*

(see boxed text, p453) in which threads are tie-dyed before weaving. Most large stores stock some fabrics naturally dyed using plant materials, an old process being revived across Isan. Prices for fabrics can be 20% to 30% cheaper (maybe 50% for less-common styles) in the weaving villages than in Bangkok shops. Sticky-rice baskets also make good souvenirs and can be bought in any ordinary market.

NAKHON RATCHASIMA PROVINCE

If you had just a single day to experience Thailand, Khorat, the original and still most commonly used name for Thailand's largest province, would be a great place to spend it. Most visitors are here to jump into the jungle at Khao Yai, Thailand's oldest national park and newest Unesco World Heritage Site. Its large size and easy access make it one of the best wildlife-watching sites in Thailand.

While Khao Yai is the soaring pinnacle of the province's tourist industry, silk and stone are solid cornerstones. Fashionistas should hit the shops in Pak Thong Chai, home of the region's silk-weaving industry, while history aficionados can soak up an evocative glimpse of the Angkor-era's heyday at the restored ruins at Phimai.

Khorat city offers little as a destination, but with a solid selection of hotels and restaurants, it makes a good base during your Isan sojourn.

Nakhon Ratchasima (Khorat)   นครราชสีมา (โคราช)

POP 215,000

Khorat doesn't wear its heart on its sleeve. Only those sporting a hefty set of rose-tinted specs will be reaching for their camera as they step off the bus in the brash gateway to the northeast. A bumper dose of urban hubbub reflects the city's affluence, and Khorat's one-time historic charm has been largely smothered under a duvet of homogenous development.

Khorat is a city that grows on you. It has a strong sense of regional identity – people call themselves *kon koh·râht* instead of *kon ee·sǎhn* – and is at its best in its quieter nooks, such as inside the east side of the historic moat, where local life goes on in its own uncompromising way.

◎ Sights & Activities

Thao Suranari Monument MONUMENT
(อนุสาวรีย์ท้าวสุรนารี; Th Rajadamnern) Thao Suranari, wife of the city's assistant governor during the reign of Rama III, is something of a Wonder Woman in these parts. Ya Mo (Grandma Mo), as she's affectionately called, became a hero in 1826 by organising a successful prisoner revolt after Chao Anou of Vientiane had conquered Khorat during his rebellion against Siam. As one version of the legend has it, she convinced the women to seduce the Lao soldiers and then the Thai men launched a surprise attack, which saved the city.

Her exploits have probably been greatly exaggerated or completely concocted – some reputable scholars suggest that she didn't even exist – to instil a sense of Thai-ness in the ethnic-Lao people of the province, but locals and visiting Thais dismiss all of this entirely and flock to the monument in adoring droves to burn incense and leave offerings of flowers and food. Those whose supplications have been honoured hire singers to perform *pleng koh-râht* (the Khorat folk song) on small stages.

Her monument sits photogenically in front of **Chumphon Gate**, the only original gate left standing: the other three are recent rebuilds. It was a part of the city walls erected in 1656 by French technicians on the orders of Ayuthaya King Narai. The little white building north of the gate that resembles the old fortifications is **Suranari Hall** (Th Chumphon; admission free; ◎9am-6pm Tue-Sun), a museum of sorts with a cool diorama and even cooler sculpted mural depicting the famous battle.

Wat Salaloi TEMPLE
(วัดศาลาลอย; Soi 1, Th Thaosura; ◎daylight hours) The city's most interesting temple was supposedly founded by Thao Suranari and her husband in 1827. Half of her ashes are interred in a small stupa here (the other half is at her monument) and so there are also singing troupes on hire to perform for her spirit here. A small statue of the heroine sits praying in the pond in front of the temple's award-winning *bòht* (chapel). Built in 1967, it resembles a Chinese junk and holds several unusual Buddha images, including one with nine faces and a large gleaming white one in a 'calming the ocean' posture. It, along with several other buildings, is decorated with Dan Kwian pottery (see p416).

Wat Phayap TEMPLE
(วัดพายัพ; Th Polsaen; ◎daylight hours) When the abbot of Wat Phayap learned that blasting for a quarry in Saraburi Province was destroying a beautiful cave, he rescued pieces of it and plastered the stalactites, stalagmites and other incredible rocks all over a room below his residence, creating a shrine like no other. Stone has since become a theme of the temple and it's now used in decoration elsewhere on the grounds.

Wat Phra Narai Maharat TEMPLE
(วัดพระนารายณ์มหาราช; Th Chomphon; ◎daylight hours) This large temple is of interest because of three holy Khmer sandstone sculptures, of which Phra Narai (Vishnu) is the holiest, that were unearthed here. To see them, follow the signs with red arrows back to the special **Naranya Temple** (◎9am-8pm) at the southeast corner. The temple's *bòht* sits on an island and there are some enormous monitor lizards living in the pond.

Maha Viravong National Museum MUSEUM
(พิพิธภัณฑสถานแห่งชาติมหาวีรวงศ์; Th Rajadamnern; admission 50B; ◎9am-4pm Wed-Sun) Though the collection at this seldom-visited museum is very small, it's also very good. There's ancient pottery – don't miss sneaking a peak at what's stored in the back – and a variety of Buddha images spanning the Dvaravati to Rattanakosin eras.

★☆ Festivals

Khorat explodes into life during the **Thao Suranari Festival**, when the city celebrates the namesake heroine. It's held annually from 23 March to 3 April and features parades, theatre and other events along Rajadamnern Rd.

⌨ Sleeping

Sansabai House HOTEL $
(☎0 4425 5144; www.sansabai-korat.com; 335 Th Suranaree; r 270-600B; ❄❀) Walk into the welcoming lobby and you half expect the posted prices to be a bait-and-switch ploy. But no, all rooms are bright and cheerful and come with good mattresses, minifridges and little balconies.

Thai Inter Hotel HOTEL $$
(☎0 4424 7700; www.thaiinterhotel.com; 344/2 Th Yommarat; r 650-750B; ❄@❀) This little hotel tries to be hip by patching together an odd mix of styles, and it pretty much pulls

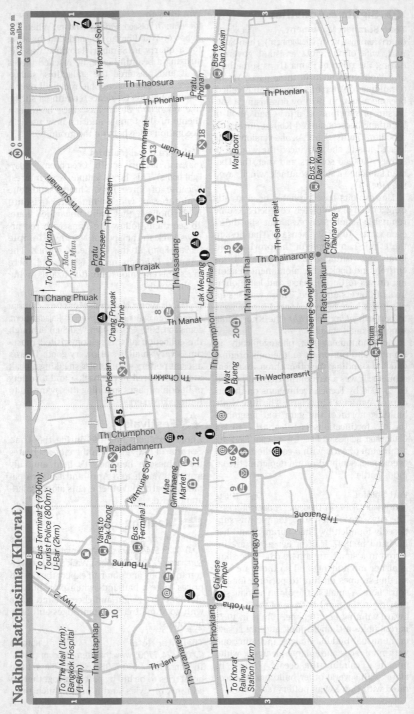

Nakhon Ratchasima (Khorat)

it off. The lobby is homey and the rooms are comfy. It's got a good (though not so quiet) location near many good restaurants and bars.

Assadang Hotel HOTEL $
(☎0 4424 2514; 315 Th Assadang; r 400-500B; ❋❄) There's no escaping the fact that this is just an old concrete box with small rooms, but a two-tone paint job and various little decorations (not to mention the dumbwaiter for your luggage) make for a nice change from the usual. The owner is very friendly.

V-One HOTEL $$$
(☎0 4434 2444; www.v-onehotelkorat.com; Th Chang Phuak; r incl breakfast 800-6780B; ❋@❄❄) The self-proclaimed 'Trendy & Boutique Hotel' is a brash mixture of colours and styles that sometimes feels more like a children's playroom than a three-star hotel. But, in trying to be different – does anybody really want a Britney Spears–themed room? – they certainly earn an A for effort. All rooms have safes and other little amenities.

Rachaphruk Grand Hotel HOTEL $$
(☎0 4426 1222; www.rachaphruk.com; Th Mittaphap; r incl breakfast 1200-1500B; ste 4500; ❋@❄❄) 'Grand' is laying it on a little thick, but this 10-storey tower in the city centre is still a decent top-end choice after all these years. The most recent renovation added furnishings that accentuate rather than hide its age. There's a fitness centre with a sauna, three restaurants and many other attached

entertainment options. Plus, wide views of the city.

Sima Thani HOTEL $$$
(☎0 4421 3100; www.simathani.com; Th Mittaphap; r incl breakfast 1650-2925B; ste 4680-17,550B; ❋@❄❄) If V-One isn't your style, this place west of the city centre offers a more standard variety of luxury.

Chaophaya Inn HOTEL $$
(☎0 4426 0555; www.chaophayainn.com, in Thai; Th Jomsurangyat; r 500-1000B; ❋@❄) This centrally located and reasonably priced place is pretty ordinary overall, but it has just enough character to boost it past the jailhouse vibe endemic in so many of Isan's midrange options.

Doctor's House HOMESTAY $
(☎08 5632 3396; 78 Soi 4, Th Seup Siri; r 200-350B; ❋) The five shared-bath guestrooms in this old wooden home are simple but clean. There are plenty of bars and restaurants here, but with a 10pm curfew you won't get to explore them properly. Bikes (50B) and motorcycles (200B) are available for hire. It's signposted down a little soi before the train tracks.

Sri Ratna Hotel HOTEL $
(no roman-script sign; ☎0 4424 3116; 7 Th Suranaree; r 180-300B; ❋) Sri Ratna trades the Doctor's House's homey vibe for a great central location. It has the ambience of an insane asylum, but the owners run it with the care and efficiency of a four-star resort.

✕ Eating

TOP CHOICE Rabieng-Pa THAI $$

(284 Th Yommarat; dishes 60-330B; ⊙dinner) The leafiest restaurant in town and the most low-key on this stretch of Yommarat Street. You'll feel like you're dining in a real forest, but it's not all about the atmosphere. The food is simply excellent and the picture menu makes ordering risk free.

Wawee Coffee CAFE $

(285 Th Mahat Thai; espresso 45B; ⊙breakfast, lunch & dinner; 🛜) Ever walked into a coffee shop and wanted to stay all day? From the lattes to the brownies and the music to the decor, this place is pretty much perfect.

Wat Boon Night Bazaar THAI $

(Th Chomphon; ⊙5.30-10pm) This night market is an excellent place for culinary exploration.

Pidaso ITALIAN $$

(☏0 4424 6700; Th Mittaphap; dishes 120-1800B; ⊙lunch & dinner; 🛜) If you want elegance with your dining experience, you'll find it at this trendy open-kitchen spot. Assuming you can actually find the restaurant, that is. It's 800m north of the Sima Thani Hotel.

Ming Ter VEGAN $

(Th Rajadamnern; dishes 30-80B; ⊙breakfast & lunch; ✐) The menu at this homey vegetarian affair is in Thai only, but since it does mock-meat versions of Thai and Chinese standards you can just order your favourites and the message will probably get through. Or, just point to something in the buffet tray.

Cabbages & Condoms THAI $

(Th Seup Siri; dishes 35-200B; ⊙lunch & dinner; ✐) This regular favourite offers a leafy terrace, a wine list (something of a rarity in Isan) and plenty of newspaper clippings celebrating the work of the nonprofit Population & Community Development Association, to-

wards which all proceeds go. It's just past the train tracks.

Gai Yang Saang Thai NORTHEASTERN THAI $

(no roman-script sign; Th Rajadamnern; whole free-range chicken 150B; ⊙breakfast, lunch & dinner) Has served some of the best *gài yâhng* (grilled chicken) in Khorat for over 40 years.

Big Chili INTERNATIONAL, THAI $$

(158/8 Th Chakkri; dishes 80-480B; ⊙dinner; 🛜) A Thai-run restaurant serving a global menu (salmon sashimi, rack of lamb, spinach lasagne, chilli dogs, Caesar salads, and even Thai-Mexican fusion such as stir-fried burritos) to mostly Thai diners.

Anego JAPANESE $$$

(62/1 Th Jomsurangyat; dishes 30-600B; ⊙dinner) Popular little place with a huge menu of Japanese dishes, plus one page of Italian pastas.

♉ Drinking & Entertainment

Khorat has a glut of good bars. Worthwhile bar-hopping destinations include those around the Th Yommarat–Th Kudan junction, Th Mahat Thai from west of Th Manat to east of Th Chainarong, and the Th Seup Siri–Soi 3 area.

Bar Nana (Th Mittaphap), at the Rachaphruk Grand Hotel, and **U-Bar** (Hwy 2), 2.5km north of the centre, have student-filled dance floors. Both get hopping around 10pm and close at 2am.

About once a week or so, the **Sima Thani Hotel** (☏0 4421 3100; Th Mittaphap) hosts *ъohng-lahng* Isan music and dance shows for tour groups, though anyone can watch.

The movie theatre at the **Mall** (☏0 4428 8288; Th Mittaphap) shows some Hollywood movies with English subtitles. There's also a child-sized water park.

🛍 Shopping

Night Bazaar Korat CLOTHING

(Th Manat; ⊙5-10pm) While it's got nothing on Chiang Mai's version, this night market, selling mostly clothes, attracts a youthful crowd and is fun to stroll through.

Mall MALL

(Th Mittaphap) This is Isan's largest and glossiest mall. Has a small branch of Asia Books.

DON'T MISS

PÀT MÈE KOH·RÂHT

One speciality you must try once is *pàt mèe koh·râht*. It's similar to *pát tai*, but boasts more flavour and is made with a local style of rice noodle (*mèe koh·râht*). It's widely available in Khorat Province, but hard to find anywhere else.

BUSES FROM TERMINAL 2

DESTINATION	FARE (B)	DURATION (HR)
Aranya Prathet (Rong Kluea Market)	190	4
Chaiyaphum	78-101	2½
Chiang Mai	435-653	12-13
Khon Kaen	118-230	3
Loei	263	6
Nang Rong	66-85	2
Nong Khai	210-420	6
Surin	90-157	4
Trat	324	8
Ubon Ratchathani	203-330	5-6
Vientiane (must have visa already)	320	6½

ℹ Information

Emergency & Medical Services
Bangkok Hospital (☑0 4442 9999; Th Mittaphap)
Tourist Police (☑0 4434 1777; Hwy 2) Opposite Bus Terminal 2.

Internet Access
Walk two or three blocks and you're bound to pass an internet cafe. Like most, **Plearnta** (Th Rajadamnern; per hr 15B; ⊙10am-midnight) stays open late.

Money
Klang Plaza 2 (Th Jomsurangyat) This shopping centre has a Bangkok Bank (changes cash only) open daily until 8pm, and an AEON ATM on the 5th floor.
Mall (Th Mittaphap) Has more extended-hours banks and another AEON ATM.

Post
Post office (Th Jomsurangyat; ⊙8.30am-10.30pm Mon-Fri, 9am-noon & 4-10.30pm Sat, 4-10.30pm Sun & holidays) Has a stamp museum.

Tourist Information
Immigration (☑0 4437 5138; ⊙8.30am-4pm Mon-Fri) Located at the *têt·sà·bahn* (city hall) in Dan Kwian.
Tourism Authority of Thailand (TAT; ☑0 4421 3666; tatsima@tat.or.th; Th Mittaphap; ⊙8.30am-4.30pm) Next to Sima Thani Hotel. Covers Khorat and Chaiyaphum Provinces.

ℹ Getting There & Away

Bus
Khorat has two bus terminals. **Terminal 1** (☑0 4424 2899; Th Burin), in the city centre, serves Bangkok and towns within Khorat Province. Buses to other destinations, plus more for Bangkok, use **Terminal 2** (☑0 4425 6006; Hwy 2), north of downtown. You never have to wait long for a bus to Bangkok (154B to 250B, three hours) since buses from most cities in Isan pass through Khorat on their way to the capital.

There are now vans to/from Ayuthaya (132B, four hours, every 30 minutes) and Lopburi (120B, 3½ hours, hourly) from Bus Terminal 2 and to Pak Chong (60B, one hour, every 20 minutes) from a roadside stop around the corner from Terminal 1.

Train
There are a lot of trains passing through **Khorat Railway Station** (☑0 4424 2044), but it's almost always faster and cheaper to take the bus. Fourteen daily trains go to/from Bangkok (3rd-class 100B, 2nd-class fan/air-con 243/325B, 1st-class sleeper upper/lower 810/1010B, most take six hours) via Ayuthaya. There are also seven Ubon Ratchathani (3rd-class 168B, 2nd-class fan/air-con 243/423B, five to six hours) and three Nong Khai (3rd-class 214B, 2nd-class air-con 368B, 5½ hours) trains.

ℹ Getting Around

There are fixed *sŏrng·tăa·ou* (pick-up truck; 8B) routes through the city, but even locals find it hard to figure them out because of the dizzying array of numbers and colours representing the many routes. Most pass the junction of Th Suranaree and Th Rajadamnern, so if you want to go somewhere just head there and ask around; someone will put you on the right one. Heading west on Suranaree, the yellow *sŏrng·tăa·ou* 1 with white and green stripes will take you past the train station, near Doctor's House – ask for *tà·nǒn sèup sì rì* – and to the tourism office, while red 12 passes the Mall. The white 15 with purple stripes and the blue-and-white 7 heading north on Rajadamnern –

you can also catch them on Th Mittaphap – go to Bus Terminal 2 (*bor kǒr sǒr sǒrng*).

Túk-túk cost between 30B and 70B to most places around town. Motorcycle taxis and sǎhm·lór (pedicabs; also spelt *sǎamláw*), both of which are common, always cost less. **Metered taxis** (📞0 4492 8678; flagfall 30B, call fee 20B) always seem to be full when they pass you on the street.

Korat Car Rental (📞08 1877 3198; www. koratcarrental.com) is a local firm with a stellar reputation. The **Sima Thani Hotel** (p416) arranges cars with drivers who speak some English for 1500B per day. Shops on Th Suranaree near Bus Terminal 1 hire motorcycles.

Around Nakhon Ratchasima

DAN KWIAN ด่านเกวียน

If you have even a small interest in ceramics, you should pay Dan Kwian a visit. Just a quick trip out of Khorat, this village has been producing pottery for hundreds of years and its creations are famous for their rough texture and rustlike hue. Only kaolin sourced from this district produces such results. Most of what's made and sold these days are cheap lawn ornaments (much of it made with cement) but there's also some attractive modern pottery plus cast reproductions of ancient Khmer sculpture. Some families in the village proper, south of the myriad shops lining the highway (turn left at the school), still use the old methods to produce their products, though the designs are modern.

Originally this was a bullock-cart stop for traders on their way to markets in old Khorat (*dàhn gweean* means 'bullock-cart checkpoint'). The ramshackle private **Kwian Museum** displays a variety of old carts from around Isan as well as some farming implements and examples of old-style pottery. The owner has died, but if the gate is open you can look around.

To get here from Khorat, hop on a bus (14B, 30 minutes) from near the southern and eastern city city gates or Terminal 2.

PAK THONG CHAI ปักธงชัย

Amphoe Pak Thong Chai became one of Thailand's most famous silk-weaving centres when Jim Thompson (see boxed text, p85) started buying silk here. Today there are almost a dozen mechanised silk factories in the district and thousands of families still work hand-looms at home in every village in the district. Pak Thong Chai is known for following the latest trends, but some shops stock traditional styles like *mát·mèe* made in other provinces.

Because Pak Thong Chai is a fairly large town, it's not nearly as fun a place to visit as other Isan silk centres such as Chonnabot (p452) or Ban Tha Sawang (see boxed text on p430), but **Macchada** (⏰8.30am-5.30pm), at the city's southern end, where you can watch weavers working, is worth seeking out if you do come. There are large highway signs directing you to the Silk Cultural Centre, but it's been closed for years.

Pak Thong Chai is 30km south of Khorat on Rte 304. Buses (30B, one hour) leave from Terminal 1 every half-hour.

BAN PRASAT บ้านปราสาท

About 3000 years ago, a primitive agricultural culture put down roots at Ban Prasat, near the banks of the Than Prasat River. It survived some 1500 years, planting rice, domesticating animals, fashioning coloured pottery, weaving cloth and, in later years, forging tools out of bronze. The secrets of this early civilisation were revealed during extensive archaeological digs completed in 1991.

Three of the **excavation pits** (admission free) with skeletons (most are replicas) and pottery left in situ are on display in the village, and a small but good **museum** (admission free; ⏰8am-4.30pm) houses some of the more interesting discoveries. It also explains what life was like in those days and in the village today. South of the museum, one family still does **silk weaving**, including raising their own worms and spinning their own thread. They welcome visitors to come by for a look.

Many families (a few of whom speak English) are part of an award-winning **homestay program** (📞08 1725 0791; per person incl 2 meals 400B) where villagers put up visitors in their homes and show them daily activities like basketry and farming. Reservations should be made at least a day in advance.

Ban Prasat is 45km northeast of Khorat, off Hwy 2, and buses (28B to 35B, 45 minutes) heading to Phimai will drop you off at the highway. A motorcycle taxi with a sidecar will zip you around to all the sites for 50B per person (including sightseeing time).

Phimai   พิมาย

The otherwise mundane little town of Phimai has one of Thailand's finest surviving Khmer temple complexes right at its heart. Reminiscent of Cambodia's Angkor Wat, Prasat Phimai once stood on an important trade route linking the Khmer capital of Angkor with the northern reaches of the realm. Phimai is an easy day trip out of Khorat, but if you prefer the quiet life, you could always make Khorat a day trip out of Phimai instead.

⊙ Sights

Phimai Historical Park   HISTORICAL SITE
(อุทยานประวัติศาสตร์พิมาย; ☑0 4447 1568; Th Anantajinda; admission 100B; ⊙7.30am-6pm) Started by Khmer King Jayavarman V (AD 968–1001) during the late 10th century and finished by his successor King Suriyavarman I (AD 1002–49), this Hindu-Mahayana Buddhist temple projects a majesty that transcends its size. It has been painstakingly reconstructed by the Fine Arts Department and is one of the most complete monuments on the circuit. It may well be wishful thinking, but the **visitor centre** (⊙8.30am-4.30pm) suggests Prasat Phimai was the model for the much grander Angkor Wat.

You enter over a cruciform **naga bridge**, which symbolically represents the passage from earth to heaven, and then through the southern gate (which is unusual since most Khmer temples face east) of the outer wall, which stretches 565m by 1030m. A raised passageway, formerly covered by a tiled roof, leads to the inner sanctum and the 28m-tall **main shrine** built of white sandstone and covered in carvings of both Buddhist and Hindu deities. At the centre of the **Brahmathat prang**, in front of the main shrine, is a replica stone sculpture of Angkor King Jayavarman VII sitting cross-legged and looking very much like a sitting Buddha. The original is in the national museum.

A free brochure provides a good overview of the complex, and guides, a few of whom speak English, lead tours; the price is open to negotiation.

Phimai National Museum   MUSEUM
(พิพิธภัณฑสถานแห่งชาติพิมาย; Th Tha Songkhran; admission 100B; ⊙9am-4pm Wed-Sun) Situated on the banks of Sa Kwan, a 12th-century Khmer reservoir, this museum houses a fine collection of Khmer sculptures from Prasat Phimai, including many exquisite lintels, and other ruins from around Lower Isan. There's also some distinctive black Phimai pottery (500 BC–AD 500) and even older ceramics from nearby Ban Prasat.

Sai Ngam   PARK
(ไทรงาม; ⊙daylight hours) A bit east of town is Thailand's largest and oldest banyan tree, a 350-plus-year-old megaflorum spread over an island in a large reservoir. The extensive system of interlocking branches and gnarled trunks makes the 'Beautiful Banyon' look like a small forest.

Other Historic Sites
Meru Bhramathat (Th Buchayan) is a toppled brick *chedi* dating back to the late Ayuthaya period (18th century). Its name is derived from a folk tale that refers to it as the cremation site of King Bhramathat.

Three city gates remain. **Pratu Chai** (Victory Gate), the one that served the road to Angkor, is the most intact. The mounded dirt ridge alongside it shows what the ramparts formerly surrounding the entire city looked like. These city walls went up in the 13th century, as did what's now known as **Kuti Rusi** (Hermit's Quarters), but was probably a healing station built by Jayavarman VII, and **Tha Nang Sa Phom** (⊙daylight hours), a laterite landing platform now on the grounds of the Fine Arts Department compound; turn right immediately after entering the gate.

✿✿ Festivals & Events

Staged in mid-November, the **Phimai Festival** celebrates the town's history, with cultural performances, sound-and-light shows and long-boat races. A smaller version of the sound-and-light show is generally held on the last Saturday of the month from October to April.

🛏 Sleeping

Old Phimai Guesthouse   GUEST HOUSE $
(☑08 0159 5363; www.phimaigh.com; Th Chomsudasadet; dm 100B, s 170B, d 200-370B; ❋🛜) This creaking wooden house tucked away down a soi is genuinely homey and attracts many backpackers. The friendly hosts can tell you all about Phimai and also run reasonably priced day trips to Phanom Rung.

Phimai Paradise   HOTEL $
(☑0 4428 7565; www.phimaiparadise.com in Thai; Th Samairujee; r 400-600B; ❋@🛜) Nothing

Phimai

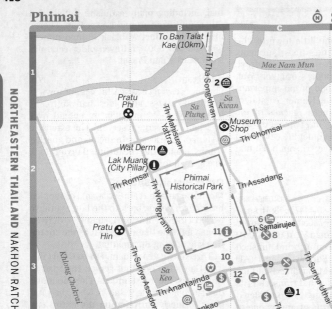

Phimai

◉ Sights
1 Meru Bhramathat C3
2 Phimai National Museum B1
3 Pratu Chai (Victory Gate) C4

🛏 Sleeping
4 Khru Pom Guesthouse C3
5 Old Phimai Guesthouse B3
6 Phimai Paradise C3

✗ Eating
7 Night Bazaar C3
8 Rabiang Mai C3

ℹ Information
9 Clock Tower C3
10 Historical Park Entrance B3
11 Visitor Center B3

ℹ Transport
12 Boonsiri Guesthouse C3

too fancy, but this newish tower has the best rooms in town.

Khru Pom Guesthouse GUEST HOUSE $
(☏0 4447 1541; Th Anantajinda; r 350-400B;
❄@🛜) This quiet and immaculate little place at the back of the block won't excite you, but it won't let you down either.

✗ Eating

The string of vendors next to Sai Ngam, open for breakfast and lunch, serve Thai and Isan basics including *pàt pímai,* which is the same as *pàt mèe koh râht* (see boxed text, p414) except it uses a softer, handmade noodle. Most restaurants in town have it on their menus too.

Rabiang Mai   THAI $

(Th Samairujee; dishes 40-200B; ⊗lunch & dinner) This semifancy place is a tad on the pricey side, but the food (mostly Thai, plus some Isan and *fa·ràng* – Western – options) is quite good.

Night Bazaar   THAI $

(Th Anantajinda; ⊗4-9pm) Small, but plenty of variety.

❶ Getting There & Away

Phimai has a bus station, but there's no need to use it since all buses pass near Pratu Chai, the clock tower and the museum on their way in and out of town.

Buses for Phimai leave from Khorat's Bus Terminal 2 (36B to 50B, 1¼ hours) every half-hour until 10pm. If you're heading north, take the Khorat bus to Ban Talat Kae (10B to 13B, 15 minutes) on the highway and catch a connection there.

❶ Getting Around

Phimai is small enough to stroll, but to see its environs (for example, Sai Ngam), hire a bike from **Boonsiri Guesthouse** (Th Chomsudasadet; per hr/day 20/60B).

Khao Yai National Park

อุทยานแห่งชาติเขาใหญ่

Up there on the podium with some of the world's greatest parks, Khao Yai (☎08 6092 6529; admission 400B) is Thailand's oldest and most visited reserve. Covering 2168 sq km, Khao Yai incorporates one of the largest intact monsoon forests remaining in mainland Asia, which is why it was named a Unesco World Heritage Site (as part of the Dong Phayayen-Khao Yai Forest Complex). The mostly English-speaking staff at the **visitor centre** (⊗8am-8pm) are very helpful.

Rising to 1351m at the summit of Khao Rom, the park's terrain covers five vegetation zones: evergreen rainforest (100m to 400m); semi-evergreen rainforest (400m to 900m); mixed deciduous forest (northern slopes at 400m to 600m); hill evergreen forest (over 1000m); and savannah and secondary-growth forest in areas where agriculture and logging occurred before it was protected.

Some 200 elephants tramp the park's boundaries. Other mammals include tigers, leopards, bears, gaur, barking deer, otters, crocodiles, various gibbons and macaques and some rather large pythons. Khao Yai also has one of Thailand's largest populations of hornbills, including the great hornbill (*nók gòk* or *nók gah·hang*), king of the bird kingdom, as well as the wreathed hornbill (*nók grahm cháhng;* literally 'elephant-jaw bird'), Indian pied hornbill (*nók kàak*) and brown hornbill (*nók ngêuak sěe nám dahn*). The park's bird list boasts 315 species.

Khao Yai has two entrances. By far the busiest is to the north in Nakhon Ratchasima Province, with most travellers passing through the town of Pak Chong. The southern entrance is in Prachinburi Province; see the boxed text, p420, for full details.

◉ Sights & Activities

There are many **viewpoints** and **salt licks** (often attracting elephants in the early morning and evening) along the roads through the park. Khao Yai also has plenty of waterfalls. Little **Nam Tok Kong Kaew**, sitting right behind the visitor centre, is the easiest to see while **Nam Tok Haew Narok**, in the far south of the park (an 800m walk from the parking area) and whose three levels combine to form a 150m drop, is the biggest. The beauty award, however, goes to 25m **Nam Tok Haew Suwat**, which scooped a starring role in Danny Boyle's film *The Beach*. It has water year-round, and you can swim in the pool at the bottom. Though easily reached by car, Haew Suwat can also be accessed by a couple of footpaths including the 8km-long Kong Kaew-Haew Suwat Trail (aka Trail 1), a somewhat challenging path that starts behind the visitor centre. There's a good chance of seeing gibbons and hornbills, and it's probably the best footpath for spotting elephants, though encounters are unlikely; the roads are better for elephant-spotting.

The **Nong Phak Chi observation tower** overlooks a little lake and a salt lick, and is one of the best wildlife-spotting spots in the park. This is the most likely place you'll see a tiger, but you have to be very lucky (like lottery-winner lucky) to do so. The shortest way (1km) to the tower starts at the Km35 pillar, and it's a wide, well-maintained path. Trekkers can get there either by a 5.4km trail from the visitor centre or a 3km path starting at Km33. The latter is better for seeing wildlife along the way and is, according to some, Khao Yai's best bird-watching walk. In the early evening deer sightings are common from the **Mo Sing To observation tower** by the visitor centre.

KHAO YAI THROUGH THE BACK DOOR

The broad swathe of Khao Yai that spreads over Nakhon Nayok and Prachinburi Provinces is known for its waterfalls and rafting, and is visited almost exclusively by locals and weekending Bangkokians. On weekdays it's nearly deserted.

Sights & Activities

The drive through the southern stretch of Khao Yai is just as beautiful as the more popular northern region, but there is more abundant wildlife, particularly elephants walking along the road at night. And visiting from the south lets you conveniently combine Khao Yai with a trip to Cambodia. **Palm Garden Lodge** (☎08 9989 4470) is in Prachinburi Province, just 12km from the entrance, and, for the most part, its day-long **park tours** (per person with 4 people 1300B) are the same as those offered by Pak Chong–based companies but with three key differences: tours visit Haew Narok waterfall (June to November, when it has water), there's the option of a night safari before leaving the park, and Klin is one of Khao Yai's few female guides.

Also in Prachinburi, near the park entrance, **Dasada** (☎0 3723 9800; www.dasada-happiness.com; Rte 3077, Km8) grows plants for the Bangkok market and puts on monthly **flower shows** (200B) in its giant greenhouse.

Most visitors to this region head to Nakhon Nayok Province where **Nam Tok Sarika** (Rte 3050; admission 200B; ⊗8am-5pm), the biggest and best known of the area's waterfalls, tumbles 200m down the edge of the mountain range in nine steps. Also lovely (and not ridiculously overpriced like Sarika) is **Nam Tok Nang Rong** (Rte 3049; per car 50B, per person 10B; ⊗8am-5pm). Both spots feature restaurants and picnic spots and places to frolic in the rivers. Water flows all year, but visiting is best from May to November. There are misty mountain views from the top of **Khun Dan Pra Kan Chon Dam** (Ta Dan Dam) near Nang Rong waterfall. On weekends, open-sided buses shuttle people across the dam for 20B.

Several businesses, including the veteran **Sarika Adventure Point** (☎08 1251 8317; www.sarikaadventurepoint.com, in Thai; Rte 3049 Km8), do leisurely rafting and kayaking trips on the Nakhon Nayok River. (They tell us there's some Class III white water in the rainy season.) The standard trip (350B per person) is 7km and 1½ hours, and you can choose

While the walks described here don't require a guide, the park recommends hiring them because, except for the short path to Nong Phak Chi, these trails aren't well trodden or well-marked. We've heard from travellers who got lost and were forced to sleep in the forest overnight. Park rangers can be hired as guides (prices negotiable) through the visitor centre. They can also lead you on longer off-trail treks for around 1000B per day (the price is negotiable). No matter where you hike, you should wear boots and long trousers. During the rainy season leeches are a problem; mosquito repellent helps keep them away.

☞ Tours

Most of the hotels and resorts around Khao Yai arrange **park tours** and this is really the ideal way to visit because a good guide will show you creatures you never would have seen on your own. The typical day-long program (1300B to 2100B per person) includes some easy walks looking for wildlife and a visit to Haew Suwat waterfall. Lunch, snacks, water and, in the rainy season, 'leech socks' (gaiters) are always included, but sometimes the park entry fee is not, so do some comparison shopping. Half-day trips (300B to 500B) typically stay outside the park to visit a cave, swim in a spring and watch a million (give or take a few hundred thousand) rare wrinkle-lipped bats disgorge from a mountain-top cave. Bird-watching, camping, trekking and other speciality tours are also available. Greenleaf Guesthouse (p421) and Khaoyai Garden Lodge (p422) and have long earned enthusiastic praise for their trips and a new player, **Bobby's Jungle Tours** (☎0 4432 8177; www.bobbysjungletourskhaoyai.com) also appears to have good guides, plus its tours finish at night so there's a better chance of encountering elephants along the park road. The park itself offers one-hour **night safaris** (☎08 1063 9241; per person 50B; ⊗7pm & 8pm), which use to mountain bike along country roads to the put-in (600B per person). For some actual adventure let them take you abseiling (2300B including park fee) down four cliffs at Than Rattana Waterfall.

Sleeping

The Nakhon Nayok area has a few upmarket resorts, but accommodation is mostly utilitarian family-run bungalows. **Phuiyara** (☑08 7059 5115; www.phuiyara.com, in Thai; r 1350-2600B, f 3200-5600B; ❄@✿), east of the dam (follow the blue signs with elephant heads, or call to have them pick you up from the van terminal), falls comfortably in between. Its 30 large bungalows are in a tree- and stream-filled garden. The weekday discount is 25% and they'll pick you up at the bus stop for free.

There's still little accommodation around the park entrance. Our favourite is the long-running **Palm Garden Lodge** (☑08 9989 4470; www.palmgalo.com; r 400-650B, bungalows 1200B; ❄@✿), 10km east of the park gate in Ban Khon Kwang. Set in a quiet garden and featuring homey fan and air-con rooms, this is a very relaxing and welcoming place. Motorcycles (250B per day) and tours are available. Be sure to say 'Hi' to the pet iguana.

Getting There & Away

Getting here without your own transport is easy, but getting around is impossible except by hitching, but that's not easy out here, especially on weekdays.

Vans from Bangkok's Victory Monument head to the dam (100B, 2½ to three hours, every 20 minutes) and for an extra 10B and 50B respectively, drivers will deliver you to Nang Rong and Sarika waterfalls. Get a phone number when they drop you off so that you can call for pick-up when you're ready to leave.

All vans to Kabinburi and some going to Aranya Prathet pass Ban Khon Kwang (100B, two hours, every 40 minutes), and will drop you 50m from Palm Garden Lodge. Prices and times to/from Aranya Prathet are the same. Buses between Aranya Prathet and Bangkok's Northeastern bus terminal also pass Ban Khon Kwang and there are five trains a day (26B to 115B, three hours) from Bangkok's Hua Lamphong station to Prachinburi town, a 150B túk-túk ride to Palm Garden.

spotlights to look for animals. There are often so many vehicles during the safari that it ruins the experience.

🛏 Sleeping

There are at least a hundred places to stay along Th Thanarat (Rte 2090), the road leading to the park, and plenty more in the not-so-pleasant gateway city of Pak Chong. Budget and some midrange places offer free transport to/from town, though usually only if you book a tour with them. All but the cheapies do weekday and off-season (April to October) discounts of 10% to 30%.

The best setting for sleeping is, of course, in the park itself. There are **campsites** (per person with own tent 30B, 2–6-person tents 150-400B) and a variety of **rooms and bungalows** (☑0 2562 0760; www.dnp.go.th/parkreserve; 2-8 people 800-3500B) around the park, often quite far from the visitor centre.

TOP CHOICE **Greenleaf Guesthouse** GUEST HOUSE $
(☑0 4436 5073; www.greenleaftour.com; Th Thanarat, Km7.5; r 200-300B; ✿) Step past the slightly chaotic common areas and you'll be surprised by the good-value rooms (with cold-water private bathrooms) at the back of this long-running family-owned place. Note that in the high season it might be 'full', if you don't book a tour.

TOP CHOICE **Kirimaya** HOTEL $$$
(☑0 4442 6000; www.kirimaya.com; Rte 3052; r incl breakfast 10,530-11,700B, ste 20,475-23,400B, pool villas 25,895B, tented villas 38,610B; ❄@✿☀) This luxury resort-spa makes an awesome first impression. Step 'through' the wooden front doors and you're greeted by a towering stilted restaurant and other Thai-Balinese fusion buildings rising from a lotus- and reed-filled pond and backed by the mountains. Rooms have genuine style

BEYOND THE FOREST

The greater Pak Chong region is a very popular escape for Bangkokians, and for many of them the national park is beside the point. The roads approaching Khao Yai from the north are lined with enough BB gun shooting ranges, sweet-corn stands, shopping malls and other tourist traps for families to stay busy all weekend without ever thinking about nature.

By far the most popular stop is **Farm Chokchai** (🖂0 4432 8386; www.farmchokchai. com; Mittaphap Hwy, Km159; ⊙9am-7pm), a 3200-hectare dairy farm overflowing with cowboy kitsch. The expanding empire now includes an ice-cream parlour, steakhouse, a souvenir shop and a safari-style tented camp (weekday/weekend per adult from 2665/3200B). There are 2½-hour **tours** (per person 250B; ⊙10am & 2pm Tue-Fri, every 20min 9am-3.40pm Sat & Sun, reservations essential) of the milking parlour, petting zoo and cowboy show.

Thailand is the pioneer of 'New Latitude Wines' and with over a dozen wineries in the area, Khao Yai area is now the epicentre of this increasingly respectable industry. Two of the leaders – **PB Valley** (🖂0 3622 6416; www.khaoyaiwinery.com; ⊙8.30am-8pm Sun-Thu, to 10pm Fri & Sat), which corked its first bottle in 1998, and **GranMonte** (🖂0 3622 7334; www.granmonte.com; ⊙9am-9pm), which got into the game three years later – lie along Pansuk–Kudkla road, the direct route from Bangkok to Khao Yai (exit Km144). Both are scenically set and offer tours (book in advance), tastings, luxury lodging and classy restaurants. They're 22.5km and 16km respectively from the park gate.

Life Park (Th Thanarat, Km19.5; per activity 160-640B; ⊙9am-6pm), at the Greenery Resort, is Khao Yai's biggest adventure park. It has go-karts, rock climbing, paintball, a bungee launch and much more.

and lots of little luxuries. We're not keen on having a golf course on the edge of the park (even one designed by Jack Nicklaus), but there's no denying this place is gorgeous. It's 7km east of the park gate. Always ask about discounts; we've seen promotional prices of 4475B for normal rooms and 7450B for pool villas.

Jungle House   HOTEL $$
(🖂0 4429 7183; www.junglehousehotel.com; Th Thanarat, Km19.5; r 800-2200B; ❉🖤) The humdrum rooms won't wow you, but from its own little patch of untamed forest to an abundance of reptiles, this older place has got the jungle vibe down pat. It even has its own elephants (30-minute rides 300B).

Hotel des Artists   HOTEL $$$
(🖂0 4429 7444; www.hotelartists.com; Th Thanarat, Km17; r incl breakfast 3500B; ❉@🖤🏊) Breaking from the Khao Yai norm, this tasteful hotel goes for French-colonial chic rather than a nature theme; though with its gorgeous mountain views out the back you won't forget where you are.

Juldis   HOTEL $$$
(🖂0 4429 7272; www.juldiskhaoyai.com; Th Thanarat, Km17; r incl breakfast 1430-4800B;

bungalows 6000B; ❉@🖤🏊) Khao Yai's original luxury lodge has kept up with the times, and though rooms are pretty plain, they're great value for this area. Juldis offers tennis courts, spa treatments and pleasant gardens.

Phuwanalee   HOTEL $$$
(🖂0 4429 7111; www.phuwanalee.com; 700m off Th Thanarat Km14; tent 4600B; r 4800-6800B, villas 18,000B; ❉🖤🏊) A great garden setting and the option of safari tents with all the same mod cons as the normal rooms make this a good, albeit expensive, choice.

Khaoyai Garden Lodge   HOTEL $
(🖂0 4436 5178; www.khaoyaigardenlodgekm7. com; Th Thanarat, Km7; r 250-2500B, f 3000B; ❉@🖤🏊) This friendly, family-run place offers a variety of rooms (the cheapest are sterile shared-bath rooms), all spread out around a garden. It's a bit worn, but it's still good value and the restaurant-lounge in front encourages interaction with your fellow guests.

✖ Eating

Each of the lodges reviewed serves food, and there are many more restaurants along Th Thanarat. The park itself has restaurants at all busy locations, including the visitor centre, campsites and some waterfalls, but even the campsite ones close around 6pm, so plan ahead.

Hi Pakchong CAFE $
(Th Trakmayon; espresso 25B; ⊘breakfast, lunch & dinner; 🛜) If for some reason you need to spend time in Pak Chong, this friendly, antique-filled coffee shop east of the train station is as pleasant a place as possible to do it.

❶ Getting There & Away

Sŏrng·tăa·ou travel the 30km from Pak Chong down Th Thanarat to the park's northern gate (40B, 45 minutes) every half-hour from 6am to 5pm. They start their journey in front of the 7-Eleven near the artistic deer – they look like giraffes – statue. It's another 14km to the visitor centre, and park guards are used to talking drivers into hauling people up there. Some also do a side business hiring motorcycles for 500B per day.

Several motorcycle shops on Pak Chong's main road do rentals for 300B per 24 hours including **Petch Motor** (📞08 1718 2400; 361/3 Th Mittaphap, at Th Tesabarn 13), a bit west of the deer statue (look for the diamonds), and **Tawiyon** (no roman-script sign; 📞0 4431 1485; 734/1-4 Th Mittaphap, at Th Tesabarn 20), a bit to the east (it has a Honda sign). Both have limited Sunday hours.

All 2nd-class buses between Bangkok (108B to 139B, 2½ hours) and Khorat (60B to 74B, one hour) stop in Pak Chong. The bus station for most Bangkok buses is west of the traffic light at Th Thesabarn 8. Most buses for Khorat (and all other points north and east) stop about 500m east of the deer statue near *dà·l àht kàak*. Board 1st-class buses to both towns across the highway from the deer statue.

There are now also vans to Bangkok's Victory Monument (160B, 2½ hours, hourly) from the traffic light and to Khorat (60B, one hour, every 20 minutes) from *dà·l àht kàak*. You can also catch vans (departing from Khorat) to Ayuthaya (90B, 2½ hours) and Lopburi (70B, two hours) across the street from *dà·l àht kàak*, but only if they happen to have empty seats when they pass through.

You can also get to Pak Chong by train from Bangkok and Khorat, but it's much faster to go by bus or van. Ayuthaya, on the other hand, has no direct bus service so the train (3rd-class 53B, 2nd-class fan/air-con 83/173B, two to three hours, 13 daily) can be a good option.

BURIRAM PROVINCE

Buriram is not a province for urban exploration. Despite hanging on to half of its historic moat, Meuang Buriram, the provincial capital and only large town, is a tough sell as a tourist destination. Buriram Province is a place to get a glimpse of the past. The countryside is chock-a-block with tradition and peppered with over 50 Khmer ruins (out of 259 in the whole country). The crowning glory is Phanom Rung, a beautifully restored complex straddling the summit of an extinct volcano. The most spectacular Angkor monument in Thailand, Phanom Rung is well worth the journey and should impress even those who've already experienced Angkor Wat in Cambodia.

Nang Rong นางรอง

POP 20,300

This workaday city is even more forgettable than Buriram, 45km to the north, but it's the most convenient base for visiting Phanom Rung. A full range of services and a good selection of hotels at least make it a friendly and comfortable one.

🛏 Sleeping & Eating

TOP CHOICE **P California Inter Hostel** GUEST HOUSE $
(📞08 1808 3347; www.pcaliforniananangrong.webs. com; Th Sangkakrit; r 250-700B; ✽@🛜) This great place on the east side of town offers bright, nicely decorated rooms with good value in all price ranges. English-speaking Khun Wicha, who's a wealth of knowledge about the area, also provides bikes, rents motorcycles (200B per day) and leads tours. A motorcycle taxi from the bus station should cost 40B.

Honey Inn GUEST HOUSE $
(📞0 4462 2825; www.honeyinn.com; 8/1 Soi Si Kun; r 250-350B; ✽@🛜) This Nang Rong veteran, 1km from the bus station, is less homey than it used to be, but with a new paint job it's still a good choice. Motorcycle hire and guided tours are also available. To find it, walk north from the bus station, cross the main road and head east until you see the sign.

Cabbages & Condoms HOTEL $$
(📞0 4465 7145; Hwy 24; r 240-1500B; ✽@) The cheapest (shared bathroom) rooms at this Population & Community Development Association–run resort, set in a garden and

ringed by several little lakes, are pretty limp. But move up the price scale (where you get large rooms with stone floors) and this is a pleasant place to stay. The restaurant is also very good. There's a clothing and shoe factory on site, opened to bring work normally found in the city to the villages. It's 6.5km west of town.

Phob Suk   THAI **$$**
(Hwy 24; dishes 50-360B; ⊙breakfast, lunch & dinner; 🖝) The picture menu at this well-known place near the bus station presents the typical mix of Thai, Isan and Chinese, but we recommend the city's famous *kǎh mǒo* (pork-rump roast).

🛈 Getting There & Away

Nang Rong's **bus terminal** (📞0 4463 1517) is on the west side of town. See p425 for transport details.

Phanom Rung Historical Park   อุทยานประวัติศาสตร์เขาพนมรุ้ง

The largest and best restored Khmer monument in Thailand, **Phanom Rung** (Phnom Rung; 📞0 4478 2715; admission 100B, bike/motorcycle/car fee 10/20/50B; ⊙6am-6pm) has a knock-me-dead location. Crowning the summit of a spent volcano (the name is derived from the Khmer words for 'big mountain'), this sanctuary sits 200m above the paddy fields, and the Dangrek Mountains on the Cambodian border are clearly visible to the southeast.

The temple was erected between the 10th and 13th centuries, the bulk of it during the reign of King Suriyavarman II (r AD 1113–50), which was the apex of Angkor architecture. The complex faces east and four times a year the sun shines through all 15 sanctuary doorways. The correct solar alignment happens during sunrise from 3 to 5 April and 8 to 10 September and sunset from 5 to 7 March and 5 to 7 October (some years are one day earlier.). The park extends its hours during these events, and locals celebrate the **Phanom Rung Fes**-tival, around the April alignment, with ancient Brahmin ceremonies and modern sound-and-light shows. Camping is allowed during this time.

Below the main sanctuary, after the long row of gift shops, an **information centre** (⊙9am-4.30pm) houses artefacts found at the site and displays about both the construction and restoration, which took 17 years. You can pick up a free informative brochure or arrange a guide (free, but tips are expected) here. Those who don't want to climb can use an upper parking lot, but the brochure isn't always available there.

Design

One of the most remarkable aspects of Phanom Rung is the **promenade** leading to the main gate. It's the best surviving example in Thailand. It begins on a slope 400m east of the main tower with three earthen **terraces**. Next comes a cruciform base for what may have been a wooden pavilion. To the right of this is a stone hall known locally as **Rohng Chang Pheuak** (White Elephant Hall) where royalty bathed and changed clothes before entering the temple complex. Flower garlands to be used as offerings in the temple may also have been handed out here. After you step down from the pavilion area, you'll come to a 160m-long promenade paved with laterite and sandstone blocks, and flanked by sandstone pillars with early Angkor style (AD 1100–80) lotus-bud tops. The promenade ends at the first and largest of three **naga bridges**. The first is flanked by 16 five-headed *naga* in the classic Angkor style.

After passing this bridge and climbing the **stairs** you come to the magnificent east gallery leading into the main sanctuary. The central **brah-sàht** has a gallery on each of its four sides and the entrance to each gallery is itself a smaller version of the main tower. The **galleries** have curvilinear roofs and false-balustrade windows. Once inside the temple walls, have a look at each of the galleries and the **gopura**, paying particular attention to the lintels over the porticoes. The craftsmanship at Phanom Rung represents the pinnacle of Khmer artistic achievement, on par with the reliefs at Angkor Wat in Cambodia.

Sculpture

The Phanom Rung complex was constructed as a Hindu monument to Shiva. Excel-

🛈 COMBO TICKET

A 150B combo ticket allows entry to both Phanom Rung and Muang Tam at a 50B discount.

VISHNU & THE KING OF POP

Phanom Rung's most famous sculpture is the **Narai Bandhomsindhu lintel**, a carving depicting a reclining Vishnu ('Phra Narai' in Thai) in the Hindu creation myth. Growing from his navel is a lotus that branches into several blossoms, on one of which sits the creator god, Brahma. Vishnu is asleep on the milky sea of eternity, here represented by a *naga* and alongside him are heads of Kala, the god of time and death. This lintel sits above the eastern gate (the main entrance) beneath the Shiva Nataraja relief.

Although it's arguably the most beautiful carving here, its fame instead comes from its role in a quarter-century-long whodunit-cum-David-versus-Goliath tale that began in 1965 when it was discovered to have been stolen. (It likely went missing several years earlier, but nobody had noticed.) In 1972 it was found on display at the Art Institute of Chicago and Thailand pressed for its return. Superstars Carabao (p735) helped the cause with their song 'Thaplang' (Lintel) featuring the line 'Take back Michael Jackson, Give us Phra Narai'. Phra Narai finally came home in 1988.

lent sculptures of both Shaiva and Vaishnava deities can be seen in the lintels and pediments over the doorways to the central monuments and in various other key points on the sanctuary exterior. On the east portico of the **mon·dòp** is a Nataraja (Dancing Shiva), which is late Baphuon or early Angkor style, while on the south entrance are the remains of Shiva and Uma riding their bull mount, Nandi. The central cell of the *brah·sàht* contains a Shivalingam (phallus image).

❶ Getting There & Away

Getting to Phanom Rung without your own vehicle seems complicated, but it's not. *Sŏrng·tăa·ou* (20B, 30 minutes, every half-hour) from in front of the old market *(nâh dà·làht go/uw)* on the east end of town and Chanthaburi-bound buses from the bus station go to Ban Ta Pek where motorcycle taxi drivers charge 200B to Phanom Rung, including waiting time. Chartering a *sŏrng·tăa·ou* at Ban Ta Pek is likely to cost a hefty 800B.

Those coming from or heading to Ubon Ratchathani (125B, five hours, hourly), Surin (60B to 70B, two hours, every half-hour), Khorat (66B to 85B, two hours, hourly), Pak Chong (104B to 140B, 2½ hours, hourly) or Bangkok (Gitjagaan Tours; 275B, five hours, hourly) have the option of getting off at Ban Tako, a well-marked turn-off about 14km east of Nang Rong, and waiting for one of the buses or *sŏrng·tăa·ou* from Nang Rong; or just taking a motorcycle taxi (300B return) all the way to Phanom Rung.

P California Inter Hostel's (p423) standard one-day tour (2340B for four people) is a good choice because as well as Phanom Rung, Muang Tam and Wat Khao Angkhan you'll get to visit a silk-weaving village.

Around Phanom Rung

PRASAT MUANG TAM ปราสาทเมืองต่ำ

Prasat Muang Tam (admission 100B; ⊘6am-6pm) is an ideal bolt-on to any visit to Phanom Rung, which is only 8km to the northwest. Dating back to the late 10th or early 11th century and sponsored by King Jayavarman V, 'Lower City' is Isan's third most interesting Khmer temple complex (after Phanom Rung and Phimai; fourth if you include Khao Phra Wihan) in terms of size, atmosphere and the quality of restoration work.

The whole complex, once a shrine to Shiva, is surrounded by laterite walls, within which are five *prang* and four lotus-filled reservoirs, each guarded by whimsical five-headed *naga*. The principal *prang* could not be rebuilt and the remaining towers, being brick, aren't nearly as tall or as beautiful as the sandstone *prang* at Phanom Rung. However, they do hold some superb lintels, including one depicting Shiva and his consort Uma riding the sacred bull, Nandi. As at Angkor Wat, the *prang* represent the five peaks of Mt Meru, the abode of the Hindu gods, and Barai Muang Tam (a 510m-by-1090m reservoir across the road) represents the surrounding ocean.

Begin your visit in the small **information centre** (admission free; ⊘8am-4.30pm). You can also enquire here about the village's **homestay** (☏08 1068 6898; per person with 2 meals 300B) program. Another overnight option is slightly pricey **Tanyaporn Homestay** (☏08 7431 3741; dm/r 150/500B; ☒), southwest of the ruins.

Around Phanom Rung

Motorcycle-taxi drivers will add Muang Tam onto a trip to Phanom Rung for another 150B.

OTHER KHMER RUINS

For those with an insatiable appetite for Khmer ruins, the area around Phanom Rung offers a smorgasbord of lesser-known sites that, taken together, create a picture of the crucial role this region once played in the Khmer empire. Even history buffs will likely find these places of only minor interest, but driving through this rice-growing region offers an unvarnished look at village life and will surely make for an enlightening trip. Note that many roads around here are in terrible shape and signage is somewhat erratic. All of the following sites, restored or stabilised to some degree by the Fine Arts Department, are free of charge and open during daylight hours.

Kuti Reusi Nong Bua Rai sits right below Phanom Rung and **Kuti Reusi Khok Meuang** is just northwest of Prasat Muang Tam, so you might as well take a peek if you're heading this way.

Little of **Prasat Khao Plaibat** is left standing. But the adventure of finding it, along with cool views of both Phanom Rung and the Dangrek Mountains on the Cambodian border, makes it worth seeking out. The seldom-used trail starts at Wat Khao Plaibat, 3km from Prasat Muang Tam. Walk around the gate next to the giant Buddha image, veer right at the *gù·dì* (monks' quarters) and slip through the barbed-wire fence. From here take the path to the right, and then a quick left up the hill and follow the strips of orange cloth tied to trees. The walk up the

hill should take less than 30 minutes if you don't get lost along the way, though it's likely you will.

Prasat Khok Ngio, 3km before Pakham, has a small museum with old pots and Buddha images uncovered around the temple and is the only one of these sites that can conveniently be reached by public transport; buses and *sŏrng·tăa·ou* heading south from Nang Rong will drop you off.

Archaeologists assume that much of the rock used to build these ancient structures came from the widely scattered **Lan Hin Dtat Ban Kruat** (Ban Kruat Quarry). It's actually more interesting for its beauty than its history. In the rainy season, stand in front of the big rock at the entrance to hear a curious echo effect from the little waterfall.

Also near Ban Kruat are **Tao Sawai** and **Tao Nai Chian**, two kilns that supplied pottery to much of the Khmer empire between the 10th and 12th centuries. Today they're little more than piles of dirt with roofs over them.

You can easily add Surin Province's **Prasat Ta Meuan** (p430) to your trip around this region. It's 55km from Phanom Rung.

WAT KHAO ANGKHAN   วัดเขาอังคาร

Although this peaceful **temple** (⊙daylight hours) atop an extinct volcano has an ancient past, as evidenced by the 8th or 9th century Dvaravati sandstone boundary markers, it's the modern constructions that make Wat Khao Angkhan worth a visit. The *bòht* and several other flamboyant buildings were erected in 1982 in an unusual nouveau-Khmer style that sort of hearkens back to the age of empire. Inside the *bòht*, the *jataka* murals, painted by Burmese artists, have English captions. The wát also hosts a Chinese-style pagoda, a 29m reclining Buddha and beautiful views of the surrounding mountains.

The temple is about 20km from either Nang Rong or Phanom Rung, and there's no public transport. The route is pretty well signposted, but if you're driving you'll have to ask directions at some junctions. A motorcycle taxi could cost as little as 200B from Ban Ta Pek and 300B from Nang Rong.

SURIN & SI SAKET PROVINCES

Surin and Si Saket Provinces are dotted with Angkor-era Khmer ruins. Most are rather modest, but for those with a history habit some are worth the effort to reach. On the other hand, Prasat Ta Meuan is very evocative and Khao Phra Wihan ranks among the northeast's best attractions, despite the Cambodian government's refusal to renovate it. The region's Khmer influence comes not only from the past, but also from the present. Over one-third of the population of these two closely related provinces is ethnically Khmer and this remains the principal language in many villages.

Besides the temples, Surin Province is home to Ban Ta Klang elephant village and some famous craft centres, while Si Saket holds two of Thailand's most unusual temples. The capital cities are rather less interesting, although Surin makes a comfortable enough base.

Surin   สุรินทร์

POP 41,200

Surin doesn't have much to say for itself until November, when the provincial capital explodes into life for the Surin Elephant Round-up, during which the city hosts giant scrums of pachyderm. You've surely never seen so many well-dressed tuskers!

◉ Sights & Activities

Surin Elephant Round-up   FESTIVAL
(admission from 80B) Surin celebrates its famous festival for 10 days, but the massive crowds come on just the last weekend for the main event, which features 300 elephants showing their skills and taking part in battle re-enactments. Arguably the festival's best event is the elephant buffet on the Friday before the big show. VIP seats, which get you closest to the action, English commentary and guaranteed shade, cost between 500B and 1000B.

Surin National Museum   MUSEUM
(พิพิธภัณฑสถานแห่งชาติสุรินทร์; ☑0 4451 3358; Th Surin-Prasat; admission free); ◎9am-4pm Wed-Sun) Displays at this well-executed museum focus on the province's Khmer ruins and Surin's three ethnic groups: Lao, Khmer and Suai, the region's renowned elephant herders. It's 4km south of town on Rte 214; catch pink *sŏrng·tăa·ou* 1 (10B) at the bus station or the clock tower by the fresh market (*dà·l àht sót*). At the time of press, an admission fee of 100B looked likely to be introduced in the near future.

Queen Sirikit Sericulture Center
(ศูนย์หม่อนไหมเฉลิมพระเกียรติสมเด็จพระนางเจ้าสิริกิติ์ พระบรมราชินีนาถ (สุรินทร์); Rte 226; admission free; ◎8am-4.30pm Mon-Fri) The easiest place to see the entire silk-making process, from larva to loom, is at this research centre 4km west of town.

San Lak Meuang   SHRINE
(ศาลหลักเมือง; Th Lak Meuang) Surin's gorgeous new city pillar shrine, just west of Th Thansarn, is a Khmer-style *prang* fronted by a copy of Phanom Rung's famous Narai Bandhomsindhu lintel (see the boxed text, p425).

LemonGrass   VOLUNTEERING
(☑08 1977 5300; www.lemongrass-volunteering. com) A well-run Surin-based outfit offering English-teaching (for children, adults and monks) and childcare placements. Bangkok-based Starfish Ventures (p39) also has a wide variety of projects in Surin.

☞ Tours

Saren Travel (☑0 4452 0174; 202/1-4 Th Thesaban 2; ◎8.30am-5pm Mon-Sat) offers tours (from 1500B per day) in and around Surin Province. Even if you pay extra for an English-speaking guide, these are great prices.

Tours from Pirom-Aree's House (p428) are very expensive, but also good.

🛏 Sleeping

Prices skyrocket during the Elephant Round-up and hotels fill up fast, so book as far in advance as possible.

Maneerote Hotel
HOTEL $$

(0 4453 9477; www.maneerotehotel.com; Soi Poi Tunggor, Th Krungsri Nai; r 400-450B; @ @) This hotel west of the fresh market scores off the charts in the high-quality-to-low-price ratio, though it's a little out of the way.

Pirom-Aree's House
GUEST HOUSE $

(0 4451 5140; Soi Arunee, Th Thungpo; s/d 120/200B) The location for this long-time budget favourite, 1km west of the city, is inconvenient but peaceful. Simple wooden shared-bath rooms and a shady garden overlook a rice paddy. Aree cooks some pretty good food and Pirom is one of the best sources of information in the region. A túk-túk from the train station costs 50B.

Kritsada Grand Palace
HOTEL $

(0 4471 3997; Th Suriyarart; r 400-450B; @ @) Sitting on a quiet side street behind săh·lah glahng (provincial hall), this stark-white tower is a bit hard to find, but that makes for a quiet downtown location. Rooms are rather plain, but good value.

Surin Majestic Hotel
HOTEL $$

(0 4471 3980; Th Jitrbumrung; r 900-1200B, ste 1800-4500B; @ @ @) Surin's top digs sit alongside the bus terminal in the heart of town. The rooms are nothing special, but good for the price and the hotel has plenty of extras, like a fitness centre.

Sang Thong Hotel
HOTEL $

(0 4451 2099; 279-281 Th Tanasan; r 100-500B; @) Though it's just an ordinary ageing cheapie, this hotel is run with jet-engine precision by an army of attentive staff. It's a short walk south of the train station, just past the fountain.

BORDER CROSSING: CHONG CHOM TO O SMACH

Because of the casino, there are plenty of minibuses (60B, 1½ hours, every 20 minutes) from Surin's bus terminal to the Cambodian border (open 6am to 6pm) at Chong Chom, where visas are available on the spot (see p770 for details). There's little transport on the Cambodian side. A seat in a 'taxi' will cost 500B for the four-hour drive to Siem Reap, but if you arrive after about 9am you probably won't find any Cambodians making the trip and may have to pay 2500B for the whole car.

Ban Donmai
HOTEL $

(no Roman-script sign; 08 9948 4181; Rte 226; r 300-500B; @) The 'Treehouse', 3km from downtown, right along the highway, is a combination of *Gilligan's Island* and your grandparents' dishevelled basement. If this sounds good, you'll love it. Boonyai and Nan, the cheerful owners, prefer that guests book at least a day in advance; in return, they'll pick you up in town for free when you arrive.

✗ Eating & Drinking

Night Market
THAI $

(Th Krungsri Nai; 5-10pm) A block south of the fountain, this good night market whips up an excellent selection of Thai and Isan dishes, including, as always, fried insects.

Tang Lak
THAI $

(Th Sirirat; dishes 49-219B; lunch & dinner;) This cute little place, popular with both Thai and *fa·ràng*, mixes fake wood and real antiques to create an old-timey feel. But it's not all about the style; the food is delicious. It's north of the Thong Tarin Hotel at the end of the road.

Kit Teung
CAFE $

(no roman-script sign; Th Sanit Nikomrut; espresso 40B; breakfast, lunch & dinner;) This bright modern place just southeast of the train station has some of the best coffee in town, but it really sets itself apart with a fun selection of Thai cakes and cookies.

Petmanee 2
NORTHEASTERN THAI $

(no roman-script sign; Th Murasart; dishes 20-80B; breakfast & lunch) This simple spot south of Ruampaet Hospital by Wat Salaloi (look for the chicken grill in front) is Surin's most famous purveyor of *sôm·đam* and *gài yâhng*. The *súp nòr mái* (bamboo shoot salad) is good too. There's no English, spoken or written, but the food is so good it's worth stumbling through an order.

Starbeam
INTERNATIONAL, THAI $$

(Th Surin Packdee; dishes 80-255B; breakfast, lunch & dinner Wed-Mon;) One of Surin's many expat hang-outs, this one has a broad menu that includes pizza, breakfast burritos and an almost-good-as-home grilled cheese. It's north of the bus station.

Larn Chang
THAI $

(199 Th Siphathai Saman; dishes 45-220B; dinner) Tasty and low-priced Thai and Isan dishes are served in and around an old

wooden house that overlooks a surviving stretch of the city moat. (The moat is now known as Sŭan Rak, 'Love Park', and couples come here to hold hands at night.) The food and the setting are lovely, especially at sunset. It's a longish walk south of the centre, on the east side of the park.

Surin Chai Kit   THAI $
(no roman-script sign; 297 Th Tanasan; dishes 25-55B; ⊗breakfast & lunch) This no-frills spot whips up tasty pan-egg breakfasts. The owners wear welcoming permagrins and give *fa·ràng* customers a handy city map. It's just to the right of the Sang Thong Hotel.

Surin's nightlife revolves around the Thong Tarin Hotel east of the bus station.

❶ Information

OTOP (Th Jitrbumrung; ⊗8am-5.30pm) Across from the Provincial Hall, this shop has the broadest selection of crafts, plus a city-specific tourist office.

Ruampaet Hospital (☎0 4451 3192; Th Thesaban 1)

Surin Plaza Mall (Th Thesaban 1) Has several banks open evenings and weekends. Located one block west of the fountain.

Tourism Authority of Thailand (TAT; ☎0 4451 4447; tatsurin@tat.or.th; Th Thesaban 1; ⊗8.30am-4.30pm) Across from Ruampaet Hospital.

❶ Getting There & Away

Bus

Frequent buses from Surin's **bus terminal** (☎0 4451 1756; Th Jitrbumrung) head to/from Bangkok (250B to 320B, seven hours). **Nakhonchai Air** (☎0 4459 5151) has a VIP service (372B, six daily). **999 VIP** (☎0 4451 5344) also has one departing daily at 9.30pm (496B). There are also buses to Ubon Ratchathani (105B to 200B, three hours, infrequently during the day), Roi Et (91B, 2½ hours, hourly), Khorat (90B to 157B, four hours, every half-hour) and Aranya Prathet (137B to 176B, six hours, three daily). Vans are the best way to Si Saket (70B, 1½ hours, every half-hour).

Train

Surin Railway Station (☎0 4451 1295) is on the line between Bangkok (3rd class 73B, 2nd-class fan/air-con 279/389B, 1st-class sleeper upper/lower 946/1146B, seven to nine hours, 10 daily) and Ubon Ratchathani (3rd class 81B, 2nd-class fan/air-con 122/150B, two to five hours, seven daily).

❶ Getting Around

Surin is very convenient for travellers; virtually everything you'll want or need is within a few blocks of the bus and train stations. If you don't want to walk, túk-túk charge around 40B for a trip within the centre. Surin also still has many cheaper pedicabs.

Pirom-Aree's House and Saren Travel hire cars.

Around Surin

BAN TA KLANG   บ้านตากลาง
To see Surin's elephants outside festival time, visit the **Elephant Study Centre** (☎0 4414 5050; admission 100B; ⊗8.30am-4.30pm) in the Suai village of Ban Ta Klang where people and pachyderms live side by side. The main attraction is the one-hour **talent show** (⊗shows at 10am & 2pm) with painting and basketball among the many tusker tricks. You can watch the stars bathe in the river (2km away) after the second show. There's also a little **museum** discussing elephants and elephant training, **elephant rides** (per 20min 200B) and a **homestay program** (per person 200B). During Visakha Bucha day (usually in May) all Suai villages in the area host **Elephant Parades**, with brightly painted pachyderms carrying the men who will enter the monkhood.

📷 **Surin Project** (☎08 4482 1210; www.surin project.org; elephant experience 12,000B) activities let you spend some quality time with Ban Ta Klang's elephants. These six-day stays are organised by the Elephant Nature Foundation, which works to improve the elephants' living conditions and provide sustainable income for their owners so they don't need to go begging on city streets. You'll work alongside the mahouts, caring for the elephants, constructing enclosures (so they won't be chained) and more. If there's space available, you can also work for just a day (1000B).

Sŏrng·tăa·ou run from Surin's bus terminal (50B, two hours, hourly) with the last one returning at 4pm. If you're driving, take Rte 214 north for 40km and follow the elephant signs down Rte 3027 for 22 more.

CRAFT VILLAGES
There are many craft villages in easy striking distance of Surin town. The province's distinct fabrics, most notably *pâh hohl* (similar to *mát·mèe*), have a Khmer influence and often use natural dyes. Surin silks aren't readily available in other parts of Thailand and prices can be 30% cheaper here.

The most famous weaving centre is **Ban Tha Sawang**.

Ban Khwao Sinarin and **Ban Chok**, next-door neighbours 18km north of Surin via Rte 214 and Rte 3036, are known for silk and silver respectively. However, these days you can buy both in each village. One of the silk specialities is *yók dòrk,* a much simpler brocade style than what's made in Ban Tha Sawang, but it still requires up to 45 foot pedals on the looms. Khun Manee, who runs **Phra Dab Suk** (☑08 9865 8720) on the main drag, takes visitors out to see silk being woven (price negotiable); he prefers that you call in advance. The silver standout is *ˈbrà keuam,* a Cambodian style of bead brought to Thailand by Ban Chok's ancestors many centuries ago. **Ban Choke Silverware Handicraft Group** (Glùm Hát·tá·gaam Krêung Ngern Bâhn Chôhk; ☑08 1309 4352), off the main road south of the police station, creates unique silver jewellery. Big blue *sŏrng·tăa·ou* to Ban Khwao Sinarin (25B, 1½ hours, hourly) park on an unnamed soi between the fountain and the train station: look for the 'Osram' signs.

The residents of **Ban Buthom** (14km out of Surin on Rte 226 on the way to Sikhoraphum) weave sturdy, unlacquered rattan baskets, including some rather flat ones that pack well.

PRASAT TA MEUAN ปราสาทตาเมือน

The most atmospheric of Surin's Khmer ruins is a series of three sites known collectively as **Prasat Ta Meuan** (admission free; ☉daylight hours) on the Cambodian border that lines the ancient route linking Angkor Wat to Phimai.

The first site, **Prasat Ta Meuan** proper, was built in the Jayavarman VII period (AD 1181–1210) as a rest stop for pilgrims. It's a fairly small monument with a two-door, 10-window sanctuary constructed of laterite blocks; only one sandstone lintel remains.

Just 300m south, **Prasat Ta Meuan Toht**, which was the chapel for a 'healing station', is a bit larger. Also built by Jayavarman VII, the ruins consist of a *gopura, mon·dòp* and main *prang,* all surrounded by a laterite wall.

Nearly 1km further on, next to the army base at the end of the road, is the largest site, **Prasat Ta Meuan Thom**. This Shiva shrine pre-dates the others by as much as two centuries. Despite a somewhat haphazard reconstruction, this one nearly justifies

the effort it takes to get here. Three *prang* and a large hall are built of sandstone blocks on a laterite base and several smaller buildings still stand inside the boundary wall. Many carvings encase the principal *prang,* although the best were pried away and sold to unscrupulous Thai dealers by the Khmer Rouge who occupied the site in the 1980s. A stairway on the southern end drops to Cambodian territory. Landmines and undetonated hand grenades still litter the thick jungle surrounding the complex; heed the 'danger' signs.

The sites begin 10.3km south of Ban Ta Miang (on Rte 224, 23km east of Ban Kruat) via a winding road used by far more cows than cars. You need your own transport to get here and a visit is just as convenient from Phanom Rung (p424) as Surin town. The ongoing border conflict has forced closure of this area at times, so check on the situation before driving all the way out here.

OTHER KHMER TEMPLE RUINS

The southern reaches of Surin Province harbour several minor Khmer ruins. The 11th-century **Prasat Ban Phluang** (admission 50B; ☉7am-6pm), 33km south of Surin, is just a solitary sandstone *prang* without its top, but some wonderful carvings (including a lintel above the entrance with the Hindu god Indra riding his elephant, Airavata; Erawan in Thai) make it worth a stop. The site sits 600m off Rte 214; the turn-off is 2.5km south of Hwy 24. Any vehicle bound for Kap Choeng or the border can drop you nearby (25B, 30 minutes).

Prasat Sikhoraphum (admission 50B; ☉7.30am-6pm) is a larger and more rewarding Khmer site 30km northeast of town. Built in the 12th century, Sikhoraphum features five brick *prang,* two of which still hold their tops, including the 32m-tall central one. Only one lintel remains, but it's a stunner. Featuring a dancing 10-armed Shiva it's in nearly pristine condition and one of the most beautiful pieces of Khmer art ever carved. Below it are the only two apsara (celestial dancers) carvings in Thailand. There's a sound-and-light show here during the Elephant Round-up. Sikhoraphum can be reached by bus (25B to 30B, one hour, hourly) or train (7B to 50B, 30 minutes) from Surin town.

If you happen to be driving to Sikhoraphum, you may as well take a 400m detour off Rte 226 for a peep at **Prasat Muang**

BAN THA SAWANG

Chansoma (☉8am-5pm) has made Ban Tha Sawang one of the most renowned silk villages in Thailand. Its exquisite brocade fabrics (pâh yók torng) incorporate threads made of real gold and silver but the weaving process is even more impressive than the finished cloth. Four (sometimes five) women, including one sitting a floor below the others, work the loom simultaneously and collectively manage over 1000 heddles. Not surprisingly, they produce just a few centimetres per day.

Many of the finished products are destined for the royal court, but you can custom order your own at an average price of 30,000B per metre. Other shops around Chansoma sell typical silks to a steady stream of Thai visitors. The village is 8km west of Surin via Rte 4026, but finding it on your own is tough since English-language signage is scattershot. Sŏrng·tăa·ou (15B, 20 minutes) run regularly from Surin's fresh market, and a túk-túk should cost between 150B and 200B.

Thi (admission free; ☉daylight hours). The three remaining brick prang are in sad shape (one looks like it's ready to topple), but they're so small they're kind of cute.

Prasat Phumpon (admission free; ☉daylight hours), a pre-Angkor Vishnu shrine dating from the 7th or 8th century, is the oldest Khmer brah·sàht in Thailand. However, that's its only claim to fame and you'll likely be disappointed by this simple brick prang. It's 9km south of Hwy 24 in Amphoe Sangkha; veer right through the village at the fork in the road.

Si Saket ศรีสะเกษ

POP 42,800

There's not a whole lot to do in the humdrum town of Si Saket, but if you're headed to Khao Phra Wihan, you may pass through. Si Saket is centred on its train station. The bus terminal is about 2km south on Th Kuang Heng and the commercial centre lies between.

Staff at the **Si Saket Tourism Information Center** (☏0 4561 1283; cnr Th Lak Muang & Th Thepa; ☉8.30am-4.30pm Mon-Fri) are enthusiastic about their province; pity they don't have more to promote.

◉ Sights

Tak Khun Ampai Panich   HISTORIC BUILDING
(บ้านขุนอำไพพาณิชย์; Th Ubon; ☉9am-7pm) The city's principal attraction is this restored wood-and-stucco Chinese-style shophouse built in 1925. It now houses an OTOP shop selling locally produced silks and crafts and a little upstairs **museum** (admission free; ☉9am-3pm) with a few antiques. It's about a 10-minute walk southeast of the train station.

Sisaket Aquarium   AQUARIUM
(ศูนย์แสดงพันธุ์สัตว์น้ำเทศบาลเมืองศรีสะเกษ; Bypass Rd; admission 30B; ☉10am-4pm Tue-Sun) The new pride and joy of Si Saket features fresh and saltwater fish species from around Thailand and two walk-through tunnels.

🛏 Sleeping & Eating

If you're pinching pence, there are several flophouses north of the train station, but there's nothing to recommend about them other than the price.

Boonsiri Boutique Hotel   HOTEL $
(☏08 1958 9915; www.boonsiriboutiquehotel.com, in Thai; Th Wichit Nakorn; r incl breakfast 480-560B; ❄🛜) One of many shiny new hotels in Si Saket, but the only one in the city centre, this unmistakable place east of the train station opted for a pink doll's-house theme in its lobby. Thankfully, the rooms are more tasteful.

Night Market   THAI $
(Th Ratchakan Rotfai 3; ☉4-11pm) There's a lot of culinary razzmatazz in this large market south of the train station.

❶ Getting There & Away

There are frequent buses to Bangkok (310B to 394B, 8½ hours) from Si Saket's **bus terminal** (☏0 4561 2500), including VIP service with **Nakhonchai Air** (☏0 4561 3191) departing at 9.15am, 9.15pm and 9.30pm (470B). Also, two companies depart from their own offices on Th Si Saket just north of the train station during the morning and evening. Vans are better than buses for Ubon Ratchathani (50B, one hour, hourly) and Surin (70B, 1½ hours, every half-hour).

There are eight daily trains from **Si Saket Railway Station** (☏0 4561 1525) to Bangkok (3rd-class 237B, 2nd-class fan/air-con 311/461B,

BORDER CROSSING: CHONG SA-NGAM TO CHOAM

This Thai–Cambodian border crossing doesn't see a lot of tourist traffic, despite the road to Siem Reap being in excellent shape, because it can't be done entirely by public transport. Visas are available; see p770 for details.

1st-class sleeper upper/lower 946/1146B, eight to 11 hours) and seven to Ubon Ratchathani (3rd class 13B, 2nd-class fan/air-con 29/50B, one hour).

Around Si Saket

KHAO PHRA WIHAN NATIONAL PARK
อุทยานแห่งชาติเขาพระวิหาร

The main attraction of this 130-sq-km **national park** (☎0 4581 8021; admission 200B, bike/motorcycle/car fee 10/20/30B) is **Khao Phra Wihan** (Preah Vihear in Khmer), one of the region's great Angkor-period monuments. Technically it's just inside Cambodia, but it's almost always visited via Thailand. Hugging the edge of a cliff on the brow of the Dangrek escarpment and accessed via a series of steep stepped *naga* approaches, the large temple complex towers 500m above the plains of Cambodia, offering both evocative ruins and dreamy views.

Claimed by both countries because of a misdrawn French map (that went unchallenged by Thailand for decades), the temple was awarded to Cambodia in a 1962 World Court ruling. Thailand's bruised pride never healed. In June 2008, as the Cambodian government sought Unesco World Heritage status for the complex, a border conflict over 4.6 sq km of land in front of the temple flared and has since led to several deadly clashes between the nations' armies and become a cause célèbre of Thailand's ultranationalist 'yellow-shirts'. This situation remains unresolved and the park is currently closed.

Renewed access to the temple may be years away – previously the Cambodians charged 200B and the Thais required a 5B border pass – though the park could reopen earlier. Its best feature is **Pha Mo-E-Daeng**, a cliff with some fabulous views of the temple and also the oldest bas-relief in Thailand. The 1000-plus-year-old carving depicts three figures sitting below a roughly cut pig (which might represent Vishnu) whose identities are an enigma to archaeologists and art historians. Although they give the general impression of representing deities, angels or kings, the iconography corresponds to no known figures in Thai, Mon or Khmer mythology. Nearby **Nam Tok Khun Sri** is a waterfall flowing (June to October only) over a cave large enough to hold an orchestra.

Landmines have been laid during the present conflict and others remain from the Khmer Rouge era, so don't stray from any well-worn paths and heed all skull-and-crossbone signs.

Sleeping

The park has four **bungalows** (☎0 2562 0760; www.dnp.go.th/parkreserve; 6 people 1000-2000B; ❋) and a **campsite** (per person with own tent 30B, 2–10-person tent hire 150-600B). Kantharalak, the nearest town with accommodation, has several simple but decent places to lay your head, including **SB Hotel** (☎0 4566 3103; Th Anan Ta Pak Dee; r 250-500B; ❋@☎) in the heart of town.

Getting There & Away

First take a bus from Si Saket (45B, 1¾ hours, every half-hour) or Ubon Ratchathani (50B, 1½ hours, every half-hour) to Kantharalak (there are also buses to Kantharalak from towns to the west along Hwy 24) and then catch a *sŏrng·tăa·ou* to Phum Saron (35B, 40 minutes, every half-hour). At Phum Saron you'll have to hire a motorcycle taxi to the park; figure on 200B return with a couple of hours waiting time. A truck will cost at least double.

OTHER KHMER RUINS

Thirty kilometres west of Si Saket via Rte 226 in Amphoe Uthumphon Phisai, **Prasat Sa Kamphaeng Yai** (admission free; ☉daylight hours), built as a shrine to Shiva, features four 11th-century *prang* and two *wí·hăhn*. The *prang,* including the main one, which was built of sandstone but restored with brick, have lost their tops, but several lintels and other Baphuon-style carvings remain. Behind the modern temple buildings are some amusing statues depicting what punishments may await people in the Buddhist version of Hell as a result of various misdeeds in this life. Hit your parents, for example, and you'll have enormous hands. Buses from Si Saket (20B, 30 minutes) and Surin (55B, 1½ hours) can drop you right nearby.

Eight kilometres west of Si Saket on the way to Kamphaeng Yai (on the north side of the highway in a temple with no sign in English) is the even more modest and completely unadorned **Prasat Sa Kamphaeng Noi** (admission free; ☺daylight hours), which, like many other Khmer ruins in the area, Angkor King Jayavarman VII commissioned as a healing station.

TEMPLES
Officially it's Wat Pa Maha Chedi Kaeo, but these days nearly everyone calls it **Wat Lan Khuat** (☺daylight hours), the 'Million Bottle Temple'. In 1982 the abbot dreamt of a *ʼbrah·sàht* in heaven made of diamonds and gems. Realising that this symbolised the need for clarity of purpose in one's life, he decided to replicate the idea as best he could on earth by covering nearly every surface of every building of his temple with glass bottles. The project would, he believed, have many benefits, including fostering cooperation within the community, encouraging younger people to come to the temple, and saving lots of money on paint. The more you look around, the less the name seems like an exaggeration. He took the theme one step further by using bottle caps to create much of the adornment. It's in Khun Han, 11km south of Hwy 24 via Rte 2111. Turn west at the roundabout in the centre of town.

Wat Phra That Rueang Rong (☺daylight hours) is another unusual temple. A previous abbot, lamenting the loss of the old ways, built the *bòht* to look like an oxcart being pulled by two giant bulls. He also created a **museum** (admission free; ☺7.30am-5.30pm) housing old tools, musical instruments and the like from the province's four cultures: Lao, Khmer, Suai and Yer. Concrete statues of people and oversized animals around the grounds offer life lessons. The *wát* is 7km north of town; take *sŏrng·tăa·ou* 2 (10B, 20 minutes) from in front of the train station.

UBON RATCHATHANI PROVINCE

This varied province, famous across Thailand for its forest temples, pushes down into the jungle-clad intersection of Thailand, Laos and Cambodia. To bolster the region's tourist profile TAT has labelled its southern reaches the 'Emerald Triangle' in recognition of its magnificent green landscapes, and drawing obvious parallels with northern Thailand's 'Golden Triangle'. Despite having plenty to entertain the rustic rover, the hoped-for hordes of visitors have failed to arrive.

Phu Chong Nayoi and Pha Taem National Parks are two of Thailand's most remote corners, and Ubon remains one of the region's more charming cities.

Ubon Ratchathani อุบลราชธานี
POP 115,000

Survive the usual knot of choked access roads and the 'Royal City of the Lotus' will reveal an altogether more attractive face. Racked up against Mae Nam Mun, Thailand's second-longest river, the historic heart of the city has a sluggish character rarely found in the region's big conurbations. There are many temples of interest that will appeal to even those suffering acute temple overload. Few cities in Thailand reward aimless wandering as richly as Ubon.

Ubon grew prosperous as a US air base during the Vietnam War era and is now a financial, educational and agricultural market centre. The nearby Thai–Lao border crossing at Chong Mek generates a small but steady stream of travellers.

☉ Sights & Activities

Wat Thung Si Meuang   TEMPLE
(วัดทุ่งศรีเมือง; Th Luang; ☺daylight hours) Wat Thung Si Meuang was built during the reign of Rama III (1824–51) and has a classic *hŏr drai* (Tripitaka hall) in excellent shape. Like many *hŏr drai*, it rests on tall, angled stilts in the middle of a pond to protect the precious scriptures (written on palm-leaf paper) from termites. It's kept open so you can look around inside. The 200-year-old murals in the little *bòht* beside the *hŏr drai* show life in that era.

Ubon Ratchathani National Museum   MUSEUM
(พิพิธภัณฑสถานแห่งชาติอุบลราชธานี; Th Kheuan Thani; admission 100B; ☺9am-4pm Wed-Sun) Occupying the former city hall, this is a very informative museum with plenty on show, from Dvaravati-era Buddhist ordination-precinct stones and a 2500-year-old Dong Son bronze drum to Ubon textiles and betelnut sets. The museum's most prized possession is a 9th-century Ardhanarisvara, a composite statue combining Shiva and his consort Uma into one being; one of just two ever found in Thailand.

Ubon Ratchathani

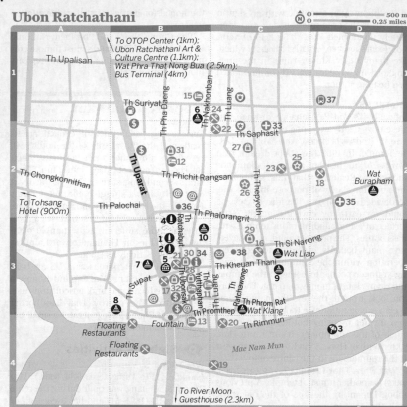

Wat Si Ubon Rattanaram TEMPLE

(วัดศรีอุบลรัตนาราม; Th Uparat; ⊙daylight hours)
The *bòht* at this important temple resembles
Bangkok's Wat Benchamabophit, but it's the
7cm-tall topaz Buddha inside that most visitors come to see. Phra Kaew Butsarakham,
as it's known, was reportedly brought here
from Vientiane at Ubon's founding and is
one of the city's holiest possessions. It sits
behind glass high up the back wall, all but
out of sight; bring binoculars if you have
them. The image directly in front of the largest Buddha is a copy.

The temple has turned a beautiful old
wooden *săh·lah* into a **museum** (admission free; ⊙9am-4pm) of religious items. The
highlight is the collection of 18th-century
đoô prá đrai̒bìdòk, gorgeous boxes used
for storing sacred palm-leaf texts. If you can
understand Thai, someone will demonstrate
the process used to paint the designs with
real gold.

Wat Ban Na Meuang TEMPLE

(วัดบ้านนาเมือง; ⊙daylight hours) Wat Sa Prasan
Suk, as it's also known, stands out from other temples in many ways. Most famously,
the *bòht* sits on a boat: a ceramic-encrusted
replica of King Rama IX's royal barge *Suphannahong*, complete with a sculpted
crew. The *wí·hăhn* also has a boat-shaped
base, this one resembling the second-most
important royal barge, *Anantanagaraj*;
and it's surrounded by an actual pond.
These were not just artistic endeavours: the
water represents our desires and the boats
represent staying above them.

The commissioner of these creations,
Luang Pu Boon Mi, died in 2001 and his
body is on display (they're waiting to finish
building a museum before cremating him)
in the *săh·lah* next to the boat *bòht*.

Finally, to reach all of these you must
pass under an immense statue of Airavata (Erawan in Thai), Hindu god Indra's

Ubon Ratchathani

three-headed elephant mount. The temple is about 4km northwest of town, and 1km off the ring road. *Sŏrng·tăa·ou* 8 passes it, but you need to tell the driver you're going here.

Wat Phra That Nong Bua　TEMPLE
(วัดพระธาตุหนองบัว; Th Thammawithi; ☉daylight hours) The richly adorned 55m *chedi* at this temple loosely resembles the Mahabodhi stupa in Bodhgaya, India. It's the only square stupa in Ubon Province unless you count the older one it was built over (you can enter to see the original between 8am and 6pm) or the four similar but smaller ones at the corners. Some of the *jataka* reliefs covering its exterior are quite expressive and two groups of four niches on each side of the *chedi* contain Buddhas standing in stylised Gupta or Dvaravati closed-robe poses. The temple is on the outskirts of town; to get there, take *sŏrng·tăa·ou* 10.

FREE **Ubon Ratchathani Art & Culture Centre**　MUSEUM
(ศูนย์ศิลปวัฒนธรรมกาญจนาภิเษกฯ; Th Jaeng Sanit; ☉8.30am-4.30pm Mon-Sat) The museum in the lower level of this striking contemporary Isan-design tower at Rajabhat University is more scattershot than the National Museum, but there are some interesting cultural displays, particularly of houses and handicrafts. There's also a whole lot of wax sculpture.

Wat Jaeng　TEMPLE
(วัดแจ้ง; Th Nakhonban; ☉daylight hours) Founded around the same time as the city, Wat Jaeng has an adorable Lan Xang–style *bòht* (built in 1887) with large *naga* eave brackets on the sides, crocodiles on the railings and Airavata along with two mythical lions atop the carved wooden facade. A travelling market fills up the *wàt* grounds every Wednesday.

Thung Si Meuang   PARK

(ทุ่งศรีเมือง) The centrepiece of this city-centre park is a huge concrete replica of a Candle Parade float (below). The humble brick obelisk in the northeast corner is the Monument of Merit, erected by former allied forces POWs (brought here for forced labour by the Japanese, who occupied Thailand during WWII) in gratitude for the secret assistance they received from ordinary Thai citizens while in the prison camps. The City Pillar Shrine (San Lak Meuang) is in the south.

Wat Supatanaram   TEMPLE

(วัดสุปัฏนาราม; Th Supat; ⊙daylight hours) Called Wat Supat for short, the unique *bòht* at this riverside temple, built between 1920 and 1936, features a Thai roof, European arches and a Khmer base. And, in contrast to other temple structures of the region, it's made entirely of stone. In front is a wooden bell, reputed to be the largest in the world.

Ko Hat Wat Tai   BEACH

(เกาะหาดวัดใต้) Picnicking families flock to this island in Mae Nam Mun during the hot, dry months from February to May when beaches rise along its shore. A makeshift bamboo bridge connects it to the northern shore and floating restaurants set up shop on the river.

✷ Festivals & Events

Ubon's famous Candle Parade (Kabuan Hae Tian) began during the reign of King Rama V when the appointed governor decided the city's rocket festival was too dangerous. The original simple designs have since grown (often with the help of styrofoam) to gigantic elaborately carved wax sculptures. The parade is part of Khao Phansaa, a Buddhist holiday marking the commencement of the Rains Retreat (Buddhist Lent) in July.

Prize-winning candles go on display along Th Si Narong next to Thung Si Meuang for a week after the parade and most of them will be parked at the city's temples at least through Ork Phansaa, the end of the Rains Retreat, three months later. Construction, also done on temple grounds, begins at least a month before the parade. The festival is very popular with Thai tourists and the city's hotels are booked out long in advance.

🛏 Sleeping

TOP CHOICE Sri Isan Hotel   HOTEL $

(☎0 4526 1011; www.sriisanhotel.com; Th Ratchabut; r 380-800B; ❄@🛜) The exception to the rule of Isan's typically uninspired budget hotels, the bright, cheerful lobby of this hotel is full of natural light streaming down through the atrium. The rooms are small and the air-conditioning takes a while to cool them down, but even the cheapest have enough charm to help you forget this. For the price, they're unbeatable. They'll pick you up at the train station or airport for 50B and from the bus station for 100B.

Sunee Grand Hotel   HOTEL $$$

(☎0 4535 2900; www.suneegrandhotel.com; Th Chayangkun; r incl breakfast 1600-3000B, ste 4250-12,500B; ❄@🛜🏊) One of the few hotels in Isan that could hold its own in Bangkok, the Sunee Grand is a stunner; and far less expensive than its peers in the capital. From the stylish light fixtures to the at-a-snap service, it will meet expectations. There's a large business centre, a piano player in the lobby and an adjacent shopping mall with a kid-sized rooftop water park.

Phadang Mansion   HOTEL $

(☎0 4525 4600; 126 Th Pha Daeng; r 500B; ❄@🛜) There are enough copies of classic paintings on the walls for this hotel to call itself a fine art gallery. You can, and should, snicker at this bit of hubris, but they're a nice touch. Rooms are boxy, but they're good and have little balconies.

Tohsang Hotel   HOTEL $$

(☎0 4524 5531; www.tohsang.com; Th Palochai; r incl breakfast 1200-1800B, ste 4000B; ❄@🛜) The tasteful decor here almost manages to hide Tohsang's age. The lobby is downright elegant while the rooms are as comfortable as they should be at these prices. They'll pick you up for free when you arrive.

Thongcome Mansion   HOTEL $

(☎08 1579 3629; Th Suriyat; r 350B; ❄❄) This little family-run place has some of Ubon's spiffiest rooms in this price range. And, because it's a new building, it doesn't suffer the quirks of older properties.

Srikamol Hotel   HOTEL $

(☎0 4524 6088; 26 Th Ubonsak; r 400B; ❄) From the chandelier in the lobby to the panelled wood doors, there are still signs from Srikamol's time as one of Ubon's best; though

WARIN CHAMRAP DISTRICT TEMPLES

The famous monk and meditation master Luang Pu Cha Suphattho, a former disciple of Luang Pu Man, known for his simple and direct teaching method, was quite a name in these parts. During his life he founded the following two well-known forest monasteries and many more around the world.

Peaceful **Wat Nong Pa Phong** (☉daylight hours) is known for its quiet discipline and daily routine of work and meditation, and some Thai-speaking Westerners live here. The wát features the golden *chedi* where Luang Pu Cha's relics are interred and a three-storey **museum** (admission free; ☉8am-4.30pm) displaying an odd assortment of items, from Luang Pu's worldly possessions to ancient artefacts to world currencies. The temple is about 10km past the river. *Sŏrng·tăa·ou* 3 gets you within 2km; a motorcycle taxi (if you can find one) should cost 20B for the final hop.

A Western-oriented wát opened in 1975 specifically for non-Thais: English is the primary language at **Wat Pa Nanachat** (www.watpahnanachat.org; ☉daylight hours). There's nothing really to see here, but visitors are welcome to drop by. A senior monk is available to answer questions most days after the 8am meal and someone will likely be around until 11am. Those with previous meditation experience are welcome to apply to stay here (write to: Guest Monk, Wat Pa Nanachat, Ban Bung Wai, Amphoe Warin Chamrap, Ubon Ratchathani 34310). Guests must follow all temple rules including eating just one meal a day and rising at 3am, and after three days men must shave their heads. A *sŏrng·tăa·ou* from Warin Market or any Si Saket bus can drop you on Rte 226, about 500m from the entrance. The wát is in the forest behind the rice fields.

those days are way behind it. It's not better than newer hotels at a similar price, but if you like it old school, you'll like this one.

River Moon Guesthouse GUEST HOUSE $
(☏0 4528 6093; 21 Th Sisaket 2; r 150-200B; @☎) This crumbling old place offers travellers something out of the ordinary. The rustic rooms, 500m from the train station, are in old railway workers' quarters and facilities are shared.

New Nakornluang Hotel HOTEL $
(☏0 4525 4768; 84-88 Th Yutthaphan; r 170-350B; ❄) Unlike River Moon, which is run down with character, this hotel is simply old. But, if you want to spend as little as possible and still be in the city centre, the cheap fan rooms are clean enough.

✕ Eating

TOP CHOICE **Jumpa-Hom** THAI $$
(Th Phichit Rangsan; dishes 55-1500B; ☉dinner; ☎) One of the loveliest and most delicious restaurants in Isan, Jumpa-Hom has a very broad set of choices including some not-so-common dishes. You can dine on a water-and-plant-filled wooden deck or in the air-con dining room, which offers a choice of tables and chairs or cushions for floor seating.

TOP CHOICE **Rung Roj** THAI $
(no roman-script sign; 122 Th Nakhonban; dishes 30-165B; ☉lunch & dinner; ☎) What this Ubon institution lacks in service, it more than makes up for with excellent food using only the freshest ingredients: the meals look straight out of a foodie magazine photo shoot. It's the restaurant with the bold plate, fork and spoon sign.

Night Market THAI $
(Th Kheuan Thani; ☉4pm-midnight) Over the past few years, Ubon's city-centre night market has grown into an excellent dining destination.

Porntip Gai Yang Wat Jaeng NORTHEASTERN THAI $
(no roman-script sign; Th Saphasit; dishes 20-130B; ☉breakfast, lunch & dinner) It looks like a tornado has whipped through this no-frills spot, but the chefs cook up a storm of their own. This is considered by many to be Ubon's premier purveyor of *gài yâhng, sôm·đam,* sausages and other Isan foods.

Risotto ITALIAN $$
(Th Phichit Rangsan; dishes 100-300B; ☉lunch & dinner) The dining room can't quite pull off an Italian vibe, but the kitchen offers a dash of *la dolce vita*. The menu has a full roster of pasta, plus salmon steak and one of the best pizzas in Isan.

Krua Ruen Pae THAI $

(no Roman-script sign; dishes 40-300B; ⊘lunch & dinner) One of several floating restaurants on the Mae Nam Mun, Krua Ruen Pae serves up tasty Thai and Isan food and a relaxed atmosphere. The *dôm kàh gài* (chicken with galangal in coconut milk) is lovely. If driving here, exit to the west and then go under the bridge.

Moon Lover CAFE $

(Th Rimmun; ⊘breakfast, lunch & dinner Tue-Sun) Enjoy coffee, smoothies and waffles with jazz and river views at this attractive little coffee shop.

U-Bake BAKERY $

(Th Phichit Rangsan; chocolate cake 55B; ⊘lunch & dinner) There are many good bakeries in town, but only U-Bake gets to share space with the lovely restaurant Jumpa-Hom.

🌿**Boon Niyon Uthayan** VEGETARIAN $

(Th Si Narong; per plate 10-20B; ⊘breakfast & lunch Tue-Sun; ⊘) Run by the ascetic Santi Asoke group, which has split from mainstream Thai Buddhism, this restaurant has an impressive vegetarian buffet under a giant roof. Most of the food is grown organically just outside the city.

Chiokee THAI $

(307-317 Th Kheuan Thani; dishes 35-120B; ⊘breakfast, lunch & dinner) A steady stream of old-timers linger over congee, tea and newspapers at this classic spot to have breakfast.

🍷 Drinking & Entertainment

U-Bar NIGHTCLUB

(Th Phichit Rangsan) While other clubs have come and gone over the years, U-Bar has long remained at the top of the heap for the college crowd, partly because the best bands from Bangkok often play here when they visit Ubon. If you go, try a Blue Kamikaze, served out of a sinister-looking slushy machine behind the bar.

e-Ba NIGHTCLUB

(Th Phichit Rangsan) A newer and more spacious club that attracts an older (but equally enthusiastic) crowd than U-Bar.

Ubon Ratchathani Art & Culture Centre CULTURAL CENTRE

(☎0 4535 2000; Th Jaeng Sanit) There are sometimes Isan music and dance performances here.

🛍 Shopping

Isan maybe be silk country, but Ubon is a cotton town. Shops selling natural-dyed, handwoven cotton clothing, bags and fabric abound. First stop should be **Camp Fai Ubon** (189 Th Thepyoth), which is signed as Peaceland. **Grass-Root** (87 Th Yutthaphan) is smaller, but also good. Although not all the cotton at **Maybe** (124 Th Si Narong; ⊘8am-7pm) is made with natural dyes, this store has the broadest selection of clothing styles.

TOP CHOICE **Rawang Thang** HANDICRAFTS

(Th Kheuan Thani; ⊘9am-9pm) There's also Ubon cotton at this shop, which sells fun and funky T-shirts, pillows, postcards, picture frames and assorted bric-a-brac, most made or designed by the friendly husband-and-wife owners. They can fill you in on all things Ubon.

Ban Khampun HANDICRAFTS

(124 Th Pha Daeng) Ubon's famous silk specialist makes some exquisite fabrics using many patterns and styles you won't find elsewhere. For two days during the Candle Festival, the owner hosts a mini cultural festival at his gorgeous home-workshop-museum just outside town.

Punchard HANDICRAFTS

(156 Th Pha Daeng; ⊘10am-9pm) Though pricey, this is the best all-round handicrafts shop in Ubon. The **Th Ratchabut branch** (⊘9am-8pm) is mostly home decor.

OTOP Center HANDICRAFTS

(Th Jaeng Sanit) A crafts mall with a varied shopping selection.

ℹ Information

Emergency & Medical Services

Tourist Police (☎0 4524 5505; Th Suriyat).

Ubonrak Thonburi Hospital (☎0 4526 0285; Th Phalorangrit) Has a 24-hour casualty department.

Internet Access

Internet cafes aren't hard to find in Ubon. **29 Internet** (Th Nakhonban; per hr 12B; ⊘24 hr) and **25 Hours** (Th Pha Daeng; per hr 15B; ⊘24 hr) are open at all hours.

Money

Ying Charoen Park (Th Ratchathani) This shopping centre across from Rajabhat University has banks that open evenings and weekends nearest to downtown.

City Mall (Th Chayangkun) In front of Sunee Grand Hotel; has an AEON ATM.

Post

Post office (Th Luang; ☺8.30am-4.30pm Mon-Fri, 9am-noon Sat, Sun & holidays)

Tourist Information

Tourism Authority of Thailand (TAT; ✆0 4524 3770; tatubon@tat.or.th; Th Kheuan Thani; ☺8.30am-4.30pm) Has helpful staff.

❶ Getting There & Away

Air

Air Asia (✆0 2515 9999; www.airasia.com) and **THAI** (✆0 4531 3340; www.thaiairways.com) each fly twice a day to Bangkok's Suvarnaphumi Airport. Air Asia's fares are as low as 1350B one way while THAI charges at least 1000B more. Air Asia also does three flights a week direct to Phuket for as little as 1450B. **Nok Air** (✆0 2900 9955; www.nokair.com) flies to Bangkok's Don Muang Airport three times a day, from 1300B.

Many travel agencies, including **Sakda Travel World** (✆0 4525 4333; www.sakdatour.com; Th Phalorangrit), sell tickets.

Bus

Ubon's **bus terminal** (✆0 4531 6085) is north of town; take *sŏrng·tăa·ou* 2, 3 or 10 to the centre. Buses link Ubon with Bangkok (385B to 473B, 8½ to 10 hours) frequently in the morning and evening, plus a few in the middle of the day. The top VIP service is offered by **999 VIP** (✆0 4531 4299), departing at 6.30pm (730B), and **Nakhonchai Air** (✆0 4526 9777) at 10.15am and 9.45pm (552B). The cross-border bus to Pakse, Laos (200B, three hours) leaves at 9.30am and 3.30pm. Vans are the best way to Si Saket (50B, one hour, hourly).

DESTINATION	FARE (B)	DURATION (HR)
Chiang Mai	590-893	17
Khon Kaen	216-252	4½
Khorat	203-330	5-6
Mukdahan	75-135	3½
Rayong	427-641	13
Roi Et	108-139	3
Sakon Nakhon	117-211	5
Surin	105-200	3
Yasothon	66-85	1½

Train

The **railway station** (✆0 4532 1588) is in Warin Chamrap; take *sŏrng·tăa·ou* 2 from Ubon. There's an overnight express train to/from Bangkok (2nd-class fan/air-con 371/551B, 1st-class sleeper upper/lower 1080/1280B) The six other departures also take 11 to 12 hours except the 5.45am (from Bangkok) and 2.50pm (from

Ubon) special express service, which takes 8½ hours. All trains also stop in Si Saket, Surin and Khorat.

❶ Getting Around

Numbered *sŏrng·tăa·ou* (10B) run throughout town. TAT's free city map marks the routes, most of which pass near its office. A *túk-túk* trip within the centre should cost from 30B to 40B. Ubon also has a few **metered taxis** (✆08 9421 6040; 35B flagfall, 15B call fee) which park at the bus station. From the airport, two car-hire counters provides rides to anywhere in town for 80B.

Chow Watana (✆08 1967 9796) Car hire with driver from 1300B per day.

Ubon Rental Cycle (✆0 4524 4708; 115 Th Si Narong) Has a few bikes for hire at 100B per day. If the office is closed, ask at the house next door.

Around Ubon Ratchathani Province

BAN PA-AO บ้านผาอ่าว
Ban Pa-Ao is a silk-weaving village, but it's best known for producing brass and bronze items using the lost-wax casting method. It's the only place in Thailand where the entire process is still done by hand. You can watch workers creating bells and bowls at **Soon Thorng Leuang Ban Pa-Ao** (☺8am-5pm) on the far side of the village. There's also a silk-weaving centre on the way into town. During our last visit the village's temple was completing a gorgeous new museum building to hold its collection of artefacts from farms and homes.

Ban Pa-Ao's **homestay program** (✆08 1076 1249; per person incl breakfast 250B) offers the chance to try your hand at both of the town's trades, though little English is spoken.

Ban Pa-Ao is 3.5km off Hwy 23. Buses to/from Yasothon pass the turn-off (20B, 20 minutes), and a motorcycle taxi from the highway should cost 20B.

PHIBUN MANGSAHAN พิบูลมังสาหาร
Thais often stop in the dusty town of Phibun Mangsahan to see a set of rapids called **Kaeng Sapheu**, just downstream of the Mae Nam Mun bridge. The rocky islets make 'Python Rapids' rise between February and May, but the shady park here is a pleasant stop year-round. It has a Chinese temple, several simple restaurants (most serving deep-fried frog skins; *năng gòp tôrt*) and a long line of souvenir shops. Many fishermen work here and they'll take you on boat trips

in little long-tails: it's 500B for a two-hour trip to an island temple. Ask at *'dăaw'* restaurant if you'd rather ride a bigger boat (500B per hour), which can hold 20 people.

The *bòht* at **Wat Phu Khao Kaew** (◷daylight hours) on the west side of town has some atypical artistic flair. The exterior is covered in tiles, the upper interior walls have reliefs of important stupas from around Thailand and a very unusual style of *yák* (temple guardian) keeps watch outside.

Villages just over the bridge as you drive toward Khong Jiam are famed for forging iron and bronze gongs, both for temples and classical Thai-music ensembles. You can watch the gong-makers hammering the flat metal discs and tempering them in rustic fires at many roadside workshops. Small gongs start at around 500B and the 2m monsters fetch as much as 200,000B. People make drums and cymbals around here too.

Visa extensions are available at Phibun Mangsahan's **immigration office** (☎0 4544 1108; ◷8.30am-noon, 1-4.30pm Mon-Fri), 1km south of the bridge on the way to Chong Mek.

🛏 Sleeping & Eating

In the centre of town, midway between the bus stop and the bridge, the friendly **Phiboonkit Hotel** (☎0 4544 1201; chompoonuch@hotmail.com; Th Phiboon; r 200-300B; ✳) is your usual, slightly chaotic, budget hotel.

Phiboon Cafe (Th Luang; ◷breakfast & lunch), a ramshackle shop right at the bridge, has made Phibun famous for *sah·lah·ʉow* (Chinese buns; 5B each). Countless shops on the highway have piggybacked on its success.

❶ Getting There & Away

Phibun's bus park behind the market serves ordinary buses (35B, one hour, every 20 minutes) to Ubon's bus station – these stop to pick up passengers at Warin Market across the river, but you may not get a seat if you board there – and *sŏrng·tăa·ou* to Chong Mek (40B, one hour, every 20 minutes). *Sŏrng·tăa·ou* (40B, 1½ hours, every half-hour) go to Talat Ban Du (Ban Du Market), near Ubon's city centre, and Khong Jiam park (40B, one hour, four each morning), near the bridge.

KAENG TANA NATIONAL PARK อุทยานแห่งชาติแก่งตะนะ

Five kilometres before Khong Jiam you can cross the Pak Mun dam to little **Kaeng Tana National Park** (☎0 4540 6888; admission 100B). After circling thickly forested Don

Tana (Tana Island), linked to the mainland by a small suspension bridge, Mae Nam Mun roils through its beautiful namesake rapids and passes below some photogenic cliffs. In the rainy season the rapids lie under water, and toward the end of the dry season naturally cut holes in the rock, similar to those at Sam Phan Bok (see boxed text, p442), emerge. Beyond the rapids and the adjacent **visitor centre** (◷8am-6pm) there are good short walks to other waterfalls and viewpoints. The 1.5km clifftop trail to **Lan Pha Phueng** viewpoint is especially serene. **Nam Tok Tad Ton** is a wide and lovely waterfall just a 300m walk from the road that you'll pass as you drive into the park from the south.

There's a **campsite** (per person with own tent 30B, 4-/8-person tent hire 150/225B) and four **bungalows** (☎0 2562 0760; www.dnp.go.th/parkreserve; 6/10 people 1000/2000B). The simple restaurant opens during the day only.

By road, the park is 14km from Khong Jiam. There's no public transport, but boats in town will take you upriver and drop you at the park for 800B. They'll wait a few hours for you to stroll around before bringing you back.

KHONG JIAM โขงเจียม

Khong Jiam sits on a picturesque peninsula at the confluence of the Mekong River and Mae Nam Mun, which the Thais call **Mae Nam Song Si** (Two-Colour River) after the contrasting currents formed at the junction. In the rainy season the multicoloured merger is visible from the shore, but the rest of the year you'll need to go out in a boat to see it properly. (Or, in April, just before the rains begin, you can walk out.) A large boat that has a sunshade and can carry 10 people costs 350B, while you'll pay 200B in a tiny boat that holds two or three. The big boats can also take you to Kaeng Tana National Park (800B) or elsewhere along the Mekong River.

Above the town is **Wat Tham Khu Ha Sawan** (◷daylight hours). The awesome views alone are worth the trip, but this well-known temple also has a unique nine-pointed *chedi,* an all-white *bòht,* an impressive orchid garden and the body of the late abbot, Luang Pu Kam, on display in a glass case atop a flamboyant altar.

Naga fireballs (see the boxed text, p465) began appearing at Khong Jiam in 2005.

🛏 Sleeping & Eating

Khong Jiam doesn't get many *fa·ràng* visitors, but it's popular with Thais, so there's an abundance of lodging. There are several simple restaurants near the Mae Nam Song Si, including two pricey ones floating on the Mekong.

Tohsang Khongjiam Resort   HOTEL $$$
(📞0 4535 1174; www.tohsang.com; r incl breakfast 2355-3885B, villas 3530-7060B, Sedhapura pool villas 12,500-14,500B; ❄@🛜🏊) The glitz and gloss at this large resort-spa are somewhat incongruous for this stretch of rural Thailand, but it holds all the aces in the posh-accommodation stakes, and the prices for the rooms are fair for what you get. The 3rd-floor rooms have the best views. There's a good restaurant and a spa and it rents bikes and kayaks. It's 3.5km from town on the south bank of the river.

Banpak Mongkhon   HOTEL $
(📞0 4535 1352; www.mongkhon.com, in Thai; Th Kaewpradit; r 250-800B, f 2500B; ❄@🛜) From the simple fan rooms to the four cute stilted wooden cottages, this place near the highway has friendly owners and lots of character, making it a great choice for any budget.

Apple Guesthouse   GUEST HOUSE $
(📞0 4535 1160; Th Kaewpradit; r 200-300B; ❄) Behind a general store, the recently spruced up Apple has wooden buildings with concrete rooms below. It's the cheapest place in town and good enough for the price.

Khong Jiam Homestay   HOMESTAY $
(📞08 7448 9399; r 500B) Talk about yin and yang – these simple wooden cottages with mattresses on the floor sit in a patch of forest right next to the Tohsang Resort. There's no food, but you can cook over a fire, or splash out and eat next door. It's often empty, but sometimes it's full with groups from Bangkok. Call when you get to town and someone will pick you up.

Baansuan Rimnam Resort   HOTEL $$$
(📞08 9792 1204; Th Rimmoon; r incl breakfast 800-1000B; ❄) This quiet, shady spot sits along Mae Nam Mun. The most expensive bungalows have terraces looking at the water through a line of trees. To get there, turn right at the school just before the temple.

ℹ Getting There & Away

All transport to town stops at the highway junction. The only direct bus to Ubon (77B, 2½ hours) leaves at 6am and returns to Khong Jiam at 2.30pm. You can also take one of the four morning *sŏrng·tăa·ou* to Phibun Mangsahan (40B, one hour) and continue from there. Buses to Bangkok (400B to 500B) leave at 7.30am (2nd class) and 4.30pm (1st class).

Apple Guesthouse has bikes (100B per day) and motorcycles (300B per day) for hire and Banpak Mongkok also rents motorcycles (200B per day).

PHA TAEM NATIONAL PARK   อุทยานแห่งชาติผาแต้ม

Up the Mekong from Khong Jiam is a long cliff named Pha Taem, the centrepiece of unheralded **Pha Taem National Park** (📞0 4531 8026; admission 200B). From the top you get an awesome bird's-eye view across the river into Laos, and you can see the first sunset in Thailand. Down below a trail passes prehistoric rock paintings dating to at least 1000 BC. Mural subjects include *blah beuk* (giant Mekong catfish), elephants, human hands, fish traps (looking much like the huge ones still used today) and geometric designs. The second viewing platform fronts the most impressive batch. A clifftop **visitor centre** (🕖7.30am-sunset) contains exhibits pertaining to the paintings and local ecology.

North of the cliff is **Nam Tok Soi Sawan**, a 25m-tall waterfall flowing from June to December. It's a 19km drive from the visitor centre and then a 500m walk, or you can hike (with a ranger) for about 15km along the top of the cliff. What the park calls **Thailand's largest flower field** (blooming November to February) lies near the falls.

The northern half of the park holds more waterfalls, ancient art and wonderful views. **Pa Cha Na Dai** cliff serves Thailand's first sunrise view (Pha Taem is about one minute behind) and amazing **Nam Tok Saeng Chan** flows through a hole cut into the overhanging rock. Scattered across the 340-sq-km park are many oddly eroded rocks, including four sites known as **Sao Chaliang**, which are mushroom-shaped stone formations similar to those found in Mukdahan's Phu Pha Thoep National Park.

Pha Taem has **campsites** (per person with own tent 30B, 2-/6-person tent hire 125/300B), **cabins** (4 people 300B) and five **bungalows** (📞0 2562 0760; www.dnp.go.th/parkreserve; 6-person bungalows with fan 1200B, 5-person with

SAM PHAN BOK

Visit Sam Phan Bok (3000 Holes) and you'll feel as much like you're visiting another planet as another country. Eons of erosion have made Swiss cheese of this narrow, rocky Mekong bend, creating the most stunning moment of the river's epic journey. The river drowns it during the rainy season, but when it's fully exposed (usually between December and May) you can explore for hours. Even in the shoulder months, when it only partly protrudes, it's still worth the trip for a look from the cliff above. Boat rides beyond Sam Phan Bok are also very rewarding. There's no shade out here, so early-morning and late-afternoon visits are best.

It's just north of Pha Taem National Park, near the village of Ban Song Khon, and there's no public transport anywhere near it. You can camp there, and a few people even hire tents. The nearest accommodation is in the village overlooking Hat Salung, a lovely stretch of river in its own right. **Song Khon Resort** (☎08 7256 1696; www.songkhonresort. com, in Thai; r 500-700B) has adequate rooms and a great location. Definitely book ahead on weekends and holidays during Sam Phan Bok season.

air-con 2000B; ✳). Vendors sell snacks and fast food near the visitor centre until about sunset.

Pha Taem is 18km from Khong Jiam via Rte 2112. There's no public transport, so the best way to get there is to hire a motorcycle in Khong Jiam (from 200B).

CHONG MEK   ช่องเม็ก

South of Khong Jiam, at the end of Rte 217, is the small border town of Chong Mek. The opening of the bridge in Mukdahan has reduced traffic on this route and stolen much of the bustle from the Chong Mek market, which used to be a big hit with Thai tourists. If you get stuck here after hours, there are several cheap guest houses north of the market.

The little bus terminal down the road from the border serves *sŏrng·tăa·ou* to Phibun (40B, one hour, every 20 minutes), vans to Ubon (100B, 1¼ hours, every half-hour) and buses to Bangkok (392B to 544B, 10 hours, five daily). There's no public transport

BORDER CROSSING: CHONG MEK TO VANGTAO

The crossing here is largely hassle free. Visas can be bought on the spot and buses wait for passengers to complete the paperwork (see p770 for details). Lao officials will probably try to extract 'stamping fees', but they're usually not too insistent. Pakse is about 45 minutes by road and if you didn't arrive on the direct bus, it's easy to catch a ride here.

between Chong Mek and Khong Jiam; either go through Phibun or hire a motorcycle taxi/ túk-túk for 200/350B.

PHU CHONG NAYOI NATIONAL PARK   อุทยานแห่งชาติภูจองนายอย

Sitting at the heart of the 'Emerald Triangle' is the little-known **Phu Chong Nayoi National Park** (☎0 4541 1515; admission 200B), one of Thailand's wildest corners and healthiest forests. Resident fauna includes elephants, tigers, Malayan sun bears, barking deer, gibbons, black hornbills and endangered white-winged ducks.

The park's primary attraction is **Nam Tok Huay Luang**, which plunges 40m over a cliff in two parallel streams. A short trail leads to the top and you can walk down 274 steps to the bottom where you can swim, though the water dries up around March. Rangers love taking visitors on short bamboo-raft trips (200B to 300B) above the falls, though water levels are too low from February to April and occasionally too high when it rains. At the far end of the 687-sq-km park, from atop **Phu Hin Drang**, there are superb views of the surrounding countryside, which looks much like the view from Pha Taem cliff (p441) but with jungle instead of the Mekong at the bottom of the valley. It's a 50km drive from the main park entrance and then a 5km hike or tractor ride.

Stargazing is superb here, so consider spending the night. There are three **bungalows** (☎0 2562 0760; www.dnp.go.th/park reserve; 4-/6-person bungalows 600/1200B) plus a **campsite** (per person with own tent 30B, 6-person tent hire 300B). Snacks and drinks are available daily and a couple of restaurants operate on weekends and holidays, but only during the day.

From Ubon catch one of the four morning buses to the town of Na Chaluai (70B, three hours) where túk-túk cost about 400B for the 20km journey to the park. You could also get off before Na Chaluai at Ban Gang Reuang, 5km from the park, and try to hitch, but traffic is light in this area.

CHAIYAPHUM PROVINCE

Travelling through Chaiyaphum Province, you're almost as likely to run into a tiger as a foreign tourist – and this is not a province with lots of tigers. Geographically it's at the heart of the country, but realistically it's a remote region that remains something of a mystery to Thais, who know only of the Siam Tulips (Dok Krachiao) that bloom a bright purple and pink in several parks around the province between June and August. For travellers, the primary appeal is the peace and quiet and sense of straying off the beaten track.

Chaiyaphum ชัยภูมิ
POP 55,500

Chaiyaphum is a bit of a nowhere town used mostly as a base for visiting surrounding attractions rather than a destination in itself. Fashionistas should head west to the silk village of Ban Khwao and the outdoorsy should hit the mountains. There are several national parks in the province, of which Tat Ton is the easiest to reach.

◉ Sights

Chaiyaphum's attractions define modest.

Just east of the city, **Prang Ku** is a small Khmer *prang* constructed during the reign of the final Angkor king, Jayavarman VII (1181–1219), as a place of worship at a 'healing station' on the route between the Angkor capital in Cambodia and Prasat Singh in Kanchanaburi Province. The Buddha figure inside the *ku* (stupa) purportedly hails from the Dvaravati period (6th to 10th centuries).

Built in 1950 as the governor's residence and now restored as a museum, **Tamnak Keeow** (Green Hall; Th Burapha; admission free; ◉9am-4pm) has ho-hum displays of pottery, *mát-mèe* cloth and photos from King Rama IX's 1955 visit. Ask the guard to find the man with the key. The nearby **Chaiyaphum**

Cultural Centre (Th Bannakan; admission free; ◉8am-4pm Mon-Sat) has mock-ups of traditional homes. Ask for the key in the room at the top of the stairs.

✹ Festivals

Chaiyaphum residents celebrate two nine-day festivals in honour of Jao Pho Phraya Lae, a Lao court official who settled this area in the 18th century and later strategically switched allegiances to Bangkok when Chao Anou from Vientiane declared war on the more powerful (and eventually victorious) Siam in the early 19th century.

The **Jao Pho Phraya Lae Fair** starts on 12 January, the date of his death, and takes place around his statue at the entrance to town. A **Jao Pho Phraya Lae Offering Ceremony** takes place during April or May at the same time as Bun Duean Hok (an Isan merit-making event) at a lakeside shrine erected where he was killed, about 3km southwest of the centre. Both events feature an elephant parade.

⊨ Sleeping

Deeprom Hotel   HOTEL **$$**
(☑0 4482 2222; www.d-promhotel.com; 339/9 Th Bannakan; r 800-900B; ste 1800B; ❄️ 🛜) With its crazy colour scheme and bold boast (the name means 'perfect'), this hotel demands attention. Rooms are less flashy, but fair for the price.

Tonkoon Hotel   HOTEL **$**
(☑0 4481 7881; 379 Th Bannakan; r 500B; ❄️ 🛜) Rooms rather resemble a college dorm; nevertheless, this spick-and-span 'mansion' standard hotel is a good choice at this price.

Siam River Resort   HOTEL **$$$**
(☑0 4481 1999; www.siamriverresort.com; Th Bannakan; r 990-2900B, bungalows 2900-5500B; ❄️@🛜🏊) Chaiyaphum's top spot is in the city centre, but hidden out of earshot of the hubbub of the city – what little there is, anyway. Guests get free use of bicycles.

Ratanasiri Hotel   HOTEL **$**
(☑0 4482 1258; 667/19 Th Non Meuang; r 200-500B; ❄️🛜) This dowdy giant is a great choice for those on a budget, but if you're planning on spending in the upper price range head for Tonkoon because rooms at Ratanasiri don't get much better as the price rises. Smiling staff make up for the lack of atmosphere and there's wi-fi in the lobby.

Chaiyaphum

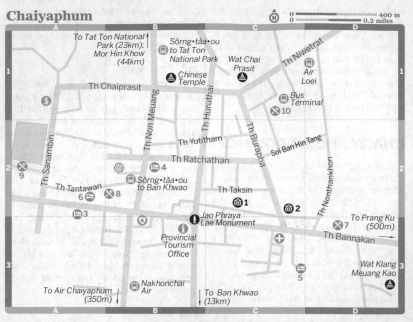

✗ Eating

Chaiyaphum's signature food is *mahm* (sour beef and liver) sausages, but they're an acquired taste and don't make it onto many menus.

Night Bazaar   THAI $
(◷4-11pm) This street market west of downtown is a better foraging destination than the night market by the bus station.

Chorragah Lahp Gory   NORTHEASTERN THAI $
(no roman-script sign; 299/21 Th Bannakan; dishes 20-80B; ◷breakfast, lunch & dinner) With its concrete floor, corrugated-metal roof and old-time foods, like the namesake *gôry* (raw beef with lemon, chilli, fish sauce and extra blood), this no-nonsense Isan eatery takes diners back to the village. The partial picture menu gets you through the language barrier.

Jae Hai Tek   VEGAN $
(no roman-script sign; Th Tantawan; dishes 25-40B; ◷breakfast & lunch; ✍) Unlike most Thai *jae* restaurants, which only have a buffet tray, this hole in the wall cooks up food to order using mock chicken, cuttlefish *(ɓlah mèuk)* and more. Either ask for your favourite dish or point to the pictures hanging on the gate.

ℹ Information

Pat Pat (Th Non Meuang; internet per hr 15B; ◷11am-10pm) Friendly internet cafe and coffee shop. English-speaking owner Bun is a good source of information about Chaiyaphum and there's a tiny book exchange.

Provincial Tourism Office (☎0 4481 1376; Th Bannakan; ◷8am-4pm)

Tesco-Lotus (Th Sanambin) Has an AEON ATM and the city centre's only bank open evenings and weekends.

ℹ Getting There & Away

Khon Kaen (58B to 81B, 2½ hours, hourly) and Khorat (78B to 101B, 2½ hours, every half-hour) buses leave from Chaiyaphum's **bus terminal** (☑0 4481 1344). So do some buses for Bangkok (196B to 252B, five hours); however, most people travel to Bangkok with **Air Chaiyaphum** (☑0 4481 1556) and **Air Loei** (☑0 4481 1446), which have their own terminals. They both charge 252B for 1st class and 294B for VIP. Air Loei also has a midnight VIP departure (392B).

Nakhonchai Air (☑0 4481 2522) runs six buses between Ubon Ratchathani (234B to 347B, seven hours, between 10.40pm and 4.40am) and Chiang Mai (370B to 716B, 11 hours, between 7.10pm and 1.10am), also from its own station. The office is back behind the orange gate.

ℹ Getting Around

A túk-túk should cost no more than 30B for any destination in town.

Around Chaiyaphum

BAN KHWAO   บ้านเขว้า

Most visitors to Chaiyaphum make a stop in the silk town of Ban Khwao, 13km to the southwest on Rte 225, where many shops sell fabric and clothing. The town is known for its low prices due to the *mát·mèe* fabrics (see boxed text, p453) being rather thin. Most weaving is now done in other villages, but several families here still have looms under their houses. Actually, these days embroidery is all the rage and many women use their sewing machines as often as their looms. The **Silk Development Centre** (no roman-script sign; admission free; ⊙8.30am-4.30pm) by the market has a small display about *mát·mèe*, but no longer arranges tours.

Sŏrng·tăa·ou to Ban Khwao (20B, 30 minutes, every 20 minutes) park near Pat Pat internet cafe in Chaiyaphum.

TAT TON NATIONAL
PARK   อุทยานแห่งชาติตาดโตน

A scenic little spot on the edge of the Laenkha mountain range, **Tat Ton National Park** (☑0 4485 3333; admission 200B) is 23km north of the city. Covering 218 sq km, Tat Ton is best known for its photogenic namesake waterfall, which is only 6m tall but stretches to 50m wide during the May-to-October rainy season. Some people think it's more beautiful from January to April, because the water is clearer then. Smaller **Tat Fah** waterfall, about 20km from Tat Ton, functions as a 20m waterslide during the rainy season.

The park has **campsites** (per person with own tent 30B, 2-/6-person tent hire 280/660B) and **bungalows** (☑0 2562 0760; www.dnp.go.th/parkreserve; 2-14 people 600-3500B), scenically situated along the river, plus several simple restaurants.

Sŏrng·tăa·ou (35B, one hour) from Chaiyaphum pass the park entrance (a hilly 1.5km walk from the falls) frequently in the morning, but there are few after 9.30am and sometimes none after 1pm, so it's usually faster to hitchhike back to town.

KHON KAEN PROVINCE

Khon Kaen Province, the gateway to Isan for those arriving from northern Thailand, serves up an interesting mix of old and new. Farming and textiles still dominate life in the countryside, while things are booming in the increasingly modern capital city.

THE STONEHENGE OF THAILAND

Mor Hin Khow (☑0 4481 0903; admission free), the most popular part of Phu Laenkha National Park, means 'hill with white rocks' in Isan, but tourism boosters decided a more creative moniker was needed and dubbed it 'The Stonehenge of Thailand'. It features a line of five natural stone pinnacles with tapered bottoms that rise to 15m and in no way resemble their namesake. Between these and the sunset-perfect **Pha Hua Nak** (Naga-head Cliff), another 2.5km up the mountain, are three more fields of less dramatic but still oddly sculpted rocks and an observation tower. It's a lovely and peaceful place to explore, and on weekdays you'll probably have it all to yourself.

Camping (2-/4-person tent hire 100/200B) at the little visitor centre is free, but bring your own food because the restaurants have limited weekend and holiday hours.

It's 21km northwest of Tat Ton National Park on a well-signposted route. There's no public transport.

Khon Kaen ขอนแก่น

POP 145,300

As the site of the northeast's largest university and an important hub for all things commercial and financial, Khon Kaen is youthful, educated and on the move. It's the kind of place that's more likely to land on a best-places-to-live list than a traveller's itinerary, but there are enough interesting attractions and good facilities to make a stop worthwhile.

Khon Kaen has ridden Isan's economic boom for all it's worth, filling the streets with traffic and draping a sterile concrete veneer over most of the town. But make no mistake, Isan's idiosyncratic appeal is still here, you just have to work a little harder to uncover it these days.

◉ Sights

BUENG KAEN NAKHON บึงแก่นนคร
This 100-hectare lake is the most pleasant place in town to spend some time, and the paths hugging its shore link quite a few interesting places. There's bike hire at the market and down along the west shore across from Wat Klang Muang Kao; the latter has two- and three-seaters (20B per hour per seat).

Wat Nong Wang TEMPLE
(วัดหนองแวง; Th Robbung; ⊙daylight hours) Down at the south end of the lake, **Phra Mahathat Kaen Nakhon** (⊙8am-6pm), the stunning stupa at the heart of this important temple, is Khon Kaen's one must-see. It features enlightening murals depicting Isan culture; various historical displays, including a collection of rare Buddha images on the 4th floor; and a 9th-floor observation deck.

Mahesak Shrine SHRINE
(ศาลเจ้าพ่อมเหศักดิ์; Th Robbung) This modern Khmer-style *prang* is dedicated to the Hindu god Indra. It's almost spooky at night.

Rim Bueng Kaen Nakhon Market MARKET
(ตลาดริมบึงแก่นนคร; Th Robbung; ⊙4-10pm) This fun little market, in the shadow of the soaring *bòht* and *chedi* of **Wat That**, features food, shopping and paint-your-own pottery stalls. During the day there are paddleboats for hire (30B per half-hour).

Khon Kaen City Museum MUSEUM
(โฮงมูนมังเมืองขอนแก่น; Th Robbung; admission 90B; ⊙9am-5pm Mon-Sat) Inside the amphitheatre, the well-done Hong Moon Mung museum provides a good introduction to Isan with

dioramas and displays going back to the Jurassic period.

Sanjao Bueng Tao Gong Ma TEMPLE
(ศาลเจ้าปึงเถ่ากงมา; Th Robbung) Sometimes called Sanjao Bueng Kaen Nakhon, this is Khon Kaen's biggest and most beautiful Chinese temple. There's a large Guan-Im (Chinese Goddess of Mercy) statue in the park across the street.

Wat Pho Ban Nontan TEMPLE
(วัดโพธิ์โนนทัน; Th Phot Thisan; ⊙daylight hours) Just off the lake, this peaceful tree-filled temple pre-dates the city and has a *săh·lah* like no other in Thailand. The ground floor is covered with ingeniously sculpted trees, animals and village scenes of people acting out old Isan proverbs.

One Pillar Pagoda SHRINE
(ศาลเจ้าเสาเดียว; Th Robbung) This replica of Hanoi's iconic temple was built by Khon Kaen's sizeable Vietnamese community. It's a good sunset-watching spot.

ELSEWHERE IN KHON KAEN

Khon Kaen National Museum MUSEUM
(พิพิธภัณฑสถานแห่งชาติขอนแก่น; Th Lang Sunratchakan; admission 100B; ⊙9am-4pm Wed-Sun) This interesting collection of artefacts spans prehistoric times to the present. Highlights are Ban Chiang pottery and a beautiful Dvaravati *săir·mah* (temple boundary marker) depicting Princess Pimpa cleaning Lord Buddha's feet with her hair. The household and agricultural displays shed light on what you'll see out in the countryside.

Wat Tham Uthayan TEMPLE
(วัดธรรมอุทยาน; Th Mittaphap; ⊙daylight hours) This peaceful temple, 10km north of the city, has many beautiful monuments, including a 23m-tall white walking Buddha image, spread across its vast grounds. It has become a well-known meditation centre because rather than teaching a formal method, Luang Po Gluai encourages people to find their own path to inner peace. Take *sŏrng·tăa·ou* 4 (15B) fron Na Muang or Prachasamoson streets.

Art & Culture University Museum MUSEUM
(หอศิลปวัฒนธรรม มหาวิทยาลัยขอนแก่น; admission free; ⊙10am-7pm) The focus of Khon Kaen University's cultural showcase is the two-storey art gallery, which features monthly installations of both student and professional work. The **Educational Museum** (admission free; ⊙8.30am-4.30pm) upstairs and in the

back provides a brief intro to Isan culture, but only if you can read Thai.

🏃 Activities

Two tour companies based in Khon Kaen can show you around town or take you across Isan.

Khon Kaen Education & Travel Programs
TOURS

(☏08 3359 9115; www.tourisaan.com) Aims a little more for leisure travellers. Some trips include quiet-water kayaking on the Nam Phong River near Ubonrat Dam.

Veena Spa
MASSAGE COURSE

(☏08 9711 8331; veenasspa@gmail.com; Soi Supatheera) Teaches Thai massage in English.

🎎 Festivals

The **Silk Fair** and **Phuk Siaw Festival** are held simultaneously over 12 days starting in late November. Centred on the *săh·lah glahng,* the festival celebrates and seeks to preserve the tradition of *pòok sèe·o* (friend bonding), a ritual union of friends during which *fài pòok kăn* (sacred threads) are tied around one's wrists. More than just a symbolic act, the friends gain a standing on par with siblings in each other's families. Other activities include a parade, Isan music and lots of shopping.

🛌 Sleeping

Piman Garden
HOTEL $$

(☏0 4333 4111; Th Glang Meuang; r 850-1250B, ste 1450-1650B; ✳@☎) Set back off the road around an attractive garden, Piman offers serenity and privacy despite its city-centre location. All come with safes and fridges plus most have balconies or porches. Even with the new higher prices, it's still a good choice.

Glacier Hotel
HOTEL $$$

(☏0 4333 4999; www.glacier-hotel.com; Soi Na Muang 25; s incl breakfast 1800-2100B, d incl breakfast 2050-2350B; ✳@☎✳) This trendy boutique hotel, shaped like a giant ice cube and sticking firmly to a white-and-blue colour code, works its 'cool' angle a bit hard, but overall it's lovely and fun. All rooms have individual designs and all the mod cons they should at these prices.

Charoenchit House
HOTEL $

(☏0 4322 7300; www.chousekhonkaen.com; Th Chuanchun; r 400-600B; ✳@☎) Viewed from the outside, you don't expect to find much

to get excited about inside these two stark white towers north of the lake. But at both the basic 400B level and attractively decorated 600B level the rooms have a fair amount of va-va-voom for the price.

KK Centrum
HOTEL $$

(☏08 1574 0507; www.kk-centrum.com; 33/17-18 Soi Supatheera; r incl breakfast 650-850B; ✳☎) What seems like an ordinary small Thai hotel sets itself apart in the details. All rooms have high-quality furnishings and the owner, who lives on site, is serious about service. It's also quiet because it's built in the back of the block.

Saen Samran Hotel
HOTEL $

(☏0 4323 9611; 55-59 Th Glang Meuang; s/d 200/250B; @☎) The city's oldest hotel is also its most charismatic, with the wooden upper floor clinging to its once-upon-a-time glory. The rooms are worn but clean and the owner is a good source of Khon Kaen advice.

Pullman Raja Orchid
HOTEL $$$

(☏0 4332 2155; www.pullmanhotels.com; off Th Prachasumran; r incl breakfast 2725-2950B, ste 3450-5450B; ✳@☎✳) A stunning lobby sets the tone for one of Isan's best hotels. This international-standard Accor-run place in the heart of the city has plenty of razzle-dazzle, including a luxurious spa and gym, a microbrewery and well-equipped rooms. Definitely pay the extra 225B to move up to the Superior level which gets you a recently renovated room and a better view.

Roma Hotel
HOTEL $

(☏0 4333 4444; Th Glang Meuang; r 230-1000B; ✳☎) A simple but effective renovation has cheered up what would otherwise be a depressing old building, making the cheaper rooms good value. Boutique rooms, costing an extra 100B, are more colourful but less tasteful, and at the upper prices you'd be better off staying elsewhere.

Grand Leo Hotel
HOTEL $

(☏0 4332 7745; 62-62/1 Th Sichant; r 350-450B; ✳) This humdrum place, around the corner from Khon Kaen's nightlife district, is functional albeit a little frumpy.

Biggie & Biggoe Place
HOTEL $$

(☏0 4332 2999; Th Robbung; r 650-800B; ✳☎) If you're in Khon Kaen to relax rather than live it up, this hotel at the foot of the lake is a good bet. Rooms are rather bland, but not bad overall.

Khon Kaen

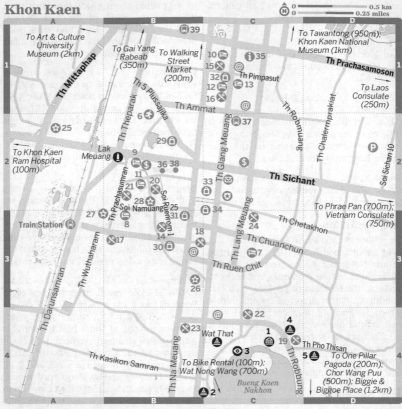

To Art & Culture
University
Museum (2km)

To Gai Yang
Rabeab
(350m)

To Walking
Street
Market
(200m)

To Tawantong (950m);
Khon Kaen National
Museum (1km)

Th Prachasamoson

Th Mittaphap

Th 5 Plussajika

Th Theparak

Th Ammat

Th Pimpasut

To Laos
Consulate
(250m)

To Khon Kaen
Ram Hospital
(100m)

Lak
Meuang

Th Glang Meuang

Th Robmuang

Th Chalermprakiat

Soi Sichan 10

Th Prachasumaran

Th Sichant

Soi Ruenrom

To Phrae Pan (700m);
Vietnam Consulate
(750m)

Th Chetakhon

Soi Namuang

Soi Ruenrom 1

Th Lang Meuang

Th Chuanchun

Train Station

Th Wuthaharam

Th Ruen Chit

Th Darunsamran

Th Na Meuang

Wat That

Th Pho Thisan

Th Kasikon Samran

To Bike Rental (100m);
Wat Nong Wang (700m)

Bueng Kaen
Nakhon

Th Robbung

To One Pillar
Pagoda (200m);
Chor Wang Puu
(500m); Biggie &
Biggoe Place (1.2km)

Eating & Drinking

Khon Kaen has a good **night market** (Th
Reunrom; ☺5pm-midnight) and the easternmost block of the Walking Street Market
(p450) is an awesome noshing destination.
There are also food vendors at Rim Bueng
Kaen Nakhon Market (p446), though people come here for the atmosphere, not the
cuisine. Another good cheap-eats choice is
the stretch of **food stalls** (Th Glang Meuang;
☺lunch & dinner) between Th Ammat and the
Roma Hotel.

TOP CHOICE Turm-Rom   THAI $

(Th Chetakhon; dishes 39-139B; ☺dinner) This
superb place combines one of the best kitchens in town with a quiet, covered garden to
create the perfect place for a night out. The
hòr mòk tá·lair (seafood curry served in a
coconut) is especially good, but in our many
visits we've never had a dud dish.

TOP CHOICE Dee Dee   THAI $

(Soi Khlong Nam; dishes 30-80B; ☺lunch) Though
it looks like just an ordinary food-to-order
shop, Khun Jaang works wonders with a
wok and the food is extraordinary. Try the
bàt mèe pát tim (egg noodles stir-fried with
red curry paste).

Chor Wang Puu   THAI $$

(no roman-script sign; Th Robbung; dishes 80-350B;
☺dinner) With wood-and-thatch dining areas
perched alongside and above a large pond,
the Crab Palace vaguely resembles a fishing
village. Naturally, fish features prominently
on the Thai, Isan and Chinese menu. It's a
beautiful spot at night, and you might even
catch a little sunset view way back behind the
lake.

Slove U   CAFE $

(Th Sri Nual; green-tea latte 40B; ☺lunch & dinner; ☏) Khon Kaen's youthful population
has spawned many good coffee shops and

Khon Kaen

this friendly closet-sized one, attractively cluttered with knick-knacks, is one of our favourites.

Hom Krun　　　　　　　　　　　THAI $
(Th Reunrom; dishes 45-199B; ☺lunch & dinner) Coffee shop by day, bar by night, the chill atmosphere and shady deck make this one of our favourite places in Khon Kaen.

Gai Yang Rabeab　　　　NORTHEASTERN THAI $
(no roman-script sign; Th Theparak; dishes 30-160B; ☺lunch) Most Thais believe Khon Kaen Province makes Thailand's best *gài yâhng* and this simple joint, serving an all-Isan menu, gets the most nods as best of the best in the city since both the owners and the chickens come from Khao Suan Kwang, the most hyped *gài yâhng* town in the province.

Tawantong　　　　　　　　　　　VEGAN $
(Th Lang Sunratchakan; dishes 25-35B; ☺breakfast & lunch; ✍) This large, all-veggie, health-food buffet sits across from the National Muse-

um. The food is so good it also gets many carnivorous diners.

Plapanoy　　　　　　　NORTHEASTERN THAI $
(no roman-script sign; Th Robbung; dishes 30-250B; ☺lunch & dinner) This large alfresco spot near Bueng Kaen Nakhon is where locals bring out-of-town guests to sample genuine Isan food. Fish is the speciality.

Restaurant Didine　　　　　INTERNATIONAL $$
(Th Prachasumran; dishes 45-355B; ☺dinner) Didine's French chef-owner whips up swanky *fa·ràng* food, such as red snapper with saffron, that you wouldn't expect to find in Khon Kaen. His Italian dishes disappoint.

Pomodoro　　　　　　　　　　　ITALIAN $$
(Soi Khlong Nam; dishes 140-320B; ☺dinner; 🔊) The best Italian in town, bar none.

Pavilion Café　　　　　　　INTERNATIONAL $$$
(Th Prachasumran; breakfast/lunch/dinner 400/460/660B; ☺breakfast, lunch & dinner)

The Pullman hotel's principal restaurant features an excellent international buffet. The nearby Kosa Hotel has a similar but smaller set-up for half the price.

First Choice
INTERNATIONAL-THAI $

(Th Pimpasut; dishes 40-250B; ⊘breakfast, lunch & dinner; 🖃🗐) The closest thing Khon Kaen has to a backpacker hostel, First Choice serves the standard guest-house menu of local and *fa·ràng* dishes, the only difference is that the Thai food isn't bad. The no-frills rooms upstairs (150B to 200B) are cheap for good reason.

Tasty Chocolat
CAFE $

(🖃0 08 9572 7997; Th Nikorn Samrann; ⊘lunch & dinner; 🗐) Isan's very own gourmet chocolate shop.

☆ Entertainment

Rad
NIGHTCLUB

(Th Prachasumran) The exuberant anchor of Khon Kaen's downtown nightlife, this is a multifaceted place with live music, DJs, karaoke, 'coyote' dancers and an alfresco restaurant.

U-Bar
NIGHTCLUB

(Soi Khlong Nam) Almost exclusively the domain of Khon Kaen University students, U-Bar is smaller than Rad, but just as loud and crowded.

Central Plaza
CINEMA

(Th Sichant) Khon Kaen's glossiest shopping mall screens movies in English and has a bowling alley.

🛍 Shopping

Khon Kaen is the best place to buy Isan handicrafts.

TOP CHOICE Walking Street Market
MARKET

(Th Na Soon Ratchakan; ⊘6-11pm Sat) In the spirit of Chiang Mai's street markets, hundreds of vendors, many of them students, gather to sell handmade handbags, T-shirts, postcards, picture frames and more; and almost nothing costs more than 150B. Dancers, musicians and other buskers work strategic corners.

Prathammakant
HANDICRAFTS

(Th Reunrom; ⊘9am-7.30pm) By far the largest and best selection of handicrafts in town, including an impressively large choice of silk, this well-known shop makes a perfect one-stop shop.

Phrae Pan
HANDICRAFTS

(131/193 Th Chatapadung) Run by the Handicraft Center for Northeastern Women's Development, this out-of-the-way store (near the Vietnamese consulate) has a superb selection of natural-dyed, handwoven silk and cotton, which is produced in nearby villages.

Souvenir
FOOD

(46/3 Th Glang Meuang; ⊘7am-8pm) Few Thai visitors leave Khon Kaen without stuffing their suitcase full of local foods: *gun chee·ang* (red pork sausages) are especially popular. *Kà·nŏm tùa* (sweets made with peanuts) and *kà·nŏm tan·yá·pêut* (sweets made with seeds) are another local speciality and this business has been making its own for nearly a century. Free samples are available.

Sueb San
HANDICRAFTS

(no roman-script sign; 16 Th Glang Meuang; ⊘8am-6.30pm Mon-Sat) More accessible than Phrae Phan, this store also stocks natural-dyed fabrics, plus some atypical handmade souvenirs.

Rin Thai Silk
HANDICRAFTS

(412 Th Na Meuang) Many locals, especially brides-to-be, looking for top-quality silk shop here.

Talat Bobae & Talat Banglamphu
MARKETS

(Th Glang Meuang) There's little here that could qualify as a souvenir, but these side-by-side markets, home to fresh foods, household goods and secondhand clothes make for good browsing.

International Books, Travel & More
BOOKS

(Soi 4, Th Sichant; ⊘9am-6pm Mon-Sat) For secondhand books.

ℹ Information

Consulates

Laos (🖃0 4324 2857; Th Prachasamoson; ⊘8am-noon & 1-4pm Mon-Fri) Visas take 15 to 30 minutes. Payment is by baht only, and at a poor exchange rate, so it's much cheaper to pay in dollars at the border.

Vietnam (🖃0 4324 2190; www.vietnamconsulate-khonkaen.org/en; 65/6 Th Chatapadung; ⊘9-11.30am & 2-4.30pm Mon-Fri) Apply in the morning and pick up in the afternoon.

Emergency & Medical Services
Khon Kaen Ram Hospital (☎0 4333 3800; Th Sichant) Has a 24-hour emergency room.
Tourist Police (☎0 4322 6195; Th Mittaphap) South of town next to HomePro.

Internet Access
Finding an internet cafe in Khon Kaen isn't too tough. Insomniacs can head to **S-Force** (Th Na Meuang; per hr 17B; ☺24hr).

Money
Khon Kaen's three largest shopping malls, **Central Plaza** (Th Sichant), **TukCom** (Th Sichant) and **Fairy Plaza** (Th Na Meuang) have banks open evening and weekend hours. Central and Fairy have AEON ATMs.

Post
Main post office (Th Glang Meuang; ☺8.30am-4.30pm Mon-Fri, 9am-noon Sat, Sun & holidays) Has a small postal museum.

Tourist Information
Immigration (☎0 4346 5242; Hwy 2; ☺8.30am-noon & 1-4.30pm Mon-Fri) North of town, near the entrance to Khon Kaen University.
Tourism Authority of Thailand (TAT; ☎0 4324 4498; tatkhkn@tat.or.th; Th Prachasamoson; ☺8.30am-4.30pm) Distributes maps of the city and can answer question about the surrounding provinces too.

Travel Agencies
Très Bien Travel (☎0 4332 2155; Pullman Raja Orchid, off Th Prachasumran; ☺8.30am-5.30pm Mon-Fri, to 2pm Sat)

❶ Getting There & Away
Air
THAI (☎0 4322 7701; www.thaiairways.com; Pullman Raja Orchid, off Th Prachasumran; ☺8am-5pm Mon-Fri) operates three daily flights between Bangkok and Khon Kaen (2600B one way).

Several hotels, including the Pullman and Piman Garden send shuttles (70B) to meet flights at Khon Kaen Airport and you don't need to be staying at the hotels to use them.

Bus
Khon Kaen is a busy transport hub and you can ride directly to nearly all cities in Isan and many beyond. A new air-conditioned bus terminal has been built on the ring road south of town, but we're skeptical that it will be operational any time soon. For now the **ordinary bus terminal** (☎0 4333 3388; Th Prachasamoson) and the **air-conditioned bus terminal** (☎0 4023 9910; Th Glang Meuang) are central and convenient. The air-con terminal should be called the '1st-class and VIP bus terminal', since 2nd-class air-con (and some 1st-class) buses use the ordinary terminal. The best VIP service to Bangkok (512B) is with **Nakhonchai Air** (☎0 2936 0009), departing at 11.15am, 11.15pm and 11.20pm, and **999 VIP** (☎0 4323 7300) at 11pm. You must already have a Lao visa to buy a ticket to Vientiane (180B, four hours, 7.45am and 3.15pm) at the air-con terminal.

BUSES FROM THE ORDINARY BUS TERMINAL

DESTINATION	COST (B)	DURATION (HR)
Chaiyaphum	58-81	2½
Khorat	118	3
Loei	129	3½
Mukdahan	155	4½
Nakhon Phanom	221	5
Nong Khai	110	3½
Phitsanulok	202-223	6
Roi Et	73-94	2½
Udon Thani	76	2

BUSES FROM THE AIR-CONDITIONED BUS TERMINAL

DESTINATION	COST (B)	DURATION (HR)
Bangkok	329-512	6-7
Chiang Mai	437-504	12
Khorat	118-230	3
Nakhon Phanom	221	5
Mukdahan	187	4
Nong Khai	139	3½
Phitsanulok	290	6
Suvarnabhumi (Airport) bus station	335	6½
Ubon Ratchathani	216-252	4½
Udon Thani	101	2

Train
There is one morning and two early-evening express trains between Bangkok (2nd-class air-con 399B, 1st-class sleeper upper/lower 968/1168B, eight hours) and **Khon Kaen Railway Station** (☎0 4322 1112). There's also a cheaper evening rapid train. Four trains to Udon Thani (3rd-class 25B, 2nd-class air-con 117B, 1½ to two hours) leave in the afternoon and early morning; only the morning trains continue to Nong Khai.

❶ Getting Around

Sŏrng·tăa·ou (9B) ply regular routes across the city. Some of the handiest (all of which pass the air-con terminal on Th Glang Meung) are line 8, which goes to Wat Nong Wang and also northwest through the university; line 10, which passes in front of the Lao and near the Vietnamese consulates (the latter is 150m north of the stoplight east of Khon Kaen Hospital); line 11, which passes the train station; and line 21 (orange), which goes out to the National Museum.

For individual rides, túk-túk are the most expensive way to get around (expect 40B to 60B for a short trip in town), but they're the method most people use because it's rare to find **metered taxis** (☎ 0 4346 5777, 0 4334 2800; 30B flagfall, 20B call fee) on the street and when you call for one you usually have to wait a long time. About the only place you're likely to find a taxis or motorcycle taxis (within town 20-30B) parked is at the bus stations and Central Plaza shopping mall.

There are many car-hire outlets around Tuk-Com mall; **Narujee** (☎ 0 4322 4220; Soi Kosa), which charges from 1200B for a car with driver, is a reliable choice.

Around Khon Kaen

CHONNABOT   ชนบท

This small town located 55km southwest of Khon Kaen is one of Thailand's most successful silk villages and is famous for producing top-quality *mát·mèe*. The **Sala Mai Thai** (no Roman-script sign; ☎ 0 4328 6160; admission free; ◷ 9am-5pm Thu-Tue) is a silk-weaving museum on the campus of Khon Kaen Industrial & Community Education College where you can learn about the entire silk-making process, and even take a turn at a loom. Out back is an exhibition hall showing the wooden contraptions devised to spin, tie, dye and weave silk by hand in the village and a large machine used in factories. A room upstairs cata-logues traditional *mát·mèe* patterns and a pair of mock-Isan houses hold various traditional household items. It's on the highway 1km west of town.

The pavilion sells silk too, but most people buy from the myriad shops on Th Sriboonruang, aka **Silk Road**, some of which also stock attractive cotton fabrics made in the nearby village of Ban Lawaan. If you get away from the centre of town, particularly to the north near the temple and school, you'll often see women working looms under their houses and they rarely mind if you stop by to take a look.

Buses bound for Nakhon Sawan, departing from Khon Kaen's ordinary bus terminal, will drop you in Chonnabot (39B, one hour, six daily). Or take a bus (30B to 40B, one hour, every half-hour) or train (9B, 30 minutes) to Ban Phai, where you can get a bus to Chonnabot (15B, 20 minutes, every hour).

PRASAT PUAY NOI   ปราสาทเปือยน้อย

The 12th-century **Prasat Puay Noi** (admission free; ◷ daylight hours) is the largest and most interesting Khmer ruin in northern Isan, though it can't compete with even some of the not-so-famous ruins further south. About the size of Buriram's Prasat Muang Tam, but less grand, the east-facing monument comprises a large central sandstone sanctuary surmounted by three partially collapsed *prang* and surrounded by laterite walls. There are still some excellent carvings intact, including Shiva riding his bull Nandi), on the pediment on the back of the 'library' and some almost lifelike *naga* on the corner of the main gate.

By public transport from Khon Kaen, catch a bus (30B to 40B, every half-hour) or train (9B, 30 minutes, 7.55am or 8.39am) to Ban Phai, then a *sŏrng·tăa·ou* to Puay Noi (35B, one hour). The last *sŏrng·tăa·ou* back to Ban Phai leaves at 2pm. If you have your own wheels, head 40km south from Khon Kaen on Hwy 2 to Ban Phai, then east on Hwy 23 (signposted to Borabu) for 11km to Rte 2301. Follow it and Rte 2297 for 24km southeast through the rural countryside to Ban Puay Noi.

PHU WIANG NATIONAL PARK   อุทยานแห่งชาติภูเวียง

Uranium miners discovered a giant patella bone in this region in 1976 and the palaeontologists who were called to investigate then unearthed a fossilised 15m-long herbivore

---

THE ORCHID PARK

If you're visiting Chonnabot between late December and early February (exact dates depend on the weather), take time for a detour to **Wat Pa Mancha Khiri** (◷ daylight hours), 11km to the west. During this time thousands of foxtail (aka Chang Kra) orchids fill the temple grounds. The local TAT office (p451) will know the exact dates.

MÁT·MÈE

Thanks to growing interest from both Thais and foreigners, the once-fading Isan tradition of *mát·mèe* has undergone a major revival and is now one of Thailand's best-known weaving styles. Similar to Indonesian *ikat*, *mát·mèe* is a tie-dye process (*mát* is 'tie' and *mèe* is 'strands') that results in a geometric pattern repeatedly turning back on itself as it runs up the fabric.

To start, the weavers string their thread (either silk or cotton) tightly across a wooden frame sized exactly as wide as the finished fabric will be. Almost always working from memory, the weavers then tie plastic (traditionally the skin of banana plant stalks was used) around bunches of strands in their desired design. The frame is then dipped in the dye (nowadays usually a chemical colour, though natural sources such as flowers and tree bark are regaining popularity), which grips the exposed thread but leaves the wrapped sections clean. The wrapping and dipping continues for multiple rounds resulting in intricate, complex patterns that come to life on the loom. The more you see of the process, the more you understand how amazing it is that the finished product turns out so beautifully.

Most of the patterns, handed down from mother to daughter, are abstract representations of natural objects such as trees and birds, but increasingly designers are working with weaving groups to create modern patterns, which invariably fetch higher prices.

later named *Phuwianggosaurus sirindhornae* after Princess Sirindhorn. Dinosaur fever followed (explaining the epidemic of model dinosaurs in Khon Kaen), more remains were uncovered and **Phu Wiang National Park** (☎0 4335 8073; admission 200B) was born.

Enclosed **excavation sites** (⊙8.30am-4.30pm), including one with a partial skeleton of *Siamotyrannus isanensis,* an early ancestor of *Tyrannosaurus rex,* can be easily reached by trails from the visitor centre or nearby parking areas. Those who want to explore further (best done by 4WD or mountain bike) will find dinosaur footprints, waterfalls and a superb viewpoint.

Phu Wiang Museum (☎0 4343 8204; ⊙9am-5pm Tue-Sun; admission free), 5km before the park, has palaeontology and geology displays, including full-size models of the dinosaur species that once lived in the area. Kids will love it. They'll also go ape over the giant photogenic dinosaur statues in nearby **Si Wiang Dinosaur Park**. Wiang Kao, the district inside the horseshoe-shaped mountains that comprise the park, is a fruit-growing area and a great place to explore by car, if you want to look at traditional village life.

The park has one 12-person **bungalow** (☎0 2562 0760; www.dnp.go.th/parkreserve; bungalows 1200B) and a **campsite** (per person with own tent 30B, 4-/6-person tent hire 400/600B). Simple food is available during the day only.

The park entrance is 90km west of Khon Kaen. Buses from Khon Kaen's ordinary bus terminal go to Phu Wiang town (40B to 50B, 1½ hours, every half-hour) where you can hire a túk-túk (400B return) or motorbike taxi (200B) for the remaining 19km to the park entrance. If you only pay for a one-way trip, you'll risk not being able to get a ride back.

NAM NAO NATIONAL PARK
อุทยานแห่งชาติน้ำหนาว

One of Thailand's most valuable nature preserves, **Nam Nao National Park** (☎0 5681 0724; admission 200B) covers nearly 1000 sq km across the Phetchabun Mountains of Chaiyaphum and Phetchabun Provinces, just beyond Khon Kaen Province. Although it covers remote territory (this remained a People's Liberation Army of Thailand stronghold until the early 1980s), Hwy 12 makes access easy.

With an average elevation of 800m, temperatures are fairly cool year-round (*ám nŏw* means 'the water feels cold') and frost occasionally occurs in December and January. Three rivers are sourced here, the Chi, Saphung and Phrom, and there are both evergreen and deciduous forest mixed with some vast bamboo groves.

The 1560-sq-km **Phu Khiaw Wildlife Sanctuary** lies adjacent to the park, so wildlife is particularly abundant; however, the animals here are more timid than at nearby Phu Kradueng National Park and so are spotted less often. Lucky visitors might spot elephants, Malayan sun bears, banteng (wild cattle), Asian jackals, barking deer, gibbons, pangolins and flying squirrels. There are even a few tigers. More than 200 species of bird, including parrots and hornbills, fly through the forest.

A fair system of hiking trails branches out from the visitor centre to several scenic overlooks. Haewsai Waterfall is 17km east of the visitor centre, while the best sunrise/morning fog (5km) and sunset (11km) viewpoints lie to the west.

There are campsites (per person with own tent 30B, 2–6-person tent hire 100-300B), a variety of bungalows (☎0 2562 0760; www.dnp. go.th/parkreserve; bungalows 4-12 people 1000-4000B) and some simple restaurants next to the visitor centre.

Hourly buses between Khon Kaen (115B, 2½ hours) and Phitsanulok travel through the park. The visitor centre is 1.5km from the highway.

BAN KHOK SA-NGA COBRA VILLAGE
หมู่บ้านงูจงอางบ้านโคกสง่า

The self-styled 'King Cobra Village' of Ban Khok Sa-Nga has a thing about snakes. Locals rear hundreds of the reptiles, and most families have some in boxes under their houses.

The custom began in 1951 when a travelling medicinal herb salesman, Ken Yongla, began putting on snake shows to attract customers. His plan was a success, and the art of breeding and training snakes has been nurtured in this village ever since. Today the King Cobra Club of Thailand puts on snake shows (donations expected; ◷8.30am-5pm) where handlers taunt snakes and tempt fate; they often lose, as the many missing fingers show. Medicinal herbs are still sold in the village.

The village is located 50km northeast of Khon Kaen via Hwy 2 and Rte 2039. Take a Kranuan bus from Khon Kaen's ordinary bus terminal to the turn-off for Ban Khok Sa-Nga (30B, one hour, every half-hour) and then take a túk-túk (20B per person) to the showgrounds.

If you're driving from Khon Kaen, consider taking the rural route that takes you past Phra That Kham Kaen (Tamarind Heartwood Reliquary), a revered *chedi* in the village of Ban Kham.

UDON THANI PROVINCE

Udon Thani
อุดรธานี

POP 227,200

Udon Thani has one foot on the highway and the other off the beaten track. The city boomed on the back of the Vietnam War as US air bases were established nearby and it subsequently became the region's primary transport hub and commercial centre. Today you have to dig deep behind its prosperous concrete veneer to find any flashes of its past. Udon sees relatively few foreign travellers, its main selling point being the abundance of Western foods and facilities preventing Isan's largest expat community from getting too homesick.

⊙ Sights

Udorn Sunshine Nursery
GARDEN
(สวนกล้วยไม้หอมอุดรซันไชน์; 127 Th Udorn-Nong Samrong; ◷8am-5pm) Ever seen a plant dance? Well, you can here. Originally earning notoriety for producing the first perfume made from an orchid, the Udon Sunshine Nursery, just northwest of town, has since developed a hybrid of *Codariocalyx motorius ohashi leguminosae* that 'dances' to music. The mature gyrant has long oval leaves, plus smaller ones of a similar shape. If you sing or talk to the plant in a high-pitched voice (saxophone or violin works even better), a few of the smaller leaves will shift back and forth. It's no hype; we've seen it ourselves, although it's much more of a waltz than a jig. The plants are most active from November to February, the cool season, and from 7am to 9.30am and 4.30pm to 6.30pm.

The plants aren't for sale. You can, however, buy Udorn Dancing Tea, made from the plant, along with the more famous Miss Udorn Sunshine orchids and perfumes. The nursery's newest product is Udorn Toob Moob Maeng Kaeng, a perfume derived from brown stink bugs.

To get here, go under the Ban Nongsamrong sign on Rte 2024, then after 150m follow the Udorn Sunshine Fragrant Orchid sign. *Sǒrng·tǎa·ou* 16 (catch it on Th Prajak in front of Central Plaza) brings you the closest, but route 6 and the 'yellow bus' get you nearby. A túk-túk from Udon's city centre should cost about 80B.

FREE **Udon Thani Provincial Museum** MUSEUM
(พิพิธภัณฑ์เมืองอุดรธานี; Th Phosri; ⊙8.30am-4.30pm Mon-Fri, 8am-4pm Sat & Sun) Filling a 1920s colonial-style building that used to be a girls' school, this museum has an interesting catch-all collection ranging from geology to handicrafts.

Nong Prajak Park PARK
(หนองประจักษ์) Udon's most popular park starts to rev up as the afternoon winds down, and there's a lot to do here, from feeding the fish to riding a bike. A bike-hire outlet on the northeast shore has one-, two- and three-seaters for 20/40/50B per hour. Much of the action takes place on the sunset-watching side of the lake, along Th Thesa. Dozens of streetside massage artists start doing rubdowns around 2pm and paint-your-own pottery shops open two hours later. Restaurants serve all day.

Sanjao Pu-Ya TEMPLE
(ศาลเจ้าปู่ย่า; Th Nittayo; ⊙daylight hours) This large, brash Chinese temple on the southern shore of Nong Bua attests to the wealth of the local Thai-Chinese merchant class. At its heart, the **Pu-Ya Shrine** houses small images of the Chinese gods Pu (Grandpa) and Ya (Grandma).

FREE **Ho Chi Minh Educational & Tourism Historical Site** MUSEUM
(แหล่งศึกษาและท่องเที่ยวเชิงประวัติศาสตร์ (โฮจิมินห์); ☎08 7437 7852; ⊙8am-5pm) During 1928 and 1929, Ho Chi Mihn used the jungle around Hong Hang village as one of his bases to train soldiers and rally Isan's sizeable Vietnamese community for his resistance against the French occupation of Vietnam. The proud local Vietnamese community have recently built a replica of his thatched-roof, mud-wall house and a big museum. Both buildings were largely empty when we visited, though we were told displays would be coming soon. Check with the tourism office to see if they have. *Bâhn lung hoh* (Uncle Ho's House), as locals call it, is 10km from Udon. Take *sǒrng·tǎa·ou* 14 (13B, 20 minutes) running south along Mukkamontri street to the junction and then follow the signs for 750m.

Festivals & Events
For the first 15 days of December, Udon celebrates the **Thung Si Meuang Fair**, with Isan cultural performances and all the usual

shopping and eating. The Pu and Ya statues from Sanjao Pu-Ya spend the first 10 days in a temporary temple in City Field. The transfers on the 1st and 10th are grand processions accompanied by a 99m dragon; there's also dragon dancing on the 5th.

Sleeping

TOP CHOICE **Much-che Manta** HOTEL $$
(☎0 4224 5222; www.much-chemanta.com; 209-211 Th Makkang; r incl breakfast 850-1500B, ste 5000B; ✴@☎☀) A lovely boutique hotel that, for our money, tops the better-known Prajaktra, with which it's inevitably compared. Creative lighting, liberal use of real wood and random splashes of colour craft a unique design while the lovely backyard restaurant features wood-fire pizzas as part of an international menu.

P & Mo Guesthouse GUEST HOUSE $
(☎08 4031 8337; arnudechbks@yahoo.co.th; 39 Th Rung Sun; r 300-400B; ✴@☎) Rooms are simple, but this friendly place gives the biggest bang for your baht in Udon. Despite fronting the bus station, it's relatively quiet.

Udon Backpackers GUEST HOUSE $
(☎08 9620 8684; www.udonbackpacker.com; 299/5 Soi Fairach 1; per person 170B; ☎) Nothing fancy here, just simple, clean rooms (cold-water showers in most) but they're *far* better than anything else in this price range. And a friendly welcome from owner Sammie is included.

City Lodge HOTEL $
(☎0 4222 4439; 83/14-15 Th Wattananuwong; r 500-600B; ✴@☎) The already colourful rooms at this British-owned property are cheered up even more with wicker furniture.

Centara HOTEL $$$
(☎0 4234 3555; www.centarahotelsresorts.com; Th Teekathanont; r/ste from 2000/5000B; ✴@☎☀) Long Udon's flagship hotel, the former Charoensri Grand has undergone a six-month renovation to keep it atop the pack. Rooms are a little small, but otherwise excellent and the full range of facilities (including a sauna, spa and fitness centre) are top-notch.

Top Mansion HOTEL $
(☎0 4234 5015; topmansion@yahoo.com; 35/3 Th Sampanthamit; r 370B; ✴@☎) This impressively spick-and-span hotel warrants consideration despite being on 'Soi Falang'.

Lotus Condotel HOTEL $
(☎0 4234 07777; 43/4 Th Thepburi; r 279-329B; ✴☎) It looks like a grain silo on the

Udon Thani

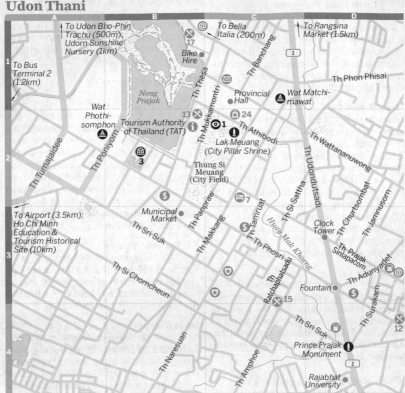

outside and feels like a hospital in the hallways; but the rooms are what matters most, and these are big, clean and priced right. But, the best feature is the neighbourhood full of university students.

✗ Eating

Udonites take their **night markets** (Th Prajak; ☺4-11pm) very seriously. The three adjoining markets in front of the train station (Centre Point, Precha and UD Bazaar) offer an impressive spread of food and a large beer garden.

Rabiang Phatchanee   THAI $
(Th Suppakitchanya; dishes 50-250B; ☺lunch & dinner) This place on the lake's east shore offers all the usual Thai dishes, but also many you've probably never tried before, such as fish-stomach salad. Eat on the shady deck or in air-conditioned dining rooms.

Bella Italia   INTERNATIONAL, THAI $$
(70/4 Th Suppakitchanya; dishes 60-600B; ☺dinner; ☏) This Italian-owned restaurant at Nong Prajak lake is as close to Italy you'll get in Isan, but the menu goes global with choices such as green curry or salmon in salsa.

Maeya   THAI $
(no Roman-script sign; 79 Th Ratchaphatsadu; dishes 45-270B; ☺lunch & dinner) One part Thai restaurant and three parts English tearoom, this labyrinth has waiters dressed in black tie and a menu stretching from ham sandwiches to wild boar in red-curry sauce. The English menu is a little cryptic: the 'rice with spit in sauce' is really 'rice with liver in sauce'.

Zirocco   THAI $$
(38/2 Th Adunyadet; dishes 59-259B; ☺dinner) This open-air Thai-style pub is the kind of place where groups of friends come to eat, drink and eat some more. If you're looking

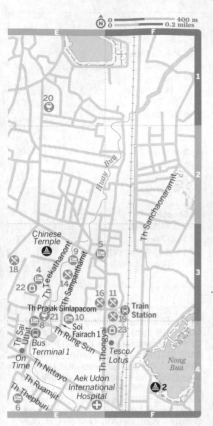

Drinking & Entertainment

The night markets offer a range of diversions. Besides dining you can shop for clothes, sing karaoke, play snooker, get a tattoo and have your fortune told. On some weekends you can watch football games on the big screen or listen to live bands.

Central Plaza (p457) screens some movies in their original English and also has a bowling alley.

Udon has the largest and most in-your-face sex tourism scene in Isan and the 'Soi Falang' (Th Sampanthamit) area is rather sleazy at night. That said, most of the people out for a night in the bars here aren't looking for extracurricular activities.

The **Bookhouse & Coffee Shop** (Soi 8, Th Adunyadet; ☺9am-9pm) is Udon's best bookstore, and one of the best in Isan. **Fuzzy Ken's** (302/10 Th Prajak; ☺10am-11pm Mon-Sat) has a smaller selection, but better location. Both shops feature food and drink and are *fa·ràng* gathering spots.

Shopping

Udon Bho-Phin Trachu   HANDICRAFTS
(no roman-script sign; Th Poniyom; ☺7am-6.30pm) There's a great selection of silk and cotton, including some natural-dyed fabrics, at this large spot northwest of Nong Prajak Lake. Look for the sign with the wooden roof.

Udon City Walking Street   MARKET
(Th Athibodi; ☺5-10pm Fri & Sat) With just a handful of vendors selling handmade items, Udon's Walking Street pales in comparison to the markets in Chiang Mai and Khon Kaen that inspired it. Still, it's got a fun, youthful atmosphere.

Central Plaza (Th Prajak; ☺11am-9pm Mon-Fri, 10am-9pm Sat & Sun) is Udon's biggest shopping mall, though strolling the open-air **UD Town** (Th Thongyai; ☺11am-10pm) is more fun.

Information

Emergency Services
Aek Udon International Hospital (☎0 4234 2555; 555/5 Th Phosri) Has a 24-hour casualty department.
Tourist Police (☎0 4221 1291; Th Naresuan)

Money
Central Plaza (Th Prajak) and **Tesco/Lotus** (UD Town) have banks that stay open late and on weekends. The latter also has an AEON ATM.

---

for a mellow night with first-rate food and a little class, Zirocco will satisfy. There's no English on the menu, but some staff can speak a little.

Gib Shop   JUICE BAR **$**
(Th Thesa; from 15B; ☺breakfast, lunch & dinner) Not all juice is created equal, and this lakeside stand proves it. Most of the fruits and veggies are organic and you can choose to have no added sugar.

Irish Clock   INTERNATIONAL **$$**
(19/5-6 Th Sampanthamit; dishes 50-420B; ☺breakfast, lunch & dinner; ☏) This wood-trimmed, Guinness-infused pub is an island of class in a sea of pick-up joints. The menu has Thai, *fa·ràng* and Indian food.

Chai Dun   THAI **$**
(no roman-script sign; 539/14 Th Phosri; buffet 60B; ☺lunch & dinner) The crowds are exhibit A for how tasty (and cheap) this all-you-can-eat buffet is.

Udon Thani

⦿ Sights
1	Pu-Ya Shrine during Thung Si Meuang Fair	C2
2	Sanjao Pu-Ya	F4
3	Udon Thani Provincial Museum	B2

⊜ Sleeping
4	Centara	E3
5	City Lodge	E3
6	Lotus Condotel	E4
7	Much-che Manta	C2
8	P & Mo Guesthouse	E4
9	Top Mansion	E3
10	Udon Backpackers	E3

⊗ Eating
11	Centre Point Night Market	F3
12	Chai Dun	D4
13	Gib Shop	B2
14	Irish Clock	E3
15	Maeya	C3
16	Precha Night Market	E3
17	Rabiang Phatchanee	B1
18	The Zirocco	E3
19	UD Bazar Night Market	F3

⦿ Drinking
20	Bookhouse & Coffee Shop	E1
21	Fuzzy Ken's	E3

⊜ Shopping
22	Central Plaza	E3
23	UD Town	F4
24	Udon City Walking Street	C2

Post

Post office (Th Wattananuwong; ⊗8.30am-4.30pm Mon-Fri, 9am-noon Sat, Sun & holidays)

Tourist Information

Tourism Authority of Thailand (TAT; ☑0 4232 5406; tatudon@tat.or.th; Th Thesa; ⊗8.30am-4.30pm) Covers Udon Thani, Nong Khai and Bueng Kan Provinces.

Udon Thani Map (www.udonmap.com) This map and its companion magazine the *Udon Thani Guide* are excellent sources of information, available free at *fa·ràng*-focused businesses.

❶ Getting There & Away

Air

THAI (☑0 2288 7000; www.thaiairways.com) and **Air Asia** (☑0 2515 9999; www.airasia.com) connect Udon Thani to Suvarnaphumi Airport in Bangkok while **Nok Air** (☑0 2900 9955; www.nokair.com) uses Don Muang airport. Regular promotional fares by the latter two keep prices around 1500B. Air Asia also has a daily direct flight to Phuket (1600B) and Nok Air goes daily direct to Chiang Mai (2500B).

Buy tickets at **On Time** (☑0 4224 7792; 539/72 Th Sai Uthit; ⊗8am-5pm Mon-Sat, to 2pm Sun), one of several travel agencies in this area.

Bus

For most destinations, including Bangkok (321B to 412B, eight to nine hours, every half-hour), buses use the downtown **Bus Terminal 1** (☑0 4222 2916; Th Sai Uthit). **Chan Tour** (☑0 4234 3403; 550B; 8 daily) and **999 VIP** (☑0 4222 1489; 641B; 9pm) have VIP service to Bangkok. Other destinations include Khorat (181B to 248B, 4½ hours, every half-hour), Sakon Nakhon (100B to 130B, 3½ hours, every half-hour), Khon Kaen (76B to 101B, two hours, every half-hour), Bueng Kan (150B, 4½ hours, 12 daily), Pattaya (365B to 585B, 11 hours, 10 daily), Suvarnabhumi (Airport) bus station (418B, eight hours, 9pm) and Vientiane (80B, two hours, six daily; you must already have a Lao visa).

Bus Terminal 2 (☑0 4221 4914), on the ring road west of the city, serves many of the same destinations plus it's the only station for western destinations such as Loei (66B to 92B, three hours, every half-hour), Phitsanulok (212B to 275B, seven hours, nine daily) and Chiang Mai (409B to 613B, 12 hours, six daily).

There are buses to Nong Khai (35B to 47B, one hour) from both terminals, but the most frequent departures are from Rangsina Market. Buses arriving from other cities sometimes drop passengers here after stopping at Bus Terminal 1.

Train

Two express trains from Bangkok (2nd-class air-con 479B, 1st-class sleeper upper/lower 1077/1277B; 10 to 11 hours) depart in the afternoon for **Udon Thani Railway Station** (☑0 4222 2061), and there's also one in the morning. Three morning trains head to Nong Khai (3rd-class 11B, 2nd-class fan/air-con 55/85B, about one hour).

ℹ Getting Around

Sŏrng·tăa·ou (10B) run regular routes across town. Route 6 (white) is handy since it runs along Th Udondutsadi past Rangsina Market and out to Bus Terminal 2. There are also two city buses (10B). The White bus follows Th Udondutsadi while the Yellow tracks Th Phosri-Nittayo, connecting the two bus terminals in the process. *The Udon Thani Map* shows all bus and *sŏrng·tăa·ou* routes.

You can rarely flag a **metered taxi** (☑0 4234 3239; 30B flagfall, 30B call fee) down on the street, but they park at Bus Terminal 1. Túk-túk (called 'skylab' here), on the other hand, are seemingly everywhere. The cost from Central Plaza to Nong Prajak Park is usually 80B. Cheaper pedicabs are also still common in Udon.

Many hotels pick guests up at the airport for free, otherwise vans to downtown cost 100B per person. There are many car-hire outlets around Central Plaza, including **Fuzzy Ken's** (☑08 6011 4627; 302/10 Th Prajak).

Around Udon Thani

BAN CHIANG   บ้านเชียง

This was once an important centre of the ancient Ban Chiang civilisation, an agricultural society that thrived in northeastern Thailand for thousands of years. Archaeological digs here have uncovered a treasure trove of artefacts dating back to 3600 BC that overturned the prevailing theory that Southeast Asia was a cultural backwater compared to China and India at the time.

What's now one of Southeast Asia's most important archaeological sites was discovered quite accidentally in 1966. Stephen Young, a student from Harvard, tripped while walking through the area and found the rim of a buried pot right under his nose. Looking around he noticed many more and speculated that this might be a burial site. He was right. Serious excavations began soon after and over a million pottery pieces and dozens of human skeletons were unearthed. The now iconic burnt-ochre swirl-design pottery (made between 300 BC and AD 200) is just one of many styles these people created over the years. Researchers also found the earliest evidence of the manufacture of metal tools – they began working bronze around 2000 BC – in the region. The area was declared a Unesco World Heritage Site in 1992.

◉ Sights

With a lack of hills and traffic, but an abundance of quaint farms and villages, the countryside around Ban Chiang is a great place to explore by bike. Lakeside Sunrise Guesthouse provides an outdated, but still helpful map.

Ban Chiang National Museum   MUSEUM
(admission 150B; ⊙8.30am-4.30pm Tue-Sun) This excellent museum exhibits a wealth of pottery from all Ban Chiang periods, plus myriad metal objects, including spearheads, sickles, fish hooks, ladles and neck rings. The displays (with English labels) offer excellent insight into the region's distant past and how its mysteries were unravelled. Hidden in back is a room showcasing the culture of the Tai Phuan people, who migrated here about 200 years ago and founded the town. One kilometre east at Wat Pho Si Nai is an original **burial ground excavation pit** (⊙8.30am-6pm), with a cluster of 52 individual burial sites dating to 300 BC. It shows how bodies were laid to rest with (infants placed inside) pottery.

Phuan Thai House   LANDMARK
About 300m southwest of the burial site (follow the signs for 'Phuan House which the King and Queen visited in 1972'), this traditional Isan house is also promoted as an attraction, but the still-lived-in houses throughout the village are more interesting.

Wat Pa Lelai   TEMPLE
(⊙daylight hours) For something completely different, visit this wát 500m north of the burial site, across the little bridge. The awesome childlike murals in the two-story building at the back are both enlightening and entertaining.

CRAFTS

Rice cultivation remains the town's primary livelihood, but selling souvenirs comes a close second. Some of the items, including Ban Chiang-style pottery, are made in the area. Walk down the road facing the museum to find a couple of touristy **pottery workshops**. One street west of the museum is a large and interesting **women's weaving group** that makes, among other things, *mát·mèe* and indigo cotton. The women's group also usually has some sticky-rice basket weavers around, though most of these are woven in the village of **Ban Dong Yen** east of Ban Chiang. To see pottery made using the ancient paddle-and-anvil method, visit **Ban Kham Or**. It's a convenient stop on your way out of town since it's right on the highway. Túk-túk cost the same as coming to

Ban Chiang from Ban Nong Mek. Visiting on your way into town isn't recommended because you'll likely wait a long time to find a lift to Ban Chiang.

🛏 Sleeping & Eating

Lakeside Sunrise Guesthouse GUEST HOUSE **$**
(📞0 4220 8167; banmai167@hotmail.com; r 250B; @) In a countryside setting yet within easy striking distance of the museum, this old wooden house is reason enough to spend the night in town. The simple rooms share a spacious verandah and bathrooms downstairs. The joyful owner speaks good English and hires out bikes (50B per day) and motorcycles (250B per day).

There are several restaurants on the road fronting the museum, one of which stays open for dinner.

❶ Getting There & Away

From Udon Thani, take a bus bound for Sakon Nakhon or Nakhon Phanom and get off at Ban Nong Mek (40B, 45 minutes), where a túk-túk will charge 60B per person for the 8km ride to Ban Chiang.

KUMPHAWAPI   กุมภวาปี

Like a little Lopburi, this otherwise ordinary town 50km southeast of Udon has a troop of monkeys living alongside its human residents. They live in the city-centre park but frequently wander beyond it to climb and lounge on buildings. After you've had enough monkey time, stroll east to Nong Han lake, which is full of lotuses and fishing rafts.

Buses to Wangsammo from Udon's Bus Terminal 1 stop in Kumphawapi (22B to 31B, one hour, every 45 minutes).

BAN NA KHA   บ้านนาข่า

Once a renowned centre for for its *kít*-patterned cotton weaving (*kít* is a diamond-grid minimal-weft brocade), Na Kha village is now one of the best fabric shopping destinations in Thailand. Downtown is a covered market with dozens of shops selling a great variety of silk and cotton from Thailand and Laos. Except at the large shops on the highway, most of the fabrics are handmade. **Maa Bah Pah Fai** (⊙6.30am-6pm), across from the temple entrance, has as good a selection as any, including some century-old *kít*.

Before leaving, take a peek at **Wat Na Ka Taewee** (⊙daylight hours), founded by a wandering monk who found a hole from which bellowed the sound and smoke of a *naga*. He plugged the hole with a rock and built the small *bòht* right in front of it. Pottery,

gold Buddha images and human skeletons unearthed during various construction projects at the temple are on display.

Udon's White Bus runs to the village, 16km north of Udon.

PHU PHRABAT HISTORICAL PARK   อุทยานประวัติศาสตร์ภูพระบาท

Steeped in mythical intrigue and peppered with bizarre rock formations, **Phu Phrabat** (📞0 4225 1350; admission 100B; ⊙8am-4.30pm) is one of Isan's highlights. Sometime around the turn of the millennium, during the Dvaravati era, local people built Hindu and Buddhist shrines alongside the many spires, whale-sized boulders and improbably balanced rocks here. But prehistoric paintings on several rock overhangs, best seen at side-by-side **Tham Woau** and **Thom Khon**, show this was probably regarded as a holy site at least 1500 years earlier. A climb beyond these rock formations to **Pha Sa Dej**, at the edge of the escarpment, ends with dramatic views of the farms and forest beyond. A web of trails meanders past all these sites and you can see them in a leisurely two hours, but it's worth spending several more. A remoter northern loop is lovely, but not well marked so it's easy to get lost.

Many of the rock formations feature in a fairy tale about a king (Phaya Kong Phan), his stunningly beautiful daughter (Nang U-sa), a hermit (Ruesi Chanta) and a love-struck prince (Tao Baros) from another kingdom. The most striking rock formation, **Hor Nang U-sa**, an overturned boot-shaped outcrop with a shrine built into it, is said to be the tower where the beautiful princess was forced to live by her overprotective father. Many of these rock formations are signposted with names in Thai and English alluding to the legend, a short version of which can be read in the museum. If you're staying at the Mut Mee Garden Guesthouse in Nong Khai (p465), you can read the entire tale.

Near the entrance is **Wat Phra Phutthabaht Bua Bok**, with its namesake Lao-style *chedi* covering a Buddha footprint. It also has some odd temple buildings in the general mood of those in the park.

There are **campsites** (per tent with own tent 20B, 2-/8-person tent hire 50B/200B) and three lovely **bungalows** (2/4/6 people 300/600/1000B) with rock-hard mattresses.

❶ Getting There & Away

The park is 65km from Udon Thani and Nong Khai, near Ban Pheu, and can be visited as a day trip from either city. *Sŏrng·tăa·ou* from Nong Khai's bus station to Ban Pheu (50B, 1½ hours) travel via Tha Bo. Vehicles from Udon's Rangsina Market continue past Ban Pheu to Ban Tiu (37B, one hour), the village at the base of the hill where a motorcycle taxi costs 50B for the final 5km climb. If you're in a hurry, túk-túk from Ban Pheu cost 200B to 300B (round trip) and motorcycle taxis are half that – some people will tell you there are no motorcycle taxis in Ban Pheu, but there are a few.

If you're using public transport, you should leave the park by 3pm for Nong Khai and 4pm for Udon.

WAT PHO CHAI SRI   วัดโพธิ์ชัยศรี

With brightly painted statuary that's even more bizarre than Nong Khai's Sala Kaew Ku, this **wát** (☺daylight hours) is a perfect add-on to Phu Phrabat and even worth a trip on its own. The life-size figures around the temple grounds are acting out scenes from Isan culture and fairy tales and demonstrating the punishment awaiting the wicked in the Buddhist version of Hell.

The temple is also home to **Luang Po Naak**, a very holy 1200-year-old Buddha image shaded by a seven-headed *naga* that locals believe is responsible for many miracles.

Also known as Wat Ban Waeng, the temple is about 5km out of Ban Pheu. A túk-túk should cost no more than 100B round trip with waiting time.

NONG KHAI PROVINCE

Lady Luck certainly smiles on the location. Occupying a narrow sweep along the banks of the Mekong, Nong Khai Province is a beautiful, intriguing region. Being on the travel route to/from Vientiane, Laos, just a short hop across the river via the Friendship Bridge, Nong Khai city is one of northeastern Thailand's most popular destinations. But long before the river was spanned, the surreal Sala Kaew Ku sculpture park was a must-see on any jaunt through the region while the towns and temples along the

---

SALA KAEW KU   ศาลาแก้วกู่

One of Thailand's most enigmatic attractions, this **sculpture park** (admission 20B; ☺8am-6pm) is a surreal journey into the mind of a mystic shaman. Built over a period of 20 years by Luang Pu Boun Leua Sourirat, who died in 1996, the park features a weird and wonderful array of gigantic sculptures ablaze with Hindu-Buddhist imagery.

As he tells his own story, Luang Pu tumbled into a hole as a child and met an ascetic named Kaewkoo who introduced him to the manifold mysteries of the underworld and set him on course to become a Brahmanic yogi-priest-shaman. Shaking up his own unique blend of Hindu and Buddhist philosophy, mythology and iconography, Luang Pu developed a large following on both sides of the Mekong in this region. In fact, his original project was on the Lao side of the river where he had been living until the 1975 communist takeover in Laos.

The park is a smorgasbord of large and bizarre cement statues of Buddha, Shiva, Vishnu and other celestial deities (as well as numerous secular figures), all born of Luang Pu's dreams and cast by workers under his direction. Some of the sculptures are quite amusing. If you're travelling with kids, they'll enjoy the serene elephant wading though a pack of anthropomorphic dogs (which teaches people not to be bothered when people gossip about them). The tallest sculpture, a Buddha seated on a coiled *naga* with a spectacular multiheaded hood, is 25m high. Also of interest is the Wheel of Life, which you enter through a giant mouth. It boils Luang Pu's philosophies down to a single, slightly baffling image. An explanation is available on the back side of the handy map to the sculpture park provided by Mut Mee Garden Guesthouse.

The main shrine building, almost as strange as the sculptures, is full of Buddha images of every description and provenance (guaranteed to throw an art historian into a state of disorientation), photos of Luang Pu at various ages and Luang Pu's corpse lying under a glass dome ringed by flashing lights.

All buses headed east pass the road leading to Sala Kaew Ku (10B), which is also known as Wat Kaek. It's about a five-minute walk from the highway. Chartered túk-túk should cost 100B to 150B return with a one-hour wait, or you can reach it by bike in about 30 minutes. The Mut Mee map shows the scenic route.

Mekong west of the capital encourage travellers to slow down.

Nong Khai หนองคาย

POP 61,500

As a major staging post for those on their way from Vientiane, Nong Khai hosts a steady stream of travellers. A clutch of excellent places to sleep and eat have sprung up to accommodate them, making this the only Isan town with a full-fledged backpacker scene, albeit a modest one. But Nong Khai's popularity is about more than just its proximity to Laos and bounty of banana pancakes. Seduced by its dreamy pink sunsets and sluggish pace of life, many visitors who mean to stay one night end up bedding down for many more.

History

Crammed between nations, Nong Khai is both a historic and physical bridgehead between Thailand and Laos. Nong Khai once fell within the boundaries of the Vientiane (Wiang Chan) kingdom, which itself vacillated between independence and tribute to Lan Xang and Siam. In 1827 Rama III gave a Thai lord, Thao Suwothamma, the rights to establish Meuang Nong Khai at the present city site, which he chose because the surrounding swamps *(nong)* would aid in the city's defence.

The area came under several attacks by *jeen hor* (Yunnanese) marauders in the late 19th century. The Prap Haw Monument (*bràhp hor* means 'defeat of the Haw') in front of the former provincial office commemorates the victims of invasions in 1874, 1885 and 1886.

In 1891, under Rama V, Nong Khai became the capital of *monthon* Lao Phuan, an early Isan satellite state that included what are now Udon, Loei, Khon Kaen, Sakon Nakhon, Nakhon Phanom and Nong Khai Provinces, as well as Vientiane. But, when western Laos was partitioned off from Thailand by the French in 1893, the French demanded that Thailand have no soldiers within 25km of the border and so the capital was moved to Udon Thani, leaving Nong Khai's fortunes to fade.

One hundred and one years later, the opening of the US$30 million, 1174m-long Saphan Mittaphap Thai-Lao (Thai-Lao Friendship Bridge) marked a new era of development for Nong Khai as a regional trade

and transport centre. The skyline has been creeping slowly upwards ever since.

◉ Sights

Tha Sadet Market MARKET

(ตลาดท่าเสด็จ; Th Rimkhong; ⏰8.30am-6pm) The most popular destination in town, almost everyone loves a stroll through this covered market. It offers the usual mix of clothes, electronic equipment, food and assorted bric-a-brac, most of it imported from Laos and China, but there are also a few shops selling quirky quality stuff. There are some floating restaurants behind the market and you can arrange boat trips here.

Wat Pho Chai TEMPLE

(วัดโพธิ์ชัย; Th Phochai; ⏰5am-6pm) Luang Po Phra Sai, a large Lan Xang–era Buddha image awash with gold, bronze and precious stones, sits at the hub of Nong Khai's holiest temple. The head of the image is pure gold, the body is bronze and the *ùt·sà·nít* (flame-shaped head ornament) is set with rubies. Due to a great number of dubious miracles people attribute to it, this royal temple is a mandatory stop for most visiting Thais.

Luang Po Phra Sai was one of three similar statues made for each of the daughters of Lao King Setthathirat, and they were taken as bounty after King Rama I sacked Vientiane in 1778. The murals in the *bòht* depict their travels from the interior of Laos to the banks of the Mekong, where they were put on rafts. A storm sent one of the statues to the bottom of the river where it remains today. It was never recovered because, according to one monk at the temple, the *naga* like having it. The third statue, Phra Soem, is at Wat Patum Wanaram next to Siam Paragon in Bangkok. Phra Sai was supposed to accompany it, but, as the murals show you, the cart carrying it broke down here, and so this was taken as a sign that it wished to remain in Nong Khai.

Nong Khai Aquarium AQUARIUM

(พิพิธภัณฑ์สัตว์น้ำจังหวัดหนองคาย; admission 100B; ⏰9am-4.30pm Tue-Sun) This big green building displays freshwater and ocean-dwelling fish from Thailand and beyond, with the giant Mekong catfish in the 'giant tank' the star attraction. It's a fun place to visit, though it's far out of town on the Khon Kaen University campus and not served by public transport.

Central Nong Khai

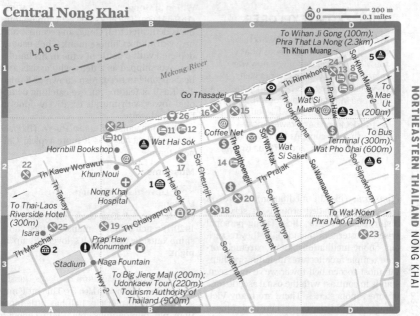

Central Nong Khai

Village Vocational Training Center CRAFT WORKSHOP

(ศูนย์ฝึกอบรมอาชีพชนบทหนองคาย; ⏱8am-5pm Mon-Sat) Run by the Good Shepherd Sisters, this workshop 7km south of town (take Hwy 2 and turn east just after the Km2 pillar) provides training and jobs for locals. It's a great place to see *mát·mèe* weaving, and it also has a pottery workshop and mushroom farm.

Wat Noen Phra Nao TEMPLE

(วัดเนินพระเนาวนาราม; ⏱daylight hours) This forest wát on the south side of town is a respected

THE MEKONG EXPLORER

Mekong River Cruises (www.cruise mekong.com) and its gorgeous boat the *Mekong Explorer* offer a new way to explore the Mekong River in Isan. Its week-long voyages between Nong Khai and Mukdahan sail November to March, and sightseeing while lounging on the deck can be as rewarding as the onshore excursions to places like That Phanom, Thailand and Tha Khaek, Laos.

vipassana (insight meditation) centre on pleasant, tree-shaded grounds. It serves as a spiritual retreat for those facing personal crises, Westerners included, if they're serious about meditation. Some extremely ornate temple architecture, including perhaps the most rococo bell tower we've ever seen, stands in contrast with the usual ascetic tone of forest monasteries. There are many Vietnamese and Chinese graves here and some of the statuary wouldn't be out of place at Sala Kaew Ku. The temple is unsigned off Rte 212, 1.5km east of the Grand Princess Hotel; turn south by the plant shop.

Phra That Klang Nam   STUPA
(พระธาตุกลางน้ำ; Th Rimkhong) The 'Holy Reliquary in the Middle of the River' (sometimes called Phra That Nong Khai) is a ruined Lao-style *chedi* submerged in the middle of the Mekong and can only be seen in the dry season when the waters lower about 13m. The *chedi* was gobbled up by the meandering Mekong in the middle of the 18th century and it toppled over in 1847. When the waters drop low enough coloured flags are fastened to it. **Phra That La Nong**, a replica erected on land, glows brightly at night.

Other Temples
Wat Lam Duan   TEMPLE
(Th Rimkhong; ⊙daylight hours) You can easily pick out this *wát* on the skyline because an immense Buddha image sits atop the *bòht*. You're welcome to climb up (shoes off) and gaze over the Mekong with it.

Wat Tung Sawang   TEMPLE
(Soi Silpakhom; ⊙daylight hours) The *bòht* here is one of the city's smallest, but the artistic flair put into the decoration makes it one of the prettiest. Nine sculptures of celestial deities sit on fanciful pedestals alongside it.

Wihan Ji Gong   TEMPLE
(Th Rimkhong) The city's newest Chinese temple is dedicated to Ji Gong, an eccentric and heavy-drinking Chinese monk – he's usually depicted with a bottle of wine in his hand – now worshipped as a deity who assists and heals people in need. Also known as Sanjao Tek-Ka-Ji, it features an eye-catching octagonal tower with murals creatively done in black and white.

The immaculate **Sanjao Pu-Ya** (Th Prab-Haw; ⊙daylight hours) is a more typical Chinese temple.

Museums
FREE **Governor's Mansion Museum**   MUSEUM
(Th Meechai; ⊙8.30am-6pm) The renovated 1929 French-colonial mansion has more shine outside than in. It's lovely lit up at night.

FREE **Nong Khai Museum**   MUSEUM
(Th Meechai; ⊙9am-4pm Mon-Fri) This little museum in the former city hall has little more than old photographs, but there's enough English labelling to make it worth a few minutes of your time, and the price is right.

Volunteering
Thailand-wide organisations Isara (p39) and Open Mind Projects (p39) are based in Nong Khai and have many opportunities here. If you're not looking for a long-term commitment you can drop by Isara's offices anytime to help out in other ways.

🎆 Festivals & Events
During Songkran (p23) the priceless image of Luang Pu Phra Sai from Wat Pho Chai (p462) is paraded around town.

Like many other cities in the northeast, Nong Khai has a **Rocket Festival** (Bun Bâng Fai), which begins on Visakha Bucha day (p24) in late May/early June, but it doesn't come close to competing with Yasothon's version (see p497).

At the end of Buddhist Lent (Ork Phansaa) in late October/early November, there are **long-boat races** on the Mekong. These correspond with the October full moon, which is when **naga fireballs** can be seen.

One particularly fun event is Nong Khai's version of the **Chinese Dragon Festival**, held over 10 days in late October and early November, with dragon dancing, acrobatics, Chinese opera and lots of firecrackers.

The **Anu Sahwaree Festival** (5 to 15 March) marks the end of the Haw rebellions and boasts the city's biggest street fair.

🛏 Sleeping

Catering to the steady flow of backpackers heading across the border, Nong Khai's budget offerings are the best in Isan.

TOP CHOICE Mut Mee Garden Guesthouse   GUEST HOUSE $

(📞0 4246 0717; www.mutmee.com; Soi Mutmee; r 150-1200B; ❄🌐) Occupying a sleepy stretch of the Mekong, Nong Khai's budget old-timer has a garden so relaxing it's intoxicating, and most nights it's packed with travellers. A huge variety of rooms (the cheapest with shared bath, the most expensive with an awesome balcony) are clustered around a thatched-roof restaurant where the owner, Julian, holds court with his grip on local legend and his passion for all things Isan. Because nobody will ever be required to vacate their room (people often stay longer than planned), only a few reservations are taken per day. There's a yoga studio in front.

Ruan Thai Guesthouse   GUEST HOUSE $

(📞0 4241 2519; 1126/2 Th Rimkhong; r 200-400B, f 1200B; ❄@🌐) Once little more than a small private home, this pleasant spot has grown with the boom time. It now boasts a variety of good-quality rooms, from simple shared-bathroom basics to a family room in a little wooden cottage. Factor in the tangle of flower-filled garden greenery and the friendly vibe and it's a winner.

GREAT BALLS OF FIRE

Mass hysteria? Methane gas? Drunken Lao soldiers? Clever monks? Or perhaps the fiery breath of the sacred *naga*, a serpent-like being that populates folkloric waterways throughout Southeast Asia. For many Lao and Thai who live by the Mekong River, it's not a matter of whether or not to believe. Since 1983 (or for ages, depending on who you ask), the sighting of the *bâng fai pá yah nâhk* (loosely translated, '*naga* fireballs') has been an annual event along the Mekong River. Sometime in the early evening, at the end of the Buddhist Rains Retreat (October), which coincides with the 15th waxing moon of the 11th lunar month, small reddish balls of fire shoot from the Mekong River and float a hundred or so metres into the air before vanishing without a trace. Most claim the *naga* fireballs are soundless, but others say a hissing can be heard if one is close enough to where they emerge from the surface of the river. People on both sides of the Mekong see the event as a sign that resident *naga* are celebrating the end of the holiday.

So what, you might ask, is the real cause behind *naga* fireballs? There are many theories. One, which aired on a Thai exposé-style TV program, claimed that Lao soldiers taking part in festivities on the other side of the Mekong were firing their rifles into the air. Interestingly, the reaction to the TV program was anger and a storm of protest from both sides of the river. Some suggest that a mixture of methane gas and phosphane, trapped below the mud on the river bottom, somehow reaches a certain temperature at exactly that time of year and is released. Many simply assume that some monks have found a way to make a 'miracle'. The latter was the premise behind a 2002 comedy film entitled *Sìp Hâh Kâm Deuan Sìp èt* (Fifteenth Waxing Moon of the Eleventh Lunar Month), released with English subtitles under the peculiar title *Mekhong Full Moon Party*.

Naga fireballs have become big business in Nong Khai Province and curious Thais from across the country converge at various spots on the banks of the Mekong for the annual show. Little Phon Phisai, the locus of fireball-watching, hosts some 40,000 guests. Special buses (30B) make the return trip to Nong Khai city and several hotels run their own buses where you'll get a guaranteed seat. Mut Mee Garden Guesthouse sails its boat there and back (2600B, including lunch and dinner).

If you don't come with the right mindset, you'll likely be disappointed. The fireball experience is more than just watching a few small lights rise from the river; it's mostly about watching Thais watching a few small lights rise from the river. And even if the *naga* doesn't send his annual greeting on the day you come (it's sometimes delayed by a day due to the vagaries of calculating the arrival of the full moon), it'll be an interesting experience.

Jumemalee Guesthouse
GUEST HOUSE $

(☑08 5010 2540; 419/1 Th Khun Muang; s 200-300B, d 300-400B, q 700B; ❄🌐) Filling two old wooden houses, Jumemalee is less lovely but more homey than its neighbour the E-San, and all rooms here have a private bathroom. The family runs the business to honour the wishes of their parents that the house never be sold. Use of bikes is free.

E-San Guesthouse
GUEST HOUSE $

(☑08 6242 1860; 538 Th Khun Muang; r 250-450B; ❄🌐) Just off the river in a small, beautifully restored wooden house ringed by a long verandah, this is a very atmospheric place to stay. The cheapest rooms share bathrooms and there are also rooms in a new building. Bikes are free.

Baan Mae Rim Nam
HOTEL $$

(☑0 4242 0256; www.baanmaerimnam.com; Mekong Promenade; r 500-700B; ❄🌐) A new hotel right on the riverfront, this bright yellow building has great rooms with balconies and river views. The 500B rooms in back, however, are less inviting.

Khiangkhong Guesthouse
HOTEL $

(☑0 4242 2870; 541 Th Rimkhong; r 300-400B; ❄@🌐) You can snag some river views from the 3rd-floor terrace (and some of the rooms) at this concrete tower that falls somewhere between guest house and hotel.

Sawasdee Guesthouse
GUEST HOUSE $

(☑0 4241 2502; www.sawasdeeguesthouse.com; 402 Th Meechai; s 160B, d 200-450B; ❄@🌐) If you could judge a hotel by its cover, this charismatic guest house in an old Franco-Chinese shophouse would come up trumps. The tidy rooms (the fan options share bathrooms) mostly lack the old-school veneer of the exterior and lobby, but at least you'll sleep well in the knowledge that you're bedded down in a little piece of living history. The owner is quite a character.

Budsabong Fine Resort
HOTEL $$$

(☑08 1666 5111; www.budsabongfineresort.com; Th Donsawan-Wattad; r incl breakfast 1600-1800B, ste 3800-4400B; ❄🌐🏊) The stark white exterior won't inspire love at first sight, but get inside and you'll find large, attractive and well-appointed rooms, many with terraces stepping right into the enormous pool. It's out in the country, beyond Sala Kaew Ku.

Thai Nongkhai Guesthouse
GUEST HOUSE $

(☑0 4241 3155; www.thainongkhai.com; 1169 Th Banthoengjit; r 450-550B; ❄@🌐) The seven rooms and bungalows here are fairly humdrum, but they are gleaming clean and the backyard location makes it pretty peaceful.

Rimkhong Guesthouse
GUEST HOUSE $

(☑08 1814 5811; 815 Th Rimkhong; s/d 150/220B) A simple place with sparse, shared-bath rooms. The owners set a sluggish pace and allow hush to prevail in the leafy courtyard.

Thai-Laos Riverside Hotel
HOTEL $$

(☑0 4246 0263; www.thailaoshotel.com, in Thai; 51 Th Kaew Worawut; r incl breakfast 700-900B; ❄🌐) This tour-bus favourite doesn't bother much with maintenance, but if you want a river view, you can do no better. And if you're into tacky hotel clubs, you'll find three of them here.

✗ Eating

TOP CHOICE Nagarina
THAI $

(☑0 4241 2211; Th Rimkhong; dishes 40-250B; ⏲lunch & dinner; 🌐🚲) As with nearly all *fa·ràng*-focused guest houses in Thailand, the Thai food at Mut Mee Garden Guesthouse is toned down and not recommended. (The Western breakfasts, on the other hand, are quite tasty.) But fear not lovers of Thai food, the kitchen of its floating restaurant turns out nothing but the real deal. It specialises in fish and often features unusual species from the Mekong. There's a sunset cruise (100B) most nights around 5pm.

TOP CHOICE Dee Dee Pohchanah
THAI $

(no roman-script sign; Th Prajak; dishes 40-230B; ⏲lunch & dinner) How good is Dee Dee? Just look at the crowds – but don't be put off by them. Despite having a full house every night, this simple place is a well-oiled machine and you won't be waiting long. Open until 2am.

Darika Bakery
THAI $

(668 Th Meechai; dishes 30-70B; ⏲breakfast & lunch) If you're an early riser, this spartan English-speaking outfit will be waiting for you from 5am with hearty egg-and-toast breakfasts, banana pancakes, baguette sandwiches and more.

Daeng Namnuang
VIETNAMESE $

(Th Rimkhong; dishes 45-180B; ⏲breakfast, lunch & dinner; 🌐) This massive river restaurant has grown into an Isan institution and hordes of out-of-towners head home with car boots and carry-on bags – there's an outlet at Udon Thani's airport – stuffed with *năam neu·ang* (pork spring rolls).

Mae Ut
VIETNAMESE **$**

(no roman-script sign; ☑0 4246 1204; Th Meechai; dishes 30-40B; ☺lunch & dinner) While Daeng Namnuang operates as much like a factory as a restaurant, this little place, serving just four items, including fried spring rolls and *khâ o gee ·ab ɓahk mŏr* (fresh noodles with pork), is more like grandma's kitchen. Look for the orange building with tables under a blue awning. English is limited.

Café Thasadej
INTERNATIONAL **$$**

(387/3 Th Bunterngjit; dishes 60-375B; ☺breakfast, lunch & dinner) Sophistication is in short supply in Nong Khai, but it oozes out of this little restaurant. Both the menu and liquor list, the latter among the best in town, go global. Gyros, Weiner schnitzel, fish and chips, lasagne, tuna salad and smoked salmon are some of the most popular options.

Nung-Len Coffee Bar
INTERNATIONAL, THAI **$**

(1801/2 Th Kaew Worawut; dishes 30-180B; ☺breakfast, lunch & dinner Mon-Sat) This petite place with an ever-smiling owner has good java and juices plus an eclectic menu of Thai and *fa·ràng* food, and even a few fusions of the two, such as 'spaghetti fried chilli with chicken'.

Saap Lah
NORTHEASTERN THAI **$**

(no roman-script sign; 897/2 Th Meechai; dishes 25-60B; ☺breakfast, lunch & dinner) For excellent *gài yâhng, sôm·đam* and other Isan foods, follow your nose to this no-frills food shop.

Mariam Restaurant
INDIAN **$**

(850/5 Th Prajak; dishes 30-80; ☺breakfast, lunch & dinner; ☑) This Muslim restaurant serves Indian (Pakistani, actually) and southern Thai food. For 120B you get three dishes, two roti and one drink.

Hospital Food Court
THAI **$**

(no roman-script sign; Th Meechai; ☺breakfast & lunch) A dozen cooks here whip up the standards.

Paradise View
THAI **$$**

(Rte 212; dishes 65-290B; ☺dinner) You can sample Isan food (it also serves Thai and Chinese) and see nearly the whole city from the Grand Paradise Hotel's open-air rooftop restaurant.

Roti Naihua
THAI **$**

(429/6 Th Rimkhong; roti 20-60B; ☺lunch & dinner; ☑) A roti supercenter with a wide choice of stuffings (blueberry jam to cashews to tuna) and showboat staff.

🍷 Drinking

Gaia
BAR

(Th Rimkhong; ☺closed Tue) Much of the Mut Mee crowd and many resident *fa·ràng* fill this laid-back lounge on the Mekong. There's a great drinks list, a chilled vibe and sometimes live music. It often hosts fundraisers for local charitable projects.

Warm Up
BAR

(Th Rimkhong) This little place rises above, both figuratively and literally, the other bars at this end of Th Rimkhong. It looks out over the river, has a free pool table and is popular with both Thais and travellers.

For something completely Thai, follow the Mekong-hugging Th Rimkhong east past Tha Sadet Market and as you approach Phra That La Nong you'll pass a bevy of restaurants and bars, some earthy, some fashionable, churning out dinner and drinks. There are some expat-owned bars around here too.

🛍 Shopping

Village Weaver Handicrafts
HANDICRAFTS

(1020 Th Prajak) This place sells high-quality, handwoven fabrics and clothing (ready made or made to order) that help fund development projects around Nong Khai. The *mát·mèe* cotton is particularly good here.

Hornbill Books
BOOKS

(Soi Mut Mee; ☺10am-7pm Mon-Sat) Buys, sells and trades English-language books. Has internet access too.

ℹ Information

Internet Access

Coffee Net (Th Bunterngjit; per hr 30B; ☺10am-9pm) Free coffee and tea while you surf.

SC Net (187 Soi Lang Wat Hai Sok; per hr 15B; ☺10am-10pm)

Medical Services

Nong Khai Hospital (☑0 4241 1504; Th Meechai)

Money

Big Jieng Mall (Hwy 2) Has several banks that are open in the evening and on weekends. It also has an AEON ATM.

BORDER CROSSING: NONG KHAI TO VIENTIANE

If you don't have a Lao visa, take a túk-túk (no more than 100B for two people from the bus station) to the **border** (⊙6.30am-10pm) where you get stamped out of Thailand. From there regular minibuses (20B) ferry passengers across the bridge to the hassle-free, but sometimes busy, Lao immigration checkpoint where 30-day visas (see p770 for details) are available. (Unless you're travelling in a large group, there's no good reason to use the visa service agencies in town.) From there it's almost 20km to Vientiane. Plenty of buses, túk-túk and taxis will be waiting for you.

If you already have your visa for Laos, there are six direct buses a day to Vientiane from Nong Khai's bus terminal (55B, one hour). There are also direct Vientiane buses from Udon Thani, Khon Kaen and Nakhon Ratchasima.

You can also go to Laos by train; though not to Vientiane. The 15-minute ride (20B to 30B, departs 9am and 2.45pm) drops you in Thanaleng (aka Dongphasay) station just over the bridge leaving you to continue to town on your own. There are immigration booths at both stations.

Post
Main post office (Th Meechai; ⊙8.30am-6pm Mon-Fri, 9am-5pm Sat, Sun & holidays)

Tourist Information
Immigration (☑0 4242 3963; ⊙8.30am-noon & 1-4.30pm Mon-Fri) South of the Friendship Bridge. Offers Thai visa extensions.

Tourism Authority of Thailand (TAT; ☑0 4242 1326; Hwy 2; ⊙8.30am-4.30pm) Inconveniently located outside of town.

Travel Agencies
Go Thasadej (☑08 1592 0164; www.go thasadej.com; Mekong Promenade; ⊙10am-8pm Mon-Sat) One of the most reliable all-round travel agents in Thailand.

ⓘ Getting There & Away

Air
The nearest airport is 55km south in Udon Thani. **Udonkaew Tour** (☑0 4241 1530; Th Pranang Cholpratan; ⊙8.30am-5.30pm) travel agency runs vans (150B per person) to/from the airport. Coming into town they'll drop you at your hotel or the bridge; going back you need to get yourself to their office. It's best to buy a ticket in advance. A private driver to the airport costs 700B at most travel agencies.

Bus
Nong Khai's **bus terminal** (☑0 4241 1612) is located just off Th Prajak, about 1.5km from the main pack of riverside guest houses. Udon Thani (35B to 47B, one hour, every half-hour) is the most frequent destination. There are also buses for Khon Kaen (110B to 139B, 3½ hours, hourly) and Nakhon Phanom (210B, 6½ hours, six daily until 12.30pm). For those travelling west along the Mekong, there are five buses to Pak Chom, and the 7.30am bus continues all the way to Loei

(130B, 6½ hours). For Chiang Mai, you have to change at Udon's Bus Terminal 2 (bor-kör-sör mài).

Bangkok buses (350B to 450B, 10 to 11 hours) are frequent in the late afternoon and early evening, but less so during the day. **Chan Tour** (☑0 4246 0205; 600B; ⊙departs 10.15am, 7.30pm, 8.45pm) and **999 VIP** (☑0 4241 2679; 700B; ⊙departs 8pm) offer VIP buses. There's also one bus direct to Suvarnabhumi (Airport) bus station (454B, nine hours, 8pm).

Train
Two express trains, one in the morning and the other in the afternoon, connect Bangkok (2nd-class air-con 498B, 1st-class sleeper upper/lower 1117/1317B, 11 to 12 hours) to **Nong Khai Railway Station** (☑0 4241 1592), which is 2km west of downtown. There's also one cheaper rapid train leaving Bangkok in the evening.

ⓘ Getting Around
Nong Khai is a great place for cycling due to the limited traffic and the nearby countryside. Many guest houses let you use bikes for free. If you need to hire one, **Khun Noui** (☑08 1975 4863; Th Kaew Worawut; ⊙8am-5pm), who sets up on the roadside across from the entrance to Mut Mee, has reliable bikes (30B per day) and motorcycles (200B).

A túk-túk between the Mut Mee area and either the bus station or bridge should be 30B to 40B.

West of Nong Khai

The people living west of Nong Khai are obsessed with **topiary**, and along Rte 211 you'll pass hedges and bushes sculpted by ambitious gardeners into everything from elephants to boxing matches. The river road

(Th Kaew Worawut), lined with floodplain fields of tobacco, tomatoes and chillies, is another option for the first stretch of the route west, though cyclists should note that it has no shoulder.

The tourism office in Nong Khai has information about village homestay programs (300B to 500B including meals) along the way, and if you stop by their office they'll help arrange your visit.

WAT PHRA THAT BANG PHUAN วัดพระธาตุบังพวน

Boasting a beautiful *chedi* that locals believe holds 29 Buddha relics, **Wat Phra That Bang Phuan** (⊙daylight hours) is one of the region's most sacred temples. Nobody knows when the first stupa was erected here, but after moving his capital from Luang Prabang to Vientiane in 1560, Lan Xang King Setthathirat commissioned grand temples to be built all around his kingdom, including a new stupa built over an older one here. Rain caused it to lean precariously and in 1970 it finally fell over. It was rebuilt in 1976–77. The current one stands 34m high on a 17-sq-metre base and has many unsurfaced *chedi* around it, giving the temple an ancient atmosphere; and it's this, much more than the main stupa, that makes a trip here rewarding.

The temple is 22km from Nong Khai on Rte 211. Take a Pak Chom-bound bus (20B, 45 minutes).

THA BO ท่าบ่อ
POP 16,000

Prosperous Tha Bo is the most important commercial centre between Nong Khai and Loei, and the covered market, which spills out to the surrounding streets, is full of locally grown products. A large Vietnamese population lives here, and they've cornered the market on noodle production. You'll see masses of *sên lék* (small rice noodles) drying in the sun on the west side of town. From about 5am to 10am you can watch people at the factories making the noodles, and then at around 2pm they start the cutting, all by hand.

It used to be mostly spring-roll wrappers laid out on the bamboo racks, but noodles are easier to make and sell so people have made the switch. Ban Hua Sai, 10km upriver just before Si Chiangmai, is now the area's spring-roll-wrapper capital.

Tha Bo is mostly a day-trip destination, but there are some cheap guest houses, if you want to spend the night.

The 'yellow bus' runs regularly between Nong Khai and Tha Bo (27B, one hour, every half-hour), taking the scenic riverside route.

Around Nong Khai

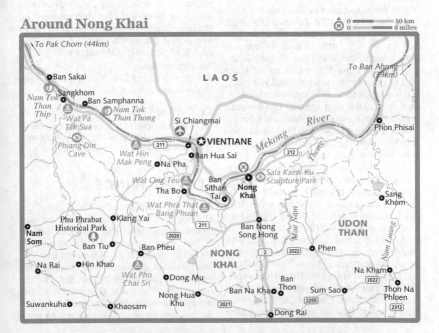

Pick it up in Nong Khai at the bus station or near the hospital on Th Meechai.

WAT HIN MAK PENG   วัดหินหมากเป้ง

Overlooking a lovely stretch of the Mekong, this vast forest temple (☺6am-7pm) is centred on a cliff rising out of the river. The very peaceful temple is highly respected because of the Thai people's continuing reverence for the founding abbot, Luang Pu Thet, who they believe reached enlightenment. Several monuments in his honour, including a glistening *chedi* housing his few earthly possessions and a lifelike wax statue, are found around the grounds. Visitors must dress politely: no shorts above the knees or sleeveless tops.

The temple is midway between Si Chiangmai and Sangkhom. Sangkhom-bound buses from Nong Khai (50B, 2¼ hours) pass the entrance, and then it's a longish walk to the buildings.

SANGKHOM   สังคม

The little town of Sangkhom, facing the Lao island of Don Klang Khong, makes a great brief stop for those following the Mekong between Nong Khai and Loei. Staring at the lovely Mekong and mountain scenery tends to dominate visitors' time here, but there are also some wonderful attractions around town.

The forest wát peering down on the town from the hills, **Wat Pa Tak Sua** (☺daylight hours), lies just 2km away as the crow flies, but is 19km to drive. (Take the turn-off across from Nam Tok Than Thong.) It has the most amazing Mekong views we know of. The sunset scene is superb and you might see the valley filled with fog on early mornings during the cold season. The footpath used by the monks every morning begins east of town just before the Km81 pillar. Follow Soi 5 past the last house and then veer right by the mango and papaya trees.

About 14km past the temple road is interesting **Phiang Din Cave** (admission by donation; ☺6am-6pm), which some locals believe is the home of a *naga* king. If you can speak Thai, you'll hear some fanciful stories. Guides lead a 30-minute route with lights or a two-hour route using torches (flashlights). On both you'll need to manoeuvre through some small, wet passages and you can't wear shoes.

Three-tiered **Nam Tok Than Thip waterfall** (admission free; ☺daylight hours), 13km west of Sangkhom (2km off Rte 211), is the largest waterfall in the area. The lower level

drops 30m and the second, easily reached via stairs, falls 100m. The 70m top drop is only barely visible through the lush forest. **Nam Tok Than Thong waterfall** (admission free; ☺daylight hours), 11km east of Sangkhom, is a wider but shorter drop. The short nature trail takes you down by the Mekong. Than Thong is more accessible than Than Thip, but can be rather crowded on weekends and holidays. Both dry up by February.

🛏 Sleeping & Eating

TOP CHOICE **Bouy Guesthouse**   GUEST HOUSE $

(☎0 4244 1065; Rte 211; r 200-280B; @) As the ever-smiling Buoy will tell you, Sangkhom's veteran lodge has just a few 'simple huts' (the cheaper ones sharing bathrooms), but they're popular for good reason. They come with hammocks and wooden decks and the riverside location, just west of town, is wonderfully relaxing. Bike/motorbike hire costs 50B/200B and river trips are available.

Poopae Ruenmaithai   HOTEL $$

(☎0 4244 1088; Rte 211; r 500-1500B; ❄@) This attractive set-up, featuring wooden walkways and decorative stonework, should have made better use of the river views, though it will definitely satisfy those who demand a certain level of comfort. The cheapest rooms, all but one of which have shared baths, are a little *Being John Malkovich,* but most people will be able to stand up straight. The restaurant is good and there's a four-person Jacuzzi for rent (200B per half-day). It's 1.5km east of downtown.

Sangkhom Away   CAFE $

(Rte 211; ☺breakfast & lunch) A fun little place in the heart of town.

❶ Getting There & Away

There are five rickety fan buses a day from Nong Khai (55B, three hours) and the earliest of those continues all the way to Loei (70B, 3½ hours).

LOEI PROVINCE

Stretching south from the sleepy arc of the Mekong River at Chiang Khan to the vast mountain plateau of Phu Kradueng National Park, Loei (meaning 'to the extreme') is a diverse, beautiful province untouched by mass tourism, despite all it has to offer. This isn't the wildest place in Thailand, but the region's tranquil national parks and nature reserves (there are far more good ones than we can feature here) can lead you to some splendid isolation. And, if you have the luck to arrive at the right time, you can balance the hush of nature with the hubbub of Dan Sai's incredible Phi Ta Khon Festival.

The terrain here is mountainous and temperatures fluctuate from one extreme to the other: it's hotter than elsewhere in Thailand during the hot season and chillier during the cold season. This is one of the few provinces in Thailand where temperatures drop below 0°C, a fact tourist brochures love to trumpet. In December and January the crisp air paints leaves red and yellow at high elevations, such as around Phu Kradueng and Phu Reua.

Loei

เลย

POP 33,000

Arrive here after a sojourn in the region's remote countryside and the capital city is little more than a reminder that concrete and congestion still exist. Not that it's a bad place, but, as the Tourism Authority of Thailand itself says, 'the city of Loei has little to hold the traveller's interest'.

◉ Sights

Loei's museums are hardly worth a special trip, but if you won't be visiting Dan Sai, there are Phi Ta Khon festival masks and photos (plus pottery and other artefacts) to see at the **Loei Museum** (Th Charoenrat; admission free; ⊗8.30am-4.30pm), above the TAT office, and the **Loei Cultural Centre** (Rte 201; admission free; ⊗8.30am-4pm), 5km north of town at Rajabhat University.

🛏 Sleeping

Sugar Guesthouse　　　　GUEST HOUSE **$**
(☏08 9711 1975; www.sugarguesthouse.blog.com; Soi 2, 4/1 Th Wisut Titep; r 180-380B; ❄@☎)
One of the cheapest places in town (the fan rooms share a bathroom) is the friendliest. The English-speaking owner arranges trips around the province at reasonable prices, or,

Loei Province

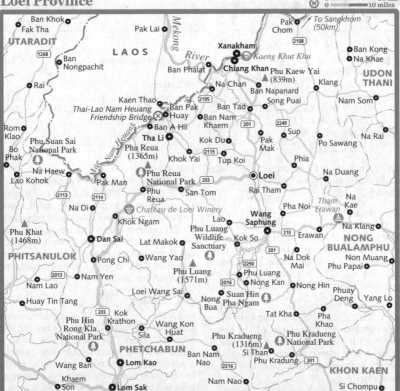

Loei

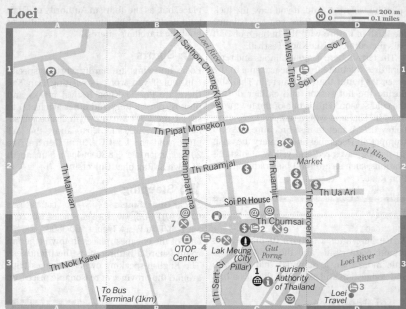

NORTHEASTERN THAILAND LOEI PROVINCE

Loei

if you'd rather get there yourself, hires bikes (50B) and motorcycles (250B). Be wary of the dog.

King Hotel HOTEL **$$**
(📞0 4281 1701; 11/8-12 Th Chumsai; r 500-1500B; ❄🛜) Fit for a king? No; though a major modernisation has given the rooms a simple but attractive style and made it a pleasant place to stay. The restaurant is good and guests can borrow bikes for free.

Phutawan Mansion HOTEL **$**
(📞0 4283 2983; http://phutawan-loei.com, in Thai; Th Nok Kaew; r 350-650B; ❄🛜) The bright newly built hotel is plain, but offers good-value rooms (they feature a fridge and quality mattresses) in a quiet, convenient location.

Loei Palace Hotel HOTEL **$**
(📞0 4281 5668; 167/4 Th Charoenrat; r 1200-2500B; ste 3500B; ❄@🛜⊠) Loei's flagship hotel sports some wedding-cake architecture, helpful staff, plenty of mod cons and usually a high vacancy rate, so ask about discounts. Wi-fi covers the first two floors only. Check out the flood marker and photos next to the reception desk to see what the city suffered in September 2002.

🍴 Eating

Baan Yai NORTHEASTERN THAI **$**
(no roman-script sign; Th Sert-Si; dishes 25-150B; ⊙lunch & dinner) This big, leafy place with a funky variety of wooden tables and chairs is a genuine Isan restaurant where the menu (no English) has entire sections for ant eggs, insects and frogs. It also serves *dtòhng mŏo*

(pork in a sour-and-spicy sauce), a dish you probably won't find elsewhere. At night there are movies and football to watch or live music.

Walking Street   NORTHEASTERN THAI $
(Th Ruamjit; ☻4-11pm) Loei's grandly named, but otherwise typical, night market is a good dining destination.

Krua Nid   THAI $
(no roman-script sign; 58 Th Charoenrat; dishes 25-40B; ☻breakfast, lunch & dinner) Fronted by a big glass buffet case, this no-frills eatery serves *hòr mòk* (soufflé-like curry steamed in banana leaves) and other central-Thai dishes. Look for the white awning.

Ban Thai   INTERNATIONAL $$
(22/58-60 Th Nok Kaew; dishes 49-370B; ☻lunch & dinner) Mr Chris, as everyone calls this restaurant, is the first choice for a fix of *fa·ràng* food. German and Italian dishes dominate the menu.

❶ Information

The **Tourism Authority of Thailand** (TAT; ☑0 4281 2812; tatloei@tat.or.th; Th Charoenrat; ☻8.30am-4.30pm) provides a good map and has helpful staff.

Internet cafes are spread around the city centre, while most banks are around Th Charoenrat, including **Krung Thai Bank** (Th Ua Ari; ☻10am-6pm), which offers convenient hours.

❶ Getting There & Away

Air
Solar Air (☑0 2535 2455; www.solarair.co.th) and **Nok Air** (☑0 2900 9955; www.nokair.com) connect Loei to Bangkok using Don Muang Airport with prices starting around 1700B. **Loei Travel** (☑0 4283 0741; www.loeitravel.com), inside the Loei Palace Hotel, sells tickets.

Bus
The most frequent service from Loei's **bus terminal** (☑0 4283 3586) is to Udon Thani (66B to 92B, three hours, every half-hour). There are also buses to Khon Kaen (129B, 3½ hours, every half-hour), Khorat (263B, six hours, hourly), Phitsanulok (139B to 178B, four hours, five daily) and Chiang Mai (409B to 526B, 10 hours, six daily). The only bus to Nong Khai (130B, 6½ hours) leaves at 6am, and it's worth catching because it follows the scenic Mekong River route. It's faster, however, to go via Udon Thani.

Buses to Bangkok (321B to 412B, 11 hours) leave hourly throughout the day and every 20 minutes in the early evening. There are VIP buses (640B) with **Air Muang Loei** (☑0 4283

2042; ☻departs 8.30pm) and **999 VIP** (☑0 4281 1706; ☻departs 9pm).

❶ Getting Around

Sŏrng·tăa·ou (10B) run from the bus station through town or you can take a túk-túk for about 30B. Airport shuttles to downtown cost 200B. The Loei Palace Hotel rents bikes (50/80B per half-/full day).

Chiang Khan   เชียงคาน

Please pardon our lamentation, but we really miss the old Chiang Khan. Virtually overnight, what was once a sleepy little-known riverside town full of traditional timber houses became a trendy destination for Thais, and now tour buses arrive daily. That said, it's far from ruined and we still think it's a good place to visit: it's just no longer great. The photogenic views of the river and the Lao mountains beyond are still there and things remain fairly peaceful in the daytime, before the evening shopping stampede begins.

◉ Sights & Activities

Temples
Like most of Chiang Khan's temples, the *ubosot* (chapel) at **Wat Si Khun Meuang** (Th Chai Khong; ☻daylight hours), which probably dates to the Rama III era, is mostly Lao-style (in particular, note the sweeping roof), but it also freely mixes central (the lotus pillars) and northern (the guardian lions) Thai stylings. It's fronted by a superb mural and there's plenty of topiary around the grounds.

Wat Mahathat (Th Chiang Khan; ☻daylight hours), in the centre of town, is Chiang Khan's oldest temple. The *bòht,* constructed in 1654, has a new roof over old walls with the faded original mural on the front.

About 2km before Kaeng Khut Khu, **Wat Tha Khaek** (☻daylight hours) is a ramshackle,

---

BORDER CROSSING: THA LI TO KAEN THAO

Foreigners can now get Lao visas (see p770 for details), at the seldom-used **Thai-Lao Nam Heuang Friendship Bridge** (☻8am-6pm) in Amphoe Tha Li, 60km northwest of Loei, but the road to Luang Prabang is rough and public transport is scarce.

NORTHEASTERN THAILAND CHIANG KHAN

700-year-old forest temple housing three 300-year-old stone Buddha images. They sit on a ledge over a larger, modern Buddha in the wát's still unfinished *bòht*.

Kaeng Khut Khu

With the mountains making an attractive backdrop, this famous bend in the Mekong is well known across Thailand. The surrounding park has a bevy of vendors selling *má·prów gàaw* (coconut candy), the local speciality. This is also a good place to try *gûng-tôrt-grôrp* (crispy fried shrimp), which looks a little like a frisbee, and *gûng đën* (dancing shrimp), little bowls of live shrimp. It's 5km downstream from town; túk-túk drivers charge 50B per person.

Boat Trips & Tours

Most guest houses arrange boat trips to Kaeng Khut Khu or further afield, and the mountain scenery makes longer trips highly recommended. Rates swing with petrol prices, but the typical 1½-hour trip in a boat that can hold 10 people costs between 800B and 1000B.

Another option is to kayak the river (1500B per person, minimum four) with **Mekong Culture & Nature Resort** (☑0 4282 1457), 1km upstream from town.

Huan Mai Sri Chiang Khan Homestay (☑0 4282 1825; www.huanmaisrichiangkhan.ob.tc, in Thai; 145 Th Chai Khong) offers an early morning tour (departing at 5am; 100B per person) that includes seeing the sunrise (and maybe a sea of fog during the cool season) from atop nearby **Phu Thok** mountain.

Bike hire generally costs 50B per day while motorcycles are between 200B and 250B. Most guest houses have free bikes for their customers.

PHI KON NAM

Similar to Dan Sai's Phi Ta Khon Festival (p476), but barely promoted, the Phi Kon Nam festival in Ban Na Sao, 7km south of Chiang Khan, is part of the village's rain-inducing Rocket Festival (Bun Bâng Fai) and coincides with Visakha Bucha (p24) in May or June. Locals believe that the souls of their cows and buffaloes wander around the village after they die, so to show respect, the villagers don wild bovine-inspired masks and colourful costumes. If you're in the area, don't miss it.

🛏 Sleeping

Chiang Khan's rocketing popularity means hotel owners have no need to price their rooms reasonably. You can usually save money by staying on a soi rather than along the river road, and most of the pricier places have weekday discounts. Also note that preserving the historic character of buildings means shared bathrooms (unless stated otherwise) and thin walls.

TOP CHOICE Poonsawasdi Hotel HOTEL $$

(☑08 0400 8777; www.poonsawasdi.com in Thai; Soi 9; r 800B; ❄ ❀ 🖭) The oldest hotel in Chiang Khan has been creatively jazzed up with coloured wood and antique furnishings, and, unlike most of the wooden oldies in town, this one still radiates historic charm inside the rooms, not just in the lobby.

TOP CHOICE Chiang Khan Guesthouse GUEST HOUSE $$

(☑0 4282 1691; www.thailandunplugged.com; 282 Th Chai Khong; s/d/tr 300/450/600B; 🖭) This traditional-style place is all creaking timber and tin roofing and the terrace sits really close to the river. Owner Pim will make you feel completely at home. She can also arrange *Ƌohng·lahng* shows (2500B) performed by local students, who keep the cash to put towards their studies.

Loogmai Guesthouse GUEST HOUSE $

(☑08 6234 0011; 112 Th Chai Khong; r 450-550B) Combining some minimalist modern artistic styling with oodles of French-colonial class, this old-school villa offers sparse but atmospheric rooms (one with private bathroom), an airy terrace with river views and a real sense of history. The owner leaves the villa at 6pm, but you get a key.

Chiang Khan Hill Resort HOTEL $$

(☑0 4282 1285; www.chiangkhanhill.com; r 800-4000B; ❄ 🖭 🖭) The best views of Kaeng Khut Khu are from the town's only resort, which overlooks the rapids. Rooms are nice for the price and the restaurant is quite good.

Tao Kae Lao Guesthouse GUEST HOUSE $$

(☑08 1311 9754; taokaelao@gmail.com; 92 Th Chai Khong; r 600-700B; ❄ ❀ 🖭) Rooms here are super simple, just mattresses on the floor, but the young Bangkokian owners put heaps of funky style into the rest of the place, making it a good spot to chill. Two rooms have river views.

Chiang Khan

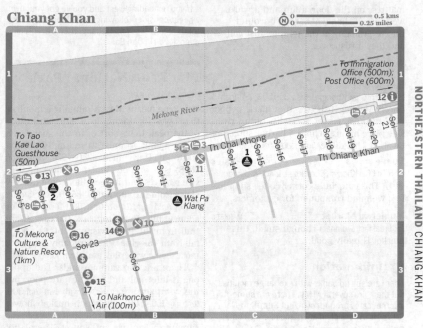

Chiang Khan

⊙ Sights
1 Wat Mahathat	C2
2 Wat Si Khun Meuang	A2

🛏 Sleeping
3 Ban Sangthong	B2
4 Chiang Khan Guesthouse	D1
5 Chiangkhan Riverview Guesthouse	B2
6 Loogmai Guesthouse	A2
7 Poonsawasdi Hotel	B2
8 Torng Sai Homestay	A2

⊗ Eating
9 Ban-Jerd-Loei	A2
10 Municipal Market	B3
11 Sum-Ran-Na	B2

ⓘ Information
12 Chiang Khan Information Center	D1
13 Hua Mai Sri Chiang Khan Homestay	A2

ⓘ Transport
14 999 VIP	B3
15 Air Muang Loei	A3
16 Phu Kradung Tours	A3
17 Sŏrng·tăa·ou to Loei & Ban Tad	A3

Chiangkhan Riverview Guesthouse GUEST HOUSE **$**
(☑08 0741 8055; www.chiangkhan.741.com; 277 Th Chai Khong; r 300-600B; ❀🛜) The most diverse choice in town, this riverside spot has rooms with fan and air-conditioning, shared and private bathrooms, and a mix of old and new construction. Some rooms have river views and the terrace is very inviting.

Ban Sangthong GUEST HOUSE **$**
(☑0 4282 1305; 162 Th Chai Khong; s/d 200/400B; @🛜) This slightly chaotic little place, stuffed with the owner's art, has the cheapest rooms on the river and an attractive little terrace.

Torng Sai Homestay GUEST HOUSE **$**
(no roman-script sign; ☑08 6227 2667; 129/3 Soi 6; s/d/tr 200/300/450B) This old wooden shophouse hasn't been gussied up like those on the riverfront. You get just a

mattress on the floor, a fan and a warm welcome. If the owners aren't around, they're probably at the temple: just call and they'll rush over.

🍴 Eating

Ban-Jerd-Loei THAI $
(187/1 Th Chai Khong; dishes 35-150B; ☺lunch & dinner) Mekong fish (try the 'black pepper fried river fish') is the speciality of this riverside place hiding behind a barber shop, but its other Thai dishes are good too.

Sum-Ran-Na CAFE $
(165 Th Chai Khong; ☺breakfast, lunch & dinner; @☜) This cute, little corner coffee shop has free wi-fi and computers for customers.

Municipal Market MARKET $
(☺breakfast & dinner) Though small, this market is really good.

ℹ Information

There are still no banks with exchange facilities, but there are several ATMs. There are some internet cafes around town, but Sum-Ran-Na (p476) is a more pleasant place to check email.
Chiang Khan Information Center (Soi 21, Th Chai Khong) This place may or may not open eventually.
Immigration (✆0 4282 1911; Soi 26, Th Chai Khong at; ☺8.30am-4.30pm Mon-Fri) For visa extensions.

ℹ Getting There & Away

Sŏrng·tǎa·ou to Loei (35B, 1¼ hours) depart about every 15 minutes in the early morning, and then whenever there are enough passengers, from a stop on Rte 201, while eight buses (34B, 45 minutes) leave from the **Nakhonchai Air** (✆0 4282 1905) terminal 300m further south. The buses continue to Khorat (297B, seven hours) via Chaiyaphum (212B, five hours).

Three companies, departing from their own offices, make the run direct to Bangkok (10 hours): **Air Muang Loei** (✆08 9842 1524; old Shell petrol station, Rte 201) at 8am and 6.30pm (479B); **999 VIP** (✆0 4282 1002; Soi 9) at 9am, 6pm, 7pm and 7.30pm (347B to 694B); and **Phu Kradung Tours** (✆08 7856 5149; Rte 201) at 6.30pm (347B).

No transport runs direct to Nong Khai. The quickest way there is via Loei and Udon Thani, but for the scenic river route take a Loei-bound *sŏrng·tǎa·ou* south to Ban Tad (20B, 30 minutes) where you can catch the bus to Nong Khai that leaves Loei at 6am. Another option is to hire a car to take you to Pak Chom (about 600B) where there are buses to Nong Khai at 10am, 1pm and 3pm.

If you're heading west and you've got your own wheels, consider following the seldom-seen back roads along Mae Nam Heuang; they'll eventually deposit you in Dan Sai.

Phu Reua National Park
อุทยานแห่งชาติภูเรือ

Phu Reua means 'Boat Mountain', a moniker that owes its origins to a cliff jutting out of the peak that's sort of in the shape of a Chinese junk. At only 121 sq km, **Phu Reua National Park** (✆0 4280 7624; admission 200B) isn't one of Thailand's most impressive reserves, but it does offer some dreamy views from the summit (1365m), reached by either a *sŏrng·tǎa·ou* or a 1km footpath. For a longer hike to the top, take the easy 2.5km trail from the lower visitor centre to 30m-tall **Nam Tok Huai Phai**, arguably the park's most scenic waterfall, and then keep going.

There are two campgrounds. The upper one is informal and facilities are poor, but the **campsites** (per person with own tent 30B, tent hire 150-450B) and rough bucket-shower **rooms** (500-700B) put you pretty close to the summit for sunrise and sunset. There's hot water, all-day electricity and wi-fi at the more attractive lower **campsite** (per person with own tent 30B, 2-/4-person tent hire 270/540B), which also has six comfortable **bungalows** (✆0 2562 0760; www.dnp.go.th/parkreserve; 4/6 people 2000/3000B) with TV and fridge. There are many small resorts below the park with cheaper prices. The restaurants at the campsites only open from September to February and sometimes weekends and holidays the rest of the year. Night-time temperatures can drop below freezing in December and January, so come prepared.

The park is 50km west of Loei on Rte 203. Buses heading west from the city can drop you in the town of Phu Reua (50B to 60B, 1½ hours), and then you'll have to hitch or charter a truck for around 500B (including a few hours' wait) to the park itself. The summit is 8km from the highway.

Dan Sai ด่านซ้าย

For 362 days a year, Dan Sai is an innocuous little town, a borderline backwater community where life revolves around a small market and a dusty main street. For the remaining three days, however, it's the site of one of the country's liveliest and loudest festivals.

Falling during the fourth lunar month, Dan Sai's **Phi Ta Khon Festival** (also called Bun Phra Wet) combines the Phra Wet Festival – during which recitations of the *Mahavessantara Jataka* (a story about one of the Buddha's past lives) are supposed to enhance the listener's chance of being reborn in the lifetime of the next Buddha – with Bun Bâng Fai (Rocket Festival). For those wishing to plunge headlong into Isan life, this curious cross between the drunken revelry of Carnival and the spooky imagery of Halloween is a must see.

The origins of the Phi Ta Khon Festival are shrouded in ambiguity, but some aspects appear to be related to tribal Tai (possibly Tai Dam) spirit cults. In fact, the dates for the festival (usually June) are divined by Jao Phaw Kuan, a local spirit medium who channels the information from the town's guardian deity. On the first day Jao Phaw Kuan performs a sacrifice to invite Phra Upakud (an enlightened monk with supernatural powers who chose to transform himself into a block of white marble to live eternally on the bottom of Mae Nam Man) to come to town. Locals then don wild costumes and masks for two days of dancing that's fuelled by *lôw kŏw* (white whisky) and full of sexual innuendo, before launching the rockets and heading to the temple to listen to sermons through the night and into the third day.

◉ Sights & Activities

FREE **Phi Ta Kon Museum**   MUSEUM
(พิพิธภัณฑ์ผีตาโขน; Th Kaew Asa; ⊙9am-5pm) Wat Phon Chai, the temple behind the big white gate, plays a major role in the Phi Ta Khon festivities, so it's an appropriate home for this museum. It has a collection of costumes worn during the celebrations, a display showing how the masks are made and video from the festival.

Wat Neramit Wiphatsana   TEMPLE
(วัดเนรมิตวิปัสสนา; ⊙daylight hours) Built on a wooded hill overlooking Phra That Si Songrak, this gorgeous (it almost looks like a Buddhist-themed resort) meditation *wát* features buildings made of unplastered laterite blocks. Famous Thai temple muralist Pramote Sriphrom spent years painting images of *jataka* tales on the interior walls of the massive *bòht*, which also hosts a copy of the Chinnarat Buddha in Phitsanulok's Wat Phra Si Ratana Mahathat (see p349). The *wát* is dedicated to the memory of the

late Luang Pu Mahaphan, a much-revered local monk.

Phra That Si Songrak   STUPA
(พระธาตุศรีสองรัก; Rte 2113; ⊙7am-5pm) The most highly revered stupa in Loei Province, this whitewashed Lao-style *chedi* stands 20m high and was built in 1560–63 on what was then the Thai–Lao border as a gesture of unity between the Lao kingdom of Wiang Chan (Vientiane) and the Thai kingdom of Ayuthaya in their resistance against the Burmese. A pavilion in front of it contains a very old chest that supposedly contains an even older carved stone Buddha about 76cm long. Despite use of the name Phra That, there are no Buddha relics here. You can't wear shoes, hats or the colour red, or carry food or open umbrellas if you climb up to the *chedi*. Down below is a modest **museum** (admission free; ⊙9am-4pm) with random artefacts donated by locals.

🛏 Sleeping & Eating

Homestay   HOMESTAY $
(✆08 9077 2080; dm/tw/tr 150/400/550B) A couple of villages just outside town have been running a successful homestay program for many years, and the families dote on *fa·ràng* guests (meals 70B). When not at work (most of the English-speaking

---

THE GARDEN OF ISAN

The Phu Reua region is famous for its flower farms and the riot of colours along the roadside makes the highway between Loei and Dan Sai one of the most scenic drives in Thailand. The cool, dry climate also allows farmers to grow a variety of crops not common in Isan, such as strawberries, coffee (the growing Coffee Bun chain is based here and its blend includes Loei-grown beans), macadamia nuts, petunias and persimmons.

One stop that most travellers with their own wheels make is **Chateau de Loei** (www.chateaudeloei.com; Rte 203 at Km60; ⊙8am-5pm), which released the first commercially produced Thai wine in 1995. It's a nickel-and-dime operation compared to the attractive and well-managed wineries around Khao Yai, but visitors are welcome to taste its wines and brandies way back in the utilitarian main building.

SUAN HIN PHA NGAM

With intriguingly warped and eroded limestone outcroppings, 'Beautiful Rock Garden' is an apt name for this hidden oasis, though Thais know it as **Kunming Meuang Thai** (สวนหินผางาม; per group 100B; ☺8.30am-5.30pm), 'Thailand's Kunming', due to its resemblance to the Stone Forest in Kunming, China. Most people just ride a tractor (10B per person one way) up to the easy-to-reach viewpoint for a quick look, but the best thing to do is walk back with your guide through the labyrinth paths. At times the route is a little rough and you need to duck through some small passageways, which creates a small sense of adventure. Plan on an hour to walk back. The site is 20km southwest of Nong Hin. There's no public transport and hitching is highly impractical.

hosts are teachers) they'll take you out to share typical daily activities. Everything can be arranged at Kawinthip Hattakham (see later).

Phunacome HOTEL $$$
(☎0 4289 2005; www.phunacomeresort.com; Rte 2013; r 3500-4900B; ❋@☎☎) This luxury resort makes the most of its country location, and the kitchen makes use of the organic rice and veggies grown on the grounds. (They make their own low-impact soaps and detergents too.) Two styles of room line a row of ponds: standard hotel rooms and some cool wood-and-thatch Isan-inspired cottages. Both are plush and lovely with nice views. The lobby has a library, massage service and restaurant with Thai and Western food. Its mascot is the buffalo and three real ones roam the grounds.

Ban Sabaaidee 2 HOTEL $
(☎08 0748 1555; Rte 2013; r 300B; ❋☎) This colourful little place 2km east of the Th Kaew Asa junction has ordinary but adequate rooms.

Dansai Resort Hotel HOTEL $
(☎0 4289 2281; Rte 2013; r 300-500B; ❋@☎) Dan Sai's most centrally located lodging has been on a building spree and now has rooms ranging from past-their-prime cold-water fan rooms to big new cottages.

Im Un THAI $
(no Roman-script sign; Rte 2013; dishes 60-150B; ☺breakfast, lunch & dinner) Thai standards and Isan favourites, such as *gaang ʻbàh* (jungle curry) and *lâhp hèt* (mushroom laap), are served under a thatched roof in a garden setting. It's on the edge of town, 900m east of the Th Kaew Asa junction.

Night Market THAI $
(Th Kaew Asa; ☺4.30-9.30pm) On the main road across from the municipal market.

🔒 Shopping

Kawinthip Hattakham SOUVENIRS
(กวินทิพย์หัตถกรรม; 75 Th Kaew Asa; ☺8am-7pm) This shop selling authentic Phi Ta Khon masks and other festival-related souvenirs makes for a fun browse. It also has bike hire (100B per day) and coffee.

❶ Information

The main road through town is Th Kaew Asa. At its north end, near the municipal market, is the **library** (☺8.30am-4.30pm Mon-Fri), which has free internet and festival displays, and the **city hall** (têt-sà-bahn; ☎0 4289 1231; www.tessaban dansai.com; ☺8.30am-4.30pm Mon-Fri), where English-speaking staff enjoy answering questions. **Krung Thai Bank** (Rte 2013; ☺8.30am-4.30pm Mon-Fri), which changes cash and travellers cheques, is on the main highway.

❶ Getting There & Away

Buses between Loei (60B, 1½ hours) and Phitsanulok (94B, three hours) stop in Dan Sai near the junction of Th Kaew Asa and Rte 2013 every couple of hours.

Sirindhorn Art Centre ศูนย์ศิลป์สิรินธร

FREE Sirindhorn Art Centre (Rte 210; ☺8am-6pm) can be found at the unlikely location of Wang Saphung, 23km south of Loei. It was built to honour Sangkom Thongmee, a famous local teacher (since retired) at the adjoining school whose students, mostly farmers' children, won thousands of awards for their work. Student works (and sometimes professional pieces) are always on display and often for sale. There's also a nice sculpture garden in front.

Tham Erawan   ถ้ำเอราวัณ

High up the side of a beautiful limestone mountain, Tham Erawan (⊙7am-6.30pm) is a large cave shrine, featuring a giant seated Buddha. Gazing out over the mountain-studded plains below, the Buddha is visible from several kilometres away and can be reached by a winding staircase of 600 steps. The views are superb, especially at sunset. More stairs and a line of lights lead you through the massive chamber and out the other side of the mountain. Be sure to get out of the cave before they turn the lights out.

The temple is along Rte 210, just across the Nong Bualamphu Province line. Buses from Loei (25B to 35B, 1¼ hours, every half-hour) to Udon Thani will drop you 2.5km away. A motorcycle taxi will shuttle you to the temple for 30B.

Phu Kradueng National Park   อุทยานแห่งชาติภูกระดึง

Capped off by its eponymous peak, **Phu Kra-dueng National Park** (☑0 4287 1333; admission 400B; ⊙trail to summit 7am-2pm Oct-May) covers a high-altitude plateau, cut through with trails and peppered with cliffs and waterfalls. Rising to 1316m, Thailand's second national park is always cool at its highest reaches (average year-round temperature 20°C), where its flora is a mix of pine forest and savannah. Various forest animals, including elephants, Asian jackals, Asiatic black bears, sambar deer, serows and white-handed gibbons inhabit the 348-sq-km park.

There's a small visitor centre at the base of the mountain, but almost everything else is up top. The main trail scaling Phu Kra-dueng is 5.5km long and takes about three to four hours to climb. It's strenuous, but not too challenging (unless it's wet) since there are steps at most of the steep parts. The hike is quite scenic and there are rest stops with food vendors about every kilometre. Once on top, it's another 3km to the main visitor centre. You can hire porters to carry your gear balanced on bamboo poles (15B per kilogram).

The 5.5km trail that passes six waterfalls in a forested valley, is the most beautiful destination; even after November, when the water has largely dried up. There are also many clifftop viewpoints, some ideal for sunrises and sunsets, scattered around the mountain.

Spending the night atop Phu Kradueng is a rite of passage for many students, so the park gets unbelievably crowded during school holidays (especially the Christmas–New Year period and from March to May). The park is closed during the rainy season (June to September) because the path to the top becomes too difficult to climb.

🛏 Sleeping & Eating

Atop the mountain there's space for 5000 people to **camp** (per person with own tent 30B, 3-/6-person tent hire 225/450B), a variety of large **bungalows** (☑0 2562 0760; www.dnp.go.th/parkreserve; bungalows 900-3600B) and many open-air eateries serving the usual stir-fry dishes. If you're arriving late, there's also camping and bungalows at the bottom and some resorts outside the entrance.

❶ Getting There & Away

Buses between Loei (50B, 1½ hours) and Khon Kaen (75B, two hours) stop in Phu Kradueng town where *sŏrng·tăa·ou* (20B per person, charters 200B) take people to the base of the mountain, 10km away.

BUENG KAN PROVINCE

Thailand's newest province officially split off from Nong Khai in 2011. It's remote and often lovely territory, and though most people travelling along the Mekong out of Nong Khai head west, there are some real rewards for bucking the trend and heading east, including one of Thailand's most amazing temples and best homestay programs.

Bueng Kan   บึงกาฬ

Little Bueng Kan is growing fast, but it's the rubber industry (40% of the province's land is now rubber-tree plantation) driving the boom rather than its new capital-city status. The only thing that qualifies as an attraction is the **Thai-Lao Market** that takes place along the Mekong on Tuesday and Friday mornings. Some of the products, such as herbs and mushrooms, sold by the Lao traders are gathered in the forest. It's also interesting to take a gander at the river during the dry season since it recedes far from Bueng Kan and reaches one of its narrowest points along the Thai–Lao border.

BORDER CROSSING: BUENG KAN TO PAKSAN

Although it's very rarely done, you can cross the border here to Paksan, but only if you already have your Lao visa (see p770 for details). The boat costs 60B per person and goes when there are eight passengers.

Not surprisingly, most travellers only stop long enough to catch connecting transport to Wat Phu Tok. If you do decide to stay, the Mekong-facing **Maenam Hotel** (0 4249 1051; 107 Th Chansin; r 350-400B; ☀@☎) is the best located place in town. It's due for some TLC (some rooms are better than others, so ask to see several), but the rooms are large and have lots of little extras. Some fancier hotels were under construction on the highway when we last visited. Just about all the restaurants on Th Chansin set up tables along the riverside promenade, but there are many bugs here.

Buses to Nong Khai (100B, 2½ hours, six daily), Nakhon Phanom (130B, three hours, six daily) and Udon Thani (150B, 4½ hours, 12 daily) park near the old clock tower.

Ban Ahong   บ้านอาฮง

Ban Ahong is a pretty riverside village 20km before Bueng Kan. **Wat Ahong Silawat** (☼daylight hours), on its eastern edge, is built amid ruddy boulders at a river bend known as *Sàdeu Námkong* (the Mekong River's Navel) because of the large whirlpool that spins here June to September. A 7m-tall copy of Phitsanulok's Chinnarat Buddha gazes over the Mekong from the building south of the *bòht* and giant Mekong catfish (*blah bèuk*) lurk in the fish pond, though they're rarely seen. It's presumed to be the deepest spot along the river and there are legends about *naga* living in underwater caves. In fact, *bâng fai pá yah nâhk* (*naga* fireballs; see the boxed text, p465) were first reported here and this is the only place where they appear in colours other than red.

The **Ahong Maekhong View Hotel** (08 6227 0465; r 500-800B; ☀) sits along the river on the temple grounds (all profits go to the temple) and does most of its business with tour groups, so it's likely you'll either find it booked out or you'll be the only guests. Each

of the 15 large rooms is well appointed and has a balcony, and the serene location makes this a great place to stay. The abbot, wanting to promote a peaceful atmosphere, requested that the rooms have no TVs. Another overnight option is the village's **homestay** (08 0755 0661; per person 200B, meals 100B), though there's barely any English spoken.

Buses between Nong Khai (100B, 2½ hours, six daily) and Bueng Kan can drop you at the temple.

Wat Phu Tok   วัดภูทอก

With its network of rickety staircases and walkways built in, on and around a giant sandstone outcrop, **Wat Phu Tok** (Isolated Mountain Temple; ☼6am-5pm, closed 10-16 April) is one of the region's wonders. The precarious paths lead past shrines and *gù·dì* that are scattered around the mountain on cliffs and in caves and provide fabulous views over the surrounding countryside. A final scramble up roots and rocks takes you to the forest on the summit, which is considered the 7th level. If you hustle and take all the short cuts you can be up and down in about an hour, but we advise against it: this is a climb that should be savoured. The quiet isolation entices monks and *mâa chee* (nuns) from all over Thailand to come meditate, so be quiet and respectful as you explore.

This forest temple used to be the domain of the famous meditation master Luang Pu Juan, a disciple of Luang Pu Man (see p488). He died in a plane crash in 1980 along with several other highly revered forest monks who were flying to Bangkok for Queen Sirikit's birthday celebration. A marble *chedi* containing Luang Pu Juan's belongings, some bone relics and fantastic exterior sculptures sits below the mountain amid a gorgeous garden.

Visitors who impress the monks by expressing some knowledge of Buddhism and meditation are permitted to stay the night in single-sex dorms at the base of the mountain.

ⓘ Getting There & Away

Túk-túk in Bueng Kan can be hired for the trip to Wat Phu Tok for 800B for the return journey plus a few hours waiting time. It's cheaper to take a bus from Bueng Kan to Ban Siwilai (20B, 45 minutes), where túk-túk drivers will do the trip for 300B to 400B. If you catch an early bus to Bueng Kan, Wat Phu Tok can be visited as a day trip from Nong Khai, although there's no need to backtrack since buses from Siwilai go to Udon Thani (140B, four hours).

If you're driving or pedalling, continue past Bueng Kan for 27km until you reach Chaiyapon, then turn right at Rte 3024, the road signed for Chet Si, and Tham Phra waterfalls. (These are in the Phu Wua Wildlife Reserve and make worthy detours, as much for the weird rocky landscape as the cascades. There's only water mid-May through December.) After 17.5km make a right and continue 4km more.

Ban Kham Pia   บ้านขามเปี้ย

Isan is flush with village homestay programs that let you delve deep into rural life; however most are aimed at Thai tour groups. But, thanks to the help of Open Mind Projects (p39) and English-speaking village-head Khun Bunleud, **Ban Kham Pia** (☑0 4241 3578, 08 7861 0601; www.thailandwildelephant trekking.com; r 200B) really knows how to welcome *fa·ràng* (meals 50B to 90B).

Another great thing about this homestay is that it's within walking distance of the 186-sq-km **Phu Wua Wildlife Reserve**, so you can add some superb treks (including sleeping in a cave) to your trip. The forest is flush with waterfalls and home to about three-dozen elephants. They're sometimes encountered on day walks from the village during the rainy season and seen almost daily from January to April during overnight stays in the 'treehouses' (not for the faint-hearted). These are in the midst of a forest clearing where monks bring sugarcane to discourage the elephants from raiding farm fields. It's about an hour's drive from the village. The standard guide fee in and around the village is 300B per day and motorcycles cost 200B per day.

Ban Kham Pia is 190km east of Nong Khai. Buses between Nong Khai (140B, 3½ hours) and Nakhon Phanom (130B, three hours) will drop you at Ban Don Chik, 3km away.

NAKHON PHANOM PROVINCE

Lao and Vietnamese influences are strong in Nakhon Phanom, a province bordered by the Mekong and full of highly revered temples. Though just about every person you see tending their fields is ethnically Thai, many wear conical Vietnamese-style straw hats. It's a region of subtleties rather than can't-miss attractions, but there are plenty of fine river views and interesting historic sites, and the colossal Wat Phra That Phanom is an enchanting talisman of Isan culture.

Nakhon Phanom   นครพนม

POP 31,700

Nakhon Phanom means 'City of Mountains', but the undulating sugarloaf peaks all lie across the river in Laos, so you'll be admiring rather than climbing them. The views are stunning, though, especially during a hazy sunrise. Nothing else in the peaceful, clean and proud city is quite as appealing as the distant row of hills, though there's plenty more to see and do for those who've come all the way out here. Most Thai visitors make some time to shop for silver at the shops near the pier.

Nakhon Phanom's temples have a distinctive style. This was once an important town in the Lan Xang Empire, and after that Thai kings sent their best artisans to create new buildings. Later a vivid French influence crossed the Mekong and jumped into the mix.

◉ Sights & Activities

Ban Na Chok   HISTORIC SITE
(บ้านนาจอก) The Vietnamese community in Ban Na Chok, about 3.5km west of town, has restored **Uncle Ho's House** (☑0 4252 2430; admission 50B; ⊙daylight hours), the simple wooden house where Ho Chi Minh stayed at times (1928–9) while planning his resistance movement. There are a few more Ho Chi Minh displays, some labelled in English, a bit to the northwest at the **community centre** (☑08 0315 4630; admission free; ⊙8am-5pm). There's a celebration of his birthday here every 19 May.

Wat Okat   TEMPLE
(วัดโอกาส; Th Sunthon Wijit; ⊙daylight hours) Predating the town, Wak Oka is home to Phra Taew and Phra Tiam, two sacred wooden Buddha images covered in gold that sit on the highest pedestal in the *wí·hǎhn*. The current Tiam (on the right) is a replica, the original was stolen in 2010, which shocked the city. The amazing mural is one of our favourites in Thailand – it's like a Thai *Where's Wally?*; try to find the backpackers – and shows the story of Phra Taew and Phra Tiam floating across the Mekong from Laos.

Nakhon Phanom

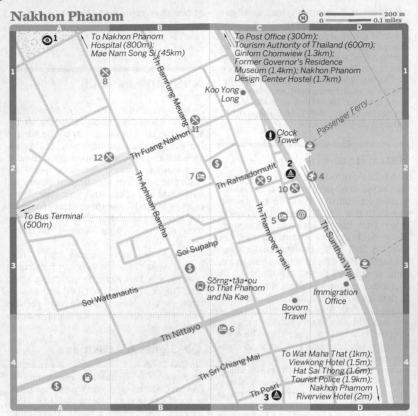

Nakhon Phanom

Wat Si Thep   TEMPLE
(วัดศรีเทพประดิษฐาราม; Th Si Thep; ☉daylight hours) This temple's *bòht* has a lot of flair. It's surrounded by statues of *têp* (angels) and has a colourful triptych on the back wall. The interior murals show the *jataka* around the upper portion and kings of the Chakri dynasty below. The French-colonial abbot's residence, built in 1921, won a preservation award.

FREE **Former Governor's Residence Museum**   MUSEUM
(จวนผู้ว่าราชการจังหวัดนครพนม (หลังเก่า); Th Sunthon Wijit; ☉10am-6pm Wed-Sun) This museum fills a beautifully restored 1925 mansion

with photos of old Nakhon Phanom, many labelled in English, while out the back are displays about the Illuminated Boat Procession (see below). If you've got questions about Nakhon Phanom, ask to speak with Bai-Tong, or find her at Luk Tan restaurant at night.

Sunset Cruise
BOAT TRIP

(per person 50B) The city runs this hour-long Mekong River cruise on *Thesaban 1*, which docks across from the Indochina Market. Snacks are served and, of course, there's karaoke.

Mekong Underwater World
AQUARIUM

(สถานที่จัดแสดงโลกของปลาแม่น้ำโขง; Rte 2033; admission 30B; ⏰9.30am-4pm Mon-Fri, 9am-4pm Sat & Sun) If you like fish, you'll like this aquarium housing Mekong River species, including *blah beuk* (giant Mekong catfish). It's 6km west of town along Hwy 22. *Sŏrng-tăa-ou* to Na Kae (20B, 15 minutes) pass by.

Wat Maha That
TEMPLE

(วัดมหาธาตุ; Th Sunthon Wijit; ⏰daylight hours) The 24m-tall, gold-and-white Phra That Nakhon *chedi* here resembles the previous *chedi* built at That Phanom (see p485).

Chom Khong Park
PARK

(สวนชมโขง; Th Ratchathan; admission free; ⏰5am-8pm) This park used to be a prison and models of prisoners sit in some of the old cells. You can also climb the guard towers.

Hat Sai Thong
BEACH

(หาดทรายทอง) From February to April, a sandbar that boosters call Golden Sand Beach, rises near the Viewkong Hotel. It's better as a place to watch fishermen than to swim.

⚔ Festivals & Events

Nakhon Phanom is famous for its **Illuminated Boat Procession** (Lái Reua Fai), a modern twist on the ancient tradition of sending rafts loaded with food, flowers and candles down the Mekong as offerings for the *naga* during **Ork Phansaa** (the end of Buddhist Lent). Today's giant bamboo rafts hold as many as 10,000 handmade lanterns, and some designers add animation to the scenes. Boat races, music competitions and other festivities run for a week, but the boats are launched only on the night of the full moon. That morning Phu Tai perform their 'peacock dance' in front of That Phanom (p485).

🛏 Sleeping

Windsor Hotel
HOTEL $

(☑0 4251 1946; 272 Th Bamrung Meuang; r 250-400B; ❉@🖲) Housed in a rather intimidating concrete block, the Windsor Hotel is nevertheless superclean, and if you can ignore the decades of age, it's a good choice. Wi-fi reaches the 1st-floor rooms and mountain views are available at the top.

Nakhon Phanom Design Center Hostel
HOSTEL $

(NDC; ☑08 5668 1780; Th Goobahtwai; dm incl breakfast & bicycle hire 350B; ❉🖲) A local architect has converted this old shophouse near the Mekong into an office-cafe-hostel. It has just two rooms and four beds, but lots of character.

iHotel
HOTEL $$

(☑0 4254 3355; Th That Phanom; r 590-1000B; ❉@🖲) The stylish 'i' mixes good mattresses, 'power showers', a backyard garden and attentive staff. On the downside, it's 5km south of town.

Viewkong Hotel
HOTEL $$

(☑0 4251 3564; www.viewkonghotel.com; Th Sunthon Wijit; r 550-900B; ste 2500B; ❉@🖲) The town's former chart-topping hotel has less pizzazz and more wear than the current champ (the Nakhon Phanom Riverview), but it's priced better and feels less cold. There's a pleasant terrace overlooking the river and it has karaoke, massage and all the other things Thai travellers can't live without. River-view rooms cost a bit extra, but are definitely worth it.

Nakhon Phanom Riverview Hotel
HOTEL $$

(☑0 4252 2333; www.nakhonphanomriverview hotel.com; Th That Phanom; r 1050-1680B, ste 3150-10,500B; ❉@🖲🏊) Though it's also showing its age and the wi-fi doesn't yet reach beyond the lobby, the Riverview has rooms with a river view and there's a lovely swimming pool. At times it drops rates to 600B.

SP Residence
HOTEL $

(☑0 4251 3500; 193/1 Th Nittayo; r 450-800B; ❉@) Plain but modern, the rooms here are less institutional than the exterior and hallways would lead you to believe.

Grand Hotel
HOTEL $

(☑0 4251 3788; 210 Th Si Thep; r 200-390B; ❉) 'Grand' it ain't, and the menagerie of animal statues in the lobby can't hide how old and spartan it is, but it's pretty clean and good for the price. The cheapest rooms on the 4th floor provide hot water and a peek at the mountains.

✖ Eating

After dinner, head to one of the laid-back, attractive bars that fill historic shophouses near the clock tower.

Indochina Market   THAI $

(Th Sunthon Wijit; ⊗breakfast, lunch & dinner) The balcony fronting the food court has choice seats that frame the mountain views.

Ginlom Chomwiew   THAI $

(no Roman-script sign; Th Sunthon Wijit; dishes 50-240B; ⊗dinner) The name of this garden spot across from the river, 'Relax and Enjoy the View', sums it up well. As for the food, do what most locals do and order some Mekong River fish such as *blàh johk sǎhm rót* (soldier river barb fish with three flavours).

Luk Tan   INTERNATIONAL, THAI $

(83 Th Bamrung Meuang; dishes 29-240B; ⊗lunch & dinner Tue-Sun) This quirky little spot does Thai-style steaks and *fa·ràng* favourites such as pizza and some of the best mashed potatoes in Thailand.

Night Market   THAI $

(Th Fuang Nakhon; ⊗4-9pm) Large and diverse, but few places to sit.

Good Morning Vietnamese & Coffee   VIETNAMESE $

(165 Th Thamrong Prasit; dishes 30-100B; ⊗ breakfast, lunch & dinner) This little corner shop has modernised with bright colours and a coffee bar, but it still serves the same family recipes, including *nǎam neu·ang* (assemble-it-yourself pork spring rolls) and

spicy Thai salads, that it has through four generations.

Baa Nang   NORTHEASTERN THAI $

(no sign; Th Aphiban Bancha; dishes 30-150B; ⊗breakfast & lunch) This simple corrugated-roof shack across from Anuban Nakhon Phanom school attracts the masses for *gài yâhng, sôm·đam* and other down-home Isan food.

ℹ Information

Bangkok Bank (Tesco-Lotus, Th Nittayo; ⊗10am-8pm) Has cash-only foreign exchange, but is open long hours.

Crab Technology (Th Si Thep; internet per hr 15B; ⊗8am-10pm)

Immigration (☑0 4251 1235; Th Sunthon Wijit; ⊗8.30am-noon & 1-4.30pm Mon-Fri) For visa extensions.

Tourism Authority of Thailand (TAT; ☑0 4251 3490; tatphnom@tat.or.th; Th Sunthon Wijit; ⊗8.30am-4.30pm) Covers Nakhon Phanom, Sakon Nakhon and Mukdahan Provinces.

ℹ Getting There & Away

Air

Nok Air (☑0 2900 9955; www.nokair.com) flies daily to/from Bangkok's Don Muang Airport (one way 2600B). Agencies such as **Bovorn Travel** (☑0 4251 2494; Th Nittayo; ⊗8am-4.30pm Mon-Fri, 8am to 1pm Sat & Sun) sell tickets. An airport shuttle drops passengers at any in-town hotel for 120B per person.

Bus

Nakhon Phanom's **bus terminal** (☑0 4251 3444; Th Fuang Nakhon) is west of the town centre. From here buses head to Nong Khai (210B, 6½ hours, six daily); Udon Thani (155B to 195B, four to five hours, every 45 minutes until 3.50pm) via Sakon Nakhon (65B to 85B, 1½ hours); Ubon Ratchathani (116B to 209B, 4½ hours, nine daily) via Mukdahan (52B to 88B, 2½

THE BI-COLOURED RIVER   แม่น้ำสองสี

If you're driving along Rte 212, take a short break at **Mae Nam Song Si**, 45km from Nakhon Phanom, where the muddy brown Mekong River meets the greenish water of Mae Nam Songkhram. The line between the two is very clear, especially when it's windy or rainy. And don't be swayed by any locals you meet along the way who tell you there's no such place in Nakhon Phanom, that you must be thinking of Mae Nam Song Si (p440) in Ubon Ratchathani. Just turn at the sign for 'The Bi-Coloured River.' This northern merger may be much less famous, but it's still pretty cool.

Suan Ahahn Paknam (no roman-script sign; ☑08 1974 4227; dishes 30-290B; ⊗lunch & dinner) is a superb little restaurant on a shaky wooden deck right at the confluence. The same family has opened a shiny new **guest house** (r 400B; ❋@) a few doors down.

hours) and That Phanom (27B to 47B, one hour). Most Bangkok (450B to 592B, 11 to 12 hours) buses depart between 7am to 8am and 4.30pm to 7pm. VIP service is offered by **999 VIP** (☑0 4251 1403) for 823B.

Sŏrng·tăa·ou to That Phanom (35B, 90 minutes, every 15 minutes until 3.30pm) park near Kasikornbank.

ℹ Getting Around

Túk-túk drivers quote 20B to 30B per person from the bus station to most places in town and 200B for the round trip to Ban Na Chok.

Nakhon Phanom's sparse traffic makes it a good place for biking. **Koo Yong Long** (☑0 4251 1118; 363 Th Sunthon Wijit; per hr/day 10/70B; ⊗8am-5pm) hires bikes.

Renu Nakhon   เรณูนคร

Renu Nakhon is a Phu Tai village known for cotton weaving, though few people in the town proper work their looms anymore. It's better to visit a nearby village, if you want to see cloth being made. The finished products, along with silk and cotton from Laos and elsewhere in Thailand, are sold in the big **handicrafts market** on the grounds of **Wat Phra That Renu Nakhon** (⊗daylight hours) as well as at a string of nearby shops. The temple's 35m-tall *tâht* closely resembles the previous *chedi* built in That Phanom and is considered very holy. Tour groups sometimes arrange Phu Tai folk dances on the stage outside the market.

The turn-off to Renu Nakhon is 8km north of That Phanom, and then it's another 7km west on Rte 2031. There's no public transport. Túk-túk drivers in That Phanom ask 300B round trip (200B for just one person) with a little waiting time for you to look at the *tâht* and do some shopping, but the final price depends on your bargaining skills. You might save a little travelling up to the junction and bargaining with a túk-túk driver there.

That Phanom   ธาตุพนม

Towering over this small, peaceful town, the spire of the colossal *chedi* at Wat Phra That Phanom is one of the region's most emblematic symbols and one of the great flagpoles of Isan identity. In comparison, the town itself, divided neatly in two with the older half next to the river, is rather forgettable.

BORDER CROSSING: NAKHON PHANOM TO THA KHAEK

The **Thai-Lao Friendship Bridge 3**, north of the city, was due to open as this book went to press. Passenger ferries will continue to link Nakhon Phanom to Tha Khaek in Laos, but they will be for locals only. Buses to Tha Khaek (70B) run between 7am and 6pm and all immigration formalities are handled at the bridge during the crossing.

◉ Sights

Wat Phra That Phanom   TEMPLE
(วัดพระธาตุพนม; Th Chayangkun; ⊗5am-8pm) This temple is a potent and beautiful place; even if you're feeling templed-out, you'll likely be impressed. At its hub is a *tâht*, more impressive than any in present-day Laos and highly revered by Buddhists from both countries. Many people believe that visiting seven times will bring them prosperity and happiness so it's something of a pilgrimage site.

The *tâht* is 53.6m high, and a five-tiered, 16kg gold umbrella laden with precious gems adds 4m more to the top. Many Thais believe that the Lord Buddha travelled to Thailand and directed that one of his breast-bone relics be enshrined in a *chedi* to be built on this very site: and so it was in 535 BC, eight years after his death. Historians date the first construction, a short stupa (there's a replica of how it may have looked in a pond in front of the temple), to around the 9th century AD and modifications have been routine since then. In 1690 it was raised to 47m and you'll find replicas of this *tâht* all over Isan. The current design went up in 1941, but it toppled during heavy rains in 1975 and was rebuilt in 1978.

Behind the surrounding cloister is a shady little park with a giant drum and to the north sits a 30m-long century-old longboat carved from a single tree. The nearby **museum** (admission free; ⊗8.30am-4pm) tells the legend (not the history) of the *tâht* and also displays a hodgepodge collection of pottery, gongs, US presidential commemorative coins and more.

Kuson Ratchadagon Street   HISTORIC SITE
(ถนนกุศลรัชฎากร) Standing high on the road in front of Phra That Phanom is an **arch**

That Phanom

That Phanom

that symbolically connects the *tâht* to the Mekong River. The block of French-Indochinese architecture between the arch and the river is reminiscent of old Saigon and a couple of the interiors are nearly museum-quality timeless. A few shops sell Vietnamese foods.

Thai-Lao Open-Border Market   MARKET
(ตลาดชายแดนไทย-ลาว; ⊙7am-2pm Mon & Thu) Hundreds of Lao cross the river to shop and sell at this biweekly market. It's mostly the same tat found in other Thai markets, but a few of the Lao traders in front of the temple sell roots, honey, bats and other forest products.

🎉 Festivals

During the **That Phanom Festival** in late January or early February, visitors descend from all over Thailand and Laos to make merit and pay respect to the *tâht*. The streets fill with market stalls, many top *mŏr lam* troupes perform and the town hardly sleeps for nine days.

🛏 Sleeping

During the That Phanom Festival rates soar and rooms are booked out well in advance. A new hotel at the riverfront promenade that was under construction when we visited looked promising.

Kritsada Rimkhong Hotel   HOTEL **$**
(📞08 1262 4111; www.ksdrimkhong-resort.com; 90 Th Rimkhong; r 350-500B; ❄@🛜) Rooms range from plain to very attractive, but all are comfy. Its restaurant uses some of the organic veggies grown on the riverbank below. If the friendly English-speaking owner is around when you call, he'll pick you up at the bus station for free.

Thatphanom Place   HOTEL **$$**
(📞0 4253 2148; thatphanomplace@gmail.com; Th Chayangkun; r 590B; ❄🛜) This lovely new (opened 2010) hotel has the best rooms in town, each featuring a unique design. If only it was near the river rather than the highway.

Saengthong Rimkhong Hotel   HOTEL **$**
(📞0 4254 1397; 507 Th Rimkhong; r 300-600B; ❄🛜) This so-so place has a mix of so-so older rooms – at this price they should have hot-water showers, but they don't – and decent newer rooms. It won't excite you, but it won't let you down either.

Chaivon Hotel   HOTEL **$**
(📞0 4254 1391; 38 Th Phanom Phanarak; r 200-300B; ❄) This green wooden hotel is pretty shabby and definitely not for everyone, but some people may enjoy a night here as it's a genuine historic relic.

🍴 Eating & Drinking

That Phanom's **Night Market** (🕐4-10pm) has a good variety of food, but few places to sit. Also, come nightfall, lots of small **riverside restaurants** (Th Rimkhong) perched on stilts and ablaze in fairy lights open their doors north of the promenade. For the most part, the biggest difference between them is the volume of the karaoke machine, so have a wander and pick your place.

Krua Kitty   THAI **$$**
(419 Soi 16; dishes 40-350B; 🕐dinner) For something almost fancy, try this open-fronted place that's popular with local bigwigs. There are classic album covers on the wall and a large menu with some dishes labelled in English.

Baan 117   CAFE **$**
(117 Soi 16; organic coffee 40B; 🕐breakfast, lunch & dinner) The welcoming husband-and-wife team, casual setting and quality beans conspire to make this the top spot in town for a cup of joe.

That's Good   THAI **$**
(37 Th Phanom Phanarak; dishes 50-100B; 🕐dinner) This bar feels like a coffee shop and looks like a grandma's living room, and by That Phanom standards, that makes it quite hip. There isn't a full menu, but there are Thai salads and fried snacks.

ℹ️ Getting There & Away

From That Phanom's new bus station, inconveniently located west of town (a túk-túk to the river should cost 30B), there are services to Ubon Ratchathani (95B to 167B, 4½ hours, hourly) via Mukdahan (26B to 45B, one hour), Udon Thani (102B to 184B, four hours, five daily) via Sakon Nakhon (35B to 65B, 1¼ hours, 10 daily) and Nakhon Phanom (27B to 47B, one hour, five daily). For Nakhon Phanom you can also take one of the frequent *sŏrng-tăa-ou* (35B, 90 minutes, every 15 minutes until 3.30pm) that park north of the *tâht*. There are a few morning buses to Bangkok (400B to 801B, 10 to 11 hours), but most depart between 5pm and 7pm and one Bangkok-bound company remains at the old bus station in town.

There's an immigration office in town, but it's only for Lao visitors on market day: nobody else is allowed to cross the river here.

SAKON NAKHON PROVINCE

Many famous forest temples sit deep in the Phu Phan mountain range that runs across Sakon Nakhon Province, and among Sakon Nakhon's famous sons are several of the most highly revered monks in Thai history, including Luang Pu (Ajahn) Man Bhuridatto, who was born in Ubon Ratchathani but died here, and his student, Luang Pu (Ajahn) Fan Ajaro. Both were ascetic *tú-dong* monks who attained high levels of proficiency in *vipassana* meditation and are widely recognised among Thais as having been *arahants* (fully enlightened beings).

Sakon Nakhon   สกลนคร

POP 68,000

Workaday Sakon Nakhon is primarily an agricultural market town and Th Ratpattana is chock-a-block with shops selling farm equipment. Although the city centre is the usual concrete mess, quiet neighbourhoods on the fringes are full of old wooden houses, and this is where you'll find the town's main attractions.

◉ Sights

Wat Pa Sutthawat — TEMPLE
(วัดป่าสุทธาวาส; ☺daylight hours) The grounds of Wat Pa Sutthawat, on the southwestern outskirts of town, are essentially a shrine to two of Thailand's best-known monks. Most famous of all is Luang Pu (Ajahn) Man Bhuridatto, who helped found the temple but didn't live here until just before his death in 1949. The final resting place of Ajahn Man's personal effects, the **Ajahn Man Museum**, looks a bit like a modern Christian church, with arches and etched-glass windows. A bronze image of Ajahn Man sits on a pedestal at the back and relics that remained after his cremation are in a glass box in front.

Luang Pu (Ajahn) Lui Chanthasaro, who died in 1989, was one of Ajahn Man's most famous students, and King Rama IX designed the *chedi* that holds the **Ajahn Lui Museum**. Ajahn Lui is represented in lifelike wax.

Both museums showcase all the monks' worldly possessions, as well as photographs and descriptions of their lives; Ajahn Man's displays, signed in English, provide a good sense of a monk's life.

Wat Phra That Choeng Chum — TEMPLE
(วัดพระธาตุเชิงชุม; Th Reuang Sawat; ☺daylight hours) The most visible highlight at Wat Phra That Choeng Chum is the 24m-high Lao-style *chedi*, which was erected in the 17th century over a smaller 11th-century Khmer *prang* and is now topped by a solid-gold umbrella. The name means 'Stupa of the Gathering of the Footprints Temple' because it was built above four Buddha footprints, which many Thais believe were left by the four incarnations of the Lord Buddha. *Lôok ní-mít* (spherical ordination-precinct markers that look like cannonballs and are buried under the regular boundary markers that surround most *bòht*) are lined up in the back.

Also on the grounds are a Lan Xang-era *bòht*, an enormous wooden bell and an octagonal *hŏr đrai* that now houses a little **museum**: If you want to look inside, ask a monk to get the key. The top of the western gate resembles the wax castles carved for Ork Phansaa (see opposite).

Wat Phra That Narai Cheng Weng — TEMPLE
(วัดพระธาตุนารายณ์เจงแวง) About 5km west of town at Ban That is a 10th- to 11th-century Khmer *prang* (named Phra That Nawaeng, a contraction of the words Narai Cheng Weng) in the early Bapuan style. Originally part of a Khmer-Hindu complex, the five-level sandstone *prang* is missing much of its top, but still features several lintels including a reclining Vishnu over its northern portico and a dancing Shiva over its eastern one. It's not very impressive or evocative, but it's the most complete Khmer ruin in the province.

To get here by public transport take *sŏrng·tăa·ou* 3 (10B) from near the market or catch it heading north on Th Ratpattana. Get off at Ban That Market and walk 500m south.

Nong Han — LAKE
(หนองหาน) Rimming the eastern and northern edges of town is 123-sq-km Nong Han, Isan's largest natural lake, which is well known among Thais due to the legend (see boxed text, opposite) surrounding it. Fishermen, who tie up their boats just east of Srinakarin Park, will take you out sightseeing, including a stop to visit the abandoned temple on **Ko Don Sawan** (Paradise Island), the lake's largest island. The going rate is around 800B. Don't copy the fishermen and swim in the lake: it's infested with liver flukes, which can cause a nasty infection known as opisthorchiasis.

The nearby Fishery Station has an **aquarium** (Th Sai Sawang; admission free; ☺9am-3pm) with fish from the lake as well as the Mekong River and Mae Nam Songkhram.

✯✯ Festivals

Ork Phansaa, the end of the Buddhist lent (late October or early November), is fervently celebrated in Sakon. The main activity is a parade featuring **wax castles**, which are then put on display in Ming Meuang Field. They can also be seen at each of the city's temples for about a month after the event.

🛏 Sleeping

Dusit Hotel — HOTEL $
(☎0 4271 1198; www.dusitsakhon.com, in Thai; Th Yuwaphattana; r 400-710B; ste 1900B; ❋@☎) This reborn old-timer has the loveliest lobby and cheeriest staff in town. The more you pay the more atmosphere you get, but each price category offers good value. The restaurant is good and the owner, Fiat, is a great source of local info.

LP Mansion — HOTEL $
(no Roman-script sign; ☎0 04271 5356; Th Prem Prida; r 250-400B; ❋@☎) LP is cheap, but not a cheapskate. Even the cheapest rooms get free coffee, Oreos and a minifridge. Rates at its older sister sleeper around the corner start at 200B.

NH The Elegant Hotel HOTEL **$$**
(☏0 4271 3338; Th Robmuang; s/d 650/700B;
❋@☎) Smart sums it up better than elegant, but that's really beside the point. What matters is that these well-appointed rooms are rock solid for the price, which includes

breakfast *and* dinner. Its biggest drawback is the noncentral location.

U-Hotel HOTEL **$$**
(☏0 4274 3033; Hwy 22; r 690-1590B; ❋@☎)
A clever design and some subtle artistic flair make this new (opened in 2010) place

---

THE LEGEND OF THE LAKE AMARALAK (PIM) KHAMHONG

Phya Khom was the ruler of Ekthita city. He had a beautiful daughter named Nang Ai whose beauty was known by everyone in every land. Prince Phadaeng of Phaphong city came to visit Nang Ai secretly, and they fell in love immediately. They spent a night together and promised that they would be rightfully married soon.

In the sixth lunar month, Phya Khom arranged a rocket-shooting contest and invited people from the surrounding lands to participate. Whoever's rocket went the highest would be rewarded with treasure and his daughter's hand in marriage. Prince Phadaeng was not invited; however, he came with a great rocket anyway knowing that he must win in order to marry Nang Ai. At the contest, Phya Khom's rocket failed to fire, as did Phadaeng's. In anger Phya Khom broke his promise and gave nothing to the winner. Phadaeng then went back to his own city with great disappointment.

While the contest was taking place, the *naga* Phangkhi, son of Suttho Naga, ruler of the underground land called Muang Badan, came in disguise to witness the beauty of Nang Ai and fell deeply in love with her.

After he returned home, he was unable to eat and sleep; so, despite his father's objection, he went back again. This time he disguised himself as a white squirrel and hid in a tree near Nang Ai's window. Once Nang Ai saw the white squirrel she wanted to have it, so she ordered a soldier to catch it for her. Unable to do so, the soldier eventually killed the squirrel with a poisoned arrow. As Phangkhi was dying he made a wish: 'May my meat be very delicious and enough to feed everyone in the city'. His wish came true and all the townspeople, except the widows who had no official duties, got a share of his meat.

When Phangkhi's followers, who witnessed his death, returned to Muang Badan and reported the news, Suttho Naga was so angry that he called in tens of thousands of soldiers to destroy Phya Khom's city. They headed off instantly to Ekthita.

Meanwhile, Phadaeng was so lovesick that he couldn't stay in his own city any longer and rode his horse back to see Nang Ai. When the two met again, she gave him a very warm welcome and offered him food cooked with squirrel meat. Phadaeng refused to eat and told Nang Ai that the squirrel was Phangkhi in disguise and that whoever ate his meat would die and their city would be destroyed.

Suttho Naga's army arrived at Ekthita by nightfall. The destruction they inflicted was so severe that the foundation of the city started to collapse. Phadaeng told Nang Ai to take the kingdom's rings, gong and drum and they fled on his horse. When Suttho Naga learned Nang Ai had run away, he began to follow her. The earth sank wherever he passed. Thinking that Suttho Naga was following the rings, gong and drum, Nang Ai threw them away but the *naga* still followed. When the horse grew tired, Suttho Naga caught up with them and grabbed Nang Ai with his tail and carried her down to Muang Badan.

The battle had caused the whole area to sink and it became a huge lake, called Nong Han. The widows who did not eat the squirrel meat were safe and the land on which their houses stood did not sink, leaving it a small island that has been called Don Hang Mai (Widow's Island) ever since.

Phadaeng returned to Phaphong, but could not bear the sadness from the loss of Nang Ai. He chose to die in order to continue to fight for her. After his death, he became a ghost leader and his army fought the *naga* in Muang Badan. The fight lasted so long that the god Indra had to come down to stop it. Ever since, Nang Ai has been waiting for Indra to decide who should be her husband.

Sakon Nakhon

worth considering by those with their own wheels. It's 5km outside town on the way to Udon Thani, across from Rajabhat University.

MJ The Majestic   HOTEL **$$**
(📞0 4273 3771; Th Khu Meuang; r 800-1440B, ste 3440B; 🏭@🛜) The cheapest rooms at Sakon's most expensive hotel are bigger than Dusit and Elegant, but not better. It's worth considering, however, if you want the full gamut of night-time entertainment (cocktail lounge, massage, snooker, karaoke) that those quieter choices don't provide.

🍴 Eating & Drinking

The **Night Plaza** (Th Khu Meuang; ⊙4-9pm), Sakon's biggest night market, has an excellent selection of food, but it's all bagged up for takeaway, so a much better option is the smaller **11 Brothers & Sisters Night Mar-**

ket (no roman-script sign; Th Sukkasem; ⊙4-9pm) where all the vendors (now more than the original 11 siblings) are related.

[TOP CHOICE] **Prachachuen**   THAI **$**
(382 Th Makkhalai; dishes 60-230B; ⊙dinner) This lovely, youthful place in an old wooden house is one of Sakon's trendiest restaurants, but it doesn't slack on the food. Whether it's the fried rice or *blah chôrn sá·mŭn·prai* (snake-head fish with herbs in chilli sauce with mango) it will be divine.

Mit Auppatam   THAI **$**
(no roman-script sign; 37 Th Sukkasem; dishes 30-180B; ⊙breakfast, lunch & dinner) This traditional place is a popular breakfast stop (with great omelettes) but it also has a big menu of curries, steaks and more. The food is so good that word reached Princess Sirindhorn, who dropped in to dine in 2008. Unfortunately, nobody here speaks English.

Sakon Nakhon

Saban Ngaa   NORTHEASTERN THAI $

(🖉Th Ratpattana; dishes 30-150B; ⊘lunch & dinner) Famous for its Isan food (but also serving Thai and Chinese), this is a great place to try local dishes such as *gaang wǎi* (rattan curry), and vegetarians have the rare chance to eat *lâhp wún sên* (spicy mungbean noodles). The atmosphere is terrible but the food is terrific.

Green Corner   INTERNATIONAL, THAI $$

(🖉Th Ratpattana; dishes 45-420B; ⊘breakfast, lunch & dinner) The top spot for *fa·ràng* food also offers Thai and Isan dishes, though many of the latter, like fried cicadas and ant's-egg omelettes, are no longer written in English on the menu.

Coffee.com   CAFE $

(Th Prem Prida; espresso 35B; ⊘lunch & dinner Mon-Sat) A cute little coffee shop.

🛍 Shopping

Mann Craft (1576 Th Sukkasem) has some beautiful fabrics and finished products dyed with indigo and other natural colorants. The **OTOP Center** (Th Sukkasem; ⊘8.30am-5pm) also sells natural-dye fabrics plus maoberry and black-ginger wines.

ℹ Information

Most banks are found along Th Sukkasem and Th Ratpattana. Branches of Bangkok Bank at **Big C** (Th Jai Phasuk) and **Tesco-Lotus** (Th Makkhalai) shopping centres open 10am to 8pm daily, though they exchange cash only. There's an AEON ATM across from Big C.

Immigration (🖉0 4271 5219; Th Jai Phasuk; ⊘8.30am-noon & 1-4.30pm Mon-Fri) For visa extensions

ℹ Getting There & Away

Air

Nok Air (🖉0 2900 9955; www.nokair.com) flies twice daily to/from Bangkok's Don Muang Airport (one way 2600B). **Phu Sakon** (🖉0 4271 2259; 332/3 Th Sukkasem; ⊘8.30am-5pm Mon-Sat) sells tickets. There's an airport shuttle to town for 150B per person.

Bus

Sakon's centrally located **bus terminal** (Th Ratpattana) serves Ubon Ratchathani (117B to 211B, five hours, nine daily), That Phanom (35B to 63B, 1¼ hours, hourly), Nakhon Phanom (65B to 85B, 1½ hours, every half-hour), Udon Thani (100B to 130B, 3½ hours, every half-hour), Khon Kaen (155B, four hours, five daily) and Bangkok (360B to 463B, 11 hours, morning and early-evening departures only).

There are also buses to Udon Thani (102B, every half-hour) and Khon Kaen (155B, five daily) from the Esso petrol station north of the bus terminal.

There are VIP bus services to Bangkok (720B, 7.30pm and 7.45pm) with **999 VIP** (🖉0 4271 2860) from a roadside stop on Th Reuang Sawat (across from Sakon Nakhon Pattana Supsa School) south of town, but you can buy tickets from its office on Th Sukkasem.

Phu Phan Mountains

Highway 213 south from Sakon Nakhon towards Kalasin crawls over the Phu Phan mountain range, which has some interesting sites on its slopes. And since buses bound for Kalasin, Mahasarakham and Khon Kaen follow this highway, reaching them is easy. Most of the road between Talat Klang Dong Sang Kaw and Somdet cuts through uninterrupted forest and is very beautiful.

PHU PHAN RAJANIWET PALACE พระตำหนักภูพานราชนิเวศน์

The grounds of the **royal family's Isan home** (☑0 4271 1550; admission free; ⊘8am-4pm), 14km south of Sakon Nakhon, are open to the public when not in use. It's quite a modest residence compared to some of their other palaces, but the gardens are beautiful and peaceful. You can only walk around the main grounds, but cars can go to the elephant corral. Visitors are not permitted to wear shorts above the knees, short dresses or revealing tops. Buses cost 20B and take 20 minutes.

PHU PHAN NATIONAL PARK อุทยานแห่งชาติภูพาน

This **national park** (☑08 1263 5029; admission free) remains relatively undeveloped and isolated. It's no surprise that the area once provided cover for the Seri Thai resistance fighters in WWII and People's Liberation Army of Thailand (PLAT) guerrillas in the 1970s. The former used **Tham Seri Thai** as an arsenal and mess hall. The 664-sq-km park is now a stomping ground for barking deer, monitor lizards, slow loris, many monkeys and a few elephants.

There are two main areas to visit. Near the visitor centre there are nice views at **Nang Mern Cliff** and you can climb down a further 1.5km to **Lan Sao Aee** plateau, which is even better for sunsets. **Nam Tok Kam Hom**, a stretch of four petite waterfalls, is 8.5km north of the visitor centre, at a wild bend in the road called **Khong Ping Ngu Curve** – named after the stacked shape snakes make when put on a skewer for grilling – that has Thailand's largest kilometre pillar. Water only runs from August to October. Between these two places, far from the highway, is the seldom-visited natural rock bridge, **Tang Pee Parn**.

Accommodation options include **campsites** (per person with own tent 30B, 2-/6-person tent hire 150/225B) and six four-person **bungalows** (☑0 2562 0760; www.dnp.go.th/parkreserve; bungalows 500-2000B; ❄).

Buses to the visitor centre cost 25B and take 45 minutes.

TALAT KLANG DONG SANG KAW ตลาดกลางดงสร้างค้อ

Twenty-five kilometres past the national park visitor centre, **Klang Dong Sang Kaw Market** stocks custard apples and other foods grown on local farms, but it's best known for products such as honey, insects, bird's nests (for good luck) and mushrooms gathered in the surrounding forest. There are also locally produced whiskies and maoberry wines.

MUKDAHAN PROVINCE

Mukdahan มุกดาหาร

POP 34,300

On the banks of the Mekong, directly opposite the Lao city of Savannakhet, Mukdahan is one of the region's more humdrum towns. The December 2006 opening of the Thai-Lao Friendship Bridge 2 formalised Mukdahan's status as a regional trade hub by connecting Thailand and Vietnam by road and gave the economy a shot in the arm; though the city doesn't feel any different than it did before.

⊙ Sights

Talat Indojin MARKET
(Indochina Market; ⊘8am-6pm) Other than the bridge, Mukdahan is best known for its riverside market, which stretches along and under the promenade. Most Thai tour groups on their way to Laos and Vietnam make a shopping stop for cheap food, clothing, assorted trinkets from China and Vietnam and silk and cotton fabrics made in Isan.

Hor Kaew Mukdahan MUSEUM
(หอแก้วมุกดาหาร; Th Samut Sakdarak; admission 20B; ⊘8am-6pm) One of the most oddly out-of-place landmarks in all of Thailand, this 65m-tall tower was built for the 50th anniversary of King Rama IX's ascension to the throne. The nine-sided base has a good museum with displays (labelled in English) on the eight ethnic groups of the province. There are great views and a few more historical displays in 'The 360° of Pleasure in Mukdahan by the Mekong' room up at the 50m level. The ball on the top holds a locally revered Buddha image supposedly made of solid silver.

Phu Manorom VIEWPOINT
(ภูมโนรมย์; ⊘6am-7pm) You can get a more organic view of Laos and the Mekong from this mountain further south. There's a nice little garden and a small temple. Tourism officials try to promote sunrise-watching here, but odds are it'll be just you and the monks.

Central Mukdahan

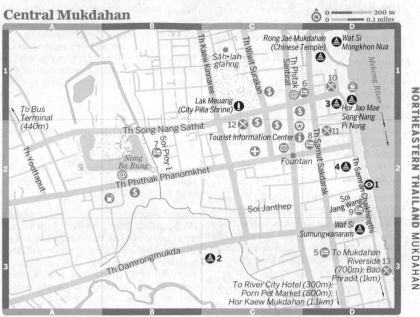

Central Mukdahan

Wat Si Mongkhon Tai TEMPLE

(วัดศรีมงคลใต้; Th Samran Chaikhongthi; ⊙daylight hours) According to one of the many legends associated with it, this temple's 2m-tall Phra Chao Ong Luang Buddha image is older than the city itself and was unearthed during Mukdahan's construction. The ceramic-encrusted northern gate was built as a gesture of friendship by the city's large Vietnamese community in 1954.

Wat Yod Kaeo Sivichai TEMPLE

(วัดยอดแก้วศรีวิชัย; Th Samran Chaikhongthi; ⊙daylight hours) This temple stands out for having its enormous Buddha inside a glass-walled wí·hǎhn, and not one, but two small chedi modelled on Phra That Phanom.

Wat Pa Silawiwet TEMPLE

(วัดป่าศิลาวิเวก; Th Damrongmukda; ⊙daylight hours) It's the hundred or so resident monkeys rather than anything religious that makes this forest temple on the edge of town worth a visit.

✨ Festivals

Besides the ordinary activities, January's **Mukdahan Thai Tribal Festival**, held for a week in the field fronting the săh·lah glahng, features dancing and other cultural activities from Mukdahan's eight ethnic groups.

🛏 Sleeping

The Riverside Hotel, which was under construction during our last visit, bears a look simply for its riverside location north of Wat Sumungwararam.

Ban Rim Suan   HOTEL $
(no Roman-script sign; ☎0 4263 2980; Th Samut Sakdarak; r 330B; ❄️@🛜) You can't call it lovely, but the owners have made some effort to liven things up here and that makes it the best budget deal in town: which is why it's almost always full by mid-afternoon. It's a tad south of the centre, but that makes it convenient for dinner and drinks along the river.

Submukda Grand Hotel   HOTEL $
(☎0 4263 3444; 72 Th Samut Sakdarak; r 400-500B; ❄️🛜) Erected at the same time as the bridge, this tower is losing its lustre, but still makes a good choice. And you can even squeeze out a river view from upper-floor balconies.

Huanum Hotel   HOTEL $
(☎0 4261 1137; Th Samut Sakdarak; r 150-350B; ❄️@🛜) A friendly old-timer that's been spruced up recently, this is the first choice of most backpackers. The cheapest rooms have cold-water showers.

Ploy Palace Hotel   HOTEL $$
(☎0 4263 1111; www.ploypalace.com; Soi Ploy 1; r 1050-1800B; ste 5500B; ❄️@🛜🏊) Rooms at this executive sleep-easy are dated, but are undergoing a slow-motion renovation: be sure to look at several before deciding. For something out of the ordinary, ask for the 8th- and 9th-floor rooms with beehives outside the windows.

River City Hotel   HOTEL $$
(☎0 4261 5444; www.rivermuk.com; Th Samut Sakdarak; r incl breakfast from 750B; ❄️@🛜🏊) With a large new tower under construction, this place is poised to unseat Ploy Palace as the best hotel in Mukdahan.

🍴 Eating

Most downtown restaurants shut their doors early, but many out along Phitak Phanomkhet Street keep the woks sizzling late into the night.

TOP CHOICE Bao Phradit   NORTHEASTERN THAI $
(no roman-script sign; Th Samran Chaikhongthi; dishes 30-200B; ⊙breakfast, lunch & dinner; 🛜) It's a bit of a trek south of the centre, but this is a real Isan restaurant with dishes like pàt pètmu/uu Ъàh (spicy stir-fried wild boar) and gaang wǎi (rattan curry). It's all served on a peaceful riverside deck. Though the English menu is a bit mysterious (it translates yam, Thai-style tangy salads, as 'review'), it's rare that a restaurant of this sort has any English at all.

TOP CHOICE Wine Wild Why?   THAI $
(Th Samran Chaikhongthi; dishes 40-150B; ⊙lunch & dinner) Housed in an atmospheric wooden building next to the river, this relaxing spot has bags of character and serves delicious Thai and Isan food, though the wine list is history. The sociable owners, transplants from Bangkok, just add to the charm.

Night Market   THAI-VIETNAMESE $
(Th Song Nang Sathit; ⊙4-9pm) Mukdahan's night market has all the Thai and Isan classics, but it's the Vietnamese vendors that set it apart. A few sell bǎhn dah (the vendors will tell you it's 'Vietnamese pizza'), which combines soft noodles, pork, spring onions and an optional egg served on a crispy cracker.

Goodmook*   INTERNATIONAL-THAI $
(414/1 Th Song Nang Sathit; dishes 60-380B; ⊙breakfast, lunch & dinner Tue-Sun; 🛜) This fun place has all the ingredients of a travellers' cafe – a mix of Thai and Western food (from đôm yam to T-bone), free wi-fi, art on the walls – except a room full of travellers, though many of those who do stop in Mukdahan longer than needed to change buses do cosy up here at some point.

Mukdahan Riverside   THAI $
(103/4 Th Samran Chaikhongthi; dishes 45-180B; ⊙lunch & dinner; 🛜) This long-popular spot offers great views from a garden terrace and a mostly Thai menu (featuring Mekong river fish, of course) that we've never heard a bad word spoken about.

Kufad   VIETNAMESE $
(no roman-script sign; 36-37 Th Samut Sakdarak; dishes 30-130B; ⊙breakfast & lunch) This simple Vietnamese cafe is rightly popular and a good choice for breakfast. The picture menu takes the guesswork out of ordering, but leaves you clueless on the prices.

ℹ️ Information

Huanam Hotel (Th Samut Sakdarak; per hr 20B; ⊙6am-11pm) The most pleasant place to check your email.

Krung Thai Bank (Th Song Nong Satit; ◷10am-7pm) The only extended-hours bank downtown.

Tourism Information Center (📞0 4261 2992; Th Phitak Phanomkhet; ◷9am-4.30pm Mon-Fri) The city tourism complex also has Thai massage and a crafts shop.

ℹ Getting There & Away

Mukdahan's **bus terminal** (📞0 4263 0486) is on Rte 212, west of town. To get there from the centre catch a yellow *sŏrng·tăa·ou* (10B, 6am to 5pm) running west along Th Phitak Phanomkhet. There are buses to Nakhon Phanom (52B to 88B, 2½ hours, every half-hour) via That Phanom (26B to 45B, one hour), Khon Kaen (155B to 187B, 4½ hours, every half-hour), Ubon Ratchathani (75B to 135B, 3½ hours, every half-hour) and Yasothon (76B to 97B, two hours, eight daily). There are also vans to Yasothon (76B, two hours, every half-hour). A few Bangkok buses (390B to 502B, 10 hours) leave during the day, but most depart between 5pm and 8pm, including **999 VIP** (📞0 4261 1478), which departs at 8am, 8pm and 8.15pm (670B).

If you're driving to Ubon Ratchathani, Rte 212 will zip you there in about three hours, but if you can spare a whole day, take the Mekong-hugging back roads through a gorgeous stretch of rural Thailand.

ℹ Getting Around

Taxi Mukdahan (📞0 4261 3666; ◷6am-midnight) charges 50B for the first 10km and 10B per kilometre if the journey is longer.

Huanam Hotel and Goodmook* restaurant hire bikes for 100B per day.

Around Mukdahan

PHU PHA THOEP NATIONAL PARK   อุทยานแห่งชาติภูผาเทิบ
Although little more than a speck of a reserve at just 48 sq km, hilly **Phu Pha Thoep National Park** (📞0 4260 1753; admission 100B) has a host of beautiful attractions; most famously large mushroom-shaped rock formations. The main rock groups sits right behind the visitor centre and wildflowers bloom around them October through December. Besides the weird rocks there are several clifftop viewpoints where pretty much only forest is visible around you. Also popular is **Nam Tok Phu Tham Phra**, a scenic waterfall (May to November only) with a grotto atop it holding hundreds of small Buddha images. It only takes a few hours on the well-marked trails to see all these sights. **Tham**

Fa Mue Daeng, a cave with 5000-year-old hand paintings, is an 8km drive from the main park area and then a 1.5km walk.

For accommodation, there's **camping** (per person with own tent 30B, 4-/6-person tent hire 300/600B) and a three-bedroom **bungalow** (📞0 2562 0760; www.dnp.go.th/parkreserve; bungalows 1800B).

The park is 15km south of Mukdahan via Rte 2034. *Sŏrng·tăa·ou* (20B, 30 minutes, every half-hour) to Don Tan, departing from Porn Pet Market, 300m north of Hor Kaew Mukdahan, pass the turn-off to the park. Hitching the last 1.3km to the visitor centre isn't tough, or you can ask the *sŏrng·tăa·ou* driver to detour off their route and take you; they will probably do it for 40B per person. Be back at the junction by 4pm to guarantee finding a *sŏrng·tăa·ou* back to town.

NORTH OF MUKDAHAN

Travelling north along the Mekong offers a lovely look at traditional Thai life and makes a fantastic bike trip. There's no single road to follow – hence the following distances may differ a bit from your trip – and the old village roads will occasionally deposit you on the new highway, but just turn left every chance you get to return to the river.

Leaving the city on Samranchaikong Rd you'll follow a long line of fish farms for about 6.5km before ducking under the 1.6km-long **Thai-Lao Friendship Bridge 2**. This is the widest reach of the Mekong along the Thai border, so this bridge stretches 400m more than Friendship Bridge 1 in Nong Khai.

You'll meet a **troop of monkeys** that resides alongside the road just before Wat Baan Sai Yai, 2.5km after the bridge.

After at least another 9km, where the greenish Mae Nam Chanot meets the muddy Mekong (you might see men unloading their fish traps here), is **Wat Mano Phirom**

(☺daylight hours), one of Mukdahan Province's oldest temples. The original *bòht*, now a *wí·hǎhn*, was built in 1756 in Lan Xang style with an elaborately carved wooden facade and large painted eave brackets. It holds many ancient Buddha images, though the elephant tusk that had eight of them carved into it, has been stolen. (Theft of Buddha images is a growing problem in Thailand.) Tourism officials are trying to promote **Hat Mano Pirom**, the beach that emerges here in the dry season, and you can now dine in a thatched-roof shelter set right in the river.

Wat Srimahapo (☺daylight hours), sometimes called Wat Pho Si, is another 4.5km north in Ban Wan Yai. You'd never expect its tiny *bòht*, built in 1916, to be worth a look, but inside, elaborately carved beams hold up the tin roof and interesting naive murals cover the walls. The monks' residence is French-colonial style.

After a further 7.5km you'll pass the modern, glass-walled **Our Lady of the Martyrs of Thailand Shrine** (☺8am-5pm, Mass at 7am Sun), locally called Wat Song Khon and often incorrectly described as the largest church in Southeast Asia. It was built in 1995 to commemorate seven Thai Catholics killed by the police in 1940 for refusing to renounce their faith. Wax sculptures of the martyrs and their ashes lie under glass at the back.

Three and a half kilometres after the church is **Kaeng Kabao**, a stretch of rocky shore and islets emerging during the dry season. A variety of restaurants have set up on and along the river here, making this a good place to refuel before heading back to Mukdahan, or continuing on for another 17km to That Phanom.

AMPHOE NONG SUNG   อำเภอหนองสูง

Whether you want to learn about a little-known culture or just want to dip your toes into village life, Nong Sung District in Mukdahan's far west is a great place to do it. Mukdahan Province has a large Phu Tai population. Of all Isan's minority groups, the Phu Tai have clung closest to their culture. Most villagers here still don traditional duds for festivals and funerals and their children do the same at school on Thursdays. The Phu Tai dialect dominates, so even if you speak fluent Thai or Isan, expect some verbal trip-ups here.

A few towns, including the weaving village of Ban Phu, 6km south of Nong Sung

town on Rte 2370, have **homestay programs** (☎08 5003 7894; per person incl meals 600B) that let you join in daily life, however English is very rare.

🍴**Thai House-Isaan** (☎08 7065 4635; www.thaihouse-isaan.com; r incl breakfast 700-1500B; ✳@✳), the easier option, is owned by a friendly Australian. It's 15km west of Nong Sung on Rte 2042. Day tours around the region cost from 900B per person (minimum two) or you can hire a bicycle (120B per day) or motorcycle (200B per day) and see things by yourself. The rooms are comfortable and well appointed, especially the Thai-style 'chalet', and the mostly organic menu covers both Thai and *fa·ràng* tastes. If you want, you can join Noi in the kitchen for a cooking lesson. Day guests are welcome.

Buses between Mukdahan and Khon Kaen can drop you in Ban Kham Pok (from Mukdahan 50B, 70 minutes, every half-hour).

YASOTHON & ROI ET PROVINCES

Yasothon and Roi Et, two of Thailand's most rural provinces, have little of interest to fast-track travellers, but they do show a side of Thailand that few people (including other Thais) ever see.

People looking to nose deeper into Isan culture will want to take a peek at Phra That Kong Khao Noi and purchase some pillows in Ban Si Than in Yasothon Province. Yasothon city saves all its gusto for the annual Rocket Festival, which completes a trifecta of Isan icons. Roi Et Province, whose capital city is the far more pleasant of the two, has a few enormous off-beat attractions, including a serious contender for Thailand's strangest temple.

Yasothon   ยโสธร

POP 23,000

Yasothon has little to offer visitors outside the official whizz-bang period of mid-May and neither looks nor acts like a capital city. In fact, it barely feels like a city at all.

◉ Sights

Yasothon has two cute little attractions that aren't worth a special trip but shouldn't be missed if you're in the area.

The heart of the **Ban Singha Tha** neighbourhood, 300m off the main road, west of Kasikornbank, is a treasure trove of classic French Indochinese shophouses, many with lovely artistic flourishes that are evidence of Yasothon's former wealth. They were built for Chinese merchants by Vietnamese labourers almost a century ago at what was then Yasothon's port, and with their historic value recently recognised, restoration work has begun.

The centrepiece of **Wat Mahathat** (Th Wariratchadet; ☉daylight hours) is a highly venerated Lao-style *chedi* said to date from AD 695 and to enshrine holy relics of Phra Anan (Ananda), the Buddha's personal attendant monk. Much more interesting, however, is the gorgeous little *hŏr đrai* (a building for storing the Tripitaka Buddhist scriptures), dating to the 1830s and restored in 2008, which sits on stilts in a pond to protect the sacred scripts from termites. If you ask a monk, he'll get the keys and let you look inside.

✿ Festivals

Rocket Festivals (Bun Bâng Fai) are held across Isan in May and June to tell Phaya Thaen, a pre-Buddhist rain god, that it's time for him to send rain; but no place celebrates as fervently as Yasothon, where the largest rockets, are 3m long and, according to the rocket-makers we talked to, packed with 500kg of gunpowder. The three-day event, held on the second weekend of May, features traditional local dances, parades, rocket contests and a lot of bawdry, drunken revelry.

🛏 Sleeping

Green Park   HOTEL **$$**
(☏0 4571 4700; Th Wariratchadet; r incl breakfast 600-800B, f 1500-2500B; ✼@🛜🏊) Though it lacks the panache of JP Emerald, we consider this much newer place the best lodging in Yasothon. You can use the adjacent health club for free. It's 1km east of the centre on the way to Mukdahan.

Baan Singha Tha Homestay   HOMESTAY **$**
(☏08 2482 6084; r per person 300B) Five families in the historic Ban Singha Tha neighbourhood now offer rooms in their homes.

JP Emerald Hotel   HOTEL **$$**
(☏0 4572 4848; www.jpemeraldhotel.com; Th Prapa; r 450B, incl breakfast 600-1650B; ✼@🛜) Yasothon's only full-service three-star hotel.

The rooms won't excite you, but they do keep up on maintenance pretty well here. Night-time diversions include snooker, coyote dancers and a disco. It's at the Roi Et end of town.

In Town Hotel   HOTEL **$**
(no Roman-script sign; ☏0 4571 3007; 614 Th Jangsanit; r 220-380B; ✼🛜) This place, on the main road, is far enough south that it almost loses the rights to its name, but for Yasothon it's far better than the budget average. The Warotohn Hotel next door is even cheaper.

Yasothon Orchid Garden   HOTEL **$**
(no Roman-script sign; ☏0 4572 1000; www.orchid-garden-hotel.com; Th Prachasamphan; r 400-450B; ✼@🛜) In the city centre, this is a plain but reasonable budget option with big rooms.

✗ Eating

Rim Chi Riverside   THAI **$**
(no Roman-script sign; dishes 30-250B; ☉lunch & dinner) Enjoy superb Isan and Thai food and bucolic Chi River views from either the tree-filled terrace or your own thatched-roof raft. This is an English-free zone, but you can't go wrong ordering *sôm·đam* or *b̆lah chôrn lui sŏo·an* (fried striped snake-head fish 'run through the garden'). It's 900m west of Krung Thai Bank.

Night Market   THAI **$**
(Th Wariratchadet; ☉4pm-midnight) East of Wat Mahathat, this is as good a place as any to sample Yasothon's famous dessert, *kà·nom wăhn lôrt chôrng* (rice noodles made with pandan served in coconut milk).

❶ Getting There & Away

Yasothon's **bus terminal** (☏0 4571 4500) is north of the city on the bypass road. A motorcycle taxi to the centre costs 50B. The main destinations are Ubon Ratchathani (66B to 85B, 1½ hours, every half-hour), Khorat (158B to 205B, four hours, every half-hour) and Khon Kaen (113B to 146B, 3½ hours, every half-hour) via Roi Et (48B to 61B, one hour). Vans are the best way to Mukdahan (76B, two hours, every half-hour). Bangkok (320B to 385B, eight to nine hours) buses leave about hourly during the day but most depart from 7pm to 10pm. There are **999 VIP buses** (☏0 4571 2965) to Bangkok (VIP 599B, 8.30pm), which stop at its downtown office by the clock tower.

Around Yasothon

PHRA THAT KONG KHAO NOI พระธาตุก่องข้าวน้อย

A rather sinister myth surrounds the **Small Sticky Rice Basket Stupa** (☉daylight hours), a brick-and-stucco *chedi* dating from the late Ayuthaya period 5km outside town towards Ubon Ratchathani. According to one legend – which is taught to school children as an example of why it's important to keep your emotions in check – a young, ravenously hungry farmer who had toiled all morning in the hot sun murdered his mother here when she brought his lunch to the fields late and in a small sticky-rice basket. The farmer, eating his lunch over his mother's dead body, realised that there was actually more sticky rice than he could manage to eat. To atone for his misdeed, he built this *chedi*.

Or perhaps not. Others say it was built by people who were travelling to Phra That Phanom to enshrine gold and gems, but got to Ban Tat Thong and learned they were too late; so they built this *chedi* instead. Some locals combine the myths and say that the repentant son was unable to build a *chedi* of his own and so joined forces with the pilgrims and they built it together.

Further complicating matters, most Yasothonians claim the real Small Rice Basket Stupa is a little further north at Ban Sadao village (7km east of Yasothon on Rte 202) in the back of **Wat Tung Sadoa**. All that remains is the base; when the original tumbled over shortly after the redeemed son's death, locals built another petite *chedi* next to it. When we asked a monk here why Thai tourists visit the other *chedi,* he simply answered, *'Gahn meuang'* (It's politics).

BAN SI THAN บ้านศรีฐาน

Residents of Ban Si Than can't leave their work behind when they go to sleep: this is a pillow-making village. All around the village (and most of those villages surrounding it) you'll see people sewing, stuffing or selling *mŏrn kít* (pillows decorated with diamond-grid *kít* patterns). The most famous style is a stiff triangle-shaped pillow used as an arm support while sitting on the floor. Most foreigners call these *mŏrn kwăhn* (axe pillow), an old name that most Thais are no longer familiar with; *mŏrn săhm lĕeam* (triangle pillow) is the common moniker nowadays. They couldn't possibly meet demand without using machine-made fabric, but the stuffing and some of the sewing is still

done by hand. Prices here are far lower than you'll pay elsewhere in Thailand, and this is also one of the few places you can buy them unstuffed (*yang mâi sài nûn;* literally 'no kapok inserted'), which makes the big ones viable as souvenirs.

If you want to see monkeys, have someone point you to **Don Ling**, 4km out of town at Ban Tao Hi.

If you want to stay here, Ban Si Than has a **homestay** (☏08 7258 1991; per person 100B, meals 50B) program. The village is 20km from Yasothon on Rte 202, then 2.5km south of Ban Nikom. Any Amnat Charoen-bound bus can drop you at the junction (20B to 25B, 45 minutes) where a motorcycle taxi will zip you in for 20B.

Roi Et ร้อยเอ็ด

POP 36,000

There has been a settlement at this spot for at least 2800 years, making this one of Isan's oldest cities. At one point, legend says, it had 11 city gates, and in ancient writing '11' was expressed as '10-plus-1'. Somehow this morphed into the city's name, which means 'one hundred one'.

Except for extensive stretches of the old city moat, Roi Et's long history hasn't followed it into the 21st century. Still, the city retains a charm and sense of identity all its own. You can't call Roi Et sleepy, but, perhaps taking its cue from the walking Buddha on the island in the city-centre lake, it does seem to move to its own urban beat.

⊙ Sights

Wat Burapha TEMPLE

(วัดบูรพา; Th Phadung Phanit; ☉daylight hours) The enormous standing Buddha towering above Roi Et's squat skyline is **Phra Phuttha Ratana Mongkon Mahamuni** (Luang Po Yai for short), the main attraction at this temple. Despite being of little artistic significance, it's hard to ignore. Head to toe he stands 59.2m, and from the ground to the tip of the *ùt·sà·nít* it's 67.8m.

Roi Et National Museum MUSEUM

(พิพิธภัณฑสถานแห่งชาติร้อยเอ็ด; Th Ploenjit; admission 100B; ☉9am-4pm Wed-Sun) This interesting museum gives equal billing to ancient artefacts and Isan culture. The 3rd floor features silk weaving, including a display showing the materials used to produce natural-dye fabrics.

Roi Et

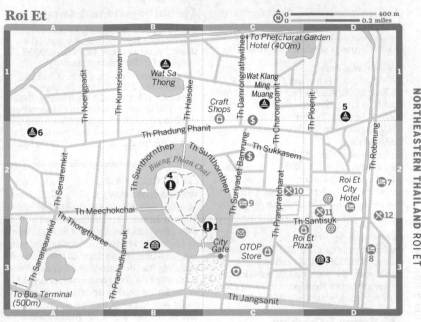

Roi Et

Bueng Phlan Chai   PARK
(บึงพลาญชัย) Walking paths criss-cross the attractive, shady island in Bueng Phlan Chai and attract the usual crowd of doting couples, students, joggers and picnickers. The beloved **walking Buddha statue** is on the north side and the **lak meuang** (city pillar) is to the south.

Wat Neua   TEMPLE
(วัดเหนือ; Th Phadung Phanit; ⊘daylight hours) This temple in the northern quarter of town has a peaceful ambience. It's known for its 1200-year-old brick *chedi* from the Dvaravati period, which has an unusual four-cornered bell-shaped form that's rare in Thailand. Also inside the central compound are some old Dvaravati *săir·mah* and a giant bodhi tree.

FREE **Roi Et Aquarium**   AQUARIUM
(สถานแสดงพันธุ์สัตว์น้ำเทศบาลเมืองร้อยเอ็ด; Th Sunthornthep; ⊘8.30am-4.30pm Wed-Sun) This little aquarium with a walk-through tunnel houses fish found around Isan.

🛏 Sleeping

Phetcharat Garden Hotel   HOTEL $$
(☏0 4351 9000; www.petcharatgardenhotel.com; Th Chotchaplayuk; r incl breakfast 540-700B, ste 1740B; ❄🛜🏊) Some chic East-meets-West styling in the open-air lobby and an enormous swimming pool earn this attractive

place several gold stars. The cheaper rooms don't capture that atmosphere and there's visible wear and tear throughout, but Phetcharat Garden is still excellent value.

Rohmintanin Park HOTEL $
(📞0 4351 6111; Th Robmuang; r incl breakfast 450-650B, ste 1200B; 🕸@🌐) This place can't quite qualify as fancy, but little decorative touches push it beyond the ordinary institutional feel so common in hotels of this price range.

Saithip Hotel HOTEL $
(no Roman-script sign; 📞0 4351 1742; Th Suriyadet Bamrung; r 240-320B; 🕸🌐) The architect added a bit of decoration to the facade and some rooms have sit-down toilets, but this is otherwise your ordinary cold-water cheapie.

Poon Petch Sportclub HOTEL $
(no Roman-script sign; 📞0 4351 6391; Th Robmuang; r 300-350B; 🕸) Though it's looking rather sorry for itself on the outside, the rooms are better than expected and come with refrigerator and balconies.

🍴 Eating & Drinking

Roi Et's nightlife district, home to several large beer gardens, runs along Th Chotchaplayuk between the canal and the Phetcharat Garden Hotel. Some more low-key tables for a tipple sit on the west side of the lake.

White Elephant INTERNATIONAL, THAI $
(Th Robmuang; dishes 60-390B; ⊙dinner) This publike place just across the old moat has a massive Thai menu, but the specialities are German, as is the owner.

Richi India Food INDIAN $
(37/1 Th Santisuk; dishes 50-250B; ⊙lunch & dinner; 🌐🍴) This colourful place looks more like a hair salon than a restaurant, and the food won't wow you, but with Indian cuisine being so rare in Isan, you take what you can get.

Night Market THAI $
(⊙3.30-11pm) By day, this big roof hosts Roi Et's municipal market, but at night it shifts gears to become the city's main night market.

ℹ️ Information

Banks are scattered around the centre, with several at the north end of Th Suriyadet Bamrung. There are several internet cafes near Roi Et Plaza department store.

ℹ️ Getting There & Away

Nok Air (📞0 2900 9955; www.nokair.com) has daily morning flights to/from Bangkok's Don Muang Airport with fares from under 2000B. The airport is 13km north of town.

Buses depart at least hourly from Roi Et's **bus terminal** (📞0 4351 1466; Th Jangsanit) to Bangkok (293B to 585B, eight hours), Khon Kaen (73B to 94B, 2½ hours), Ubon Ratchathani (108B to 139B, three hours), and Surin (91B, 2½ hours). The bus terminal is 1km from the city centre. Túk-túk charge 40B to 50B to the lake.

Around Roi Et

WAT PA NON SAWAN วัดป่าโนนสวรรค์
Making Sala Kaew Ku (p461) feel like a Thomas Kinkade creation, **Wat Pa Non Sawan** (admission free; ⊙daylight hours) is home to hundreds of colourful sculptures ranging from merely peculiar to 'what-the...?!' Whether it's the immense dragons, *wâi*ing turtles, Hindu gods, gruesome scenes of hell or the lonely polar bear, this place is sure to make you think as well as smile, which is exactly the point of it all. Also note the use of pots in many of the sculptures, a theme chosen because this is a pottery-making region. With all this spectacle around, the Bollywood songs played over the loudspeakers seem perfectly normal.

Be sure to say sà·wà·dee to the octogenarian abbot who inspired it all. He lives and greets visitors on the ground floor of the tower; inside Hanuman's mouth.

The temple is 30km east of Roi Et and buses can drop you at Thung Khao Luang (25B, 30 minutes), where a motorcycle taxi for the last 8km will cost 60B.

PHRA MAHA CHEDI CHAI MONGKHON พระมหาเจดีย์ชัยมงคล
Far from finished, the **Phra Maha Chedi Chai Mongkhon** (admission free; ⊙6.30am-6pm) is already a sight to behold. At its heart is a gleaming white *chedi* rising a symbolic 101m, making it one of the tallest in Thailand. It's encircled by a 101m-wide building and sits on 101 *râi* (16 hectares) of land. Inside is a riot of gold paint and mirrored tiles, and, depending on your tastes, it's either beautiful or gaudy; but either way you're sure to love it. The *chedi* sits atop a mountain that's sometimes called **Isan Buddhist Park**. Another 8km down the forest-clad road from the *chedi* is the **Northeast Botany in Literature Park**, a quiet botanical garden featuring plants mentioned in

important Thai stories. Two kilometres further on is **Pha Mok Mi Wai** cliff, which is a viewpoint for the sea of fog that forms most mornings during the cool season.

The *chedi* is 80km northwest of Roi Et city near Nong Phok. It's a pain to get there without your own wheels. From Roi Et take a *sŏrng·tǎa·ou* to Phon Thong (40B, one hour, every half-hour) and then catch one of the Khon Kaen-Amnat Charoen buses to *brà·doo kong* (Kong Gate) in Ban Tha Saat (25B, 30 minutes, hourly). Then it's 5km uphill. Hitching is usually easy.

KU PHRA KOH NA   กู่พระโคนา

Fifty kilometres southeast of Roi Et town are the minor Khmer ruins of **Ku Phra Koh Na** (admission free; ☉daylight hours), an 11th-century Hindu shrine. The Baphuon-style temple comprises three brick *prang* facing east from a sandstone base surrounded by a sandstone-slab wall that once had four gates. The middle *prang* was replastered in 1928 and Buddha niches were added. The attached Buddha footprint shrine is fronted by original *naga* sculptures. The two other *prang* have been restored (though they still look like they might tumble any time) in their original forms. The northern *prang* has a reclining Phra Narai (Vishnu) lintel over the main door while the lintel above the northern false door of the other *prang* shows Kali.

The ruins themselves are neither impressive nor well restored, but it's interesting to see how they've been incorporated into the modern temple. And if that doesn't thrill you, spend your time watching the hundreds of monkeys living here.

Surin-bound buses from Roi Et can drop you off at Wat Ku (40B, one hour), as it's known locally, which is 6km south of Suwannaphum on Rte 214.

SA KAEW PROVINCE

Not a part of Isan, either culturally or geographically, but also markedly distinct from the nearby coastal provinces, seldom-travelled Sa Kaew feels like a lost land. Many small Khmer ruins litter the sparsely populated countryside, but with Angkor Wat beckoning, none are worth the time or effort to reach.

Aranya Prathet   อรัญประเทศ
POP 15,800

The border town of Aranya Prathet (aka Aran) is known to Thais mostly for smuggling and gambling. (The casinos are over the border in Poipet.) For travellers, it's the busiest border crossing for trips to Angkor Wat and few actually stop here longer than needed to get their passport stamped. Though really, as border towns go, it's not that bad.

If you do spend a little time, **Talat Rong Kluea** (☉8am-8pm) is worth exploring. It's mainly thrift-store tat and cheap Chinese-made junk – for those seeking secondhand sunglasses and counterfeit Converse, it's the place to be – but the Rong Kluea experience isn't about what's being sold, it's about seeing the caravans of Cambodian traders pushing huge handcarts through a market so vast that many of the Thais coming here rent bikes (20B per day) and motorcycles (100B per three hours) to go shopping.

BORDER CROSSING: ARANYA PRATHET TO POIPET

The Cambodian border is open 7am to 8pm daily. There are many persistent scammers trying to get you to buy your Cambodia visa through them, but no matter what lies they tell you, there's absolutely no reason to get visas at the Cambodian consulate or anywhere else. Doing so costs more and takes longer. Don't even show your passport to anyone before Thai immigration and don't change money. Just make a beeline for the border.

After getting stamped out of Thailand follow the throng to Cambodian immigration: find the 'Visa on Arrival' sign if you don't have a visa already (see p770 for visa details). Weekday mornings you can finish everything in 10 to 20 minutes, but arrive after noon and it could take an hour or more. Weekends and holidays, when many Thais arrive to gamble and foreign workers do visa runs, are also very busy.

The best way to continue on to Siem Reap is by taxi. See Lonely Planet's *Cambodia* guide for information.

🛏 Sleeping & Eating

There are hotels at the border, but staying in town is much more pleasant.

Indochina Hotel   HOTEL $$
(☑0 3723 2588; www.indochina-hotel.net; Th Thanavithee; r incl breakfast 900-1280B; ❄🛜🌊) Better than anything you'd expect to find in Aran, this quiet place north of the city is built around a palm-lined swimming pool; pool-view rooms are worth the extra 140B.

Mob Coffee   HOTEL $
(☑0 3723 1839; r 380B; ❄🛜) The bright, clean rooms at this little place inside the bus station – there aren't many buses, so it's not noisy – are among the best value in the city.

Market Motel   HOTEL $
(☑0 3723 2302; www.aranyaprathethotel.com; 105/30-32 Th Ratuthit; r 250-700B; ❄@🛜🌊) Rooms here aren't as good as Mob's, but the vibe is much better...and there's a swimming pool.

A small **night market** (⊙4pm-2am) rings a little reservoir just east of the Market Motel.

ⓘ Getting There & Around

Buses from Bangkok's 'Mo Chit' (207B, 4½ hours), 'Ekamai' (200B, four hours) and Suvarnaphumi Airport (187B, three hours) bus stations plus the vans from Victory Monument (230B, four hours, every half-hour) go all the way to the border, so there's no need to stop in Aranya Prathet city. There's rumour of direct bus service all the way to Siem Reap, but we think it's unlikely to happen soon.

Two daily trains also make the run from (5.55am and 1.05pm) and to (6.40am and 13.55pm) Bangkok's Hua Lamphong Station (3rd class 48B, six hours) to the city, where you'll either need to take a sŏrng·tăa·ou (15B), motorcycle taxi (60B) or túk-túk (80B) the final 6km to the border.

The through-service bus trips sold on Khao San Rd and elsewhere in Thailand seem cheap and convenient, but they haven't been nick-named 'scam buses' for nothing. By using them you're agreeing to let people hassle you and rip you off. Read **Tales of Asia** (www.talesofasia. com/cambodia-overland.htm) for the juicy details.

Aran also has buses to Chantaburi (150B, four hours, hourly) and Khorat (190B, four hours, six daily) from the bus terminal, and Surin (137B to 176B, six hours, three daily) from a stop to the north.

Sa Kaew   สระแก้ว

The provincial capital isn't much more than an overgrown village that in and of itself presents no compelling (or even trifling) reason to stop. But a couple of little known parks beyond the town beckon intrepid travellers.

Khao Chakan is an isolated 240m-tall mountain pocked with caves and inhabited by a horde of greedy monkeys who follow visitors waiting for handouts. One of the caves, reached by a long staircase, pokes straight through the heart of the mountain like a keyhole while others release their resident bats in a seemingly endless gush starting at dusk. It's 17km south of town on Rte 317 and, lucky for you, buses back to Sa Kaew (20B, 30 minutes, hourly) pass the mountain during the night; to be sure of getting a ride, walk to the village and wait for them there rather than at the entrance to the park.

Running along the southern escarpment of the Khorat Plateau, **Pang Sida National Park** (☑0 3724 3775; admission 200B) is known for waterfalls and butterflies. Some of both can be seen at the visitor centre 27km north of Sa Kaew. The waterfalls are most beautiful August to October. Butterfly flocks are impressive year-round, but are largest May to July.

There's **camping** (per person with own tent 30B, 2-person tent hire 200B) and **bungalows** (☑0 2562 0760; www.dnp.go.th/parkreserve; bungalows 600-1200B; ❄). In the morning, sŏrng·tăa·ou from Sa Kaew's market can deliver you to the visitor centre (40B, one hour), but there are none after 10am. A motorcycle taxi from town should cost about 300B for a short visit and 1000B all day.

For those intending to sleep in Sa Kaew, the **Travel Hotel** (no Roman-script sign; ☑0 3724 1024; Th Suwannasorn; r 380-550B; ❄🛜) is an ugly building with adequate rooms in a perfect location.

For transport information, see opposite: virtually all vehicles leaving there pass through Sa Kaew on the way to Bangkok, minus about 45 minutes and 20% of the price.

Hua Hin & the Southern Gulf

Best Places to Eat

» Rang Yen Garden, Cha-am (p511)

» Night Market, Hua Hin (p511)

» Sang Thai Restaurant, Hua Hin (p519)

» Rim Lom, Prachuap Khiri Khan (p529)

Best Places to Stay

» Baan Bayan, Hua Hin (p519)

» Away Hua Hin, Pranburi (p523)

» Brassiere Beach, Pranburi (p523)

» Aow Noi Sea View, Prachuap Khiri Khan (p528)

» Proud Thai Beach Resort, Ban Krut (p530)

Why Go?

Known as the 'royal' coast, the upper southern gulf has long been the favoured retreat of the Bangkok monarchy and elite. Each Thai king, dating from Rama IV, has found an agreeable spot to build a royal getaway. Today domestic tourists flock to this coast in the same pursuit of leisure as well as to pay homage to the revered kings whose palaces-away-from-palace are now open to the public. Rarely does culture and coast meet with such proximity and collaboration.

Indeed this is the country's surf-and-turf destination offering historic sites, pleasant provincial life, jungle-filled parks and long sandy beaches all within an easy commute from Bangkok. That most backpackers suffer a gruelling trip further south to the built-up Samui islands is a great mystery to anyone who has walked for kilometres along Hua Hin's powdery white sands. The one blemish is that there are few reefs (so little to no diving and snorkelling) and as a result the water takes more of an Atlantic greyish hue than a tropical azure.

When to Go

The best time to visit is during the hot and dry season (February to June). From July to October (southwest monsoon) and October to January (northeast monsoon) there is occasional rain and strong winds; but the region tends to stay drier than the rest of the country during the monsoon period because of a geographic anomaly.

During stormy periods, stinging jellyfish are often carried close to shore making swimming hazardous. Thais get around this by swimming fully clothed.

Hua Hin & the Southern Gulf Highlights

1 Exploring the hilltop palace and underground caves of **Phetchaburi** (p505)

2 Strolling the long blonde coastline of **Hua Hin** (p512) dotted with wave-jumping kiteboarders.

3 Eating and shopping (and eating some more) at Hua Hin's **Night Market** (p519)

4 Escaping into the wild depths of **Kaeng Krachan National Park** (p509) and spotting gibbons and wild elephants.

5 Letting the kids run around all day in their bathing suits at **Dolphin Bay** (p523)

6 Making the popular pilgrimage to **Khao Sam Roi Yot National Park** (p524) to see the illuminated cave shrine of Tham Phraya Nakhon.

7 Motorcycling between curvaceous bays and limestone peaks in **Prachuap Khiri Khan** (p526)

8 Being a beach bum on kicked-back **Hat Bang Saphan Yai** (p530)

Phetchaburi (Phetburi)

เพชรบุรี

POP 46,600

An easy escape from Bangkok, Phetchaburi should be on every cultural traveller's itinerary. It has temples and palaces like Ayuthaya, outlying jungles and cave shrines like Kanchanaburi and access to the coast (unlike either of the two). The town offers a delightful slice of provincial life with busy markets, old teak shophouses and visiting groups of Thai students who work up the courage to say 'hello' to the few foreigners in town.

Historically Phetchaburi is a visible timeline of kingdoms that have migrated across Southeast Asia. During the 11th century, the Khmer empire settled in, though their control was relatively short-lived. As Khmer power diminished, Phetchaburi became a strategic royal fort during the Thai-based Sukhothai and Ayuthaya kingdoms. During the stability of the Ayuthaya kingdom, the upper peninsula flourished and Phetchaburi thrived as a 17th-century trading post between Burma and Ayuthaya. The town is often referred to as a 'Living Ayuthaya', since the equivalent of the many relics that were destroyed in the former kingdom's capital are still intact here.

◉ Sights & Activities

For such a small town, Phetchaburi has a number of historic temples that keep Thai tourists busy for the day. The most noteworthy are included below.

Phra Nakhon Khiri Historical Park
HISTORIC SITE

(อุทยานประวัติศาสตร์พระนครคีรี; ☑0 3240 1006; admission 150B; ☺8.30am-5pm) This national historical park sits regally atop Khao Wang (Palace Hill) surveying the city with subdued opulence. Rama IV (King Mongkut) built the palace and surrounding temples in 1859 to be used as a retreat from Bangkok. The hilltop location allowed the king to pursue his interest in astronomy and stargazing.

The palace was built in a mix of European and Chinese styles and each breezy hall is furnished with royal belongings. Cobblestone paths lead from the palace through the forested hill to three summits, each topped by a chedi. The white spire of Phra That Chom Phet skewers the sky and can be spotted from the city below.

There are two entrances to the site. The front entrance is across from Th Ratwithi and involves a strenuous footpath that passes a troop of unpredictable monkeys. The back entrance is on the opposite side of the hill and has a tram (one way adult/child 40B/free; ☺8.30am-5.30pm) that glides up and down the summit. This place is a popular school-group outing and you'll be as much of a photo-op as the historic buildings.

A Monday night market lines the street in front of Khao Wang with the usual food and clothing stalls.

Wat Mahathat Worawihan
TEMPLE

(วัดมหาธาตุวรวิหาร; Th Damnoen Krasem) Centrally located, gleaming white Wat Mahathat is a lovely example of an everyday temple with as much hustle and bustle as the busy commercial district around it. The showpiece is a five-tiered Khmer-style *prang* (Khmer-style stupa) decorated in stucco relief, a speciality of Phetchaburi's local artisans. Inside the main *wí·hǎhn* (shrine hall or sanctuary) are contemporary murals, another example of the province's thriving temple craftsmanship. The tempo of the temple is further heightened with the steady beat from traditional musicians and dancers who perform for merit-making services.

After visiting the temple, follow Th Suwanmunee through the old teak house district filled with the smells of incense from religious paraphernalia shops.

Wat Kamphaeng Laeng
TEMPLE

(วัดกำแพงแลง; Th Phokarang) Back before Siam had defined itself as an independent entity, the Angkor (Khmer) kingdom stretched from present-day Cambodia all the way to the Malay peninsula. To mark their frontier conquests, the Khmers built ornate temples in a signature style that has been copied throughout Thai history. This Khmer remnant is believed to date back to the 12th century and was originally Hindu before the region's conversion to Buddhism. There is one intact sanctuary flanked by two smaller shrines and deteriorating sandstone walls. Though it isn't the most remarkable example of Khmer architecture, it is a peaceful place to snap a few arty pictures.

Tham Khao Luang
CAVE

(ถ้ำเขาหลวง; ☺8am-6pm) About 4km north of town is Tham Khao Luang, a dramatic stalactite-filled chamber that is one of Thailand's most impressive cave shrines and a favourite of Rama IV. The cave is accessed

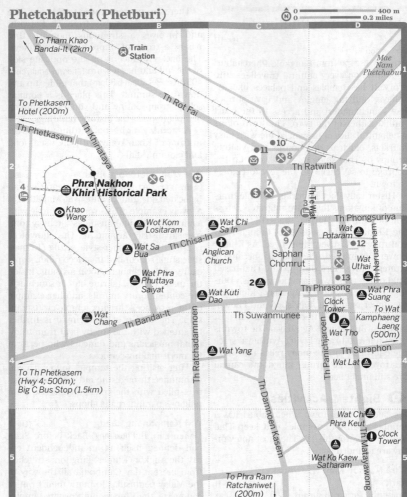

HUA HIN & THE SOUTHERN GULF

through a steep set of stairs. It's central Buddha figure is often illuminated with a heavenly glow when sunlight filters in through the heart-shaped skylight. On the opposite end of the chamber is a row of sitting Buddhas casting repetitive shadows on the undulating cavern wall.

According to the guides, Rama IV built the stone gate that separates the main chamber from a second chamber as a security measure for a couple who once lived in the cave. A figure of a prostrate body in the third chamber is said to represent the cycle of life and death but it hasn't experienced a peaceful resting place as bandits destroyed much of it in search of hidden treasures. Deeper in the cave is supposedly a rock formation that looks like Christ on the cross but our literal eyes couldn't spot it. (Thais are especially imaginative at spotting familiar forms in cave stalactites.)

Around the entrance to the cave you'll meet brazen monkeys looking for handouts. Guides are available for hire near the car park though they aren't always forthcoming about their fees (usually 100B per person).

You'll need to arrange transport here from town (around 150B roundtrip).

Phetchaburi (Phetburi)

Tham Khao Bandai-It   CAVE
(ถ้ำเขาบันไดอิฐ; donation appreciated; ⊘9am-4pm)
This hillside monastery, 2km west of town, sprawls through several large caverns converted into simple Buddha shrines and hermit meditation rooms. English-speaking guides (tip appreciated) lead tours through the caves, mainly as a safety precaution from the monkeys. One cavern contains a significant population of bats, and guides will instruct you not to look up with your mouth open (a good rule for everyday life).

Phra Ram Ratchaniwet   HISTORIC SITE
(พระรามราชนิเวศน์; Ban Peun Palace; ☑0 3242 8083; admission 50B; ⊘8am-4pm Mon-Fri). An incredible art deco creation 1km south of town, construction of this royal summer palace began in 1910 at the behest of Rama V (who died just after the project was started). It was designed by German architects, who used the opportunity to showcase contemporary innovations in construction and interior design. The structure is typical of the early 20th century, a period that saw a Thai passion for erecting European-style buildings in an effort to keep up with the 'modern' architecture of its colonised neighbours.

The outside of the two-storey palace is not too exciting, but inside there are spacious sun-drenched rooms decorated with exquisite glazed tiles, stained glass, parquet floors and plenty of wrought-iron details. The double-spiral staircase provides a debutante's debut and the king's personal bathroom was state-of-the-art.

Hat Puak Tian   BEACH
(หาดปึกเตียน) Locals come to this dark-sands beach, 20km southeast of Phetchaburi, on weekends to eat seafood and frolic in the surf. Another modest attraction is the literary role this beach played in the Thai epic poem *Phra Aphaimani,* written by Sunthorn Phu. A partially submerged statue of a giant woman standing offshore with an outstretched hand and a forlorn expression depicts a character from the poem who disguised herself as a beautiful temptress to win the love of the hero and imprison him on this beach. But he discovers her treachery (and her true ugliness) and with the help of a mermaid escapes to Ko Samet (a nicer beach so maybe he was on to something).

You'll need private transport to reach this beach.

🎊 Festivals & Events

Phra Nakhon Khiri Fair   CULTURAL
Centred on Khao Wang, this provincial-style celebration takes place in early April and lasts nine days. Phra Nakhon Khiri is festooned with lights, there are traditional dance performances, craft and food displays and a beauty contest.

🛏 Sleeping

Phetchaburi is seriously lacking in accommodation, especially in the budget range, since most people visit as a daytrip from Hua Hin or Cha-am. Pity that there isn't more of a guest-house scene here since it is an ideal place for cultural tourists overwhelmed by Bangkok.

Sun Hotel   HOTEL **$$**
(☑0 3240 0000; www.sunhotelthailand.com; 43/33 Soi Phetkasem; r 800-1500B; ❄@⊛) The best of an uninspiring bunch, the Sun Hotel

PHETCHABURI SIGHTSEEING

Some of the city's best sights are outside of town but don't let the distance deter you. Hire a *sŏrng·tǎa·ou* (passenger pick-up truck) for the day (usually around 400B) to hit all the highlights. **Rabieng Rim Nam** (☎0 3242 5707; 1 Th Chisa-In; 950B per person for 4 people), a guest house and restaurant, also runs day tours with an English-speaking guide.

sits opposite the back entrance to Phra Nakhon Khiri. It has large, comfortable rooms with functional bathrooms and professional staff. There's a pleasant cafe downstairs; internet and wi-fi are available for a fee.

Jomklow Hotel HOTEL $
(☎0 3242 5398; 1 Th Te Wiat; r 180B) A multistorey hotel in need of a serious makeover has very, very basic jail-cell style rooms.

Phetkasem Hotel HOTEL $
(☎0 3242 5581; 86/1 Th Phetkasem; r 200-400B; ✳) Another candidate for an extreme makeover, the Phetkasem has rundown rooms with broken down furniture but at least there is a roof over your head.

Eating

Surrounded by palm sugar plantations, Phetchaburi is famous for Thai sweets, including *kà·nŏm môr gaang* (egg custard) and the various 'golden' desserts made from egg yolks to portend good fortune. Nearby fruit orchards produce refreshingly aromatic *chom·pôo Phet* (Phetchaburi rose apple), pineapples and golden bananas.

Day Market MARKET $
A good spot for people-watching and local noshing, the day market, north of the clock tower, has food stalls on the perimeter serving the usual noodle dishes as well as specialities such as *kà·nŏm jeen tôrt man* (thin noodles with fried spicy fishcake) and the hot-season favourite *kôw châa pét·bù·ree* (moist chilled rice served with sweetmeats).

Rabieng Rim Nam INTERNATIONAL $
(☎0 3242 5707; 1 Th Chisa-In; dishes 40-180B; ☺breakfast, lunch & dinner) This riverside restaurant serves up terrific food and a lot of tourist information in English – a rarity in this town – and organises tours. Sadly the

affiliated guest house is just too decrepit to recommend.

Khon Toy Restaurant THAI $
(soi behind Sun Hotel; dishes from 35B; ☺lunch & dinner) This open-air restaurant is shielded from the street by a screen of greenery. Inside is a simple but busy kitchen that does a brisk business in evening takeaway meals. Everything is stir-fried and tasty.

Jek Meng THAI $
(85 Th Ratwithi; dishes 50-80B; ☺lunch & dinner) Dishes up big, piping-hot bowls of noodles and fried rice. Look for the black-and-white chequered tablecloths.

Na & Nan THAI $
(Th Damnoen Kasem; dishes 40-60B; ☺lunch & dinner) Another friendly noodle place along a strip of casual restaurants in the centre of town. Their *gŏo·ay dĕe·o gài* (chicken noodles) comes southern style with a whole chicken drumstick.

❶ Information

There's no formal information source in town, but Rabieng Rim Nam is a great resource for both Phetchaburi and Kaeng Krachan National Park. The Sun Hotel has wi-fi and one terminal (per hr 100B).

Main post office (cnr Th Ratwithi & Th Damnoen Kasem)

Police station (☎0 3242 5500; Th Ratwithi) Near the intersection of Th Ratchadamnoen.

Siam Commercial Bank (2 Th Damnoen Kasem) Other nearby banks also offer foreign exchange and ATMs.

Telephone office (cnr Th Ratwithi & Th Damnoen Kasem; ☺7am-10pm) Upstairs at the post office.

❶ Getting There & Away

The stop for buses to Bangkok is beside the night market. There are services to/from Bangkok's Southern (Sai Tai Mai) station (120B, two hours; hourly morning departures). Across the street is a minivan stop with services to Bangkok's Victory Monument (80B) and Southern station (100B).

Ordinary buses to Cha-am (40B) and Hua Hin (50B) stop in town near Th Matayawong.

Most southbound air-conditioned buses and minivans stop out of town on Th Phetkasem in front of the Big C department store. Destinations include Cha-am (50B, 40 minutes, frequent departures) and Hua Hin (50B, two hours). Motorcycle taxis await and can take you into town for around 50B.

KAENG KRACHAN NATIONAL PARK อุทยานแห่งชาติแก่งกระจาน

Wake to the eerie symphony of gibbon calls as the early morning mist hangs limply above the forest canopy. Hike through lush forests to spot elephant herds and other wildlife at the communal watering holes. Or sweat through your clothes as you summit the park's highest peak. At 3000 sq km, Thailand's largest **national park** (☑0 3245 9293; www.dnp.go.th; admission 200B; ☺visitors centre 8.30am-4.30pm) is surprisingly close to civilization but shelters an intense tangle of wilderness that sees few tourists. Two rivers (Mae Nam Phetchaburi and Mae Nam Pranburi), a large lake and abundant rainfall keep the place green year-round. Animal life is abundant and includes wild elephants, deer, gibbons, boars, dusky langurs and wild cattle.

This park also occupies an interesting overlapping biozone for birds as the southernmost spot for the northern species and the northernmost for the southern species. There are about 400 species of birds, including hornbills as well as pheasants and other ground-dwellers.

Activities

Hiking is the best way to explore the park. Most of the trails are signed and branch off of the main road. The **Nam Tok Tho Thip** trail starts at the Km36 marker and continues for 4km to an 18-tiered waterfall. **Phanoen Thung** is the park's highest point and can be summited via a 6km hike that starts at the Km27 marker. Note that some trails, including the one to Phanoen Thung, are closed during the rainy season (August to October).

The twin waterfalls of **Pa La-U Yai** and **Pa La-U Noi** in the southern section of the park are popular for daytrippers on minivan tours from Hua Hin. It's also possible to organise mountain biking in the park from Hua Hin.

Tourist infrastructure in Kaeng Krachan is somewhat limited and the roads can be rough. The park rangers can help arrange camping-gear rental, food and transport. There are crowds on weekends and holidays but weekdays should be people free. The best months to visit are between November and April. **Rabieng Rim Nam** (☑0 3242 5707; 1 Th Chisa-In, Phetchaburi; from 1950B per person for 4 people) arranges trekking and birding tours that range from one day to multiple days if you don't want to figure out the logistics yourself.

Sleeping & Eating

There are various **bungalows** (☑0 2562 0760; www.dnp.go.th/parkreserve; bungalows from 1200B) within the park, mainly near the reservoir. These sleep from four to six people and are simple affairs with fans and fridges. There are also **camp sites** (per person 60-90B), including a pleasant grassy one near the reservoir at the visitors centre and a modest restaurant. Tents can be rented at the visitors centre.

On the road leading to the park entrance are several simple resorts and bungalows. About 3.5km before reaching the visitors centre, **A&B Bungalows** (☑08 9891 2328; r from 700B) is scenic and popular with bird-watching groups. There is a good restaurant here that can provide you with a packed lunch.

Getting There & Away

Kaeng Krachan is 52km southwest of Phetchaburi, with the southern edge of the park 35km from Hua Hin. If you have your own vehicle, drive 20km south from Phetchaburi on Hwy 4 to the town of Tha Yang. Turn right (west) and after 38km, you'll reach the visitors centre. You use the same access road from Tha Tang if coming south from Hua Hin.

You can also reach the park by **minivan** (☑08 9231 5810; one-way 100B) from Phetchaburi; they don't travel to a fixed schedule so have your hotel call to make arrangements. Alternatively you can catch a *sŏrng·tăa·ou* (pick-up trucks; 80B, 1½ hours, 6am to 2pm) from Phetchaburi (near the clock tower) to the village of Ban Kaeng Krachan, 4km before the park. From the village, you can charter transport to the park. You can also charter your own *sŏrng·tăa·ou* all the way to the park but you'll need to haggle.

Minivan tours also operate from Hua Hin.

Frequent rail services run to/from Bangkok's Hua Lamphong station. Fares vary depending on the train and class (3rd class 84B to 144B, 2nd class 188B to 358B, three hours).

❶ Getting Around

Motorcycle taxis go anywhere in the town centre for 40B to 50B. *Sŏrng·tǎa·ou* cost about the same. It's a 20-minute walk (1km) from the train station to the town centre.

Rabieng Rim Nam (p508) hires out bicycles (120B per day) and motorbikes (250B per day).

Cha-am   ชะอำ

POP 72,341

At weekends and on public holidays, Cha-am is a beach getaway for working-class families and Bangkok students. Neon-painted buses (called '*chor ching cha*') deliver young holidaymakers, firmly in party mode, fuelled by thumping techno music. It is a 100% Thai-style beach party with eating and drinking marathons held around umbrella-shaded beach chairs and tables. Entertainment is provided by the banana boats that zip back and forth eventually making a final jack-knife turn that throws the passengers into the sea. Applause and giggles usually follow from the beachside audience.

Cha-am sees only a few foreigners, usually older Europeans who winter here instead of more expensive Hua Hin. And the beach sees even fewer bathing suits since most Thais frolic in the ocean fully clothed. This isn't the spot to meet a lot of young travellers or even a good option for families of young children who might be overwhelmed by paparazzi-like Thais in holiday mode. But for everyone else, Cha-am's beach is wide and sandy, the grey-blue water is clean and calm, the people-watching is superb and the prices are some of the most affordable anywhere on the coast.

★ Festivals & Events

Crab Festival   FOOD

In February, Cha-am celebrates one of its local marine delicacies: blue crabs. Food stalls, concerts, and lots of neon turn the beachfront into a pedestrian party.

Gin Hoy, Do Nok, Tuk Meuk   FOOD

You really can do it all at this annual festival held in September. The English translation means 'Eat Shellfish, Watch Birds, Catch Squid' and is a catchy slogan for all of Cha-am's local attractions and fishing traditions. Mainly it is a food festival showcasing a variety of shellfish but there are also bird-watching events at nearby sanctuaries and squid-fishing demonstrations.

ANIMAL ENCOUNTERS

Modern sensibilities have turned away from circus-like animal attractions but many well-intentioned animal lovers curious to see Thailand's iconic creatures (such as elephants, monkeys and tigers) unwittingly contribute to an industry that is poorly regulated and exploitative. Animals are often illegally captured from the wild and disfigured to be less dangerous (tigers often have their claws and teeth removed), they are acquired as pets and then neglected or inhumanely confined, or they are abandoned when they are too sick or infirm to work.

Wildlife Friends Foundation Thailand runs a **wildlife rescue centre** (☏0 3245 8135; www.wfft.org; Wat Khao Luk Chang, 35km northwest of Cha-am) that adopts and cares for abused and abandoned animals. Most of these animals are wild creatures that can't return to the wild due to injuries or lack of survival skills. The centre cares for 400 animals, including bears, tigers, gibbons, macaques, loris and birds. There is also an affiliated elephant rescue program that buys and shelters animals being used as street beggars.

The centre offers a **full access tour** (5000B for six people) that introduces the animals and discusses their rescue histories. The tour includes a visit with the elephants (but no rides are offered) and hotel transfer from Hua Hin or Cha-am.

Those looking for a more intimate connection with the animals can volunteer to help at the centre. An average day could involve chopping fruits and vegetables to feed sun bears, cleaning enclosures and rowing out to the gibbon islands with a daily meal. Volunteers are required to stay a minimum of two weeks and work a full (usually 6.30am to 6.30pm) six days a week. Contact the centre or visit the **volunteer website** (www.wildlifevolunteer.org) for prices and details.

🛏 Sleeping

Cha-am has two basic types of accommodation: apartment-style hotels along the beach road (Th Ruamjit) and more expensive 'condotel' developments (condominiums with a kitchen and operating under a rental program). Expect a discount on posted rates for weekday stays.

The northern end of the beach (known as Long Beach) has a wider, blonder strip of sand and sees more foreign tourists, while the southern end is more Thai. Th Narathip divides the beach into north and south and the beach road (Th Ruamjit) soi are numbered in ascending order in both directions from this intersection.

Charlie House
GUEST HOUSE **$$**
(☑0 3243 3799; 241/60-61, Soi 1 North, Th Ruamjit; r 650-800B; ❄🤶) This cheery place boasts a lime-green lobby and colourful rooms that are fun to return to after a day of people-watching. Don't confuse it with institutional Charlie Place or Charlie TV on the same soi.

Cha-am Mathong Guesthouse
GUEST HOUSE **$$**
(☑08 1550 2947; www.chaammathongcom; cnr Th Ruamjit & Soi 3 South; r 600-800B; ❄) Clean and convenient with all the mod cons, Mathong won't win any awards for hand-holding but you get a lot of bang for your baht.

Dee Lek
GUEST HOUSE **$$**
(☑0 3247 0396; www.deelek.com; 225/30-33 Soi Long Beach, Th Ruamjit; r 1200-1500B; ❄🤶) Popular with Scandinavians, Dee Lek has roomy rooms with spacious bathrooms and upholstered European-style furniture.

Casa Papaya
HOTEL **$$$**
(☑0 3247 0678; www.casapapayathai.com; 810/4 Th Phetkasem; r 3000-5000B; ❄❄) This quirky spot is right on the beach in between Cha-am and Hua Hin and garners fans with its homely and hospitable atmosphere. The beachfront and sea-view bungalows have rooftop decks to enjoy the sunlight (or the moonlight), and inside there are king-size beds and bathrooms in wonderfully brave colours.

🍴 Eating

From your beach chair you can wave down the itinerant vendors selling barbecued and fried seafood or order from a menu of nearby beachfront restaurants. At the far northern end of the beach, seafood restaurants with reasonable prices can be found at the fishing pier.

🔝 Rang Yen Garden
THAI **$**
(☑0 3247 1267; 259/40 Th Ruamjit; dishes 60-180B; ⊗lunch & dinner Nov-Apr) This lush garden restaurant is a cosy and friendly spot to feel at home after a day of feeling like a foreigner. It serves up Thai favourites and is only open in the high season.

Bella Pizza
ITALIAN **$$**
(Soi Bus Station, Th Ruamjit; dishes 150-200B; ⊗lunch & dinner) There are enough foreigners in town to warrant a pizza restaurant and this pie shop makes everyone happy. Plus there's a curious international pedigree: the Thai owner worked in Sweden at a pizza restaurant.

Poom Restaurant
SEAFOOD **$$**
(☑0 3247 1036; 274/1 Th Ruamjit; dishes 120-250B; ⊗lunch & dinner) Slightly more expensive than other nearby beach restaurants, but worth it for the fresh seafood served under tall sugar palms. It appears to be the restaurant of choice for weekending Thais – always a good sign.

Pla Too Restaurant
SEAFOOD **$$**
(☑032 508175; dishes 150-250B; ⊗lunch & dinner) Thanks to the smells from the kitchen, you'll be hungry just walking from the car park to the sprawling beachfront restaurant, beloved by Thais and foreigners alike. It is near the Courtyard Marriott in between Cha-am and Hua Hin.

ℹ Information

Phetkasem Hwy runs through Cha-am's busy town centre, which is about 1km away from the beach. The town centre is where you'll find the main bus stop, banks, the main post office, an outdoor market and the train station.

You'll find plenty of banks along Th Ruamjit with ATMs and exchange services.

Only Chaam (www.onlychaam.com) is an online blog and website about visiting Cha-am.

Communications Authority of Thailand (CAT; Th Narathip) For international phone calls.

Post office (Th Ruamjit) On the main beach strip.

Tourism Authority of Thailand (TAT; ☑0 3247 1005; tatphet@tat.or.th; 500/51 Th Phetkasem; ⊗8.30am-4.30pm) On Phetkasem Hwy, 500m south of town. The staff speak good English.

ℹ️ Getting There & Away

Buses stop on Phetkasem Hwy near the 7-Eleven store at the intersection of Th Narathip. Frequent bus services operating to/from Cha-am include the following:

Bangkok's Southern (Sai Tai Mai) station (150B, three hours)

Phetchaburi (50B, 40 minutes)

Hua Hin (50B, 30 minutes).

Minivans to Bangkok's Victory Monument (160B, 2½ hours, hourly 7am to 5.30pm) leave from Soi Bus Station, in between Th Ruamjit and Th Chao Lay. Other minivan destinations include Hua Hin (120B) and Phetchaburi (100B). A private taxi to Hua Hin will cost 500B.

The **train station** (Th Narathip) is west of Phetkasem Hwy. From Bangkok's Hua Lamphong station five daily trains go to Cha-am (40B to 150B, four hours) and continue on to Hua Hin. Cha-am is listed in the timetable only in Thai as 'Ban Cha-am'.

ℹ️ Getting Around

From the city centre to the beach it's a quick motorcycle (30B) or *sŏrng·tăa·ou* (40B) ride. Some drivers will try to take you to hotels that offer commissions instead of the one you requested.

You can hire motorcycles for 300B per day all along Th Ruamjit. Cruisy bicycles are available everywhere for 20B per hour or 100B per day, and are a good way to get around.

Hua Hin   หัวหิน

POP 98,896

Thailand's original beach resort is no palmfringed castaway island and arguably it is all the better for it. Instead it is a delightful mix of city and sea with a cosmopolitan ambience, lively markets, tasty street eats, long wide beaches and fully functional city services (meaning no septic streams bisect the beach like those *other* places).

Hua Hin traces its aristocratic roots to the 1920s when Rama VI (King Vajiravudh) and Rama VII (King Prajadhipok) built summer residences here to escape Bangkok's stifling climate. The most famous of the two is **Phra Ratchawang Klai Kangwon** (Far from Worries Palace), 3km north of town and which is still a royal residence today and so poetically named that Thais often invoke it as a city slogan. Rama VII's endorsement of Hua Hin and the construction of the southern railway made the town *the* place to be for Thai nobility who built their own summer residences beside the sea.

In the 1980s the luxury-hotel group Sofitel renovated the town's grand dame hotel that in turn sparked overseas tourism. Today all the international hotel chains have properties in Hua Hin, and a growing number of wealthy expats retire to the nearby housing estates and condominiums. Middle-class and high-society Thais from Bangkok swoop into town on weekends, making parts of the city look a lot like upper Sukhumvit.

There's a lot of money swirling around, which unnecessarily scares off baht-minded backpackers. Because this is a bustling Thai town, seafood is plentiful and affordable, there's cheap public transport for beach hopping and it takes a lot less time and effort (and money) to get here from Bangkok than to the southern islands. So quit wasting your time everywhere else and hurry up to Hua Hin beach.

⊙ Sights

The city's beaches are numerous, wide and long; swimming is safe, and Hua Hin continues to enjoy some of the peninsula's driest weather. During stormy weather, watch out for jellyfish.

HUA HIN TOWN   เมืองหัวหิน

A former fishing village, Hua Hin town retains its roots with an old teak shophouse district bisected by narrow soi, pier houses that have been converted into restaurants and guest houses and a busy fishing pier still in use today. South of the harbour is a rocky headland that inspired the name 'Hua Hin', meaning 'Stone Head'. In the commercial heart are busy markets and all the modern conveniences you forgot to pack.

Hat Hua Hin   BEACH

(หาดหัวหิน; public access via eastern end of Th Damnoen Kasem) When viewed from the main public entrance, Hua Hin's beach might seem like a lot of hype. Initially you meet a pleasant but not stunning stretch of sand punctuated by round, smooth boulders and bordered here by the Sofitel resort, which nearly kisses the high tide mark. Don't be dismayed; this is the people-watching spot. Visiting Thais come here to photograph their friends wading ankle-deep in the sea and pony rides are offered to anyone standing still.

But if you're after swimming and sunbathing continue south to where the 5km-long beach stretches into a Buddha-adorned headland (Khao Takiab). The sand is a fine white powder that is wide and long and the sea is a calm grey-green. Instead of coconut trees, resort towers line the interior of the beach but this is a minor distraction for long uninterrupted walks. Access roads lead to Th Phetkasem, where you can catch a green *sŏrng·tăa·ou* back to town.

Hua Hin Train Station
HISTORIC SITE

(สถานีรถไฟหัวหิน; Th Liab Tang Rot Fai) An iconic piece of local architecture, the red-and-white pavilion that sits beside Hua Hin's train station once served as the royal waiting room during the reign of Rama VI. It was the railway that made Hua Hin's emergence as a tourist destination possible for the Bangkok-based monarchy and the city's elite. In the early 20th century, the four-hour journey between Hua Hin and Bangkok was a transportation revolution. That was before the emergence of speeding minivan drivers fuelled by energy drinks.

NORTH HUA HIN

The summer residences of the royal family and minor nobility dot the coast northward from Hua Hin's fishing pier toward Cha-am.

Hat Hua Hin Neua
BEACH

(หาดหัวหินเหนือ; North Hua Hin Beach; public access paths off of Th Naebkehardt) Genteel but modest Thai-Victorian garden estates bestowed with ocean-inspired names, such as 'Listening to the Sea House', line this end of the coast. The current monarchy's palace lies about 3km north of town but visitors are only allowed on the **grounds** (◷5.30-7.30am & 4-7pm; ID required). On weekends, Th Naebkehardt is the preferred getaway for Bangkok Thais, some of whom still summer in the old-fashioned residences while others come to supper in the houses that have been converted into restaurants.

FREE Plearn Wan
NOTABLE BUILDING

(เพลินวาน; ☑0 3252 0311; www.plearnwan.com; Th Phetkasem btw Soi 38 & 40) More of an art installation than a commercial enterprise, Plearn Wan is a vintage village containing stylized versions of old-fashioned shophouses that once occupied the Thai-Chinese districts of Bangkok and Hua Hin. There's a pharmacy selling (well actually displaying) roots, powders and other concoctions that Thai grandmothers once used; a music store specialising in the crooner era of the 1950s and 1960s; and other bygone shops and attractions that pre-date the arrival of 7-Eleven. It would be a tourist trap if it

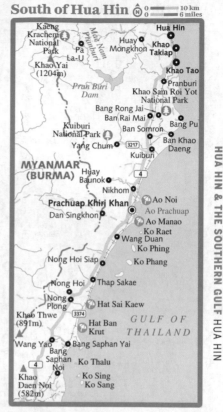

South of Hua Hin

charged an admission fee but most visitors just wander the grounds snapping photos without making any impulse purchases. If you want to support this bit of nostalgia, there are retro souvenirs and snack shops.

Phra Ratchaniwet Mrigadayavan
HISTORIC SITE

(พระราชนิเวศน์มฤคทายวัน; ☑0 3250 8443; admission 30B; ◷9am-4.30pm) With a breezy seaside location 10km north of Hua Hin, this summer palace was built during the reign of Rama VI (King Vajiravudh) in 1923 as a health-promoting retreat for the king who suffered from rheumatoid arthritis. The court's Italian architect built the palace to maximise air circulation and admire the sea. The result is a series of interlinked teak houses with tall shuttered windows and patterned fretwork built upon stilts forming a shaded ground-level boardwalk. It is functional and elegant without excessive opulence. Surrounding the palace is a beautiful

Hua Hin

garden with statuesque trees, some nearing a century old. A traditional Thai orchestra helps transport visitors' imaginations backwards in time.

The palace is located within the grounds of Camp Rama VI, a military post, and you need to check in at the gate. It is easiest to come via private transport but you can also catch a Hua Hin to Cha-am bus and ask to be dropped off at the turn-off to the palace. There are often motorcycle taxis waiting that will take you the remaining 2km.

INLAND OF HUA HIN

Baan Silapin ART GALLERY
(บ้านศิลปิน; ☑032534830; www.huahinartistvillage. com; Th Hua Hin-Pa Lu-U; ☺10am-5pm Tue-Sun) Local painter Tawee Kase-ngam established this artist collective in a shady grove 4km west of Th Phetkasem. The galleries and studio spaces highlight the works of 21 artists, many of whom opted out of Bangkok's

fast-paced art world in favour of Hua Hin's more relaxed atmosphere and its scenic landscape of mountains and sea. Outlying clay huts shelter the playful sculptures of Nai Dee and Mae A-Ngoon. Khun Nang, a skilful and charismatic teacher, leads **art classes** (9.30am-11.30am; 300/200B adult/child) for adults on Tuesday and Thursday and for children on Saturday.

Hua Hin Hills Vineyard VINEYARD
(ไร่องุ่นหัวหินฮิลล์ วินยาร์ด; ☑08 1701 8874; www.huahinhillsvineyard.com; Th Hua Hin-Pa Lu-U; ☺10am-6pm) Part of the New Latitudes wine movement (see the boxed text, p516), this vineyard is nestled in a scenic mountain valley 45km west of Hua Hin. The loamy sand and slate soil feeds several Rhone grape varieties that are used in their Monsoon Valley wine label.

You can spend the day here learning about viticulture in a tropical climate on a **vineyard tour** (free; ☺1 & 4pm), doing a **wine**

Hua Hin

tasting (290B for 3 samples) or eating at the picturesque **Sala Wine Bar & Bistro** (dishes 200-500B). There is also a pétanque course, mountain-biking trails and elephant riding.

A vineyard shuttle leaves the affiliated **Hua Hin Hills Wine Cellar store** (☑0 3252 6 351, Market Village, Th Phetkasem, South Hua Hin) at 10.30am and 3pm and returns at 1.30pm and 6pm; return ticket is 200B.

KHAO TAKIAB เขาตะเกียบ

About 7km south of Hua Hin, Monumental Chopstick Mountain guards the southern end of Hua Hin beach and is adorned with a giant standing Buddha. Atop the 272m mountain is a Thai-Chinese temple (**Wat Khao Lat**) and many resident monkeys who are not to be trusted – but the views are great. On the southern side of Khao Takiab is **Suan Son Pradipath** (Sea Pine Garden), a muddy beach maintained by the army and popular with weekending Thais. Green *sŏrng·tǎa·ou* go all the way from Hua Hin to Khao Takiab village, where you'll find loads of simple Thai eateries.

The new and stylish **Cicada Market** (Th Phetkasem; ⊙4-11pm Fri & Sat, 4-10pm Sun) is an outdoor market still moulting in the food and shopping category, but it has found its niche on Friday nights when live bands hit the stage and the vibe is mellow and arty. You can catch a green *sŏrng·tǎa·ou* (20B; from 6am to 9pm) from Hua Hin Night Market; a hired túk-túk will cost 150B one-way.

🏃 Activities

There are many travel agencies in town offering day trips to nearby national parks. Unless you're in a group, you may have to wait until enough people sign up for the trip of your choice.

Hua Hin Adventure Tour (☑0 3253 0314; www.huahinadventuretour.com; Th Naebkehardt) offers more somewhat active excursions including kayaking trips in the Khao Sam Roi Yot National Park and mountain biking in Kaeng Krachan National Park.

NEW ATTITUDES TOWARDS WINE

Common wisdom would tell you that tasty wine grapes don't grow alongside coconut trees. But advances in plant sciences and a global palette for wines has changed all of that and ushered in the geographic experiment dubbed New Latitude Wines, produced from grapes grown outside the traditional 30- to 50-degree parallels.

The New Latitudes' main challenge is to replicate the wine-producing grapes preferred climate as best as possible. That means introducing a false dormancy or winter period through pruning, regulated irrigation and companion planting of grasses to prevent soil loss during the rainy season. If you're familiar with viticulture in the Old World, you'll be shocked to see all the cultivation rules Thai vineyards successfully break.

Wine experts have yet to crown a New Latitude that surpasses the grand dames but they do fill a local niche. Siam Winery, the parent company of Hua Hin Hills Vineyard (see p514), aims to produce wines that pair with the complex flavours of Thai food. The vineyard grows columbard, chenin blanc, muscat, shiraz and sangiovese grapes, among others, and typically the citrus-leaning whites are a refreshing complement to the fireworks of most Thai dishes.

Because of the hot climate, a wine drinker's palette is often altered. The thinner wines produced in Thailand tend to have a more satisfying effect than the bold chewy reds that pair well with a chilly spring day. Drinking red wine in Thailand has always been a challenge because the heat turns otherwise leathery notes straight into vinegar. To counteract the tropical factor, break yet another wine rule and chill reds in the refrigerator to replicate 'cellar' temperature as close as possible.

Kiteboarding

Adding to the beauty of Hua Hin beach are the airborne kites (attached to a wave board) that seem to sail among the puffy clouds. Hua Hin is an ideal kiteboarding spot: it has a long, consistent windy season. Winds blow from the northeast from October to December and from the southeast from January to March. In 2010 Hua Hin hosted the Kiteboarding World Cup.

Kiteboarding Asia   KITEBOARDING
(☑08 8230 0016; www.kiteboardingasia.com; South Hua Hin; beginner courses 11,000B) This 10-year old company operates four beachside shops that rent equipment and teach lessons. The three-day introductory course teaches beginners the physical mechanics of the sport, and the instructor recommends newbies come when the winds are blowing from the southeast (January to March) and the sea is less choppy.

Golf

Home to the country's first golf course, Hua Hin continues to be an international and domestic golfing destination.

Hua Hin Golf Centre   GOLF
(☑0 3253 0476; www.huahingolf.com; Th Selakam; ⊘noon-10pm) The friendly staff at this pro shop can steer you to the most affordable, well-maintained courses where the mon-

keys won't try to run off with your balls. The company also organises golf tours and rents equipment.

Black Mountain Golf Course   GOLF
(☑0 3261 8666; www.bmghuahin.com; green fees 2500B) The city's newest course is currently everyone's favourite. About 10km west of Hua Hin, the 18-hole course was carved out of jungle and an old pineapple plantation and it retains some natural creeks used as water hazards. The 2009 and 2010 Asian PGA tour was held here.

Cycling

Cycling is a scenic and affordable option for touring Hua Hin's outlying attractions, especially since hiring a taxi to cover the same ground is ridiculously expensive. Don't be spooked by the busy thoroughfares; there are plenty of quiet byways where you can enjoy the scenery.

Hua Hin Bike Tours   CYCLING
(☑08 1173 4469; www.huahinbiketours.com; 4/34 Soi Hua Hin 96/1, Th Phetkasem, South Hua Hin; tours 1500-2500B) A husband-and-wife team (see the boxed text, p518) operates this cycling company that leads half-, full-, and multiday tours to a variety of attractions in and around Hua Hin. Pedal to the **Hua Hin Hills Vineyard** (p514) for some well-earned refreshment, tour the coastal byways south

of Hua Hin, or ride among the limestone mountains of **Khao Sam Roi Yot National Park** (p524). They also rent premium bicycles (500B per day) for independent cyclists and can recommend routes. The same couple also leads long-distance charity and corporate bike tours across Thailand; visit the parent company **Tour de Asia** (www.tour deasa.org) for more information.

🔁 Courses

Buchabun Art & Crafts Collection COOKING (☎08 1572 3805; www.thai-cookingcourse.com; 22 Th Dechanuchit; courses 1500B) Aspiring chefs should sign up for a half-day Thai cooking class that includes a market visit and recipe book. They only run it if several people are interested.

✸ Festivals & Events

King's Cup Elephant Polo Tournament ELEPHANT RACING Polo with a Thai twist, this annual tournament involving elephant mounts instead of horses takes place on the scenic grounds of the Anantara Hua Hin resort in September. It might not be as fast-paced as its British cousin but it is a charitable event that raises money for elephant-welfare issues.

Hua Hin Jazz Fest JAZZ In honour of the king's personal interest in the genre, the city that hosts royal getaways also hosts an annual jazz festival featuring Thai and international performers. All events are free and usually occur in June.

Fringe Festival THEATRE Organised by the Patravadi Theatre, a renowned avant-garde performance space in Bangkok, this modern arts festival is held at its sister location, **Vic Hua Hin** (☎0 3282 7814; www.vichuahin.com; 62/70 Soi Hua Na Nong Khae, South Hua Hin). Running from January to March, there are a host of dance, music and comedy performances from local and international artists as well as multinational collaborations.

🛏 Sleeping

Most budget and midrange options are in town occupying multistorey buildings in the old shophouse district. It is an atmospheric setting with cheap tasty food nearby but you'll have to 'commute' to the beach, either by walking to north Hua Hin beach (best at low tide) or catching a *sŏrng·tăa·ou* to the southern end of Hua Hin beach.

The top-end options are beachfront resorts sprawling south from the Sofitel. All the international brands have a presence in Hua Hin but we've only listed unique and local options for a more intimate experience.

Hua Hin Town

Pattana Guest House GUEST HOUSE **$** (☎0 3251 3393; 52 Th Naresdamri; r 350-550B; ✳) Tucked away down a soi, this simple teak house has a lovely garden filled with little reading nooks. The rooms are small and basic but adequate and the family who runs it is friendly and artistic.

Tong-Mee House GUEST HOUSE **$** (☎0 3253 0725; 1 Soi Raumpown, Th Naebkehardt; r 450-550B; ✳@) Hidden away in a quiet residential soi, this smart guest house is the best value in town. The rooms are small but well kept and have balconies.

Supasuda Guest House GUEST HOUSE **$** (☎0 3251 3618; www.spghouse.com; 1/8 Th Chomsin; r 800-1000B; ✳☎) Large rooms come with mermaid murals and hot showers. The more expensive ones have verandahs and a bit of road noise. Guests have access to the common terrace.

Ban Somboon GUEST HOUSE **$** (☎0 3251 1538; 13/4 Soi Hua Hin 63, Th Phetkasem; r 950-1200B; ✳) With family photos decorating the walls and a compact garden, this place is like staying at your favourite Thai auntie's house. This is a very quiet, centrally located soi with several other good-value guest houses.

Baan Tawee Suk GUEST HOUSE **$** (☎0 89459 2618; 43/8 Th Poonsuk; r 800B; ✳☎) This new multistorey guest house is fresh and clean with all the mod cons. Rooms are a little cramped so leave the super-sized luggage at home.

Sirima GUEST HOUSE **$** (☎0 3251 1060; Th Naresdamri; r 550B; ✳) The best of the old-style pier guest houses, Sirima has a pretty exterior with stained glass and polished wood. A long hallway leads to a common deck overlooking the water. Rooms come in various degrees of quality but the tile-floored ones are better.

My Place Hua Hin HOTEL **$$** (☎0 32514 1112; www.myplacehuahin.com; 17 Th Amnuaysin, Th Phetkasem; r 1850-2200B; ✳☎) A small well-maintained hotel in the heart of the city – it might sound commonplace but

My Place actually delivers on what turns out to be a tall order.

Euro-Hua Hin City Hotel YHA   HOSTEL **$**
(☑0 3251 3130; 5/15 Th Sasong; r 250-800B; ❄) Just like any large hostel back home, this place feels both comfortable and institutional. All rooms have air-con, even the somewhat cramped dorms. There are also single and double private rooms and all accommodation includes breakfast. Add 50B to these prices if you don't belong to HI.

Baan Chalelarn Hotel   HOTEL **$$**
(☑0 3253 1288; www.chalelarnhuahin.com; 11 Th Chomsin; r 1200-1300B; ❄@) Chalelarn has a beautiful lobby with wooden floors, while the big rooms are equipped with king-size beds. Verandahs and breakfast are all part of the perks.

Araya Residence   HOTEL **$$**
(☑0 3253 1130; www.araya-residence.com; 15/1 Th Chomsin; r 1500-2000B; ❄@) Wood and concrete are combined to create a rustic yet modern feel at this pseudo-stylish hotel. The rooms are spacious and comfortable though the hotel is a little tatty around the edges.

Also recommended:

Fat Cat Guesthouse   GUEST HOUSE **$**
(☑08 6206 2455; 8/3 Th Naresdamri; r 300-900B; ❄) The rooms with fan occupy a separate building down a residential soi and some have fantastic views of the city.

Fulay Guesthouse   GUEST HOUSE **$**
(☑0 3251 3145; www.fulayhuahin.net; 110/1 Th Naresdamri; r 430-980B; ❄🛜) An old-style pier guest house, with good beds, newish bathrooms and flowering plants in the common area.

Baan Oum-or Hotel   HOTEL **$$**
(☑0 3251 5151; 77/18-19 Soi 63, Th Phetkasem; r 1000-1500B; ❄) The rooms are big and bright and there are only seven of them so book ahead.

LOCAL KNOWLEDGE

SIRANEE (GAE) MEESITH, CO-OWNER HUA HIN BIKE TOURS

I am from a very small village surrounded by rice farms, water buffalos and such. It is a bit boring sometimes but Bangkok, where I went to university, is extreme. Hua Hin is in between. It is a relaxing little town but still has places to go: peaceful beaches, mountains, caves and activities (biking, kiteboarding or swimming in the ocean). There are also shopping, bakeries, cafes and loads of good seafood restaurants.

BEST BEACH

Hua Hin beach is beautiful with white sand from the Hilton Hotel, south all the way to Khao Takiap.

BEST BIKE RIDE

I enjoy cycling outside of the centre of Hua Hin where there are so many small roads and dirt trails with beaches to visit, mountain viewpoints, clean air and plenty of sunshine. You can't see all this by car and cycling is also good exercise and environmentally friendly to help keep Hua Hin beautiful and clean.

FAVOURITE OUTING FOR OUT-OF-TOWNERS

Tham Phraya Nakhon is an amazing cave in Khao Sam Roi Yot National Park that has a Thai-style pavilion inside with a statue of Rama V. Three of Thailand's kings have visited this cave and two have signed the wall of the cave. Getting to the cave is also part of the attraction because it is inside a mountain that requires trekking up a 430m jungle trail reached by taking a boat from a nearby beach or hiking over another small mountain. Plus there are nearby inexpensive and excellent Thai seafood restaurants too.

SECRET SPOT

Eighteen Below Ice Cream (Th Naebkehardt, North Hua Hin) is owned by a young couple: the wife used to be a Thai actress and the husband is a Belgian pastry chef who makes amazing ice cream and pastries. They started out just selling to the finer hotels in Hua Hin but later decided to turn their home into a lovely garden cafe. Many Thai people from Bangkok go there on weekends but most foreigners have no idea the place exists.

All Nations Guest House GUEST HOUSE $
(☑0 3251 2747; 10-10/1 Th Dechanuchit; r 500-800B; ✸) Has slightly dingy rooms but at a decent price with enough noise protection.

Hua Hin Beaches

TOP CHOICE Baan Bayan HOTEL $$$
(☑0 3253 3540; www.baanbayan.com; 119 Th Phetkasem, South Hua Hin; r 4000-11,000B; ✸✸✸) A colonial beach house built in the early 20th century, Baan Bayan is perfect for travellers seeking a luxury experience without the overkill of a big resort. The airy, high-ceilinged rooms are painted a relaxing buttery yellow, the staff are attentive and the location is absolute beachfront.

Green Gallery Bed & Breakfast HOTEL $$
(☑0 3253 0487; www.greenhuahin.com; 3/1 Soi Hua Hin 51, Th Naebkehardt, North Hua Hin; r 1200B; ✸✸) Just as cute as candy, this small hotel occupies a converted colonial-style beach house. Individually decorated rooms reflect a hip artiness that defines urban Thai style. You're also a short walk to north Hua Hin beach.

Rahmahyah Hotel GUEST HOUSE $$
(☑0 3253 2106; 113/10 Soi Hua Hin 67, Th Phetkasem, South Hua Hin; r from 1000B; ✸✸✸) Across the street from Market Village, about 1km south of town, is a small guest house enclave tucked between the high-end resorts, with beach access. The Rahmahyah is the best of the bunch with professional staff and clean functional rooms. The front rooms get a lot of highway noise.

Baan Laksasubha HOTEL $$$
(☑032514525; www.baanlaksasubha.com; Th 53/7 Naresdamri; r 4200-7900B; ✸✸✸) Next door to the Sofitel, this petite resort, owned by a Bangkok aristocrat, specialises in family-friendly cottages. The decor is so crisp and subdued that it is almost plain, meandering garden paths lead past the pool to the beach and there's a dedicated kid's room with toys and books. The taxi drivers will understand you better if you say 'baan lak-su-pah'.

Veranda Lodge HOTEL $$$
(☑032533678; 113 Soi Hua Hin 67, Th Phetkasem, South Hua Hin; www.verandalodge.com; r 3000-5000B; ✸✸✸) Beachfront without the whopping price tag, this top-end hotel has a variety of options, from modern hotel rooms to luxurious garden bungalows.

Sofitel Centara Grand Resort and Villas HOTEL $$$
(☑0 3251 2021; www.sofitel.com; 1 Th Damnoen Kasem; r from 5500B; ✸@✸) The historic Railway Hotel, Hua Hin's first seaside hotel, was restored to suit modern beachgoers with expansive grounds, a spa and sporting facilities and colonial or new world rooms.

Anantara Resort & Spa HOTEL $$$
(☑0 3252 0205; www.huahin.anantara.com; r from 7500B; Th Phetkasem; ✸✸✸) Anantara's self-contained resort, 4.5km north of Hua Hin, is designed to invoke a traditional Thai village with a low-key but luxurious ambience. An experiential resort, there are spa facilities, water sports and cultural activities.

Chiva-Som International Health Resort HOTEL $$$
(☑0 3253 6536; www.chivasom.com; 74/4 Th Phetkasem, South Hua Hin; 3-night packages from 68,310B; ✸✸) When a getaway isn't enough, there's Chiva-Som, for overworked, overstressed (and just maybe overpaid) business folk and celebrities. Health and wellness services include nutrition consultation, yoga and fitness classes, massage of every variety as well as detox programs.

✕ Eating

Night Market SEAFOOD $
(Th Dechanuchit btw Th Phetkasem & Th Sasong; dishes from 60B; ◷5pm-midnight) An attraction that rivals the beach, Hua Hin's night market tops locals' lists of favourite spots to eat. Ice-packed displays of spiny lobsters and king prawns appeal to the big-spenders but the simple stir-fry stalls are just as tasty. Try pàt pŏng gà·rèe 'boo (crab curry), gûng tôrt (fried shrimp) and hŏy tôrt (fried mussel omelette). In between, souvenir stalls cater to Thai's favourite digestive activity: shopping.

Sang Thai Restaurant THAI $
(Th Naresdamri; dishes 120-350B; ◷lunch & dinner) One of many beloved pier-side restaurants, Sang Thai soaks in the view and specialises in whole steamed fish that arrives still sizzling to your table.

Jek Pia Coffeeshop SEAFOOD $
(51/6 Th Dechanuchit; dishes 80-160B; ◷lunch & dinner) More than just a coffee shop, this 50-year-old restaurant is another culinary destination specialising in an extensive array of stir-fried seafood dishes. If it is too full to get a seat, you can order from the same

menu at the sukiyaki restaurant further south on Th Naebkehardt.

Hua Hin Koti
SEAFOOD $$

(☑0 3251 1252; 16/1 Th Dechanuchit; dishes 80-250B; ⊙lunch & dinner) Across from the Night Market, this Thai-Chinese restaurant is a national culinary luminary. Thais adore the fried crab balls, while foreigners swoon over *đôm yam gûng* (shrimp soup with lemongrass). And everyone loves the spicy seafood salad *(yam tá-lair)* and deep-fried fish with ginger.

Th Chomsin Food Stalls
THAI $

(cnr Th Chomsin & Th Naebkhardt; dishes from 30B; ⊙lunch & dinner) If you're after 100% authentic eats, check out the food stalls that congregate at this popular lunch corner. Though the setting is humble, Thais are fastidious eaters and use a fork (or their fingers with a pinch of *kôw něe·o*) to remove the meat from the bones of *gài tôrt* (fried chicken) rather than putting teeth directly to flesh.

Sofitel Cafe & Tea Corner
CAFE $$

(1 Th Damnoen Kasem; dishes 80-150B; ⊙breakfast & lunch) It is customary to pay homage to a city's grand dame hotel with a spot of tea and the Sofitel obliges with this refined tea room occupying the grounds of the former Railway Hotel. The cafe is serenaded by classical music and cooled by sea breezes, perfect for thumbing the newspaper and sipping your stimulants with an aristocratic air. There are also a few historic photos and memorabilia earning it the unlikely designation of 'museum'. The real draw, though, is the hotel's topiary garden filled with gigantic clipped shrubs depicting elephants, giraffes and geese.

Chatchai Market
THAI $

(Th Phetkasem; ⊙daylight hours; dishes from 30B) The city's day market resides in an historic building built in 1926 with a distinctive seven-eaved roof in honour of Rama VII. There are the usual market refreshments: morning vendors selling *ƀah·tôrng·gŏh* (Chinese-style doughnuts) and *gah·faa boh·rahn* (ancient-style coffee spiked with sweetened condensed milk); as well as all-day noodles with freshly made wontons; and the full assortment of fresh tropical fruit.

World News Coffee
CAFE $

(130/2 Th Naresdamri; dishes 70-150B; ⊙breakfast, lunch & dinner; @) This Starbucks-esque cafe serves baked goods and lots of different cof-

fees. You can surf the web for 50B per hour and there are magazines and newspapers to complement your first cup of the day.

🍷 Drinking & Entertainment

Drinking in Hua Hin is still stuck in the '90s: sports bars or hostess bars – and sometimes you can't tell the difference. But the onslaught of weekending Bangkok Thais has kicked up the sophistication factor. Apart from these, also consider Cicada Market in Khao Takiab (see p515).

No Name Bar
BAR

(Th Naresdamri) Past the Chinese shrine that sits on the rocky headland is this cliffside restaurant and bar that drinks in the ocean along with all the alcoholic adult beverages.

Hua Hin Brewing Company
BAR

(33 Th Naresdamri) Though there's no longer any beer brewed here, the spacious outdoor deck is a mature spot to watch the passing parade on Th Naresdamri.

Mai Tai Cocktail & Beer Garden
BAR

(33/12 Th Naresdamri) Recession-era prices are on tap at this convivial outdoor terrace made for people-watching and beer-drinking.

O'Neill's Irish Pub
IRISH BAR

(5 Th Phunsuk) Pretty authentic for being so far from the Blarney Stone, O'Neill's does cheap draught specials and live sports on several tellies.

El Murphy's Mexican Grill & Steakhouse
BAR

(25 Soi Selakam, Th Phunsuk) Every sports bar has an international gimmick and this comfy spot marries Mexico and Ireland. Come in to enjoy a tall one, the live band and an unlikely assortment of tourists and expats.

Music Room
LIVE MUSIC

(Soi Hua Hin 32, Th Phetkasem, North Hua Hin) The place to be for weekending Thais, the Music Room features live bands of every imaginable genre as well as theme parties and a local collection of celebrities.

ℹ Information

Emergency
Tourist police (☑0 3251 5995; Th Damnoen Kasem)

Internet Access
Internet access is available all over Hua Hin, in guest houses and cafes.

KEEPING UP WITH THE BANGKOK THAIS

On weekends, a different kind of tidal system occurs in Hua Hin. Bangkok professionals flow in, filling up hotels and restaurants on Th Naebkehardt, washing over the night market or crowding into nightclubs. And then come Sunday they clog the roadways heading north, obeying the pull of the upcoming work week.

Their presence is so pronounced that there is an irresistible urge to join them. And because of restaurant features on Thai TV or food magazines, everyone goes to the same places. So don your designer sunglasses and elbow your way to a table at one of these popular spots in North Hua Hin:

Sôm·đam Stand
FOOD STALL

(Th Naebkehardt; dishes 50-80B; ☺lunch) Across from Iammeuang Hotel is a sôm·đam stand that easily wipes out the country's supply of green papayas in one weekend. We couldn't even elbow our way to a seat before they packed up for the day.

Eighteen Below Ice Cream
ICE CREAM

(Th Naebkehardt; dishes 160B; closed Wed) At the end of the road behind Baan Talay Chine Hotel, this gourmet ice cream shop is run by a trained chef and specialises in rich and creamy flavours.

Baan Itsara
SEAFOOD

(Th Naebkehardt; dishes from 160B; ☺lunch & dinner) Overpriced in our opinion, Baan Itsara is a must-be-seen spot that does 'inter' versions of Thai seafood dishes. Squid with basil comes with pine nuts so it is more like a pesto than the traditionally spicy Thai version.

Jae Siam
NOODLES

(Th Naebkehardt; dishes 30-50B; ☺lunch & dinner) If you've lost track of the days of the week, cruise by this open-air noodle shop, next to Evergreen Hotel, where Hua Hin civil servants pack in on weekdays and Bangkok Thais come on weekends. The shop is famous for gŏo·ay đĕe·o mŏo đŭn (stewed pork noodles) and gŏo·ay đĕe·o gài đŭn (stewed chicken noodles).

Internet Resources
Tourism Hua Hin (www.tourismhuahin.com) A cursory intro to the site with a good run-down on the outlying area.

Hua Hin Observer (www.observergroup.net) An expat-published magazine available online.

Medical Services
Hospital San Paolo (☏0 3253 2576; 222 Th Phetkasem) Just south of town with emergency facilities.

Bangkok Hospital Hua Hin (☏0 3261 6800; www.bangkokhospital.com/huahin; Th Phetkasem btw Soi Hua Hin 94 & 106;) The latest outpost of the luxury hospital chain; it's in South Hua Hin.

Money
There are exchange booths and ATMs on Th Naresdamri and banks on Th Phetkasem.

Post & Telephone
Main post office (Th Damnoen Kasem) Includes the CAT office for international phone calls.

Tourist Information
TAT office (☏0 3251 3885; 39/4 Th Phetkasem; ☺8.30am-4.30pm) Staff here speak English and are quite helpful; the office is north of town near Soi Hua Hin 70.

Municipal Tourist Information Office (☏0 3251 1047; cnr Th Phetkasem & Th Damnoen Kasem; ☺8.30am-4.30pm Mon-Fri) Provides maps and information about Hua Hin. There's another branch (☏0 3252 2797; Th Naebkehardt; 9am-7.30pm Mon-Fri, 9.30am-5pm Sat & Sun) near the clock tower.

Travel Agencies
Tuk Tours (☏0 3251 4281; www.tuktours.com; 33/5 Th Phunsuk) Helpful, no-pressure place that can book activities and transport all around Thailand.

ℹ Getting There & Away
Air
The **airport** (www.huahinairport.com) is 6km north of town but only has charter services through **Nok Mini** (☏0 2641 4190; www.nokmini.com).

Bus

Hua Hin's long-distance **bus station** (Th Phetkasem btw Soi Hua Hin 94 & 98) is south of town and serves the following destinations:

Chiang Mai (785B, 12 hours, three daily departures)

Prachuap Khiri Khan (65B, 1½ hours)

Phuket (856B, nine hours, one nightly departure)

Surat Thani (480B, seven hours, two daily departures)

Ubon Ratchathani (1200B, 13 hours, one daily departure)

Buses to Bangkok (160B, three hours, every two hours from 8am to 9pm) also leave from a bus company's in-town **office** (Th Sasong), near the Night Market.

Ordinary buses depart from a **station** (cnr Th Phetkasem & Th Chomsin), north of the market, and destinations include **Cha-am** (50B, 30 minutes) and **Phetchaburi** (50B, 1½ hours).

Lomprayah (☑0 3253 3739; Th Narasdamri) offers a bus-boat combination from Hua Hin to Ko Tao (1000B, 8½ hours; one morning and one night departure).

Minivans

Minivans to Bangkok's Sai Tai Mai (Southern) bus station and Victory Monument (180B, three hours, every 30 minutes from 4am to 8pm) leave from an office on Th Naebkehardt. A direct service to Victory Monument leaves from an office on the corner of Th Phetkasem and Th Chomsin.

Train

There are frequent trains running to/from Bangkok's Hualamphong station (2nd class 212-302B, 3rd class 94-154B, four hours) and other stations on the southern railway line.

ⓘ Getting Around

Green *sŏrng·tăa·ou* depart from the corner of Th Sasong & Th Dechanuchit, near the Night Market and travel south on Th Phetkasem to Khao Takiab (20B). Pranburi-bound buses depart from the same stop.

Túk-túk fares in Hua Hin are outrageous and start at a whopping 100B and barely budge from there. Motorcycle taxis are much more reasonable (40B to 50B) for short hops.

Motorcycles (250B to 500B per day) can be hired from shops on Th Damnoen Kasem. **Thai Rent A Car** (☑0 2737 8888; www.thairentacar. com) is a professional car-rental agency with competitive prices, a well-maintained fleet and hotel drop-offs.

Hua Hin to Pranburi

South of Hua Hin are a series of beaches framed by dramatic headlands that make great daytrips when Hua Hin beach feels too urban.

HAT KHAO TAO   หาดเขาเต่า

About 13km south of Hua Hin, a barely inhabited beach stretches several kilometres south from Khao Takiab to Khao Tao (Turtle Mountain). It is blissfully free of civilization: there are no high rises, no beach chairs, no sarong sellers and no horseback riders.

The mountain has a sprawling temple dedicated to almost every imaginable deity: Buddha, Khun Yin (Chinese goddess of Mercy), Vishnu and even the Thai kings. Follow the trail toward the oceanfront to hike up to the Buddha on the hill.

To get here take a Pranburi bus from Hua Hin and ask to be dropped off at the turnoff for Khao Tao (20B); a motorcycle taxi can take you to the temple (20B). Getting back to the highway might be tricky as return transport is rare; you can always walk or flag down a ride as people are usually coming and going from the temple.

HAT SAI NOI   หาดทรายน้อย

About 20km south of Hua Hin, a scenic cove, Hat Sai Noi, drops off quickly into the sea providing a rare opportunity for deep-water swimming. Nearby are all the amenities: simple seafood restaurants and even small guest houses. For ideal seclusion, come on a weekday. The beach is south of Khao Tao on a lovely road that passes a reservoir and is lined with bougainvillea and limestone cliffs. To get here follow the same directions for Khao Tao but instruct the motorcycle taxi to take you to Hat Sai Noi (60B); getting back to the highway will be difficult but inquire at one of the restaurants for assistance.

Pranburi & Around

POP 75,571

Continuing along the highway south from Hua Hin leads to the country 'suburb' of Pranburi district, which has become the *in-the-know* coastal alternative for Bangkok Thais. Some even go so far as to call it the 'Thai Riveria'. Yet locally the fishing village and nearby beaches are known by a more humble name: **Pak Nam Pran** (mouth of the Pranburi River), designating only its geographic location.

A coastal road separates a string of small villa-style resorts from the beach and with each successive rainy season the ocean claims more sand than its fair share requiring the installation of a bulkhead along parts of the long coastline. Since the primary clientele are Thai, the disappearing beach is of minor consequence. Instead most domestic tourists come for sea views and the village's primary product: dried squid. In the mornings the squid boats dock in the river, unloading their catch and beginning the process of sun-drying. It is a pungent but interesting affair with large drying racks spread out across town.

Bordering the river is an extensive mangrove forest, protected by the **Pranburi Forest Park** (☏0 3262 1608; admission free). Within the park is a wooden walkway that explores the mangroves from the perspective of a a mud-dweller, a sea-pine lined beach and accommodation facilities. The park also offers boat trips along the river and small canals.

The coastal road provides a pleasant trip to **Khao Kalok** (Skull Mountain), a mammoth headland that shelters a beautiful bay on the southern side. This southern beach is wide and sandy and far removed from the hubbub of Hua Hin and even from Pak Nam Pran for that matter, though it does get busy on weekends. Lazying along this stretch are several secluded boutique resorts that would be ideal for honeymooners or folks looking to 'get away from it all' without having to go too far.

The next southern bay is often called **Dolphin Bay**, because of the seasonal visit from bottlenose dolphins and finless porpoise from February to May. Sculpted, jungle-covered islands sit scenically off-shore and the beach is wide and unhindered. This area is a family favourite because the resorts are value-oriented, traffic is minimal and nightlife is non-existent. You're also a few kilometres from the northern entrance to Khao Sam Roi Yot National Park (see p524 for more information).

🛏 Sleeping & Eating

It is mainly high, high-end here but not all of the beach resorts sufficiently earn the price tag so be discerning when making online reservations for places not listed here. That said, this area has some of the best seaside boutiques in Thailand that wholeheartedly deserve a splash-out occasion.

TOP CHOICE **Away Hua Hin** HOTEL $$$
(☏0891446833; www.away-huahin.com; south of Khao Kalok; r from 5000B; ✱☀📶) A boutique resort without pretence, Away has reconstructed seven antique teak houses, many from northern Thailand, to this coastal patch of paradise and outfitted them with large cosy beds and stylish bathrooms. The affable owners, a Thai-Australian family, set a homey mood where breakfast is enjoyed at a common table in the 'big' house providing instant camaraderie with worldly friends. Some villas provide extreme privacy while others accommodate families.

La a natu Bed & Bakery HOTEL $$$
(☏0 3268 9941; www.laanatu.com; south of Khao Kalok; r from 5000B; ✱📶) Turning the humble Thai rice village into a luxury experience is all the rage in the boutique hotel world but La a natu does it with a little more panache than most. The thatched roof villas growing on stilts from cultivated rice paddies have rounded modern corners and a Flintstone-esque playfulness to their design. Each villa is extremely private but evocative of traditional rustic lifestyles with living quarters on the ground floor and often steep, ladder-like stairs leading to the sleeping area. And then there's the semiprivate beach right at your doorstep.

Dolphin Bay Resort HOTEL $$
(☏0 3255 9333; www.dolphinbayresort.com; Dolphin Bay; r from 1500B; ✱@☀) The resort that defined Dolphin Bay as a family-friendly retreat offers a low-key holiday camp ambience with a variety of standard issue, value-oriented bungalows and apartments. The grounds are large enough for kids to roam safely, there are two large pools and the nice sandy beach is just across the street. The gang will love it.

Brassiere Beach HOTEL $$$
(☏0 3263 0555; www.brassierebeach.com; Dolphin Bay; r from 5000B; ✱) A delicious combination of privacy and personality, these nine stucco villas abut the mountains of Khao Sam Roi Yot National Park and face a secluded beach, 100m from the nearest paved road. The rooms have an uncluttered Mexican-villa style, some with roof decks and most with open-air showers. Though the prude in you might mispronounce it, Brassiere Beach deserves your support.

Khao Kalok Restaurant
THAI $

(dishes 60-150B; ☺lunch & dinner) At the southern base of the mountain, this open-air restaurant provides a front-row view of the moored fishing boats. Tasty dishes, like *gaang kĕe·o wăhn* (green curry), *ɓlah mèuk gà·prow* (squid stir-fried with basil) and even the standard *pàt pàk roo·am* (stir-fried vegetables) arrive at a leisurely pace.

Also recommended:

Pranburi Forest Park
CAMPING GROUND $

(☑0 32621608, Pak Nam Pran; tent site & gear rental 300B) A popular spot for 'freshy' (university freshmen) parties, the forest park has a shaded oceanfront camping ground, basic bungalows (1000/2000B for 6/12 people) and a restaurant. No fires allowed.

Pineapple Resort
GUEST HOUSE $

(☑0 81933 9930; Pak Nam Pran; r 500-600B; ✷) A little dishevelled, Pineapple's basic concrete bungalows sit about 50m from the beach but provides a cheap retreat in the land of luxury.

Palm Beach Pranburi
HOTEL $$

(☑0 3263 1966; www.palmbeachpranburi.com; Pak Nam Pran; r from 1500B; ✷☀) A solid midranger surrounded by neighbours who think they're boutique.

The Beach House
GUEST HOUSE $

(☑08 7164 6307; Pak Nam Pran; r 500-800B; ✷☏) One of the cheapest options around, this guest house caters to young kite-boarders who allot their funds toward the sport instead of lodging.

❶ Getting There & Around

Pranburi is about 35km south of Hua Hin and accessible by ordinary bus from Hua Hin's Night Market (20B). You'll be dropped off on the highway where you can catch a *sŏrng·tăa·ou* to Pak Nam Pran. There is also a minivan service from Bangkok's Victory Monument to Pranburi (180B); if you're going to Dolphin Bay (sometimes referred to as Khao Sam Roi Yot Beach), you'll have to negotiate an additional fare with the driver (usually 100B).

If you want to explore the area, you'll need to rent a motorbike as public transport isn't an option.

Khao Sam Roi Yot National Park
อุทยานแห่งชาติเขาสามร้อยยอด

Towering limestone outcrops form a rocky jigsaw-puzzled landscape at this 98-sq-km park (☑0 3282 1568; adult/child 200/100B), which means Three Hundred Mountain Peaks. There are also caves, beaches and coastal marshlands to explore for outdoor enthusiast and bird-watchers. With its proximity to Hua Hin, the park is well travelled by daytrippers and contains a mix of public conservation land and private shrimp farms, so don't come expecting remote virgin territory.

Rama IV and a large entourage of Thai and European guests came here on 18 August 1868 to see a total solar eclipse (apparently predicted by the monarch himself) and to enjoy a feast prepared by a French chef. Two months later the king died from malaria, contracted from mosquito bites inflicted here. Today the risk of malaria in the park is low, but the mosquitoes can be pesky.

The **Khao Daeng Visitors Centre** in the southern end of the park has the largest collection of tourist information and English-speaking rangers. Maps are handed out at the entrance gates.

Travel agencies in Hua Hin run daytrips. **Hua Hin Bike Tours** (☑08 1173 4469; www.huahinbiketours.com; tours 1500-2500B) offers cycling and hiking tours.

◉ Sights & Activities

The following are listed in geographic order north to south because the maps provided at the park checkpoints are often in Thai.

Tham Kaew
CAVE

(ถ้ำแก้ว) Not a popular daytrippers' stop, Tham Kaew is a series of underground chambers and narrow passageways accessed by a steep scramble 128m up the mountain. Stalactites and limestone formations here glitter with calcite crystals (hence the cave's name, 'Jewel Cave') are plentiful. You can hire lamps from the booth at the footpath's entrance, and exercise caution as the path can be slippery and dangerous.

Tham Phraya Nakhon & Hat Laem Sala
CAVE

(ถ้ำพระยานคร/หาดแหลมศาลา) The park's most popular attraction is this revered cave sheltering a royal *săh·lah* (often spelt *sala;* meeting hall) built for Rama V in 1890 that is often bathed in streams of light.

BIRDS OF A FEATHER

Because the park is at the intersection of the East Asian and Australian migration routes, as many as 300 migratory and resident bird species have been recorded at Khao Sam Roi Yot National Park, including yellow bitterns, cinnamon bitterns, purple swamphens, water rails, ruddy-breasted crakes, bronze-winged jacanas, grey herons, painted storks, whistling ducks, spotted eagles and black-headed ibises. Thung Sam Roi Yot is one of only two places in the country where the purple heron breeds.

Waterfowl are most commonly seen in the cool season. November to March are the best waterfowl-watching months. The birds come from as far as Siberia, China and northern Europe to winter here. Common places for bird-watchers are the Mangrove Centre, Khlong Khao Daeng and even some of the beaches.

Thai Birding (www.thaibirding.com) provides more in-depth information about the park's bird species and where to spot them.

The cave is accessed by a walking trail from picturesque **Hat Laem Sala**, a sandy beach flanked on three sides by limestone hills and casuarinas. The beach hosts a small visitors centre, restaurant, bungalows and camp sites. The cave trail is 450m long and is steep, rocky and at times slick so don't wear your ballet flats. Once there you'll find two large caverns with sinkholes – the meeting hall is the second of the two.

Reaching Laem Sala requires alternative travel since there is no road connection. It is reached by boat from Bang Pu (300B return), which sits beachfront from the turn-off from Tham Kaew. Alternatively you can follow the steep footpath from Bang Pu for a 20-minute hike to the beach.

Tham Sai   CAVE
(ถ้ำไทร) This cave sits at the end of a 280m hillside trail and features a large single cavern filled with stalactites and stalagmites. Be careful of steep drop-offs inside and slippery footings. Usually only the more adventurous types undertake this one. Villagers rent out lamps near the cave mouth. It is just north of Hat Sam Phraya.

Hat Sam Phraya   BEACH
(หาดสามพระยา) This shady casuarina-lined beach is about 1km long and is a pleasant stop for a swim after a sweaty hike. There is a restaurant and toilets.

Khao Daeng   HIKING
(เขาแดง) The turn-off to the trail winds through towering mountains promising a rewarding hike. The 30-minute step trail that leads to the top of Khao Daeng delivers spectacular views of limestone cliffs against a jagged coastline.

Khlong Khao Daeng   BIRDING
(คลองเขาแดง) You can hire a boat at Wat Khao Daeng for a cruise (400B, 45 minutes) along the canal in the morning or afternoon. Before heading out, chat with your prospective guide to see how well they speak English. Better guides will know the English names of common waterfowl and point them out to you.

Mangrove Walk   NATURE TRAIL
Located behind the visitors centre in the southern end of the park is a wooden boardwalk that circumnavigates a mangrove swamp popular for bird-watching and crab spotting. There are guides available for hire from the centre depending on availability and English-language ability.

Thung Sam Roi Yot   BIRDING
(ทุ่งสามร้อยยอด) The country's largest freshwater marsh is recognized as a natural treasure and provides an important habitat for songbirds and water birds, amphibians and other wetland species. It sits in the western corner of the park accessible from Hwy 4 (Th Phetkasem) at the Km275.6 marker; hold on to your entrance fee ticket to avoid having to pay again.

🛏 Sleeping & Eating

The **National parks department** (☑ 0 2562 0760; www.dnp.go.th/parkreserve; tent site 60-90B, bungalows 1200-1400B) hires out bungalows (sleeping up to six people) at Hat Laem Sala and at the visitors centre; advance reservations required. You can pitch a tent at campsites near the Khao Daeng viewpoint, Hat Laem Sala or Hat Sam Phraya. There are basic restaurants at all these locations.

WHERE THE ELEPHANTS ARE

Want to see herds of wild elephants enjoying an evening bath surrounded by the sounds of the jungle? Though urbanised Thailand seems hundreds of kilometres away from such a natural state, **Kuiburi National Park** (☑0 3264 6292; Hwy 3217; adult/child 200/100B), southwest of Khao Sam Roi Yot National Park, shelters one of the country's largest herds of wild elephants (estimated at over 140 animals). The park provides an important habitat link between the rugged Myanmar (Burma) border and Kaeng Krachan National Park, forming one of the largest intact forest tracts in Southeast Asia. The herds can frequently be found bathing at the watering ponds near the Pa Yang substation, which is equipped with wildlife-viewing platforms.

Trekking and elephant-spotting tours include English-speaking guides and transport and can be arranged through the park headquarters.

Bungalow **accommodation** (www.dnp.th.go/parkreserve; bungalows 1800B) is available for overnight stays with advance reservations.

There are also private resorts within 4km of the park at Dolphin Bay; see Pranburi & Around (p528) for more information.

❶ Getting There & Away

The park is about 40km south of Hua Hin, and best visited by vehicle. There are two main entrances into the park. The turn-off for the northern entrance is at Km256 marker on Hwy 4 (Th Phetkasem). The southern entrance is off the Km286.5 marker.

If you don't have your own wheels and don't want to take a tour from Hua Hin, you can get a minivan from Bangkok's Victory Monument to Pranburi (180B) and then hire a motorcycle to tour the park independently. You can also negotiate with the minivan driver to drop you off at the entrance to the park but then you won't have transport into the park.

Prachuap Khiri Khan

ประจวบคีรีขันธ์

POP 86,870

A sleepy seaside town, Prachuap Khiri Khan feels like you've finally arrived in southern Thailand. The pace is supremely relaxed, Muslim headscarves are common and the broad bay is a tropical blue punctuated by bobbing fishing boats. Usually you have to travel to the southern Andaman to find the honeycombed limestone mountains that saddle Prachuap's scenic bays. All in all it is a slice of everything nice – pretty coastal scenery and laid-back provincial-style living.

In recent years, more and more expats have been defecting to Prachuap from the overbuilt Samui archipelago bringing with them the travellers' amenities that the town was lacking. Now it is a lot less lonely but just as enjoyable. Attractions, with a small 'a', include climbing to a hill-top temple, taking a leisurely motorbike ride to the excellent beaches north and south of town, or just enjoying some of Thailand's freshest (and cheapest) seafood.

Prachuap Khiri Khan, and specifically Ao Manao, was one of seven points on the gulf coast where Japanese troops landed on 8 December 1941 during their invasion of Thailand. Several street names around town commemorate the skirmish that ensued afterwards: Phithak Chat (Defend Country), Salachip (Sacrifice Life) and Suseuk (Fight Battle).

◉ Sights & Activities

Khao Chong Krajok   VIEWPOINT

(เขาช่องกระจก) At the northern end of town, Khao Chong Krajok ('Mirror Tunnel Mountain', so named for the mountain-side hole that seemingly reflects the sky) provides a beloved Prachuap tradition: climbing to the top, dodging ill-behaved monkeys and enjoying a cascading view of a curlicue coastline. A long flight of stairs soiled by the partly wild monkeys leads to a mountain-top **temple** established by Rama VI. From here there are perfect views of the town and the bay and even the border with Myanmar, just 11km away. Don't bring food, drink or plastic bags with you as the monkeys will assume it is a prize worth nipping.

Ao Prachuap   BAY

(อ่าวประจวบ) The town's crowning feature is Ao Prachuap (Prachuap Bay), a gracefully curving bay outlined by an oceanfront esplanade. In the cool hours of the morning and evening, locals run, shuffle or promenade along this route enjoying the ocean breezes and sea music. On Friday and Saturday evenings, the esplanade hosts a **Walking Street market** (Th Chai Thaleh; ⏱from 5pm), selling food, souvenirs and clothes.

North of Khao Chong Krajok, just over the bridge, the bay stretches peacefully to a toothy mountain scraper with less commercial activity than its in-town counterpart. There is a nice sandy beach here though it does lack in privacy due to its proximity to passing motorists. Nonetheless, weekending Thais often visit because there is no bulkhead and it is a pleasant beachcombing spot. At the far northern end is a traditional fishing village decorated with colourful wooden trawlers and a visible sense of hard work and a hand-made life.

Wat Ao Noi   TEMPLE

(วัดอ่าวน้อย) From Ao Prachuap, follow the coastal road 8km north as it skirts through the fishing village and flower-filled lanes to reach this beautiful teak **temple** that straddles two bays (Ao Noi and Ao Khan Kradai). Limestone mountains pose photogenically in the background, while a dramatic nine-headed naga protects the temple's exterior. Inside are unique bas-relief murals depicting the *jataka* stories (Buddha's previous lives).

The temple grounds are forested with a variety of fruit trees (jackfruit, pomegranate, mango and rose apple) and a lotus pond filled with ravenous fish, eager to be feed by merit-makers. You'll catch an unpleasant odour nearby indicating that the temple is in the business of raising swiftlets for the profitable edible bird's nest industry; don't try to steal any nests or eggs as the fine and punishment (five years' imprisonment and 500,000B) are severe.

A craggy limestone mountain (Khao Khan Kradai) shelters the temple from the coast and contains a locally famous cave temple, known as **Tham Phra Nawn** (Sleeping Buddha Cave). The cave is accessible via a concrete trail that leads up and around the side of the hill providing scenic views of Ao Khan Kradai and the foothills beyond. It is blissfully quiet and the forested hill is dotted with blooming cactus clinging to the craggy rocks. Inside the cave is a small cavern leading to a larger one that contains the eponymous reclining Buddha. If you have a torch (flashlight) you can proceed to a larger second chamber also containing Buddha images.

Prachuap Khiri Khan

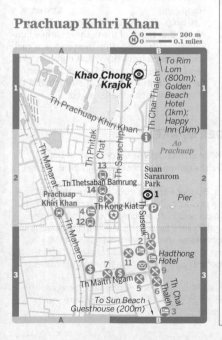

Ao Manao   SWIMMING

(อ่าวมะนาว) On weekends, locals head to Ao Manao, 4km south of town, an island-dotted bay ringed by a clean sandy beach. It is within Wing 5 of a Thai air-force base and each and every week the beach is given a military-grade clean up. There are the usual beach amenities: a restaurant and rentable beach chairs, umbrellas and inner tubes. En route to the beach you'll pass Thailand's Top Guns relaxing on a nearby golf course and driving range. You enter the base through a checkpoint on Th Suseuk from town; you may need to show your passport. The beach closes at 8pm.

🛏 Sleeping

You can always find a cosy place to stay near the sea as many of the oceanfront residences rent out rooms. Just cruise down Th Chai Thaleh and see who has a vacancy sign out. In recent years, Prachuap has even gained a few full-fledged guest houses.

IN TOWN

Maggie's Homestay   GUEST HOUSE $
(✆08 7597 9720; 5 Soi Tampramuk; r 150-600B; ❄@) In the old-fashioned backpacker tradition, lovely owner Maggie oversees an eclectic collection of travellers who call her house home. Simple rooms occupy a converted house with a shady garden and shared kitchen facilities.

Yuttichai Hotel   GUEST HOUSE $
(✆0 3261 1055; 115 Th Kong Kiat; r 160-400B; ❄@) One of Prachuap's original guest houses, Yuttichai has simple budget rooms (with cold-water showers) close to the train station. The cheapest rooms share bathrooms. If you

don't stay here, at least stop by their old-style Thai-Chinese cafe popular with the 'men in brown' (police).

Sun Beach Guesthouse   GUEST HOUSE $$
(✆0 3260 4770; www.sunbeach-guesthouse.com; 160 Th Chai Thaleh; r 700-1000B; ❄❄🛜) With hotel amenities and guest-house hospitality, Sun Beach is a superb midranger. Its neoclassical styling and bright-yellow paint liven things up, while the rooms are super-clean and come with large verandahs.

Prachuap Beach Hotel   HOTEL $$
(✆0 3260 1288; 123 Th Suseuk; r 650-1100B; ❄🛜) Crisp white linens and splashy accent walls add a bit of flair to this multistorey number. One side has fabulous sea views, while the other has decent, though not exciting, mountain views.

OUT OF TOWN

🏆 **Aow Noi Sea View**   HOTEL $$
(✆0 3260 4440; www.aownoiseaview.com; Ao Noi; r 600-800B; ❄) North of town, this three-storey hotel is Prachuap's best beachfront option. With pretty Ao Noi beach at your doorstep, you'll enjoy sea breezes, rooms with large bathrooms and a homey ambience complete with linen drying on the line outside.

Happy Inn   GUEST HOUSE $
(✆0 3260 2082; 149-151 Th Suanson; r 250-500B) About 1km north of town, these simple bungalows (with cold-water showers) face each other along a brick drive that ends next to a pleasant forested canal. You are right across the road from Ao Prachuap's beach and the staff are sweet and soft-spoken.

DETOUR: DAN SINGKHON BORDER MARKET

A mere 12km southwest of Prachuap Khiri Khan is the Burmese border town of Dan Singkhon. Once a strategic military point, Dan Singkhon now hosts a lively border market beloved by locals for its many bargains.

Beginning at dawn on Saturday mornings, Burmese appear from a bend in the road just beyond the checkpoint, pushing handcarts piled high with the usual trinkets, market goods and plants. Short-term tourists might be befuddled as to what will fit in a suitcase but locals and expats make frequent buying trips here for orchids, the market's specialty, and hardwood furniture. Even if you come to window-shop, the market has a festive vibe, with music blaring, colourful umbrellas lining the road and thatched 'sales booths' hidden under palms. You'll need to arrive well before noon to enjoy it, as the market closes at midday.

To get to Dan Singkhon from Prachuap Khiri Khan with your own vehicle, head south on Hwy 4. After several kilometres you'll see a sign for Dan Singkhon; from here you'll head west about 15km before reaching the border.

Golden Beach Hotel   HOTEL $$
(☎0 3260 1626; www.goldenbeachprachuap.com;
113-115 Th Suanson; r 500-1200B; ❋❄) Near
Happy Inn, Golden Beach is a comfortable
midrange option across from Ao Prachuap's beach. Some rooms have generous
picture windows providing a marine sleeping companion.

✗ Eating

Restaurants in Prachuap are cheap and
tasty and Western food is popping up at little restaurants on Th Chai Thaleh. The **day
market** (Th Maitri Ngam; ☉daylight hours) is
the place to get pineapples fresh from the
orchards; ask the vendor to cut it for you.
Across the street is a **Muslim chicken stall**
(Th Maitri Ngam; dishes 40-60B; ☉dinner) that
does some of the crispiest fried chicken in
the country. The **night market** (Th Kong Kiat;
☉5-9pm) is small and has the usual stir-fry
stalls.

⬚TOP CHOICE Rim Lom   SEAFOOD $$
(5 Th Suanson; dishes 120-220B; ☉lunch & dinner) We still dream about this meal on a
bright sunny day surrounded by lunching
civil servants. The *pàt pǒng gà·rèe ⁊oo* (crab
curry) comes with big chunks of sweet crab
meat and the *yam ta-lair* (seafood salad) is
spicy, zesty and festooned with seafood.

Phloen Samut   SEAFOOD $$
(44 Th Chai Thaleh; dishes 80-200B; ☉lunch & dinner) One of a few seafood restaurants along
the promenade, Phloen Samut is conveniently located in town though locals complain that the food needs improvement.

Ma Prow   INTERNATIONAL $$
(48 Th Chai Thaleh; dishes 80-200B; ☉lunch & dinner) An airy wooden pavilion across from the
beach, Ma Prow cooks up excellent *⁊lah
sǎm·lee dàat dee·o* (a local specialty of whole
sun-dried cotton fish that is fried and served
with mango salad). The tamarind fish dish is
another favourite with foreigners and locals.

Ning's Guesthouse Restaurant   INTERNATIONAL $
(Th Chai Thaleh; dishes 40-120B; ☉breakfast, lunch
& dinner) Decorated in a playful Rasta-style
mood, Ning is an early riser serving Western
breakfasts before anyone else is awake. She
continues cooking through the day too.

Suan Krua   VEGETARIAN $
(Soi Tampramuk; dishes 30-60B; ☉lunch) Next
door to Maggie's Homestay, this vegetarian restaurant cooks fast and furiously
for a limited time only and then it closes
until the next day. Be here promptly and
hungrily.

ℹ Information
Bangkok Bank (cnr Th Maitri Ngam & Th
Sarachip)
Police station (Th Kong Kiat) Just west of Th
Sarachip.
Post office (cnr Th Maitri Ngam & Th
Suseuk)
Thai Farmers Bank (Th Phitak Chat) Just north
of Th Maitri Ngam.
Tourist office (☎0 3261 1491; Th Chai Thaleh;
☉8.30am-4.30pm) At the northern end of
town. The staff speak English and are very
helpful.

ℹ Getting There & Away
There are hourly air-conditioned buses that
leave from Th Phitak Chat to the following
destinations:
Bangkok (170B, five hours)
Cha-am (100B, two hours)
Hua Hin (100B, 1½ hours)
Phetchaburi (140B, three hours)

Minivans leave from the corner of Th Thetsaban
Bamrung and Th Phitak Chat to the following
destinations:
Bangkok (250B)
Ban Krut (70B, one hour)
Bang Saphan Yai (80B, 1½ hours)
Chumphon (180B, 3½ hours)
Hua Hin (80B)

Long-distance buses to southern destinations
(such as Phuket and Krabi) stop at the new bus
station, 2km northwest of town on the main
highway; motorcycle taxis will take you for 40B
to 50B.

The train station is on Th Maharat; there are
frequent services to/from Bangkok (1st class
768B, 2nd class 210-425B, 3rd class 168B; six
hours).

ℹ Getting Around
Prachuap is small enough to get around on
foot, but you can hop on a motorcycle taxi
around town for 20B to 30B. To reach outlying
destinations, Ao Noi and Ao Manao it is 100B
to 150B.

You can hire motorbikes for 250B per day. The
roads in the area are very good and it's a great
way to see the surrounding beaches.

Ban Krut & Bang Saphan Yai บ้านกรูด/บางสะพานใหญ่

POP 4275/ 68,344

What a nice surprise to find these lovely low-key beaches (80km to 100km south of Prachuap Khiri Khan, respectively) so close to civilization but so bucolic. Dusk falls softly through the coconut trees and the sea is a crystalline blue lapping at a long sandy coastline. No high-rises, no late-night discos, and no speeding traffic to distract you from a serious regimen of reading, swimming, eating and biking.

Though both beaches are pleasantly subdued, they are also well known by Thais and Ban Krut, in particular, hosts bus tours as well as weekending families. During the week you'll have the beaches largely to yourself and a few long-tail boats.

Check out the websites **Ban Krut Info** (www.bankrutinfo.com) and **Bang Saphan Guide** (www.bangsaphanguide.com) for local information on the area.

Ban Krut is a divided into two beaches by a temple-topped headland. To the north is **Hat Sai Kaew**, which is remote and private with only a few resorts in between a lot of jungle. To the south is **Hat Ban Krut**, with a beachfront road and a string of bungalow-style resorts and restaurants on the interior side of the road. Both are golden-sand beaches with clear, calm water but Hat Ban Krut is slightly more social and easier to get around without private transport.

Bang Saphan Yai, 20km south of Ban Krut, fits that most famous beach cliché: It is Thailand 15 years ago before pool villas and package tourists pushed out all the beach bums. Once you settle into a simple beachfront hut, you probably won't need shoes and the days will just melt away. Islands off the coast, including **Ko Thalu** and **Ko Sing**, offer good snorkelling and diving from the end of January to mid-May.

🛏 Sleeping & Eating

Ban Krut

You'll struggle to find true budget options here, but if you visit on a weekday you should secure a discount. In Hat Ban Krut, bicycles (100B per day) and motorcycles (300B per day) can be hired to run errands in town, and most accommodation options arrange snorkelling trips to nearby islands. If you stay in Hat Sai Kaew you'll need private transport.

TOP CHOICE Proud Thai Beach Resort　　GUEST HOUSE $$

(☏08 9682 4484; www.proudthairesort.com; Hat Ban Krut; r 700-1200B; ❄) Well-maintained bungalows in a flower-filled garden come with porches and morning coffee delivered by the affable owner.

NaNa Chart Baan Kruit　　HOTEL $$

(☏0 3269 5525; www.thailandbeach.com; Hat Sai Kaew; dm 490B, r 800-2600B; ❄❄) Technically it is a hostel, but NaNa Chart easily qualifies as a resort with a variety of bungalows on a barely inhabited beach. The cheapest are wooden huts with shared bathroom, and the ritzy beachfront ones have most of the mod-cons. The resort caters to large groups so expect some company. Hostel members (200B for three-year membership) receive discounted rates.

Bayview Beach Resort　　HOTEL $$$

(☏0 3269 5566; www.bayviewbeachresort.com; Hat Sai Keaw; r 1700-4800B; ❄❄) A great choice for families, Bayview has handsome bungalows with large verandahs amid shady grounds. There's a beachside pool and a kid-friendly wading pool as well as a small playground. The resort also has meeting facilities for groups and conventions.

Kasama's Pizza　　PIZZARIA $$

(Hat Ban Krut; dishes from 150B; ⊙lunch & dinner) An expats' favourite, this open-air spot near the main road to town does praiseworthy New York–style pizzas in coconut territory.

Bang Saphan Yai

The beach is 6km south of the town of Bang Saphan Yai. Accommodation is a mix of high-end pool villas on the south side of Why Not Bar and basic beach huts to the north.

Roytawan　　GUEST HOUSE $

(r from 300B, 🕾) Smack dab on the beach, this bare-bones operation is run by a sweet local family. The bungalows provide basic shelter and the resident roosters kindly sleep until daybreak. The restaurant is fab too. If you continue north from here you'll find similar set-ups.

Patty Hut　　GUEST HOUSE $

(☏08 6171 1907; r 300-700B; ❄) This funky spot behind the Coral Hotel is 300m from the beach. It is a collection of wooden bungalows ranging from simple to simpler.

Suan Luang Resort GUEST HOUSE $
(✆0 3281 7031; www.suanluang.com; bungalows 480-680B; ❇) The most professional of the guest houses, Suan Luang is run by a friendly family and has wooden bungalows around an interior garden. You're 700m from the beach, though. The excellent restaurant serves Thai and French food, and there are day trips to waterfalls and parks on offer.

Coral Hotel HOTEL $$
(✆0 3281 7121; www.coral-hotel.com; r 1525-5580B; ❇@❇) This upmarket hotel is right on the beach and has all the resort amenities, including organised diving and snorkelling tours. The rooms probably don't deserve to be priced this high but competition in this category is low.

ⓘ Getting There & Around

Because public transport around here is either nonexistent or limited; be sure to take a bus that stops in town instead of on the highway, an inconvenient and expensive distance from the beaches. When booking transport, don't confuse Bang Saphan Yai with Bang Saphan Noi, which is a fisherman's village 15km further south.

From Bangkok's Southern (Sai Tai Mai) station buses go to Ban Krut (275B, departs 12.30pm, six hours) and Bang Saphan Yai (275B, hourly, six hours); in Bangkok, use **Bangsaphan Tour** (✆08 7829 7752).

Frequent minivans run from Prachuap Khiri Khan to Ban Krut (70B) and Bang Saphan Yai (80B).

Many seasoned visitors prefer to take the train for closer proximity to the beaches. There are several daily options but the sprinter train (special express No 43) is one of the fastest. It leaves Bangkok's Hua Lamphong station at 8am and arrives in Ban Krut (445B) at 12.45pm and Bang Saphan Yai (450B) at 1pm. You can also hop on an afternoon train to Chumphon with plenty of time to spare before the ferry to Ko Tao.

A motorcycle taxi from town to the beaches should cost 40B to 70B. Talk to your hotel or guest house about arranging transport back to town for your onward travel.

Chumphon ชุมพร
POP 55,835

Chumphon is a transit town funnelling travellers to and from Ko Tao or westward to Ranong or Phuket.

While there's not a lot to do while you wait, the surrounding beaches are good places to step off the backpacker bandwagon for a few days. **Hat Thung Wua Laen** (15km north of town) is a pretty beach with easy public transport to Chumphon and plenty of traveller amenities.

For a transit hub, Chumphon is surprisingly unconsolidated. You'll need to rely on the travel agencies (p533) to book tickets, provide timetables and point you to the right bus stop; fortunately agents in Chumphon are a dedicated lot.

☆ Festivals & Events

Chumphon Marine Festival CULTURAL
From mid-March to the end of April, Hat Thung Wua Laen hosts a variety of events including folk-art exhibits, shadow-puppet performances and a food display.

Chumphon Traditional Boat Race CULTURAL
To mark the end of Buddhist Lent in October (Ork Phansaa), traditional long-tail boats race each other on the Mae Nam Lang Suan (Lang Suan River), about 60km south of Chumphon. Other merit-making activities coincide with the festival.

🛏 Sleeping

Since most people overnighting in Chumphon are backpackers, accommodation is priced accordingly.

In Town

TOP CHOICE **Suda Guest House** GUEST HOUSE $
(✆0 7750 4366; 8 Soi Bangkok Bank; r 230-500B; ❇) Suda, the friendly English-speaking owner, maintains her impeccable standards in six rooms with wooden floors and a few nice touches that you wouldn't expect for the price. It's very popular so phone ahead.

San Tavee New Rest House GUEST HOUSE $
(✆0 7750 2147; 4 Soi Bangkok Bank; r 200-300B) If Suda's, two doors down is full, check the four rooms here. They're small but clean, and have fans and shared bathroom.

Farang Bar GUEST HOUSE $
(✆0 7750 1003; 69/36 Th Tha Taphao; r 150-300B; @) A backpacker dive, Farang Bar has ramshackle rooms next door to its bar (naturally) catering mainly to travellers who get deposited here by buses from Bangkok's Th Khao San. Day-use showers (20B) decorated in round pebbles give an unexpected (and unintentional, we're sure) spa-like feel. The restaurant isn't worth bothering about, though.

Chumphon

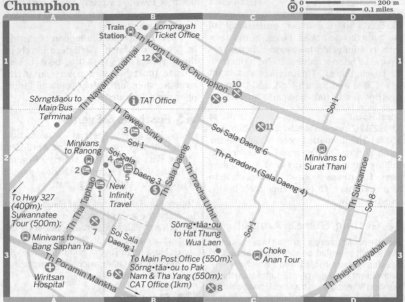

Chumphon

Sleeping

Eating

Morakot Hotel HOTEL $$
(0 7750 2999; 102-112 Th Tawee Sinka; r 800-950B; ☀) The multistorey lime-green building has recently received a fresh upgrade making it a solid midrange choice for provincial VIPs.

Chumphon Gardens Hotel HOTEL $
(0 7750 6888; 66/1 Th Tha Taphao; r 500B; ☀) Spacious rooms including cable TV are a great distraction while you hang around and wait.

Out of Town

Chumphon Cabana Resort & Diving Centre HOTEL $$$
(0 7756 0245; www.cabana.co.th; Hat Thung Wua Laen; r 1800-2700B; ☀☀) Though the rooms

are in need of an upgrade, Chumphon Cabana has done a great job upgrading its environmental profile. Inspired by the King's environmental sustainability speech, the owner reconfigured the resort to look to the past for instructions on how to be green. The grounds are devoted to raising the resort's own food with rice fields, hydroponic vegetable gardens and a chicken farm. Waste water is recycled through water-hyacinth ponds. And their efforts are used to instruct others.

If you don't stay here, at least enjoy some homegrown food at **Rabieng Talay**, the resort's affiliated restaurant.

View Resort BUNGALOWS
(Hat Thung Wua Laen, r 650-1000B; ✳) The nicest of a few simple bungalow operations on Hat Thung Wua Laen.

MT Resort HOTEL $$
(✏0 7755 8153; www.mtresort-chumphon.com; Hat Tummakam Noi; r 950-1500B; ✳) This friendly spot on a quiet beach beside the Lomprayah ferry pier is a good place to break your journey before or after Ko Tao. Free kayaks are provided to explore offshore islands and the mangroves of the nearby Mu Ko Chumphon National Park. Call to organise a transfer from Chumphon.

✖ Eating & Drinking

Chumphon's night market (Th Krom Luang Chumphon) is excellent, with a huge variety of food options and good people-watching. There are two day markets (Th Tha Taphao & Th Pracha Uthit).

Khanom Jeen Restaurant THAI $
(Th Sala Daeng; dishes 60B; ⊙breakfast & lunch) Next to Fame Restaurant, this hole-in-the-wall eatery is locally famous for its spicy bowls of kà·nŏm jeen (rice noodles served with a spicy fish sauce). Add your own touch with condiments of holy basil, sliced cucumber and pickled vegetables.

Ban Yang Na CAFE $
(Th Sala Daeng; dishes from 40B; ⊙breakfast & lunch; ✳) This air-conditioned cafe provides a nice retreat from the heat plus the usual caffeine and bakery treats.

Papa Seafood SEAFOOD $$
(2-2/1 Th Krom Luang Chumphon; dishes 80-200B; ⊙lunch & dinner) The food (mainly seafood, obviously) is good, without being exceptional, but it's a popular local hang-out. Next door is Papa 2000 where you can dance off dinner.

Fame Restaurant INTERNATIONAL $
(188/20 Th Sala Daeng; dishes 80-220B; ⊙breakfast, lunch & dinner) A farang (foreigner) depot, Fame does a little bit of everything; cooks up Western breakfasts and Thai stir-fries, books ferry tickets and rents out day-use showers. It's open from before the crack of dawn until late at night.

Ocean Shopping Mall INTERNATIONAL $$
(off of Th Sala Daeng; dishes 150-250B; ⊙lunch & dinner) It isn't a culinary destination but Chumphon's shopping mall has air-con and chain restaurants for cool and convenient layover noshing.

❶ Information

There are banks along Th Sala Daeng with exchange facilities and ATMs.

Bangkok Bank (Th Sala Daeng) Has an ATM.

CAT office (Th Poramin Mankha) About 1km east of the post office.

Main post office (Th Poramin Mankha) In the southeastern part of town.

New Infinity Travel (✏0 7757 0176; 68/2 Th Tha Taphao; ⊙8am-10pm; @) A great travel agency with knowledgeable and friendly staff; they'll also sell you paperbacks and rent you one of four rooms.

TAT (✏0 7750 1831; 111/11-12 Th Tawee Sinkha; ⊙9am-4.30pm) Hands-out maps and brochures but not always up-to-date on transport information.

Wiratsin Hospital (✏0 7750 3238; Th Poramin Mankha) Privately owned; handles emergencies.

❶ Getting There & Away

Air

Solar Air (✏0 7755 8212; www.solarair.co.th) flies to Bangkok (once daily, one hour, 2900B).

Boat

You have many boat options for getting to Ko Tao (p571), though departure times are limited to mainly morning and night. Most ticket prices include pier transfer. If you buy a combination ticket, make sure you have a ticket for both the bus and the boat.

Slow boat (250B, six hours, midnight) – the cheapest, slowest and most scenic option as everyone stretches out on the open deck of the fishing boat with the stars twinkling overhead. This boat doesn't run in rough seas or inclement weather.

Car ferry (350B, six hours, 11pm Mon-Sun) – a more comfortable ride with bunk or mattress options available on board.

Songserm express boat (450B, three hours, 7am) – faster, morning option leaving from Tha Talaysub, about 10km from town.

Lomprayah catamaran (600B, 1¾ hours, 7am & 1pm) – a popular bus-boat combination that leaves from Tha Tummakam, 25km from town; the ticket office is beside Chumphon train station.

Bus

The main bus terminal is on the highway, an inconvenient 16km from Chumphon. To get there you can catch a sŏrng·tăa·ou (50B) from Th Nawamin Ruamjai. You'll have to haggle with the opportunistic taxi drivers for night transit to/ from the station; no matter what they tell you, it shouldn't cost more than 200B.

There are several in-town bus stops to save you a trip out to the main bus station. **Choke Anan Tour** (☏ 0 7751 1757; soi off of Th Pracha Uthit), in the centre of town, has daily departures to the following destinations:

Bangkok's Southern (Sai Tai Mai) station (375B to 550B, eight hours, five departures)

Hat Yai (370B; seven hours; four departures)

Phuket (320B; 3½ hours; four departures)

Ranong (320B; two hours; four departures)

Suwannatee Tour (☏ 0 7750 4901), 700m southeast of train station road, serves the following destinations:

Bangkok's Southern (Sai Tai Mai) station (270B to 405B 2nd class-VIP buses, three departures)

Cha-am (175B)

Hua Hin (170B)

Phetchaburi (205B)

Prachuap Khiri Khan (120B)

Minivan companies are numerous and depart from individual offices throughout town (see the Chumphon map):

Surat Thani (170B, three hours, every hour) Departs from an unnamed soi on Th Krom Luang Chumphon; the soi is east of an optical shop.

Bang Saphan Yai (120B, two hours, two afternoon departures) Leaves from Th Poramin Mankha, near the hospital.

Ranong (120B, 2½ hours, every hour 7am to 3pm) Departs from Th Tha Taphao; arrives at Ranong bus station (not in the town).

Train

There are frequent services to/from Bangkok (2nd class 292B to 382B, 3rd class 235B, 7½ hours). Overnight sleepers range from 440B to 770B.

Southbound rapid and express trains – the only trains with 1st and 2nd class – are less frequent and can be difficult to book out of Chumphon from November to February.

❶ Getting Around

Sŏrng·tăa·ou and motorcycle taxis around town cost 40B and 20B respectively per trip. *Sŏrng·tăa·ou* to Hat Thung Wua Laen cost 30B.

Motorcycles can be rented at travel agencies and guest houses for 200B to 250B per day. Car hire costs around 1500B per day from travel agencies.

Ko Samui & the Lower Gulf

Includes »

Best Places to Eat

» Dining On The Rocks (p550)

» Five Islands (p551)

» The Whitening (p582)

Best Places to Stay

» Six Senses Samui (p546)

» Anantara Bo Phut (p547)

» L'Hacienda (p547)

» Sarikantang (p561)

» The Sanctuary (p566)

Why Go?

The Lower Gulf features Thailand's ultimate island trifecta: Ko Samui, Ko Pha-Ngan and Ko Tao. This family of spectacular islands lures millions of tourists every year with their powder-soft sands and emerald waters. Ko Samui is the oldest brother, with a business-minded attitude towards vacation. High-class resorts operate with Swiss efficiency as uniformed butlers cater to every whim. Ko Pha-Ngan is the slacker middle child with tangled dreadlocks and a penchant for hammock-lazing and all-night parties. Baby Ko Tao has plenty of spirit and spunk – offering high-adrenaline activities, including world-class diving and snorkelling.

Travellers seeking something a bit more off the radar than these island brethren will find a thin archipelago of pin-sized islets just beyond. Known as Ang Thong Marine National Park, this ethereal realm of greens and blues offers some of the most picture-perfect moments in the entire kingdom.

When To Go

From February to April celebrate endless sunshine after the monsoon rains have cleared. From June to August – which conveniently coincides with the Northern Hemisphere's summer holidays – are some of the most inviting months in the region, with relatively short drizzle spells.

From October to December torrential monsoon rains rattle hot-tin roofs like anxious fingernails, as room rates drop significantly to lure a few optimistic beach-goers

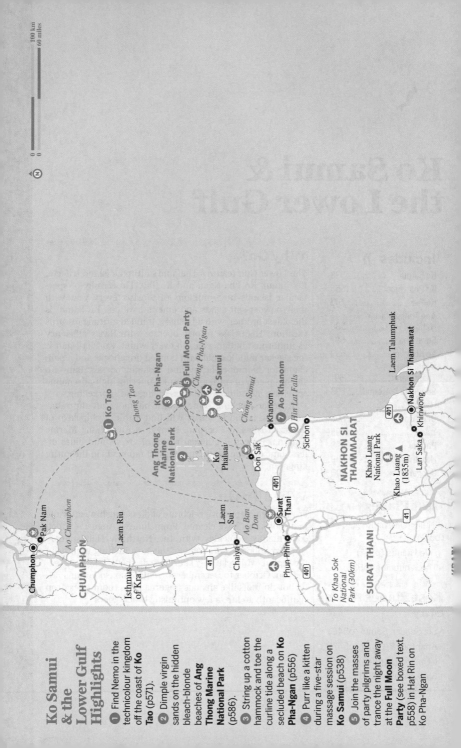

Ko Samui & the Lower Gulf Highlights

1 Find Nemo in the technicolour kingdom off the coast of **Ko Tao** (p571).

2 Dimple virgin sands on the hidden bleach-blonde beaches of **Ang Thong Marine National Park** (p586).

3 String up a cotton hammock and toe the curline tide along a secluded beach on **Ko Pha-Ngan** (p556).

4 Purr like a kitten during a five-star massage session on **Ko Samui** (p538).

5 Join the masses of party pilgrims and trance the night away at the **Full Moon Party** (see boxed text, p558) in Hat Rin on Ko Pha-Ngan.

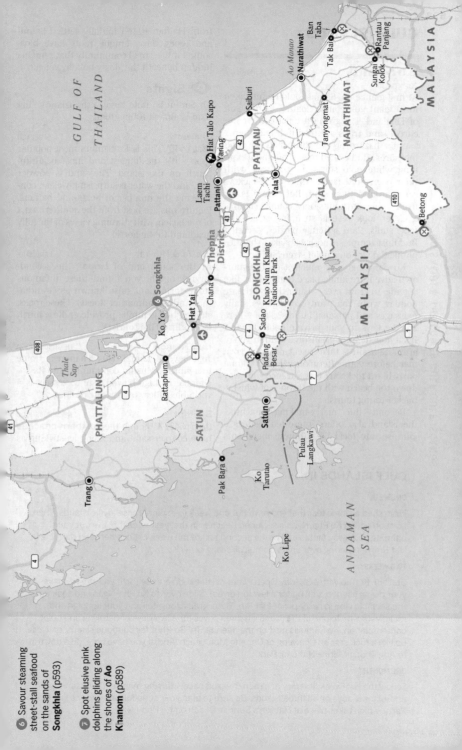

GULF OF THAILAND

MALAYSIA

Ban Taba
Rantau Panjang
Narathiwat
Tak Bai
Sungai Kolok
Tanyongmat
NARATHIWAT
Ao Manao
Saiburi
Hat Talo Kapo
Yaring
PATTANI
42
YALA
Laem Tachi
Pattani
Yala
410
43
Betong

Songkhla
SONGKHLA
Thepha District
Chana
42
Hat Yai
Khao Nam Khang National Park
Ko Yo
Sadao
4
Padang Besar
MALAYSIA
408
Rattaphum
4
1
PHATTALUNG
Thale Sap
7
41
SATUN
Trang
4
Satun
Pak Bara
Ko Tarutao
Pulau Langkawi
ANDAMAN SEA
Ko Lipe

6 Savour steaming street-stall seafood on the sands of **Songkhla** (p593)

7 Spot elusive pink dolphins gliding along the shores of **Ao Khanom** (p589)

GULF ISLANDS

Ko Samui
เกาะสมุย

POP 40,230

At first glance, Ko Samui could be mistaken for a giant golf course floating in the Gulf of Thailand. The greens are perfectly manicured, sand traps are plentiful, and there's a water hazard or two thrown in for good measure. Middle-aged men strut about donning white polo shirts that contrast with their cherry-red faces, while hired lackeys carry around their stuff. But Samui is far from being an adults-only country club – a closer look reveals steaming street-side food stalls, 2am jetsetter parties, secreted Buddhist temples, and backpacker shanties plunked down on a quiet stretch of sand.

Ko Samui is very much a choose-your-own-adventure kinda place that strives, like a genie, to grant every visitor their ultimate holiday wish. You want ocean views, daily massages and personal butlers? Poof – here are the keys to your private poolside villa. It's a holistic aura-cleansing vacation you're after? Shazam – take a seat on your yoga mat before your afternoon colonic. Wanna party like a rockstar? Pow – trance your way down the beach with the throngs of whisky-bucket-toting tourists.

Beyond the merry-making machine, the island also offers interested visitors a glimpse into local life. Chinese merchants from Hainan Island initially settled Samui and today these unique roots have blossomed into a small community that remains hidden beneath the glossy holiday veneer.

◉ Sights

Ko Samui is quite large – the island's ring road is almost 100km total.

Chaweng
BEACH

(Map p540) This is Ko Samui's most popular spot – it's the longest and most beautiful beach on the island. The sand is powder soft, and the water is surprisingly clear, considering the number of boats and bathers. Picture ops are best from the southern part of the beach, with stunning views of the hilly headland to the north.

Hin-Ta & Hin-Yai
LANDMARK

At the south end of **Lamai**, the second-largest beach, you'll find these infamous stone formations (also known as Grandfather and Grandmother Rocks). These rocks, shaped like genitalia provide endless mirth to giggling Thai tourists.

Hua Thanon
NEIGHBOURHOOD

Just beyond Lamai, Hua Thanon is home to a vibrant Muslim community, and its anchorage of high-bowed fishing vessels is a veritable gallery of intricate designs.

Bo Phut
NEIGHBOURHOOD

(Map p542) Although the **northern beaches** have coarser sand and aren't as striking as

---

GULF ISLANDS IN...

ONE WEEK

First, shed a single tear that you have but one week to explore these idyllic islands. Then start on one of Ko Pha-Ngan's secluded beaches in the west or east to live out your ultimate castaway fantasies. For the second half of the week choose between partying in Hat Rin, pampering over on Ko Samui, or diving on li'l Ko Tao.

TWO WEEKS

Start on Ko Tao with a 3½-day Open Water certification course (or, if you already have your diving licence, sign up for a few fun dives). Slide over to Ko Pha-Ngan and soak up the sociable vibe in party-prone Hat Rin. Then, grab a long-tail and your luggage and make your way to one of the island's hidden coves for a few days of detoxing and quiet contemplation. Ko Samui is next on the agenda. Try Bo Phut for boutique sleeps, or live it up like a rock star on Chaweng or Choeng Mon beach. And, if you have time, do a day trip to Ang Thong Marine National Park.

ONE MONTH

Follow the two-week itinerary at a more relaxed pace, infusing many extra beach-book-and-blanket days on all three islands. Be sure to plan your schedule around the Full Moon Party, which takes place at Hat Rin's Sunrise Beach on Ko Pha-Ngan.

Ko Samui

0 ————— 5 km
0 ————— 2.5 miles

To Ko Pha-Ngan (25km)
To Ko Pha-Ngan (15km); Ko Tao (62km)
Wat Na Phalan
Laem Na Phra Lan
Ban Bang Po
Ban Tai
Ao Bang Po
Laem Yai
Hat Mae Nam
Laem Sai
Ban Mae Nam
Hat Bo Phut
Hat Ang Thong
Ban Bo Phut
▲(467m)
Na Thon
Tourist Police
Ban Lipa Yai
▲(465m)
Samui Hospital
Immigration Office
Nam Tok Hin Lat
Wat Hin Lat
Ban Lipa Noi
Khao Pom (630m)
Ban Saket
Khao Phlu (565m)
Laem Chon Khram
Nam Tok Na Muang
Ao Thong Yang
Thong Yang
Ban Thurian
Nam Tok Wang Saotong
Ao Taling Ngam
Ban Taling Ngam
Wat Khunaram
Khao Khwang (410m)
Wat Samret
Ao Phangkka
Ban Bang Kao
Ban Phang Ka
Ban Thong Krut
Khao Thaleh
Laem Hin Khom
Ao Thong Krut
Ao Bang Kao
Wat Laem Saw
Laem Set
GULF OF THAILAND
Laem Saw
Ko Taen
To Ko Mat Sum (2km)

Ko Som
Wat Plai Laem
Ao Samrong
Wat Phra Yai
Hat Choeng Mon
Ko Fan Yai
Big Buddha Beach
Hyperbaric Chamber
Bandon International Hospital
Airport
Ko Matlang
Chaweng Lake
Samui International Hospital
Hat Chaweng
Hat Chaweng Noi
Coral Cove
Ban Lamai
Ao Thong Ta Khian
Hat Lamai
Laem Nan
Samui Aquarium & Tiger Zoo
Hat Na Thian
GULF OF THAILAND

To Surat Thani (76km)

To Ang Thong Marine National Park (31km)

To Don Sak (30km); Khanom (35km)

the beaches in the east, they have a laid-back vibe and stellar views of Ko Pha-Ngan. Bo Phut stands out with its charming Fisherman's Village; a collection of narrow Chinese shophouses that have been transformed into trendy resorts and boutique hotels.

Nam Tok Na Muang
WATERFALL
(Map p539) At 30m, this is the tallest waterfall on Samui and lies in the centre of the island about 12km from Na Thon. The water cascades over ethereal purple rocks, and there's a great pool for swimming at the base. This is the most scenic – and somewhat less frequented – of Samui's falls. There are two other waterfalls in the vicinity: a smaller waterfall called **Na Muang 2**, and, thanks to recently, improved road conditions, the high drop at **Nam Tok Wang Saotong** (Map p539). These chutes are situated just north of the ring road near Hua Thanon.

Wat Hin Lat
TEMPLE
(Map p539; ☎0 7742 3146) On the western part of Samui, near the waterfalls of the same name, is a meditation temple that teaches daily *vipassana* courses.

Nam Tok Hin Lat
WATERFALL
(Map p539) Near Na Thon, this is worth visiting if you have an afternoon to kill before taking a boat back to the mainland. After a mildly strenuous hike over streams and boulders, reward yourself with a dip in the pool at the bottom of the falls. Keep an eye out for the Buddhist temple that posts signs with spiritual words of moral guidance and enlightenment. Sturdy shoes are recommended.

Wat Laem Saw
TEMPLE
(Map p539) For temple enthusiasts, Wat Laem Saw, at the southern end of Samui near Ban Phang Ka, has an interesting, highly venerated old Srivijaya-style stupa.

Hat Chaweng

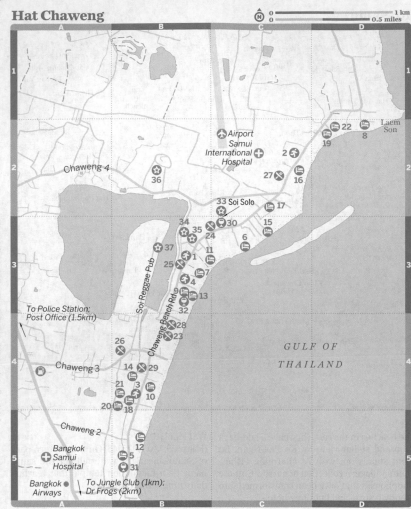

Wat Phra Yai
TEMPLE

(Temple of the Big Buddha; Map p539) At Samui's northern end, on a small rocky island linked by a causeway, is Wat Phra Yai. Erected in 1972, the modern Buddha (sitting in the Mara posture) stands 15m high and makes an alluring silhouette against the tropical sky and sea. Nearby, a new temple, **Wat Plai Laem** (Map p539), features an enormous 18-armed Buddha.

Wat Khunaram
TEMPLE

(Map p539) Several temples have the mummified remains of pious monks, including Wak Khunaram, which is south of Rte 4169 between Th Ban Thurian and Th Ban Hua. Its monk, Luang Phaw Daeng, has been dead for over two decades but his corpse is preserved sitting in a meditative pose and sporting a pair of sunglasses.

Wat Samret
TEMPLE

(Map p539) At Wat Samret, near Th Ban Hua, you can see a typical Mandalay sitting Buddha carved from solid marble – a common sight in India and northern Thailand, but not so common in the south.

Hat Chaweng

🏃 Activities

Diving

If you're serious about diving, head to Ko Tao and base yourself there for the duration of your diving adventure. If you're short on time and don't want to leave Samui, there are plenty of operators who will take you to the same dive sites (at a greater fee, of course). Try to book with a company that has its own boat (or leases a boat) – it's slightly more expensive, but you'll be glad you did it. Companies without boats often shuttle divers on the passenger catamaran to Ko Tao, where you board a second boat to reach your dive site. These trips are arduous, meal-less and rather impersonal.

Certification courses tend to be twice as expensive on Ko Samui as they are on Ko Tao, this is largely due to use of extra petrol, since tiny Tao is significantly closer to the preferred diving locations. You'll drop between 16,000B and 22,000B on an Open Water certification, and figure between 3200B and 6200B for a diving day trip depending on the location of the site.

Ko Samui's hyperbaric chamber is at Big Buddha Beach (Hat Bang Rak).

100 Degrees East   DIVING
(☏0 7742 5936; www.100degreeseast.com; Bang Rak) Highly recommended.

Diveristy   DIVING
(Map p540; ☏0 7741 3196; www.diveristy.nl; Hat Chaweng) Based at the Amari Hotel.

Samui Planet Scuba   DIVING
(SIDS; Map p540; ☏0 7723 1606; samuiplanet scuba@planetscuba.net; Hat Chaweng)

Other Activities

Blue Stars   KAYAKING, SNORKELLING
(Map p540; ☏0 7741 3231; www.bluestars.info; trips 2600B) For those interested in snorkelling and kayaking, book a day trip to the stunning Ang Thong Marine Park. Blue Stars, based in Hat Chaweng on Ko Samui, offers guided sea-kayak trips in the park.

Football Golf   SPORT
(☏08 9771 7498; ⏰9am-6.30pm) At Choeng Mon there's a strange combustion called 'football golf' where you 'putt' your football

Bo Phut

Bo Phut

into a rubbish-bin-sized hole. It's great for the kids and each game (300B) comes with a complimentary soft drink. It's a par 66.

Namuang Safari Park　　THEME PARK
(Map p539; ☎0 7742 4098) Located near Na Muang Falls, Namuang has safari options and packages galore. Adventure tours (from 900B) vary in length and can include elephant trekking, monkey shows, 4WD rides and even a visit to a rubber plantation to drain the trees (now that's excitement). Prices include hotel transfer.

Samui Aquarium & Tiger Zoo　　THEME PARK
(Map p539; ☎0 7742 4017; adult/child 750/450B; ⏰9am-6pm) The Samui Aquarium & Tiger Zoo features the standard array aquariums and tigers, as well as a large aviary. It's a pleasant diversion for the kids, though some of the cages and tanks are noticeably rundown. The tiger show is at 2.30pm and the sea lion spectacle starts at 1.30pm. The

admission includes the use of the large on-site swimming pool.

Spas & Yoga
Competition for Samui's five-star accommodation is fierce, which means that the spas are of the highest calibre. For top-notch pampering, try the spa at Anantara Bo Phut, or the Hideaway Spa at the Six Senses Samui. The Spa Resort in Lamai is the island's original health destination, and is still known for its effective 'clean me out' fasting regime.

Yoga Thailand　　YOGA & SPA
(☎0 7792 0090; www.yoga-thailand.com; Phang Ka; retreats from €680; ✱@🤶) Secreted away along the southern shores, Yoga Thailand is ushering in a new era of therapeutic holidaying with its state-of-the-art facilities and dedicated team of trainers. Accommodation is located in a comfy apartment block up the street while yoga studios, wellness centres and a breezy cafe sit calmly along the shore.

Tamarind Retreat THAI MASSAGE
([Z]0 7723 0571; www.tamarindretreat.com) Tucked far away from the beach within a silent coconut-palm plantation, Tamarind's small collection of villas and massage studios is seamlessly incorporated into nature: some have granite boulders built into walls and floors, others offer private ponds or creative outdoor baths.

Health Oasis Resort YOGA & SPA
([Z]0 7742 0124; www.healthoasisresort.com) If you're lookin' to get 'cleansed', whether it's your aura or your colon, then you've happened upon the right place. New Age is all the rage at the Health Oasis. Guests can choose from a variety of healing packages involving everything from meditation to fasting. Bungalows are modern and receive plenty of sunshine. There's also a vegetarian restaurant on site, of course.

Absolute Sanctuary YOGA & SPA
([Z]0 7760 1190; www.absoluteyogasamui.com) What was once a friendly yoga studio has blossomed into a gargantuan wellness complex featuring plenty of accommodation and an exhaustive menu of detox and wellness programs.

Courses

**Samui Institute of Thai
Culinary Arts** COOKING
(SITCA; Map p540; [Z]0 7741 3434; www.sitca.net; Hat Chaweng) If you're contemplating a Thai cooking course, SITCA is the place to do it. It has daily Thai-cooking classes and courses in the aristocratic Thai art of carving fruits and vegetables into intricate floral designs. Lunchtime classes begin at 11am, while dinner starts at 4pm (both cost 1950B for a three-hour course with three or more dishes). Included is an excellent tutorial about procuring ingredients in your home country. Of course you get to eat your projects, and even invite a friend along for the meal. Complimentary DVDs with Thai cooking instruction are also available so you can practise at home.

Sleeping

'Superior', 'standard', 'deluxe', 'standard deluxe', 'deluxe superior', 'superior standard' – what does it all mean? Trying to decode Samui's obnoxious hotel lingo is like trying to decipher the ancient Maya language. The island's array of sleeping options is overwhelming – we've compiled a list of our fa-

vourites, but the following inventory is by no means exhaustive.

If you're looking to splurge, there is definitely no shortage of top-end resorts sporting extravagant bungalows, charming spas, private infinity pools, and first-class dining. Bo Phut, on the island's northern coast, has a charming collection of boutique lodging – the perfect choice for midrange travellers. Backpack-toting tourists will have to look a little harder, but budget digs do pop up once in a while along all of the island's beaches.

Private villa services have become quite popular in recent years. Rental companies often advertise in the various tourist booklets that circulate on the island.

This large section is organised as follows: we start on the popular east coast with Chaweng and Lamai, then move anticlockwise around the island covering the smaller beaches.

CHAWENG

TOP
CHOICE **Jungle Club** BUNGALOWS $$
(Map p540; [Z]08 1894 2327; www.jungleclubsamui.com; bungalows 800-4500B; ✱@☎❄) The perilous drive up the slithering dirt road is totally worthwhile once you get a load of the incredible views from the top. This isolated mountain getaway is a huge hit among locals and tourists alike. There's a relaxed back-to-nature vibe – guests chill around the stunning horizon pool or tuck themselves away for a catnap under the canopied roofs of an open-air *săh·lah* (often spelt *sala;* hall). Call ahead for a pick-up – you don't want to spend your precious jungle vacation in a body cast. Taxis from the main road cost 50B; it's 100B from central Chaweng.

TOP
CHOICE **Library** RESORT $$$
(Map p540; [Z]0 7742 2767; www.thelibrary.name; r from 13,300B; ✱@☎❄) This place is too cool for school, which is ironic since it's called 'The Library'. The entire resort is a sparkling white mirage accented with black trimming and slatted curtains. Besides the futuristic iMac computer in each page (rooms are called 'pages' here), our favourite feature is the large monochromatic wall art – it glows brightly in the evening and you can adjust the colour depending on your mood. Life-size statues are engaged in the act of reading, and if you too feel inclined to pick up a book, the on-site library houses an impressive assortment of colourful art and design books. The large rectangular pool is not to

be missed – it's tiled in piercing shades of red, making the term 'bloodbath' suddenly seem appealing.

Tango Beach Resort RESORT $$
(Map p540; ☎0 7742 2470; www.tangobeachsamui.com; r 1600-4600B; ❄@🖥🛏) A midrange all-star, Tango features a string of bungalows arranged along a teak boardwalk that meanders away from the beach.

Centara Grand RESORT $$$
(Map p540; ☎0 7723 0500; www.centralhotels resorts.com; r 8900-19,500B; ❄@🖥🛏) Centara is a massive, manicured compound in the heart of Chaweng, but the palm-filled property is so large that you can safely escape the streetside bustle. Rooms are found in a hotel-like building that is conspicuously Western in theme and decor. Grown-ups can escape to the spa, or one of the four restaurants, and leave the children at the labyrinth of swimming pools under the watchful eye of an in-house babysitter.

Baan Chaweng Beach Resort RESORT $$$
(Map p540; ☎0 7742 2403; www.baanchaweng beachresort.com; bungalows 3500-7000B; ❄@🖥🛏) A pleasant option for those who want top-end luxury without the hefty bill, Baan Chaweng is one of the new kids on the block and is keeping the prices relatively low. The immaculate rooms are painted in various shades of peach and pear, with teak furnishings that feel both modern and traditional.

Muang Kulay Pan Hotel RESORT $$$
(Map p540; ☎0 7723 0849-51; www.kulaypan.com; r 4200-15,000B; ❄@🖥🛏) No, that's not a rip in the wallpaper – it's all part of the design concept. The architect cites a fusion between Zen and Thai concepts, but we think the decor is completely random. The seaside grounds have been purposefully neglected to lend an additional sense of chaos to this unique resort.

Baan Haad Ngam RESORT $$$
(Map p540; ☎0 7723 1500; www.baanhaadngam.com; bungalows 6400-14,000B; ❄@🖥🛏) Vibrant Baan Haad Ngam shuns the usual teak and tan – every exterior is painted an interesting shade of green – like radioactive celery. It's sassy, classy and a great choice if you've got the dime.

Pandora Boutique Hotel RESORT $$
(Map p540; ☎0 7741 3801; www.pandora-samui.com; r 2700-4900B; ❄🖥🛏) As adorable as it is memorable, Pandora looks like it just fell out of a comic book – maybe *Tintin and the Mystery of Surprisingly Cheap Accommodation in Chaweng*? Rooms are outfitted with cheerful pastels, wooden moulding, and the occasional stone feature.

Kirikayan Boutique Resort RESORT $$$
(☎0 7733 2299; www.kirikayan.com; r from 5295B; ❄@🖥🛏) Simple whites, lacquered teak and blazing red accents set the colour scheme at this hip address along Chaweng's southern sands. Wander past thick palm trunks and sky-scraping foliage to find the relaxing pool deck at the back.

Ark Bar RESORT $$
(Map p540; ☎0 7742 2047; www.ark-bar.com; bungalows 1500B; ❄🖥🛏) You'll find two of every creature at Ark Bar – hardcore partiers, chilled out hippies, teenagers, forty-somethings, even Canadians. Lately, the perennially popular resort has started to shift gears – higher-end digs is now the name of the game.

Chaweng Garden Beach RESORT $$
(Map p540; ☎0 7796 0394; www.chawenggarden.com; r from 1850-8500B; ❄@🖥🛏) A popular 'flashpacker' choice, this campus of accommodation has a large variety of room types serviced by an extra-smiley staff.

Nora Chaweng HOTEL $$
(Map p540; ☎0 7791 3666; www.norachawengho tel.com; r from 2100B; ❄@🖥🛏) Nora Chaweng is not on the beach, but this newer addition to the Chaweng bustle has swankily designed rooms, an inviting on-site pool and a relaxing spa studio.

Loft Samui HOSTEL $
(Map p540; ☎0 7741 3420; www.theloftsmui.com; r from 590B; ❄@🖥) A newer budget operation in Chaweng, the Loft is giving has-beens such as the Wave a run for their money with cheap digs furnished by a couple of quirky details – adobe styling and savvy built-ins. It seems to be quite popular with travelling Israelis.

Akwa GUEST HOUSE $
(Map p540; ☎08 4660 0551; www.akwaguest house.com; r from 700B; ❄@🖥) A charming B&B-style sleeping spot, Akwa has a few funky rooms decorated with bright colours. Expect teddy bears adorning each bed, quirky bookshelves stocked with DVDs and cartoon paintings all over.

Queen Boutique Resort HOTEL $

(Map p540; ☎0 7741 3148; queensamui@yahoo.com; r from 800-1200B; ❀@☎) Despite the less-than-friendly staff, Queen offers up boutique sleeps for backpacker prices. Make sure, however, that you get a room with tiled floors; the ones with scuffed linoleum are far less appealing.

Baan Samui RESORT $$

(Map p540; ☎0 7723 0965; www.see2sea.com; r from 8240B; ❀@☎⛵) In sharp contrast to the austere Library next door, Baan Samui is a campus of colourful beachside units. If the Flintstones had a holiday ranch house, it would probably look something like this.

Samui Hostel HOSTEL $

(Map p540; ☎08 9874 3737; dm 180B; ❀@) It doesn't look like much from the front, but the dorm rooms here are surprisingly spic and span. It's a great place for solo travellers on a tight budget, although couples should know that a private double room can be scouted in Chaweng for around 400B.

P Chaweng HOTEL $

(Map p540; ☎0 7723 0684; r 400-600B, ste 1000B; ❀@) This vine-covered cheapie doesn't even pretend to be close to the beach, but the pink-tiled rooms are spacious and squeaky clean (minus a couple of bumps and bruises on the wooden furniture). Pick a room facing away from the street – it seems a tad too easy for someone to slip through an open window and pilfer your stuff.

LAMAI

TOP CHOICE Rocky Resort RESORT $$$

(☎0 7741 8367; www.rockyresort.com; Hua Thanon; r 4890-17,000B; ❀☎⛵) Our favourite spot in Lamai (well, actually just south of Lamai), Rocky finds the right balance between an upmarket ambience and an unpretentious, sociable atmosphere. During the quieter months the prices are a steal, since ocean views abound, and each room has been furnished with beautiful Thai-inspired furniture that seamlessly incorporates a modern twist. The pool has been carved in between a collection of boulders mimicking the rocky beach nearby (hence the name).

Banyan Tree Koh Samui RESORT $$$

(☎0 7791 5333; www.banyantree.com/en/samui/overview; villas from 23,000B; ❀@☎⛵) Phuket's most prestigious address has set up a sister property along the secluded northern sands of Lamai. Occupying an entire bay, this sprawling homage to over-the-top luxury sports dozens of villas hoisted above the foliage by spider-like stilts. Golf carts zip around the grounds carrying jetsetters between the myriad dining venues and the gargantuan spa (which sports a relaxing rainforest simulator, no less).

Samui Jasmine Resort RESORT $$$

(☎0 7723 2446; 131/8 Moo 3; r & bungalows 3800-5000B; ❀☎⛵) Smack dab in the middle of Lamai beach, pleasant Samui Jasmine is a great deal. Go for the lower-priced rooms – most have excellent views of the ocean and the crystal-coloured lap pool. The design scheme features plenty of varnished teak and also frilly accessories such as lavender pillows.

Spa Resort BUNGALOWS $$

(☎0 7723 0855; www.spasamui.com; Lamai North; bungalows 800-2800B; ❀☎) This health spa has a bevy of therapeutic programs on offer, and no one seems to mind that the lodging is cheap by Lamai's standards. Programs include colonics, massage, aqua detox, hypnotherapy and yoga, just to name a few. The bathrooms leave a bit to be desired, but who needs a toilet when you're doing a weeklong fast? Accommodation tends to book up quickly, so it's best to reserve in advance (via email). Nonguests are welcome to partake in the programs.

iBed HOSTEL $

(☎0 7745 8760; www.ibedsamui.com; dm/s 550/1100B) The sleekest hostel on the island (if not all of Thailand), iBed has all the accoutrements of an Apple-sponsored space station: personal TVs at each bed, smooth coats of paint, bleach-white linens, and plenty of polished concrete. The wide verandahs, ample common space and mod kitchen foster a sociable vibe during the busier months.

Lamai Wanta RESORT $$

(☎0 7742 4550, 0 7742 4218; www.lamaiwanta.com; r & bungalows 1954-4800B; ❀@☎⛵) The pool area feels a bit retro, with its swatch book of beige- and blue-toned tiles, but in the back there are modern motel rooms and bungalows that have fresh coats of white paint. On the inside, rooms tread a fine line between being minimal and sparse. Lamai Wanta is located towards the south end of Lamai – be on the look out for the resort's small sign; it's located down a small beachside soi.

Amarina Residence   GUEST HOUSE **$**
(www.amarinaresidence.com; r 900-1200B) Although the lobby is unusually dark compared to most tropical foyers, the rooms upstairs are sun-drenched and sport tasteful light-wood furnishing.

Beer's House   BUNGALOWS **$**
(🖉0 7723 0467; 161/4 Moo 4 Lamai North; bungalows 200-550B) These tiny shade-covered bungalows are lined up right along the sand. Some huts have a communal toilet, but all have plenty of room to sling a hammock and laze the day away.

New Hut   BUNGALOWS **$**
(🖉0 7723 0437; newhut@hotmail.com; Lamai North; huts 200-500B) New Hut is a rare beachfront cheapie with tiny-but-charming A-frame huts.

NORTHERN BEACHES

Ko Samui's northern beaches have the largest range of accommodation. Choeng Mon has some of the most opulent resorts in the world, while Mae Nam and Bang Po cling to their backpacker roots despite the recent construction of several flash pads. Bo Phut, in the middle, is the shining star in Samui's constellation of beaches.

Choeng Mon

TOP CHOICE Six Senses Samui   RESORT **$$$**
(🖉0 7724 5678; www.sixsenses.com/hideaway-samui/index.php; bungalows from 18,000B; ✱@🛜🏊) This hidden bamboo paradise is worth the once-in-a-lifetime splurge. Set along a rugged promontory, Six Senses strikes the perfect balance between opulence and rustic charm, and defines the term 'barefoot elegance'. Most of the villas have stunning concrete plunge pools and offer magnificent views of the silent bay below. The regal, semi-outdoor bathrooms give the phrase 'royal flush' a whole new meaning. Beige golf buggies move guests between their hidden cottages and the stunning amenities strewn around the property – including a world-class spa and two excellent restaurants.

Tongsai Bay   RESORT **$$$**
(🖉0 7724 5480-5500; www.tongsaibay.co.th; ste 11,000-30,000B; ✱🛜🏊) For serious pampering, head to this secluded luxury gem. Expansive and impeccably maintained, the hilly grounds make the cluster of bungalows look more like a small village. Golf carts whiz around the vast landscape transporting guests to various activities (such as

massages) or dinner. All the extra-swanky split-level suites have day-bed rest areas, gorgeous romantic decor, stunning views, large terraces and creatively placed bathtubs (you'll see). Facilities include salt- and freshwater pools, a tennis court, the requisite spa, a dessert shop and also several restaurants.

Sala Samui   RESORT **$$$**
(🖉0 7724 5888; www.salasamui.com; bungalows US$360-1100; ✱@🛜🏊) Look out folks, these guys mean business – they quote their room rates in US dollars instead of baht. Is the hefty price tag worth it? Definitely. The design scheme is undeniably exquisite – regal whites and lacquered teaks are generously lavished throughout, while subtle turquoise accents draw on the colour of each villa's private plunge pool.

Imperial Boat House Hotel   RESORT **$$$**
(🖉0 7742 5041-52; www.imperialhotels.com; Hat Choeng Mon; r 4000-5500B, boat ste 6000-6700B; ✱🛜🏊) This sophisticated retreat has a three-storey hotel and several free-standing bungalows made from imported-teak rice barges whose bows have been transformed into stunning patios. Oxidised copper cannons blast streams of water into the boat-shaped swimming pool.

Ô Soleil   BUNGALOWS **$**
(🖉0 7742 5232; r & bungalows from 400B; ✱) One of the cheaper beachfront properties on the island, old Ô Soleil offers a scatter of bungalows and semidetached rooms extending inland from the sand. It's a very casual affair, so be sure to safely store your valuables.

Big Buddha Beach (Bang Rak)

This area gets its moniker from the huge golden Buddha that acts as overlord from the small nearby quasi-island of Ko Fan. Its proximity to the airport means lower prices at the resorts.

Samui Mermaid   RESORT **$**
(🖉0 7742 7547; www.samui-mermaid.info; r 400-2500B; ✱@🛜🏊) Samui Mermaid is a great choice in the budget category because it feels like a full-fledged resort. There are two large swimming pools, copious beach chairs, two lively restaurants and every room has cable TV. The landing strip at Samui's airport is only a couple of kilometres away, so sometimes there's noise, but free airport transfers sweeten the deal.

Shambala

BUNGALOWS $

(☑0 7742 5330; www.samui-shambala.com; bungalows 600-1000B; ❄️📶) While surrounding establishments answer the call of upmarket travellers, this laid-back, English-run place is a backpacking stalwart with a subtle hippy feel. There's plenty of communal cushion seating, a great wooden sun-deck, and the bungalows are bright and roomy. Staff doles out travel tips and smiles in equal measure.

Ocean 11

GUEST HOUSE $$

(☑0 7741 7118; www.o11s.com; bungalows 1900-3200B; ❄️📶) A little slice of luxury at a very reasonable price, Ocean 11's apartments are a steal (get it?!). Silly film references aside, this mellow spot with cottagey, Med-style decor is a great midrange getaway along a relatively quiet patch of sand.

Bo Phut

The beach isn't breathtaking, but Bo Phut has the most dynamic lodging in all of Samui. A string of vibrant boutique cottages starts deep within the clutter of Fisherman's Village and radiates outward along the sand.

TOP CHOICE Anantara

RESORT $$$

(Map p542; ☑0 7742 8300; www.anantara.com; r 4000-18,000B; ❄️@📶🏊) Anantara's stunning palanquin entrance satisfies every fantasy of a far-flung oriental kingdom. Low-slung torches spurt plumes of unwavering fire, and the residual smoke creates a light fog around the fanned palm fronds higher up. Clay and copper statues of grimacing jungle creatures abound on the property's wild acreage, while guests savour wild teas in an open-air pagoda, swim in the lagoon-like infinity-edged swimming pool, or indulge in a relaxing spa treatment. The new wing of adjacent white-washed villas brings the resort up to another level of opulence.

TOP CHOICE L'Hacienda

GUEST HOUSE $$

(Map p542; ☑0 7724 5943; www.samui-hacienda. com; r 1400-3500B; ❄️📶🏊) Polished terracotta and rounded archways give the entrance a Spanish mission motif. Similar decor permeates the eight adorable rooms, which sport loads of personal touches such as pebbled bathroom walls and translucent bamboo lamps. There's a charming surprise waiting for you on the roof, and we're pretty sure you'll love it as much as we did.

Zazen

RESORT $$$

(Map p542; ☑0 7742 5085; www.samuizazen.com; r 6010-17,200B; ❄️@📶🏊) What was once a simple place has now transformed into the boutique-iest boutique resort on Samui – every inch of this charming getaway has been thoughtfully and creatively designed. It's 'Asian minimalism meets modern Rococo' with a scarlet accent wall, terracotta goddesses, a dash of feng shui, and a generous smattering of good taste. Guests relax poolside on comfy beach chairs gently shaded by canvas parasols. The walk-in prices are scary, so it's best to book in advance.

Lodge

HOTEL $$

(Map p542; ☑0 7742 5337; www.apartmentsamui. com; r 1400-2500B; ❄️📶🏊) Another great choice in Bo Phut, the Lodge feels like a colonial hunting chalet with pale walls and dark wooden beams jutting across the ceiling. Every room has scores of wall hangings and a private balcony overlooking the beach. The 'pent-huts' on the top floor are very spacious. Reservations are a must – this place always seems to be full.

Ibis Bo Phut

HOTEL $$

(Map p542; ☑0 7791 4800; www.ibishotel.com/ thailand; r from 1600B; ❄️@📶🏊) The biggest resort on the island, the brand new Ibis still has that new car smell in its shiny, efficient rooms. Families will love the children's bunk beds and the grassy grounds perfect for a game of tag. If you're looking for a resort with traces of Thai character, this is not the place for you.

B1 Villa Spa

APARTMENTS $$$

(Map p542; ☑0 7742 7268; www.b1villa.com; ste 2800-7000B; ❄️📶🏊) There's a refreshing burst of character at this inn-style option along the beach in Fisherman's Village. Each room displays a unique collection of wall art, and has been given a special moniker – the 2nd-storey spaces are named after the stars in Orion's belt. Oh, and it's B1 as in 'B1 with yourself', get it?

Khuntai

GUEST HOUSE $

(Map p542; ☑0 7724 5118; r 400-850B; ❄️) This clunky orange guest house is as cheap as decent rooms get on Samui. A block away from the beach, on the outskirts of Fisherman's Village, Khuntai's 2nd-floor rooms are drenched in afternoon sunshine and feature outdoor lounging spots.

Mae Nam & Bang Po

W Retreat Koh Samui
RESORT $$$

(☎0 7791 5999; www.starwoodhotels.com/whotels; r from 23,000B; ❈@☎☀) A bejewelled 'W' welcomes guests as they drive up the curling road to the lobby, and upon arrival jaws immediate drop whilst staring out over the glittering infinity pools and endless horizon. The trademark 'W glam' is palpable throughout the resort, which does its darnedest to fuse an urban vibe with tropical serenity. It'll be a while before this new resort finds its groove, so until then we recommend coming by for the Sunday brunch (2500B) or a sunset cocktail at Woo Bar.

Napasai By Orient Express
RESORT $$$

(☎0 7742 9200; www.napasai.com; r from 9200B; ❈@☎☀) Gorgeously manicured grounds welcome weary travellers as they glide past grazing water buffalo and groundsmen donning cream-coloured pith helmets. A generous smattering of villas dot the expansive landscape – all sport traditional Thai-style decorations, from the intricately carved wooden ornamentation to streamers of luscious local silks.

Maenam Resort
BUNGALOWS $$

(☎0 7742 5116; www.maenamresort.com; bungalows 1400-3000B; ❈@☎) Palm-bark cottages are set in several rows amid a private, jungle-like garden. They're decked out in a mix of wicker and wooden furnishings, and vary in price according to their distance from the beach. Suites are a steal for families.

Harry's
BUNGALOWS $$

(☎0 7742 5447; www.harrys-samui.com; bungalows 1200-3000B; ❈☀) Arriving at Harry's feels like entering sacred temple grounds. Polished teak wood abounds in the lobby and the classic pitched roofing reaches skyward. The concrete bungalows, stashed in a verdant garden, do not retain the flamboyant architectural theme out front, but they're cute and comfortable nonetheless.

Coco Palm Resort
BUNGALOWS $$

(☎0 7742 5095; bungalows 1200B; ❈☀) The bungalows at Coco Palm have been crafted with tonnes of rattan. A rectangular pool is the centrepiece along the beach – and the price is right for a resort-like atmosphere.

Shangrilah
BUNGALOWS $

(☎0 7742 5189; bungalows 300-2000B; ❈) A backpacker's Shangri La indeed – these are some of the cheapest huts around and they're in decent condition.

WEST COAST

Largely the domain of Thai tourists, Samui's west coast doesn't have the most picturesque beaches, but it's a welcome escape from the east-side bustle.

InterContinental Samui Baan Taling Ngam Resort
RESORT $$$

(☎0 7742 9100; www.ichotelsgroup.com/intercontinental; r from 6300B; ❈@☎☀) Unlike most of Samui's five-star digs, Baan Taling Ngam has been designed in a 'classic Thai' theme. Luxuriously appointed guest accommodation contains custom-made Thai-style furnishings and the service here is impeccable. As it's not right on the beach, a shuttle service transports guests back and forth; airport and ferry transfers are also provided.

Am Samui
BUNGALOWS $$

(☎0 7723 5165; www.amsamuiresort.com; bungalows from 1100B; ❈☎☀) Cast modesty aside, spread your curtains wide, and welcome sunshine and sea views in through your floor-to-ceiling windows. Lounge-worthy porch furniture further contributes to the comfy, casual vibe established at the open-air restaurant and pool.

SOUTH COAST

The southern end of Ko Samui is spotted with rocky headlands and smaller sandy coves. The following options are all well worth the baht, in fact, these resorts represent some of our favourite places to stay on the island.

Easy Time
BUNGALOWS $$

(☎0 7792 0110; www.easytimesamui.com; Phang Ka; r from 1950B; ❈@☎☀) Safely tucked away from the throngs of tourists, this little haven – nestled inland around a serene swimming pool – is a great place to unwind. Duplex villa units and a chic dining space create an elegant mood that is refreshingly unpretentious.

Elements
RESORT $$$

(☎0 7791 4678; www.elements-koh-samui.com; Phang Ka; r 5540-21,500B; ❈@☎☀) A refreshing twist on the modern boutique sleep, Elements occupies a lonely strand of palm-studded sand. Rooms are arranged in condo-like blocks, each one featuring an eye-pleasing blend of Thai and West styling. Hidden villas dot the path down to the fire-coloured restaurant and ocean-side lounge area.

✗ Eating

If you thought it was hard to pick a place to sleep, the island has even more options when it comes to dining. From roasted crickets to beluga caviar – Samui's got it and is not afraid to flaunt it.

Influenced by the mainland, Samui is peppered with *kôw gaang* (rice and curry) shops, usually just a wooden shack displaying large metal pots of southern Thai-style curries. Folks pull up on their motorcycles, lift up the lids to survey the vibrantly coloured contents, and pick one for lunch. *Kôw gaang* shops are easily found along the Ring Rd (Rte 4169) and sell out of the good stuff by 1pm. Any build-up of local motorcycles is usually a sign of a good meal in progress.

The upmarket choices are even more numerous and although Samui's swank dining scene is laden with Italian options, visitors will have no problem finding flavours from around the globe. Lured by high salaries and spectacular weather, world-class chefs regularly make an appearance on the island.

CHAWENG

Dozens of the restaurants on the 'strip' serve a mixed bag of local bites, international cuisine, and greasy fast food. For the best ambience, get off the road and head to the beach, where many bungalow operators set up tables on the sand and have glittery fairy lights at night.

TOP CHOICE **Samui Institute of Thai Culinary Arts**   THAI $$$
(SITCA; Map p540; ☎0 7741 3434; course 1950B; ☺lunch & dinner Mon-Sat) Go one better than savouring a traditional Thai meal: cook it yourself!

Laem Din Market   MARKET $
(Map p540; dishes from 30B; ☺4am-6pm, night market 6pm-2am) A busy day market, Laem Din is packed with stalls that sell fresh fruits, vegetables and meats and stock local Thai kitchens. Pick up a kilo of sweet green oranges or wander the stalls trying to spot the ingredients in last night's curry. For dinner, come to the adjacent night market and sample the tasty southern-style fried chicken and curries.

Gringo's Cantina   MEXICAN $$
(Map p540; dishes 140-280B; ☺dinner) Wash down a Tex-Mex classic with a jug of sangria or a frozen margarita. We liked the *chimichangas* (mostly because we like saying *chimichanga*). There are burgers, pizzas and vegie options too, for those who don't want to go 'south of the border'.

Page   ASIAN FUSION $$$
(Map p540; dishes 180-850B; ☺breakfast, lunch & dinner) If you can't afford to stay at the ultraswanky Library, have a meal at its beachside restaurant. The food is expensive (of course) but you'll receive glances from the beach bums on the beach as they try to figure out if you're a jetsetter or movie star. Lunch is a bit more casual and affordable, but you'll miss the designer lighting effects in the evening.

Prego   ITALIAN $$$
(Map p540; www.prego-samui.com; mains 200-700B; ☺dinner) This smart ministry of culinary style serves up fine Italian cuisine in a barely-there dining room of cool marble and modern geometry. Reservations are accepted for seatings at 7pm and 9pm.

Dr Frogs   STEAKHOUSE $$$
(off Map p540; mains 380-790B; ☺lunch & dinner) Perched atop a rocky overlook, Dr Frogs combines incredible ocean vistas with delicious international flavours (namely Italian and Thai favourites). Delectable steaks and crab cakes, and friendly owners, put this spot near the top of our dining list.

Betelnut@Buri Rasa   ASIAN FUSION $$$
(Map p540; mains 600-800B; ☺dinner) Fusion can be confusing, and often disappointing, but Betelnut will set you straight. Chef Jeffrey Lords claims an American upbringing and European culinary training, but most importantly he spent time in San Francisco, where all good food is born. The menu is a pan-Pacific mix of curries and chowder, papaya and pancetta.

Zico's   BRAZILIAN $$$
(Map p540; menu 790B; ☺dinner) This palatial *churrascaria* puts the *carne* in Carnival. Vegetarians beware – Zico's is an all-you-can-eat Brazilian meat-fest complete with saucy dancers sporting peacock-like outfits.

Khaosan Restaurant & Bakery   INTERNATIONAL $
(Map p540; dishes from 60B; ☺breakfast, lunch & dinner) From *filet mignon* to flapjacks and everything in between, this chow house is popular with those looking for a cheap nosh. Hang around after your meal and catch a newly released movie on the big TV. It's everything you'd expect from a place called 'Khaosan'.

Wave Samui INTERNATIONAL $

(Map p540; dishes from 60B; ☉breakfast, lunch & dinner) Everyone says that Samui is going upmarket, but the most crowded restaurants at dinnertime are still the old-fashioned budget spots, like this one. This jack-of-all trades (guest house-bar-restaurant) serves honest food at honest prices and fosters a travellers' ambience with an in-house library and a popular happy hour (3pm to 7pm).

LAMAI

As Samui's second-most populated beach, Lamai has a surprisingly limited assortment of decent eateries when compared to Chaweng next door. The Tesco Lotus is a great place to pick up snacks for a beachside picnic. Most visitors, however, dine wherever they're staying.

Rocky's INTERNATIONAL $$$

(dishes 300-800B; ☉lunch & dinner) Easily the top dining spot on Lamai, Rocky's gourmet dishes are actually a bargain when you convert the baht into your native currency. Try the signature beef tenderloin with blue cheese – it's like sending your tastebuds on a Parisian vacation. On Tuesday evenings, diners enjoy a special Thai-themed evening with a prepared menu of local delicacies. Rocky's is located at the like-named resort just south of Lamai.

Lamai Day Market MARKET $

(dishes from 30B; ☉6am-8pm) The Thai equivalent of a grocery store, Lamai's market is a hive of activity, selling food necessities and takeaway food. Visit the covered area to pick up fresh fruit or to see vendors shredding coconuts to make coconut milk. Or hunt down the ice-cream seller for homemade coconut ice cream. It's next door to a petrol station.

Hua Thanon Market MARKET $

(dishes from 30B; ☉6am-6pm) Slip into the rhythm of this village market slightly south of Lamai; a window into the food ways of southern Thailand. Vendors shoo away the flies from the freshly butchered meat and housewives load bundles of vegetables into their baby-filled motorcycle baskets. Follow the market road to the row of food shops delivering edible Muslim culture: chicken biryani, fiery curries or toasted rice with coconut, bean sprouts, lemongrass and dried shrimp.

NORTHERN BEACHES

Some of Samui's finest establishments are located on the northern coast. Boho Bo Phut has several trendy eateries to match the string of yuppie boutique hotels.

Choeng Mon & Big Buddha Beach (Bang Rak)

TOP CHOICE Dining On The Rocks ASIAN FUSION $$$

(☎0 7724 5678; reservations-samui@sixsenses.com; Choeng Mon; menus from 2200B; ☉dinner) Samui's ultimate dining experience takes place on nine cantilevered verandahs of weathered teak and bamboo that yawn over the gulf. After sunset (and a glass of wine), guests feel like they're dining on a wooden barge set adrift on a starlit sea. Each dish on the six-course prix-fixe menu is the brainchild of the experimental cooks who regularly experiment with taste, texture and temperature. If you're celebrating a special occasion, you'll have to book well in advance if you want to sit at 'table 99' – the honeymooners' table – positioned on a private terrace. Dining On The Rocks is located at the isolated Six Senses Samui.

BBC INTERNATIONAL $$

(Big Buddha Beach; dishes 60-200B; ☉breakfast, lunch & dinner) No, this place has nothing to do with *Dr Who* – BBC stands for Big Buddha Café. It's popular with the local expats, the international menu is large, and there are exquisite ocean views from the patio.

Antica Locanda ITALIAN $$

(www.anticasamui.com; dishes 170-280B; ☉dinner) This friendly trattoria has pressed white tablecloths and caskets of Italian wine. Try the *vongole alla marinara* (clams in white wine) and don't forget to check out the succulent specials of the day.

If you're waiting for a ferry in Bang Rak consider stopping by one of the following:

Catcantoo BBQ $$

(http://catcantoo.net; mains 90-350B; ☉breakfast, lunch & dinner) Enjoy bargain-basement breakfast (99B) in the morning, succulent ribs at noon, or shooting some pool later in the day.

Pae Chuan Chim THAI $

(mains 30-40B; ☉breakfast & lunch) Without an ounce of atmosphere to speak of, this open-air noodle-scooping haunt is popular with locals who break for lunch to reenergise. Located next to the hyperbaric chamber.

Bo Phut

Shack Bar & Grill
STEAKHOUSE $$$

(Map p542; www.theshackgrillsamui.com; mains 480-780B; ☺dinner) With hands down the best steaks on the island, the Shack imports the finest cuts of meat from Australia and slathers them in a rainbow of tasty sauces from red wine to blue cheese. Booth seating and jazz over the speakers give the joint a distinctly Western vibe, though you'll find all types of diners come here to splurge.

Zazen
ASIAN FUSION $$$

(Map p542; dishes 550-850B, set menu from 1300B; ☺lunch & dinner) The chef describes the food as 'organic and orgasmic', and the ambient 'yums' from elated diners definitely confirm the latter. This romantic dining experience comes complete with ocean views, dim candle lighting and soft music. Reservations recommended.

Starfish & Coffee
THAI $$

(Map p542; mains 130-180B; ☺breakfast, lunch & dinner) This streamer-clad eatery was probably named after the Prince song, since we couldn't find any starfish on the menu (there's loads of coffee though). Evenings feature standard Thai fare and sunset views of rugged Ko Pha-Ngan.

Villa Bianca
ITALIAN $$

(Map p542; dishes from 200B; ☺lunch & dinner) Another fantastic Italian spot on Samui, Villa Bianca is a sea of crisp white tablecloths and woven lounge chairs. Who knew wicker could be so sexy?

Karma Sutra
INTERNATIONAL $$

(Map p542; mains 130-260B; ☺breakfast, lunch & dinner) A haze of purples and pillows, this charming chow spot in the heart of Bo Phut's Fisherman's Village serves up international and Thai eats listed on colourful chalkboards. Karma Sutra doubles as a clothing boutique.

Mae Nam & Bang Po

Angela's Bakery
BAKERY, INTERNATIONAL $$

(Mae Nam; dishes 80-200B; ☺breakfast & lunch) Duck through the screen of hanging plants into this beloved bakery, smelling of fresh bread and hospitality. Angela's sandwiches and cakes have kept many Western expats from wasting away in the land of rice.

Bang Po Seafood
SEAFOOD $$

(Bang Po; dishes from 100B; ☺dinner) A meal at Bang Po Seafood is a test for the tastebuds. It's one of the only restaurants that serves traditional Ko Samui fare (think of it as island roadkill, well, actually it's more like local sea-kill): recipes call for ingredients such as raw sea urchin roe, baby octopus, sea water, coconut, and local turmeric.

WEST COAST

The quiet west coast features some of the best seafood on Samui. Na Thon has a giant **day market** on Th Thawi Ratchaphakdi – it's worth stopping by to grab some snacks before your ferry ride.

TOP CHOICE Five Islands
SEAFOOD $$$

(www.thefiveislands.com; Taling Ngam; dishes 150-500B, tours 3000-6500B; ☺lunch & dinner) Five Islands defines the term 'destination dining' and offers the most unique eating experience on the island. Before your meal, a traditional longtail boat will take you out into the turquoise sea to visit the haunting Five Sister Islands where you'll learn about the ancient and little-known art of harvesting bird nests to make bird's-nest soup, a Chinese delicacy. This perilous task is rewarded with large sums of cash – a kilo of nests is usually sold for 100,000B to restaurants in Hong Kong (yup, that's five zeros). The lunch tour departs around 10am, and the dinner program leaves around 3pm. Customers are also welcome to dine without going on the tour and vice versa.

About Art & Craft Café
VEGETARIAN $$

(Na Thon; dishes 80-180B; ☺breakfast & lunch) An artistic oasis in the midst of hurried Na Thon, this cafe serves an eclectic assortment of healthy and wholesome food, gourmet coffee and, as the name states, art and craft, made by the owner and her friends. Relaxed and friendly, this is also a gathering place for Samui's dwindling population of bohemians and artists.

🍸 Drinking & Entertainment

Samui's biggest party spot is, without a doubt, noisy Chaweng. Lamai and Bo Phut come in second and third respectively, while the rest of the island is generally quiet, as the drinking is usually focused around self-contained resort bars.

CHAWENG & LAMAI

Making merry in Chaweng is a piece of cake. Most places are open until 2am and there are a few places that go strong all night long. Soi Green Mango has loads of girly bars. Soi Colibri and Soi Reggae Pub are raucous as well.

KO SAMUI & THE LOWER GULF KO SAMUI

POP'S CULTURE: LIFE AS A LADYBOY

Pop, age 45, is what Thais call a *gà·teu·i*, usually referred to as a 'ladyboy' in English. Thailand's transgender population is the subject of many debates and conversations, especially among tourists. Although tolerance is widespread in Buddhist Thailand, concealed homophobia prevails – for *gà·teu·i*, this can be a challenging life, with the entertainment and sex industries the only lucrative career avenues open. We spent the day with Pop and got the skinny on what life was really like as a member of Thailand's oft-talked-about 'third sex'.

LET'S START WITH A QUESTION THAT MANY TOURISTS IN THAILAND WOULD LIKE TO ASK: WHY DOES THERE SEEM TO BE SO MANY GA-TEU-I IN THAILAND?

Well, that's like asking me why I am a ladyboy! I have no idea. I didn't ask to have these feelings. I think the more important thing to notice is why there are so many ladyboys in the cabaret or sex industry. First, however, let me start by staying that the word *gà·teu·i* is the informal way of saying 'person with two sexes'; the term *pôo yǐng kâhm pêt* is generally more polite. Also, *gà·teu·i* is strictly reserved for people who still have male body parts but dress as female, so I am not technically *gà·teu·i* anymore.

Most tourists think that there are tonnes of ladyboys in Thailand because they are in places that many tourists visit. Yes, some ladyboys want to be cabaret dancers, just like some women want to be cabaret dancers, but most of them don't. These types of jobs are the only ones available to ladyboys, and the pay is lousy. Life is not as 'Hollywood' for a ladyboy as it may seem on stage. Most ladyboys don't have the chance to have a job that is respected by the community. We are not allowed to become doctors or psychologists and most corporations do not allow ladyboy employees because they don't want *gà·teu·i* to be associated with their company's image. Since many of us cannot have proper jobs, many ladyboys drop out of school at a young age , and lately this educational gap in the culture has become huge. Ladyboys work in the sex industry because they aren't given the opportunity to make a lot of money doing something else. I feel like a second-class citizen; we are not allowed to use male *or* female bathrooms! I used to have to climb 14 flights of stairs to use the special ladyboys' bathroom at my old job! Also, Thai law states that my ID cards and passport must always have an 'M' for male because the definition of a female in Thailand is someone who can bear children. It's hard for me to leave the country because my passport says 'male' but I look like a female. They will never let me through security because it looks like a fraudulent passport.

WHEN DID YOU FIRST REALISE THAT YOU MIGHT BE A TRANSGENDER PERSON?

I realised that I was different when I was about six years old. I always wanted to dress up like my sister and would get upset when my parents dressed me in boy's clothing. It felt wrong being in boy's clothes. I felt good in my sister's outfits.

HOW DOES ONE TELL THE DIFFERENCE BETWEEN A LADYBOY AND A WOMAN ON THE STREET?

Sometimes it's really hard to tell...sometimes a ladyboy can be more beautiful than a woman! There is no set way to figure it out, unless you ask them for their ID card. These days, doctors are really starting to perfect the operations, and the operations are expensive – mine was 150,000B! I had the 'snip', then I had breast implants, my Adam's apple was shaved off, and I also had a nose job (I didn't like my old nose anyways). Other operations available include silicone implants in the hips, jaw narrowing, cheekbone shaving and chin sculpting – to make it rounder. But before anyone can have an operation, you have to have a psych evaluation. The operation was extremely painful. I spent seven days in the hospital

Beach Republic   LOUNGE
(www.beachrepublic.com; 176/34 Moo 4 Hat Lamai) Recognised by its yawning thatch-patched awnings, Beach Republic would be the perfect spot to shoot one of those MTV Spring Break episodes. There's an inviting wading pool, comfy lounge chairs and an endless cocktail list.

Q-Bar   LOUNGE
(Map p540; www.qbarsamui.com; Hat Chaweng) Overlooking Chaweng Lake, Q-Bar is a little piece of Bangkok nightlife planted among the

and it took me about two months to fully recover. Younger patients tend to heal faster – I was about 40 years old when I had the operation.

WHY DIDN'T YOU HAVE THE OPERATION EARLIER? AND HOW HAVE YOUR HANDLED THE TRANSITION?

I didn't 'change' earlier because I didn't want to give up my job, and I knew that after the operation I would be forced to quit. I was working as a software instructor at a university, and university teachers are not allowed to be transgender. I also waited until my father passed away so that it would be easier on my family when I made the transition.

Well, contrary to what some tourists believe, no family particularly *wants* a transgender child, even a family with only boys. Some of my close friends no longer speak to their families. My mother was always very comforting. A month before my operation she told me 'you will always be my child, but never lie to anyone about who you are – accept who you are'. I have two adopted sons who are now quite grown-up, and after I made the change, they bought me presents on Mother's Day instead of Father's Day – I thought that was very sweet. My father, on the other hand, was never very supportive. When he found I was sleeping with men, he...well...let's put it this way, he practised his *moo·ay thai* [also spelt *muay thai*] boxing on me.

HOW DID YOU FEEL WHEN YOU WOKE UP AFTER THE OPERATION? HOW HAS LIFE BEEN SINCE THE OPERATION?

I woke up with a big smile. Life is great. I am happy that I can be on the outside what I am on the inside – I can stop feeling sad every time I look down! Finding a job after my surgery was hard. I wrote on my CV 'transgender post-op' so that there would be no surprises in the interview, but I never heard back from any companies. Oh, actually one company asked me to come for an interview, but they spent the meeting asking me inappropriate questions about my personal life. It was very disheartening. I finally found a queer-friendly company, where I am employed as a hospitality software implementer, meaning that I go around to hotels around Thailand and teach front-desk staff how to use the hotel's computer system. I adore my job.

Now that my surgery is far behind me, I have to take female hormones regularly until I die. I take a pill twice per week, but some male-to-females take one injection per month (I hate needles). Some people have a bad reaction to the medication at first. I have had friends that got a lot of pimples and got really fat. Sometimes it takes a while before you find the right amount of hormones. Besides the hormones, there is a certain amount of... maintenance...that needs to take place in order to keep my new parts working. Put it this way, when you get your ears pierced, if you don't regularly wear earrings...well... Anyways, my aunt, who moved to the United States, asked me if I wanted to move too, but I am happy in Thailand. Even though transgender individuals don't have a lot of rights, I'm not convinced that it is that much better anywhere else.

AND FINALLY, WHAT DO YOU FEEL IS THE BIGGEST MISCONCEPTION ABOUT GÀ·TEU·I IN THAILAND?

This is an easy question. The biggest misconception is that we are all promiscuous whores and liars. Like any human being, we are just looking for love. It is true that many ladyboys do try to trick the people around them, but this is because they are afraid of being rejected for who they really are. Also, many of them lie because they desperately want to be real women, but they will never be real women. I know that – that's why I always show the real me – I am comfortable with who I am. I wish everyone else would be too.

As told to Brandon Presser.

coconut trees. The upstairs lounge opens just before sunset, treating cocktail connoisseurs to various highbrow tipples and a drinkable view of southern Chaweng – mountains, sea and sky. After 10pm, the night-crawlers descend upon the downstairs club where DJs spin the crowd into a techno amoeba. A taxi there will cost between 200B and 300B.

Ark Bar BAR
(Map p540; www.ark-bar.com; Hat Chaweng) The 'it' destination for a Wednesday-night romp on Samui. Drinks are dispensed from the

multicoloured bar draped in paper lanterns, and guests lounge on pyramidal pillows strewn down the beach. The party usually starts around 4pm.

Christy's Cabaret CABARET

(Map p540; Hat Chaweng) This flashy joint offers free *gà·teu·i* (ladyboys, also spelt *kàthoey*) cabaret every night at 11pm and attracts a mixed clientele of both sexes. Other ladyboys loiter out front and try to drag customers in, so to speak.

Good Karma BAR

(Map p540; Hat Chaweng) Open all day, this snazzy lounge lures the hip 'hi-so' (Thai high society) crowd with canopied daybeds and a hidden pond.

Bar Solo BAR

(Map p540; Hat Chaweng) A sign of things to come, Bar Solo has future-fitted Chaweng's outdoor beer halls into an urban setting with sleek cubist decor and a cocktail list that doesn't scream holiday hayseed. The evening drink specials lure in the front-loaders preparing for a late, late night at the dance clubs on Soi Solo and Soi Green Mango.

Tropical Murphy's IRISH BAR

(Map p540; Hat Chaweng) A popular *fa·ràng* (foreigner) joint, Tropical Murphy's dishes out steak-and-kidney pie, fish and chips, lamb chops and Irish stew (mains 50B to 300B). Come night-time, the live music kicks on and this place turns into the most popular Irish bar on Samui (yes, there are a few).

Green Mango BAR

(Map p540; Hat Chaweng) This place is so popular it has an entire soi named after it. Samui's favourite power drinking house is very big, very loud and very faràng. Green Mango has blazing lights, expensive drinks and masses of sweaty bodies swaying to dance music.

Reggae Pub BAR

(Map p540; Hat Chaweng) This fortress of fun sports an open-air dance floor with music spun by foreign DJs. It's a towering two-storey affair with long bars, pool tables and a live-music stage. The whole place doubles as a shrine to Bob Marley.

Mint BAR

(Map p540; Hat Chaweng) The scene on Green Mango Soi is too entertaining to keep the crowds corralled in this stylish club on or-dinary nights. But the Mint is able to lure a few DJ heavyweights for a Samui spin on extraordinary nights. Watch the entertainment listings for special events.

NORTHERN & WEST COAST BEACHES

Woo Bar LOUNGE

(Mae Nam) The W Retreat's signature lobby bar gives the word 'swish' a whole new meaning with cushion-clad pods of seating plunked in the middle of an expansive infinity pool that stretches out over the infinite horizon. This is, without a doubt, the best place on Samui for a sunset cocktail.

Nikki Beach LOUNGE

(www.nikkibeach.com/kohsamui; Lipa Noi) The acclaimed luxury brand has brought its international *savoir faire* to the secluded west coast of Ko Samui. Expect everything you would from a chic address in St Barts or St Tropez: haute cuisine, chic decor and gaggles of jetsetters. Themed brunch and dinner specials keep the masses coming throughout the week, and sleek bungalow accommodation is also on offer.

Pier LOUNGE

(Map p542; Bo Phut) This sleek black box sticks out among Bo Phut's narrow Chinese tenements. It's the hippest address in Fisherman's Village, sporting multilevel terraces, a lively bar, and plenty of wide furniture to lounge around on and watch the rickety fishing vessels pull into the harbour.

Gecko Village CLUB

(Map p542; Bo Phut) For electronica fans, Gecko Village is the original maven of beats. It's a beachfront bar and resort that has used its London connections to lure international DJs to Samui paradise. The New Year's Eve parties and Sunday sessions are now legendary thanks to the big names that grace the turntables.

Billabong Surf Club BAR

(Map p542; Bo Phut) Billabong's all about Aussie Rules football – it's playing on the TV and the walls are smothered with memorabilia from Down Undah. There are great views of Ko Pha-Ngan and hearty portions of ribs and chops to go with your draught beer.

ⓘ Information

Dangers & Annoyances

As on Phuket, the rate of road accident fatalities on Samui is quite high. This is mainly due to the large number of tourists who rent motorcycles only to find out that the winding roads, sudden tropical rains and frenzied traffic can be lethal. If you decide to rent a motorcycle, protect yourself by wearing a helmet, and ask for one that has a plastic visor. Even if you escape unscathed from a riding experience, we've heard reports that some shops will claim that you damaged your rental and will try to extort you for some serious cash.

Beach vendors are registered with the government and should all be wearing a numbered jacket. No peddler should cause an incessant disturbance – seek assistance if this occurs.

Emergency

Tourist police (Map p539; ☎0 7742 1281, emergency 1155) Based at the south of Na Thon.

Immigration Offices & Visas

Located about 2km south of Na Thon is Ko Samui's **Immigration Office** (Map p539; ☎0 7742 1069; ☺8.30am-noon & 1-4.30pm Mon-Fri). Officials here tend to issue the minimum rather than maximum visa extensions. During our visits here we've watched dozens of tourists wait through exhausting lines only to get curtly denied an extension for no particular reason. On a particularly bad day expect extensions to take the entire afternoon. See p766 for more details on visas.

Internet Access

There are countless places all over the island for internet access, even at the less popular beaches. Prices range from 1B to 2B per minute. Keep an eye out for restaurants that offer complimentary wi-fi service. Most accommodation offers a wi-fi connection; ironically you'll pay extra for it at high-end hotels.

Media & Maps

The Siam Map Company puts out quarterly booklets including a *Spa Guide, Dining Guide*, and an annual directory, which lists thousands of companies and hotels on the island. Its *Siam Map Company Samui Guide Map* is fantastic, free, and easily found throughout the island. Also worth a look is the *Samui Navigator* pamphlet. **Essential** (www.essential-samui) is a pocket-sized pamphlet focused on promoting Samui's diverse activities. *Samui Guide* looks more like a magazine and features mostly restaurants and attractions.

Medical Services

Ko Samui has four private hospitals, all near Chaweng's Tesco-Lotus supermarket on the east coast (where most of the tourists tend to gather). The government hospital in Na Thon has seen significant improvements in the last couple of years but the service is still a bit grim because

funding is based on the number of Samui's legal residents (which doesn't take into account the many illegal Burmese workers).

Bandon International Hospital (Map p542; ☎0 7742 5840, emergency 0 7742 5748)

Bangkok Samui Hospital (Map p540; ☎0 7742 9500, emergency 0 7742 9555) Your best bet for just about any medical problem.

Hyperbaric Chamber (Map p539; ☎0 7742 7427; Big Buddha Beach) The island's dive medicine specialists.

Samui International Hospital (Map p540; ☎0 7742 2272; www.sih.co.th; Hat Chaweng) Emergency ambulance service is available 24 hours and credit cards are accepted. Near the Amari Resort in Chaweng.

Money

Changing money isn't a problem on the east and north coasts, and in Na Thon. Multiple banks and foreign-exchange booths offer daily services and there's an ATM every couple of hundred metres. You should not have to pay credit card fees as you do on neighbouring Ko Tao.

Post

In several parts of the island there are privately run post-office branches charging a small commission. You can almost always leave your stamped mail with your accommodation.

Main post office (Map p539; Na Thon) Near the TAT office; not always reliable.

Tourist information

Essential (www.essential-samui) A pocket-sized pamphlet focused on promoting Samui's diverse activities.

Samui Guide (www.samuiguide.com) This guide looks more like a magazine and features mostly restaurants and attractions.

Samui Navigator (www.samuinavigaot.com) This pamphlet is also worth a look.

Siam Map Company (www.siammap.com) Puts out quarterly booklets including guides to spas and dining spots, and an annual directory, which lists thousands of companies and hotels on the island. Its *Siam Map Company Samui Guide Map* is fantastic, free and easily found throughout the island.

TAT office (Map p539; ☎0 7742 0504; Na Thon; ☺8.30am-4.30pm) At the northern end of Na Thon; this office is friendly, helpful and has handy brochures and maps – although travel agents throughout the island can provide similar information.

ⓘ Getting There & Away

Air

Samui's airport is located in the northeast of the island near Big Buddha Beach. **Bangkok**

Airways (www.bangkokair.com) operates flights roughly every 30 minutes between Samui and Bangkok's Suvarnabhumi Airport (50 minutes). Bangkok Air also flies direct from Samui to Phuket, Pattaya, Chiang Mai, Singapore and Hong Kong. **Firefly** (www.fireflyz.com.my) operates direct flights from Samui to Kuala Lumpur's Subang airport.

There is a **Bangkok Airways Office** (Map p540; ✆0 7742 0512-9) in Chaweng and another at the **airport** (✆0 7742 5011). The first (at 6am) and last (10pm) flights of the day are always the cheapest.

During the high season, make your flight reservations far in advance as seats often sell out. If the Samui flights are full, try flying into Surat Thani from Bangkok and taking a short ferry ride to Samui instead. Flights to Surat Thani are generally cheaper than a direct flight to the island, although they are much more of a hassle.

Boat

To reach Samui, the four main piers on the mainland are Ao Ban Don, Tha Thong, Don Sak and Khanom – Tha Thong (in central Surat) and Don Sak being the most common. On Samui, the three oft-used ports are Na Thon, Mae Nam and Big Buddha. Expect complimentary taxi transfers with high-speed ferry services.

There are frequent boat departures between Samui and Surat Thani. The hourly Seatran ferry is a common option. Ferries take one to five hours, depending on the boat. A couple of these departures can connect with the train station in Phun Phin (for a nominal extra fee). The slow night boat to Samui leaves from central Surat Thani each night at 11pm, reaching Na Thon around 5am. It returns from Na Thon at 9pm, arriving at around 3am. Watch your bags on this boat.

There are almost a dozen daily departures between Samui and Ko Pha-Ngan. These leave from the Na Thon, Mae Nam or Big Buddha pier and take from 20 minutes to one hour. The boats departing from Big Buddha service Hat Rin, and the other boats alight at Thong Sala. From the same piers, there are also around six daily departures between Samui and Ko Tao. These take 1¼ to 2½ hours.

Bus & Train

A bus-ferry combo is more convenient than a train-ferry package for getting to Ko Samui because you don't have to switch transportation in Phun Phin. However, the trains are much more comfortable and spacious – especially at night. If you prefer the train, you can get off at Chumphon and catch the Lomprayah catamaran service the rest of the way.

❶ Getting Around

Motorbikes You can rent motorcycles (and bicycles) from almost every resort on the island. The going rate is 200B per day, but for longer periods try to negotiate a better rate.

Sŏrng·tăa·ou Drivers of *sŏrng·tăa·ou* love to try to overcharge you, so it's always best to ask a third party for current rates, as they can change with the season. These vehicles run regularly during daylight hours. It's about 50B to travel between beaches, and no more than 100B to travel halfway across the island. Figure about 20B for a five-minute ride on a motorcycle taxi.

Taxis On Samui service is quite chaotic due to the plethora of cabs. In the past taxi fares were unwieldy; these days prices are more standardised across the islands (though fares are still ridiculously inflated compared to Bangkok). Taxis typically charge around 500B for an airport transfer. Some Chaweng travel agencies can arrange minibus taxis for less.

Ko Pha-Ngan   เกาะพะงัน

POP 11,000

In the family of southern Gulf islands, Ko Pha-Ngan sits in the crystal sea between Ko Samui, its business-savvy older brother, and little Ko Tao, the spunky younger brother full of dive-centric energy. Ko Pha-Ngan is a chilled out middle child who is a beach bum with tattered dreadlocks, a tattoo of a Chinese serenity symbol, and a penchant for white nights and bikini-clad pool parties.

The scenic cape of Hat Rin has long been the darling destination of this laid-back paradise. Sunrise Beach started hosting the world-famous Full Moon parties long before Alex Garland's *The Beach* inspired many to strap on a rucksack. Today, thousands of visitors still flock to the island's sands for an epic trance-a-thon fuelled by adrenaline and a couple of other substances...

But like any textbook teenager, this angst-ridden island can't decide what it wants to be when it grows up. Should the party personality persist or will the stunning and secluded northern beaches finally come out from under Hat Rin's shadow?

While Pha-Ngan's slacker vibe and reputation will no doubt dominate for years to come, the island is secretly starting to creep upmarket. Every year, tired old shacks are being replaced by crisp modern abodes. In Hat Rin, you will be hard-pressed to find a room on Sunrise Beach for less than 1000B. Soon, the phrase 'private infinity pool' and 'personal butler' will find a permanent place

Ko Pha-Ngan

in the island's lexicon, replacing 'pass the dutch' and 'another whiskey bucket please'. But don't fret just yet – the vast inland jungle continues to feel undiscovered, and there are still plenty of secluded bays in which you can string up a hammock and watch the tide roll in.

◉ Sights

For those who tire of beach-bumming, this large jungle island has many natural features to explore including mountains, waterfalls and, most importantly, some of the most spectacular beaches in all of Thailand.

Beaches & Waterfalls

There are many waterfalls throughout the island's interior, four of which gush throughout the year.

Nam Tok Than Sadet   WATERFALL
These falls feature boulders carved with the royal insignia of Rama V, Rama VII and Rama IX. King Rama V enjoyed this hidden spot so much that he returned over a dozen times between 1888 and 1909. The river waters of Khlong Than Sadet are now considered sacred and used in royal ceremonies. Also near the eastern coast, **Than Prawet** is a series of chutes that snake inland for approximately 2km.

Nam Tok Phaeng   WATERFALL
In the centre of the island, Nam Tok Phaeng is protected by a national park; this waterfall is a pleasant reward after a short, but rough, hike. Continue the adventure and head up to **Khao Ra**, the highest mountain on the island at 625m. Those with eagle-eyes will spot wild crocodiles, monkeys, snakes, deer and boar along the way, and the **viewpoint** from the top is spectacular – on a clear day you can see Ko Tao. Although the trek isn't arduous, it is very easy to lose one's way, and we *highly* recommend hiring an escort in Ban

THE TEN COMMANDMENTS OF FULL MOON FUN

No one knows exactly when or how these crazy parties got started – many believe it began in 1987 or 1988 as someone's 'going away party', but none of that is relevant now. Today, thousands of bodies converge monthly on the kerosene-soaked sands of Sunrise Beach for an epic trance-a-thon. Crowds can reach an outrageous 40,000 partiers during high season, while the low season still sees a respectable 5000 pilgrims.

If you can't make your trip coincide with a full moon but still want to cover yourself in fluorescent paint, fear not – enterprising locals have organised a slew of other reasons to get sloshed. There are Black Moon Parties (at Ban Khai), Half Moon Parties (at Ban Tai) and Moon-set Parties (at Hat Chaophao) just to name a few.

Some critics claim that the party is starting to lose its carefree flavour, especially since the island's government is trying to charge a 100B entrance fee to partygoers. Despite the disheartening schemes hatched by money-hungry locals, the night of the Full Moon is still the ultimate partying experience, so long as one follows the unofficial Ten Commandments of Full Moon fun:

» Thou shalt arrive in Hat Rin at least three days early to nail down accommodation during the pre-Full Moon rush of backpackers (see p561).

» Thou shalt double-check the party dates as sometimes they coincide with Buddhist holidays and are rescheduled.

» Thou shalt secure all valuables, especially when staying in budget bungalows.

» Thou shalt savour some delicious fried fare in Chicken Corner before the revelry begins.

» Thou shalt wear protective shoes during the sandy celebration, unless thou want a tetanus shot.

» Thou shalt cover thyself with swirling patterns of neon body paint.

» Thou shalt visit Magic Mountain or the Rock for killer views of the heathens below.

» Thou shalt not sample the drug buffet, nor shalt thou swim in the ocean under the influence of alcohol.

» Thou shalt stay in a group of two or more people, especially if thou art a woman, and especially when returning home at the end of the evening.

» Thou shalt party until the sun comes up and have a great time.

Madeua Wan (near the falls). The local guides have crude signs posted in front of their homes, and, if they're around, they'll take you up to the top for 500B. Most of them only speak Thai.

Hat Khuat
BEACH

Also called Bottle Beach, Hat Khuat is a classic fave. Visitors flock to this shore for a relaxing day of swimming and snorkelling – some opt to stay the night at one of the several bungalow operations along the beach. For additional seclusion, try the isolated beaches on the east coast, which include **Than Sadet**, **Hat Yuan**, **Hat Thian** and the teeny **Ao Thong Reng**. For additional enchanting beaches, consider doing a day trip to the stunning **Ang Thong Marine National Park** (p586).

Wát

Remember to change out of your beach clothes when visiting one of the 20 wát on Ko Pha-Ngan. Most temples are open during daylight hours.

The oldest temple on the island is **Wat Phu Khao Noi**, near the hospital in Thong Sala. While the site is open to visitors throughout the day, the monks are only around in the morning. **Wat Pho**, near Ban Tai, has a **herbal sauna** (admission 50B; ☑3-6pm) accented with natural lemongrass. The **Chinese Temple** is believed to give visitors good luck. It was constructed about 20 years ago after a visiting woman had a vision of the Chinese Buddha, who instructed her to build a fire-light for the island. **Wat Khao Tham**, also near Ban Tai, sits high on a hill and has resident female monks. At the temple there is a bulletin board detailing a meditation retreat taught by an American-Australian couple. For additional information, write in advance to Wat Khao Tham, PO Box 8, Ko Pha-Ngan, Surat Thani 84280.

🏃 Activities

Diving & Snorkelling

With Ko Tao, the high-energy diving behemoth, just a few kilometres away, Ko Pha-Ngan enjoys a much quieter, more laid-back diving scene focused on fun diving rather than certifications. A recent drop in Open Water certification prices has made local prices competitive with Ko Tao next door. Group sizes tend to be smaller on Ko Pha-Ngan since the island has less divers in general.

Like the other islands in the Samui Archipelago, Pha-Ngan has several small reefs dispersed around the island. The clear favourite snorkelling spot is **Ko Ma**, a small island in the northwest connected to Ko Pha-Ngan by a charming sandbar. There are also some rock reefs of interest on the eastern side of the island.

A major perk of diving from Ko Pha-Ngan is the proximity to **Sail Rock** (Hin Bai), the best dive site in the Gulf of Thailand and a veritable beacon for whale sharks. This large pinnacle lies about 14km north of the island. An abundance of corals and large tropical fish can be seen at depths of 10m to 30m, and there's a rocky vertical swim-through called 'The Chimney'.

Dive shops on Ko Tao sometimes visit Sail Rock, however the focus tends to be more on swallow reefs (for newbie divers) and the shark-infested waters at Chumphon Pinnacle. The most popular trips departing from Ko Pha-Ngan are three-site day trips which stop at **Chumphon Pinnacle**, Sail Rock and one of the other premiere sites in the area (see boxed text p573). These three-stop trips cost from around 3650B to 3800B and include a full lunch. Two-dive trips to Sail Rock will set you back around 2350B to 2500B.

The following list includes the main operators on the island with a solid reputation.

Reefers   DIVING
(🖉08 6471 4045; www.reefersdiving.com) Based at Shiralea (p564), this is one of the newer outfits on the island. Vic, the owner, and his gaggle of instructors are chilled and professional. Recommended.

Lotus Diving   DIVING
(🖉0 7737 4142; www.lotusdiving.net) This dive centre has top-notch instructors, and owns not one, but two beautiful boats (that's two more vessels than most of the other operations on Ko Pha-Ngan). Trips can be booked at their office in Chalok Lam, or at the Backpackers Information Centre (p570). Recommended.

Haad Yao Divers   DIVING
(🖉08 6279 3085; www.haadyaodivers.com) Established in 1997, this dive operator has garnered a strong reputation by maintaining European standards of safety and customer service.

Other Activities

Hiking and snorkelling day trips to **Ang Thong Marine National Park** (p586) generally depart from Ko Samui, but recently tour operators are starting to shuttle tourists from Ko Pha-Ngan as well. Ask at your accommodation for details about boat trips as companies often come and go due to unstable petrol prices.

Many of the larger accommodation options can hook you up with a variety of aquatic equipment such as jet skis and kayaks, and the friendly staff at Backpackers Information Centre (p570) can attend to any of your other water-sports needs.

Wake Up   WAKEBOARDING
(🖉08 7283 6755; www.wakeupwakeboarding.com; ☺Jan-Oct) Jamie passes along his infinite wakeboarding wisdom to eager wannabes at his small water sports school in Chalok Lam. Fifteen minutes of 'air time' will set you back 1500B (2500B for 30 minutes), which is excellent value considering you get one-on-one instruction. Kite-boarding, wake-skating and waterskiing sessions are also available, as are round-the-island day trips (2000B per person; a six-person quorum needed).

Eco Nature Tour   TOUR
(🖉08 4850 6273) This exceedingly popular oufit offers a 'best of' island trip, which includes elephant trekking, snorkelling and a visit to the Chinese temple, a stunning viewpoint and Phang waterfall. The day trip, which costs 1500B, departs at 9am and returns around 3pm. Bookings can be made at its office in Thong Sala or at the Backpackers Information Centre. **Pha-Ngan Safari** (🖉0 7737 4159, 08 1895 3783) offers a similar trip for 1900B.

🛏 Sleeping

Ko Pha-Ngan's legendary history of laid-back revelry has solidified its reputation as *the* stomping ground for the gritty backpacker lifestyle. Recently, however, the island is starting to see a shift towards a more upmarket clientele. Many local mainstays have collapsed their bamboo huts and constructed newer, sleeker accommodation aimed at the ever-growing legion of 'flashpackers'.

On other parts of the island, new tracts of land are being cleared for Samui-esque five-star resorts. But backpackers fear not; it'll still be many years before the castaway lifestyle goes the way of the dodo. For now, Ko Pha-Ngan can revel in its three distinct classes of lodging: pinch-a-penny shacks, trendy midrange hang-outs, and blow-the-bank luxury.

Hat Rin sees a huge number of visitors compared to the rest of the island. Party pilgrims flock to this picturesque peninsula for the legendary festivities, and although most of them sleep through the daylight hours, the setting remains quite picturesque despite the errant beer bottle in the sand. The southern part of Sunrise Beach is starting to reek of kerosene due to the nightly fire-related shenanigans at Drop-In Bar – needless to say it's best to sunbathe at the quieter northern part of the sand.

Pha-Ngan also caters to a subculture of seclusion-seekers who crave a deserted slice of sand. The northern and eastern coasts offer just that – a place to escape.

The following sleeping options are organised into five sections: we start in Hat Rin, move along the southern coast, head up the west side, across the northern beaches and down the quiet eastern shore.

HAT RIN

The thin peninsula of Hat Rin features three separate beaches. Hat Rin Nok (Sunrise Beach) is the epicentre of Full Moon tomfoolery, Hat Rin Nai (Sunset Beach) is the less impressive stretch of sand on the far side of the tiny promontory, and Hat Seekantang (also known as Hat Leela), just south of Hat Rin Nai, is a smaller, more private beach. The three beaches are linked by Ban Hat Rin (Hat Rin Town) – a small inland collection of restaurants and bars.

Needless to say, the prices listed here are meaningless during periods of maximum lunar orbicularity. Also, during Full Moon events, bungalow operations expect you to stay for a minimum number of days (around four or five). If you plan to arrive the day of the party (or even the day before), we strongly suggest booking a room in advance, or else you'll probably have to sleep on the beach (which you might end up doing anyway). Full Mooners can also stay on Samui and take one of the hourly speedboat shuttles (from 550B) to access the festivities.

TOP **Sarikantang** RESORT **$$$**
CHOICE
(Map p560; ☎0 7737 5055; www.sarikantang.com; Hat Seekantang; bungalows 1400-6200B; ❋🛜🌊) Don't get too strung out over trying to pronounce the resort's name – you can simply call this place 'heaven'. Cream-coloured cabins, framed with teak posts and lintels, are sprinkled among swaying palms and crumbling winged statuettes. Inside, the rooms look like the set of a photo shoot for an interior design magazine.

Pha-Ngan Bayshore Resort RESORT **$$**
(Map p560; ☎0 7737 5227; www.phanganbayshore. com; Hat Rin Nok; r 1700-3200B; ❋@🛜🌊) After a much-needed overhaul in 2009, this hotel-style operation has primed itself for the ever-increasing influx of flashpackers in Hat Rin. Sweeping beach views and a giant swimming pool make Pha-Ngan Bayshore one of the top addresses on Sunrise Beach.

Seaview Sunrise BUNGALOWS **$**
(Map p560; www.seaviewsunrise.com; Hat Rin Nok; r 500-800; ❋🛜) As far as budget digs are concerned, this is the only solid option for Full Moon revellers who want a sleeping spot within inches of the tide. Huts are sturdy and perfectly utilitarian. The polished wooden interiors are splashed with the occasional burst of neon paint from the ghosts of parties past. Try for a bungalow away from the small canal to avoid the mosquitos.

Palita Lodge BUNGALOWS **$$**
(Map p560; ☎0 7737 5172; www.palitalodge.com; Hat Rin Nok; bungalows 1800-5900B; ❋🛜🌊) Smack in the heart of the action, Palita is a tribute to the never-ending party that is Hat Rin's Sunrise Beach. Spacious concrete bungalows, with wooden accents and modern design elements, are neatly pressed together on this beachy wedge of sand and shrubs. Week-long bookings are a must during Full Moon revelry.

Delight GUEST HOUSE **$**
(Map p560; ☎0 7737 5527; www.delightresort. com; Ban Hat Rin; r 700-2200B; ❋🛜🌊) Tucked behind the bright yellow Kodak sign in

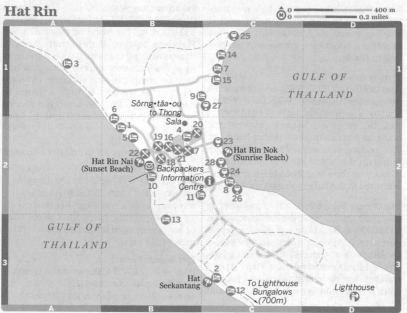

Hat Rin

Hat Rin

🛏 Sleeping
1 Blue Marine B2
2 Cocohut Village C3
3 Coral Bungalows A1
4 Delight B2
5 Friendly Resort B2
6 Neptune's Villa B2
7 Palita Lodge C1
8 Paradise Bungalows C2
9 Pha-Ngan Bayshore
   Resort B1
10 Rin Beach Resort B2
11 Same Same B2
12 Sarikantang C3
13 Sea Breeze Bungalow B3
14 Seaview Sunrise C1
15 Tommy Resort C1

🍴 Eating
16 Lazy House B2

17 Little Home B2
18 Lucky Crab B2
   Mama Schnitzel .... (see 20)
19 Monna Lisa B2
20 Mr K B2
21 Nic's B2
22 Om Ganesh B2
   Same Same Burger .... (see 11)

🍷 Drinking
23 Cactus Bar C2
24 Drop-In Bar C2
25 Mellow Mountain C1
26 Rock C2
27 Sunrise C1
28 Zoom/Vinyl C2

🎭 Entertainment
   Club Paradise .... (see 8)
   Tommy .... (see 15)

the centre of Hat Rin, Delight offers some of the best lodging around. Spic-and-span hotel rooms come with subtle designer details (such as peacock murals) and are sandwiched between an inviting swimming pool and a lazy lagoon peppered with lily pads.

Cocohut Village　RESORT $$$
(Map p560; ☏0 7737 5368; www.cocohut.com; Hat Seekantang; bungalows 2800-12,000B; ❈@🌐☒) This super-social place is the unofficial gathering spot for vacationing Israelis. In fact, Cocohut is so happenin' that guests might

forget that they are just up the street from the brouhaha on Sunrise Beach. The priciest lodging options, such as the cliff villas and beachfront bungalows, are some of the best bets in Hat Rin.

Tommy Resort RESORT $$
(Map p560; ☎0 7737 5215; www.phangantommyresort.com; Hat Rin Nok; r 1490-8000B; ❄@≋) Tommy is a trendy address in the heart of Hat Rin, striking a balance between chic boutique and carefree backpacker hang-out. The rectangular swimming pool charges things up, since every other man-made body of water on the island looks like it was manufactured at the kidney-shaped pool factory.

Sea Breeze Bungalow BUNGALOWS $$
(Map p560; ☎0 7737 5162; Ban Hat Rin; bungalows 500-8000B; ❄≋) Sea Breeze gets a good report card from our readers, and we agree; the labyrinth of secluded hillside cottages is an ideal hammocked retreat for any type of traveller. Several bungalows, poised high on stilts, deliver stunning views of Hat Rin and the sea.

Lighthouse Bungalows BUNGALOWS $
(off Map p560; ☎0 7737 5075; www.lighthousebungalows.com; Hat Seekantang; bungalows 300-1200B) Hidden at the far end of Hat Rin, this low-key collection of humble huts gathers along a sloping terrain punctuated by towering palms. To access this secluded resort, walk through Leela Beach Bungalows (don't bother stopping) and follow the wooden boardwalk as it curves to the left (southeast) around the sea-swept boulders.

Coral Bungalows RESORT $
(Map p560; ☎0 7737 5023; www.coralhaadrin.com; Hat Rin Nai; bungalows 500-1000B; ❄@≋) This party-centric paradise has firmly planted its flag in 'Backpackerland' as the go-to spot for a booze-addled rompfest. By day, sun-worshippers straddle beachside chaises. Then, by night, like a vampire, Coral transforms into a sinister pool-party machine fuelled by one too many vodka Red Bulls.

Same Same GUEST HOUSE $
(Map p560; ☎0 7737 5200; www.same-same.com; Ban Hat Rin; r 500-800B; ❄🛜) Although still a super-sociable spot for Scandinavians during the Full Moon madness, Same Same is but a faint flicker of what it used to be – especially during the quieter parts of the month.

Paradise Bungalows BUNGALOWS $
(Map p560; ☎0 7737 5244; Hat Rin Nok; bungalows 300-1200B; ❄) The world-famous Full Moon Party was hatched at this scruffy batch of bungalows, and the place has been living on its name fame ever since. The backpackers keep on coming to wax nostalgic, although the grounds are starting to look more like a junkyard now that the family has divvied up to land into several small 'resorts'. Paradise lost.

Stroll down Sunset Rd to find the following:

Neptune's Villa RESORT $$
(Map p560; ☎0 7737 5251; http://neptunesvilla.net; Hat Rin Nai; r from 2000B; ❄) An old favourite among travellers, Neptune's is an ever-expanding spot with a mixed bag of accommodation spread across several motel-style units.

Rin Beach Resort RESORT $$
(Map p560; ☎0 7737 5112; www.rinbeachresort.com; Hat Rin Nai; bungalows 1200-10,000B; ❄🛜≋) Giant amphorae, spewing forth gushes of water, welcome weary travellers as they tumble off the wooden ferry. Cottages are bright and airy with dark cherry-wood accents and colourful sutra paintings.

Friendly Resort RESORT $$
(Map p560; ☎0 7737 5167; friendly_resort@hotmail.com; Hat Rin Nai; r from 1000B; ❄🛜≋) Looking out over the pier, Friendly has a tangle of accommodation wrapped around a small central pool.

Blue Marine BUNGALOWS $
(Map p560; ☎0 7737 5079; www.bluemarinephangan.com; Hat Rin Nai; bungalows 600-1200B; ❄🛜) Prim concrete bungalows topped by shimmering blue-tiled roofs.

SOUTHERN BEACHES

The accommodation along the southern coast is the best bang for your baht on Ko Pha-Ngan. There are fleeting views of the islands in the Ang Thong Marine National Park; however, the southern beaches don't have the postcard-worthy turquoise waters you might be longing for. This section starts at the port in Thong Sala and follows the coast east towards Hat Rin.

Ban Tai

The waters at Ban Tai tend to be shallow and opaque, especially during low season, but lodging options are well-priced compared to other parts of the island, and you're not too far from Hat Rin.

TOP CHOICE Coco Garden BUNGALOWS $

(📞0 7737 7721, 08 6073 1147; www.cocogardens.com; bungalows 450-1250B; ❄️🛜) The best budget spot along the southern coast, Coco Garden one-ups the nearby resorts with well-manicured grounds and sparkling bungalows that are almost pathologically clean.

B52 BUNGALOWS $$

(www.b52-beach-resort-phangan.info; bungalows 1650-4000B; ❄️🛜🏊) Find your very own love shack at B52's campus of Thai-styled bungalows sporting plenty of thatch, polished concrete floors and rustic tropical tree trunks.

Milky Bay Resort RESORT $$$

(📞0 7723 8566; http://milkybaythailand.com; bungalows 2300-13,200B; ❄️@🛜🏊) Milky white walls, which permeate the grounds, are peppered with large black stones resembling the spots on a cow. These bovine bulwarks snake through the resort linking the airy, thatched bungalows to the sea.

Ban Khai

Like Ban Tai, the beaches aren't the most stunning, but the accommodation is cheap and there are beautiful views of Ang Thong Marine National Park in the distance.

Boom's Cafe Bungalows BUNGALOWS $

(📞0 7723 8318; www.boomscafe.com; bungalows 400-1000B;❄️) Staying at Boom's is like visiting the Thai family you never knew you had. The friendly owners lovingly tend their sandy acreage and dote on the contented clientele. No one seems to mind that there's no swimming pool, since the curling tide rolls right up to your doorstep. Boom's is located at the far eastern corner of Ban Khai, near Hat Rin.

Mac Bay BUNGALOWS $

(📞0 7723 8443; bungalows 500-1500B; ❄️🏊) Home to the Black Moon Party (another lunar excuse for Ko Pha-Ngan to go wild), Mac Bay is a sandy slice of Ban Khai where even the cheaper bungalows are spic and span. At beer o'clock, grab a shaded spot on the sand and watch the sun dance amorphous shadows over the distant islands of Ang Thong Marine Park.

Morning Star BUNGALOWS $$

(📞0 7737 7756; www.morningstar-resort.info; bungalows 1600-5390B; ❄️🛜🏊) This collection of

wooden and concrete jungle cottages has spotless interiors; some rooms are furnished with noticeably ornate dressers and vanities, others have subtle dark-wood trimming. A dozen white wooden beach chairs orbit the adorable kidney-bean-shaped pool.

WEST COAST BEACHES

Now that there are two smooth roads between Thong Sala and Chalok Lam, the west coast has seen a lot of development. The atmosphere is a pleasant mix between the east coast's quiet seclusion and Hat Rin's sociable vibe, although some of the beaches along the western shores (particularly towards the south) aren't as picturesque as the other parts of the island.

Ao Nai Wok to Si Thanu

Close to Thong Sala, the resorts peppered along this breezy strip mingle with patches of gnarled mangroves. Despite the lack of appealing beaches, the prices are cheap and the sunsets are memorable.

TOP CHOICE Chills Resort RESORT $$

(📞08 9875 2100; www.chillsresort.com; Ao Srithanu; r from 1200B; ❄️🛜🏊) Set along a stunning and secluded stretch of stony outcrops, Chills' cluster of delightfully simple-but-modern rooms all have peaceful ocean views letting in plenty of sunlight and sea breezes. The natural rock-pool perched along the breakers is the perfect place to swig an afternoon cocktail while watching the sunset.

TOP CHOICE Shambhala Bungalow Village BUNGALOWS $

(📞08 9875 2100; www.shambhala-phangan.com; Ao Nai Wok; bungalows 600-1200B; ❄️🛜) Rather than bulldozing tired old beachside bungalows, the owners of Shambhala have lovingly restored a batch of huts and added loads of personal touches that make this not only a memorable place to stay, but also a very comfortable one for those with small coffers. Expect fresh linen, carved wood, artistic lighting and neatly designed bathrooms.

Loy Fa BUNGALOWS $

(📞0 7737 7319; loyfabungalow@yahoo.com; Ao Srithanu; bungalows 300-800B; ❄️) Loy Fa scores high marks for its friendly, French-speaking Thai staff, charming gardens and sturdy huts guarding sweeping ocean views. Modern bungalows tumble down the promontory onto an uberprivate sliver of ash-coloured sand.

Grand Sea Resort
RESORT $$

(☎0 7737 7777; www.grandsearesort.com; Ao Nai Wok; bungalows 1200-3000B; ✸🛜🌐) A good choice for those wanting a bit of sand close to Thong Sala, Grand Sea feels like a collection of wooden Thai spirit houses.

Hat Chaophao

Like Hat Yao up the coast, this rounded beach is lined with a variety of bungalow operations. There's an inland lake further south, and a 7-Eleven to cure your midnight munchies.

Sunset Cove
BUNGALOWS $$

(☎0 7734 9211; www.thaisunsetcove.com; bungalows 1200-3580B; ✸@🛜🌐) There's a feeling of Zen symmetry among the forested assortment of boutique bungalows; the towering bamboo shoots are evenly spaced along the cobbled paths weaving through brush and boulders. The beachside abodes are particularly elegant, sporting slatted rectangular windows and barrel-basined bathtubs.

Pha-Ngan Paragon
BUNGALOWS $$$

(☎08 4728 6064; www.phanganparagon.com; bungalows 2250-13,100B; ✸@🛜🌐) A tiny hideaway with seven rooms, the Paragon has decor that incorporates stylistic elements from ancient Khmer, India and Thailand, without forfeiting any modern amenities. The 'royal bedroom' deserves a special mention – apparently the canopied bed has been imported from Kashmir.

Hat Yao & Hat Son

One of the busier beaches along the west coast, Hat Yao sports a swimmable beach, numerous resorts and a few extra services such as ATMs and convenience stores.

Shiralea
BUNGALOWS $

(☎08 0719 9256; www.shiralea.com; Hat Yao; bungalows 500B; ✸🛜🌐) Although this batch of fresh-faced poolside bungalows is not right on the beach (about 100m away), you'll be hard-pressed to find a better deal on the island. Reefers, the on-site dive outfit offers world-class diving at your doorstep, and don't forget to ask the friendly owner where the name Shiralea comes from – we're pretty sure you'll be quite surprised.

Haad Yao Bay View Resort
RESORT $$$

(☎0 7734 9193; www.haadyao-bayviewresort.com; Hat Yao; r & bungalows 1500-7000B; ✸@🛜🌐) Still sparkling after a facelift in 2008, this conglomeration of bungalows and hotel-style accommodation looks like a tropical mirage on Hat Yao's northern headland. Vacationers, in various states of undress, linger around the large turquoise swimming pool catching rays and Zs. Others nest in their private suites amid polished hardwood floors and wicker daybeds.

Haad Son Resort
RESORT $$

(☎0 7734 9104; www.haadson.info; Hat Son; bungalows 1000-8000B; ✸@🛜🌐) The word 'complex' has a double meaning at this vast resort; we suggest leaving a trail of breadcrumbs along the serpentine paths if you ever want to find the way back to your room. The poshest rooms aren't worth the baht, so go for the budget digs; they're simple, but you'll have access to all of the on-site amenities.

Tantawan Bungalows
BUNGALOWS $

(☎0 7734 9108; www.tantawanbungalow.com; Hat Son; bungalows 450-550B; 🌐) This charming teak nest, tucked among jungle fronds, is dripping with clinking chandeliers made from peach coral and khaki-coloured seashells. Guests can take a dip in the trapezoidal swimming pool or enjoy the sunrise on their small bamboo porches. Don't forget to try the tasty on-site restaurant. Diners sit in a sea of geometric cushions while gobbling up some of the tastiest Thai and French-inspired dishes on the island.

High Life
BUNGALOWS $

(☎0 7734 9114; www.highlifebungalow.com; Hat Yao; bungalows 500-2000B; ✸🛜🌐) We can't decide what's more conspicuous: the dramatic ocean views from the infinity-edged swimming pool, or the blatant double entendre in the resort's name. True to its moniker, the 25 bungalows, of various shapes and sizes, sit on a palmed outcropping of granite soaring high above the cerulean sea. Advance bookings will set you back an extra 200B.

Haad Yao See Through Boutique Resort
HOTEL $$

(☎0 7734 9315; www.haadyao.net; Hat Yao; r from 1750B; ✸🛜) After a slice of Hat Yao beach was cut up among brothers, 'See Through' came into existence along a thin tract of land. Rooms are decorated with a vibrant swatchbook of yellows, greens and reds, however the exterior – an imposing block of polished concrete – looks more construction site than boutique chic.

Hat Salad

Hat Salad is our favourite beach on the west coast, and it isn't short on quality digs set along the inviting sand.

Cookies Salad   RESORT $$
(☑0 7734 9125, 08 3181 7125; www.cookies-phangan.com; bungalows 1500-3000B; ☀) The resort with a tasty name has delicious Balinese-styled bungalows orbiting a two-tiered lap pool tiled in various shades of blue. Shaggy thatching and dense tropical foliage gives the realm a certain rustic quality, although you won't want for creature comforts.

Green Papaya   BUNGALOWS $$$
(☑0 7737 4182; www.greenpapayaresort.com; bungalows 3600-8500B; ✴@☎☀) The polished wooden bungalows at Green Papaya are a clear standout along the lovely beach at Hat Salad, however they come at quite a hefty price.

Salad Hut   BUNGALOWS $$
(☑0 7734 9246; www.saladhut.com; bungalows 1400-4000B; ✴@☎☀) Wholly unpretentious yet sharing a beach with some distinctly upscale options, this small clutch of Thai-style bungalows sits but a stone's throw from the rolling tide. Watch the sun gently set below the waves from your lacquered teak porch.

Salad Beach Resort   BUNGALOWS $$
(☑0 7734 9149; www.phangan-saladbeachresort.com; bungalows 1900-4900B; ✴@☎☀) A full-service retreat along the sands of Salad. Room decor employs an unusual palette of colours, but the grounds are tasteful and understated – especially around the pool.

Ao Mae Hat

The northwest tip of the island has excellent ocean vistas, and little Ko Ma is connected to Pha-Ngan by a stunning sandbar.

Royal Orchid   BUNGALOWS $
(☑0 7737 4182; royal_orchid_maehaad@hotmail.com; bungalows 300-800B; ✴@) Handsome backpacker bungalows are arranged like a zipper along a slender garden path – most have fleeting views of the serene beach and idyllic sandbar that extends to scenic Ko Ma offshore.

NORTHERN BEACHES

Stretching from Chalok Lam to Thong Nai Pan, the dramatic northern coast is a wild jungle with several stunning and secluded beaches – it's the most scenic coast on the island.

Chalok Lam (Chaloklum) & Hat Khom

The cramped fishing village at Chalok Lam is like no other place on Ko Pha-Ngan. The conglomeration of teak shanties and huts is a palpable reminder that the wide-reaching hand of globalisation has yet to touch some parts of the world. Sŏrng·tǎa·ou ply the route from here to Thong Sala for around 100B per person. There's a dirt road leading from Chalok Lam to Hat Khom, and water taxis are available as well (50B to 100B).

Malibu   BUNGALOWS $
(☑0 7737 4013; Chalok Lam; bungalows 300-1300B; ✴) The casual vibe around the large backyard beach (over the lagoon bridge) sets Malibu apart from the other budget bungalows around Chalok Lam. A drink-wielding hut, stationed on the private sandbar, lures guests of every ilk. The cheapest huts are a bit rough around the edges, although the new round bungalow-like concoctions are overpriced.

Mandalai   HOTEL $$$
(☑0 7737 4316; www.mymandalai.com; Chalok Lam; r 2750-5600B; ✴☀) Like an ash-white Riyadh from a distant Arabian land, this small boutique hotel quietly towers over the surrounding shantytown of fishermen's huts. Floor-to-ceiling windows command views of tangerine-coloured fishing boats in the bay, and there's an intimate wading pool hidden in the inner cloister.

Bottle Beach (Hat Khuat)

This isolated dune has garnered a reputation as a low-key getaway, and has thus become quite popular. During high season, places can fill up fast so it's best to try to arrive early. Grab a long-tail taxi boat from Chalok Lam for 50B to 120B (depending on the boat's occupancy).

Bottle Beach II   BUNGALOWS $
(☑0 7744 5156; bungalows 350-500B) At the far eastern corner of the beach, this is the spot where penny pinchers can live out their castaway fantasies.

Smile   BUNGALOWS $
(☑08 1956 3133; smilebeach@hotmail.com; bungalows 400-700B) At the far western corner of the beach, Smile features an assortment of wooden huts that climb up a forested hill. The two-storey bungalows (700B) are our favourite.

Thong Nai Pan

The pair of rounded bays at Thong Nai Pan looks a bit like buttocks; Ao Thong Nai Pan Yai (*yai* means 'big') is the southern half, and Ao Thong Nai Pan Noi (*noi* means 'little') curves just above. These beaches have been increasing in popularity over the last few years, as bamboo bungalows are being razed to make room for elaborate resorts.

Anantara Rasananda RESORT $$$
(☑0 7723 9555; www.rasananda.com; villas from 5000B; ✳@☎☁) Rasananda represents the future of Ko Pha-Ngan. This attempt at five-star luxury is a sweeping sand-side property with a smattering of semi-detached villas – many bedecked with private plunge pools. A savvy mix of modern and traditional *săh-lah* styling prevails, and new Anantara management means that this high-end stalwart is here to stay.

Dolphin BUNGALOWS $
(bungalows 500-1400B;✳☎) This hidden retreat gives yuppie travellers a chance to rough it in style, while granola-types will soak up every inch of the laid-back charm. Quiet afternoons are spent lounging on the comfy cushions in one of the small pagodas hidden throughout the jungle. Lodging is only available on a first-come basis.

Longtail Beach Resort BUNGALOWS $
(☑0 7744 5018; www.longtailbeachresort.com; bungalows 390-1150B; ✳☎) Effortlessly adorable, and one of the last remaining batches of beach bungalows in the area, Longtail offers backpackers a taste of Pha-Ngan's past with its charming thatch-and-bamboo abodes.

EAST COAST BEACHES

Robinson Crusoe, eat your heart out. The east coast is the ultimate hermit hang-out. For the most part you'll have to hire a boat to get to these beaches, but water taxis are available in Thong Sala and Hat Rin.

Than Sadet & Thong Reng

Mai Pen Rai BUNGALOWS $
(☑0 7744 5090; www.thansadet.com; bungalows 600B; @) *Mai pen rai* is the Thai equivalent of 'don't worry, be happy', which isn't too surprising since this bay elicits nothing but sedate smiles. Bungalows mingle with Plaa's next door on the hilly headland, and sport panels of straw weaving with gabled roofs.

Treehouse BUNGALOWS $
(treehouse.kp@googlemail.com; bungalows from 200B) The legendary backpacker hang-out of

Ko Chang (the big Ko Chang) has recently set up shop along the secluded waters of Thong Reng. Follow the cheery plastic flowers over the hill from Than Sadet to find uberbasic digs drenched in bright shades of paint.

Hat Thian

TOP CHOICE The Sanctuary BUNGALOWS $$
(☑08 1271 3614; www.thesanctuarythailand.com; dm 200B, bungalows 450-5450B) If you're looking for Alex Garland's mythical beach, this is about as close as it gets. A friendly enclave promoting relaxation, the Sanctuary is an inviting haven offering splendid lodgings while also functioning as a holistic retreat (think yoga classes and detox sessions). Accommodation, in various manifestations of twigs, is scattered around the resort, married to the natural surroundings. You'll want to Nama-stay forever.

Beam Bungalows BUNGALOWS $
(☑0 7927 2854; bungalows 300-700B) Beam is set back from the beach and tucked behind a coconut palm grove. Charming wooden huts have dangling hammocks out front, and big bay windows face the ocean through the swaying palms.

Hat Yuan

Hat Yuan has a few bungalow operations, and is quite secluded as there are no roads connecting this little beach to Hat Rin down the coast.

Barcelona BUNGALOWS $
(☑0 7737 5113; bungalows 300-700B) Solid wood huts come in two shades: natural wood or creamy white. They climb up the hill on stilts behind a palm garden and have good vistas and jovial staff.

✗ Eating

Ko Pha-Ngan is no culinary capital, especially since most visitors quickly absorb the lazy lifestyle and wind up eating at their accommodation. Those with an adventurous appetite should check out the island's centre of local commerce, Thong Sala.

HAT RIN

This bustling 'burb has the largest conglomeration of restaurants and bars on the island, yet most of them are pretty lousy. The infamous Chicken Corner is a popular intersection stocked with several faves such as **Mr K Thai Food** (Map p560; Ban Hat Rin; dishes 30-80B) and **Mama Schnitzel** (Map p560;

Ban Hat Rin; dishes 40-100B), which promise to cure any case of the munchies, be it noon or midnight.

Lazy House INTERNATIONAL $$
(Map p560; Hat Rin Nai; dishes 90-270B; ⊘lunch & dinner) Back in the day, this joint was the owner's apartment – everyone liked his cooking so much that he decided to turn the place into a restaurant and hang-out spot. Today, Lazy House is easily one of Hat Rin's best places to veg out in front of a movie with a scrumptious shepherd's pie.

Little Home THAI $
(Map p560; Ban Hat Rin; mains from 40B; ⊘breakfast, lunch & dinner) With no design aesthetic whatsoever, Little Home woos the masses with cheap, flavourful Thai grub that's gobbled up with alacrity among wooden tables and flimsy plastic chairs.

Monna Lisa ITALIAN $$
(Map p560; Hat Rin Nai; pizza & pasta from 200B; ⊘breakfast, lunch & dinner) The best spot in Hat Rin for a pizza, Monna Lisa is a relatively new operation run by a team of friendly Italians. The mushroom and ham pizza practically knocked our socks off – as did the homemade truffle pasta.

Nic's INTERNATIONAL $$
(Map p560; Ban Hat Rin; mains 80-280B; ⊘dinner) A dizzying realm of polished concrete and coloured pillows, Nic's – at the back of Hat Rin's lake – slings tasty pizzas and tapas every evening. Slurp a Singha during the 6pm-to-8pm happy hour.

Lucky Crab SEAFOOD $$
(Map p560; Hat Rin Nai; dishes 100-400B; ⊘lunch & dinner) Lucky Crab is your best bet for seafood in Hat Rin. Rows of freshly caught creatures are presented nightly atop miniature longtail boats loaded with ice. Once you've picked your prey, grab a table inside amid dangling plants and charming stone furnishings.

Om Ganesh INDIAN $$
(Map p560; Hat Rin Nai; dishes 70-190B; ⊘breakfast, lunch & dinner) Customers meditate over curries, biryani rice, roti and lassis though the local expats joke that every dish tastes the same. Platters start at 350B.

Same Same Burger BURGER $$
(Map p560; www.same-same.com; Hat Rin Nai; burgers 180-230B; ⊘lunch & dinner) Owned by the folks who run the backpacker digs with

the *same same* name, this bright-red burger joint is the *same same* as McDonald's (except pricier).

SOUTHERN BEACHES
On Saturday evenings from 4pm to 10pm, a side street in the eastern part of Thong Sala becomes **Walking Street** – a bustling pedestrian zone mostly filled with locals hawking their wares to other islanders. There's plenty on offer, from clothing to food. Be sure to try the delicious red prok with gravy (40B) at Lang Tang – you'll find it in glass cases next to a large English sign saying 'Numpanich'.

Night Market MARKET $
(Thong Sala; dishes 25-180B; ⊘dinner) A heady mix of steam and snacking locals, Thong Sala's night market is a must for those looking for a dose of culture while nibbling on a low-priced snack. The best place to grab some cheap grub is the stall in the far right corner with a large white banner. Hit up the vendor next door for tasty seafood platters, such as red snapper served over a bed of thick noodles. Banana pancakes and fruit smoothies abound for dessert.

Kaito JAPANESE $$
(Thong Sala; dishes from 130B; ⊘dinner Thu-Mon) Authentic Japanese imports are the speciality here – slurp an Asahi while savouring your tangy seaweed salad and *tonkatsu* (pork cutlet). The upstairs level has cosy cushion seating while the main sitting area is flanked with *manga* and pocket-sized Japanese novels.

Mason's Arms BRITISH $$
(Thong Sala; mains 160-350B; ⊘lunch & dinner) Suddenly, a clunky structure emerges from the swaying palms; it's a Tudor-style manse, plucked directly from Stratford-upon-Avon and plunked down in the steamy jungle. This lodge-like lair is one blood pudding away from being an official British colony. The fish 'n' chips is a local favourite.

Pizza Chiara ITALIAN $$
(Thong Sala; pizzas 180-320B; ⊘lunch & dinner) The quintessential chequered tablecloths confirm it (in case you didn't guess from the name): Pizza Chiara is all about tasty Italian fare. Go for the Pizza Cecco smothered with prosciutto, salami, mushrooms and *cotto* cheese.

Ando Loco MEXICAN $
(Ban Tai; mains from 59B; ⊘dinner) This outdoor Mexican hang-out looks like an animation

cell from a vintage Hanna-Barbera cartoon, with assorted kitschy accoutrements such as papier-mâché cacti. Down a super-sized margarita and show your skills on the beach volleyball court. Ando Loco closes during low season (around September to December).

OTHER BEACHES

TOP CHOICE Sanctuary HEALTH FOOD **$$**
(Hat Thian; mains from 130B) Forget what you know about health food: the Sanctuary's restaurant proves that wholesome eats can also be delicious. Enjoy a tasty parade of plates – from Indian pakoras to crunchy Vietnamese spring rolls – as an endless playlist of music (undoubtedly the island's best) wafts overhead. Don't forget to wash it all down with a shot of neon-green wheatgrass. Yum!

Cucina Italiana ITALIAN **$$**
(Jenny's; Chalok Lam; pizza 180B; ☉dinner) Cucina Italiana has a cult following on Ko Pha-Ngan. The friendly Italian chef is passionate about his food, and creates all of his dishes from scratch. On Thursday and Sunday you can order unlimited toppings on your oven-roasted pizza for only 180B.

Peppercorn STEAKHOUSE **$$**
(www.peppercornphangan.com; Sri Thanu; mains 160-400; ☉2-10pm Mon-Sat) Escargot and succulent steaks in a rickety jungle cottage? You bet. Peppercorn may be tucked in the brush away from the sea, but that shouldn't detract foodies from seeking out one of Pha-Ngan's best attempts at highbrow international cuisine.

Cookies Salad THAI **$$**
(Hat Salad; mains from 100B; ☉breakfast, lunch & dinner) Worth tracking down if you're staying on the west coast, this casual restaurant, perched atop a cliff on the south side of Hat Salad, offers a stunning assortment of Thai treats (don't miss the Penang curry) and unique smoothies (including a rich nutella swirl). Sadly cookie salads are not on offer.

🍷 Drinking

Every month, on the night of the full moon, pilgrims pay tribute to the party gods with trance-like dancing, wild screaming and glow-in-the-dark body paint. The throngs of bucket-sippers and fire twirlers gather on the infamous Sunrise Beach (Hat Rin Nok) and party until the sun replaces the moon in the sky.

A few other noteworthy spots can be found around the island for those seeking something a bit mellower.

HAT RIN
Hat Rin is the beating heart of the legendary Full Moon fun, and the area can get pretty wound up even without the influence of lunar phases. When the moon isn't lighting up the night sky, partygoers flock to other spots on the island's south side. See the boxed text on p558 for details. The following party venues flank Hat Rin's infamous Sunrise Beach from south to north.

Rock BAR, CLUB
(Map p560) Great views of the party from the elevated terrace on the far south side of the beach.

Club Paradise BAR, CLUB
(Map p560) Paradise basks in its celebrity status as the genesis of the lunar *loco*-motion.

Drop-In Bar BAR, CLUB
(Map p560) This dance shack blasts the chart toppers that we all secretly love. The other nights of the year are equally as boisterous.

Zoom/Vinyl BAR, CLUB
(Map p560) An ear-popping trance venue.

Cactus Bar BAR, CLUB
(Map p560) Smack in the centre of Hat Rin Nok, Cactus pumps out a healthy mix of old school tunes, hip-hop and R&B.

Sunrise BAR, CLUB
(Map p560) A newer spot on the sand where trance beats shake the graffiti-ed walls.

Tommy BAR, CLUB
(Map p560) One of Hat Rin's largest venues lures the masses with black lights and trance music blaring on the sound system. Drinks are dispensed from a large ark-like bar.

Mellow Mountain BAR, CLUB
(Map p560) Also called 'Mushy Mountain' (you'll know why when you get there), this trippy hang-out sits at the northern edge of Hat Rin Nok delivering stellar views of the shenanigans below.

OTHER BEACHES
Eagle Pub BAR
(Hat Yao) At the southern end of Hat Yao, this drink-dealing shack, built right into the rock face, is tattooed with the neon graffiti of virtually every person who's passed out on the

lime green patio furniture after too many *caipirinhas*.

Jam
BAR

(Hin Wong; www.thejamphangan.com) It's DIY live music at this friendly nightspot on the west coast. Saturday nights are open mic, and the rest of the week you'll usually catch a few locals jamming on their guitars.

Pirates Bar
BAR

(Hat Chaophao) This wacky drinkery is a replica of a pirate ship built into the cliffs. When you're sitting on the deck and the tide is high (and you've had a couple drinks), you can almost believe you're out at sea. These guys host the well-attended Moon Set parties, three days before Hat Rin gets pumpin' for the Full Moon fun.

Sheesha Bar
BAR

(Chalok Lam) The antithesis of grungy Hat Rin, Sheesha Bar swaps buckets of Samsung for designer drinks. The enticing patchwork of beige sandstone and horizontal slats of mahogany fit right in with the arabesque Mandalai Hotel across the street (owned by the same family).

Flip Flop Pharmacy
BAR

(Thong Nai Pan) This open-air bar on the sands of Thong Nai Pan is the area's preferred hang-out spot.

Amsterdam
BAR

(Ao Plaay Laem) Near Hat Chaophao on the west coast, Amsterdam attracts tourists and locals from all over the island, who are looking for a chill spot to watch the sunset.

ℹ Information

Dangers & Annoyances

Some of your fondest vacation memories may be forged on Ko Pha-Ngan; just be mindful of the following situations that can seriously tarnish your experience on this hot-blooded jungle island.

DRUGS You're relaxing on the beach when suddenly a local walks up and offers you some local herb at a ridiculously low price. 'No thanks,' you say, knowing that the penalties for drug use in Thailand are fierce. But the vendor drops his price even more and practically offers you the weed for free. Too good to be true? Obviously. As soon as you take a toke, the seller rats you out to the cops and you're whisked away to the local prison where you must pay a wallet-busting fine. This type of scenario happens all the time on Ko Pha-Ngan so it's best to avoid the call of the ganja.

Here's another important thing to remember: your travel insurance does not cover any drug-related injury or treatment. Drug-related freak-outs *do* happen – we've heard first-hand accounts of partiers slipping into extended periods of delirium. Suan Saranrom (Garden of Joys) Psychiatric Hospital in Surat Thani has to take on extra staff during full-moon periods to handle the number of *fa·ràng* who freak out on magic mushrooms, acid or other abundantly available hallucinogens.

WOMEN TRAVELLERS Female travellers should be extra careful when partying on the island. We've received many reports about drug- and alcohol-related rape (and these situations are not limited to Full Moon parties). Another disturbing problem is the unscrupulous behaviour of some of the local motorcycle taxi drivers. Several complaints have been filed about drivers groping female passengers; there are even reports of severe sexual assaults.

MOTORCYCLES Ko Pha-Ngan has more motorcycle accidents than injuries incurred from Full Moon tomfoolery. Nowadays there's a system of paved roads, but much of it is a labyrinth of rutty dirt-and-mud paths. The island is also very hilly, and even if the road is paved, it can be too difficult for most to take on. The *very* steep road to Hat Rin is a perfect case in point. The island now has a special ambulance that trolls the island helping injured bikers.

Emergency

Main police station (Map p557; ☎ 0 7737 7114, 191) Located about 2km north of Thong Sala. The police station in Hat Rin (near Hat Rin school) will not let you file a report; to do so you must go to Thong Sala. Local police have been known to charge 200B to file a report. Do not pay this – it should be free. Note that if you are arrested you do have the right to an embassy phone call; you do not have to agree to accept the 'interpreter' you are offered.

Internet Access

Hat Rin and Thong Sala are the main centres of internet activity, but every beach with development now offers access. Rates are generally 2B per minute, with a 10B to 20B minimum and discounts if you stay on for more than an hour. Places offering a rate of 1B per minute usually have turtle-speed connections.

Laundry

If you got fluorescent body paint on your clothes during your full-moon romp, don't bother sending them to the cleaners – the paint will never come out. Trust us, we tried. For your other washing needs, there are heaps of places that will gladly wash your clothes. Prices hover around 40B per kilo, and express cleanings shouldn't be more than 60B per kilo.

Medical Services

Medical services can be a little crooked in Ko Pha-Ngan – expect unstable prices and under-qualified doctors. Many clinics charge a 3000B entrance fee before treatment. Serious medical issues should be dealt with on nearby Ko Samui.

Ko Pha-Ngan Hospital (Map p557; ☎0 7737 7034; Thong Sala; ☻24hr) About 2.5km north of Thong Sala; offers 24-hour emergency services.

Money

Thong Sala, Ko Pha-Ngan's financial 'capital', has plenty of banks, currency converters and several Western Union offices. Hat Rin has numerous ATMs and a couple of banks at the pier. There are also ATMs in Hat Yao, Chaloklum and Thong Nai Pan.

Post

Main post office (Map p560; ☻8.30am-4.30pm Mon-Fri, 9am-noon Sat) In Thong Sala; there's a smaller office right near the pier in Hat Rin.

Tourist information

There are no government-run Tourist Authority of Thailand (TAT) offices on Ko Pha-Ngan, instead tourists get their information from local travel agencies and brochures. Most agencies are clumped around Hat Rin and Thong Sala. Agents take a small commission on each sale, but collusion keeps prices relatively stable and standardised. Choose an agent you trust if you are spending a lot of money – faulty bookings do happen on Ko Pha-Ngan, especially since the island does not have a unit of tourist police.

Several mini-magazines also offer comprehensive information about the island's accommodation, restaurants, activities and Full Moon Parties. Our favourite option is the pocket-sized **Phangan Info** (www.phangan.info).

Backpackers Information Centre (Map p560; ☎0 7737 5535; www.backpackersthailand.com; Hat Rin) A must for travellers looking to book high-quality tours (diving, live-aboards, jungle safaris etc) and transport. Not just for backpackers, it's an expat-run travel agency that offers peace of mind with every purchase – travellers are provided with the mobile phone number of the owners should any problems arise. It also runs the Crystal Dive shop next door.

Websites

Backpackers Thailand (www.backpackersthailand.com) Everything you need to know about Ko Pha-Ngan, from booking accommodation to finding out the Full Moon schedule. Doubles as a vast resource for the whole country as well.

❶ Getting There & Away

As always, the cost and departure times are subject to change. Rough waves are known to cancel ferries between the months of October and December.

Bangkok, Hua Hin & Chumphon

The Lomprayah and Seatran Discovery service has bus-boat combination packages that depart from Bangkok and pass through Hua Hin and Chumphon. It is also quite hassle-free to take the train from Bangkok to Chumphon and switch to a ferry service (it works out to be about the same price and the train is comfier if you get a couchette). Travellers can also opt for the slightly cheaper government bus to Bangkok. For additional information about travelling through Chumphon see p533.

Ko Samui

There are around a dozen daily departures between Ko Pha-Ngan and Ko Samui. These boats leave throughout the day from 7am to 6pm and take from 20 minutes to an hour. All leave from either Thong Sala or Hat Rin on Ko Pha-Ngan. The *Haad Rin Queen* goes back and forth between Hat Rin and Big Buddha Beach on Samui.

Ko Tao

Ko Tao-bound Lomprayah ferries depart from Thong Sala on Ko Pha-Ngan at 8.30am and 1pm and arrive at 9.45am and 2.15pm. The Seatran service departs from Thong Sala at 8.30am and 2pm daily. Taxis depart Hat Rin for Thong Sala one hour before the boat departure. The cheaper-but-slower Songserm leaves Ko Pha-Ngan at 12.30pm and alights at 2.30pm.

Surat Thani & the Andaman Coast

Combination boat-bus tickets are available at any travel agency. Simply tell them your desired destination and they will sell you the necessary links in the transport chain. Most travellers will pass through Surat Thani as they swap coasts. There are approximately six daily departures between Ko Pha-Ngan and Krabi on the Raja Car Ferry, Songserm or Seatran. These boats leave from Thong Sala throughout the day from 7am to 8pm. Every night, depending on the weather, a night boat runs from Surat, departing at 11pm. Boats in the opposite direction leave Ko Pha-Ngan at 10pm. Visit **Backpackers Thailand** (www.backpackersthailand.com) to get detailed departure times for additional Andaman destinations.

❶ Getting Around

Motorbikes You can rent motorcycles all over the island for 150B to 250B per day. Always wear a helmet – it's the law on Ko Pha-Ngan, and local policemen are starting to enforce it. If you plan on riding over dirt tracks it is imperative that you rent a bike comparable to a Honda MTX125 – gearless scooters cannot make the journey. Bicycle rentals are discouraged unless you're fit enough to take on Lance Armstrong.

Sŏrng·tăa·ou Pick-up trucks and *sŏrng·tăa·ou* chug along the island's major roads and the riding rates double after sunset. Ask your accommodation about free or discount transfers when you leave the island. The trip from Thong Sala to Hat Rin is 100B; further beaches will set you back around 150B.

Water taxi Long-tail boats depart from Thong Sala, Chalok Lam and Hat Rin, heading to a variety of far-flung destinations such as Hat Khuat (Bottle Beach) and Ao Thong Nai Pan. Expect to pay anywhere from 50B for a short trip, and up to 300B for a lengthier journey. You can charter a private boat ride from beach to beach for about 150B per 15 minutes of travel.

Ko Tao

เกาะเต่า

POP 1382

First there was Ko Samui, then Ko Pha-Ngan; now, the cult of Ko Tao ('Ko Taoism' perhaps?) has emerged along Thailand's crystalline Gulf coast. Today, thousands of visitors come to worship the turquoise waters offshore, and quite often they stay. The secret to Ko Tao's undeniable appeal? Simple: although the island is only 21 sq km, tiny Tao sure knows how to pack it in – there's something for everyone, and nothing is in moderation. Diving enthusiasts cavort with sharks and rays in a playground of tangled neon coral. Hikers and hermits can re-enact an episode from *Lost* in the dripping coastal jungles. And when you're Robinson Crusoe-ed out, hit the pumpin' bar scene that rages on until dawn.

Many years have passed since the first backpacker came to the scrubby island and planted a flag in the name of self-respecting shoestring travellers everywhere (hello pizza parlours and ladyboy shows), but fret not, there's still plenty of time to join the tribe. Ko Tao has several years to go before corporate resort owners bulldoze the remaining rustic cottages, and visitors start discussing stockholdings rather than sea creatures spotted on their latest dive.

🏃 Activities

Diving

Never been diving before? Ko Tao is *the* place to lose your scuba virginity. The island issues more scuba certifications than any-

where else in the world. The shallow bays scalloping the island are the perfect spot for newbie divers to take their first stab at scuba. On shore, over 40 dive centres are ready to saddle you up with some gear and teach you the ropes in a three-and-a-half-day Open Water certification course. We know, we know, homework on a holiday sucks, but the intense competition among scuba schools means that certification prices are unbeatably low, and the standards of service are top notch, as dozens of dive shops vie for your baht.

It's no surprise that this underwater playground has become exceptionally popular with beginners; the waters are crystal clear, there are loads of neon reefs, and temperatures feel like bathwater. The best dive sites are found at offshore pinnacles within a 20km radius of the island (see the boxed text p573), but seasoned scubaholics almost always prefer the top-notch sites along the Andaman Coast. The local marine wildlife includes groupers, moray eels, batfish, bannerfish, barracudas, titan triggerfish, angelfish, clownfish (Nemos), stingrays, reef sharks, and frequent visits by almighty whale sharks.

When you alight at the pier in Mae Hat, swarms of touts will try to coax you into

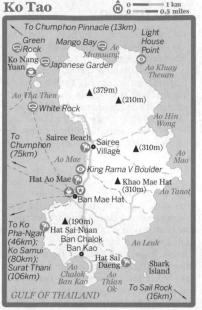

Ko Tao

ZERO TO HERO

It's the oldest story in the book: 'I came to Ko Tao on vacation and six months later I'm still here!' Seems like the island's magical magnetic energy catches hold of everyone, so don't be surprised if you too find yourself altering plane tickets.

For those of you who anticipate embracing the castaway lifestyle, consider going from 'Zero to Hero' as they call it on Ko Tao. Over the last few years, several of the savvier diving operators started package deals where you can go from scuba newbie to pro over the course of a couple of months. You'll graduate through four levels of diving certifications, 'intern' as a divemaster at your dive school, then take a stab at the instructor program. Prices hover around 80,000B and include all the bells and whistles necessary to turn you into a fish. Accommodation is not included.

staying at their dive resort with promises of a 'special price for you' – some touts even start accosting tourists on the boat ride over to the island. There are dozens of dive centres on Ko Tao, so it's best to arrive armed with the names of a few reputable schools. If you aren't rushed for time, consider relaxing on the island for a couple of days before making any diving decisions – you will undoubtedly bump into swarms of scubaphiles and instructors who will gladly offer their advice and opinions. Remember: the success of your diving experience (especially if you are learning how to dive) will largely depend on how much you like your instructor. There are other factors to consider as well, like the size of your diving group, the condition of your equipment, and the condition of the dive sites, to name a few.

For the most part, diving prices are somewhat standardised across the island, so there's no need to spend your time hunting around for the best deal. A **PADI** (www.padi.com) Open Water certification course costs 9800B; an **SSI** (www.ssithailand. com) Open Water certificate is slightly less (9000B) because you do not have to pay for instructional materials. An Advanced Open Water certification course will set you back 8500B, a rescue course is 9500B and the Divemaster program costs a cool 25,000B. Fun divers should expect to pay roughly 1000B per dive, or around 7000B for a 10-dive package. These rates include all dive gear, boat, instructors/guides and snacks. Discounts are usually given if you bring your own equipment. Be wary of dive centres that offer too many price cuts – safety is paramount, and a shop giving out unusually good deals is probably cutting too many corners.

Most dive schools will hook you up with cheap – or even free – accommodation. Almost all scuba centres offer gratis fan rooms for anyone doing beginner coursework.

Expect large crowds and booked-out beds throughout the months of December, January, June, July and August, and a monthly glut of wannabe divers after every Full Moon Party on Ko Pha-Ngan next door. If you are planning to do 'diving detox' after a Full Moon romp, make sure you purchase your ferry tickets at least two days before the eve of the lunar lunacy – boats sell out quickly.

The following dive schools are among the best operators on the island; they all do their bit to help keep Ko Tao a pristine place.

Ban's Diving School   DIVING
(Map p574; ☑0 7745 6466; www.amazingkohtao. com; Sairee Beach) A well-oiled diving machine and relentlessly expanding conglomerate, Ban's certifies more divers per year than any other scuba school in the world and refurbishments in 2009 have given it a five-star feel. Classroom sessions tend to be conducted in large groups, but there's a reasonable amount of individual attention in the water. A breadth of international instructors means that students can learn to dive in their native tongue. The affiliated resort (p577) is quite popular with party-seekers.

Big Blue Diving   DIVING
(Map p574; ☑0 7745 6415, 0 7745 6772; www. bigbluediving.com; Sairee Beach) If Goldilocks were picking a dive school, she'd probably pick Big Blue – this midsize operation (not too big, not too small) gets props for fostering a sociable vibe while maintaining a high standard of service. Divers of every

ilk can score dirt-cheap accommodation at their resort (p578).

Buddha View
DIVING

(☏0 7745 6074; www.buddhaview-diving.com; Chalok Ban Kao) Another big dive operation on Ko Tao, Buddha View offers the standard fare of certification and special programs for technical diving (venturing beyond the usual parameters of recreational underwater exploration). Discounted accommodation is available at its friendly resort (p579).

Crystal Dive
DIVING

(Map p574; ☏0 7745 6107; www.crystaldive.com; Mae Hat) Crystal is the Meryl Streep of diving operators, winning all the awards for best performance year after year. It's one of the largest schools on the island (and around the world), although high-quality instructors and intimate classes keep the school feeling quite personal. Multilingual staff members, air-conditioned classes and two on-site swimming pools sweeten the deal. Highly recommended.

New Heaven
DIVING

(☏0 7745 6587; www.newheavendiveschool.com; Chalok Ban Kao) The owners of this small diving operation dedicate a lot of their time to preserving the natural beauty of Ko Tao's underwater sites by conducting regular reef checks and contributing to reef restoration efforts. A special CPAD research diver certification program is available in addition to the regular order of programs and fun dives.

Scuba Junction
DIVING

(Scuba J; Map p574; ☏0 7745 6164; www.scuba-junction.com; Sairee Beach) A groovy new storefront and a team of outgoing instructors lure travellers looking for a more intimate dive experience. Scuba Junction guarantees a maximum of four people per diving group.

Snorkelling

Snorkelling is a popular alternative to diving, although scuba snobs will tell you that

---

DIVE SITES AT A GLANCE

In general, divers don't have a choice as to which sites they explore. Each dive school chooses a smattering of sites for the day depending on weather and ocean conditions. Deeper dive sites such as Chumphon Pinnacle are usually visited in the morning. Afternoon boats tour the shallower sites such as Japanese Gardens. Recently, two large vessels have been sunk off the coast, providing scubaphiles two new wreck dives. Divers hoping to spend some quality time searching for whale sharks at Sail Rock should join one of the dive trips departing daily from Ko Pha-Ngan.

» **Chumphon Pinnacle** (36m maximum depth), 13km west of Ko Tao, has a colourful assortment of sea anemones along the four interconnected pinnacles. The site plays host to schools of giant trevally, tuna and large grey reef sharks. Whale sharks are known to pop up once in a while.

» **Green Rock** (25m maximum depth) is an underwater jungle gym featuring caverns, caves and small swim-throughs. Rays, grouper and triggerfish are known to hang around. It's a great place for a night dive.

» **Japanese Gardens** (12m maximum depth), between Ko Tao and Ko Nang Yuan, is a low-stress dive site perfect for beginners. There's plenty of colourful coral, and turtles, stingray and pufferfish often pass by.

» **Mango Bay** (16m maximum depth) might be your first dive site if you are putting on a tank for the first time. Lazy reef fish swim around as newbies practice their skills on the sandy bottom.

» **Sail Rock** (34m maximum depth), best accessed by Ko Pha-Ngan, features a massive rock chimney with a vertical swim-through, and large pelagics like barracuda and kingfish. This is one of the top spots in southeast Asia to see whale sharks.

» **Southwest Pinnacle** (33m maximum depth) offers divers a small collection of pinnacles that are home to giant groupers and barracudas. Whale sharks and leopard sharks are sometimes spotted (pun partially intended).

» **White Rock** (29m maximum depth) is home to colourful corals, angelfish, clown fish and territorial triggerfish. Another popular spot for night divers.

Mae Hat & Sairee Beach

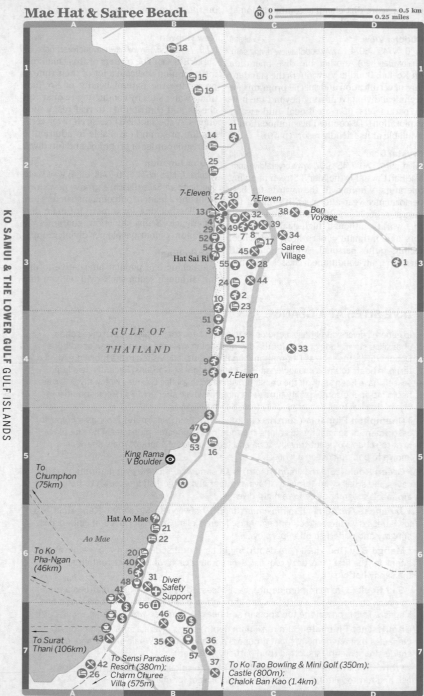

Mae Hat & Sairee Beach

strapping on a snorkel instead of an air tank is like eating spray cheese when there's Camembert on the table. Orchestrating your own snorkelling adventure is simple, since the bays on the east coast have small bungalow operations offering equipment rental for between 100B and 200B per day.

Most snorkel enthusiasts opt for the do-it-yourself approach on Ko Tao, which involves swimming out into the offshore bays or hiring a longtail boat to putter around further out. Guided tours are also available and can be booked at any local travel agency. Tours range from 500B to 700B (usually including gear, lunch and a guide/boat captain) and stop at various snorkelling hotspots around the island. **Laem Thian** is popular for its small sharks, **Shark Island** has loads of fish (and ironically no sharks), **Hin Wong** is known for its crystalline waters, and **Light House Point**, in the north, offers a dazzling array of colourful sea anemones. Dive schools will usually allow snorkellers on their vessels for a comparable price – but it's only worth snorkelling at the shallower sites such as Japanese Gardens. Note that dive boats visit the shallower sites in the afternoons.

Freediving
Over the last couple of years freediving (exploring the sea using breath-holding techniques rather than scuba gear) has grown rapidly in popularity. Several small schools

have opened up across the island. We recommend the capable staff at **Apnea Total** (Map p574; ☑08 7183 2321; www.apnea-total.com; Sairee Beach) who have earned several awards in the freediving world and possess a special knack for easing newbies into this heart-pounding sport. The student-teacher ratio of three to one also ensures plenty of attention to safety. Also worth a special mention is **Blue Immersion** (Map p574; ☑08 7682 1886; www.blue-immersion.com; Sairee Beach) run by friendly Akim, a martial arts expert and a freediving pro – he is one of the first people in the world to freedive below 100m. Freediving prices are standardised across the island as well – a 2½-day SSI beginner course will set you back 5500B.

Technical Diving & Cave Diving

Well-seasoned divers and hardcore Jacques Cousteaus should contact **Tech Thailand** (www.techthailand.com) if they want to take their underwater exploration to the next level and try a technical dive. According to PADI, tec diving, as it's often known, is 'diving other than conventional commercial or recreational diving that takes divers beyond recreational diving limits'. Technical diving exceeds depths of 40m and requires stage decompressions, and a variety of gas mixtures are often used in a single dive.

Several years ago, Tech Thailand's old boat, MS *Trident*, made a name for itself in the diving community after successfully locating dozens of previously undiscovered wrecks in the Gulf of Thailand. Its most famous discovery was the USS *Lagarto,* an American naval vessel that sank during WWII. The gulf has long been an important trading route and new wrecks are being discovered all the time, from old Chinese pottery wrecks to Japanese *marus* (merchant ships). In 2011 the *Trident* was purposefully sunk off the coast of Ko Tao to create an artificial reef. A miscalculation with the explosives has left the wreck a bit too deep for beginners.

Recently, cave diving has taken Ko Tao by storm, and the most intrepid scuba buffs are lining up to make the half-day trek over to Khao Sok National Park (p611). Beneath the park's main lake lurks an astonishing submarine world filled with hidden grottos, limestone crags and skulking catfish. In certain areas divers can swim near submerged villages that were flooded in order to create a reservoir and dam. Most cave-diving trips depart from Ko Tao on the afternoon boat service and return to the island on the after-noon boat service of the following day. Overnight stays are arranged in or near the park.

Stop by Buddha View (p573) on Saturdays for a free introduction into the world of technical diving, or hit the waters with the Tech Thailand team on 'wreck Wednesdays'. If you aren't diving with Buddha View or Master Divers, your dive school of choice can easily help you get sorted.

Underwater Photography & Videography

If your wallet is already full of PADI certification cards, consider renting an underwater camera or enrolling in a marine videography course. Many scuba schools hire professional videographers to film Open Water certifications, and if this piques your interests, you could potentially earn a few bucks after completing a video internship. Your dive operator can put you in touch with any of the half-dozen videography crews on the island. We recommend **ACE Marine Images** (Map p574; ☑0 7745 7054; www.acemarineimages.com; Sairee Beach), one of Thailand's leading underwater videography studios. Their interactive eight-dive course (30,000B) includes an independent diver certification and one-on-one instruction in the editing room. **Deep Down Productions** (☑08 7133 4102; www.deepdown-productions.com) and **Oceans Below** (☑08 6060 1863; www.oceansbelow.net) offer videography courses and internships that are a bit easier on the pocketbook.

Other Activities

TOP CHOICE **Flying Trapeze Adventures** ACROBATICS
(FTA; Map p574; ☑08 0696 9269; www.flyingtrapezeadventures.com; Sairee Beach; ☾4-8pm, lessons at 4pm, 5pm & 6pm) Find out if you're a great catch while donning a pair of hot pink tights during a one-hour group trapeze lesson (950B). Courses are taught by super-friendly Gemma and her posse of limber sidekicks, who take you from circus neophyte to soaring savant in four jumps or less. Bookings are best done over the phone, or you can show up at one of the nightly demos, which start at 7.30pm. Participants must be at least six years old.

Goodtime Adventures TOURS
(Map p574; ☑08 7275 3604; www.gtadventures.com; Sairee Beach; ☾noon-late) Although most activities on Ko Tao revolve around the sea, the friendly crew at Goodtime Adventures offer a wide variety of land-based ac-

tivities to get the adrenaline pumping. Hike through the island's jungly interior, swing from rock to rock during a climbing and abseiling session (from 2000B), or unleash your inner daredevil during an afternoon of cliff jumping. Goodtime also offers accredited boating certifications, and at the time of research they were setting up a groovy zipline course on neighbouring Ko Nang Yuan. The Goodtime office, along the Sairee sands, doubles as a friendly cafe serving an assortment of international nibbles (including dip coffee!)

Shambhala
YOGA

(Map p574; ☎08 4440 6755; Sairee Beach) Ko Tao's only full-time yoga centre is housed in beautiful wooden *săh·lah* located on the forested grounds of Blue Wind (see p577) in Sairee Beach. The two-hour classes, led by Kester, the energetic yogi, cost 300B.

Ko Tao Bowling & Mini Golf
BOWLING, MINIGOLF

(off Map p574; ☎0 7745 6316; ☺noon-midnight) Located on the main road between Mae Hat and Chalok Ban Kao, Ko Tao Bowling & Mini Golf has several homemade bowling lanes where the employees reset the pins after every frame (300B per hour). The 18-hole minigolf course has a landmark theme – putt your ball through Stonehenge or across the Golden Gate Bridge.

🛏 Sleeping

If you are planning to dive while visiting Ko Tao, your scuba operator will probably offer you free or discounted accommodation to sweeten the deal. Some schools have on-site lodging, while others have deals with nearby bungalows. It's important to note that you only receive your scuba-related discount on the days you dive. So, for example, if you buy a 10-dive package, and decide to take a day off in the middle, your room rate will not be discounted on that evening. Also, a restful sleep is important before diving, so scope out these 'great room deals' before saying yes – some of them are one 'roach away from being condemned.

There are also many sleeping options that have absolutely nothing to do with the island's diving culture. Ko Tao's secluded eastern coves are dotted with stunning retreats that still offer a true getaway experience, but these can be difficult to reach due to the island's dismal network of roads. You can often call ahead of time and arrange to be picked up from the pier in Mae Hat.

Note that Ko Tao is not Ko Samui – if you are looking for impeccable service and perfect five-star standards you will not find it here...yet.

SAIREE BEACH
Giant Sairee is the longest and most developed strip on the island, with a string of dive operations, bungalows, travel agencies, minimarkets and internet cafes. The narrow 'yellow brick road' stretches the entire length of the beach (but watch out for motorcycles).

Blue Wind
BUNGALOWS $

(Map p574; ☎0 7745 6116; bluewind_wa@yahoo.com; bungalows 300-1000B; ❄🛜) Hidden within a clump of bodacious lodging options, Blue Wind offers a breath of fresh air from the high-intensity dive resorts strung along Sairee Beach. Sturdy bamboo huts are peppered along a dirt trail behind the beachside bakery. Large, tiled air-conditioned cabins are also available, boasting hot showers and TVs.

Ban's Diving Resort
RESORT $$

(Map p574; ☎0 7745 6466; www.amazingkohtao.com; r 500-2500B; ❄@🛜🏊) This dive-centric party palace offers a wide range of quality accommodation from basic backpacker digs to sleek hillside villas. Post-scuba chill sessions happen on Ban's prime slice of beach, or at one of the two swimming pools tucked within the strip of jungle between the two motel-like structures. Evenings are spent at the Fish Bowl bar downing international cuisine and 'buckets' in equal measure.

Place
VILLA $$$

(www.theplacekohtao.com; villas 4000-7000B) Honeymooners will delight in this unique option – two private luxury villas nestled in the leaf-clad hills with sweeping ocean views down below. A private plunge pool comes standard – naturally – and private chef services are available for those who choose to remain in their love nest instead of sliding down to Sairee for restaurant eats.

Ko Tao Cabana
BUNGALOWS $$$

(Map p574; ☎0 7745 6250; www.kohtaocabana.com; bungalows 2600-11,800B; ❄@🛜🏊) This prime piece of beachside property offers timber-framed villas and crinkled white adobe huts dotted along the boulder-strewn beach. Bric-a-brac cheers the colourful bungalows – stone gnomes greet you with a naughty smirk as you shower in the roofless bathrooms. The newly constructed private villas are one of the more upscale options on the island, though they're a bit rough around the edges compared to the five-star behemoths on Ko Samui.

Big Blue Resort
BUNGALOWS $

(Map p574; ☎0 7745 6050; www.bigbluediving.com; r 400-1000B; ❄@) This scuba-centric resort has a summer camp vibe – diving classes dominate the daytime, while evenings are spent en masse, grabbing dinner or watching fire twirling. Both the basic fan bungalows and motel-style air-con rooms offer little when it comes to views, but who has the time to relax when there's an ocean out there to explore?

Sairee Cottage
BUNGALOWS $$

(Map p574; ☎0 7745 6126; saireecottage@hotmail. com; bungalows 400-1500B;❄) The air-con bungalows are hard to miss since they've been painted in various hues of fuchsia. Low prices mean low vacancy rates – so arrive early to score one of the brick huts facing out onto a grassy knoll.

Bow Thong
BUNGALOWS $

(Map p574; ☎0 7745 6266; bungalows from 600B; ❄☎) A member of the quieter northern section of silky Sairee Beach, Bow Thong has a cluster of comfortable bungalows, if you're looking to be near the waves and aren't affiliated with a dive school.

Sunset Buri Resort
BUNGALOWS $$

(Map p574; ☎0 7745 6266; bungalows 700-2500B; ❄@☎) A long beach-bound path is studded with beautiful white bungalows featuring enormous windows and flamboyant temple-like roofing. The kidney-shaped pool is a big hit, as are the large beach recliners sprinkled around the resort.

Koh Tao Coral Grand Resort
BUNGALOWS $$$

(Map p574; ☎0 7745 6431; www.kohtaocoral.com; bungalows 3350-6950B; ❄☎) The plethora of pink facades at this family-friendly option feels a bit like Barbie's dream Thai beach-house. Cottage interiors are coated in cheery primary colours framed by white truncated beams while pricier digs have a more distinctive Thai flavour, boasting dark lacquered mouldings and gold-foiled art.

Seashell Resort
BUNGALOWS $$

(Map p574; ☎0 7745 6299; www.seashell-resort. com; bungalows 450-3800B; ❄☎) Several bungalows have ocean views from their porches (a rarity in Sairee), while others sit in a well-maintained garden of colourful vegetation

and thin palm trunks. Seashell welcomes divers and nondivers alike.

In Touch Resort
BUNGALOWS $$

(Map p574; ☎0 7745 6514; bungalows 500-1200B; ❄☎) Older bungalows are a mishmash of bamboo and dark wood, while several rounded air-con rooms have a cave theme – it's all very *Flintstones,* except the shower nozzle hasn't been replaced with the trunk of an elephant.

Koh Tao Backpackers
HOSTEL $

(Map p574; ☎08 8447 7921; www.kohtaobackpack ers.com; dm 300B; ❄☎) No-frills bunk beds for serious penny pinchers.

MAE HAT

All ferry arrivals pull into the pier at the busy village of Mae Hat. Accommodation is spread throughout, but the more charming options extend in both directions along the sandy beach.

North of the Pier

Regal Resort
RESORT $$

(Map p574; ☎0 7745 6007; www.kohtaoregal.com; r 1500-4900B; ❄@☎) Home to the most inviting swimming pool on the island, sparkling white Regal proudly sits along the sands of Mae Hat. Set slightly away from the pier, this is a solid option for travellers seeking a sprinkle of air-con and ocean views from their balcony.

Crystal Dive Resort
BUNGALOWS $$

(Map p574; ☎0 7745 6107; www.crystaldive.com; bungalows 800-1500B; ❄❄) The bungalow and motel-style accommodation at Crystal is reserved for its divers, and prices drop significantly for those taking courses. Guests can take a dip in the refreshing pool when it isn't overflowing with bubble-blowing newbie divers.

Montra Resort & Spa
RESORT $$$

(Map p574; ☎0 7745 7057; www.kohtaomontra. com; r 4000-12,800B; ❄@☎) A newer address virtually at the Mae Hat pier, Montra is an upmarket affair with all the modern bells and whistles. The hotel structure is rather imposing when compared to the scatter of humble bungalows next door.

Mr J Bungalow
BUNGALOWS $

(Map p574; ☎0 7745 6066; bungalows 250-1000B) Even though Mr J tried to charge us 50B for his business card, we still think he's well worth the visit. The eccentric owner entangles guests in a philosophical web while tending to his flock of decent bungalows. Ask him about reincarnation if you want to hear some particularly twisted conjectures.

South of the Pier

Charm Churee Villa RESORT $$$
(off Map p574; ☑0 7745 6393; www.charmchureevilla.com; bungalows 3700-18,700B; ❄@❄) Tucked gently under sky-scraping palms, the luxuriant villas of Charm Churee are dedicated to the flamboyant spoils of the Far East. Gold-foiled oriental demigods pose in arabesque positions, with bejewelled eyes frozen in a Zen-like trance. Staircases, chiselled into the rock face, dribble down a palmed slope revealing teak huts strewn across smoky boulders. The villas' unobstructed views of the swishing indigo waters are charming.

Sensi Paradise Resort RESORT $$$
(Map p574; ☑0 7745 6244; www.sensiparadise.com; bungalows 2100-700B; ❄❄❄) There are one too many geckos in the bathroom to call this place 'natural chic', but if you like to be at one with nature then you'll appreciate that these rustic cottages are somehow simultaneously upscale. Friendly caretakers and several airy teak *săh·lah* add an extra element of charm.

Utopia Suites APARTMENTS $$
(Map p574; ☑0 7745 6729; r/ste from 600/2000B, monthly from 20,000B) Utopia is located in the charming fishing village, just a stone's throw from the pier. The beachside apartment-style accommodation is perfect for families and small groups. Ask about discounts for extended stays.

The following sleeping spots are located further south and can be accessed by a quick ride in a boat taxi:

Sai Thong Resort BUNGALOWS $$
(☑0 7745 6868; Hat Sai Nuan; bungalows 400-900B; ❄) As the rush of Mae Hat dwindles away along the island's southwest shore, Sai Thong emerges along sandy Hat Sai Nuan. Bungalows, in various incarnations of weaving and wood, have colourful porch hammocks and palm-filled vistas. Guests frequent the restaurant's relaxing sun deck – a favourite spot for locals too.

Tao Thong Villa BUNGALOWS $
(☑0 7745 6078; Ao Sai Nuan; bungalows from 500B) Very popular with long-termers seeking peace and quiet, these funky, no-frills bungalows have killer views. Tao Thong ac-

tually straddles two tiny beaches on a craggy cape about halfway between Mae Hat and Chalok Ban Kao.

CHALOK BAN KAO

Ao Chalok, about 1.7km south of Mae Hat by road, is the third-largest concentration of accommodation on Ko Tao, but can feel a lot more crowded because the beach is significantly smaller than Sairee and Mae Hat. The beach itself isn't tops as low tides are often muddy.

Ko Tao Resort RESORT $$$
(☑0 7745 6133; www.kotaoresort.com; r & bungalows from 2500B; ❄@❄❄) The entrance is a throwback to the days when taste and architecture weren't particularly synonymous (the '70s perhaps?), but inside everything's thoroughly modern and the facilities themselves fit the true definition of a resort. Rooms are split between 'pool side' and 'paradise zone' – all are well stocked, water sports equipment is on offer, and there are several bars primed to serve an assortment of fruity cocktails. 'Chalok Harbour', a new addition, features an extra dining option and additional chaise seating along a spacious pier.

Chintakiri Resort RESORT $$$
(☑0 7745 6133; www.chintakiri.com; r & bungalows 2900-4000B; ❄@❄) Perched high over the gulf waters overlooking Chalok Ban Kao, Chintakiri is one of Ko Tao's newer luxury additions as the island furtively creeps up-market. Rooms are spread around the inland jungle, and sport crisp white walls with lacquered finishing.

Buddha View Dive Resort BUNGALOWS $$
(☑0 7745 6074; www.buddhaview-diving.com; r 300-1500B; ❄) Like the other large diving operations on the island, Buddha View offers its divers discounted on-site digs in a super-social atmosphere. If you plan on staying a while, ask about the 'Divers Village' across the street, which offers basic accommodation from around 4000B per month.

New Heaven Resort BUNGALOWS $$
(☑0 7745 6422; newheavenresort@yahoo.co.th; r & bungalows 1200-3900B) Just beyond the clutter of Chalok Ban Kao, New Heaven delivers colourful huts perched over impossibly clear waters. A steep path of chiselled stone tumbles down the shrubby rock face revealing views ripped straight from the pages of *National Geographic*.

Freedom Beach
BUNGALOWS $

(☑0 7745 6596; bungalows 400-1500B; ❄) On its own secluded beach at the eastern end of Ao Chalok, Freedom feels like a classic backpacker haunt, although there's a variety of accommodation to suit various humble budgets. The string of bungalows (from wooden shacks to sturdier huts with air-con) links the breezy seaside bar to the resort's restaurant high on the cliff.

Viewpoint Resort
BUNGALOWS $$

(☑0 7745 6666; www.kohtaoviewpoint.com; bungalows 800-1300B) A hot-shot architect from Bangkok allegedly designed this friendly, family-run retreat at the end of civilisation. Cottages are spartan but airy and well maintained. Some have partial sea views; others quietly sit in a gorgeous hillside garden that thrums with cicadas at night.

Also worth a look:

Tropicana
GUEST HOUSE $

(☑0 7745 6167; www.koh-tao-tropicana-resort.com; r from 400) Low-rise hotel units peppered across a garden campus that provide fleeting glimpses of the ocean between fanned fronds and spiky palms.

JP Resort
GUEST HOUSE $

(☑0 7745 6099; r from 400B) A colourful menagerie of prim motel-style rooms stacked on a small scrap of jungle across the street from the sea.

EAST COAST BEACHES
The serene eastern coast is, without a doubt, one of the best places in the region to live out your island paradise fantasies. The views are stunning; beaches are silent, yet all of your creature comforts are 10 minutes away. Accommodation along this coast is organised from north to south.

Hin Wong
A sandy beach has been swapped for a boulder-strewn coast, but the water is crystal clear. The road to Hin Wong is paved in parts, but sudden sand pits and steep hills can toss you off your motorbike.

Hin Wong Bungalows
BUNGALOWS $

(☑0 7745 6006; bungalows from 300B) Pleasant wooden huts are scattered across vast expanses of untamed tropical terrain – it all feels a bit like *Gilligan's Island* (minus the millionaire castaways). A rickety dock, jutting out just beyond the breezy restaurant, is the perfect place to dangle your legs and watch schools of black sardines slide through the cerulean water.

View Rock
BUNGALOWS $

(☑0 7745 6548/9; viewrock@hotmail.com; bungalows 300-400B) When coming down the dirt road into Hin Wong, follow the signs as they lead you north of Hin Wong Bungalows. View Rock is precisely that: views and rocks; the hodgepodge of wooden huts, which looks like a secluded fishing village, is built into the steep crags offering stunning views of the bay.

Tanote Bay (Ao Tanot)
Tanote Bay is more populated than some of the other eastern coves, but it's still rather quiet and picturesque. It is the only bay on the east coast that is accessible by a decent road. Discounted taxis (around 100B) bounce back and forth between Tanote Bay and Mae Hat; ask at your resort for a timetable.

Poseidon
BUNGALOWS $

(☑0 7745 6735; poseidonkohtao@hotmail.com; bungalows from 300B) Poseidon keeps the tradition of the budget bamboo bungalow alive with a dozen basic-but-sleepable huts scattered near the sand.

Family Tanote
BUNGALOWS $$

(☑0 7745 6757; bungalows 700-3500) As the name suggests, this scatter of hillside bungalows is run by a local family who take pride in providing comfy digs to solitude seekers. Strap on a snorkel mask and swim around with the fish at your doorstep, or climb up to the restaurant for a tasty meal and pleasant views of the bay.

Ao Leuk & Ao Thian Ok

Jamahkiri Resort & Spa
RESORT $$$

(☑0 7745 6400; www.jamahkiri.com; bungalows 6900-13,900B) The flamboyant decor at this whitewashed estate is decidedly focused around tribal imagery. Wooden gargoyle masks and stone fertility goddesses abound amid swirling mosaics and multi-armed statues. Feral hoots of distant monkeys confirm the overarching jungle theme, as do the thatched roofs and tiki-torched soirees. The resort's seemingly infinite number of stone stairways can be a pain, so it's a good thing Ko Tao's most luxurious spa is located on the premises.

KO NANG YUAN
Photogenic Ko Nang Yuan, just off the coast of Ko Tao, is easily accessible by the Lom-

prayah catamaran, and by water taxis that depart from Mae Hat and Sairee.

Ko Nangyuan Dive Resort BUNGALOWS $$$
(☑0 7745 6088; www.nangyuan.com; bungalows 1200-9000B; ❀⬤) Although the obligatory 100B tax to access the island is a bit off-putting (as is the 100B water taxi ride each way), Nangyuan Dive Resort is nonetheless a charming place to stay. The rugged collection of wood and aluminium bungalows winds its way across three coolie-hat-like conical islands connected by an idyllic beige sandbar. The resort also boasts the best restaurant on the island, but then again, it's the only place to eat...

Eating

With super-sized Samui lurking on the horizon, it's hard to believe that quaint little Ko Tao holds its own in the gastronomy category. Most resorts and dive operators offer on-site dining, and stand-alone establishments are multiplying at lightning speed in Sairee Beach and Mae Hat. The diverse population of divers has spawned a broad range of international cuisine, including Mexican, French, Italian, Indian and Japanese. On our quest to find the tastiest Thai fare on the island, we discovered, not surprisingly, that our favourite local meals were being dished out at small, unnamed restaurants on the side of the road.

SAIREE BEACH

Darawan INTERNATIONAL $$
(Map p574; mains 160-400B; ☺lunch & dinner) Like a top-end dining venue plucked from the posh shores of Samui nearby, regal Darawan is the island's newest place to take a date. Perched atop the trees at the back of Ban's sprawling resort, the yawning outdoor balcony offers beautiful views of the setting sun (come around 6pm). Designer lighting, efficient waiters and a tasty 'wagyu' burger seal the deal.

Barracuda Restaurant & Bar ASIAN FUSION $$
(Map p574; mains 180-380B; ☺dinner) A wonderful addition to Ko Tao's ever-expanding dining scene, Barracuda offers a refined selection of seafood and gourmet bites. The owner, a masterful chef with many years in the biz, makes an earnest attempt to use only locally sourced ingredients to enhance his fusion faves. The seafood platter is a steal at 395B – wash down your meal with

a mojito and head next door to watch the owner's boyfriend perform in the ladyboy cabaret.

ZanziBar SANDWICHES $
(Map p574; sandwiches 90-140B; ☺breakfast, lunch & dinner) The island's outpost of sandwich yuppie-dom slathers a mix of unpronounceable condiments betwixt two slices of wholegrain bread.

Blue Wind Bakery INTERNATIONAL $
(Map p574; mains 50-120B; ☺breakfast, lunch & dinner) This beachside shanty dishes out Thai favourites, Western confections and freshly blended fruit juices. Enjoy your thick fruit smoothie and flaky pastry while reclining on tattered triangular pillows.

Chopper's Bar & Grill INTERNATIONAL $$
(Map p574; dishes 60-200B; ☺breakfast, lunch & dinner) So popular that it's become a local landmark, Chopper's is a two-storey hang-out where divers and travellers can widen their beer belly. There's live music, sports on the big-screen TVs, billiards and a cinema room. Friday nights are particularly popular; the drinks are 'two for one', and dishes are half-priced as well. Cheers for scored goals are interspersed with exaggerated chatter about creatures seen on the day's dive.

Kanya THAI $
(Map p574; mains 60-130B; ☺breakfast, lunch & dinner) Tucked at the back of Sairee Village on the road to Hin Wong, four-table Kanya serves an assortment of international dishes, but you'll be missing out if you stray from the delectable array of home-cooked Thai classics – the *dôm yam 'blah* is divine.

Café Corner CAFE $$
(Map p574; snacks & mains 30-120B; ☺breakfast & lunch) Prime real estate, mod furnishings, and tasty iced coffees have made Café Corner a Sairee staple over the last few years. Swing by at 5pm to stock up for tomorrow morning's breakfast; the scrumptious baked breads are buy-one-get-one-free before being tossed at sunset.

Big Blue East THAI, INTERNATIONAL $$
(Map p574; dishes 70-250B; ☺breakfast, lunch & dinner) Big Blue Resort's busy chow house, located about 2m from the crashing tide, dispatches an assortment of Thai and international eats, including tasty individual pizzas. The joint fills up around sunset with divers chuckling at the daily dive bloopers shown on the big-screen TV.

Ally the Pancake Man
CREPES **$**

(Map p574; pancakes from 20-40B; ⊙lunch & dinner) Stop by the 7-Eleven beside Big Blue Resort to check out Ally The Pancake Man as he dances around – like an Italian chef making pizza – while cooking your tasty snack. The 'banana Nutella' is a fave.

Krua Thai
THAI **$**

(Map p574; dishes 50-120B; ⊙lunch & dinner) Popular with the tourists who want their food 'faráng spicy' rather than 'Thai spicy', Krua Thai offers a large assortment of classic favourites served in a well-maintained storefront.

El Gringo
MEXICAN **$$**

(Map p574; dishes 80-150B; ⊙breakfast, lunch & dinner) As if there aren't already enough nicknames for white people in Thailand. The self-proclaimed 'funky Mexican joint' slings burritos of questionable authenticity in both Sairee Beach and Mae Hat. Delivery available.

MAE HAT

TOP CHOICE ### Whitening
INTERNATIONAL **$$**

(Map p574; dishes 160-300B; ⊙dinner) Although it looks like a pile of forgotten driftwood during the day, this beachy spot falls somewhere between being a restaurant and being a chic seaside bar – foodies will appreciate the tasty twists on indigenous and international dishes while beertotalers will love the beachy, bleached-white atmosphere that hums with gentle lounge music. Dine amid dangling white Christmas lights while keeping your bare feet tucked into the sand. This is the top spot on the island for a celebratory dinner. And the best part? It's comparatively easy on the wallet.

Café del Sol
INTERNATIONAL **$$**

(Map p574; dishes 70-320B; ⊙breakfast, lunch & dinner; @📶) Even the pickiest eater will be satisfied with the menu's expansive selection of 'world cuisine'. Located just steps away from the pier, this is our favourite breakfast spot on the island – go for the 'Del Sol breakfast' (delicious fruit salad, yoghurt and coffee) with a scrumptious spinach omelette on the side. Lunch and dinner dishes range from hearty pepper hamburgers to homemade pasta, though prices tend to be quite inflated.

Zest Coffee Lounge
CAFE **$**

(Map p574; dishes 70-190B; ⊙breakfast & lunch; 📶) Indulge in the street-cafe lifestyle at Zest – home to the best cup of joe on the island. Idlers can nibble on *ciabatta* sandwiches or sticky confections while nursing their creamy caffe latte. There's a second branch in Sairee, although we prefer this location.

Safety Stop Pub
INTERNATIONAL **$**

(Map p574; mains 60-250B; ⊙breakfast, lunch & dinner; 📶) A haven for homesick Brits, this pier-side restaurant and bar feels like a tropical beer garden. Stop by on Sundays to stuff your face with an endless supply of barbecued goodness, and surprisingly the Thai dishes aren't half bad!

Pranee's Kitchen
THAI **$**

(Map p574; dishes 50-120B; ⊙breakfast, lunch & dinner; 📶) An old Mae Hat fave, Pranee's serves scrumptious curries and other Thai treats in an open-air pavilion sprinkled with lounging pillows, wooden tables and TVs. English movies (with hilariously incorrect subtitles) are shown nightly at 6pm.

Food Centre
THAI **$**

(Map p574; mains from 30B; ⊙breakfast, lunch & dinner) An unceremonious gathering of hot tin food stalls, Food Centre – as it's come to be known – lures lunching locals with veritable smoke signals rising up from the concrete parking lot abutting Mae Hat's petrol station. You'll find some of the island's best papaya salad here.

Greasy Spoon
BREAKFAST **$**

(Map p574; English breakfast 120B; ⊙breakfast & lunch) Although completely devoid of character, Greasy Spoon stays true to its name offering a variety of heart-clogging breakfast treats: eggs, sausage, stewed vegies and chips (their speciality) that'll bring a tear to any Brit's eye.

Tattoo Bar & Restaurant
BURGERS **$$**

(Map p574; mains 150B) Just 30m south of the Whitening (at the edge of the fishing village), Tattoo is a casual affair with a cosy area for TV watching. If you're hungry, try the massive Aussie burger, homemade meat pies and sausage rolls.

Farango's
PIZZA **$$**

(Map p574; dishes 80-230B; ⊙lunch & dinner) Ko Tao's first faràng restaurant spins tasty pizzas and other signature Italian fare. Free delivery. There's a second location on the outskirts of Sairee Village.

LEARNING THE LOCAL LINGO

Due to the steady influx of international visitors, English is spoken just about everywhere; however, the locals on this scuba-savvy island regularly incorporate diving sign-language symbols into common parlance – especially at the bars.

Here are a few gestures to get you started:

» **I'm OK** Make a fist and tap the top of your head twice

» **Cool** Bring together the tips of your index finger and thumb forming an 'O'

» **I'm finished/I'm ready to go** Hold your hand tight like a karate chop and quickly swing it back and forth perpendicular to your neck.

CHALOK BAN KAO

Long Pae   STEAKHOUSE **$$$**
(mains 100-430B; ☺dinner) Situated off the radar from most of the island's tourist traffic, 'Uncle Pae' sits on a scruffy patch of hilly jungle with distant views of the sea down below. The speciality here is steak, which goes oh-so well with a generous smattering of pan-Asian appetisers.

New Heaven Restaurant   INTERNATIONAL **$$**
(mains 60-350B; ☺lunch & dinner) The best part about New Heaven Restaurant is the awe-inducing view of Shark Bay (Ao Thian Ok) under the lazy afternoon moon. The turquoise waters below are so translucent that the curving reef is easily visible from your seat. The menu is largely international, and there are nap-worthy cushions tucked under each low-rise table.

Koppee   CAFE **$$**
(mains 60-180B; ☺breakfast, lunch & dinner) A clone of some of the sleeker cafes in Mae Hat and Sairee, white-washed Koppee serves scrumptious international fare including a variety of home-baked desserts.

🍸 Drinking & Entertainment

After diving, Ko Tao's favourite pastime is drinking, and there's definitely no shortage of places to get tanked. In fact, the island's three biggest dive centres each have bumpin' bars – **Fish Bowl** (Map p574), **Crystal Bar** (Map p574) and **Buddha On The Beach** in Chalok Bak Kao – that attract swarms of travellers and expats alike. It's well worth stopping by even if you aren't a diver. Fliers detailing upcoming parties are posted on various trees and walls along the island's west coast (check the two 7-Elevens in Sairee). Also keep an eye out for posters touting 'jungle parties' held on nondescript patches of scrubby jungle in the centre of the island.

In addition to the following options, several places already reviewed (p581), such as Choppers and Safety Stop Pub, double as great hang-out joints for a well-deserved post-dive beer.

Just remember: don't drink and dive.

Castle   CLUB
(off Map p574; www.thecastlekohtao.com; Mae Hat) Located along the main road between Mae Hat and Chalok Ban Kao, the Castle has quickly positioned itself as the most loved party venue on the island, luring an array of local and international DJs to its triad of parties each month.

Fizz   BAR
(Map p574; Sairee Beach) Recline on mattress-sized pillows and enjoy designer cocktails while listening to Moby, or Enya, mixed with hypnotic gushes of the rolling tide.

Lotus Bar   BAR
(Map p574; Sairee Beach) Lotus is the de facto late-night hang-out spot along the northern end of Sairee. Muscular fire twirlers toss around flaming batons, and the drinks are so large there should be a lifeguard on duty.

Dragon Bar   LOUNGE
(Map p574; Mae Hat) This bar caters to those seeking snazzy, cutting-edge surroundings. There is a happening 'communist chic' retro styling throughout, and everything's dimly lit, moody and relaxing. Dragon Bar is rumoured to have the best cocktails on the island.

Office Bar   BAR
(Map p574; Sairee Beach) With graffiti proudly boasting 'No Gaga, and no Black Eyed F*^#*# Peas', this hexagonal hut lures regulars with grunge beats and rickety wooden seats.

Diza   BAR
(Map p574; Sairee Beach) Once a tatty shack that blasted music as it sold pirated DVDs, Diza has evolved into a casual hang-out at the crossroads of Sairee Village. Locals lounge

on plastic chairs as they slurp their beer and people-watch.

Clumped at the southern end of Sairee Beach, **AC Party Pub** (Map p574), **In Touch** (Map p574) and **Maya Bar** (Map p574) take turns reeling in the partiers throughout the week.

🛍 Shopping

Although most items are cheap when compared to prices back home, diving equipment is a big exception to the rule. On Ko Tao you'll be paying Western prices plus shipping plus commission on each item (even with 'discounts') so it's better to do your scuba shopping at home or on your computer.

If you're having trouble scrubbing the sea salt out of your hair, stop by **Avalon** (Map p574; Mae Hat; ⏰10am-7pm Mon-Sat) for some locally made (and ecofriendly) body and hair care products.

ℹ Information

The ubiquitous *Koh Tao Info* booklet lists loads of businesses on the island and goes into some detail about the island's history, culture and social issues.

Dangers & Annoyances

There's nothing more annoying than enrolling in a diving course with your friends and then having to drop out because you scraped your knee in a motorcycle accident. The roads on Ko Tao are horrendous, save the main drag connecting Sairee Beach to Chalok Ban Kao. While hiring a moped is extremely convenient, this is not the place to learn how to drive. The island is rife with abrupt hills and sudden sand pits along gravel trails. Even if you escape unscathed from a riding experience, scamming bike shops may claim that you damaged your rental and will try to extort you for some serious cash.

Travellers should also be aware that mosquito-borne dengue fever (and a similar but less-severe cousin) is a real and serious threat. The virus can spread quickly due to tightly packed tourist areas and the small size of the island.

Emergency

Police station (Map p574; 📞0 7745 6631) Between Mae Hat and Sairee Beach along the rutty portion of the beachside road.

Internet Access

Rates are generally 2B per minute, with a 20B minimum and discounts if you log on for one hour or longer. You may find, however, that certain useful tourism websites have been firewalled at internet cafes affiliated with travel agencies. The larger dive schools on the island usually have a wireless connection available for laptop-toting travellers.

Medical Services

All divers are required to sign a medical waiver before exploring the sea. If you have any medical condition that might hinder your ability to dive (including mild asthma), you will be asked to get medical clearance from a doctor on Ko Tao. If you're unsure about whether or not you are fit to dive, consider seeing a doctor before your trip as there are no official hospitals on the island, and the number of qualified medical professionals is limited. Also, make sure your traveller's insurance covers scuba diving. On-island medical 'consultations' (and we use that term very lightly) cost 300B. There are several walk-in clinics and mini-hospitals scattered around Mae Hat and Sairee. All serious medical needs should be dealt with on Ko Samui. If you are diving, ask your outfitter to point you in the proper direction of medical advice.

Diver Safety Support (Map p574; 📞08 1083 0533; kohtao@sssnetwork.com; Mae Hat; ⏰on call 24hr) Has a temporary hyperbaric chamber and offers emergency evacuation services.

Money

There are 24-hour ATMs at the island's 7-Elevens. There's also a cluster of ATMs orbiting the ferry docks at Mae Hat. There is a money exchange window at Mae Hat's pier and a second location near Choppers in Sairee. There are several banks near the post office in Mae Hat, at the far end of town along the island's main inland road. They are usually open from 9am to 4pm on weekdays. Almost all dive schools accept credit cards, however there is usually a 3% or 4% handling fee.

Post

Post office (Map p574; 📞0 7745 6170; ⏰9am-5pm Mon-Fri, 9am-noon Sat) A 10- to 15-minute walk from the pier; at the corner of Ko Tao's main inner-island road and Mae Hat's 'down road'.

Tourist Information

There's no government-run TAT office on Ko Tao. Transportation and accommodation bookings can be made at most dive shops or at any of the numerous travel agencies, all of which take a small commission on services rendered.

Bon Voyage (Sairee Beach) Run by the kind Ms Jai, a Ko Tao native, this is a great place to make your transport connections and update your blog beneath cool blasts of air-con. It's located along the road connecting Sairee Beach and Hin Wong.

Websites

Koh Tao Online (www.kohtaoonline.com)
An online version of the handy *Koh Tao Info* booklet.

ℹ Getting There & Away

As always, the cost and departure times are subject to change. Rough waves are known to cancel ferries between the months of October and December. When the waters are choppy we recommend taking the Seatran rather than the Lomprayah catamaran if you are prone to seasickness. The catamarans ride the swell, whereas the Seatran cuts through the currents as it crosses the sea. Note that we highly advise purchasing your boat tickets *several* days in advance if you are accessing Ko Tao from Ko Pha-Ngan after the Full Moon Party.

Bangkok, Hua Hin & Chumphon

Lomprayah's new air service, **Solar Air** (www.lomprayah.com), jets passengers from Bangkok's Don Muang airport to Chumphon once daily in each direction from Monday to Saturday. Upon arriving in Chumphon, travellers can make a seamless transfer to the catamaran service bound for Ko Tao.

Bus-boat package tickets from Bangkok are available from travel agencies all over Bangkok and the south. Buses switch to boats in Chumphon and Bangkok-bound passengers can choose to disembark in Hua Hin (for the same price as the Ko Tao–Bangkok ticket).

If you are planning to travel through the night, the train's couchettes are a much more comfortable option than the bus. Travellers can plan their own journey by taking a boat to Chumphon, then making their way to Chumphon's town centre to catch a train up to Bangkok (or any town along the upper southern gulf); likewise in the opposite direction.

From Ko Tao, the high-speed catamaran departs for Chumphon at 10.15am and 2.45pm (1½ hours), the Seatran leaves the island at 4pm (two hours), and a Songserm fast boat makes the same journey at 2.30pm (three hours). There may be fewer departures if the swells are high.

There's also a midnight boat from Chumphon arriving early in the morning. It returns from Ko Tao at 11pm.

Ko Pha-Ngan

The Lomprayah catamaran offers a twice-daily service, leaving Ko Tao at 9.30am and 3pm and arriving on Ko Pha-Ngan around 10.50am and 4.10pm. The Seatran Discovery Ferry offers an identical service. The Songserm Express Boat departs daily at 10am and arrives on Ko Pan-Ngan at 11.30am. Hotel pick-ups are included in the price.

Ko Samui

The Lomprayah catamaran offers a twice-daily service, leaving Ko Tao at 9.30am and 3pm and arriving on Samui around 11.30am and 4.40pm. The Seatran Discovery Ferry offers an identical service. The Songserm Express Boat departs daily at 10am and arrives on Samui at 12.45pm. Hotel pick-ups are included in the price.

Surat Thani & the Andaman Coast

If you are heading to the Andaman Coast and do not want to stop on Ko Pha-Ngan or Ko Samui along the way, there are two routes you can take. The first, and more common, approach is through Surat Thani. First, board a Surat-bound boat (the Songserm or the night ferry, unless you want to change ships) then transfer to a bus upon arrival. The night boat leaves Ko Tao at 8.30pm. Daily buses to the Songserm Express Boat depart from Surat Thani at 8am and arrive at 2.30pm. Return passengers leave Ko Tao at 10am and arrive in Surat Thani at 4.30pm.

The second option is to take a ferry to Chumphon on the mainland and then switch to a bus or train bound for the provinces further south.

ℹ Getting Around

Sŏrng·tăa·ou In Mae Hat *sŏrng·tăa·ou*, pick-up trucks and motorbikes crowd around the pier as passengers alight. If you're a solo traveller, you will pay 100B to get to Sairee Beach or Chalok Ban Kao. Groups of two or more will pay 50B each. Rides from Sairee to Chalok Ban Kao cost 80B per person, or 150B for solo tourists. These prices are rarely negotiable, and passengers will be expected to wait until their taxi is full unless they want to pay an additional 200B to 300B. Prices double for trips to the east coast, and the drivers will raise the prices when rain makes the roads harder to negotiate. If you know where you intend to stay, we highly recommend calling ahead to arrange a pick up. Many dive schools offer free pick-ups and transfers as well.

Motorbikes Renting a motorcycle is a dangerous endeavour (see Dangers & Annoyances, opposite) if you're not sticking to the main, well-paved roads. Daily rental rates begin at 150B for a scooter. Larger bikes start at 350B. Discounts are available for weekly and monthly rentals. Try **Lederhosenbikes** (Map p574; ✆08 1752 8994; www.lederhosenbikes.com; Mae Hat; ⏰8.30am-6pm Mon-Sat). Do not rent all-terrrain-vehicles (ATVs) or jet skis – they are unsafe.

Water taxis Boat taxis depart from Mae Hat, Chalok Ban Kao and the northern part of Sairee Beach (near Vibe Bar). Boat rides to Ko Nang Yuan will set you back at least 100B. Long-tail boats can be chartered for around 1500B per day, depending on the number of passengers carried.

Ang Thong Marine National Park

อุทยานแห่งชาติหมู่เกาะอ่างทอง

The 40-some jagged jungle islands of Ang Thong Marine National Park stretch across the cerulean sea like a shattered emerald necklace – each piece a virgin realm featuring sheer limestone cliffs, hidden lagoons and perfect peach-coloured sands. These dream-inducing islets inspired Alex Garland's cult classic *The Beach,* about dope-dabbling backpackers.

February, March and April are the best months to visit this ethereal preserve of greens and blues; crashing monsoon waves means that the park is almost always closed during November and December.

◉ Sights

Every tour stops at the park's head office on **Ko Wua Talap**, the largest island in the archipelago. The island's **viewpoint** might just be the most stunning vista in all of Thailand. From the top, visitors will have sweeping views of the jagged islands nearby as they burst through the placid turquoise water in easily anthropomorphised formations. The trek to the lookout is an arduous 450m trail that takes roughly an hour to complete. Hikers should wear sturdy shoes and walk slowly on the sharp outcrops of limestone. A second trail leads to **Tham Bua Bok**, a cavern with lotus-shaped stalagmites and stalactites.

The **Emerald Sea** (also called the Inner Sea) on **Ko Mae Ko** is another popular destination. This large lake in the middle of the island spans an impressive 250m by 350m and has an ethereal minty tint. You can look but you can't touch; the lagoon is strictly off-limits to the unclean human body. A second dramatic **viewpoint** can be found at the top of a series of staircases nearby.

The naturally occurring stone arches on **Ko Samsao** and **Ko Tai Plao** are visible during seasonal tides and weather conditions. Because the sea is quite shallow around the island chain, reaching a maximum depth of 10m, extensive coral reefs have not developed, except in a few protected pockets on the southwest and northeast sides. There's a shallow coral reef near Ko Tai Plao and Ko Samsao that has decent but not excellent snorkelling. There are also several novice dives for exploring shallow caves and colourful coral gardens and spotting banded sea snakes and turtles. Soft powder beaches line **Ko Tai Plao**, **Ko Wuakantang** and **Ko Hintap**.

☞ Tours

The best way to experience Ang Thong is by taking one of many guided tours departing from Ko Samui and Ko Pha-Ngan. The tours usually include lunch, snorkelling equipment, hotel transfers and (with fingers crossed) a knowledgeable guide. If you're staying in luxury accommodation, there's a good chance that your resort has a private boat for providing group tours. Some midrange and budget places also have their own boats, and if not, they can easily set you up with a general tour operator. Dive centres on Ko Samui and Ko Pha-Ngan offer scuba trips to the park, although Ang Thong doesn't offer the world-class diving that can be found around Ko Tao and Ko Pha-Ngan.

Due to the tumultuous petrol prices, tour companies tend to come and go like the wind. Ask at your accommodation for a list of current operators.

🛏 Sleeping

Ang Thong does not have any resorts; however, on Ko Wua Talap the national park has set up five bungalows, each housing between two and eight guests. Campers are also allowed to pitch a tent in certain designated zones. Advance reservations can be made with the **National Parks Services** (☏0 7728 6025; www.dnp.go.th; bungalows 500-1400B). Online bookings are possible, although customers must forward a bank deposit within two days of making the reservation.

❶ Getting There & Around

The best way to reach the park is to catch a private day-tour from Ko Samui or Ko Pha-Ngan (located 28km and 32km away, respectively). The islands sit between Samui and the main pier at Don Sak; however, there are no ferries that stop off along the way.

The park officially has an admission fee (adult/child 400/200B), although it should be included in the price of every tour (ask your operator if you are unsure). Private boat charters are also another possibility, although high petrol prices will make the trip quite expensive.

SURAT THANI PROVINCE

Surat Thani

อำเภอเมืองสุราษฎร์ธานี

POP 128,990

Known in Thai as 'City of Good People', Surat Thani was once the seat of the ancient Srivijaya empire. Today, this busy junction has become a transport hub that indiscriminately moves cargo and people around the country. Travellers rarely linger here as they make their way to the deservedly popular islands of Ko Samui, Ko Pha-Ngan and Ko Tao.

🛏 Sleeping

For a comfy night in Surat, escape the grimy city centre and hop on a *sŏrng·tăa·ou* heading towards the Phang-Nga district. When you climb aboard, tell the driver 'Tesco-Lotus', and you'll be taken about 2km to 3km out of town to a large, box-like shopping centre. A handful of hotel options orbit the mall and have reasonable prices and refreshingly modern amenities.

Options in the downtown area are cheaper, but they tend to offer 'by the hour' service, so things can get a bit noisy as clients come and go. If you're on a very tight budget, consider zipping straight through town and taking the night ferry to reach your island destination.

100 Islands Resort & Spa RESORT $
(☎0 7720 1150; www.roikoh.com; 19/6 Moo 3, Bypass Rd; r 590-1200B; 🕸@🛜🏊) Across the street from the suburban Tesco-Lotus, 100 Islands is as good as it gets in Thailand for under 600B. This teak palace looks out of place along the highway, but inside, the immaculate rooms surround an overgrown garden and lagoon-like swimming pool.

Wangtai Hotel HOTEL $$
(☎0 7728 3020; www.wangtaisurat.com; 1 Th Talad Mai; r 790-2000B; 🕸@🛜🏊) Across the river from the TAT office, Wangtai tries its best to provide a corporate hotel atmosphere. Polite receptionists and tux-clad bellboys bounce around the vast lobby, and upstairs, rooms have unmemorable furnishings, but there are good views of the city.

🍴 Eating

For foodstuffs, go to the **night market** (Sarn Chao Ma; Th Ton Pho) to enjoy fried, steamed, grilled or sautéed delicacies. There are additional evening food stalls near the departure docks for the daily night boats to the islands, a seafood market at Pak Nam Tapi, and an afternoon **Sunday market** (🕙4-9pm) near the TAT office. During the day many food stalls near the downtown bus terminal sell *kôw gài òp* (marinated baked chicken on rice).

Crossroads Restaurant INTERNATIONAL $$
(Bypass Rd; dishes 50-200B; 🕙lunch & dinner) Located southwest of Surat across from the Tesco-Lotus mall, Crossroads has a quaint bluesy vibe enhanced by dim lighting and live music. Try the oysters – Surat Thani is famous for its giant molluscs, and the prices are unbeatable.

ℹ Information

Th Na Meuang has a bank on virtually every corner in the heart of downtown. If you're staying near the 'suburbs', the Tesco-Lotus has ATMs as well.

Boss Computer (per hr 20B; 🕙9am-midnight) The cheapest internet connection around. Located near the post office.

Post office (☎0 7727 2013, 0 7728 1966; Th Talat Mai; 🕙8.30am-4.30pm Mon-Fri, 8.30am-12.30pm Sat) Across from Wat Thammabucha. The local One Tambon One People (OTOP) craft house is located inside.

Siam City Bank (Th Chonkasem) Has a Western Union office.

Taksin Hospital (☎0 7727 3239; Th Talat Mai) The most professional of Surat's three hospitals. Just beyond the Talat Mai Market in the northeast part of downtown.

TAT office (☎0 7728 8817; tatsurat@samart.co.th; 5 Th Talat Mai; 🕙8.30am-4.30pm) Friendly office southwest of town. Distributes plenty of useful brochures and maps, and staff speak English very well.

ℹ Getting There & Away

In general, if you are departing Bangkok or Hua Hin for Ko Pha-Ngan or Ko Tao, consider taking the train or a bus-boat package that goes through Chumphon rather than Surat. You'll save time, and the journey will be more comfortable. Travellers heading to/from Ko Samui will most likely pass through. If you require any travel services, try **Holiday Travel** (Th Na Meuang) or **Pranthip Co** (Th Talat Mai) – both are reliable and English is spoken.

Air

Although flights from Bangkok to Surat Thani are cheaper than the flights to Samui, it takes quite a bit of time to reach the gulf islands from the airport. In fact, if you are attempting to fly back

Surat Thani

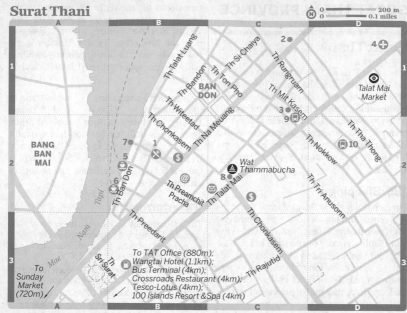

KO SAMUI & THE LOWER GULF SURAT THANI PROVINCE

Surat Thani

to Bangkok from the gulf islands, you'll probably have to leave your beachside bungalow the evening before your flight and spend the night in Surat. Not ideal. If you want to fly through Surat, there are daily shuttles to Bangkok on **Thai Airways International** (THAI; ☎0 7727 2610; 3/27-28 Th Karunarat).

Boat

In the high season travellers can usually find bus-boat services to Ko Samui and Ko Pha-Ngan directly from the Phun Phin train station (which is 14km west of Surat). These services don't cost any more than those booked in Surat Thani and can save you some serious waiting time. There are also several ferry and speedboat operators that connect Surat Thani to Ko Tao, Ko Pha-Ngan and Ko Samui. Most boats – such

as the Raja and Seatran services – leave from Don Sak (about one hour from Surat; bus transfers are included in the ferry ticket) although the Songserm leaves from the heart of Surat town. Be warned that the Raja service can be a very frustrating experience, especially for travellers who are tight on time. The boat trip usually takes around 90 minutes to Ko Samui and 2½ hours to Ko Pha-Ngan, although oftentimes the captain will cut the engines to half propulsion, which means that the journey can take up to five hours.

From the centre of Surat there are nightly ferries to Ko Tao (eight hours, departs at 10pm), Ko Pha-Ngan (seven hours, departs at 10pm) and Ko Samui (six hours, departs at 11pm). These are cargo ships, not luxury boats, so bring food and water and watch your bags.

Bus & Minivan

The most convenient way to travel around the south, frequent buses and minivans depart from two main locations in town known as Talat Kaset 1 and Talat Kaset 2. Talat Kaset 1, on the north side of Th Talat Mai (the city's main drag) offers speedy service to Nakhon. This is also the location of Pranthip Co, one of the more trustworthy agencies in town. Buses to Phun Phin also leave from Talat Kaset 1. At Talat Kaset 2, on the south side of Th Talat Mai, you'll find frequent transportation to Hat Yai and minibuses to Nakhon, Trang, Khanom and Krabi. Andaman-bound buses (usually destined for Phuket) depart every hour from 7am to 3.30pm, stopping at Takua Pa for those who want to access Khao Sok National Park. The 'new' bus terminal (which is actually a few years old now, but still referred to as new by the locals) is located 7km south of town on the way to Phun Phin. This hub services traffic to and from Bangkok.

Train

When arriving by train you'll actually pull into Phun Phin, a cruddy town 14km west of Surat. From Phun Phin, there are buses to Phuket, Phang-Nga and Krabi – some via Takua Pa, a junction city further west and the stopping point for Khao Sok National Park. Transport from Surat moves with greater frequency, but it's worth checking the schedule in Phun Phin first – you might luck out and save yourself a slow ride between towns.

If you plan on travelling during the day, go for the express railcars. Night travellers should opt for the air-con couchettes. Odd-numbered trains are travelling from Bangkok south – even-numbered trains are travelling in the opposite direction. Trains passing through Surat stop in Chumphon and Hua Hin on their way up to the capital, and in the other direction you'll call at Trang, Hat Yai and Sungai Kolok before hopping the border. The train station at Phun Phin has a 24-hour left-luggage room that charges around 20B a day. The advance ticket office is open from 6am to 6pm daily (with a nebulous one-hour lunch break somewhere between 11am and 1.30pm).

ⓘ Getting Around

Air-conditioned vans to/from Surat Thani airport cost around 70B per person and they'll drop you off at your hotel.

To travel around town, *sŏrng·tăa·ou* cost 10B to 30B (it's 15B to reach Tesco-Lotus from the city centre), while *săhm·lór* (also spelt *săamláw*; three-wheeled vehicles) charge between 20B and 40B.

Fan-cooled Orange buses run from Phun Phin train station to Surat Thani every 10 minutes (15B, 25 minutes). For this ride, taxis charge a cool 200B for a maximum of four people, while share-taxis charge 100B per person. Other taxi rates are posted just north of the train station (at the metal pedestrian bridge).

NAKHON SI THAMMARAT PROVINCE

Ao Khanom   อ่าวขนอม

Little Khanom, halfway between Surat Thani and Nakhon Si Thammarat, quietly sits along the blue gulf waters. Overlooked by tourists who flock to the jungle-islands nearby, this pristine region, simply called Khanom, is a worthy choice for those seeking a serene beach setting unmarred by enterprising corporations.

⊙ Sights

The most unique feature in Khanom are the **pink dolphins** – a rare albino breed with a stunning pink hue. They are regularly seen from the old ferry pier and the electric plant pier around dawn and dusk.

WORTH A TRIP

WÁT SUAN MOKHAPHALARAM

Surrounded by lush forest, **Wát Suan Mokkhaphalaram** (Wat Suanmokkh; www.suan mokkh.org), whose name means 'Garden of Liberation', charges 2000B for a 10-day program that includes food, lodging and instruction (although technically the 'teaching' is free). English retreats, run by the International Dhamma Hermitage, begin on the first day of every month and registration takes place the afternoon before. Founded by Ajan Buddhadasa Bhikkhu, arguably Thailand's most famous monk, the temple's philosophical teachings are ecumenical in nature, comprising Zen, Taoist and Christian elements, as well as the traditional Theravada schemata.

For details on reaching the temple, located 7km outside of Chaiya, check out www. suanmokkh-idh.org/idh-travel.html.

The area is also home to a variety of pristine geological features including **waterfalls** and **caves**. The largest of the falls, known as **Samet Chun**, has tepid pools for cooling off, and great views of the coast. To reach the falls, head south from Ban Khanom and turn left at the blue Samet Chun sign. Follow the road for about 2km and after crossing a small stream, take the next right and hike up into the mountain following the dirt road. After about a 15-minute walk, listen for the waterfall and look for a small trail on the right. The scenic **Hin Lat Falls** is the smallest cascade, but it's also the easiest to reach. There are pools for swimming and several huts providing shade. It's located south of Nai Phlao.

There are also two beautiful caves along the main road (Hwy 4014) between Khanom and Don Sak. **Khao Wang Thong** has a string of lights guiding visitors through the network of caverns and narrow passages. A metal gate covers the entrance; stop at the house at the base of the hill to retrieve the key (and leave a small donation). Turn right off the main highway at Rd 4142 to find **Khao Krot Cave**, which has two large caverns, but you'll have to bring a torch (flashlight).

For a postcard-worthy vista of the undulating coastline, head to **Dat Fa Mountain**, located about 5km west of the coast along Hwy 4014. The hillside is usually deserted, making it easy to stop along the way to snap some photos.

🛏 Sleeping & Eating

In the last few years, there has been talk of further developing Khanom's beaches into a more laid-back alterative to the islands nearby. The area is still far from booming, but large-scale development is on the cards. A recent surge in gulf oil rigging has meant that developers are eyeing Khanom as a potential holiday destination for the nearby workers.

There are enough options here that pre-booking isn't a must – in fact we advise checking out a few places before picking a spot to crash. Many of the resorts see very few customers and the constant disuse (not regularly flushing the toilets etc) means that some rooms are dank as the relentless jungle reclaims them. It's best to stay away from the large hotels and stick to beachside bungalow operations.

For some cheap eats, head to **Kho Khao Beach** at the end of Rd 4232. You'll find a steamy jumble of BBQ stands offering some tasty favourites such as *mŏo nám đòk* (spicy pork salad) and *sôm đam* (spicy green papaya salad). On Wednesday and Sunday there are markets further inland near the police station.

JATUKHAM RAMMATHEP

If you've spent more than 24 hours in Thailand, you've probably seen a Jatukham Rammathep dangling around someone's neck – these round amulets are everywhere.

The bearers of the Jatukham Rammathep are supposed to have good fortune and protection from any harm. The origin of the amulet's name remains a mystery, although a popular theory suggests that Jatukham and Rammathep were the aliases of two Srivijayan princes who buried relics under Nakhon's Wat Phra Mahathat some 1000 years ago.

A notorious Thai police detective first wore the precious icon, and firmly believed that the guardian spirits helped him solve a particularly difficult murder case. He tried to popularise the amulet, but it wasn't a market success until his death in 2006. Thousands of people attended his funeral, including the crown prince, and the Jatukham Rammathep took off.

The talismans are commissioned at the Mahathat temple, and in the last several years, southern Thailand has seen a spike in economic activity. The first amulet was sold in 1987 for 39B, and today, over 100 million baht are spent on the town's amulets every *week*. The desire for these round icons has become so frenzied that a woman was crushed to death on the temple grounds during a widely publicised discount sale (she was not wearing her talisman).

Every day, trucks drive along Nakhon's main roads blaring loud music to promote new shipments. These thumping beats have started to shake the ground beneath the temple, and the repeated hammering has, in an ironic metaphor, bent the main spire of Wat Mahathat.

Racha Kiri
RESORT $$$

(☑0 7530 0245; www.rachakiri.com; bungalows 3500-12,500B; ❋🛜🏊) Khanom's upscale retreat is a beautiful campus of rambling villas. The big price tag means no crowds, which can be nice, although the resort feels like a white elephant when the property isn't being used as a corporate retreat.

Talkoo Beach Resort
BUNGALOWS $$

(☑0 7552 8397; bungalows 1470B; ❋🏊) This charming operation has dozens of snazzy white cottages featuring quirky fixtures such as sinks made from hollowed-out tree trunks. This is the best lodging option in the vicinity.

Suchada Villa
BUNGALOWS $

(☑0 7552 8459; bungalows 800B; ❋) Right along the main road, Suchada is recognisable by its cache of brightly coloured bungalows. Rooms are cute and clean with quirky designer details such as strings of shells dangling in front of the bathroom doors.

ℹ Information

The police station and hospital are located just south of Ban Khanom at the junction leading to Kho Khao Beach. There's a 7-Eleven (with an ATM) in the heart of Ban Khanom.

ℹ Getting There & Away

From Surat Thani, you can catch any Nakhon-bound bus and ask to be let off at the junction for Khanom. Catch a motorcycle taxi (70B) the rest of the way. You can get a share taxi from Nakhon Si Thammarat's share-taxi terminal to Khanom town for 85B.

From Khanom town you can hire motorcycle taxis out to the beaches for about 60B. There are three separate bus stops in the vicinity. Ask your driver to stop near the fruit market or the hospital, as these are the closest stops to the beach.

Nakhon Si Thammarat
อำเภอเมืองนครศรีธรรมราช

POP 117,100

The bustling city of Nakhon Si Thammarat (usually shortened to 'Nakhon') won't win any beauty pageants. However, travellers who stop in this historic town will enjoy a decidedly cultural experience amid some of the most important wát in the kingdom.

Hundreds of years ago, an overland route between the western port of Trang and the eastern port of Nakhon Si Thammarat functioned as a major trade link between Thailand and the rest of the world. This ancient influx of cosmopolitan conceits is still palpable today, and can be found in the recipes of local cuisine, or housed in the city's temples and museums.

⊙ Sights

Most of Nakhon's commercial activity (hotels, banks and restaurants) takes place in the northern part of the downtown. South of the clock tower, visitors will find the city's historic quarter with the oft-visited Wat Mahatat. Th Ratchadamnoen is the main thoroughfare and teems with cheap *sŏrng·tǎa·ou* heading in both directions.

Wat Phra Mahathat Woramahawihaan
TEMPLE

(Th Si Thamasok) The most important wát in southern Thailand, Wat Phra Mahathat Woramahawihaan (simply known as Mahathat) is a stunning campus boasting 77 *chedi* (stupa) and an imposing 77m *chedi* crowned by a gold spire. According to legend, Queen Hem Chala and Prince Thanakuman brought relics to Nakhon over 1000 years ago, and built a small pagoda to house the precious icons. The temple has since grown into a rambling site, and today, crowds gather daily to purchase the popular Jatukham amulets (see opposite). Don't miss the modest ceramics museum inside.

Shadow Puppets
MUSEUM

(Th Si Thamasok Soi 3) Traditionally, there are two styles of local shadow puppet: *năng đà·lung* and *năng yài*. At just under 1m tall, the former feature movable appendages and parts (including genitalia); the latter are nearly life-sized, and lack moving parts. Both are intricately carved from cow hide. Suchart Subsin's puppet house has a small museum where staff can demonstrate the cutting process. Short shows can be performed for visitors for a nominal fee.

National Museum
MUSEUM

(Th Ratchadamnoen; admission 30B; ⊙9am-4pm Wed-Sun) When the Tampaling (also known as Tambralinga) kingdom traded with merchants from Indian, Arabic, Dvaravati and Champa states, the region around Nakhon became a melting pot of crafts and art. Today, many of these relics are on display behind the run-down facade of the national museum.

DON'T MISS

KHAO LUANG NATIONAL PARK

Known for its beautiful mountain and forest walks, cool streams, waterfalls and or-chards, **Khao Luang National Park** (อุทยานแห่งชาติเขาหลวง; ☎ 0 7530 9644-7; adult/child 400/200B) surrounds the 1835m peak of Khao Luang. This soaring mountain range reaches up to 1800m, and is covered in virgin forest. An ideal source for streams and rivers, the mountains show off impressive waterfalls and provide a habitat for a plethora of bird species – this place is a good spot for any budding ornithologist. Fans of flora will also get their kicks here; there are over 300 species of orchid in the park, some of which are found nowhere else on earth.

Park bungalows can be rented for between 600B and 1000B per night, and sleep six to 12 people. **Camping** is permitted along the trail to the summit. To reach the park, take a *sŏrng·tăa·ou* (around 25B) from Nakhon Si Thammarat to the village of Khiriwong, at the base of Khao Luang. The entrance to the park and the offices of the Royal Forest De-partment are 33km from the centre of Nakhon on Rte 4015, an asphalt road that climbs almost 400m in 2.5km to the office and a further 450m to the car park.

Sleeping & Eating

Nakhon is a great place to sample cuisine with a distinctive southern twist. In the evening, Muslim food stands sell delicious *kôw mòk gài* (chicken biryani), *má·dà·bà* (*murdabag;* Indian pancake stuffed with chicken or vegetables) and roti. Several tasty options cluster around Bovorn Bazaar on Th Ratchadamnoen.

Nakorn Garden Inn   GUEST HOUSE $
(☎ 0 7532 3777; 1/4 Th Pak Nakhon; r 445B; ✳) The motel-style Nakorn Garden Inn offers a pleasant alternative to the usual cement cube. Rooms are encased in exposed crim-son brick and set around a sandy garden. Each unit is identical, sporting a TV and fridge; try to score a room that gets plenty of sunlight.

Twin Lotus Hotel   HOTEL $$
(☎ 0 7532 3777; www.twinlotushotel.net; 97/8 Th Phattanakan Khukhwang; r 1400-1600B; ✳🕸≋) Its age is starting to show, but Twin Lotus is still a nice spot for a little pampering while visiting Nakhon. This 16-storey behemoth sits a couple of kilometres southeast of the city centre.

Khrua Nakhon   THAI $$
(Bovorn Bazaar; dishes 60-200B; ⊙breakfast & lunch) This joint has a great selection of traditional Nakhon cuisine. Order a shar-ing platter, which comes with five types of curry (including an unpalatable spicy fish sauce), or try the *kôw yam* (southern-style rice salad). There's one at a second location in Robinson Ocean Mall.

Rock 99   INTERNATIONAL $
(1180/807 Bavorn Bazaar; dishes 40-130B; ⊙din-ner) The choice *fa·ràng* hang-out in Nakhon, Rock 99 has a good selection of internation-al fare – from taco salads to pizzas (avoid the Thai fare though). There's live music on Wednesday, Friday and Saturday nights, but expect to bump into friendly expats almost all the time.

ℹ Information

Several banks and ATMs hug Th Ratchadamnoen in the northern end of downtown. There is an English-language bookstore on the 3rd floor of Robinson Ocean shopping mall.

Bovorn Bazaar (Th Ratchadamnoen) A mall housing a few internet cafes.

Police station (☎1155; Th Ratchadamnoen) Opposite the post office.

Post office (Th Ratchadamnoen; ⊙8.30am-4.30pm)

TAT office (☎ 0 7534 6515) Housed in a 1926-vintage building in the northern end of the Sanam Na Meuang (City Park). Has some useful brochures in English. The local OTOP craft house is just a block away on the west side of Sanam Na Meuang Park.

ℹ Getting There & Away

Air Several small carriers such as Nok Air, Air Asia and Orient Thai Airlines (plus Thai Airways) fly from Bangkok to Nakhon everyday. There are about six daily one-hour flights.

Trains There are two daily train departures from Bangkok to Nakhon (stopping through Hua Hin, Chumphon and Surat Thani along the way). They are both 12-hour night trains leaving at 5.35pm and 7.15pm. These trains continue on to Hat Yai and Sungai Kolok.

Bus Buses from Bangkok depart either between 6am and 8am, or between 5.30pm and 10pm. There are about seven daily departures. Ordinary buses to Bangkok leave from the bus terminal, but a couple of private buses leave from booking offices on Th Jamroenwithi, where you can also buy tickets. The journey takes 12 hours.

When looking for minivan stops to leave Nakhon, keep an eye out for small desks along the side of the downtown roads (minivans and waiting passengers may or may not be present nearby). It's best to ask around as each destination has a different departure point. Krabi and Don Sak minivans are grouped together – just make sure you don't get on the wrong one. Stops are scattered around Th Jamroenwithi, Th Wakhit and Th Yommarat.

❶ Getting Around

Sŏrng·tăa·ou run north–south along Th Ratchadamnoen and Th Si Thammasok for 10B (a bit more at night). Motorcycle-taxi rides start at 20B and cost up to 50B for longer distances.

SONGKHLA PROVINCE

Songkhla's postal code is 90210, but this ain't no Beverly Hills! The province's two main commercial centres, Hat Yai and Songkhla, are not usually affected by the political turmoil plaguing the cities further south. Intrepid travellers will be able to count the number of other tourists on one hand as they wander through local markets, savour Muslim-Thai fusion cuisine and relax on breezy beaches.

Songkhla & Around สงขลา

POP 90,780

'The great city on two seas' lends itself perfectly to the click of a visitor's camera; however, slow-paced Songkhla doesn't see much in the way of foreign tourist traffic. Although the town hasn't experienced any of the Muslim separatist violence plaguing the provinces further south, it's still catching the same bad press. This is a darn shame, since it's the last safe city where travellers can experience the unique flavour of Thailand's predominately Muslim Deep South.

The population is a mix of Thais, Chinese and Malays, and the local architecture and cuisine reflect this fusion at every turn.

◉ Sights

National Museum   MUSEUM

(พิพิธภัณฑสถานแห่งชาติสงขลา; Th Wichianchom; admission 150B; ⊙9am-4pm Wed-Sun, closed public holidays) The 1878 building that now houses the **national museum** was originally built in a Chinese architectural style as the residence of a luminary. This museum is easily the most picturesque national museum in Thailand and contains exhibits from all Thai art-style periods, particularly the Srivijaya. Also on display are Thai and Chinese ceramics and sumptuous Chinese furniture owned by the local Chinese aristocracy.

Hat Samila   BEACH

(หาดสมิหลา) If museums aren't your style, head to the beach. The residents have begun taking better care of the strip of white sand along Hat Samila, and it is now quite pleasant for strolling or flying a kite (a local obsession). A bronze **Mermaid sculpture**, depicted squeezing water from her long hair in tribute to Mae Thorani (the Hindu-Buddhist earth goddess), sits atop some rocks at the northern end of the beach. Locals treat the figure like a shrine, tying the waist with coloured cloth and rubbing the breasts for good luck. Next to that are the **Cat and Rat sculptures**, named for the Cat and Rat Islands (Ko Yo and Ko Losin). Fragments of a dragon statue are sliced up and placed around the city. The **Nag Head** (dragon head), which shoots water into the ocean, is said to bring prosperity and fresh water – it's a popular meeting spot for locals.

Ko Yo   ISLAND

(เกาะยอ) A popular day trip from Songkhla, this island in the middle of Thale Sap is actually connected to the mainland by bridges and is famous for its cotton-weaving industry. There's a roadside market selling cloth and ready-made clothes at excellent prices.

If you visit Ko Yo, don't miss **Wat Phrahorn Laemphor**, with its giant reclining Buddha, and check out the **Thaksin Folklore Museum** (☑0 7459 1618; admission 100B; ⊙8.30am-4.30pm), which actively aims to promote and preserve the culture of the region, and is a must-see. The pavilions here are reproductions of southern Thai–style houses and contain folk art, handicrafts and traditional household implements.

If you have kids in tow, try the following:

Songkhla Zoo
ZOO

(สวนสัตว์สงขลา; Khao Rup Chang; adult/child 30/5B; ⊘9am-6pm) Enjoy cuddling with baby tigers.

Songkhla Aquarium
AQUARIUM

(สงขลาอะควาเรียม; www.songkhlaaquarium.com; adult/child 150/80B; ⊘9am-5pm Wed-Mon) Point at clownfish at this flashy new attraction.

🛏 Sleeping & Eating

Songkhla's hotels tend to be lower priced than other areas in the gulf, which makes going up a budget level a relatively cheap splurge.

For quality seafood, head to the street in front of the BP Samila Beach Hotel – the best spot is the restaurant directly in the roundabout. If market munching is your game, you'll find a place to sample street food every day of the week. On Sundays try the bustling market that encircles the Pavilion Hotel. Monday, Tuesday and Wednesday feature a night market (which closes around 9pm) near the local fish plant and bus station, and the Friday-morning market sits diagonally opposite the City Hall.

BP Samila Beach Hotel
HOTEL $$

(☏0 7444 0222; www.bphotelsgroup.com; 8 Th Ratchadamnoen; r 1680-2500B; ✳@☀☒) A landmark in quaint Songkhla, the city's poshest address is actually a really good deal – you'd pay nearly double for the same amenities on the islands. The beachfront establishment offers large rooms with fridges, satellite TVs and a choice of sea or mountain views (both are pretty darn good).

Green World Palace Hotel
HOTEL $$

(☏0 7443 7900-8; 99 Th Samakisukson; r 1000-1200B; ✳@☀☒) When expats say that sleeping in Songkhla is a steal, they're not lying – Green World is the proof. This classy affair boasts chandeliers, a spiralling staircase in the lobby and a 5th-floor swimming pool with views. Rooms are immaculate and filled with all the mod cons of a hotel twice the price.

Khao Noy
CURRY SHOP $

(☏0 7431 1805; 14/22 Th Wichianchom; dishes 30-50B; ⊘breakfast & lunch Thu-Tue) Songkhla's most lauded *rãhn kôw gaang* (curry shop) serves up an amazing variety of authentic southern-style curries, soups, stir-fries and salads. Look for the glass case holding several stainless-steel trays of food just south of the sky-blue Chokdee Inn.

ℹ Information

Banks can be found all over town.

Indonesian Consulate (☏0 7431 1544; Th Sadao)

Malaysian Consulate (☏0 7431 1062; 4 Th Sukhum)

Police station (☏0 7432 1868; Th Laeng Phra Ram) North of the town centre.

Post office (Th Wichianchom) Opposite the market; international calls can be made upstairs.

ℹ Getting There & Around

Trains From Songkhla you'll have to go to Hat Yai to reach most long-distance destinations in the south (trains no longer pass through town).

Buses The government bus station is located a few hundred metres south of the Viva Hotel. Three 2nd-class buses go daily to Bangkok, stopping in Chumphon, Nakhon Si Thammarat and Surat Thani, among other places. For Hat Yai, buses and minivans take around 40 minutes, and leave from Th Ramwithi. *Sŏrng·tăa·ou* also leave from here for Ko Yo.

Hat Yai
หาดใหญ่

POP 157,400

Welcome to backcountry Thailand's version of big city livin'. Songkhla Province's liveliest town has long been a favourite stop for Malaysian men on their weekend hooker tours. These days Hat Yai gladly shakes hands with globalisation – Western-style shopping malls stretch across the city, providing local teenagers with a spot to loiter and middle-aged ladies with a place to do their cardio.

Tourists usually only get a glimpse of the city's winking commercial lights from the window of their train carriage as they connect the dots along the peninsula, but those who decide to explore will be rewarded with excellent local cuisine (the city has hundreds of restaurants), shopping (DVDs anyone?) and an evening bar scene that brilliantly mixes cosy pubs and bouncing discothequcs.

🛏 Sleeping & Eating

Hat Yai has dozens of hotels within walking distance of the train station. The city is the unofficial capital of southern Thailand's cuisine, offering Muslim roti and curries, Chinese noodles and dim sum, and fresh Thai-style seafood from both the gulf and Andaman coasts. On Th Niyomrat, between Niphat Uthit 1 and 2, starting at Tamrab

Muslim, is a string of casual and inexpensive Muslim restaurants open from about 7am to 9pm daily. Meals at these places cost between 20B to 60B.

The **night market** (Th Montri 1) boasts heaps of local eats including several stalls selling the famous Hat Yai-style deep-fried chicken and *kà·nŏm jeen* (fresh rice noodles served with curry), as well as a couple of stalls peddling grilled seafood.

Regency Hotel
HOTEL **$$**

(☑0 7435 3333-47; www.theregencyhatyai.com; 23 Th Prachathipat; r 798-5680B; ✳@✳) This beautiful hotel has that grand old-world charm that's so very rare nowadays. Rooms in the old wing are smaller (and cheaper) and feature attractive wood furnishings, while the new wing boasts amazing views.

Sor Hueng 3
THAI **$**

(☑08 1896 3455; 79/16 Th Thamnoonvithi; dishes 30-120B; ⊘dinner) This popular local legend with branches all over town prepares heaps of delicious Thai-Chinese and southern Thai faves. Simply point to whatever looks good or order something freshly wok-fried from the extensive menu.

❶ Information

Immigration Office (Th Phetkasem) Near the railway bridge, it handles visa extensions.

TAT Office (tatsgkhla@tat.or.th; 1/1 Soi 2, Th Niphat Uthit 3) Very helpful staff here speak excellent English and have loads of info on the entire region.

Tourist police (Th Niphat Uthit 3; ⊘24hr) Near the TAT office.

❶ Getting There & Away

Air

Thai Airways International (THAI; 182 Th Niphat Uthit 1) operates eight flights daily between Hat Yai and Bangkok.

Nearly all of the low-cost airlines now operate flights to and from Bangkok:

Air Asia (www.airasia.com) Daily flights from Hat Yai to Bangkok and Kuala Lumpar.

Nok Air (www.nokair.com) Daily flights between Hat Yai and Bangkok's Don Muang Airport.

Bus

Most interprovincial buses and south-bound minivans leave from the bus terminal 2km southeast of the town centre, while most north-bound minivans now leave from a minivan terminal 5km west of town at Talat Kaset, a 60B túk-túk ride from the centre of town. Buses link Hat Yai to almost any location in southern Thailand.

Prasert Tour (Th Niphat Uthit 1) conducts minibuses to Surat Thani (4½ hours, 8am to 5pm), and **Cathay Tour** (93/1 Th Niphat Uthit 2) can also arrange minivans to many destinations in the south.

Train

There are four overnight trains to/from Bangkok each day, and the trip takes at least 16 hours. There are also seven trains daily that run along the east coast to Sungai Kolok and two daily trains running west to Butterworth and Padang Besar, both in Malaysia.

There is an advance booking office and left-luggage office at the train station; both are open 7am to 5pm daily.

❶ Getting Around

An **Airport Taxi Service** (☑0 7423 8452; 182 Th Niphat Uthit 1) makes the run to the airport four times daily (80B per person, 6.45am, 9.30am, 1.45pm and 6pm). A private taxi for this run costs 280B.

Sŏrng·tăa·ou run along Th Phetkasem (10B per person). Túk-túk and motorcycle taxis around town cost 20B to 40B per person.

DEEP SOUTH

Yala
ยะลา

POP 65,000

Landlocked Yala feels quite different from the neighbouring towns. The city's gaping boulevards and well-organised street grid feels distinctly Western, especially since Yala is predominantly a university town.

Yala's biggest attraction is **Wat Kuha Pi Muk** (also called Wat Na Tham or Cave-front Temple), 8km west of town on the road connecting Yala to Hat Yai (Rte 409). This Srivijaya-period cave temple features a reclining Buddha that dates back to AD 757. A statue of a giant guards the temple's entrance, and inside small natural openings in the cave's roof let in the sun's rays to illuminate a variety of ancient Buddhist cave drawings. Wat Kuha Pi Muk is one of the most important pilgrimage points in southern Thailand.

Take a breather from wát ogling and check out what is known as the largest mail box in Thailand, built in the township of Betong in 1924. Betong also functions as a legal, but inconvenient, border crossing to

TROUBLE IN THE DEEP SOUTH

Background   *Patrick Winn*

Thailand's southernmost frontier is lush, green and prone to violence. Though the three provinces in Thailand's deep south were conquered by the Siamese kingdom more than 100 years ago, a regional insurgency still kicks and screams for independence.

Armed separatists dream of reclaiming 'Patani', a Qatar-sized Muslim sultanate that perished long before today's insurgents were even born. Along with much of the Malay-Indonesian archipelago, the region absorbed Islamic beliefs from 13th-century Arab traders. The kingdom existed for about 500 years until 1902, when it was seized by Buddhist Siam and carved into three provinces: Yala, Narathiwat, Pattani and parts of neighbouring Satun.

But the deep south has never truly assimilated with Thailand. After a relative lull of violence in the 1980s and '90s, the independence struggle is now raging harder than ever.

Deaths have reached 4600 since 2004, a year marking the revival of violent struggle. Despite separatists' semi-secret peace talks with the Royal Thai Army, few expect the low-grade civil war to end anytime soon.

Killings occur at a daily clip. Shock tactics rival those of insurgents in Iraq or Pakistan. Beheadings of monks and kids are recurrent. Teachers, seen as agents of cultural assimilation, are shot dead en route to morning lessons. Rubber farmers are gunned down with AK-47 fire simply for having good relations with Buddhist neighbours.

The separatists are also growing more sophisticated and savvy. Their roadside bombs were once built from Tupperware, C-4 and rusty nails. They have since graduated to radio-control detonators and complex attacks, which first wipe out unlucky civilians and then responding bomb squads with secondary bombs planted nearby.

What compels insurgents to such extremes? According to separatists, they must resist 'Siamese Infidels' forcing Buddhist culture down their throats. As far back as 1939, the Thai state shut down the region's Islamic schools and Qu'ranic sharia law courts. The local Yawi dialect was forbidden in government offices.

Locals still bemoan the indignity of visiting government bureaus where imported officials can't speak their local tongue. The army also enforces a 'state of emergency' – essentially martial law – that limits the rights of those arrested. Muslim groups complain that men are falsely accused and never come home. Powerful positions, from army officers to police chiefs to mayors, are typically held by Thai Buddhists and not local Muslims.

Two army scandals have helped galvanise disdain for the Thai state: the Tak Bai and Krue Sae events of 2004. The former saw roughly 80 Muslim protesters in the town of Tak Bai, Narathiwat, stacked in a truck's sweltering cargo hold until they suffocated. In the latter incident, troops stormed a mosque called Krue Sae in Pattani and gunned down more than 30 suspected insurgents. The alleged separatists were armed with knives and a single gun. The army insists both incidents were accidental.

Perhaps the separatists' most unique feature is their ironclad code of silence. Thai soldiers say combating the insurgency is akin to fighting ghosts. The self-proclaimed 'Patani Mujahedin' run what one academic calls a network without a core: a patchwork of village-based cells operating independently.

The various resistance groups share common ideals but no common leader. Accounts vary, but the various networks are believed to control roughly 8000 separatists. Unlike al-Qaeda or the Taliban, they seldom claim responsibility for attacks, preferring silence to glory.

Leaflets scattered around victims' corpses are the insurgents' preferred method of communication. One typical screed reads: 'Make violence brutally. Attack the Buddhist Thais. We know that the Buddhist Thais do not like violence and love peace. When the Buddhist Thais cannot stand, they will surrender.'

As intended, killings have stoked Buddhist flight en masse. In parts of the army's so-called 'red zone', vestiges of the Thai state control, such as schools and even postal routes, are few and far between. Monks dare not go on alms runs without M-16-gripping soldiers at their sides. At times, according to some experts, as many as 25% of the deep south's villages have at some point fallen under de facto insurgency control.

The insurgency is noted for its reluctance to attack targets outside the deep south, which is likely the reason the conflict attracts scant global interest. The greater region offers targets that, if attacked, would deal great damage to the psyche of Thailand and its tourists.

But separatists have left alone the backpacker beaches of Krabi, Phuket's resorts and even Bangkok, the heart of the Thai authority. Likewise, insurgents appear uninterested in joining forces with al-Qaeda or Islamic terror groups in Pakistan or Indonesia.

One senior member of the oldest insurgent group, the Patani United Liberation Organization, has insisted the insurgency will never solicit outside help. Though speaking only for one of several factions, he claims post-revolution Patani will warmly welcome Western tourists to its pristine beachfront.

But for now, the violence has strangled regional tourism. Even if separatists are only out to harm Thai Buddhists and Muslim collaborators, marketplace bombs kill indiscriminately. Hotels classy enough to satisfy tourists have also come under attack; these are the same hotels favoured by high-ranking officers.

The only reliable stream of tourism comes from Malaysian men travelling north for booze and rented female company. Still, given a spate of explosions outside dodgy nightclubs, they do so at a pronounced risk.

But no matter how much blood the 'Patani Mujahedin' spill, they are unlikely to secure their stated goal: an independent Islamic state.

Though most Thais view the deep south as a different planet, heavy nationalism imbued in Thai schools has bred a population incapable of stomaching territorial loss. An authority figure who backed ceding Thai soil would risk political suicide. And though the Bangkok press chronicles daily killings in detail, the insurgency remains an afterthought to voters convinced terror will never creep outside the deep south.

Instead of Thai surrender, some version of autonomy is a more reasonable, but still distant, hope for insurgents and their sympathisers. Sporadic talks between Thai military officials and separatists in exile have taken place since the late 2000s. However, the army's faith is shaken each time insurgency heads try to prove their authority through ceasefires that are ignored by rebels on the ground.

So a vexing question remains for Thailand's military: how do you negotiate with a network with no core?

Patrick Winn is the Southeast Asia correspondent for the Global Post foreign news agency

Should You Go?

Although it's possible to visit the region, the insurgency has stifled tourism in the deep south to the extent that tourist infrastructure – hotels, restaurants, transportation and activities – is minimal. And the threat of violence means that exploring the area's largely pristine and uninhabited beaches – ostensibly most travellers' reason for visiting the region – can't generally be recommended.

To date, tourists have not been targeted, but the haphazard nature of the insurgency makes it difficult to predict which way the situation will turn (and bombs kill indiscriminately). If you plan to visit the region and want to know the situation on the ground, the authorities suggest contacting the local Tourist Police or TAT, but you'll have to be prepared for pessimistic spiel. Generally speaking, travel in Pattani and Narathiwat in the early morning and late evening is discouraged, and independent travel via rented motorcycle carries considerable risk. While in urban areas, it's probably also a good idea not to linger around parked motorcycles, as they have been used to carry remote-controlled bombs.

Austin Bush, author of the Deep South section of this chapter

KO SAMUI & THE LOWER GULF YALA

Malaysia; contact Yala's **immigration office** (📞0 7323 1292) or see the boxed text, p600 for details.

🛏 Sleeping & Eating

The lack of tourism means great bargains for a comfy bed.

Chang Lee Hotel   HOTEL $
(📞0 7324 4600; www.yalasirichot.4t.com; 318 Th Sirirot; s & d 400-460B; 🌬) A 15-minute walk from the train station, the Chang Lee has plush rooms that cater to business travellers. Facilities include a karaoke nightclub and coffeeshop.

Although inland, Yala has several excellent seafood restaurants – there's a cluster around Th Pitipakdee and Th Sribumrung. Rice and noodle stalls abound near the train station.

ℹ Getting There & Around

Buses to Hat Yai (150B, 2½ hours) stop several time a day on Th Sirirot, outside the Prudential TS Life office. Across the street is the stop for other short- to medium-distance buses north. Yala's train station has four daily departures for Bangkok (193B to 1675B, 18 to 22 hours) and seven for Sungai Kolok (41B to 917, two to three hours).

Pattani   ปัตตานี

POP 118,000

Like a rebellious child that can never get along with his stepmother, Pattani has never quite adjusted to Thai rule. It was once the heart and soul of a large Muslim principality that included the nearby provinces of Yala and Narathiwat. Although today's political situation has stunted the area's development, Pattani has a 500-year history of trading with the world's most notorious imperial powerhouses. The Portuguese established a trading post here in 1516, the Japanese passed through in 1605, the Dutch in 1609, and the British flexed their colonial muscle in 1612.

Yet despite the city's interesting past, there's little of interest in Pattani except its access to some decent nearby beaches. Unfortunately, the ongoing insurgency (see the boxed text, p596) has made all but a handful of these sandy destinations unsafe for the independent traveller.

◉ Sights

The Mae Nam Pattani (Pattani River) acts as a divider between the older town to the east and the newer town to the west. Along Th Ruedi you can see what is left of old Pattani architecture – the Sino-Portuguese style that was once so prevalent in this part of southern Thailand. On Th Arnoaru there are several very old, but still quite intact, Chinese-style homes.

Thailand's second-largest mosque is the **Matsayit Klang** (Th Naklua Yarang), a traditional structure with a green hue that is probably still the south's most important mosque. It was built in the 1960s.

If it weren't for the political unrest, Pattani could be one of the better beach destinations in the region. Unfortunately, exploring much of the area independently is not a safe option at this time, and there are plenty of pretty beaches further north that are perfectly safe.

Locals frequent **Laem Tachi**, a sandy cape that juts out over the northern end of Ao Pattani. It can be reached by boat taxi from Pattani pier. **Hat Talo Kapo**, 14km east of Pattani near Yaring Amphoe, is another hot spot. And although it's technically in Songkhla Province, **Thepha district**, 35km northwest of Pattani, is the most developed beach destination in the area. There you'll find a few slightly aged resorts that cater mostly to middle-class Thais. At **Hat Soi Sawan**, near the Songkhla–Pattani border, several families have set up informal beachfront restaurants that are popular with weekend visitors. To reach Thepha, hop on any Songkhla-bound bus from Pattani (or vice versa); mention the name of your resort and you'll be deposited at the side of the road for the brief walk to the beach.

🛏 Sleeping & Eating

PATTANI TOWN

CS Pattani Hotel   HOTEL $$
(📞0 7333 5093; www.cspattanihotel.com; 299 Moo 4, Th Nong Jik; r/ste incl breakfast 1000-1500/2500-3500B; 🌬@🛜🏊) If you are spending the night in Pattani, you might as well enjoy it. The CS Pattani features a gorgeous colonial lobby, two pools, an excellent restaurant, a sauna and steam room...the list goes on. It's located about 2km west of the centre of town.

Palace Hotel   HOTEL $
(📞0 7334 9171; 10-12 Pipit Soi Talattewiwat 2; r 200-700B; 🌬) Despite its location in a grubby soi near the town market, the rooms here, in particular those with air-con on the lower floors, are neat and comfortable.

Satay Jao Kao
MUSLIM-THAI $

(37/20 Th Udomwithi; dishes 20-30B; ☺10am-6pm) This well-respected open-air restaurant serves beef satay local style with cubes of rice and a sweet dipping sauce. Several other restaurants along Th Udomwithi come highly recommended by Pattani's Muslim foodies.

THEPHA DISTRICT

Sakom Cabana
RESORT $$

(☑0 7431 8065; 136 Moo 4, Tambon Sakom; r 600-800B; ✳) Located about 40km from Pattani town, this basic resort features a clean compound with several attractive wooden duplex bungalows a short walk from the beach.

ℹ Information

There are several banks along the southeastern end of Th Pipit, near the Th Naklua Yarang intersection.

Internet cafe (cnr Th Peeda Talattewiwat 2 & Th Pipit; per hr 20B) Near Palace Hotel.

Pattani Hospital (☑0 7332 3411-14; Th Nong Jik)

Police station (☑0 7334 9018; Th Pattani Phirom)

ℹ Getting There & Around

Minivans are the region's most popular mode of transport and there are frequent daytime departures to Hat Yai (100B, 1½ hours), Narathiwat (100B, two hours), Songkhla (90B, 1½ hours) and Sungai Kolok (130B, 2½ hours) at various terminals around Pattani town. Ask at your hotel for the departure points. Buses to Bangkok (594B to 1187B, 15 to 16 hours) depart from the station near the CS Pattani Hotel. Local taxis can take you anywhere in town for 10B per person.

Narathiwat
นราธิวาส

POP 109,000

Sitting on the banks of the Bang Nara River, Narathiwat is probably the most Muslim large city in Thailand. Some of the Sino-Portuguese buildings lining the riverfront are over a century old, and some pleasant beaches are just outside town. Unfortunately the security situation in this part of the country (see the boxed text, p596) has suffocated the little tourism that this region used to see. Be sure to check the latest situation before travelling to Narathiwat.

⊙ Sights

Towards the southern end of Th Pichitbamrung stands **Matsayit Klang**, a wooden mosque built in the Sumatran style. It was reputedly built by a prince of the former kingdom of Pattani over a hundred years ago.

Just north of town is **Hat Narathat**, a 5km-long sandy beach fronted by towering pines, which serves as a veritable public park for locals. The beach is only 2km from the town centre – you can easily walk there or take a săhm·lór.

Five kilometres south of town, **Ao Manao** used to be a popular sun and sand destination, but today it's increasingly the stomping ground of local fishermen.

The tallest seated-Buddha image in southern Thailand is at **Wat Khao Kong**, 6km southwest on the way to the train station in Tanyongmat. The image is 17m long and 24m high, and made of reinforced concrete covered with tiny gold-coloured mosaic tiles that glint magically in the sun.

🛏 Sleeping & Eating

Most of the town's accommodation is located on and around Th Puphapugdee along the Bang Nara River.

Tanyong Hotel
HOTEL $$

(☑0 7351 1477; 16/1 Th Sophaphisai; r incl breakfast 900-1700B; ✳🛜) A few decades ago this was undoubtedly Narathiwat's most upscale hotel, but the passing of time has rendered it a convenient and competent, although slightly overpriced, choice.

Ocean Blue Mansion
HOTEL $

(☑0 7351 1109; 297 Th Puphapugdee; r 350-1500B; ✳) This hotel/apartment is the only one in town to really take advantage of the riverfront view. Rooms include a huge fridge and cable TV.

Jay Sani
MUSLIM-THAI $

(50/1 Th Sophaphisai; dishes 30-60B) This is where locals go for excellent Thai-Muslim food. Point to whatever curry or stir-fry looks good, but be sure not to miss the sublime beef soup.

Ang Mo
CHINESE, THAI $

(cnr Th Puphapugdee & Th Chamroonnara; dishes 30-80B; ☺lunch & dinner) This exceedingly popular Chinese restaurant is both cheap and tasty, and has even fed the likes of members of the Thai royal family.

BORDER CROSSING: SUNGAI KOLOK TO RANTAU PANJANG

The Thai **border** (⊘5am-9pm) is about 1km from the centre of Sungai Kolok or the train station. After completing border formalities, cross the bridge to the Malaysian border post, and then to an informal transport centre, where a share taxi to Kota Bharu, the capital of Malaysia's Kelantan State, will cost about RM$8 per person (about 80B) or about RM$40 to charter the whole car yourself. The ride takes around 40 minutes. There are also buses to Kota Bharu for RM$4.50, taking about an hour.

It's possible to continue south by the so-called 'jungle train', but the closest station is at Pasir Mas, located along taxi/bus routes to Kota Bharu.

Tak Bai, also in Narathiwat, and Betong, further south in Yala, are also legal crossing points for foreign tourists, but the abundance of transport and other infrastructure makes Sungai Kolok–Rantau Panjang the area's most convenient crossing point.

ⓘ Information

The **Tourism Authority of Thailand office** (TAT; ☑nationwide call centre 1672, Narathiwat 0 7352 2411) is inconveniently located a few kilometres south of town, just across the bridge on the road to Tak Bai.

ⓘ Getting There & Around

Air Asia (☑nationwide call centre 02 515 9999; www.airasia.com; Narathiwat Airport) and **Nok Air** (☑nationwide call centre 1318; www.nokair. co.th; Narathiwat Airport) each operate a daily flight to and from Bangkok (from 1790B, 90 minutes).

Air-con buses to Bangkok and Phuket and most minivans leave from the **bus terminal** (☑0 7351 1552) 2km south of town on Th Rangae Munka. Buses to Phuket (530B, 12 hours), which originate in Sungai Kolok, pass Narathiwat three times daily at 7am, 9am and 6.30pm, and continue via Pattani, Hat Yai, Songkhla, Trang, Krabi and Phang-Nga. Buses to Bangkok (669B to 1296B, 15 hours) depart several times during the day.

Minivans heading to Hat Yai (150B, three hours), Pattani (100B, two hours), Songkhla (150B, two hours), Sungai Kolok (70B, one hour) and Yala (100B, 1½ hours) generally leave on an hourly basis from 5am to 5pm.

Narathiwat is small enough to navigate by foot, although motorcycle taxis only charge 20B to get around.

Sungai Kolok   สุไหงโกลก

POP 70,000

Although Narathiwat is officially the provincial capital, it's a skinny wimp compared to its bigger and brasher sibling, Sungai Kolok. This soulless border town is the main southern coastal gateway between Malaysia and Thailand, and the primary industries here revolve around border trade and catering to weekending Malaysian men who are often looking for sex. Every night Soi Phuthon and the small strip behind the Marina Hotel come alive with booming bars that make Pattaya or Patong look sedate in comparison.

🛏 Sleeping & Eating

If you must stay the night in Sungai Kolok, there's a large assortment of hotels to choose from – most cater to the 'by-the-hour' clientele.

Unfortunately, despite the mix of cultures and emphasis on tourism, Sungai Kolok is definitely not a culinary destination. A small **night market** unfolds next to the immigration office – exceptionally good and cheap eats can be got at the stall in the centre that only has Chinese writing.

Genting Hotel   HOTEL $$

(☑0 7361 3231; 250 Th Asia 18; r 620-720B, ste 1520B; ❄🛜🏊) Geared towards the conference trade, the Genting comes equipped with a pub and a karaoke lounge. There are some good, only slightly scuffed, midrange rooms, and it's away from the seedier areas.

Merlin Hotel   HOTEL $

(☑0 7361 8111; 68 Th Charoenkhet; r 480-700B; ❄) Don't let the lobby fool you – the rooms here are very plain indeed, but the Merlin's a good choice if you need a cheap room with a view.

ⓘ Information

In addition to the one at the border, there is an **immigration office** (☑0 7361 1231; Th Charoenkhet; ⊘8.30am-4.30pm Mon-Fri) across from the Merlin Hotel. A tourist police office sits at the border. There are plenty of banks with

ATMs in town as well as foreign-exchange booths, which are open during border-crossing hours.

CS Internet (Th Asia 18; internet per hr 20B; ⊙10am-9pm) Across from the Genting Hotel.

ℹ Getting There & Away

Bus & Minivan

The long-distance **bus station** (☎0 7361 2045) is located east of downtown, from where there are three daily air-con buses for the 18-hour trip to Bangkok (720B to 1400B) between 9pm and 10pm. There are two early-morning buses that head to Phuket (580B), stopping in Krabi (460B) along the way. Minivans to Narathiwat (80B, one hour) depart on the half-hour from across from the train station. Minivans heading to Pattani (130B, 2½ hours), Yala (90B) and Hat Yai (180B,

four hours) depart hourly during daylight hours, from in front of the Genting Hotel.

Train

Two daily trains connect Sungai Kolok to Bangkok (200B to 1753B, about 20 hours, departures at 11.30am and 2.20pm). Local trains also make stops in Surat Thani, Nakhon Si Thammarat and Hat Yai; to check timetables and prices for other destinations contact the **State Railway of Thailand** (☎nationwide call centre 1690; www.railway.co.th) or look at their website.

ℹ Getting Around

Motorcycle taxis zoom around town – it'll cost you around 30B to make the ride between the city centre and the border.

Phuket & the Andaman Coast

Best Places to Eat

» Trang Night Market (p676)

» Rum Jungle (p634)

» Ka Jok See (p631)

» Tatonka (p647)

Best Places to Stay

» Six Senses Hideaway (p621)

» Mom Tri's Villa Royale (p635)

» Indigo Pearl (p649)

» Sukorn Beach Bungalows (p683)

» Pak-up Hostel (p652)

Why Go?

The Andaman is Thailand's turquoise coast, that place on a 'Travel to Paradise' poster that makes you want to leave your job and live in flip-flops…forever. And for once, the beauty exceeds the hype. White beaches, cathedral-like limestone cliffs, neon corals and hundreds of jungle-covered isles extend down the Andaman Sea from the border of Myanmar to Malaysia. Photographs haven't yet fully captured the array of blues and greens, let alone the soft fingers of humidity on the skin or the feel of the world's softest sands between your toes. For this, you'll need to visit.

The catch is, the destination is no secret and the beaches are becoming more crowded with backpackers, package tourists and everyone in between. Flashy resorts are pushing out the bamboo shacks and authenticity now hides in the backroads. But your poster dream is still here – if you're willing to look.

When to Go

May to October is the rainy season. At this time, the sea swells kick up surf, many resorts close and others slash their prices. The Vegetarian Festival is held in late September or October and involves parades of pierced-faced worshippers, endless firecrackers and great meatless food.

December to January is the high season for tourism. Prices soar, and accommodation and transport need to be booked in advance.

RANONG PROVINCE

The first piece in the Andaman's puzzle of coastal provinces is the least-populated region in Thailand and also its most rainy, with up to eight months of showers per year. As a result, Ranong's forests are lush and green, but it means that it's swampy near the mainland coast where beaches are almost nonexistent.

Ranong Town

POP 24,500

On the eastern bank of the Sompaen River's turbid, tea-brown estuary, the frontier town of Ranong is a short boat ride – or a filthy swim – from Myanmar. This border town par excellence (shabby, frenetic, slightly seedy) has a thriving Burmese population (keep an eye out for men wearing traditional *longyi;* Burmese sarong), a clutch of hot springs and some tremendous street food.

Today the town is basking in the transit tourism to Ko Phayam more than the visa runs it was once known for (visas given at the border are only given for two weeks now). Meanwhile, more and more dive operators specialising in live-aboard trips to the Surin or Similan Islands and Burma Banks are establishing themselves here, adding a pinch of an expat feel.

⊙ Sights & Activities

Ranong lacks the sophistication of your standard spa town, but you can sample the waters at sacred, outdoor **Rakswarin Hot Springs** (Th Petchkasem; admission free; ⊗8am-5pm), 2km east of town, and where there are pools hot enough to boil eggs (65°C); it's thought to possess miraculous healing powers.

Siam Hot Spa (☑0 7781 3551; www.siamhotsparanong.com; 73/3 Th Petchkasem), opposite the public springs, offers a more sterilised mineral-bath experience. You can dip into a jacuzzi (600B) or standard tubs (300B), and pair it with a salt scrub (550B) or a massage (200B).

Live-aboard diving trips to world-class bubble-blowing destinations, including the Burma Banks and the Surin and Similan Islands, are all the rage in Ranong. Try

---

BORDER CROSSING: RENEWING VISAS AT VICTORIA POINT

The dusty, tumbledown port at the southernmost tip of mainland Myanmar was named Victoria Point by the British, but is known as Ko Song (Second Island) by the Thais. The Burmese appellation, Kawthoung, is most likely a corruption of the Thai name. Most travellers come here to renew their visas, but the place also makes an interesting day trip.

The easiest way to renew your visa is to opt for one of the 'visa trips' (from 1000B per person including visa fees) offered by travel agencies in Ranong – check out Pon's (p607) – but it's relatively easy to do the legwork yourself.

When the Thailand–Myanmar border is open, boats to Kawthoung leave from the pier at Saphan Plaa (Pla Bridge, about 5km from the centre of Ranong). Take *sŏrng·tǎa·ou* (small pickup truck, also spelt *sǎwngthǎew*) 2 from Ranong (20B) to the pier, where captains of long-tail boats will lead you to the immigration window then to their boat (per person one-way/return 100/200B). When negotiating your price, confirm whether it is per person or per ride, and one-way or return. At the checkpoint, you must inform the authorities that you're a day visitor – in which case you will pay a fee of US$10 (it must be a crisp bill, you can get one from harbour touts for about 500B). The only big hassles come from 'helpers' on the Myanmar side who offer to do everything from carrying your day pack to collecting forms and then ask for hefty tips.

It's possible to stay overnight in one of Victoria Point's dingy, overpriced hotels but note that this is a rough town and lone women in particular may not feel safe. If you have a valid Myanmar visa in your passport, you'll be permitted to stay for up to 28 days.

If you're just coming to renew your Thai visa, the whole process will take a minimum of two hours. Bear in mind when you are returning to Thailand that Myanmar's time is 30 minutes behind Thailand's. This has caused problems in the past for returning visitors who got through Burmese immigration before its closing time only to find the **Thai immigration office** (⊗8.30am-4.30pm) closed. It's a good idea to double-check Thai immigration closing hours when leaving the country – if you don't get stamped in you'll have to return to Myanmar again the next day.

Phuket & the Andaman Coast Highlights

❶ Cavort with curious pufferfish amid the fiery-coloured coral of the **Trang Islands** (p680)

❷ Scale a limestone cliff then recuperate in the blissful jade waters of **Railay** (p657)

❸ Float in a sea of lapis lazuli while gazing at the limestone crags of **Ko Phi-Phi** (p662)

❹ Traipse through the veritable Jurassic Park of **Khao Sok National Park** (p611)

❺ Snorkel over healthy coral reefs by day and chill at low-key reggae bars at night on **Ko Lipe** (p687)

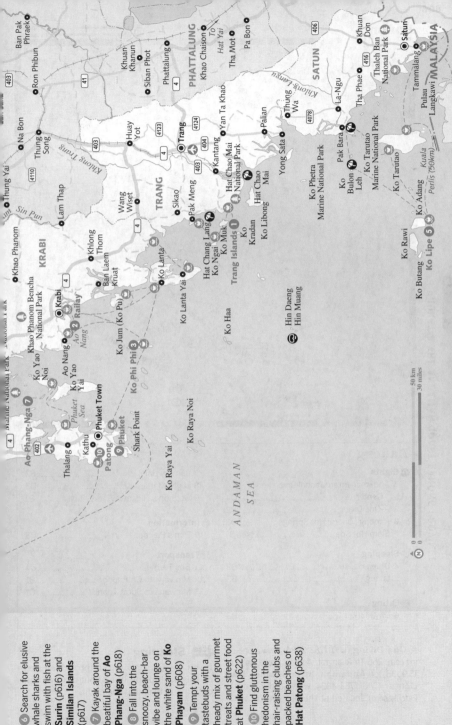

6 Search for elusive whale sharks and swim with fish at the **Surin** (p616) and **Similan Islands** (p617)

7 Kayak around the beatiful bay of **Ao Phang-Nga** (p618)

8 Fall into the snoozy, beach-bar vibe and lounge on the white sand of **Ko Phayam** (p608)

9 Tempt your tastebuds with a heady mix of gourmet treats and street food at **Phuket** (p622)

10 Find gluttonous hedonism in the hair-raising clubs and packed beaches of **Hat Patong** (p638)

Ranong

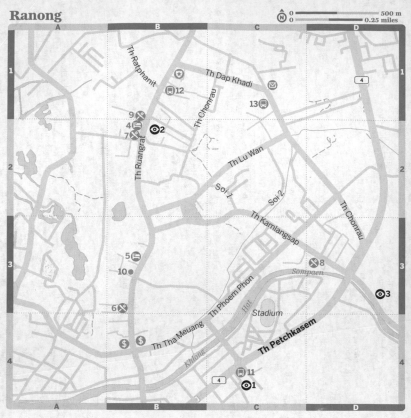

Ranong

A-One-Diving (☎0 7783 2984; www.a-one-div ing.com; 256 Th Ruangrat; 4-night packages from 15,900B) or **Andaman International Dive Center** (☎0 7783 4824; www.aidcdive.com; Th Petchkasem), located at the bus station.

🛏 Sleeping

If you are doing a visa run through an agency, they'll ship you in and out of town without having to spend the night.

Luang Poj   GUEST HOUSE $
(☑0 7783 3377, 08 7266 6333; luangpoj@gmail.
com; 225 Th Ruangrat; r 500B;❄🌐) Luang Poj is
a gorgeous remodel of Ranong's first hotel: a
1920s-era building. Most rooms are windowless and all share warm-water bathrooms
and are decorated in a signature colour (we
like the purple room). It's further highlighted with modern flair: think Indian art, bird-
cages, one-of-a-kind light fixtures and retro
photography.

Dhala House   GUEST HOUSE $
(☑0 7781 2959; http://dahla.siam2web.com; 323/5
Th Ruangrat; r 400-500B; ❄🌐) The Dhala has
cute, concrete bungalows with tiled floors
and pebbled tile bathrooms; the bungalows
line a garden and are set off the main drag.
It has got the friendliest vibe in town and
management will happily arrange a late
check-out if you're on a visa run.

✕ Eating & Drinking

Ranong has a lively, young and very local
drinking scene involving lots of karaoke.

On Th Kamlangsap, there is a **night market** not far from Hwy 4 that sells great Thai
dishes at low prices. The **day market** on Th
Ruangrat offers inexpensive Thai and Burmese meals.

Jammy Bar   THAI, INTERNATIONAL $$
(Th Ruangrat; dishes from 69B; 🌐) The indoor-
outdoor garden is vaguely Balinese and is
the best-looking dining area in town. Luck-
ily the food is great too: the Thai dishes are
fantastic as are the stranger choices includ-
ing grilled ostrich (229B) or local beef (129B).
There's live music on weekend nights.

Sophon's Hideaway   THAI & INTERNATIONAL $$
(☑0 7783 2730; Th Ruangrat; mains 80-250B;
☺10am-midnight; 🌐) This expat favourite has
everything, including internet access, a free
pool table, a pizza oven, full bar, water features and rattan furnishings aplenty.

ℹ Information

Internet can be found along Th Ruangrat for 20B
per hour and there's a cluster of ATMs at the Th
Tha Meuang and Th Ruangrat intersection.
Main post office (Th Chonrau; ☺9am-4pm
Mon-Fri, to noon Sat)

ℹ Getting There & Away
Air
Ranong Air (☑0 7783 2222; www.ranongair.
com) runs four flights per week between Ranong

and Bangkok (one-way 2800B), Phuket (one-way
2300B) and Hat Yai (one-way 2800B). Book
flights at Pon's Place.

Bus
The bus terminal is on Th Petchkasem 1km from
town, though some Bangkok-bound buses stop
at the main market. *Sŏrng·tǎa·ou 2* (blue) passes
the terminal. Some bus services are shown in
the table:

DESTINATION	PRICE	DURATION
Bangkok	240-680B	10hr
Chumphon	100B	3hr
Hat Yai	410B	5hr
Khao Lak	150B	3½hr
Krabi	200-300B	6hr
Phang-Nga	150B	5hr
Phuket	240B	5-6hr
Surat Thani	100-180B	4-5hr

Minivans head to Surat Thani (250B, 3½ hours,
four times daily) and Chumphon (120B, three
hours, hourly from 6am to 5pm); see the map for
departure locations.

ℹ Getting Around

Motorcycle taxis will take you almost anywhere
in town for 20B, to the hotels along Th Petchkasem for 25B and to the pier (for 50B) for boats
to Ko Chang, Ko Phayam and Myanmar. Pon's
Place can assist with motorcycle and car rentals
and offers shuttle vans from its office to the ferry
docks for 50B.

Ko Chang   เกาะช้าง

If you're looking for the big Ko Chang,
you've come to the wrong place. But if your
suitcase is overflowing with novels and
you're seeking a silent stretch of sand on
which to read them, then welcome! Unlike

PON'S PLACE: RANONG'S TOURISM EXPERT

Pon's Place (☑08 1597 4549; www.
ponplace-ranong.com; Th Ruangrat;
☺7.30am-midnight) is the go-to spot in
Ranong for everything from Western
breakfasts (from 40B) to Ranong Air
bookings. Pon himself is a friendly guy
with his phone essentially attached
to his head, as he micromanages his
Ranong tourism empire. If you need
help with anything, stop here first.

most of the Andaman's islands, Ko Chang enjoys its back-to-basics lifestyle – there are no ATMs, internet (2B per minute) is found only at Cashew Resort on Ao Yai and there's no rush for more development.

When you're done with your book, spend your time exploring the island's tiny village 'capital' (and we use that word lightly), or wind your way around on one of the dirt trails. Sea eagles, Andaman kites and hornbills all nest here, and, if you're lucky, you'll catch sight of them floating above the mangroves.

Bungalow operators can arrange boat trips to Ko Phayam (p608) and other nearby islands for around 200B per person (including lunch) in a group of six or more. Dive trips are also possible. **Aladdin Dive Cruise** (☑0 7782 0472; www.aladdindivecruise.de), on Ko Chang, runs PADI courses and offers a range of live-aboard dive safaris.

🛏 Sleeping & Eating

Ao Yai is the main beach where you'll find most lodging options and there are a few more places tucked away on Ao Tadaeng, to the south, which is linked to Ao Yai via a short walking track. More isolated options can be found on the beaches to the north and far south of the island. All guest houses have restaurants that also welcome nonguests.

Crocodile Rock   GUEST HOUSE $
(☑08 0533 4138; tonn1970@yahoo.com; Ao Yai; bungalows 250-450B) Outstanding bamboo bungalows hover on Ao Yai's serene southern headland with superb bay views through gentle foliage. Its classy kitchen turns out homemade yoghurt, breads, cookies, good espresso and a variety of veggie and seafood dishes.

Sawasdee   GUEST HOUSE $
(☑08 6906 0900, 08 1803 0946; www.sawadeekohchang.com; Ao Yai; bungalows 350-600B) The A-frame wooden bungalows have vented walls to keep things cool and every option has sunken bathrooms painted bright colours, and hammocks on the terraces.

Sunset Bungalows   GUEST HOUSE $
(☑08 4339 5224, 08 0693 8577; Ao Yai; bungalows 250-400B) Sweet wooden bungalows with bamboo decks and attached Thai-style bathrooms sit back in the trees along Ao Yai's best stretch of beach.

Mama's   GUEST HOUSE $
(☑0 7782 0180, 08 0530 7066; mamasbungalows@yahoo.com; Ao Tadaeng; huts 250-300B) One of three good choices on Ao Tadaeng, Mama's is tucked into a pretty corner on a rocky, hibiscus-laden hillside.

❶ Getting There & Away

From central Ranong Town, take a *sŏrng·tăa·ou* (25B) or a shuttle run by most guest houses (50B) to Saphan Plaa. Three long-tail boats (150B) and two speedboats (350B) leave daily from mid-October to May. All stop on the island's west coast beaches.

A taxi boat service connecting Ko Chang and Ko Phayam runs on weekdays only from Koh Chang Resort on Ao Yai. This boat (per person 150B each way, one hour) leaves Ko Chang at 10am and returns at 4pm.

Ko Phayam   เกาะพยาม

Technically part of Laem Son National Park (p609), little Ko Phayam is a beach-laden isle that – for now – is managing to go mainstream while still holding onto its soul. Spectacular beaches are dotted with beach bungalows and the wooded interior has some rudimentary concrete motorbike paths. Fauna in the area includes wild pigs, monkeys and snakes, and look for sea eagles, toucans and hornbills. The one 'village' on the island, where you will also find the main pier and a majestic golden Buddha at **Wat Phayam**, caters mostly to tourists but hit it during a festival (such as the Cashew Festival in April) and you'll see that islanders still have a firm attachment to their homeland.

The main drawback of Ko Phayam is that the snorkelling isn't great but the Surin Islands are relatively close and you can hop on live-aboard dive expeditions or speedboat transfers. For dive trips and PADI courses contact **Phayam Divers** (☑08 6995 2598; www.phayamlodge.com; Ao Yai).

🛏 Sleeping & Eating

Electricity is often only available from sunset to 10pm or 11pm. Most resorts are open year-round and have attached eateries serving Thai fare that are also open to nonguests. Every strip of sand has its low-key, driftwood beach bar.

oPP Land   HOTEL $
(☑08 1678 4310; www.payampplandbeach.com; Ao Hin-Khow; bungalows 650B) This is a stunning ecolodge, north of the pier on the

little-visited windward side of the island. The stylish concrete bungalows are powered by the wind and sun and have terraces that overlook the sea. The owners have set up an organic garden, make their own all-natural laundry detergent and treat the sewage with a cutting-edge grey-water system.

Chomjan Resort
HOTEL **$**

(☑08 5678 4166; www.chomjanresort.com; Ao Khao Kwai; bungalows 500-800B) One of the most comfortable places on this beach; tidy concrete bungalows are up on a beachside slope and have sea views through mature trees. All have terraces with lounging cushions and open-to-sky bathrooms. The restaurant here serves excellent Thai fare.

Starlight Bungalows
GUEST HOUSE **$**

(☑08 1978 5301; http://sites.google.com/site/starlightbungalows/; Ao Khao Kwai; bungalows 500-650B) American-Thai run; choose from high-ceiling spacious wooden huts or small bamboo ones further back in the trees. The social vibe here is as fab as the food – Pom the cook regularly wins local Thai-food cook-offs.

Bamboo Bungalows
GUEST HOUSE **$$**

(☑0 7782 0012; www.bamboo-bungalows.com; bungalows 550-1500B; ❄⚡) This is a very popular and social beachfront property with a lush garden and a lounge-restaurant with hammocks and cool log swings out the front. Bungalows range from sagging bamboo jobs to fairly luxurious peaked-roof cottages that have tiled floors, ceiling fans and outdoor rain showers.

Mr Gao
HOTEL **$**

(☑0 7787 0222; www.mr-gao-phayam.com; Ao Khao Kwai; bungalows from 250B; ⛆) The varnished wood or bamboo bungalows are a hit with activity-oriented couples and families. It has 24-hour electricity and kayak rental, and arranges transport and multiday trips to the Surin Islands (see p616).

Aow Yai Bungalows
GUEST HOUSE **$**

(☑0 7787 0216, 08 9819 8782; bungalows 300-600B) This is the thatched bamboo bungalow pioneer that started it all here in the late 1980s. Choose between small wooden and bamboo bungalows in the palm grove and a larger beachfront model on the southern end of Ao Yai.

ℹ Getting There & Around

There are daily ferries from Ranong's Saphan Plaa to Ko Phayam's main pier (150B, 1½ to two hours) at 9am and 2pm, and speedboats (350B, 45 minutes) at 10am and 2.30pm. From Ko Phayam back to Ranong the boats run at 9am and 1pm. Long-tail–boat charters to Ko Chang are 1200B, or you can take the taxi boat (150B, one hour) that departs from the main pier at 4pm on weekdays only.

A motorcycle taxi from the pier to the main beaches costs 50B to 80B per person each way depending on the beach. Motorbike and bicycle rentals are available in the village, and from most of the larger resorts.

Laem Son National Park

อุทยานแห่งชาติแหลมสน

This **national park** (☑0 7786 1431; www.dnp.go.th; adult/child 200/100B) covers 315 sq km. It includes about 100km of Andaman Sea coastline – the longest protected shore in the country – and more than 20 islands. Much of the coast here is edged with mangroves and laced with tidal channels, which are home to various species of birds, fish, deer and monkeys. Sea turtles nest on Hat Praphat.

KO PHAYAM'S BEACHES

Ko Phayam has many small beaches but these two long stretches of sandy bliss are where most folk end up:

» **Ao Khao Kwai (Buffalo Bay)** is a golden white cove with jungled bluffs and a rock reef offshore – it's the most stunning location on the island. Lovers of peace and quiet head here along with some hippies and the occasional German package tourist. It's a terrific swimming beach, too, except at low tide, when the sea recedes leaving mud flats on the southern end.

» **Ao Yai** is long, wide and chilled out yet social, attracting everyone from gap-year backpackers to glam-packing couples to young families to retirees. The surf kicks up in the fringe and low seasons and you can rent boogie boards and surfboards at guest houses along the beach. At other times the swimming is great here and the island's best snorkelling (don't expect much) is found off **Leam Rung**, Ao Yai's northernmost point.

ANDAMAN DISCOVERIES COMMUNITY-BASED TOURISM

Andaman Discoveries (☏08 7917 7165; www.andamandiscoveries.com; Khuraburi), formerly Northern Andaman Tsunami Relief, runs highly recommended community-based tours of one to seven days, including to Ban Talae Nok, a historic fishing village surrounded by tropical forest and mangroves, just down the road from 6km of uninhabited beach. There's an award-winning homestay here featuring cultural and handicraft activities, and fishing and snorkelling trips to uninhabited islands. Pair it with a visit to Laem Son and its warm-hearted residents, who also offer handicraft and sustainable-agriculture demonstrations.

Andaman Discoveries also manages three community-service projects: a learning centre for children of Burmese migrant workers; an orphanage outside of Khao Lak; and a school for disabled children in Phuket. Volunteer placement is available, and whatever you decide to do, it will be an unforgettable experience.

The most accessible beach is the gorgeous 3km white sweep of **Hat Bang Ben**, where the park headquarters are located. Look south and peninsulas jut out into the ocean like so many fingers hiding isolated coves accessible only by long-tail boat. All of the beaches are said to be safe for swimming year-round. From here you can also see several islands, including the nearby Ko Kam Yai, Ko Kam Noi, Mu Ko Yipun, Ko Khang Khao and, to the north, Ko Phayam. Park staff arrange boat trips to any of these islands for 1500B to 1800B depending upon the destination. If there is a prettier sunset picnic spot on the north Andaman coast, we missed it.

🛏 Sleeping & Eating

The following accommodation is at Hat Bang Ben. **Camping** (per person 80B) is allowed anywhere among the casuarinas (pay at the park office just inside the park entrance) or you can rent a tent from 150B per night.

Wasana Resort   GUEST HOUSE **$**
(☏0 7786 1434; bungalows 400-750B; ❄🖥) The Wasana is a family-run ring of cosy bungalows wrapping around the colourful on-site restaurant. The owners, a Dutch-Thai couple, have plenty of great ideas for exploring Laem Son (ask about the stunning 10km trek around the headland) and can take you out on a day trip to the islands.

National Park Bungalows   BUNGALOWS **$$**
(☏0 2562 0760; reserve@dnp.go.th; bungalows with fan 1200B, houses with air-con 1600B; ❄) Choose from basic fan-cooled bungalows and bigger houses with air-con. The on-site restaurant serves three meals per day.

ℹ Getting There & Away

The turn-off for Laem Son National Park is about 58km from Ranong down Hwy 4 (Petchkasem Hwy), between the Km 657 and Km 658 markers. Buses heading south from Ranong can drop you off here (ask for Hat Bang Ben). Once you're off the highway, however, you'll have to flag down a pickup truck going towards the park. If you can't get a ride all the way, it's a 10km walk from Hwy 4 to the park entrance.

Boats out to other various islands can be chartered from the park's visitors centre; the general cost is 1200B to 1500B per day.

PHANG-NGA PROVINCE

Wounds take a long time to heal, but Phang-Nga is finally on the mend. Although tales are still being told about the 2004 tsunami, there's a palpable sense of progress as hot spots such as Khao Lak return to the well-trodden route.

From November to April the water is very clear, the sun shines and soda-white beaches beckon. In the rainy season, however, many places shut down and the area can feel a bit haunted.

Ko Phra Thong & Ko Ra   เกาะพระทอง/เกาะระ

Legend has it that many centuries ago, pirates docked and buried a golden Buddha beneath the sands at Ko Phra Thong, translated as 'Golden Buddha Island'. The legendary statue has never been found but Ko Phra Thong's modern-day treasures are its endless sandy beaches, mangroves, vast birdlife and rare orchids.

Nearby and even quieter is golden beach and mangrove-encircled Ko Ra. This small isle is a mountainous jungle with an impressive array of wildlife (including leopard cats, flying lemurs, scaly anteaters and slow loris) and has a welcoming local population of fisherfolk.

Locals of Tung Dap village on the southern tip of Ko Phra Thong have requested that tourists not visit their area, so please be respectful and avoid this corner.

🛏 Sleeping

TOP CHOICE **Golden Buddha Beach Resort**   BUNGALOWS $$$
(✆08 1892 2208; www.goldenbuddharesort.com; bungalows 3100-14,000B) The area's poshest resort attracts a stream of yoga aficionados keen for a spiritual getaway. Accommodation is in naturalistic-chic privately owned wooden houses rented out short- or long-term. There's also a dive centre.

Ko Ra Eco-Resort   BUNGALOWS $$
(✆08 9867 5288, 08 5280 5507; www.thaiecolodge. com; bungalows 1100-1900B) Nestled in the trees on a small private beach, this older place is under new, activity-oriented management. Everything from meditation retreats to spectacular wildlife hikes and diving and snorkelling tours – including to the relatively nearby Surin Islands – is available.

ℹ Getting There & Away

There are no regular boats to Ko Phra Thong or Ko Ra, but you could theoretically charter a long-tail from the Kuraburi pier for around 1500B each way – boatmen are hard to find. It's far better and cheaper to contact your resort in advance to arrange transport.

Khao Sok National Park
อุทยานแห่งชาติเขาสก

If your leg muscles have atrophied after one too many days of beach-bumming, consider venturing inland to the wondrous Khao Sok National Park. Many believe this lowland jungle – the wettest spot in Thailand – to be over 160 million years old, making it one of the oldest rainforests on the globe. It features dramatic limestone formations and waterfalls that cascade through juicy thickets drenched with rain. A network of dirt trails snakes through the quiet park, allowing visitors to spy on the exciting array of indigenous creatures.

The best time of year to visit is between December and April – the dry season. During the June to October wet season, trails can be extremely slippery, flash flooding is common and leeches come out in force. On the other hand, animals leave their hidden reservoirs throughout the wet months, so you're more likely to stumble across big fauna.

◉ Sights & Activities

Khao Sok's vast terrain makes it one of the last viable habitats for large mammals. During the wetter months you may happen upon bear, boar, gaur, tapirs, gibbons, deer, wild elephants and perhaps even a tiger. There are more than 300 bird species, 38 bat varieties and one of the world's largest flowers, the rare *Rafflesia kerrii*, which is found only in Khao Sok (within Thailand). These giant flowers can reach 80cm in diameter.

Chiaw Lan, created in 1982 by an enormous shale-clay dam called Ratchaprapha (Kheuan Ratchaprapha or Chiaw Lan), sits about an hour's drive (65km) east of the visitors centre. The limestone outcrops protruding from the lake reach a height of 960m, over three times higher than the formations in the Phang-Nga area.

Tham Nam Thalu cave contains striking limestone formations and subterranean streams, while Tham Si Ru features four converging passageways used as a hideout by communist insurgents between 1975 and 1982. The caves can be reached on foot from the southwestern shore of the lake. You can rent boats from local fishermen to explore the coves, canals, caves and cul-de-sacs along the lakeshore.

Elephant trekking, kayaking and rafting are popular park activities. The hiking is also excellent, and you can arrange park tours from any guest house in or around the park. Various trails you can hike independently from the visitors centre lead to the

ℹ KHAO SOK TOURS

Tours in and around Khao Sok can be up to 50% cheaper when booked at guest houses or travel agents near the park itself. Tours booked from further-afield destinations such as Phuket or Khao Lak will include higher-priced transport and tour-agent commissions.

waterfalls of **Sip-Et Chan** (4km), **Than Sa-wan** (9km) and **Than Kloy** (9km), among other destinations. The park office hands out free trail maps.

🛏 Sleeping & Eating

The road leading into the park is lined with simple, charming guest houses and all offer a variety of park tours and guide services, while some are located a short distance from the road; minibuses travel along this road. We recommend going on a two-day, one-night trip (2500B per person) to Chiaw Lan where you sleep in floating huts on the lake and go on variety of canoe and hiking excursions.

Most guest houses have their own eateries (also open to nonguests) and there are a few restaurants on the road as well.

Art's Riverview Jungle Lodge
GUEST HOUSE **$$**

(☎08 6470 3234; http://krabidir.com/artsriverviewlodge; bungalows 650B) In a monkey-filled jungle bordering a river with a natural limestone cliff-framed swimming hole, this is the prettiest location in Khao Sok. Wood bungalows are simple but big; all have river views.

Morning Mist Resort
HOTEL **$$**

(☎08 9971 8794; www.khaosokmorningmistresort.com; bungalows 650-1000B; ❀) One of the more comfortable choices. All of the clean, tiled, fan-cooled bungalows have balconies and the most expensive overlook the river.

Jungle Huts
GUEST HOUSE **$**

(☎0 7739 5160; www.khao-sok-junglehuts.com; huts 300-1200B) Basic but good-value huts sit in a forest of fruit trees near a river or high up on stilts connected by a vertiginous walkway.

Tree Tops River Huts
GUEST HOUSE **$$**

(☎08 7283 2133; www.treetopsriverhuts.com; bungalows 540-1900B; ❀) Right at the park entrance, solid but ageing bungalows are high on stilts in the trees overlooking the river.

ℹ Information

The **park headquarters** (☎0 7739 5025; www.khaosok.com; park admission 200B) and visitors centre are 1.8km off Rte 401, close to the Km 109 marker.

There's an ATM outside the Morning Mist Mini-Mart and internet is available near the park entrance for 2B per minute.

ℹ Getting There & Around

Minivans to Surat Thani (250B, one hour), Krabi (300B, two hours) and a handful of other destinations leave daily from the park. Otherwise, from Surat catch a bus going towards Takua Pa or from the Andaman coast, take a Surat Thani–bound bus. Buses drop you off along the highway (Rte 401), 1.8km from the visitors centre. If guest house touts don't meet you, you'll have to walk to your chosen nest (from 50m to 2km).

To explore Chiaw Lan lake on your own, charter a long-tail (2000B per day) at the dam's entrance.

Khao Lak & Around   เขาหลัก

Hat Khao Lak is a beach for folks who shun the glitz of Phuket's bigger resort towns, but still crave comfort, shopping and plenty of facilities. With warm waves to frolic in, long stretches of golden sand backed by forested hills, and easy day trips to the Similan and Surin Islands, Khao Sok and Khao Lak/Lam Ru National Parks or even

---

TSUNAMI EARLY WARNING SYSTEM

On the morning of 26 December 2004, an earthquake off the coast of the Indonesian island of Sumatra sent enormous waves crashing against much of Thailand's Andaman coast, claiming around 8000 lives and causing millions of dollars of damage to homes and businesses. In 2005 Thailand officially inaugurated a national-disaster–warning system, which was created in response to the country's lack of preparedness in 2004. The Bangkok-based centre anticipates that a tsunami warning can be issued within 30 minutes of the event being detected by existing international systems.

If there is another tsunami, it's expected that the public will be warned via the nationwide radio network, Channel 5 army TV network, the state-operated TV pool and SMS messages. For non-Thai speakers, the centre has installed warning towers along the high-risk beachfront areas that will broadcast announcements in various languages accompanied by flashing lights. The **call centre** (☎1860) also handles questions and tips from the public regarding potential or unfolding disasters.

Phuket, the area is a central base for exploring the North Andaman – above and below the water.

About 2.5km north of Hat Khao Lak, **Hat Bang Niang** is an even quieter version of sandy bliss with skinnier beaches but fewer people. Khao Lak proper (also called Khao Lak Town locally) – a hodgepodge of restaurants, tourist markets and low-rise hotels along a grey highway – isn't exactly eye-catching, but it is convenient.

◉ Sights

Khao Lak/Lam Ru National Park   NATIONAL PARK
(🕿0 7642 0243; www.dnp.go.th; adult/child 100/50B; ⊙8am-4.30pm) The area immediately south of Hat Khao Lak has been incorporated into the vast 125-sq-km **Khao Lak/Lam Ru National Park**, a collage of sea cliffs, 1000m-high hills, beaches, estuaries, forested valleys and mangroves. Wildlife includes hornbills, drongos, tapirs, gibbons, monkeys and Asiatic black bears. The visitors centre, just off Hwy 4 between the Km 56 and Km 57 markers, has a very nice open-air restaurant on a shady slope overlooking the sea. From the restaurant you can take a fairly easy 3km round-trip nature trail that heads along the cape and ends at often-deserted Hat Lek beach.

Khlong Thap Liang   NATURE RESERVE
Guided hikes along the coast or inland can be arranged through many tour agencies in town, as can long-tail boat trips up the scenic **Khlong Thap Liang** estuary. The latter trip affords opportunities to view mangrove communities of crab-eating macaques.

Between Khao Lak and Bang Sak is a network of sandy **beach trails** – some of which lead to deserted beaches – which are fun to explore on foot or by rented motorcycle. Most of the hotels in Khao Lek Town rent motorbikes for 250B per day.

Boat 813   MONUMENT
In an open field nearly 1km from shore, this boat is a testament to the force of the 2004 Boxing Day Tsunami. Nearly 10 years later, it remains the region's most prominent reminder of the disaster. There's an information booth nearby with a tsunami timeline in both Thai and English. It's a 50B *sŏrng·tăa·ou* ride between here and Khao Lak.

Khao Lak

🏃 Activities

Diving & Snorkelling
Diving or snorkelling day excursions to the Similan and Surin islands are immensely popular, but if you can, opt for a live-aboard trip. Since the islands are around 60km from the mainland (about three hours by boat), if you do opt for a live-aboard you'll have a more relaxing trip and experience the islands

sans day-trippers. All dive shops offer live-aboard trips from around 10,000/19,000B for two-/three-day packages and day trips for 4900B to 6500B.

On these miltiday trips, you'll wake up with the dawn and slink below the ocean's surface up to four times each day in what's commonly considered to be one of the top 10 diving realms in the world. While both the Similan and Surin Islands (p616) have experienced vast coral bleaching recently, **Richelieu Rock** is still the *crème de la crème* of the region's sites and **Ko Bon** and **Ko Ta Chai** are two other good sites due to the traffic of giant manta rays.

Although geared towards divers, all dive shops welcome snorkellers who can hop on selected dive excursions or live-aboards for a discount of around 40%; otherwise, tour agencies all around town offer even cheaper snorkelling trips to the Similan Islands for around 2700B. PADI Open Water certification courses cost anywhere from 10,000B to 18,000B depending upon where you dive. You can go on a 'discover scuba' day trip to the Similans for around 6000B to 6500B.

Recommended dive shops:

Wicked Diving
DIVING
(0 7648 5868; www.wickeddiving.com) An exceptionally well-run and environmentally conscious outfit that runs diving and snorkelling overnight trips offering a range of live-aboard options including Whale Sharks & Mantas, Turtle & Reefs and Sharks & Rays conservation trips, run in conjunction with **Ecocean** (www.whaleshark.org). It does all the PADI courses, too.

Similan Diving Safaris
DIVING
(0 7648 5470; www.similan-diving-safaris.com) The speciality here is the high-quality four-day live-aboard (18,800B all-inclusive) that regularly attracts return customers. Knowledgeable staff and amazing food sweeten the deal. As far as live-aboards are concerned, this is probably the best bang for your baht. Day trips are also available.

Big Blue
DIVING
(0 7648 5544; www.bigbluekhaolak.com) Japanese and Swedish owned; its speedboat, live-aboard and dive instructors are among the best in Khao Lak.

Sea Dragon Diver Centre
DIVING
(0 7648 5614; www.iq-dive.com) (0 7648 5420; www.seadragondivecenter.com; Th Phetkasem)

One of the older operations in Khao Lak, Sea Dragon has maintained high standards throughout the years.

Sleeping

For the cheapest sleeps in town, head to Sea Dragon Diver Center (p614) and ask about the dorm beds at Tiffy's Café, which go for 180B per night.

Sarojin
HOTEL $$$
(0 7642 7900-4; www.sarojin.com; Hat Pakarang; r 12,500-22,250B; ❄@☎☒) A quiet retreat 15km north of Khao Lak with a Japanese-meets-modern-Thai style, the service here is stellar and the setting is elegant and intimate. The very private spa (treatments from 2300B), which takes in views of coconut groves and is nestled at the edge of the mangroves, is one of the best on the Andaman coast. We especially love the pool with its stylish lounging huts that hover above the crystal-blue water, and a cooking class takes place on the banks of the Takuapa River, where you can watch water buffalo stroll by. No kids allowed.

Nangthong Beach Resort
HOTEL $$
(0 7648 5911; www.nangthong2.com; r 2000-2200B, bungalows 2500-3000B; ❄@☎☒❀) The best choice in Khao Lak proper has large, well-appointed rooms, and even larger bungalows, with ceramic-tile floors, dark-wood furnishings, a burgeoning garden, impeccable service and the best stretch of sand in town.

La Flora Resort
HOTEL $$$
(0 7642 8000; www.lafloraresort.com; r 5700-7700B, villas 9000-10,500B; ❄@☎☒❀) On gorgeous Hat Bang Niang, this resort exudes barefoot class; it's both elegant and supremely relaxing. Cabana-style villas are large and modern with sexy beachfront infinity pools and there's a kid-friendly pool in the centre of things. Rooms have marble floors, ceramic sinks, striking modern art, mp3 docks and aromatherapy diffusers.

Le Meridian
HOTEL $$$
(0 7642 7500; www.lemeridien.com; Hat Bang Sak; r from 5220B, villas from 11,200B; ❄@☎☒) A four-star megaresort, its 243 rooms and 20 villas are the only nests on Hat Bang Sak, 20km north of Khao Lak. It lacks the boutique touch and five-star service of the Sarojin, but it is slightly cheaper and is certainly

majestic, sprawling nearly all the way from the highway to the sea.

Nangthong Bay Resort
HOTEL **$$**

(☑0 7648 5088; www.nangthong.com; r 200-3000B; ❄@☎☲⊛) Until its sister property (the Nangthong Beach Resort) opened, this was the best midranger on the beach. The rooms are designed with a sparse black-and-white chic decor. The cheapest rooms are set back from the beach, but are fantastic value. Grounds are lush and service is excellent.

Greenbeach
HOTEL **$$**

(☑0 7648 5845; greenbeach_th@yahoo.com; bungalows 1300-2300B; ❄⊛) On an excellent stretch of Khao Lak beach and extending back into a garden, this place has a warm family-style soul. The wooden bungalows have glass doors, air-con and fan, shady terraces and views of a towering, ancient banyan tree. Even the cheapest rooms have sea views.

Fasai House
GUEST HOUSE **$**

(☑0 7648 5867; r 500-700B; ❄@) The best budget choice in Khao Lak, Fasai has immaculate motel-style rooms and smiling staff members who coyly giggle like geishas.

Khao Lak/Lam Ru National Park Bungalows
BUNGALOWS **$**

(☑0 2562 0760; reserve@dnp.go.th; bungalows 800-2000B) There is a handful of four- and six-bed bungalows in the national park. Standards are basic, but the setting will suit those after an eco-experience.

Khaolak Banana Bungalows
BUNGALOWS **$**

(☑0 7648 5889; www.khaolakbanana.com; r 500-1200B; ❄⊛) These adorable little bungalows have swirls painted on the cement floors and sun-filled indoor-outdoor bathrooms. A cute pool with deckchairs sweetens the deal.

Walker's Inn
GUEST HOUSE **$**

(☑0 7648 5668; Th Petchkasem; r 400-750B; ❄☎) Its big but plain and ageing tiled rooms with air-con and hot showers sit above a pub. It's friendly and popular with backpackers.

✘ Eating & Drinking

This is no culinary capital, but there are a few local haunts where tourists congregate to rehash the day's diving yarns. Early-morning divers will be hard-pressed to find a place to grab a bite before 8.30am.

TOP CHOICE Mama's Restaurant
RESTAURANT **$$**

(Th Petchkasem; dishes 60-300B) Nobody, and we do mean nobody, does seafood better than Mama, who's set up across from Boat 813. Her fish cakes are insane, so is the barracuda sautéed in yellow curry.

Phu Khao Lak
RESTAURANT **$$**

(Th Petchkasem; dishes 80-240B; ◷breakfast, lunch & dinner) With its cloth tables spilling to the edges of a lawn at the southern end of the Khao Lak strip, this place is hard to miss. And you shouldn't because there's a huge menu of Western and Thai dishes here with ample descriptions, all cooked to perfection.

Pinocchio
RESTAURANT **$$$**

(☑0 7644 3079; 67/61 Th Hat Bang Niang, Hat Bang Niang; mains 240-480B) This beautiful candle-lit garden restaurant features a huge stone pizza oven, imported wine and cheese, tremendous sourdough bread, even better pizza, homemade pasta, and gelato.

Happy Snapper
BAR

(Th Petchkasem) Here's a bar stocked with good liquor, with a map of the world on the ceiling, the tree of life on the wall and a rockin' house band on stage six nights a week in the high season, led by the owner, a Bangkok-born bass legend.

❶ Information

For diving-related emergencies, call the **SSS Ambulance** (☑08 1081 9444), which rushes injured persons down to Phuket for treatment. The ambulance can also be used for car or motorcycle accidents. There is also one nurse in Bang Niang who caters to diving related injuries.

There are numerous travel agencies scattered about – the best is **Khao Lak Land Discoveries** (☑0 7648 5411; www.khaolaklanddiscovery.com; Th Phetkasem).

❶ Getting There & Away

Any bus running along Hwy 4 between Takua Pa (50B, 45 minutes) and Phuket (100B, two hours) will stop at Hat Khao Lak if you ask the driver.

Khao Lak Discoveries runs hourly minibuses to/from Phuket International Airport (600B, one hour 15 minutes). Alternately you can take a taxi (1200B) or tell a Phuket-bound bus-driver to let you off at the 'airport' – you'll get let off at an intersection where motorcycle taxis to the airport (10 minutes) cost 100B.

Surin Islands Marine National Park อุทยานแห่งชาติหมู่เกาะสุรินทร์

The five gorgeous islands that make up this **national park** (www.dnp.go.th; admission 400B; ☺mid-Nov–mid-May) sit about 60km offshore, a measly 5km from the Thai–Burma marine border. Healthy rainforest, pockets of white-sand beach in sheltered bays and rocky headlands that jut into the ocean characterise these granite-outcrop islands. The clearest of water makes for great marine life, with underwater visibility often up to 35m. The islands' sheltered waters also attract *chow lair* (also spelt *chao leh*) – sea gypsies – who live in a village onshore during the monsoon season from May to November. Around here they are known as Moken, from the local word *oken* meaning 'saltwater'.

Ko Surin Nuea (north) and Ko Surin Tai (south) are the two largest islands. Park headquarters and all visitor facilities are at Ao Chong Khad on Ko Surin Nuea, near the jetty. Khuraburi is the jumping-off point for the park. The pier is about 9km north of town, as is the mainland **national park office** (☎0 7649 1378; ☺8am-5pm) with good information, maps and helpful staff.

Khuraburi is the jumping-off point for the park. The pier is about 9km north of town, as is the mainland **national park office** (☎0 7649 1378; ☺8am-5pm), with good information, maps and helpful staff.

◉ Sights & Activities

Several tour operators run day tours from Khao Lak and Khuruburi (2900B including food and park lodging) to the park. The best in safety, service and value is **Greenview** (☎0 7640 1400; Khuraburi pier). Agencies dealing with diving in Hat Khao Lak (p613), Phuket (p622) and Ranong (p607) are the most convenient options for booking liveaboard dive trips. Transfers from the place of purchase are always included.

Diving & Snorkelling

Dive sites in the park include **Ko Surin Tai** and **HQ Channel** between the two main islands. **Richelieu Rock** (a seamount 14km southeast) is also technically in the park and happens to be one of, if not the, best, dive sites on the Andaman coast. Whale sharks are sometimes spotted here during March and April. There's no dive facility in the park

itself, so dive trips (four-day live-aboards around 20,000B) must be booked from the mainland; see Getting There & Away (p617), and the diving sections for Khao Lak (p616) and Ranong (p603), for more information.

Snorkelling isn't as good as it used to be due to recent bleaching of the hard corals but you'll still see fish and soft corals. Two-hour snorkelling trips (per person 80B, gear per day 150B) leave the park headquarters at 9am and 2pm daily. Expect to be in the company of mostly Thais who swim fully clothed. If you'd like a more serene snorkelling experience, charter your own long-tail from the national park (half day 1000B), or better yet, directly from the Moken themselves in **Ban Moken** (Moken Village). The most beautiful, vibrant soft corals we saw were at **Ao Mae Yai**, an enormous North Island bay around the corner from Chong Khod. The best section of reef is between the white buoys along the northern peninsula. There are more fish off tiny **Ko Pajumba**, but the coral isn't in great shape. **Ao Suthep**, off the South Island, has vast schools of iridescent fish and shallow blue holes with milky bottoms.

Wildlife & Hiking

Around park headquarters you can explore the forest fringes, looking out for crab-eating macaques and some of the 57 resident bird species, which include the fabulous Nicobar pigeon, endemic to the Andaman islands. Along the coast you're likely to see the Brahminy kite soaring and reef herons on the rocks. Twelve species of bat live here, most noticeably the tree-dwelling fruit bats (also known as flying foxes).

A rough-and-ready **walking trail** winds 2km along the coast, through forest and back down to the beach at **Ao Mai Ngam**, where there's camping facilities and its own canteen. At low tide it's easy to walk along the coast between the two campsites.

Village Tour

Ban Moken at Ao Bon on the South Island welcomes visitors. Post-tsunami, Moken have settled in this one sheltered bay where a major ancestral worship ceremony (Loi Reua) takes place in April. The national park offers a **Moken Village Tour** (per person 300B). You'll stroll through the village where you should ask locals for permission to hike the 800m **Chok Madah trail** over the jungled hills to an empty beach. Tours depart at 9.15am and must be reserved the day before.

You can also organise a ride over from the park's HQ (per person 100B). If you do visit the village, bring cash to buy handicrafts to help support its economy. There's also a clothing donation box at park headquarters for the Moken, so this is a good, responsible place to lighten your load.

🛏 Sleeping & Eating

Park accommodation is decent, but because of the island's short, narrow beaches it can feel seriously crowded when full (around 300 people). Book online at www.dnp.go.th or with the mainland **national park office** (🕿 0 7649 1378; ⊙8am-5pm) in Khuraburi. The clientele is mostly Thai, giving the place a lively holiday-camp feel. You can camp on both Ao Chong Klod and Ao Mae Ngam. The former has the more spectacular beach, the latter fills up last, is more secluded and with its narrow white-sand shallow bay, it feels a bit wilder. There are no bungalows on Ao Mae Ngam.

Bungalows (2000B) have wood floors and private terraces, as well as private terracotta bathrooms and fans that run all night. **Tents** (2-/4-person 300/450B, bedding per person 60B) are available for rent or you can pitch your own **tent** (per night 80B). There's generator power until 10pm.

A park **restaurant** (dishes from 80B, set menus 170-200B) serves decent Thai food.

ℹ Getting There & Away

Tour operators use speedboats (return 1600B, one hour one-way) that leave around 9am and honour open tickets. A cheaper 'big boat' that had been docked for over two years when we passed, may start service again during the lifetime of this book.

Similan Islands Marine National Park อุทยานแห่งชาติหมู่เกาะสิมิลัน

Known to divers the world over, beautiful **Similan Islands Marine National Park** (www.dnp.go.th; admission 400B; ⊙Nov-May) is 60km offshore. Its smooth granite islands are as impressive above water as below, topped with rainforest, edged with white-sand beaches and fringed with coral reefs. Unfortunately recent coral bleaching has killed of many of the hard corals but soft corals are still intact, the fauna is there and it remains a lovely place to dive.

Two of the nine islands, Island 4 (Ko Miang) and Island 8 (Ko Similan), have ranger stations and accommodation; park headquarters and most visitor activity centres are on Island 4. 'Similan' comes from the Malay word *sembilan*, meaning 'nine', and while each island is named, they're more commonly known by their numbers. Recently, the park was expanded to included Ko Bon and Ko Tachai, both have remained unscathed by coral bleaching, making them some of the better diving and snorkelling areas.

Hat Khao Lak is the jumping-off point for the park. The pier is at Thap Lamu, about 10km south of town.

⊙ Sights & Activities

Diving & Snorkelling

The Similans offer diving for all levels of experience, at depths from 2m to 30m. There are rock reefs at **Ko Payu** (Island 7) and divethroughs at **Hin Pousar** (Elephant Head), with marine life ranging from tiny plume worms and soft corals to schooling fish and whale sharks. There are dive sites at each of the six islands north of Ko Miang; the southern part of the park (Islands 1, 2 and 3) is off-limits to divers and is a turtle nesting ground. No facilities for divers exist in the national park itself, so you'll need to take a dive tour. Dive outfits in Hat Khao Lak (p613) and Phuket (p622) book dive trips (three-day live-aboards from around 14,500B).

You can hire snorkelling gear (per day 100B) from the park headquarters. Day-tour operators usually visit three or four different snorkelling sites. Plenty of tour agencies in Hat Khao Lak offer snorkelling-only day/overnight trips from around 3000/5000B.

Wildlife & Hiking

The forest around the park headquarters on Ko Miang (Island 4) has a couple of walking trails and some great wildlife. The fabulous Nicobar pigeon, with its wild mane of grey-green feathers, is common here. Endemic to the islands of the Andaman Sea, it's one of some 39 bird species in the park. Hairy-legged land crabs and fruit bats (flying foxes) are relatively easily seen in the forest, as are flying squirrels.

A small **beach track** with information panels leads 400m to a tiny, pretty snorkelling bay. Detouring from it, the **Viewpoint Trail** – 500m or so of steep scrambling – has panoramic vistas from the top. A 500m walk to **Sunset Point** takes you through forest to a smooth granite platform facing – obviously – west.

On Ko Similan (Island 8) there's a 2.5km forest hike to a **viewpoint**, and a shorter, steep scramble off the main beach to the top of **Sail Rock** (aka Balance Rock).

Sleeping & Eating

Accommodation in the park is available for all budgets. Book online at www.dnp.go.th or with the mainland **national park office** (☏ 0 7645 3272) at Hat Khao Lak. Tour agents in Hat Khao Lak also arrange overnight to multiday trips that include transport, food and lodging at the park – these cost little more than it would to go solo.

On Ko Miang there are sea-view **bungalows** (r 2000B; 🌀) with balconies; two dark five-room wood-and-bamboo **longhouses** (r 1000B) with fans, and **tents** (2-/4-person 300/450B). There's electricity from 6pm to 6am.

Tents are also available on Ko Similan. You can pitch your own **tent** (per night 80B) on either island.

A **restaurant** (dishes 100-150B) near the park headquarters serves simple Thai food.

Getting There & Away

There's no public transport to the park but theoretically independent travellers can book a speedboat transfer (return 1700B, 1½ hours one way) with a Hat Khao Lak snorkelling operator, though they much prefer that you join the snorkelling tour and generally discourage independent travel to the Similans.

Agencies in Khao Lak (p613) and Phuket (p662) book day/overnight tours (from around 3000/5000B) and dive trips (three-day liveaboards from around 15,000B) – this is about how much you would pay if you tried to get to the islands on your own steam. You can try to link up with a dive trip and pay for the excursion sans diving equipment, but operators will only cooperate if their boats are relatively empty.

Phang-Nga Town & Ao Phang-Nga

พังงา/อ่าวพังงา

POP 9700

With turquoise bays peppered with craggy limestone rock towers, brilliant-white beaches and tumbledown fishing villages, Ao Phang-Nga is one of the region's most spectacular landscapes. Little wonder then that it was here, among the towering cliffs and swifts' nests that James Bond's nemesis, Scaramanga (*The Man with the Golden Gun*), chose to build his lair. Wanted assassins with goals of world domination would not be recommended to hide out here nowadays, since the area is swarming with tourists in motorboats and sea kayaks nearly year-round. Much of the bay, and some of the coastline, has now been incorporated into the Ao Phang-Nga Marine National Park (p619).

Sights & Activities

Phang-Nga is a scruffy town with not much going for it, backed up against sublime limestone cliffs. There isn't a whole lot to see or do unless you happen to be here during the annual **Vegetarian Festival** (see the boxed text, p618) in late September or October.

Boat Tours

About 8.5km south of the town centre is Tha Dan. From here, you can charter boats to see half-submerged **caves**, oddly shaped islands and **Ko Panyi**, a Muslim village on stilts. There are tours to the well-trod **Ko Phing Kan** ('James Bond Island'; see p620) and **Ao Phang-Nga Marine National Park** (500B per person for a two- to three-hour tour); see p619 for more information. Takua Thung, another pier area about 10km further west of Tha Dan, also has private boats for hire at similar prices to tours. The park office, inside Ao Phang-Nga Marine National Park (p619), also offers boat tours.

Although it can be a pain to haggle with boatmen, it's nice to create your own itinerary. Of course, it's easier (and cheaper) to go with an organised tour through an agency in town. **Sayan Tours** (☏ 0 7643 0348; www.sayantour.com) has been doing tours of Ao Phang-Nga for many years now, and continues to receive good reviews from travellers. Half-/full-day tours cost from 700/1000B per person and include **Tham Lawt** (a large water cave), Ko Phing Kan and Ko Panyi, among other destinations. For an extra 300B you can add a bit of kayaking. It also offers a **river-rafting trip** (per person 1600B) to the Son Pat Waterfall 25km south of Phang-Nga, and tours to nearby destinations, including **Sa Nang Manora Forest Park**.

Sleeping & Eating

Phang-Nga doesn't have much in the way of quality sleeping and most folks choose to swing by on a day trip. Several food stalls on the main street of Phang-Nga sell delicious *kà·nŏm jeen* (thin wheat noodles) with chicken curry, *nám yah* (spicy ground-fish curry) or *nám prík* (spicy sauce). There's a morning market open from 5am to 10am daily and a small night market on Tuesday, Wednesday and Thursday evenings, located just south of Soi Lohakit.

Phang-Nga Inn   HOTEL **$$**
(☏0 7641 1963; 2/2 Soi Lohakit, Phang-Nga; r 400-1500B;☼) This converted residential villa features heavy wood staircases, louvred cabinets and peaceful gardens. It's well furnished, there's a little eatery and the staff are gracious.

Phang-Nga Guest House   GUEST HOUSE **$**
(☏0 7641 1358; Th Petchkasem, Phang-Nga; r 250-380B;☼) Nothing fancy. Just a clean block of cheap and cherry-tiled rooms in the otherwise drab centre of town.

❶ Getting There & Away

Phang-Nga's bus terminal is located just off the main street on Soi Bamrung Rat. Bangkok buses to/from Phang-Nga include VIP class (912B, 12 hours, one daily), 1st class (552B, 12 to 13 hours, two daily) and 2nd class (441B, 12 hours, three to four daily).

There are several other bus services available:

DESTINATION	PRICE	FREQUENCY	DURATION
Hat Yai	300B	2 daily	6hr
Krabi	74B	frequent	1½hr
Phuket	85B	frequent	1½hr
Ranong	170B	4 daily	5hr
Surat Thani	150B	frequent	3hr
Trang	240B	frequent	3½hr

Around Phang-Nga

AO PHANG-NGA MARINE NATIONAL PARK   อุทยานแห่งชาติอ่าวพังงา
Established in 1981 and covering an area of 400 sq km, **Ao Phang-Nga Marine National Park** (☏0 7641 1136; www.dnp.go.th; admission 200B; ☺8am-4pm) is noted for its classic karst scenery. There are over 40 islands with huge vertical cliffs, some with caves that are accessible at low tide and lead into hidden *hôrngs* (lagoons surrounded by solid rock walls). The bay itself is composed of large and small tidal channels including Khlong Ko Phanyi, Khlong Phang-Nga, Khlong Bang Toi and Khlong Bo Saen. These channels run through vast mangroves in a north–south direction and today are used by fisherfolk

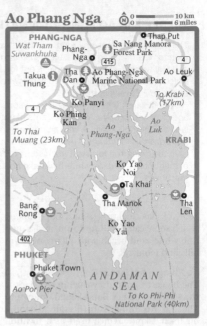

and island inhabitants as aquatic highways. These mangroves are the largest remaining primary mangrove forests in Thailand.

In the peak season the bay can become a package-tourist superhighway. But if you explore in the early morning (best done from Ko Yao Noi or Ko Yao Yai) or stay out a bit late, you'll find a slice of beach, sea and a limestone karst to call your own. The best way to experience the park is by kayak.

◉ Sights & Activities

John Gray's Seacanoe   SEA KAYAKING
(☏0 7622 6077; www.johngray-seacanoe.com) John Gray was the first kayak outfitter in the bay and remains the most ecologically minded. He's constantly clamouring for more protection for his beloved *hôrngs* among local national-park rangers and their supervisors in Bangkok. His **Hong By Starlight day trip** (per person 3950B) dodges the crowds, involves plenty of sunset paddling and will introduce you to Ao Phang-Nga's famed bio-luminescence once night falls. See also p622.

Ko Nok & Ko Klui   ISLANDS
Set halfway between Phuket and Krabi, these two islands are far enough from tour epicentres that you'll usually have them to yourself. **Ko Klui**, the big island north of Ko

WILDLIFE IN AO PANG-NGA NATIONAL PARK

The marine limestone environment here favours a long list of reptiles, including Bengal monitor lizards, flying lizards, banded sea snakes, dogface water snakes, shore pit vipers and Malayan pit vipers. Keep an eye out for a two-banded monitor (*Varanus salvator*), which looks like a crocodile when seen swimming in the mangrove swamp and can measure up to 2.2m in length.

Amphibians in the Ao Phang-Nga region include marsh frogs, common bush frogs and crab-eating frogs. Avian residents of note are helmeted hornbills (the largest of Thailand's 12 hornbill species, with a body length of up to 127cm), the edible-nest swiftlets (*Aerodramus fuciphagus*), white-bellied sea eagles, ospreys and Pacific reef egrets.

In the mangrove forests and on some of the larger islands reside over 200 species of mammals, including white-handed gibbons, serows, dusky langurs and crab-eating macaques.

Yao Noi, has tidal access to a huge *hôrng*, which some call the **Blue Room**, and a pristine white-sand beach with plenty of hornbills and monkeys.

Ko Phing Kan (James Bond Island) ISLAND
The biggest tourist drawcard in the park is the so-called 'James Bond Island', known to Thais as **Ko Phing Kan** (literally 'Leaning on Itself Island'). Once used as a location setting for *The Man with the Golden Gun*, the island is now full of vendors hawking coral and shells that should have stayed in the sea.

ⓘ Getting There & Around

If you have your own vehicle, drive about 6km south on Hwy 4 from the centre of Phang-Nga, turn left onto Rte 4144 (the road to Tha Dan) and travel 2.6km to the park headquarters. Without your own transport you'll need to take a *sŏrng·tăa·ou* to Tha Dan (30B).

From the park office, you can hire a boat (1500B, maximum four passengers) for a three-hour tour of the surrounding islands.

Ko Yao
เกาะยาว

With mountainous backbones, unspoilt shorelines, a large variety of birdlife and a population of friendly Muslim fisherfolk, **Ko Yao Yai** and **Ko Yao Noi** are laid-back vantage points for soaking up Ao Phang-Nga's beautiful scenery. The islands are part of the Ao Phang-Nga National Park (p619) but are most easily accessed from Phuket.

Please remember to respect the beliefs of the local Muslim population and wear modest clothing when away from the beaches.

◉ Sights & Activities

Despite being the relative pipsqueak of the Ko Yao Islands, Ko Yao Noi is the main population centre, with fishing, coconut farming and tourism sustaining its small, year-round population. Bays on the east coast recede to mud flats at low tide but the beaches are still splendid.

Ko Yao Yai is far less developed than Ko Yao Noi; it offers an even more remote and wild getaway. Villagers are still pleasantly surprised to see tourists pedalling their bicycles or buzzing by on rented motorbikes.

Cycling
Bring along or rent (200B per day from most guest houses) a mountain bike if you want to explore each of the islands' numerous dirt trails, or join up with Phuket's **Amazing Bike Tours** (☑08 7263 2031; www.amazingbiketoursthailand.com; day trip 2900B). Or, if you like the idea of cycling but think it's too darn hot, rent an ecofriendly electric bicycle (220B per day) from **Eco Island Vehicles** (☑08 6476 1143; Ko Yao Noi), whose staff will pick you up at your Ko Yao Noi hotel; they also rent mountain bikes (200B).

Diving & Snorkelling
Half-day three-island snorkelling tours (1700B, maximum six passengers) through Ao Phang-Nga are easily organised from any guest house or with long-tail captains on the beaches. **Koh Yao Diver** (☑08789 575 517; http://kohyaodiver.com) leads dive trips from both islands.

Rock Climbing
Mountain Shop Adventures (☑08 9971 0380, 08 4841 1540; www.themountainshop.org; Tha Khao) offers full-day rock climbing trips

around Ko Yao Noi from 2500B, as well as fishing, snorkelling and kayak trips. There are over 150 climbs on Ko Yao Noi and owner Mark has routed most of them himself – many trips involve boat travel to get to remote limestone cliff faces. Beginner to advanced trips are available.

🛏 Sleeping & Eating

TOP CHOICE Six Senses Hideaway HOTEL **$$$**
(☏0 7641 8500; www.sixsenses.com/hideaway-yao noi; Ko Yao Noi; r 32,000-400,000B; ✳@☲) This swanky five-star property – where 56 hillside pool villas (and their tremendous spa) have been built to resemble an old *chow lair* village – doesn't disappoint. Views of distant limestone formations are jaw-dropping; its Thai kitchen is tantalising; and its commitment to sustainability is unparalleled among global five-star chains.

Elixir HOTEL **$$$**
(☏08 7808 3838; www.elixirresort.com; Ko Yao Yai; bungalows 8000-25,500B; ✳@☲) The first of Yao Yai's two four-star resorts offers tasteful beachfront and hillside peaked-roof villas steeped in classic Thai style. There are dark-wood floors and high ceilings, indoor and outdoor showers, and ceramic-bowl sinks. It's set on a private beach, where you'll also find a common pool, dive centre, massage pagodas and spectacular sunsets over Phuket.

Koyao Island Resort HOTEL **$$$**
(☏0 1606 1517; www.koyao.com; Ko Yao Noi; villas 7000-13,200B; ✳@☲) Its open-concept thatched bungalows offer serene views across a palm-shaded garden and infinity pool to a skinny white beach. We love the elegant, near safari-esque feel of the villas here with their fan-cooled patios and indoor-outdoor bathrooms.

Thiwson Beach Resort GUEST HOUSE **$$**
(☏08 1737 4420; www.thiwsonbeach.com; Ko Yao Yai; bungalows 800-3000B; ✳🕭) Easily the cleanest, and sweetest, of Ko Yao Yai's bungalow properties. Here are proper wooden bungalows with polished floors, outdoor baths, and wide patios facing the best beach on the island. Beachfront bungalows are the largest, but fan rooms are tremendous value.

Lom Lea GUEST HOUSE **$$**
(☏0 7659 7486; www.lomlae.com; Ko Yao Noi; bungalows 2000-5500B; 🕭) Stylish, naturalist wooden bungalows are fronted by a stun-

ning and secluded beach with views of Phang-Nga's signature karst islands. There's a dive centre, a good restaurant and plenty of activities on offer.

Paradise Hotel HOTEL **$$$**
(☏08 1892 4878; www.theparadise.biz; Ko Yao Noi; r from 7500B; ☲) Tucked into a private cove on the far north, and accessible only by long-tail boat or by a winding, rutted earthen road, stay at this ageing place for its exceptionally beautiful and remote location.

Sabai Corner Bungalows GUEST HOUSE **$**
(☏0 7659 7497; www.sabaicornerbungalows.com; Ko Yao Noi; bungalows 500-2000B) Tucked into a rocky headland, the wooden and bamboo bungalows here are full of character and blessed with gorgeous views.

ℹ Information

In Ta Khai, the largest settlement on Ko Yao Noi, there's a 7-Eleven with an attached ATM, and another ATM around the corner at Government Savings Bank.

On Ko Yai Yai, the only ATM is out of the way near the Klong Hia Pier, so you'd be wise to carry plenty of cash.

ℹ Getting There & Away

From Phuket

For Ko Yao Noi, hourly long-tails (150B, 20 minutes) or three daily speedboats (200B, 20 minutes) leave Tha Bano Rong north of Phuket Town between 7.30am and 5.40pm.

To Ko Yao Yai, catch a speedboat or ferry from Tha Rasada near Phuket Town. Ferries depart at 8.30am, 10.30am and 2pm (one hour, 100B). Speedboats (30 minutes, 150B) make the run at 4pm and 5pm. On Fridays the schedule shifts to accommodate prayer times.

From Krabi

There are four 'express' boats (450B, 1½ hours) and two speedboats (600B, 45 minutes) per day from Krabi's Tha Len pier to Ko Yao Noi piers at Tha Manok and Tha Khao.

From Phang-Nga

From Tha Sapan Yao in Phang-Nga there's a 7.30am ferry to Ko Yao Noi continuing to Ko Yao Yai (200B, two hours) that makes an excellent budget cruise of Ao Phang-Nga. It leaves Ko Yao Noi for the return trip at 1pm.

ℹ Getting Around

To get from Ko Yao Noi to Ko Yao Yai, catch a shuttle boat from Tha Manok (100B to 150B, 15 minutes) to Tha Klong Hia. On the islands, you can travel by túk-túk (pronounced đúk đúk'; motorised transport) for about 150B per ride or rent a motorbike from most guest houses for around 250B per day. It's around 70B to 100B for túk-túk transport to the resorts.

PHUKET ISLAND ภูเก็ต

POP 83,800

The reigning granddaddy of Thailand beach vacations, Phuket Province features one giant island – the Andaman's drop zone of quintessential tropical fun.

The island of Phuket has long been misunderstood. First of all, the 'h' is silent. Ahem. And second, Phuket doesn't feel like an island at all. It's so huge (it's the biggest in the country) that you rarely get the sense that you're surrounded by water, which is probably the reason why the 'Ko' (meaning 'island') has been dropped from its name. Dubbed the 'pearl of the Andaman' by marketing execs, this is Thailand's original flavour of tailor-made fun in the sun.

The island's 'sin city' of Patong is the biggest town and busiest beach. It's the ultimate gong show where podgy beach-aholics sizzle off their hangovers and go-go girls play ping-pong...without paddles... But ultimately the island's affinity to luxury far outshines its other stereotypes. Jet-setters come through in droves, getting pummelled during swanky spa sessions and swigging sundowners at one of the many fashion-forward nightspots. And you don't have to be an heiress to tap into Phuket's trendy to-do list. There's deep-sea diving, high-end dining, white beaches that beckon you and your book – whatever your heart desires.

🏃 Activities

Diving & Snorkelling

Phuket enjoys an enviable central location for diving. The much-talked-about Similan Islands sit to the north, while dozens of dive sites orbit Ko Phi-Phi (p662) and Ko Lanta (p671) to the south. Of course, this means that trips from Phuket to these awesome destinations cost slightly more than from places closer to the sites since you'll be forking over extra dough for petrol. Most operators on Phuket take divers to decent sites orbiting the island, such as Ko Raya Noi and Ko Raya Yai (also called Ko Racha Noi and Ko Racha Yai) to the south; however, these spots rank lower on the wow-o-meter. The reef off the southern tip of Raya Noi is particularly good for experienced divers. It's a deep site where soft corals cling to boulders, around which pelagic fish species roam. Manta and marble rays are also frequently glimpsed here, and if you're lucky, you may even see a whale shark.

There are heaps of 'dive' shops here – at last count there were over 100, though most of them are the equivalent of a booking agency. The more serious ones often operate their own boat(s) while others send you off with another operator, so ask if you've got any concerns.

Typical one-day dive trips to nearby sites cost around 3500B, including two dives and equipment. Nondivers (and snorkellers) are often permitted to join these dive trips for a significant discount. PADI Open Water certification courses cost around 15,000B for three days of instruction and equipment.

Snorkelling is best along Phuket's west coast, particularly at the rocky headlands between beaches. Mask, snorkel and fins can be rented for around 250B a day. As with scuba diving, you'll find better snorkelling, with greater visibility and variety of marine life, along the shores of small outlying islands such as Ko Raya Yai and Ko Raya Noi.

As elsewhere in the Andaman Sea, the best diving months are December to May, when the weather is good and the sea is smooth and clear.

Recommended diving and snorkelling centres on Phuket include **Sun Fun Divers** in both Patong (p639) and Kata (see Map p636), **Oi's Longtail** (p651) in Hat Nai Yang, and **Dive Asia** in Hat Karon (p635).

Another outfit well worth checking out is **Offspray Leisure** (☑08 1894 1274; www.offsprayleisure.com; 43/87 Chalong Plaza, Chalong; dive trips from 2950B), a dive and snorkelling excursion company specialising in small-load, intimate trips to the reefs around Ko Phi-Phi.

Sea Kayaking

Several companies based on Phuket offer canoe tours of scenic Ao Phang-Nga (see p618). Kayaks can enter semisubmerged caves inaccessible to long-tail boats. A day paddle costs from 3950B per person including meals, equipment and transfer; many outfits also run all-inclusive, three-day (from 13,700B) or six-day (from 27,100B) kayak/camping trips.

Ko Phuket

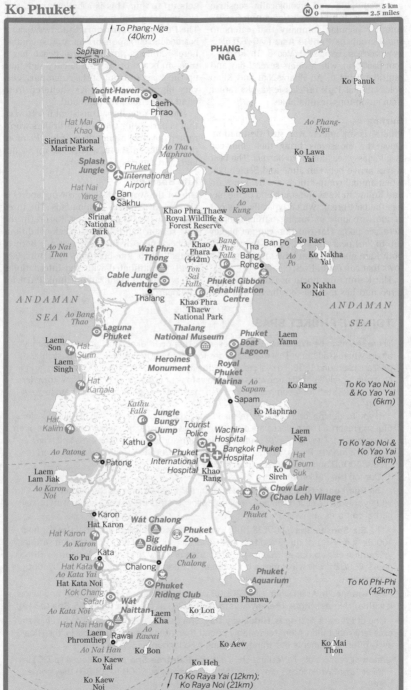

A reputable and ecologically sensitive company is **John Gray's Seacanoe** (p629). Another popular company that caters to small groups is **Paddle Asia** (☎0 7621 6145; www.paddleasia.com; 9/71 Moo 3, Th Rasdanusorn, Ban Kuku), which offers several day and multiday trips to Ao Phang-Nga and Khao Sok National Park on classic kayaks rather than sit-on-tops or inflatables.

Surfing

Phuket is an undercover surf destination. Once the monsoons bring their midyear swell, glassy seas fold into barrels. The best waves arrive between June and September, when annual competitions are held in Kata and Kalim. In Kata, the south end of the bay has the best break, which typically tops out at 2m; a couple of surfing outfits operate here, see p635. Hat Nai Han can get bigger (up to 3m) near the yacht club. Be warned, both Kata and Nai Han have vicious undertows that can claim lives.

Hat Kalim, just north of Patong, is sheltered and has a consistent break that also gets up to 3m. This is a hollow wave, and is considered the best break on the island. The **Phuket Boardriders Club** (www.phuket boardriders.com) sponsors an August contest here. Kamala's northernmost beach has a nice 3m beach break, and Laem Singh, just up the coast in front of the Amanpuri, gets very big and fast, plus it's sheltered from wind by the massive headland.

Hat Nai Yang has a consistent if soft wave that is perfect for veteran boardriders who'd rather not take a pounding. It breaks more than 200m offshore, swells get up to 3m high and there is no undertow.

Kite Boarding

One of the world's fastest growing sports is also one of Phuket's coming fads. The three best spots are Hat Nai Yang, Karon (in the low season) and Rawai (ideal conditions for beginners in the high season). Both of Phuket's two kite-boarding operators (see p648) are affiliated with the International Kiteboarding Organization (think PADI for kite boards).

TOP FIVE PHUKET SPAS

There seems to be a massage shop on every corner on Phuket. Most are low-key family affairs where traditional Thai massage goes for about 250B per hour, and a basic mani-pedi costs around 150B – a real steal. The quality of service at these places varies, and changes rapidly as staff turnover is high. Go with your gut instinct or ask fellow travellers or your hotel staff for recommendations. No matter where you choose, it's hard to go wrong.

If you're looking for a more Westernised spa experience, head to one of Phuket's plentiful spa resorts. These places are often affiliated with a ritzy hotel (but nearly all are open to nonguests). They are *haute couture* affairs with sumptuous Zen designs and huge treatment menus. Prices vary depending on location, but treatments generally start at around 1000B and go up and up from there.

Our top five Phuket spa picks:

» The **Bua Luang Spa** (p649), at the Anantara Phuket, combines the best of Thai and Ayurvedic healing traditions. Why not follow that turmeric body scrub with a Thai herbal compress massage?

» The **Six Senses Spa** (☎0 7638 1010; www.sixsenses.com; 100 Th Viset, Hat Rawai; r from 4000B; ✿@🔊✿), at the Evason Phuket Resort, is sublimely back-to-nature in setting, yet cutting edge as far as treatments are concerned. Try the Energising Journey (three hours, 7600B), which includes a body toner, an Energiser massage, followed by foot acupressure.

» Get wrapped in Asian white clay (2000B) or detoxifying seaweed (2500B) and follow it with a Tri Phase Stone Therapy Massage (2900B) at the **Sala Resort & Spa** (p649).

» One of Phuket's first spas, **Hideaway Day Spa** (p646) in Ao Bang Thao still enjoys an excellent reputation. More reasonably priced than many hotel counterparts, the Hideaway offers treatments in a tranquil setting by a lagoon.

» Another reasonable, refreshing choice is the **Raintree Spa** at Sino House (p630) in Phuket Town. When locals crave spa therapy (massages 500B to 1000B) they come here.

Yachting

Phuket is one of Southeast Asia's main yachting destinations, and you'll find all manner of craft anchored along its shores – from 80-year-old wooden sloops to the latest in high-tech motor cruisers.

Marina-style facilities with year-round anchorage are presently available at a few locations:

Phuket Boat Lagoon   MARINA
(✆0 7623 9055; fax 0 7623 9056) Located at Ao Sapam, about 10km north of Phuket Town on the eastern shore. It offers an enclosed marina with tidal-channel access, serviced pontoon berths, 60- and 120-tonne travel lifts, a hard-stand area, plus a resort hotel, laundry, coffee shop, fuel, water, repairs and maintenance services.

Royal Phuket Marina   MARINA
(✆0 7637 9397; www.royalphuketmarina.com) The US$25 million Royal Phuket Marina is located just south of Phuket Boat Lagoon. It's more luxurious with shiny new townhouses, upscale restaurants and a convention centre overlooking 190 berths.

Yacht Haven Phuket Marina   MARINA
(✆0 7620 6704; www.yacht-haven-phuket.com) This marina is at Laem Phrao on the northeastern tip of Phuket. The Yacht Haven boasts 130 berths with deep-water access, and a scenic restaurant. It also does yacht maintenance.

Port clearance is rather complicated; the marinas will take care of the paperwork (for a fee, of course) if notified of your arrival in advance. Expect to pay from 17,000B per day for a high-season, bareboat charter.

For more information on yacht charters (both bareboat and crewed), contact the following:

Asia Marine (www.asia-marine.net; Yacht Haven Phuket Marina)

Tawan Cruises (✆08 8194 3234; www.tawancruises.com)

If you're interested in a more affordable sailing trip, seek out **Phuket Sail Tours** (✆08 7897 0492; www.phuketsailtours.com; Ao Por). Its day trips through Ao Phang-Nga (3000B all-inclusive) come highly recommended.

Horse Riding

Phuket offers horse riding in Rawai (p635).

⬥ Courses

Popular Thai cooking classes are held in Kata (p635), Phuket Town (p629), Ko Sireh (p633) and Patong (p639).

☞ Tours

It's not hard to find elephant rides and 4WD tours of the island's interior, though none of those will win their way into the hearts of animal rights activists or environmentalists, so why not take a bike ride? **Amazing Bike Tours** (✆0 7628 3436; www.amazingbiketoursthailand.asia; 32/4 Moo 9, Th Chaofa, Chalong; day trips from 1600B), Phuket's best new adventure outfitter, leads small groups on half-day bicycle tours through the Khao Phra Thaew Royal Wildlife & Forest Reserve, and it offers terrific day trips around Ko Yao Noi and the gorgeous beaches and waterfalls of Thai Muang in nearby Phang-Nga province.

Phuket for Children

There's plenty for kids to do on Phuket. And while the seedier face of the sex industry is on full show in Patong (we wouldn't bring our kids there, although many people do), the rest of the island is fairly G-rated.

Elephant treks are always a big hit with kids, with the best options available on the Kata-Hat Nai Han road. **Phuket Aquarium** (p633) and a visit to the tiny **Phuket Gibbon Rehabilitation Centre** (p650) are also terrific animal-themed activities that are sure to please.

The main family-flogged feature of Phuket is **Phuket Fantasea** (p644), which is a pricey extravaganza of animals, costumes, song, special effects, pyrotechnics, and a lousy dinner.

Dino Park (p637) in Karon is a park with a maze of caves, lagoons and dinosaur statues where kids can play minigolf.

The biggest water park in Thailand is **Splash Jungle** (Map p623; ✆0 7637 2111; www.splashjunglewaterpark.com; Mai Khao; adult/child 5-12yr/child under 5yr 1500/750B/free), which has a wave pool, a play pool including tipping buckets and water cannons, 12 very cool water slides for all ages, a sauna and bar for mum and dad; the price includes pick-up at your resort.

Volunteering

Soi Dog Foundation (✆08 7050 8688; www.soidog.org) is a well-organised unit aimed at sterilising, providing medical care for and

PHUKET'S MOO·AY TAI EXPLOSION *ADAM SKOLNICK*

Over the past few years, spurred in no small part by the increasing global presence and popularity of Mixed Martial Arts, several *moo·ay tai* (also spelled *muay thai;* Thai boxing) gyms catering to international male and female athletes have sprouted off the beach in Phuket. Based on the original *moo·ay tai* camp concept, fighters live and train on site with seasoned *moo·ay tai* professionals.

The whole thing started with Pricha 'Tuk' Chokkuea and his gym, **Rawai Muay Thai** (✆08 1476 9377; www.rawaimuaythai.com; 43/42 Moo 7, Th Sai Yuan). He and former business partner Danny Avison, a Phuket-based triathlete, decided to train tourists as a fundraising mechanism so Tuk could also train impoverished, up-and-coming Thai fighters, without dipping deeply into their fight purse (the traditional *moo·ay tai* business model, and something Tuk always resented). For years his was the only gym around, but in Rawai alone there are now more than half-a-dozen gyms.

The best new gym is Avison's **Promthep Muay Thai Camp** (✆08 5786 2414; www. promthepmuaythai.com; 91 Moo 6, Soi Yanui). In addition to training fighters, Avison has a tremendous multisport cross-training weight-loss program. Wherever you enter the ring, be warned: this is no wussie watered-down-for-Westerners theme-park ride. Prepare to sweat, cringe, grapple and bleed. If you're the real deal, maybe you'll even win a fight under the Bang-la Stadium lights?

feeding stray dogs. Volunteers are needed for feeding the dogs but it's just as helpful to donate funds towards the projects. Check the website for updates and details.

ℹ Information

Dangers & Annoyances

During the May to October monsoon, large waves and fierce undertows can make it too dangerous to swim. Dozens of annual drownings occur every year on Phuket's beaches, especially on Laem Singh, Kamala and Karon. Red flags are posted to warn bathers of serious rip tides.

Keep an eye out for jet skis when you are in the water. Although in 1997 the Phuket governor declared jet skis illegal, enforcement of the ban is another issue.

Renting a motorcycle can be a high-risk proposition. Thousands of people are injured or killed every year on Phuket's highways. If you must rent one, make sure you at least know the basics and wear a helmet.

There have been recent late-night motorbike muggings and stabbings on the road leading from Patong to Hat Karon, and on the road between Kata and the Rawai–Hat Nai Han area. There have been a few recent random sexual assaults on women, as well. Women should think twice before sunbathing topless (a big no-no in Thailand anyway) and alone, especially on an isolated beach, and it can be dangerous to go for a jog alone at night or early in the morning.

Medical Services

Local hospitals are equipped with modern facilities, emergency rooms and outpatient-care clinics. Both of the following, which are near Phuket Town, have hyperbaric chambers:

Bangkok Phuket Hospital (Map p623; ✆0 7625 4425; www.phukethospital.com; Th Yongyok Uthit) Reputedly the favourite with locals.

Phuket International Hospital (Map p623; ✆0 7624 9400; www.phuketinternationalhospital.com; Th Chalermprakiat) International doctors rate this hospital as the best on the island.

Tourist Information

The weekly English-language *Phuket Gazette* publishes information on activities, events, dining and entertainment around the island, as well as the latest scandals. It can be accessed online at www.phuketgazette.net.

Websites

Jamie's Phuket (www.jamie-monk.com) A fun insider's blog written by a long-time Phuket expat resident with excellent photos and travel tips.

One Stop Phuket (www.1stopphuket.com) A user-friendly travel guide and internet-booking referral service.

Phuket Dot Com (www.phuket.com) Offers a sophisticated compendium of many kinds of information, including accommodation on the island.

ℹ Getting There & Away

Air

Phuket International Airport (☏0 7632 7230) is 30km northwest of Phuket Town; it takes around 45 minutes to an hour to reach the southern beaches from here.

Some regional airline carriers:

Air Asia (www.airasia.com) Serves Phuket beautifully. In addition to several daily flights to Bangkok (around 1480B), it also flies direct to Hong Kong (5000B), Chiang Mai (1600B), Singapore (1400B), Bali (2730B) and other destinations.

Bangkok Airways (off Map p628; ☏0 7622 5033; www.bangkokair.com; 58/2-3 Th Yaowarat) Has daily flights to Ko Samui (2380B) and Bangkok (1725B) and more.

Nok Air (www.nokair.com) Links Phuket with Bangkok.

THAI (Map p628; ☏0 7621 1195; www.thaiair ways.com; 78/1 Th Ranong, Phuket Town) Operates around seven daily flights to Bangkok (from around 3000B) with connections to/from several other cities in Thailand, as well as international destinations.

Several other international airlines fly to Phuket and have offices in Phuket Town including the following:

Dragonair (Map p628; ☏0 7621 5734; Th Phang-Nga, Phuket Town)

Korean Airlines (☏0 7621 6675; 1/8-9 Th Thungkha, Phuket Town)

Malaysia Airlines (off Map p628; ☏0 7621 6675; 1/8-9 Th Thungkha, Phuket Town)

Silk Air (Map p628; ☏0 7621 3891; www.silk air.com; 183/103 Th Phang-Nga, Phuket Town)

Ferry & Speedboat

Tha Rasada, north of Phuket Town, is the main pier for boats to Ko Phi Phi (for more information see p668) with connections to Krabi, Ko Lanta, the Trang Islands, Ko Lipe and even as far as Langkawi Island in Malaysia (where there are further ferry connections to Penang).

For quicker service to Krabi and Ao Nang via the Ko Yao islands, boats leave from Tha Bang Bong north of Tha Rasada; see p668 for more details.

Minivan

Travel agencies all around Phuket island sell tickets (which include the ferry fare) for air-conditioned minivans down to Ko Samui and Ko Pha-Ngan. Air-conditioned minivan services to Krabi, Ranong, Trang, Surat Thani and several other locations are also available. Prices are slightly higher than the buses, which all stop in Phuket Town (see p632).

ℹ Getting Around

Local transport around Phuket is terrible. The systems in place make tourists either stay on their chosen beach, rent a car or motorbike (which can be hazardous) or take overpriced private car 'taxis' or túk-túk. There are *sŏrng·tăa·ou* that run to the beaches from Phuket Town but often you'll have to go via Phuket Town to get from one beach to another (say Hat Surin to Hat Patong) and this can take hours.

See the Getting Around sections of individual locations on Phuket Island for taxi and *sŏrng·tăa·ou* details.

Phuket Town
เมืองภูเก็ต

POP 94,325

Long before tourist T-shirts or flip-flops, Phuket was an island of rubber trees, tin mines and cash-hungry merchants. Attracting entrepreneurs from as far away as the Arabian Peninsula, China, India and Portugal, Phuket Town was a colourful blend of cultural influences, cobbled together by tentative compromise and cooperation. Today the city is proof of the island's historical soul. Wander down streets clogged with Sino-Portuguese architecture housing arty coffeeshops, galleries, wonderful inexpensive restaurants and hip little guest houses; peek down alleyways to find Chinese Taoist shrines shrouded in incense smoke.

But the town is not just some lost-in-time cultural archive. Bubbling up throughout the emerging Old Town is an infusion of relevant art, music and food that attract a very hip crowd both foreign and Thai. Investors have finally caught on

ℹ **METERED TAXIS**

To escape Phuket's 'taxi mafia' (an organization of overpriced chartered cars that are often the only means of transport in the beach areas) get the phone number of a metered taxi and use the same driver throughout your stay in Phuket. The easiest way to do this is to take a metered taxi from the airport (one of the only places where you'll find them) when you arrive then take down your driver's phone number. Metered taxis are found about 50m to the right as you exit the arrivals hall.

Phuket Town

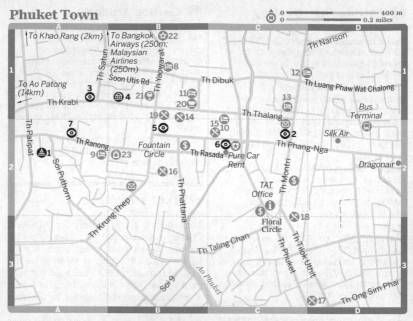

Phuket Town

Sights
1 Jui Tui Temple A2
2 Old Post Office Building C2
3 Phra Phitak Chyn Pracha
   Mansion A1
   Phuket Philatelic Museum .... (see 2)
4 Phuket Thaihua Museum B1
5 Shrine of the Serene Light B2
6 Standard Chartered Bank C2
7 THAI Office A2
   The Raintree Spa .... (see 12)

Activities, Courses & Tours
   Blue Elephant Restaurant &
   Cookery School .... (see 3)

Sleeping
8 Casa 104 .... B1
9 Chinotel A2
10 D's Corner & Guesthouse C2
11 Phuket 346 .... B1

12 Sino House C1
13 Sleep Sheep Phuket Hostel C1

Eating
14 China Inn B1
15 Cook C2
16 Ka Jok See B2
17 La Gaetana D3
18 Uptown Restaurant C3
19 Wilai B1

Drinking
20 Bo(ok)hemian B1
21 Saneha B1

Entertainment
22 Timber Hut B1

Shopping
23 Day Market B2

that culture, not just slinky beaches and girly bars, is a commodity. Old shophouses and homes, once left to rot, are being bought up and restored, resulting in flash-forward-gentrification.

If you're on a budget, Phuket Town has the best lodging bargains on the island. From here you can hop on regular *sŏrng·tăa·ou* to any of Phuket's beaches (which will take between 30 minutes and 1½ hours; see p633) for more details.

⊙ Sights

Sino-Portuguese architecture
HERITAGE ARCHITECTURE

Stroll along the streets of Thalang, Dibuk, Yaowarat, Ranong, Phang-Nga, Rasada and Krabi for a glimpse of some of the best architecture on offer. Soi Romanee off Th Thalang is the most ambient area of town. The most magnificent examples of buildings are the **Standard Chartered Bank** (Th Phang-Nga), Thailand's oldest foreign bank; the **THAI office** (Th Ranong); and the **old post office building**, which now houses the **Phuket Philatelic Museum** (Th Montri; admission free; ⊙9.30am-5.30pm). The best-restored residential properties are found along Th Dibuk and Th Thalang. The fabulous **Phra Phitak Chyn Pracha Mansion** (9 Th Krabi) has been restored and turned into a branch of the upscale Blue Elephant restaurant chain and a cookery school.

Shrine of the Serene Light
SHRINE

(ศาลเจ้าแสงธรรม; Saan Jao Sang Tham; ⊙8.30am-noon & 1.30-5.30pm) A handful of Chinese temples inject some added colour into the area but the Shrine of the Serene Light, tucked away at the end of a 50m alley near the Bangkok Bank of Commerce on Th Phang-Nga, is a cut above the rest. You'll see Taoist etchings on the walls, the vaulted ceiling stained from incense plumes, and the altar is always alive with fresh flowers and burning candles. The shrine is said to have been built by a local family in the mid-1880s.

Khao Rang
VIEWPOINT

(เขารัง; Phuket Hill; off Map p628) For a bird's-eye view of the city, climb up pretty Khao Rang, northwest of the town centre. It's at its best during the week, when the summit is relatively peaceful, but keep an eye out for the mobs of snarling dogs.

Phuket Thaihua Museum
MUSEUM

(พิพิธภัณฑ์ภูเก็ตไทยหัว; 28 Th Krabi; admission 200B; ⊙9am-5pm) This flashy new museum, set in an old Sino-Portuguese home, is filled with photos and exhibits on Phuket's history. The last room is covered in photos of local dishes – and if this makes you hungry, info on where to find the food stalls is listed.

⚐ Activities & Courses

TOP CHOICE / John Gray's Seacanoe
SEA KAYAKING

(off Map p628; ☑0 7625 4505-7; www.johngray-seacanoe.com; 124 Soi 1, Th Yaowarat) The original, still the most reputable and by far the most ecologically sensitive sea-kayaking company on the island. Like any good brand in Thailand, his 'Seacanoe' name and itineraries have been frequently copied. He's north of Phuket Town.

Blue Elephant Restaurant & Cookery School
COOKING SCHOOL

(☑0 7635 4355; www.blueelephant.com; 96 Th Krabi, Phuket Town; half-day class 2800B) Phuket's newest cookery school is in the stunning restored 1903 Sino-Portuguese style **Phra Phitak Chyn Pracha Mansion** (see p629). There are a variety of options from short group lessons to five-day private training (78,000B). Morning classes take in a market visit.

⚐ Festivals & Events

The **Vegetarian Festival** (see p618) is Phuket's most important event. The TAT office in Phuket prints a helpful schedule of events for the festival.

WORTH A TRIP

BIG BUDDHA

Set on a hilltop just northwest of Chalong circle and visible from almost half of the island, the **Big Buddha** (พระใหญ่; Map p623) has the best view on Phuket. Once you're up here, pay your respects at the golden shrine, then step up to Big Buddha's glorious plateau where you can peer into Kata's bay, glimpse the shimmering Karon strand and, on the other side, survey the serene Chalong harbour where the channel islands look like pebbles.

Of course, you'll be forgiven if you disregard the view for a few minutes to watch local craftsmen put the finishing touches on their 60 million baht Buddha, dressed in Burmese alabaster. Over the last 20 years construction on Phuket hasn't stopped, so it means something when locals refer to the Big Buddha project as Phuket's most important development in the last 100 years.

Sleeping

Phuket Town is the cheapest place on the island to get some 'zzz's and is a treasure trove of budget lodging. Head out to the beaches for more midrange and top-end options.

Sino House   HOTEL **$$**
(☑ 0 7623 2494; www.sinohousephuket.com; 1 Th Montri; r 2000-2500B; ❄ @) Shanghai style meets *Mad Men* chic at this impressive Old Town offering. The rooms here are massive with modern furnishings, fantastic hand-made ceramic basins and quarter-moon shower tubs in their bathrooms. There's an on-site **Raintree Spa** (see p624) and long-term rates (18,000B per month) are available.

VEGETARIAN FESTIVAL

Loud popping sounds like machine-gun fire fill the streets, the air is nearly opaque with grey-brown smoke and men and women traipse along blocked-off city roads, their cheeks pierced with skewers and knives or, more surprisingly, lamps and tree branches; some of the flock have blood streaming down their fronts or open lashes across their backs. No this isn't a war zone, this is the **Vegetarian Festival**, one of Phuket's most important festivals, centred in Phuket Town.

The festival, which takes place during the first nine days of the ninth lunar month of the Chinese calendar – usually late September or October – celebrates the beginning of 'Taoist Lent', when devout Chinese abstain from eating meat. But more obvious to the outsider are the daily processions winding their way through town with floats of ornately dressed children and ladyboys (*gà·teu·i*, also spelt *kàthoey*), near armies of flag-bearing colour-coordinated young people and, most noticeably, men and women engaged in outrageous acts of self-mortification. Shopowners along Phuket's central streets set up altars in front of their shopfronts offering nine tiny cups of tea, incense, fruit, firecrackers, candles and flowers to the nine emperor gods invoked by the festival.

Those participating as mediums bring the nine deities to earth by entering into a trance state, piercing their cheeks with an impressive variety of objects, sawing their tongues or flagellating themselves with spiky metal balls. Whatever form the self-flagellation takes, the mediums (primarily men) walk in procession, stopping at shop-front altars, where they pick up the offered fruit. They also drink one of the nine cups of tea, grab some flowers to stick in their waistbands or set strings of firecrackers alight. The shop owners and their families stand by with their palms together in a *wâi* gesture, out of respect for these mediums who are temporarily possessed by deities. Surreal and overwhelming hardly describes it.

In Phuket Town, the festival activities are centred around five Chinese temples, with the **Jui Tui temple** on Th Ranong the most important, followed by **Bang Niew** and **Sui Boon Tong** temples. There are also events at temples in the nearby towns of **Kathu** (where the festival originated) and **Ban Tha Reua**. If you stop by the procession's starting point early enough in the morning, you may see a surprisingly professional, latex-glove-clad crew piercing the devotee's cheeks – not for the faint-hearted. Other ceremonies occur throughout the festival at the temples and can include firewalking and knife-ladder climbing. Beyond the headlining gore, fabulous vegetarian food stalls line the side streets offering a perfect opportunity to sample cheap local treats and strike up interesting conversations with the locals.

The **TAT office** (p632) in Phuket prints a helpful schedule of events for the Vegetarian Festival each year. The festival also takes place in Trang, Krabi and other southern Thai towns.

Oddly enough, there is no record of these sorts of acts of devotion associated with Taoist Lent in China. The local Chinese claim the festival was started by a theatre troupe from China that stopped off in Kathu around 150 years ago. The story goes that the troupe was struck seriously ill because the members had failed to propitiate the nine emperor gods of Taoism. The nine-day penance they performed included self-piercing, meditation and a strict vegetarian diet.

For more info, visit www.phuketvegetarian.com.

Phuket 346   GUEST HOUSE $$
(📞08 7281 1898; www.phuket346.com; 15 Soi Romanee; r 1300B; ❄) On charming Soi Romanee, this romantic old shophouse has been exquisitely restored to look like a cosy art gallery. Rooms have white-patterned wallpaper and the occassional bright-coloured wall decorated with modern art. Downstairs are fish ponds and a streetside cafe where jazz is played.

Casa 104   GUEST HOUSE $$
(📞0 7622 1268; 104 Th Yaowarat; r from 1000B; ❄🔑) This is a stunning renovation of a 100-year-old shophouse with burgundy walls, dangling chandeliers, bouquets of bamboo and peacock feathers, and early days' swing on the sound system. And that's just the lobby bar. Guestrooms are more sparse and windowless, but still elegant with white concrete floors, rain showers and original art-nouveau fixtures.

Chinotel   HOTEL $$
(📞0 7621 4455; www.chinotelphuket.com; 133-135 Th Ranong; r 1380-1780B; ❄@🔑) It has super-comfortable, clean, new, compact rooms with style – there's a bit of brick, a dash of bamboo and a brightly painted wall or two. Add a TV, fridge, hot-water bathroom and convenient location and you have a gem.

Sleep Sheep Phuket Hostel   HOSTEL $
(📞0 7621 6464; www.sleepsheepphuket.com; 243-245 Soi Dtac Shop; r 650B; ❄@🔑) In an alleyway off Th Thalang, this relatively modern place has big, brightly painted rooms with hot-water bathrooms and an uncommonly friendly staff; plus it smells like freshly laundered sheets.

D's Corner & Guesthouse   GUEST HOUSE $
(📞08 3590 4828; 132 Th Thalang; r 380-700B; ❄@) Huge, airy and clean rooms in this spacious guest house are hidden off the road down an unlikely hallway. The welcome is mediocre but the place is great value. Skip your free toast and eat breakfast at the Malaysian roti cafe next door.

🍴 Eating

There's good food in Phuket Town, and meals here cost a lot less than those at the beach.

TOP CHOICE Ka Jok See   THAI, INTERNATIONAL $$$
(📞0 7621 7903; kajoksee@hotmail.com; 26 Th Takua Pa; dishes 180-480B; ☺dinner Tue-Sun) Dripping Old Phuket charm and creaking under the weight of the owner's fabulous trinket collection, this atmospheric little eatery offers great food, top-notch music and – if you're lucky – some sensationally camp cabaret.

La Gaetana   INTERNATIONAL $$$
(📞0 7625 0523; 352 Th Phuket; dishes 200-450B; ☺lunch Mon, Tue & Fri, dinner Tue-Sun) An irresistibly intimate five-table restaurant, La Gaetana has black concrete floors, colourful walls and stemware, an open kitchen in the courtyard and a superb Italian menu. Think duck breast carpaccio followed by osso bucco.

TOP CHOICE Cook   ITALIAN THAI $
(📞0 7625 8375; 101 Th Phang-Nga; dishes 60-120B) The Thai owner-chef used to cook Italian at a megaresort, so when he opened this ludicrously inexpensive Old Town cafe he fused the two cultures. So, order the sensational green curry pizza with chicken, or the pork curry coconut-milk pizza, and fall in love.

China Inn   THAI FUSION $$
(Th Thalang; dishes 80-250B) The organics movement meets Phuket cuisine at this turn-of-the-century shophouse. There's red curry with crab, a host of veggie options, homemade yoghurt and fruit smoothies with organic honey. There's also a gallery here with textiles, carvings and clothes from Myanmar and Laos.

Uptown Restaurant   THAI $
(Th Tilok Uthit; dishes 30-60B; ☺10am-9pm) This classic, breezy Chinese-style cafe may not look fancy, but look around and you'll notice mounted photos of Thai celebrities who have stopped by to slurp the spectacular noodles.

Wilai   THAI $
(14 Th Thalang; dishes from 65B; ☺breakfast & lunch) Wilai serves Phuket soul food. It does Phuketian *pàt tai* with some kick to it, and a fantastic *mèe sua,* noodles sautéed with egg, greens, prawns, chunks of sea bass, and squid. Wash it down with fresh chrysanthemum juice.

🍷 Drinking & Entertainment

This is where you can party like a local. Bars buzz until late, patronised almost exclusively by Thais and local expats.

PHUKET & THE ANDAMAN COAST PHUKET TOWN

Timber Hut
CLUB

(✆0 7621 1839; 118/1 Th Yaowarat; admission free; ⊙6pm-2am) Thai and expat locals have been filling this old clubhouse every night for nearly 20 years. They gather at long wooden tables on two floors, converge around thick timber columns, swill whiskey, and sway to live bands that swing from hard rock to funk to hip-hop with aplomb.

Saneha
BAR

(✆08 1892 1001; Th Yaowarat; ⊙6pm-late) A fun upscale bohemian joint lit by seashell chandeliers, with plenty of dark corners where you can sip, snuggle, snack, and dig that soulful acoustic crooner on stage.

Bo(ok)hemian
CAFE

(✆0 7625 2854; 61 Th Thalang; ⊙9am-10pm; 🛜) Every town should have a coffee house this cool. The split-level open design feels both warm and leading edge. It has wi-fi, used books for sale, gourmet coffee and tea, and damn good chocolate cake.

🛍 Shopping

There are some fabulous bohemian-chic boutiques scattered throughout the Old Town selling jewellery, women's fashions, fabrics and souvenirs. Some whimsical art galleries tucked behind charming Chinese shopfronts are mostly found on Th Yaowarat.

Day Market
MARKET

(Th Ranong) This market near the town centre traces its history back to the days when pirates, Indians, Chinese, Malays and Europeans traded in Phuket. You might still find some fabrics from Southeast Asia, though it mostly sells food now.

ℹ Information

There are numerous internet cafes and ATMs around Th Phuket, Th Ranong, Th Montri and Th Phang-Nga.

Main post office (Th Montri; ⊙8.30am-4pm Mon-Fri, 9am-noon Sat)

Police (✆191, 0 7622 3555; cnr Th Phang-Nga & Th Phuket)

TAT office (✆0 7621 2213; www.tat.or.th; 73-75 Th Phuket; ⊙8.30am-4.30pm) Has maps, information brochures, a list of standard *sŏrng·tăa·ou* fares out to the various beaches, and the recommended charter costs for a vehicle.

ℹ Getting There & Around

To/From the Airport

Despite what airport taxi touts would like you to believe, a bright-orange **government airport bus** (www.airportbusphuket.com; tickets 85B) runs between the airport and Phuket Town via the Heroines Monument about every hour between 6am and 7pm. There's also a minibus service at the airport that will take you into Phuket Town for 150B per person. Services to Patong, Kata and Karon beaches cost 180B if there are enough passengers. Chartered cars between the airport and Phuket Town cost 500B; between the airport and beaches is 700B to 1000B. Metered taxis should cost no more than 550B (including airport tax) to anywhere around the island.

Bus

You'll find the **bus terminal** (✆0 7621 1977) just to the east of the town centre, within walking distance of the many hotels. Services from here include the following:

DESTINATION	BUS TYPE	FARE	DURATION
Bangkok	2nd class	487B	15hr
	air-con	626B	13-14hr
	VIP	974B	13hr
Hat Yai	air-con	556B	6-7hr
Ko Samui	air-con	430B	8hr (bus/boat)
Krabi	ordinary	95B	4hr
	air-con	145B	3½hr
Phang-Nga	ordinary	120B	2½hr
Ranong	ordinary	209B	6hr
	air-con	270B	5hr
Surat Thani	ordinary	195B	6hr
	air-con	240B	5hr
Trang	air-con	240B	5hr

Car

There are cheap car-rental agencies on Th Rasada near **Pure Car Rent** (✆0 7621 1002; www.purecarrent.com; 75 Th Rasada), which is a good choice. Suzuki jeeps go for about 1200B per day (including insurance), though in the low season the rates can go down to 750B. And if you rent for a week or more, you should get a discount.

The rates are always better at local places than at the better-known international firms, though you may be able to get deals with the familiar companies if you reserve in advance.

Motorcycle

You can rent motorcycles on Th Rasada near Pure Car Rent, or from various places at the beaches. Costs are anywhere from 200B to 300B per day, and can vary depending on the season. Bigger bikes (over 125cc) can be rented at shops in Patong, Kata, Rawai and Karon.

Sŏrng·tăa·ou & Túk-túk

Large bus-sized *sŏrng·tăa·ou* run regularly from Th Ranong near the day market to the various Phuket beaches (25B to 40B per person) – see the respective destinations for details. These run from around 7am to 5pm; outside these times you have to charter a túk-túk to the beaches, which will set you back 500B to Patong, 500B to Karon and Kata, 340B to 400B for Rawai and 600B to Kamala. You'll have to bargain. Beware of tales about the tourist office being 5km away, or that the only way to reach the beaches is by taxi, or even that you'll need a taxi to get from the bus terminal to the town centre (it is more or less in the town centre). For a ride around town, túk-túk drivers should charge 100B to 200B.

Motorcycle taxis around town cost 30B.

Ko Sireh
เกาะสิเหร่

This tiny island, 4km east of the district capital and connected to the main island by a bridge, is known for its *chow lair* (also spelt *chao leh*) village and a hilltop reclining Buddha at **Wat Sireh**.

The largest settlement of *chow lair* in Thailand is little more than a poverty-stricken cluster of tin shacks on stilts, plus one seafood restaurant. The Urak Lawoi, the most sedentary of the three *chow lair* groups, are found only between the Mergui Archipelago and the Tarutao-Langkawi Archipelago, and speak a creolised mixture of Malay and Mon-Khmer.

A single road loops the island, passing a few residences, prawn farms, lots of rubber plantations and a bit of untouched forest. On the east coast there's a public beach called **Hat Teum Suk**, as well as a terrific cooking school, the **Phuket Thai Cookery School** (0 7625 2354; www.phuketthaicookeryschool.com; Ko Sireh; courses per day from 2500B; 8.30am-5pm). Here you can get intimate with aromatic Thai spices at this popular cooking school set on a quiet seafront plot on Ko Sireh's east coast. Courses can last up to six hours. The school provides hotel pickups, market tours and a cookbook.

Laem Phanwa
แหลมพันวา

Laem Phanwa is a gorgeous, wooded, elongated cape, jutting into the sea south of Phuket. At the tip of the cape, **Phuket Aquarium** (Map p623; 0 7639 1126; www.phuketaquarium.org; adult/child 100/50B; 8.30am-4.30pm) displays a varied collection of tropical fish and other marine life. Experience it with a stroll along the walk-through tunnel.

The beaches and coves are rustic and protected by rocky headlands and mangroves. The sinuous coastal road is magic. If you just can't leave, check into the recently renovated **Cape Panwa Hotel** (0 7639 1123; www.capepanwa.com; 27 Moo 8, Th Sakdidej; r from 6100B;), a four-star, family-friendly stunner perched on 400m of secluded white sand.

The **seafood restaurants** along the Laem Phanwa waterfront are a great place to hang out and watch the pleasure skiffs and painted fishing boats passing by.

To get to the cape in your own vehicle, take Rte 4021 south and then turn down Rte 4023 just outside Phuket Town.

Rawai
ราไวย์

Now this is a place to live, which is exactly why Phuket's rapidly developing south coast is teeming with retirees, Thai and expat entrepreneurs, and a service sector that, for the most part, moved here from somewhere else.

The region is not just defined by its beaches but by the lush coastal hills that rise steeply and tumble into the Andaman Sea forming **Laem Promthep**, Phuket's southernmost point. These hills are home to pocket neighbourhoods and cul de sacs that are knitted together by just a few roads. So even with the growth you can feel nature, especially when you hit the beach.

Sights & Activities

Hat Nai Han, with its crescent of white sand backed by causarinas, bobbing yachts, seafront temple Wat Nai Han and monsoon-season surf break, is the best beach in the area, but there are smaller, hidden beaches that are just as beautiful. **Hat Rawai** lacks Nai Han's good looks. It's just a rocky longtail and speedboat harbour, which makes it the perfect place to open up a seafood grill.

There's a string of them here. All are locally owned and equally delicious.

Rawai is a fine place to learn how to kite board (see p648).

Long-tail and speedboat charters are available from Hat Rawai. Destinations include the quiet snorkelling islands of Ko Bon (long-tail/speedboat 800/2000B, Coral Island (1200/3000B) and Ko Kai (4000/8000B). Maximum six passengers.

Phuket Riding Club (☑ 0 7628 8213; www.phuketridingclub.com; 95 Th Viset, Rawai) offers one-hour (per person 800B) and two-hour (1500B) rides in the jungle around Rawai and along nearby beaches.

Rawai also offers *moo•ay tai* (also spelt *muay Thai*) courses (see p626).

🛏 Sleeping

All the lodging in lovely Hat Nai Han is reached via a skinny, rutted paved road that begins from the Phuket Yacht Club parking lot (yes you can drive past the guard) – or charter a long-tail from Rawai for 500B.

Vijitt   HOTEL $$$
(☑ 0 7636 3600; www.vijittresort.com; 16 Moo 2, Th Viset, Hat Nai Han; villas from 7800B; ❋) Arguably the area's most elegant property is sprinkled with deluxe villas that boast limestone floors, large bathtubs, outdoor showers, and gorgeous sea views from private terraces. Its stunning, black-bottom infinity pool overlooks Friendship Beach.

Ao Sane Bungalows   HOTEL $
(☑ 0 7628 8306, 08 1326 1687; 11/2 Moo 1, Th Viset, Hat Nai Han; bungalows 600-850B; ❋) The rickety cold-water, fan-cooled wooden bungalows are on a secluded beach, with million-dollar views of Ao Sane and Ao Nai Han. There's a beachside restaurant, dive centre and an old-hippie vibe.

Royal Phuket Yacht Club   HOTEL $$$
(☑ 0 7638 0200; www.royalphuketyachtclub.com; 23/3 Moo 1, Th Viset, Hat Nai Han; r from 6800B; ❋@☒) Still a destination for many a transcontinental yachty, there's an air of old-world elegance here, especially in its fabulous lobby-bar spinning with ceiling fans. Rooms feature large terraces – and stunning bay views – and there's every creature comfort you could imagine somewhere on-site. If you can snag one of the low-season discounts, it really is excellent value.

✗ Eating & Drinking

Besides the restaurants listed here, there are a dozen tasty **seafood grills** roasting fresh catch along the roadside at the northern end of Hat Rawai.

TOP CHOICE Rum Jungle   RESTAURANT $$$
(☑ 0 7638 8153; 69/8 Th Sai Yuan; meals 300-500B; ☉dinner, closed Sun) The best restaurant in the area and one of the best in all of Phuket is family run and spearheaded by a terrific Aussie chef. The New Zealand lamb shank is divine, as are the steamed clams, and the pasta sauces are all made from scratch. Everything – including the Pampero rocks – is served under a thatched roof to an exceptional world-beat soundtrack.

Nikita's   BAR
(☑ 0 7628 8703; Hat Rawai; ☉11am-late) Overlooking the sea on Phuket's south coast, Nikita's is a pleasant, open-aired place to hang out, with coffee drinks, green teas, a nice selection of shakes, and cocktails. If you're hungry you can order from the attached restaurant, Baan Rimlay (wood-fired pizzas from 200B).

❶ Getting There & Away

Rawai is about 18km south of Phuket Town. *Sŏrng·tăa·ou* (30B) run from Phuket's fountain circle at Th Ranong – some continue on to Hat Nai Han, but not all of them so ask first. The túk-túk trip from Rawai to Nai Han is a hefty 200B.

You can hire taxis (which are actually just chartered cars) from Rawai and Hat Nai Harn to the airport (700B), Patong (500B) and Phuket Town (500B).

Hat Kata   หาดกะตะ

Kata attracts a lively crowd with its shopping and busy beach without the seedy hustle endemic to Patong up the coast. While you might not find a secluded strip of sand, you will find plenty to do and plenty of easy-going folks to clink beers with.

There's surfing here in the shoulder and wet seasons, some terrific day spas and fantastic food. The beach is actually divided in two by a rocky headland, and the road between them is home to Phuket's original millionaire's row. Hat Kata Yai is on the north end, while the more secluded Hat Kata Noi unfurls to the south. Both offer soft golden sand and attract a bohemian crowd.

The main commercial street of Th Thai Na is perpendicular to the shore and has most of the restaurants and shops, along with some cheaper places to stay.

◉ Sights & Activities

The small island of **Ko Pu** is within swimming distance of the shore (if you're a strong swimmer); on the way are some OK coral reefs. Be careful of rip tides; heed the red flags and don't go past the breakers. **Dive Asia** (☑0 7633 0598; www.diveasia.com; 24 Th Karon, Kata) is a recommended dive outfit; there is a second location at 623 Th Karon near Karon Beach.

Both Hat Kata Yai and Hat Kata Noi offer decent **surfing** from April to November. Board rental costs 100B to 150B for one hour or 300B to 600B for the whole day. Try the following:

Phuket Surf (☑08 7889 7308, 08 1684 8902; www.phuketsurf.com) On Hat Kata Yai's southern cove, near the best break; offers surf lessons starting at 1500B for a half-day, as well as board rentals for 100/300B per hour/day. Check its website for more info about local surf breaks.

Phuket Surfing (☑0 7628 4183; www.phuket surfing.com) Just in front of Phuket Surf and sharing a roof with Nautilus Dive, it rents boards by the hour for 100B to 150B.

If you're looking for an alternative to the St Tropez–esque south Kata crush, make a left turn (west) just before the main road rises up and heads towards Karon, continue past the cluster of Thai-food joints and you'll find a gorgeous stretch of Kata beach in the secluded, rocky north end (ie Hat Kata Yai) where long-tails bob in the tide. There are beach chairs and umbrellas for rent along with snorkel gear. And cold beverages are just a lazy wave away.

➔ Courses

Kata Hot Yoga YOGA CLASS
(☑0 7660 5950; www.katahotyoga.com; 217 Th Khoktanod; per class 420B). Crave more heat? Consider taking a class here; they are held three times a day.

Mom Tri's Cooking Class COOKERY SCHOOL
(☑0 7633 0015; www.boathousephuket.com; 2/2 Th Kata (Patak West), Hat Kata; per person per day/weekend 2200/3500B) Offers a fantastic weekend Thai cooking class with its renowned chef, Rattana.

🛏 Sleeping

The following are average prices for the high season (May to October). Like Patong, it's getting harder and harder to find anything under 1000B during the high season, but prices drop radically when tourism is down.

The best deals in town can be found on Th Kata (aka the new road).

TOP CHOICE **Mom Tri's Villa Royale** HOTEL $$$
(☑0 7633 3568; www.villaroyalephuket.com; ste incl breakfast from 12,500B; ✳@🛰🏊) Tucked away in a secluded Kata Noi location with the grandest of views, Villa Royale is a supremely romantic place with fabulous food. Unwind in beautiful rooms straight out of the pages of *Architectural Digest* and guiltless pleasures include the attached **Spa Royale** and a saltwater pool – if you prefer a tamer version of the real thing – which is just steps away.

Sawasdee Village HOTEL $$$
(☑0 7633 0979; www.phuketsawasdee; 38 Th Ked Kwan; bungalows 6500-8500B; ✳@🛰🏊) This is a boutique resort with a lush, opulent but compact footprint built in classic Thai style. Ornate, peaked-roof bungalows have wood floors, beamed ceilings and doors open onto a thick tropical landscape laced with *koi* (carp) canals and gushing with waterfalls. Not to mention those Buddhist art installations. Throw in its quality spa and this place is unique and inviting in every way.

Caffe@Caffe GUEST HOUSE $$
(☑0 7628 4005; www.caffeatcaffe.com; 100/60-61 Th Kata; r 1800B; ✳🛰) Tiled rooms with gold-coloured wallpaper alternated with white painted walls, striped duvets, mini-balconies, fridges and TVs make this place as comfy as it is hip. It's in a three-storey building with a modern cafe downstairs.

Mom Tri's Boathouse HOTEL $$$
(☑0 7633 0015; www.boathousephuket.com; 2/2 Th Kata (Patak West); r 9600-25,000B; ✳🛰🏊) For Thai politicos, pop stars, artists and celebrity authors, the intimate boutique Boathouse is still the only place to stay on Phuket. Rooms are spacious and gorgeous, some sporting large breezy verandahs. Critics complain that the Boathouse is a bit stiff-lipped and old-fashioned for this century, but no-one can deny that the main reason to stay here is for the food. The on-site

restaurant, Boathouse Wine & Grill (p636), is among the best on the island.

Honey Resort
HOTEL **$$**

(☎0 7633 0938; www.honeyresort.com; 100/69 Th Kata; r 3400-3900B; ❄️🛜) This place has spacious new rooms with (tasteful!) wood panelling to spare. All rooms have daybeds, built-in dressers, desks, bathtubs and marble washbasins. There's free wi-fi and flat-screen TVs, too. Promotional rates can be absurdly low, but even the rack rates are a good deal.

Katathani Resort & Spa
HOTEL **$$$**

(☎0 7633 0124; www.katathani.com; 14 Th Kata Noi; r from 7800B; ❄️🛜🏊) Taking over a huge portion of lush, relatively quiet Hat Kata Noi, this glitzy spa resort offers all the usual trimmings in stylish surrounds. It features a spa, a handful of pools and heaps of space. Excellent low-season deals are often available here.

Sugar Palm Resort
HOTEL **$$**

(☎0 7628 4404; www.sugarpalmphuket.com; 20/10 Th Kata; r incl breakfast 3700-5200B; ❄️@🛜🏊) It's a 'chic chill-out world' at the Sugar Palm, as this Miami-meets-Thailand-style resort claims. Rooms, decorated in urban whites, blacks and lavender, are exceptional value and sublimely comfy, and all surround a black-bottomed, U-shaped pool. It's a block to the beach in the heart of Kata's lively shopping and restaurant strip.

Fantasy Hill Bungalow
HOTEL **$**

(☎0 7633 0106; fantasyhill@hotmail.com; 8/1 Th Patak; r with fan/air-con 450/800B; ❄️) Sitting in a lush garden on a hill, the older but well-maintained bungalows here are great value. The place is peaceful but central and the staff supersweet. Angle for a corner room with air-con and a view.

✖ Eating

There's some surprisingly classy food in Kata, though you'll be paying for it. For cheaper eats, head to Th Thai Na and to the cluster of affordable, casual seafood restaurants on Th Kata (Patak West) near the shore.

Boathouse Wine & Grill
MEDITERRANEAN **$$$**

(☎0 7633 0015; www.boathousephuket.com; 2/2 Th Kata (Patak West); mains 450-950B; ⊙breakfast, lunch & dinner) The perfect place to wow a fussy date, the Boathouse is the pick of the bunch for most local foodies. The atmos-

Hat Karon & Hat Kata

phere can be a little stuffy – this is the closest Phuket gets to old-school dining – but the Mediterranean fusion food is fabulous, the winelist expansive and the sea views sublime.

TOP CHOICE Capannina
ITALIAN **$$**

(☎0 7628 4318; capannina@fastmail.fm; 30/9 Moo 2, Th Kata; mains 200-700B) Everything here – from the pastas to the sauces – is made fresh and you can taste it. The ravioli and gnocchi are memorable, the risotto comes highly recommended, and it has great pizzas, calzones and veal Milanese, too. It gets crowded during the high season, so you may want to reserve ahead.

Oasis
FUSION **$$$**

(☎0 7633 3423; Th Kotanod; meals 350-600B) Two restaurants in one, the top shelf is an Asian-fusion tapas bar blessed with live jazz. The lower level is a candlelit fine-dining pa-

Hat Karon & Hat Kata

tio restaurant where you can sample fresh barracuda fillet with a sun-dried herb crust while you watch the oblong paper lanterns swing in the trees.

Thai Kitchen THAI $
(Th Thai Na; meals 80B; ⊙breakfast, lunch & dinner) Good rule of thumb: if a humble, roadside cafe is packed with Thai people, you can be certain that the food will rock. Its green curry (warning: your nose will run) and glass-noodle dishes are superb. It's just down the road from, ahem, 'Pussy Bar'.

🍸 Drinking

Kata's nightlife tends to be pretty mellow.

Ska Bar BAR
(⊙till late) At Kata's southernmost cove, tucked into the rocks and seemingly intertwined with the trunk of a grand old banyan tree, is our choice for oceanside sundowners. The Thai bartenders add to Ska's funky Rasta vibe, and the canopy dangles with buoys, paper lanterns and the flags of 10 countries.

Ratri Jazztaurant BAR
(✆0 7633 3538; Kata Hill; ⊙6pm-midnight) Hang out on the hillside terrace, listen to live jazz, watch the sun go down and enjoy delicious Thai food (dishes 145B to 345B). Now *this* is a vacation.

❶ Information

There are plenty of ATMs along Kata's main drag.
Post office (⊙9am-4.30pm Mon-Fri, to noon Sat) On Rte 4028, at the end of Th Thai Na.

❶ Getting There & Around

Sŏrng·tăa·ou to both Kata and Karon (per person 25B) leave frequently from the day market on Th Ranong in Phuket from 7am to 5pm. The main *sŏrng·tăa·ou* stop in Kata is in front of Kata Beach Resort.

Taxis from Kata go to Phuket Town (600B), Patong (600B) and Karon (200B).

Motorbike rentals (per day 300B) are widely available.

Hat Karon หาดกะรน

Karon is like Patong and Kata's love child: It's chilled-out, a touch glamorous and a tad cheesy with some sleazy corners. There are two megaresorts and package tourists aplenty here but there's still more sand space per capita than either Patong or Kata. The further north you go the more chic and beautiful the beach gets, culminating at the northernmost edge, accessible from a rutted road that extends past the vendors and food stalls, where the water is like turquoise glass.

Back within the inland network of streets and plazas you'll find a blend of good local food, more Scandinavian signage than seems reasonable, low-key girly bars, T-shirt vendors and lovely **Karon Park**, with its artificial lake and mountain backdrop. Fronting the whole mess is a fine stretch of sand.

Jurassic Park meets minigolf at **Dino Park** ([⁂]0 7633 0625; www.dinopark.com; Th Patak West, Karon; adult/child 240/180B; ☺10am-midnight), a bizarre park on the southern edge of Hat Karon. It's a maze of caves, lagoons, leafy gardens, dinosaur statues and, of course, putting greens.

🛏 Sleeping

Mövenpick　　　　　　HOTEL **$$$**
([⁂]0 7639 6139; www.moevenpick-hotels.com; 509 Th Kata (Patak West); r from 5900B, villas from 7000B; ❋�wifi☀) Grab a secluded villa and choose from a private plunge pool or outdoor rainforest shower; alternatively chill in the cubelike rooms with huge floor-to-ceiling glass windows in the ultramodern hotel. Besides a prime location across the street from a pretty beach, the Mövenpick offers a big pool with swim-up bar, a spa, and an alfresco restaurant and bar.

Karon Beach Resort　　　　HOTEL **$$$**
([⁂]0 763 3006; www.katagroup.com; 51 Th Kata (Patak West); r from 7500B; ❋wifi☀) Perched on the south end of Hat Karon, there are some elegant touches here. From the Buddhist sculpture in the jasmine-scented halls to the crown mouldings, wood furnishings, ceramic tiles and cushy duvets in the rooms, to those luscious sea views from the balcony.

In On The Beach　　　　　HOTEL **$$**
([⁂]0 7639 8220; www.karon-inonthebeach.com; 695-697 Moo 1, Th Patak; r from 3500B; ❋@wifi☀) This is a sweet, tasteful inn on Karon Park. The location is sublime, and the rooms – think of marble floors, wi-fi, air-con and ceiling fans, horseshoe-shaped pool – and come with sea views. With substantial low-season discounts, this is the perfect surf lair.

Andaman Seaview Hotel　　HOTEL **$$$**
([⁂]0 7639 8111; www.andamanphuket.com; 1 Soi Karon, Th Kata (Patak West); r from 4800B; ❋wifi☀🛈) The design here is sort of Cape Cod with sky-blue-and-white exterior and checkerboard marble floors in the lobby. Overall, there's a family vibe. The rooms have a turn-of-the-20th-century-Americana theme with marble tables, antiquated ceiling fans, art-deco-ish bathroom tiles and white-shutter cabinet doors. There's a bubbling kids pool and an adult pool.

Kangaroo Guesthouse　　GUEST HOUSE **$**
([⁂]0 7639 6517; 269/6-9 Karon Plaza; r 800B; ❋wifi) Basic, but very clean, sunny tiled rooms with hot water, air-con, a cute breakfast nook, and balconies overlooking a narrow, slightly seedy soi.

🍴 Eating & Drinking

There are a few cheap Thai and seafood places off the roundabout at the north end of Hat Kata (including a number of beachside seafood houses under one louvred roof 100m north of it) and a similar group on the main road near the southern end of Hat Karon.

[TOP CHOICE] Pad Thai Shop　　　THAI **$**
(Th Patak East; dishes 40B; ☺breakfast, lunch & dinner) On the busy main road behind Karon, just north of the tacky Ping Pong Bar, is this glorified food stand where you can find rich and savoury chicken stew (worthy of rave reviews in its own right), and the best *pàt tai* on planet earth: spicy and sweet, packed with prawns, tofu, egg and peanuts, and wrapped in a fresh banana leaf. You will be grateful. It closes at around 7pm.

Bai Toey　　　　　　　THAI **$$**
([⁂]08 1691 6202; Soi Old Phuket; meals 200B-250B) This is a charming Thai bistro with shaded outdoor patio and indoor seating. It has the traditional curry, stir-fry and noodle dishes, but you'd do well to sample its Thai-style grilled beef. It's a sliced fillet brushed in oyster sauce, served with sticky rice (200B).

Nakannoi　　　　　　　　BAR
([⁂]08 7898 5450; Karon Plaza; ☺5pm-1am) It's a boho arthouse hideaway with original canvases on the walls, found-art (including antique motorcycles and bicycles) decor, a concrete island bar and a permanent bandstand, where the owner jams with his mates after 8pm almost every night.

❶ Getting There & Away

For details on transport to Karon, see Getting There & Around, p637.

Hat Patong　　　　หาดป่าตอง

Sun-seared Scandinavians in bad knock-off T-shirts, beach-buzzing wave runners, a complete disregard for managed development, and an ability for turning the midlife

GAY PRIDE IN PHUKET

Although there are big gay-pride celebrations in Bangkok and Pattaya, the **Phuket Gay Pride Festival** is considered by many to be the best in Thailand, maybe even Southeast Asia. It usually happens between February and April but whenever it blooms, the whole island – but Patong specifically – is packed with (mostly male) revellers from all over the world.

The main events of the four-day weekend party are a huge beach-volleyball tournament and, of course, the Grand Parade, featuring floats, cheering crowds and beautiful costumes in the streets of Patong. In recent years, the festival has also included social-responsibility campaigns against child prostitution, substance abuse and for HIV awareness.

Any other time of year, the network of streets that link the Royal Paradise Hotel with Th Rat Uthit in Patong is where you'll find Phuket's gay pulse; check out the **Boat Bar** (p643).

For updates on future festivals or for more information about the scene in general, go to www.gaypatong.com.

crisis into a full-scale industry (sorry, Viagra, Patong was here first) make Patong rampant with unintentional comedy.

A place of concrete and silicone, and moral and gender bending, Patong is a simply a free for all. Anything, from a Starbucks 'venti latte' to an, ahem, companion for the evening is available for the right price. And while that's true about dozens of other, phonier, destinations, Patong doesn't try to hide what it is. It is what it is. And that's refreshing in a way.

Of course, that doesn't mean you're going to like it. But when you arrive you'll take one look at the wide, white-sand beach and its magnificent crescent bay, and you'll understand how all this started. Today this town is much more of a city than Phuket Town and it's the centre of Phuket's action.

Diving and spa options abound, as well as upscale dining, streetside fish grills, campy cabaret, Thai boxing, dusty antique shops and one of Asia's coolest shopping malls.

Activities & Courses

Sea Fun Divers DIVING
(0 7634 0480; www.seafundivers.com; 29 Soi Karon Nui, Patong) This is an outstanding and very professional diving operation. Its standards are extremely high and the service is impeccable. There's an office at the Le Meridien resort in Patong, and a second location at the Katathani Resort.

Pum Thai Cooking School COOKERY SCHOOL
(0 7634 6269; www.pumthaifoodchain.com; 204/32 Tha Rat Uthit, Hat Patong) This restaurant chain (three locations in Thailand and two in France) holds several daily one- to six-hour classes (per person 4650B). Longer classes begin with a market tour and end with a meal.

Sleeping

It's getting pretty difficult to find anything in Patong costing less than 1000B from about November to April (the period that corresponds to the prices listed in this book), but outside this time period rates drop by 40% to 60%.

BYD Lofts HOTEL **$$$**
(0 7634 3024; www.bydlofts.com; 5/28 Th Rat Uthit; apt 4900-11,500B;) If style and comfort are more important to you than beachfront (although it's only a minute's walk to the beach), look no further. Urban-style apartments with lots of white (floors, walls, blinds) and sharp lines feel angelic compared with the seedy world of Patong on the streets below. There's a day spa, a rooftop pool and an excellent restaurant on the premises.

TOP CHOICE Burasari HOTEL **$$$**
(0 7629 2929; www.burasari.com; 18/110 Th Ruamchai; r 2700-9300B;) It's a lovely maze of swimming pools and waterfalls, etched columns, cushion-strewn lounges and bars. Rooms are more simple but chic with flat screen TVs, queen-sized beds and bamboo accents. The **Naughty Radish** cafe here serves outrageous customisable salads (from 180B) and the best smoothies (120B) on Phuket.

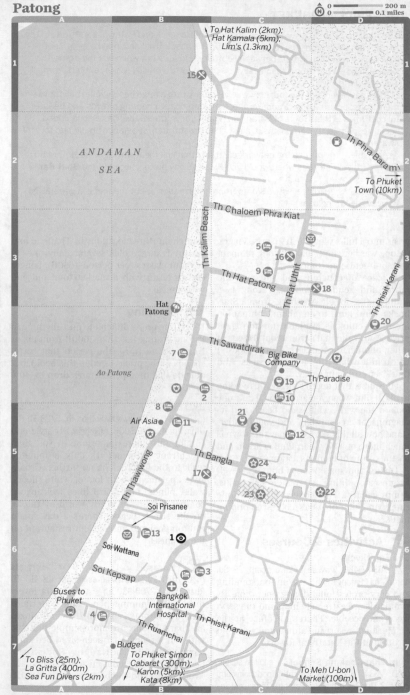

Patong

N ⬆

0 —————— 200 m
0 —————— 0.1 miles

To Hat Kalim (2km);
Hat Kamala (5km);
Lim's (1.3km)

ANDAMAN
SEA

Th Phra Barami

To Phuket
Town (10km)

Th Chaloem Phra Kiat

Th Kalim Beach

Th Hat Patong

Th Rat Uthit

Th Phisit Karani

Hat
Patong

Th Sawatdirak

Big Bike
Company

Th Paradise

Ao Patong

Air Asia

Th Bangla

Th Thawiwong

Soi Prisanee

Soi Wattana

Soi Kepsap

Buses to
Phuket

Bangkok
International
Hospital

Th Phisit Karani

Th Ruamchai

Budget

To Bliss (25m);
La Gritta (400m);
Sea Fun Divers (2km)

To Phuket Simon
Cabaret (300m);
Karon (5km);
Kata (8km)

To Meh U-bon
Market (100m)

PHUKET & THE ANDAMAN COAST PHUKET ISLAND

Patong

TOP CHOICE **Baipho, Baithong & Sala Dee** GUEST HOUSE **$$**

(☏0 7629 2074, 0 7629 2738; www.baipho.com, www.baithong.com, www.saladee.com; 205/12-13 & 205/14-15 Th Rat Uthit 200 Pee; r 1800-3300B; ❄☎) These three arty guest houses are all on the same little soi under the same friendly and organised management. Rooms and common areas are filled with Buddha imagery and Zen-spa-type trimmings mingling with modern art and urban touches. The dimly lit, nestlike rooms are all unique so ask to see a few if possible. **The Lounge**, downstairs at Baithong, serves cocktails and very good Italian and Thai food as well as gourmet snacks. Guests can use the pool at the unsightly Montana Grand Phuket next door.

La Flora HOTEL **$$$**

(☏0 7634 4241; www.laflorapatong.com; 39 Th Thawiwong; r from 9500B; ❄☎☸) Here's where clean lines and minimalist decor spill onto Patong beach. Rooms are large with wood furnishings (check out that floating desk), flat-screen TV and DVD, bathtub and shower. The minibar is stocked with complimentary soft drinks, and there's a huge lap pool.

Newspaper HOTEL **$$**

(☏0 7634 6276; www.newspaperphuket.com; 125/4-5 Th Paradise; r 2500-5000B; ❄☎) One of Patong's classiest three-star inns and easily the most stylish and sophisticated on this gay-friendly block of bars and cafes. Rooms have upscale tile floors, bedside lanterns, dark-wood furnishings and understated feature walls. It's frequently booked, so reserve ahead.

The Belle Resort HOTEL **$$**

(☏0 7629 2782; www.thebelleresort.com; 104/31-33 Soi Prisanee; r from 1800B; ❄☎☸) Simple, upscale Zen design, dimly lit rooms with wood floors, lots of glass and soft beds, make this a stylish choice. It's on a quiet street of Italian restaurants near the beach and in the heart of the action.

Baan Pronphateep HOTEL **$$**

(☏0 7634 3037; baanpronphateep.com; 168/1 Th Thawiwong; r 1600-2100B; ❄) Banyan tree shaded and nestled down a secluded little soi, this is a quiet and simple three-star choice. Rooms are spacious and come with a full-sized fridge and a private patio.

Casa Jip GUEST HOUSE **$**

(☏0 7634 3019; www.casajip.com; 207/10 Th Rat Uthit; r from 700B; ❄) Italian run and great value, this place has very big, if simple, rooms with comfy beds and a taste of Thai style. You get cable TV and there's even a breakfast room service.

Patong Backpacker Hostel   HOSTEL **$**
(☑0 7625 6680; www.phuketbackpacker.com; 167
Th Ranong; dm 300-450B, r 1200B; ❄️🛜) This is a
great location near the beach and the owner
offers info on all the best, cheapest places
to eat in town. Dorm prices vary depending
on the number of beds in the room (three to
10). The top floor is the brightest but dorm
rooms on the lower floors each have their
own attached bathroom. Skip the overpriced
room.

Some other options:

Bliss   HOTEL **$$$**
(☑0 7629 2098; www.theblissphuket.com; 40 Th
Thawiwong; ste from 15,000B; ❄️🛜🏊) A sleek,
new all-suite resort. The suites are 90 sq
m with a full-sized living room and master
bedroom with wood floors, two flat-screen
TVs, a lap pool, a Jacuzzi and a blooming
garden on the terrace. Low-season dis-
counts make it worth the splurge.

Impiana Phuket Cabana   HOTEL **$$$**
(☑0 7634 0138; www.impiana.com; 41 Th Thawi-
wong; r from 7000B; ❄️🛜🏊) Cabana-style
and plumb on the best part of the beach,
the rooms here are laden with chic and
creature comforts and are close to all the
action.

Merrison Inn   HOTEL **$$**
(☑0 7634 0383; www.merrisoninn.com; 5/35 Th
Hat Patong; r 1300B; ❄️🛜) Polished concrete
floors, terrazzo bathrooms, wall-mounted
flat-screen TVs, queen-sized beds and
more than a little Asian kitsch make this
place a real bargain.

Yorkshire Hotel   HOTEL **$$**
(☑0 7634 0904; www.theyorkshirehotel.com;
169/16 Soi Saen Sabai; r 1800-2300; ❄️@🛜)
About as Thai as a plate of Yorkshire pud.
There's a flicker of B&B charm here and
the rooms are sleek.

✖️ Eating

Patong has stacks of restaurants and the
trick is to steer around the watered-down
Thai and poorly executed Western food clog-
ging most main drags. The most glamorous
restaurants are in a little huddle above the
cliffs on the northern edge of town.

Bargain seafood and noodle stalls pop
up across town at night – try the lanes on
and around Th Bangla, or venture over to

the **Patong Food Park** (Th Rat Uthit; ⏰4pm-
midnight) once the sun drops.

Baan Rim Pa   THAI **$$$**
(☑0 7634 4079; Th Kalim Beach; dishes 215-475B)
Stunning Thai food is served with a side or-
der of spectacular views at this institution.
Standards are high, with prices to match,
but romance is in the air, with candlelight
and piano music aplenty. Book ahead and
tuck in your shirt.

Lim's   THAI **$$$**
(☑0 7634 4834; 28 Th Phrabaramee, Soi 7; meals
300-600B; ⏰6pm-midnight) Lim's is 500m
north (uphill) from the coast road to Kamala. It's a modern, moulded-concrete dining
room and lounge serving upscale Thai cuisine. When celebrities land in Phuket, most
spend at least one evening here.

Mengrai Seafood   SEAFOOD **$$**
(Soi Tun; meals 120-300B) Located down a
sweaty, dark soi off Th Bangla is a wonderful
food court serving fresh, local food. The stalls
towards the end of the soi serve daily curries
that local expats swear by. This restaurant
specialises in (very) fresh fish, prawns and
mussels.

Chicken Rice Briley   THAI **$**
(Patong Food Park, Th Rat Uthit; meals 35-45B;
⏰breakfast & lunch) The only diner in the Pa-
tong Food Park to offer sustenance when
the sun shines. Steamed chicken breast
is served on a bed of rice with a bowl of
chicken broth with crumbled bits of meat
and bone, and roast pork. Dip in the fantas-
tic chilli sauce. There's a reason it's forever
packed with locals.

Ninth Floor   INTERNATIONAL **$$$**
(☑0 7634 4311; 47 Th Rat Uthit; mains 290-1990B;
⏰dinner) Come on up to the 9th floor of the
Sky Inn Condotel building where you can
watch the sea of lights spread through sliding floor-to-ceiling glass doors. This is the
highest open-air restaurant on the island,
but the perfectly prepared steaks and chops
are what made it a Patong institution.

🍷 Drinking

Some visitors may find that Patong's bar
scene is enough to put them off their *pàt tai*,
but if you're in the mood for plenty of beer,
winking neon and short skirts, it is certainly
worth sampling.

Th Bangla is Patong's beer and bar-girl
mecca and features a number of spectacular,

go-go extravaganzas, where you can expect the usual mix of gyrating Thai girls and often red-faced Western men. The music is loud (expect techno), the clothes are all but nonexistent and the decor is typically slapstick with plenty of phallic imagery. That said, the atmosphere is more carnival than carnage and you'll find plenty of Western women pushing their way through the throng to the bar.

Two Black Sheep PUB
(0895 921 735; www.twoblacksheep.net; 172 Th Rat Uthit; ⊙11am-2am) Owned by a fun Aussie couple (he's a musician, she's a chef), this old-school pub is a great find. It has good grub and live music nightly. From 8pm to 10pm there's an acoustic set, then Chilli Jam, the house band, gets up and rocks till the last call. And it bans bar girls, which keeps everything at a PG (Parental Guidance) level.

JP's Restaurant & Bar BAR
(0 7634 3024; www.bydlofts.com; 5/28 Th Hat Patong; ⊙10.30am-11.30pm) This hipster indoor-outdoor lounge definitely brings a touch of style and panache to Patong. There's a low-slung bar, the outdoor sofa booths are cush, happy hour (with free tapas) starts at 10pm and there are weekly DJ parties.

La Gritta BAR
(0 7634 0106; www.amari.com; 2 Th Meun-ngern; ⊙10.30am-11.30pm) A spectacular, modern restaurant in the town's southwest that doesn't fit in with the ageing bones of this once-great property, but who cares? With tiered booths, massive yet muted light boxes and a deck that is just centimetres above the boulder-strewn shore, there is no better place for a sunset cocktail.

Monte's BAR
(Th Phisit Karani; ⊙11am-midnight) Now this, my friends, is a tropical pub. There's a thatched roof, a natural-wood bar, dozens of orchids and a flat screen for ballgames. The barflies swarm on Fridays for Monte's famous Belgian-style mussels, and on the weekends he fires up the grill.

Boat Bar GAY BAR
(0 7634 2206; www.boatbar.com; 125/20 Th Rat Uthit) Phuket's original gay nightspot and still its only disco, is usually jumping with a lively, mostly gay crowd. Make sure to arrive before the midnight cabaret!

☆ Entertainment

Cabaret and Thai boxing are something of a speciality here.

Phuket Simon Cabaret CABARET
(0 7634 2011; www.phuket-simoncabaret.com; Th Sirirach; admission 700-800B; ⊙performances 7.30pm & 9.30pm nightly) About 300m south of town, this cabaret offers entertaining transvestite shows. The 600-seat theatre is grand, the costumes are gorgeous and the ladyboys (gà·teu·i) are convincing. The house is often full – book ahead.

Sound Phuket CLUB
(0 7636 6163; www.soundphuket.com; Jung Ceylon complex, Unit 2303, 193 Th Rat Uthit; admission varies; ⊙10pm-4am) When internationally renowned DJs come to Phuket these days, they are usually gigging amid the rounded, futuristic environs of Patong's hottest (and least sleazy) nightclub. If top-shelf DJs are on the decks, expect to pay up to 300B entry fee.

Rock City CLUB
(Th Rat Uthit; www.rockcityphuket.com; ⊙9pm-late) Let the grunge begin! This dark den of rock lives on the glory of AC/DC, Metallica and Guns N' Roses tribute bands. On Tuesday, Friday and Sunday, rockers channel music by the Red Hot Chili Peppers, the Rolling Stones, U2 and Bon Jovi in one International Rock City Party (1000B) with free cocktails and beer before 11pm, so get there early and keep it rockin'.

Bangla Boxing Stadium THAI BOXING
(0 7282 2348; Th Phisit Karani; admission 1000-1500B; ⊙9-11.30pm Tue, Wed, Fri & Sun) Old name, new stadium, same game: a packed line-up of competitive moo·ay tai (Thai boxing) bouts.

Jung Ceylon CINEMA
(Th Rat Uthit) You can catch new Hollywood releases in pristine, amphitheatre-style cinemas at the shopping mall.

ⓘ Information

There are internet cafes, and banks with ATM and currency-exchange facilities across the town.
Post office (Th Thawiwong; ⊙9am-4.30pm Mon-Fri, to noon Sat)
Tourist police (1699; cnr Th Thawiwong & Th Bangla)

ⓘ Getting There & Around

Air Asia (☎0 7634 1792; www.airasia.com; 39 Th Thawiwong; ⊙9am-9pm) has an office in town.

Túk-túk circulate around Patong for 50B to 100B per ride. There are numerous places to rent 125cc motorbikes and jeeps. **Big Bike Company** (☎0 7634 5100; 106 Th Rat Uthit) rents proper motorcycles (500B to 1000B per day). Keep in mind that the mandatory-helmet law is strictly enforced in Patong, where roadblocks/checkpoints can spring up at a moment's notice. **Budget** (☎0 7629 2389; 44 Th Thawiwong; ⊙9am-4pm) has an office in the Patong Merlin Hotel.

Sŏrng·tăa·ou to Patong from Phuket Town leave from Th Ranong, near the day market and fountain circle; the fare is 25B. The after-hours charter fare is 500B. *Sŏrng·tăa·ou* then drop off and pick up passengers at the southern end of Patong beach. From here you can hop on a motorbike taxi (20B to 30B per ride), flag down a túk-túk (prices vary widely) or walk till your feet hurt.

Hat Kamala   หาดกมลา

A chilled-out hybrid of Hat Karon and Hat Surin, calm but fun Kamala tends to lure a mixture of longer-term lower-key partying guests, a regular crop of Scandinavian families, and young couples. The bay is magnificent, turquoise and serene with shore breakers that lull you to sleep. Palms and pines mingle on the leafy and rocky northern end where the water is a rich emerald green and the snorkelling around the rock reef is pleasant, while new resorts are ploughed into the southern bluffs above the gathering long-tails. The entire beach is backed with lush rolling hills, which one can only hope are left alone...forever. And it's the only beach on Phuket with a walking path lined with this many restaurants, resorts and shops. Ditch the motorbike and step into Kamala bliss.

◉ Sights & Activities

Local beach boffins will tell you that **Laem Singh**, just north of Kamala, is one of the best capes on the island. Walled in by cliffs, it has no road access so you have to park your vehicle on the headland and clamber down a narrow path, or you could charter a long-tail (1000B) from Hat Kamala. It gets crowded.

Phuket Fantasea   THEMED THEATRE **$$**
(☎0 7638 5000; www.phuket-fantasea.com; admission with/without dinner 1900/1500B; ⊙6-11.30pm Fri-Wed) This is a US$60 million 'cultural

theme park' located just east of Hat Kamala. Despite the billing, there aren't any rides, but there is a show that takes the colour and pageantry of Thai dance and combines this with state-of-the-art light-and-sound techniques that rival anything found in Las Vegas (think 30 elephants). All of this takes place on a stage dominated by a full-scale replica of a Khmer temple. Kids especially will be captivated by the spectacle but it is over-the-top cheesy, and cameras are forbidden.

🛏 Sleeping & Eating

Layalina Hotel   HOTEL **$$$**
(☎0 7638 5942; www.layalinahotel.com; r incl breakfast 5500-7700B; ✳@☎☂) Nab one of the split-level suites with very private rooftop terraces at this small boutique hotel for romantic sunset views over white sand and blue sea. The decor is simple, Thai and chic, with fluffy white duvets and honey-toned wood furniture. Room rates include a one-hour couple's massage at the on-site spa. The pool is ridiculously small – but that turquoise ocean *is* only steps away.

Cape Sienna Hotel   HOTEL **$$$**
(☎0 7633 7300; www.capesienna.com; r 8500-10,130B; bungalows 4350-5600B; ✳@☎☂) This flashy, romantic hotel dominates the southern headland and offers magnificent azure bay views from the lobby and a pool. Rooms are modern, with plenty of clean, fresh lines and all the amenities. No kids allowed.

Clear House   HOTEL **$$**
(☎0 7638 5401; www.clearhousephuket.com; r 1300B; ✳☎) Shabby chic with a mod twist, whitewashed rooms have pink feature walls, plush duvets, flat-screen TVs, wi-fi and huge pebbled baths. This place just feels good.

Rockfish   FUSION **$$**
(☎0 7627 9732; 33/6 Th Kamala Beach; dishes 150-1000B; ⊙breakfast, lunch & dinner) Perched above the river mouth and the bobbing long-tails, with beach, bay and mountain views, is Kamala's best dining room. It rolls out gems such as braised duck breast with kale, and prosciutto-wrapped scallops.

ⓘ Getting There & Away

To catch a regular *sŏrng·tăa·ou* from Kamala to Patong costs 50B per person, while a *sŏrng·tăa·ou* charter (starting in the evenings) costs 250B.

Hat Surin   หาดสุรินทร์

Like that hot boy or girl in school who also happens to have style, soul, a fun personality and wealthy parents, Hat Surin is the kind of place that can inspire (travel) lust in anyone who meets her/him. With a wide, blonde beach, water that blends from pale turquoise in the shallows to a deep blue on the horizon and two lush, boulder-strewn headlands, Surin could easily attract tourists on looks alone. Ah, but there are stunning galleries, five-star spa resorts and wonderful beachfront dining options, too. So by the time you're done swimming, sunbathing, snacking at local fish grills and sipping cocktails at barefoot-chic beach clubs, don't be surprised if you've fallen in love.

🛏 Sleeping

Hat Surin is home to some of Phuket's classiest resorts but there's little available for people with small budgets. To experience one of Phuket's most exclusive hotels (and celebrity magnets) stay at the over-the-top luxurious **Amanpuri Resort** (☑0 7632 4333; www.amanresorts.com; villas US$925-8050; ❄@☌).

TOP
CHOICE **The Surin Phuket**   HOTEL **$$$**
(☑0 7662 1579; www.thesurinphuket.com; r 17,000-58,000B; ❄☌☌) Almost any place located on a private beach this quiet and stunning would have be a top pick. But The Surin's (previously 'The Chedi') bungalows, with naturalistic wooden exteriors that hide beneath the hillside foliage, and earthy, luxurious interiors, make the site that much better. You'll have to be in decent shape for walking around the resort, since it can be quite a hoof up hills and over wooden walkways to get to many of the bungalows. It received an extensive renovation mid-2011 so should be even better by the time you get there.

TOP
CHOICE **Twin Palms**   RESORT **$$$**
(☑0 7631 6500; www.twinpalms-phuket.com; r 6100-38,800B; ❄@☌☌) This is the Audrey Hepburn of Phuket's hotels – it's classic yet completely contemporary. There's a pervasive feeling of space with minimalist, artsy swimming pools everywhere that are fringed by delicate white frangipani. Even the simplest rooms are extra spacious and have oversized bathrooms, sublimely comfortable

beds and a supreme sense of calm. It's a few minutes' walk to the beach. Expats from all over Phuket can be found eating the island's most popular **brunch** (open noon to 2pm; buffet 1300B) here on Sunday.

Benyada Lodge   HOTEL **$$**
(☑0 7627 1261; www.benyadalodge-phuket.com; r 2800-3500B; ❄@☌☌) Chic, modern rooms – with black louvred closets, terracotta-tiled bathrooms and silk, pastel-coloured throw pillows scattered in the lounging corner – are a great bargain for this area. The service is stellar. Take in the sunset and have a dip in the pool at the rooftop bar or it's only a few minutes' walk to the beach.

Capri Hotel   HOTEL **$$**
(☑0 7627 0597; www.phukethotelcapri.com; r 900-1500B; ❄☌) Here's your slice of Italy with pillars everywhere and Mediterranean-style painted archways over the bathrooms in the cute, bright rooms. The best nests have pink-painted wrought-iron balconies overlooking a not-very-European, but quiet street. Add the Italian bistro downstairs and it's a fantastic bargain.

🍴 Eating & Drinking

There are plenty of excellent restaurants in and around Surin. For cheap seafood, your first stop should be the numerous, fun and delicious seafront dining rooms.

TOP
CHOICE **Taste**   FUSION **$$**
(☑08 7886 6401; tapas 160-225B) The best of a new breed of urban-meets-surf eateries along the beach. Dine indoors or alfresco on meal-sized salads, perfectly cooked fillet mignon or a variety of Thai-Mediterranean starters and mains. Service is outstanding and there's an enticing attached gallery selling Tibetan, Nepali and local jewellery and art.

Catch   FUSION **$$$**
(☑0 7631 6500; mains 250-450B) Slip on your breeziest linen to dine at this draped, cabana-style eatery right on the beach. It's part of Twin Palms, even though it's not attached, and has all the same classy attributes as the hotel in both ambience and cuisine.

Stereo Lab   BAR, CLUB
(☑08 9218 0162; www.stereolabphuket.com; Hat Surin; ◷11am-2am) It offers a bar, dance floor, and unbroken sea views. Special events feature known international DJs.

Northern Beaches

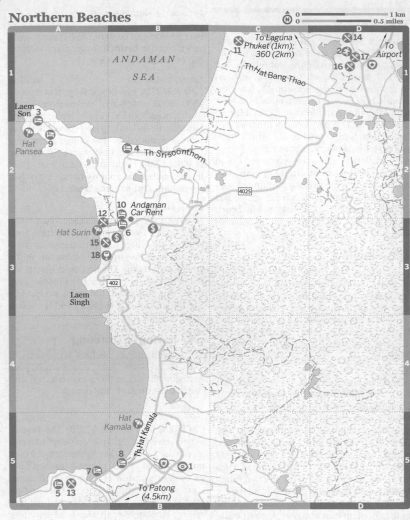

ℹ Information

There is an ATM at Surin Plaza, just east of the beach on Rte 4025. Internet access is available at most hotels for 1B per minute.

ℹ Getting There & Away

A regular *sǒrng·tǎa·ou* from Phuket Town's Th Ranong to Hat Surin costs 35B per person, while túk-túk or *sǒrng·tǎa·ou* charters cost 450B.

Rent cars from **Andaman Car Rental** (☎0 7662 1600; www.andamancarrent.com; ◷9am-9pm), opposite the entrance to Twin Palms. Vehicles can be rented from 1400B per day.

Ao Bang Thao อ่าวบางเทา

Almost as large and even more beautiful than Patong Bay, the stunning, 8km white-sand sweep of Ao Bang Thao has several personalities. The southern half is home to a sprinkling of three-star bungalow resorts. Further inland you'll find an old fishing village laced with canals along with a number of upstart villa subdivisions. Don't be alarmed if you see a herd of water buffalo grazing just 100m from a gigantic construction site.

Northern Beaches

Smack in the centre of it all is the somewhat absurd Laguna Phuket complex – a network of five four- and five-star resort properties and an ageing shopping mall knitted together by an artificial lake, patrolled by tourist shuttle boats, and a paved nature trail. But in the north Mother Nature asserts herself once more, and a lonely stretch of powder -white sand and tropical blue extends past all the bustle and change, and delivers the kind of peace you imagined when you booked your trip.

The **Hideaway Day Spa** (☑08 1750 0026; www.phuket-hideaway.com; 382/33 Th Srisoontorn, Chergtalay) has an excellent reputation. It offers traditional Thai massage, sauna and mud body wraps in a tranquil wooded setting at the edge of a lagoon. Treatments start at 1500B. It also has its own line of spa products.

🛏 Sleeping

Laguna Phuket is home to five luxury resorts, an 18-hole golf course and 30 restaurants. Guests at any one of the resorts can use the dining and recreation facilities at all of them. Frequent shuttle buses make the rounds of all the hotels, as do pontoon boats (via the linked lagoons).

TOP CHOICE Banyan Tree Phuket   HOTEL **$$$**
(☑0 7632 4374; www.banyantree.com; villas from 25,000B; ✳@☎☞) One of Phuket's finest hotels, and the first to introduce bungalows with their own private pool, the Banyan Tree Phuket (in Laguna Phuket) is an oasis of sedate, understated luxury. Accommodation is

in villas – and, as long as you're here, the onsite spa should not be missed.

Angsana Laguna Phuket   HOTEL **$$$**
(www.angsana.com; see website for prices; ✳@☎☞☞) Gated away in Laguna Phuket, the Sheraton Grande Laguna underwent extensive renovation to be rebranded as the Angsana Laguna Phuket opening in December 2011. The gigantic hotel will appeal to a lively, active crowd. It features a gigantic 323m-long pool, water-sports facilities galore and well over 400 rooms.

Andaman Bangtao Bay Resort   HOTEL **$$$**
(☑0 7627 0246; www.andamanbangtaobayresort. com; bungalows 3900-5900B; ✳☎☞) Every bungalow has a sea view and there's a summer-camp vibe at this pleasant little resort. The design is very Thai, with woodcarvings on the walls and coconuts hanging from the eaves of the roofs, but for this price we expected a little more luxury.

🍴 Eating

Many of Phuket's finest eateries are found just outside Laguna's main gate, and there are even more at the seafood-oriented beach cafes south of the Banyan Tree Phuket.

TOP CHOICE Tatonka   INTERNATIONAL **$$$**
(☑0 7632 4349; Th Srisoonthorn; dishes 250-300B; ⊙dinner Thu-Tue) This is the home of 'globetrotter cuisine', which owner-chef Harold Schwarz developed by taking fresh local products and combining them with Europe, Colorado and Hawaii cooking techniques. The eclectic, tapas-style selection includes creative vegetarian and seafood dishes and

such delights as Peking duck pizza (220B). There's also a tasting menu (750B per person, minimum two people), which lets you try a little of everything. Call ahead during the high season.

Siam Supper Club INTERNATIONAL **$$$**
(☑0 7627 0936; Hat Bang Thao; dishes 180-450B) One of the hippest spots on Phuket where the 'infamous' come to sip cocktails, listen to jazz and eat an excellent meal. The menu is predominantly Western with gourmet pizzas, seafood *cioppino* and hearty mains such as veal tenderloin with wild mushrooms on truffle mash. Don't miss the insane cheesecake.

Babylon Beach Club ITALIAN & THAI **$$$**
(☑08 1970 5302; Hat Bang Thao; dishes 120-850B; ☀) Accessible by dirt road are the seaside, polished, whitewashed environs of the Babylon Beach Club. Under new Italian management, lunch is more casual 'beach fare' such as burgers and salads while dinner gets more lavish with mains such as prawn and asparagus risotto.

Tawai THAI **$$$**
(☑0 7632 5381; Moo 1, Laguna Resort Entrance; mains 180-300B) Set in a lovely old house decorated with traditional art is this gem of a Thai kitchen, serving classics like roast duck curry and pork *lâhp*. A free shuttle service is available to and from the Laguna hotels.

Chaba THAI **$$$**
(☑0 7627 1580; Moo 1, Laguna Resort Entrance; meals 400-800B) Upscale Thai served with flair on the lagoon just outside the Laguna gates. Just point, it will steam, grill or fry it.

❶ Getting There & Away

A *sŏrng·tăa·ou* between Ao Bang Thao and Phuket Town's Th Ranong costs 25B per person. Túk-túk charters are 700B.

Sirinat National Park
อุทยานแห่งชาติสิรินาถ

Comprising the beaches of Nai Thon, Nai Yang and Mai Khao, as well as the former Nai Yang National Park and Mai Khao wildlife reserve, **Sirinat National Park** (☑0 7632 8226; www.dnp.go.th; admission 200B; ⏰8am-5pm) encompasses 22 sq km of coastal land, plus 68 sq km of sea.

The whole area is a 15-minute or less drive from Phuket International Airport, which makes it particularly convenient for a first stop.

◉ Sights & Activities

If you're after a lovely arc of fine golden sand, away from the buzz of Phuket busyness, **Hat Nai Thon** is it. Swimming is quite good here except at the height of the monsoon, and there is some coral near the headlands at either end of the bay.

Hat Nai Yang's bay is sheltered by a reef that slopes 20m below the surface – which makes for both good snorkelling in the dry season and fantastic surfing in the monsoon season. Along the dirt road at the very southern end is a seemingly endless strip of seafood restaurants, beach bars and, oddly enough, tailor shops. It's all refreshingly rough around the edges.

Oi's Longtail (☑08 1978 5728; 66 Moo 3, Hat Nai Yang; tours 1600B) specialises in two-hour snorkelling tours of the reefs around Ko Waeo. It's located at the Bank restaurant, opposite the long-tail boat harbour.

Hat Nai Yang is a great place to go kite boarding. Two fine operators with offices here:

Kiteboarding Asia KITE BOARDING
(☑08 1591 4594; www.kiteboardingasia.com; lessons from 4000B) Its main office is on Hat Nai Yang, but it has a kiosk on the south end of Hat Karon (see Map p636) that's open in the low season. It also offers lessons off Rawai's Friendship Beach.

Kite Zone KITE BOARDING
(☑0833 952 005; www.kitesurfingphuket.com; beginner lessons from 1100B) With locations in Nai Yang and Rawai, it is the younger, hipper of the two schools, with a tremendous perch on Friendship Beach. Courses range in length from an hour to five days.

About 5km north of Hat Nai Yang is **Hat Mai Khao**, Phuket's longest beach. Sea turtles lay their eggs here between November and February. Take care when swimming, as there's a strong year-round undertow. Except on weekends and holidays you'll have this place almost to yourself.

🛏 Sleeping & Eating

HAT NAI THON หาดในทอน
Naithonburi HOTEL **$$$**
(☑0 7620 5500; www.naithonburi.com; Moo 4, Th Hat Nai Thon; r 3500-4500B) A mellow megaresort if ever there was one. Yes, it has 222

rooms, but it rarely feels too crowded. Rooms are spacious with terracotta tile floors, Thai silks on the bed and private balconies. The enormous pool is lined with lounges and daybeds. Its **Chao Lay Bistro** (mains from 180B) is as swank as Nai Thon gets.

Naithon Beach Resort — HOTEL $$$

(☎0 7620 5379; www.phuket-naithon.com; 23/31 Moo 4, Th Hat Nai Thon; cottages 3300B; ☺Nov-May; ✲) Aka Woody's Paradise, small polished wood chalets with slate bathrooms are tucked into the south end of Hat Nai Thon, 10 steps from the sand.

HAT NAI YANG & HAT MAI KHAO หาดในยาง/หาดไม้ขาว

Anantara Phuket — HOTEL $$$

(☎0 7633 6100; www.phuket.anantara.com; 888 Moo 3, Tumbon Mai Khao; villas from 35,000B; ✲@ᴥ✉) Phuket's newest all-villa property opens onto a serene lotus-filled lagoon that extends to the beach. Luxurious, classic Thai pool villas are connected to the lobby, bars, restaurants and the beach, by old timber boardwalks that wind beneath swaying palms. It also offers the **Bua Luang Spa** (see p624) and the hotel's **Sea Fire Salt Restaurant** is worth a romantic splurge even if you're not staying here.

TOP CHOICE Indigo Pearl — HOTEL $$$

(☎0 7632 7006; www.indigo-pearl.com; r 6800-26,250B; ✲@ᴥ✉) One of the most unique and hip of Phuket's high-end resorts takes its design cues from the island's tin-mining history – although it sounds weird, this industrial theme melded with tropical luxe creates a spectacularly soothing place to stay. Hardware, such as vices, scales and other mining tools, is used in the decor to the tiniest detail – even the toilet-paper rolls are big bolts – and the common lounge areas are infused with indigo light. The gardens are modern and lush and surround a pool that looks like an oasis with a big waterfall.

Sala Resort & Spa — HOTEL $$$

(☎0 7633 8888; www.salaphuket.com; 333 Moo 3, Tambon Maikhao; r from 11,550B; villas from 15,750B; ✲@ᴥᴥ) This uberstylish, boutique property is a blend of Sino-Portuguese and art-deco influences with mod flair. Even 2nd-storey rooms have outdoor bathrooms. The black-granite infinity pool at the beachfront is gorgeous, and the bar area includes cushy, circular sofa lounges. It's the kind of place that makes everyone feel like a celebrity. It also offers spa services.

Nai Yang Beach Resort — HOTEL $$

(☎0 7632 8300; www.naiyangbeachresort.com; 65/23-24 Th Hat Nai Yang; r from 3600B; ✲@ᴥ ᴥᴥ) This workhorse of a midranger is as clean as it is busy and dominates causarina-lined Hat Nai Yang. The lowest-end rooms are fan cooled, while higher-end ones sport modern Thai style and are quite chic.

JW Marriott Phuket Resort & Spa — HOTEL $$$

(☎0 7633 8000; www.marriott.com; r from 6800B; ✲@ᴥᴥᴥ) So big there's a free shuttle to get around it, the Marriott wends its way around swimming pools and lily ponds along a steep light-gold beach – at night it's lit by flaming torches. Rooms are elegant with big bathrooms, hardwoods and sea views.

Sirinat National Park — CAMPING, BUNGALOWS $-$$

(☎0 7632 7152; reserve@dnp.go.th; campsites 30B, bungalows 1000-2000B) There are campsites (bring your own tent) and large, concrete bungalows at the park headquarters on a gorgeous, shady, white-sand bluff. Check in at the visitors centre or book online.

Rimlay Bungalows — GUEST HOUSE $

(☎08 9646 0239; andaman-car@hotmail.com; 90 Moo 5 Nai Yang; bungalow 500B, r 800-1800B) Spread over two properties, the bamboo bungalows are miniscule and basic while fan-cooled or air-conditioned rooms are tiled, have attached hot-water bathrooms and are great value.

ⓘ Getting There & Away

If you're coming from the airport, a taxi costs about 200B. There is no regular *sŏrng·tăa·ou*, but a túk-túk charter from Phuket Town costs about 800B.

Khao Phra Taew Royal Wildlife & Forest Reserve อุทยานสัตว์ป่าเขาพระแทว

Phuket's not all sand and sea. In the north of the island, this park protects 23 sq km of virgin island rainforest (evergreen monsoon forest). There are some pleasant hikes over the hills and a couple of photogenic waterfalls: **Nam Tok Ton Sai** and **Nam Tok Bang Pae**. The falls are at their most impressive during the rainy season between June and

November. The highest point in the park is **Khao Phara** (442m). Because of its royal status, the reserve is better protected than the average national park in Thailand.

A German botanist discovered a rare and unique species of palm in Khao Phra Taew in the mid-1900s. Called the white-backed palm or *langkow* palm, the fan-shaped plant stands 3m to 5m tall and is found only here and in Khao Sok National Park (p611).

Nowadays resident mammals are limited to humans, pigs, monkeys, slow loris, langurs, civets, flying foxes, squirrels, mousedeer and other smaller animals. Watch out for cobras and wild pigs.

Park rangers may act as guides for hikes in the park on request; payment for services is negotiable.

Phuket Gibbon Rehabilitation Centre
ANIMAL SHELTER

(Map p623; ☑0 7626 0492; www.gibbonproject. org; donations encouraged; ☺9am-4pm) A tiny sanctuary in the park near Nam Tok Bang Pae, it is open to the public. Financed by donations (1500B will care for a gibbon for a year), the centre adopts gibbons that have been kept in captivity in the hopes they can be reintroduced to the wild. The centre also has volunteer opportunities that include providing educational information to visitors, cleaning cages and feeding the animals as well as tracking the released animals.

Cable Jungle Adventure Phuket
ZIP LINES

(☑08 1977 4904; 232/17 Moo 8, Th Bansuanneramit; per person 1950B; ☺9am-6pm) If you're the thrill-seeking sort, harness up at this maze of eight zip lines, linking cliffs to ancient trees, tucked away in hills. The zips range from 6m to 23m above the ground and the longest run is 100m. Closed-toe shoes are a must.

To get to Khao Phra Taew from Phuket Town by vehicle, take Th Thepkasatri north about 20km to Thalang District and turn right at the intersection for Nam Tok Ton Sai, which is 3km down the road. Some travel agencies run day tours to the park.

Thalang District
อำเภอถลาง

A few hundred metres northeast of the famous **Heroines Monument** in Thalang District on Rte 4027, and about 11km northwest of Phuket Town, is **Thalang National Museum** (Map p623; ☑0 7631 1426; admission 30B; ☺8.30am-4pm). The museum contains five exhibition halls chronicling southern themes such as the history of Thalang-Phuket and the colonisation of the Andaman Coast, and describing the various ethnicities found in southern Thailand. The legend of the 'two heroines' (memorialised on the nearby monument), who supposedly drove off an 18th-century Burmese invasion force by convincing the island's women to dress as men, is also recounted in detail. The focal point of one hall is the impressive 2.3m-tall statue of Vishnu, which dates to the 9th century and was found in Takua Pa early in the 20th century.

Also in Thalang District, about 5km north of the crossroads near Thalang town, is **Wat Phra Thong** (Map p623; admission by donation; ☺dawn-dusk), Phuket's 'Temple of the Gold Buddha'. The image is half buried so that only the head and shoulders are visible. According to local legend, those who have tried to excavate the image have become very ill or encountered serious accidents. The temple is particularly revered by Thai-Chinese, many of whom believe the image hails from China. During the Chinese New Year pilgrims descend from Phang-Nga, Takua Pa and Krabi.

KRABI PROVINCE

When travellers talk about the amazing Andaman, they are probably talking about Krabi, with its trademark karst formations curving along the coast like a giant limestone fortress. Rock-climbers will find their nirvana in Railay, while castaway wannabes should head to Ko Lanta, Ko Phi-Phi or any of the other 150 islands swimming off the bleach-blonde shores.

Krabi Town
กระบี่

POP 27,500

Krabi Town is majestically situated among impossibly angular limestone karsts jutting from the mangroves but midcity you're more likely to be awestruck by the sheer volume of guest houses and travel agencies packed into this compact, quirky little town. Western restaurants are ubiquitous, as are gift shops that all sell the same ole trinkets. Yet if you hang out a while, you'll also see that there's a very real provincial scene going on in between the cracks.

Th Utarakit is the main road into and out of Krabi and most places of interest are on the soi that branch off it.

👁 Sights & Activities

Wat Tham Seua   TEMPLE
(วัดถ้ำเสือ) Wat Tham Seua (Tiger Cave Temple) is a sprawling hill and cave temple complex 8km northwest of Krabi that's an easy day trip from Krabi Town. The best part of the grounds can be found by following a loop trail through a little forest valley behind the ridge where the *bòht* (central sanctuary) is located. You'll find several limestone caves hiding Buddha images, statues

and altars. Troops of monkeys cackle from the trees. Back near the park entrance you'll come to a gruellingly steep 1237-stair case leading to a 600m karst peak. The fit and fearless are rewarded with a Buddha statue, a gilded stupa and spectacular views. Motorcycle taxis or túk-túk to the wát from Krabi cost 100B each way; a *sǒrng·tǎa·ou* from Th Utarakit is 50B. Please, please dress appropriately when visiting the wát by covering shoulders to knees.

Sea Kayak Krabi   KAYAKING
(📞0 7563 0270; www.seakayak-krabi.com; 40 Th Ruen Rudee) It offers a wide variety of sea-kayaking tours, including to Ao Thalane

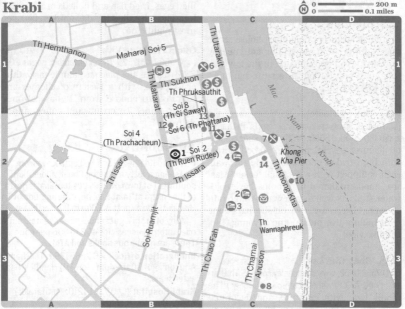

(half/full day 900/1500B), which has looming sea cliffs; Ko Hong (full day 1800B), famed for its emerald lagoon; and Ban Bho Tho (full day 1700B), which has sea caves with 2000- to 3000-year-old cave paintings. All rates include guides, lunch, fruit and drinking water.

☞ Tours

Various companies offer day trips to Khlong Thom, about 45km southeast of Krabi on Hwy 4, taking in some nearby hot springs and freshwater pools. Expect to pay around 1000B to 1200B, including transport, lunch and beverages; bring a swimsuit and good walking shoes. Various other 'jungle tour' itineraries are available.

🛏 Sleeping

Krabi has an exceptional guest-house scene that continues to improve, but go to nearby Ao Nang if you crave luxury. In the low season, guest-house room prices can plummet to as low as 150B.

TOP CHOICE Pak-up Hostel   HOSTEL $
(☎0 5611 955; www.pakuphostel.com; 87 Th Utarakit; dm 180-200B, d 600B; ❄🐶) This snazzy hostel features several uberhip 10-bed dorms with big wooden bunks built into the wall, each equipped with a personal locker. Massive, modern shared bathrooms have coldwater stalls as well as a few hot-water rain showers. There are two on-site bars (one with nightly live music) and a young, hip, clublike vibe.

TOP CHOICE Chan Cha Lay   GUEST HOUSE $
(☎0 7562 0952; www.chanchalay.com; 55 Th Utarakit; r 400-700B, r without bathroom 250B; ❄) The rooms here with en suite, and decorated in gorgeous Mediterranean blues with polished-concrete semioutdoor bathrooms, are Krabi's most stylish and comfortable. The shared-bathroom, fan-only rooms are plain, but spotless with firm beds.

K Guesthouse   GUEST HOUSE $
(☎0 7562 3166; Kguesthouse@yahoo.com; 15-25 Th Chao Fan; r 150-600B; ❄@🐶) This is a Wild West–looking place with varnished wooden rooms that line a second-storey verandah that overlooks the street. Cow heads on the walls and easy socialising in the downstairs cafe add to the frontier appeal.

✕ Eating & Drinking

TOP CHOICE Night market   THAI $
(Th Khong Kha; meals 20-50B) The most popular and pleasant place for an evening meal is near the Khong Kha pier. Menus are in English but the food is authentic: try papaya salad, fried noodles, *dôm yam gûng* (prawn and lemon-grass soup) and sweet milky Thai desserts.

Day Market   THAI $
(Th Sukhon; meals 20-60B) This market is even more Thai than the night market. Among the tropical-fruit stands are simmering curry pots, and banquet trays of steaming noodles with fried squid, sautéed beef, devilled eggs, fried fish and boiled corn. Eat daring. Though called the day market, it's open most nights too.

Cucina Italiana Viva   ITALIAN $$
(☎0 7563 0517; 29 Th Phruksauthit; pizzas 200-260B) This is the place to sample tasty, thin-crust pizza, with a variety of cheeses and toppings to choose from. It has calzones, Italian wine, ice cream and coffee, and it delivers.

ℹ Information

Ferries to Ko Phi-Phi and Ko Lanta leave from a passenger jetty at Khlong Chilat, about 4km southwest of town. Krabi's bus terminal is north of the centre at Talat Kao, near the junction of Th Utarakit. The airport is 17km to the northeast.

Many of Krabi's guest houses and restaurants offer internet access for 40B to 60B per hour. There are numerous banks and ATMs.

Immigration office (☎0 7561 1350; Th Chamai Anuson; ⊙8.30am-4pm Mon-Fri) Handles visa extensions.

Krabi Hospital (☎0 7561 1210; Th Utarakit) About 1km north of town.

Post office (Th Utarakit) Just south of the turn-off to Khong Kha pier.

ℹ Getting There & Away

Air

Most domestic carriers offer flights between Bangkok and Krabi International Airport (one-way around 4400B, 1¼ hours). **Bangkok Air** (www.bangkokair.com) has a daily service to Ko Samui for around 3800B.

Boat

Boats to Ko Phi-Phi and Ko Lanta leave from the passenger pier at Khlong Chilat, about 4km southwest of Krabi. Travel agencies will arrange free transfers when you buy a boat ticket with them.

The largest boat operator is **PP Family Co** (☎0 7561 2463; www.phiphifamily.com; Th Khong Kha), which has a ticket office right beside the pier in town. In high season there are boats to Ko Phi-Phi (300B, 1½ hours) at 9am, 10.30am, 1.30pm and 3pm while in low season the schedule is reduced to two boats per day.

From November to May, there is only one daily boat to Ko Lanta (350B, two hours) leaving Krabi's Khlon Chilat pier at 11.30am. These can also stop at Ko Jum (one hour), where long-tails shuttle you to shore (though you'll pay the full 350B). During the wet season, you can only get to Ko Lanta by frequent air-conditioned vans (300B, 2½ hours), which also run throughout the high season.

If you want to get to Railay, long-tail boats leave from Krabi's Khong Kha pier to Hat Rai Leh East (150B, 45 minutes) from 7.45am to 6pm. The boatmen will wait until they can fill a boat with 10 people before they leave; if you're antsy to go before then, you can charter the whole boat for 1500B.

To get to Phuket or the Ko Yao Islands, the quickest route is with direct boats from the pier at Ao Nang (see p653). *Sŏrng·tăa·ou* run between the two piers for 50B or a taxi costs 300B to 400B.

Bus

The **Krabi bus terminal** (☎0 7561 1804; cnr Th Utarakit & Hwy 4) is in nearby Talat Kao, about 4km north of Krabi. Air-conditioned government buses leave for Bangkok (720B, 12 hours) at 7am, 4pm and 5.30pm. There's a very plush 24-seat VIP bus to Bangkok (1100B) departing at 5.30pm daily. From Bangkok's southern bus terminal, buses leave at 7.30am and between 7pm and 8pm. Regular, air-conditioned government buses from Talat Kao also service Hat Yai (170B, three hours), Phuket (145B, 3½ hours), Surat Thani (140B, 2½ hours) and Trang (90B, two hours).

Minivan

Minivans are booked through travel agencies in town. Prices can vary widely; shop around to get an idea. Some sample fares are Ao Leuk (80B, one hour), Hat Yai (350B, three hours), Ko Lanta (350B, 1½ hours) and Phuket (350B, three hours). Minivans leave when full.

Sŏrng·tăa·ou

Sŏrng·tăa·ou run from the bus station to central Krabi and on to Hat Noppharat Thara (40B), Ao Nang (60B) and the Shell Cemetery at Ao Nam Mao (80B). There are services from 6am to 6.30pm. In the high season there are more-frequent services until 10pm for a 10B surcharge. For Ao Luk (80B, one hour) there are frequent *sŏrng·tăa·ou* from the corner of Th Phattana

and Th Phruksauthit; the last service leaves at around 3pm.

❶ Getting Around

Central Krabi is easy to explore on foot, but the bus terminal and airport are both a long way from the town centre. A taxi from the airport to town will cost 400B. In the reverse direction, taxis cost 350B, while motorcycle taxis cost 300B. Agencies in town can arrange seats on the airport bus for 120B. *Sŏrng·tăa·ou* between the bus terminal and central Krabi cost 40B.

Car & Motorcycle

Hiring a vehicle is an excellent way to explore the countryside around Krabi. Most of the travel agencies and guest houses in town can rent you a Yamaha motorbike for around 200B per day. **Yellow House** (☎0 7562 2809; Th Chao Fah) has a gleaming fleet of Yamahas and provides helmets. A few of the travel agencies along Th Utarakit rent out small 4WDs for 1200B to 1800B per day.

Ao Nang
อ่าวนาง

POP 12,400

Granted, you're not breaking ground, but there's still plenty to like about Ao Nang, a beach town that's unabashedly devoted to tourism. It all starts with the beaches, framed by limestone headlands tied together by narrow strips of golden sand. In the dry season, the sea glows a lovely turquoise hue; in the wet season rip tides stir up the mocha shallows. If you're hankering for a swim in crystalline climes at any time of year, you can easily book a trip to the local islands that dot the horizon.

Ao Nang is compact, easy to navigate, and with the onrush of attractive, midrange development, accommodation standards are especially high, with substantial discounts possible. It's not nearly as cheap (or as authentic) as Krabi town, but it's cleaner and sunnier; it's also much better value than what you'll find in Phuket. There's plenty to do (mangrove tours? snorkelling trips?); it's only a 40-minute trip from Krabi airport, and a smooth 20-minute long-tail boat ride from stunning Railay. It's no wonder this beach is increasingly popular with travellers of every ilk.

◉ Sights

Shell Cemetery
NATURE RESERVE

(สุสานหอย; admission 50B; ⊙8.30am-4.30pm) About 9km east of Ao Nang at the western end of Ao Nam Mao is the **Shell Cemetery**,

KHAO PHANOM BENCHA NATIONAL PARK

This 50-sq-km **park** (อุทยานแห่งชาติเขาพนมเบญจา; ☑0 7566 0716; adult/child under 14yr 200/100B) protects a dramatic area of virgin rainforest along the spine of 1350m-high Khao Phanom Bencha, 20km north of Krabi. The park is full of well-signed trails to scenic waterfalls, including the 11-tiered **Huay To Falls**, 500m from the park headquarters. Nearby and almost as dramatic are Huay Sadeh Falls and Khlong Haeng Falls. On the way into the park you can visit **Tham Pheung**, a dramatic cave with shimmering mineral stalactites and stalagmites. The numerous trails that wend through the area are excellent for hiking.

Many bird-spotters come here to see white-crowned and helmeted hornbills, argus pheasants and the extremely rare Gurney's pitta. Local guides aren't absolutely necessary here, considering the well-marked trails. But visitors who hire guides tend to spot more wildlife, and have a deeper experience in general.

There is no public transport to the park, but it's easy to get here from Krabi by hired motorcycle; follow the signposted turn-off from Hwy 4. Park your motorcycle by the park headquarters. Alternatively, you can hire a túk-túk for around 600B round-trip.

also known as Gastropod Fossil or Su-San Hoi. Here you can see giant slabs formed from millions of tiny 75-million-year-old fossil shells. There's a small **visitors centre** (admission 50B; ☉8.30am-4.30pm), with geological displays and various stalls selling snacks. *Sŏrng·tăa·ou* from Ao Nang cost 30B.

🏃 Activities

Loads of activities are possible at Ao Nang, and children under 12 typically get a 50% discount.

Kayaking

Several companies offer kayaking tours to mangroves and islands around Ao Nang. Popular destinations include the scenic sea lagoon at Ko Hong (1500B to 1800B) to view collection points for sea-swallow nests (spurred by demand for bird's-nest soup). There are also trips to the lofty sea cliffs and wildlife-filled mangroves at Ao Thalane (half/full day 500/800B) and to the sea caves and 2000- to 3000-year-old paintings at Ban Bho Tho (half/full day 700/900B). Rates will vary slightly, but always include lunch, fruit, drinking water, sea kayaks and guides.

Diving & Snorkelling

Ao Nang has numerous dive schools offering trips to local islands, including Ko Si, Ko Ha, Yava Bon and Yava Son. It costs about 3200B for two dives. Ko Mae Urai is one of the more unique local dives, with two submarine tunnels lined with soft and hard corals. Other trips run further afield to King Cruiser (three dives 4700B) and Ko Phi-Phi (two dives 3900B). A PADI Open Water course will set you back 14,900B to 16,000B. Reliable dive schools include **Ao Nang Divers** (☑0 7563 7244; www.aonang-divers.com) and **Poseidon Dive Center** (☑0 7563 7263; www.poseidon-diving.com). Most dive companies can also arrange snorkelling trips in the area.

Cycling

Take a Tour de Krabi by hooking up with **Krabi Eco Cycle** (☑0 7563 7250; www.krabiecocycle.com; 41/2 Muu 5; half-/full-day tour 800/1700B). The recommended full-day 15.5km pedal takes you through rubber plantations, small villages, hot springs and, finally, a cooler dip at the aptly named Emerald Pool. Lunch is included on all tours except the half-day bike-only tour.

🎓 Courses

Krabi Thai Cookery School COOKERY SCHOOL (☑0 7569 5133; www.thaicookeryschool.net; 269 Moo 2, Ao Nang, Rte 4204) About 10km from Ao Nang between Wat Sai Thai and Ao Nam Mao, this school offers one-day Thai-cooking courses from 1000B; transfers are included in the price.

👉 Tours

Any travel agency worth its salt can book you on one of the popular four- or five-island tours for around 2200B. The **Ao Nang Long-tail Boat Service** ☑0 7569 5313; www.aonangboatco-op.com) offers private charters for up to six people to Hong Island (2500B) and Bamboo Island (3800B), and the standard five-island tour, of course. You can also book half-day trips to Poda and Chicken

Islands (1700B, four hours) for up to four people.

Several tour agencies offer tours to **Khlong Thom**, including visits to freshwater pools, hot springs and the **Wat Khlong Thom Museum**; the price per adult/child is 1200/900B. So-called 'mystery tours' visit local snake farms, rural villages, crystal pools and rubber, pineapple, banana and papaya plantations, and cost around 900/450B per adult/child. Tour agencies also offer trips to attractions around Ao Phang-Nga and to a number of dubious animal shows.

You can also arrange day tours to Ko Phi-Phi on the **Ao Nang Princess** (adult/child 1400/1000B). The boat leaves at 9am from the Hat Noppharat Thara National Park headquarters and visits Bamboo Island, Phi-Phi Don and Phi-Phi Leh. Free transfers from Ao Nang to Hat Noppharat Thara are included in the price.

🛏 Sleeping

Prices at all these places drop by 50% during the low season. There is a handful of under-1000B spots lining the main road about 3km from the beach.

Golden Beach Resort   HOTEL $$$
(☑0 7563 7870-74; www.goldenbeach-resort.com; r 3900-6100B, bungalows 5100-8100B; ❀❄) This sprawling, unpretentious resort dominates the southernmost 400m of Ao Nang's beachfront – the best part of the beach. It's made up of large hotel blocks and stylish white-cement, wood-trimmed bungalows arranged in garden foliage around a big pool. It's only verging on hip but it definitely feels good to be here. Check the website for specials.

Somkiet Buri Resort   HOTEL $$
(☑0 7563 7320; www.somkietburi.com; r 17100-6200B; ❀❄) This place just might inspire you to slip into a yoga pose. The lush jungle grounds are filled with ferns and orchids, while lagoons, streams and meandering wooden walkways guide you to the 26 large and creatively designed rooms. A great swimming pool is set amid it all – balconies either face this pool or a peaceful pond. The service is first-rate.

Red Ginger Chic Resort   HOTEL $$$
(☑0 7563 7777; www.redgingerkrabi.com; 88 Moo 3; r 6300-10,900B; ❀❄❄) Fashionable and colourful with detailed tiles, large paper lanterns, and a frosted-glass bar in the lob-

by. Large rooms feature elegant wallpaper, modern furnishings and large balconies overlooking an expansive pool. Expect discounts of up to 50% in the low season.

Ao Nang Cliff Resort   HOTEL $$$
(☑0 7562 6888; www.aonangcliffbeach.com; r 4500-7500B; ❀❄❄) Think sunken bedrooms, daybeds, duvets, and rain showers. The best-situated rooms have cliff and sea views, and the pool outside the lobby is stunning. If you come in the low season you can grab a room for 2500B.

Verandah   HOTEL $$
(☑0 7563 7454; www.theverandahaonang.com; r incl breakfast 1700-2300B; ❀@) Solid value right in the middle of things, the rooms here are simple, spacious and immaculate, with tiled floors, minifridge, hot water, satellite TV and safety boxes. The price includes breakfast and guests are welcome to use the pool at nearby Peace Laguna Resort.

Apasari   HOTEL $$
(☑0 7563 7188; www.apasari.com; r 1800-5800B; ❀@❄) One of a handful of stylish new midrangers on Ao Nang's newest boulevard. Rooms have high-end tiled floors, built-in desks and wardrobes, and flat-screen TVs. All rooms have balconies overlooking the lap pool. It's exceptional value in the low season.

Dream Garden   HOTEL $
(☑0 7563 7338; r 950-1200B; ❀@) Walk through the entrance of a dingy travel agency, past a stylish polished cement spa effusing scents of lemon-grass to a two-storey block of plain but clean and large tiled rooms with hot water, wood furnishings and small terraces.

Phra Nang Inn   HOTEL $$$
(☑0 7563 7130; www.phrananghotels.com; r incl breakfast 4000-9000B; ❀@❄) It's an artistic explosion of rustic coconut wood, bright orange and purple paint, and plenty of elaborate Thai tiles. There are two pools, and a second, similarly designed branch is across the road from the original.

J Hotel   HOTEL $
(☑0 7563 7878; j_hotelo@hotmail.com; r from 800B; ❀@) J Hotel is an old standby that caters well to backpackers. Large, bright rooms have new tiled floors, built-in desks, wardrobes and satellite TV, but some smell a bit musty. Sniff well before you commit.

Bernie's Place
HOTEL $

(☑0 7563 7093; r 300-700B;❄) The staff look and act like they're sleepwalking but rooms are big and bright with ceiling fans and some have sea views from a common verandah. The dark downstairs bar offers protein-packed, backpacker-priced buffets (all you can eat for 250B).

✗ Eating

Ao Nang is full of mediocre restaurants serving overpriced Italian, Scandanavian, Indian, Thai and fast food. For superbudget meals, a few stalls pop up at night on the road to Krabi (near McDonald's). You'll find *roti* (pancakes), *gài tôrt* (fried chicken), hamburgers and the like. Another 100m up the road (and across the street) you'll find decent priced, tasty Thai fare in a row of bamboo-hut-style restaurants.

TOP CHOICE Soi Sunset
SEAFOOD $$

(☑0 7569 5260; Soi Sunset; dishes 60-400B; ☺lunch & dinner) At the western end of the beach is this narrow pedestrian-only alley housing several romantic seafood restaurants with gorgeous views of an island-dotted ocean. They all have model ice boats at the entrance showing off the day's catch and smiling staff to beckon you in to take a seat. One of the best (and most popular) is Krua Ao Nang at the end of the strip.

Jeanette's Restaurant
SWEDISH, THAI $$

(☑08 9474 6178; www.jeanettekrabi.com; dishes 120-450B; ☺breakfast, lunch & dinner) The most popular place in town thanks to its signature bench seating, ink-blot art on the walls and traditional Thai menu augmented with Swedish hits (that apple pie does sound good).

☗ Drinking & Entertainment

Have a drink – there's no shortage of bars in Ao Nang.

Aonang Krabi Muay Thai Stadium
THAI BOXING

(☑0 7562 1042; admission 800B, ringside 1200B) If you get tired of the beach bars and video movies on the strip, this place has boisterous *moo·ay tai* (Thai boxing) bouts two days a week (check current schedules at any travel agent in town) from 8.45pm. A free *sŏrng·tăa·ou* runs along the strip at Ao Nang, collecting punters before the bouts.

Last Café
CAFE, BAR

(☺11am-7pm) At the far southern end of Hat Ao Nang is this barefoot beach cafe, with cold beer and cool breezes. Come here for a welcome blast of Ao Nang natural.

Amy's Bar
BAR

(☺11am-2am) Give Amy's points for its floral retro hippy design, which comes with flat screens streaming live football games, billiards and the ladies who love them. It's one of several pubs on this soi, which runs perpendicular to the cliff.

❶ Information

All the information offices, including **Ao Nang Visitor Center** (☑0 7562 8221), on the strip, are private tour agencies, and most offer international calls and internet access for around 1B per minute.

Several banks have ATMs and foreign-exchange windows (open from 10am to 8pm) on the main drag.

❶ Getting There & Around

Bus, Car & Minivan

Sŏrng·tăa·ou run to/from Krabi (50B, 20 minutes) starting at the Krabi bus terminal (add 10B to the fare) via Th Maharat, the Khong Kha pier in Krabi and on to Hat Noppharat Thara, Ao Nang and finally the Shell Cemetery. From Ao Nang to Hat Noppharat Thara or the Shell Cemetery it's 20B.

Airport buses to and from Ao Nang cost 80B to 100B and leave throughout the day. Private taxis from the airport cost about 800B. Minibuses go to destinations all over the south including Phuket (350B to 400B, three to four hours), Pak Bara (300B, 3½ hours) and Ko Lanta (400B, two hours).

Dozens of places along the strip rent out small motorcycles for 150B to 200B. Budget Car Hire charges around 1600B.

Boat

Boats to Railay's Hat Rai Leh West are run by **Ao Nang Long-tail Boat Service** (☑0 7569 5313; www.aonangboatco-op.com) and rates are 80B per person from 7.30am to 6pm or 150B per person from 6pm to 6am. It's a 15-minute journey – boats leave when there are a minimum six people or you can charter the whole boat by paying for the equivalent of six people.

Ferries and speedboats leave from the nearby pier at Hat Noppharat Thara (see p668) to Ko Phi Phi, Ko Lanta, Phuket and the Ko Yao Islands.

Around Ao Nang

HAT NOPPHARAT THARA
หาดนพรัตน์ธารา

North of Ao Nang, the golden beach goes a bit more *au naturel* as it curves around a headland for 4km, until the sea eventually spills into a natural lagoon at the Hat Noppharat Thara National Park headquarters. Here scores of long-tails mingle with fishing boats and speedboats against a stunning limestone backdrop. The small **visitors centre** has displays on coral reefs and mangrove ecology, labelled in Thai and English.

Several resorts falsely advertise a 'central Ao Nang' location – so if you don't like reading fine print, you might end up sleeping out here (and you might prefer it anyway).

🛏 Sleeping

Sala Talay Resort & Spa   HOTEL **$$$**
(☑0 7581 0888; www.salatalay.com; r 10,000-29,000B; ✷@☒) This beautiful new hotel is all moulded concrete, wood and stone. Rooms have polished concrete floors, walls and washbasins, DVD players and flat-screen TVs. Online rates are significantly lower than our listed rack rates outside the peak season.

Sabai Resort   HOTEL **$$**
(☑0 7563 7791; www.sabairesort.com; bungalows 1300-2200B; ✷@☒) This is the most professionally run of the area's bungalow properties. The tiled-roof bungalows are fan cooled with pebbled concrete patios overlooking a palm-shaded swimming pool, and a flower garden.

Government bungalows   BUNGALOWS **$**
(☑0 7563 7200; bungalows 800B-1000B) These wooden, fan-cooled bungalows across the street from the beach are rustic yet well maintained and a terrific budget choice. Prices don't go up in the high season, but you'd better book ahead. Check in at national park headquarters near the harbour.

Around the national park headquarters there are several **restaurants** serving snacks such as fried chicken and papaya salad.

ℹ Getting There & Away

Sŏrng·tăa·ou between Krabi and Ao Nang stop in Hat Noppharat Thara; the fare is 40B from Krabi or 10B from Ao Nang. From November to May the *Ao Nang Princess* runs between Hat Nop-pharat Thara National Park headquarters and Ko Phi-Phi (400B, two hours). The boat leaves from the national park jetty at 9am, returning from Ko Phi-Phi at 3.30pm. It also stops at Railay's Hat Rai Leh West. This boat can also be used for day trips to Ko Phi-Phi. During the high season there's also a direct boat to Phuket, leaving from the same pier (450B) via Ko Lanta at 10.30am and 3.30pm (450B).

A faster alternative to Phuket is to take the *Green Planet* speedboat (950B, 1¼ hours) to Bang Rong Pier, north of Phuket Town via Ko Yao Noi and Koh Yao Yai (both 450B, 45minutes). The boat leaves Hat Noppharat Thara at 11am and 4pm and transport to your Phuket accommodation is included in the fare.

Railay
ไร่เล

Krabi's fairy-tale limestone crags come to a dramatic climax at Railay (also spelled Rai Leh), the ultimate jungle gym for rock-climbing fanatics. This quiet slice of paradise fills in the sandy gaps between each craggy flourish, and although it's just around the bend from chaotic tourist hustle in Ao Nang, the atmosphere here is nothing short of laid-back, Rasta-Thai haven.

◉ Sights

At the eastern end of Hat Phra Nang is **Tham Phra Nang** (Princess Cave), an important shrine for local fishermen. Legend has it that a royal barge carrying an Indian princess foundered in a storm here during the 3rd century BC. The spirit of the drowned princess came to inhabit the cave, granting favours to all who came to pay respect. Local fishermen – Muslim and Buddhist – place carved wooden phalluses in the cave as offerings in the hope that the spirit will provide plenty of fish.

About halfway along the path from Hat Rai Leh East to Hat Phra Nang, a crude path leads up the jungle-cloaked cliff wall to a hidden lagoon known as **Sa Phra Nang** (Holy Princess Pool). There's a dramatic viewpoint over the peninsula from the nearby cliff top, but be warned that this is a strenuous hike with some serious vertigo-inducing parts.

Above Hat Railay East is another large cave called **Tham Phra Nang Nai** (Inner Princess Cave; adult/child 40/20B; ⊙5am-8pm), also known as Diamond Cave. A wooden boardwalk leads through a series of caverns full of beautiful limestone formations but, with shifting rain patterns, the water is gone and with it the illuminated effects that won the diamond moniker. But even in monochrome conditions, it's still worth a stroll.

🏃 Activities

Rock Climbing

With nearly 500 bolted routes, ranging from beginner to challenging advanced climbs, all with unparalleled cliff-top vistas, it's no surprise that Railay is among the top climbing spots in the world. You could spend months climbing and exploring – and many people do. The newest buzz is deep-water soloing where climbers free-climb ledges over deep water – if you fall you will most likely just get wet, so even daring beginners can give this a try.

Most climbers start off at **Muay Thai Wall** and **One, Two, Three Wall**, at the southern end of Hat Rai Leh East, which have at least 40 routes graded from 4b to 8b on the French system. The mighty **Thaiwand Wall** sits at the southern end of Hat Rai Leh West and offers a sheer limestone cliff with some of the most challenging climbing routes.

Other top climbs: **Hidden World** (some classic routes for intermediate climbers), **Wee's Present Wall** (an overlooked 7c+ gem), **Diamond Cave** (another beginner-to-intermediate favourite) and **Ao Nang Tower** (a three-pitch climbing wall reached only by long-tail).

The going rate for climbing courses is 800B to 1000B for a half day and 1500B to 2000B for a full day. Three-day courses (6000B) will involve lead climbing, where you clip into bolts on the rock face as you ascend. Experienced climbers can rent gear sets from any of the climbing schools for 800/1300B for a half/full day – the standard set consists of a 60m rope, two climbing harnesses and climbing shoes. If you're planning to climb independently, you're best off bringing your own gear from home; be sure to bring plenty of slings and quickdraws, chalk (sweaty palms are inevitable in the tropics) and a small selection of nuts and cams as back-up for thinly protected routes. If you forget anything, some climbing schools sell a small range of imported climbing gear but they might not have exactly what you need or the right size. A woven rattan mat (available locally for 100B to 150B) will help keep the sand out of your gear.

Several locally published books detail climbs in the area, but *Rock Climbing in Thailand* (US$40), by Elke Schmitz and Wee Changrua, is one of the more complete guides. Recommended climbing shops:

Highland Rock Climbing CLIMBING OUTFIT (📞08 0693 0374; chaow_9@yahoo.com; Hat Rai Leh East) If you're bunking on the mountain, the owner of this outfit is the man to climb with.

Hot Rock CLIMBING OUTFIT (📞0 7562 1771; www.railayadventure.com; Hat Rai Leh West) Has a very good reputation and is owned by one of the granddaddies of Railay climbing.

King Climbers CLIMBING OUTFIT (📞0 7563 7125; www.railay.com; Hat Rai Leh East) One of the biggest, oldest, most reputable and commercial schools.

Wee's Climbing School CLIMBING OUTFIT (📞08 1149 9745; www.tonsai basecamp; Hat Ton Sai) Arguably the most professional outfit in the area.

Water Sports & Other Activities

Several **dive** operations in Railay run trips out to Ko Poda and other dive sites. Two local dives at outlying islands costs about 2000B while a three- or four-day PADI Open Water dive course is 12,000B.

Full-day, multi-island **snorkelling** trips to Ko Poda, Chicken Island and beyond can be arranged through any of the resorts for about 1800B (maximum six people) or you can charter a long-tail (half/full day 1700/2200B) from Hat Railay West beach. If you just want to snorkel off Railay, most resorts can rent you a mask set and fins for 100B to 150B each.

Flame Tree Restaurant (Hat Rai Leh West) rents out **sea kayaks** for 200B per hour or 800B per day. Overnight trips to deserted islands can be arranged with local boat owners, but you'll need to bring your own camping gear and food.

Railay Thai Cookery School (Rai Leh Headlands; 📞08 4096 4994; courses 1200B), right below Railay Phutawan Resort Restaurant, offers five-hour courses in a lovely semioutdoor setting at 8.30am and 2.30pm daily.

🛏 Sleeping & Eating

HAT RAI LEH WEST

Railay West is beautiful and developers know it – you'll only find midrange and top-end resorts around here. Rates drop by 30% in the low season. You can't go wrong with any of the resorts' restaurants.

Railay

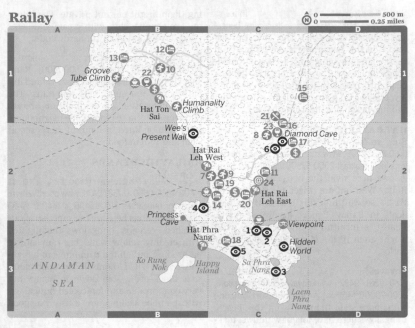

Railay

◉ Sights

◉ Activities, Courses & Tours

◉ Sleeping

◉ Eating

◉ Drinking

◉ Information

Railay Bay Resort & Spa   HOTEL **$$$**
(☎0 7562 2570-2; www.railaybayresort.com; bungalows 3700-17,800B; ✳@☒) The amoeba-shaped blue pool here faces onto the best bit of the beach so you can switch between salt and fresh water. Elegant bungalows with big windows, white walls and rustic-chic timber terraces run right across the peninsula to Hat Railay East via gorgeously planted grounds. Bungalows on the east side are older, with dark-tinted windows, and are the least expensive.

Sand Sea Resort
HOTEL $$

(☏0 7562 2608; www.krabisandsea.com; bungalows 1950-5950B; ✳@☎) The lowest-priced resort on this beach offers everything from ageing fan-only bungalows to newly remodelled cottages with every amenity. There's a peaceful karst-view, foliage-enclosed pool – if you're able to tear yourself away from that sublime beach out the front, that is.

HAT RAI LEH EAST

Sunrise Tropical Resort
HOTEL $$

(☏0 7562 2599; www.sunrisetropical.com; bungalows incl breakfast 2500-5750B; ✳@☎☎) Bungalows here rival the better ones on Hat Railay West but are priced for Hat Rai Leh East – so we think this is one of the best deals in Railay. Expect hardwood floors, Thai-style furniture, lush bathrooms with bright aqua tiles and private balconies or patios.

Anyavee
HOTEL $$

(☏0 7581 9437; www.anyavee.com; bungalows 2800-7000B; ✳@☎) A quirky resort but one with more style than most on this beach. Bungalows here have lots of windows, making them bright but not private. The interiors are country chic, with cream-and-beige plaid duvets and plenty of hardwoods.

Rapala Rockwood Resort
HOTEL $

(☏08 4191 5326; bungalows 500-750B) Ramshackle bamboo bungalows have verandahs, bathrooms, mosquito nets and fans. The delightful location atop a hill means breezes and views of the sea (and your neighbours). The cushion-lined restaurant here serves Thai and Indian food.

RAILAY HIGHLANDS

TOP CHOICE Railay Phutawan Resort
HOTEL $$

(☏08 4060 0550, 0 7581 9478; www.phuritvalleyresort.com; bungalows 1140-1940B; r 1640B; @✳) The best options here are the super-spacious polished cement bungalows highlighted with creamy yellow walls, big rain-shower bathrooms and all the trimmings of a high-end resort. Tiled rooms in an apartment-style block are a step down in luxury but very comfortable and fan-cooled bungalows with bamboo ceilings are musty but good value.

WHERE TO STAY IN RAILAY

There are four beaches around Railay or you can choose to stay up on the headland. It's only about a five-minute walk between Hat Rai Leh East, Hat Rai Leh West, Hat Phra Nang and the headlands. Hat Ton Sai is more isolated and to get to the other beaches you'll need to take a long-tail (50B) or hike – it takes about 20 minutes to scramble over the rocks from Hat Railay West.

» **Hat Rai Leh East** is the most developed beach. The shallow, muddy bay lined with mangroves is not appetising for swimming, but the beach is lined with hotels and guest houses, and those headlands and limestone cliffs are miraculous.

» **Hat Rai Leh West** is a near-flawless white wonder and the best place to swim, join an afternoon pick-up football game or just watch the sun go down. Tastefully designed midrange resorts are sprinkled throughout, and long-tail boats pick up and drop off here to/from nearby Ao Nang.

» **Hat Phra Nang** is quite possibly one of the world's most beautiful beaches, with a crescent of pale, golden sand, framed by karst cliffs carved with caves. Those distant limestone islets peeking out of the cerulean sea are Chicken (Ko Hua Khwan) and Poda islands. Rayavadee, the peninsula's most exclusive resort, is the only one on this beach but anyone can drop a beach towel.

» **Hat Ton Sai** is the grittier climbers' retreat. The beach here isn't spectacular, but with so many good climbs all around, most people don't mind. Bars and bungalows are nestled in the jungle behind the beach and it's a lively, fun scene.

» **The Railay Headlands** catch sea breezes and, since it's the most recent place to be developed, feels like a frontier with plantations, jungle and some very friendly locals. To get here you'll have to walk about 500m from either Hat Rai Leh West or East. From Hat Rai Leh West follow 'Walking Street,' veer left onto a dirt path then follow the signs to Ya-Ya Bar. From Hat Rai Leh East turn right on the cement road accessible via the beachside Diamond Cave Restaurant.

Railay Cabana   GUEST HOUSE **$**
(☑0 7562 1733, 08 4057 7167; bungalows 350-600B) Superbly located high in the hills in a bowl of karst cliffs, this is your hippie tropical mountain hideaway. Simple, clean thatched-bamboo bungalows are surrounded by mango, mangosteen, banana and guava groves. The only sounds are birds chirping and children laughing.

TOP
CHOICE **Railay Phutawan**
Resort Restaurant   THAI, WESTERN
(meals 80-180B; ⊙breakfast, lunch & dinner) Amid dense jungle and karst cliffs, it's best to dine here during the day to appreciate the view. Try to get one of the intimate shaded booths at the jungle's edge.

HAT PHRA NANG   หาดถ้ำพระนาง

TOP
CHOICE **Rayavadee**   HOTEL **$$$**
(☑0 7562 0740-3; www.rayavadee.com; pavilions 22,300-39,900B, villas 72,000-128,000B; ❄🐾🌐🏊) This exclusive resort has sprawling banyan-tree- and flower-filled grounds navigated by golf buggies. The two-storey, mushroom-domed pavilions are filled with antique furniture and every mod con – as well as the occasional private jacuzzi, swimming pool or butler service. Two restaurants grace Hat Phra Nang (one is half inside an illuminated cave) and nonguests can stop in for pricey but divine Thai or Mediterranean meals.

HAT TON SAI   หาดต้นไทร
Countryside Resort   HOTEL **$**
(☑08 5473 9648; countryside-resort.com; cabins 850B; ❄@🌐) This is a UK-owned property with attractive solar-powered cabins. There are high ceilings, lace curtains and ceiling fans. Top-row nests have insane karst views, and you'll love Ewok-faced Ollie, the property mascot.

Paasook   HOTEL **$**
(☑08 9645 3013; bungalows 300-800B) Definitely the most stylish budget establishment on Ton Sai: wooden bungalows have elongated floor-to-ceiling windows and concrete floors. The gardens are lush, management is friendly and there's a rustic-chic outdoor restaurant, perfect for steamy evenings.

Mountain View Resort   HOTEL **$$**
(☑0 7562 2610-3; bungalows 1300-1900B; ❄) This place is bright, cheery and immaculate with mint-green walls, tiled floors and crisp sheets in lodge-like environs. Some rooms are slightly musty, so sniff around.

🍸 Drinking

There's a bunch of places on the beaches where you can unwind and get nicely inebriated.

Chillout Bar   BAR **$**
(Hat Ton Sai) Right on the beach and with several levels of decks, this is where the bigger name Thai and international bands play when they're in town. At other times, it's the ideal place to lounge with a beer.

Highland Rock Climbing   CAFE **$**
(☑08 0693 0374; Railay Headlands) Part climbing school, part cafe, this place is cobbled from driftwood and dangling with orchids. The owner, Chaow, sources his beans from sustainable farms in Chiang Rai, and serves the best coffee on the peninsula.

Ya-ya Bar   BAR **$**
(Railay Headlands) The Ya-ya Bar has an awesome setting under a massive climbing wall. Bob Marley looms like a patron saint. Mojitos (160B) are poured liberally. There's also a Thai boxing ring with courses on demand offered at 500B per hour.

ℹ️ Information

There are two ATMs along Hat Rai Leh East. On Hat Ton Sai there is one ATM near the Ton Sai Bay Resort. Several of the bigger resorts can change cash and travellers cheques.

For minor climbing injuries there's a small **clinic** at Railay Bay Resort.

Wi-fi availability will depend on where you stay. If you lack the hardware, try **Phra Nang Tours & Travel** (internet per min 1B) on the east beach.

ℹ️ Getting There & Around

Long-tail boats to Railay run from Khong Kha pier in Krabi and from the seafronts of Ao Nang and Ao Nam Mao. Boats between Krabi and Hat Rai Leh East leave every 1½ hours from 7.45am to 6pm when they have six to 10 passengers (150B, 45 minutes). Chartering the whole boat costs 1500B.

Boats to Hat Rai Leh West or Hat Ton Sai from Ao Nang cost 80B (15 minutes) from 7.30am to 6pm or 150B at other times; boats don't leave until six to eight people show up. Private charters cost 800B. During exceptionally high seas the boats from Ao Nang and Krabi stop running, but you may still be able to get from Hat Rai Leh East to Ao Nam Mao (100B, 15 minutes), where you can pick up a *sŏrng·tăa·ou* to Krabi or Ao Nang.

From October to May the *Ao Nang Princess* runs from Hat Noppharat Thara National Park headquarters to Ko Phi-Phi with a stop at Hat Rai Leh West. Long-tails run out to meet the boat at around 9.15am from in front of the Sand Sea Resort in Hat Rai Leh West. The fare to Ko Phi-Phi from Railay is 350B.

Ko Phi-Phi Don เกาะพีพีดอน

Oh, how beauty can be a burden. Like Marilyn Monroe, Phi-Phi Don's stunning looks have become its own demise. Everyone wants a piece of her. Though not exactly Hollywood, this is Thailand's Shangri-la: a hedonistic paradise where tourists cavort in azure seas and snap pictures of longtails puttering between craggy cliffs. With its flashy, curvy, blonde beaches and bodacious jungles it's no wonder that Phi-Phi has become the darling of the Andaman coast. And, like any good starlet, this island can party hard all night and still look like a million bucks the next morning. Unfortunately, nothing can withstand this glamorous pace and unless limits are set, Phi-Phi is in for an ecological crash.

Ko Phi-Phi Don is practically two islands joined together by a narrow isthmus flanked by the stunning **Ao Ton Sai** and **Ao Lo Dalam** on either side. Boats dock at the large concrete pier at Ao Ton Sai and a narrow path, crammed full of tour operators, bungalows, restaurants, bars and souvenir shops, stretches east along the beach towards **Hat Hin Khom**. The maze of small streets in the middle of this sandbar is equally packed and is known as **Tonsai Village** (or the Tourist Village). The swimmer-friendly **Hat Yao** (Long Beach) faces south and has some of Phi-Phi Don's best coral. The beautifully languid and long eastern bays of **Hat Laem Thong** and **Ao Lo Bakao** are reserved for several top-end resorts, while the smaller bays of **Hat Phak Nam** and **Hat Rantee** play host to a few simple, low-key bungalow affairs.

◉ Sights & Activities

The strenuous and sweaty climb to Phi-Phi's **viewpoint** is a rewarding short hike. The path up the mountain begins near Spider Monkey and wends its way up a steep crag – most people will need to stop for a short break (don't forget to bring some water), but once you reach the top you'll be treated to postcard-worthy views of the twin bays, soaring karst formations and quiet Ko Phi-Phi Leh off in the distance.

Diving

Crystal-clear Andaman water and abundant marine life make the perfect recipe for top-notch scuba. Popular sights include the **King Cruiser Wreck**, sitting a mere 12m below the surface; **Anemone Reef**, teeming with hard corals and clownfish; **Hin Bida**, a submerged pinnacle attracting turtles and large pelagic fish; and **Ko Bida Nok**, with its signature karst massif luring leopard sharks. Hin Daeng and Hin Muang (p671), about 70km south, are expensive ventures from Ko Phi-Phi – it's cheaper to link up with a dive crew in Ko Lanta.

An Open Water certification course costs around 12,900B, while the standard two-dive trips cost from 3200B. Trips out to Hin Daeng/Hin Muang will set you back 5500B. A couple of diving companies:

Adventure Club DIVING
(Map p664; ☑08 1970 0314; www.phi-phi-adventures.com) Our favourite diving operation on the island runs an excellent assortment of educational, ecofocused diving, hiking and snorkelling tours. You won't mind getting up at 6am for the much-loved shark-watching snorkel trips on which you're guaranteed to cavort with at least one reef shark.

Blue View Divers DIVING
(Map p663; ☑0 7581 9395; www.blueviewdivers.com) Focuses on community involvement and beach clean-ups (its latest effort cleared up 700 tonnes of rubbish) and is the only shop to offer dives from a long-tail.

Snorkelling

A popular snorkelling destination is **Ko Mai Phai** (Bamboo Island), 5km north of Phi-Phi Don. There's a shallow area here where you may see small sharks. Snorkelling trips cost between 600B and 2400B, depending on whether you travel by long-tail or motorboat. There is also good snorkelling along the eastern coast of **Ko Nok**, near Ao Ton Sai, and along the eastern coast of **Ko Nai**. If you're going on your own, most bungalows and resorts rent out a snorkel, mask and fins for 150B to 200B per day.

Rock Climbing

Yes, there are good limestone cliffs to climb on Ko Phi-Phi, and the views are spectacular. The main climbing areas are **Ton Sai Tower**, at the western edge of Ao Ton Sai, and **Hin Taak**, a short long-tail boat ride around the bay. There are some good climbing shops on the island and most places charge around

Ko Phi-Phi Don

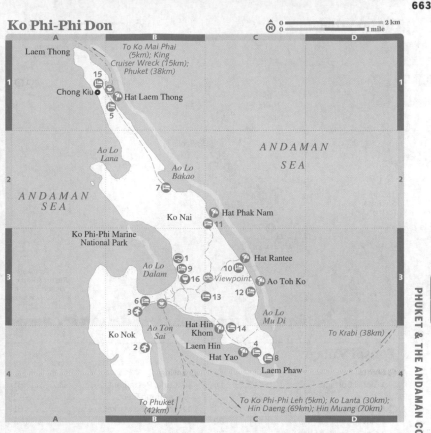

Ko Phi-Phi Don

Activities, Courses & Tours

1	Blue View Divers	B3
2	Hin Taak	B4
3	Ton Sai Tower	B3

Sleeping

4	Beach Resort	C4
5	Holiday Inn Phi Phi Island	B1
6	Mama Beach Residence	B3
7	Phi Phi Island Village	B2
8	Phi-Phi Hill Resort	C4

9	PP Viewpoint Resort	B3
10	Rantee Hut	C3
11	Relax Beach Resort	C2
12	Toh Ko Beach Resort	C3
13	Uphill Cottage	C3
14	Viking Natures Resort	C4
15	Zeavola	A1

Drinking

16	Sunflower Bar	B3

1000B for a half-day of climbing or 1500B to 2000B for a full day, including instruction and gear. **Spider Monkey** (Map p664; ☎0 7581 9384; www.spidermonkeyclimbing.com) is run by Soley, one of the most impressive climbers on Phi-Phi. One of the bigger outfits around is **Cat's Climbing Shop** (Map p664; ☎08 1787 5101; www.catclimbingshop.com) in the tourist village. Cat's gets good reports for safety and service.

Courses

Thai-food fans can take cooking courses at the recommended **Pum Restaurant & Cooking School** (Map p664; ☎08 1521 8904;

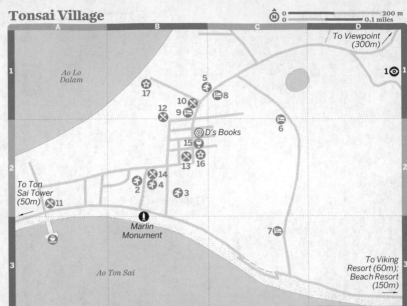

Tonsai Village

www.pumthaifoodchain.com; classes 450-4650B) in the tourist village. You'll learn to make some of the excellent dishes that are served in its restaurant and go home with a great cookbook.

☞ Tours

Ever since Leo smoked a spliff in Alex Garland's *The Beach,* Ko Phi-Phi Leh (see p668) has become somewhat of a pilgrimage site. Aside from long-tail boat tours to this island and to Ko Mai Phai (Bamboo Island),

tour agencies can arrange sunset tours to Monkey Bay and the beach at Wang Long (600B). Adventure Club (see p671) is a good choice.

🛏 Sleeping

Finding accommodation on this ever-popular island has never been easy and you can expect serious room shortages at peak holiday times. Masses of touts meet incoming boats and, while often annoying, can make your life easier.

Be sure you lock the door while you sleep and close all the windows when you go out. Break-ins can be a problem.

TONSAI VILLAGE   บ้านต้นไทร
The flat, hourglass-shaped land between Ao Ton Sai and Ao Lo Dalam is crowded with loads of lodging options.

TOP CHOICE **Mama Beach Residence**   HOTEL **$$**
(Map p663; ☑08 8443 1363, 0 7560 1365; www. mama-beach.com; r 2500-3800B; ✱@✿) Popular with French travellers, this is an uncommonly chic block-style hotel right on the best part of Ao Ton Sai beach. Mod-con-equipped rooms have large white tiled floors, sea-view terraces with relaxing wood deck furniture, and bathrooms with stone sinks and showers bordered with loose seashells. Seaside yoga classes (1¼ hours, 400B) are offered several nights a week at 6pm.

PP Viewpoint Resort   HOTEL **$$**
(Map p663; ☑0 7560 1200, 0 7561 8111; www. phiphiviewpoint.com; bungalows 1700-3500B; ✱✱✿) At the far northeastern end of Ao Lo Dalam, wooden bungalows sit high on stilts and enjoy awesome views. There is a small swimming pool that practically drops into the ocean below and a glass-walled tower with 360-degree views where you can pamper yourself with a Thai massage. The Ao Dalam party can be heard up here so bring earplugs.

Chunut House   GUEST HOUSE **$$**
(Map p664; ☑0 7560 1227; www.phiphichunut house.com; bungalows 2500-3500B; ✱✿) On a quiet path away from the bazaar of the tourist village, this place is refreshingly tranquil. Spacious wooden and bamboo bungalows are dripping with naturalistic mobiles, planters and crafty touches, and have clean tiled bathrooms.

The White   GUEST HOUSE **$$**
(Map p664; ☑0 7560 1300; www.whitephiphi. com; r 1500-1800B; ✱@✿) Geared towards the 'flashpacker' crowd, The White has two comfy and surprisingly quiet locations in Tonsai Village – the better being The White 2 that has a few rooftop suites with patios. Squeaky clean rooms, decked out with TVs and safes, are very white (of course) with hip touches such as black-and-white tiled hot-water bathrooms.

Uphill Cottage   GUEST HOUSE **$**
(Map p663; ☑0 7560 1124, 08 6553 2316; www. phiphiuphillcottage.com; r 700-1500B; ✱✿) Rooms are basic but big and clean, and you can only faintly hear the noise from the tourist-centre party. Aptly named, this place is (surprise!) up on a hill near the viewpoint path. Rooms have terraces with views over town and a hint of the sea.

Oasis Guesthouse   GUEST HOUSE **$**
(Map p664; ☑0 7560 1207; r 900B; ✱) It's worth the walk up the side road east of the village centre to find this cute guest house with wooden shutters and surrounded by trees. The innkeeper can be surly, but freshly painted rooms have sparkling bathrooms. It's first come, first serve only.

Rock Backpacker   HOSTEL **$**
(Map p664; ☑08 1607 3897; dm 300B, r 400-600B) A proper hostel on the village hill, with clean dorms lined with bunk beds, tiny private rooms, an inviting restaurant-bar and a rugged, graffiti-scrawled exterior.

ⓘ **SLEEPING (OR TRYING TO) ON KO PHI-PHI**

Noise pollution on Phi-Phi is bad and centred around central Ao Ton Sai and Ao Dalam – although don't expect an early night on Hat Hin Khom either. At the time of writing bars had a 2am curfew in Ao Dalam and 1.30am in Ton Sai – that are more or less observed – but that doesn't stop inebriated revellers from making plenty of other noises (door slamming seems to be a late-night island pastime).

The most peaceful accommodation can be found on the following:

» Phi-Phi's east coast

» The back road that connects the southeast end of Ao Ton Sai with Ao Lo Dalam (and passes Chunut House)

» The hill near the road up to the viewpoint

» The far western section of Ao Ton Sai

» Hat Yao

Of course, the best option may be to simply grab a bucket and join the scrum.

HAT HIN KHOM
หาดหินคม

This area has a few small white-sand beaches in rocky coves that are relatively quiet. It's about a 15-minute jungle walk from both Hat Yao and the Ao Ton Sai bustle.

Viking Natures Resort
HOTEL $$

(Map p663; ☑08 3649 9492; www.vikingnaturesresort.com; bungalows 1000-6500B; ☎) OK it's funky (in all senses of the word), but the wood, thatch and bamboo bungalows here are dreamily creative and stylish with lots of driftwood, shell mobiles and hammock-decked lounging spaces with outrageous views of Ko Phi-Phi Leh. All bungalows have mosquito nets and balconies, but the cheaper rooms don't have their own bathrooms.

HAT YAO
หาดยาว

You can either walk here in about 30 minutes from Ton Sai via Hat Him Khom or take a long-tail (100B to 150B) from Ton Sai pier. This long stretch of pure-white beach is perfect for swimming and well worth the walk but don't expect to have it to yourself – it's popular with families and sporty types playing volleyball.

Phi-Phi Hill Resort
GUEST HOUSE $$

(Map p663; ☑0 7561 8203; www.phiphihill.com; bungalows 700-2000B; ❋@) High up in a very quiet plantation of mostly fruit trees, this simple resort spans the island's southern bluff so you can watch the sun rise on one side and set on the other. The best deals are the big, clean wooden fan-cooled cold-water bungalows on the sunset side. It closes from May to October.

Beach Resort
HOTEL $$$

(Map p663; ☑0 7561 8268; phiphithebeach.com; bungalows 3450-5350B; ❋≋) An expanding class act with a tiny pool and chic bar, this place swarms with package tourists looking for (and finding) comfort. The elegant teak, Thai-style bungalows grace a manicured jungle hillside with stunning views of Ko Phi-Phi Leh.

HAT RANTEE & AO TOH KO

Still fairly low-key, this series of small, remote grey-gold beaches has good snorkelling. You can either get here by long-tail from Ao Ton Sai pier (300B – although most resorts provide free pick-up if you reserve and the return trip is 150B) or by making the strenuous 45-minute hike over the viewpoint.

Toh Ko Beach Resort
GUEST HOUSE $$

(Map p663; ☑08 1537 0528; www.tohkobeachresort.com; bungalows 1000-2800B; @☎) All alone on white, mellow Ao Toh Ko, there's a summer-camp camaraderie here. Simple, wooden or bamboo fan-cooled bungalows are perched on a hill and have stone baths and mosquito nets.

Rantee Hut
GUEST HOUSE $

(Map p663; ☑08 9741 4846; bungalows 700-1000B) The basic Rantee Hut stands out for its groovy sea-view restaurant strewn with lounging cushions and seeping mellow reggae tunes.

HAT PHAK NAM & AO LO BAKAO

Hat Phak Nam is a gorgeous white-sand beach is nestled on the same bay as a small fishing hamlet. To get here, either charter a long-tail from Ao Ton Sai for around 500B (150B by shared taxi boat upon your return), or make the very sweaty one-hour hike over the viewpoint.

The fine stretch of palm-backed sand of **Ao Lo Bakao**, ringed by dramatic hills, is one of Phi-Phi's most lovely, with offshore views over aqua bliss to Bamboo and Mosquito Islands. Phi-Phi Island Village arranges transfers for guests but on your own a charter from Ao Ton Sai will cost 800B.

TOP CHOICE Relax Beach Resort
HOTEL $$

(Map p663; ☑08 1083 0194, 08 9475 6536; www.phiphirelaxresort.com; bungalows 1400-4400B; ❋@≋) There are 47 unpretentious but pretty Thai-style bungalows with wood floors, two-tiered terraces with lounging cushions and mosaic bathrooms in the newest nests. All are rimmed by lush jungle – there's a good restaurant and breezy bar, and it's worked by incredibly charming staff who greet and treat you like family.

Phi-Phi Island Village
HOTEL $$$

(Map p663; ☑0 7636 3700; www.ppisland.com; bungalows 7200-21,500B; ❋☎≋) This place really is a village unto itself: its whopping 100 bungalows take up much of the beachfront with palms swaying between them. Facilities vary from the family-friendly and casual to romantic dining experiences and pampering spa treatments. It adds up to good living with a whiff of old-school luxury if you have the means.

HAT LAEM THONG   หาดแหลมทอง

The beach here is long, white and sandy with a small *chow lair* (sea gypsy) rubbish-strewn settlement at the north end. Despite the upmarket offerings here the beach is really busy and all the hotels are packed together. A long-tail charter from Ao Ton Sai costs 800B. Operators can also arrange transfers.

Holiday Inn Phi-Phi Island   HOTEL $$$

(Map p663; ☑0 7562 7300; www.phiphi.holidayinn. com; bungalows 8297-10,400B; ❄☎≋) This is your standard Thailand-issue Holiday Inn – comfortable, white-concrete-with-dark-rim-chic and filled with active types milling around the pool. The restaurant has a gorgeous alfresco deck with sea views.

Zeavola   HOTEL $$$

(Map p663; ☑0 7562 7000; www.zeavola.com; bungalows 9900-26,900B; ❄@☎≋) Hibiscus-lined pathways lead to shady teak bungalows with sleek, distinctly Asian indoor-outdoor floorplans. Each comes with glass walls on three sides (with remote-controlled bamboo shutters for privacy), beautiful 1940s fixtures and antique furniture, a patio and impeccable service.

Eating

Most of the resorts, hotels and bungalows around the island have their own restaurants. Ao Ton Sai is home to some reasonably priced restaurants but don't expect haute cuisine.

Local Food Market   THAI $

(Map p664; Ao Ton Sai; ❂breakfast, lunch & dinner) The cheapest and most authentic eats are at the market. A handful of local stalls huddle on the narrowest sliver of the isthmus and serve up scrumptious *pàt tai,* fried rice, *sôm·đam* (spicy green papaya salad) and smoked catfish.

Le Grand Bleu   FUSION $$$

(Map p664; ☑08 1979 9739; mains 195-695B; ❂lunch & dinner) This place serves Thai-Euro fusion set in a charming wooden house just off the main pier. It serves French and Aussie wines, and you can get your duck wok-fried with basil or oven-roasted and caramelised with mango.

Unni's   WESTERN $$

(Map p664; mains around 120B; ❂breakfast, lunch & dinner) Come here for lunch to dine on homemade bagels topped with everything from smoked salmon to meatballs. There are also massive salads, Mexican food, tapas, cocktails and more.

Garlic Restaurant   THAI $

(Map p664; ☑08 3502 1426; dishes 45-95B; ❂breakfast, lunch & dinner) A bright shacklike place that's always packed with happy travellers chowing terrific, not-too-spicy Thai food.

Papaya   THAI $

(Map p664; ☑08 7280 1719; Ton Sai Village; dishes 80-300B) The food here is cheap, tasty and spicy. You'll get some real-deal Thai food served in heaping portions. It has basil and chilli, all the curries and *đŏm yam,* too.

🍸 Drinking & Entertainment

A rowdy nightlife saturates Phi-Phi. Buckets of cheap whiskey and Red Bull, and sticky-sweet cocktails make this the domain for spring-break wannabes and really bad hangovers. The truth is if you're nesting within earshot of the wild happenings you may as well enjoy the chaos.

TOP CHOICE Sunflower Bar   BAR

(Map p663; Ao Lo Dalam) Poetically ramshackle, this driftwood gem is still the chillest bar in Phi-Phi. Destroyed in the tsunami, the owner rebuilt it with reclaimed wood. The long-tail booths are named for the four loved ones he lost in the flood.

Reggae Bar   BAR

(Map p664; Tourist Village) You haven't experienced Phi-Phi's nightlife until you've watched tourists beat the crap out of each other in this rowdy bar's Thai-boxing ring. Both contestants get a free bucket to ease the pain.

Slinky Bar   CLUB

(Map p664; Ao Lo Dalam) This was the beach dance floor of the moment when we visited. Expect the standard fire show, buckets of candy juice and throngs of folk mingling, flirting and flailing to throbbing bass on the sand.

Breakers   BAR

(Map p664; Ton Sai Village; ❂11am-2am; ☎) A sports bar as good for TV football as it is for people-watching and great food. The burgers (200B to 240B) and steaks are awesome and the buffalo-wings starter-plate sampler can feed a handful of pint-swillers.

ⓘ Information

ATMs and internet shops (per minute 2B) are spread thickly throughout the tourist village but aren't available on the more remote eastern beaches. Wi-fi is available at **D's Bookshop** (Map p664; ⏱7am-10pm) in the heart of the tourist village. It also sells new and used fiction, and pours a decent espresso (50B).

ⓘ Getting There & Away

Ko Phi-Phi can be reached from Krabi, Phuket, Ao Nang, Railay and Ko Lanta. Most boats moor at Ao Ton Sai, though a few from Phuket use the isolated northern pier at Laem Thong. The Phuket and Krabi boats operate year-round, while the Ko Lanta and Ao Nang boats only run in the October to April high season.

Boats depart from Krabi for Ko Phi-Phi (300B, 1½ hours) at 9am and 3.30pm, while from Ao Nang (350B, 1½ hours) there's one boat at 3.30pm each day. From Phuket, boats leave at 9am, 2.30pm and 3pm and return from Ko Phi-Phi at 9am, 1.30pm and 3pm (400B, 1¾ to two hours). Boats to Ko Lanta leave Phi-Phi at 11.30am and 2pm and return from Ko Lanta at 8am and 1pm (300B, 1½ hours). For Railay (350B, 1¼ hours), take the Ao Nang–bound ferry.

ⓘ Getting Around

There are no roads on Phi-Phi Don so transport on the island is mostly by foot, although long-tails can be chartered at Ao Ton Sai for short hops around Ko Phi-Phi Don and Ko Phi-Phi Leh.

Long-tails leave from the Ao Ton Sai pier to Hat Yao (100B to 150B), Laem Thong (800B), Hat Rantee (500B) and Viking Cave (on Ko Phi-Phi Leh; 500B). Chartering speedboats for six hours costs around 6500B, while chartering a long-tail boat costs 1200B for three hours or 2500B for the whole day.

Ko Phi-Phi Leh   เกาะพีพีเล

Rugged Phi-Phi Leh is the smaller of the two Phi-Phi islands and is protected on all sides by soaring cliffs. Coral reefs crawling with marine life lie beneath the crystal-clear waters and are hugely popular with day-tripping snorkellers. Two gorgeous lagoons await in the island's interior – **Pilah** on the east coast and **Ao Maya** on the west coast. In 1999 Ao Maya was controversially (the film crew reportedly trashed it) used as the setting for the filming of *The Beach,* based on the popular novel by Alex Garland.

At the northeastern tip of the island, **Viking Cave** (Tham Phaya Naak) is a big collection point for swifts' nests. Nimble col-lectors scamper up bamboo scaffolding to gather the nests. Before ascending, they pray and make offerings of tobacco, incense and liquor to the cavern spirits. This cave gets its misleading moniker from 400-year-old graf-fiti left by Chinese fishermen.

There are no hotels on Phi-Phi Leh and most people come here on one of the lu-dicrously popular day trips out of Phi-Phi Don. Tours last about half a day and include snorkelling stops at various points around the island, with detours to Viking Cave and Ao Maya. Long-tail trips cost 800B; by mo-torboat you'll pay around 2400B. Expect to pay a 400B national-park day-use fee upon landing.

It is possible to camp on Phi-Phi Leh through **Maya Bay Camping** (☏08 6944 1623; www.mayabaycamping.com; per person 2100B). It offers action-packed overnight trips that include kayaking, snorkelling, lunch, dinner, and sleeping bags under the stars.

Ko Jum & Ko Si Boya   เกาะจำ (ปู)/เกาะศรีบอยา

Like Lanta's two baby brothers, Ko Jum (the northern hilly part is called Ko Pu) and Ko Si Boya eagerly wait for tourists to come and play on their streamers of white sand. The islands share a relaxed ambience where travellers can wander around friendly Mus-lim fishing villages or fill up their vacation days with afternoons of blissful nothingness.

🛏 Sleeping & Eating

Limited transport forces most resorts to close between June and October. Most accommo-dation options have on-site restaurants.

TOP CHOICE Koh Jum Beach Villas   VILLAS **$$$**
(☏08 6184 0505; www.kohjumbeachvillas.com; Hat Yao; villas 6000-16,000B; 🛜🄐) Spacious wood-en homes with plenty of lush decks with cushioned seating are spread along a lus-cious nub of Hat Yao. Houses are privately owned and rented out by the night and the community is devoted to keeping the place as environmentally and socially responsible as possible.

Oon Lee Bungalows   GUEST HOUSE **$–$$**
(☏08 7200 8053; www.koh-jum-resort.com; bun-galows 500-3800B) This Crusoe-chic, Thai-French family-run resort is nestled on a deserted white beach on the Ko Pu part of Ko Jum. Wooden stilted bungalows are in

a shady garden and plenty of activities, including some of the island's best hiking, are on offer. The fusion restaurant here is reason enough for a visit.

Woodland Lodge GUEST HOUSE $
(✆08 1893 5330; www.woodland-koh-jum.com; Hat Yao; bungalows 800-1000B) This place has tasteful, clean huts with shiny, polished wood floors and verandahs. The exceptionally friendly British-Thai owners can organise boat trips and fishing and have an excellent, sociable restaurant.

Siboya Resort HOTEL $
(✆0 7561 8026, 08 1979 3344; www.siboyabungalows.com; bungalows 200-1200B; @ 🛜) OK, Ko Siboya's beach isn't spectacular. But the mangrove setting is wild and full of life, and the wood bungalows are large and tasteful. No wonder ever-smiling, secretive, European and Canadian 50-somethings flock here like it's the menopausal version of Alex Garland's *The Beach*.

ℹ Getting There & Away

From December to April, boats between Krabi and Ko Lanta can drop you at Ko Jum (400B, one hour). In November and May, only the early-morning boat will make the stop. Ko Si Boya can also be accessed by a 3pm boat (100B) from Ban Laem Kruat, a village about 30km southeast of Krabi, at the end of Rte 4036. Boats to Ko Si Boya leave from Laem Hin (50B), north of Ban Laem Kruat throughout the day.

Ko Lanta เกาะลันตา
POP 20,000

Long and thin, and covered in bleach-blonde tresses, Ko Lanta is Krabi's sexy beach babe. The largest of the 50-plus islands in the local archipelago, this relaxing paradise effortlessly caters to all budget types with its west-coast parade of peach sand – each beach better than the next. The northern beaches are busy but fun and things get more and more mellow as you head southbound.

Ko Lanta is relatively flat compared to the karst formations of its neighbours, so the island can be easily explored by motorbike (bicycles involve long distances and high temperatures). A quick trip around reveals a colourful crucible of cultures – fried-chicken stalls sit below slender minarets, creaking *chow lair* villages dangle off the island's side, and small Thai *wát* hide within green-brown tangles of curling mangroves.

Ko Lanta is technically called Ko Lanta Yai, the largest of 52 islands in an archipelago protected by the Ko Lanta Marine National Park. Almost all boats pull into Ban Sala Dan, a dusty two-street town at the northern tip of the island.

◉ Sights

Ban Ko Lanta (Old Town) TOWN
Halfway down the eastern coast, **Ban Ko Lanta** (Lanta Old Town) was the original port and commercial centre for the island, and provided a safe harbour for Arabic and Chinese trading vessels sailing between Phuket, Penang and Singapore.

Some of the gracious and well-kept wooden stilt houses and shopfronts here are more than 100 years old. Pier restaurants offer up fresh catch and have views over the sea. There's a small afternoon market on Sunday, and if you're looking for sturdy, attractive handmade leather goods, stop by **Lanta Leather** (✆08 5046 6410; ⊙8am-8pm); for quality hammocks don't miss **Hammock House** (✆0 4847 2012; www.jumbohammock.com; ⊙10am-5pm) where you can also pick up its fabulous *Lanta Biker's Map* full of off-the-beaten-path recommendations.

If you crave information on culture, head south and stop by the **Chao Leh Museum** (Ban Sanghka-U), where you'll find a complex of traditionally lashed bamboo homes, engaging oil canvases and exhibits detailing the *chow lair's* myths, music and ceremonies. To find the museum look for the houseboat jutting from the hillside across the road from the sea.

Ko Lanta Marine National Park NATIONAL PARK
(อุทยานแห่งชาติเกาะลันตา; adult/child 400/200B) Established in 1990, this marine national park protects 15 islands in the Ko Lanta group, including the southern tip of Ko Lanta Yai. The park is increasingly threatened by the runaway development on the western coast of Ko Lanta Yai. The other islands in the group have fared slightly better – **Ko Rok Nai** is still very beautiful, with a crescent-shaped bay backed by cliffs, fine coral reefs and a sparkling white-sand beach. Camping is permitted on Ko Rok Nok and nearby **Ko Haa**, with permission from the national-park headquarters. On the eastern side of Ko Lanta Yai, **Ko Talabeng** has some dramatic limestone caves that you can visit on sea-kayaking tours. The national-park fee applies if you visit any of these islands.

Ko Lanta

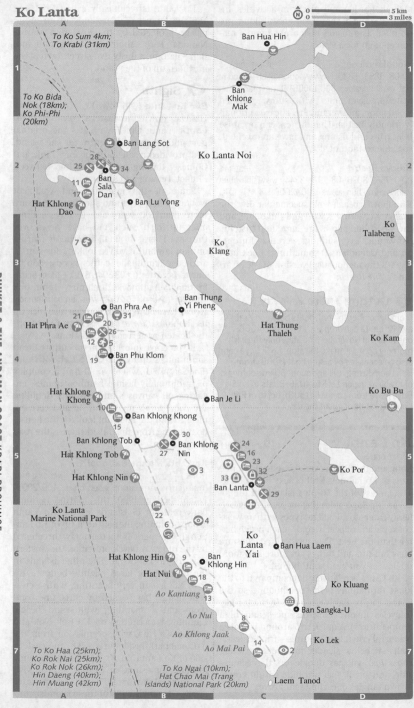

To Ko Sum 4km;
To Krabi (31km)

To Ko Bida
Nok (18km);
Ko Phi-Phi
(20km)

Ban Hua Hin

Ban
Khlong
Mak

Ban Lang Sot

Ko Lanta Noi

Ban
Sala
Dan

Ban Lu Yong

Hat Khlong
Dao

Ko
Klang

Ko
Talabeng

Ban Phra Ae

Ban Thung
Yi Pheng

Hat Phra Ae

Ban Phu Klom

Hat Thung
Thaleh

Ko Kam

Hat Khlong
Khong

Ban Je Li

Ko Bu Bu

Ban Khlong Khong

Ban Khlong Tob

Ban Khlong
Nin

Hat Khlong Tob

Ko Por

Hat Khlong Nin

Ban Lanta

Ko Lanta
Marine National Park

Ko
Lanta
Yai

Ban Hua Laem

Hat Khlong Hin

Ban
Khlong Hin

Hat Nui

Ko Kluang

Ao Kantiang

Ban Sangka-U

Ao Nui

Ko Lek

Ao Khlong Jaak

To Ko Haa (25km);
Ko Rok Nai (25km);
Ko Rok Nok (26km);
Hin Daeng (40km);
Hin Muang (42km)

Ao Mai Pai

To Ko Ngai (10km);
Hat Chao Mai (Trang
Islands) National Park (20km)

Laem Tanod

Ko Lanta

PHUKET & THE ANDAMAN COAST KO LANTA

The **national-park headquarters** is at Laem Tanod, on the southern tip of Ko Lanta Yai, reached by a steep and corrugated 7km dirt track from Hat Nui; túk-túk can take you there. There are some basic hiking trails and a **scenic lighthouse**, and you can hire long-tails here for island tours during the low season.

Tham Khao Maikaeo   CAVE
(ถ้ำเขาไมแก้ว) Monsoon rains – pounding away at limestone cracks and crevices for millions of years – have created this complex of forest caverns and tunnels. There are chambers as large as cathedrals, dripping with stalactites and stalagmites, and tiny passages that you have to squeeze through on hands and knees. There's even a subterranean pool you can take a chilly swim in. Sensible shoes are essential and getting totally covered in mud is almost guaranteed.

Tham Khao Maikaeo is reached via a guided trek through the jungle. A local family runs treks to the caves (with torches) for around 200B. The best way to get here is by rented motorcycle, or most resorts can arrange transport.

Close by, but reached by a separate track from the dirt road leading to the marine national park headquarters, **Tham Seua** (Tiger Cave) also has interesting tunnels to explore; elephant treks run up here from Hat Nui.

🏃 Activities
Diving & Snorkelling
Some of Thailand's top spots are within arm's reach of Ko Lanta. The best diving can be found at the undersea pinnacles called **Hin Muang** and **Hin Daeng**, about 45 minutes away by speedboat. These world-class dive sites have lone coral outcrops in the middle of the sea, and act as important feeding stations for large pelagic fish such as sharks, tuna and occasionally whale sharks and manta rays. Hin Daeng is considered by many to be Thailand's second-best dive site after Richelieu Rock, near the Burmese border (p662). The sites around **Ko Haa** have consistently good visibility, with depths of 18m to 34m, plenty of marine life and a

cave known as 'the Cathedral'. There are also trips to the King Cruiser Wreck, Anemone Reef and Ko Phi-Phi.

Trips out to Hin Daeng/Hin Muang cost around 5000B to 6000B, while trips to Ko Haa tend to be around 3500B to 4500B. PADI Open Water courses will set you back around 14,000B to 17,000B.

Numerous tour agencies in the main tourist areas can organise snorkelling trips out to Ko Rok Nok, Ko Phi-Phi and other nearby islands.

Scubafish DIVING
(⌂0 7566 5095; www.scuba-fish.com) One of the best dive operations on the island is located at Baan Laanta Resort (p674) on Ao Kantiang; there's also a small second office at the Narima resort. Unlike some of the large and impersonal operators based in Ban Sala Dan, Scubafish runs personal and personable programs tailored to one's needs, including the Liquid Lense underwater photography program. The three-day dive packages (9975B) are quite popular.

Other reliable dive companies include the following:

Blue Planet Divers DIVING
(⌂0 7566 2724; www.blueplanetdivers.net; Ban Sala Dan) The only school that specialises in free diving instruction.

Lanta Diver DIVING
(⌂0 7568 4208; www.lantadiver.com; Ban Sala Dan)

Dive & Relax DIVING
(⌂08 4842 2191; www.diveandrelax.com; Hat Phra Ae) In the Lanta Castaway Beach Resort.

Courses

Time for Lime COOKING
(⌂0 7568 4590; www.timeforlime.net) On Hat Khlong Dao, this place has a huge, professional kitchen with plenty of room to run amok. It offers cooking courses with a slightly more exciting selection of dishes than most cookery schools in Thailand; five-hour courses cost 1800B with substantial discounts if you take more than one class. Profits from the school help finance Lanta Animal Welfare (see p673).

Sleeping

Ko Lanta is home to many long stretches of beach packed with accommodation. Some resorts close down for the May-to-October low season, others drop their rates by 50%

or more. Resorts usually have their own restaurants and tour-booking facilities that can arrange island snorkelling, massages, tours and motorcycle rental.

HAT KHLONG DAO หาดคลองดาว
This is an outstanding 2km stretch of white sand with no rocks – perfect for swimming. Unfortunately garbage does accumulate when the tides shift. Locals say it comes from Phi-Phi. And they say it disdainfully.

TOP CHOICE **Costa Lanta** HOTEL $$$
(⌂0 7566 8168; www.costalanta.com; r from 6200B; ✳@🗲🗲) Here are incredibly Zen abodes nestled in a coconut-palm garden laced with tidal canals at the north end of Hat Khlong Dao. Everything from the floors to the walls and the washbasins is polished concrete and the barn doors of each cabana open on two sides to maximise air flow. The restaurant is stunning, as is the black spill-over pool on the edge of the sand. Discounts are available if booked through its website. The low-season rates are a steal.

Maya Beach Resort HOTEL $$$
(⌂0 7568 4267; mayalanta.com; r 4300B; ✳@🗲🗲) Ignore the Best Western affiliation if you can, because this place has attractive, large, Ikea-chic rooms on two floors. There are louvred railings on the terrace, Buddhist shrines on the sand and a pool that blends with the nearby sea.

HAT PHRA AE หาดพระแอ
The beach at Hat Phra Ae (Long Beach) is only mediocre, but the ambience is lively. A large travellers' village has set up camp and there are loads of *fà·ràng*-oriented restaurants, beach bars, internet cafes and tour offices.

Relax Bay HOTEL $$
(⌂0 7568 4194; www.relaxbay.com; bungalows 1200-2500B; ✳🗲) This gorgeous French-run place is spread out over a tree-covered headland near a small beach. Its wooden bungalows sit on stilts with large decks, or for a more unique experience sleep in a sea-view luxury tent perched over the rocks on a wooden platform.

Sanctuary GUEST HOUSE $
(⌂08 1891 3055; sanctuary_93@yahoo.com; bungalows 600-1200B) The original Phra Ae resort is still a delightful place to stay. There are artistically designed wood-and-thatch bungalows with lots of grass and a hippie-

JUNIE KOVACS & LANTA ANIMAL WELFARE

Founder: Lanta Animal Welfare, which rescues animals, organises sterilisation and vaccination campaigns, and offers local sensibility and education.

WHY ARE THERE SO MANY STRAYS?

Many guest houses get puppies or kittens for the tourist season because the guests like them. Once the season is over the animals get abandoned on backroads.

HOW TO HELP.

Volunteers are needed short or long term to walk dogs, help with fundraising campaigns, helping out volunteer vets, catching strays and so on. If you fall in love with an animal we can help with the paperwork to bring it home with you! Soi Dog (see p625) on Phuket is another great place where you can help and every little bit counts. Donations are also greatly appreciated since we get no help from the government.

As told to Celeste Brash.

ish atmosphere that's low-key and friendly. The restaurant offers Indian and vegetarian eats and the Thai usuals. It also holds yoga classes.

Hutyee Boat GUEST HOUSE $
(☑08 3633 9723; bungalows 350-400B) A hidden hippie paradise of big, solid bungalows with tiled bathrooms and minifridges in a forest of palms and bamboo. It's behind Nautalus Bungalows.

Somewhere Else GUEST HOUSE $
(☑08 1536 0858; bungalows 400-1000B; ☎) Big octagonal bamboo huts grace a shady lawn right on a very social and lounge-worthy stretch of beach.

HAT KHLONG KHONG หาดคลองโขง
This is thatched-roof, Rasta-bar bliss with plenty of beach -volleyball games, moon parties and the occasional well-advertised mushroom shake (imbibe at own risk). Still, it's all pretty low-key and all ages are present. The beach goes on forever in either direction.

TOP CHOICE **Bee Bee Bungalows** GUEST HOUSE $
(☑08 1537 9932; www.beebeebungalows; bungalows 400-800B; ✽@☎) One of the best budget spots on the island, Bee Bee's superfriendly staff care for a dozen creative bamboo cabins – every one is unique and a few are up on stilts in the trees. The on-site restaurant has a library of tattered paperbacks to keep you busy while you wait for your delicious Thai staples.

Lanta Darawadee HOTEL $$
(☑0 7566 7094; www.lantadarawadee.com; bungalows incl breakfast 1000-1600B; ✽☎☎) If you're

digging the Hat Khlong Khong scene but can't live without air-con, here's a great-value option right on the beach. It's bland but the new, clean rooms have good beds, terraces, minifridges and TVs. The water is solar heated and rates include breakfast.

HAT KHLONG NIN หาดคลองนิน
After Hat Khlong Tob, the main road heading south forks: head left for the inland road which runs to the east coast, go right and the country road hugs the coastline for 14km to the tip of Ko Lanta. The first beach here is lovely, white Hat Khlong Nin. There are lots of small, inexpensive guest houses at the north end of the beach that are usually attached to restaurants – it's easy to get dropped off here then shop around for a budget place to stay.

Sri Lanta HOTEL $$
(☑0 7566 2688; www.srilanta.com; cottages from 3000B; ✽@☎) At the southern end of the beach, this decadent resort consists of minimalist, naturalistic wooden villas in wild gardens stretching from the beach to a landscaped jungle hillside. There's a very stylish beachside area with a restaurant, infinity pool and private drapery-swathed massage pavilions. The resort strives for low environmental impact by using biodegradable products and minimising energy use and waste.

AO KANTIANG อ่าวกันเตียง
A superb sweep of sand backed by mountains is also its own self-contained little village complete with minimarts, internet cafes, motorbike rental and restaurants. Much of the beach here is undeveloped although

there are lots of sailboats and motorboats anchored in the bay. It's far from everything; if you land here don't expect to move much.

Phra Nang Lanta HOTEL $$$

(☑0 7566 5025; lanta@vacation village.co.th; studios 6000B; ❄@☎☜) The gorgeous Mexican-style adobe concrete studios are huge and straight off the pages of an architectural mag. Interiors are decorated with clean lines, hardwoods and whites accented with bright colours. Outside, flowers and foliage climb over bamboo lattice sunshades and the pool and lush restaurant-bar look over the beautiful beach.

Baan Laanta Resort & Spa HOTEL $$$

(☑0 7566 5091; www.baanlaanta.com; bungalows from 3500B; ❄@☜) Landscaped grounds wind around stylish wooden bungalows and a pool that drops off to a stretch of white sandy beach. The room's centrepiece is a futon-style bed on a raised wooden platform under a gauzy veil of mosquito netting.

Kantiang Bay View Resort HOTEL $-$$

(☑0 7566 5049; kantiang bay.net; bungalows 500-2000B; ❄@) Choose between the cheap, rickety, not-exactly-spotless wooden-and-bamboo bungalows or the more expensive, candy-coloured tiled rooms with minifridge. The bamboo-clad restaurant serves decent, *fa·ràng*-friendly Thai dishes.

AO KHLONG JAAK & LAEM TANOD อ่าวคลองจาก/แหลมโตนด

The splendid beach at Ao Khlong Jaak is named after the inland waterfall.

La Laanta HOTEL $$$

(☑0 7566 5066; www.lalaanta.com; bungalows 2800-6200B; ❄@☜☎☜) This is barefoot elegance at its finest. Owned and operated by a young, hip, English-speaking Thai-Vietnamese couple, this is the grooviest spot on the entire island. Thatched bungalows have polished-concrete floors, platform beds, floral-design motifs and decks overlooking a pitch of sand, which blends into a rocky fishermen's beach. Set down a rutted dirt road, it's also the closest resort to the marine national park.

Andalanta Resort HOTEL $$$

(☑0 7566 5018; www.andalanta.com; bungalows 2600-6900B; ❄@☎) You'll find beach-style, modern air-conditioned bungalows (some with a loft) and simple fan-cooled ones; all face the sea. The garden is a delight, there's

an ambient restaurant and the waterfall is just a 30- to 40-minute walk away.

Mu Ko Lanta Marine National Park Headquarters CAMPING GROUND $

(☑in Bangkok 0 2561 4292; camping with own tent per person 30B, with tent hire 300-400B) The secluded jungle grounds of the national-park headquarters are a wonderfully serene and wild place to camp. There are toilets and running water, but you should bring your own food. You can also get permission for camping on Ko Rok or Ko Haa here. National-park entry fees apply (see p669). The road to the marine national-park headquarters fords the *klong* (canal), which can get quite deep in the wet season.

BAN KO LANTA บ้านเกาะลันตา

There are a handful of inns open for business on Lanta's oft-ignored, wonderfully dated and incredibly rich Old Town.

Mango House GUEST HOUSE $$

(☑0 7569 7181; www.mangohouses.com; suites 2000-2500B; ☉Oct-April) These 100-year-old Chinese teak pole houses and former opium den are stilted over the harbour. The original time-worn wood floors are still intact, ceilings soar and the house-sized rooms are decked out with satellite TVs, DVD players and ceiling fans. The restaurant is just as sea-shanty-chic and serves Thai and Western dishes with panache.

Sriraya GUEST HOUSE $

(☑0 7569 7045; r with shared bathrooms 500B) Sleep in a simple but beautifully restored, thick-beamed Chinese shophouse. Walls are black and the sheets are white. Angle for the street-front balcony room that overlooks the old town's ambient centre.

✖ Eating

Ban Sala Dan has plenty of restaurants and minimarts. Don't miss the seafood restaurants along the northern edge of the village. With tables on verandahs over water, they offer fresh seafood sold by weight (which includes cooking costs).

Beautiful Restaurant SEAFOOD $$

(☑0 7569 7062; Ban Ko Lanta; mains 100-200B) This is the best of the Old Town's seafood houses. Tables are scattered on four piers that extend into the sea. The fish is fresh and exquisitely prepared.

Lanta Seafood   SEAFOOD **$$**

(✆0 7566 8411; Ban Sala Dan) The best option of the seafood-by-weight options. Order the *blah tôrt kà mîn* – it's white snapper rubbed with fresh, hand-ground turmeric and garlic, then deep fried.

Red Snapper   FUSION **$$**

(✆0 7885 6965; tapas/mains from 70/235B; ⏰dinner) A Dutch-run tapas restaurant on the roadside in Ao Phra Ae, the garden setting is romantic and the duck breast with shitake mushrooms comes highly recommended.

🍷 Drinking & Entertainment

If you're looking for roaring discotheques, pick another island. If you want a more low-key bar scene with music wafting well into the night, then head to Ao Phra Ae, where you'll find a cluster of fun spots such as **Opium**, **Earth Bar** and **Reggae House**.

ℹ Information

Ban Sala Dan village has a number of internet cafes (1B per minute), travel agencies, dive shops and motorcycle rental joints. There are five 7-Elevens spread along the island's west coast – each one has an ATM.

Ko Lanta Hospital (✆0 7569 7085) It's 1km south of Ban Ko Lanta (Old Town).

Police station (✆0 7569 7017) North of Ban Ko Lanta.

ℹ Getting There & Away

Most people come to Ko Lanta by boat or air-conditioned minivan. If you're coming under your own steam, you'll need to use the frequent **vehicle ferries** (motorcycle 20B, car/4WD 75/150B; ⏰7am-8pm) between Ban Hua Hin and Ban Khlong Mak (Ko Lanta Noi) and on to Ko Lanta Yai.

Boat

There are two piers at Ban Sala Dan. The passenger jetty is about 300m from the main strip of shops; vehicle ferries leave from a second jetty that's several kilometres further east.

There is one passenger ferry connecting Krabi's Khlong Chilat pier with Ko Lanta departing from Ko Lanta at 8am (400B, two hours) and returning from Krabi at 11am. It also stops at Ko Jum (for the full 400B fare).

Boats between Ko Lanta and Ko Phi-Phi technically run year-round, although service can peter out in the low season if there are too few passengers. Ferries usually leave Ko Lanta at 8am and 1pm (300B, 1½ hours); in the opposite direction boats leave Ko Phi-Phi at 11.30am and 2pm. From here you can transfer to ferries to Phuket.

WORTH A TRIP

KO LANTA'S MARKETS

» Sunday day market at Ban Sala Dan

» Sunday evening/Monday morning market in Old Town

» Tuesday/Wednesday market in Ban Je Li

» Saturday market near Ban Khlong Nin

From around 21 October to May, you can join a four-island snorkelling tour to the Trang Islands and hop off with your bags at any destination you choose (350B) – bring your swimsuit. Boats stop on Ko Ngai (two hours), Ko Muk (three hours) and Ko Kradan (four hours).

There are also several speedboats that go from Ko Lanta to the Trang islands, the fastest being the **Satun-Pak Bara Speedboat Club** (✆0 7475 0389, 08 2433 0114; www.tarutaolipeisland.com) that stops in Ko Ngai (650B, 30 minutes), Ko Muk (900B, one hour) and Ko Bulon Leh (1600B, two hours) then continues on to Ko Lipe (1900B, three hours).

Tigerline (✆08 1092 8800; www.tigerline travel.com), a high-speed ferry, runs between Ban Sala Dan on Ko Lanta and Ko Lipe (1400B, four hours), stopping at Ko Ngai (500B, 30 minutes), Ko Kradan (750B, 1½ hours) and Ko Muk (750B, two hours). The service leaves at 1pm. The next day the same boat makes the return trip from Ko Lipe departing at 9am and arriving in Ban Sala Dan after noon.

Minivan

Minivans run year-round and are your best option from the mainland. Daily minivans to Krabi airport (280B, 1½ hours) and Krabi Town (250B, 1½ hours) leave hourly between 7am and 3.30pm. From Krabi, minivans depart hourly from 8am till 4pm.

Minivans to Phuket (350B, four hours) leave Ko Lanta every two hours or so, but are more frequent in the high season. There are also several daily air-conditioned minivans to Trang (250B, 2½ hours) and less frequent services to Khao Lak (650B, six hours), Ko Samui (650B including boat ticket) and other popular destinations.

ℹ Getting Around

Most resorts send vehicles to meet the ferries – a free ride *to* your resort. In the opposite direction expect to pay 80B to 250B. Alternatively, you can take a motorcycle taxi from opposite the 7-Eleven in Ban Sala Dan; fares vary from 50B to 250B depending on distance.

Motorcycles (250B per day) can be rented all over the island. Unfortunately, very few places provide helmets and none provide insurance, so take extra care on the bumpy roads.

Several places rent out small 4WDs for around 1600B per day, including insurance.

TRANG PROVINCE

With its own set of jagged jungly karst formations and lonely islets in the crystalline sea, Trang feels like 'Krabi Lite'. Travellers are getting wise to the province's charms, and the region is experiencing a tourist boom like neighbouring Krabi did several years back. Trang's shining stars are the constellation of fabled offshore isles known simply as the Trang Islands.

Trang Town ตรัง

POP 64,700

Most visitors to Trang are in transit to nearby islands, but if you're an aficionado of culture, Thai food or markets, plan to stay a day or more. It's an easy-to-manage town where you can get lost in wet markets by day and hawker markets and late-night Chinese coffee shops by night; at nearly any time of the year, there's likely to be some minor festival that oozes local colour.

Most of the tourist facilities lie along the main drag, Th Praram VI, between the clock tower and the train station.

Sights

Trang is more of a business centre than a tourist town. Wat Tantayaphirom (Th Tha Klang) has a huge white *chedi* (stupa) enshrining a footprint of the Buddha that's mildly interesting. The Chinese Meunram Temple, between Soi 1 and Soi 3, sometimes sponsors performances of southern Thai shadow theatre. It's also worth strolling around the large wet and dry markets on Th Ratchadamnoen and Th Sathani.

Activities & Tours

Tour agencies around the train station and along Th Praram VI offer various tours around Trang Province. Boat trips to Hat Chao Mai National Park and the Trang Islands start at 750B plus national-park fees. There are also sea-kayaking tours to the gorgeous Tham Chao Mai mangrove forests (650B). Snorkelling trips on private

long-tails to Ko Rok (3500B, maximum four people) and trips to local caves and waterfalls (1800B, maximum three people) by private car can also be arranged by most agencies.

For a cultural fix you can spend a day hiking in the Khao Banthat Mountains to visit villages of the Sa Kai mountain people (2500B, maximum two people).

Sleeping & Eating

Trang is famous for its *mŏo yâhng* (crispy barbecued pork) and *ráhn go·bíi* (coffee shops) that serve real filtered coffee. You can find *mŏo yâhng* in the mornings at some coffee shops or by weight at the wet market on Th Ratchadamnoen. To really get into the local scene get to a dim-sum depot early in the morning and stay out late at the coffee shops along Th Ratsada.

Sri Trang Hotel   HOTEL $
(0 7521 8122; www.sritrang.com; 22-26 Th Praram VI; r 450-690B; ❄️☎️) There is a range of fan-cooled and air-conditioned rooms in this renovated 60-year-old building with high ceilings, a winding wood staircase, groovy paint jobs, and wi-fi throughout. There's also a hang-out-able cafe-bar downstairs.

Rua Rasada Hotel   HOTEL $$$
(0 7521 4230; www.ruarasadahotel.com; 188 Th Pattalung; r incl breakfast from 2700B; ❄️☎️🏊) Trang's slickest choice is a 10-minute (25B) túk-túk ride from the train station. The chic rooms have large tiles, comfortable beds and a dusky blue, dark mauve-and-grey colour scheme. It's a five-minute walk to Robinson's Shopping Mall and Cinema City.

Koh Teng Hotel   HOTEL $
(0 7521 8148; 77-79 Th Praram VI; r 180-380B; ❄️) The Koh Teng is the undisputed king of backpacker digs in Trang. If you're feeling optimistic, the huge, windowlit rooms here have an adventuresome kind of shabby charm to them; if not, the grunge factor might get you down.

TOP CHOICE **Night market**   MARKET $
(btwn Th Praram VI & Th Ratchadamnoen; meals around 30B; ⊙dinner) The best night market on the Andaman coast will have you salivating over bubbling curries, fried chicken and fish, *pàt tai* and an array of Thai desserts. Go with an empty stomach and a sense of adventure. On Friday and Saturday nights

Trang Province

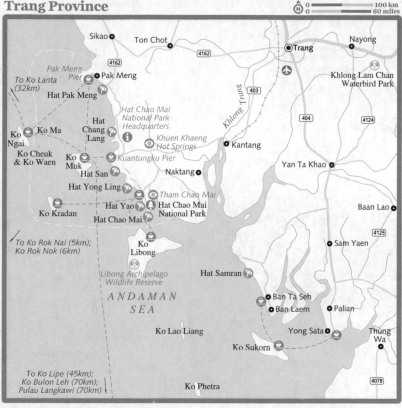

there's a second night market right in front of the train station.

Asia Ocha
THAI **$**

(Th Kantang; meals from 30B; ⊙breakfast, lunch & dinner) In business since the mid-1940s, this place serves filtered coffee to an all-Thai clientele who sit at vintage marble tables in this antiquated building. Don't miss the food either – the roast duck is delectable.

ℹ Information

You'll find several internet cafes and various banks with ATMs and foreign-exchange booths on Th Praram VI.

My Friend (☎0 7522 5984; 25/17-20 Th Sathani; per hr 30B) Has the best 24-hour internet cafe in town.

Post office (cnr Th Praram VI & Th Kantang) Also sells CAT cards for international phone calls.

ℹ Getting There & Away

Air

Nok Air (www.nokair.com) and **Orient Thai Airways** (www.orient-thai.com) operate daily flights from Bangkok (Don Muang airport) to Trang (around 1500B one-way).

The airport is 4km south of Trang; minivans meet flights and charge 60B to get to town. In the reverse direction a taxi or túk-túk will cost 80B to 100B.

Bus

Buses leave from the Trang **bus terminal** (Th Huay Yot). Air-conditioned buses from Trang to Bangkok cost 600B to 680B (12 hours, morning and afternoon). More comfortable are the VIP 24-seater buses that leave at 5pm and 5.30pm (1050B). From Bangkok, VIP/air-conditioned buses leave between 6.30pm and 7pm.

Other services:

Hat Yai (110B, three hours, frequent departures)

Krabi (115B, two hours, frequent departures)

Trang

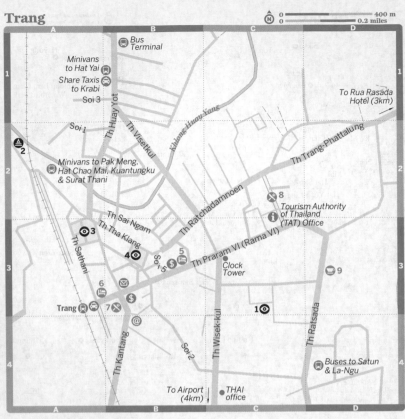

Phang-Nga (180B, 3½ hours, hourly)

Phuket (240B, five hours, hourly)

Satun (120B, three hours, frequent departures)

Minivan & Share Taxi

Hourly vans heading to Surat Thani (180B, 2½ hours), with connections to Ko Samui and Ko Pha-Ngan, leave from a **depot** (Th Tha Klang) just before Th Tha Klang crosses the railway tracks. Several daily air-conditioned minivans between Trang and Ko Lanta (250B, 2½ hours) leave from the travel agents across from the train station. There are shared taxis to Krabi (180B, two hours) and air-conditioned minivans to Hat Yai (160B, two hours) from offices just west of the Trang bus terminal.

Local transport is mainly by air-conditioned minivan rather than *sŏrng·tăa·ou*. Minivans leave regularly from the depot on Th Tha Klang for Pak Meng (70B, 45 minutes), Hat Chao Mai (80B, one hour) and Kuantungku pier (100B, one hour) for onward boat travel.

Train

Only two trains go all the way from Bangkok to Trang: the express 83 and the rapid 167, which both leave from Bangkok's Hua Lamphong station in the afternoon and arrive in Trang the next morning.

From Trang, trains leave in the early and late afternoon. Fares are around 1480B/831B for a 1st-/2nd-class air-conditioned sleeper and 285B for 3rd class.

ⓘ Getting Around

Túk-túk and their drivers mill around near the train station and should charge about 30B for local trips, or 250B per hour. Motorbike taxis charge the same price.

Motorcycles can be rented at travel agencies for about 200B per day. Most agencies can also help you arrange car rental for around 1400B per day.

Trang

Trang Beaches

Think of limestone karsts rising from steamy palm-studded valleys and swirling seas. Trang's beaches are mostly just jumping-off points to the islands but if you have the time, stop and enjoy the scenery.

HAT PAK MENG & HAT CHANG LANG
หาดปากเมง/หาดฉางลาง

Thirty-nine kilometres west of Trang in Sikao District, Hat Pak Meng is the main jumping-off point for Ko Ngai. There's a wild-looking stretch of coastline here, and though the beach is scruffy, the backdrop – jutting limestone karsts on all sides that rival the best of Railay and Phi-Phi – is spectacular. The main pier is at the northern end of the beach and there are several seafood restaurants with deck chairs under casuarinas where Rte 4162 meets the coast.

Tour agencies at the jetty organise one-day boat tours to Ko Muk, Ko Cheuk, Ko Ma and Ko Kradan for 900B to 1000B per person (minimum three people), including lunch and beverages. There are also snorkelling day tours to Ko Ngai (750B) and Ko Rok (1200B to 1400B, plus national-park fees). Mask and snorkel sets and fins can be rented by the pier for 50B each.

Hat Chang Lang is the next beach south from Hat Pak Meng and it continues the casuarina-backed beach motif. At the southern end of Hat Chang Lang, where the beachfront road turns inland, is the headquarters of **Hat Chao Mai National Park** (⊉0 7521 3260; adult/child under 14yr 200/100B; ⊗6am-6pm).

The 231-sq-km park covers the shoreline from Hat Pak Meng to Laem Chao Mai and encompasses the islands of Ko Muk, Ko Kradan and Ko Cheuk plus a host of small islets. In various parts of the park you may see endangered dugong and rare black-necked storks, as well as more common species such as sea otters, macaques, langurs, wild pigs, pangolins, little herons, Pacific reef egrets, white-bellied sea eagles and monitor lizards.

Tours and long-tail charters from Ko Muk and Ko Kradan can get you to the park.

⊨ Sleeping

Anantara Sikao　　　　　　　HOTEL $$$
(⊉0 7520 5888; www.sikao.anantara.com; r 5400-15,400B; ❋⊛⊠) Set on the northern edge of Hat Chang Leng, Anantara's glamorous yet hip vibe has refreshed these old bones (it was once an Amari Resort). Deluxe oceanfront rooms have wood floors, floating desks, flat-screen TVs and amazing views of Pak Meng's signature karsts. There are impressive timber columns and Balinese wood furnishings in the lobby, and the view from its Acqua restaurant is jaw dropping. Take the free shuttle to its guests-only beach club on seductive Ko Kradan.

National Park Headquarters　CAMPING, CABINS $
(⊉0 7521 3260; www.dnp.go.th/index_eng.asp; camping with own tent free, with tent hire 300B, cabins 800-1000B) Simple cabins sleep up to six people and have fans. You can also camp under the casuarinas. There's a restaurant and a small shop here, too.

❶ Getting There & Away

There are several daily boats from Pak Meng to Ko Ngai (400B) at 10am, returning from Ko Ngai at 9am. A long-tail charter is 1200B.

Regular air-conditioned minivans from Th Kha Klang in Trang run to Hat Pak Meng (80B, 45 minutes) and Chao Mai (100B, one hour). Or you can charter a taxi from Trang for around 800B.

The Chao Mai National Park headquarters is about 1km off this road, down a clearly signposted track.

HAT YAO
หาดยาว

A rickety, scruffy fishing hamlet just south of Hat Yong Ling, Hat Yao is sandwiched between the sea and imposing limestone cliffs, and sits at the mouth of a thick mangrove estuary. A rocky headland at the southern end of Hat Yao is pockmarked with caves and there's good snorkelling around the island immediately offshore. The best beach in the area is the tiny **Hat Apo**, hidden away among the cliffs. **Tham Chao Mai** is a vast cave full of crystal cascades and impressive stalactites and stalagmites that can be explored by a chartered boat.

Just south of the headland is the Yao pier, the main departure point for Ko Libong and the midpoint in the Tigerline chain that connects Ko Lipe to Ko Lanta.

Sleeping & Eating

Haad Yao Nature Resort (☎08 1894 6936; www.trangsea.com; r 500-1200B, bungalows 800B; ❄@), set in the harbour, is run by the Lifelong Learning Foundation, an ecological and educational NGO led by enthusiastic naturalists. This place offers a variety of environment-focused tours in the Hat Yao area. It has large cottages with wide terraces, TV and DVD, simpler motel-style rooms and a few overwater bungalows.

Along the beach, north of the limestone headland, is a collection of wooden seafood restaurants selling cheap Thai meals. There is also a handful of tasty restaurants on the harbour.

Getting There & Around

From here, you can take a regular long-tail boat to Ko Libong (50B, 20 minutes) or charter a long-tail to Ko Libong (800B, 20 minutes) or Ko Muk (1500B, one hour). *Sŏrng·tăa·ou* to Trang (70B, one hour) leave when full from the pier and meet arriving boats. **Tigerline** (☎08 1092 8800; www.tigerlinetravel.com) is the area's high-speed ferry service, which docks in Hat Yao for lunch on its way between Lanta (750B, 2½ hours) and Lipe (750B, 2½ hours).

Trang Islands

The mythical Trang Islands are the last iteration of the Andaman's iconic limestone peaks before they tumble into the sea like sleeping giants. Shrouded in mystery and steeped in local legend, these stunning island Edens are home to roving *chow lair* and technicolour reefs.

KO NGAI เกาะไหง (ไห)

The long, blonde, wind-swept beach along the developed east coast of Ko Ngai (often called Ko Hai) extends into blue water with a sandy bottom (perfect for children) that ends at a reef drop-off with excellent snorkelling. Coral and clear waters actually encircle the entire densely forested island – it's a stunning place. With no indigenous population living here, several spiffy resorts have the whole island to themselves. There are two dive centres (dives from 1500B), mask and snorkel sets and fins can be rented from resorts for 60B each, sea kayaks rent for around 150B per hour, or you can take half-day snorkelling tours of nearby islands (850B per person). Internet at the big resorts is slow and costs 100B to 150B per hour.

Even though it's technically a part of Krabi Province, the island's mainland link is with Pak Meng.

Sleeping

Most places are decidedly midrange and come with restaurants and 24-hour electricity. The boat pier is at Koh Ngai Resort, but if you book ahead resorts on the other beaches will arrange transfers.

Coco Cottages HOTEL $$
(☎08 1693 6457, 08 9724 9225; www.coco-cottage.com; bungalows 1650-4700B; ❄📶) As the name suggests, cottages are coconut extravaganzas with thatched roofs, coconut-wood walls and lit with coconut-shell lanterns. Grab a sea-view fan bungalow if you can.

Ko Hai Seafood GUEST HOUSE $$
(☎08 1367 8497; r 1200B; ❄@≋) These solid bamboo bungalows are easily the most charming budget choice on the beach. The owners are happy, fun and laid-back plus they have one of the best kitchens on the island.

Ko Hai Camping CAMPING GROUND $
(☎08 1970 9804; seamoth2004&yahoo.com; tent 600B) Big, clean fan-cooled tentalos on the beach have shared bathrooms and are run by friendly Tu, who also manages the adjacent Sea Moth Dive Center.

Getting There & Away

Ko Ngai Villa runs the daily boats from Hat Pak Meng to Ko Ngai at 10am (400B, 1½ hours), returning from Ko Ngai between 9am (400B, 1½ hours). You can also privately charter a long-tail to and from Pak Meng for 1200B, as well as Ko Muk (1200B) and Ko Kradan (1500B).

In the high season, the **Tigerline** (☎08 1092 8800; www.tigerlinetravel.com) high-speed ferry runs between Ban Sala Dan (750B, 30 minutes) on Ko Lanta and Ko Lipe (1400B, four hours) stopping at the pier on nearby Ko Muk. **Satun Pakbara Speedboat Club** (☎0 7475 0389, 08 2433 0114; www.tarutaolipeisland.com) is the more direct and comfortable choice from Ko Lanta (650B, 30 minutes). Or you can charter a long-tail to Lanta for 2000B.

KO MUK
เกาะมุก

Motoring into Ko Muk is unforgettable whether you land on the sugary white-sand bar of Hat Sivalai or spectacular Hat Faràng (aka Hat Sai Yao, aka Charlie's Beach) where jade water kisses a perfect beach. Unfortunately, the lodging options aren't tremendous; there's a steady stream of Speedo-clad package tourists tramping the beach, and even more in the speedboats that buzz in from Ko Lanta. Still, the west-coast sunsets are glorious, it's easy to hop from here to any and every island in the province, and you may feel Ko Muk's topography stir something deep and wild in your primordial soul.

Hat Faràng is where most of the action is – a blend of travellers and package tourists revelling in calm more than party. Hat Sivalai and Hat Lodung are both a short walk from the main pier. If you're facing the sea at the pier, humble, local-flavoured Hat Lodung is to your left after a stilt *chao lair* village and some mangroves; stunning Hat Sivilai wraps around the peninsula to the right.

☉ Sights & Activities
Good snorkelling opportunities lie offshore and the archipelago's star attraction, Tham Morakot (Emerald Cave), hides at the northern end of the island. This cave is a limestone tunnel that leads 80m to a mint-green sea lagoon (pirates once hid treasure here). Inside, you swim part of the way in pitch-blackness, to a small, concealed white-sand beach surrounded by lofty limestone, with a chimney that lets in a piercing shaft of light around midday. The cave features on most tour itineraries so it gets ridiculously crowded in high season. Rent a kayak (per hour/day 150/500B) or charter a long-tail (300B) to visit on your own early in the morning or late in the afternoon, but watch the tides – you can't go in at high tide.

Between Ko Muk and Ko Ngai are the small karst islets of Ko Cheuk and Ko Waen, which have good snorkelling and small sandy beaches.

Princess Divers (☏08 6270 9174) is located at Charlie Beach resort and the independent Chill Out Divers is right behind Charlie Beach Resort. Both are recommended and offer one/two dives for 1800/2600B and PADI courses from 10,900B. Chill Out Divers also offers yoga classes (250B to 400B) on the beach.

Koh Muk Nature Resort rents out mountain bikes (per day 150B) with maps for self-guided island tours.

🛏 Sleeping

Sivalai
HOTEL $$$
(☏08 9723 3355; www.komooksivalai.com; Hat Sivalai; bungalows incl breakfast 5000-8000B; ✵) Straddling an arrow-shaped peninsula of white sand and surrounded by views of karst islands and the mainland, this location is mind-bogglingly sublime. Elegant thatched-roof cottages are almost encircled with glass doors so you can let in as much of the view as you want.

Pawapi Resort
GUEST HOUSE $$
(☏08 9669 1980; www.pawapi.com; Hat Sivalai; bungalows incl breakfast 2600B) The upscale bamboo bungalows here hover on stilts

---

REMARKABLE RUBBER TREES

If you ever wondered where the bounce in your rubber comes from, wonder no further: unlike money, it grows on trees. All over the Trang region, particularly on the islands floating off its coast, you are likely to come across tracts of rubber-tree plantations.

Rubber trees produce the milky liquid known as latex in vessels that grow within the bark of the tree. The trees are 'tapped' by making a thin incision into the bark at an angle parallel with the latex vessels (note that latex isn't the tree's sap). A small cup collects the latex as it drips down the tree. New scores are made every day – you can see these notched trees and collection cups throughout the region.

Latex from multiple trees is collected, poured into flat pans and mixed with formic acid, which serves as a coagulant. After a few hours, the very wet sheets of rubber are wrung out by squishing them through a press. They're then hung out to dry. You'll see these large, yellowish pancakes drying on bamboo poles wherever rubber trees are grown. The gooey ovals are then shipped to processing plants where they are turned into rubber as we know it.

about 1.5m off the ground so that breezes ventilate the room from all sides and the insanely gorgeous view sits 180 degrees in front of you.

Charlie Beach Resort   HOTEL **$$**
(☑0 7520 3281/3; www.kohmook.com; Hat Faràng; bungalows 1200-3100B; ❋@) There's a bunch of different bungalow options, ranging from basic beach shacks to three-star, air-conditioned cottages at this sprawling resort, which dominates the beach and is linked by sandy paths. Skip the restaurant, though.

Sawasdee Resort   GUEST HOUSE **$**
(☑08 1508 0432; www.kohmook-sawadeeresort. com; Hat Faràng; bungalows 800B) Unremarkable wooden bungalows with terraces are right on the quiet shady north end of Hat Faràng. You're paying for the location – which is sublime.

Ko Mook Garden Resort   GUEST HOUSE **$**
(☑08 1748 384, 08 1798 7805; Hat Lodung; bungalows 300B, r 500B) The wooden rooms here are large while the bamboo bungalows are small and basic. Staying here means you're with a local family who take guests snorkelling, lend out bikes and give out detailed maps of all the island's secret spots.

❶ Getting There & Away

Boats to Ko Muk leave from the pier at Kuantungku. There are four daily departures at 8am, 10am, noon and 3pm (100B to 300B, 30 min-

NICE DAY FOR A WET WEDDING

Every Valentine's Day, Ko Kradan is the setting for a rather unusual wedding ceremony. Around 35 brides and grooms don scuba gear and descend to an underwater altar amid the coral reefs, exchanging their vows in front of the Trang District Officer. How the couples manage to say, 'I do,' underwater has never been fully explained, but the ceremony has made it into the *Guinness Book of Records* for the world's largest underwater wedding. Before and after the scuba ceremony, the couples are paraded along the coast in a flotilla of motorboats. If you think this might be right for your special day, visit the website www.trangonline.com/underwaterwedding.

utes) that make the return trip to the mainland an hour later; the early morning ferry is the cheapest. Minibuses to/from Trang (200B, one hour) meet the boats. A chartered long-tail from Kuantungku to Ko Muk (600B, 30 minutes) and from Ko Muk to either Pak Meng or Hat Yao is around 1200B (45 minutes to one hour).

Long-tail charters to Ko Kradan (600B, 30 minutes) and Ko Ngai (1000B, one hour) are easily arranged on the pier or at Rubber Tree Bungalow or Ko Yao Restaurant on Hat Faràng.

From November to May, Ko Muk is one of the stops on the speedboats connecting Ko Lanta and Ko Lipe; see p691 for details.

KO KRADAN   เกาะกระดาน

Kradan is doted with slender, silky whitesand beaches, bathtub-warm shallows and limestone karst views. There are pristine hard and soft corals just off the south coast and a small but lush tangle of remnant jungle inland. Development is happening fast and while there are now many places to stay on Kradan, all except a select few are overpriced and lack soul.

For internet and boat tickets go to Kradan Beach Resort, the biggest spread of mediocre bungalows on the main beach.

🛏 Sleeping

Seven Seas Resort   HOTEL **$$$**
(☑08 2490 2442; www.sevenseasresorts.com; r 6600-7600B, bungalows 11,750-15,600B; ❋@☎❄) This small luxury resort has ultraslick rooms with enormous beds that could sleep four (if you're into that). Beach bums will adore this stretch of sand where cotton hammocks link the curling mangroves. The breezy restaurant, hugging the jet-black infinity pool, serves a mix of Western dishes and excellent southern-style curries. Overall, it's a tad pricey, but the amazing staff more than make up for it.

Paradise Lost   GUEST HOUSE **$–$$**
(☑08 9587 2409; www.kokradan.wordpress.com; dm 250B. bungalows 900-1600B, with shared bathrooms 700B) One of the first places built on Kradan and still one of the best, this groovy, inland US-owned bungalow property has easy access to the island's more remote beaches. Small bamboo nests have solid wood floors and shared bathrooms. Larger bungalows are all wood and have private facilities, and dorms are on an open verandah. The guest house's kitchen (dishes 120B to 1800B) is the best on the island.

ℹ Getting There & Away

Daily **BOATS** to Kuantungku leave at 9am and noon; tickets include the connecting minibus to Trang (450B). A chartered long-tail from Kuantungku will cost around 800B one-way (45 minutes to one hour); you can also charter boats from Kradan to other islands within the archipelago.

Tigerline (☏08 1092 8800; www.tigerline travel.com) connects Kradan with Ko Lanta (750B, 1½ hours) and Hat Yao (750B, one hour). **Patpailin Ferry** goes to Ko Muk and Ko Ngai (both 500B) then continues on to Ko Lanta.

KO LIBONG   เกาะลิบง

Thais believe that if you wear the tears of the dugong as perfume, you'll attract your soul mate. Perhaps this is why Trang's largest island, while lessvisited than its neighbours, receives a subset of offbeat tourists, as Ko Libong is known for its fertile beds of sea grass (the rare dugong's habitat) more than its beaches. The island is home to a small Muslim fishing community and has a few resorts on the isolated western coast.

On the eastern coast of Ko Libong at **Laem Ju Hoi** is a large area of mangroves protected by the Thai Botanical Department as the **Libong Archipelago Wildlife Reserve** (☏0 7525 1932). The grass-filled sea channels here are one of the dugong's last habitats in Thailand, and around 40 of them graze on the sea grass that flourishes in the bay. The nature resorts in Hat Yao (p679) and on Ko Libong (the reserve is not far from the Libong Beach Resort) offer dugong-spotting tours by sea kayak, led by trained naturalists, for around 1000B. Sea kayaks can also be rented at most resorts for 200B per hour.

🛏 Sleeping

Libong Beach Resort   HOTEL **$**
(☏0 7522 5205; www.libongbeachresort.com; bungalows 500-800B; ✳@) This is the only place on the island that's open year-round – rates drop considerably in the low season. There are several options from bland slap-up shacks behind a murky stream to beachfront – and very comfortable – varnished wood-and-thatch chalets. The resort offers a slew of trips, motorbike rental (300B) and internet access (per hour 100B). There's also a dive centre (two dives 3500B) open during the high season.

ℹ Getting There & Away

Long-tail boats to Ban Ma Phrao on the east coast of Ko Libong leave regularly from Hat Yao (20 minutes) during daylight hours for 50B per person; the long-tail jetty at Hat Yao is just west of the newer Yao pier. On Ko Libong, motorcycle taxis run across to the resorts on the west coast for 100B. A chartered long-tail directly to the resorts will cost 800B each way.

KO LAO LIANG   เกาะเหลาเลียง

Ko Lao Liang is actually two islands right next to each other: Ko Laoliang Nong, the smaller of the two where the only resort is found, and the larger Ko Laoliang Pi, where there's a small fishermen's settlement. The islands are stunning, vertical karst formations with small white-sand beaches, clear water and plenty of coral close to shore.

The only place to stay is **Laoliang Island Resort** (☏08 4304 4077; www.laoliangresort.com; per person 1500B), which is rock-climbing-orientated. Lodging here is in comfy tents equipped with mattresses and fans and there are plenty of activities on offer, including snorkelling, climbing and sea kayaking. At night there's a small bar and the restaurant fires up its seafood barbecue regularly – it's like summer camp for grown-ups (although kids are happy here too). Rates include all meals, snorkel gear and sea kayaks.

Tigerline (☏08 1092 8800; www.tigerlinetrav el.com) stops just off Ko Lao Liang between Ko Lanta (1400B, 2½ hours) and Ko Lipe (750B, 2½ hours).

KO SUKORN   เกาะสุกร

Sukorn is a cultural paradise of tawny beaches, light-green sea, black-rock headlands and stilted shack neighbourhoods that are home to about 2800 Muslim fisherfolk – their rice fields, watermelon plots and rubber plantations unfurl on narrow concrete roads. Cycle past fields occupied only by water buffalo, through pastel villages where folk are genuinely happy to see you, and sleep soundly through deep, black nights. Sukorn's simple stillness is breathtaking, its authenticity a tonic to the road-weary soul.

With few hills, stunning panoramas, lots of shade and plenty of opportunities to meet locals, renting a bike (150B) is the best way to see the island. Covering up is an absolute must when you leave the beach – be respectful of the locals.

🛏 Sleeping

TOP CHOICE **Sukorn Beach Bungalows**   HOTEL **$$**
(☏0 7520 7707, 08 1647 5550; www.sukorn-island -trang.com; bungalows 1000-2500B; ✳🛜) Easily the most professionally run place on this island, the concrete-and-wood bungalows

MU KO PHETRA MARINE NATIONAL PARK อุทยานแห่งชาติหมู่เกาะเภตรา

Often outshone by the Ko Tarutao Marine National Park next door, **Mu Ko Phetra Marine National Park** (☎0 7478 1582; adult/child 400/200B) is a stunning chain of small islands that includes Ko Khao Yai, Ko Lao Liang (p683), Ko Bulon Leh (see p685) and 19 other jungle-clad towers of limestone. The largest island here is **Ko Khao Yai**, which has several pristine beaches suitable for swimming, snorkelling and camping, and a rock formation resembling a Gothic castle.

The park headquarters, east of Pak Bara, has a small visitors centre and an over-the-water restaurant, plus a nature trail through the forest. **Accommodation** (r 600N, 3-9-person bungalows 800-1500B) is available, and with permission, camping is possible on many of the uninhabited islands in the park. Park fees only apply if you visit the islands offshore.

all have comfy verandahs and a long swimming beach out the front from which you can watch the sun set over outlying islands. The friendly Dutch and Thai owners are chock-full of information, arrange excellent island-hopping tours, and offer guided tours of Sukorn (per person 350B). Oh, and the food (mains 180 to 300B) is the best in the Trang Islands.

Sukorn Cabana　　　　　　　HOTEL $$
(☎08 9724 2326; www.sukorncabana.com; bungalows 800-1300B; ❄@) Sloping landscaped grounds dotted with papaya, frangipani and bougainvillea hold large and clean bungalows with thatched roofs, varnished-wood interiors and plush verandahs. The gorgeous beach has stunning views over Ko Phetra.

❶ Getting There & Away

The easiest way to get to Sukorn is by private transfer from Trang available through the resorts for 1750B per person. The cheapest way is to take a *sǒrng·tǎa·ou* from Trang to Yan Ta Khao (40 minutes, 60B) then transfer to Ban Ta Seh (45 minutes, 40B) where long-tails (50B) leave from the pier when full.

Otherwise book a private taxi or *sǒrng·tǎa·ou* from Trang to Ban Ta Seh (800B), where you can charter a long-tail to Ban Saimai (200B), the main village on Ko Sukorn. The resorts are a 20-minute walk or 50B motorcycle taxi ride from Ban Saimai. You can also charter long-tails directly to the beach resorts (750B).

From Ko Sukorn you can charter long-tails to Ko Lao Liang (1750B) – where you can meet the high-speed **Tigerline** (☎08 1092 8800; www.tigerlinetravel.com) ferry that connects Lanta with Lipe and serves all islands in between – including Ko Kradan, Ko Ngai or Ko Muk (1400B).

SATUN PROVINCE

Until recently, Satun was mostly overlooked, but that's all changed thanks to the dynamic white sands of Ko Lipe – a one-time backpacker secret turned mainstream beach getaway. Beyond Ko Lipe the province still hardly rates a blink of the eye as visitors rush north to Ko Lanta or south to Pulau Langkawi, Malaysia. This means, of course, that they miss the untrammelled beaches and sea caves on Ko Tarutao, the rugged trails and ribbon waterfalls of Ko Adang and the rustic beauty of Ko Bulon Leh.

Pak Bara ปากบารา

The small fishing community of Pak Bara is the main jumping-off point for the islands in the Ko Phetra and Ko Tarutao Marine National Park. The peaceful town has some decent sleeping options and great seafood, but unless you arrive after the boats have gone there's no pressing reason to stick around.

The main road from La-Ngu terminates at the pier where there are several travel agencies, internet cafes, cheap restaurants and shops selling beach gear. There's a huge new **visitors centre** (☎0 7478 3485) for Ko Tarutao Marine National Park just back from the pier (under construction when we passed), where you can book accommodation and obtain permission for camping. Travel agencies here can arrange tours to the islands in the national park.

Travellers planning to visit the quieter islands of the Ko Tarutao National Park should stop by the **park headquarters** (☎0 7478 3485) just behind the pier, where you can book accommodation and obtain permission for camping. Travel agencies at the pier will gladly sell you a ticket to wherever you want to go, and many of these businesses also offer kayaking and snorkelling day trips (from 1500B).

If you get stuck in town, there are a couple of places to stay, including **Best House Resort** (☑0 7578 3058; bungalows 600B; ☒), which is the closest to the pier. If you're waiting for a speedboat to one of the islands, there are a few Muslim restaurants huddling around the pier – the best one is next to Andrew Tour. There's one ATM next to Adang Seatours on the main drag.

ⓘ Getting There & Away

There are hourly buses between 7am and 4pm from Hat Yai to the pier at Pak Bara (90B, 2½ hours). Coming from Satun, you can take an ordinary bus towards Trang and get off at La-Ngu (60B, 30 minutes), continuing by *sŏrng·tăa·ou* to Pak Bara (20B, 15 minutes).

Air-conditioned minivans leave hourly for Hat Yai (150B, two hours) from travel agencies near Pak Bara pier. There are also minivans to Trang (200B, 1½ hours), which connect to numerous destinations such as Krabi (450B, four hours) and Phuket (650B, six hours).

From 21 October to the end of May there are several speedboats to Ao Pante Malacca on Ko Tarutao and on to Ko Lipe. Boats depart from Pak Bara at 10am, 11am and 12.30pm (return 1200B, 1½ hours); in the reverse direction boats leave from Ko Lipe at 9.30am, 10am, 12.30pm and 1.30pm. From 16 November these boats also stop at Ko Adang for the same price. For Ko Bulon Leh, boats depart at 12.30pm, arriving in Ko Bulon Leh one hour later (return 800B), before buzzing on to Ko Lipe. If you miss the Bulon boat, you can easily charter a long-tail from local fishermen (1500B to 2000B, 1½ hours). During the wet season, services to Ko Lipe are dependent on the weather and demand, but are usually cut back to three times per week.

Ko Bulon Leh   เกาะบุโหลนเล

Floating in the sea between the Trang Islands and Ko Tarutao Marine Park, Ko Bulon Leh (also called Bulon) is surrounded by crystal-clear waters that mingle with its powder-soft beaches. The island is in that perfect state of limbo where it's developed enough to offer comfortable facilities, yet not so popular that you have to fight for your own patch of sand.

The exceptional **beach** extends along the east coast from Bulone resort, and around the northeast cape. Bulon's wild coastal beauty is accessible amid coral-gravel–laden

blue **Ao Panka Yai** on the southern coast. There's good snorkelling around the western headland, and if you follow the trails through remnant jungle and rubber plantations you'll wind your way to **Ao Muang** (Mango Bay), where you'll find a *chow lair* squid-fishing camp. **Ao Panka Noi**, accessible form the path leading down from Viewpoint Resort, is another fishing village with long-tails docking on a fine gravel beach. Here you'll find beautiful karst views and a clutch of simple restaurants.

Bulone Resort also offers internet (per minute 3B), and battery-charging services for laptops (50B) and digital cameras (10B).

🍴 Sleeping & Eating

Most places here shut down in the rainy season (May to October). There are a few local restaurants and a small shop in the Muslim village next to Bulon Viewpoint.

Marina Resort   HOTEL **$**
(☑08 1598 2420, 08 5078 1552; bungalows 500-1000B) Log-built and shaggy with stilted decks, louvred floors and high ceilings, thatched huts never looked or felt so good. There's a kitchen serving tasty food attached to an inviting patio restaurant with cushioned floor seating.

Bulone Resort   HOTEL **$$**
(☑08 6960 0468; www.bulone-resort.com; bungalows 1250-1650B) Perched on the northeast cape with access to two exquisite stretches of white sand, these cute wooden bungalows have the best beachside location on Bulon. Queen-sized beds come with iron frames and ocean breezes.

Chaolae Homestay   GUEST HOUSE **$**
(bungalows 300B) Fantastic-value classy bungalows have varnished wood interiors, thatched roofs and polished cement bathrooms (with squat toilets). It's blissfully quiet, run by a lovely *chow lair* family and is steps away from decent snorkelling at Ao Panka Yai.

ⓘ Getting There & Away

The boat to Ko Bulon Leh (400B) leaves from Pak Bara at 12.30pm daily if there are enough takers. Ship-to-shore transfers to the beach by long-tail cost 50B – save yourself from sweat and ask to get dropped off on the beach closest to your resort. In the reverse direction, the boat moors in the bay in front of Pansand Resort at around 9am. You can charter a long-tail from Pak Bara for 1500B to 2000B.

From November to May there are two daily speedboats (600B, one hour) from Ko Bulon Leh to Ko Lipe in Ko Tarutao Marine National Park. Boats, which originate in Ko Lanta and make stops in the Trang Islands, depart from in front of the Pansand resort at 1pm and 3pm.

Ko Tarutao Marine National Park อุทยานแห่งชาติหมู่เกาะตะรุเตา

Like with any good secret, it's only a matter of time before someone lets the cat out of the bag. In this case, that someone was a producer from *Survivor,* America's eminent reality show, who chose this stunning marine park for the fifth instalment of the hit series. Fortunately, stringent Thai law has protected **Ko Tarutao Marine National Park** (☎0 7478 1285; adult/child 400/200B; ☻Nov–mid-May) from preying developers – the marine national park is still one of the most exquisite and unspoiled regions in Thailand.

The massive archipelago features myriad coral reefs, and 51 islands covered with well-preserved virgin rainforest teeming with dusky langurs, crab-eating macaques, mouse deer, wild pigs, sea otters, fishing cats, water monitors, tree pythons, hornbills and kingfishers.

The park officially closes in the low season (May to October), when virtually all boats stop running.

KO TARUTAO เกาะตะรุเตา

Most of Ko Tarutao's whopping 152 sq km is covered in dense, old-growth jungle that rises sharply up to the park's 713m peak. Mangrove swamps and impressive limestone cliffs circle much of the island, and the western coast is lined with quiet white-sand beaches.

Tarutao has a sordid history that partly explains its great state of preservation today. Between 1938 and 1948, more than 3000 Thai criminals and political prisoners were incarcerated here, including interesting inmates such as So Setabutra, who compiled the first Thai-English dictionary while imprisoned on the island. During WWII food supplies were severely depleted and hundreds of prisoners died from malaria. The prisoners and guards mutinied, taking to piracy in the nearby Strait of Malacca until they were suppressed by British troops in 1944.

There's internet (80B per hour) and wi-fi (50B per hour) at the Ao Pante Malacca Information Centre.

⊙ Sights & Activities

The overgrown ruins of the camp for political prisoners can be seen at **Ao Taloh Udang**, in the southeast of the island, reached via a long overgrown track. The prison camp for civilian prisoners was over on the eastern coast at **Ao Taloh Waw**, where the big boats from Satun's Tammalang pier now dock.

Next to the park headquarters at Ao Pante Malacca, a steep trail leads through the jungle to **Toe-Boo Cliff**, a dramatic rocky outcrop with fabulous views towards Ko Adang and the surrounding islands.

Ao Pante Malacca has a lovely alabaster beach shaded by pandanus and casuarinas. If you follow the large stream flowing inland through here, you'll reach **Tham Jara-Khe** (Crocodile Cave), once home to deadly saltwater crocodiles. The cave is navigable for about 1km at low tide and can be visited on long-tail tours from the jetty at Ao Pante Malacca.

Immediately south of Ao Pante Malacca is **Ao Jak**, which has another fine sandy beach; and **Ao Molae**, which also has fine white sand and a ranger station with bungalows and a camp site. A 30-minute boat ride or 8km walk south of Ao Pante is **Ao Son**, an isolated sandy bay where turtles nest between September and April. You can camp here but there are no facilities. Ao Son has decent snorkelling, as does **Ao Makham**, further south. From the small ranger station at Ao Son you can walk inland to **Lu Du Falls** (about 1½ hours) and **Lo Po Falls** (about 2½ hours).

⊨ Sleeping & Eating

There's accommodation both at Ao Pante Malacca and Ao Molae open mid-November to mid-May. The biggest spread of options is at Ao Pante Malacca, conveniently near all the facilities, where there are **bungalows** (800-1000B), simple **longhouse rooms** (550B) with shared bathrooms sleeping up to four people, and **camp sites** (with/without tent rental 375/150B). Ao Molae is more quiet and isolated – and arguably prettier. Rather swanky one- and two-room **duplexes** (r 600-1000B) are right on the beach. Accommodation can be booked at the **park office** (☎0 7478 3485) in Pak Bara.

Camping (sites with/without tent rental 255/ 30B) is permitted under casuarinas at Ao Molae and Ao Taloh Waw, where there are toilet and shower blocks, and on the wild beaches of Ao Son, Ao Makham and Ao Taloh Udang, where you will need to be self-sufficient. Note that local monkeys have a habit of going into tents and destroying or eating everything they find inside – so shut everything tight.

There are **canteens** (dishes 40-120B; ⏰7am-2pm & 5-9pm) at Ao Pante Malacca and Ao Molae. The food is satisfying and tasty but you can only find beer at Ao Molae.

❶ Getting There & Around

Boats connecting Pak Bara and Ko Lipe stop at Ko Tarutao along the way; see p685 for detailed information.

With a navigable river and long paved roads, the island lends itself well to self-propulsion: hire a kayak (per hour/day 100B/300B) or mountain bike (50/200B) – or if it's just too damned hot, charter a vehicle (per day 600B). Long-tails can be hired for trips to Ao Taloh Udang (2000B), Ao Taloh Wow (1500B), and Tham Jara-Khe or Ao Son for around 800B each.

If you're staying at Ao Molae, take a park car (per person 60B) from the jetty at Ao Pante Malacca.

KO LIPE

เกาะหลีเป๊ะ

Ko Lipe is this decade's poster child for untamed development in the Thai Islands. Blessed with two wide white-sand beaches separated by jungled hills, and within spitting distance of protected coral reefs, a few years ago the island was only spoken about in secretive whispers. But then the whispers became small talk, which quickly turned into a roar – you know, the kind generally associated with bulldozers. The biggest losers in all this have been the 700-strong community of *chow lair* villagers who sold land to a Thai developer.

Yet, given this upheaval, there's still plenty to love about Lipe. The gorgeous white-sand crescent of Hat Pattaya on the southern coast has some terrific beach bars, seafood and a party vibe during the high season.

KO LIPE'S METAMORPHOSIS *ADAM SKOLNICK*

Ko Lipe began to change in earnest around 2005 when the sandy cross-island trail was smothered in concrete. However, the seeds of change were planted more than a decade earlier when a Phi-Phi developer named Ko Kyiet approached local *chow lair* (sea gypsy) families about their ancestral land. Although deals were struck, they were never completed. Enter Ko Pi Tong, a Satun native who, according to Kun Pooh of Pooh's Bar and Pooh's Bungalows – a long-time local and one of Lipe's tourism leaders – made his money on the ecologically dubious and lucrative enterprise of collecting swifts' nests.

'Pi Tong is like Robin Hood', said Pooh. 'He paid what Kyiet owed the locals plus interest.' Indeed, Tong went back to the *chow lair* families, most of who didn't have proper documentation for their land, and offered them lump sums of cash. They accepted, which means that technically this was all legal and that they participated in their own plight, but it isn't quite that simple.

When Kyiet negotiated the initial deals, he allowed the *chow lair* to keep a slice of their ancestral land. But Tong bought almost everything. Kun Pan, an elder, who lives in the new cordoned-off *chow lair* village on the hillside above Sunset Beach, explained the situation.

'Before, we had the whole island, we all lived on the beach', said Pan, a silver-haired fishermen with deep lines worn into his leathery brow. 'My brother and I, we not want to sell. The police come and take us to Satun. They said we had no land rights.'

Pooh disputes Pan's claim. He suggests the seaman is confused because 'Tong let [local people] live on the land he bought from them for years'. Tong evicted them relatively recently.

According to Pooh, Tong is now selling the land for many times the purchase price. Clearly, Tong has brought commerce, jobs, infrastructure and wealth into what once was a southern Thai backwater. Plus, some *chow lair* families held out, kept their land and launched successful businesses, such as Daya Resort, on their own – a fact that seems to contradict Pan's story. Still, it's hard not to notice that the vast majority of *chow lair* appear left out of the recent prosperity.

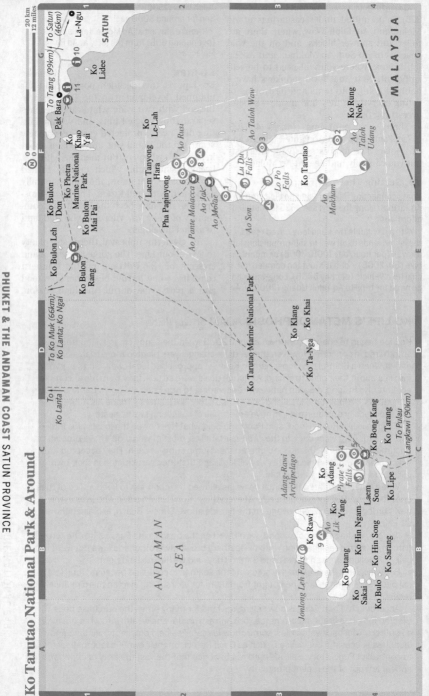

Ko Tarutao National Park & Around

20 km
12 miles

MALAYSIA

SATUN

La-Ngu
To Satun (46km)
To Trang (99km)

Ko Lidee

Pak Bara
To Trang (99km)

Ko Bulon Don

Ko Phetra Marine National Park

Ko Bulon Mai Pai

Ko Bulon Leh

Ko Bulon Rang

To Ko Muk (66km);
Ko Lanta; Ko Ngai

To Lanta
Ko Lanta

A N D A M A N   S E A

Jonlong Leh Falls

Ko Rawi

Ao Lik Ko Yang

Ko Hin Ngam

Ko Butang

Ko Sakai

Ko Bulo

Ko Hin Song

Ko Sarang

Adang-Rawi Archipelago

Ko Adang

Pirate's Falls

Laem Son

Ko Lipe

Ko Bong Kang

Ko Tarang

To Pulau Langkawi (90km)

Ko Klang

Ko Ta-Nga   Ko Khai

Ko Tarutao Marine National Park

Laem Tanyong Hara

Pha Papinyong

Ao Punte Malacca

Ao Jak

Ao Motae

Ao Son

Ao Rusi

Ko Le-Lah

Ao Taloh Waw

Lu Du Falls

Lo Po Falls

Ao Makham

Ko Tarutao

Ao Taloh Udang

Ko Rung Nok

MALAYSIA

Khao Yai

Ko Tarutao National Park

Windswept **Sunrise Beach**, another sublime long stretch of sand, juts to the north where you'll have spectacular Ko Adang views. A drawback of both of the busy beaches is the preponderance of long-tails that crowd out swimmers. **Sunset Beach**, with its golden sand, gentle jungled hills and serene bay that spills into the Adang Strait, has an altogether different feel and retains Lipe's wild soul. In between there's an ever-expanding concrete maze of cafes, travel agencies, shops and salons, but with more resorts opting to stay open year-round.

There are no banks or ATMs on the island, though several of the bigger resorts can change travellers cheques, cash or give advances on credit cards – all for a hefty fee. Internet is available along the cross-island path for 3B per minute and a few places behind Sunrise Beach charge 2B per minute.

🏃 Activities

There's good coral all along the southern coast and around **Ko Kra**, the little island opposite Sunrise Beach. Most resorts rent out mask and snorkel sets and fins for 50B each, and can arrange four-point long-tail snorkel trips to Ko Adang and other coral-fringed islands for around 1500B. The best way to see the archipelago is to hire a local *chow lair* captain. **Islander Sea Sports** (☏08 7294 9770; per hr/day 100/600B) rents brand-new kayaks on Hat Pattaya.

Divers with a Lipe bias will tell you that there are dozens of sites in the area. What they won't tell you is that the visibility can be pretty hit-and-miss – sometimes the water is crystal-clear, at other times hard currents drag in clouds of sand. Nevertheless, Ko Lipe is a chilled-out place to do some scuba – there aren't zillions of divers (like on Phuket or Ko Tao) and the reefs are comparatively unharmed. The region's top dive spots include **Eight Mile Rock**, a submerged pinnacle that lures large pelagic fish; the **Yong Hua Shipwreck**, now covered in marine growth; and **Ko Bu Tang**, with its aptly named Stingray City site. There are also pleasant diving spots dotting the channel between Ko Adang and Ko Rawi.

Most diving schools run trips from early November to mid-May and charge around 2700B for a two-dive excursion. A PADI Open Water course will set you back around 12,800B.

The following dive operators are recommended, and use proper boats rather than long-tails:

Forra Diving   DIVING
(☏08 4407 5691; www.forradiving.com) Friendly French-run school with an office on both Sunrise and Pattaya Beaches.

Ocean Pro   DIVING
(☏08 9733 8068; www.oceanprodivers.net) Professional and knowledgeable staff run a seamless operation.

🛏 Sleeping

Most, but not all, resorts on Ko Lipe close from May to October, when the boats don't run as frequently.

Ko Lipe

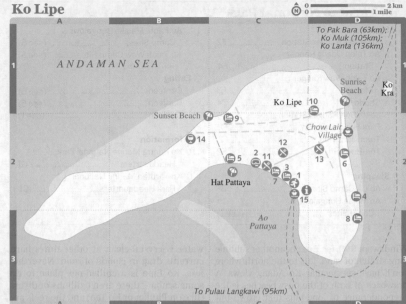

ANDAMAN SEA

To Pak Bara (63km);
Ko Muk (105km);
Ko Lanta (136km)

Sunrise Beach
Ko Kra
Ko Lipe 10
Sunset Beach 9
14
Chow Lair Village
12
2 11 13
5 3 6
7 1
Hat Pattaya 15
4
8
Ao Pattaya

To Pulau Langkawi (95km)

Ko Lipe

Activities, Courses & Tours
Forra Diving ....(see 7)
Forra Diving ....(see 6)
1 Islander Sea Sports C2
2 Ocean Pro C2

Sleeping
3 Blue Tribes C2
4 Castaway Resort D2
5 Daya Resort C2
6 Forra Dive D2
7 Forra Dive2 .... C2
8 Idyllic Resort D3
9 Porn Resort C2
10 South Sea D1

Eating
11 Nong Bank Restaurant C2
12 Pee Pee Bakery C2
13 Pooh's Bar D2

Drinking
14 Mia Luna B2

Information
15 Bundhaya Resort C2
Immigration Office ....(see 15)

Transport
Speedboat Departure Office ....(see 15)

TOP CHOICE Castaway Resort HOTEL $$$
(☎08 3138 7472; www.castaway-resorts.com;
Sunrise Beach; bungalows 3500-5000B; @☎)
The roomy wood bungalows with hammock-
laden terraces, cushions everywhere, over-
head fans and fabulous, modern-meets-
naturalistic bathrooms are the most chic on
Lipe. It's also one of the most environmental-
ly friendly – with solar hot water and lights.

TOP CHOICE Daya Resort HOTEL $
(☎0 7472 8030; Hat Pattaya; bungalows 500-
1000B) One of the few places that's still lo-
cally run, the striped bungalows here are
your standard slap-up wooden affairs but
the beach is fantastic, the flowery back gar-
den charming, and the restaurant has the
absolute best and cheapest seafood grill on
the island...and that's saying something.

Idyllic Resort
HOTEL $$$

(☎08 1802 5453; www.idyllicresort.com; Sunrise Beach; bungalows 6300-15,000B; ✳@🛜🛁) High design has arrived on Lipe. With slanted roofs, concrete-and-glass walls, flat-screen TVs, a shingled exterior and floating decks out the front, the digs are more like futuristic pods than beach bungalows.

Blue Tribes
HOTEL $$

(☎08 6285 2153; www.bluetribeslipe.com; Hat Pattaya; bungalows 1200-1700B; ✳@) One of Pattaya's more attractive small resorts, its best nests are the two-storey thatched wooden bungalows with downstairs living rooms and top-floor bedrooms that have sliding doors opening to sea views.

Forra Dive
HOTEL $$

(☎08 0545 5012; www.forradiving.com; Sunrise Beach; bungalows 800-1000B) Announced by 17 flags that whip in the eastward breeze, this place captures the look of Lipe's pirate spirit with a range of bamboo bungalows and lofts. The best are large with indoor-outdoor bathrooms and hammock-strung terraces. Divers get 25% off lodging and there's a second location, Forra Dive 2, with similar bungalows on Hat Pattaya.

South Sea
GUEST HOUSE $

(☎08 0544 0063, 08 1678 9903; Sunset Beach; bungalows 350B) Inland from Sunset beach, this sunny flower-and-shell-mobile-filled compound has tiny bamboo huts with small sleeping mats and attached semioutdoor Thai-style bathrooms.

Porn Resort
HOTEL $

(☎08 9464 5765; Sunset Beach; bungalows 500-750B) This collection of weathered bungalows with hard beds is the only resort on imperfect yet golden and swimmable Sunset Beach. It's rustic but the best deal on Lipe for a terrace on private beachfront.

✖ Eating & Drinking

Hat Pattaya's resorts put on nightly fresh seafood barbeques and Daya's (see earlier) is arguably the best. Cheap eats are best found at the roti stands and small Thai cafes along Walking Street.

For drinking, driftwood-clad Rasta bars are found on all beaches. At least some things never change.

Nong Bank Restaurant
RESTAURANT $$

(Hat Pattaya; dishes 80-120B; ⊙breakfast, lunch & dinner) This place serves point-and-grill seafood and a superb yellow curry with crab (120B), with a half-dozen tables scattered beneath a tree on the white sand.

Pooh's Bar
RESTAURANT, BAR $

(☎0 7472 8019; www.poohlipe.com) This massive complex was built by a Lipe pioneer and includes bungalows, a dive shop and several restaurants. It's a very popular local expat hang-out, especially in the low season. Each night it projects films onto its big screen.

Pee Pee Bakery
BAKERY $

(Hat Pattaya; dishes from 80B; ⊙breakfast, lunch & dinner) The best breakfasts on Lipe include homemade breads and pastries and great people-watching as you dine. A full American set costs 240B.

Mia Luna
BAR

(Hat Pattaya) This is a pirate bar of hanging painted bouys, driftwood seating and hammocks. It's isolated on its own nugget of white sand near Bila Beach and a short walk over the hill from Hat Pattaya.

❶ Getting There & Away

From 21 October through the end of May, several speedboats run from Pak Bara (see p684) to Ko Lipe via Ko Tarutao or Ko Bulon Leh at 9.30am, 11am, 12.30pm and 2pm (550B to 650B, 1½ hours); in the reverse direction boats leave at 9.30am, 10am, 12.30pm and 1.30pm. Low-season transport depends on the weather but there are usually three direct boats per week. A boat charter to Ko Lipe from Pak Bara is a hefty 4000B each way.

Tigerline (☎08 1092 8800; www.tigerline travel.com) offers the cheapest high-speed ferry service to Ko Lanta (1500B, 5½ hours), stopping at Ko Muk (1400B, 3½ hours), Ko Kradan (1400B, four hours) and Ko Ngai (1400B, 4½ hours). It departs from Ko Lipe's Pattaya Beach at 9.30am.

> ### BORDER CROSSING: KO LIPE TO PULAU LANGKAWI
>
> Both of Ko Lipe's speedboat companies also offer daily trips to Pulau Langkawi (1200B, one hour) in Malaysia; departure is at 7.30am, 10.30am and 4pm. Be at the immigration office at the Bundhaya Resort early to get stamped out. In reverse, boats leave from Pulau Langkawi for Ko Lipe at 7.30am, 9.30am and 2.30pm Malay time.

PHUKET & THE ANDAMAN COAST KO TARUTAO MARINE NATIONAL PARK

Satun-Pak Bara Speedboat Club (☏0 7475 0389, 08 2433 0114; www.tarutaolipe island. com) has a daily, more comfortable speedboat that departs from Ko Lipe for Ko Lanta (1900B, three hours) at 9am also stopping at Ko Bulon Leh (600B, one hour), Ko Muk (1400B, two hours) and Ko Ngai (1600B, 2½ hours). The same boat makes the return trip from Ko Lanta at 1pm.

No matter which boat you end up deciding to use, you will have to take a long-tail shuttle (per person 50B) to and from the floating pier at the edge of the bay.

Ko Adang & Ko Rawi
เกาะอาดัง/เกาะราวี

The island immediately north of Ko Lipe, **Ko Adang** has brooding, densely forested hills, white-sand beaches and healthy coral reefs. Lots of snorkelling tours make a stop here. Inland are a few short jungle trails and tumbling waterfalls, including the ramble up to **Pirate's Falls**, which is rumoured to have been a freshwater source for pirates. There are great views from **Chado Cliff**, above the main beach, where green turtles lay their eggs between September and December.

Ko Rawi, a long rocky, jungled ellipse 11km west of Ko Adang, has first-rate beaches and large coral reefs offshore. Camping at Ao Lik is allowed, with permission from the national-park authorities. Excellent snorkelling spots include the northern side of **Ko Yang** and tiny **Ko Hin Ngam**, which has underwater fields of giant clams, vibrant anemones and striped pebble beaches. A legend has it that the stones are cursed and anyone who takes one away will experience bad luck until the stone is returned to its source. Even a short stop on the island will cost you the park's entrance fee (adult/child 200/100B).

Park accommodation on Ko Adang is located near the ranger station at Laem Son. There are new and attractive **bungalows** (3-9 people 600-1800B), scruffier **longhouses** (3-bed r 300B) with attached bathrooms and facilities for **camping** (sites per person 30B, with tent hire 250B). A small canteen provides good Thai meals.

Long-tails from Ko Lipe will take you to Ko Adang and Ko Rawi for 50B per person, although you might have to do a little bargaining.

Satun
สตูล
POP 33,400

Lying in a steamy jungle valley surrounded by limestone cliffs, and framed by a murky river, isolated Satun is a relaxing coastal town where tourism is limited to visa-run traffic, which flows in both directions.

⊙ Sights

The **Ku Den Museum** (Satun National Museum; Soi 5, Th Satun Thanee; admission 20B; ◷8.30am-4.30pm Wed-Sun), housed in a lovely old Sino-Portuguese mansion, is an excellent museum that was constructed to house King Rama V during a royal visit. When the king failed to show up, the governor snagged the roost. The building has been lovingly restored and the exhibits feature dioramas with soundtracks covering every aspect of southern Muslim life.

⬛ Sleeping & Eating

Sinkiat Thani Hotel   HOTEL **$**
(☏0 7472 1055; www.sinkiathotel.thport.com; 50 Th Burivanich; r 680B; ❉@) This ageing tower is central, a bit run-down, but certainly clean enough. It has amazing city and jungle views through smudged windows on top floors. Plus it's right next to On's Restaurant.

On's   THAI, WESTERN **$**
(☏0 7473 0469, 08 1097 9783; 48 Th Burivanich; dishes 80-150B; ◷8am-late; @📶) With its bamboo, sarong-draped tables, leafy front porch and tasty Thai and Western dishes, this is

---

BORDER CROSSING: SATUN TO KUALA PERLIS OR PULAU LANGKAWI

Boats to Malaysia leave from Tammalang pier, 7km south of Satun. Large long-tail boats run at 9.30am and 4:30pm dily to Kuala Perlis in Malaysia (300B one-way, one hour). From Malaysia the fare is M$30.

For Pulau Langkawi in Malaysia, boats leave from Tammalang pier at 9.30am, 1.30pm and 4pm daily (300B, 1½ hours). In the reverse direction, boats leave from Pulau Langkawi at 8.30am, 12.30pm and 3pm and cost M$27. Keep in mind that Malaysia is one hour ahead of Thai time.

Satun

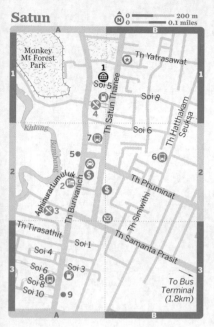

the place to hang in Satun (which explains the yachtie barflies).

Chinese and Muslim bites can be scouted on Th Burivanich and Th Samanta Prasit. Try the 'red pork' with rice at the Chinese food stalls or the southern-style roti offered at most Muslim restaurants (around 50B each). Satun's popular **night market** (off Th Satun Thanee) comes to life around 5pm and serves great Thai curries.

ℹ Getting There & Away

Boat

There's a high-season service to Ko Lipe that departs at 11.30am daily (650B, 1½ hours; December to May). Enquire about tickets at the pier, 7km south of town, or at On's (p692).

Bus

Buses leave from the **bus terminal** (Th Samanta Prasit), 2km east of the town centre. Air-conditioned services to Bangkok (800B to 1200B, 14 hours) leave at 7am, 7.30am, 3pm and 4pm. Air-conditioned buses to Trang (110B, 1½ hours) leave hourly. There are also a few daily buses to Krabi (220B, four hours) and Phuket (360B, seven hours). Buses to Hat Yai (70B, two hours) and local buses without air-con to Trang (90B, two hours) will stop and pick up passengers on Th Satun Thanee.

Minivan & Share Taxi

There are regular minivans to the train station in Hat Yai (80B, one hour) from a depot south of Wat Chanathipchaloem on Th Sulakanukoon. Occasional minivans run to Trang, but buses are much more frequent. If you're arriving by boat at Tammalang pier, there are direct air-con minivans to Hat Yai and Hat Yai airport (90B).

ℹ Getting Around

Small orange sŏrng·tăa·ou to Tammalang pier (for boats to Malaysia) cost 40B and leave from the 7-Eleven on Th Sulakanukoon 40 minutes before ferry departure. A motorcycle taxi from the same area costs 60B.

Understand Thailand

population per sq km

THAILAND USA UK

≈ 32 people

Thailand Today

Political Stability?

After a five-year period of political instability initiated by the 2006 coup d'état, Thailand has reached a political plateau with the 2011 general election. Ousted prime minister Thaksin Shinawatra's politically allied party, Puea Thai, won a clear majority of parliamentary seats, and his sister Yingluck Shinawatra, a political novice, was elected prime minister. She is Thailand's first female prime minister and this is the fifth straight electoral win for a Thaksin-backed political party. The people have clearly spoken and so far there has been no resistance from opposition groups or the military.

Prime minister Yingluck's first days in office set about fulfilling campaign promises, such as raising the national minimum wage to 300B per day (a 30% increase), extending symbolic olive branches to the monarchy and the military and pledging to work towards national reconciliation. Her appointments for the important cabinet-level positions of security and defence sidestepped hardliners in favour of two candidates who are believed to straddle the political/military divide.

The next question mark in Yingluck's administration is if or when she will issue a pardon for Thaksin to return from exile. Currently he is barred from politics until 2012 and is evading a two-year prison term. So far Thaksin has publicly stated that he has no plans to return to Thailand, though this statement was made from Japan where he appeared to be on a diplomatic appointment. During the campaign, Thaksin described his sister as his 'clone' and spoke of an indeterminate future when he would return to the country. According to an *Asia Time*'s article (August 25, 2011), the government was described by a source as operating like a family business with Yingluck as the figurehead and Thaksin as the CEO.

Thailand's political protestors are divided into red and yellow colour-coded camps and they swap anti-government positions depending on which group holds the prime minister's chair.

Do & Don'ts

» Do take off your shoes when entering a home or temple. Be careful where you put your feet (considered filthy in Thailand).

» Don't criticise the monarchy.

» Do smile: it puts Thais at ease.

» Don't argue or get visibly angry; you'll cause embarrassment.

» Stand respectfully for the national anthem (unless you're inside a home or building other than a theatre).

» Dress modestly (cover to the elbows and ankles) for visits to temples or buildings associated with the monarchy.

Top Films

Uncle Boonmee Who Can Recall His Past Lives (ApichatTop pong Weerasethakul; 2010) Winner of Cannes 2010 Palm d'Or.

Bangkok Traffic Love Story (Adisorn Tresirikasem; 2009) Romantic comedy with public-transit message.

belief systems
(% of population)

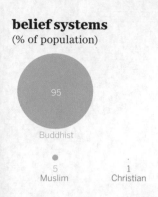

95
Buddhist

5
Muslim

1
Christian

if Thailand were 100 people

75 would be Thai
14 would be Chinese
11 would be Other

Regardless of the division of power, Thais in general seem fatigued from the previous years' political distress, which undermines a deep-seated sense of a unified 'Thai-ness' and a cultural aversion to displays of violence and anger. Bangkokians, especially, are exhausted by the hassles of traffic jams and road closures that accommodate the seemingly endless exercise of freedom of assembly.

During the height of the 2010 crisis, the Western press was intrigued by the apparent class divide that defined the two political sides: the proletariat (pro-Thaksin) Red Shirts and the aristocratic (anti-Thaksin) Yellow Shirts. But Thai intellectuals feel this is an over-simplification of the situation and that the lines aren't as clearly drawn. In the middle of the extremes are the uncolour coded Thais who have sympathies with both sides. They might agree with the Red Shirts on the grounds of restoring democracy and disapproving of the military's and the court's meddling in politics, but they are sceptical of the Red Shirts' unquestioning loyalty to Thaksin.

For the political troubles in Thailand's south, see the boxed text, p596.

» Population: 66.7 million

» GDP: $580.3 billion

» GDP per capita: US$8700

» Unemployment: 1.2%

» Education spending: 4.1% of GDP

The Ageing King

Thais don't often discuss the topic openly but many are worried about their beloved monarch, King Bhumibol Adulyadej (Rama IX). Now in his mid-80s, he is the world's longest-serving king and is respected, and virtually worshipped, by his subjects. But as the king's health has declined, his role in society has diminished. He has been hospitalised for nearly two years and his public appearances are so rare that they make laudatory coverage in Thai national news.

In King Bhumibol's more active years, he was viewed as a stabilising force in times of political crisis. But he has not exercised that role during

Top Books

Agrarian Utopia (Uruphong Raksasad; 2009) The daily rhythms and financial struggles of farmers in northern Thailand.
White Buffalo (Shinoret Khamwandee; 2011) A man returns to his Isan village to find that all the local ladies love Western men.

Very Thai (Philip Cornwell-Smith) Colourful photos and essays on Thailand's quirks.
Chronicle of Thailand (William Warren) History of the last 50 years.

the most recent political troubles, which are partly due to the impending power vacuum that will result after his passing and the power-consolidating efforts of then-prime minister Thaksin. Beginning in 2006, the anti-Thaksin faction adopted the colour yellow, which is the colour associated with the king's birthday, to signal their allegiance with the political interests of the monarchy.

Losing the king will be a national tragedy: he has ruled for more than 60 years and defined through his life what many regarded as the modern Thai man (educated, family-oriented, philanthropic and even stylish). The heir apparent, his son the Crown Prince Vajiralongkorn, has assumed many of the royal duties his father previously performed but the ongoing political problems complicate a smooth transfer of crown from father to son.

Teflon Economy

From an economic perspective, you'd never know that Thailand is so politically divided. The former Asian tiger economy has moved into the new millennium as a Teflon economy: misfortune doesn't seem to stick. Outside forces – the global recession, a weakening US dollar – had some negative effects on the economy. In 2008 to 2009, manufacturing and exports, which constitute about half of GDP, took a dip but rebounded a year later with a growth rate that rivalled the boom times of the mid-1990s. With or without democracy, investors remain confident in the country, and tourism continues to grow despite the bloody Bangkok clashes in 2010. High growth is expected for 2011, meaning that unemployment remains relatively low and that Thais continue to experience stable and increasing standards of living. Modernisation marches on.

Thais who want to show that they love the king but don't want to claim a political identity now wear pink shirts as a neutral colour. On his most recent public appearance, the king himself also wore a pink shirt.

History & Politics

History

Thai history begins as a story of migrants heading into a frontier land claimed by distant empires for trade, forced labour and patronage. Eventually the nascent country develops its own powerful entities that unite feuding localities and begins to fuse a national identity around language, religion and monarchy. The kings resist colonisation from the expansionist Western powers on its border only to cede their absolute grip on the country when challenged from forces within. Since the transition to a constitutional monarchy in 1932, the military predominately rules the country with a few democratic hiccups in between.

Ancient History

Little evidence remains of the cultures that existed in Thailand before the middle of the 1st millennium AD. *Homo erectus* fossils in Thailand's northern province of Lampang date back at least 500,000 years, and the country's most important archaeological site is Ban Chiang, outside of Udon Thani, which provides evidence of one of the world's oldest agrarian societies. It is believed that Mekong River Valley and Khorat Plateau were inhabited as far back as 10,000 years ago by farmers and bronze-workers. Cave paintings in Pha Taem National Park near Ubon Ratchathani date back some 3000 years.

Early Empires

Starting in the 1st millennium, the 'Tai' people, considered to be the ancestors of the contemporary Thais, began migrating in waves from southern China into present-day Southeast Asia. These immigrants spoke Tai-Kadai, said to be the most significant ethno-linguistic group in Southeast Asia. Some settled in the river valleys of modern-day Thailand while others chose parts of modern-day Laos and the Shan state of Myanmar.

TIMELINE	4000–2500 BC	6th–11th centuries	9–13th centuries
	Prehistoric people develop pottery, rice cultivation and bronze metallurgy in northeastern Thailand.	Dvaravati establish city-states in central Thailand.	Angkor extends control across parts of Thailand.

They settled in villages as farmers, hunters and traders and organised themselves into administrative units known as *meu·ang,* under the rule of a lord, that became the building block of the Tai state. Over time, the Tai expanded from the northern mountain valleys into the central plains and northeastern plateau, where there existed several important trading centres ruled by various indigenous and 'foreign' empires, including the Mon-Dvaravati, Khmer (Cambodia) and Srivijaya (Malay).

Relief carvings at Angkor Wat depict Tai mercenaries serving in Khmer armies. The Khmer called them 'Syam'. The name was transliterated to 'Siam' by the English trader James Lancaster in 1592.

Dvaravati

The Mon dominated parts of Burma, western Thailand and into the central plains. In the 6th to 9th centuries, the Dvaravati culture emerged as a distinct Buddhist culture associated with the Mon people. Little is known about this period but it is believed that Nakhon Pathom might have been the centre, and that overland trade routes and trading outposts extended west to Burma, east to Cambodia, north to Chiang Mai and Laos, and towards the northeast, as evidenced by findings of distinctive Dvaravati Buddha images, temples and stone inscriptions in Mon language.

The Dvaravati was one of many Indian-influenced cultures that established themselves in Southeast Asia, but scholars single out the Dvaravati because of its artistic legacy and the trade routes that might have provided an early framework for what would become the core of the modern-day Thai state.

Khmer

While the Dvaravati are an historical mystery, the Khmers were Southeast Asia's equivalent of the Roman Empire. This kingdom became famous for its extravagant sculpture and architecture and had a profound effect on the art and religion of the region. Established in the 9th century, the Khmer kingdom built its capital in Angkor (modern-day Cambodia) and expanded westward across present-day central and northeastern Thailand. Administrative centres anchored by Angkor-style temples were built in Lopburi (then known as Lavo), Sukhothai and Phimai (near Nakhon Ratchasima) and linked by road to the capital.

The Khmer's large-scale construction projects were a symbol of imperial power in its frontier and examples of the day's most advanced technologies. Khmer elements – Hinduism, Brahmanism, Theravada Buddhism and Mahayana Buddhism – mark this period in Thailand.

Srivijaya

While mainland Thailand was influenced by forces from the north and west, the Malay peninsula was economically and culturally fused to cultures further south. Between the 8th and 13th centuries, the Malay penin-

10th century

Arrival of Tai peoples in Thailand.

1240–1438

Approximate dates of Sukhothai kingdom.

» Ruins at Sukhothai Historical Park

sula was under the sway of the confederation of the Srivijaya which controlled maritime trade between the South China Sea and Indian Ocean. The Srivijaya capital is believed to have been in Palembang on Sumatra.

Of the series of Srivijaya city-states that grew to prominence along the Malay peninsula, Tambralinga established its capital near present-day Nakhon Si Thammarat and adopted Buddhism in the 13th century, while the states further south fell under the influence of Islam, creating a religious boundary which persists to this day. Remains of Srivijaya culture can be seen around Chaiya and Nakhon Si Thammarat. Many art forms of the Srivijaya kingdom, such as *năng đà·lung* (shadow play) and *lá·kon* (classical dance-drama), remain today.

Emerging Tai Kingdoms

In the 13th century, the regional empires started to decline and prosperous Tai city-states emerged with localised power and military might. The competing city-states were ultimately united into various kingdoms that began to establish a Thai identity. Scholars recognise Lanna, Sukhothai and Ayuthaya as the unifying kingdoms of the period.

Lanna

The Lanna kingdom, based in northern Thailand, dates its formation to the upper Mekong River town of Chiang Saen in the middle of the 12th century by King Mengrai, who settled the bickering between neighbouring towns by conquering them. He then migrated south to Chiang Mai (meaning 'new city') in 1292 to establish his capital. The king was a skilled diplomat and forged important alliances with potential rivals, such as King Ngam Muang of Phayao and King Ramkhamhaeng of Sukhothai; a bronze statue commemorating this confederation stands in Chiang Mai today. King Mengrai is also credited for successfully repulsing the Mongol invasions in the early 14th century.

The Lanna kingdom is also recognised for its royal patronage of the Sinhalese tradition of Theravada Buddhism that is now widely practised in Thailand and of the distinctive northern Thai culture that persists in the region. The Lanna kingdom didn't experience an extensive expansion period as it was plagued by dynastic intrigues and wars with rival powers.

Sukhothai

During the 13th century, several principalities in the central plains united and wrested control from the dying Khmer empire, making their new capital at Sukhothai (meaning 'Rising of Happiness'). Thais consider Sukhothai the first true Thai kingdom and the period is recognised as an artistic and cultural awakening.

Top History Reads

» *Thailand: A Short History* (2003) by David K Wyatt

» *A History of Thailand* (2009) by Chris Baker and Pasuk Phongpaichit

» *Chronicle of Thailand: Headlines Since 1946* (2010) by William Warren

1283	1292	1351–1767	1511
Early Thai script invented by King Ramkhamhaeng of Sukhothai.	Chiang Mai becomes the capital of Lanna.	Reign of Ayuthaya.	Portuguese found foreign mission in Ayuthaya, followed by other European nations.

Ancient Sites

» Ayuthaya Historical Park

» Sukhothai Historical Park

» Chiang Saen Historical Park

» Lopburi Khmer ruins

» Nakhon Si Thammarat National Museum

» Phimai Historical Park

HISTORY & POLITICS HISTORY

The most revered of the Sukhothai kings was Ramkhamhaeng, who is credited for developing the modern Thai writing system, which is based on Indian, Mon and Khmer scripts. He also established Theravada Buddhism as the official religion.

In its prime, the Sukhothai kingdom extended as far as Nakhon Si Thammarat in the south, to the upper Mekong River Valley in Laos and to Bago (Pegu) in southern Burma. For a short time (1448–86), the Sukhothai capital was moved to Phitsanulok, but by that time another star was rising in Thailand, the kingdom of Ayuthaya.

Ayuthaya

In the mid-14th century, the Ayuthaya kingdom began to dominate Chao Phraya River basin during the twilight of the Khmer period. It survived for 416 years, defining itself as Siam's most important early kingdom with an expansive sphere of influence (including much of the former Khmer empire) and a fundamental role in organising the modern Thai state and social structure.

With a strategic island location formed by encircling rivers, Ayuthaya grew wealthy through international trade during the 17th century's age of commerce and fortified itself with superior Portuguese-supplied firearms and mercenaries. The river system connected to the Gulf of Thailand and to the hinterlands as well.

This is the period when Western traders 'discovered' Southeast Asia and Ayuthaya hosted many foreign settlements. Accounts by foreign visitors mention Ayuthaya's cosmopolitan markets and court. In 1690 Londoner Engelbert Campfer proclaimed, 'Among the Asian nations, the kingdom of Siam is the greatest'.

Ayuthaya adopted Khmer court customs, honorific language and ideas of kingship. The monarch styled himself as a Khmer *devaraja* (divine king) rather than Sukhothai's *dhammaraja* (righteous king); Ayuthaya

FRIENDS OF THE KING

In the 1680s many foreign emissaries were invited to Ayuthaya by King Narai, who was keen to acquire and consume foreign material, culture and ideas. His court placed orders for spyglasses, hourglasses, paper, walnut trees, cheese, wine and marble fountains. He joined the French Jesuits to observe the eclipse at his palace in Lopburi and received a gift of a globe from France's King Louis XIV.

In the 1680s, Narai recruited the services of the Greek adventurer Constantine Phaulkon, who was later accused of conspiring to overthrow the ailing king. Instead, the accusers led a coup and executed Constantine.

1688	1767	1768	1782
King Narai dies and is followed by the Palace Revolution and the expulsion of the French.	Ayuthaya is sacked by the Burmese.	King Taksin establishes a new capital in Thonburi.	Founding of the Chakri dynasty and Bangkok as the new capital.

continued to pay tribute to the Chinese emperor, who rewarded this ritualistic submission with generous gifts and commercial privileges.

The glories of Ayuthaya were interrupted by the expansionist Burmese. In 1569 the city had fallen to the great Burmese king, Bayinnaung, but regained independence under the leadership of King Naresuan. Then, in 1765, Burma's ambitious and newly established Kongbaung dynasty pushed eastward to eliminate Ayuthaya as a political and commercial rival. Burmese troops laid siege to the capital for a year before destroying it in 1767. The city was devastated, its buildings and people wiped out. The surrounding areas were deserted. So chilling was this historic sacking and razing of Ayuthaya that the perception of the Burmese as ruthless foes and aggressors still persists in the minds of many Thais to this day.

The Bangkok Era

With Ayuthaya in ruins, the line of succession of the kings was broken and chaos ensued. A former general, Taksin, claimed his right to rule, handily defeating potential rivals, and established his new capital in Thonburi, a settlement downriver from Ayuthaya with better access to trade. Consolidating his power, King Taksin, the son of a Chinese father and Thai mother, strongly promoted trade with China.

Towards the end of his 15 years on the throne, the king was deposed in 1782 by the military. One of the coup organisers, Chao Phraya Chakri assumed the throne as King Yot Fa (Rama I) and established the Chakri dynasty, which still rules today. The new monarch moved the capital across Chao Phraya River to modern-day Bangkok.

The first century of Bangkok rule focused on rebuilding what had been lost when Ayuthaya was sacked. Surviving knowledge and practices were preserved or incorporated into new laws, manuals of government practice, religious and historical texts and literature. At the same time, the new rulers transformed their defence activities into expansion by means of war, extending their influence in every direction. Destroying the capital cities of both Laos and Cambodia, Siam contained Burmese aggression and made a vassal of Chiang Mai. Defeated populations were resettled and played an important role in increasing the rice production of Siam, much of which was exported to China.

Unlike the Ayuthaya rulers who identified themselves with the Hindu god Vishnu, the Chakri kings positioned themselves as defenders of Buddhism. They undertook compilations and Thai translations of essential Buddhist texts and constructed many royal temples.

In the meantime, a new social order and market economy was taking shape in the mid-19th century. Siam turned to the West for modern scientific and technological ideas and reforms in education, infrastructure and legal systems. One of the great modernisers, King Mongkut (Rama

HISTORY & POLITICS HISTORY

King Naresuan is portrayed as a national hero and became a cult figure, especially worshipped by the Thai army. His story inspired a high-budget, blockbuster film trilogy, *King Naresuan*, by filmmaker Chatrichalerm Yukol, funded in part by the Thai government.

Landmarks of the Bangkok Era

» Wat Arun

» Wat Phra Kaew & Grand Palace

» Dusit Palace Park

1851–68	**1855**	**1868–1910**	**1874**
Reign of King Mongkut (Rama IV) and a period of Western influence.	Bowring Treaty concluded between Siam and Britain stimulating the Thai economy and granting extraterritorial rights to British subjects in Siam.	Reign of King Chulalongkorn (Rama V) and increased European imperialism in neighbouring countries.	Slavery is abolished.

IV) never expected to be king. Before his ascension he had spent 27 years in the monastery, founding the Thammayut sect based on the strict disciplines of the Mon monks. During his monastic career, he became proficient in Pali, Sanskrit, Latin and English and studied Western sciences.

During his reign (1851–68), Siam concluded treaties with Western powers that integrated the kingdom into the world market system, ceded royal monopolies and granted extraterritorial rights to British subjects.

Mongkut's son, King Chulalongkorn (Rama V) was to take much greater steps in replacing the old political order with the model of the nation-state. He abolished slavery and the corvée system (state labour), which had lingered on ineffectively since the Ayuthaya period. Chulalongkorn's reign oversaw the creation of a salaried bureaucracy, a police force and a standing army. His reforms brought uniformity to the legal code, law courts and revenue offices. Siam's agricultural output was improved by advances in irrigation techniques and increasing peasant populations. Schools were established along European lines. Universal conscription and poll taxes made all men the king's men.

In 'civilising' his country, Chulalongkorn relied greatly on foreign advisers, mostly British. Within the royal court, much of the centuries-old protocol was abandoned and replaced by Western forms. The architecture and visual art of state, like the new throne halls, were designed by Italian artists.

Like his father, Chulalongkorn was regarded as a skilful diplomat and is credited for successfully playing European powers off one another to avoid colonisation. In exchange for independence, Thailand ceded territory to French Indochina (Laos in 1893, Cambodia in 1907) and British Burma (three Malayan states in 1909). In 1902, the former Pattani kingdom was ceded to the British, who were then in control of Malaysia, but control reverted back to Thailand five years later. (The Deep South region continues to consider itself an occupied land by the Thai central government – see p709.)

Siam was becoming a geographically defined country in a modern sense. By 1902, the country no longer called itself Siam but Prathet Thai (the country of the Thai) or Ratcha-anachak Thai (the kingdom of the Thai). By 1913, all those living within its borders were defined as 'Thai'.

Democracy vs Military

In 1932 a group of young military officers and bureaucrats calling themselves Khana Ratsadon (People's Party) mounted a successful, bloodless coup which marked the end of absolute monarchy and introduced a constitutional monarchy. The leaders of the group were inspired by the democratic ideology they had encountered during their studies in Europe.

In the years after the coup, rival factions (royalists, military, civilians) struggled for the upper hand in the new power regime. Even the People's

> In 1868 King Mongkut (Rama IV) abolished a husband's right to sell his wife or her children without her permission. The older provision, it was said, treated the woman 'as if she were a water buffalo'.

1890	1893
Siam's first railway connects Bangkok with Nakhon Ratchasima.	French blockade Chao Phraya River over disputed Indochina territory, intensify threat of colonisation.

» Wat Arun on the Chao Phraya River, Bangkok

Party was not unified in its vision of a democratic Thailand and before general elections were held the military-wing of the party seized control of the government. The leader of the civilian wing of the People's Party, Pridi Phanomyong, a French-educated lawyer, was forced into exile in 1933 after introducing a socialist-leaning economic plan that angered the military generals. King Prajathipok (Rama VII) abdicated in 1935 and retired to Britain. Thailand's first popular election was held in 1937 for half of the seats in the People's Assembly, the newly instated legislative body. General Phibul Songkhram, one of the leaders of the military faction of the People's Party, became prime minister, a position he held from 1938 to 1944 and again from 1948 to 1957.

Phibul's regime coincided with WWII and was characterised by strong nationalistic tendencies centering on 'nation' and 'Thai-ness'. He collaborated with the Japanese and allowed them to use Thailand as a staging ground for its invasion of other Southeast Asian nations. By siding with the Japanese, the Phibul government was hoping to gain international leverage and reclaim historical territory lost during France's expansion of Indochina. Thailand intended to declare war on the US and Britain during WWII. But Seni Pramoj, the Thai ambassador in Washington and a member of Seri Thai (the Thai Liberation Movement), refused to deliver the formal declaration of war, thus saving Thailand from bearing the consequences of defeated-nation status. Phibul was forced to resign in 1944 and was tried for war crimes.

In an effort to suppress royalist sentiments, Ananda Mahidol, the nephew of the abdicated king, was crowned Rama VIII in 1935, though he was only 10 years old and spent much of his childhood studying abroad. After returning to Thailand, he was shot dead under mysterious circumstances in his bedroom in 1946. In the same year, his brother, His Majesty Bhumibol Adulyadej (pronounced *phuumíphon adunyâdèt*) was appointed as the ninth king of the Chakri dynasty, going on to become the longest-reigning king in Thai history, as well as the world's longest-reigning, living monarch.

For a brief period after the war, democracy flourished: full elections for the people's assembly were held and the 1946 constitution sought to reduce the role of the military and provide more democratic rights. And it all lasted until the death of King Ananda, the pretext the military used to return to power with Phibul at the helm.

Military Dictatorships

In 1957 Phibul's successor General Sarit Thanarat subjected the country to a true military dictatorship: abolishing the constitution, dissolving the parliament and banning all political parties. In the 1950s, the US directly involved itself in Southeast Asia, attempting to contain communist

Phibul Song-khram changed the name of the country in 1939 from 'Siam' to 'Prathet Thai' (or 'Thailand' in English); it was considered an overt nationalistic gesture intended to unite all the Tai-speaking people.

PRATHET THAI

1902	1909	1913	1916
Siam annexes Yala, Pattani and Narathiwat from the former sultanate of Pattani.	Anglo-Siamese Treaty outlines Siam's boundaries.	King Vajiravudh requires all citizens to adopt surnames.	The first Thai university, Chulalongkorn University, is established.

expansion in the region. In the context of the Cold War, the US government gave economic and military support to the Sarit government and continued that relationship with subsequent military dictators, Thanom Kittikachorn and Praphat Charusathien, who controlled the country from 1964 to 1973. They negotiated a package of economic deals with the USA in exchange for allowing the development of US military bases in Thailand to support the war in Vietnam.

By 1973, an opposition group of left-wing activists, mainly intellectuals and students, along with peasants, workers and portions of the middle class, organised political rallies demanding a constitution from the military government. On 14 October that year the military brutally suppressed a large demonstration in Bangkok, killing 77 people and wounding more than 800. The event is commemorated by a monument on Th Ratchadamnoen Klang in Bangkok, near the Democracy Monument. King Bhumibol stepped in and refused to support further bloodshed, forcing Thanom and Praphat to leave Thailand.

In the following years, the left-oriented student movement grew more radical, creating fears among working-class and middle-class Thais of home-grown communism. In 1976 Thanom returned to Thailand (ostensibly to become a monk) and was received warmly by the royal family. In response, protestors organised demonstrations at Thammasat University against the perceived perpetrator of the 14 October massacre. Rightwing, anti-communist civilian groups clashed with the students, resulting in bloody violence. In the aftermath, many students and intellectuals were forced underground, and joined armed communist insurgents –

> Thailand has had 17 constitutions, all rewritten as a result of 18 (this number is debatable) coups. Each reincarnation seeks to allocate power within the branches of government with a bias for the ruling interest (military, royalist or civilian) and against their political foes.

LIBERAL COUNTERWEIGHT

Pridi Phanomyong (1900–83) was a French-educated lawyer and a civilian leader in the 1932 revolution and People's Party. His work on democratic reforms in Thailand was based on constitutional measures and attempts to restrict by law military involvement in Thai politics. He supported nationalisation of land and labour, state-led industrialisation and labour protection. In 1934, he founded Thammasat University. He also served as the figurehead of Seri Thai (the resistance movement against WWII Japanese occupation of Thailand) and was Thai prime minister (1946).

Though acknowledged as a senior statesman, Pridi Phanomyong was a controversial figure and a major foe of Phibul and the military regimes. He was accused of being a communist by his critics and forced out of the country under suspicion of regicide. Since the thawing of the Cold War, his legacy has been re-examined and recognised its democratic efforts and the counterbalancing effects it had on military interests. He was named one of Unesco's great personalities of the 20th-century world in 2000.

<table>
<tr><td>**1917**</td><td>**1932**</td><td>**1939**</td><td>**1941**</td></tr>
<tr><td>Siam sends troops to join the Allies in WWI.</td><td>Bloodless coup ends absolute monarchy.</td><td>The country's English name is officially changed from Siam to Thailand.</td><td>Japanese forces enter Thailand during WWII.</td></tr>
</table>

known as the People's Liberation Army of Thailand (PLAT) – based in the jungles of northern and southern Thailand.

Military control of the country continued through the 1980s. The government of the 'political soldier', General Prem Tinsulanonda, enjoyed a period of political and economic stability. Prem dismantled the communist insurgency through military action and amnesty programs. But the country's new economic success presented a challenging rival: prominent business leaders who criticised the military's role in government and their now-dated Cold War mentality. Communists, they maintained, should be business partners, not enemies.

It's Just Business

In 1988, Prem was replaced in fair elections by Chatichai Choonhavan, leader of the Chat Thai Party, who created a government dominated by well-connected provincial business people. His government shifted power away from the bureaucrats and set about transforming Thailand into an 'Asian Tiger' economy. But the business of politics was often bought and sold like a commodity and Chatichai was overthrown by the military on grounds of extreme corruption. This coup demarcated an emerging trend in Thai politics: the Bangkok business community and educated classes siding with the military against Chatichai, his provincial business-politicians and their money politics approach to governance.

In 1992, after reinstating elections, an unelected military leader inserted himself as prime minister. This was met with popular resistance and the ensuing civilian-military clash was dubbed 'Black May'. Led by former Bangkok mayor, Chamlong Srimuang, around 200,000 protestors (called the 'mobile phone mob', representing their rising urban affluence) launched a mass demonstration in Bangkok that resulted in three nights of violence with armed soldiers. On the night of 20 May, King Bhumibol called an end to the violence.

After Black May, a new wave of democracy activists advocated for constitutional reforms. For most of the 1990s, the parliament was dominated by the Democrat Party, which represented the urban middle class and business interests. Its major base of support came from the southern Thai population centres. Formerly port towns, these were now dominated by tourism and exports (rubber, tin and fishing). On the other side of the spectrum were the former pro-military politicians based in the central plains and the people of the agrarian northeast in new provincial towns who focused on state-budget distribution to their provinces. These political lines exist today.

In 1997, the boom years went bust and the Asian economic crisis unfolded. The country's economy was plagued by foreign-debt burdens, an overextension in the real-estate sector and a devalued currency. Within

Prem Tinsu-lanonda serves as lifelong head of the Privy Council of King Bhumibol and is believed to be the architect of the 2006 coup.

1945	1946	1957	1959
WWII ends; Thailand cedes seized territory from Laos, Cambodia and Malaysia.	King Bhumibol Adulyadej (Rama IX) ascends the throne; Thailand joins the UN.	Sarit Thanarat leads a coup that introduces military rule that lasts until 1973.	The first tourist authority created.

months of the crisis, the Thai currency plunged from 25B to 56B per US$1. The International Monetary Fund (IMF) stepped in to impose financial and legal reforms and economic liberalisation programs in exchange for more than US$17 billion to stabilise the Thai currency.

In the aftermath of the crisis, the Democrats returned to power uncontested, but were viewed as ineffective as the economy worsened.

Thaksinocracy

In 2000, the economic slump began to ease and business interests eclipsed the military as the dominant political force. The telecommunications billionaire and former police officer, Thaksin Shinawatra, through his Thai Rak Thai (TRT or 'Thai Loving Thai') party, capitalised on the rising nationalism and won a majority in the elections of 2001. Self-styled as a CEO-politician, Thaksin swiftly delivered on his campaign promises for rural development, including agrarian debt relief, village capital funds and cheap health care.

Thanks to the 1997 constitutional reforms designed to strengthen the prime minister's position, his was one of Thai history's most stable elected governments. The surging economy and his bold, if strong-arm, leadership won an outright majority in 2005, effectively introducing one-party rule. His popularity among the working class and rural voters was immense.

In 2006 Thaksin was accused of abusing his powers and of conflicts of interest, most notably in his family's sale of their Shin Corporation to the Singaporean government for 73 billion baht (US$1.88 billion), a tax-free gain thanks to telecommunications legislation that he had helped craft. Demonstrations in Bangkok called for his ousting and on 19 September 2006, the military staged a bloodless coup that forced Thaksin into exile. The TRT Party was dissolved by court order and party executives were barred from politics for five years. As promised, the interim government held general elections in December, returning the country to civilian rule, but the outcome was unsatisfactory to the military and the Bangkok upper- and middle-classes when Thaksin's political allies won a majority and formed a government led by Samak Sundaravej.

Demonstrations against the Thaksin-aligned government were led by Chamlong Srimuang (Black May activist and former Bangkok governor) and Sondhi Limthongkul (a long-time business and political rival of Thaksin's). Their group, the People's Alliance for Democracy (PAD), earned the nickname 'Yellow Shirts' because they wore yellow (the king's birthday colour) to express their royalist allegiances; it was believed that Thaksin was so successfully consolidating power during his tenure that he had designs on the throne or at least in interrupting royal succession.

Without the job of being absolute, King Bhumibol had to find new work so he started the Royal Project Foundation in 1969 to help struggling farmers. The foundation's most lauded effort was eradication of opium cultivation among the northern hill tribes.

1965	1968	1973	1976
Thailand hosts US military bases during the Vietnam War.	Thailand is a founding member of the Association of Southeast Asian Nations (ASEAN).	Thai students, workers and farmers demonstrate for the reinstallation of a democratic government.	Violent suppression of student movement by the military.

In September 2008, Samak Sundaravej was unseated by the Constitutional Court on a technicality: while in office, he hosted a TV cooking show that the court found to be a conflict of interest. Still not politically satisfied, the Yellow Shirts seized control of Thailand's main airports, Suvarnabhumi and Don Muang, for a week in November 2008 until the military manoeuvred a silent coup and another favourable court ruling that further weakened Thaksin's political proxies. Through last-minute coalition building, Democrat Abhisit Vejjajiva was elected in a parliamentary vote, becoming Thailand's 27th prime minister.

Thaksin supporters organised their own counter-movement as the United Front for Democracy Against Dictatorship, better known as the 'Red Shirts'. Supporters hail mostly from the north and northeast, and include anti-coup, pro-democracy activists as well as die-hard Thaksin fans. There is a degree of class struggle, with some Red Shirts expressing bombastic animosity towards the aristocrats. The Red Shirts most provocative demonstration came in 2010 after Thailand's Supreme Court ordered the seizure of US$46 billion of Thaksin's assets after finding him guilty of abusing his powers as prime minister. Red Shirts occupied Bangkok's central shopping district for two months and demanded the dissolution of the government and reinstatement of elections. Protest leaders and the government were unable to reach a compromise and in May 2010 the military used forced to evict the protestors, resulting in bloody clashes where 91 people were killed and a smouldering central city (US$1.5 billion of crackdown-related arson damage was estimated).

In 2011, general elections were held and Thaksin's politically allied Puea Thai party won a parliamentary majority with Thaksin's sister Yingluck Shinawatra elected as prime minister. For more information, on this see p696.

> Thaksin was the first prime minister in Thai history to complete a four-year term of office.

Troubles in the Deep South

Starting in 2001, Muslim separatist insurgents have been waging a low-scale war against the central government in Thailand's southernmost provinces of Pattani, Narathiwat and Yala. These three provinces once comprised the area of the historic kingdom of Patani until it was conquered by the Chakri kings. Under King Chulalongkorn, the traditional ruling elite were replaced with central government officials and bureaucrats from Bangkok. During WWII, a policy of nation-building set out to transform the multi-ethnic society into a unified and homogenous Thai Buddhist nation. This policy was resisted in the Deep South and gave birth to a strong separatist movement fighting for the independence of Patani. In the 1980s and '90s, the assimilation policy was abandoned and then-prime minister Prem promised support for Muslim cultural

» Military response to student protests, 1976

1979

After three years of military rule, elections and parliament restored.

1980

Prem Tinsulanonda's government works to undermine the communist insugency movement and eventually ends it with a political solution.

rights and religious freedoms. He also offered amnesty to the armed insurgents and implemented an economic development plan for the historically impoverished region.

The Thaksin regime took another approach to the region, which still ranks among the most economically and educationally depressed in the country. Greater central control was exerted and was viewed as a thinly disguised policy to break up the traditional stronghold of the Democrat Party. The policy succeeded in weakening relations between the local elite, Southern voters and the Democrats who had served as their representative in parliament. However, it did not take into consideration the sensitive and tenacious Muslim culture of the Deep South. In 2002, the government dissolved the long-standing inspectorate and the Army-run joint civilian-police-military border security office – a unit often lauded for maintaining peace and stability and providing a communication link between the Thai government and the southern Muslims. In its place the Thai provincial police assumed control of security though they lacked perceived moral authority and support of the local population. In 2004, the government responded harshly to demonstrations that resulted in the Krue Se Mosque and Tak Bai incidents, which together cost the lives of at least 180 Muslims, many of them unarmed civilians. In 2005, martial law was declared in the area.

For more information on the conflict in the Deep South, see the boxed text, p596.

It was widely believed that the 2006 coup, led a by a Thai-Muslim general, could potentially settle the violence in the south but that has not come to pass. Bombings and shootings continue and the region has become a no-go zone.

TROUBLE IN THE TEMPLE FRONTIER

In 2008 Cambodia successfully petitioned Unesco to list the ancient Khmer temple of Khao Phra Wihan ('Preah Vihear' in Cambodian; see p432) as an official World Heritage Site. Remote and seemingly insignificant, the temple has long been a contentious issue between Cambodia and Thailand. A 1969 International Court of Justice case awarded Cambodia ownership of the temple, but both countries lay claim to a 4.6-sq-km area surrounding it. Four years since the Unesco decision, troops have been deployed to the border and periodically exchange fire.

Running up to the Thai general election of 2011, border tensions increased partly due to competing political interests in both countries. Cambodian leader Hun Sen is viewed as a Thaksin ally and was accused of using the dispute to make the Abhiset government look weak. Meanwhile anti-Thaksin groups in Thailand were accused of exploiting the issue as a nationalistic wedge to discredit pro-Thaksin sentiments. The struggle seems to have fizzled with the Puea Thai electoral win and a 2011 Thai-Cambodian border committee meeting resulted in an official statement of future cooperation.

1988	1991-2	1997	2001
Chatichai Choonhavan becomes first elected PM since 1976; trade opens with Indochina.	General Suchinda attempts to seize power; King Bhumibol intervenes to halt civil turmoil surrounding 'Black May' protests.	Asian economic crisis; passage of historic 'people's constitution'.	Telecommunications tycoon, Thaksin Shinawatra is elected prime minister.

Politics

Government

Much of the political drama that has unfolded since the 2006 coup involves a long-standing debate about how to structure Thailand's legislative body and, ultimately, who gets greater control. The National Assembly (or parliament of Thailand) currently has 630 members divided into two chambers (House of Representatives and the Senate) with a mix of seats being popularly elected and elected by party vote. The ratio of seats being popularly elected changes with each replacement constitution. The 1997 constitution, dubbed the People's Constitution, called for both chambers to be fully elected by popular vote. This power to the people paved the way for Thaksin and his well-loved Thai Rak Thai party to gain nearly complete control. The military and the elites have since rescinded such a popular structure, often arguing that full democratic representation doesn't work in Thailand.

When Thai voters go to the polls they cast a ballot for the constituency MP (member of parliament) and for their preferred party, the results of which are used to determine individual winners and proportional representation outcomes for the positions assigned by party vote.

The prime minister is the head of the government and is elected via legislative vote by the majority party. Under the current constitution, the prime minister must be a sitting MP.

Voting in Thailand is compulsory for all eligible citizens (over the age of 18) but members of the clergy are not allowed to vote. Voter turnout for national elections has steadily increased since the new millennium with 78% of registered voters casting ballots in 2007. Charges of vote-buying typically accompany every election. Anecdotally, local party leaders make their rounds through the villages handing out money for the promise of a vote. In some cases, villagers will accept money from competing parties and report that they have no loyalty at the ballot box.

The ballots include a 'no' vote if the voter wishes to choose 'none of the above'. It is also common to 'spoil' the ballot, or disqualify it, by writing on it or defacing it. During the 2005 general election a large number of ineligible ballots contained anti-Thaksin messages.

Media

Southeast Asian governments are not typically fond of uncensored media outlets, but Thailand often bucked this trend throughout the 1990s, even ensuring press freedoms in its 1997 constitution, albeit with fairly broad loopholes. That era came to an end with the ascension of Thaksin Shinawatra, a telecommunications billionaire, at the beginning of the 21st century. With Thaksin winning the prime ministership and his party holding a controlling majority, the press encountered the kind of censor-

The Democrat Party (Phak Prachathipat) founded in 1946 is now the longest-surviving political party in Thailand.

2004	2006	2008	2008
Indian Ocean tsunami kills over 5000 people in Thailand and damages tourism and fishing industries; Muslim insurgency reignites in Deep South.	King Bhumibol celebrates 60th year on the throne; Thaksin government overthrown in a coup and prime minister forced into exile.	Cambodia successfully petitions Unesco to list Phra Wihan as a World Heritage Site, reigniting border tensions with Thailand.	Yellow Shirt, pro-royalist activists seize Bangkok's international airports, causing weeklong shut-down.

Page 712

HISTORY & POLITICS POLITICS

SIGNS OF ELECTION

Preceding an election, Thai candidates paper the roadways and electricity poles with political billboards and signs. Traditional posters show the candidate posing seriously in an official uniform but recent trends include ad-like approaches with catchy slogans and evocative imagery.

Always a trendsetter, Chuvit Kamolvisit, former brothel owner turned political whistle-blower, won over voters with his 2011 'Angry Man' campaign ads, featuring him in grimacing and glaring poses expressing frustration and anger with the government. (Incidentally, one of his first acts in office was to expose an illegal Bangkok casino run by high-ranking police.)

Residents complain about the signs' obstruction of traffic but signmakers like the boost in business. All candidate posters are vulnerable to vandalism or theft, but the plastic ones are particularly desired as a makeshift sunshade or roof patch.

ship and legal intimidation not seen since the 1970s era of military dictatorships. The government filed a litany of defamation lawsuits against individuals, publications and media groups who printed embarrassing revelations about the Thaksin regime.

After the 2006 ousting of Thaksin, the media managed to retain its guarantees of press freedoms in the new constitution, but this was a 'paper promise' that did little to rescue the press from intimidation, lawsuits and physical attacks. Sweeping powers to ensure national security, often invoked against the press, were added to the emergency powers laws that went into effect after the coup.

Press intimidation in Thailand is made easier because of the country's lèse majesté laws – causing offence against the dignity of the monarchy – which carries a jail term of between three and 15 years. Often the media exercises self-censorship with regard to the monarchy, mainly out of respect for the crown, but also out of fear that political enemies will file lèse majesté charges.

Filing of lèse majesté charges has increased since 2006, mainly against political rivals, but also against journalists and even average citizens. Charges have been filed against a Thai Facebook user who posted a negative comment about the king and an overseas Thai who posted translations of a banned book about the king on his blog.

Publications that the government views as presenting an unflattering role of the monarchy are often banned. Several critical issues of *The Economist* have been banned since 2006. Internet censorship is also on the rise and so-called Red Shirt (pro-Thaksin) radio stations based in the northeast have been shut down by the government.

2010
Red Shirt, pro-Thaksin activists occupy central Bangkok for two months; military crackdown results in 91 deaths.

2011
Puea Thai party wins general election; Yingluck Shinawatra becomes Thailand's first female prime minister.

» Red-shirt protesters at Democracy Monument, Bangkok

Festivals

There is no better way to tap into Thailand's traditional folkways than to attend a festival, be it a provincial parade or a national shindig. In addition, festivals give Thais an excuse to do their two favourite pastimes: socialise and eat (which are never mutually exclusive).

Loi Krathong festival (p358), Chiang Mai

FELIX HUG/LONELY PLANET IMAGES ©

Top Festivals

Thailand's festivals are vibrant affairs in which religion and culture take to the streets. Traditional dance and music are features, as are some modern twists on the old ways.

Loi Krathong

1 This elegant festival alights the night with small boats adorned with flowers and lit candles set adrift in waterways across the country. The offerings thank the river goddess for irrigation and transport. Sukhothai (p358) is famous for this tradition.

Vegetarian Festival

2 Inherited from Chinese immigrants, this nine-day holiday from meat is lovingly practised in Bangkok and other Thai cities with historic Chinese populations. Food stalls with yellow banners turn the usual meaty stir-fry into a soy-based meal. In Phuket, the festival (p618) has a self-mortification parade.

Long-Tail Boat Races

3 In ancient times, long-tail boats, powered by up to 50 men, would race during end-of-rainy season celebrations (Ork Phansaa). A survivor of that era is the International Swan Boat Race (p164), held in Ayuthaya, that pits international and domestic teams.

Hua Hin Jazz Festival

4 To honour the king's jazz interest, this two-day festival assembles domestic and international ensembles to jam on the beach. Music-lovers lay out a beach blanket and listen as the waves lap in time (p517).

Candle Parade Festival, Ubon Ratchathani

5 During Khao Phansaa (Buddhist Lent), merit-makers donate essential and ceremonial items (such as candles) to the temples. In Ubon Ratchathani, the simple candle offerings became huge wax sculptures that are paraded through the town (p436).

Clockwise from top left
1. Launching lanterns for Loi Krathong, Chiang Mai 2. Self-mortification during the Vegetarian Festival, Phuket 3. Long-tail boat race during Ork Phansaa, Sakon Nakhon 4. Hua Hin Jazz Festival

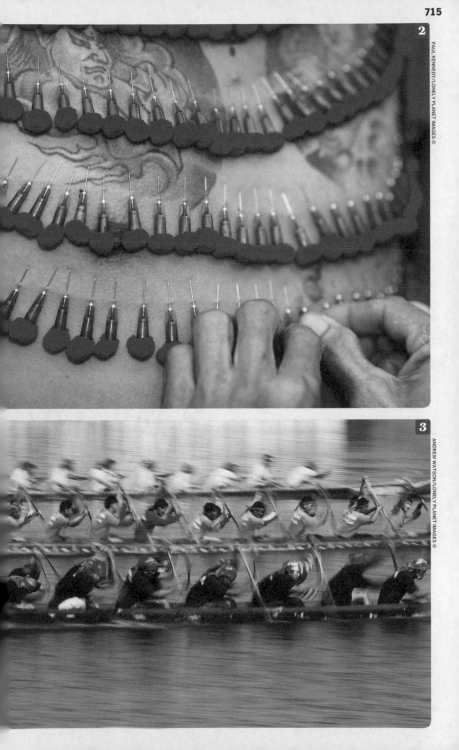

Songkran

Water mayhem ushers in the traditional Thai New Year in mid-April. It is a time of cleansing, renewal and loading up pick-up trucks with beds armed with super soakers to douse other water warriors.

Thailand's most famous festival didn't start out as a water war. Once upon a time it was a quiet festival of house cleaning, resolutions and temple festivities. Traditionally the temple's primary Buddha was ceremoniously bathed, often by being paraded about as the faithful dutifully splashed water on it. In fact water 'splashing' (not 'shooting') is a common component of New Year's festivals throughout Southeast Asia and even parts of China. Afterwards water might be sprinkled on the hands of elderly family members or playfully splashed on friends as a way of wishing them luck. The cleansing powers of water also offers refreshment during the hottest time of the year.

It isn't hard to imagine how the splashing water custom would eventually evolve into a throwing, launching and soaking wet party. Luck is said to be measured by how doused (not soused or drunk) you are and so those roving water-hurling bands are just wishing you a whole lot of luck in the year to come.

TOP SONGKRAN SPOTS

» **Bangkok** (p104) Head to Th Khao San for serious water battles.

» **Chiang Mai** (p258) Line up along the moat to splash and be splashed.

» **Ayuthaya** (p165) and **Sukhothai** Tame and traditional versions for Songkran purists.

Clockwise from top left
1. Having fun, Bangkok 2. Hill-tribe girls at a Songkran ceremony, Wat Phra That Doi Suthep, Chiang Mai 3. Incense and candle offerings during Songkran celebrations at Sanam Luang, Bangkok

2

ANDREW WATSON/LONELY PLANET IMAGES ©

Buddhist Lent

July to October, one of the holiest periods of the Buddhist calendar, coincides with the rainy season. It is a period of reflection, meditation and religious observances.

The start of Khao Phansaa (Buddhist Lent) is observed on the first day of the waning moon in the eighth lunar month. This is the traditional time for young men to enter the monkhood and earn merit for their family and maturity for themselves. Thai men who have not yet become monks are often viewed as 'unripe'. Buddhist Lent is also known as the rains retreat, when monks withdraw into the monastery. The practice dates to the historical Buddha when monks were itinerant preachers and foul weather made travel difficult. The start of the rains also initiated the planting season and the potential for trampling on young seedlings was a concern.

Many merit-making activities define this period for the laity. Buddhist faithful present the monks with once-useful offerings of candles and lamp oil, which have now become symbols of spiritual illumination.

The end of Buddhist lent (three lunar months later) is known as Ork Phansaa. The temples observe the *gà·tǐn* ceremony, in which new robes are given to the monks by merit-makers. Folk practices herald the end of the rains with long-tail-boat races.

RICHARD VAN KESTEREN/ALAMY ©

TOP BUDDHIST LENT FESTIVALS

» **Ubon Ratchathani's Candle Parade Festival** (p436) Elaborate wax candles become religious works of art.

» **Nong Khai's Naga Fireballs** (p465) Mysterious gaseous balls rise out of the Mekong River.

» **Nakhon Phanom's Illuminated Boat Festival** (p483) Electrified boats turn the Mekong River into a mini-disco.

Clockwise from top left & following page
1. Loi Krathong offerings **2.** *Moo·ay tai* dancer at Ork Phansaa parade, Sakon Nakhon **3.** The Candle Festival during Khao Phansaa, Ubon Ratchathani **4.** Long-tail-boat races, Ork Phansaa festivities, Sakon Nakhon **5.** Loi Krathong, Chiang Mai **6.** Vegetarian Festival, Phuket

The People & Culture

Thailand's cohesive national identity provides a unifying patina for ethnic and regional differences that evolved through historical migrations and geographic kinships with ethnically diverse neighbours.

Ethnic Makeup

Some 75% of the citizens of Thailand are ethnic Thais, providing a superficial view of sameness. But subtle regional differences do exist. In the central plains (Chao Phraya delta), Siamese Thais united the country through its historic kingdoms and promulgated its culture and language. Today the central Thai dialect is the national standard and Bangkok exports unified culture through popular media and standardised education.

The northeast (Isan) has always stood apart from the rest of the country, sharing closer ethnic and cultural ties with Laos and the Thai Lao people. The Isan dialect differs from central Thai, folk beliefs vary and even the local ingredients in *sôm·dam* (spicy papaya salad) mark a cultural shift: *sôm·dam* Lao contains field crabs, while standard *sôm·dam* contains peanuts. In the northeastern provinces that border Cambodia, there is a distinct Khmer influence as many families migrated across the border during historical tumult. A minority tribe, known as Suay lives near Surin and Khorat (Nakhon Ratchasima) and are traditional elephant mahouts; with the expansion of the elephant-tourism business many Suay people have relocated across the country for job opportunities.

Thai Pak Tai people define the characteristics of the south. The dialect is a little faster than standard Thai, the curries are a lot spicier, and there

Thailand Demographics

» Population: 66.7 million

» Fertility rate: 1.6

» Percentage of people over 65: 9.2%

» Urbanisation rate: 34%

» Life expectancy: 73 years

THE INVISIBLE BURMESE

Due to the ongoing dysfunction of the Myanmar state, there is an increasing exodus of Burmese to Thailand. Approximately 150,000 people have entered the kingdom as political and ethnic refugees but the vast majority are economic migrants (estimated at two to three million but less than half are documented). They fill the low-level jobs – fish-processing, construction, domestic and factory work – that used to employ unskilled northeastern Thai labourers. In part, many Thais believe that the country needs this imported workforce as the population is ageing faster than it is reproducing.

However, the emerging immigration 'situation' has not been dealt with as swiftly by the government as the private sector. Because many of the Burmese immigrants are residing and working in the country illegally, they are subjected to exploitative relationships with employers that many activists describe as modern-day slavery. The Burmese can't return home due to persecution by the military regime and they can't turn to the Thai authorities in cases of workplace abuse because they would face deportation.

A MODERN PERSPECTIVE ON THE HILL TRIBES

Hill tribes tend to have among the lowest standards of living in Thailand. Although it could be tempting to correlate this quality of life with traditional lifestyles, their situation is compounded, in most cases, by not having Thai citizenship. Without the latter, they don't have the right to own land, educate their children, earn a minimum wage or access health care. In the last decades some members of hill-tribe groups have been issued Thai identification cards, which enable them to access national programs (in theory, though, extra 'fees' might prevent families from being able to afford public schooling and health care). Other hill-tribe families have received residency certificates that restrict travel outside of an assigned district, in turn limiting access to job opportunities associated with a mobile modern society.

Furthermore, the Thai government has pursued a 30-year policy of hill-tribe relocation, often moving villages from fertile agricultural land to infertile land, in turn removing the tribes from a viable subsistence system in which tribal customs were intact to a market system in which they can't adequately compete and in which tribal ways have been fractured.

In the past decade, the expansion of tourism into the mountainous regions of the north presents a complicating factor to the independence of hill-tribe villages. City speculators will buy land from hill-tribe farmers for fairly nominal sums only to be resold, usually to resorts, for much higher costs if the documentation of ownership can be procured. (In many cases the hill-tribe farmer doesn't own the land rights and has very little bargaining power when approached by outsiders.) The displaced farmer and his family might then migrate to the city, losing their connection to their rural and tribal lifestyle with few resources to succeed in the lowland society.

is more mixing of Muslim folk beliefs into the regional culture thanks to the geographic proximity to Malaysia and the historic Muslim population.

If you were to redraw Thailand's borders according to ethnicity and culture, northern Thailand would be united with parts of southern China and northern Myanmar. The traditional homeland of the Tai people was believed to be the Yunnan region of China. There are also many subgroups, including the Shan (an ethnic cousin to the Thais who settled in the highlands of Burma) and the Tai Lü (who settled in Nan and Chiang Rai province as well as the Vietnam highlands).

People of Chinese ancestry – second- or third-generation Hakka, Teochew, Hainanese or Cantonese – make up 14% of the population. Bangkok and the nearby coastal areas have a large population of immigrants from China who came for economic opportunities in the early to mid-20th century. In northern Thailand there is also a substantial number of Hui-Chinese Muslims who emigrated from Yunnan in the late 19th century.

China and Thailand have long been linked through trade, migration and cultural commonalities. Many families have intermarried with Thais and have interwoven traditional Chinese customs into the predominant Thai culture. Historically wealthy Chinese introduced their daughters to the royal court as consorts, developing royal connections and adding a Chinese bloodline that extends to the current king. The mercantile centres of most Thai towns are run by Thai-Chinese families and many places in the country celebrate Chinese festivals such as the annual Vegetarian Festival.

The second-largest ethnic minority are the Malays (4.6%), most of whom reside in the provinces of the Deep South. The remaining minority groups include smaller percentages of non-Thai-speaking people such as the Vietnamese, Khmer, Mon, Semang (Sakai), Moken (*chow lair;* also spelt *chao leh;* people of the sea, or 'sea gypsies'), Htin, Mabri, Khamu

Many NGOs in Chiang Mai and Chiang Rai work with hill-tribe communities to provide education, health care and advocacy efforts. The Mirror Foundation (http://themirror foundation.org/cms/) and Association for Akha Education (www.akhathai.org) are two long-running NGOs that accept volunteers.

and a variety of hill tribes. A small number of Europeans and other non-Asians reside in Bangkok and the provinces.

Hill Tribes

Ethnic minorities in the mountainous regions of northern Thailand are often called 'hill tribes', or in Thai vernacular, *chow kŏw* (mountain people). Each hill tribe has its own language, customs, mode of dress and spiritual beliefs.

Most are of seminomadic origin, having come from Tibet, Myanmar, China and Laos during the past 200 years or so. They are 'fourth-world' people in that they belong neither to the main aligned powers nor to the developing nations. Rather, they have crossed and continue to cross national borders, often fleeing oppression by other cultures, without regard for recent nationhood.

Language and culture constitute the borders of their world. Some groups are caught between the 6th and 21st centuries, while others are gradually being assimilated into modern life. Many tribespeople are also moving into lowland areas as montane lands become deforested.

Akha (I-kaw)

Population: 70,000
Origin: Tibet
Present locations: Thailand, Laos, Myanmar, Yunnan
Economy: dry rice, corn, beans, peppers
Belief system: animism with an emphasis on ancestor worship; some groups are Christian
Cultural characteristics: The Akha are among the poorest of Thailand's ethnic minorities and reside mainly in Chiang Mai and Chiang Rai provinces, along mountain ridges or steep slopes 1000m to 1400m in altitude. They're regarded as skilled farmers but are often displaced from arable land because of government intervention. The well-known Akha Swing Ceremony takes place from mid-August to mid-September, between rice planting and harvest time. Akha houses are constructed of wood and bamboo, usually atop short wooden stilts and roofed with thick grass. At the entrance of every traditional Akha village stands a simple wooden gateway consisting of two vertical struts joined by a lintel. Akha shamans affix various charms made from bamboo strips to the gateway to prevent malevolent spirits from entering. Standing next to each village gateway are the crude wooden figures of a man and a woman, each bearing exaggerated sexual organs, in the belief that human sexuality is abhorrent to the spirit world.

Akha are focused on family ties and will recite their personal genealogies upon first meetings to determine a shared ancestor.

Their traditional clothing consists of a headdress of beads, feathers and dangling silver ornaments.

The Tribal Research Institute in Chiang Mai recognises 10 different hill tribes but there may be up to 20. Hill tribes are increasingly integrating into the Thai mainstream and many of the old ways are disappearing.

Hmong (Mong or Maew)

Population: 151,000
Origin: south China
Present locations: south China, Thailand, Laos, Vietnam
Economy: rice, corn, cabbages, strawberries
Belief system: animism
Cultural characteristics: The Hmong are Thailand's second-largest hill-tribe group and are especially numerous in Chiang Mai Province

with smaller enclaves in the other northern Thai provinces. They usually live on mountain peaks or plateaus above 1000m. Kinship is patrilineal and polygamy is permitted.

Hmong tribespeople wear simple black jackets and indigo or black baggy trousers with striped borders (White Hmong) or indigo skirts (Blue Hmong) and silver jewellery. Sashes may be worn around the waist, and embroidered aprons draped front and back. Most women wear their hair in a bun.

Karen (Yang or Kariang)

Population: 420,000
Origin: Myanmar
Present locations: Thailand, Myanmar
Economy: rice, vegetables, livestock
Belief system: animism, Buddhism, Christianity, depending on the group
Cultural characteristics: The Karen are the largest hill-tribe group in Thailand and number about 47% of the total tribal population. They

tend to live in lowland valleys and practise crop rotation rather than swidden agriculture. Their numbers and proximity to mainstream society have made them the most integrated and financially successful of the hill-tribe groups. Karen homes are built on low stilts or posts, with the roofs swooping quite low. There are four distinct Karen groups – the Skaw (White) Karen, Pwo Karen, Pa-O (Black) Karen and Kayah (Red) Karen.

Thickly woven V-neck tunics of various colours are typically worn (though unmarried women wear white). Kinship is matrilineal and marriage is monogamous.

Lahu (Musoe)

Population: 103,000
Origin: Tibet
Present locations: south China, Thailand, Myanmar
Economy: dry rice, corn
Belief system: theistic animism; some groups are Christian
Cultural characteristics: The Thai term for this tribe, *moo·seu*, is derived from a Burmese word meaning 'hunter', a reference to their skill in the forest. The Lahu tend to live at about 1000m altitude and can be found in remote areas of Chiang Mai, Chiang Rai and Tak provinces. They typically live in mixed ethnic villages and are an ethnically diverse group with five main subsets: Red Lahu (the most numerous Lahu group in Thailand), Black Lahu, White Lahu, Yellow Lahu and Lahu Sheleh. Houses are built of wood, bamboo and grass, and usually stand on short wooden posts. Lahu food is probably the spiciest of all the hill-tribe cuisines.

Traditional dress consists of black-and-red jackets with narrow skirts worn by women; bright green or blue-green baggy trousers worn by men.

Lisu (Lisaw)

Population: 55,000
Origin: Tibet
Present locations: Thailand, Yunnan
Economy: rice, corn, livestock
Belief system: animism with ancestor worship and spirit possession
Cultural characteristics: Lisu villages are usually in the mountains at an elevation of about 1000m and occur in eight Thai provinces: Chiang Mai, Chiang Rai, Mae Hong Son, Phayao, Tak, Kamphaeng Phet, Sukhothai and Lampang. Patrilineal clans have pan-tribal jurisdiction, which makes the Lisu unique among hill-tribe groups (most of which have power centred with either a shaman or a village headman). Homes are built on the ground and consist mostly of bamboo and thatched grass.

The women wear long multicoloured tunics over trousers and sometimes black turbans with tassels. Men wear baggy green or blue pants pegged in at the ankles.

Mien (Yao)

Population: 35,500
Origin: central China
Present locations: Thailand, south China, Laos, Myanmar, Vietnam
Economy: dry rice, corn
Belief system: animism with ancestor worship, Taoism, Buddhism and Christianity
Cultural characteristics: The Mien are highly skilled at crafts such as embroidery and silversmithing. They settle near mountain springs at between 1000m and 1200m with a concentration in Nan, Phayao and Chiang Rai provinces and a few communities in Chiang Mai, Lampang and Sukhothai. Migration into Thailand increased during the American War era when the Mien collaborated with the CIA against Pathet Lao forces; 50,000 Mien refugees were resettled in the US. The Mien are heavily influenced by Chinese traditions and they use Chinese characters to write their language. Kinship is patrilineal and marriage is polygamous. Houses are built at ground level, out of wood or bamboo thatch.

Women wear trousers and black jackets with intricately embroidered patches and red furlike collars, along with large dark-blue or black turbans. Men wear black tunics and black pants.

The Thai Character

Much of Thailand's cultural value system is hinged upon respect for the family, religion and monarchy. Within that system each person knows his or her place and Thai children are strictly instructed in the importance of group conformity, respecting elders and suppressing confrontational views. In most social situations, establishing harmony often takes a leading role and Thais take personal pride in making others feel at ease.

Sà·nùk

The Lahu people are known for their strict adherence to gender equality.

In general, Thais place high value on *sà·nùk*, which means 'fun'. It is often regarded as a necessary underpinning of anything worth doing. Even work and studying should have an element of *sà·nùk*, otherwise it automatically becomes drudgery. This doesn't mean Thais don't want to work, but they labour best as a group, so as to avoid loneliness and ensure an element of playfulness. Nothing condemns an activity more than *mâi sà·nùk* (not fun). The back-breaking work of rice farming, the tedium of long-distance bus driving, the dangers of a construction site: Thais often mix their job tasks with a healthy dose of socialising. Watch these workers in action and you'll see them flirting with each other, trading insults or cracking jokes.

Saving Face

Thais believe strongly in the concept of saving face, ie avoiding confrontation and endeavouring not to embarrass themselves or other people (except when it's *sà·nùk* to do so). The ideal face-saver doesn't bring up negative topics in conversation, doesn't express firm convictions or opinions, and doesn't claim to have an expertise. Agreement and harmony are considered to be the most important social graces.

While Westerners might think a heated discussion OK, Thais avoid such confrontations and regard any instance where voices are raised as rude and potentially volatile. Losing your temper causes a loss of face for those present and Thais who have been crossed may react in extreme ways.

Minor embarrassments, such as tripping or falling, might elicit giggles from a crowd of Thais. In this case they aren't taking delight in your mishap, but helping you save face by laughing it off.

Status & Obligation

All relationships in traditional Thai society – and those in the modern Thai milieu as well – are governed by social rank defined by age, wealth, status and personal or political position. The elder position is called *pôo yài* (literally the 'big person') and is used to describe parents, bosses, village heads, public officials etc. The junior position is called *pôo nóy* (little person) and describes anyone who is subservient to the *pôo yài*. Although this tendency towards social ranking is to some degree shared by many societies around the world, the Thai twist lies in the set of mutual obligations linking the elder to the junior.

Pôo nóy are supposed to show obedience and respect (together these concepts are covered by the single Thai term *greng jai*) towards the elder. Those with junior status are not supposed to question or criticise those with elder status be it in the office, the home or the government. In the workplace, this means younger staff members are not encouraged to speak during meetings and are expected to do their bosses' bidding.

In return *pôo yài* are obligated to care for or 'sponsor' the *pôo nóy*. It is a paternalistic relationship in which *pôo nóy* can ask for favours involving money or job access. *Pôo yài* reaffirm their rank by granting requests when possible; to refuse would be to risk a loss of face and status.

The protocol defined by the social hierarchy governs almost every aspect of Thai behaviour within family units, business organisations, schools and the government. Elected or appointed officials occupy one of the highest rungs on the social ladder and often regard themselves as caretakers of the people, a stark contrast to the democratic ideal of being the voice of the people. The complicated personal hierarchy in Thailand often prevents collaboration, especially between those with competing status. This is why Bangkok has several modern-art museums with somewhat anaemic collections rather than one consolidated powerhouse.

Most foreign visitors will interact with a simplified version of this elder-junior relationship in the form of *pêe* (elder sibling) and *nórng* (younger sibling). All Thais refer to each other using familial names. Even people unrelated by blood quickly establish who's *pêe* and who's *nórng*. This is why one of the first questions Thais ask new acquaintances is 'How old are you?'.

The famous Thai smile comes in part from their desire to enjoy themselves and lighten the load of daily life.

The Thai equivalent of giving someone the middle finger is to show them the bottom of the foot.

THE NICKNAME GAME

At birth Thai babies are given auspicious first names, often bestowed by the family patriarch or matriarch. These poetic names are then relegated to bureaucratic forms and name cards, while the child is introduced to everyone else by a one-syllable nickname. Thai nicknames are usually playful and can be inspired by the child's appearance (Moo, meaning 'pig', if he/she is chubby) or a favourite pastime (Toon, short for 'cartoon' for avid TV-watchers). Girls will typically be named Lek or Noi (both of which means 'small'). Some parents even go so far as imprinting their interests on their children's names: Golf (as in the sport) and Benz (as in the car).

Lifestyle

Individual lifestyles vary according to family background, income and geography. In many ways Bangkok is its own phenomenon where upper- and middle-class Thais wake up to an affluent and increasingly Westernised world with all the mod cons: smartphones, fast food, K-pop music and fashion addictions. The amount of disposable income in Bangkok is unparalleled elsewhere in the country and to some degree is a source of contempt for the rest of the country, which views the capital as excessively materialistic.

The economic boom years of the 2000s aided the ascent of the working class, some of whom have migrated to commercial and tourism cities where they could earn enough to pay off debts and catapult their children from labourers to professionals. Many also thank former prime minister Thaksin's populist measures for providing economic relief to this beleaguered sector of the society.

Young Thais are opportunity migrants, leaving small villages and small towns for job prospects in the service industry or the big cities. They form their own urban tribes in their adopted cities and return home for holidays. Regardless of the job, most Thais send a portion of their pay home to their parents or to support dependent children left behind to be raised in the village.

The official year in Thailand is reckoned from 543 BC, the beginning of the Buddhist Era, so that AD 2011 is BE 2554, AD 2012 is BE 2555 etc.

More traditional family units and professions can be found in the provincial capitals across the country. The civil servants – teachers and government employees – make up the backbone of the Thai middle class and live in nuclear families in terrace housing estates outside the city centre. Some might live in the older in-town neighbourhoods filled with front-yard gardens growing papayas, mangoes and other fruit trees. The business class lives in the city centre, usually in apartments above shopfronts, making for an easy commute but a fairly urban life. In the cool hours of the day, the wage earners and students head to the nearest park to jog, play badminton or join in the civic-run aerobics classes.

One of the best places to view the Thai 'lifestyle' is at the markets. Day markets sell kitchen staples as well as local produce and regional desserts. Night markets are good for dinner and people-watching as few Thais bother to cook for themselves.

Though fewer people toil in the rice paddies than in the past, the villages still survive on the outskirts of the urban grid. Here life is set to the seasons, the fashions are purchased from the market and if the water buffaloes could talk they'd know all the village gossip.

From a demographic perspective Thailand, like most of Asia, is greying. Women pursue careers instead of husbands; unmarried women now

SOCK IT TO ME

Sometimes called Siamese football in old English texts, đà·grôr is a homegrown sport that involves fancy footwork and a woven rattan ball. Players typically stand in a circle (the size depends on the number of players) and simply try to keep the ball airborne by kicking it between each other. Points are scored for style, difficulty and variety of kicking manoeuvres. This form of the game is often played by friends wherever there's a little room: a vacant lot, school playground and sandy beaches.

A popular variation on đà·grôr – and the one used in intramural or international competitions – is played like volleyball, with a net, but with only the feet and head permitted to touch the ball. It's amazing to see the players perform aerial pirouettes, spiking the ball over the net with their feet. Another variation has players kicking the ball into a hoop 4.5m above the ground – basketball with feet, and no backboard!

Đà·grôr was introduced to the Southeast Asian Games by Thailand, and international championships tend to alternate between the Thais and Malaysians.

comprise 30% of the population (plus they start to outnumber men in their 30s). Successful government-sponsored family-planning efforts and professional opportunities have reduced the fertility rate so successfully – from six children in the 1960s to 1.6 children today – that analysts are now warning of future labour shortages and overextended pension systems.

Religion

Religion is alive and well in Thailand and colourful examples of daily worship can be found on nearly every corner. Walk the streets early in the morning and you'll see the solemn procession of Buddhist monks, with shaved heads and orange-coloured robes, engaged in *bin·dá·bàht*, the daily house-to-house alms food gathering.

Although the country is predominantly Buddhist, the minority religions often practise alongside one another. The green-hued onion domes of the mosques mark a neighbourhood as Muslim in pockets of Bangkok and in southern towns. In urban centres, large rounded doorways inscribed with Chinese characters and flanked by red paper lanterns marked *săhn jôw*, Chinese temples dedicated to the worship of Buddhist, Taoist and Confucian deities.

Buddhism

Approximately 95% of Thai people are Theravada Buddhists, a branch of Buddhism that came from Sri Lanka during the Sukhothai period.

The ultimate end of Theravada Buddhism is *nibbana* ('nirvana' in Sanskrit), which literally means the 'blowing out' or extinction of all grasping and thus all suffering *(dukkha)*. Effectively, *nibbana* is also an end to the cycle of rebirths (both moment-to-moment and life-to-life) that is existence.

In reality, most Thai Buddhists aim for rebirth in a 'better' existence rather than the supramundane goal of *nibbana*. The concept of rebirth is almost universally accepted in Thailand, even by non-Buddhists.

The idea of reincarnation also provides Thais with a sense of humility and interconnectedness. They might observe a creepy-crawly in the bushes and feel that perhaps they too were once like that creature or that a deceased relative now occupies a non-human body. Reflecting Thailand's social stratification, reincarnation is basically a reward or punishment. Live a good life and be reborn higher up the social ladder or behave badly throughout your life and come back in a lowlier form, such as an insect.

The new generation's upward mobility has erased some of the over-reliance on fate as a key to success but even cosmopolitan types still adhere to the Buddhist theory of karma, expressed in the Thai proverb *tam dee, dâi dee; tam chôoa, dâi chôoa* (good actions bring good results; bad actions bring bad results). A good person can improve their lot in life today and in future lives by making merit *(tam bun)*: offering food and donations to the monks and performing regular worship at the local wát. Merit-making can also result in success in business, academic tests, finding love, getting pregnant and a host of other concerns.

The Buddhist hierarchy in Thailand is made up of the Tiratana (Triple Gems) – the Buddha, the *dhamma* (the teachings) and the *sangha* (the Buddhist community). The Buddha, in his myriad sculptural forms, is found on a high shelf in the most understated roadside restaurants as well as in expensive Bangkok hotels. The *dhamma* is chanted morning and evening in every temple and taught to every Thai citizen in primary school. The *sangha* is the orange-robed monks, who carry on the day-to-day business of the religion. In temple architecture, the three-tiered roof represents the Triple Gems.

Historically the Thai king has occupied a revered position in Thai Buddhism, often viewed as semi-divine. Thai royal ceremonies remain almost exclusively the domain of Brahman priests, bestowed with the

Lifestyle Statistics

» Average age for marriage for a Thai man/woman: 27/24 years

» Minimum daily wage in Bangkok: 206B

» Entry-level government salary: 9000B per month

Thailand is often touted as the rice basket of the world; it produces 20 million tonnes per year, dividing the crop in half for domestic consumption and export.

duty of preserving the three pillars of Thai nationhood, namely sovereignty, religion and the monarchy.

Thai Buddhism has no particular Sabbath day but there are holy days *(wan prá)*, which occur every seventh or eighth day depending on phases of the moon. There are also religious holidays, typically marking important events in the Buddha's life. During these holy days Thais will go to the temple to listen to teachings, make merit and circumnavigate the main sanctuary three times.

Merit-Making

Thais visit temple for spiritual enlightenment as well as cultural entertainment. They might make a dedicated day trip to an important temple or include a merit-making stop en route to another outing. During these visits, merit-making is an individual ritual rather than the congregational affair. Worshippers buy offerings such as lotus buds, incense and candles and present these symbolic gifts to the temple's primary Buddha image. The flowers are placed on the altar, and the worshipper kneels (or stands, in the case of outdoor altars) before the Buddha image with three lit incense sticks placed between the palms in a prayerlike gesture. The head is bowed towards the floor and the hands are then raised between the heart and the forehead three times before the incense is planted at the altar. A square of thin gold paper is then affixed to the Buddha image.

Other merit-making activities include offering food to the temple *sangha*, meditating (individually or in groups), listening to monks chanting *suttas* (Buddhist discourse), and attending a *têht* or *dhamma* talk by the abbot or another respected teacher.

Monks & Nuns

Socially, every Thai male is expected to become a monk *(bhikkhu* in Pali; *prá* or *prá pík·sù* in Thai) for a short period in his life, optimally between the time he finishes school and the time he starts a career or marries. A family earns great merit when one of its sons 'takes robe and bowl'. Traditionally, the length of time spent in the *wát* is three months, during the *pan·săh* (Buddhist lent), which begins in July and coincides with the rainy season. However, nowadays men may spend as little as a week to accrue merit as monks. Most temporary ordinations occur under the age of 20 years old, when a man may enter the *sangha* as a 10-vow novice *(nairn)*.

Monks are required to shave their heads, eyebrows and any facial hair during their residence in the monastery as a sign of renouncing worldly concerns. They are also required to live an ascetic life free of luxury and eat one meal per day (sometimes two, depending on the temple traditions). Monks who live in the city usually emphasise study of the Buddhist scriptures, while those who opt for the forest temples tend to emphasise meditation. Fully ordained monks perform funeral and marriage rites, conduct sermons and instruct monastic teachings.

In rural areas, the monastery is also a social institution, providing charity outreach to the sick and the poor. Male children can enter the monastery and receive a free education, a tradition that was more prevalent before the advent of the public-schooling system. Monks also take on social-justice and environmental causes; a number of revered monks have protested dam-building, or wrapped trees in sacred cloth to prevent illegal logging.

In Thai Buddhism, women who seek a monastic life are given a minor role in the temple that is not equal to full monkhood. A Buddhist nun is known as *mâa chee* (mother priest) and lives as an *atthasila* (eight-precept) nun, a position traditionally occupied by women who had no other place in society. Thai nuns shave their heads, wear white robes and take

Reincarnation is a popular topic in Thai movies and books; in the movie *Citizen Dog*, the male lead receives unsolicited advice from his deceased grandmother who has been reborn as a gecko.

Spiritual Readings

» *Being Dharma: The Essence of the Buddha's Teachings* (2001; Ajahn Chah)

» Access to Insight (www. accesstoinsight. org)

» *Thai Folk Wisdom: Contemporary Takes on Traditional Proverbs* (2010; Tulaya Pornpiriyakulchai and Jane Vejjajiva)

» *Sacred Tattoos of Thailand* (2011; Joe Cummings)

HOUSES OF THE HOLY

Many homes or inhabited dwellings in Thailand have an associated 'spirit house', built to provide a residence for the plot of land's *prá poom* (guardian spirits). Based on animistic beliefs that predate Buddhism, guardian spirits are believed to reside in rivers, trees and other natural features and need to be honoured (and placated). The guardian spirit of a particular plot of land is the supernatural equivalent of a mother-in-law, an honoured but sometimes troublesome family member. To keep the spirits happily distracted, Thais erect elaborate dollhouse-like structures on the property where the spirits can 'live' comfortably separated from human affairs. To further cultivate good relations and good fortune, daily offerings of rice, fruit, flowers and water are made to the spirit house. If the human house is enlarged the spirit house must also be enlarged, so that the spirits do not feel slighted. Spirit houses must be consecrated by a Brahman priest.

care of temple chores. Generally speaking, *mâa chee* aren't considered as prestigious as monks and don't have a function in the merit-making rituals of lay people.

Islam

At around 4% of the population, Muslims make up Thailand's largest religious minority, living side by side with the Buddhist majority. There are some 3000 mosques in Thailand – over 200 in Bangkok alone. Of these mosques, 99% are associated with the Sunni branch of Islam (in which Islamic leadership is vested in the consensus of the Ummah, or Muslim community), and 1% with the Shi'ite branch (in which religious and political authority is given to descendants of the Prophet Mohammed).

Islam was introduced to Thailand's southern region between AD 1200 and 1500 through the influence of Indian and Arab traders and scholars. To this day, most of Thailand's Muslims reside in the south, concentrated in the regions of Pattani, Narathiwat, Satun and Yala. These southerners trace their heritage to the former Kingdom of Pattani, an Islamic kingdom whose territory straddled the present-day border between Thailand and Malaysia. Accordingly, the south shares both a border and a cultural heritage with its predominantly Muslim neighbour, Malaysia. Indeed, most of Thailand's southern Muslims are ethnically Malay and speak Malay or Yawi (a dialect of Malay written in the Arabic script) in addition to Thai. These cultural differences, coupled with a perception of religious and linguistic discrimination, have led to a feeling of disconnection from the Buddhist majority in some parts of the Muslim-dominated south.

The Theravada school is often called the southern school because it travelled from the Indian subcontinent to Southeast Asia, while Mahayana Buddhism was adopted throughout the northern regions of Nepal, Tibet, China and the rest of east Asia.

Arts

Thailand has an intensely visual culture and an appreciation of beauty that infuses audacious temple buildings, humble old-fashioned houses and the high arts developed for the royal court.

Architecture

Most striking of Thailand's architectural heritage are the Buddhist temples, which dazzle in the tropical sun with wild colours and soaring rooflines. A classic component of temple architecture is the presence of one or more *chedi* (stupa), a mountain-shaped monument that pays tribute to the enduring stability of Buddhism. Many contain relics of important kings or the historical Buddha.

Thai temples rely heavily on Hindu-Buddhist iconography as artistic flourishes and instructional guides. *Naga,* a mythical serpentlike creature, guarded Buddha during meditation and is often depicted in entrance railings and outlining roof gables. On the tip of the roof is the *chôr fáh:* a golden bird-shaped silhouette suggesting flight.

The lotus bud is another sacred motif that is often used to decorate the tops of the temple gates, verandah columns and the spires of Sukhothai-era *chedi*. Images of the Buddha often depict him meditating in a lotus blossom-shaped pedestal. It carries with it a reminder of the tenets of Buddhism. The lotus can bloom even in a rancid pond, illustrating the capacity for religious perfection to flourish even in unlikely situations.

Thais began mixing traditional architecture with European forms in the late 19th and early 20th centuries. The port cities of Thailand, including Bangkok and Phuket, acquired fine examples of Sino-Portuguese architecture – buildings of stuccoed brick decorated with an ornate facade – a style that followed the sea traders during the colonial era. This style is often referred to as 'old Bangkok' or 'Ratanakosin'.

Bangkok's relatively modern skyscrapers are textbook examples of postmodern dos and don'ts. In the 1960s and '70s the trend in modern Thai architecture, inspired by the European Bauhaus movement,

THAILAND'S ARTISTIC PERIODS

PERIOD	TEMPLE & CHEDI STYLES	BUDDHA STYLES	EXAMPLES
Dvaravati Period (7th–11th Centuries)	Rectangular-based *chedi* with stepped tiers	Indian influenced ; thick torso, large hair curls, arched eyebrows (like flying birds), protruding eyes, thick lips and flat nose.	Phra Pathom Chedi, Nakhon Pathom; Lopburi Museum, Lopburi; Wat Chama Thewi, Lamphun
Srivijaya Period (7th–13th Centuries)	Mahayana-Buddhist style temples; Javanese-style *chedi* with elaborate arches	Indian influenced; heavily ornamented, humanlike features and slightly twisted at the waist.	Wat Phra Mahathat Woramahawihaan and National Museum, Nakhon Si Thammarat
Khmer Period (9th-11th Centuries)	Hindu-Buddhist temples; corn-cob shaped *prang* (Khmer-styled *chedi*)	Buddha meditating under a canopy of the seven-headed *naga* and atop a lotus pedestal.	Phimai Historical Park, Nakhon Ratchasima; Phanom Rung Historical Park, Surin
Chiang Saen-Lanna Period (11th–13th Centuries)	Teak temples; square-based *chedi* topped by gilded umbrella; also octagonal-based *chedi*	Burmese influences with plump figure, round, smiling face and footpads facing upwards in meditation pose.	Wat Phra Singh, Chiang Mai; Chiang Saen National Museum, Chiang Saen
Sukhothai Period (13th–15th Centuries)	Khmer-inspired temples; slim-spired *chedi* topped by a lotus bud	Graceful poses, often depicted 'walking', no anatomical human detail.	Sukhothai Historical Park, Sukhothai
Ayuthaya Period (14th–18th Centuries)	Classical Thai temple with three-tiered roof and gable flourishes; bell-shaped *chedi* with tapering spire	Ayuthaya-era king, wearing a gem-studded crown and royal regalia.	Ayuthaya Historical Park, Ayuthaya
Bangkok-Ratanakosin Period (19th Century)	Colourful and gilded temple with Western-Thai styles; mosaic-covered *chedi*	Reviving Ayuthaya style.	Wat Phra Kaew, Wat Pho and Wat Arun, Bangkok

HANDMADE ART

Thailand has a long tradition of handicrafts, often regionally and even village specific. Ceramics include the greenish celadon products, red-earth clay pots of Dan Kwian, and central Thailand's *ben·jà·rong* or 'five-colour' style. *Ben·jà·rong* is based on Chinese patterns while celadon is of Thai origin.

Northern Thailand has long produced regionally distinctive lacquerware thanks to the influence of Burmese artisans.

Each region in Thailand has its own silk-weaving style. In ancient times woven textiles might have functioned much like business cards do today – demarcating tribal identity and sometimes even marriage status. Today, village weaving traditions continue but have become less geographically specific.

moved towards a stark functionalism – the average building looked like a giant egg carton turned on its side. When Thai architects began experimenting with form over function during the building boom of the mid-1980s, the result was high-tech designs such as ML Sumet Jumsai's famous 'Robot Building' on Th Sathon Tai in Bangkok. Rangsan Torsuwan, a graduate of Massachusetts Institute of Technology (MIT), introduced the neoclassic (or neo-Thai) style.

Traditional Painting & Sculpture

Thailand's artistic repository remains mainly in the temples where Buddha sculptures and murals communicate a visual language of the religion. These Buddha images trace Thailand's historical and artistic evolution from a conquered backwater to a sovereign nation. The period when the country first defined its own artistic style was during the Sukhothai era, famous for its graceful and serene Buddha figures.

Temple murals are the main form of ancient Thai art. Always instructional in intent, murals often depict the *jataka* (stories of the Buddha's past lives) and the Thai version of the Hindu epic *Ramayana*. Lacking the durability of other art forms, pre-20th-century religious painting is limited to very few surviving examples. The earliest examples are found at Ayuthaya's Wat Ratburana but Bangkok has some of the best surviving examples.

The development of Thai religious art and architecture is broken into different periods or schools defined by the patronage of the ruling capital. The best examples of a period's characteristics are seen in the variations of the *chedi* shape and in the features of the Buddha sculptures. The works from the various artistic periods differ in the depiction of Buddha's facial features, the top flourish on the head, the dress and the position of the feet in meditation.

Contemporary Art

Adapting traditional themes to the secular canvas began around the turn of the 20th century as Western influence surged in the region. In general, Thai painting favours abstraction over realism and continues to preserve the one-dimensional perspective of traditional mural paintings. There are two major trends in Thai art: the updating of religious themes and tongue-in-cheek social commentary. Some artists overlap the two.

Italian Corrado Feroci is often credited as the father of modern Thai art. He was first invited to Thailand by Rama VI in 1923 and built Bangkok's Democracy Monument and other monuments in Bangkok.

In the 1970s Thai artists tackled the modernisation of Buddhist themes through abstract expressionism. Leading works in this genre include the colourful surrealism of Pichai Nirand and the mystical pen-and-ink drawings of Thawan Duchanee. Receiving more exposure overseas than

Recommended Arts Reading

» *The Thai House: History and Evolution* (2002; Ruethai Chaichongrak)

» *The Arts of Thailand* (1998; Steve Van Beek)

» *Flavours: Thai Contemporary Art* (2005; Steven Pettifor)

» *Bangkok Design: Thai Ideas in Textiles & Furniture* (2006; Brian Mertens)

» *Buddhist Temples of Thailand: A Visual Journey Through Thailand's 40 Most Historic Wats* (2010; Joe Cummings)

at home, the work of Montien Boonma uses the ingredients of Buddhist merit-making, such as gold leaf, bells and candle wax, to create pieces.

Politically motivated artwork defines a parallel movement in Thai contemporary art. In Thailand's rapidly industrialising society, many artists watched as rice fields became factories, the forests became asphalt and the spoils went to the politically connected. Manit Sriwanichpoom is best known for his Pink Man on Tour series, in which he depicted artist Sompong Thawee in a pink suit with a pink shopping cart amid Thailand's most iconic attractions. Vasan Sitthiket is more blatantly controversial and uses mixed-media installations to condemn the players he views as corrupt. His works have been banned in Thailand and criticised as anti-Thai.

In the 1990s there was a push to move art out of museums and into public spaces. An artist and art organiser, Navin Rawanchaikul started his 'in-the-streets' collaborations in his hometown of Chiang Mai and then moved his ideas to Bangkok where he filled the city's taxi cabs with art installations, a show that literally went on the road. His other works have a way with words, such as the mixed-media piece *We Are the Children of Rice (Wine)* (2002) and his rage against the commercialisation of museums in his epic painting entitled *Super (M)art Bangkok Survivors* (2004). This piece was inspired by the struggles of the Thai art community, which protested against the efforts to turn the Bangkok Art and Culture Centre into a shopping 'experience' instead of a museum.

Thai sculpture is often considered to be the strongest of the contemporary arts. Khien Yimsiri creats elegant human and mythical forms out of bronze. Manop Suwanpinta moulds the human anatomy into fantastic shapes that often intersect with technological features, such as hinged faces that open to reveal inanimate content. Kamin Lertchaiprasert explores the subject of spirituality and daily life in his sculptures, which often include a small army of papier-mâché figures. His *Ngern Nang* (Sitting Money) installation included a series of figures made from discarded paper bills from the national bank embellished with poetic instructions on life and love.

Music

Throughout Thailand you'll find a diversity of musical genres and styles, from the serene court music that accompanies classical dance-drama to the chest-thumping house music played at dance clubs.

Classical Music

The classical orchestra is called the *pèe pâht* and was originally developed to accompany classical dance-drama and shadow theatre, but these days can be heard in straightforward performances at temple fairs and tourist attractions. The ensemble can include from five to more than 20 players. Prior to a performance the players offer incense and flowers to the *dà·pohn*.

The standard Thai scale divides the eight-note octave into seven fulltone intervals, with no semitones. Thai scales were first transcribed by the

Art Museums & Galleries

» National Museum, Bangkok

» Bangkok Art and Culture Centre

» 100 Tonson Gallery, Bangkok

» H Gallery, Bangkok

» Kathmandu Photo Gallery, Bangkok

TRADITIONAL INSTRUMENTS

» *pèe* – high-pitched woodwind, often heard at Thai-boxing matches

» *rá·nâht èhk* – bamboo-keyed percussion that resembles a xylophone

» *kórng wong yài* – tuned gongs arranged in a semicircle

» *dà·pohn (tohn)* – a double-headed hand-drum

» *pĭn* – four-stringed instrument plucked like a guitar

» *sor* – slender bowed instrument with a coconut-shell soundbox

» *klòo·i* – wooden flute

Thai-German composer Peter Feit (also known by his Thai name, Phra Chen Duriyang), who composed Thailand's national anthem in 1932.

Lôok Tûng & Mǒr Lam

The bestselling modern musical genre in Thailand is *lôok tûng* (literally 'children of the fields'), which dates to the 1940s. Analogous to country and western music in the USA, it's a genre that appeals to working-class Thais. Subject matter almost always cleaves to tales of lost love, tragic early death, and the dire circumstances of farmers who work day in and day out and are still in debt. The plaintive singing style ranges from sentimentality to anguish and singers are often backed by Las Vegas–style showgirl dancers.

dà·pohn (tohn)

Mǒr lam is Thailand's blues; it's a folk tradition firmly rooted in the northeast of Thailand and is based on the songs played on the Lao-Isan *kaan* (a wind instrument devised of a double row of bamboo-like reeds fitted into a hardwood soundbox). The oldest style is most likely to be heard at a village gathering and has a simple but insistent bass beat and is often sung in Isan dialect. It has traditionally had a 'country bumpkin' image, but *mǒr lam* has jumped the generational fence and now has an electrified pop version and seriously silly side.

rá·nâht èhk

As economic migrants from across the country have moved to Bangkok, the two genres have begun to merge. Contemporary singers regularly cross from one style to another with a few songs in between.

Thailand's most famous *lôok tûng* singer was Pumpuang Duangjan, who received a royally sponsored cremation when she died in 1992 and a major shrine at Suphanburi's Wat Thapkradan. Gravelly voiced Siriporn Ampaipong helped carry the tradition afterwards and is still beloved. The new *lôok tûng* princess is Tai Orathai, a college graduate who can vibrate those dramatic notes with rivers of feeling.

pèe

Jintara Poonlarp is a current fixture in the constellation; she's quite nouveau with a trendy haircut and Bangkok-style fashions instead of the farm-girl look. Mike Pirompon excels with the oh-so-sad ballads and Rock Salaeng puts the rock-and-roll in *lôok tûng*.

Thai Rock & Pop

The 1970s ushered in the politically conscious folk rock of the USA and Europe, which the Thais dubbed *pleng pêu·a chee·wít* ('songs for life'). Chiefly identified with the Thai band Caravan, this style defined a major contemporary shift in Thai music. Songs of this nature have political and environmental topics rather than the usual love themes. During the authoritarian dictatorships of the '70s many of Caravan's songs were officially banned. Another longstanding example of this style, Carabao mixed in rock and heavy metal and spawned a whole generation of imitators.

sor

Thailand also has a thriving teen-pop industry – sometimes referred to as T-pop – centred on artists chosen for their good looks, which often means they are half-Thai, half-*fà·ràng* and sport English names. Thailand's king of pop is Thongchai 'Bird' Mcintyre (also known as Pi Bird). His first album came out in 1986 and he has followed up with an album almost every year since. With Madonna's staying power coupled with a nice-guy persona, he is very popular with Thais in their 30s and 40s.

The current crop of pop stars are imitating Korean pop stars (Japan pop, or J-pop, is out). Girly Berry is a group of attractive, young songstresses with a signature dance move (see it on YouTube), essential for pop groups.

klòo·i

The 1990s gave birth to an alternative pop scene – known as 'indie' – pioneered by the independent record label Bakery Music. During indie's heyday, Modern Dog, composed of four Chulalongkorn University graduates, orchestrated the generation's musical coming of age. Another indie fixture was Loso (from 'low society' as opposed to 'hi-so' or socialites), which

kórng wong yài

LOOKING FOR LIVE MUSIC?

Bangkok is the source for a nightly dose of live music with clubs specialising in cover bands, jazz and rock jam sessions and DJ spin scenes. The Hua Hin Jazz Festival is a well-regarded affair and the Pattaya International Music Festival recruits domestic and international talent. Pai has hosted a reggae festival that complements the town's hippie-haven reputation. Chiang Mai has a small collection of live-music venues, including a cosy 'songs-for-life' club that was once the mainstay of the musical scene.

Music Sources

» E Thai Music (www.ethaimusic. com) is an online music store with transliterated lyrics

» 365 Jukebox (www.365jukebox. com) tracks popular hits on Thai radio stations, including Fat FM 104.5 (alt-rock), Seed FM 97.5 (T-pop), and Luk Thung FM95.0 (lôok tûng and mŏr lam)

Thailand Playlist

» That Song (Modern Dog)

» The Sound of Siam: Leftfield Luk Thung, Jazz & Molam in Thailand 1964–1975 (Soundway Records compilation)

» Made in Thailand (Carabao)

» Best (Pumpuang Duangjan)

» Romantic Comedy (Apartment Khunpa)

updated Carabao's affinity for Thai folk melodies and rhythms. But the past decade has moved these bands into 'classic' rock status and Bakery Music was bought by a conglomerate. The alt scene lives on in Abuse the Youth, Class A Cigarettes, Slur, Tattoo Colour and Apartment Khunpa and a host of bands influenced by punk, reggae and other international genres.

The revived disco sound of Groove Riders has brought down the tempo but upped the funky factor. Their hit 'Disco' has become a wedding-song staple. Hugo Chakrabongse was a popular Thai TV actor and minor royal when he gave it all up for music. He has since resurfaced in the US as a songwriter for Beyoncé and was recently signed to Jay-Z's record label.

Dance & Theatre

Thailand's high arts have been in decline since the palace transitioned from a cloistered community. Some of the endangered art forms have been salvaged and revived. Folk traditions have a broader appeal, though the era of village stage shows is long gone.

Thailand's most famous dance-drama is kŏhn, which depicts the Ramakian, the Thai version of India's Ramayana. Dancers wear elaborate costumes and some characters are masked. The central story revolves around Prince Rama's search for his beloved Princess Sita, who has been abducted by the evil 10-headed demon Ravana and taken to the island of Lanka.

Every region has its own traditional dance style performed at temple fairs and provincial parades. School-aged children often take traditional Thai dance lessons. Occasionally temples will also provide shrine dancers, who are commissioned by merit-makers to perform.

Most often performed at Buddhist festivals, lí-gair is a gaudy, raucous theatrical art form thought to have descended from drama rituals brought to southern Thailand by Arab and Malay traders. It contains a colourful mix of folk and classical music, outrageous costumes, melodrama, slapstick comedy, sexual innuendo and up-to-date commentary.

Puppet theatre also enjoyed royal and common patronage. Lá·kon lék (little theatre) used marionettes of varying sizes for court performances similar to kŏhn. Two to three puppet masters are required to manipulate the metre-high puppets by means of wires attached to long poles. Stories are drawn from Thai folk tales, particularly Phra Aphaimani, and occasionally from the Ramakian.

Shadow-puppet theatre – in which two-dimensional figures are manipulated between a cloth screen and a light source at night-time performances – has been a Southeast Asian tradition for perhaps five centuries originally brought to the Malay Peninsula by Middle Eastern traders. In Thailand it is mostly found in the south. As in Malaysia and Indonesia, shadow puppets in Thailand are carved from dried buffalo or cow hides (năng).

Cinema

When it comes to Thai cinema, there are usually two concurrent streams: the movies that are financially successful and the movies that are considered cinematically meritorious. Only occasionally do these overlap.

Popular Thai cinema ballooned in the 1960s and '70s, especially when the government levied a tax on Hollywood imports thus spawning a home-grown industry. The majority of films were cheap action flicks that were often dubbed *nám nôw* (stinking water), but the fantastic, even nonsensical, plots and rich colours left a lasting impression on modern-day Thai filmmakers, who have inserted these elements into modern contexts.

Thai cinema graduated into international film circles in the late '90s early '00s, thanks in part to director Pen-Ek Ratanaruang and his gritty and engrossing films, including *Ruang Rak Noi Nid Mahasan* (Last Life in the Universe; 2003). Apichatpong Weerasethakul is Thailand's leading *cinéma-vérité* director and continues to receive accolades at Cannes, most recently winning the Palme d'Or for *Uncle Boonmee Who Can Recall His Past Lives* (2010).

Thai cinema remains largely escapist fare though there are oftentimes sociological commentaries rather than overt political messages. A film-festival favourite, *Mundane History* (Jao Nok Krajok; 2009), directed by up-and-comer Anocha Suwichakornpong, is a family drama about a paralysed man and his friendship with his male nurse. The plot is nonlinear and a critique of Thailand's stratified society. Other trends in Thai cinema include movies dealing with homosexuality, including the critically acclaimed *The Love of Siam* (Rak Haeng Siam; 2009), directed by Chukiat Sakveerakul, which was Thailand's submission to the Oscars that year.

The big studios like to back ghost stories, horror flicks, historic epics, sappy love stories and camp comedies. Elaborate historical movies serve a dual purpose: making money and promoting national identity. Criticised as a propaganda tool, the *Legend of King Naresuan* epic, which comprises four instalments, focuses on the Ayuthaya-era king who repelled an attempted Burmese invasion. Each chapter (three have been released so far) has been a box-office winner.

Despite more daring storytelling, Thai cinema censors are still dedicated to their jobs and often ban or cut out scenes that contain objectionable subject matter. In 2007 the film board introduced a rating system (five levels indicated by appropriate age of viewer) that takes some of the guesswork out of what is allowed.

Literature

The written word has a long history in Thailand, dating back to the 11th or 12th century when the first Thai script was fashioned from an older Mon alphabet. The 30,000-line *Phra Aphaimani,* composed by poet Sunthorn Phu in the late 18th century, is Thailand's most famous classical literary work. Like many of its epic predecessors around the world, it tells the story of an exiled prince who must complete an odyssey of love and war before returning to his kingdom in victory.

Of all classical Thai literature, however, *Ramakian* is the most pervasive and influential in Thai culture. The Indian source, *Ramayana,* came to Thailand with the Khmers 900 years ago, first appearing as stone reliefs on Prasat Hin Phimai and other Angkor temples in the northeast. Eventually the Thais developed their own version of the epic, which was first written down during the reign of Rama I. This version contained 60,000 stanzas and was a quarter longer than the Sanskrit original.

Although the main themes remained the same, the Thais embroidered the *Ramayana* with more biographical detail on arch-villain Ravana (called Thotsakan, or '10-necked' in the *Ramakian*) and his wife Montho. Hanuman, the monkey god, differs substantially in the Thai version in his flirtatious nature (in the Hindu version he follows a strict vow of chastity). One of the classic *Ramakian* reliefs at Bangkok's Wat Pho depicts Hanuman clasping a maiden's bared breast as if it were an apple.

Thai Movies

» *Fun Bar Karaoke* (1997), directed by Pen-Ek Ratanaruang

» *Yam Yasothon* (2005), directed by Petchtai Wongkamlao

» *Fah Talai Jone* (Tears of the Black Tiger; 2000), directed by Wisit Sasanatieng

» *Mekhong Sipha Kham Deuan Sip-et* (Mekong Full Moon Party; 2002), directed by Jira Malikul

Recommended Fiction

» *The Lioness in Bloom: Modern Thai Fiction about Women* (translated by Susan Fulop Kepner)

» *Four Reigns* (Kukrit Pramoj)

» *Bangkok 8* (John Burdett)

» *Fieldwork: A Novel* (Mischa Berlinski)

Eating in Thailand

There's an entire universe of amazing dishes once you get beyond 'pad thai' and green curry, and for many visitors food is one of the main reasons for choosing Thailand as a destination. Even more remarkable, however, is the love for Thai food among the locals: Thais become just as excited as tourists when faced with a bowl of well-prepared noodles or when seated at a renowned hawker stall. This unabashed enthusiasm for eating, not to mention an abundance of fascinating ingredients and influences, has generated one of the most fun and diverse food scenes anywhere in the world.

Kids may have a problem adjusting to Thai food; see the boxed text, p46 for some information on how to deal with this.

Appon's Thai Food (www.khiewchanta.com) features more than 800 authentic and well-organised Thai recipes – many with helpful audio recordings of their Thai names – written by a native Thai.

The Four Flavours

Simply put, sweet, sour, salty and spicy are the parameters that define Thai food, and although many associate the cuisine with spiciness, virtually every dish is an exercise in balancing these four tastes. This balance might be obtained by a squeeze of lime juice and a glug of fish sauce, or a tablespoon of fermented soybeans and a strategic splash of vinegar. Bitter also factors into many Thai dishes, and often comes from the addition of a vegetable or herb. Regardless of the source, the goal is the same: a favourable balance of four clear, vibrant flavours.

Staples & Specialities

Rice & Noodles

Rice is so central to Thai food culture that the most common term for 'eat' is *gin kôw* (literally, 'consume rice') and one of the most common greetings is *Gin kôw rěu yang?* (Have you consumed rice yet?). To eat is to eat rice, and for most of the country, a meal is not acceptable without this staple.

SOMETHING'S FISHY

Westerners might scoff at the all-too-literal name of this condiment, but for much of Thai cooking, fish sauce is more than just another ingredient, it is the ingredient.

Essentially the liquid obtained from fermented fish, fish sauce takes various guises depending on the region. In northeastern Thailand, discerning diners prefer a thick, pasty mash of fermented freshwater fish and sometimes rice. Elsewhere, where people have access to the sea, fish sauce takes the form of a thin liquid extracted from salted anchovies. In both cases the result is highly pungent, but generally salty (rather than fishy) in taste, and used much the same way as the saltshaker is in the West.

NOODLE MIXOLOGY

If you see a steel rack containing four lidded glass bowls or jars on your table, it's proof that the restaurant you're in serves *gŏo·ay đĕe·o* (rice noodle soup). Typically these containers offer four choices: *nám sôm prík* (sliced green chillies in vinegar), *nám plah* (fish sauce), *prík pòn* (dried red chilli, flaked or ground to a near powder) and *nám·đahn* (plain white sugar).

In typically Thai fashion, these condiments offer three ways to make the soup hotter – hot and sour, hot and salty, and just plain hot – and one to make it sweet.

The typical noodle-eater will add a teaspoonful of each one of these condiments to the noodle soup, except for the sugar, which in sweet-tooth Bangkok usually rates a full tablespoon. Until you're used to these strong seasonings, we recommend adding them a small bit at a time, tasting the soup along the way to make sure you don't go overboard.

There are many varieties of rice in Thailand and the country has been among the world leaders in rice exports since the 1960s. The highest grade is *kôw hŏrm má·lí* (jasmine rice), a fragrant long grain that is so coveted by neighbouring countries that there is allegedly a steady underground business in smuggling out fresh supplies. Residents of Thailand's north and northeast eat *kôw nĕe·o*, 'sticky rice', a glutinous short-grained rice that is cooked by steaming, not boiling. In Chinese-style eateries, *kôw đôm*, 'boiled rice', a watery porridge sometimes employing brown or purple rice, is a common carb.

Rice is customarily served alongside main dishes like curries, stir-fries or soups, which are lumped together as *gàp kôw* (with rice). When you order plain rice in a restaurant you use the term *kôw plòw*, 'plain rice' or *kôw sŏoay*, 'beautiful rice'.

> Thailand is the world's leading exporter of rice, and in 2010 exported 9.03 million tonnes of the grain.

You'll find four basic kinds of noodle in Thailand. Hardly surprising, given the Thai fixation on rice, is the overwhelming popularity of *sên gŏo·ay đĕe·o*, noodles made from rice flour mixed with water to form a paste, which is then steamed to form wide, flat sheets. The sheets are folded and sliced into various widths.

Also made from rice, *kà·nŏm jeen*, is produced by pushing rice-flour paste through a sieve into boiling water, much the way Italian-style pasta is made. *Kà·nŏm jeen* is a popular morning market meal that is eaten doused with various spicy curries and topped with a self-selection of fresh and pickled vegetables and herbs.

The third kind of noodle, *bà·mèe*, is made from wheat flour and egg. It's yellowish in colour and is sold only in fresh bundles.

Finally there's *wún·sên*, an almost clear noodle made from mung-bean starch and water. Often sold in dried bunches, *wún·sên* (literally 'jelly thread') is prepared by soaking in hot water for a few minutes. The most common use of the noodle is in *yam wún sên,* a hot and tangy salad made with lime juice, fresh sliced *prík kêe nŏo* (tiny chillies), shrimp, ground pork and various seasonings.

> *Thai Food* by David Thompson is widely considered the most authoritative English-language book on Thai cooking. Thompson's latest book, *Thai Street Food*, focuses on less formal street cuisine.

Curries & Soups

In Thai, *gaang* (it sounds somewhat similar to the English 'gang') is often translated as 'curry', but it actually describes any dish with a lot of liquid and can thus refer to soups (such as *gaang jèut*) as well as the classic chilli paste-based curries for which Thai cuisine is famous. The preparation of the latter begins with a *krêu·ang gaang,* created by mashing, pounding and grinding an array of fresh ingredients with a stone mortar and pestle to form an aromatic, extremely pungent-tasting and rather thick paste. Typical ingredients in a *krêu·ang gaang*

(CON)FUSION CUISINE

A popular dish at restaurants across Thailand is *kôw pàt à·me·rí·gan,* 'American fried rice'. Taking the form of rice fried with ketchup, raisins and peas, sides of ham and deep-fried hot dogs, and topped with a fried egg, the dish is, well, every bit as revolting as it sounds. But at least there's an interesting history behind it: American fried rice apparently dates back to the Vietnam War era, when thousands of US troops were based in northeastern Thailand. A local cook apparently decided to take the ubiquitous 'American Breakfast' (also known as ABF, fried eggs with ham and/or hot dogs, and white bread, typically eaten with ketchup) and make it 'Thai' by frying the various elements with rice.

This culinary cross-pollination is only a recent example of the tendency of Thai cooks to pick and choose from the variety of cuisines at their disposal. Other (significantly more palatable) examples include *gaang mát·sà·màn,* 'Muslim curry', a now classic blend of Thai and Middle Eastern cooking styles, and the famous *pàt tai,* essentially a blend of Chinese cooking methods and ingredients (frying, rice noodles) with Thai flavours (fish sauce, chilli, tamarind).

include dried chilli, galangal, lemon grass, kaffir lime zest, shallots, garlic, shrimp paste and salt.

Another food celebrity that falls into the soupy category is *ôôm yam,* the famous Thai spicy and sour soup. Fuelling the fire beneath *ôôm yam*'s often velvety surface are fresh *prík kêe nŏo* (tiny chillies) or, alternatively, half a teaspoonful of *nám prík pŏw* (a roasted chilli paste). Lemon grass, kaffir lime leaf and lime juice give *ôôm yam* its characteristic tang.

Stir-Fries & Deep-Fries

The simplest dishes in the Thai culinary repertoire are the various stir-fries *(pàt),* introduced to Thailand by the Chinese, who are world famous for being able to stir-fry a whole banquet in a single wok.

The list of *pàt* dishes seems endless. Many cling to their Chinese roots, such as the ubiquitous *pàt pàk bûng fai daang* (morning glory flash-fried with garlic and chilli), while some are Thai-Chinese hybrids, such as *pàt pèt* (literally 'hot stir-fry'), in which the main ingredients, typically meat or fish, are quickly stir-fried with red curry paste.

Tôrt (deep-frying in oil) is mainly reserved for snacks such as *glôo·ay tôrt* (deep-fried bananas) or *pò·pée·a* (egg rolls). An exception is *plah tôrt* (deep-fried fish), which is a common way to prepare fish.

Hot & Tangy Salads

Standing right alongside curries in terms of Thai-ness is the ubiquitous *yam,* a hot and tangy 'salad' typically based around seafood, meat or vegetables.

Lime juice provides the tang, while the abundant use of fresh chilli generates the heat. Most *yam* are served at room temperature or just slightly warmed by any cooked ingredients. The dish functions equally well as part of a meal, or on its own as *gàp glâam,* snack food to accompany a night of boozing.

Perhaps the zenith of this style of cooking is northeastern Thailand's *sôm·ôam* (see the boxed text, p741).

Nám Prík

Although they're more home than restaurant food, *nám prík,* spicy chilli-based 'dips', are, for the locals at least, among the most emblematic of all Thai dishes. Typically eaten with rice and steamed or fresh vegetables and herbs, they're also among the most regional of Thai dishes, and

Maintained by a Thai woman living in the US, She Simmers (www.shesimmers.com) is a good source of recipes that cover the basics of Thai cooking.

you could probably pinpoint the province you're in by simply looking at the *nám prík* on offer.

Fruits

Being a tropical country, Thailand excels in the fruit department. *Má·môo·ang* (mangoes) alone come in a dozen varieties that are eaten at different stages of ripeness. Other common fruit include *sàp·pà·rót* (pineapple), *má·lá·gor* (papaya) and *đaang moh* (watermelon), all of which are sold from ubiquitous vendor carts and accompanied by a dipping mix of salt, sugar and ground chilli.

Sweets

English-language Thai menus often have a section called 'Desserts', but the concept takes two slightly different forms in Thailand. *Kŏrng wăhn*, which translates as 'sweet things', are small, rich sweets that often boast a slightly salty flavour. Prime ingredients for *kŏrng wăhn* include grated coconut, coconut milk, rice flour (from white rice or sticky rice), cooked sticky rice, tapioca, mung-bean starch, boiled taro and various fruits. Egg yolks are a popular ingredient for many *kŏrng wăhn* – including the ubiquitous *fŏy torng* (literally 'golden threads') – probably influenced by Portuguese desserts and pastries introduced during the early Ayuthaya era (see the boxed text, p743).

Thai sweets similar to the European concept of pastries are called *kà·nŏm*. Probably the most popular type of *kà·nŏm* in Thailand are the bite-sized items wrapped in banana leaves, especially *kôw đôm gà·tí* and *kôw đôm mát*. Both consist of sticky rice grains steamed with *gà·tí* (coconut milk) inside a banana-leaf wrapper to form a solid, almost taffy-like mass.

Although foreigners don't seem to immediately take to most Thai sweets, two dishes few visitors have trouble with are *rođi*, the backpacker staple 'banana pancakes' slathered with sugar and condensed milk, and *ai·đim gà·tí*, Thai-style coconut ice cream. At more traditional shops, the ice cream is garnished with toppings such as kidney beans or sticky rice, and is a brilliant snack on a sweltering Thai afternoon.

Regional Variations

One particularly unique aspect of Thai food is its regional diversity. Despite having evolved in a relatively small area, Thai cuisine is anything but a single entity, and takes a slightly different form every time it crosses a provincial border.

Central Thai food is the most ubiquitous and refined Thai cuisine, and has been greatly influenced by both royal court cuisine and foreign cooking styles, from Chinese to Malay/Muslim. Sweet and rich flavours rule

Keep up with the ever-changing food scene in Bangkok by following the dining section of CNNGo's Bangkok pages (www. cnngo.com/ bangkok/eat) and BK's restaurant section (http:// bk.asia-city.com/ restaurants).

THE CULT OF SÔM·ĐAM

Green papaya salad, known in Thai as *sôm·đam*, probably has its origins in Laos, but is today one of the most popular dishes in Thailand. It is made by taking strips of green unripe papaya and bruising them in a clay or wood mortar along with garlic, palm sugar, green beans, tomatoes, lime juice, fish sauce and a typically shock-inducing amount of fresh chillies. *Sôm·đam low*, the 'original' version of the dish, employs heartier chunks of papaya, sliced eggplants, salted field crabs, and a thick unpasteurised fish sauce known as *þlah ráh*. Far more common in Bangkok is *đam tai*, which includes dried shrimp and peanuts, and is seasoned with bottled fish sauce. In other riffs on the dish, the papaya can be replaced with green mango, cucumber or long beans. Almost always made by women, *sôm·đam* is also primarily enjoyed by women, often as a snack rather than an entire meal – the intense spiciness provides a satisfying mental 'full'.

A THAI PILSNER PRIMER

We relish the look of horror on the faces of Thailand newbies when the waitress casually plunks several cubes of ice into their pilsners. Before you rule this supposed blasphemy out completely, there are a few reasons why we and the Thais actually prefer our beer on the rocks.

First, despite all the alleged accolades displayed on most bottles, Thai beer does not possess the most sophisticated bouquet in the world and is best drunk as cold as possible. Also, if you haven't already noticed, the weather in Thailand is often extremely hot, another reason it makes sense to maintain your beer at maximum chill. And lastly, domestic brews are generally quite high in alcohol and the ice helps to dilute this, preventing dehydration and one of those infamous Beer Chang hangovers the next day. Taking these theories to the extreme, some places in Thailand serve something called *beea wún*, 'jelly beer', beer that has been semi-frozen until it reaches a deliciously slushy and refreshing consistency.

However, a brief warning: it's a painfully obvious sign you've been in Thailand too long if you put ice in your draught Hoegaarden.

in central Thai dishes, which often feature ingredients such as coconut milk, freshwater fish and meats.

Northeastern Thai food is undoubtedly Thailand's most rustic regional cooking style, and is most likely indicative of what the ethnic Tai people have been eating for hundreds, if not thousands of years. Spicy, tart flavours and simple cooking methods such as grilling and soups dominate the northeastern kitchen, in which the predominant carb is sticky rice. Because many northeastern Thais are migratory workers, their cuisine is available in simple stalls in virtually every corner of the country.

The most obscure regional cooking style in Thailand is undoubtedly northern-style cooking. Also based around sticky rice, meat, in particular pork, bitter/hot flavours and deep-frying play important roles in the northern Thai kitchen. Given the north's elevation and climate, northern Thai food is probably the most seasonal of regional Thai cuisines. For more on northern cuisine, see the boxed text, p304.

Southern Thai cooking is arguably the spiciest of Thailand's regional cooking styles. It can also be very salty, and not surprisingly, given the south's coastline, seafood plays a large role. Turmeric provides many southern Thai dishes with a yellow/orange hue, and many southern Thai meals are accompanied by a platter of fresh herbs and vegetables as a way of countering their heat. Thailand's south is also a good place to sample Muslim-Thai cooking, which is probably Thailand's sweetest cuisine.

Written, photographed and maintained by the author of this chapter, www. austinbush photography. com/category/ foodblog details food and dining in both Bangkok and provincial Thailand.

Drinks

Coffee, Tea & Fruit Drinks

Thais are big coffee drinkers, and good-quality arabica and robusta are cultivated in the hilly areas of northern and southern Thailand. The traditional filtering system is nothing more than a narrow cloth bag attached to a steel handle. This type of coffee is served in a glass, mixed with sugar and sweetened with condensed milk – if you don't want either, be sure to specify *gah·faa dam* (black coffee) followed with *mâi sài nám·dahn* (without sugar).

Black tea, both local and imported, is available at the same places that serve real coffee. *Chah tai* derives its characteristic orange-red colour from ground tamarind seed added after curing.

Fruit drinks appear all over Thailand and are an excellent way to rehydrate after water becomes unpalatable. Most *nám pŏn·lá·mái* (fruit juices) are served with a touch of sugar and salt and a whole lot of ice. Many foreigners object to the salt, but it serves a metabolic role in helping the body to cope with tropical temperatures.

Beer & Spirits

There are several brands of beer in Thailand, ranging from domestic brands (Singha, Chang, Leo) to foreign-licensed labels (Heineken, Asahi, San Miguel) – all largely indistinguishable in terms of taste and quality. For more on how the Thais drink their beer, see the boxed text, p742.

Domestic rice whisky and rum are favourites of the working class, struggling students and family gatherings as they're more affordable than beer. Once spending money becomes a priority, Thais often upgrade to imported whiskies. These are usually drunk with lots of ice, soda water and a splash of coke. On a night out, buying a whole bottle is the norm in most of Thailand. If you don't finish it, it will simply be kept at the bar until your next visit.

Can I Drink the Ice?

Among the most common concerns we hear from first-time visitors to Thailand is about the safety of the country's ice. If it's your first time in Thailand, keep in mind that you are that you're exposing yourself to an entirely different cuisine and a new and unfamiliar family of bacteria and other bugs, so it's virtually inevitable that your body will have a hard time adjusting.

On the good side, in most cases this will mean little more than an upset tummy that might set you back a couple hours. You can avoid more serious setbacks, at least initially, by trying to frequent popular restaurants/vendors where dishes are prepared to order, and only drinking bottled water.

And the ice? We've been lacing our drinks with it for years and have yet to trace it back to any specific discomfort.

Where to Eat & Drink

Prepared food is available just about everywhere in Thailand, and it shouldn't come as a surprise that the locals do much of their eating outside the home. In this regard, as a visitor, you'll fit right in.

Bangkok's Top 50 Street Food Stalls, by Chawadee Nualkhair, also functions well as a general introduction and guide to Thai-style informal dining.

Thai Hawker Food by Kenny Yee and Catherine Gordon is an illustrated guide to recognising and ordering street food in Thailand.

MUITO OBRIGADO

Try to imagine a Thai curry without the chillies, *pàt tai* without the peanuts, or papaya salad without the papaya. Many of the ingredients used on a daily basis by Thais are recent introductions courtesy of European traders and missionaries. During the early 16th century, while Spanish and Portuguese explorers were first reaching the shores of Southeast Asia, there was also subsequent expansion and discovery in the Americas. The Portuguese in particular were quick to seize the exciting new products coming from the New World and market them in the East, thus most likely having introduced such modern-day Asian staples as tomatoes, potatoes, corn, lettuce, cabbage, chillies, papayas, guavas, pineapples, pumpkins, sweet potatoes, peanuts and tobacco.

Chillies in particular seem to have struck a chord with Thais, and are thought to have first arrived in Ayuthaya via the Portuguese around 1550. Before their arrival, the natives got their heat from bitter-hot herbs and roots such as ginger and pepper.

And not only did the Portuguese introduce some crucial ingredients to the Thai kitchen, but also some enduring cooking techniques, particularly in the area of sweets. The bright-yellow duck egg and syrup-based treats you see at many Thai markets are direct descendants of Portuguese desserts known as *fios de ovos* ('egg threads') and *ovos moles*. And in the area surrounding Bangkok's Church of Santa Cruz, a former Portuguese enclave, you can still find *kà·nŏm fa·ràng,* a bunlike snack baked over coals.

Open-air markets and food stalls are among the most popular places where Thais eat. In the mornings stalls selling coffee and Chinese-style doughnuts spring up along busy commuter corridors. At lunchtime, midday eaters might grab a plastic chair at yet another stall for a simple stir-fry, or pick up a foam box of noodles to scarf down at the office. In most small towns, night markets often set up in the middle of town with a cluster of vendors, metal tables and chairs, and some shopping as an after-dinner mint.

There are, of course, restaurants (*ráhn ah·hǎhn*) in Thailand that range from simple food stops to formal affairs. Lunchtime is the right time to point and eat at the *ráhn kôw gaang* (rice-and-curry shop), which sells a selection of premade dishes. The more generic *ráhn ah·hǎhn đahm sàng* (food-to-order shop) can often be recognised by a display of raw ingredients – Chinese kale, tomatoes, chopped pork, fresh or dried fish, noodles, eggplant, spring onions – for a standard repertoire of Thai and Chinese dishes. As the name implies, the cooks attempt to prepare any dish you can name, a slightly more difficult operation if you can't speak Thai.

Thai Food Master (www.thaifoodmaster.com), maintained by a longtime foreign resident of Thailand, contains helpful step-by-step photos that illustrate the making of a variety of Thai dishes.

Vegetarians & Vegans

Vegetarianism isn't a widespread trend in Thailand, but many of the tourist-oriented restaurants cater to vegetarians. That doesn't mean that all Thais are monogamous carnivores; there are, however, home-grown practices of vegetarianism and veganism rooted in a strict interpretation of Buddhism made popular by Bangkok's ex-Governor Chamlong Srimuang. Now there are several nonprofit *ráhn ah·hǎhn mang·sà·wí·rát* (vegetarian restaurants) in Bangkok (see the boxed text, p121) and several provincial capitals where the food is served buffet-style and is very inexpensive. Dishes are almost always 100% vegan (ie no meat, poultry, fish or fish sauce, dairy or egg products).

During the Vegetarian Festival, celebrated by Chinese Buddhists in October, many restaurants and street stalls in Bangkok, Phuket and in the Chinese business districts of most Thai towns go meatless for one

---

TASTY TRAVEL

Thailand's cuisine is intensely regional and virtually every town is associated with a specific dish that's unavailable (or at least not as tasty) outside the city limits. To help you look (and eat) like a local, we've listed a few of the more ubiquitous regional specialities:

» **Ayuthaya**: *gǒo·ay đěe·o reu·a* ('boat noodles') Rice noodles served with a dark, intense spice-laden broth.

» **Chiang Mai**: *nám prík nùm* and *kâab mǒo* (roast chilli 'dip' and deep-fried pork crackling) Available at virtually every market in the city, the two dishes go wonderfully together, ideally accompanied by par-boiled veggies and sticky rice.

» **Hat Yai**: *gài tôrt hàht yài* This city's namesake fried chicken is marinated in a dried-spice mixture, which gives it a distinctive red hue.

» **Khon Kaen**: *gài yâhng* Marinated free-range chicken (*gài bâhn*) grilled over hot coals – a northeastern speciality said to be best in this town.

» **Lampang**: *kôw đaan* Deep-fried sticky rice cakes drizzled with palm sugar are a popular treat in this northern town.

» **Nong Khai**: *nǎam neu·ang* This Vietnamese dish of balls of pork served with rice paper wrappers and a basket of herbs has found a home in northeastern Thailand.

» **Phetchaburi**: *kôw châa* This odd but delicious Mon dish of chilled fragrant rice served with sweet/savoury sides is said to be best in this central Thai town.

» **Trang**: *mǒo yâhng* Roast pig, skin and all, typically eaten as part of a dim sum brunch, is a speciality of this southern town.

BEYOND THE STREET STALL

Read any food magazine article about eating in Thailand, and you will inevitably find gushing references to the glories of the country's street food. While much of the food sold from mobile carts and streetside stalls is indeed very tasty, it certainly isn't the case that *only* street food is good. In fact, in our research, we've found that the best places to eat are anything but mobile, but rather are the long-standing, family-owned restaurants typically found in aged Sino-Portuguese shophouses. The cooks at such places have likely been serving the same dish, or limited repertoire of dishes, for several decades, and really know what they're doing. The food may cost slightly more than on the street, but the setting is usually more comfortable and hygienic, not to mention the fact that you're eating a piece of history. While such restaurants rarely have English-language menus, you can usually point to a picture or dish. If that fails, turn to p785 and practise your Thai.

So do indulge in a street cart or two – they're a fun part of the Thailand experience – but be sure to try a few old-school restaurants as well.

month. Other easy, though less common, venues for vegetarian meals include Indian restaurants, which usually feature a vegetarian section on the menu.

The phrase 'I'm vegetarian' in Thai is *pŏm gin jair* (for men) or *dì·chăn gin jair* (for women). Loosely translated this means 'I eat only vegetarian food', which includes no eggs and no dairy products – in other words, total vegan.

Habits & Customs

Like most of Thai culture, eating conventions appear relaxed and informal but are orchestrated by many implied rules.

Whether at home or in a restaurant, Thai meals are always served 'family-style', that is from common serving platters, and the plates appear in whatever order the kitchen can prepare them. When serving yourself from a common platter, put no more than one spoonful onto your plate at a time. Heaping your plate with all 'your' portions at once will look greedy to Thais unfamiliar with Western conventions. Another important factor in a Thai meal is achieving a balance of flavours and textures. Traditionally, the party orders a curry, a steamed or fried fish, a stir-fried vegetable dish and a soup, taking great care to balance cool and hot, sour and sweet, salty and plain.

Originally Thai food was eaten with the fingers, and it still is in certain regions of the kingdom. In the early 1900s, Thais began setting their tables with fork and spoon to affect a 'royal' setting, and it wasn't long before fork-and-spoon dining became the norm in Bangkok and later spread throughout the kingdom. To use these tools the Thai way, use a serving spoon, or alternatively your own, to take a single mouthful of food from a central dish, and ladle it over a portion of your rice. The fork is then used to push the now food-soaked portion of rice back onto the spoon before entering the mouth.

If you're not offered chopsticks, don't ask for them. Thai food is eaten with fork and spoon, not chopsticks. When *fa·ràng* (Westerners) ask for chopsticks to eat Thai food, it only puzzles restaurant proprietors. Chopsticks are reserved for eating Chinese-style food from bowls, or for eating in all-Chinese restaurants. In either case you will be supplied with chopsticks without having to ask. Unlike their counterparts in many Western countries, restaurateurs in Thailand won't assume you don't know how to use them.

The Sex Industry in Thailand

Thailand has had a long and complex relationship with prostitution that persists today. It is also an international sex-tourism destination, a designation that began around the time of the Vietnam War. The industry targeted to foreigners is very visible with red-light districts in Bangkok, Phuket and Pattaya, but there is also a more clandestine domestic sex industry and myriad informal channels of sex-for-hire.

Prostitution is technically illegal in Thailand. However, laws against prostitution are often ambiguous and unenforced, and economic motivations provide a steady supply of workers. Some analysts argue that the high demand for sexual services in Thailand means that there is litle likelihood of the industry being curtailed; however, limiting abusive practices within the industry is the goal of activists and government agencies.

It is difficult to determine the number of sex workers in Thailand, the demographics of the industry or its economic strength. This is because there are many indirect forms of prostitution, because the illegality of the industry makes research difficult, and because different organisations use different approaches to collect data. In 2003 measures to legalise prostitution cited the Thai sex industry as being worth $US4.3 billion (about 3% of GDP), employing roughly 200,000 sex workers. A study conducted in the same year by Thailand's Chulalongkorn University estimated 2.8 million sex workers, of which 1.98 million were adult women, 20,000 were adult men and 800,000 were children, defined as any person under the age of 18.

History & Cultural Attitudes

Prostitution has been widespread in Thailand since long before the country gained a reputation among international sex tourists. Throughout Thai history the practice was accepted and common among many sectors of the society, though it has not always been respected by the society as a whole.

Due to international pressure from the United Nations, prostitution was declared illegal in 1960, though entertainment places (go-go bars, beer bars, massage parlours, karaoke bars and bath houses) are governed by a separate law passed in 1966. These establishments are licensed and can legally provide nonsexual services (such as dancing, massage, a drinking buddy); sexual services occur through these venues but they are not technically the businesses' primary purpose.

With the arrival of the US military forces in Southeast Asia during the Vietnam War era, enterprising businesspeople adapted the existing framework to suit foreigners, in turn creating an international sex-tourism industry that persists today.

Created by a sex-workers' advocacy group, This is Us: EMPOWER Foundation National Museum (☑0 2526 8311; 57/60 Th Tiwanon, Nonthaburi; open weekdays) leads visitors through the history and working conditions of sex workers in Thailand.

In 1998 the International Labour Organisation, a United Nations agency, advised Southeast Asian countries, including Thailand, to recognise prostitution as an economic sector and income generator. It is estimated that one-third of the entertainment establishments are registered with the government and the majority pay an informal tax in the form of police bribes. One bar manager we spoke with said that they pay 5000B per month to the police.

Economic Motivations

Regardless of their background, most women in the sex industry are there for financial reasons: many find that sex work is one of the highest paying jobs for their level of (low) education, and they have financial obligations (be it dependents or debts). The most comprehensive data on the economics of sex workers comes from a 1993 survey by Kritaya Archavanitkul. The report found that sex workers made a mean income of 17,000B per month (US$18 per day), the equivalent of a mid-level civil servant job, a position acquired through advance education and family connections. At the time of her study, most sex workers had not completed high school.

The International Labor Organisation, however, estimates a Thai sex workers' salary at US$9 a day, or the average wage of a Thai service-industry worker.

These economic factors provide a strong incentive for rural, unskilled women (and to a lesser extent, men) to engage in sex work.

As with many in Thai society, a large percentage of sex workers' wages are remitted back to their home villages to support their families (parents, siblings and children). Khun Kritaya's 1993 report found that between 1800B and 6100B per month were sent back home to rural communities. The remittance-receiving households typically bought durable goods (TVs and washing machines), bigger houses and motorcycles or automobiles. Their wealth displayed their daughters' success in the industry and acted as free inducement for the next generation of sex workers.

Anecdotally, rural families have been known to put pressure on their female children to become prostitutes when debts begin to mount. The bar manager we interviewed said that she tried to return home after a stint as a sex worker in Pattaya but her mother chastised her saying, 'Everyone can do this, so can you.'

Working Conditions

The unintended consequence of prostitution prohibitions is the lawless working environment it creates for women who enter the industry. Sex work becomes the domain of criminal networks that are often involved in other illicit activities and circumvent the laws through bribes and violence.

HIV/AIDS

Thailand was lauded for its rapid and effective response to the AIDS epidemic through an aggressive condom-use campaign in the 1990s. Infection rates of female sex workers declined to 5% by 2007 but rates have recently doubled among informal sex workers (street prostitutes and freelancers). Analysts warn that the country is on the verge of a resurgence as public education efforts have declined and cultural attitudes towards sex have changed. Of the country's 610,000 people living with HIV/AIDS, intravenous drug users make up the largest portion (30% to 50% in 2007).

THE SEX INDUSTRY IN THAILAND ECONOMIC MOTIVATIONS

Sex workers are not afforded the rights of other workers: there is no minimum wage; no required vacation, sick leave or break time; no deductions for social security or employee-sponsored health insurance and no legal redress.

Bars can set their own punitive rules that fine a worker if she doesn't smile enough, arrives late or doesn't meet the drink quota. EMPOWER reported that many sex workers will owe money to the bar at the end of the month through these deductions. In effect, these women have to pay to be prostitutes and the fines disguise a pimp relationship.

Through lobbying efforts pro-sex worker groups, such as EMPOWER, hope that lawmakers will recognise all workers at entertainment places (including dish washers and cooks as well as 'working girls') as employees subject to labour and safety protections.

Other commentators (such as the Coalition Against Trafficking in Women; CATW) argue that legalising prostitution is not the answer, because such a move would legitimise a practice that is always going to be dangerous and exploitative for the women involved. Instead, these groups focus on how to enable the women to leave prostitution and make their way into different types of work.

Organisations working across borders to stop child prostitution include ECPAT (End Child Prostitution & Trafficking; www. ecpat.net) and its Australian affiliate Child Wise (www. childwise.net).

Child Prostitution & Human Trafficking

According to ECPAT (End Child Prostitution & Trafficking), there are currently 30,000 to 40,000 children involved in prostitution, though estimates are unreliable. According to Chulalongkorn University, the number of children may be as as high as 800,000.

In 1996 Thailand passed a reform law to address the issue of child prostitution (defined into two-tiers: 15 to 18 years old and under 15). Fines and jail time are assigned to customers, establishment owners and even parents involved in child prostitution (under the old law only prostitutes were culpable.) Many countries also have extraterritorial legislation that allows nationals to be prosecuted in their own country for such crimes committed in Thailand.

Urban job centres such as Bangkok, Chiang Mai and Pattaya and border towns such as Mae Sai and Mae Sot have large populations of displaced and marginalised people (Burmese immigrants, ethnic hill-tribe members and impoverished rural Thais). Children of these fractured families often turn to street begging, which is often an entryway into prostitution usually through low-level criminal gangs.

The Coalition Against Trafficking in Women (CATW; www. catwinternational. org) is a non-governmental organization that works internationally to combat prostitution and trafficking in women and children.

Thailand is also a conduit and destination for people trafficking (including children) from Myanmar, Laos, Cambodia and China. According to the United Nations, human trafficking is a crime against humanity and involves recruiting, transporting, transferring, harbouring and receiving a person through force, fraud or coercion for purposes of exploitation. In 2007 the US State Department labelled Thailand as not meeting the minimum standards of prevention of human trafficking.

It is difficult to obtain reliable data about trafficked people, including minors, but a 1997 report on foreign child labour, by Kritaya Archwanitkul, found that there were, 16,423 non-Thai prostitutes working in the country and that 30% were children under the age of 18 (a total of 4900). Other studies estimated that there were 100,000 to 200,000 foreign-born children in the Thai workforce but these figures do not determine the type of work being done.

Responsible travellers can help to stop child-sex tourism by reporting suspicious behaviour on a dedicated hotline (☏1300) or reporting the individual directly to the embassy of the offender's nationality.

Environment & Wildlife

Thailand spans a distance of 1650km from its northern tip to its southern tail, a distance that encompasses 16 latitudinal degrees and a variety of ecological zones, making it one of the most environmentally diverse countries in Southeast Asia.

The Land

Thailand's odd shape is often likened to the head of an elephant with the shaft of the trunk being the Malay peninsula and the head being the northern mountains. Starting at the crown of the country, northern Thailand is dominated by the Dawna-Tenasserim mountain range, a southeast-trending extension of the Himalayan mountains. Dropping into the central region, the topography mellows into rice-producing plains fed by rivers that are as revered as the national monarchy. Thailand's most exalted river is Chao Phraya, which is formed by the northern tributaries of Ping, Wang, Yom and Nan – a lineage as notable as any aristocrat's. The country's early kingdoms emerged around Chao Phraya basin, still the seat of the monarchy today. The river delta is in cultivation for most of the year.

Tracing the contours of Thailand's northern and northeastern border is another celebrated river: Mekong. As the artery of Southeast Asia, Mekong both physically separates and culturally fuses Thailand with its neighbours. It is a workhorse river that has been dammed for hydroelectric power and swells and contracts based on the seasonal rains. In the dry season, riverside farmers plant vegetables in the muddy floodplain, harvesting their crops before the river reclaims its territory.

The landscape of Thailand's northeastern border is occupied by the arid Khorat Plateau rising some 300m above the central plain. This is a hardscrabble land where the rains are meagre, the soil is anaemic and the red dust stains as stubbornly as the betel nut chewed by the ageing grandmothers.

The kingdom's eastern rivers dump their waters into the Gulf of Thailand, a shallow basin off the neighbouring South China Sea. The warm, gentle gulf is an ideal cultivation ground for coral reefs. On the other side of its long slender 'trunk' is the Andaman Sea, a splendid tropical setting of stunning blue waters and dramatic limestone islands. Onshore, the peninsula is dominated by some final remaining stands of rainforest and ever-expanding rubber and palm-oil plantations.

Flora & Fauna

In the northern half of Thailand, most indigenous species are classified zoologically as Indo-Chinese, referring to fauna originating from mainland Asia, while that of the south is generally Sundaic, typical of peninsular Malaysia, Sumatra, Borneo and Java. There is also an interesting overlap that provides habitat for plants and animals from both zones starting in Uthai Thani and extending south to the gulf region around Prachuap Khiri Khan.

Thailand is particularly rich in birdlife, with over a thousand recorded resident and migrating species, approximately 10% of the world's bird species. The cool mountains of northern Thailand are populated by montane species and migrants with clear Himalayan affinities such as flycatchers and thrushes. The arid forests of Khao Yai National Park in northeastern Thailand are a favourite for hornbills. Marshland birds prefer the wetlands of the central region, while Sundaic species such as Gurney's Pitta flock to the wetter climate of southern Thailand.

Besides abundant birdlife, visitors to the country's national parks are most likely to spot monkeys. Thailand is home to five species of macaque, four species of the smaller leaf-monkey and three species of gibbons. Although they face the same habitat loss as other native species, monkeys sometimes survive in varying states of domestication with humans. The long-armed gibbons were once raised alongside children in rural villages, and macaques can be found living in small wooded patches or unused temples in population centres.

Other species found in the kingdom's parks and sanctuaries include gaur (Indian bison), banteng (wild cattle), serow (an Asiatic goat-antelope), sambar deer, muntjac (barking deer), mouse deer and tapir – to name a few.

Thailand has six venomous snakes: the common cobra, king cobra, banded krait, green viper, Malayan viper and Russell's pit viper. Although the relatively rare king cobra can reach up to 6m in length, the nation's largest snake is the reticulated python, which can reach a whopping 10m.

The country's many lizard species include two common varieties – đúk·gaa, a reclusive and somewhat homely gecko heard in the early evening coughing its name; and jîng·jòk, a spirited house lizard that is usually spotted on ceilings and walls chasing after bugs. The black jungle monitor, which looks like a miniature dinosaur, lives in some of the southern forests.

The oceans are home to hundreds of species of coral, and the reefs created by these tiny creatures provide the perfect living conditions for hundreds of species of fish, crustaceans and tiny invertebrates. You can find the world's smallest fish (the 10mm-long goby) and the largest (the 18m-long whale shark), plus reef denizens such as clownfish, parrotfish, wrasse, angelfish, triggerfish and lionfish. Deeper waters are home to grouper, barracuda, sharks, manta rays, marlin and tuna. You might also encounter turtles, whales and dolphins.

Thailand's most famous animals are also its most endangered. The Asian elephant, a smaller cousin to the African elephant, once roamed the forests of Indochina in great herds. But the wild elephant faces extinction due to habitat loss and poaching. The population of wild elephants in Thailand is estimated at about 1000.

Reclusive wild tigers stalk the hinterlands between Thailand and Myanmar but in ever-decreasing numbers. It is difficult to obtain an accurate count but experts estimate that around 200 to 300 wild tigers remain in Thailand. Although tiger hunting and trapping is illegal, poachers continue to kill the cats for the overseas wildlife trade.

The rare dugong (also called manatee or sea cow), once thought extinct in Thailand, survives in a few small pockets around Trang, but is increasingly threatened by habitat loss and the lethal propellers of tourist boats.

Wild National Parks

» Kaeng Krachan, Phetchaburi Province

» Western Forest Complex, Kanchanaburi Province

» Kuiburi National Park, Prachuap Khiri Khan Province

The Mekong River rivals the Amazon River in terms of biodiversity and shelters endangered and newly discovered species, such as the Khorat big-mouthed frog, which uses fangs to catch prey.

MEKONG RIVER

The remaining jungles of Thailand can be divided into two forest types: monsoon (with a distinct dry season of three months or more) and rainforest (where rain falls more than nine months per year). The most heavily forested provinces are Chiang Mai and Kanchanaburi.

Monsoon forests in the northern parts of the country are comprised of deciduous trees, which are green and lush during the rainy season but dusty and leafless during the dry season. Teak is one of the most highly valued monsoon forest trees, but it now exists only in limited quantities.

In southern Thailand, where rainfall is plentiful and distributed evenly throughout the year, forests are classified as rainforests with a few areas of monsoon forest. One remarkable plant found in some southern forests is *Rafflesia kerrii,* a squat plant with a huge flower that reaches 80cm across; you can see it at Khao Sok National Park near Surat Thani.

Thailand is home to nearly 75 coastal mangrove species: small salt-tolerant trees that provide an incubator for many coastal fish and animal species. Reforestation programs of mangrove areas have gained in popularity thanks to their protective role in the 2004 Asian tsunami.

Orchids are Thailand's most exquisite native flora. There are over 1100 native species and they cover a variety of habitat: some are ground dwellers, while others anchor high up in trees and still others cling to rocky outcrops.

Queen Sirikit Botanic Garden, outside of Chiang Mai, shelters local and native species, including a beautiful collection of orchids and lotus.

Environmental Issues

Deforestation

Thailand has put enormous pressure on its ecosystems through cultivation of land into cities and farms. Natural forest cover now makes up about 28% of the kingdom's land area as compared to 70% some 50 years ago. The rapid depletion of the country's forests coincided with the shift towards industrialisation, urbanisation and commercial logging. Although these statistics are alarming, forest loss has slowed since the turn of the millennium to about 0.4% per year.

In response to environmental degradation, the Thai government created a large number of protected areas, starting in the 1970s, and set a goal of 40% forest cover by the middle of this century. In 1989 all logging was banned in Thailand following disastrous mudslides in Surat Thani Province that buried villages and killed more than a hundred people.

ENCOUNTERS WITH ELEPHANTS

Thailand's emblematic animal has had many career changes from beast of burden and war machine to tourist attraction. Today visitors can have close encounters with elephants as a mahout-in-training or from a wildlife-viewing platform.

Ban Ta Klang Spend time with elephants and their mahouts in this traditional elephant herding village in northeastern Thailand (p429)

Elephant Nature Park Watch pachyderms enjoy a semi-wild retirement after a lifetime of work at this unique sanctuary, outside Chiang Mai (p253)

Kuiburi National Park Wild elephants congregate in the evenings at salt ponds in this national park, southwest of Hua Hin (see the boxed text, p526)

Elephantstay Programme In the former royal capital, the Ayuthaya Elephant Palace runs a mahout-training program to preserve the ancient tradition (see the boxed text, p164)

Thai Elephant Conservation Center The country's official retirement home for elephants offers an array of educational elephant activities, from one-day visits to mahout training (p307)

It is now illegal to sell timber felled in the country, but this law is frequently flouted by local populations living near forest complexes and by well-connected interests.

A corollary problem to deforestation is habitat loss. Wildlife experts agree that the greatest danger faced by Thai fauna and flora is neither hunting nor the illegal wildlife trade but habitat loss. Species that are notably extinct in Thailand include the kouprey (a type of wild cattle), Schomburgk's deer and the Javan rhino, but innumerable smaller species have also disappeared with little fanfare.

> Bangkok has been sinking at a rate of 10cm annually and some scientists estimate that the city may face submersion within 20 years due to rising sea levels.

Flooding

Seasonal flooding is a common natural occurrence in some parts of Thailand due to the nature of the monsoon rains. But the frequency of record-level floods has increased in recent years. In 2010, the rainy season came several months late and transformed reservoirs in Nakhon Ratchasima Province from parched pits into overflowing disaster zones, creating 50-year flood conditions. Swollen rivers and prolonged downpours then extended flooding through the central plains and south all the way to Hat Yai. There were 177 deaths and a massive disaster relief response that lasted for several months after waters subsided. Another record flood occurred in 2006 with 46 affected provinces, mainly in the north, and again in 2008 along Mekong.

In 2011, a two-week period of heavy rainfall several months prior to the start of the rainy season caused flooding in southern Thailand, including the beach resorts. Tourists were stranded until flights and boat

ILLEGAL WILDLIFE TRADE

Thailand is a signatory to the UN Convention on International Trade in Endangered Species (Cites), but the country remains an important transport link and marketplace for the global wildlife trade, which is the third-largest black-market activity after drugs and arms dealing. Endangered animals and animal parts are poached from local forests or smuggled from neighbouring countries through Thailand en route to the lucrative markets of China or the US. Despite police efforts, Bangkok's Chatuchak Market contains a clandestine exotic species section.

Though the country's efforts to stop the trade are more impressive than those of its neighbours, corruption and weak laws hinder law enforcement. In 2011, a United Arab Emirates national was arrested at Bangkok's Suvarnabhumi airport with a suitcase full of drugged wildlife (leopard and bear cubs and baby gibbons). According to investigators, the smuggler did not possess the suitcase until after he had passed through immigration, suggesting an airport collaborator. Through political connections, the smuggler was released from jail and allowed to leave the country, facing no criminal charges or fines. Even if the case was prosecuted the maximum fines would have been minimal compared to the profit margin on the sale of the animals. Another complicating factor is that Thai law allows the trade of wild species bred in captivity, designed ostensibly to take the pressure off wild populations. Most agree that the real solution isn't harsher penalties but decline in demand. Without buyers, there will be no trade.

On a small scale, several NGOs work on the attendant problems. **WARF** (Wild Animal Rescue Foundation of Thailand; www.warthai.org) was started by a Bangkok housewife who converted her backyard into a makeshift sanctuary for unwanted wild pets some 30 years ago. Today the NGO works with the forestry department on sting operations, job-skills training and educational workshops in Thai public schools. Some of the students who attend WARF workshops have parents who are poachers and WARF hopes that the message of conservation (and maybe even a little environmental peer pressure) will be brought home to those students. With better education and job training, WARF hopes to dissuade future poachers and to turn current poachers into conservationists.

transport could resume. Even worse, months of heavy rainfall followed, and the ensuing devastating floods (also 50-year flood conditions) inundated many parts of Thailand, killing hundreds and affecting tens of millions of people. By late October, the residents of Bangkok were engaged in a desperate struggle to keep as much of the floodwaters out of the city as possible. Despite their efforts, many residential and industrial areas of Bangkok became flooded and as this book went to print, the flooding was not expected to dissipate for four to six weeks. Many refuge centres were set up including at Don Muang airport, which was converted into a tent city.

There are a myriad of suspected reasons for these extreme weather patterns. Many environmental experts attribute human alteration of natural flood barriers and watercourses and deforestation as potential causes. Increased incidents of flooding along Mekong is often linked to upstream infrastructure projects, such as dams and removal of rapids for easier navigation, and increasing human populations along the river that infringe on forested floodplains and wetlands. Another emerging component is the role of climate change in the increase of seasonal rains.

Coastal & Marine Degradation

Thailand's coastal region has experienced higher population and economic growth than the national average and the majority of the country's manufacturing industry is located along the eastern seaboard and the upper Gulf of Thailand. With increased population comes increased environmental pressure.

Soil erosion is a major coastal problem. According to the World Bank, Thailand is losing 2 sq km from its coastline every year. This is in part due to coastal development (construction of jetties, breakwaters, oceanfront hotels and roads), land subsiding (due to groundwater depletion) and to rising sea levels. Accurate data is lacking on coastal water quality but analysts admit that wastewater treatment facilities are outpaced by the area's population and that industrial wastewater is often insufficiently treated.

Coastal degradation puts serious pressure on Thailand's diverse coral reef system and marine environment. It is estimated that about 50% of Thailand's coral reefs are classified as highly threatened, indicating a disproportionate number of dead coral to living coral, according to a World Bank 2006 environmental report. The 2010 global bleaching phenomenon, in which El Nino weather conditions contributed to warmer sea temperatures, exacerbated the health of Thailand's reefs. The Thai government closed to tourism 18 areas in seven marine parks that had experienced widespread bleaching. It is unclear if these reefs, which were 80% affected, will recover.

The overall health of the ocean is further impacted by large-scale fishing, an important part of the Thai economy. Fisheries continue to experience declining catches and an industry once dominated by small family fisherfolk has now shifted to big commercial enterprises that can go into deeper waters and devote more resources to a profitable catch.

The town of Pranburi maintains a thriving fishing industry. Trawlers pull up at the mouth of the river where workers unload their catch and set the fish out to dry on racks spread across town. Thais think the smell is heavenly.

ENVIRONMENT & WILDLIFE ENVIRONMENTAL ISSUES

Survival Guide

Directory A-Z

Accommodation

Thailand offers a wide variety of accommodation from cheap and basic to pricey and luxurious. Accommodation rates listed in this book are high-season prices. Icons are included to indicate internet access, wi-fi, swimming pools or air-con availability. If there isn't an air-con icon, assume that there's only a fan.

A two-tiered pricing system has been used in this book to determine budget category (budget, midrange, top end). In big cities and beach resorts, rates under 1000B are budget, under 3000B are midrange, with top end over 3000B. For small towns, rates under 600B are budget, under 1500B are midrange and top end over 1500B.

In places where spoken English might be limited, it is handy to know the following: *hôrng pát lom* (room with fan) and *hôrng aa* (room with air-con).

Guest Houses

Guest houses are generally the cheapest accommodation in Thailand and can be found all along the backpacker trail. In areas like the northeast and parts of the southeast, guest houses (as well as tourists) are not as widespread.

Rates vary according to facilities and location. In small towns between 150B to 200B are about the cheapest rates around and usually have shared bathroom and a rickety fan. Private facilities, air-con and sometimes a TV can be had for 600B to 800B. But prices are much higher in the beach resorts, where a basic fan room starts at 700B to 800B. Many guest houses make their bread and butter from their on-site restaurants that serve the classic backpacker fare (banana pancakes and fruit shakes). Although these restaurants are convenient and a good way to meet other travellers, don't measure Thai food based on these dishes.

Most guest houses cultivate a travellers' ambience with friendly knowledgeable staff and book exchanges. But there are also plenty of guest houses with grumpy, disgruntled, clerks who let customers know that they dislike their jobs.

Increasingly, guest houses can handle advance reservations, but due to inconsistent cleanliness and quality it is advisable to always look at a room in person before committing. In tourist centres, if your preferred place is full, there are usually alternatives nearby. Guest houses typically only accept cash payments.

Hotels

In provincial capitals and small towns, the only options are often older Thai-Chinese hotels, once the standard in all of Thailand. Most cater to Thai guests and English is usually limited.

These hotels are multistorey buildings and might offer a range of rooms from midrange options with private bathrooms, air-con and TV to cheaper ones with shared bath facilities and a fan. In some of the older hotels, the toilets are squats and the 'shower' is a *klong* jar (a large terracotta basin from which you scoop out water for bathing). Although the Thai-Chinese hotels have got tonnes of accidental retro charm, unless the establishment has been recently refurbished, we've found that they are too old and worn to represent good value compared to the guest houses.

In recent years, there has been a push to fill the budget gap for ageing backpackers or young affluent travellers who want the ambience of a guest house with the comforts of a hotel. Now in major

---

BOOK ACCOMMODATION ONLINE

For more accommodation reviews and recommendations by Lonely Planet authors, check out the online booking service at www.lonelyplanet.com/thailand. You'll find the true, insider lowdown on the best places to stay. Reviews are thorough and independent. Best of all, you can book online.

tourist towns, 'flashpacker' hotels have dressed up the utilitarian options of the past with stylish decor and more creature comforts.

International chain hotels can be found in Bangkok, Chiang Mai, Phuket and other high-end beach resorts. Many of these upscale resorts incorporate traditional Thai architecture with modern minimalism.

Most top-end hotels and some midrange hotels add a 7% government tax (VAT) and an additional 10% service charge. The additional charges are often referred to as 'plus plus'. A buffet breakfast will often be included in the room rate. If the hotel offers a Western breakfast, it is usually referred to as 'ABF', meaning 'American breakfast'.

Midrange and chain hotels, especially in major tourist destinations, can be booked in advance and some offer internet discounts through their websites or online agents. They also accept most credit cards, but only a few deluxe places accept American Express.

National Parks Accommodation

Most national parks have bungalows or campsites. Bungalows typically sleep as many as 10 people and rates range from 800B to 2000B, depending on the park and the size of the bungalow. These are popular with extended Thai families who bring enough provisions to survive the Apocalypse. A few parks also have *reu·an tăa·ou* (longhouses).

Camping is available at many parks for 60B to 90B per night. Some parks rent tents and other sleeping gear, but the condition of the equipment can be poor.

Reservations for all park accommodation must be made in advance through the **central booking system** (☎0 2561 0777; web2.dnp. go.th/parkreserve). Do note that reservations for campsites and bungalows are

handled on different pages within the website.

Business Hours

The following are standard hours for different types of businesses in Thailand. Reviews in this book list only variations from these standards. All government offices and banks are closed on public holidays (see p758).

Banks 9.30am to 3.30pm Monday to Friday; ATMs accessible 24 hours.

Bars 6pm to midnight (officially); closing times vary due to local enforcement of curfew laws; bars close during elections and certain religious public holidays.

Clubs (discos) 8pm to 2am; closing times vary due to local enforcement of curfew laws; clubs close during elections and certain religious public holidays.

Government offices 8.30am to 4.30pm Monday to Friday; some close for lunch (noon to 1pm), while others are open Saturday (9am to 3pm).

Live-music venues 6pm to 1am; closing times vary due to local enforcement of curfew laws; clubs close during elections and certain religious public holidays.

Restaurants 10am to 10pm; some specialise in morning meals and close by 3pm.

Stores local stores: 10am to 6pm daily; department stores 10am to 8pm daily. In some small towns, local stores close on Sunday.

Customs Regulations

The **customs department** (www.customsclinic.org) maintains a helpful website with specific information about customs regulations. Thailand allows the following items to enter duty free:

» reasonable amount of personal effects (clothing and toiletries)
» professional instruments
» 200 cigarettes
» 1L of wine or spirits

Thailand prohibits the import of the following items:

» firearms and ammunition (unless registered in advance with the police department)
» illegal drugs
» pornographic media

When leaving Thailand, you must obtain an export licence for any antique reproductions or newly cast Buddha images (except personal amulets). Submitting two front-view photos of the object(s), a

---

COMMISSION HASSLES

In the popular tourist spots you'll be approached, sometimes surrounded, by touts or transport drivers who get a commission from the guest house for bringing in potential guests. While it is annoying for the traveller, this is an acceptable form of advertising among small-scale businesses in Thailand. As long as you know the drill, everything should work out in your favour. Touts get paid for delivering you to a guest house or hotel (whether you check in or not). Some places refuse to pay commissions so in return the touts will steer customers away from those places (saying it is closed or burned down). In less scrupulous instances, they'll tell you that the commission-paying hotel is the one you requested. If you meet with resistance, call the guest house for a pick-up as they are often aware of aggressive business tactics.

photocopy of your passport, along with the purchase receipt and the object(s) in question, to the **Department of Fine Arts** (☏0 2628 5032). Allow four days for the application and inspection process to be completed.

Electricity

Thailand uses 220V AC electricity; power outlets most commonly feature two-prong round or flat sockets.

220V/50Hz

220V/50Hz

Climate

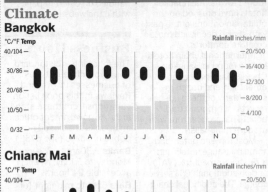

Bangkok

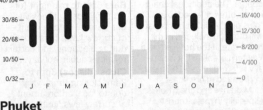

Chiang Mai

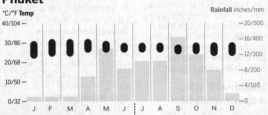

Phuket

Embassies & Consulates

Foreign embassies are located in Bangkok; some nations also have consulates in Chiang Mai, Phuket or Pattaya.

Australia (Map p90; ☏0 2344 6300; www.thailand. embassy.gov.au; 37 Th Sathon Tai, Bangkok)

Cambodia (☏0 2957 5851-2; 518/4 Pracha Uthit/Soi Ramkamhaeng 39, Bangkok)

Canada Bangkok (Map p90; ☏0 2636 0540; www.thailand. gc.ca; 15th fl, Abdulrahim Bldg, 990 Th Phra Ram IV); Chiang Mai Consulate (☏0 5385-0147; 151 Superhighway, Tambon Tahsala)

China Bangkok (☏0 2245 7044; www.chinaembassy.or.th; 57 Th Ratchadaphisek); Chiang Mai Consulate (Map p240;

☏0 5327 6125; 111 Th Chang Lor, Tambon Haiya)

Denmark (Map p90; ☏0 2343 1100; www.ambbangkok. um.dk; 10 Soi 1, Th Sathon Tai; Bangkok) Consulates in Phuket and Pattaya.

France (Map p82; ☏0 2657 5100; www.ambafrance-th.org; 35 Soi 36, Th Charoen Krung); Bangkok Visa & Culture Services (Map p90; ☏0 2627 2150; 29 Th Sathon Tai); Chiang Mai Consulate (Map p240; ☏0 5328 1466; 138 Th Charoen Prathet) Consulates also in Phuket & Surat Thani.

Germany (Map p90; ☏0 2287 9000; www.bangkok.diplo. de; 9 Th Sathon Tai, Bangkok)

India (Map p92; ☏0 2258 0300-6; indianembassy.in.th; 46 Soi Prasanmit/Soi 23, Th Sukhumvit); Bangkok Visa Application Centre (Map p92; ☏02 6652 9681; www.ivac-th.

com; Glass Haus Bldg, 15th fl, suite 1503, Th Sukhumvit); Chiang Mai Consulate (✆0 5324 3066; 33/1 Th Thung Hotel, Wat Gate)

Indonesia (Map p86; ✆0 2252 3135; www.kemlu.go.id/ bangkok; 600-602 Th Phetch-aburi, Bangkok)

Ireland (Map p90; ✆0 2677 7500; www.irelandinthailand. com; 28th fl, Q House, Th Sathon Tai, Bangkok) Consu-late only; the nearest Irish embassy is in Kuala Lumpur.

Israel (Map p92; ✆0 2204 9200; bangkok.mfa.gov.il; Ocean Tower 2, 25th fl, 25 Soi 19, Th Sukhumvit, Bangkok)

Japan (Map p90; ✆0 2207 8500; www.th.emb -japan.go.jp; 177 Th Withayu/ Wireless Rd); Chiang Mai Consulate (✆0 5320 3367; 104-107 Airport Business Park, Th Mahidon)

Laos (✆0 2539 6678; www. bkklaoembassy.com; 502/1-3 Soi Sahakarnpramoon, Pracha Uthit/Soi 39, Th Ramkamhaeng, Bangkok)

Malaysia (Map p90; ✆0 2629 6800; 35 Th Sathon Tai, Bangkok) Also has a consu-late in Songkhla.

Myanmar (Burma; Map p82; ✆0 2233 2237; www.mofa. gov.mm; 132 Th Sathon Neua, Bangkok)

Nepal (✆0 2391 7240; www. immi.gov.np; 189 Soi 71, Th Sukhumvit, Bangkok)

Netherlands (Map p86; ✆0 2309 5200; www.netherland sembassy.in.th; 15 Soi Tonson, Th Ploenchit, Bangkok)

New Zealand (Map p86; ✆0 2254 2530; www.nzembassy. com; 14th fl, M Thai Tower, All Seasons Pl, 87 Th Withayu/ Wireless Rd, Bangkok)

Philippines (Map p92; ✆0 2259 0139; www.philembassy-bangkok.net; 760 Th Sukhum-vit, Bangkok)

Russia (Map p82; ✆0 2234 9824 www.thailand.mid.ru; 78 Soi Sap, Th Surawong, Bangkok) Also consulates in Pattaya and Phuket.

Singapore (Map p82; ✆0 2286 2111; www.mfa.gov.sg/

bangkok; 129 Th Sathon Tai, Bangkok)

South Africa (Map p90; ✆0 2659 2900; www.saem bbangkok.com; 12A fl, M Thai Tower, All Seasons Place, 87 Th Withayu/Wireless Rd, Bangkok)

Spain (Map p92; ✆0 2661 8284; es.embassyinformation. com; 23 fl, Lake Ratchada Of-fice Complex, 193 Th Ratchadaphisek, Bangkok)

Switzerland (Map p86; ✆0 2674 6900; www.eda.admin.ch/ bangkok; 35 Th Withayu/Wire-less Rd, Bangkok)

UK Bangkok (Map p86; ✆0 2305 8333; ukinthailand.fco.gov. uk; 14 Th Withayu/Wireless Rd); Chiang Mai Consulate (Map p240; ✆0 5326 3015; British Council, 198 Th Bamrungrat) Consulate also in Pattaya.

USA Bangkok (Map p86; ✆0 2205 4049; http://bangkok. usembassy.gov; 95 Th With-ayu/Wireless Rd); Chiang Mai Consulate (Map p240; ✆0 5310 7777; 387 Th Wichay-anon)

Vietnam (Map p86; ✆0 2251 5836-8; www.vietnamembassy-thailand.org; 83/1 Th Withayu/ Wireless Rd, Bangkok)

Gay & Lesbian Travellers

Thai culture is relatively toler-ant of both male and female homosexuality. There is a fairly prominent gay and les-bian scene in Bangkok, Pat-taya and Phuket. With regard to dress or mannerism, les-bians and gays are generally accepted without comment. However, public displays of affection – whether hetero-sexual or homosexual – are frowned upon. Utopia (www. utopia-asia.com) posts lots of Thailand information for gay and lesbian visitors and publishes a guidebook to the kingdom for homosexuals.

Holidays

Government offices and banks close on the following days.

1 January New Year's Day

February (date varies) Makha Bucha Day, Buddhist holy day

6 April Chakri Day, com-memorating the founder of the Chakri dynasty, Rama I

13–14 April Songkran Festival, traditional Thai New Year and water festival

5 May Coronation Day, commemorating the 1946 coronation of HM the King and HM the Queen

1 May Labour Day

May/June (date varies) Visakha Bucha, Buddhist holy day

July (date varies) Asahna Bucha, Buddhist holy day

12 August Queen's Birthday

23 October Chulalongkorn Day

October/November (date varies) Ork Phansaa, the end of Buddhist 'lent'

5 December King's Birthday

10 December Constitution Day

31 December New Year's Eve

Insurance

A travel-insurance policy to cover theft, loss and medical problems is a good idea. Poli-cies offer differing medical-expense options. There is a wide variety of policies available, so check the small print. Be sure that the policy covers ambulances or an emergency flight home.

Some policies specifically exclude 'dangerous activi-ties', which can include scuba diving, motorcycling or even trekking. A locally acquired motorcycle licence is not valid under some policies.

You may prefer a policy that pays doctors or hospi-tals directly rather than you having to pay on the spot and claim later. If you have to claim later make sure you keep all documentation.

Worldwide travel insur-ance is available at www. lonelyplanet.com/travel_ services. You can buy, extend and claim online anytime

– even if you're already on the road.

See p776 for recommendations on health insurance and p774 for details on vehicle insurance.

Internet Access

You'll find plenty of internet cafes just about everywhere. The going rate is anywhere from 40B to 120B an hour, depending on how much competition there is. Connections tend to be pretty fast and the machines are usually well maintained. Wireless access (wi-fi) is usually available in most hotels and guest houses though staff aren't adept at fixing downed services. Wi-fi signal strength deteriorates in the upper floors of a multistorey building so check to see if your floor has a nearby router.

Legal Matters

In general, Thai police don't hassle foreigners, especially tourists. They generally go out of their way to avoid having to speak English with a foreigner especially regarding minor traffic issues.

One major exception is drugs, which most Thai police view as either a social scourge against which it's their duty to enforce the letter of the law, or an opportunity to make untaxed income via bribes.

If you are arrested for any offence, the police will allow you the opportunity to make a phone call to your embassy or consulate in Thailand, if you have one, or to a friend or relative if not. There's a whole set of legal codes governing the length of time and manner in which you can be detained before being charged or put on trial, but a lot of discretion is left to the police. In the case of foreigners the police are more likely to bend these codes in your favour. However, as with police worldwide, if you don't

show respect you will make matters worse.

Thai law does not presume an indicted detainee to be either 'guilty' or 'innocent' but rather a 'suspect', whose guilt or innocence will be decided in court. Trials are usually speedy.

The **tourist police** (☏1155) can be very helpful in cases of arrest. Although they typically have no jurisdiction over the kinds of cases handled by regular cops, they may be able to help with translations or with contacting your embassy. You can call the hotline number 24 hours a day to lodge complaints or to request assistance with regards to personal safety.

Maps

ThinkNet (www.thinknet.co.th) produces high-quality, bilingual city and country maps, including interactive-map CDs. For GPS users in Thailand, most prefer the Garmin units and the associated map products that are accurate and fully routed.

Money

The basic unit of Thai currency is the baht. There are 100 satang in one baht; coins include 25-satang and 50-satang pieces and baht in 1B, 2B, 5B and 10B coins. Older coins have Thai numerals only, while newer coins have

Thai and Arabic numerals. The 2B coin is similar in size to the 1B coin but it is gold in colour. The two satang coins are typically only issued at supermarkets where prices aren't rounded up to the nearest baht.

Paper currency is issued in the following denominations: 20B (green), 50B (blue), 100B (red), 500B (purple) and 1000B (beige).

ATMs & Credit/Debit Cards

Debit and ATM cards issued by a bank in your own country can be used at ATMs around Thailand to withdraw cash (in Thai baht only) directly from your account back home. ATMs are widespread throughout the country and can be relied on for the bulk of your spending cash. You can also use ATMs to buy baht at foreign-exchange booths at some banks.

Thai ATMs now charge a 150B foreign-transaction fee on top of whatever currency conversion and out-of-network fees your home bank charges. That means that ATMs are now a lot more expensive to use than in the past. Before leaving home, shop around for a bank account that has free international ATM usage and reimburses fees incurred at other institution's ATMs.

Aeon is the only bank that we know of in Thailand that doesn't charge the 150B usage fee on foreign accounts but their distribution of national ATMs is somewhat limited and often located in Big C stores.

Credit cards as well as debit cards can be used for purchases at some shops, hotels and restaurants. The most commonly accepted cards are Visa and MasterCard. American Express is typically only accepted at high-end hotels and restaurants.

To report a lost or stolen credit/debit card, call the following hotlines in Bangkok:

American Express (✆0 2273 5544)

MasterCard (✆001 800 11887 0663)

Visa (✆001 800 441 3485)

Changing Money

Banks or the rarer private moneychangers offer the best foreign-exchange rates. When buying baht, US dollars are the most accepted currency, followed by British pounds and euros. Most banks charge a commission and duty for each travellers cheque cashed.

Current exchange rates are printed in the *Bangkok Post* and the *Nation* every day, or you can walk into any Thai bank to see a daily rate chart.

See p18 for some information on the cost of travel in Thailand.

Foreign Exchange

As of 2008, visitors must declare arriving or departing with an excess of US$20,000. There are also certain monetary requirements for foreigners entering Thailand; demonstration of adequate funds varies per visa type but typically does not exceed a traveller's estimated trip budget. Rarely will you be asked to produce such financial evidence, but be aware that such laws do exist. The **Ministry of Foreign Affairs** (www.mfa.go.th) can provide more detailed information.

It's legal to open a foreign-currency account at any commercial bank in Thailand. As long as the funds originate from out of the country, there aren't any restrictions on maintenance or withdrawal.

Tipping

Tipping is not generally expected in Thailand. The exception is loose change from a large restaurant bill; if a meal costs 488B and you pay with a 500B note, some Thais will leave the 12B change. It's not so much a tip as a way of saying 'I'm not so money grubbing as to grab every last baht'.

At many hotel restaurants or other upmarket eateries, a 10% service charge will be added to your bill. When this is the case, tipping is not expected. Bangkok has adopted some standards of tipping, especially in restaurants frequented by foreigners.

Photography

Thais are gadget fans and they readily snap pics with cameras or camera phones. Memory cards for digital cameras are generally widely available in the more popular formats and available in the electronic sections of most shopping malls. In the tourist areas, many internet shops have CD-burning software if you want to offload your pictures. Alternatively, most places have sophisticated enough connections that you can quickly upload digital photos to a remote storage site.

Be considerate when taking photographs of the locals. Learn how to ask politely in Thai and wait for an embarrassed nod. In some of the regularly visited hill-tribe areas be prepared for the photographed subject to ask for money in exchange for a picture. Other hill tribes will not allow you to point a camera at them.

Post

Thailand has a very efficient postal service and local postage is inexpensive. Typical provincial post offices keep the following hours: 8.30am to 4.30pm weekdays and 9am to noon on Saturdays. Larger main post offices in provincial capitals may also be open for a half-day on Sundays.

Most provincial post offices will sell do-it-yourself packing boxes. Don't send cash or other valuables through the mail.

Thailand's poste restante service is generally very reliable, though these days few tourists use it. When you receive mail, you must show your passport and fill out some paperwork.

Safe Travel

Although Thailand is not a dangerous country to visit, it is smart to exercise caution, especially when it comes to dealing with strangers (both Thai and foreigners) and travelling alone. In reality, you are more likely to be ripped off or have a personal possession surreptitiously stolen than you are to be physically harmed.

Assault

Assault of travellers is rare in Thailand, but it does happen. Causing a Thai to 'lose face' (feel public embarrassment or humiliation) can sometimes elicit an inexplicably strong and violent reaction. Oftentimes alcohol is the number one contributor to bad choices and worse outcomes.

Women, especially solo travellers, need to be smart and somewhat sober when interacting with the opposite sex, be they Thai or *fa·ràng* (foreigner) Opportunists pounce when too many whisky buckets are involved. Also be aware that an innocent flirtation might convey firmer intentions to a recipient who does not share your culture's sexual norms.

Border Issues & Hot Spots

Thailand enjoys much better relations with its neighbours and most land borders are fully functional passages for goods and people. However, the ongoing violence in the Deep South (see the boxed text, p596) has made the crossing at Sungai Kolok into Malaysia completely off limits and the entire Muslim-majority provinces (Yala, Pattani and Narathiwat) should be avoided by casual visitors.

Cross-border relations between Thailand and Myanmar have significantly normalised though borders are subject to closing without warning. Borders are usually closed due to news-making events, like Myanmar's 2010 elections, so keeping abreast of current events prior to arriving at the border will prevent potential problems.

The long-contested area at Khao Phra Wihan (known as 'Preah Vihear' in Cambodia), along the Thai-Cambodian border, is still a source of military clashes and should be avoided until a lasting peace is found.

Check with your government's foreign ministry for current travel warnings.

Druggings & Drug Possession

It is illegal to buy, sell or possess opium, heroin, amphetamines, hallucinogenic mushrooms and marijuana in Thailand. Belying Thailand's anything-goes atmosphere are severely strict punishments for possession and trafficking that are not relaxed for foreigners. Possession of drugs can result in at least one year or more of prison time. Drug smuggling – defined as attempting to cross a border with drugs in your possession – carries considerably higher penalties, including execution.

Scams

Thais can be so friendly and laid-back that some visitors are lulled into a false sense of security, making them vulnerable to scams of all kinds. Bangkok is especially good at long-involved frauds that dupe travellers into thinking that they've made a friend and are getting a bargain on highly valuable gem stones (which are actually pretty, sparkling glass).

Follow Tourism Authority of Thailand's (TAT) number-one suggestion to tourists: *Disregard all offers of free shopping or sightseeing help from strangers*. These invariably take a commission from your purchases. See the boxed text, p142, for more information.

Theft & Fraud

Exercise diligence when it comes to your personal belongings. Ensure that your room is securely locked and carry your most important effects (passport, money, credit cards) on your person. Take care when leaving valuables in hotel safes.

Follow the same practice when you're travelling. A locked bag will not prevent theft on a long-haul bus.

When using a credit card, don't let vendors take your credit card out of your sight to run it through the machine. Unscrupulous merchants have been known to rub off three or four or more receipts with one purchase. Sometimes they wait several weeks – even months – between submitting each charge receipt to the bank, so that you can't remember whether you'd been billed by the same vendor more than once.

To avoid losing all of your travel money in an instant, use a credit card that is not directly linked to your bank account back home so that the operator doesn't have access to immediate funds.

Contact the **tourist police** (☏1155) if you have any problems with consumer fraud.

Touts & Commissions

Touting is a longtime tradition in Asia, and while Thailand doesn't have as many touts as, say, India, it has its share. In Bangkok, túk-túk drivers, hotel employees and bar girls often take new arrivals on city tours; these almost always end up in high-pressure sales situations at silk, jewellery or handicraft shops.

Touts also steer customers to certain guest houses that pay a commission. Travel agencies are notorious for talking newly arrived tourists into staying at badly located, overpriced hotels.

Some travel agencies often masquerade as TAT, the government-funded tourist information office. They might put up agents wearing fake TAT badges or have signs that read TAT in big letters to entice travellers into their offices where they can sell them bus and train tickets for a commission. Be aware that the official TAT offices do not make hotel or transport bookings. If such a place offers to do this for you then they are a travel agent not a tourist information office.

When making transport arrangements, talk to several travel agencies to look for the best price, as the commission percentage varies greatly between agents. Also resist any high-sales tactics from an agent trying to sign you up for everything: plane tickets, hotel, tours etc. The most honest Thais are typically very low-key and often sub-par salespeople.

Shopping

Many bargains await you in Thailand but don't go shopping in the company of touts, tour guides or friendly strangers as they will inevitably take a commission on anything you buy, thus driving prices up beyond an acceptable value and creating a nuisance for future visitors.

Antiques

Real Thai antiques are increasingly rare. Today most dealers sell antique reproductions or items from Myanmar. Bangkok and Chiang Mai are the two centres for the antique and reproduction trade.

Real antiques cannot be taken out of Thailand without a permit. No Buddha image, new or old, may be exported without the permission of the Department of Fine Arts. See p756 for information.

Ceramics

Many kinds of hand-thrown pottery, old and new, are available throughout the kingdom. Bangkok is full of modern ceramic designs while Chiang Mai sticks to traditional styles. Ko Kret and Dan Kwian are two traditional pottery villages.

Clothing

Clothes tend to be inexpensive in Thailand but readymade items are not usually cut to fit Westerners' body types. Increasingly, larger-sized clothes are available in metropolitan malls or tourist centres. Markets sell cheap everyday items and are handy for picking up something when everything else is dirty. For chic clothes, Bangkok and Ko Samui lead the country with design-minded fashions. Finding shoes that fit larger feet is also a problem. The custom of returns is not widely accepted in Thailand, so be sure everything fits before you leave the store.

Thailand has a long sartorial tradition, practised mainly by Thai-Indian Sikh families. But this industry is filled with cut-rate operators and commission-paying scams. Be wary of the quickie 24-hour tailor shops; they often use inferior fabric and have poor workmanship. It's best to ask longtime foreign residents for a recommendation and then go for two or three fittings.

Fake Goods

In Bangkok, Chiang Mai and other tourist centres there's a thriving black-market street trade in fake designer goods. No one pretends they're the real thing, at least not the vendors. Technically it is illegal for these items to be produced and sold and Thailand has often been pressured by intellectual-property enforcement agencies to close down the trade. Rarely does a crackdown by the police last and often the vendors develop more surreptitious means of distribution, further highlighting the contraband character of the goods. In the Patpong market, for example, a vendor might show you a picture of a knock-off watch, you pay for it and they go around the corner to fetch it. They usually come back but you'll wait long enough to wonder.

Furniture

Rattan and hardwood furniture items are often good purchases and can be made to order. Chiang Mai is the country's primary furniture producer with many retail outlets in Bangkok. Due to the ban on teak harvesting and the subsequent exhaustion of recycled teak, 70% of export furniture produced in Thailand is made from parawood, a processed wood from rubber trees that can no longer be used for latex production.

Gems & Jewellery

Thailand is a leading exporter of gems and ornaments, rivalled only by India and Sri Lanka. Although rough-stone sources in Thailand have decreased dramatically, stones are now imported from Myanmar, Sri Lanka and other countries to be cut, polished and traded.

Although there are a lot of gem and jewellery stores in Thailand, it has become so difficult to dodge the scammers that the country no longer represents a safe and enjoyable place to buy these goods. It is better just to window shop.

Lacquerware

Chiang Mai is known for gold-on-black lacquerware. Lacquerware furniture and decorative items were traditionally made from bamboo and teak but these days mango wood might be used as the base. If the item is top quality, only the frame is bamboo and horse or donkey hairs will be wound round it. With lower-quality lacquerware, the whole object is made from bamboo. The lacquer is then coated over the framework and allowed to dry. After several days it is sanded down with ash from rice husks, and another coating of lacquer is applied. A high-quality item may have seven layers of lacquer. The piece is then engraved and painted and polished to remove the paint from everywhere except in the engravings. Multicoloured lacquerware is produced by repeated applications.

From start to finish it can take five or six months to produce a high-quality piece of lacquerware, which may have as many as five colours. Flexibility is one characteristic of good lacquerware: a well-made bowl can have its rim squeezed together until the sides meet without suffering damage. The quality and precision of the engraving is another thing to look for.

Textiles

The northeast is famous for *mát·mèe* cloth – a thick cotton or silk fabric woven from tie-dyed threads, similar to Indonesia's *ikat* fabrics. Surin Province is renowned for its *mát·mèe* silk often showcasing colours and geometric patterns inherited from Khmer traditions.

In the north, silks reflect the influence of the Lanna weaving traditions, brought to Chiang Mai and the surrounding mountains by the various Tai tribes.

Fairly nice *bah·dé* (batik) is available in the south in patterns that are more similar to the batik found in Malaysia than in Indonesia.

Each hill tribe has a tradition of embroidery that has been translated into the modern marketplace as bags and jewellery. Much of what you'll find in the marketplaces has been machine made, but there are many NGO cooperatives that help villagers get their handmade goods to the consumers. Chiang Mai and Chiang Rai are filled with handicraft outlets.

Telephone

The telephone country code for Thailand is ☑66 and is used when calling the country from abroad. All Thai telephone numbers are preceded by a '0' if you're dialling domestically (the '0' is omitted when calling from overseas). After the initial '0', the next three numbers represent the provincial area code, which is now integral to the telephone number. If the initial '0' is followed by an '8', then you're dialling a mobile phone.

International Calls

If you want to call an international number from a telephone in Thailand, you must first dial an international access code plus the country code followed by the subscriber number.

In Thailand, there are various international access codes charging different rates per minute. The standard direct-dial prefix is ☑001; it is operated by CAT and is considered to have the best sound quality; it connects to the largest number of countries but is also the most expensive. The next best is ☑007, a prefix operated by TOT with reliable quality and slightly cheaper rates. Economy rates are available with ☑007, ☑008 and ☑009; both of which use Voice over Internet Protocol (VoIP), with varying but adequate sound quality.

The following are some common international country codes: ☑61 Australia, ☑44 UK and ☑1 US.

Many expats use **DeeDial** (www.deedial.com), a direct-dial service that requires a prepaid account managed through the internet. The cheapest service they offer is the 'ring-back' feature, which circumvents local charges on your phone.

There are also a variety of international phonecards available through **CAT** (www.cthai.com) offering promo-

tional rates of less than 1B per minute.

Dial ☑100 for operator-assisted international calls or reverse-charges (collect) call. Alternatively, contact your long-distance carrier for their overseas operator number, a toll-free call, or try ☑001 9991 2001 from a CAT phone and ☑1 800 000 120 from a TOT phone.

Mobile Phones

The easiest phone option in Thailand is to acquire a mobile (cell) phone equipped with a local SIM card.

Thailand is on the GSM network and mobile phone providers include AIS, DTAC and True Move.

You have two hand-phone options: you can buy a mobile phone in Thailand at one of the urban shopping malls or phone stores near the markets in provincial towns. Or you can use an imported phone that isn't SIM-locked (and one that supports the GSM network). To get started buy a SIM card of a particular carrier (AIS and DTAC are most popular), which includes an assigned telephone number. Once your phone is SIM-enabled you can buy minutes with prepaid phonecards. SIM cards and refill cards (usually sold in 300B to 500B denominations) can be bought from 7-Elevens throughout the country.

There are various promotions but rates typically hover at around 1B to 2B per minute anywhere in Thailand and between 5B and 9B for international calls. SMS is usually 3B per message, making it the cheapest 'talk' option.

If you don't have access to a private phone you can use a somewhat old-fashioned way to call overseas through a service called Home Country Direct, available at some post offices and CAT centres throughout the country.

Calling overseas through phones in most hotel rooms usually incurs additional surcharges (sometimes

3G HERE WE COME, MAYBE?

Thailand's telecommunications companies and state-owned agencies have been wrangling over the 3G (mobile broadband platform) for so many years that the new-generation technology has since been surpassed by 4G. Thailand is the only Asean country not to have the service despite a huge number of smartphone users. In 2010 and 2011, contracts to operate the services were awarded and then suspended by the courts, approval to import equipment has been delayed and now it looks like 2012 might be the year of 3G, maybe.

as much as 50% over and above the CAT rate); however, sometimes local calls are free or at standard rates. Some guest houses will have a mobile phone or landline that customers can use for a per-minute fee for overseas calls.

There are also a variety of public payphones that use prepaid phonecards for calls (both international and domestic) and, less common, coin-operated pay phones for local calls. Using the public phones can be a bit of a pain: they are typically placed beside busy thoroughfares where traffic noise is a problem.

Time

Thailand's time zone is seven hours ahead of GMT/UTC (London). At government offices and local cinemas, times are often expressed according to the 24-hour clock, e.g. 11pm is written '23.00'.

Toilets

Increasingly, the Asian-style squat toilet is less of the norm in Thailand. There are still specimens in rural places, provincial bus stations, older homes and modest restaurants, but the Western-style toilet is becoming more prevalent and appears wherever foreign tourists can be found.

If you encounter a squat, here's what you should know.

You should straddle the two footpads and face the door. To flush use the plastic bowl to scoop water out of the adjacent basin and pour into the toilet bowl. Some places supply a small pack of toilet paper at the entrance (5B), otherwise bring your own stash or wipe the old-fashioned way with water.

Even in places where sit-down toilets are installed, the septic system may not be designed to take toilet paper. In such cases there will be a waste basket where you're supposed to place used toilet paper and feminine hygiene products. Some modern toilets also come with a small spray hose – Thailand's version of the bidet.

Tourist Information

The government-operated tourist information and promotion service, **Tourism Authority of Thailand** (TAT; www.tourismthailand.org), was founded in 1960 and produces excellent pamphlets on sightseeing, accommodation and transport. TAT's head office is in Bangkok and there are 22 regional offices throughout the country. Check the destination chapters for the TAT office in the towns you're planning to visit.

The following are a few of TAT's overseas information offices; check TAT's website for contact information in

Hong Kong, Taipei, Seoul, Tokyo, Osaka, Fukuoka, Stockholm and Rome.

Australia (☑02 9247 7549; www.thailand.net.au; Level 2, 75 Pitt St, Sydney, NSW 2000)

France (☑01 53 53 47 00; 90 Ave des Champs Élysées, 75008 Paris)

Germany (☑069 138 1390; www.thailandtourismus.de; Bethmannstrasse 58, D-60311, Frankfurt/Main)

Malaysia (☑603 216 23480; www.thaitourism.com.my; Suite 22.01, Level 22, Menara Lion, 165 Jalan Ampang, Kuala Lumpur, 50450)

Singapore (☑65 6235 7901; c/o Royal Thai Embassy, 370 Orchard Rd, 238870)

UK (☑020 7925 2511; www.tourismthailand.co.uk; 3rd fl, Brook House, 98-99 Jermyn St, London SW1Y 6EE)

USA (☑323 461 9814; 1st fl, 611 North Larchmont Blvd, Los Angeles, CA 90004)

Travellers with Disabilities

Thailand presents one large, ongoing obstacle course for the mobility impaired. With its high curbs, uneven footpaths and nonstop traffic, Bangkok can be particularly difficult. Many streets must be crossed via pedestrian bridges flanked with steep stairways, while buses and boats don't stop long enough even for the fully abled. Rarely are there any ramps or other access points for wheelchairs.

A number of more expensive top-end hotels make consistent design efforts to provide disabled access to their properties. Other deluxe hotels with high employee-to-guest ratios are usually good about accommodating the mobility impaired by providing staff help where building design fails. For the rest, you're pretty much left to your own resources.

Counter to the prevailing trends, **Worldwide Dive &**

Sail (www.worldwidediveand sail.com) offers live-aboard diving programs for the deaf and hard of hearing.

Some organisations and publications that offer tips on international travel include the following:

Accessible Journeys (www. disabilitytravel.com)

Mobility International USA (www.miusa.org)

Society for Accessible Travel & Hospitality (www. sath.org)

Visas

The **Ministry of Foreign Affairs** (www.mfa.go.th) oversees immigration and visas issues. Check the website or the nearest Thai embassy or consulate for application procedures and costs.

Tourist Visas & Exemptions

The Thai government allows tourist-visa exemptions for 41 different nationalities, including those from Australia, New Zealand, the USA and most of Europe, to enter the country without a prearranged visa.

For those arriving in the kingdom by air, a 30-day visa is issued without a fee. For those arriving via a land border, the arrival visa is 15 days.

Without proof of an onward ticket and sufficient funds for one's projected stay any visitor can be denied entry, but in practice this is a formality that is rarely checked.

If you plan to stay in Thailand longer than 30 days (or 15 days for land arrivals), you should apply for the 60-day Tourist Visa from a Thai consulate or embassy before your trip. Contact the nearest Thai embassy or consulate to obtain application procedures and determine fees for tourist visas.

Non-Immigrant Visas

The Non-Immigrant Visa is good for 90 days and is intended for foreigners entering the country for business, study, retirement and extended family visits. There are multiple-entry visas available in this visa class; you're more likely to be granted multiple entries if you apply at a Thai consulate in Europe, the US or Australia than elsewhere. If you plan to apply for a Thai work permit, you'll need to possess a Non-Immigrant Visa first.

Visa Extensions & Renewals

If you decide you want to stay longer than the allotted time, you can extend your visa by applying at any immigration office in Thailand. The usual fee for a visa extension is 1900B. Those issued with a standard stay of 15 or 30 days can extend their stay for seven to 10 days (depending on the immigration office) if the extension is handled before the visa expires. The 60-day tourist visa can be extended by up to 30 days at the discretion of Thai immigration authorities.

Another visa-renewal option is to cross a land border. A new 15-day visa will be issued upon your return and some short-term visitors make a day trip out of the 'visa run'. See the destination chapters for land border information and border formalities.

If you overstay your visa, the usual penalty is a fine of 500B per day, with a 20,000B limit. Fines can be paid at the airport or in advance at an immigration office. If you've overstayed only one day, you don't have to pay. Children under 14 travelling with a parent do not have to pay the penalty.

Foreign residents in Thailand should arrange visa extensions at the immigration office closest to their in-country address.

Volunteering

There are many wonderful volunteering organisations in Thailand that provide meaningful work and cultural engagement. **Volunteer Work Thailand** (www.volunteer workthailand.org) maintains a database of opportunities. For more information see p37. Also see individual destination chapters.

Women Travellers

Women face relatively few problems in Thailand. With the great amount of respect afforded to women, an equal measure should be returned.

Thai women, especially the younger generation, are showing more skin than in the recent past. That means almost everyone is now

THAILAND'S IMMIGRATION OFFICES

The following are two immigration offices where visa extensions and other formalities can be addressed. Remember to dress in your Sunday best when doing official business in Thailand and do all visa business yourself (don't hire a third party). For all types of visa extensions, bring along two passport-sized photos and one copy each of the photo and visa pages of your passport.

» **Bangkok immigration office** (☎0 2141 9889; Bldg B, Bangkok Government Center, Th Chaeng Wattana; ⊙9am-noon & 1-4.30pm Mon-Fri)

» **Chiang Mai immigration office** (Map p236; ☎0 5320 1755-6; Th Mahidon; ⊙8.30am-4.30pm Mon-Fri)

dressing like a bar girl and you can wear spaghetti strap tops and navel-bearing shirts (if only they were still trendy) without offending Thais' modesty streak. But to be on the safe side, cover up if you're going deep into rural communities. And certainly cover up if visiting temples.

Attacks and rapes are not common in Thailand, but incidents do occur, especially when an attacker observes a vulnerable target: a drunk or solo woman. If you return home from a bar alone, be sure to have your wits about you. Avoid accepting rides from strangers late at night or travelling around in isolated areas by yourself – common sense stuff that might escape your notice in a new environment filled with hospitable people.

While Bangkok might be a men's paradise to some, foreign women are finding their own Romeos on the Thai beaches. As more couples emerge, more Thai men will make themselves available. Women who aren't interested in such romantic encounters should not presume that Thai men have merely platonic motives. Frivolous flirting could unintentionally cause a Thai man to feel a loss of face if attention is then diverted to another person and, in some cases where alcohol is involved, the spurned man may become unpleasant or even violent.

Transport

GETTING THERE & AWAY

Flights, tours and rail tickets can be booked online at www.lonelyplanet.com/bookings.

Entering the Country

Entry procedures for Thailand, by air or by land, are straightforward: you'll have to show your passport (see p766 for information about visa requirements); and you'll need to present completed arrival and departure cards. Blank arrival and departure cards are usually distributed on the incoming flight or, if arriving by land, can be picked up at the immigration counter.

You do not have to fill in a customs form on arrival unless you have imported goods to declare. In that case, you can get the proper form from Thai customs officials at your point of entry. See p761 for Thai customs information about minimum funds requirements.

Air

Airports

Bangkok is Thailand's primary international and domestic gateway. There are also smaller airports throughout the country serving domestic and sometimes inter-regional routes.

Suvarnabhumi International Airport (BKK; ☎ 0 2132 1888) Receives nearly all international flights and most domestic flights. It is located in Samut Prakan – 30km east of Bangkok and 110km from Pattaya. The airport name is pronounced *sù·wan·ná·poom*.

Don Muang Airport (DMK; ☎ 0 2535 1111) Bangkok's second airport is still used for domestic flights operated by Nok Air and Orient Thai (formerly One-Two-Go). Be aware of this when booking connecting flights on these airlines.

Phuket International Airport (HKT; ☎ 0 7632 7230) International Asian destinations include Hong Kong, Singapore and Bali on Air Asia. Direct charter flights from Europe are also available.

Chiang Mai International Airport (CNX; www.chiangmaiairportonline.com) International Asian destinations include Kuala Lumpur, Taipei and Singapore.

Airlines

The following airlines fly to and from Bangkok.

Air Asia (☎ 0 2515 9999; www.airasia.com)

Air Berlin (☎ 0 2236 9779; www.airberlin.com)

Air Canada (☎ 0 2670 0400; www.aircanada.com)

Air China (☎ 0 2634 8991; www.fly-airchina.com)

Air France (☎ 0 2610 0808; www.airfrance.fr)

CLIMATE CHANGE & TRAVEL

Every form of transport that relies on carbon-based fuel generates CO_2, the main cause of human-induced climate change. Modern travel is dependent on aeroplanes, which might use less fuel per kilometre per person than most cars but travel much greater distances. The altitude at which aircraft emit gases (including CO_2) and particles also contributes to their climate change impact. Many websites offer 'carbon calculators' that allow people to estimate the carbon emissions generated by their journey and, for those who wish to do so, to offset the impact of the greenhouse gases emitted with contributions to portfolios of climate-friendly initiatives throughout the world. Lonely Planet offsets the carbon footprint of all staff and author travel.

Air New Zealand (☎0 2235 8280; www.airnewzealand.com)

Bangkok Airways (☎1771; www.bangkokair.com)

British Airways (☎0 2627 1701; www.britishairways.com)

Cathay Pacific Airways (☎0 2263 0606; www.cathay pacific.com)

China Airlines (☎0 2250 9898; www.china-airlines.com)

Delta Airlines (☎0 2660 6900; www.delta.com)

Emirates (☎0 2664 1040; www.emirates.com)

Eva Air (☎0 2269 6288; www.evaair.com)

Garuda Indonesia (☎0 2679 7371; www.garuda -indonesia.com)

Gulf Air (☎0 2254 7931; www.gulfairco.com)

Japan Airlines (☎0 2649 9520; www.jal.co.jp)

Jetstar Airways (☎0 2267 5125; www.jetstar.com)

KLM-Royal Dutch Airlines (☎0 2610 0800; www.klm.com)

Korean Air (☎0 2620 6900; www.koreanair.com)

Lao Airlines (☎0 2236 9822; www.laoairlines.com)

Lufthansa Airlines (☎0 2264 2400; www.lufthansa.com)

Malaysia Airlines (☎0 2263 0565; www.mas.com.my)

Myanmar Airways International (☎0 2261 5060; www.maiair.com)

Nepal Airlines (☎0 2266 7146; www.nepalairlines.com.np)

Orient Thai (☎1126; www.flyorientthai.com)

Philippine Airlines (☎0 2263 0565; www.philippineair lines.com)

Qantas Airways (☎0 2236 2800; www.qantas.com.au)

Royal Brunei Airlines (☎0 2637 5151; www.bruneiair.com)

Scandinavian Airlines (☎0 2645 8200; www.flysas.com)

Singapore Airlines (☎0 2353 6000; www.singaporeair.com)

South African Airways (☎0 2635 1410; www.flysaa.com)

Thai Airways International (☎0 2288 7000; www.thaiair.com)

United Airlines (☎0 2353 3939; www.ual.com)

Vietnam Airlines (☎0 2655 4137; www.vietnamair.com.vn)

Tickets

In some cases – when travelling to neighbouring countries or to domestic destinations – it is still convenient to use a travel agent in Thailand. The amount of commission an agent will charge often varies so shop around to gauge the discrepancy in prices. Paying by credit card generally offers protection, because most card issuers provide refunds if you can prove you didn't get what you paid for. Agents who accept only cash should hand over the tickets straightaway and not tell you

to 'come back tomorrow'. After you've made a booking or paid your deposit, call the airline and confirm that the booking was made.

Air fares during the high season (December to March) can be expensive.

Land

Thailand shares land borders with Laos, Malaysia, Cambodia and Myanmar. Travel between all of these countries can be done by land via sanctioned border crossings. With improved highways, it is also becoming easier to travel from Thailand to China. See p770 for specific border crossing immigration points and transport summaries.

Bus, Car & Motorcycle

Road connections exist between all of Thailand's neighbours, and these routes can be travelled by bus, shared taxi and private car. In some cases, you'll take a bus to the border point, pass through immigration and then pick up another bus or shared taxi on the other side. In other cases, especially when crossing the Malaysian border, the bus will stop for immigration formalities and then continue to its destination across the border.

Train

Thailand's and Malaysia's state railways meet at Butterworth (93km south of the Thai–Malaysian border), which is a transfer point to Penang (by boat) or to Kuala Lumpur and Singapore (by Malaysian train).

There are several border crossings for which you can take a train to the border and then switch to automobile transport on the other side. The Thai–Cambodian border crossing of Aranya Prathet to Poipet and the Thai–Lao crossing of Nong Khai to Vientiane are two examples.

TRAVELLING BY BOAT TO/FROM THAILAND

You can cross into and out of Thailand via public boat from the Andaman coast to the Malaysian island of Langkawi.

All foreign-registered private vessels, skippers and crew must check in with the relevant Thai authorities as soon as possible after entering Thai waters. Although major ports throughout Thailand offer port check-ins, most leisure-boating visitors check in at Phuket, Krabi, Ko Samui, Pranburi or Pattaya. Before departing from Thailand by boat, you must also check out with immigration, customs and the harbourmaster.

Another rail line travels to the Malaysian east coast border town of Sungai Kolok, but because of ongoing violence in Thailand's Deep South we don't recommend this route for travellers.

Border Crossings

CAMBODIA

Cambodian tourist visas are available at the border for US$20, though some borders charge 1200B. Bring a passport photo and try to avoid some of the runner boys who want to issue a health certificate or other 'medical' paperwork for additional fees.

Aranya Prathet to Poipet (p501) The most direct land route between Bangkok and Angkor Wat.

Hat Lek to Krong Koh Kong (p217) The coastal crossing for travellers heading to/from Ko Chang/ Sihanoukville.

Pong Nam Ron to Pailin (p212) A backdoor route from Ko Chang (via Chanthaburi) to Battambang and Angkor Wat.

Several more remote crossings include O Smach to Chong Chom (periodically closed due to fighting at Khao Phra Wihan) and Chong Sa to Ngam Choam, but they aren't as convenient as you'll have to hire private transport (instead of a shared taxi) on the Cambodian side of the border.

CHINA

With an increase in infrastructure the interior of southern China is now linked with Laos and northern Thailand, making it possible to travel somewhat directly between the two countries. You'll need to arrange your Chinese visa prior to departure, ideally in Bangkok or Chiang Mai.

It was once also possible to travel overland from the Thai town of Mae Sai through Myanmar and across the border near Mong La to the

---

BICYCLE TRAVEL IN THAILAND

For travelling just about anywhere outside Bangkok, bicycles are an ideal form of local transport – cheap, nonpolluting and slow moving enough to allow travellers to see everything. Bicycles can be hired in many locations, especially guest houses, for as little as 50B per day, though they aren't always high-quality. A security deposit isn't usually required.

Bicycle touring is also a popular way to see the country, and most roads are sealed and have roomy shoulders. Because duties are high on imported bikes, in most cases you'll do better to bring your own bike to Thailand rather than purchase one here. No special permits are needed for bringing a bicycle into the country, although it may be registered by customs – which means if you don't leave the country with your bicycle, you'll have to pay a customs duty. It's advisable to bring a well-stocked repair kit.

Chinese town of Daluo, but this border has been closed since 2005.

Chiang Khong to Mengla (p333) The China–Thailand highway (Rte 3) was a former opium smuggling trail that has been modernised into a major transnational shipping route. The 1800km of paved road between Kunming, in China's Yunnan Province, to Bangkok is still missing one vital link: the fourth Thai-Lao Friendship Bridge (at Chiang Khong-Huay Xai) across the Mekong River, which is projected to be completed in 2014. Meanwhile the crossing is done by boat and buses leave from the Lao town of Huay Xai.

Chiang Saen to Jinghong (p329) A slow boat travels along the Mekong River from northern Thailand to China's Yunnan Province.

LAOS

It is fairly hassle free to cross into Laos from northern Thailand and northeastern Thailand. Lao visas (US$30 to US$42) can be obtained on arrival and applications require a passport photo.

Nong Khai to Vientiane (p468) The first Thai-Lao

Friendship Bridge spans this section of the Mekong River and is the main transport gateway between the two countries. Nong Khai is easily reached by train or bus from Bangkok.

Chiang Khong to Huay Xai (p333) A popular crossing that links northern Thailand and Chiang Mai with Luang Prabang via boat.

Mukdahan to Savannakhet (p495) The second Thai-Lao Friendship Bridge provides a trilateral link between Thailand, Laos and Vietnam.

Nakhon Phanom to Tha Khaek (p485) The third Thai-Lao Friendship Bridge is scheduled for completion in late 2011.

Chong Mek to Vangtao (p442) On the Thai side, the border is best accessed via Ubon Ratchathani and is a good option for transiting to Pakse (on the Lao side). Remote crossings include Bueng Kan to Paksan (p480; Lao visas must be arranged in advance), Tha Li to Kaen Thao (p473; requires chartered transport) and Ban Huay Kon to Muang Ngeun (p348).

Air-Fares & Train Routes Map

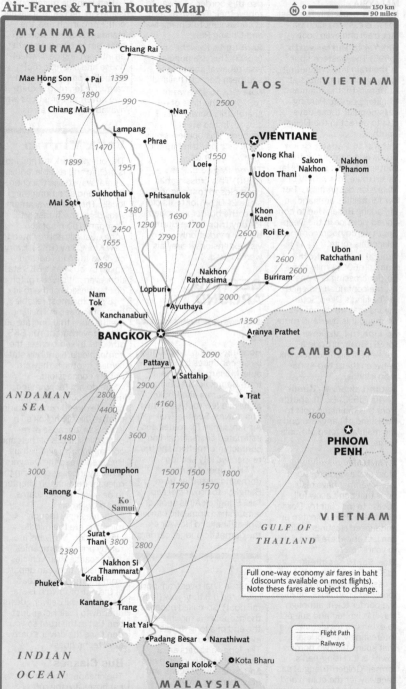

Full one-way economy air fares in baht (discounts available on most flights). Note these fares are subject to change.

— — — Flight Path
———— Railways

MALAYSIA

Malaysia, especially the west coast, is easy to reach via bus, train and even boat.

Hat Yai to Butterworth (p595) The western spur of the train line originating in Bangkok terminates at Butterworth, the mainland transfer point to Penang. Less popular these days due to unrest in the Deep South.

Hat Yai to Padang Besar Buses originate out of the southern transit town of Hat Yai en route to a variety of Malaysian destinations. Border formalities are handled at Padang Besar. Due to continued violence in the Deep South we do not recommend taking this route.

Sungai Kolok to Kota Bahru (p600) While this border crossing is a possibility, the continued violence in Thailand's Deep South means that we do not recommend this overland route.

Ko Lipe to Langkawi (p691) Boats provide a convenient high-season link between these two Andaman islands.

Satun-Langkawi/Kuala Perlis (p692) Boats shuttle from this mainland port to the island of Langkawi and the mainland town of Kuala Perlis.

MYANMAR

Most of the land crossings into Myanmar have restrictions that don't allow full access to the country. Border points are also subject to unannounced closures, which can last anywhere from a day to years.

Mae Sai to Tachileik (p322) This is the only crossing through which foreigners can travel beyond the border town, although travel is limited and subject to extensive regulations. Interestingly, the bridge that spans the two border towns is Lo Hsing-han's former 'Golden Triangle' passageway for the opium and heroin trade. Many travellers use this border as a way to renew their Thai visas as it is convenient to Chiang Mai and Chiang Rai.

Ranong to Kawthoung (p603) This is a popular visa-renewal point in the southern part of Thailand.

Mae Sot to Myawadi (p375) At the time of research this border was closed. In the event it reopens, this border is only open as a day trip into the Myawadi market.

Three Pagodas Pass (p190) This crossing has been closed to foreigners since 2006. Prior to its closure, the border was open for day trips to the Burmese border market only and no visa extensions/renewals were issued.

GETTING AROUND

Air

Hopping around the country by air continues to be affordable. Most routes originate from Bangkok, but Chiang Mai, Ko Samui and Phuket all have a few routes to other Thai towns. See the Thai Air-fares map for routes and estimated costs; for airline contact information, see the respective city sections.

THAI operates many domestic air routes from Bangkok to provincial capitals. Bangkok Air is another established domestic carrier. Orient Thai and Nok Air are the domestic budget carriers.

Boat

The true Thai river transport is the *reu·a hǎhng yow* (long-tail boat), so-called because the propeller is mounted at the end of a long drive shaft extending from the engine. The long-tail boats are a staple of transport on rivers and canals in Bangkok and neighbouring provinces.

Between the mainland and islands in the Gulf of Thailand or the Andaman Sea, the standard craft is a wooden boat, 8m to 10m long, with an inboard engine, a wheelhouse and a simple roof to shelter passengers and cargo. Faster, more expensive hovercraft or jetfoils are available in tourist areas.

Bus & Minivan

The bus network in Thailand is prolific and reliable, and is a great way to see the countryside and sit among the locals. The Thai government subsidises the Transport Company *(bò·rí·sàt kŏn sòng)*, usually abbreviated to Baw Khaw Saw (BKS). Every city and town in Thailand linked by bus has a BKS station, even if it's just a patch of dirt by the side of the road.

By far the most reliable bus companies in Thailand are the ones that operate out of the government-run BKS stations. In some cases the companies are entirely state owned, in others they are private concessions.

We do not recommend using bus companies that operate directly out of tourist centres, like Bangkok's Th Khao San, because of repeated instances of theft and commission-seeking stops. Be sure to read the Dangers & Annoyances sections in the relevant destination chapters to be aware of bus scams and problems.

Increasingly though, minivans are the middle-class option. Minivans are run by private companies and because their vehicles are smaller they can depart from the market (instead of the out-of-town bus stations) and will deliver guests directly to their hotel. Just don't sit in the front so you don't see the driver's daredevil techniques!

Bus Classes

The cheapest and slowest buses are the *rót*

	Aranya Prathet	Ayuthaya	Bangkok	Chiang Mai	Chiang Rai	Chumphon	Hat Yai	Hua Hin	Khon Kaen	Mae Hong Son	Mae Sai	Mukdahan	Nakhon Ratchasima	Nakhon Sawan	Nong Khai	Phitsanulok	Phuket	Sungai Kolok	Surat Thani	Tak	Trat
Ayuthaya	246																				
Bangkok	275	79																			
Chiang Mai	844	607	685																		
Chiang Rai	1014	777	775	191																	
Chumphon	727	531	452	1138	1308																
Hat Yai	1268	1072	993	1679	1849	555															
Hua Hin	458	262	183	869	1039	269	810														
Khon Kaen	432	397	440	604	774	902	1443	633													
Mae Hong Son	1013	767	800	225	406	1298	1839	1029	829												
Mae Sai	1082	845	746	259	68	1376	1917	1107	842	474											
Mukdahan	601	524	680	917	1087	1029	1570	760	313	1142	1155										
Nakhon Ratchasima	239	204	257	744	914	709	1250	440	193	969	982	320									
Nan	816	609	663	323	208	1139	1603	886	558	514	263	1000	760								
Nong Khai	598	563	516	720	890	1068	1609	799	166	945	958	347	359	1755							
Phitsanulok	535	298	420	309	479	829	1370	560	295	578	547	608	435	728	411						
Phuket	1125	929	862	1536	1706	412	474	667	1300	1696	1774	1427	1107	276	1466	1227					
Sungai Kolok	1555	1359	1210	1966	2136	842	287	1097	1730	2126	2204	1857	1357	1462	1896	1657	761				
Surat Thani	927	731	635	1338	1508	214	401	469	1102	1498	1576	1229	909	1288	1268	1029	286	791			
Tak	581	335	435	280	460	866	1407	597	441	432	528	754	544	354	557	146	1264	1694	1066		
Trat	285	392	313	999	1169	765	1306	496	717	1397	1237	886	524	996	883	690	1163	1593	965	727	
Ubon Ratchathani	444	367	620	881	1051	872	1413	603	277	1106	1119	157	163	1091	443	572	1270	1700	1072	707	729

tam·má·dah (ordinary fan buses) that stop in every little town and for every waving hand along the highway. Only a few of these ordinary buses, in rural locations or for local destinations, still exist since most have been replaced by air-con buses.

The bulk of the bus service is faster, more comfortable air-con buses, called *rót aa* (air bus). Longer routes offer at least two classes of air-con buses: 2nd class and 1st class; the latter have toilets. 'VIP' and 'Super VIP' buses have fewer seats so that each seat reclines further; sometimes these are called *rót norn* (sleeper bus).

It is handy to bring along a jacket, especially for long-distance trips, as the air-con can make the cabin cold.

The service on these buses is usually quite good and on certain routes sometimes includes a beverage service and video, courtesy of an 'air hostess', a young woman dressed in a polyester uniform.

On overnight journeys the buses usually stop somewhere en route for 'midnight kôw đôm', when passengers are awakened to get off the bus for a free meal of rice soup.

Reservations

You can book air-con BKS buses at any BKS terminal. Ordinary (fan) buses cannot be booked in advance. Privately run buses can be booked through most hotels or any travel agency, but it's best to book directly through a bus office to be sure that you get what you pay for.

Car & Motorcycle

Driving Licence

Short-term visitors who wish to drive vehicles (including motorcycles) in Thailand need an International Driving Permit.

Fuel & Spare Parts

Modern petrol (gasoline) stations are in plentiful supply all over Thailand wherever there are paved roads. In more-remote, off-road areas *ben·sin/nám·man rót yon* (petrol containing benzene) is usually available at small roadside or village stands. All fuel in Thailand is unleaded, and diesel is used by trucks and some passenger cars. In 2007, Thailand introduced several alternative fuels, including gasohol (a blend of petrol and ethanol that comes in different octane levels, either 91% or 95%) and compressed natural gas, used by taxis with bifuel capabilities. For news and updates about fuel options, and other car talk, see the website of **BKK Auto** (www.bkkautos.com).

Hire & Purchase

Cars, jeeps and vans can be rented in most major cities and airports from local companies as well as international chains. Local companies tend to have cheaper rates than the international chains, but their fleets of cars tend to be older and not as well maintained. Check the tyre treads and general upkeep of the vehicle before committing.

Motorcycles can be rented in major towns and many smaller tourist centres from guest houses and small mum-and-dad businesses. Renting a motorcycle in Thailand is relatively easy and a great way to independently tour the countryside. For daily rentals, most businesses will ask that you leave your passport as a deposit. Before renting a motorcycle, check the vehicle's condition and ask for a helmet (which is required by law).

Many tourists are injured riding motorcycles in Thailand because they don't know how to handle the vehicle and are unfamiliar with road rules and conditions. Drive slowly, especially when roads are slick, to avoid damage to yourself and to the vehicle, and be sure to have adequate health insurance. If you've never driven a motorcycle before, stick to the smaller 100cc step-through bikes with automatic clutches. Remember to distribute weight as evenly as possible across the frame of the bike to improve handling.

Insurance

Thailand requires a minimum of liability insurance for all registered vehicles on the road. The better hire companies include comprehensive coverage for their vehicles. Always verify that a vehicle is insured for liability before signing a rental contract; you should also ask to see the dated insurance documents. If you have an accident while driving an uninsured vehicle, you're in for some major hassles.

Road Rules & Hazards

Thais drive on the left-hand side of the road (most of the time!). Other than that, just about anything goes, in spite of road signs and speed limits.

The main rule to be aware of is that right of way goes to the bigger vehicle; this is not what it says in the Thai traffic law, but it's the reality. Maximum speed limits are 50km/h on urban roads and 80km/h to 100km/h on most highways – but on any given stretch of highway you'll see various vehicles travelling as slowly as 30km/h and as fast as 150km/h. Speed traps are common along Hwy 4 in the south and Hwy 2 in the northeast.

Indicators are often used to warn passing drivers about oncoming traffic. A flashing left indicator means it's OK to pass, while a right indicator means that someone's approaching from the other direction. Horns are used to tell other vehicles that the driver plans to pass. When drivers flash their lights, they're telling you not to pass.

In Bangkok traffic is chaotic, roads are poorly signposted and motorcycles and random contra flows mean you can suddenly find yourself facing a wall of cars coming the other way.

Outside of the capital, the principal hazard when driving in Thailand, besides the general disregard for traffic laws, is having to contend with so many different types of vehicles on the same road – trucks, bicycles, túk-túk ('pronounced *dúk dúk*; motorised transport) and motorcycles. This danger is often compounded by the lack of working lights. In village areas the vehicular traffic is lighter but you have to contend with stray chickens, dogs and water buffaloes.

Hitching

Hitching is never entirely safe in any country and we don't recommend it. Travellers who decide to hitch should understand that they are taking a small but potentially serious risk. Hitching is rarely seen these days in Thailand, so most passing motorists might not realise the intentions of the foreigner standing on the side of the road with a thumb out. Thais don't 'thumb it'; instead when they want a ride they wave their hand with the palm facing the ground. This is the same gesture used to flag a taxi or bus, which is why some drivers might stop and point to a bus stop if one is nearby.

In some of the national parks where there isn't public transport Thais are often willing to pick up a passenger standing by the side of the road.

Local Transport

City Bus & Sŏrng·tăa·ou

Bangkok has the largest city-bus system in the country, while Udon Thani and a few other provincial capitals have some city bus services. The etiquette for riding public buses is to wait at a bus stop and hail the vehicle by waving your hand palm-side downward. You typically pay the fare once you've taken a seat or, in some cases, when you disembark.

Elsewhere, public transport is provided by *sŏrng·tăa·ou* (a small pick-up truck outfitted with two facing rows of benches for passengers). They sometimes operate on fixed routes, just like buses, but they may also run a share-taxi service where they pick up passengers going in the same general direction. In tourist centres, *sŏrng·tăa·ou* can be chartered just like a regular taxi, but you'll need to negotiate the fare beforehand. You can usually hail a *sŏrng·tăa·ou* anywhere along its route and pay the fare when you disembark.

Depending on the region, *sŏrng·tăa·ou* might also run a fixed route from the centre of town to outlying areas or even points within the provinces. Sometimes these vehicles are larger six-wheeled vehicles (sometimes called *'rót hòk lór'*).

Mass Transit

Bangkok is the only city in Thailand to have an above-ground and underground light-rail public transport system. Known as the Skytrain and the Metro, respectively, both systems have helped to alleviate the capital's notorious traffic jams.

Motorcycle Taxi

Many cities in Thailand have *mor·deu·sai ráp jăhng* (100cc to 125cc motorcycles) that can be hired, with a driver, for short distances. If you're empty-handed or travelling with a small bag, they can't be beaten for transport in a pinch.

In most cities, you'll find motorcycle taxis clustered near street intersections, rather than cruising the streets looking for fares. Usually they wear numbered jerseys. Fares tend to run from 10B to 50B, depending on distance and you'll need to establish the price beforehand. The exception is in Bangkok where the soi motorcycle taxis are a standard 10B.

Taxi

Bangkok has the most formal system of metered taxis. In other cities, a taxi can be a private vehicle with negotiable rates. You can also travel between cities by taxi but you'll need to negotiate a price as few taxi drivers will run a meter for intercity travel.

Tours

Many operators around the world can arrange guided tours of Thailand. Most of them simply serve as brokers for tour companies based in Thailand. The better tour companies build their own Thailand itineraries from scratch and choose their local suppliers based on which best serve these itineraries. Many are now offering 'voluntourism' programs, which means that you might buy lunch for an orphanage, visit a hospital or teach an English class in addition to sightseeing. Also see Volunteering (p766) if you're looking for alternative travelling experiences.

Asian Trails (www.asiantrails.info) Tour operator that runs programs for overseas brokers; trips include a mix of on- and off-the-beaten-path destinations.

Hands Up Holidays (www.handsupholidays.com) Volunteer tourism and village sightseeing programs.

Intrepid Travel (www.intrepidtravel.com) Specialises in small-group travel geared towards young people.

Isan Explorer (www.isanexplorer.com) Custom tours to the northeast.

I-to-I (www.i-to-i.com) Volunteer tourism and gap-year programs.

Mekong Cruises (www.cruisemekong.com) Float down the mighty river aboard an elegant vessel.

Orient Express (www.orient-express.com) High-end luxury tours of common and uncommon places in Thailand.

Spice Roads (www.spiceroads.com) Variety of regional cycling programs.

Tiger Trails (www.tigertrailthailand.com) Nature, culture and strenuous trekking tours around Chiang Mai and northern Thailand.

Tour de Thailand (www.tourdethailand.com) Charity bike ride organiser covering touring routes throughout the country.

SĂHM·LÓR & TÚK-TÚK

Săhm·lór are three-wheeled pedicabs that are typically found in small towns where traffic is light and old-fashioned ways persist.

The modern era's version of the human-powered săhm·lór is the motorised túk-túk. They're small utility vehicles, powered by screaming engines (usually LPG-powered) and a lot of flash and sparkle.

With either form of transport the fare must be established by bargaining before departure. In tourist centres, túk-túk drivers often grossly overcharge foreigners so have a sense of how much the fare should be before soliciting a ride. Hotel staff are helpful in providing reasonable fare suggestions.

Readers interested in pedicab lore and design may want to have a look at Lonely Planet's hardcover pictorial book, *Chasing Rickshaws*, by Lonely Planet founder Tony Wheeler.

Tours with Kasma Loha-Unchit (www.thaifoodand travel.com) Thai cookbook author offers personalised 'cultural immersion' tours of Thailand.

Train

Thailand's train system connects the four corners of the country and is most convenient as an alternative to buses for the long journey north to Chiang Mai or south to Surat Thani. The train is also ideal for short trips to Ayuthaya and Lopburi from Bangkok where traffic is a consideration.

The 4500km rail network is operated by the **State Railway of Thailand** (SRT; ☎1690; www.railway.co.th) and covers four main lines: the northern, southern, north-eastern and eastern lines. All long-distance trains originate from Bangkok's Hua Lamphong station.

Classes

The SRT operates passenger trains in three classes – 1st, 2nd and 3rd – but each class varies considerably depending on whether you're on an ordinary, rapid or express train.

First Class – Private cabins define the 1st-class carriages, which are available only on rapid, express and special-express trains.

Second Class – The seating arrangements in a 2nd-class, non-sleeper carriage are similar to those on a bus, with pairs of padded seats, usually recliners, all facing towards the front of the

train. On 2nd-class sleeper cars, pairs of seats face one another and convert into two fold-down berths. The lower berth has more headroom than the upper berth and this is reflected in a higher fare. Children are always assigned a lower berth. Second-class carriages are found only on rapid and express trains. There are air-con and fan 2nd-class carriages.

Third Class – A typical 3rd-class carriage consists of two rows of bench seats divided into facing pairs. Each bench seat is designed to seat two or three passengers, but on a crowded rural line nobody seems to care. Express trains do not carry 3rd-class carriages at all. Commuter trains in the Bangkok area are all 3rd class.

Costs

Fares are determined on a base price with surcharges added for distance, class and train type (special express, express, rapid, ordinary). Extra charges are added if the carriage has air-con and for sleeping berths (either upper or lower).

Reservations

Advance bookings can be made from one to 60 days before your intended date of departure. You can make bookings in person from any train station. Train tickets can also be purchased at travel agencies, which usually add a service charge to the ticket price. If you are planning long-distance train travel from outside the country, you should email the **State Rail-**

way of Thailand (passenger -ser@railway.co.th) at least two weeks before your journey. You will receive an email confirming the booking. Pick up and pay for tickets an hour before leaving at the scheduled departure train station.

It is advisable to make advanced bookings for long-distance sleeper trains between Bangkok and Chiang Mai or from Bangkok to Surat Thani, especially around Songkran in April and peak tourist-season months of December and January.

For short-distance trips you should purchase your ticket at least a day in advance for seats (rather than sleepers).

Partial refunds on tickets are available depending on the number of days prior to your departure you arrange for a cancellation. These arrangements can be handled at the train station booking office.

Station Services

You'll find that all train stations in Thailand have baggage-storage services (or 'cloak rooms'). Most stations have a ticket window that will open between 15 and 30 minutes before train arrivals. There are also newsagents and small snack vendors, but no full-service restaurants.

Most train stations have printed timetables in English; although this isn't always the case for smaller stations. Bangkok's Hua Lamphong station is a good spot to load up on timetables.

Health

Health risks and the quality of medical facilities vary depending on where and how you travel in Thailand. The majority of the major cities and popular tourist areas are well developed with adequate and even excellent medical care. However, travel to remote rural areas can expose you to some health risks and less adequate medical care.

Travellers tend to worry about contracting exotic infectious diseases when visiting the tropics, but such infections are far less common than problems with pre-existing medical conditions such as heart disease, and accidental injury (especially as a result of traffic accidents).

Visitors to Thailand becoming ill in some way is common, however. Respiratory infections, diarrhoea and dengue fever are particular hazards in Thailand. Fortunately most common illnesses can be prevented or are easily treated.

The following advice is a general guide and does not replace the advice of a doctor trained in travel medicine.

BEFORE YOU GO

Pack medications in clearly labelled original containers and obtain a signed and dated letter from your physician describing your medical conditions, medications and syringes or needles. If you have a heart condition, bring a copy of your electrocardiography (ECG) taken just prior to travelling.

If you take any regular medication bring double your needs in case of loss or theft. In Thailand you can buy many medications over the counter without a doctor's prescription, but it can be difficult to find the exact medication you are taking.

Insurance

Even if you're fit and healthy, don't travel without health insurance – accidents do happen. You may require extra cover for adventure activities such as rock climbing or diving, as well as scooter/motorcycle riding. If your health insurance doesn't cover you for medical expenses abroad, ensure you get specific travel insurance. Most hospitals require an upfront guarantee of payment (from yourself or your insurer) prior to admission. Inquire before your trip about payment of medical charges and retain all documentation (medical reports, invoices etc) for claim purposes.

Vaccinations

Specialised travel-medicine clinics are your best source of information on which vaccinations you should consider taking. Ideally you should visit a doctor six to eight weeks before departure, but it is never too late. Ask your doctor for an International Certificate of Vaccination (otherwise known as the yellow booklet), which will list all the vaccinations you've received. The **Centers for Disease Control** (CDC; www.cdc.gov) has a traveller's health section that contains recommendations for vaccinations. The only vaccine required by international regulations is yellow fever. Proof of vaccination will only be required if you have visited a country in the yellow-fever zone within the six days prior to entering Thailand. If you are travelling to Thailand from Africa or South America you should check to see if you require proof of vaccination.

Medical Checklist

Recommended items for a personal medical kit include the following:

» antifungal cream, eg Clotrimazole

» antibacterial cream, eg Muciprocin

» antibiotic for skin infections, eg Amoxicillin/Clavulanate or Cephalexin

» antibiotics for diarrhoea include Norfloxacin, Ciprofloxacin or Azithromycin for bacterial diarrhoea; for giardiasis or amoebic dysentery take Tinidazole

» antihistamine – there are many options, eg Cetrizine for daytime and Promethazine for night

» antiseptic, eg Betadine

» antispasmodic for stomach cramps, eg Buscopan

» contraceptives

» decongestant

» DEET-based insect repellent

» oral rehydration solution for diarrhoea (eg Gastrolyte), diarrhoea 'stopper' (eg Loperamide) and antinausea medication

» first-aid items such as scissors, Elastoplasts, bandages, gauze, thermometer (but not one with mercury), sterile needles and syringes (with a doctor's letter), safety pins and tweezers

» hand gel (alcohol based) or alcohol-based hand wipes

» ibuprofen or another anti-inflammatory

» indigestion medication, eg Quick Eze or Mylanta

» laxative, eg Coloxyl

» migraine medicine – for migraine suffers

» paracetamol

» Permethrin to impregnate clothing and mosquito nets if at high risk

» steroid cream for allergic/itchy rashes, eg 1% to 2% hydrocortisone

» sunscreen, sunglasses and hat

» throat lozenges

» thrush (vaginal yeast infection) treatment, eg Clotrimazole pessaries or Diflucan tablet

» Ural or equivalent if you are prone to urine infections

IN TRANSIT

Deep Vein Thrombosis

Deep vein thrombosis (DVT) occurs when blood clots form in the legs during long trips such as flights, chiefly because of prolonged immobility. The longer the journey, the greater the risk. Though most blood clots are reabsorbed uneventfully, some may break off and travel through the blood vessels to the lungs, where they can cause life-threatening complications.

The chief symptom of DVT is swelling or pain of the foot, ankle or calf, usually but not always on one side. When a blood clot travels to the lungs, it may cause chest pain and difficulty in breathing. Travellers with any of these symptoms should immediately seek medical attention.

To prevent the development of DVT on long flights you should walk about the cabin, perform isometric compressions of the leg muscles (ie contract the leg muscles while sitting) and drink plenty of fluids (nonalcoholic). Those at higher risk should speak with a doctor about extra preventive measures.

Jet Lag & Motion Sickness

Jet lag is common when crossing more than five time zones; it results in insomnia, fatigue, malaise or nausea. To avoid jet lag try drinking plenty of fluids (nonalcoholic) and eating light meals. Upon arrival, seek exposure to natural sunlight and readjust your schedule. Some people find melatonin helpful but it is not available in all countries.

Sedating antihistamines such as dimenhydrinate (Dramamine) or Prochlorperazine (Phenergan) are usually the first choice for treating motion sickness. Their main side effect is drowsiness. A herbal alternative is ginger. Scopolamine patches are considered the most effective prevention.

IN THAILAND

Availability & Cost of Health Care

Bangkok is considered the nearest centre of medical excellence for many countries in Southeast Asia. Private hospitals are more expensive than other medical facilities but offer a superior standard of care and English-speaking staff. Such facilities are listed under Information in the city and some other sections of this book. The cost of health care is relatively cheap in

---

FURTHER READING

» **International Travel & Health** (www.who.int/ith) Health guide published by the World Health Organization (WHO).

» **Centers for Disease Control & Prevention** (www.cdc.gov) Country-specific advice.

» Your home country's Department of Foreign Affairs or the equivalent; register your trip, a helpful precaution in the event of a natural disaster.

» *Healthy Travel – Asia & India* (by Lonely Planet) Includes pretrip planning, emergency first aid, and immunisation and disease information.

» *Traveller's Health: How to Stay Healthy Abroad* (by Dr Richard Dawood) Considered the 'health bible' for international holidays.

» *Travelling Well* (by Dr Deborah Mills) Health guidebook and website (www.travellingwell.com.au).

» *Healthy Living in Thailand* (published by the Thai Red Cross) Recommended for long-term travellers.

Thailand compared to most Western countries.

Self-treatment may be appropriate if your problem is minor (eg traveller's diarrhoea), you are carrying the appropriate medication and you are unable to attend a recommended clinic or hospital.

Buying medication over the counter is not recommended, because fake medications and poorly stored or out-of-date drugs are common.

Infectious Diseases

Cutaneous Larva Migrans

This disease, caused by dog or cat hookworm, is particularly common on the beaches of Thailand. The rash starts as a small lump, and then slowly spreads like a winding line. It is intensely itchy, especially at night. It is easily treated with medications and should not be cut out or frozen.

Dengue Fever

This mosquitoborne disease is increasingly problematic throughout Southeast Asia, especially in the cities. As there is no vaccine it can only be prevented by avoiding mosquito bites. The mosquito that carries dengue is a daytime biter, so use insect-avoidance measures at all times. Symptoms include high fever, severe headache (especially behind the eyes), nausea and body aches (dengue was previously known as 'breakbone fever'). Some people develop a rash (which can be very itchy) and experience diarrhoea. The southern islands of Thailand are particularly high-risk areas. There is no specific treatment, just rest and paracetamol – do not take aspirin or ibuprofen as they increase the risk of haemorrhaging. See a doctor to be diagnosed and monitored.

Dengue can progress to the more severe and life-threatening dengue haemorrhagic fever, however this is very uncommon in tourists. The risk of this increases substantially if you have previously been infected with dengue and are then infected with a different serotype.

Hepatitis A

The risk in Bangkok is decreasing but there is still significant risk in most of the country. This food- and waterborne virus infects the liver, causing jaundice (yellow skin and eyes), nausea and lethargy. There is no specific treatment for hepatitis A. In rare instances, it can be fatal for those over the age of 40. All travellers to Thailand should be vaccinated against hepatitis A.

Hepatitis B

The only sexually transmitted disease (STD) that can be prevented by vaccination, hepatitis B is spread by body fluids, including sexual contact. In some parts of Thailand up to 20% of the population are carriers of hepatitis B, and usually are unaware of this. The long-term consequences can include liver cancer, cirrhosis and death.

HIV

HIV is now one of the most common causes of death in people under the age of 50 in Thailand. Always practise safe sex; avoid getting tattoos or using unclean syringes.

Influenza

Present year-round in the tropics, influenza (flu) symptoms include high fever, muscle aches, runny nose, cough and sore throat. Flu is the most common vaccine-preventable disease contracted by travellers and everyone should consider vaccination. There is no specific treatment, just rest and paracetamol. Complications such as bronchitis or middle-ear infection may require antibiotic treatment.

Leptospirosis

Leptospirosis is contracted from exposure to infected surface water – most commonly after river rafting or canyoning. Early symptoms are very similar to the flu and include headache and fever. It can vary from a very mild ailment to a fatal disease. Diagnosis is made through blood tests and it is easily treated with Doxycycline.

Malaria

There is an enormous amount of misinformation concerning malaria. Malaria is caused by a parasite transmitted by the bite of an infected mosquito. The most important symptom of malaria is fever, but general symptoms such as headache, diarrhoea, cough or chills may also occur – the same symptoms as many other infections. A diagnosis can only be made by taking a blood sample.

Most parts of Thailand visited by tourists, particularly city and resort areas, have minimal to no risk of malaria, and the risk of side effects from taking antimalarial tablets is likely to outweigh the risk of getting the disease itself. If you are travelling to high-risk rural areas (unlikely for most visitors), seek medical advice on the right medication and dosage for you.

Travellers are advised to prevent mosquito bites by taking these steps:

» use a DEET-containing insect repellent on exposed skin; natural repellents such as citronella can be effective, but must be repeatedly applied

» sleep under a mosquito net, ideally impregnated with Permethrin

» choose accommodation with screens and fans

» impregnate clothing with Permethrin in high-risk areas

» wear long sleeves and trousers in light colours

RARE BUT BE AWARE

» Avian Influenza – Most of those infected have had close contact with sick or dead birds.

» Filariasis – A mosquitoborne disease that is common in the local population; practise mosquito-avoidance measures.

» Hepatitis E – Transmitted through contaminated food and water and has similar symptoms to hepatitis A; can be a severe problem in pregnant women. Follow safe eating and drinking guidelines.

» Japanese B Encephalitis – Viral disease transmitted by mosquitoes, typically occurring in rural areas; vaccination is recommended for travellers spending more than one month outside cities or for long-term expats.

» Meliodosis – Contracted by skin contact with soil. Affects up to 30% of the local population in northeastern Thailand. The symptoms are very similar to those experienced by tuberculosis (TB) sufferers. There is no vaccine but it can be treated with medications.

» Strongyloides – A parasite transmitted by skin contact with soil; common in local population. It is characterised by an unusual skin rash – a linear rash on the trunk which comes and goes. An overwhelming infection can follow. It can be treated with medications.

» Tuberculosis – Medical and aid workers and long-term travellers who have significant contact with the local population should take precautions. Vaccination is recommended for children spending more than three months in Thailand. The main symptoms are fever, cough, weight loss, night sweats and tiredness. Treatment is available with long-term multidrug regimens.

» Typhus – Murine typhus is spread by the bite of a flea; scrub typhus is spread via a mite. Symptoms include fever, muscle pains and a rash. Following general insect-avoidance measures and doxycycline will also prevent them.

» use mosquito coils
» spray your room with insect repellent before going out for your evening meal

Measles

This highly contagious viral infection is spread through coughing and sneezing. Most people born before 1966 are immune as they had the disease in childhood. Measles starts with a high fever and rash and can be complicated by pneumonia and brain disease. There is no specific treatment. Ensure you are fully vaccinated.

Rabies

This uniformly fatal disease is spread by the bite or lick of an infected animal – most commonly a dog or monkey. You should seek medical advice immediately after any animal bite and commence post-exposure treatment. Having a pretravel vaccination means the postbite treatment is greatly simplified.

If an animal bites you, gently wash the wound with soap and water, and apply iodine-based antiseptic. If you are not prevaccinated you will need to receive rabies immunoglobulin as

soon as possible, followed by five shots of vaccine over 28 days. If prevaccinated you need just two shots of vaccine given three days apart.

STDs

Sexually transmitted diseases most common in Thailand include herpes, warts, syphilis, gonorrhoea and chlamydia. People carrying these diseases often have no signs of infection. Condoms will prevent gonorrhoea and chlamydia but not warts or herpes. If after a sexual encounter you develop any rash, lumps, discharge or pain when passing urine seek immediate medical attention. If you have been sexually active during your travels have an STD check on your return home.

Typhoid

This serious bacterial infection is spread through food and water. It gives a high and slowly progressive fever, severe headache, and may be accompanied by a dry cough and stomach pain. It is diagnosed by blood tests and treated with antibiotics. Vaccination is recommended for all travellers spending more than a week in Thailand, or travelling outside of the major cities. Be aware that vaccination is not 100% effective so you must still be careful with what you eat and drink.

Traveller's Diarrhoea

Traveller's diarrhoea is by far the most common problem affecting travellers – up to 50% of people will suffer from some form of it within two weeks of starting their trip. In over 80% of cases, traveller's diarrhoea is caused by a bacteria (there are numerous potential culprits), and responds promptly to treatment with antibiotics.

Here we define traveller's diarrhoea as the passage of more than three watery bowel movements within 24 hours, plus at least one other symptom such as vomiting, fever, cramps, nausea or feeling generally unwell.

Treatment consists of staying well hydrated; rehydration solutions such as Gastrolyte are the best for this. Antibiotics such as Norfloxacin, Ciprofloxacin or Azithromycin will kill the bacteria quickly.

Loperamide is just a 'stopper' and doesn't get to the cause of the problem. It can be helpful, for example if you have to go on a long bus ride. Don't take Loperamide if you have a fever, or blood in your stools. Seek medical attention quickly if you do not respond to an appropriate antibiotic.

Giardia lamblia is a parasite that is relatively common in travellers. Symptoms include nausea, bloating, excess gas, fatigue and intermittent diarrhoea. 'Eggy' burps are often attributed solely to giardiasis. The treatment of choice is Tinidazole, with Metronidazole being a second-line option.

Amoebic dysentery is very rare in travellers but may be misdiagnosed by poor-quality labs. Symptoms are similar to bacterial diarrhoea. You should always seek reliable medical care if you have blood in your diarrhoea. Treatment involves two drugs; Tinidazole or Metronidazole to kill the parasite in your gut and then a second drug to kill the cysts. If left untreated complications, such as liver abscesses, can occur.

Environmental Hazards

Food

Eating in restaurants is the biggest risk factor for contracting traveller's diarrhoea. Ways to avoid it include eating only freshly cooked food, and avoiding food that has been sitting around in buffets. Peel all fruit and cook vegetables. Eat in busy restaurants with a high turnover of customers.

Heat

Many parts of Thailand are hot and humid throughout the year. For most people it takes at least two weeks to adapt to the hot climate. Prevent swelling of the feet and ankles as well as muscle cramps caused by excessive sweating by avoiding dehydration and excessive activity in the hot hours of the day.

Heat stroke is a serious medical emergency and requires immediate medical treatment. Symptoms come on suddenly and include weakness, nausea, a hot dry body with a body temperature of over 41°C, dizziness, confusion, loss of coordination, fits and eventually collapse and loss of consciousness.

Insect Bites & Stings

Bedbugs live in the cracks of furniture and walls and then migrate to the bed at night to feed on you. You can treat the itch with an antihistamine. Lice inhabit various parts of your body but most commonly your head and pubic area. Transmission is via close contact with an infected person. They can be difficult to treat and you may need numerous applications of an antilice shampoo such as Permethrin. Pubic lice are usually contracted from sexual contact.

Ticks are contracted when walking in rural areas. They are commonly found behind the ears, on the belly and in armpits. If you have had a tick bite and experience symptoms such as a rash at the site of the bite or elsewhere, fever or muscle aches you should see a doctor. Doxycycline prevents tick-borne diseases.

Leeches are found in humid rainforest areas. They do not transmit any disease but their bites are often intensely itchy for weeks afterwards and can easily become infected. Apply an iodine-based antiseptic to any leech bite to help prevent infection.

Bee and wasp stings mainly cause problems for people who are allergic to them. Anyone with a serious allergy should carry an injection of adrenaline (eg an Epipen) for emergencies. For others, pain is the main problem – apply ice to the sting and take painkillers.

Parasites

Numerous parasites are common in local populations in Thailand, but most of these are rare in travellers. The two rules to follow to avoid parasitic infections are to wear shoes and to avoid eating raw food, especially fish, pork and vegetables. A number of parasites are transmitted via the skin by walking barefoot, including strongyloides, hookworm and cutaneous *larva migrans*.

Skin Problems

Prickly heat is a common skin rash in the tropics, caused by sweat being trapped under the skin. Treat by taking cool showers and using powders.

Two fungal rashes commonly affect travellers. The first occurs in the groin, armpits and between the toes. It starts as a red patch that slowly spreads and is usually itchy. Treatment involves keeping the skin dry, avoiding chafing and using an antifungal cream such as Clotrimazole or Lamisil. The fungus *Tinea versicolor* causes small and light-coloured patches, most commonly on the back, chest and shoulders. Consult a doctor.

Cuts and scratches become easily infected in humid climates. Immediately wash all wounds in clean water and apply antiseptic. If you develop signs of infection, see a doctor. Coral cuts can easily become infected.

Snakes

Though snake bites are rare for travellers, there are over

85 species of venomous snakes in Thailand. Always wear boots and long pants if walking in an area that may have snakes. First aid in the event of a snake bite involves 'pressure immobilisation' using an elastic bandage firmly wrapped around the affected limb, starting at the hand or foot (depending on the limb bitten) and working up towards the chest. The bandage should not be so tight that the circulation is cut off, and the fingers or toes should be kept free so the circulation can be checked. Immobilise the limb with a splint and carry the victim to medical attention. It is very important that the victim stays immobile. Do not use tourniquets or try to suck the venom out.

The Thai Red Cross produces antivenom for many of the poisonous snakes in Thailand.

Sunburn

Even on a cloudy day sunburn can occur rapidly. Use a strong sunscreen (at least factor 30), making sure to reapply after a swim, and always wear a wide-brimmed hat and sunglasses outdoors. Avoid lying in the sun when the sun is at its highest in the sky (10am to 2pm). If you become sunburnt stay out of the sun until you have recovered, apply cool compresses and take painkillers for the discomfort. One per cent hydrocortisone cream applied twice daily is also helpful.

Travelling With Children

Thailand is relatively safe for children from a health point of view. It is wise to consult a doctor who specialises in travel medicine prior to travel to ensure your child is appropriately prepared. A medical kit designed specifically for children includes paracetamol or Tylenol syrup for fevers, an antihistamine, itch cream, first-aid supplies, nappy-rash treatment, sunscreen and insect repellent. It is a good idea to carry a general antibiotic (best used under medical supervision) – Azithromycin is an ideal paediatric formula used to treat bacterial diarrhoea, as well as ear, chest and throat infections.

Good resources are the Lonely Planet publication *Travel with Children,* and for those spending longer away Jane Wilson-Howarth's book *Your Child's Health Abroad* is excellent.

Women's Health

Pregnant women should receive specialised advice before travelling. The ideal time to travel is in the second trimester (16 and 28 weeks), when pregnancy-related risks are at their lowest.

JELLYFISH STINGS

Box jellyfish stings range from minor to deadly. A good rule of thumb, however, is to presume a box jelly is dangerous until proven otherwise. There are two main types of box jellyfish – multitentacled and single-tentacled.

Multitentacled box jellyfish are present in Thai waters – these are potentially the most dangerous and a severe envenomation can kill an adult within two minutes. They are generally found on sandy beaches near river mouths and mangroves during the warmer months.

There are many types of single-tentacled box jellyfish, some of which can cause severe symptoms known as the Irukandji syndrome. The initial sting can seem minor; however severe symptoms such as back pain, nausea, vomiting, sweating, difficulty breathing and a feeling of impending doom can develop between five and 40 minutes later. There has been the occasional death reported from this syndrome as a result of high blood pressure causing strokes or heart attacks.

There are many other jellyfish in Thailand that cause irritating stings but no serious effects. The only way to prevent these stings is to wear protective clothing, which provides a barrier between human skin and the jellyfish.

First Aid for Severe Stings

For severe life-threatening envenomations the first priority is keeping the person alive. Stay with the person, send someone to call for medical help, and start immediate CPR if they are unconscious. If the victim is conscious douse the stung area liberally with vinegar – simple household vinegar is fine – for 30 seconds. For single-tentacled jellyfish stings pour vinegar onto the stung area as above; early application can make a huge difference. It is best to seek medical care quickly in case any other symptoms develop over the next 40 minutes.

Australia and Thailand are now working in close collaboration to identify the species of jellyfish in Thai waters, as well as their ecology – hopefully enabling better prediction and detection of the jellyfish.

Thanks to Dr Peter Fenner for the information in this boxed text.

Avoid rural travel in areas with poor transport and medical facilities. Most of all, ensure travel insurance covers all pregnancy-related possibilities, including premature labour.

Malaria is a high-risk disease in pregnancy. Advice from the WHO recommends that pregnant women do *not* travel to those areas with Chloroquine-resistant malaria. None of the more effective antimalarial drugs is completely safe in pregnancy.

Traveller's diarrhoea can quickly lead to dehydration and result in inadequate blood flow to the placenta. Many of the drugs used to treat various diarrhoea bugs are not recommended in pregnancy. Azithromycin is considered safe.

In Thailand's urban areas, supplies of sanitary products are readily available. Your personal birth-control option may not be available so bring adequate supplies. Heat, humidity and antibiotics can all contribute to thrush. Treatment of thrush is with antifungal creams and pessaries such as Clotrimazole. A practical alternative is one tablet of fluconazole (Diflucan). Urinary-tract infections can be precipitated by dehydration or long bus journeys without toilet stops; bring suitable antibiotics for treatment.

Language

WANT MORE?
For in-depth language information and handy phrases, check out Lonely Planet's *Phrasebook Name*. You'll find it at **shop .lonelyplanet.com**, or you can buy Lonely Planet's iPhone phrasebooks at the Apple App Store.

Thailand's official language is effectively the dialect spoken and written in central Thailand, which has successfully become the lingua franca of all Thai and non-Thai ethnic groups in the kingdom.

In Thai the meaning of a single syllable may be altered by means of different tones. In standard Thai there are five: low tone, mid tone, falling tone, high tone and rising tone. The range of all five tones is relative to each speaker's vocal range, so there is no fixed 'pitch' intrinsic to the language.

» **low tone** – 'Flat' like the mid tone, but pronounced at the relative bottom of one's vocal range. It is low, level and has no in-flection, eg bàht (baht – the Thai currency).

» **mid tone** – Pronounced 'flat', at the relative middle of the speaker's vocal range, eg dee (good). No tone mark is used.

» **falling tone** – Starting high and falling sharply, this tone is similar to the change in pitch in English when you are emphasising a word, or calling someone's name from afar, eg mâi (no/not).

» **high tone** – Usually the most difficult for non-Thai speakers. It's pronounced near the relative top of the vocal range, as level as possible, eg máh (horse).

» **rising tone** – Starting low and gradually rising, sounds like the inflection used by English speakers to imply a question – 'Yes?', eg sǎhm (three).

The Thai government has instituted the Royal Thai General Transcription System (RTGS) as a standard method of writing Thai using the Roman alphabet. It's used in official documents, road signs and on maps.

However, local variations crop up on signs, menus etc. Generally, names in this book follow the most common practice.

In our coloured pronunciation guides, the hyphens indicate syllable breaks within words, and some syllables are further divided with a dot to help you pronounce compound vowels, eg mêu·a·rai (when).

The vowel a is pronounced as in 'about', aa as the 'a' in 'bad', ah as the 'a' in 'father', ai as in 'aisle', air as in 'flair' (without the 'r'), eu as the 'er' in 'her' (without the 'r'), ew as in 'new' (with rounded lips), oh as the 'o' in 'toe', or as in 'torn' (without the 'r') and ow as in 'now'.

Most consonants correspond to their English counterparts. The exceptions are b (a hard 'p' sound, almost like a 'b', eg in 'hip-bag'); d (a hard 't' sound, like a sharp 'd', eg in 'mid-tone'); ng (as in 'singing'; in Thai it can occur at the start of a word) and r (as in 'run' but flapped; in everyday speech it's often pronounced like 'l').

BASICS

The social structure of Thai society demands different registers of speech depending on who you're talking to. To make things simple we've chosen the correct form of speech appropriate to the context of each phrase.

When being polite, the speaker ends his or her sentence with kráp (for men) or kâ (for women). It is the gender of the speaker that is being expressed here; it is also the common way to answer 'yes' to a question or show agreement.

The masculine and feminine forms of phrases in this chapter are indicated where relevant with 'm/f'.

Hello.	สวัสดี	sà-wàt-dee
Goodbye.	ลาก่อน	lah gòrn
Yes.	ใช่	châi
No.	ไม่	mâi
Please.	ขอ	kŏr
Thank you.	ขอบคุณ	kòrp kun
You're welcome.	ยินดี	yin dee
Excuse me.	ขออภัย	kŏr à-pai
Sorry.	ขอโทษ	kŏr tôht

How are you?
สบายดีไหม — sà-bai dee măi

Fine. And you?
สบายดีครับ/ค่ะ — sà-bai dee kráp/
แล้วคุณล่ะ — kâ láa·ou kun lâ (m/f)

What's your name?
คุณชื่ออะไร — kun chêu à-rai

My name is ...
ผม/ดิฉันชื่อ... — pŏm/dì-chăn chêu ... (m/f)

Do you speak English?
คุณพูดภาษา — kun pôot pah-săh
อังกฤษได้ไหม — ang-grìt dâi măi

I don't understand.
ผม/ดิฉันไม่ — pŏm/dì-chăn mâi
เข้าใจ — kôw jai (m/f)

ACCOMMODATION

Where's a ...?	... อยู่ที่ไหน	... yòo têe năi
campsite	ค่ายพักแรม	kâi pák raam
guesthouse	บ้านพัก	bâhn pák
hotel	โรงแรม	rohng raam
youth hostel	บ้าน เยาวชน	bâhn yow-wá-chon

Do you have a ... room?	มีห้อง ... ไหม	mee hôrng ... măi
single	เดี่ยว	dèe·o
double	เตียงคู่	đee·ang kôo
twin	สองเตียง	sŏrng đee·ang

air-con	แอร์	aa
bathroom	ห้องน้ำ	hôrng nám
laundry	ห้องซักผ้า	hôrng sák pâh
mosquito net	มุ้ง	múng
window	หน้าต่าง	nâh đàhng

Question Words

What?	อะไร	à-rai
When?	เมื่อไร	mêu·a-rai
Where?	ที่ไหน	têe năi
Who?	ใคร	krai
Why?	ทำไม	tam-mai

DIRECTIONS

Where's ...?
... อยู่ที่ไหน — ... yòo têe năi

What's the address?
ที่อยู่คืออะไร — têe yòo keu à-rai

Could you please write it down?
เขียนลงให้ได้ไหม — kĕe·an long hâi dâi măi

Can you show me (on the map)?
ให้ดู (ในแผนที่) — hâi doo (nai păan têe)
ได้ไหม — dâi măi

Turn left/right.
เลี้ยวซ้าย/ขวา — lée·o sái/kwăh

It's ...	อยู่ ...	yòo ...
behind	ที่หลัง	têe lăng
in front of	ตรงหน้า	đrong nâh
near	ใกล้ๆ	glâi glâi
next to	ข้างๆ	kâhng kâhng
straight ahead	ตรงไป	đrong bai

EATING & DRINKING

I'd like (the menu), please.
ขอ (รายการ — kŏr (rai gahn
อาหาร) หน่อย — ah-hăhn) nòy

What would you recommend?
คุณแนะนำอะไรบ้าง — kun náa-nam à-rai bâhng

That was delicious!
อร่อยมาก — à-ròy mâhk

Cheers!
ไชโย — chai-yoh

Please bring the bill.
ขอบิลหน่อย — kŏr bin nòy

I don't eat ...	ผม/ดิฉัน ไม่กิน ...	pŏm/dì-chăn mâi gin ... (m/f)
eggs	ไข่	kài
fish	ปลา	blah
red meat	เนื้อแดง	néu·a daang
nuts	ถั่ว	tòo·a

Key Words

bar	บาร์	bah
bottle	ขวด	kòo·at
bowl	ชาม	chahm
breakfast	อาหารเช้า	ah-hăhn chów
cafe	ร้านกาแฟ	ráhn gah-faa
chopsticks	ไม้ตะเกียบ	mái đà-gèe·ap
cold	เย็น	yen
cup	ถ้วย	tôo·ay
dessert	ของหวาน	kŏrng wăhn
dinner	อาหารเย็น	ah-hăhn yen
drink list	รายการ เครื่องดื่ม	rai gahn krêu·ang dèum
fork	ส้อม	sôrm
glass	แก้ว	gâa·ou
hot	ร้อน	rórn
knife	มีด	mêet
lunch	อาหาร กลางวัน	ah-hăhn glahng wan
market	ตลาด	đà-làht
menu	รานการ อาหาร	rai gahn ah-hăhn
plate	จาน	jahn
restaurant	ร้านอาหาร	ráhn ah-hăhn
spicy	เผ็ด	pèt
spoon	ช้อน	chórn
vegetarian (person)	คนกินเจ	kon gin jair

Signs

ทางเข้า	Entrance
ทางออก	Exit
เปิด	Open
ปิด	Closed
ที่ติดต่อสอบถาม	Information
ห้าม	Prohibited
ห้องสุขา	Toilets
ชาย	Men
หญิง	Women

with	มี	mee
without	ไม่มี	mâi mee

Meat & Fish

beef	เนื้อ	néu·a
chicken	ไก่	gài
crab	ปู	boo
duck	เป็ด	bèt
fish	ปลา	blah
meat	เนื้อ	néu·a
pork	หมู	mŏo
seafood	อาหารทะเล	ah-hăhn tá-lair
squid	ปลาหมึก	blah mèuk

Fruit & Vegetables

banana	กล้วย	glôo·ay
beans	ถั่ว	tòo·a
coconut	มะพร้าว	má-prów
eggplant	มะเขือ	má-kĕu·a
fruit	ผลไม้	pŏn-lá-mái
guava	ฝรั่ง	fa-ràng
lime	มะนาว	má-now
mango	มะม่วง	má-môo·ang
mangosteen	มังคุด	mang-kút
mushrooms	เห็ด	hèt
nuts	ถั่ว	tòo·a
papaya	มะละกอ	má-lá-gor
potatoes	มันฝรั่ง	man fa-ràng
rambutan	เงาะ	ngó
tamarind	มะขาม	má-kăhm
tomatoes	มะเขือเทศ	má-kĕu·a têt
vegetables	ผัก	pàk
watermelon	แตงโม	đaang moh

Other

chilli	พริก	prík
egg	ไข่	kài
fish sauce	น้ำปลา	nám blah
ice	น้ำแข็ง	nám kăang

noodles	เส้น	sên
oil	น้ำมัน	nám man
pepper	พริกไทย	prík tai
rice	ข้าว	kôw
salad	ผักสด	pàk sòt
salt	เกลือ	gleu·a
soup	น้ำซุป	nám súp
soy sauce	น้ำซีอิ๊ว	nám see·éw
sugar	น้ำตาล	nám đahn
tofu	เต้าหู้	đow hôo

Drinks

beer	เบียร์	bee·a
coffee	กาแฟ	gah-faa
milk	นมจืด	nom jèut
orange juice	น้ำส้ม	nám sôm
soy milk	น้ำเต้าหู้	nám đow hôo
sugar-cane juice	น้ำอ้อย	nám ôy
tea	ชา	chah
water	น้ำดื่ม	nám dèum

EMERGENCIES

| Help! | ช่วยด้วย | chôo·ay dôo·ay |
| Go away! | ไปให้พ้น | bai hâi pón |

Call a doctor!
เรียกหมอหน่อย   rêe·ak mŏr nòy

Call the police!
เรียกตำรวจหน่อย   rêe·ak đam·ròo·at nòy

I'm ill.
ผม/ดิฉันป่วย   pŏm/dì-chăn bòo·ay (m/f)

I'm lost.
ผม/ดิฉัน
หลงทาง   pŏm/dì-chăn
          lŏng tahng (m/f)

Where are the toilets?
ห้องน้ำอยู่ที่ไหน   hôrng nám yòo têe năi

SHOPPING & SERVICES

I'd like to buy ...
อยากจะซื้อ ...   yàhk jà séu ...

I'm just looking.
ดูเฉย ๆ   doo chěu·i chěu·i

Can I look at it?
ขอดูได้ไหม   kŏr doo dâi măi

How much is it?
เท่าไร   tôw-rai

That's too expensive.
แพงไป   paang bai

Can you lower the price?
ลดราคาได้ไหม   lót rah-kah dâi măi

There's a mistake in the bill.
บิลใบนี้ผิด   bin bai née pìt ná
นะครับ/ค่ะ   kráp/kâ (m/f)

TIME & DATES

What time is it?
กี่โมงแล้ว   gèe mohng láa·ou

morning	เช้า	chów
afternoon	บ่าย	bài
evening	เย็น	yen
yesterday	เมื่อวาน	mêu·a wahn
today	วันนี้	wan née
tomorrow	พรุ่งนี้	prûng née

Monday	วันจันทร์	wan jan
Tuesday	วันอังคาร	wan ang-kahn
Wednesday	วันพุธ	wan pút
Thursday	วันพฤหัสฯ	wan pá-réu-hàt
Friday	วันศุกร	wan sùk
Saturday	วันเสาร์	wan sŏw
Sunday	วันอาทิตย์	wan ah-tít

TRANSPORT

Public Transport

bicycle rickshaw	สามล้อ	săhm lór
boat	เรือ	reu·a
bus	รถเมล์	rót mair
car	รถเก๋ง	rót gĕng
motorcycle taxi	มอร์เตอร์ไซค์	mor-đeu-sai
ráp jâhng
plane	เครื่องบิน	krêu·ang bin
train	รถไฟ	rót fai
túk-túk	ตุ๊ก ๆ	đúk đúk

Numbers

1	หนึ่ง	nèung
2	สอง	sŏrng
3	สาม	săhm
4	สี่	sèe
5	ห้า	hâh
6	หก	hòk
7	เจ็ด	jèt
8	แปด	bàat
9	เก้า	gôw
10	สิบ	sìp
11	สิบเอ็ด	sìp-èt
20	ยี่สิบ	yêe-sìp
21	ยี่สิบเอ็ด	yêe-sìp-èt
30	สามสิบ	săhm-sìp
40	สี่สิบ	sèe-sìp
50	ห้าสิบ	hâh-sìp
60	หกสิบ	hòk-sìp
70	เจ็ดสิบ	jèt-sìp
80	แปดสิบ	bàat-sìp
90	เก้าสิบ	gôw-sìp
100	หนึ่งร้อย	nèung róy
1000	หนึ่งพัน	nèung pan
10,000	หนึ่งหมื่น	nèung mèun
100,000	หนึ่งแสน	nèung săan
1,000,000	หนึ่งล้าน	nèung láhn

When's the ... bus?	รถเมล์คัน ... มาเมื่อไร	rót mair kan ... mah mêu·a rai
first	แรก	râak
last	สุดท้าย	sùt tái
next	ต่อไป	dòr bai

A ... ticket, please.	ขอตั๋ว ...	kŏr đŏo·a ...
one-way	เที่ยวเดียว	têe·o dee·o
return	ไปกลับ	bai glàp

I'd like a/an ... seat.	ต้องการ ที่นั่ง ...	đôrng gahn têe nâng ...
aisle	ติดทางเดิน	đìt tahng deun
window	ติดหน้าต่าง	đìt nâh đàhng

platform	ชานชาลา	chan-chah-lah
ticket window	ช่องขายตั๋ว	chôrng kăi đŏo·a
timetable	ตารางเวลา	đah-rahng wair-lah

What time does it get to (Chiang Mai)?
ถึง (เชียงใหม่) กี่โมง — tĕung (chee·ang mài) gèe mohng

Does it stop at (Saraburi)?
รถจอดที่ (สระบุรี) ไหม — rót jòrt têe (sà-rà-bù-ree) măi

Please tell me when we get to (Chiang Mai).
เมื่อถึง (เชียงใหม่) กรุณาบอกด้วย — mêu·a tĕung (chee·ang mài) gà-rú-nah bòrk dôo·ay

I'd like to get off at (Saraburi).
ขอลงที่(สระบุรี) — kŏr long têe (sà-rà-bù-ree)

Driving & Cycling

I'd like to hire a/an ...	อยากจะ เช่า ...	yàhk jà chôw ...
4WD	รถโฟร์วีล	rót foh ween
car	รถเก๋ง	rót gĕng
motorbike	รถ มอร์เตอร์ไซค์	rót mor-đeu-sai

I'd like ...	ต้องการ ...	đôrng gahn ...
my bicycle repaired	ซ่อมรถ จักรยาน	sôrm rót jàk-gà-yahn
to hire a bicycle	เช่ารถ จักรยาน	chôw rót jàk-gà-yahn

Is this the road to (Ban Bung Wai)?
ทางนี้ไป (บ้านบุ่งหวาย) ไหม — tahng née bai (bâhn bùng wăi) măi

Where's a petrol station?
ปั๊มน้ำมันอยู่ที่ไหน — bám nám man yòo têe năi

Can I park here?
จอดที่นี่ได้ไหม — jòrt têe née dâi măi

How long can I park here?
จอดที่นี่ได้นานเท่าไร — jòrt têe née dâi nahn tôw-rai

I need a mechanic.
ต้องการช่างรถ — đôrng gahn châhng rót

I have a flat tyre.
ยางแบน — yahng baan

I've run out of petrol.
หมดน้ำมัน — mòt nám man

Do I need a helmet?
ต้องใช้หมวก กันน็อกไหม — đôrng chái mòo·ak gan nórk măi

This glossary includes Thai, Pali (P) and Sanskrit (S) words and terms frequently used in this guidebook. For definitions of food and drink terms, see p785.

ah·hǎhn – food

ah·hǎhn bàh – 'jungle food', usually referring to dishes made with wild game

ajahn – *(aajaan)* respectful title for 'teacher'; from the Sanskrit term *acarya*

amphoe – *(amphur)* district, the next subdivision down from province

amphoe meu·ang – provincial capital

AUA – American University Alumni

bâhn – *(ban)* house or village

baht – *(bàat)* the Thai unit of currency

bàht – a unit of weight equal to 15g; rounded bowl used by monks for receiving alms food

bai sěe – sacred thread used by monks or shamans in certain religious ceremonies

ben·jà·rong – traditional five–coloured Thai ceramics

BKS – Baw Khaw Saw (Thai acronym for the Transport Company)

BMA – Bangkok Metropolitan Authority; Bangkok's municipal government

bodhisattva (S) – in Theravada Buddhism, the term used to refer to the previous lives of the Buddha prior to his enlightenment

bòht – central sanctuary in a Thai temple used for the monastic order's official business, such as ordinations; from the Pali term *uposatha (ubohsòt)*; see also *wí·hǎhn*

bòr nám rórn – hot springs

Brahman – pertaining to Brahmanism, an ancient religious tradition in India and the predecessor of Hinduism; not to be confused with 'Brahmin', the priestly class in India's caste system

BTS – Bangkok Transit System (Skytrain); Thai: *rót fai fáh*

bah·đé – batik

bàk đâi – southern Thailand

bèe·pâht – classical Thai orchestra

bohng·lahng – northeastern Thai marimba (percussion instrument) made of short logs

CAT – CAT Telecom Public Company Limited

chedi – see *stupa*

chow – folk; people

chow lair – *(chow nám)* sea gypsies

chow nah – farmer

CPT – Communist Party of Thailand

doy – mountain in the Northern Thai dialect; spelt 'Doi' in proper names

đà·làht – market

đà·làht nám – water market

đam·bon – *(tambol)* precinct, next governmental subdivision under *amphoe*

đròrk – *(trok)* alley, smaller than a soi

fa·ràng – a Westerner (person of European origin); also guava

gà·teu·i – *(kàthoey)* Thailand's 'third gender', usually cross-dressing or transsexual males; also called ladyboys

gopura (S) – entrance pavilion in traditional Hindu temple architecture, often seen in Angkor-period temple complexes

góo·ay hâang – Chinese-style work shirt

grà·bèe grà·borng – a traditional Thai martial art employing short swords and staves

gù·đì – monk's dwelling

hàht – beach; spelt 'Hat' in proper names

hǐn – stone

hǒr đrai – a Tripitaka (Buddhist scripture) hall

hǒr glorng – drum tower

hǒr rá·kang – bell tower

hôrng – *(hong)* room; in southern Thailand this refers to semi-submerged island caves

hôrng tǎa·ou – rowhouse or shophouses

Isan – *(ee·sǎhn)* general term used for northeastern Thailand

jataka (P) – *(chah·dòk)* stories of the Buddha's previous lives

jeen – Chinese

jeen hor – literally 'galloping Chinese', referring to horse-riding Yunnanese traders

jôw meu·ang – principality chief; *jôw* means lord, prince or holy being

kaan – reed instrument common in northeastern Thailand

kàthoey – see *gà·teu·i*

klorng – canal; spelt 'Khlong' in proper nouns

kǒhn – masked dance–drama based on stories from the Ramakian

kon ee·sǎhn – the people of northeastern Thailand; *kon* means person

kǒw – hill or mountain; spelt 'Khao' in proper names

KMT – Kuomintang

KNU – Karen National Union

kràbìi–kràbawng – see *grà·bèe grà·borng*

ku – small *chedi* that is partially hollow and open

kúay hâeng – see *góo·ay hâang*

kùtì – see *gù·dì*

lăam – cape; spelt 'Laem' in proper names

làk meu·ang – city pillar

lá·kon – classical Thai dance-drama

lék – little, small (in size); see also *noi*

lí·gair – Thai folk dance-drama

longyi – Burmese sarong

lôok tûng – Thai country music

lôw kŏw – white whisky, often homemade rice brew

lôw tèu·an – illegal (homemade) whisky

mâa chee – Thai Buddhist nun

mâa nám – river; spelt Mae Nam in proper names

Mahanikai – the larger of the two sects of Theravada Buddhism in Thailand

mahathat – *(má·hăh tâht)* common name for temples containing Buddha relics; from the Sanskrit–Pali term *mahadhatu*

má·noh·rah – Southern Thailand's most popular traditional dance-drama

masjid – *(mát·sà·yìt)* mosque

mát·mèe – technique of tie-dyeing silk or cotton threads and then weaving them into complex patterns, similar to Indonesian *ikat*; the term also refers to the patterns themselves

metta (P) – *(mêt·đah)* Buddhist practice of loving-kindness

meu·ang – city or principality

mon·dòp – small square, spired building in a *wát*; from Sanskrit *mandapa*

moo·ay tai – *(muay thai)* Thai boxing

mŏr lam – an Isan musical tradition akin to *lôok tûng*

mŏrn kwăhn – wedge-shaped pillow popular in northern and northeastern Thailand

MRTA – Metropolitan Rapid Transit Authority, Bangkok's subway system; Thai: *rót fai fáh đâi din*

naga (P/S) – *(nâhk)* a mythical serpent-like being with magical powers

ná·kon – city; from the Sanskrit-Pali *nagara*; spelt 'Nakhon' in proper nouns

nám – water

nám đòk – waterfall; spelt 'Nam Tok' in proper nouns

năng đà·lung – Thai shadow play

neun – hill; spelt 'Noen' in proper names

ngahn têt·sà·gahn – festival

nibbana (P/S) – nirvana; in Buddhist teachings, the state of enlightenment; escape from the realm of rebirth; Thai: *níp·pahn*

noi – *(nóy)* little, small (amount); see also *lék*

nôrk – outside, outer; spelt 'Nok' in proper names

ow – bay or gulf; spelt 'Ao' in proper nouns

pâh ka·máh – cotton sarong worn by men

pâh mát·mèe – *mát·mèe* fabric

pâh sîn – cotton sarong worn by women

pâhk glahng – central Thailand

pâhk něua – northern Thailand

pâhk tâi – see *pàk đâi*

pĕe – ghost, spirit

pin – small, three-stringed lute played with a large plectrum

pìi·phâat – see *pèe·pâht*

pík·sù – a Buddhist monk; from the Sanskrit *bhikshu*, Pali *bhikkhu*

PLAT – People's Liberation Army of Thailand

pleng koh·râht – Khorat folk song

pleng pêu·a chee·wít – 'songs for life', Thai folk-rock music

ponglang – see *bohng·lahng*

poo kŏw – mountain

pôo yài bâhn – village chief

prá – an honorific term used for monks, nobility and Buddha images; spelt 'Phra' in proper names

prá krêu·ang – amulets of monks, Buddhas or deities worn around the neck for spiritual protection; also called *prá pim*

prá poom – earth spirits or guardians

prang – *(brahng)* Khmer-style tower on temples

prasada – blessed food offered to Hindu or Sikh temple attendees

prasat – *(brah·sàht)* small ornate building, used for religious purposes, with a cruciform ground plan and needlelike spire, located on temple grounds; any of a number of different kinds of halls or residences with religious or royal significance

PULO – Pattani United Liberation Organization

râi – an area of land measurement equal to 1600 sq metres

reu·a hăhng yow – long-tail boat

reu·an tăa·ou – longhouse

reu·sĕe – an ascetic, hermit or sage (Hindi: *rishi*)

rót aa – blue-and-white air-con bus

rót bràp ah·gàht – air-con bus

rót fai fáh – Bangkok's Skytrain system

rót fai tâi din – Bangkok's subway system

rót norn – sleeper bus

rót tam·má·dah – ordinary (non air-con) bus or train

rót too·a – tour or air-con bus

săh·lah – open-sided, covered meeting hall or resting place; from Portuguese term *sala*, literally 'room'

săhm·lór – three-wheeled pedicab

săhn prá poom – spirit shrine

săm·nák sŏng – monastic centre

săm·nák wí·bàt·sà·nah – meditation centre

samsara (P) – in Buddhist teachings, the realm of rebirth and delusion

sangha – (P) the Buddhist community

satang – *(sà·đahng)* a Thai unit of currency; 100 satang equals 1 baht

sèe yâak – intersection, often used to give driving directions

sĕmaa – boundary stones used to consecrate ground used for monastic ordinations

serow – Asian mountain goat

sêua môr hôrm – blue cotton farmer's shirt

soi – lane or small street

Songkran – Thai New Year, held in mid-April

sŏo·an ah·hăhn – outdoor restaurant with any bit of foliage nearby; literally 'food garden'

sŏrng·tăa·ou – (literally 'two rows') common name for small pick-up trucks with two benches in the back, used as buses/taxis; also spelt '*săwngthăew*'

SRT – State Railway of Thailand

stupa – conical-shaped Buddhist monument used to inter sacred Buddhist objects

sù·săhn – cemetery

tâh – pier, boat landing; spelt 'Tha' in proper nouns

tâht – four–sided, curvilinear Buddha reliquary, common in Northeastern Thailand; spelt 'That' in proper nouns

tâht grà·dòok – bone reliquary, a small *stupa* containing remains of a Buddhist devotee

tàlàat náam – see *đà·làht nám*

tâm – cave; spelt 'Tham' in proper nouns

tam bun – to make merit

tambon – see *đam·bon*

TAT – Tourism Authority of Thailand

têt·sà·bahn – a governmental division in towns or cities much like municipality

THAI – Thai Airways International; Thailand's national air carrier

thammájàk – Buddhist wheel of law; from the Pali *dhammacakka*

Thammayut – one of the two sects of Theravada Buddhism in Thailand; founded by King Rama IV while he was still a monk

thanŏn – *(tà·nŏn)* street; spelt 'Thanon' in proper noun and shortened to 'Th'

T-pop – popular teen-music

tràwk – see *đròrk*

trimurti (S) – collocation of the three principal Hindu deities, Brahma, Shiva and Vishnu

Tripitaka (S) – Theravada Buddhist scriptures; (Pali: *Tipitaka*)

tú·dong – a series of 13 ascetic practices (for example eating one meal a day, living at the foot of a tree) undertaken by Buddhist monks; a monk who undertakes such practices; a period of wandering on foot from place to place undertaken by monks

túk–túk – *(đúk–đúk)* motorised săhm·lór

ùt·sà·nít – flame-shaped head ornament on a Buddha

vipassana (P) – *(wí·bàt·sà·nah)* Buddhist insight meditation

wâi – palms–together Thai greeting

wan prá – Buddhist holy days, falling on the days of the main phases of the moon (full, new and half) each month

wang – palace

wát – temple–monastery; from the Pali term *avasa* meaning 'monk's dwelling'; spelt 'Wat' in proper nouns

wá·tá·ná·tam – culture

wát bàh – forest monastery

wí·hăhn – *(wihan, viharn)* any large hall in a Thai temple, usually open to laity; from Sanskrit term *vihara*, meaning 'dwelling'

Yawi – traditional language of Malay parts of Java, Sumatra and the Malay Peninsula, widely spoken in the most southern provinces of Thailand; the written form uses the classic Arabic script plus five additional letters

yài – big

yâhm – shoulder bag

behind the scenes

SEND US YOUR FEEDBACK

We love to hear from travellers – your comments keep us on our toes and help make our books better. Our well-travelled team reads every word on what you loved or loathed about this book. Although we cannot reply individually to postal submissions, we always guarantee that your feedback goes straight to the appropriate authors, in time for the next edition. Each person who sends us information is thanked in the next edition – and the most useful submissions are rewarded with a free book.

Visit **lonelyplanet.com/contact** to submit your updates and suggestions or to ask for help. Our award-winning website also features inspirational travel stories, news and discussions.

Note: We may edit, reproduce and incorporate your comments in Lonely Planet products such as guidebooks, websites and digital products, so let us know if you don't want your comments reproduced or your name acknowledged. For a copy of our privacy policy visit lonelyplanet.com/privacy.

OUR READERS

Many thanks to the travellers who used the last edition and wrote to us with helpful hints, useful advice and interesting anecdotes:

A Emily Abbey, Abi, Anglade, Nidhi Akkaravivat, Henk Allebosch, Birgit Allmendinger, Pascal Ancher, Niels Andeweg, Sandro Antoniol, Armando, Georgina Arrambide, David Arrizon, Anton Asche, Ramin Assemi, Vallee Audree, Silas Aumell, Jayne Azzopardi, **B** Hervé B, Reinier Bakels, Eric Bakker, Anne Balamuth, Kunigunde Baldauf, Colin Barrow, Koen Bart, Gavin Bartle, Antony Barton, Hannah Battersby, Malcolm Battle, Nick Baum, Gill Beaumont, RV Beck, Angelika Berger, Simon Bevan-Davies, Jenny Birch, Daphne Bloem, Jiraporn Boonnark, Paolo Borraccetti, Maaike Bosschart, Nic Boulton, Dawn Bragg, Rogier Brand, Brett, Catherine Brien, James Briggs, Christian Brinch, Mark Brown, Oli Brown, Linda Bruce, Werner Bruyninx, Arabella Buchanan, Lisa Bunnak, Nikki Buran, KJ Busbroek, Jihi & Andrew Bustamante, **C** Dalila Calabrese, Daniel Cao, Jordan Carnwath, Michael Carroll, Kevin Carty, Casper, Oswald & Rosalind Johnen, Thomas A. Mayes, Nelson Chen, Rachel Clewlow, Isabel Clough, Constance Cluset, Pierre-Jean Cobut, Dawn Marie Cooper, Sofie Coucke, Terry Crossley, Philip Crosson, Ashley Crowther, **D** Carl Danzig, Neil Davies,

Daniel Davis, Charlotte De Koning, Eva De Jonckheere, Serge Desforges, Jean-Nicolas Dewaide, Emma Dhesi, Claudio Digennaro, Fredrik Divall, Peter Domcek, Daniel Donatelli, Missy Downey, Sophie Dubus, Jean Duggelby, **E** Mark Eckenrode, Glenn Edwards, Thor Egil Tonnessen, Christof Engl, Matt and Eileen Erskine, **F** Michael Falvella, Betina Faurschou Jensen, Rob Ferrara, Yung Fierens, Christian Fischer, Andrea Fisher, Suz Flach, Marloes Fortuijn, Charles Froeschle, **G** Uschi Gaida, Pierre Gallant, Julien Gamba, Stefan Gerke, Jack Gilead, Steve Gillatt, Marcos González Cabanas, Henrike Gootjes, Dianna Graham, Geraldine Grant, Connie Green, Dave Green, Tom Green, Julie Groves, Mattiassg Grufberg, Tom Grundy, **H** Jesse Halperin, Joe Hammes, Pisit Hanvinyanan, Jamie Harling, Ronan Heeney, Cynthia Heiner, Max Henkle, Helen Henry, Hermann, Hubris18, Menard, Micahel, Michelle, Ramin, Sartorial, Christian Herwig, James Hodgson, Anne Hof, Mark Hoppe, Kevin Hunt, Ken Hyde, **I** Ambre Iris, Idoia Iturbe, Bjornar Ivarsen, **J** Esther Jackson, Kent Jakobsen, Dawon Jeong, Tracy Johnston, **K** Roozbeh Kaboli, Marta Kaminska, Kan7, Karin, Gijs Kattenpoel Oude Heerink, Chad Keenan, Chris Kelly, Rob Kerr, Douwe Kiela, Ilse Kijlstra, Anouk Korfage, David Kos, Suzanne Kuiper, Joep Kusters, Peter Ole Kvint, **L** Anique Landre, Renate Lang, Marius

Laudan, Marije Laverman, Kristel Leconte, Melissa Leo, Arnoud Levenga, Alona Lisitsa, Jenny Little, Paul Lombart, Maik Long, Matthew Losee, Jade Lynch, **M** Lisa Machin, Ellen Macro, Andrew Maiorano, Zowie March, Mark, Alex Marques, Deborah Martell, Sebastien Maury, Philip McGarvey, Cath McGowan, Larry McGrath, David Mehler, Tamar Meijers, Carla Mensink, Lukas Messikommer, Lynda Miller, Alex Moore, Andrew Morecroft, Alan Morison, Jan Mulder, Karina Mullen, Andy Murdock, **N** Kavindra Nethsingha, Elisabeth Nielsen, Sarah-Jayne Nolan, Alexander Nowikow, **O** Joanne Oakes, Sean Offord, Colleen O'Flynn, Ben Ogden, Esther Oliveros, Bjoern Olsson, Jose Olsthoorn, Petra O'Neill, **P** Lyle Paul, Paul and Kumari Pease, Annika Pedersen, Laura Perkins, Rein Peter Vos, Guus Peters, Katrin Plichta, Jan Polatschek, Jenny Popoff, Kathrine Pratt, Erik Pravica, Steph Price, **R** Alan Ramsay, Tim Rawson, Stefano Razio, Paul Reardon, Jouni Remes, Richard Kendrick, Helen Richardson, Adam Ridley, Adrian Robert, Ivor Roberts, Philip and Helen Robinson, Jeffrey Rogers, Patrick Roman, Roee and Ofra Rotman, Robert Rozenberg, Samuele Rudelli, Karin Ruetsche, **S** Claire Sadler Penn, Naparporn Sai-Ngern, Brett Samuels, Komson Sander Nijboer-Puthitanont, Bret Sauels,

Michelle Scaman, Johann Schmid, Ninalaurent Schmiter, Florian Schneider, Linda and Patrick Schneider and Sproll, Dorle Schreiber, Stephen Scott, William Seager, Alex Shields, Helen Shih, Reesa Simmonds, Joshua Singh, Jay Slangen, Kelly Sloane, Lisa Smieja, James Smith, Kristina Solheim, Bianca Son, Natalie Spink, Bart Steegmans, Leonard Storchevoy, Matthea Stoter, Gabi Suchantke-Rackner, Kathryn Sweeney, Steve Syder, **T** Norbert Taatgen, Ginny Tang, Hans Henrik Ter-Borch, Wieke Ter Weijde, Kris Terauds, Jenelle Theodore, Andy Thomas, Allan Thomson, Fred Tiedemann Croese, Claire Toepfer, Rebecca Tofield, **U** Oliver Uhl, **V** Adriaan Van Der Ploeg, Ankie Van Der Put, Arie Van Oosterwijk, Dave Van Duren, Emma Van Bergeijk, Guus Van Der Hoorn, Ilona Van Breugel, Irene Van Baarsen, Josine Van Der Wal, Kim Van Oudheusden, Raymond Van Den Berg, Sonja Van Der Lely, Viola Van Alphen, Diana Vancea, Peter Voelger, Alexandra Von Muralt, **W** Timmy Waiyarat, Sandra Walkert, Anthony Warren, Liu Way, Gerard Weegerink, Erica Wijarnako, David Wilcox, China Williams, Konstantin Willmann, Danielle Wolbers, Eddie Wooldridge, Ed Wright, Heuionalani Wyeth, **Y** Scott Yelin, Katy Young, Jennifer Yuill, **Z** Robert Zackowski, Adrienne Zinn, Anke Zylmann

AUTHOR THANKS

China Williams

Thanks ever so much to Nong who was a wonderful second mother to Felix and a good 'wife' to me. Many thanks to Lisa on Ko Chang and Chris and Gae in Hua Hin for showing me around. To Ted and co-author Mark for dressing up Pattaya. Felix sends his love to the gals at Seven Hotel (Kan, Goong and Pa too). To Mason and Jane for the brain dump and welcome dinner; Joe and Kong for coffee talk; and Ruengsang for her savoir-faire. And to my husband who survived so long without us; it is good to be home. Final shout-out to the co-authors and the Lonely Planet crew.

Mark Beales

Huge thanks to Ilaria for inviting me back to update the Central chapter and many thanks to China for her excellent help and advice. In Lopburi, the wonderful Kook from TAT was a star, as were all her TAT colleagues, while in Kanchanaburi, Bill at Hellfire Pass was incredibly helpful. Finally, thanks to my dad, Ted, for his constant encouragement and support.

Tim Bewer

A hearty *kòrp jai lǎi lǎi dêu* to the perpetually friendly people of Isan who rarely failed to live up to their reputation for friendliness

and hospitality when faced with my incessant questions. In particular Chommanaad Booanree, Julian Wright, June Niampan, Netwaroon (Banjo) Khempila, Sujirat Janpan, and Tanawan (Veena) Puntace all provided great help and good company. And a special thanks to Jookbang for a whole lot of things.

Celeste Brash

Huge thanks to my husband Josh and my kids who I missed so much on this extra-long trip. In Phuket thanks to Celine Masson, Lauren Ladky, Jade in Surin and Aleksander Bochenek; fellow Lonely Planet authors Adam Skolnick, Brandon Presser, Lisa Dunford and Greg Bloom for expert support; to Bodhi Garrett, master of the best places and to Starlight on Phayam and Dick on Sukorn. And China and Ilaria for keeping this crazy book together.

Austin Bush

Thanks to talented Lonely Planeters Ilaria Walker, David Connolly and Bruce Evans; dedicated coordinating author China Williams; and the kind folks on the ground in Thailand including Joe Cummings, Greg Glachant, Craig Harrington, Richard Hermes, Natchaphat Itthi-chaiwarakom, Maher Satter, David Thompson, Pailin Wedel and Patrick Winn.

Alan Murphy

Many people in Chiang Mai helped on this project including contributing writers Reiko Harima and Jackie Pollock who did a fantastic job. Also a big thanks to my friend Laddawan who had some great tips on local eateries. And lastly I want to acknowledge all the local people who took the time out to speak with me during research; your time was much appreciated.

Brandon Presser

As always, a big thank you to the Bambridges for the best home away from home on the planet. Special thanks also to Matt Bolton, Dena DiOrio, Crystal, and Joanne. At Lonely Planet, props to Ilaria Walker, China Williams, Bruce Evans, and my exceptional co-authors.

ACKNOWLEDGMENTS

Climate map data adapted from Peel MC, Finlayson BL & McMahon TA (2007) 'Updated World Map of the Köppen-Geiger Climate Classification', *Hydrology and Earth System Sciences*, 11, 163344.

Bestselling guide to Thailand – source: Nielsen BookScan, Australia, UK and USA, January 2011 to October 2011.

Cover photograph: The Marble Temple is the tourist name for 'Wat Benchamabophit', Paul Chesley, Getty Images.

Many of the images in this guide are available for licensing from Lonely Planet Images: www.lonelyplanetimages.com.

THIS BOOK

This 14th edition of Thailand was coordinated by Lonely Planet veteran and Thailand guru China Williams. She wrote the Plan your Trip and Understand (with the exception of Food and Drink) chapters, the Survival Guide and the Hua Hin & the Southern Gulf and the Ko Chang & Eastern Seaboard chapters. China was assisted by an extraordinary group of Thailand aficionados: Mark Beales (Central Thailand), Tim Bewer (Northeastern Thailand), Celeste Brash (Phuket & the Andaman Coast), Austin Bush (Bangkok, Northern Thailand, Deep South and Eating in Thailand), Alan Murphy (Chiang Mai) and Brandon Presser (Ko Samui & the Lower Gulf and part of the Responsible Travel chapter). The Health chapter is based on that supplied by Trish Batchelor.

For the previous edition, Brandon Presser worked on the Phuket & Andaman Coast chapter,

Catherine Bodry did the Hua Hin & Southern Gulf and Ko Chang & Eastern Seaboard chapters and China Williams updated the Chiang Mai chapter.

This guidebook was commissioned in Lonely Planet's Melbourne office, and produced by the following:

Commissioning Editor
Ilaria Walker
Coordinating Editor
Evan Jones
Coordinating Cartographer Peter Shields
Coordinating Layout Designer Wendy Wright
Managing Editors Bruce Evans, Brigitte Ellemore
Managing Cartographer David Connolly
Managing Layout Designer Jane Hart
Assisting Editors Alice Barker, Jackey Coyle, Victoria Harrison, Anne Mulvaney, Charlotte Orr, Helen Yeates

Assisting Cartographers Andras Bogdanovits, Andrew Smith, Andy Rojas, Corey Hutchison, Hunor Csutoros, Jane Chapman, Jennifer Johnston, Ildiko Bogdanovits, Karen Grant, Mick Garrett
Assisting Layout Designers Adrian Blackburn, Nicholas Colicchia, Paul Iacono
Cover Research Naomi Parker
Internal Image Research Rebecca Skinner
Illustrator Wendy Wright
Language Content Annelies Mertens

Thanks to Elin Berglund, Helen Christinis, Brendan Dempsey, Ryan Evans, Chris Girdler, Briohny Hooper, Corey Hutchison, Shawn Low, Alison Lyall, Wayne Murphy, Trent Paton, Averil Robertson, John Taufa, Juan Winata, Gerard Walker

NOTES

NOTES

NOTES

index

802

INDEX B–C

how to use this book

These symbols will help you find the listings you want:

- 👁 Sights
- 🐚 Beaches
- 🏃 Activities
- 🎓 Courses
- 👉 Tours
- 🎊 Festivals & Events
- 🛏 Sleeping
- 🍴 Eating
- 🍸 Drinking
- ☆ Entertainment
- 🛍 Shopping
- ℹ Information/Transport

These symbols give you the vital information for each listing:

- 📞 Telephone Numbers
- 🕐 Opening Hours
- Ⓟ Parking
- 🚭 Nonsmoking
- ❄ Air-Conditioning
- @ Internet Access
- 📶 Wi-Fi Access
- 🏊 Swimming Pool
- 🥗 Vegetarian Selection
- 📖 English-Language Menu
- 👪 Family-Friendly
- 🐾 Pet-Friendly
- 🚌 Bus
- ⛴ Ferry
- Ⓜ Metro
- Ⓢ Skyway
- 🚊 Tram
- 🚆 Train

Look out for these icons:

TOP CHOICE — Our author's recommendation

FREE — No payment required

🌿 — A green or sustainable option

Our authors have nominated these places as demonstrating a strong commitment to sustainability – for example by supporting local communities and producers, operating in an environmentally friendly way, or supporting conservation projects.

Reviews are organised by author preference.

Map Legend

Sights
- 🏖 Beach
- 🔺 Buddhist
- 🏰 Castle
- ✝ Christian
- 🕉 Hindu
- ☪ Islamic
- ✡ Jewish
- ❶ Monument
- 🏛 Museum/Gallery
- ☯ Ruin
- 🍷 Winery/Vineyard
- 🐾 Zoo
- ⦿ Other Sight

Activities, Courses & Tours
- 🤿 Diving/Snorkelling
- 🛶 Canoeing/Kayaking
- ⛷ Skiing
- 🏄 Surfing
- 🏊 Swimming/Pool
- 🚶 Walking
- 🏄 Windsurfing
- ➕ Other Activity/Course/Tour

Sleeping
- 🛏 Sleeping
- ⛺ Camping

Eating
- 🍴 Eating

Drinking
- ☕ Drinking
- ☕ Cafe

Entertainment
- 🎭 Entertainment

Shopping
- 🛍 Shopping

Information
- 🏦 Bank
- 🏢 Embassy/Consulate
- ➕ Hospital/Medical
- @ Internet
- 👮 Police
- ✉ Post Office
- 📞 Telephone
- 🚻 Toilet
- ℹ Tourist Information
- • Other Information

Transport
- ✈ Airport
- ⊗ Border Crossing
- 🚌 Bus
- ➕🚠➕ Cable Car/Funicular
- 🚲 Cycling
- ⛴ Ferry
- Ⓜ Metro
- 🚝 Monorail
- Ⓟ Parking
- ⛽ Petrol Station
- 🚕 Taxi
- 🚉 Train/Railway
- 🚊 Tram
- • Other Transport

Routes
- Tollway
- Freeway
- Primary
- Secondary
- Tertiary
- Lane
- Unsealed Road
- Plaza/Mall
- Steps
- Tunnel
- Pedestrian Overpass
- Walking Tour
- Walking Tour Detour
- Path

Geographic
- 🛖 Hut/Shelter
- 🔆 Lighthouse
- 👁 Lookout
- 🔺 Mountain/Volcano
- 🌴 Oasis
- 🌳 Park
-)(Pass
- 🌳 Picnic Area
- 🏞 Waterfall

Population
- ★ Capital (National)
- ◉ Capital (State/Province)
- ● City/Large Town
- • Town/Village

Boundaries
- — — — International
- — — — State/Province
- — — — Disputed
- — — Regional/Suburb
- Marine Park
- Cliff
- Wall

Hydrography
- River, Creek
- Intermittent River
- Swamp/Mangrove
- Reef
- Canal
- Water
- Dry/Salt/Intermittent Lake
- Glacier

Areas
- Beach/Desert
- + + + Cemetery (Christian)
- × × × Cemetery (Other)
- Park/Forest
- Sportsground
- Sight (Building)
- Top Sight (Building)

Celeste Brash

Phuket & the Andaman Coast Celeste first arrived in Thailand as a student of Thai language, history and culture at Chiang Mai University. She's come back to the country many times since and has done the gamut from wild nights on Ko Phang-Ngan to weeks of silence at Wat Suanmok. Her award-winning travel stories have appeared in *Travelers' Tales* books and she's been published in a slew of newspapers and magazines from the *LA Times* to *Islands* magazine. Celeste has lost count of how many Lonely Planet guides she's contributed to but her heart is irrevocably stuck on Southeast Asia, and Thailand is her first love. When not dragging her husband and two children to exotic places, she and her family live in Portland, Oregon. Find her on the web at www.celestebrash.com.

Read more about Celeste at:
lonelyplanet.com/members/Celeste

Austin Bush

Bangkok, Northern Thailand, Deep South section, Eating in Thailand Austin came to Thailand in 1998 on a language scholarship at Chiang Mai University. The lure of city life and a need for employment and spicy food eventually led Austin to Bangkok. And city life, employment and spicy food have managed to keep him there since. But escaping Bangkok, particularly for the mountains of Northern Thailand, is one of his favourite things about contributing to this particular guide. A native of Oregon and a freelance writer and photographer who often focuses on food, samples of Austin's work can be seen at www.austinbushphotography.com.

Read more about Austin at:
lonelyplanet.com/members/Austin

Alan Murphy

Chiang Mai Province Alan discovered Southeast Asia sometime in the mid-1990s when he travelled extensively around the region. Since then he has returned to live and work as a volunteer in Chiang Mai, advocating for the rights of migrant workers around the Mekong region. Among other journalistic endeavours, Alan has written and updated guidebooks for Lonely Planet since 1999, and loves the opportunity to get under the skin of a new destination. This was his first time working on the *Thailand* guide and he was very happy to be assigned Chiang Mai – a city with a real heart and a fantastic diversity of people. It seems more like home every time he returns.

Read more about Alan at:
lonelyplanet.com/members/Alan

Brandon Presser

Ko Samui & the Lower Gulf, part of Responsible Travel chapter Growing up in a land where bear hugs are taken literally, this wanderlust-y Canadian always craved swaying palms and golden sand. A trek across Southeast Asia as a teenager was the clincher — he was hooked, returning year after year to scuba dive, suntan, and savour spoonfuls of spicy *sôm·dam* (spicy papaya salad). After leaving his job at the Louvre, Brandon picked up his pen and rucksack, and became a full-time freelance travel writer. He's since contributed to over 20 Lonely Planet titles from *Iceland* to *Thailand* and many 'lands' in between.

Read more about Brandon at:
lonelyplanet.com/members/Brandon

OUR STORY

A beat-up old car, a few dollars in the pocket and a sense of adventure. In 1972 that's all Tony and Maureen Wheeler needed for the trip of a lifetime – across Europe and Asia overland to Australia. It took several months, and at the end – broke but inspired – they sat at their kitchen table writing and stapling together their first travel guide, *Across Asia on the Cheap*. Within a week they'd sold 1500 copies. Lonely Planet was born.

Today, Lonely Planet has offices in Melbourne, London and Oakland, with more than 600 staff and writers. We share Tony's belief that 'a great guidebook should do three things: inform, educate and amuse'.

OUR WRITERS

China Williams

Coordinating Author, Hua Hin & the Southern Gulf, Ko Chang & Eastern Seaboard Oh Thailand, it appears we're growing old together. China first came to Thailand to teach English in Surin way back in 1997, a few months prior to the country's currency crisis. Since then she has shuttled across the Pacific to work on various Thailand guidebooks for nine years. This is her third trip with her son, who is now four years old. Be assured that all the beaches in the upper gulf and eastern seaboard have been kid-tested and mother-approved, including the wholesome bits of prostitute-city Pattaya. China lives in Catonsville, Maryland (USA) with her husband, Matt, and son, Felix.

Read more about China at:
lonelyplanet.com/members/China

Mark Beales

Central Thailand After receiving a scholarship to study journalism, Mark worked as a reporter for 13 years. In 2004 he swapped the chilly shores of England for the sunnier coasts of Thailand. As well as being a freelance writer, Mark has worked as a teacher and TV presenter. Highlights on this trip included waking up to a giant hornbill attempting to prise open the door of his tree-top cabin and meeting an impossibly cute one-day-old elephant in Ayuthaya. When Mark isn't on the road, he teaches English at an international school in Rayong. For more on Mark's work, visit www.markbeales.com.

Read more about Mark at:
lonelyplanet.com/members/Mark

Tim Bewer

Northeastern Thailand While growing up, Tim didn't travel much except for the obligatory pilgrimage to Disney World and an annual summer week at the lake. He's spent most of his adult life making up for this, and has since visited more than 70 countries, including most of those in Southeast Asia. After university he worked as a legislative assistant before quitting to backpack around West Africa. It was during this trip that he decided to become a freelance travel writer and photographer, and he's been at it ever since. When he isn't shouldering a backpack somewhere he lives in Khon Kaen, Thailand, where he jointly runs the Isan Explorer (www.isanexplorer.com) tour company.

Read more about Tim at:
lonelyplanet.com/members/Tim

OVER PAGE MORE WRITERS

Published by Lonely Planet Publications Pty Ltd
ABN 36 005 607 983
14th edition – Feb 2012
ISBN 978 1 74179 714 5
© Lonely Planet 2012   Photographs © as indicated 2012
10 9 8 7 6 5 4 3 2 1
Printed in China

Although the authors and Lonely Planet have taken all reasonable care in preparing this book, we make no warranty about the accuracy or completeness of its content and, to the maximum extent permitted, disclaim all liability arising from its use.